"Value-packed, accurate, and comprehensive..."
—*Los Angeles Times*

"Unbeatable..."—*The Washington Post*

LET'S GO:
SPAIN & PORTUGAL

is the best book for anyone traveling on a budget. Here's why:

No other guidebook has as many budget listings.

In Barcelona, we found 32 hotels or hostels for under $22 a night. In the countryside we found hundreds more. We tell you how to get there the cheapest way, whether by bus, plane, or thumb, and where to get an inexpensive and satisfying meal once you've arrived. There are hundreds of money-saving tips for everyone plus lots of information on student discounts.

LET'S GO researchers have to make it on their own.

Our Harvard-Radcliffe researchers travel on budgets as tight as your own—no expense accounts, no free hotel rooms.

LET'S GO is completely revised every year.

We don't just update the prices, we go back to the places. If a charming café has become an overpriced tourist trap, we'll replace the listing with a new and better one.

No other budget guidebook includes all this:

Coverage of both the cities and the countryside; directions, addresses, phone numbers, and hours to get you there and back; in-depth information on culture, history, and the people; listings on transportation between and within regions and cities; tips on work, study, sights, nightlife, and special splurges, city and regional maps; and much, much more.

LET'S GO is for anyone who wants to see Spain and Portugal on a budget.

Books by Let's Go, Inc.

Let's Go: Europe
Let's Go: Britain & Ireland
Let's Go: France
Let's Go: Germany, Austria & Switzerland
Let's Go: Greece & Turkey
Let's Go: Israel & Egypt
Let's Go: Italy
Let's Go: London
Let's Go: Paris
Let's Go: Rome
Let's Go: Spain & Portugal

Let's Go: USA
Let's Go: California & Hawaii
Let's Go: Mexico
Let's Go: New York City
Let's Go: The Pacific Northwest, Western Canada & Alaska
Let's Go: Washington, D.C.

LET'S GO:
The Budget Guide to
SPAIN & PORTUGAL
1993

Nell Eisenberg
Editor

Jane Yeh
Assistant Editor

Written by
Let's Go, Inc.
a wholly owned subsidiary of
Harvard Student Agencies, Inc.

PAN BOOKS
London, Sydney and Auckland

Helping Let's Go

If you have suggestions or corrections, or just want to share your discoveries, drop us a line. We read every piece of correspondence, whether a 10-page letter, a tacky Elvis postcard, or, as in one case, a collage. All suggestions are passed along to our researcher/writers. Please note that mail received after May 5, 1993 will probably be too late for the 1994 book, but will be retained for the following edition. Address mail to:

Let's Go: Spain & Portugal
Let's Go, Inc.
1 Story Street
Cambridge, MA 02138

In addition to the invaluable travel advice our readers share with us, many are kind enough to offer their services as researchers or editors. Unfortunately, the charter of Let's Go, Inc. and Harvard Student Agencies, Inc. enables us to employ only currently enrolled Harvard students.

Published in Great Britain 1993 by Pan Books Ltd
Cavaye Place, London SW10 9PG
9 8 7 6 5 4 3 2 1

Published in the United States of America
by St. Martin's Press, Inc.

LET'S GO: SPAIN & PORTUGAL. Copyright © 1993 by Let's Go, Inc., a wholly owned subsidiary of Harvard Student Agencies, Inc.
Maps by David Lindroth, copyright © 1993, 1992, 1991, 1990, 1989, 1986 by St. Martin's Press, Inc.

ISBN: 0 330 32700 3

Let's Go: Spain & Portugal is written by the Publishing Division of Let's Go, Inc., 1 Story Street, Cambridge, Mass. 02138

Let's Go® is a registered trademark of Let's Go, Inc.

Printed and bound in the United States of America
on recycled paper with biodegradable soy ink.

This book is sold subject to the condition that it shall not, by way of trade or otherwise, be lent, re-sold, hired out or otherwise circulated without the publisher's prior consent in any form of binding or cover other than that in which it is published and without a similar condition including this condition being imposed on the subsequent purchaser.

Editor	Nell Eisenberg
Assistant Editor	Jane Yeh
Managing Editor	July Belber
Publishing Director	Paul C. Deemer
Production Manager	Mark N. Templeton
Office Coordinator	Bart St. Clair
Office Manager	Anne E. Chisholm

Researcher-Writers

Morocco, Andalucía	Mark Burns
Galiza, Euskadi, Asturias, Cantabria, Castilla y León (except Ávila, Salamanca, Segovia, and Soria)	Kristina Cordero
Catalunya (except Costa Brava, Girona, and Catalan Pyrenees), València, Illes Baleares, Murcia, Andalucía	Rachel Geman
Madrid, Castilla-La Mancha, Ávila, Salamanca Segovia, Extremadura, Andalucía	Andrew Hallman
La Rioja, Navarra, Aragón, Costa Brava Girona, Catalan Pyrenees, Soria	Anna More
Portugal	Joseph E. Mullin III

Sales Group Manager	Tiffany A. Breau
Sales Group Representatives	Frances Marguerite Maximé
	Breean T. Stickgold
	Harry J. Wilson
Sales Group Coordinator	Aida Bekele
President	Brian A. Goler
C.E.O.	Michele Ponti

Acknowledgments

Six people researched and wrote this book, two helped edit it, and a number of others worked on the project.

Researcher-Writers

Mark Burns: Mark used his uncanny friendliness to its full advantage, winning friends throughout southern Spain and Morocco, and overhauling accommodations and food sections based on their advice. Due to strange airline mishaps, Mark is the only SPAM R-W who made it to all three countries.

Kristina Cordero: *La Reina de I.P.* (PI queen) is not a human, but a robot dressed up in a Kristina Cordero suit, programmed to sleuth out Practical Information at three times mortal speed. No robot could write such flawless Let's Go-ish prose, however, nor have such appreciation for tabloid journalism and El Corte Inglés. Kristina's exhaustive research (supplemented by Alfredo, and Pablo, and Ramón, and José Antonio, and Francisco, and Manchu, and Jesus, and Luchita....) made possible much-needed expansion in Northwest Spain.

Rachel Geman: Hilarious and astute in her writing, tirelessly conscientious in her research, Rachel never flagged on her killer, record-length itinerary down the entire eastern coast of Spain. She sacrificed sleep, peace of mind, and the company of her friends to get the job done—and done with excellence. We can't be grateful enough to repay her (we just wish we could've paid her more).

Andy Hallman: Product of *Let's Go* nepotism, Andy did Madrid research that puts city guides to shame. He still holds the record for longest copy batch (119 pages), best Europe highlighting (his green early work), and most detailed description of the *menú del dia* (sublime).

Anna More: Ever-competent Anna More is the ideal R-W for panicky, overprotective editors. Bypassing the three-week blues entirely, she faxed back RENFE maps at the last second and whizzed warp-speed through dozens of Pyrenean towns. I only wish I could have given her a longer itinerary.

Joseph E. Mullin: Sprightly coxswain Joe Mullin hopped from town to town on his grueling itinerary that challenged Rachel's for difficulty. Straight-from-the-hip Joe never used a superfluous word and his native knowledge of things Portuguese was invaluable.

Editors

Jane Yeh: Jane's brilliant creativity and her courage in the face of six official languages (plus countless regional dialects) would impress the Knights Templar, while her high-tech expertise and high-speed efficiency make glorious Poliscar look like an ill-tuned heap of rubble. Probably the only assistant editor on earth who could both mastermind New Faster Format and endure my constant fishiness, goddess Jane ate up a mammoth copy pile, and spat back pages of luscious, geniusy prose.

July Belber: Managing editor and fellow deviant, July knew exactly when I should fight for The Unsavory, and when I should shut up and work. Though she couldn't get our couch back, she mysteriously nabbed the good room and stuck around until the bitter end, even when I blubbered from exhaustion.

Others

In the "laid back room" [read: zoo] of 1 Story Street, Elijah, Muneer, Kayla, David, Alex, Mike, Jane, and July hung a cleaver from the ceiling and acted freaky. Thanks to Publishing Director Pete Deemer for the earplugs, Production Manager Mark Templeton for the bone font, Managing Editor Chris Caps for map wizardry and Mexico Editor René Celaya for SPAM phone checking, even as he was approaching deadline. Ex-SPO Editor Michael Armstrong Roche set a high standard for the guide and showered me with an unending barrage of hints and advice. Jenny Davidson, third member of the evil SPAM house, somehow caught errors in languages she doesn't speak as she proofread almost the entire book.

I spent time outside of work this spring and summer (all 10 minutes of it) with friends and family who tried to get my head out of Iberia. Thanks to Ari (for sense), Kate (for political savvy and that iced coffee feeling), Sue (for encouragement), Jessica Robinson Saalfield (for on-site detective work), Sarah (for commiseration), and my loyal and sympathetic family (for everything). To Mike C. Vazquez and his love pentagon I say thanks for not cutting me out of the loop. I only wish that I could have given more support this summer to St. Julia Booms, woman of bat instinct, primate might, and superhuman strength.

—NE

Above all, this book belongs to **Nell Eisenberg,** whose generosity, humor, and grace were the only good things about this job, and to whom I'm infinitely grateful. As editor she devoted all of her energy and spirit to making the book the very best it could be, working longer hours than anyone in the office. The thought and care she put into everything she did—from the first tearsheet to the last regional intro; her brilliant writing and editing; her genius for clearer, faster format; and her unswerving dedication, I salute. I couldn't have worked for anyone cooler. Kisses to **Jenny Davidson,** the Mata Hari of industrial espionage and proofreader *extraordinaire,* who read more than three-quarters of this book with a peerless eagle eye. I am thankful for her intrinsic kindness, consideration, and intelligence, and for giving me a home for the summer. Her presents made the last weeks far more bearable.

A cornucopia of thanks to **Mark Templeton,** whose thankless task was to install and debug a new computer network and software office-wide; and to Bart St. Clair and the whole office for humoring me during those 14-hour workdays. ¡Kudos! to **René Celaya** for help with Spanish and **Muneer Ahmad** and **Gary Bass** for advice on Morocco. **Andrew Kaplan's** kind gift saved me in the darkest of hours. Intellectual debts to my professors at Harvard, who gave me whatever knowledge I have of Spanish history and art history.

As usual, **Karen Cinorre** was my lifeline and my savior throughout. **Helen Wingard Hill's** hilarious correspondence and sympathetic ear brightened many, many days. Last but not least, thanks to my parents, for whose constant and generous support I am endlessly grateful.

—JYY

About Let's Go

A generation ago, Harvard Student Agencies, a three-year-old non-profit corporation dedicated to providing employment to students, was doing a booming business booking charter flights to Europe. One of the extras offered to passengers on these flights was a 20-page mimeographed pamphlet entitled *1960 European Guide,* a collection of tips on continental travel compiled by the HSA staff. The following year, students traveling to Europe researched the first full-fledged edition of *Let's Go: Europe,* a pocket-sized book with tips on budget accommodations, irreverent write-ups of sights, and a decidedly youthful slant.

Throughout the 60s, the series reflected the times: a section of the 1968 *Let's Go: Europe* was entitled "Street Singing in Europe on No Dollars a Day." During the 70s *Let's Go* evolved into a large-scale operation, adding regional European guides and expanding coverage into North Africa and Asia. In the 80s, we launched coverage of the United States, developed our research to include concerns of travelers of all ages, and finetuned the editorial process that continues to this day. The early 90s saw the introduction of *Let's Go* city guides.

1992 has been a big year for us. We are now Let's Go, Incorporated, a wholly owned subsidiary of Harvard Student Agencies. To celebrate this change, we moved from our dungeonesque Harvard Yard basement to an equally dungeonesque third-floor office in Harvard Square, and we purchased a high-tech computer system that allows us to typeset all of the guides in-house. Now in our 33rd year, *Let's Go* publishes 17 titles, covering more than 40 countries. This year *Let's Go* proudly introduces two new entries in the series: *Let's Go: Paris* and *Let's Go: Rome.*

But these changes haven't altered our tried and true approach to researching and writing travel guides. Each spring 90 Harvard University students are hired as researcher-writers and trained intensively during April and May for their summer tour of duty. Each researcher-writer then hits the road for seven weeks of travel on a shoestring budget, researching six days per week and overcoming countless obstacles in the quest for better bargains.

Back in Cambridge, Massachusetts, an editorial staff of 32, a management team of six, and countless typists and proofreaders—all students—spend more than six months pushing nearly 8000 pages of copy through a rigorous editing process. By the time classes start in September, the typeset guides are off to the printers, and they hit bookstores world-wide in late November. Then, by February, next year's guides are well underway.

A NOTE TO OUR READERS

The information for this book is gathered by Let's Go's researchers during the late spring and summer months. Each listing is derived from the assigned researcher's opinion based upon his or her visit at a particular time. The opinions are expressed in a candid and forthright manner. Other travelers might disagree. Those traveling at a different time may have different experiences since prices, dates, hours, and conditions are always subject to change. You are urged to check beforehand to avoid inconvenience and surprises. Travel always involves a certain degree of risk, especially in low-cost areas. When traveling, especially on a budget, you should always take particular care to ensure your safety.

America's No. 1 Tour Operator To Spain

WHEN YOU THINK

SPAIN

THINK WELCOME TOURS INTERNATIONAL
hispanidad holidays inc.

1. Low Cost Airfares.
2. Group and Special Tours.
3. Independent Services –
   Hotels • Paradors • Cars.
4. Escorted Tours –
   Year-round Departures.
5. Experienced Staff.
6. Personalized Attention.

OUR 19TH YEAR

GROUPS AND SPECIAL ARRANGEMENTS:
· Incentives and Conventions · Sport Packages · Youth and Education Programs · Special Events · Pilgrimages · Congresses or Meetings

We are the group travel specialists to Spain, Portugal, Morocco and Mexico. Feel free to contact us. We will give you complete quotations and suggestions without obligations.

AMERICA'S
NO. 1
TOUR OPERATOR
TO SPAIN

 **WELCOME** TOURS INTERNATIONAL
hispanidad holidays inc.

99 Tulip Avenue • Floral Park, NY 11001
(516) 488-4700 • 1 (800) 274-4400

CONTENTS

List of Maps xv

General Introduction 1
   Geographical Organization 2
   Planning Your Trip 2
   When To Go 2
   Documents 2
   Money 7
   Insurance 10
   Packing 11
   Health 15
   Safety 16
   Specific Concerns 17
   Alternatives to Tourism 21
   Useful Addresses 24
   Getting There 27
   From North America 27
   From Europe 30
   Customs 32

SPAIN 36
   Once There 36
   Tourist Offices 36
   Embassies and Consulates 36
   Getting Around 37
   Accommodations 42
   Food and Drink 44
   Communications 46
   More Money 48
   Life and Times 49
   Language(s) 49
   History 49
   Art 52
   Architecture 53
   Literature 53
   Reading Matter 53
   The Media 54

Madrid 56
   Orientation 56
   Practical Information 57
   Accommodations 66
   Food 71
   Sights 75
   Entertainment 84

Near Madrid 92
   El Escorial 92
   Sierra de Guadarrama 96
   Alcalá de Henares 97
   Aranjuez 98

Castilla-La Mancha 100
   Toledo 100
   Almagro 106
   Cuenca 107
   Guadalajara 109
   Sigüenza 110

Castilla y León 111
   Segovia 111
   Avila 116
   Salamanca 119
   Near Salamanca 125
   Zamora 126
   León 128
   Valladolid 132
   Palencia 136
   Burgos 140
   Soria 146

Galiza (Galicia) 149
   Santiago de Compostela 150
   Rías Baixas (Bajas) 155
   Rías da Costa da Morte (Rías
     de la Costa de la Muerte) ... 162
   A Coruña (La Coruña) 164
   Rías Altas 168

Asturias and Cantabria 171
   Oviedo 172
   Picos de Europa 176
   Santander 180
   Cantabrian and Asturian
     Coast 185

**Euskadi (País Vasco, Basque
Country)** 189
   Bilbo (Bilbao) 190
   Gernika (Guernica ....) 194
   Lekeitio (Lequeitio) 196

CONTENTS

Donostia (San Sebastián) 197
Vitoria-Gasteiz 207

La Rioja and Navarra 211
Logroño 211
Haro 215
Pamplona 216
Near Pamplona 221
Estella 222
Navarrese Pyrenees 224

Aragón 229
Zaragoza 230
Tarazona 235
La Ruta del Vino: Muel,
   Cariñena, Daroca 236
Teruel 237
Huesca 242
Aragonese Pyrenees 243

Catalunya (Catalonia) 252
Barcelona 253
Costa Brava 282
Girona (Gerona) 293
Catalan Pyrenees 298
Costa Daurada (Costa
   Dorada) 304
Tarragona 305

**Illes Baleares
(Balearic Islands)** 310
Mallorca 311
Menorca 322
Eivissa (Ibiza) 328

València 333
València 334
Morella 341
Xàtiva (Játiva) 342
Gandía 344
Alacant (Alicante) 345
Costa Blanca 349

Murcia 351
Murcia 351
Lorca 354

Andalucía 355

Sevilla 355
Osuna 373
Córdoba 374
Jaén 381
Ubeda 383
Baeza 385
Cazorla 386
Granada 387
Sierra Nevada 397
Málaga 400
Costa del Sol 404
Antequera 410
Ronda 412
Algeciras 416
Gibraltar 418
Tarifa 421
Véjer de la Frontera 422
Cádiz 423
Costa de la Luz 426
Jerez de la Frontera 430
Arcos de la Frontera 432

Extremadura 434
Cáceres 435
Plasencia 438
Trujillo 440
Guadalupe 443
Badajoz 445
Mérida 447
Los Pueblos Blancos 449

PORTUGAL 452
Once There 452
Tourist Offices 452
Embassies and Consulates 452
Getting Around 452
Accommodations 455
Food and Drink 457
Communications 458
More Money 459
Life and Times 460
History 460
Art 462
Architecture 462
Literature 462
Music 463

Lisboa (Lisbon) 464

Orientation and Practical Information	464
Accommodations and Camping	468
Food	470
Sights	472
Entertainment	476

Estremadura 478
- Sintra 478
- Estoril and Cascais 481
- Setúbal 482
- Óbidos 484
- Peniche 486
- Caldas da Rainha 488
- Nazaré 489

Beira Alta and Beira Baixa 493
- Coimbra 494
- Leiria 498
- Batalha 499
- Fátima 500
- Figueira da Foz 502
- Aveiro 504
- Viseu 506

Douro and Minho 508
- Porto (Oporto) 508
- Braga 512
- Guimarães 517
- Barcelos 518
- Viana do Castelo 519
- Vila Nova de Cerveira 521

Trás-Os-Montes 523
- Bragança 523
- Vila Real 525

Ribatejo and Alentejo 527
- Santarém 527
- Tomar 530
- Évora 533
- Elvas 536
- Portalegre 539

Beja 542

Algarve 545
- Faro 545
- Lagos 549
- Sagres 551
- Olhão 553
- Tavira 553
- Vila Real de Santo António ... 554

MOROCCO 556
- Once There 556
- Tourist Offices 556
- Embassies and Consulates 557
- Orientation 557
- Getting Around 557
- Accommodations 559
- Food and Drink 560
- Communications 561
- More Money 562
- Additional Concerns 563
- Festivals and Holidays 564
- Life and Times 565
- History 565
- Literature 567
- Reading Matter 568
- Tangier 569
- Asilah 574
- Fes 576
- Rabat 583
- Casablanca 587
- El-Jadida 589
- Essaouria 592
- Marrakech 594

GLOSSARY 602
- General 602
- Food, Drink, and Restaurant Terms 604

APPENDICES 606

INDEX 613

In case you're having trouble learning the value of a peseta.

There's nothing to worry about if your money supply has taken a little siesta. With Western Union, you can receive money from the States within minutes, in case the situation arises. Plus it's already been converted into pesetas.

Just call our number in Barcelona, 343 301 12 12, or the United States, 1-800-325-6000, and then pick up your money at any Western Union location. Olé.

WESTERN UNION | MONEY TRANSFER®

© 1992 Western Union Financial Services, Inc.

List of Maps

Regional Transport	34-5
Spain	38-9
Madrid	58-9
Barcelona	254-5
València	335
Sevilla	356-7
Córdoba	375
Granada	388
Portugal	453
Lisboa	466-7
Morocco	556
Fes	577
Marrakech	595

WITH OUR RAIL PASSES YOU'LL HAVE UP TO 70% MORE MONEY TO WASTE.

With savings of up to 70% off the price of point to point tickets, you'll be laughing all the way to the souvenir stand. Rail passes are available for travel throughout Spain and Portugal or any other part of Europe and we'll even help you fly there. So all you'll have to do is leave some extra room in your suitcase. To learn more call **1-800-4-EURAIL** (1-800-438-7245). *Rail Europe*

Rail Europe, P.O. Box 10383, Stamford, CT 06904.

LET'S GO: SPAIN AND PORTUGAL

Using Let's Go

Let's Go introduces the budget traveler to Spain, Portugal, and Morocco. Our researchers travel on a shoestring budget, so their concerns are the same as yours: how to travel, sleep, eat, sightsee, and enjoy evenings in the most economical way possible. *Let's Go* is primarily a reference book; our priority is to list accurate practical information, transport information, and inexpensive restaurants and accommodations. This edition of *Let's Go: Spain & Portugal* has a streamlined faster format, with most of the information in easily scannable quick-reference listings.

In the section Planning Your Trip, we guide you through the gobs of tasks that need to get done before you go. The contents are: Documents (how to apply for passports, visas, student IDs, youth hostel memberships); Money (the pros and cons of traveler's checks, credit cards, and ATMS and how to send money); Packing; Health; Insurance; Safety; and Specific Concerns (tips and resources about diets, drugs, gay and lesbian travelers, senior travelers, travelers with children, and women travelers). This section also explains how to arrange a job overseas or study programs at a foreign university. The Useful Addresses section lists addresses and phone numbers for tourist offices, embassies, and consulates of Spain, Portugal, and Morocco in your home country, not to mention listings of travel services, the agencies to consult about any travel question.

In Getting There, we exhaust the possibilities for traveling to Spain and Portugal inexpensively, whether by plane, train, bus, or ferry. We unravel mysterious customs regulations country by country.

For each country, the Once There section provides practical information about Getting Around, Accommodations, Food and Drink, Communications, and More Money. Addresses of tourist offices and of your home country's embassy and consulates are included. Next comes Life and Times, accounts of each country's history, art, architecture, and literature. At the back of the book, the Glossary and Appendix are flip-to references for translations of Castilian, Catalan, Galician, and Portuguese words and more country-specific practical information.

For each town we cover, Orientation and Practical Information sections describe the town's accessibility from other points in the country, the layout of the town, how to get into the city center from the train and/or bus station, and the addresses and phone numbers of the local tourist office; the currency exchange; the telephone and post offices (with their telephone and postal codes); the train and bus stations; taxi services; car, bicycle, and moped rental; the police; and the emergency telephone number. We list schedules and fares of every mode of transportation in, out of, and around the town. For larger cities, *Let's Go* also provides a map and information about airports, student travel offices, American Express offices, hospitals, bookstores, gay and lesbian resources, public toilets, and laundromats. With your purse in mind, the Accommodations and Food sections offer ranked lists of lodgings, supermarkets, and restaurants. After accommodations is a write-up of each town's Sights, in readable (sometimes slanged-out) prose. In addition to Iberia's well-known attractions, *Let's Go* describes offbeat and unusual sights that other guides tend to ignore. Finally, each section concludes with Entertainment: nightlife, festivals, and a description of possible daytrips in the countryside nearby.

Geographical Organization

Let's Go: Spain & Portugal divides Iberia into 22 regions. Small neighboring regions are sometimes grouped together. The chapters on Spain are arranged geographically in two clockwise spirals, a tight one around Madrid embracing the two Castillas—many towns there are often visited on daytrips from Madrid—and a larger one moving from the Castillas northwest to Galiza and round the periphery, winding up in Extremadura, the customary point of entry to Portugal. Portugal's scheme takes the reader from Lisboa north through Estremadura—the region most intimately bound with the capital—along the coast to the northern frontier, then south through the central plains, wrapping it up in the Algarve. This method most closely reflects the peninsula's transportation network, and therefore the natural flow of travelers from one region to the next.

Planning Your Trip

When To Go

Traveling during the **off-season** (or "low season," *temporada baja*) means sparser crowds and lower prices for accommodations and transportation. Accommodations will also be easier to find, as the lack of tourists leaves more rooms vacant. And since off-season coincides with the academic year, the university towns spring to life. However, some small and tourist-oriented towns virtually shut down in off-season. Tourist offices and sights maintain shorter hours, some restaurants close, and seaside resorts empty out. Overcast skies and cold temperatures in certain regions may make traveling unpleasant.

High season (*temporada alta*) in Spain and Portugal is summer (roughly June-Sept.) for coastal and interior regions. For mountainous ski resorts, winter is high season. In many places, high season includes **Semana Santa** (Holy Week, starting the Sunday before Easter Sunday) and famous festival days too. In August most of Europe goes on holiday, leaving behind scores of closed restaurants, lodgings, and offices.

To further complicate life, parts of Spain observe a "mid-season" between the high and low, charging prices between the extremes.

Documents

Apply early for travel documents to save yourself needless headaches. Some agencies have backlogs.

Passports

You must have a valid passport to enter and leave Spain, Portugal, and Morocco. If your current passport bears an Israeli stamp you should apply for a new one before traveling to Morocco—it's Arab League policy not to admit Israeli and South African citizens or holders of passports with Israeli stamps. Carry your passport with you at all times. In all three countries (Spain, Portugal, and Morocco), the police have the right to stop you and demand to see it.

Before you leave, you should photocopy your entire passport. Keep the copy, as well an extra proof of citizenship (expired passport or a birth certificate), in a separate part of your baggage. It's also wise to leave a copy with a relative or friend back home. While a copy doesn't serve as a substitute for a valid passport, it speeds the process of replacing one.

If you lose your passport while traveling, notify the local police and the nearest consulate of your home government immediately. Your consulate will be able to issue you a new passport or temporary traveling papers.

U.S.

U.S. citizens may apply for a passport, valid for 10 years (5 yrs. if under 18), at any one of several thousand **federal courts** or **post offices** authorized to accept passport applications, or at a **U.S. Passport Agency** (Boston, Chicago, Honolulu, Houston, Los Angeles, Miami, New Orleans, New York, Philadelphia, San Francisco, Seattle, Stamford, CT, and Washington, DC). Parents must apply in person for children under 13. You must apply in person if this is your first passport, if you're under 18, or if your current passport is more than 12 years old or was issued before your 18th birthday.

For a U.S. passport, you must submit the following: (1) a completed application; (2) proof of U.S. citizenship (a certified birth certificate, naturalization papers, or a previous passport); (3) identification bearing your signature and either your photo or a personal description (e.g., an unexpired driver's license or passport); and (4) two identical, recent passport (2 in. by 2 in.) photographs. Bring items (1-4) and US$65 (under 18 US$40) in the form of a check (cashier's, traveler's, certified, or personal) or money order. Passport Agencies alone accept cash.

You can **renew** your passport by mail (or in person) for US$55. Your old passport will serve as both (2) and (3) and must be enclosed with the application and photos.

Processing usually takes two to three weeks if you apply in person at a Passport Agency, three to four weeks at a court or post office. *File your application as early as possible.* The Passport Agency recommends applying between August and December. You may pay for express-mail return of your passport. For **rush service,** if you have proof of departure within five working days (e.g., an airline ticket), the Passport Agency will issue a passport while you wait (and wait, and wait). Arrive at dawn.

Overseas, a U.S. consulate can usually issue new passports, given proof of citizenship. For more **information,** call the U.S. Passport Information's 24-hr. recording (tel. (202) 647-0518) or contact the Passport Agency nearest you.

Canada

Canadian citizens may apply in person for a five-year passport at one of 26 **regional offices** (addresses are in the telephone directory), or at a Canadian diplomatic mission if residing in the U.S. By mail, send the application to the Passport Office, Department of External Affairs, Ottawa, Ont. K1A 0G3. Applications are available at post offices, most travel agencies, and passport offices.

You must submit (1) a completed application; (2) original documentary evidence of Canadian citizenship; and (3) two identical photographs, both signed by the holder and one certified by a "guarantor" from an approved list who has known you for at least two years. Children may be included on a parent's passport. The fee is CDN$35, paid in cash, certified cash, money order, or bank draft.

Processing takes five days if you're applying in person and three weeks if by mail. For more **information,** check the free booklet *Bon Voyage, But...,* available from any passport office.

U.K.

There are two types of British passport. For a **Full British Passport,** valid for 10 years (5 yrs. if under 16), apply in person or by mail at any passport office (London, Liverpool, Newport, Peterborough, Glasgow, Belfast). You must submit: (1) a completed application; (2) a birth certificate and marriage certificate (if applicable); and (3) two identical, recent photos signed by a guarantor. The fee is £15. Children under 16 and a spouse who doesn't have a passport may be included on your passport. Processing takes four to six weeks.

For a **Visitor's Passport**, valid for one year in Western Europe only, apply in person at major post offices. You must bring identification and two identical photos. The fee is £7.50.

Ireland

Irish citizens may apply for their first 10-year passport by mail to one of two **passport offices:** Setanta Centre, Molesworth St., Dublin 2 (tel. (1) 711 633); and 1A South Mall, Cork, County Cork (tel. (021) 272 525). You must send (1) a completed long application; (2) a birth certificate; and (3) 2 identical photos. Applications are available at local guard stations and the passport offices. To **renew**, send your (1) a complete short application; (2) your expired passport; and (3) 2 identical photos. The fee is £45.

Australia

Apply at a **post office, passport office,** or Australian diplomatic mission if overseas. Parents must apply for unmarried children under 18. You must submit (1) a completed form; (2) proof of citizenship (birth certificate, expired passport issued after November 22, 1984, or citizen certificate from the Dept. of Immigration); (3) proof of your present name; (4) more ID (driver's license, credit card, etc.); and (5) 2 identical, recent photos signed as instructed in the application. The fee is adjusted every three months. Also, travelers over 11 pay a departure tax when leaving the country. Processing takes two weeks. For more **information,** call (008) 02 60 22 or 13 23 32, or consult any post office.

New Zealand

Applications are available at the local Link Centre, travel agency, or New Zealand Representative. Apply by mail; you must submit (1) a completed application; (2) proof of citizenship; (3) proof of identity; and (4) 2 certified photos. The fee is NZ$56.25, if under 16 NZ$25.30 (NZ$110 and NZ$49.50 if overseas). Processing takes three weeks, but **rush service** is available in emergency. For more **information,** write to New Zealand Passport Office, Documents of National Identity Division, P.O. Box 10-526, Wellington (tel. (04) 474 81 00).

Visas

A visa is a stamp in your passport by a foreign government allowing you to stay in their country for a specified period of time. **American, Canadian, and British citizens** need only a passport to remain in Spain for 90, Portugal for 60, and Morocco for 90 days. **New Zealand citizens** may remain in Spain for 30 days, Portugal for 60 days, and Morocco for 90 days.

If you want to stay for longer, apply for a visa at the country's embassy or consulate in your home country well before your departure (see Useful Addresses: Embassies and Consulates for addresses). Unless you're a student, extending your stay once abroad is more difficult. You must contact the country's immigration officials or local police well before your time is up, although in Portugal you may apply to the *Serviço de Estrangeiros* seven days prior to your original date of expiration. You must show sound proof of financial resources.

For more **information,** send for the U.S. government pamphlet *Foreign Visa Requirements*. Mail a check for US$0.50 to Consumer Information Center, Dept. 454V, Pueblo, CO 81009 (tel. (719) 948-3334). If you don't want to deal with federal bureaucracy, contact **Visa Center, Inc.,** 507 Fifth Ave., Suite 904, New York, NY 10017 (tel. (212) 986-0924). This organization secures visas for travel to and from all possible countries. The service charge varies; the average cost for a U.S. citizen is US$12-15 per visa.

Student and Youth Identification

The **International Student Identity Card (ISIC)** is the most widely accepted form of student identification. The card gets discounts for archaeological sights, theaters, museums, accommodations, and train, ferry, and airplane travel. The ISIC also provides medical/accident insurance of up to US$3000 plus US$100 coverage per day of in-hospital care for up to 60 days. In addition, cardholders have access to a toll-free Traveler's Assistance hotline whose multilingual staff can provide help in medical, legal, and financial emergencies overseas. In many cases, an ordinary student ID from your college will be honored for student discounts as well.

In **Spain,** students with identification are entitled to free admission to state museums and monuments, as well as discounts on international train tickets. In **Portugal,** cardholders receive comparable benefits. In **Morocco,** cardholders get discounts on some Royal Air Maroc flights.

Among the student travel offices that issue ISICs are Council Travel, Let's Go Travel, and Student Travel Network in the U.S.; Travel CUTS in Canada; and any of the organizations under the auspices of the International Student Travel Confederation (ISTC) around the world (see Useful Addresses: Travel Services for addresses). When you apply for the card, pick up a copy of the *International Student Travel Guide,* listing by country some of the discounts available. You can also write to CIEE for a copy.

To apply, supply in person or by mail: (1) current, dated proof of your degree-seeking student status (a letter on school stationery signed and sealed by the registrar, a photocopied grade report, or a Bursar's receipt with school seal indicating full payment for fall 1992, spring 1993, or summer 1993 sessions); (2) a 1 1/2 x 2" photo with your name printed on the back; and (3) the name, address, and phone number of a beneficiary (in the event of the insured's death payment will be made to the beneficiary). You must be at least 12 years old. The 1993 card is valid from Sept. 1992 through Dec. 1993. The fee is US$15.

The US$16 **International Teacher Identity Card (ITIC)** offers identical discounts in theory, but because of its recent introduction many establishments are reluctant to honor it. The application process is the same as for an ISIC.

Federation of International Youth Travel Organizations (FIYTO) issues its own discount card to those who aren't students but are under 26. Also known as the **International Youth Card,** the FIYTO card offers many of the same benefits as the ISIC. Most organizations that sell the ISIC also sell the International Youth Card. To apply, bring (1) proof of birthdate (copy of birth certificate or passport); and (2) a passport-sized photo. The fee is US$10, CDN$12, or £4. For more **information**, contact CIEE (see Useful Addresses: Travel Services) or FIYTO at 81 Islands Brygge, DK-2300

Discounts aren't just for students anymore.

Get the International Youth Card and get reduced airfares, discounts, insurance, and traveler's assistance worldwide.

Call (212) 661-1414, ext. 1109 for more information
or contact any Council Travel office. (See inside front cover.)

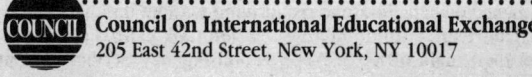

Council on International Educational Exchange
205 East 42nd Street, New York, NY 10017

Copenhagen S, Denmark (tel. (01) 54 60 80). Their free annual catalog lists over 4000 discounts, including airfares, for cardholders.

Hostelling Organizations

> Hostelling International Membership In fall 1992, the International Youth Hostel Federation (IYHF) changed its name to Hostelling International (HI). As the conversion will take some time, you may still see the IYHF name.

A one-year Hostelling International (HI) membership allows you to stay at youth hostels all over Spain, Portugal, and Morocco at unbeatable prices. And you don't need to be a youth; those over 25 pay only slightly more money for a bed. Obtaining a membership card before you leave home will save you time and trouble, and may be cheaper depending on currency exchange rates. (In Spain 1800ptas; in Portugal 3000$.) HI cards are rarely sold on the spot at youth hostels, and only in Spain are they commonly sold at TIVE travel agencies; so you may want to have one before you arrive. For more details on youth hostels, see Once There: Accommodations for each country.

HI cards are available from some travel agencies, including Council Travel, Let's Go Travel, and STA Travel (see Useful Addresses: Travel Services), and from the following organizations:

Hostelling International (HI), headquarters at 9 Guessens Rd., Welwyn Garden City, Herts, AL8 6QW, England (tel. (0707) 33 24 87).

American Youth Hostels (AYH), P.O. Box 37613, Washington, DC 20013-7613 (tel. (202) 783-6161). Fee US$25, under 18 US$10, over 54 US$15. The *Guide to Budget Accommodations, Vol 1: Europe and the Mediterranean* (US$11) lists up-to-date information on HI hostels. Also information on summer positions as group leaders. Distributes the International Youth Hostel Handbook Vol. I and II ($10.95).

Hostelling International—Canada (HIC), National Office, 1600 James Naismith Dr., #608, Gloucester, Ont. K1B 5N4 (tel. (613) 748-5638). Fee CDN$25 plus tax, under 18 CDN$12 plus tax.

Youth Hostels Association of England and Wales (YHA), 14 Southampton St., Covent Garden, London WC2E 7HY (tel. (071) 836 1036). Fee £8.90, ages 16-20 £4.70.

An Óige (Irish Youth Hostel Association), 39 Mountjoy Sq., 1 (tel. (01) 36 31 11; fax (01) 36 58 07). Fee £7.50, under 18 £4.

Australian Youth Hostels Association (AYHA), Level 3, 10 Mallett St., Camperdown, New South Wales, 2050 Australia (tel. (02) 565 1699). Fee AUS$40, renewal AUS$24. Under 18: AUS$12; AUS$12.

Youth Hostels Association of New Zealand, P.O. Box 436, corner of Manchester and Gloucester St., Christchurch 1 (tel. 79 99 70). Fee NZ$34, renewal NZ$24. Under 18: NZ$12; NZ$12.

To reserve spaces in high season, obtain an **International Booking Voucher** from any national youth hostel association (in your home country or the country you'll be visiting) and send it to the desired hostel four to eight weeks in advance of your stay. N.B.: This preapplication is why school groups get dibs on rooms when they breeze into town. If your plans are firm enough to allow it, pre-booking is wise.

International Driving Permit and Insurance Certificate

An **International Driving Permit** is officially required to drive in Spain, unless you have a valid driver's license from an EEC country. Although not required in Portugal and Morocco, where you can drive with a valid American or Canadian license for up to three months, the permit smooths out difficulties with foreign police officers and is an additional piece of identification. However, the permit isn't required at most car rental agencies, so you can choose to risk driving without one.

The **American Automobile Association (AAA)** sells permits at all of their offices. Contact their main office at AAA Travel Agency Services Department, 1000 AAA

Drive (mail stop 100), Heathrow, FL 32746 (tel. (800) 222-4357). In Canada, the **Canadian Automobile Association (CAA)** sells permits at their branch offices. Their main office is at Toronto Head Office, 2 Carlton St., Toronto, Ont. M5B 1K4 (tel. (416) 964-3170). You must submit (1) a completed application; (2) two recent passport-sized photos; (3) a valid U.S. or Canadian driver's license (which must always accompany the International Driving Permit). The fee is US$10 (€DN$14). You must be over 18.

Standard insurance is covered by most credit cards. If you rent, lease, or borrow a car, you'll need a **green card,** or **International Insurance Certificate**, to *prove* that you have liability insurance. Get it through the car **rental agency;** most of them include coverage in their prices. If you lease a car, get a green card through the dealer. Some travel agents offer the card, and it's available at the border. If you have auto insurance that applies abroad, you'll still need a green card to certify this to foreign officials. Inquire at the Foreign Motoring Services division of AAA or CAA (see addresses above).

Money

The information in this book was researched in the summer of 1992. Since then, prices may have risen by as much as 5-15%. The exchange rates listed (see Appendix) were compiled in early September. Since rates fluctuate considerably, check them before you go in a national newspaper.

For information on banking hours, Value-Added Tax (VAT), and tipping in Spain, Portugal, and Morocco, see Once There: More Money for each country.

Currency and Exchange

In Spain the unit of currency is the *peseta* (pta); in Portugal, the *escudo* ($); in Morocco, the *dirham* (dh).

Before leaving home, buy about US$75 in the currency of the first country you'll visit to save time and money at the airport—the poor exchange rate at home banks still beats that at an airport.

Once there, shop around at **banks** for the best rates. Commission charges sometimes outweigh a good exchange rate. Conversion charges are usually calculated by bulk sum rather than percentage, so it's preferable to convert infrequently and in large amounts. On the other hand, don't convert more than is safe to carry around. For typical banking hours in Spain, Portugal, and Morocco, see the Appendix.

In Portugal, banks in larger cities often have high-tech. **automatic exchange machines.** Like ATMs, these machines provide 24-hour service. Simply insert American bills, and *escudos* pop out. In Spain, large airports have these machines, but they are otherwise rare.

Traveler's Checks

Traveler's checks are the safest way to carry money, can be replaced if lost or stolen, and may save you money (since commission charges are nonexistent or lower than for currency). Most banks and several agencies sell checks, usually at face value plus a 1% commission.

Although some low-cost establishments don't accept checks as payment, you can change them in for currency at American Express offices and most banks. If you bring checks, you need bring almost no cash from your home country (but it's still useful to have a bit for emergencies). The major brands of checks (such as American Express, Visa, Thomas Cook/MasterCard) are recognized across Spain and Portugal. In Morocco most banks recognize major checks, but many smaller hotels and restaurants only accept American Express.

If your checks are lost or stolen, expect red tape and delays. To expedite the refund process, keep your check receipts in a safe place separate from your checks. Also leave the check numbers with a loved one at home. To help identify which checks are missing, record check numbers before you go and tick them off every time you cash some.

When you buy your checks, ask for a list of refund centers. Most importantly, keep a separate stash of cash or checks for emergencies.

American Express (in the U.S. and Canada tel. (800) 221-7282); in the U.K. (088) 52 13 13; in Australia, New Zealand, and the S. Pacific (02) 886 06 89; from elsewhere collect (801) 964 66 65). Checks in 7 currencies with 1% commission, none for AAA members. Check for Two, a new option, allows two people traveling together to sign for one set of checks. Many offices cash AmEx checks without commission and have their own travel agency. Call for (or pick up at travel agencies) their free booklet *Traveler's Companion,* which lists every AmEx office in the world. Call their **Global Assist hotline** (in the U.S. (800) 554-2639; from elsewhere collect (202) 783-7474) for medical and legal referrals, weather information, urgent message relay, and other travel emergencies.

Bank of America (in the U.S. tel. (800) 227-3460); from elsewhere collect (415) 624-5400). Checks in US$ only with 1% commission. **Travel Assistance hotline** (in the U.S. tel. (800) 368-7878; from elsewhere collect (202) 347-7113) offers free legal and medical assistance, urgent message relay, lost document services, translator/interpreter referral, and up to US$1000 advanced to a medical facility for prompt treatment (tel. (01) 629 74 66).

Barclays Bank (in the U.S. and Canada tel. (800) 221-2426; in the U.K. (202) 67 12 12; from elswhere collect (212) 858-8500). Checks in US$, CDN$, British pounds, and German marks with 1% commission.

Citicorp (in the U.S. and Canada tel. (800) 645-6556; from elsewhere collect (813) 623-1709). Checks in US$, British pounds, German marks, and Japanese yen with 1-2.5% commission. **Travel Assist Hotline** (tel. (800) 523-1199) is a slightly abridged version of Europe Assistance Worldwide's Travel Assist program.

MasterCard International (in the U.S. and Canada tel. (800) 223-7373; from elsewhere collect (212) 974-5696). Checks in 11 currencies with 1% commission. Available also from **Thomas Cook** (tel. same as MasterCard).

Visa International (in the U.S. and Canada tel. (800) 227-6811; from elsewhere collect (415) 574-7111). Checks in 13 currencies. Commission depends on the issuing bank.

Credit Cards

While many low-cost establishments don't honor credit cards, they can still be invaluable. Pay by credit card whenever possible, since credit cards get the best exchange rate of all.

Moreover, major credit cards instantly extract cash advances from banks and ATMs throughout Western Europe in the local currency (albeit with hefty charges). Some cards enable you to cash personal checks. If traveler's checks are lost or stolen, credit cards provide cash until the checks are replaced. Credit cards also offer an array of services, from insurance to emergency assistance. If a family member has a credit card, an additional card can be issued in your name, with bills (and an extra fee) going to your beloved.

American Express, MasterCard, and Visa are the most welcomed cards. In Europe, **MasterCard** is called Eurocard, while **Visa** is called Carte Bleue; however, their logos are the same. In Spain, Visa is far more widely accepted than MasterCard. AmEx may be the best choice, since branch offices throughout the world offer all kinds of services tailored to the needs of travelers. Call the credit card company to find out where your card is accepted and where ATMs accept it (see Traveler's Checks for phone numbers).

American Express. Membership fee $55 per year. Personal checks up to US$1000 (US$5000 with Gold Card) cashed and mail held for cardholders. Purchase Protection Plan insures most purchases for 90 days against theft or accidental damage (up to $1000). Special benefits for student cardholders include vouchers for discount airfares within the continental U.S (tel. (800) 695-9900). See Traveler's Checks for additional services.

MasterCard and Visa. Issued by individual banks, each of which determine their card's membership fees and benefits.

ATMs

Most ATMs (automatic teller machines) in Europe belong to the **Cirrus** network (tel. (800) 424-7787). ATMs accept either major credit cards or "cash cards" from your lo-

Don't forget to write.

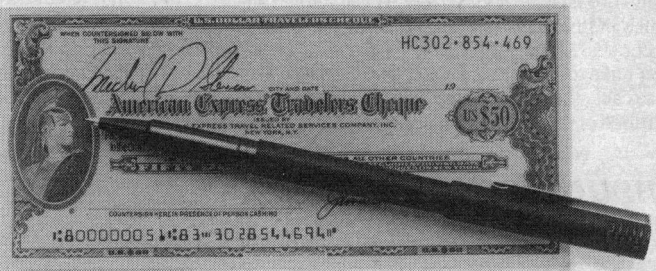

Now that you've said, "Let's go," it's time to say, "Let's get American Express® Travelers Cheques." Because when you want your travel money to go a long way, it's a good idea to protect it. So before you leave, be sure and write.

© 1992 American Express Travel Related Services Company, Inc.

cal bank. For withdrawals in the local currency, both cards offer better exchange rates than banks or traveler's checks. But whereas credit cards charge a hefty fee for each transaction, cash cards don't. Beware—in Europe ATMs often don't accept personal identification numbers (PINs) longer than 4 digits, so have yours changed before you leave home. If your credit card has no PIN, have the credit card company assign you one.

Sending Money Abroad

American Express cardmembers can cash personal **checks** that are sent to them at any AmEx office. Outside AmEx offices, cashing a check in a foreign currency takes weeks and a US$30 fee to clear. If you have a **credit card,** someone back home can deposit money to your account, so that you can then withdraw it from an ATM. Otherwise, money can be **wired** to you through AmEx or Western Union.

American Express, MoneyGram Customer Service (in the U.S. tel. (800) 543-4080; in Canada tel. (800) 933-3278). Their MoneyGram Service wires money (to Spain in 10min.). If you have an AmEx Optima card, you can wire by phone; otherwise, go in person to an AmEx office. The money is disbursed in AmEx traveler's checks (in US$). The charge is US$45 to send US$500; US$70 to send US$1000. Not every AmEx office will handle MoneyGrams.

Western Union (in the U.S. tel. (800) 325-6000, 325-4176). Takes 2-5 business days. If you have a MasterCard or Visa, you can cable up to the credit limit of the card by phone. Otherwise, go in person to a Western Union office with cash or a cashier's check (no money orders). Money arrives at the central telegram office (or sometimes at a large commercial bank). You can pick it up by showing proof of ID. The charge is US$65 to send US$500; US$75 to send US$1000. In Spain and Portugal, Western Union reaches only really big cities; in Morocco, only Casablanca.

Money can also be **cabled** from bank to bank. Both sender and receiver must have accounts at the respective banks. The sender must give exact information, including passport number and the recipient bank name and address. Send through an international bank that has an office in your home country; local banks are slower. Transfer takes from one day to a week; the fee is usually a flat US$20-30.

In life or death emergencies, the **State Department's Citizens Emergency Center,** Dept. of State, 2201 C St. NW, Washington, DC 20520 (tel. (202) 647-5225; at night, Sun., and holidays tel. (202) 647-4000), will send U.S. citizens money. For a fee of about US$25, they'll send the money within hours to the nearest consular office. They don't like to send sums greater than US$500. The quickest way to have the money sent is to cable the money to the State Department through Western Union; or to bring cash, certified check, bank draft, or money order to the State Department.

Insurance

When buying travel, theft/loss, accident, or health insurance, beware of unnecessary coverage—your current policies might extend to travel-related concerns. **Medicare's** foreign travel coverage is limited to Canada and Mexico. **Canadians** are protected by their home province's health insurance plan; check with the provincial Ministry of Health or Health Plan Headquarters. **Homeowners' insurance** (or that of your family) often covers theft while traveling and loss of documents (passport, plane ticket, railpass, etc.) up to about US$500. **AmEx cardholders** receive automatic car rental and flight insurance on purchases made with the card.

University term-time medical plans often cover summer travel. The **ISIC, ITIC,** and **FIYTO card** provide US$3000 worth of accident insurance plus US$100 per day for up to 60 days of in-hospital care coverage. CIEE also offers an inexpensive **Trip-Safe** package for cardholders that doubles coverage of medical treatment, accident, and charter flights missed due to illness. If you're ineligible for these cards, Trip-Safe extends coverage of the insurance you have.

File insurance claims upon return home. Keep all relevant documents (such as police reports, doctor's statements, receipts). Check the time limit on filing to make sure that you'll be returning home in time to secure reimbursement. The following firms offer insurance programs; almost all cover trip cancellation and medical expenses in some form.

>**Access America, Inc.,** 6600 W. Broad St., P.O. Box 90310, Richmond, VA 23620 (tel. (800) 284-8300). 24-hr. hotline. Covers trip cancellation/interruption, theft, loss of luggage, on-the-spot hospital admittance costs, and emergency medical evacuation.
>
>**ARM Coverage, Inc.,** P.O. Box 310, 120 Mineola Blvd., Mineola, NY 11501 (tel. (800) 323-3149 or (516) 294-0220). Quite comprehensive Carefree Travel policy. 24-hr. hotline. Covers theft, loss of luggage, and injury.
>
>**Travel Assistance International,** 1133 15th St. NW, #400, Washington, DC 20005 (tel. (800) 821-2828). Travel packages include medical and travel insurance, medical and legal referrals, and lost passport/visa assistance. 1-yr. policy (US$150) covers all trips under 90 days.
>
>**Travel Guard International,** 1145 Clark St., Stevens Point, WI 54481 (tel. (800) 782-5151). Their slick Travel Guard Gold policy covers trip cancellation/interruption, penalty waiver, baggage delay, and accidental death and dismemberment. Fee is 8% of your trip cost. Their Scholar Care policy (US$291 per yr.) is tailored to students and teachers spending a year or semester abroad.

Packing

Pack light. Set out everything you think you'll need, eliminate half, and take more money. Once you're on the road you'll be thankful. Portly luggage marks you as a tourist, and if your luggage is too unwieldy you're liable to start blubbering. You can buy anything you need in Europe.

Luggage

Decide what kind of luggage is best suited for your trip.

>**Internal-frame backpack**: Ideal if you're planning to hike over a lot of ground or camp; get one with several external compartments. Some of them convert into a more normal-looking suitcase, for when you feel like looking normal. More cumbersome, an **external-frame** pack offers added support, distributes weight better, and allows for a sleeping bag to be strapped on. External-frame packs have been known to get caught and mangled in airline baggage conveyors; tie down any loose parts to minimize risk. In any case, get a pack with a strong, padded hip belt to transfer the weight from your weary shoulders to your legs. Quality packs cost anywhere from US$125 to US$300.
>
>**Light suitcase, carry-on/overnight bag, or large shoulder bag:** Best suited for people who plan to stay in cities and large towns and don't want to stand out as budget tourists.
>
>**Daypack or bookbag:** Bring a smaller bag in addition to a larger pack or suitcase. Make sure it's big enough to hold lunch, camera, water bottle, and *Let's Go*. Frees you up from your larger pack, which you can store in a locker or leave in a hotel. Get one with secure zippers and closures.

Clothing and Footwear

Bring few, but comfortable clothes; many people recommend mix-and-matchables. Keep accessories to a minimum.

>**In general:** Dark-colored clothes show dirt less than light ones; a small (not brightly colored) print also hides stains and spots. Loose garments which can be layered are more versatile. Sturdy cotton-blend pants or a longish skirt are appropriate in more situations than are jeans, and are faster-drying to boot. For women, the longer skirt is an excellent option, being cooler, looser, and more non-tourist-looking than pants or shorts. Bring non-wrinkling, quick-drying clothes that you can wash in a sink (laundromats are very expensive and may be hard to find). When traveling in summer, natural fibers and cotton blends are the coolest choices; synthetics trap heat.
>
>**Conservative clothes:** Dress codes are extremely important for both men and women. Running shorts, cut-offs, tank and tube tops, and T-shirts mark the tourist. Bare shoulders and bare knees are considered immodest, especially in the countryside. Churches, synagogues, and other places of worship often refuse admission to visitors who have not bothered to cover up. Worse, if you look like a ragamuffin, locals may zap you with the evil eye (especially in small towns); you'll

Don't let bad water ruin your trip.

One out of two world travelers will get sick. Drinking contaminated water is the number one cause. PŪR water purifiers make the water safe to drink.

You're planning a great trip—investing lots of time and money. You don't want to miss a thing. But you worry. You've heard stories. Will you get sick? Is any water really safe? Will you be out enjoying the day as planned? Or will you be spending your days with cramps and diarrhea, hoping the medications will work?

Don't let bad drinking water turn your trip-of-a-lifetime into a nightmare. Wherever you travel, before you drink the local water, purify it with PŪR™ water purifiers—The only ones that instantly remove Giardia and eliminate all other microorganisms including bacteria and viruses. PŪR water purifiers are affordable, lightweight, and easy to use.

Don't let bad water ruin your trip. Make sure it's safe. Make sure it's PŪR. For more information or to order,

Call 1-800-845-PURE

Water Purifiers

"My fellow travelers experienced stomach upset and worse while I was completely fine."
—Ellen R. Benjamin, Ph.D.

© 1992 PŪR, a division of Recovery Engineering, Inc., 2229 Edgewood Avenue South, Minneapolis, MN 55426

need four Marías (only one need be a virgin) to remove it. (Also, see Specific Concerns: Women Travelers.)

Walking shoes: A must, whether you're in the city or the country. Sneakers or sandals fall apart faster than you can say "bocadillo." Sturdy, rubber-soled shoes made for walking (not for tennis, basketball, or running) will serve you best. Always break in your shoes and/or hiking boots before you go to avoid agonizing blisters.

Socks: A double pair of socks—thin polypropylene for a lining and light wool outside—will cushion and keep dry your feet. Polypropylene dries very fast and allows your feet to breathe.

Don't forget: Raingear and a light sweater or jacket, even in summer. Gloves and thermal underwear are handy, perhaps necessary, in winter.

Miscellaneous

You'll find the following miscellaneous items valuable.

umbrella	Ziploc bags (for damp clothes, soap, food)
petite alarm clock	waterproof matches
sun hat	moleskin (for blisters)
needle and thread	safety pins
sunglasses	a personal stereo (Walkperson) with headphones
pocketknife	notebook and pens
plastic water bottle	pocket English-language phrasebook
small flashlight	string (makeshift clothesline and lashing material)
towel	rubber squash ball (universal plug for sinks without stoppers)

An all-purpose **first-aid kit** includes: bandages, aspirin, medications for motion sickness and diarrhea, mild antiseptic soap, antibiotic ointment such as Bacitracin, mosquito repellent, an antihistamine, sunscreen, and lip balm.

Stores in Europe stock most **toiletries**. Still, a **cold-water soap** always comes in handy (what could be more *a propos* than all-natural Dr. Bronner's Castile Soap, sold at camping stores, usable for anything from washing clothes, bathing, and shampooing to brushing your teeth). Tampons and contact-lens fluids tend to be expensive, so bring some. Don't expect to find your preferred brand of condoms (see Health below).

If planning to stay in youth hostels, make the requisite **sleepsack** yourself (instead of paying the hostel's linen charge). Fold a full size sheet in half the long way, then sew it closed along the open long side and one of the short sides.

If you must bring electrical appliances you'll need a **converter**. North American current runs at 110 volts AC, while in Europe most outlets are 220V AC. Also, as European outlets are made for 2 round prongs, you'll need an **adapter**. Converters and adapters are sold at many hardware stores. If you don't feel like going to the hardware store, order a converter or the free pamphlet *Foreign Electricity is No Deep Dark Secret* by mail, write to the Franzus Company, Murtha Industrial Park, P.O. Box 142, Beacon Falls, CT 06403 (tel. (203) 723-6664).

Film is expensive in Europe. Despite disclaimers, airport security X-rays can fog film. A lead-lined pouch, sold at camera stores, protects film. Pack it in your carry-on luggage, since airline people use higher-intensity X-rays on checked luggage. Although developing is inexpensive and fast in Spain, the use of non-standard chemicals sometimes does weird things; try to wait to develop your pictures until you get home.

Have your laptop or notebook **computer** and disks hand-inspected at the airport, lest stray X-rays erase their memory.

English-language books, whether novels or *Let's Go,* are expensive overseas and don't exist in smaller towns. If you decide to pack books for your trip, try used bookstores; you can buy novels for a dollar or two, then chuck them when you're on the road so that you're not loaded down. People you meet on the road may want to swap books with you; some of your books may still be on the travelers' circuit ten, maybe twenty years from now.

The entire *Let's Go* series is quite elusive in Spain, Portugal, and Morocco. If you're planning to travel to more countries it's wise to buy the guides back home (we're not pulling your leg; we don't work on commission). In our Orientation and Practical Information listings for each town, we'll tell you where English-language books are sold.

Camping

Purchase **equipment** before you leave. As a rule, prices drop in fall when stores clear out their old merchandise.

Backpacks: See Luggage above.

Synthetic-filled sleeping bag: Cheaper, more durable, and faster drying than a down-filled one. Bags are rated according to the lowest temperature in which they can be used. A three-season bag (US$110; down-filled US$135) keeps you warm even below freezing point. A less hard-core bag costs about US$40.

Pads: A cushion between your soft body and the hard ground. An **ensolite pad** (US$10-15) is warmer than the foam kind and keeps you warm and dry. A **Thermarest air mattress** (US$40) is a deluxe ensolite pad and air mattress that virtually inflates itself; like sleeping on air. Regular air mattresses start at US$50.

Stuff bags: To store your sleeping bag and pad. They're usually included in the price of a sleeping bag.

Tents: Expensive, but crucial if you plan to camp a lot. Last year's models are often drastically reduced. Get one with a rain fly and bug netting. For two people, a two-person tent (US$100) is a bit tight; consider a four-person model (US$130).

Tarpaulin or **plastic groundcloth:** To put under the tent.

Campstoves: Don't rely on campfire cooking; some regions restrict fires. Simple stoves (US$40-125) burn butane or white gas. Also bring a mess kit and a battery-operated lantern.

Other: Waterproof matches; insect repellent; calamine lotion; and water-purification pills.

The following **organizations** provide advice and/or supplies.

Campmor, 810 Rte. 17 N, P.O. Box 997-LG92, Paramus, NJ 07653-0997 (tel. (800) 526-4784). Name-brand equipment at low prices.

L.L. Bean, 1 Casco St., Freeport, ME 04033 (tel. (800) 221-4221; customer service tel. (800) 341-4341). Equipment and preppy outdoor clothing favored by rich northeastern Americans, but ultra-

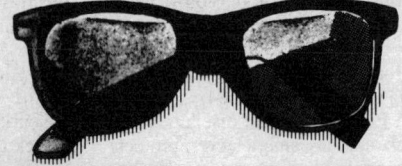

ISRAEL
COME SEE FOR YOURSELF

Find out about a wide variety of exciting programs for college students:

- KIBBUTZ
- UNIVERSITY STUDY
- SUMMER TOURS
- ARCHAEOLOGICAL DIGS
- INTERNSHIPS
- POST GRAD
- YESHIVA
- VOLUNTEER

Just call for more information:
ISRAEL UNIVERSITY CENTER/USD AZYF
110 East 59th Street, 3rd Floor, New York, NY 10022
(212) 339-6941   1-800-27 ISRAEL
We Fly El Al Israel Airlines!
STUDY, TRAVEL, WORK OPPORTUNITIES

stocked, high-quality, and chock-full of information. Call or write for their free catalog. Open 24 hrs.

National Campers and Hikers Association, Inc., 4804 Transit Rd., Bldg. 2, Depew, NY 14043-4906 (tel. (716) 668-6242). Sells the International Camping Carnet, required at some European campgrounds (US$30 includes membership in their association). Also has a short bibliography of camping travel guides and a list of camping stores in major European cities.

Recreational Equipment, Inc. (REI), Sumner, WA 98302 (tel. (800) 426-4840). Long-time outdoor equipment cooperative favorite of outdoorsy northwestern types. Lifetime membership (not required) US$10. Sells *Europa Camping and Caravanning* (US$13), an encyclopedic listing of campsites in Europe.

Health

See Packing: Miscellaneous above for a suggested compact **first-aid kit**.

If you wear **glasses** or **contact lenses,** take an extra pair along. It's wise to leave a copy of your prescription with someone at home so you can have a new pair sent if disaster strikes. Contact wearers should pack plenty of lens solution, as it may be difficult to find in Europe. Pack these things in your carry-on bag.

If you'll be taking any **medication** while traveling, obtain a full supply before you leave, since matching your prescription with a foreign equivalent is a total nightmare and if you pop a strange variant of your favorite drug you may freak out. Always carry up-to-date prescriptions (including the medication's trade name, manufacturer, chemical name, and dosage) and a statement from your doctor. If you use **birth control pills**, definitely stock up. **Condoms** are in stores under the name of *preservativo* in Spain and are often over-the-counter, usually in pharmacies. (See Once There: Stores: Pharmacies for each country.) However, you may feel more comfortable using your old-reliable American condoms.

Consult your doctor regarding hepatitis, cholera, and typhoid **shots** as well as malaria pills. In Morocco, watch any open sores, scratches, cuts, or mosquito bites: heat and iffy sanitation conditions increase the likelihood of infection.

Food poisoning can spoil your trip. In Spain you can pretty well do as you would in your home country. In some areas of Portugal and throughout Morocco, street vendors sell aged or otherwise fishy food; avoid unpeeled fruits and vegetables, particularly hard-to-wash leafy greens. Drink plenty of bottled fluids.

In Morocco, drinking water from the village pump is a serious risk; you may want to rely on bottled or boiled water. Insist on breaking the plastic seal on the bottle yourself before paying to make sure you're not getting tap water. Please remember, if you can't drink the water, you can't suck the ice. For information on **diabetic travelers,** see Specific Concerns: Specific Diets.

Overexposure to **sun** is always dangerous. In summer, residents of Spain, Portugal, and Morocco frequently restrict their activities during the hottest parts of the day. Follow their example and drink plenty of liquids to avoid unnecessary fatigue, sunburn, and heat stroke. Soothe a case of **prickly heat** (strange rash) by bathing frequently, dusting with talcum powder, and keeping cool. Wear that sun hat, sunglasses, and SPF 30 **sunscreen** unless you want to look like the Queen Mother when you're 35.

If you have a medical condition that can't easily be recognized (diabetes, allergies to antibiotics, epilepsy, heart conditions, *sidus inverses*) you should buy the potentially lifesaving **Medic Alert identification tag.** This internationally recognized tag indicates the condition and provides the number of Medic Alert's 24-hr. hotline, through which medical personnel can obtain information about your medical history. Lifetime membership, which includes a steel tag, costs US$35. Contact Medic Alert Foundation International, P.O. Box 1009, Turlock, CA 95381-1009 (tel. (800) 432-5378; emergency (209) 634-4917).

In remote areas you may have difficulty finding emergency medical care. The **International Association for Medical Assistance to Travelers (IAMAT)** is a non-profit organization that provides medical care to travelers by doctors trained in Europe or North America. It charges according to a set payment schedule. There's no charge for membership, though they want you to give them money since IAMAT relies on voluntary contributions. Members receive qualified medical assistance from English-speaking physicians and a mountain of paraphernalia: an ID card, an international directory of IAMAT physicians, a chart detailing advisable immunizations for 200 countries and territories, and charts noting areas of risk for malaria and other diseases. Wait, there's more—IAMAT also tells members how to take preventitive measures against infectious diseases. People who donate at least US$25 also get a packet of 24 World Climate Charts, advice on recommended seasonal clothing and sanitary conditions of water, milk, and food in 140 cities around the world. Send for their booklets *How to Adjust to the Heat, How to Adapt to Altitude,* and *How to Avoid Traveler's Diarrhea.* Contact IAMAT in the U.S. at 417 Center St., Lewiston, NY 14092 (tel. (716) 754-4883); in Canada at 40 Regal St., Guelph, Ont. N1K 1B5 (tel. (519) 836-0102).

American, Canadian, and British embassies and consulates and AmEx offices can also help find English-speaking doctors. Full payment in cash before checkout (sometimes before treatment) is virtually the rule at most European hospitals.

Safety

The **emergency police number** is: 091 in Spain, 115 in Portugal, and 19 in Morocco. Memorize it.

To avoid falling prey to thieves and hustlers, always look like you know what's up. Keep money and valuables with you at all times, especially while you're sleeping, perhaps in a **moneybelt** or **neck pouch** or stuffed in your bra or pinned to your underclothes. On the cutting edge of theft-proof bodywear is the **leg pouch.** Thieves can easily slip into your moneybelt on a crowded bus, but it's much harder to get into your pants. If you're carrying a zippered backpack, use a small lock. Be wary—sneaky crooks have been known to slit open backpacks and purses with razorblades while their victims are spacing out.

In major cities, watch out for thieves who are fast and professional. Remember that **pickpockets** come in all shapes and sizes and are in on some unbelievable rackets. Because pros can unzip a bag in just a few seconds, wear yours with the opening against your body. Threading a safety pin or keyring through both zippers on a pack makes it difficult to open quickly and prevents it from slipping open accidentally.

Never leave valuables unattended, even during the day. If you plan to sleep outside or don't want to carry everything with you, store your gear at a train or bus station. (See Appendix: Luggage Storage.)

Overnight **trains** are favorite hangouts for petty criminals. Always steer clear of empty train compartments, particularly at night. Size potential berth-mates up carefully and avoid fishy ones. If you have a compartment on a train and you are sure the train won't be stopping, sleep with the window open; berths have been known to be gassed and burgled. In a couchette, try to reserve a top bunk when you buy your ticket; the awkward height may deter theives. Don't check luggage on trains, especially if switching trains en route.

Make photocopies of all **important documents,** including your passport, identification, credit cards, and traveler's check serial numbers. Keep one set in your luggage and leave another set with friends at home. Although copies won't substitute for lost or stolen documents, they'll expedite replacements.

In **Morocco,** solo travelers may be singled out for harassment. Firmly saying *imshi* (go away) will sometimes stop hecklers. Don't tolerate any prolonged harassment, even if it means protesting loudly; passers-by will generally come to your assistance if you yell. Invitations to a home-cooked Moroccan meal or friendly directions to a bargain rug dealer are possible lures into a huge scam. (See Morocco: Once There: Hustlers and Guides.)

For more information, see Specific Concerns: **Women Travelers.**

Specific Concerns (Alphabetically)

Diets

Diabetic

People with diabetes should consult the *Ticket to Safe Travel,* a booklet put out by the **American Diabetes Association,** 1660 Duke St., Alexandria, VA 22314 (tel. (800) 232-3472). The ADA can also give you a wallet-size ID card with information on diabetes.

Halal

For halal food, look under "halal" in the yellow pages of phone books, where shops and restaurants (if they exist) will be listed. In large cities, try the Muslim quarters.

Kosher

The prospects aren't so good in Spain, Portugal, and Morocco. For **information** about kosher food abroad, consult *The Jewish Travel Guide* (US$11.50, US$1.50 postage), which lists kosher restaurants, synagogues, and other Jewish institutions in over 80 countries. Write to **Sephor-Herman Press, Inc.,** 1265 46th St., Brooklyn, NY 11219 (tel. (718) 972-9010). In the U.K., order it from **Jewish Chronicle Publications,** 25 Furnival St., London EC4A 1JT, United Kingdom.

Vegetarian

Spain, Portugal, and Morocco can be a vegetarian's paradise. Virtually every town has a local **market,** where produce is fresh and inexpensive (under each city see Food for addresses and hours). Vegetarian restaurants are quite common in larger cities and tourist resorts *(Let's Go* lists many of the best). Contact the following for more information.

North American Vegetarian Society, P.O. Box 72, Dolgeville, NY 13329 (tel. (518) 568-7970).

The Vegetarian Society of the U.K., Parkdale, Dunham Rd., Altrincham, Cheshire WA14 4QG, England (tel. 06 (19) 28 07 03).

Drugs

Don't buy drugs and never carry drugs across borders. The horror stories about drug busts in Europe and North Africa are grounded in fact. Every year, hundreds (nobody really knows how many, but it's a lot) of travelers are arrested in foreign countries for illegal possession, use, and trafficking of drugs. About forty percent of those arrested are charged with possession of a tiny amount of marijuana (as little as a single seed). Some countries—Morocco—are especially severe in their treatment of those arrested on dope-related charges.

Although plenty of locals may be using hashish, this openness is an illusion. In **Morocco** dealers often work for the police. In one racket, a drug dealer sells to a foreign visitor, heads straight for the police, describes the patron in detail, collects a fee for information, and gets the goods back when the buyer is arrested.

Your government is completely powerless in the judicial system of a foreign country. Consular officers can only visit a prisoner, provide a list of attorneys, and inform family and friends. Once you leave your home country, you are not covered by its laws. The legal codes in some countries, including Morocco, provide for guilt by association; *you* may be charged if your companions are found in possession of illegal drugs. This is scary stuff—the burden of proof usually lies on the accused to prove her or his innocence; and many countries will not give you the benefits of jury trial, bail, or parole.

For more **information** on the subject of drugs overseas, send for the free pamphlet *Travel Warning on Drugs Abroad* from the Bureau of Consular Affairs, Public Affairs #5807, Dept. of State, Washington, DC 20520 (tel. (202) 647-1488). Enclose a stamped, self-addressed envelope.

Gay and Lesbian Travelers

In Spain and Portugal, the legal minimum age for sexual intercourse is 18. Some consider the gay scene in **Spain** the most open in Europe; in the major cities (Madrid, Barcelona) people are quite tolerant. Eivissa (Ibiza) and Cádiz also have thriving gay communities. The encyclopedic **Guía Gay Visado,** written in Spanish and sold in Barcelona and gay bookstores elsewhere, is the only Spain-specific guide to gay and lesbian entertainment. It has annually-updated listings for cities across Spain. (As of fall 1992, the English translation had been seized by U.S. Customs, hence wasn't sold in the U.S.; bookstores in London weren't been able to get it either. Contact the nearest gay bookstore for an update.)

Portugal, on the other hand, some consider rather conservative. Gay people should exercise discretion, especially in less urban areas. In **Morocco,** both civil and Islamic law prohibit the practice of homosexuality.

Under each major city in *Let's Go*, see Orientation and Practical Information: Gay and Lesbian Services for bookstores, hotlines, and information specific to individual cities. Also, check kiosks and bookstores in each city you visit for local publications and services.

>**Are You Two Together?** (US$18). Mostly travel essays with useful information on Western European capitals and gay resorts. Humorously written by a lesbian couple. Covers both lesbian and gay male travelers, but better for lesbians.
>
>**Ferrari Publications,** P.O. Box 35575, Phoenix, AZ 85069 (tel. (602) 863-2408). Publishes *Places of Interest* (US$12.95), *Places for Women* (US$9), *Places for Men* (US$12.95), and *Inn Places: USA and Worldwide Gay Accommodations* (US$14.95).
>
>**Gay's The Word,** 66 Marchmont St., London WCIN 1AB, England (tel. (71) 278 76 54). Full of information; periodicals for gay and lesbian travelers. Prints bimonthly review. Open Mon-Fri. 11am-7pm, Sat. 10am-6pm, Sun. and Bank Holidays 2-6pm.
>
>**Giovanni's Room,** 345 S. 12th St., Philadelphia, PA 19107 (tel. (215) 923-2960). Bookstore with an enormous range of gay travel guides, including all those mentioned here. Big mail order business worldwide. Shipping costs US$3.50 per book in the U.S.
>
>**Metro Man 1993.** A new guide for gay men covering major cities worldwide. In German and English; published by a German company.
>
>**Odysseus Guide 1991**: USA and International (US $18), Odysseus Enterprises, P.O. Box 7695, Flushing, NY. A good accommodations guide.
>
>**Open Leaves,** 71 Cardigan St., Carlton, Victoria 3053, Australia. Carries some of the guides listed here.
>
>**Renaissance House,** Box 292, Village Station, New York, NY 10014-0292 (tel. (212) 674-0120). Distributes *Spartacus International Gay Guide* (see below), as well as other gay guides and resources.
>
>**Spartacus International Gay Guide** (US$27.95), Bruno Gmünder Publishing, 100 E. Biddle St., Baltimore, Maryland 21202 (tel. (301) 727-5677; fax (301) 727-5998). One of the oldest and most popular guides for gay men. Lists bars, clubs, bathhouses, cruising areas, restaurants, hotels, bookstores, and hotlines worldwide. Some complain that it's only scantily updated and isn't hip enough.
>
>**Women Going Places** (US$14), 9-11 Kensington High St., London W8, England. Also distributed by Inland Book Company, P.O. Box 121261, East Haven, CT 06512 (tel. (203) 467-4257). Annually revised international guide for lesbians (and all women) that lists women-owned and -operated enterprises, local lesbian, feminist, and gay info numbers, bookstores, restaurants, hotels, and meeting places. Formerly called *Gaia's Guide*.

Senior Travelers

In **Spain,** only Spanish seniors receive a discount on train fares with RENFE's *Tarjeta Dorada* (Gold Card). However, Spanish national museums and monuments are free to the Queen Mother and seniors of any nationality. **Portugal** offers similar transportation discounts. Generally, discounts may be limited to national or EEC citizens.

In many cases, student discounts are available to senior citizens as well. An **HI card** is US$15 if you're over 54. (See Documents: Hostelling International Membership above.) Always ask if there are discounts for seniors. The following organizations and publications provide information on services and discounts for senior travelers.

American Association of Retired Persons (AARP), Special Services Dept., 601 E St. NW, Washington, DC 20049 (tel. (800) 227-7737; for travel info (202) 434-2277). Membership open to anyone over 49 (US$8). AARP Travel Services gives benefits to members and their spouses. Also, discounts on hotels, motels, and car rental and sightseeing companies.

Bureau of Consular Affairs, Superintendent of Documents, U.S. Government Printing Office, Washington, DC 20402 (tel. (202) 783-3238). Information on passports, visas, health, and currency. Send for *Travel Tips for Older Americans* ($1). Allow 4 wks. for delivery.

Elderhostel, 75 Federal St., 3rd fl., Boston, MA 02110 (tel. (617) 426-7788). Weeklong residential academic programs (US$1500-5000) at colleges in over 40 countries in Europe and the Americas. Fee includes room, board, tuition, and extracurriculars. Must be over 59 to enroll; companions must be over 49.

Gateway Books, 13 Bedford Cove, San Rafael, CA 94901 (tel. (415) 454-5215). Publishes Adele and Gene Malott's *Get Up and Go: A Guide for the Mature Traveler* (US$10.95, postage $1.90), which recommends places to visit and general budgeting hints.

National Council of Senior Citizens, 1331 F St. NW, Washington, DC 20004 (tel. (202) 347-8800). Annual (US$12) or lifetime (US$150) membership provides supplemental Medicare insurance as well as discounts on hotels, car rentals, and travel agents.

Pilot Books, 103 Cooper St., Babylon, NY 11702 (tel. (516) 422-2225). Publishes *The International Health Guide for Senior Citizen Travelers* (US$4.95) and newly-revised *The Senior Citizens' Guide to Budget Travel in Europe* (US$5.95). Postage for each book US$1.

Travelers with Children

Avoid hassles by booking rooms in advance and planning sightseeing stops that your children will enjoy; a day spent admiring the Velázquez paintings in the Prado will probably result in frazzled nerves for both adults and kids.

LEARN SPANISH IN SPAIN

★SALAMANCA - The university city where people speak standard Spanish.

★INTENSIVE COURSES - 2 to 32 weeks all year round. Small class sizes.

★Prices starting at 74.000 pts./4 weeks. Includes: 20 hrs. class/week, room & activities.

★Homestay/shared apartment.

Quality language school in a fiendly, professional atmosphere.

For further information contact
Paseo de Carmelitas, 57 - 37002 Salamanca (Spain)
Tel. 34 23 - 26 73 34 - Fax 34 23 - 26 89 62

Travel with Children (US$11, postage US$1.50), available from **Lonely Planet Publications,** 115 Filbert St., Oakland, CA 94607 (tel. (800) 229-0122 or (510) 893-8555); and P.O. Box 617, Hawthorn, Victoria 3122, Australia. *Sharing Nature with Children* (US$6.95) and *Backpacking with Babies and Small Children* (US$8.95) are available from **Wilderness Press,** 2440 Bancroft Way, Berkeley, CA 94704 (tel. (800) 443-7227).

Travelers with Disabilities

Accessibility varies widely. Guidebooks and booklets don't have accurate information about ramps, door widths, and elevator dimensions. The best method is to directly ask restaurants, hotels, railways, and airlines about their facilities. Rail is usually the most convenient form of travel. Call **Rail Europe** (tel. (800) 848-7245 or (800) 438-7245) for information on discounted rail travel.

The customary six-month quarantine on all animals, including **guide dogs** is a serious pain in the butt. Spain and Morocco require an international health and inoculation certificate for pets; for Spain, this document must be certified at the Spanish consulate. Owners must usually obtain an import license, bring documentation of the animal's rabies, distemper, and contagious hepatitis inoculations, and provide a veterinarian's letter attesting to the pet's health. The following organizations provide more information.

American Foundation for the Blind, 15 W. 16th St., New York, NY 10011 (tel. (800) 232-5463 or (212) 620-2147). Info, travel books, and ID cards (US$10) for the blind. ID card can also be ordered by phone (Product Center tel. (800) 829-0500). Call Mon.-Fri. 8:30am-4:30pm EST.

Disability Press, Ltd., Applemarket House, 17 Union St., Kingston-upon-Thames, Surrey KT1 1RP, United Kingdom (tel. 08 15 49 63 99). Publishes the *Disabled Traveller's International Phrasebook* (£1.75), a compilation of useful phrases in most European languages.

Federation of the Handicapped, 211 W. 14th St., New York, NY 10011 (tel. (212) 206-4200). Tours and an annual summer trip for members. Annual membership US$4.

The Guided Tour, 613 W. Chelterham Ave., Suite 200, Melrose Park, PA 19126-2414 (tel. (215) 782-1370; fax (215) 635-2637). Year-round full-time travel program for developmentally and learning-disabled adults; also trips for travelers with physical disabilities.

Mobility International, U.S.A. (MIUSA), P.O. Box 3551, Eugene, OR 97403 (voice and TDD tel. (503) 343-1284); and 228 Burough High St., London SE1 1JX, United Kingdom. Annual membership US$20. Information on travel programs, organized tours, accommodations, and study abroad. Contacts in over 30 countries. Sells *A World of Options: A Guide to International Educational Exchange, Community Service and Travel for Persons with Disabilities* (US$14, non-members US$16).

Travel Information Service, Moss Rehabilitation Hospital, 1200 W. Tabor Road, Philadelphia, PA 19141 (tel. (215) 456-9600). Booklets (US$5) on sights, accommodations, transport, and accessibility in specific European cities.

Twin Peaks Press, P.O. Box 129, Vancouver, WA 98666 (tel. (800) 637-2256; orders only tel. (800) 637-2256). Publishes *Directory for Travel Agencies for the Disabled* (US$12.95), *Travel for the Disabled* (US$19.95), and *Wheelchair Vagabond* (US$14.95). Add US$2 shipping and handling for the first book ordered, US$1 for each additional book.

Women Travelers

Women traveling alone—particularly those who look foreign—often must deal with unwarranted harrassment. You've probably heard it all before, but here it is again: a litany of **precautions**. Walk as if you know where you are going, avoid eye contact (sunglasses are indispensible), meet all advances and catcalls with silence, and, if still troubled, walk or stand near older women or couples until you feel safe. Ask for directions from women or couples rather than men. Keep spare change handy for telephones and emergency bus and taxi fares. Carry a whistle or large stick on your person. A Walkman or headphones clearly show that you are not listening (no one has to know that it's not even on). If someone starts following you, tell a policeman if possible; tell anyone, and you'll often frighten your pursuer away. Alternatively, walk to the police station. In any situation that becomes threatening, don't hesitate to call for help. Memorize the **emergency police number** (091 for Spain; 115 for Portugal; 19 for Morocco).

Unfortunately, wearing tighter or more revealing **clothes** means more annoying hassle from macho pigs in the streets. Below-the-knee hemlines, culottes, or pants reduce harrassment. Furthermore, obviously American garb (sweatshirts, college t-shirts, sneakers, hiking shorts, even jean jackets) tends to draw hecklers.

Budget **accommodations** sometimes mean more risk than savings. Avoid dives and the city outskirts in favor of university dorms or youth hostels. Centrally located accommodations are usually safest to return to after dark.

For more **information** on safety and health, consult the *Handbook for Women Travelers* (£4.95) by Gemma Moss, available from **Piatkus Publishers,** 5 Windmill St., London W1 1P 1HF, England (tel. (01) 631 07 10).

In **Morocco,** where Islamic culture requires women to be veiled and secluded even in their own homes, a solo female tourist may feel like more of a freak and a reject than ever before. Strolling arm in arm with another woman, a common European and North African practice, can lessen the risk of harassment or violence. Particularly in the larger inland cities, expect other, subtler forms of discrimination, such as being refused a room in a hotel that isn't full; proprietors would rather not be responsible for your well-being. Many bars refuse to admit women. Again, the best response to most harassment is none at all; any reply may be interpreted as encouragement.

Finally, see the general information listed under Safety (above).

Alternatives to Tourism

Study

Foreign students study in **Spain** both through U.S. university programs and in courses organized by Spanish universities or language centers for foreign students. If your language skills are good, you can enroll directly in a Spanish university. U.S. citizens

---

STUDY IN SPAIN
THE CENTER FOR CROSS-CULTURAL STUDY
SEVILLE, SPAIN

ACADEMIC YEAR, SEMESTER, JANUARY TERM
AND SUMMER PROGRAMS
24 YEARS OF EXCELLENCE IN SPANISH STUDIES
FOR U.S. COLLEGE STUDENTS
Language, liberal arts, business, education, outside study

FOR COMPLETE INFORMATION, WRITE OR CALL:

In the United States:	In Spain:
Director, CC-CS	CC-CS
219 Strong Street, Box L	Calle Harinas, 18
Amherst, MA 01002	41001 Sevilla, Spain
Tel: (413) 549-4543	Tel: (011-34-5) 422-4107

who are considering enrolling as regular students in a Spanish university should write for *General Information About Higher Education in Spain* and *Study in Spain,* two information packets available from the **U.S. consulate** in Barcelona (see Spain: Once There: Useful Addresses). Talk to counselors at your college.

All universities in **Portugal** are open to foreign students. Contact individual institutions for specifics. Foreigners can enter language-study programs at the **University of Lisboa's** Faculdade de Lengua e Cultura, Cidade Universitária, 1699 Lisboa CODEX (tel. 76 51 62), and the **University of Coimbra's** Faculdade de Artes, Largo da Porta Ferrea, 3049 Coimbra CODEX (tel. 255 51, 255 52, or 255 53).

For more **information** on study abroad, contact the following organizations.

> **Council on International Educational Exchange (CIEE).** For address, phone number, and more details see Useful Addresses: Travel Services. A good place to start. Heaps of info on study abroad.
>
> **American Field Service Intercultural Programs,** 313 E. 43rd St., New York, NY 10017 (tel. (800) 237-4636 or (212) 949-4242). High school (ages 15-18) exchange program in over 55 countries.
>
> **American Institute of Foreign Study (AIFS),** 102 Greenwich Ave., Greenwich, CT 06830 (tel. (800) 727-2437). Arranges study at European universities. Separate division for high school students (tel. (617) 421-9575). Summer programs last 3-12 wks.
>
> **Central Bureau for Educational Visits and Exchanges,** Seymour Mews House, Seymour Mews, London W1H 9PE, England (tel. (71) 486 51 01). Publishes *Study Holidays* (mailed to U.K. £8.95, to mainland Europe £10.40, to elsewhere £13.95) and *Home from Home* (£7.99, £9.49, £11.99), an annual guide to homestays, termstays, and exchanges. These also sold by IIE (see below).
>
> **Education Office of Spain,** 150 Fifth Ave., Suite 918, New York, NY 10011 (tel. (212) 741-5144, 741-5145). 1350 Connecticut Ave. NW, Suite 1050, Washington, DC 20036 (tel. (202) 452-0004). Much information on study in Spain.
>
> **Experiment in International Living,** School for International Training, College Semester Abroad Admissions, Box 676, Kipling Rd., Brattleboro, VT 05302 (tel. (800) 451-4465, (800) 336-1616, or (802) 257-7751). Offers 15-week programs for sophomores, juniors, and seniors. Most U.S. colleges will transfer credit from SIT. Minimal financial aid available.
>
> **Institute for International Education (IIE),** 809 United Nations Plaza, New York, NY 10017-3580 (tel. (212) 883-8200). Sells *Basic Facts on Foreign Study* (free); the annual *Academic Year Abroad* (US$39.95, postage US$3), listing over 2000 programs; and *Vacation Study Abroad* (US$31.95, postage US$3), listing over 1400 programs. Publishes *Financial Resources for International Study,* which lists over 600 foundations providing money to undergrad, grad, and post-grad students, sold by Peterson's Guides (for address see Work and Volunteering below). Also sells books by the Central Bureau for Educational Visits and Exchanges (see above).
>
> **UNESCO,** Unipub Co., 4611-F Assembly Dr., Lanham, MD 20706 (tel. (800) 274-4888). Publishes *Study Abroad* (US$24, postage US$2.50).

Work and Volunteering

The employment situation in Spain, Portugal, and Morocco is grim for citizens and worse for foreigners. Getting a **work visa** is extremely difficult. Jobs in restaurants and bars are good sources of under-the-table income. In rural areas, you might try working on farms.

Teaching English is another source of official and unofficial employment in Spain and Portugal, and probably the only one in Morocco. Some English-language schools arrange work permits for employees. Inquire at language and private schools. Try posting signs in markets and message boards stating that you're a native speaker; scan the classified of local papers, where residents advertise for language instruction. The U.S. State Dept. **Office of Overseas Schools** (Rm. 245 SA-29, Dept. of State, Washington, DC 20522-2902 (tel. (703) 875-7800) maintains a list of elementary and secondary schools abroad, and agencies that arrange placement for teaching abroad. In Portugal, contact the **American Language Institute,** Av. Duque de Loulé, 22-10, Lisboa.

Summer positions as **tour group leaders** are available with **Hostelling International/American Youth Hostels (AYH),** P.O. Box 37613, Washington, DC 20013-7613 (tel. (202) 783-6161). You must be at least 21, take a nine-day training course (US$295, room and board included; in Washington, DC US$395), and lead a group in the U.S. before taking one to Europe. The **Experiment in International Living (EIL)**, P.O. Box 676, Kipling Rd., Brattleboro, VT 05302 (tel. (800) 451-4465 or (802) 257-7751), requires you to be at least 24 and have leadership ability and extensive overseas experience. Applications are due in late November for summer positions. **CIEE** also has group leader positions available; contact the International Voluntary Projects division (see Useful Addresses: Travel Services for address).

International work camps allow volunteers to live and work together on two- to four-week community projects. Room and board are spartan.

For **information** on these and other work options, look up some of the following sources.

>**Addison Wesley,** 1 Jacob Way, Reading, MA 01867 (tel. (800) 447-2226). Sells the general guide *International Jobs: Where They Are, How to Get Them* (US$12.95).
>
>**Archaeological Institute of America,** 675 Commonwealth Ave., Boston, MA 02215 (tel. (617) 353-9361). *The Archaeological Fieldwork Opportunities Bulletin* (US$8.50, non-members US$10.50, postage US$3) lists international digs every Jan.
>
>**CIEE,** Work Abroad Dept., 205 E. 42nd St., New York, NY 10017 (tel. (212) 661-1414). Operates a reciprocal work program (US$150) in Spain during the summer months for college and university students who are U.S. citizens and possess intermediate facility in Spanish (at least 2 years of college-level Spanish). They assist you with job-hunting and finding accommodations, but you must secure your own job. Positions available include unskilled work at hotels, shops, and restaurants. Also sells assorted guides about work and volunteer programs abroad (see Useful Addresses: Travel Services for titles and prices).
>
>**Interexchange Program,** 161 Sixth Ave., New York, NY 10003 (tel. (212) 924-0446). Write for their catalogs listing work abroad options in Europe.
>
>**International Association for the Exchange of Students for Technical Experience (IAESTE),** a division of Association for International Practical Training (AIPT), 10 Corporate Ctr., Suite 250, 10400 Little Patuxent Parkway, Columbia, MD 21044 (tel. (410) 997-2200). Internship exchange

Study in Seville Spain

Emphases in Liberal Arts and International Business

Courses available in Spanish and in English

Fluency in Spanish not required

All courses approved by UW-Platteville and validated on an official UW-Platteville transcript

$4325 per semester for Wisconsin and Minnesota residents

$4575 per semester for non-residents
Costs include: Tuition and Fees
 Room and Board
  in Spanish Homes
 Fieldtrips

All financial aid applies

For further information contact
Study Abroad Programs
308 Warner Hall
University of Wisconsin-Platteville
1 University Plaza
Platteville, WI 53818-3099
(608) 342-1726
University of Wisconsin-Platteville

programs for science, engineering, math, architecture, and agriculture students who have completed sophomore year. Applications (US$75) due Dec. 10 for summer placement.

International Schools Services (ISS), 15 Roszel Rd., P.O. Box 5910, Princeton, NJ 08543 (tel. (609) 452-0990). Free newsletter *Newslinks*. Their Educational Staffing Dept. coordinates placement of teachers in international and American schools and publishes the booklet *Your Passport to Teaching and Administrative Opportunities Abroad*.

Peterson's Guides, 202 Carnegie Center, P.O. Box 2123, Princeton, NJ 08543-2123 (tel. (800) 338-3282). Distributes *The Directory of Overseas Summer Jobs* (US$10.95), which lists 50,000 openings worldwide; *Work Your Way Around the World* (US$12.95); and *The Au Pair and Nanny's Guide to Working Abroad* (US$10.95). Also sells *The ISS Directory of Overseas Schools* (US$34.95), published by ISS (see above).

Tagus Turismo Juvenil. Paid and volunteer work in Portugal. (See Useful Addresses: Travel Services).

Volunteers for Peace, 43 Tiffany Rd., Belmont, VT 05730 (tel. (802) 259-2759). A workcamp organization that publishes the *International Workcamp Directory* (US$10 postpaid), which covers 37 countries and a free newsletter. Placement is quick; reservations are generally confirmed within 3 wks. Registration fee (US$125) for camps in Western Europe.

World Trade Academy Press, 50 E. 42nd St., #509, New York, NY, 10017 (tel. (212) 697-4999). Publishes *Directory of American Firms Operating in Foreign Countries* (US$195 and in libraries) and excerpts of listings of American firms in specific countries (US$10-15 per country). Also publishes *Looking For Employment in Foreign Countries* (US$16.50).

Useful Addresses

The organizations and publications listed below can help you put your travel ideas together.

Tourist Offices

National tourist offices are valuable sources of information, but often don't answer faxes. Make your inquiries as specific as possible. For addresses of tourist offices in Spain, Portugal, and Morocco, turn to Once There: Tourist Offices for each country.

National Tourist Office of Spain

U.S.: 665 Fifth Ave., **New York**, NY 10022 (tel. (212) 759-8822). 845 N. Michigan Ave., **Chicago**, IL 60611 (tel. (312) 642-1992). San Vicente Plaza Bldg., 8383 Wilshire Blvd., #960, **Beverly Hills**, CA 90211 (tel. (213) 759-8822). 1221 Brickell Ave., #1850, **Miami**, FL 33131 (tel. (305) 358-1992).

Canada: 102 Bloor St. W., 14th fl., Toronto, Ont. M5S 1M8 (tel. (416) 961-3131).

U.K.: 57-58 St. James St., London SW1A ILD (tel. (71) 499 11 69).

Australia: 203 Castlereagh St., #21A, P.O. Box A685, Sydney South, NSW 2000 (tel. (2) 264-7966).

Portuguese National Tourist Office

U.S.: 590 Fifth Ave., New York, NY 10036 (tel. (212) 354-4403).

Canada: 60 Bloor St. W., Suite 1005, Toronto, Ont. M4W 3B8 (tel. (416) 921-7376).

U.K.: 22/25A Sackville St., London W1X 1DE (tel. (71) 494 14 41).

Moroccan National Tourist Office

U.S.: 20 E. 46th St., #1201, **New York**, NY 11017 (tel. (212) 557-2520). 421 N. Rodeo Dr., #7, Rodeo Terrace, **Beverly Hills**, CA 90210 (tel. (213) 271-8939). P.O. Box 22662, Moroccan Pavilion, Epcot Center, **Lake Buena Vista**, FL 32830 (tel. (407) 827-5337).

Canada: 2001 rue Université, #1460, Montreal, Que. PQ H3A 2A6 (tel. (514) 842-8111; fax (514) 842-5316; telex 055-62191).

U.K.: 174 Regent St., London W1R GHB (tel. (71) 437 00 73).

Australia: 11 West St. N., Sydney, NSW 2060 (tel. 95 767 170).

Embassies and Consulates

Note that you should direct questions concerning visas and passports to consulates, not embassies (whose function is solely diplomatic). For addresses of your home country's embassies and consulates in Spain, Portugal, and Morocco, turn to Once There: Embassies and Consulates for each country.

Embassy and Consulate General of Spain

U.S.: Embassy, 2700 15th St. NW, Washington, DC 20009 (tel. (202) 265-0190). **Consulate,** 150 E. 58th St., 16th fl., New York, NY 10155 (tel. (212) 355-4080, 355-4090).

Canada: Embassy, 350 Sparks St., #802, Ottawa, Ont. KIR 7S8 (tel. (613) 237-2193, 237-2194).

U.K.: Embassy, Portland House, 16th fl., Stag Place, London SW1E 5SE (tel. (71) 235 55 55). **Consulate,** 20 Draycott Pl., London SW3 2RZ (tel. (71) 581 59 21, 581 59 22, or 581 59 23).

Australia and New Zealand: Embassy, 15 Arkana St., Yarralumla, ACT 2600 (tel. (6) 73 35 55, (6) 73 38 45). Mailing address: P.O. Box 256, Canberra, Woden ACT 2606. **Consulate,** 34 Market St., 24th fl., Sydney, NSW 2000 (tel. (2) 261 24 33, (2) 261 24 43). Mailing address, P.O. Box E441, St. James, NSW 2000.

Embassy and Consulate General of Portugal

U.S.: Embassy, 2125 Kalorama Rd. NW, Washington, DC 20008 (tel. (202) 328-8610). **Consulates,** 630 Fifth Ave., #655, New York, NY 10111 (tel. (212) 246-4580, 246-4582). Others in Boston, Los Angeles, New Bedford, Newark, Providence, San Francisco, San Juan (Puerto Rico), and the Dominican Republic.

Canada: Embassy, 645 Highland Park Dr., Ottawa, Ont. K1Y OB8 (tel. (613) 729-2270). **Consulates,** 2020 University Ave., Suite 1725, Montreal, Que. 838 285 (tel. (514) 499-0359). 121 Richmond St. W., Suite 701, Toronto, Ont. M5H 2K1 (tel. (416) 360-8260, 360-8261).

U.K.: Embassy, 11 Belgrave Sq., London SW1X 8PP (tel. (71) 235 53 31). **Consulate,** same as above.

Australia and New Zealand: Embassy, 23 Curgoa Circuit, O'Malley, Canberra, ACT 2606 (tel. (6) 290 17 33). **Consulate in Australia,** 132 Ocean St., Edgecliff, NSW 2027 (tel. (2) 326 13 44). Mailing address, G.P.O. Box 4219, Sydney, NSW 2001. **Consulate in New Zealand,** 4749 Fort St., Oakland.

Embassy and Consulate of the Kingdom of Morocco

U.S.: Embassy, 1601 21st St. NW, Washington, DC 20009 (tel. (202) 462-7979). **Consulate,** 437 Fifth Ave., 10th fl., New York, NY 10016 (tel. (212) 758-2625).

Canada: Embassy, 38 Range Rd., Ottawa, Ont. K1N 814 (tel. (613) 236-7391).

U.K.: Embassy, 49 Queens Gate Garden, London SW7 5NE (tel. (71) 581 50 01).

Travel Services

These organizations help with booking flights and acquiring railpasses, student ID cards, and HI memberships.

Council on International Educational Exchange (CIEE), 205 E. 42nd St., New York, NY 10017 (tel. (212) 661-1414). Information on academic work, voluntary service, and professional opportunities abroad. Administers ISIC, FIYTO, and ITIC cards. Write for *Student Travels*, CIEE's new biannual travel magazine for college students (free, postage $1). Also available are *Work, Study, Travel Abroad: The Whole World Handbook* ($12.95, postage $1.50); *Going Places: The High School Student's Guide to Study, Travel, and Adventure Abroad* ($13.95, postage $1.50); and *Volunteer! The Comprehensive Guide to Voluntary Service in the U.S. and Abroad* ($8.95, postage $1.50).

Council Travel, one of CIEE's 2 budget subsidiaries. Their 38 offices across the U.S. sell Eurail and individual country railpasses, guidebooks, travel gear, discounted flights, ISIC, FIYTO, and ITIC cards, and HI (IYHF) memberships. Publishes *Budget Traveller* newsletter. Offices include 205 E. 42nd St., **New York,** NY 10017 (tel. (212) 661-1450); 729 Boylston St., Suite 201, **Boston,**

MA 02116 (tel. (617) 266-1926); 1093 Broxton Ave., **Los Angeles**, CA 90024 (tel. (310) 208-3551); 1153 N. Dearborn St., **Chicago**, IL 60610 (tel. (312) 951-0585); 919 Irving St., **San Francisco**, CA 94122 (tel. (415) 566-6222); 2000 Guadalupe St., **Austin**, TX 78705 (tel. 512 472-4931). Other offices in Europe and Asia include the **U.K.:** 28A Poland St., London W1V 3DB (tel. (71) 437 77 67). (See Getting There: From North America for information on **Council Charter**, CIEE's air travel division.)

Educational Travel Centre (ETC), 438 N. Frances St., Madison, WI 53703 (tel. (608) 256-5551). Flight information, HI (IYHF) cards, and railpasses. Write or call for a free copy of their travel newsletter *Taking Off*.

International Student Travel Confederation (ISTC). Issues ISICs. **U.S.:** CIEE/Council Travel (see above). **Canada:** Travel CUTS (see address below). **U.K.:** London Student Travel, 52 Grosvenor Gardens, London SW1 W0AU (tel. (71) 730 34 02). **Ireland:** USIT, Ltd., Acton Quay, O'Connell Bridge, Dublin 2 (tel. (1) 77 88 43). **Australia:** SSA/STA Travel (see address below). **New Zealand:** New Zealand Student Travel, Courtenay Chambers, 2nd fl., 15 Courtenay, Wellington (tel. (04) 85 05 61).

Let's Go Travel Services, Harvard Student Agencies, Inc., Thayer Hall-B, Harvard University, Cambridge, MA 02138 (tel. (617) 495-9649). Railpasses, HI (IYHF) memberships, ISICs, International Teacher ID cards, FIYTO cards, guidebooks (including every *Let's Go*), maps, bargain flights, and a complete line of budget travel gear. All items available by mail; call or write for a catalog.

Rail Europe Inc., 226 Westchester Ave., White Plains, NY 10604 (tel. (800) 438-7245; tel. (914) 682-5172 in NY, NJ, CT). Sells all Eurail products and passes, national railpasses, and point-to-point tickets. Up-to-date information on all rail travel in Europe, but their number is continually busy.

STA Travel, 17 E. 45th St., New York, NY 10017 (tel. (800) 777-0112) or (212) 986-9643); 7202 Melrose Ave., Los Angeles, CA 90046 (tel. (213) 934-8722). **U.K.:** 74 and 86 Old Brompton Rd., London SW7 3LQ (tel. (71) 937 99 21 for European travel; tel. (71) 937 99 71 for North American travel). **Australia:** 222 Faraday St., Melbourne, Victoria 3053 (tel. (33) 47 69 11). **New Zealand:** 10 High St., Auckland (tel. (9) 309 99 95). Bargain flights, railpasses, insurance, ISICs, and HI cards.

Tagus Turismo Juvenil, Pr. Londres, 9B, 1000 Lisboa (tel. (1) 89 15 31). R. Guedes de Azevedo, 34-36 C, 4000 Porto (tel. (2) 208 27 63). (See Portugal: Once There: Tourist Offices for more locations.) Portugal's youth travel agency. Information on workcamps and *au pair* positions, discount transportation, HI cards, student residences, camping, and study visits in Portugal. English spoken.

Travel CUTS (Canadian Universities Travel Service), 187 College St., Toronto, Ont. M5T 1P7 (tel. (416) 979-2406). Offices throughout Canada. **U.K.:** 295-A Regent St., London W1R 7YA (tel. (71) 637 31 61). Discount flights, Eurailpasses, ISIC, FIYTO cards. Runs the Canadian Work Abroad Programme and arranges adventure tours. Their newspaper, *The Canadian Student Traveler*, is free at all offices and on Canadian campuses.

Publications

Forsyth Travel Library, 9154 W. 57th St., P.O. Box 2975, Shawnee Mission, KS 66201 (tel. (800) 367-7984 or (913) 384-3440). Mail-order service that stocks a vast range of city, area, and country maps, as well as rail and ferry travel guides. Sole North American distributor of the *Thomas Cook European Timetable* (US$24.95, postage US$4), covering all Europe. Write or call for free newsletter and catalog.

Travelling Books, P.O. Box 77114, Seattle, WA 98177 (tel. (206) 367-5848). Provides mail order service through comprehensive catalogue. Specializes in travel books, maps, language aids, and accessories for the independent traveler. Free catalogue.

Wide World Books and Maps, 1911 N. 45th St., Seattle, WA 98105 (tel. (206) 634-3453). Useful free catalog listing the most recent guidebooks for every part of the world. Open Mon.-Fri. 10am-7pm, Sat. 10am-6pm, Sun. noon-5pm.

Getting There

From North America

Most major airlines maintain an incomprehensible and sometimes completely random fare structure; prices vary according to the day of the week, month of the year, amount of time spent abroad, and date of reservation. When planning your trip, try to keep your schedule and itinerary flexible.

A flight to London, Frankfurt, Brussels, or Luxembourg can cost considerably less than a direct flight to Madrid or Lisboa. In fact, flying to London is usually the cheapest way across the Atlantic, though special fares to other cities (Amsterdam, Brussels) can cost even less.

Off-season fliers enjoy lower fares. Peak season rates begin on May 15 or June 1 and run until around September 15. "Midweek" (Mon.-Thurs.) flights run about US$30 cheaper.

Usually it's less expensive to fix a return date when purchasing your ticket, even if you pay to change it later. "Open return" and one-way tickets are pricey.

Don't hesitate to comparison shop. Since commissions are smaller on cheaper flights, some agents may be less than eager to help you find the best deal. In addition, check the travel section of the Sunday *New York Times* and other major papers for incredibly cheap (but erratic) fares. Consult **student travel agencies** such as Council Travel, Travel CUTS, and Let's Go Travel (see Planning Your Trip: Useful Addresses: Travel Services). They offer special deals to students that aren't available to regular travel agents.

Commercial Airlines

Flying with a commercial airline is the most expensive option, but the most flexible, reliable, and comfortable one as well. Look into smaller carriers such as **Virgin Atlan-**

LEARN A LANGUAGE, LIVE A LANGUAGE!

Eurocentres offers high-quality intensive courses in Spanish in our centres in Madrid and Barcelona.

We offer courses of 2 to 12 weeks, consisting of 30 hours' instruction per week, with optional classes in Business, Literature, Life and Culture. We arrange Homestay Accommodation for you with carefully-selected families, so you can learn the language faster - and also learn about the culture of the people and the country.

If you would like further information about courses in Europe, please contact us for a FREE brochure. Call TOLL-FREE 1-800-648-4809 or write:

Eurocentre Alexandria
101 N.Union St., Alexandria, VA 22314
Fax: (703) 684-1495

EUROCENTRES

tic and **Icelandair** that may undercut the fares of large airlines. Most airlines offer price cuts for advance purchase.

> **Icelandair** (tel. (800) 233-5500): **Get Up And Go** fare from New York to Luxembourg (round-trip Mon.-Thurs. $598, Fri.-Sun. $658). Reservations can be made no more than 3 days before departure. Changes cost US$125.
>
> **Virgin Atlantic** (tel. (800) 862-8621): **Instant Purchase Plan** (New York to London round-trip US$750). Reservations can be made no more than 10 days before departure.

If you're abnormally flexible, some airlines offer **three-day advance purchase youth fares,** available only within three days of departure; return dates are open. You must be under 25. Most airlines no longer offer standby fares, and the few that do are only in summer. Call individual companies for the latest information.

The major airlines offer viable budget options in the form of **Advanced Purchase Excursion (APEX)** fares. These provide confirmed reservations and "open-jaw" tickets, which allow you to arrive and depart from different cities. For APEX, reservations must be made 21 days in advance with 7- to 14-day minimum and 60- to 90-day maximum stay limitations. You'll be heavily penalized for cancellation and change of reservation. For summer travel, book APEX fares early.

Charter Flights

Charter flights are the most economical option, especially in high season. You can book some charters up to the last minute, but most summer flights fill up months in advance. Later in the season, companies start having trouble filling their planes and either cancel flights or offer special prices. Charters allow you to mix and match arrival and departure points in Europe. Once you've made reservations, however, the flexibility ends. You must choose your departure and return dates when you book and will lose money if you cancel within 14 to 20 days of departure.

Charters are inconvenient, inevitably delayed, and require long layovers. In addition, most companies reserve the right to cancel flights until 48 hours before departure; ask a travel agent about your charter company's reliability. In 1993 a host of Spanish companies now operating as ticket wholesalers will be authorized to operate their own charter services.

> **Council Charter,** 205 E. 42nd St., New York, NY 10017 (tel. (212) 661-0311 or (800) 800-8222). A subsidiary of CIEE, Council Charter is among the oldest and most reliable of charter companies. Flights to most major European cities can be purchased through any **Council Travel** office in the U.S. or by calling the New York number.
>
> **Travel CUTS** (see Planning Your Trip: Useful Addresses: Travel Services).
>
> **Unitravel** (tel. (800) 325-2222). Well-established company with discounted fares on major airlines. Departures from over 70 cities. Call and request their memo listing all flights departing from your city. Open Mon.-Fri. 8am-8pm, Sat. 8am-6pm.

Discount Clubs and Consolidators

Discount clubs and ticket consolidators proffer savings on charter flights, commercial flights, and tour packages by acting as clearinghouses for unsold tickets, available three weeks to a few days before departure. Check the travel section of the newspaper (best is the *New York Times*). Clubs generally charge yearly dues of US$30-50. Study with care their often Byzantine contracts—you may prefer not to stop over in Luxembourg for 11 hours.

> **Access International** (tel. (800) 825-3633 or (212) 465-0707).
>
> **Air Hitch,** 2901 Broadway, #100, New York, NY 10025 (tel. (212) 864-2000). No membership fee. For the truly flexible. You choose a date range in which you want to travel and a number of possible destinations; they place you with 90% certainty in a vacant spot with as little as 2 days' notice. One-way flights to Europe from the East Coast about US$169.
>
> **Bargain Air,** 655 Deep Valley Drive #355, Rolling Hills, CA 90274 (tel. (800) 347-2345); in CA tel. (310) 377-6349; fax (310) 877-1824).

Always travel with a friend.

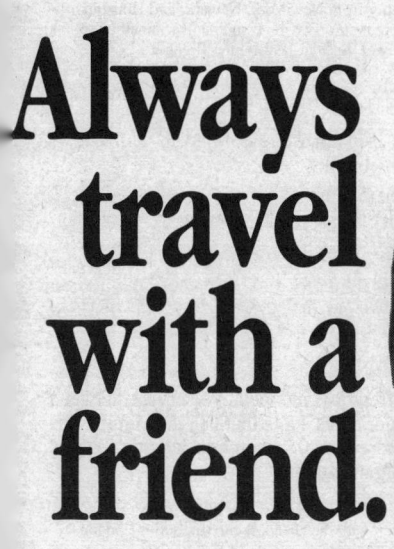

Get the International Student Identity Card, recognized worldwide.

For information call toll-free **1-800-GET-AN-ID**, or contact any Council Travel office. (See inside front cover.)

Council on International Educational Exchange
205 East 42nd Street, New York, NY 10017

Discount Travel International, Ives Bldg., #205, 114 Forrest Ave., Narberth, PA 19072 (tel. (215) 668-7184). Membership US$45.

Moment's Notice (tel. (212) 486-0503; hotline (212) 750-9111).

Travel Avenue, 641 West Lake #201, Chicago, IL 60606-3691 (tel. (800) 333-3335).

Worldwide Discount Travel Club, 1674 Meridian Ave., Miami Beach, FL 33139 (tel. (305) 534-2082). Membership US$50.

Courier Flights

Intrepids who pack light might consider flying to Europe as couriers. Although they seem fishy, many courier companies are quite well established. Here's how it works: a company hires you as a courier, uses your checked luggage space for freight, and lets you bring on your own carry-on luggage. Fares vary wildly. Most companies offer single round-trip tickets leaving from New York with fixed-length (usually short) stays. The following are courier companies and information resources. Check the travel section of a major newspaper for more courier companies.

NOW Voyager, 74 Varick St., #307, New York, NY 10013 (tel. (212) 431-1616). The major courier service, arranging flights all over the world, mainly from New York, Newark, and Houston. Registration US$50 for first-time couriers and a visit to their office in person. Doll yourself up to look responsible. Flights US$199-500, off-season lower. Special last-minute flights to London and Paris as low as US$150.

Halbert Express, 147-05 176th St., Jamaica, NY 11434 (tel. (718) 656-8189).

Thunderbird Press, 5930-10 W. Greenway Blvd., Suite 112H, Glendale, AZ 85306 (tel. (800) 345-0096. Sells the *Courier Air Travel Handbook* (US$10.70).

Travel Unlimited, P.O. Box 1058, Allston, MA 02134-1058. Distributes a comprehensive, monthly newletter that details all possible options for courier travel. An invaluable source of cheap fares. 1 yr. subscription US$25 (outside of the U.S. US$35).

From Europe

Plane

Iberia, TAP Air, and **Royal Air Maroc** offer fast, inexpensive service between Madrid, Lisboa, and Casablanca, plus other major cities. Note that baggage limitations for intra-European flights is a low 20kg (as opposed to 70 lbs. on transatlantic flights). For more **information,** contact the following organizations.

Air Travel Advisory Bureau, Strauss House 41-45, Goswell Rd., London EC1V 7DN, United Kingdom (tel. (071) 636 29 08). Puts travelers in touch with the cheapest carriers out of London for free.

Council Travel, 31, rue St. Augustin, Paris 75002. 28A Poland St., London WIV 3DB (tel (71) 437 77 67).

STA Travel, 74 and 86 Old Brompton Rd., London SW7 3LQ, United Kingdom (tel. (71) 937 99 21).

Train

If you ride an overnight train in a regular coach seat, you probably won't get a wink of sleep all night. A better option is a sleeping berth in a **couchette** car. (See Planning Your Trip: Safety for safety tips on trains.) For more **information,** order *Camp Europe by Train* (US$12.95), a thorough guide to train travel from Forsythe Travel Library (see Planning Your Trip: Useful Addresses: Publications).

BIJ

BIJ (Billet International de Jeunesse) tickets are a raving bargain if you're under 26. They cut up to 25% off regular second-class fares on international routes and are valid on virtually all trains. When you buy the ticket, you specify both destination and route, then have the option of stopping anywhere along the route for up to two months.

BIJs are sold *only in Europe,* at student travel agencies and **Eurotrain** outlets—in the U.K. at 52 Grosvenor Gardens, London SW1 W0AU (tel. (71) 730 85 18).

Eurail

If you're planning much travel outside Spain, Portugal, or Morocco consider buying a **Eurailpass.** Before you do, make sure it'll save you money. Add up the second-class fares for the major routes you plan to cover, then deduct 25% if you're eligible for BIJ tickets. Watch out for supplements—on trains that require reservations (usually any but the slowest), the railpass requires you to pay an additional fee. Even with a Eurailpass, reservations are required for trips between major cities and covering distances over 250km. Within Spain, Portugal, and Morocco, train fares are low enough to make a railpass unnecessary. As no national railpass exists in these countries, Eurail is your only "pass" option.

Eurailpasses are valid in 17 European countries (including Spain and Portugal, excluding Morocco and the U.K.) and entitle you to passage on some ferries and reduced fares on others. If under 26, a one-month **Eurail Youthpass** costs US$470; an adult one-month **Eurailpass** costs US$680. The **Eurail Flexipass** is US$280 for five days' travel in a 15-day period; US$610 for 14 days' travel in a one-month period.

Eurailpasses are sold *only outside of Europe.* They're available through Council Travel, Let's Go Travel, Travel CUTS, and other travel agencies (see Planning Your Trip: Useful Addresses: Travel Services). They can be replaced only if you've bought Eurail-brand insurance on them—you can no longer simply fill out a validation slip.

Note: The **InterRail** pass (similar to Eurail but valid in Morocco) is dead.

Bus

In general, bus travel is far more comfortable in Europe than in North America. (Incidentally, buses can travel from the U. K. to Iberia via ferry.) Call the office of travel

---

Discounted Flights to

Spain & Portugal

from **$232** each * way

Also Available:

Amsterdam, Athens, Barcelona, Berlin, Brussels, Budapest, Cairo, Copenhagen, Dusseldorf, Edinburgh, Frankfurt, Geneva, Glasgow, Hamburg, Helsinki, Istanbul, Lisbon, London, Madrid, Milan, Moscow, Munich, Nice, Oslo, Paris, Prague, Rome, Stockholm, Stuttgart, Tel Aviv, Venice, Vienna, Zurich

♦ Nationwide Departures on Major Scheduled Airlines!
♦ One Ways, Open Jaws and Long Stays available!
♦ All payments held in an escrow account for your protection!
♦ Mastercard, VISA, Discover & American Express accepted!
♦ Flight Times available at time of booking!

UniTravel® 800-325-2027

Reliable Low Cost Travel Since 1968

* NYC/MAD midweek low season Instant Purchase fare.

agencies, such as Council Travel, STA Travel, and Travel CUTS in the city you're departing from.

> **Euroline Buses,** 52 Grosvenor Gardens, London SW1W 0AU (tel. (71) 730 82 35). Expresses from London to over 100 destinations, including many in Spain and Portugal. To Madrid one-way £75, return £130; off-season one-way £69, return £124.
>
> **Magic Bus,** 20 Filellinon St., Syntagma, Athens, Greece (tel. (1) 323 74 71). Cheap, direct service between major cities in Europe. Ask for their student discounts.
>
> **Spain-Based Companies: ALSA** (tel. (1) 468 19 27) and **Auto Transporte Julia, S.A.** (tel. (1) 468 37 99, 468 38 13). They connect Madrid with Portugal, France, Italy, Switzerland, and Belgium. **Iberbus-Linebus** (tel. (1) 467 25 65, 467 28 57). Links Spain, France, Italy, Belgium, and Holland.

Ferry

The cheapest way to get to Morocco by ferry is from Algeciras, Spain. Several boat lines run between Spain and Tangier. Frequent ferries connect Málaga and the Canary Islands to Tangier.

Customs

Don't be alarmed by customs procedures. Customs officials may snoop through your most personal possessions both when you enter and leave Spain, Portugal, or Morocco and upon return home. The rules for importing and exporting are exceedingly complicated.

Imports

First, there's an **allowance** on what you can bring into a country. Anything exceeding the allowance must be **declared** and is charged a **duty.** All three countries permit up to 200 cigarettes and one still and one movie camera, with 10 rolls of film per camera. Note that it's illegal to import Moroccan *dirhams*.

> **Spain:** In place of 200 cigarettes, you're allowed 50 cigars or 250g of tobacco. One bottle of wine and one of hard liquor.
>
> **Portugal:** Two liters of wine and one of hard liquor.
>
> **Morocco:** In place of 200 cigarettes, you're allowed 400g of tobacco. One bottle of wine and one of hard liquor. 0.25 liter of eau de cologne.

Before leaving home you should make a list of the serial number, model, make, and/or description of any expensive items, especially foreign-made ones, that you're bringing into the country. (Canadian citizens should do this on the Y-38 forms provided by the customs offices.) Have your list stamped by a customs official prior to departure in order to prove that you really did buy that valuable Spanish belt in Macy's, not Madrid.

Exports

On leaving a country, you must **declare** all articles acquired abroad; keep receipts for everything that you bought. Note that items bought at duty-free shops are *not* exempt from duty when you return home. However, only the truly profligate budget traveler will exceed the maximum allowances and be compelled to deal closely with customs officials.

Also note that it's illegal to export **Moroccan dirhams.** On leaving Morocco, you may convert 50% of the *dirhams* in your possession (100% if you've been in the country less than 48 hrs.) by presenting exchange slips (to prove they were purchased at the official rate) to an authorized bank at your point of departure. Save your receipts as proof each time you change money, and try not to end up with too many extra *dirhams*.

U.S. citizens can import (bring home) US$400 worth of goods **duty-free** every 30 days; the next US$1000 is subject to a 10% tax. Duty-free goods must be for personal or household use (which includes gifts) and cannot include more than 100 cigars, 200 cigarettes, and one liter of alcohol. (You must be 21 or older to bring liquor into the U.S.) All duty-free items must accompany you; you may not mail them home. Beyond your US$400 allowance, certain manufactured goods purchased in **Morocco** may be duty-free under the Generalized System of Preferences (GSP). For more information, write for the brochure *GSP and the Traveler* from the U.S. Customs Service, 1301 Constitution Ave., Washington, DC 20229 (tel. (202) 566-8195).

> **Banned:** Non-prescription drugs and narcotics, many foods, plant and animal products, pornography, lottery tickets, and harmful items (guns, knives, bombs, etc.) To avoid problems when carrying prescription drugs, make sure the bottles are clearly marked and have the prescription ready to show the customs officer.
>
> **Mailing things home:** You can mail home unsolicited gifts duty-free if they're worth less than US$50. If you send back parcels worth more than US$50, the Postal Service will collect a duty plus a handling charge from the recipient. You may not mail alcohol, tobacco, or perfume into the U.S. Mark the package "unsolicited gift" and indicate the nature of the item and its retail value. To mail home personal belongings of U.S. origin, mark the package "American goods returned."
>
> **Information:** The brochure *Know Before You Go* provides general customs information. Ask for item 477Y and enclose 50 cents to R. Woods, Consumer Information Center, Pueblo, CO 81009. *Traveler's Tips on Bringing Food, Plant, and Animal Products into the United States* is available from the Animal and Plant Health Inspection Service, U.S. Dept. of Agriculture, Attn: Public Information, Washington, DC 20250.

Canadian citizens may bring back goods **duty-free** with a maximum value of CDN$300 every year after at least one week away; anything more valuable will be taxed at 20%. If you're 16 or older, you may import 200 cigarettes, 50 cigars, 1kg loose tobacco, and 1.1 liters of alcohol. (The minimum age for liquor and tobacco importation varies by province.) All duty-free items must accompany you; you may not mail them home.

> **Banned:** Pretty much the same as for U.S. citizens. If you're traveling home via the U.S., remember that painkillers containing codeine (over-the-counter in Canada but illegal in the stodgy U.S.) may not be brought into the U.S.
>
> **Mailing things home:** You can mail home unsolicited gifts duty-free if they're worth less than CDN$40. You may not mail alcohol or tobacco. Mark packages as explained for U.S. citizens above.
>
> **Information:** For the booklets *I Declare/ Je Déclare* and *Bon Voyage, But...*, contact External Affairs, Communications Branch, Mackenzie Ave., Ottawa, Ont. K1A OL5 (tel. (613) 957-0275).

British citizens can import £32 of goods **duty-free**, including 200 cigarettes, 100 cigarillos, 50 cigars, 250g tobacco, two liters of table wine plus either one liter over 44 proof *or* two liters of alcohol under 44 proof. (You must be over 16 to import liquor or tobacco.) Allowances are about 50% higher for goods bought in EEC countries. For **information**, contact Her Majesty's Customs and Excise Office, New King's Beam House, 22 Upper Ground, London SE1 9PJ (tel. (71) 382 54 68).

Irish citizens can import IR£34 of goods **duty-free,** including the same amount of tobacco products allowed British citizens and either one liter of alcohol over 44 proof or two liters of alcohol under 44 proof. For **information,** contact Division 1, Office of the Revenue Commissioners, Dublin Castle, Dublin 1 (tel. (1) 679 27 27).

Australian citizens can import AUS$400 (under 18 AUS$200) of goods **duty-free**, including 250g of tobacco (i.e., 250 cigarettes) and one liter of alcohol. (You must be 18 to import either.) You may not export over AUS$5000 without filing a special form with customs. For **information,** see the booklet *Customs Information for All Travelers,* available at Australian consulates and offices of the Collector of Customs.

New Zealand citizens can import NZ$700 of goods **duty-free**, including 200 cigarettes, 50 cigars, or a combination thereof equaling 250g; 4.5 liters of beer or wine; and 1.125 liters of hard liquor. For information, see the booklets *New Zealand Customs Guide for Travellers* and *If You're Not Sure About It, DECLARE IT,* available at customs offices.

Getting There

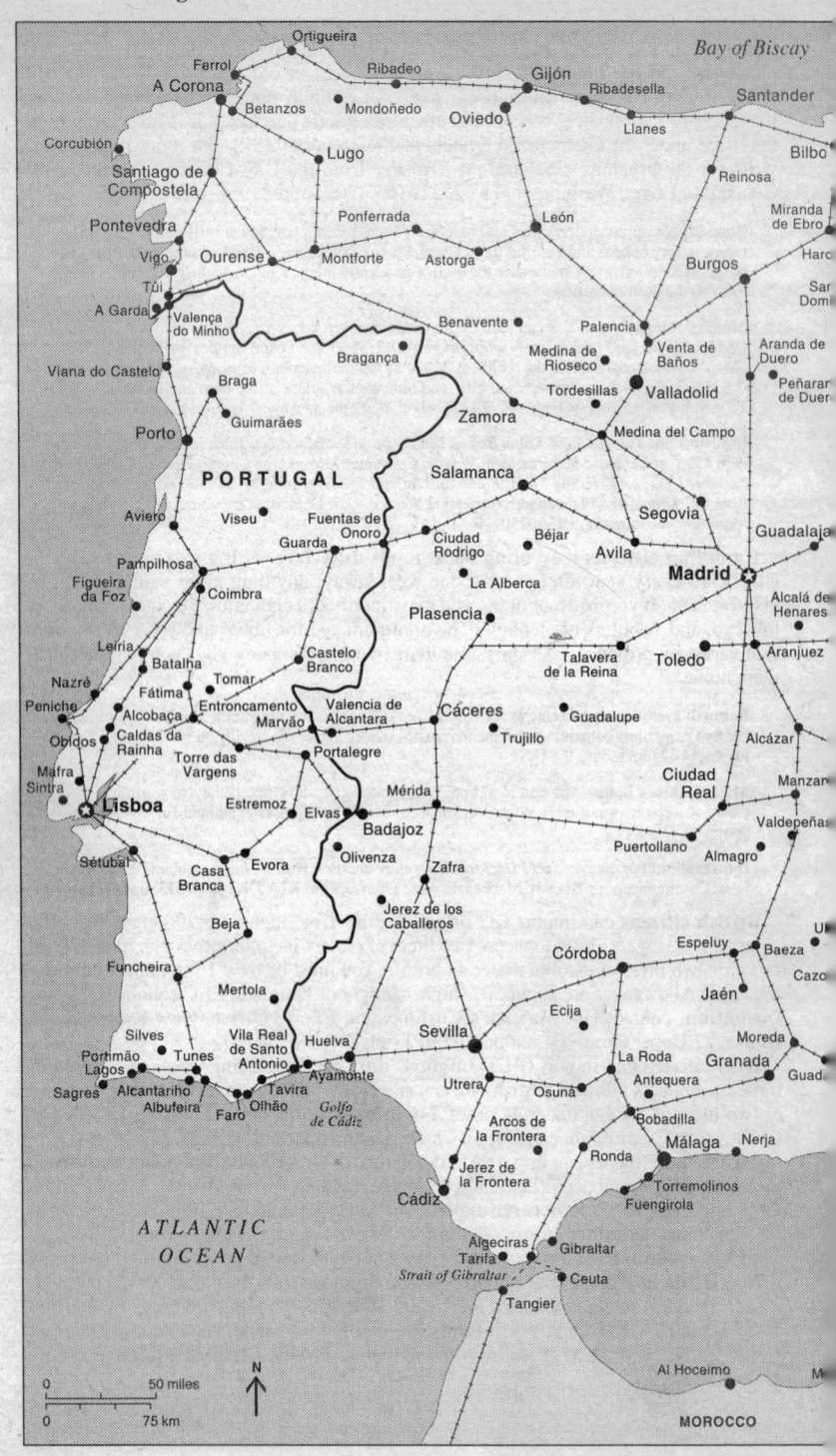

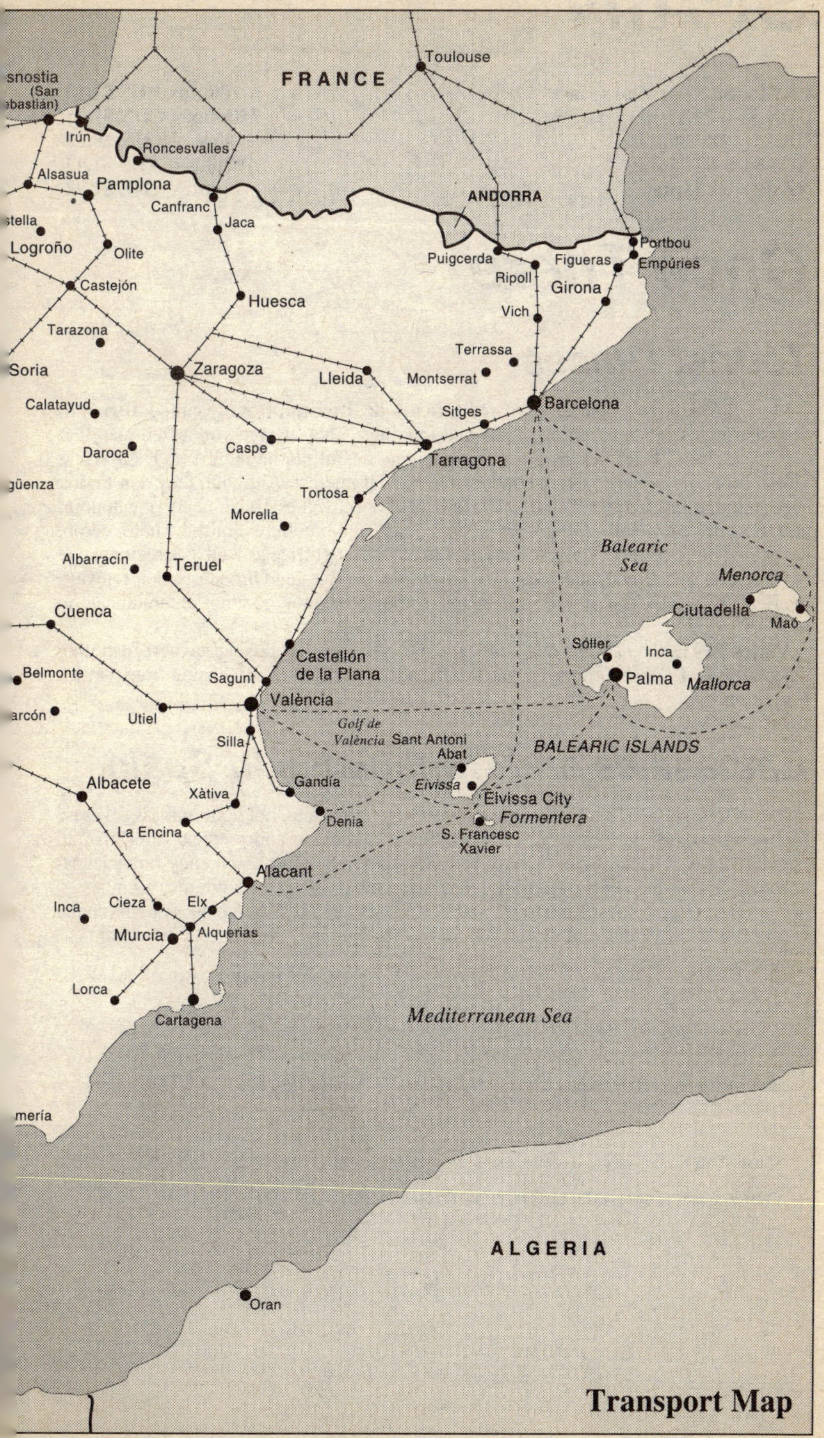

Transport Map

SPAIN

US $1 = 88.59 pesetas (ptas)
CDN $1 = 79.81ptas
UK £1 = 180.80ptas
AUS $1 = 69.76ptas
NZ $1 = 52.11ptas

100ptas = US $1.13
100ptas = CDN $1.25
100ptas = UK £0.55
100ptas = AUS $1.43
100ptas = NZ $1.92

Once There

Tourist Offices

Most towns have a centrally located **Oficina de Turismo** (fondly called **Turismo**) that distributes information on sights and lodgings. They'll give you a free map that usually includes brief descriptions of sights and useful phone numbers. Their sleek, glossy brochures cater to every conceivable special interest. Although they don't book accommodations, many a Turismo keeps lists of approved establishments or can point you to a *casa particular*. Often they'll stock maps and brochures for the whole region, if not the whole country. Larger cities tend to have a city office as well as a regional one (with regional, national, and some city info); their services and brochures don't always overlap. In smaller towns, the staff, maps, and/or brochures may not communicate in English.

Viajes TIVE, the national chain of student travel agencies, are everywhere, peddling discount travel tickets, churning out ISICs and HI cards, and dispensing transport information.

Embassies and Consulates in Spain

If you're seriously ill or in trouble, contact your consulate, not your embassy (whose function is solely diplomatic). They provide legal advice and medical referrals and contact relatives back home. In extreme cases, they may offer emergency financial assistance. Embassies are in Madrid; consulates (subdivisions of a country's embassy) are in other major cities. Embassies and consulates keep regular business hours: open from Monday to Friday, out to lunch from 1:30 to 3pm, and closed by 5:30 or 6pm.

U.S. Embassy: C. Serrano, 75, Madrid 28006 (tel. (1) 577 40 40). **Consulate,** Barcelona, Via Laietana, 33, 4th fl. (tel. (3) 319 95 50).

Canadian Embassy: Edificio Goya, C. Núñez de Balboa, 35, Madrid 28001 (tel. (1) 431 43 00 or 578 04 17). **Consulate,** Via Augusta, 125, ATICO 3A, Barcelona 08006 (tel. (3) 209 06 34).

British Embassy: C. Marqués de Encinares, 16, 2nd fl., Madrid 28029 (tel. (1) 308 52 01). **Consulate,** Pl. Nueva 8, DP DO Seville (tel. (5) 422 88 75); Alameda Urquijo, 2, 9th fl., Bilbo (tel. (94) 415 76 00).

Australian Embassy: Po. Castellana, 143, Madrid 28046 (tel. (1) 579 04 28).

New Zealand Embassy: Pl. Lealtad, 2, 3rd fl., Madrid 28014 (tel. (1) 523 02 26; fax (1) 523 01 71).

Getting Around

Train

Spanish trains are clean, somewhat punctual, and reasonably priced, although they don't run to some small towns. If you encounter problems, it'll be mainly at border stops, where you must change trains because of different rail gauges (although this by product of Franco's isolationism is slowly being undone). The **Viajes TIVE** travel agencies help untangle the complex, swiftly changing world of Spanish rail.

RENFE

Spain's national railroad system is **RENFE** (**RE**d **N**acional de los **F**errocarriles **E**spañoles). Below are explanations of the numerous types of RENFE train service, ranked by convenience. Bag on any *tranvía, semidirecto,* or *correo* train—these are ludicrously slow and are now uncommon.

> **AVE** (*Alta Velocidad Española*): Shiny new high-speed trains that run on European gauge tracks. Although AVE trains now only dart between Madrid and Sevilla (hitting on Ciudad Real and Córdoba en route), service to Barcelona and eventually Paris is in the works. AVE soars above other trains in comfort and price, not just speed. Headsets bring movies or music to your ears, while train attendants bring newspapers, a drink, and a snack. It's like an airplane, only with human-size seats and legroom.
>
> **Talgo:** Generally the best choice. Elegant, low-slung trains zip passengers in air-conditioned compartments. May (or may not) be faster than *regional* (see below) but more comfortable, and costs about twice as much.
>
> **Electro**: Very comfortable and quick, but less so than *talgo* due to more intermediate stops.
>
> **Expreso**, **Estrella**, and **Rápido**: The first 2 are usually equipped with sleeping cars. All 3 vary greatly in speed.
>
> **Cercanía**: Commuter trains that radiate from larger cities to suburbs and nearby *pueblos*, making frequent stops and usually lacking A/C.
>
> **Regional:** Similar to *cercanías,* they circulate through smaller towns.

RENFE also offers a number of discounts. Unfortunately, no youth railpass exists (not even the old *Tarjeta Joven).* ¡Beware of **red days** (holidays), which add 10% to your fare!

> **Blue days:** Most every day except for holidays and Friday and Saturday afternoons. On blue days round-trip tickets are discounted 12%; 20% for those under 26 with a *Carnet Joven de la Comunidad*, the Spanish citizen's youth ID. Youth IDs from other nations (especially EEC ones) sometimes work; if you're under 26, this is your only hope.
>
> **Cheque-trem purchasing option:** 50,000ptas worth of train travel for 42,500ptas. Only viable if you're planning to travel *a lot.*
>
> **BIJ tickets:** For international routes. Inquire at travel agencies. (For more info, see Getting There: From Europe: Train.)
>
> **Tarjeta Dorada:** Only Spanish citizens or residents of at least 6 months are eligible. 40% discounts on all fares to travelers over 60.
>
> **Family Pass:** Gives extra discounts to families on blue days.

Buy tickets within 60 days of departure at RENFE travel offices, RENFE train stations, and authorized travel agencies. RENFE will refund 85% (75% on "red days") of the ticket price for cancellation up to 15 minutes before train departure.

Unless you plan to spend every moment switching between trains, don't bother with the meticulously complete, 400+ page **Guía RENFE** (at train station bookstores, 1000ptas). This timetable doesn't list prices for any trains except AVE. It also lacks info on international routes.

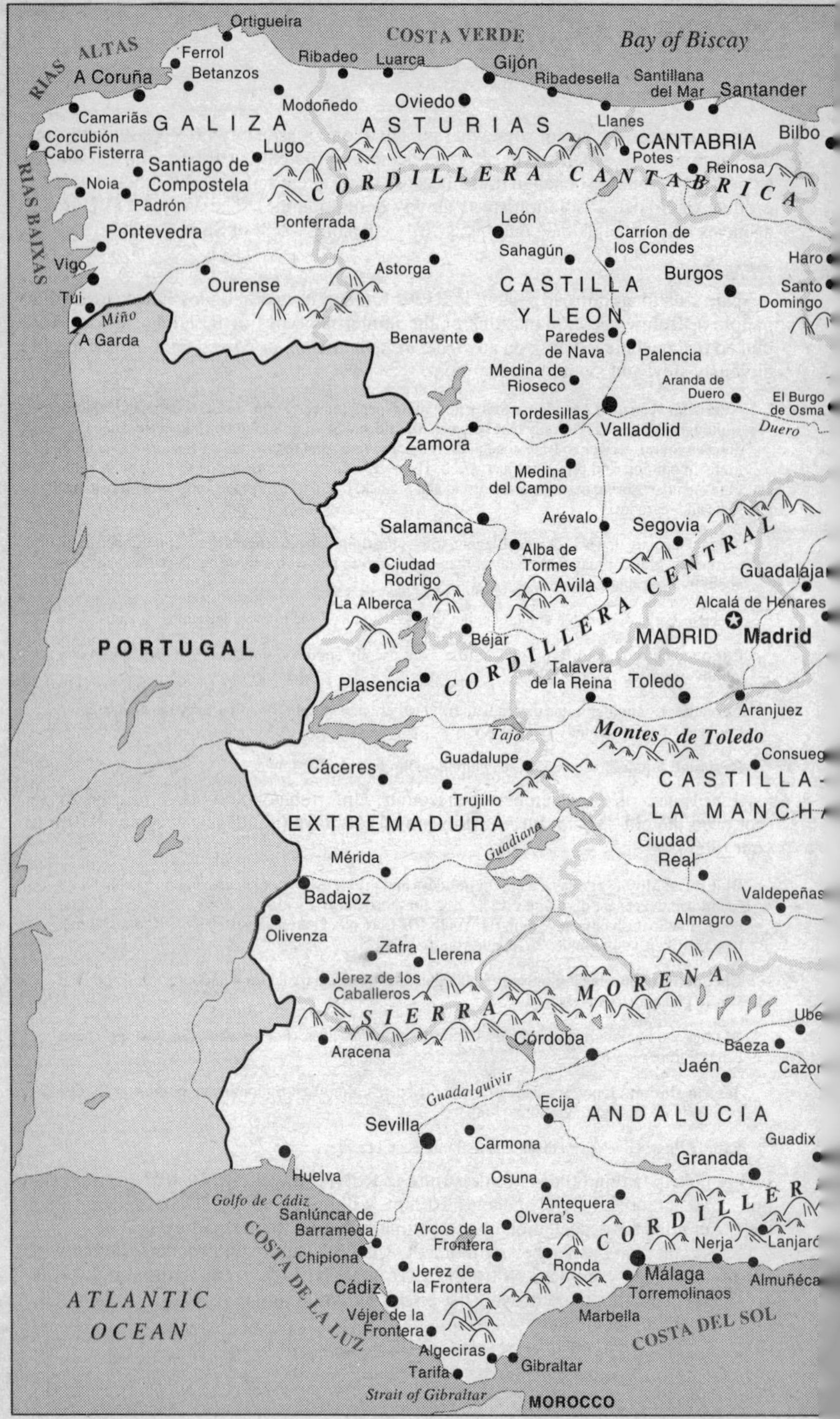
COSTA VERDE
Bay of Biscay
RIAS ALTAS
RIAS BAIXAS
Ortigueira
Ferrol
A Coruña
Betanzos
Ribadeo
Luarca
Gijón
Ribadesella
Santillana del Mar
Santander
Bilbo
Modoñedo
Oviedo
Camariñas
Corcubión
Cabo Fisterra
GALIZA
ASTURIAS
Llanes
CANTABRIA
Potes
Reinosa
Lugo
Santiago de Compostela
Noia
Padrón
CORDILLERA CANTABRICA
Pontevedra
Ponferrada
León
Carrion de los Condes
Sahagún
Vigo
Astorga
Haro
Ourense
CASTILLA Y LEON
Burgos
Santo Domingo
Tui
Miño
A Garda
Benavente
Paredes de Nava
Palencia
Medina de Rioseco
Aranda de Duero
El Burgo de Osma
Tordesillas
Valladolid
Duero
Zamora
Medina del Campo
Salamanca
Arévalo
Segovia
Alba de Tormes
Ciudad Rodrigo
Avila
CORDILLERA CENTRAL
La Alberca
Alcalá de Henares
Béjar
MADRID
Madrid
PORTUGAL
Plasencia
Talavera de la Reina
Toledo
Aranjuez
Tajo
Montes de Toledo
Cáceres
Guadalupe
Trujillo
EXTREMADURA
Guadiana
Ciudad Real
Mérida
Badajoz
Valdepeñas
Almagro
Olivenza
Zafra
Llerena
Jerez de los Caballeros
SIERRA MORENA
Aracena
Córdoba
Baeza
Jaén
Guadalquivir
Ecija
ANDALUCIA
Sevilla
Carmona
Guadix
Granada
Huelva
Osuna
Golfo de Cádiz
Antequera
Sanlúncar de Barrameda
Olvera's
Arcos de la Frontera
CORDILLERA
Nerja
Chipiona
Ronda
Málaga
Jerez de la Frontera
Torremolinaos
Cádiz
COSTA DE LA LUZ
Marbella
ATLANTIC OCEAN
Véjer de la Frontera
COSTA DEL SOL
Algeciras
Gibraltar
Tarifa
Strait of Gibraltar
MOROCCO

FRANCE
Donostia
Hondarribia
Irún
Roncesvalles
NAVARRA
Pamplona
Sangüesa
Tafalla
Olite
Logroño
RIOJA
Ansó
Jaca
Aínsa
Loarre
Huesca
PIRINEOS
ANDORRA
Seu d'Urgell
Puigcerdà
Ripoll
Portbou
Empúries
Figueras
Palafrugell
CATALUNYA
Vic
Girona
Tossa de Mar
Tudela
Ebro
Soria
Tarazona
Zaragoza
Lleida
Montserrat
Terrassa
COSTA BRAVA
Barcelona
Calatayud
Cariñera
ARAGON
Daroca
Vilanova i la Geltrú
Sitges
Tarragona
Sigüenza
Tajo
Tortosa
COSTA DAURADA
N
Balearic Sea
Morella
Albarracín
Teruel
Mora de Rubieios
Peñíscola
TO MENORCA
Alcúdia
Cuenca
Castelló de la Plana
Inca
Palma
Manacor
Belmonte
Sagunt
Golf de València
Mallorca
Alarcón
Júcar
VALENCIA
València
COSTA DEL AZAHAR
Cullera
Sant Antoni Abat
ILLES BALEARES
Santa Eulària des Riu
Eivissa
Eivissa City
Albacete
Gandía
Xàtiva
Denia
Formentera
Villena
Alcoi
Calp
S. Francesc Xavier
Menorca
Alacant
Ciutadella
Maò
COSTA BLANCA
Elx
Orihuela
MURCIA
Murcia
Manga del Mar Menor
Lorca
Cartagena
Mediterranean Sea
Almería
COSTA DE ALMERIA
0 50 miles
0 75 km
ALGERIA

FEVE and Eurail

The only other train company in Spain is **FEVE** (*Ferrocarril de Vía Estrecha*), actually a conglomeration of private companies which has short runs between northern towns not served by RENFE. Service is notoriously erratic and slow, and stations are typically far from the center of town.

Eurail no longer sells its Spanish Rail Pass; you can either deal with RENFE's discounts or get a Eurailpass. Those with Eurailpasses must pay a small fee to make reservations on trains in Spain. (For more information, see Getting There: From Europe: Train.)

Bus

With train fares becoming more expensive and discounts being eliminated, many avant-garde budgeteers have switched to bus as their preferred mode of transport. Bus routes are far more exhaustive than the rail network, are the only public transportation to isolated areas, and almost always cost less. Standards of comfort are quite high, especially on longer journeys. Buses are usually slightly slower than the equivalent trains; but highway improvements and expansions have cut travel time between major cities by as much as 50% in the past few years. A glowing example is the Sevibus Madrid-to-Sevilla line with service at least four times per day (6 1/2 hr., 2000ptas). By contrast, a *talgo* train is just one hour faster, and a second-class fare costs over 5000ptas.

Spain has no national bus line, just a multitude of private companies. This lack of centralization makes trip planning an ordeal. **Viajes TIVE** or the main information window at the bus station can help. Bus companies have worked it so that only one or two companies will serve a destination; their coverage rarely overlaps. In many cities, each bus company has its own station from which buses arrive and depart. Note that Auto-Res/Cunisa, S.A. offers a *tarjeta joven* (**youth pass;** see details below).

Some, but hardly all, of the major companies (based in Madrid) are listed below. Plenty of regional companies have cities other than Madrid as their nucleus or bypass Madrid entirely.

ALSA (tel. (1) 468 19 27). Provides service between Madrid and Asturias, Galicia, and Castilla-León; and international service to Portugal, France, Italy, Switzerland, and Belgium. **Auto Transporte Julia, S.A.** (tel. (1) 468 37 99 or 468 38 13) also has service to these countries. **Iberbus-Linebus** (tel. (1) 467 25 65 or 467 28 57) goes to France, Italy, Belgium, and Holland.

Samar, S.A. (tel. (1) 468 42 36). Runs east from Madrid to Guadalajara, Zaragoza, Lérida, and Andorra (France); and south to Málaga, Granada, and Algeciras.

Enatcar (tel. (1) 527 99 27 or 467 35 77). Many routes in new buses from Madrid to Andalucía (Granada, Málaga, Algeciras), Valencia (Alicante), and Catalunya (Barcelona).

Sevibus, S.A. (tel. (1) 530 44 17). Between Madrid and Sevilla (including Huelva and Ayamonte) in festive-hued buses, complete with free drink and headsets for the movie or music.

Continental-Auto (tel. (1) 356 23 07). Runs to many *pueblos* of interest near Madrid, including Toledo, Guadalajara, and Alcalá de Henares.

Auto-Res/Cunisa, S.A. (tel. (1) 551 72 00). The workhorse of Spanish buses, though still comfortable, goes west from Madrid into southern Castilla y León and Extremadura; and from Madrid to Sevilla, Valencia, and its nearby beaches. They offer a *tarjeta joven* (youth pass, 200ptas) for those under 26, good for 10% discounts on normal fares.

Plane

Given the substantial distances between Spanish cities, you might consider flying if you're pressed for time (or rich). **Iberia,** Spain's major national airline, flies out of hubs Madrid and Barcelona on both international and domestic routes. **Aviaco,** a subsidiary of Iberia, covers only domestic routes. Prices at Aviaco and charter companies such as Air España (Palma), Aviación y Comercio (Madrid), and Euskal Air (Vitoria) are often lower than Iberia's.

Tarifas-minis are special Iberia and Aviaco fares. Available only on certain days, they cost about 60% of the normal price for round-trip, tourist-class tickets. Travelers under 24 can sometimes get an additional discount. You must buy your ticket at least three days in advance and travel round-trip (although you can take a circuitous route). There are no refunds or exchanges. Check with travel agencies such as Viajes TIVE on the latest *mini* offers.

Car

A car brings freedom, flexibility, and handsome scenery at a cost. Spain has recently improved its highway system, so that major cities are connected by four-lane *autopistas* with plenty of service stations (although service stations still aren't common on back roads). The Spanish AAA is called the **Real Automóbil Club.**

Gas comes in super (97 octane), normal (92 octane), and diesel; an increasing number of gas stations provide unleaded. Prices are astronomical by North American standards, about US$4 per gallon.

Speeders beware: police can "photograph" the speed and license plate of your car, issuing you a ticket without even pulling you over. Don't cruise in the passing lane—it provokes the ire of police and fellow motorists alike. Officially you need an **international driver's license** to drive in Spain (see Planning Your Trip: Documents). For touring through picturesque local areas, the leaflets on *rutas turísticas*—available at tourist offices—suggest routes but are low on practical information.

The ridesharing agency **Adedo,** C. Estudios, 9, Madrid (tel. (1) 265 65 65), helps match drivers and passengers. Membership costs 1500ptas for drivers, 3500ptas for passengers. Membership for one trip costs only 500ptas; international trips cost 1000ptas. Insurance is included in the fee. Call at least two days in advance.

Renting a car in Spain is considerably cheaper than in many other European countries, although tax on rentals can be as much as 12%. Spain's largest national car rental company is **Atesa.** Another major rental company is **Europcar,** whose U.S. affiliate is National Car Rental. You'll find **Avis, Hertz,** and other major companies in cities and airports. Rates start at about US$200 per week (not including insurance and tax), but local companies may be cheaper. It's cheaper (for some reason) to reserve your rental in the U.S. before coming to Spain. Most companies require you be at least 21 and to have had a driver's license for at least one year. The following companies offer information on reservations.

Auto-Europe, P.O. Box 1097, Camden, ME 04843 (in the U.S. and Canada tel. (800) 223-5555; elsewhere (207) 236-8235; fax (207) 236-4724).

Avis (tel. (800) 331-1212). You must reserve while still in the U.S.

Europe By Car, 1 Rockefeller Pl., New York, NY 10020 (tel. (800) 223-1516 or (212) 581-3040). Student and faculty discounts.

Hertz Rent-A-Car (tel. (800) 654-3131).

Kemwel Group, 106 Calvert St., Harrison, NY 10528-3199 (tel. (800) 678-0678 or (914) 835-5454). Rents, leases, and sells most makes of cars. The good rental rates are even lower if reservations are made.

National Car Rental (tel. (800) 227-7368).

Moped and Bicycle

Touring by **moped** is a breezy way to see the country. Mopeds cruise at an easy 40mph and don't use much gas. They can be dangerous in rain and on rough roads or gravel, so always wear a helmet and don't pack a huge, unwieldy, unbalancing backpack. Rental agencies reside in most cities (US$20-25 per day, less in coastal areas where tourist rentals are more common).

Bicycling is a gloriously active mode of transport that allows you to see the country close up. Even experienced cyclists should think twice about pedaling through central and southern Iberia in the scorching summer (the north is cooler and less crowded).

Back roads in flatlands and coastal areas are the best for bike touring; beware of more mountainous regions. Bicycles aren't permitted on toll highways.

The first thing to buy is a sturdy bike helmet, difficult to find in some areas of Spain. You'll also need a tough bike lock (the best are made by Kryptonite and cost US$35-US$50), a strong pump, and various spare parts and tools. Wise cyclists bring along a basic bike repair book and the relevant gadgetry.

Airlines count a bicycle as your second free piece of checked luggage. As a third piece, it'll cost US$85 each way. The bike can't weigh over 70 lbs. and must be boxed (normally boxes are available at the airport). Policies vary, so call individual airlines.

A number of books about biking in Europe recommend scenic and cyclable roads. *Europe by Bike: 18 Tours Geared for Discovery,* by Karen and Terry Whitehill (The Mountaineers Press, Seattle $10.95), is a fairly accurate aid for planning your trip and outfitting your bike.

Hitchhiking

> Let's Go does not recommend hitching as a means of travel; the information presented below and throughout the book is not intended to do so.

Hitchers report that Castilla and Andalucía offer little more than a long, hot wait and that hitchhiking out of Madrid—in any direction—is virtually impossible. The Mediterranean coast and the islands are supposedly more promising. Approaching people for rides at gas stations near highways and rest stops reportedly gets results.

The dangers of hitchhiking should not be underestimated. Drivers have raped, sexually assaulted, and killed passengers. If you choose to solicit a ride, avoid doing it alone. Experienced hitchers sit in the front, and never get in the back seat of a two-door car. If the driver begins to harass them, they ask firmly to be let out. They report that, in an emergency, opening the door on the road may surprise a driver enough to slow down. Pretending you're about to vomit may also help, they say.

Ferry

Ferrying to Spain's Mediterranean and Atlantic islands is scenic, romantic, and sunny. **Transmediterránea** is the major player between the Balearic Islands (Illes Baleares) and the Canaries; also investigate smaller companies such as **ISNASA**. Don't forget to ask about discount fares. During high season, make reservations and expect overcrowding. Buy your ticket at least an hour prior to departure to avoid paying a surcharge on board.

Couchettes are good deals on overnight trips. A *silla,* the least expensive option, is a deck chair. A *butaca,* good for sleeping and sunning alike, is more akin to an airplane seat.

Accommodations

Youth Hostels

The **Red Española de Albergues Juveniles (REAJ),** the Spanish Hostelling International (HI) affiliate, runs about 100 youth hostels year-round and over 140 in summer. A bargainous bed costs 600-700ptas per night, about half the cost of a single in most other accommodations. Rates are slightly higher for guests 26 or older (i.e. over 25). Hostels are typically some distance away from the town center. Early curfews are common and enforced lockouts may cramp your style if you club-hop. As they're often brimming with school groups, don't expect much privacy. To reserve a bed in high season (July and August), obtain an **International Booking Voucher** from REAJ (or your home country's HI affiliate) and send it to the desired hostel four to eight weeks in advance of your stay.

To stay in a hostel, an **HI card** (1800ptas) is almost always required. Rarely sold on the spot, they're ubiquitous at Viajes TIVE, other travel agencies, and REAJ offices.

Also mandatory is a **sleepsack,** so either bring your own or rent one from the hostel—in listings we'll write "Sheets 200ptas." (To make a cheap sleepsack, see Planning Your Trip: Packing.) Youth hostels are not to be confused with posh *albergues nacionales,* ritzy government-run establishments in out-of-the-way places.

For **information** such as hostel addresses, contact REAJ, C. José Ortega y Gasset, 71, Apartado 208, Madrid 28006 (tel. (1) 401 95 01). (See also Planning Your Trip: Documents: HI Membership.)

Pensiones and Hostales

Accommodations have many an alias in Spain; each name indicates a specific type of establishment. All legally registered establishments must display a blue plaque identifying their category. The outlaws (terms no longer registered with Turismo, hence not required to fulfill its standards) are *fondas* and *casa de huéspedes.* Many cities are swamped in high season (see Accommodations sections under specific cities); make reservations or start searching for lodgings early in the day.

Cheapest and barest are **hospe dajes.** The categories next higher in quality are **pensiones,** then **hostales,** then **hostal-residencias** (all three similar in amenities), the staples of many a budget traveler. *Hostales* must have sinks in the bedrooms, while *hostal-residencias* verge on *hotel* poshness. These are rated by the government on a two-star system; even one-star places in this category are usually very comfortable. Note that *pensiones, casas de huéspedes,* and *casas* are basically boarding houses, often lacking heat, having curfews, and fonder of long-term guests *(estables).* The highest-priced accommodations are **hoteles**, far beyond the reach of budget travelers.

Pensión completa (full board: breakfast, lunch, dinner) usually costs about 2000ptas; **pensión media** (half-board: breakfast, dinner) is only sometimes offered. **"Full bath"** or **"bath"** refers to a shower and toilet, while "shower" means just a shower stall. Most rooms that *Let's Go* lists have winter heating, as it can get cold in Spain (particularly the mountainous north).

Before handing over your passport, ask to see a room and verify the price, which proprietors are required by law to post prominently in every room and by the main entrance. Minimum and maximum prices are fixed according to the facilities, but don't expect these to correspond exactly to low and high seasons. Prices can be undercut, but not legally exceeded. It's illegal for establishments to discriminate against people who don't eat breakfast; don't pay for breakfast if you don't eat it. Haggling for prices in small inns is still acceptable. Single rooms may be hard to come by, and solo travelers should be prepared to pay for a double.

If you run into trouble when it's time to pay, ask for the **libro de reclamaciones** (complaint book), which by law must be produced on demand. The argument will usually end immediately, since all complaints must be forwarded to the authorities within 48 hours and hotelkeepers are penalized for overcharging. As many tourist offices keep lists of accommodations, report any problems to them; tourist officials may offer to call the establishment for you to resolve disputes.

Camping

Campgrounds are the cheapest genre of accommodations. The government regulates campgrounds on a three-class system, rating and pricing them by the quality of amenities. All campgrounds must post fees within view of the entrance and are required by law to provide sinks, showers, and toilets. The ritzier ones have a playground, grocery store, cafe/restaurant, post office, car wash, and/or hairdresser. In high season, make reservations and arrive early. Information on official camping areas is available from most tourist offices. Tourist offices stock the **Guía de Campings,** a fat guide to all official campgrounds in Spain.

Alternative Accommodations

In some regions tourist authorities are aggressively promoting alternate types of accommodations to help deal with insufficient accommodations in larger cities and to bolster tourism in rural areas.

Casas particulares (private residences): May be the only choice in less touristed towns. Tourist offices keep lists of residences. Restaurant proprietors and bartenders often supply names and directions.

Casas rurales (rural cottages) and **Casas rústicas** (farmhouses): Referred to in official publications as *agroturismo*. Most popular in Euskadi (Basque Country). Overnight rates range from 1000 to 2500ptas.

Refugios: Rustic huts in the mountains. You usually have to walk to them. Write to the Federación Nacional de Montañismo, Alberto Aguilera, 3, 28015 Madrid (tel. (1) 445 13 82 or 445 14 38) for more information.

Colegios Mayores (state university student dorms): Open to travelers in summer; the Consulate General of Spain (see Planning Your Trip: Useful Addresses) has more information. Private universities also rent out rooms in their **residencias** (dorms). Ask local tourist offices for more information.

Monasteries—Benedictine and Cistercian—and **Convents:** Peaceful lodgings in somewhat rural settings. Where else can you enjoy Gregorian chants and austere Romanesque and Gothic architecture? Don't expect luxury; they're functioning religious institutions, not hotels. Silence, prayer, and seclusion are the rule. Lodgings are usually single-sex and visitors are expected to respect the ways of the Order. Several monasteries refuse to charge, instead suggesting a donation (about 1500ptas). Both the national and local tourist offices keep lists with directions, telephone numbers, rules, and suggested donations. Reservations generally must be made well in advance.

Paradores Nacionales: The pride of the Spanish tourist industry. Castles, palaces, convents, and historic buildings that have been converted into luxurious hotels. At least 10,000ptas for a double, if not more. The national tourist office has volumes on the subject.

Food and Drink

Spaniards prize fresh ingredients and sauces that don't overpower a dish. Their gastronomic tradition is an ancient, influential, and varied one; chefs are known to scour medieval and Renaissance recipe collections for "new" ideas.

Each region has developed its own gorgeous repertoire of dishes based on indigenous produce, meats, and fish. While the most well known Spanish dishes—*paella, gazpacho,* and *tortilla española*--are from València, Andalucía, and Castilla respectively, the most sophisticated and varied cuisines on the peninsula were developed in Euskadi, Navarra, Catalunya, and Galiza.

Typical Fare

Coastal areas prepare their catches distinctively and deliciously. The Basques are undisputed masters of *bacalao* (cod), *calamar en su tinta* (squid in its own ink), *sopa de pescado* (fish soup), and mouthwatering *angulas a la bilbaína* (baby eels in garlic, shoveled down with oversized wood forks so the critters won't slide off a metal surface). In Galiza, they drool over *empanadas* (pies) filled with uncommonly good *gambas* (jumbo shrimp), *veiras* (scallops), *mejillones* (mussels), and *santiaguiños* (spider crabs). Catalunya is the home of *zarzuela,* a seafood and tomato bouillabaise, and its own version of *langosta* (lobster). Catalunya is also famed for its juxtapositions of sweet and sour flavors, as in *oca con peras* (goose with pears). Menorcan mayonnaise was the precursor of Miracle Whip (and named for the capital Maó (Mahón). Chefs of the Illes Baleares stir up a variety of fish stews, while Andalusians are masters of the light touch in fried fish. Mallorca's *ensaimada,* angel's hair pastry smothered in powdered sugar, sweetens up breakfast throughout the mainland.

València's menu makes innovative use of rice; its *paella,* the saffron-seasoned dish made with meat, fish, poultry, vegetables, or snails is an international celebrity (there are over 200 variants throughout the region). In the north, Asturias warms to *fabada* (bean stew) and finishes it off with *queso cabrales* (blue cheese). Landlocked Castilla churns out dense *cocido* (stew) of meats, sausage, and chickpeas, as well as *chorizo,* an ugly but savory little sausage seasoned with paprika and garlic. For pork lovers, impossibly tender (such that it can be sliced with a plate) *cochinillo asado al horno* (roast suckling pig) is a glutton's delight. Culinary adventurers shouldn't miss Navarra's quirky *perdiz con chocolate* (partridge in chocolate). Smoked or cured meats are described as *serrano,* while grilled meats are *asado.*

Two delightful English-language **reference books** on Spanish foods and wines are Penelope Casas's *The Foods and Wines of Spain* and *Tapas.* Campsa, the petrochemicals company, publishes an excellent, regularly updated guide to Spanish restaurants called *Guía Campsa.* Also see our **Glossary of Food and Restaurant Terms** in the back of the book.

Meals and Dining Hours

Spaniards start their day with a continental breakfast of coffee or thick, liquid chocolate and *bollos* (rolls) or *churros* (lightly fried fritters). *Café solo* means black coffee; add a splash of milk and it's *café cortado.* For something like café au lait, order *café con leche*—what most Spaniards quaff at breakfast.

As in the rest of Europe, dinner ("lunch" to Americans) is served at midday, between 2 and 3pm. The midday meal traditionally consists of several courses: an *entremés* (appetizer) of soup or another starter; a main course of meat or fish with vegetable or *ensalada* (salad); and a dessert of fruit and *queso* (cheese), or perhaps a sweet. Often you must order the vegetable separately (the combination platter is rarer here than in the U.S.). In family-style restaurants, they may automatically set out a lettuce and tomato salad before a group of diners.

Supper at home is light and devoured around 8pm. Only speed freaks can wait to eat out; supper out begins any time after 9pm, usually at 10pm, and is a light, three-course meal.

Restaurants

Some restaurants are "open" from 8am until 1 or 2am; but most serve meals from 1:30 or 2pm to 4pm only, and in the evening from 8 until 11pm or midnight. Eating at the bar is always cheaper than at tables. Usually the check isn't brought to your table unless you request it. You can leave the proper amount on the table or pay at the register, then leave.

Each city's tourist office rates its *restaurantes* with a row of forks, five forks indicating luxury. *Cafeterías* are rated by a row of up to three cups. All cafeterias and one- and two-fork establishments are in the budget range. Prices for a full meal range from about 800ptas in the cheapest bar-restaurants to perhaps 1800ptas in a four-forker.

Dining options for misers are three: 1) **Platos combinados** (combination platters) include a main course and side dishes on a single plate, plus bread and sometimes beverage. 2) **Menú del día**—two dishes, bread, wine/beer/mineral water, and dessert—costs roughly 700-1100ptas. (This generally means choosing one dish from Group A and one from Group B.) Spanish workers, from blue-collars to CEOs, usually settle into a favorite restaurant, ordering the *menú* every day at lunch. The food ranges from decent to superb, and the dishes are the most typically Spanish—but you'll be full when the dust clears. *Lentejas* (lentils), *cocido* (stew with chickpeas), *sopa* (soup), *paella, pollo* (chicken) in all its forms, seafood, and *patatas* (potatoes) tend to always turn up on menus. 3) **A la carte** is a written menu from which you order separate entrees.

Tapas

Grazed upon or just snarfed down at bars, **tapas** (named for the *tapa* or sausage slice that used to be placed atop a wine glass to keep flies out) are ever so conducive to convivial good spirits. Sêek out these varied delights in *tascas* that specialize in given varieties (in many bars, regrettably, they're not made on the premises). A *tasca,* often also called a **taberna,** is a bar or pub that serves *tapas* at a counter or a few tables in back.

Tabernas are generally open noon to 4pm and 8pm 'til midnight or 2am. **Mesones** are *tabernas* that serve at tables only. Those who don't speak Spanish can indicate their *tapa* of choice by pointing at the array on (or behind) the counter. Some *tapas* terms:

Pinchos are bite-size samples stabbed by a toothpick.

Tapas are regular appetizer-like servings.

Raciónes may be equal to an entree in size.

Bocadillos are *tapas* served as a sandwich on a hunk of thick bread—often a viable substitute for lunch.

Your fork may find its way into the following: *champiñones al ajillo* (mushrooms in garlic sauce), *jamón serrano* (smoked ham), *atún* or *bonito* (tuna), *merluza* (hake), *calamares fritos* (fried squid), *chorizo* (spicy sausage), *gambas* (shrimp), *boquerones* (smelts), *ternera* (veal), *lomo* (pork), *judías verdes* (green beans), and *lenguado* (sole).

Drinks

Wash down your *tapas* with a draft beer (request *cerveza del país* for uniformly excellent Spanish beer), a glass of wine (**vino** *blanco* is white, *vino tinto* red, *vino rosado* blush), or sherry (*jerez*). The *vino de la casa* (house wine) makes an economical, often delicious choice.

Perhaps the most famous of Spanish wines is **jerez** (sherry), which hails—and takes its name—from Jerez in Andalucía. Tipple the dry *fino* and *amontillado* as aperitifs, or finish off a rich supper with the sweet *oloroso* and *dulce*. The *manzanilla* produced in Sanlúcar (near Cádiz) has a slight salty aftertaste, which some ascribe to the salt-impregnated soil of this coastal area.

The region around Córdoba presses the delicious dry wines Montilla and Morilas. La Rioja's vintages, Castilla's Valle del Duero (e.g., Vega Sicilia, strictly for Prime Ministers) labels, and Catalunya's whites and *cavas* (champagnes) are world-famous. But even Lord Peter Wimsey would deem local wines and liqueurs uniformly fine. You might down some Tenerife from the Islas Canarias (Canary Islands) or the full-bodied reds from Cariñena near Zaragoza. Also for swigging are the fresh young Ribeiro and more delicate Albariño from Galiza, the muscatel of Málaga, and **sidra** (alcoholic cider) from Asturias and Euskadi (see Donostia/San Sebastián: Food). Spanish **sangría**, a red-wine punch, stirs in sliced peaches and oranges, seltzer, and sugar; a dash of brandy supplies the kick. A lighter option is *tinto de verano,* a cold summer drink of red wine and carbonated mineral water.

A **caña** is a normal-sized beer, a **tubo** a large (served in a tall cylindrical glass). The blanket term for beer is **cerveza**. A mixed drink in a wine glass is generically called a **bica** or **copa**. A refreshing blend of beer and *gaseosa* (sweetened seltzer, resembling 7-Up) is called a *clara*. In entertainment listings, look under the *Ir ve de Copas* heading for late-night places to drink.

Spain whips up numerous non-alcoholic quenchers, most notably **horchata de chufa** (a cooling orgeat made from pressed almonds), and the crushed-ice *granizados*. Toast your shady spot on a *terraza* (outdoor café) with *blanco y negro* (white and black, i.e., ice cream and coffee float). The Spanish take on *batidos* (milkshakes) is wickedly creamy.

Communications

Mail

The most reliable way to send a message is actually via telegram (see below); the least is by surface mail, which may take over two months. Mail sent from small towns takes longer than from major cities. Stamps are sold at post offices, hotels, and tobacconists. (Identify a tobacconist by the brown sign with yellow lettering and an icon of a tobacco leaf; they always have postal scales).

Air mail: *Por avión.* Takes 10-14 business days to reach the U.S. and Canada; faster to the U.K. and Ireland; slower to Australia and New Zealand. Postage for a letter 83ptas.

Surface mail: *Por barco.* Takes one month or more. Considerably less expensive than air mail.

Postcards: *Postales.* Take even longer than letters. Postage 83ptas.

Registered or express mail: *Registrado* or *certificado.* The most reliable way to send a letter or parcel home. Takes 4-7 business days. Postage for a letter 500ptas.

Overnight mail: *Postal Expres.* Promises overnight delivery but inevitably takes 2-3 business days. Postage 5000ptas.

General Delivery mail: *Lista de Correos.* Letters or packages held for pick-up. Letters should be addressed as follows: LAST NAME, First Name; Lista de Correos; City Name; Postal Code; COUNTRY; AIR MAIL. When you pick it up, always ask for mail under both your first and last name to make sure it hasn't been misfiled. You can have mail forwarded to another Lista de Correos address if you must leave town whilst expecting mail. Takes 2 wks. Usually no charge for pick-up.

American Express: Mail (no packages) for cardholders may be sent to some AmEx offices, where it'll be held. This service may be less reliable than Lista de Correos. A directory of which offices hold mail can be had from any AmEx office, or contact their main office at 65 Broadway, New York, NY 10006 (tel. (800) 528-4800). They'll keep mail for one to three months after receipt.

Telegraph

A telegram *(telegrama),* the most reliable means of communication, costs the same as a three-minute international call. Telegraph offices are inside **post offices.** A message of 10-15 words costs about US$15.

Fax

Most Spanish **post offices** have fax services. Some photocopy shops and some telephone offices *(Telefónica)* also offer fax service, but they charge more than the post office (whose rates are regulated by the government), and faxes can only be sent, not received. The word for fax is the same in Spanish.

Throughout Spain, the price at post offices is standardized. (Prices not including IVA.) To send to North America: 1320ptas for the first page, 1100ptas each additional page. To receive: 330ptas for the first page, 194ptas each additional page.

Telephone

Country Code: 34.

Local Operator: 009.

Local Police Emergency: 091.

Guardia Civil: 062.

Phone booths are marked by signs that say *Teléfono público* or *Locutorio.* Most bars also have pay phones. Local calls cost 15ptas. A three-minute call to anywhere in Spain is 100ptas. **Phonecards** in 1000 and 2000ptas denominations are more convenient than feeding coin after coin into a pay phone; they're sold at tobacconists (although mysteriously they're often sold out).

Direct-dialing from a phone booth is the cheapest way to make international calls. It can take up to 30 seconds after you dial to make the connection. Call the operator beforehand to get an idea of how much your call will be. Then dial 07, wait for the high-pitched dial tone, then it's: country code + city code + phone number. Handy calling cards let you make calls even when you don't have a pocket full of coins, but their rates are higher.

AT&T calling card: To call the U.S., dial 900 99 00 11, then give the operator the number you want to reach and your calling card number. In Spain, you can use your AT&T calling card to use the "Dedicated Phone Line" at the Madrid airport and the Madrid Colón *Telefónica.* This allows you to contact a U.S. operator directly and be charged at U.S. rates. Call (800) 874-4000 for information about this.

MCI calling card: To call the U.S., dial 900 99 00 14, then give the operator the number you want and your calling card number. The system isn't perfect, so you may have to press a special button in the phone booth rather than dialing the number above.

Collect calls *(cobro revertido)* are billed according to pricier person-to-person *(persona a persona)* rates but may still be cheaper than calls from hotels. Amaze your friends by making collect calls from a non-public phone! (1) Dial 005. (2) State the number and your name. (3) Hang up the phone. (4) The phone magically rings when your call has been accepted.

Telefónica is a central phone office, for local, non-local, and international calls, where you take a number and then sit down in comfort. The doting staff does the legwork—service you'll be paying extra for. Offices are generally crowded. Some are open 24 hrs. Visa credit cards are accepted.

Overseas Access is a telephone service offered by EurAide, P.O. Box 2375, Naperville, IL 60567 (tel. (708) 420-2343). European travelers pay a registration fee (US$15) and a weekly (US$15) or monthly (US$40) fee. Anyone who wants to get in touch with you calls a "home base" in Munich and leaves a short message (US$1 per min.); you get the message by calling the home base as often as you like. Calls to Munich from Iberia are obviously cheaper than overseas calls. If you buy a Eurailpass from them, the initial fee is waived and the monthly rate is US$25.

More Money

The smallest denomination of paper currency, apart from the rare 500ptas bill, is 1000ptas. Coins come in 1, 5, 10, 25, and 100ptas.

In summer, **banking hours** are Monday through Friday 9am-2pm; in winter, banks are also open Saturday 9am-1pm. The odd bank is open for an afternoon session too. Banks charge a minimum of 500-750 ptas for currency exchange.

El Corte Inglés

This Spanish department store chain exchanges currency from Monday to Saturday 10am-8pm at competitive rates: 1% commission (250ptas min. charge) on traveler's checks; 2% commission (500ptas min. charge) on currency. Located in the heart of larger cities close to subway or bus stops, El Corte Inglés also gives out free, excellent, indexed street maps. This multi-purpose Spanish retailing giant offers many conveniences to the traveler: pay phones, English-language novels and guidebooks, interpreters, a beauty salon, eateries, quick photo developing, and their very own travel agency. They've got it all.

Value-Added Tax (VAT)

The Value-Added Tax (VAT; in Spain **IVA**) is a sales tax levied on all goods and services in the European Economic Community, at a rate that depends on the item. Stores, restaurants, and lodgings include IVA in posted prices, unless otherwise noted. In Spain the basic rate is 6-10%. Ask at stores and tourist offices about IVA refunds—a rare possibility with many restrictions (e.g., hefty minimum amount spent). The tax on accommodations and other "services" is not refundable. Prices quoted in *Let's Go* include VAT except where noted.

Tipping

Most restaurants add a service charge to your bill. It's customary to round off the sum to the next highest unit of currency and leave the change as a tip. In Spain you should generally tip 5%, more if the service is exceptional. Everyone else deserves a tip too: barpeople 25ptas, train or airport porters 100-150ptas per bag, taxi drivers 10% of the meter fare, hotel porters 100-150ptas, parking lot attendants 15-25ptas, cloakroom attendants 25-100ptas, shoeshiners 25ptas, movie theater ushers 25ptas, washroom attendants 25ptas, and hotel chambermaids 65-100ptas per day (optional).

Life and Times

Language(s)

Spain has four official languages: Castilian (Spanish), Catalan, Galician, and Basque. The latter are not dialects of Castilian; in fact, all are subdivided into dialects of their own. Other than the universally spoken Castilian, Catalan is the most widespread of these, never having lost its prestige among the elite classes. It is spoken in Catalunya and the Baleares, less extensively in València. Galician—related to Portuguese—is the language of the once-Celtic northwest corner, more prevalent in the countryside than in the cities (although it's now spreading among the young). Basque is almost entirely confined to the rural citizens of Euskadi and northern Navarra, the regions near France.

All four languages have long-established standardized grammars and all (but for Basque) ancient literary traditions. They're being saved from death by regional television broadcasts, strong native film industries, and extensive schooling in these languages. For more details about Catalan, Galician, and Basque, see their respective regional introductions.

Although Spanish is pronounced differently from country to country in Latin America, the Castilian spoken in Spain differs most in the pronunciation of "c" before "e" or "i". **Note:** *Let's Go* **provides a glossary and pronunciation guide in the back of the book for all terms used recurrently throughout the text.**

History

Way Back

Spain was colonized by a succession of civilizations—Basque (here to this day), Tartesian, Iberian, Celtic, Greek, Phoenician, and Carthaginian—long before the Romans stomped in (the 2nd century BC). The **Romans** left scraps of their language, architecture, magnificent roads (to this day the routes they built are the most efficient way between any two towns), and their techniques for the irrigation and care of grapes, olives, and wheat. A slew of Germanic tribes, including the Swabians (in Galiza) and the Vandals, swept over the peninsula, but only the **Visigoths** established a hold after converting to Christianity. Their influence has been exaggerated by the Orthodox Right (nicknamed the *godos* or Goths), who apotheosized their reign as a period of Christian purity and national unity (hence the predilection in the Middle Ages and among some sectors today for Visigothic names such as Guzmán and Gonzalo).

The Moors and the Reconquista

There's nothing more biased than to speak of "Spaniards" and "Moors," as the Moors (and for that matter the Jews of Spain) are as Spanish as their Christian neighbors. Muslim civilization and culture reached its Iberian pinnacle under the Caliphate of Córdoba, which controlled most of the peninsula through the 10th century. The Cordoban dictator Almanzor snuffed out all opposition within his court and undertook a series of flashy military campaigns that climaxed with the ruthless destruction of Santiago de Compostela, a Christian holy city, in 997.

The **Reconquista** ("reconquering," referring to the Christian conquest and expulsion of the Moors) is something of a historical figment, presenting a united Christian front where in fact there was factionalism, and a monolithic march south where there were long periods of peaceful coexistence. Rather, the turning point came when Almanzor died, leaving a power vacuum in Córdoba. The Caliphate holdings shattered into petty states called *taífas*. From that moment on the Christians had the upper hand, first under the leadership of the Kingdom of Léon, followed by that of the tough Castilians. Christian policy was official toleration of Muslims and Jews, a tactic that fostered a syncretic culture whose style of art is called **Mudejar**.

The Jews

In 1369 Enrique de Trastámara defeated his half-brother Pedro el Cruel (a legendary Richard III type) at Montiel, inaugurating the Trastámara dynasty that was to spawn Isabel la Católica. Seemingly overnight, toleration was substituted by Christian rigidity à la 14th-century France. The pogroms of 1391 started soon after, when thousands of Jews were massacred and many more converted. This produced a *Converso* (the word for a converted Jew) culture in which Jews, if they converted, could rise to the highest ranks of political, ecclesiastical, and intellectual institutions and hook up with the Christian aristocratic and merchant classes. The Catholic saint Teresa of Avila (1515-1582) is perhaps the most famous *Converso* in Spanish history. This led to a paradoxical situation in which a "tainted" upper class desperately sought to deny its Semitic heritage by devising false genealogies, among other tactics. *Converso* culture is neither entirely Jewish nor Christian.

The Catholic Monarchs

In 1469, the marriage of **Fernando** de Aragón **and Isabel** de Castilla (a.k.a. Ferdinand and Isabella) joined Iberia's two mightiest Christian kingdoms. By 1492, the unstoppable duo had captured Granada (the last Moorish stronghold) and had shipped off Columbus, among others, to explore (read: exploit) the New World. The couple's strong leadership would make the Spanish Empire the most powerful in the world by the next century. Following Christian Europe's example, the Catholic Monarchs introduced the evil **Inquisition**. Unlike the Italian Inquisition, the Spanish version was deployed to strengthen the authority of both the state and the Church.

The **expulsion** (or forced conversion) **of the Jews** in 1492 was remarkable because it was late by European standards (postdating England's and France's by two centuries) and because of the sheer numbers of native Jews that were kicked out. Such a drastic policy was all the more shocking given the fairly tolerant tradition of religious *convivencia* (coexistence) that had lasted until then.

The Habsburgs and the Golden Age

The daughter of Fernando and Isabel, Juana La Loca (the Mad), married Felipe el Hermoso (the Fair), scion of the powerful Habsburg dynasty. Ms. Crazy and Mr. Handsome spawned **Carlos V** (Charles V, 1516-1556), who reigned supreme over an immense empire—what is today the Netherlands, Belgium, part of Germany, Austria, Spain, and the colonies in the Americas. As the last Holy Roman Emperor, Carlos embroiled Spain in a war with France; as a cultured absolutist monarch and art patron of superb taste, he nabbed Titian as his court painter. The austere but grand emperor was a trendsetter too; he introduced to Spain the Habsburg fashion of wearing all black—the first time in history black clothing was hip. (The fashion spread to the Netherlands as well and would last through three generations.)

But trouble was a-brewing in the Netherlands (then called the Low Countries and Flanders). After Carlos V conveniently died, his son **Felipe II** (Philip II, 1556-1598) was left holding the bag—a bag full of rebellious colonies. This stick-in-the-mud ruler was even more of a paper-pusher and fanatic Catholic than his father, controlling the country with an iron fist and jumpstarting the Inquistion. He even managed to snag Portugal when the king died in 1580. One year later the Dutch, led by Amsterdam, declared their independence from Spain. Poor greedy Felipe began a war with the Protestants, then provoked yet another with England (a country of non-Catholics) soon after. The latter ground to a halt when the Spanish Armada was creamed by Sir Francis

Drake in 1588. Felipe retreated to his grim, newly built palace (El Escorial) and blubbered in his somber quarters when nobody was watching.

Felipe III (1598-1621) was a spoiled playboy who was having too much fun to bother running a big, centralized nation, so he let his adviser, the Duque de Lerma (Duke of Lerma) pull the strings. The ace puppetmaster was loathed by the rest of the court (and still is by historians). Inconveniently for them both, the **Thirty Years' War** broke out all over Europe and sapped Spain's resources. Charming Felipe expelled a total of almost 300,000 Moors during his reign.

Mustachioed wall-flower **Felipe IV** (1621-1665) held the country together through his long, tumultuous reign. Fighting with the Dutch had its ups (the successful siege of Breda, commemorated in the Velázquez painting) and its downs (the final independence of the Netherlands and truce-signing in 1848). In the early years, the Conde Duque de Olivares (Count-Duke Olivares), yet another schemey, ambitious adviser, manipulated impressionable young Felipe. Eventually the king's somber blood came to the fore, and he carried out his duties free of undue influence. Emulating his great-grandfather Carlos V, he was a discerning patron of art (Velázquez, Lope de Vega, Caldéron) and architecture (the Buen Retiro in Madrid), and donned the very plainest black clothes (all made of the most luxurious fabrics, of course). War with France was ended with the marital union of his daughter and Louis XIV. After Felipe's death the country fell into disarray. Ironically, in an economically and culturally bankrupt Spain, once-thriving and parasitic Castilla was the region most deeply wounded by the Golden Age.

The Bourbons and the Nineteenth Century

The 1713 Treaty of Utrecht seated **Felipe V,** a Bourbon grandson of Louis XIV, on the Spanish throne. The king built extravagant palaces (to ape Versailles in France) like mad and cultivated a flamboyant, decadent court of debauchery. Despite his example, the Bourbons who followed Felipe were able administrators who began to regain control of the Spanish American trade lost to northern Europeans. They were also great patrons and entrepreneurs, responsible for scores of new canals, roads, and resettlement schemes, and for agricultural reform and encouragement of industry, the sciences, and the arts (through centralized academies). **Carlos III** goes down in history as Madrid's all-time best mayor for his radical transformation of the capital. Spain's standing in the world had recovered sufficiently that it could team up with France to secure the U.S.'s independence from Britain, chiefly through a succession of victories engineered in the southern states by Captain Gálvez. The next monarch, **Carlos IV,** is best known as the ugly guy in countless portraits by Goya.

This recovery period was shattered by the Napoleonic occupation and the subsequent restoration of arch-reactionary Fernando VII, supported by Wellington in his bid to revoke the highly progressive Constitución de Cádiz of 1812. As a result of Fernando's ineptitude, and partly inspired by the Liberal ideas embodied in that constitution, most of Spain's Latin American empire finally threw off the yoke during the first quarter of the 19th century. Parliamentary Liberalism was restored in 1833 upon Fernando VII's death and dominated Spanish politics with brief interruptions until the advent of Primo de Rivera's mild dictatorship in the 1920s.

The 19th century was a period of rapid industrialization in some regions and great demographic growth in all, with resources pumped into the now virtually colony-less country. In the world of art, Catalunya thrived in its *Renaixença* (Renaissance), producing the **Modernista** movement in architecture and design, led by the brilliantly creative Antoni Gaudí.

Recent History

In April 1931 King Alfonso XIII left Spain in ignominy and the Second Republic was born. Republican Liberals and Socialists established safeguards for farmers and industrial workers, granted women's suffrage (oh, thank you) and religious liberty, and chipped away at the influence of the military. The national euphoria of the Republic's first days faded fast. The 1933 elections broke the Republican-Socialist coalition and gave increased power to rightist and Catholic parties in the parliamentary *Cortes.* Military dissatisfaction and the rise of a new Fascist wing, the *Falange,* further polarized national politics. By 1936, the Radicals, Anarchists, Socialists, and Republicans had formed a loosely federated **Popular Front** to win the next elections. But then **Generalisímo Francisco Franco** grabbed command of the Spanish army and, aided by militarist uprisings inside Spain, plunged the nation into Civil War.

The three-year **Civil War** ignited worldwide ideological passions. Civil War is actually a misnomer for what was an outright German-Italian invasion; Germany and Italy dumped masses of troops, supplies, and munitions straight into Franco's lap. Franco's *Falangista* Republic soon controlled all major population and industrial centers. On the other side, the Popular Front coalition was abandoned by the West and had only the International Brigade for outside support. Even the aid from Stalinist Russia waned as the Spanish left insisted on ideological autonomy. Given these odds, it's amazing the anti-Franco resistance held out for even three years, proof in itself that most Spaniards rejected Fascism.

Brain-drain followed on the heels of Franco's victory, as leading scientists, artists, and intellectuals emigrated en masse from totalitarian Spain. Worker dissatisfaction, student unrest, regional discontent, and international isolation characterized the first decades of the Franco dictatorship. A number of anarchist and nationalist groups, most notably the separatist Basque ETA, resisted the dictatorship through violent terrorist acts. As Franco aged, he attempted to smooth international relations by joining NATO and encouraging tourism, but the "national tragedy" did not officially end until Franco's death in 1975.

King Juan Carlos, grandson of Alfonso XIII and a Franco protegé, sensed the national mood and undid much of Franco's damage. In 1978, under centrist premier Adolfo Suárez, the Spanish adopted a new constitution in a national referendum that led to the restoration of parliamentary government and regional autonomy.

Charismatic **Felipe González** led the PSOE (Spanish Socialist Worker's Party) to victory in the 1982 elections. González opened the Spanish economy and hobnobbed with mainstream politicians, overseeing Spain's integration into the European Economic Community in 1986. Despite his support for continued membership in NATO and unpopular economic policies, González was reelected in 1986 and continued a program of massive public investment. Inflation has been tamed and unemployment substantially reduced; Spain's long stretch of startling economic growth has catapulted its economy to the front ranks of the industrialized world.

Art

Spanish painting flowered in the Golden Age, at the height of the Spanish Empire (roughly 1492-1650). Toledo's adopted Greek **El Greco** (1540-1640) developed an eccentric, elongated style. Court painter **Diego Velázquez** (1599-1660) created illusionistic poached eggs, hermeneutic conundrums, and slews of royal portraits. Meanwhile, **José Ribera** (1591-1652) and **Bartolomé Murillo** (1617-1682) specialized in popular, saccharine religious works. Under the Bourbons, **Francisco de Goya** (1746-1828) painted unflattering portraits of royalty and protests against the Napoleonic occupation of Spain.

20th-century Spanish artists (often living in France) led a number of movements. **Pablo Picasso** (1881-1973) inaugurated his "Blue Period" while in Barcelona. With his French cohort Georges Braque, he pioneered Cubism. His 1937 *Guernica* portrays the bombing of that city during the Spanish Civil War. Catalunyan **Joan Miró** (1904-1983) explored playful, colorful abstract compositions. Fellow Catalan and mustachioed person **Salvador Dalí** (1904-1991) was a major player in Surrealism. His self-important autobiography (a precursor of the Warhol Diaries) is *Diary of a Genius.* **Josep Maria Sert** (1874-1945) also made his mark in painting with larger mural works.

Architecture

Scattered **Roman ruins**—aqueducts, temples, theaters—lie principally in Tarragona, Segovia, and Mérida. Since the **Moors'** religion banned representations of humans and animals, they channeled their brilliance into spectacular buildings and ornately patterned surfaces (cf. the Alhambra in Granada and the Mesquita in Córdoba). Islamic and Christian influences melded in the **Spanish Romanesque** style, whose heavy stone monasteries and churches, such as Salamanca's *catedral*, proliferated in the 11th and 12th centuries.

Christians under Muslim rule created the **Mozarabic** fad. But after the Reconquista, it was Muslims who developed the truly novel **Mudejar** style, combining the Gothic and the Islamic in the Alcazars at Sevilla and Segovia. Toledo, center of Spain's Jewish culture, boasts some of the oldest **synagogues** in the world.

The embarrassing riches of the New World funded the **Plateresque** ("in the manner of a silversmith") movement, a flash variant of Gothic—unrestrained gold and silver and intricate ornamentation was on every surface in Plateresque Salamanca. Influenced by the Italians, Jaén's Andrés de Vandelvira pioneered the **Spanish Renaissance** style, as seen in fundamentalist Felipe II's El Escorial. The pendulum swung back to opulence in 17th- and 18th-century Baroque, in Spain taking the form of the compressed ornament, shells, and garlands of the **Churrigueresque** style (named after José Benito Churriguera, though he was not a major architect of this overwrought style). Flamboyant examples include the altar of Toledo's cathedral.

In the late 19th and early 20th centuries, Catalan **Modernista** burst on the scene at Barcelona, led by quirky genius **Antonio Gaudí, Luis Domènich i Montaner,** and **José Puig y Caldafalch.** Modernista buildings take the notion of freedom seriously, swooping wildly about with voluptous curves and unexpected textures. The new style took some inspiration from Mudejar relics, but relied heavily on the inspiration of organic natural forms and human imagination.

Literature

The 12th-century **Cantar de Mío Cid** (Song of my Cid) is Christian Spain's oldest surviving epic poem. This dramatic tale of the Reconquista is the first major work written in Castilian. The Golden Age on paper took many forms: the **picaresque novel** *(Lazarillo de Tormes, Guzmán de Alfarache);* **St. Teresa of Avila's** mystic religious encounters; the drama of **Calderón de la Barca** and **Lope de Vega. Miguel de Cervantes'** *Don Quixote de la Mancha* is perhaps the most famous work of Spanish literature, telling the quixotic tale of the hapless don and his loyal sidekick Sancho Panza.

Modern literature begins with the **Generación del '98,** a group led by **Miguel de Unamuno** (essayist and professor at Salamanca) and cultural critic **José Ortega y Gasset** who wrote after the country's defeat in the Spanish-American War. In the 20th century, the Nobel Committee has honored playwright and essayist **Jacinto Benavente y Martínez,** poet **Vicente Aleixandre,** and novelist **Camilo José Cela** (author of *La Familia de Pascal Duarte).*

Reading Matter

History

H.V. Livermore's *The Origins of Spain and Portugal* is a good one-volume history reaching back to the pre-Roman era. In *The Structure of Spanish History,* Américo Castro opened the door to a reevaluation of the Jewish part in Spanish culture. For a delightful survey of the fun Catholic Monarchs' and Habsburgs' eras, read J. H. Elliott's *Imperial Spain 1469-1714.* Raymond Carr has documented the modern era well in *Spain, 1808-1939,* as has Pablo Fusi with *Spain: Dictatorship to Democracy.*

Art and Architecture

The best bibliographies and accounts of political, architectural, and art history are in *The Blue Guide*—especially learned and reliable since it's written by specialists. The standard work on Spanish architecture is Bernard Bevan's *History of Spanish Architecture*. *Palace For a King*, by J. H. Elliott and Christopher Brown, is a page-turner about the building of Felipe IV's Buen Retiro in Madrid. Fred Licht's collection of essays, *Goya*, is a must-read for fans of that artist.

Literature

A good survey of Spanish literature (in 8 volumes) is *A Literary History of Spain*, directed by R.O. Jones. Gerald Brenan's *The Literature of the Spanish People* is a comprehensive, opinionated history. N.D. Shergold's *History of the Spanish Stage* is a splendidly documented backstage account of Spain's brilliant Golden Age (16th-17th century) drama.

City Guides

The best architecture guides to Madrid are Guerra de La Vega's excellent, multi-volume illustrated series and the Madrid Colegio de Arquitectos' two-volume *Guía* (in Spanish). Francisco Azorín's *Leyendas y Anécdotas del Viejo Madrid* outlines an entertaining walking tour of the capital that incorporates (duh) legends and anecdotes. *Michael's Guide to Madrid* also sketches out walking tours of the capital (in English). The *Insight City Guide* series has an excellent volume on Barcelona written by long-term residents.

Other

In good bookstore travel sections you'll find books devoted to specialized aspects of travel in Spain such as the *paradores,* country inns, the rural countryside, wilderness areas, and flora and fauna.

Guía de la España Templaría, by Juan Atienza, is a priceless travel guide that covers only the mysterious hideaways of the Knights Templar. The masterpiece is widely available in Spain and is (sniff) in Spanish only.

Ever since Washington Irving took up residence in Granada and wrote *Tales of the Alhambra,* American and British authors have been inspired by Spanish landscapes. The undisputed classics on Spain are 20th-century Bloomsbury-Circle-expatriate Gerald Brenan's *The Face of Spain* and *South from Granada*. The latter divulges amazing folklore from the Las Alpujarras villages (including a foolproof formula for removing the evil eye) in the Sierra Nevada. Richard Ford's lyrical three-volume *Handbook for Travelers in Spain* (1845) is another favorite.

The Media

For Visitors Only

Spain's tourist industry is superbly organized; national and regional governments publish excellent **brochures** and **pamphlets** on highly specialized subjects, usually in English as well as Spanish. Choose from photo-riddled booklets on camping, hunting, fishing, water and snow sports, other recreational activities (such as horse riding and kayaking), the national parks, foods and wines, accommodations in monasteries and country cottages, art and architecture, crafts, festivals, and more.

Lookout magazine contains classifieds and regular features on taxes, work permits, and sundry practical matters. It's published in English on the Costa del Sol (and available on newsstands in larger cities). Their publishing house also has a full line of books on the foods and wines of Spain, gardening, etc.

The Spanish Ministerio del Interior and national tourist office distribute a pamphlet called *Living in Spain* which explains foreigners' rights and responsibilities, regulations governing residence and work, and special services available to them.

Newspapers

ABC is the oldest national daily paper and has a somewhat conservative bent. *El País* has perhaps the largest readership and is the most professional of the bunch. *El Mundo* is a left-wing, younger rag that's critical of the government. *Diario 16* is also critical but more moderate. The same publishers put out a popular newsweekly *Cambio 16*.

Television

The state-run channels, à la the U.K.'s BBC, are called TVE1 and La2. The private national stations are Tele5 and Antena3. In Madrid, the local autonomous network is TeleMadrid (TM3). Plus is a subscription network for which you pay a fee.

News is on at 3 and 8:30pm on most stations. Programming includes well-dubbed American movies, sports (including bullfights), steamy Latin American *telenovelas* or *culebrones* (soaps/miniseries), *concursos* (game shows), and kitschy three-hour variety-show extravaganzas. Newspapers publish listings and schedules.

Madrid

The city's air (which 19th-century European princesses came to sniff when pregnant) has been likened to champagne, but it's Madrid's boundless energy and hyperactive imagination that makes visitors swoon. Trapped smack in the hot, dry Castilian plain, residents of Spain's First City frig and frug with abandon amid broad, leafy boulevards, grandiose Renaissance and Neoclassical monuments, sumptuous mansions, sidewalk *terrazas*, and endless theaters, museums, and cafés.

Madrid has perfected the trick of transcending daily reality. The city clearly confuses night with day; eye-burning spotlights, together with the perpetual stream of automobile and pedestrian traffic, blur the distinction between 4am and 4pm. The sea is nowhere near the city, but a flotilla of overnight refrigerated transport ensure it some of the freshest seafood in Europe. The absence of a seafront promaenade doesn't keep citizens from enjoying the Costas' summer *terrazas* and *chiringuitos* that line the city's boulevards. Even the Manzanares, a creek pretending to be a river according to Lope de Vega, is sufficient excuse to build Renaissance and Baroque bridges worthy of the Guadalquivir or even the Seine.

Although it witnessed the coronation of Fernando and Isabel, Madrid was of no great importance until paper-pushing Habsburg Felipe II plunked down the Spanish court here permanently in 1561—an unlikely choice of capital considering the city's distance from vital ports and rivers. Yet from that moment on, the city became the seat of wealth, and culture, and imperial glory, watching over Spain's 16th- and 17th-century Golden Age of literature (Quevedo, Larra), art (Velázquez, Goya), and architecture. Today's Madrid owes much of its Neoclassical flair, from the Palacio Real in the west to the Museo del Prado in the east, to the 18th-century urban renewal of Bourbon Felipe V.

Passionately hostile to Franco's nationalists, the center was the last city to fall save for València. Since then Madrid has kept up a furious pace. The capital of contemporary Spanish cultural life, surpassing Barcelona as the country's manufacturing and financial center, the city is anything but a museum piece.

Orientation

The epicenter of Madrid is the **Puerta del Sol,** an intersection where eight streets meet—notice the "Kilometro 0" marker on the sidewalk in front of the police station. Sol is *the* transportation hub of the city: below ground, three metro lines (blue #1, red #2, yellow #3) converge and transport people to within walking distance of any point in the city; above ground, buses, and taxis swarm. Moreover, from Sol, most sights, museums, restaurants, *hostales,* and nightclubs are under a half-hour's walk away. Sol itself is packed with restaurants, *cafeterías, hostales,* shops, and services of all kinds.

Four major streets conduct traffic in and out of Sol. With your back to the clock tower on the **police station** (a good landmark):

1) The street leading traffic out of Sol (on the far left) is **Calle del Arenal.** Calle del Arenal runs into **Calle de Bailén** at its other end (in front of the Plaza de Oriente and Palacio Real). A right turn on Bailén leads to **Plaza de España**, with **Parque del Oeste** to the left and a view over the Casa del Campo beyond it (30min.). **Paseo del Pintor Rosales** and its many *terrazas* border the park, the western edge of Madrid's *centro* (city center).

2) The street leading traffic into Sol is **Calle Mayor** (on the near left). Down this street is the **Plaza Mayor.** The municipal tourist office is on the far side of the plaza. C. Mayor ends at C. Bailén, across from an under-construction church (next to the Palacio Real). A left onto C. Bailén moves away from the big building scene over a *viaducto* into **La Latina,** Madrid's oldest neighborhood (on the left after crossing the bridge; 20min.).

3) At Sol, the continuation of C. Mayor emerges from the other side of the intersection, now called **Carrera San Jerónimo** (on your near right). Plaza Canalejas is just down the street; **Calle Príncipe** leads out of the right of the plaza to **Plaza Santa Ana** and a zone of quality restaurants, bars, and *terrazas*. Continuing downhill with C. San Jerónimo, you come to the **Plaza de las Cortes**. C. San Jerónimo ends at the wide **Paseo del Prado**, across from the **Museo del Prado** (20min.).

4) The last of the big four avenues is **C. Alcalá** (on your far right), which lets traffic into the intersection. Down this street are "bank palaces," including the imposing Banco de España at the foot of the slope, ending at **Plaza de la Cibeles** and Po. Prado. Take the pedestrian underpass to reach the Palacio de Comunicaciones (post office palace) on the other side of Po. Prado. Beyond the post office is **Plaza de la Indepencia** and the **Parque del Retiro** (30min.). Calle Serrano, lined with chic designer stores, leads out from the other side of the plaza, stretching north to form the western border of a posh residential *barrio* called **Salamanca**.

South of Sol, amidst a tangle of streets, is **Calle de Atocha**, which runs downhill to train filled **Estachión de Atocha**. South of C. Atocha lies the *barrio* **Arganzuela**.

North of Sol, bounded by the **Gran Vía**, is a major shopping area: El Corte Inglés (see Practical Information) and many other shops, *cafeterías*, bars, and hotels fill this area. **C. Montera**, the one street with car traffic amidst these pedestrian *calles*, leads from Sol to the massive Gran Vía and the eponymous Metro stop. To the left, Gran Vía runs by **Plaza de Callao** and heads downhill to Pl. España (20min.). Past Pl. España, the Gran Vía becomes C. Princesa, stretching uphill through the residential **Argüelles** and collegiate **Moncloa** *barrios*. Even farther north is the **Ciudad Universitaria** (1-1 1/2 hr.).

One of the most important roads leading off the Gran Vía to the north, in both traffic volume and tourist interest, is **C. Fuencarral**. *Hostales* and shops pack this narrow street. It also forms the eastern border of **Malasaña**, a lively middle-class *barrio* where Madridites get down at night. Parallel to C. Fuencarral is C. Hortaleza, which heads into the working-class *barrio* **Chueca**, full of inexpensive restaurants, nightclubs, and *hostales*. North of these two zones, Madrid is increasingly modern, gentrified, and residential.

If Puerta del Sol is the heart of Madrid, then the single long avenue named in turn **Paseo Prado, Recoletos,** and **Castellana** is its spine. This extended *paseo* moves from historical and cultural sights northwards into various financial and business centers, governmental ministries, skyscrapers, and the Estadio Santiago Bernabéu.

Madrid is extremely safe compared to other major European cities, but the Puerta del Sol, Plaza 2 de Mayo in Malasaña, Plaza de Chueca, and Pl. España (to a lesser extent) are particularly intimidating late at night. Generally, avoid the parks and quiet residential areas when it's dark.

Practical Information

Note: At the time of publication, the Telefónica (state telephone company) was in the midst of replacing Madrid phone numbers beginning with a 2 with a 5. If we list a phone number beginning with 2 and you can't get through, dial the number starting with a 5. And if we list the first digit of a phone number as 5 and you don't reach what you're trying to call, the number may not have been converted yet—try a 2.

Getting There

By Plane

All flights land at the **Aeropuerto Internacional de Barajas**, in the town of the same name a half-hour by car northeast of Madrid. The simplest and cheapest way to get into town is the **Bus-Aeropuerto** (look for EMT signs just outside the doors), which stops every 15 minutes outside the national and international terminals (275ptas).

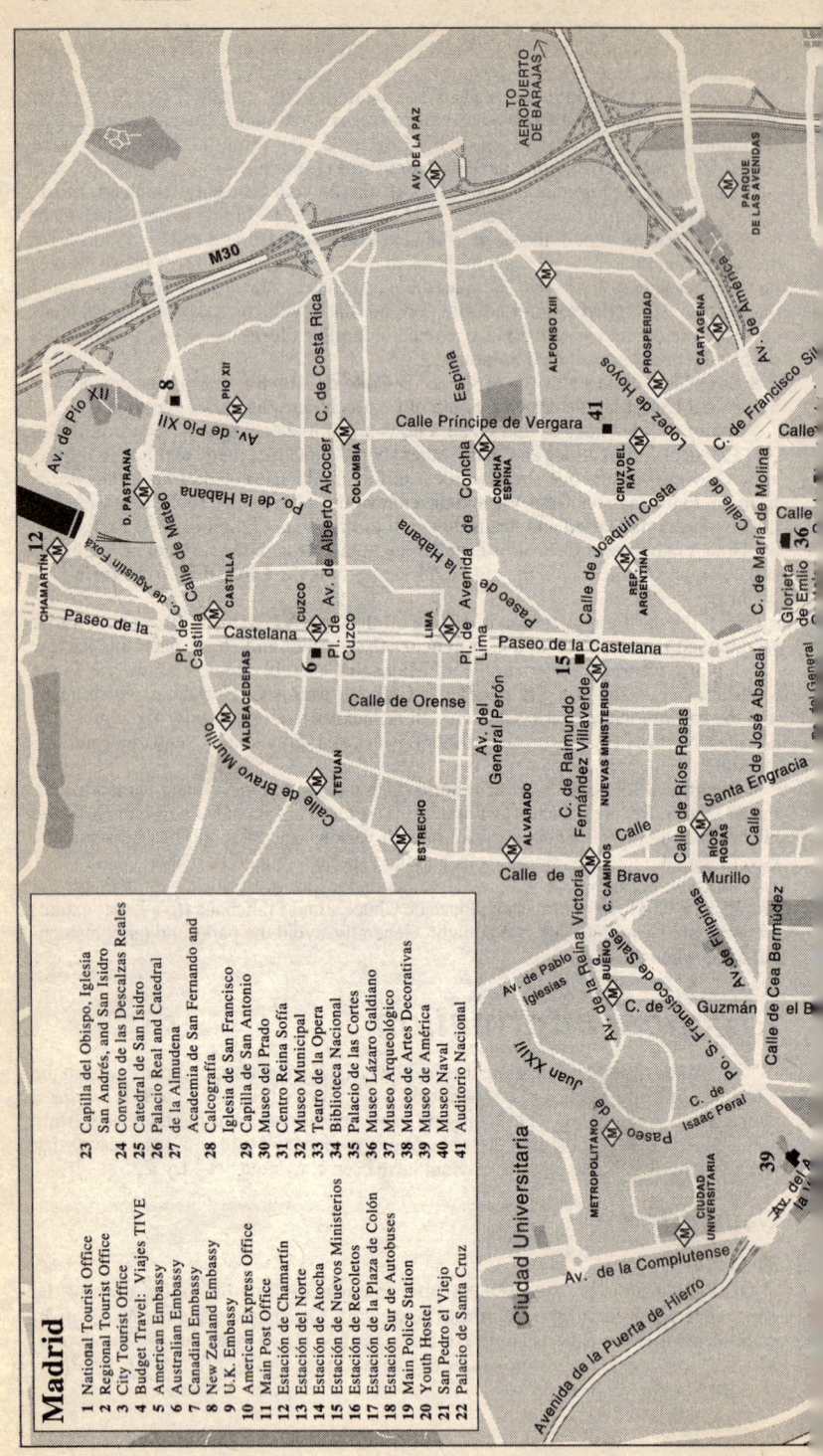

Madrid

1. National Tourist Office
2. Regional Tourist Office
3. City Tourist Office
4. Budget Travel: Viajes TIVE
5. American Embassy
6. Australian Embassy
7. Canadian Embassy
8. New Zealand Embassy
9. U.K. Embassy
10. American Express Office
11. Main Post Office
12. Estación de Chamartín
13. Estación del Norte
14. Estación de Atocha
15. Estación de Nuevos Ministerios
16. Estación de Recoletos
17. Estación de la Plaza de Colón
18. Estación Sur de Autobuses
19. Main Police Station
20. Youth Hostel
21. San Pedro el Viejo
22. Palacio de Santa Cruz
23. Capilla del Obispo, Iglesia San Andrés, and San Isidro
24. Convento de las Descalzas Reales
25. Catedral de San Isidro
26. Palacio Real and Catedral de la Almudena
27. Academia de San Fernando and Calcografía
28. Iglesia de San Francisco
29. Capilla de San Antonio
30. Museo del Prado
31. Centro Reina Sofía
32. Museo Municipal
33. Teatro de la Opera
34. Biblioteca Nacional
35. Palacio de las Cortes
36. Museo Lázaro Galdiano
37. Museo Arqueológico
38. Museo de Artes Decorativas
39. Museo de América
40. Museo Naval
41. Auditorio Nacional

Practical Information 59

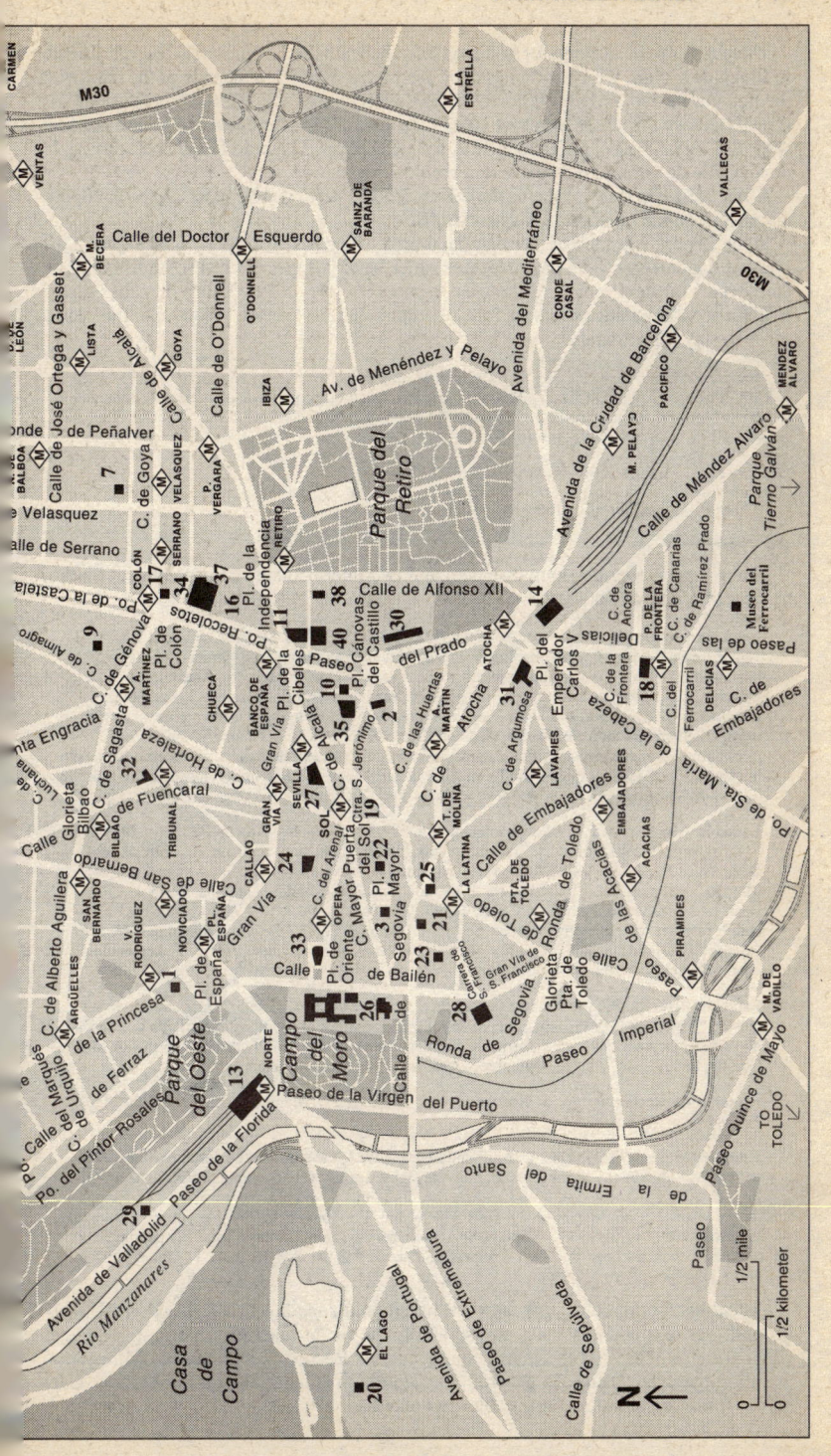

The bus from the airport stops underground beneath the Jardines del Descrubrimento in **Plaza de Colón,** which is on Paseo de Recoletos. Exit from the side of the park with the noisy waterfall and you'll be on Paseo de Recoletos. The "Colón" metro station is directly across the street. Alternatively, it's a 15- to 20-minute walk to Puerta del Sol: walk left down Paseo de Recoletos to the next plaza, Plaza de la Cibeles; turn right down Calle de Alcalá, and bear left at the next fork.

A fleet of taxis waits at the airport. The ride to Puerto del Sol costs 2000-2500ptas, depending on the number of bags and traffic.

In the airport, a branch of the regional tourist office (see Tourist Office below) in the international arrivals area has maps and other basics. (Open Mon.-Fri. 8am-8pm, Sat. 8am-1pm.) In the airport and the Bus-Aeropuerto stop in Pl. Colón, branches of the Brújula accommodations service (see Accommodations Service below) can find you a place to stay immediately.

Iberia: Pl. Canovas, 4 (tel. 585 85 85). Open Mon.-Fri. 9am-7pm, Sat. 9am-2pm. Branch office at C. Princesa, 2 (tel. 585 81 59). Metro: Pl. España. Other branches throughout the city generally open Mon.-Fri. 9am-7pm, Sat. 9am-1pm. Telephone reservations 8am-10pm (domestic flights 411 10 11, international flights 463 99 66).

American Airlines: C. Pedro Texeira, 8 (tel. 597 20 68).

TWA: Pl. Colón, Torres de Jerez (tel. 410 60 12).

By Train

Three *largo recorrido* (long distance) and two intermediate stations connect Madrid to the rest of the world.

Estación Chamartín: Agustín de Foxá (tel. 323 21 21, 232 15 15). Metro: Chamartín, line #8 (1 stop from Pl. Castilla stop on blue line #1). Bus #5 runs to and from Sol (45min.); the stop is just beyond the lockers. Chamartín services towns throughout Spain (Albacete, Alacant, Barcelona, Bilbao, Cádiz, Cartagena, Córdoba, Irún, Málaga, Santander, Sevilla, Soria, Zaragoza), Portugal, and France (with connections at the French border). In addition to these *largo recorrido* destinations, all *cercanías* trains can be boarded here (see *cercanías* below). Chamartín has a tourist office, currency exchange, accommodations service, post office, telephones, car rental, lockers, bookstores, *cafeterías,* police—not to mention the astrology booth at ticket sales and the roller-disco-bowl-a-rama right next door beyond the lockers. Ticket windows open 6:45am-11:35pm.

Estación Atocha: Av. Ciudad de Barcelona (tel. 527 31 60). Metro: Atocha-Renfe (on blue line #1). To walk to Sol, follow C. Atocha uphill (35min.) and turn right on C. Carretas at Pl. Benavente. Newly-renovated Atocha has expanded its service from small towns in Castilla-La Mancha, Andalucía, and Extremadura to include Valéncia, Granada, Córdoba, Cuenca, Ciudad Real, Badajoz, Mérida, Almeria, Cádiz, Toledo, and Salamanca. Also AVE (Alta Velocidad Española) service to Sevilla via Córdoba. Service to Portugal. For '93 the city is planning several art galleries, boutiques, restaurants, and cafés to complement the shiny new station. Ticket windows open 6:30am-11:30pm.

Estación Príncipe Pío (or Norte): Po. del Rey, 30 (tel. 247 00 00). Metro: Opera by way of extension "Norte" (follow signs in either direction). The smallest of the 3 *largo recorrido* stations—no services beyond ticket sales, arrivals, and departures. Trains from here head northwest to A Coruña, León, Lugo, Oviedo, Ourense, Salamanca, Valladolid, and Zamora.

Estación de Recoletos: Po. de Recoletos, 4 (tel. 232 15 15). Metro: Colón. Follow the signs. Trains every 5-10min.

Estación Nuevos Ministerios: C. Raimundo Fernández Villaverde, on the corner with Po. Castellana. Metro: Nuevos Ministerios. Follow the signs. Trains every 5-10min. **RENFE Main Office:** C. Alcalá, 44 (tel. 530 02 02), where Gran Vía hits C. Alcalá. Metro: Banco de España. Arrive when it opens to avoid long waits. Open Mon.-Fri. 10am-8pm. Sample one-way *expreso* fares to: Avila (8 per day, 2hr., 965ptas); Segovia (8 per day, 2hr., 540ptas); Toledo (9 per day, 1hr., 480ptas); Cuenca (6 per day, 3hr., 1230ptas); Salamanca (3 per day, 3 1/2 hr., 1175ptas); Lisboa (11hr., 4530pta); Paris (17-19hr., 11,450pta).

Cercanías (commuter train) fares are based on a zone layout à la London's Underground. Self-explanatory, easy-to-use automatic ticket machines are in all stations. Chamartín, Atocha, and the intermediate stations Recoletos and Nuevos Ministerios are all in the center zone. To get from one station to another, the fare is 125ptas. *Cercanías* trains are slow, uncomfortable, and may lack A/C.

Regional or **regional-expres** trains cost only a little more and get there twice as fast. Sample one-way fares to: Alcalá de Henares 230ptas; Guadalajara 340ptas; El Escorial 265ptas; Aranjuez 265ptas (trains leave every 15-30min.).

By Bus

Numerous private companies serve Madrid, each with its own station. Buses depart from and arrive back to each station, usually passing through the central **Estación Sur de Autobuses** en route. Countless buses of all different flavors are packed in the large exhaust-stained hangar. Getting off here is convenient for services and transport into the center of Madrid. To get to the metro stop (Palos de la Frontera, yellow line #3), go downstairs to the main floor filled with bars, shops, ticket windows, telephones; the entrance is in the corner with the information window. The metro from here runs straight to Sol.

> **Estación Empresa Ruíz:** Rda. Atocha, 12 (tel. 468 08 50). Metro: Atocha.
>
> **Estación La Sepulvedana:** Po. de la Florida, 3 (tel. 247 52 61). Metro: Norte (take extension from Opera to the train station). To Avila (3 per day, 2hr.; 780ptas, round-trip 1100ptas) and Segovia (14 per day, 1 1/2 hr.; 655ptas, round-trip 1125ptas).
>
> **Estación Herranz:** C. Fernández de los Ríos (tel. 543 81 67), on the corner with C. Isaac Peral. Metro: Moncloa. To El Escorial (about every hr., 1hr., 315ptas) continuing to Valle de los Caídos (leaves El Escorial 3:15pm, returns 5:30pm; 20min.; from Madrid one-way 575ptas, from Escorial round-trip 200ptas).

By Rideshare and Thumb

Associación Para el Auto-stop Compartido, C. Estudios, 9 (tel. 265 65 65) arranges shared journeys. People also check the jam-packed message boards at HI hostels and the TIVE travel agency for ridesharing offers.

Hitchhiking route information is also available by calling 441 72 22. Not popular or safe, we surely don't recommend it. The following national routes emanate from Madrid: N-I (north) for Burgos and Irún; N-II (northeast) for Zaragoza and Barcelona; N-III (east) for Cuenca and València; N-IV (south) for Aranjuez, Alicant, and Andalucía; N-V (west) for Badajoz; N-VI (northwest) for Avila, Sierra de Guadarrama, Segovia, Salamanca, and Galiza; E-4 (west) for Extremadura and Portugal; 401 (southeast) for Toledo and connecting country road to Consuegra.

Getting Around

Maps

Both the *Plano de Madrid* and the *Plano de los Transportes*, free at the city tourist office, are necessary and quite sufficient. If you're a map freak or planning to do some heavy-duty back alley exploration, buy the red Almax *Madrid y extrarradio* map (550ptas). It's thoroughly indexed and complete with a metro plan, a sketchy bus plan, and a long list of addresses and phone numbers (from Academia Real de Bellas Artes to Zoo).

Metro

Clearly the easiest and most convenient way to get around, the Metro is especially enjoyable if you are a troll or a vampire who can't bear to see the light of day. Trains run frequently; only Sundays and late at night will you wait more than five minutes. A cheery green timer hanging above the platform tells how long it's been since the last one departed. The free, compact *Plano del Metro* (available at any ticket booth) is easier to use than the unwieldy *Plano de los Transportes*.

Ten lines connect 120 stations throughout Madrid. The various lines are referred to by color and number. Metro rides cost 125ptas; the super-bargain *billete de diez* (ticket of 10 rides) costs 490ptas. Monthly passes must be bought before the first day of the month. For more details, call 435 22 66 and 552 49 00 (general metro information lines) or ask at any ticket booth.

Trains run from 6am until 1:30am. Regarding safety, the trains are usually well-traveled—they don't run late enough (in Madrid time) to be deserted. Crime in the Metro stations is fairly rare, and women usually feel safe traveling alone. As usual, use common sense and avoid empty cars. Ride in the first car where the conductor sits (always at the far left end of the platform) if you feel uncomfortable. Some stations, particularly those that handle two or more lines, have long tunnels and series of escalators; exercise caution here and stick with people. The Chueca, Gran Vía, Sol, Tirso de Molina, La Latina, and Plaza de España stations surface in areas which are somewhat intimidating after midnight. On the whole, the metro is clean, efficient, and worry-free.

Bus

The extensive city bus system (150 routes) can be frustrating to novices. Finding the route you want and its corresponding stops is easy enough with the *Plano de los Transportes,* but unless you know what your destination looks like or ask your neighbor to alert you, you'll have a hard time knowing when to get off the bus.

The fare is 125ptas. A 10-ride *bonobus* pass, sold at newsstands and tobacco shops, costs 490ptas. Buses run from 6am until midnight. Between midnight and 3am, 11 nocturnal buses travel from Sol and Pl. Cibeles to the outskirts every half hour; after that, hourly until 5am. Nocturnal buses (numbered N1-N11) are indicated on a special section on the *Plano.* There are N stops all along the marked routes, not just in Sol and Pl. Cibeles. For information on buses call Empresa Municipal de Transportes (EMT) at 401 99 00.

Taxi

Taxis, taxis everywhere—white with a diagonal red stripe on their side. A green *libre* sign in the window or a lit green light indicates availability. Taxis are affordable for groups of two to four people, and particularly useful late at night when only nocturnal buses run.

The base fare is 140ptas, plus 65ptas per km. Common supplements include: to or from the airport (300ptas); luggage charge (50ptas per bag); on Sundays and holidays (150ptas); at night (11pm-6am, 150ptas). The fare from the city center to the airport is about 2000ptas (cheaper from Pl. Colón, more from Sol or Pl. España). To Estación Chamartín from Pl. Colón costs about 1500ptas.

Before getting in, you might ask for an estimate, but generally taxi drivers aren't trying to cheat passengers. (If the fare is over 3000ptas, you're probably being ripped off.) If you have a complaint or think you've been overcharged, demand a *recibo oficial* (official receipt) and *hoja de reclamaciones* (complaint form), which the driver is required to supply. Take down the license number, route taken, and fare charged. Drop off the forms and information at City Hall, Pl. Villa, 4 (tel. 447 07 15) to possibly get a refund.

Radio Taxi: tel. 447 51 80.

Tele Taxi: tel. 445 90 08.

Car Rental

Don't do it unless you're planning to zoom out of Madrid. Traffic is congested and parking a nightmare. Tobacco shops sell parking permits. To find out if your car has been towed or merely stolen, call 458 75 12.

You must be over 21 and have an International Driver's License and major credit card (or leave a deposit equal to the estimated rental fee). A tiny Fiat I costs about 50,000ptas per week (including insurance) plus 35ptas per km. Gas isn't included in the price.

Atesa: C. Orense, 83 (tel. 570 46 09). Metro: Tetuán. C. Francisco leads to C. Orense. Open Mon.-Fri. 8am-8pm, Sat.-Sun. 9am-1pm. Also at the airport (tel. 205 86 60). Open 7am-midnight.

Autos Bravo: C. Toledo, 136 (tel. 474 80 75). Metro: Puerta de Toledo.

Avis: Gran Vía, 60 (tel. 547 20 48). Open Mon.-Fri. 8am-7pm, Sat.-Sun. 9am-1pm. Also at the airport (tel. 305 42 74). Open 7am-midnight.

Moped Rental

Popular with Madrid's young residents, mopeds are fleet and easy to park. A lock and helmet are needed. One store is **Motocicletas Antonio Castro**, C. Conde Duque, 13 (tel. 542 06 57), at Santa Cruz de Marcenado. (Metro: San Bernardo.) A 49cc Vespino is 2850ptas per day plus 13% IVA. A 250cc Yamaha is 6700ptas per day plus 13% IVA. Prices include mileage and insurance but not gas; the deposit is 6000ptas. You must be at least 18 and have a driver's license and passport. (Open Mon.-Fri. 8am-2pm and 5-8pm, Sat. 9am-1:30pm.)

Tourist Office

There's no such thing as a national tourist office; use the provincial/regional offices for regional information and the municipal office for Madrid information. If you're vague, the English-speaking staff will give you the basics and dispose of you quickly. If you've specific questions, be politely persistent and the staff will unearth fact sheets galore.

Municipal: Pl. Mayor, 3 (tel. 266 54 77). Metro: Sol. Cramped and crowded. Hands out *Plano de Madrid* and *Plano de los Transportes del Centro de Madrid*, along with slightly outdated *Guía de Madrid* and the always helpful monthly guide to activities, *En Madrid. VIP Madrid,* ostensibly a guide for businesspeople, is packed with useful listings and information on Spanish customs. The transport map is the only one not in English. Open Mon.-Fri. 10am-8pm, Sat. 10am-2pm.

Regional/Provincial Office of the Comunidad de Madrid: C. Princesa, 1, Torre de España (tel. 541 23 25), entrance faces Pl. España. Metro: Pl. España. Brochures about, transport info to, and maps of towns in the Comunidad. Also has brochures about towns throughout Spain; campsites; highways; daytrips; *paradores.* A **2nd office** is at C. Duque Medinaceli, 2 (tel. 429 49 51), just off Pl. Cortes. Metro: Sol. It's closed for repairs and expected to open in '93—when the office at C. Princesa will take its turn at renovation. Call before going to either. Open Mon.-Fri. 9am-7pm, Sat. 9:30am-1:30pm. More offices at **Estación Chamartín** (tel. 315 99 76; open Mon.-Fri. 8am-8pm, Sat. 8am-1pm) and the **airport,** in the international arrivals area (tel. 305 86 56; open same hrs. as Chamartín).

Tours

Choose your tour carefully; a number of those that advertise in *hostales* and travel agencies are blitzkrieg excursions, not worth the expense.

Descubre Madrid: run by the Patronato Municipal de Turismo, C. Mayor, 69 (tel. 588 29 06), under the arch and the first door on the right. Open Mon.-Fri. 9am-1pm. Even if you only know a little Spanish, these guided tours (3-4hr.) are an excellent way to see the city; they're targeted primarily at residents, not tourists and don't cost much money. Over sixty tours each season (March-July and Sept.-Jan.) cover topics ranging from masterpieces in the Prado to medieval archaeology to music. Walking tours 330ptas. Bus tours 660ptas. Package of 3 walking and 3 bus tours 2530ptas. Package of 2 walking and 2 bus tours 2200ptas. Students, retired people, and under 25: 265ptas; 550ptas; 1650ptas; 1430ptas. Prices include monument and museum admission charges. Details also at the municipal tourist office.

Accommodations Service

Brújula: Torre de Madrid, 6th floor (tel. 248 97 05), at Pl. España. Open Mon.-Fri. 9:30am-1:30pm and 4-7pm, Sat. 9:30am-1:30pm. Also at Estaciones Chamartín (tel. 315 78 94) and Atocha (tel. 228 26 84), Estación Sur de Autobuses in Pl. Colón (tel. 275 96 80), and in the airport (all open 8am-9pm). They make reservations for anywhere in Spain free of charge except for the long-distance calls. You provide the location and price range; they plug it into their magic computer. You must go in person. Since it's a private company and they aren't charging you, they extract a commission from the hotel or *hostal*, so prices may be slightly inflated. Not every establishment is signed up with Brújula (no youth hostels). Nevertheless, it's a good deal and convenient to have a bed secured when you've just arrived in town.

Budget Travel

Viajes TIVE: C. Fernando el Católico, 88 (tel. 543 02 08, 543 74 12). Metro: Moncloa. Branch office at José Ortega y Gasset, 71 (tel. 401 95 01). Metro: Lista. What *Let's Go* dreams about at night. Sponsored and run by the Comunidad de Madrid, so no commissions are added in—hence the lowest prices in town. Some English spoken. Discount airfares and ticket sales. Organized group excursions and language classes. Thriving message board with rides, cheap tickets, and apartment sharing notices. General lodgings and student residence infomation. BIJ train tickets. InterRail pass for 1 month of train travel (under 26 31,000ptas). ISIC 500ptas. FIYTO (good for RENFE discounts) 500ptas. HI cards 1800ptas. Round-trip bus fares to: Barcelona (4200ptas); Granada (3550ptas); Albacete (2875ptas); Paris (13,610ptas); Lisboa (7550ptas); Munich (29,250ptas). Both open Mon.-Fri. 9am-2pm, Sat. 9am-noon. Arrive early.

Embassies and Consulates

U.S. Embassy: C. Serrano, 75 (tel. 577 40 00). **Consulate,** same address (tel. 576 34 00). Open Mon.-Fri. 9am-1:30pm and 3-6pm.

Canadian Embassy and Consulate: C. Núñez de Balboa, 35 (tel. 431 43 00).

British Embassy: C. Fernando el Santo, 16 (tel. 319 02 00). **Consulate,** C. Marqués de la Ensenada, 16 (tel. 308 52 01).

Australian Embassy and Consulate: Po. Castellana, 143 (tel. 579 04 28).

New Zealand Embassy and Consulate: Pl. Lealtad, 2, 3rd fl. (tel. 523 02 26).

Money

For currency exchange, American Express has the best rates, especially if you have their traveler's checks. Banks do it (1-2% commission, 500ptas min. charge), El Corte Inglés does it (see Other: El Corte Inglés below), even four- and five-star hotels do it. Places open on weekends and as late as 2am, such as Exact Change, Cambios-Uno, and Chequepoint, are rip-offs. They charge no commission and have small (250-300ptas) minimum charges but their rates are outrageous; many are at Sol and on the Gran Vía.

American Express: Pl. Cortes, 2, Madrid 28014 (tel. 322 55 00; 24-hr. cardholder services tel. 572 03 03; 24-hr. lost checks toll-free tel. 900 99 44 26; fax 429 21 78). The travel agency and other cardholder services are around the right corner of the building when you face it. In addition to currency exchange (dollars to pesetas only; 1% cash and 2% traveler's check commission; no commission on American Express traveler's checks; no min. charge), they'll hold mail for cardholders and check users. In an emergency, AmEx cashes personal checks up to US$1000 for cardholders only. Express Cash machine. Open Mon.-Fri. 9am-5:30pm, Sat. 9am-noon.

Communications

Post Office: Palacio de Comunicaciones, Pl. Cibeles (tel. 521 81 95). Information open Mon.-Fri. 8am-9pm. Open for stamps Mon.-Fri. 9am-10pm, Sat. 9am-2pm, Sun. 10am-1pm; for certified mail Mon.-Fri. 9am-10pm, Sat. 9am-2pm, Sun. 10am-1pm; for Lista de Correos Mon.-Fri. 9am-8pm, Sat. 9am-2pm; for **telegrams** 24 hrs. Telegram assistance available Mon.-Fri. 9am-9pm. To send telegrams by phone call 522 20 00. Door H for telegrams, telex, and telephones. Door K for *Postal Expres.* **Postal Code:** 28070.

Telephones: Telefónica, Gran Vía, 30, at C. Valverde. Metro: Gran Vía. Direct-dial lines to the U.S. (phone #9, long lines in the evening). Open 9am-midnight. Also a **branch** at C. Virgen de los Peligros, 19. Open 9am-10pm. The **Palacio de Comunicaciones** (above) is infinitely quieter. Enter door H, next to the gold mailboxes on Po. Prado. Calls over 500ptas can be charged to a credit card. Open Mon.-Fri. 8am-midnight, Sat.-Sun. and holidays 8am-10pm. Long-distance calls may also be placed at **Po. Recoletos, 43,** off Pl. Colón. Open Mon.-Fri. 9am-10pm, Sat.-Sun. and holidays 10am-9pm. **Telephone Code:** 91.

Emergency, Health, and Help

General Information Line: tel. 010. Run by the Ayuntamiento, they'll tell you anything about Madrid, from the address of the nearest police station to a zoo's hours. Spanish only.

Emergency: tel. 091, 092.

Police: Puerta del Sol, 7 (tel. 221 65 16). Also at C. Luna, 29 (tel. 521 04 11).

Fire: tel. 080.

Ambulance: Red Cross (tel. 522 22 22).

Hospital: Most are in the north and east ends. These are all public hospitals and will treat you whether or not you can pay in advance. If your Spanish is poor, try **Anglo-American Medical Unit,** Conde de Aranda, 1, 1st fl. (tel. 435 18 23), to the left. Metro: Serrano. Doctors, dentists, optometrists. Run partly by British and Americans. Regular personnel on duty 9am-8pm, but assistance is available at all hours. *Not* an emergency clinic. **Hospital Clínico San Carlos,** Pl. Cristo Rey (tel. 544 17 05). Metro: Moncloa. **Hospital General Gregorio Marañón,** C. Dr. Esquerdo, 46 (tel. 586 80 00). Metro: O'Donnell. **Hospital Santa Cristina,** C. O'Donnell, 59 (tel. 573 62 00). Metro: O'Donnell. Run by *Insalud,* Spain's National Health Institute.

Late-Night Pharmacy: tel. 098, or check *Farmacias de Guardia* listings in local papers to find pharmacies open after 8pm. Contraceptive products sold over the counter in most Spanish pharmacies and at **Profilácticos,** C. Fuencarral, 6.

Crisis Lines: Poison Control (tel. 262 04 20). **AIDS Information Hotline** (tel. 445 23 28). **Alcoholicos Anónimos** (Spanish, tel. 532 30 30). **Women's Medical Issues Hotline** (tel. 730 49 01, 419 94 41). English here is poor. Open Mon.-Fri. 3:30-6:30pm. **Sociedad Sexológica de Madrid** for information and advice on sexual matters (tel. 522 25 10). **English-Language Helpline** for practical information and confidentiality from trained volunteers 7-11pm. Answering machine other hours (tel. 559 13 93).

Other

El Corte Inglés: C. Preciados, 3 (tel. 532 18 00). Metro: Sol. C. Goya, 76 (tel. 577 71 71). Metro: Goya. C. Princesa, 42 (tel. 542 48 00). Metro: Argüelles. C. Raimundo Fernández Villaverde, 79 (tel. 556 23 00). Metro: Nuevos Ministerios. As always, they've got a **map. Currency exchange:** 1% commission on cash (250ptas min. charge); 2% commission on traveler's checks (500ptas min. charge). They also offer novels and guidebooks in English; haircutting; both cafeteria and restaurant; and **telephones.** Cheap, excellent **supermarket.** Open Mon.-Sat. 10am-9pm.

Luggage Storage: Estaciones de Chamartín and Atocha. Automatic lockers for backpacks 300ptas per day, for large packs and suitcases 500ptas per day. Open 7:30am-11:30pm. **Estacíon Sur de Autobuses.** Bags checked (75ptas per bag per day). Lockers also at the airport-bus terminal beneath Pl. Colón.

Lost Property: Pl. Legazpi, 7 (tel. 588 43 46). Metro: Legazpi. Also at **Almacén de Objetos Perdidos,** C. Santa Engracia, 120 (tel. 441 02 11). Metro: Ríos Rosas. The latter holds lost items 2 yrs. For objects lost on the **metro,** check at Retiro station (tel. 435 22 66).

Message Boards: Very full one at **Librería Turner** bookstore (below) offers language *intercambios* with natives, language instruction, and apartment sharing information. Lines form outside just before it opens (10am and 5pm). **TIVE** travel agency (above) also has a board brimful with cheap travel tickets and ridesharing offers. At **Albergue Juvenil Santa Cruz (HI)** (see Accommodations below), the same types of notices but less of them.

English Bookstore: Librería Turner, C. Genova, 3 (tel. 319 09 26). Classics and the very latest. Guidebooks. **Booksellers,** C. José Abascal, 48 (tel. 442 79 59). Rather expensive, but a vast array.

Library: Bibliotecas Populares, C. Felipe el Hermoso, 4 (tel. 445 98 45), for information. Metro: Cuatro Caminos and Puerta de Toledo. These lamentable public libraries are small, crowded, and lack A/C. The new one at Puerta de Toledo is the only exception. They'll issue you a card on the spot (passport necessary, 500ptas). The **Biblioteca Nacional** isn't open for reading or browsing. Entrance only to scholars doing doctorate and post-doctorate research. To use the facilities, bring letters of recommendation and a project proposal.

English-Language Periodicals: Dailies and weeklies available at kiosks on the Gran Vía, Paseos Prado, Recoletos, and Castellana, and around Puerta del Sol. **Women's Services: Librería de Mujeres Women's Center,** C. San Cristóbal, 17 (tel. 521 70 43), near Pl. Mayor. Concerts, readings, lectures, political activities, and international bookstore. Some English spoken. **Women's Groups,** C. Barquillo, 44, 1st floor (tel. 419 36 89). For information, call after 8pm.

Gay and Lesbian Services: Librería El Galeón, C. Sagasta, 7. Metro: Bilbao. A gay bookstore that carries the *Guía Gay Visado,* an annually-updated list of gay and lesbian entertainment throughout Spain. For lesbian and gay club listings, *El Mundo's* Friday supplement *Metropoli* stands out from other papers' and from the *Guía del Ocio.*

Cultural Center: Washington Irving Center, Marqués de Villa Magna, 8 (tel. 435 69 22). Large selection of U.S. magazines. Occasional photography exhibits. Library open Mon.-Fri. noon-7pm. **British Cultural Center,** Almagro, 5 (tel. 419 12 50). Library open Mon.-Fri. 9am-1pm and 3-6pm; in off-season Mon.-Thurs. 9am-7pm, Fri. 9am-3pm.

Youth Organization: Instituto de la Juventud, C. José Ortega y Gasset, 71 (tel. 401 13 00).

Religious Services: Centro Islámico, C. Alonso Cano, 3. Metro: Iglesia. **Mezquita de Madrid,** on the M-30 near Av. América. The largest mosque in Western Europe. **Sinagoga Beth Yaacov,** C. Balmes, 3 (tel. 445 98 43 or 445 98 35), near Pl. Sorolla. Metro: Iglesia. Also small chapel, two social halls, room for Sun. classes, mikvah, library, and facilities for kosher catering. Kosher restaurant can be blocked off if you call ahead. **Church of England,** C. Hermosilla, 45. Metro: Velázquez. **North American Catholic Church,** Av. Alfonso XIII, 165. Metro: Puente de Vallecas, off Av. Peña Prieta.

Laundromat: Lavandería Donoso Cortés, C. Donoso Cortés, 17 (tel. 446 96 90). Metro: Quevedo. Self-service. Wash and dry 350ptas per 5kg. Soap 60ptas. Open Mon.-Fri. 8:30am-7:30pm, Sat. 8:30am-1pm. **Lavandería Marcenado,** C. Marcenado, 15 (tel. 416 68 71). Metro: Prosperidad. Full service. Wash and dry 600ptas per 5kg. Open Mon.-Fri. 9:30am-1:30pm and 4:30-8pm, Sat. 9:30am-1:30pm. **Lavandería Maryland,** Meléndez Valdés, 52 (tel. 243 30 41). Go through passage to the mall out back. Metro: Argüelles. Self-service or they'll do it while you wander. Self-service wash and dry 600ptas per 5kg, full service 860ptas.

Toilets: Public ones at any El Corte Inglés, Galerías Preciados, or McDonald's; in the Retiro; a pay cabin around the corner from *Telefónica* at Pl. Colón (often out of order).

Publications About Madrid

En Madrid: Monthly calendar of events. Available free at municipal tourist office.

Guía del Ocio: Weekly entertainment paper with listings of concerts, exhibits, cinema, restaurants, bars, clubs, sports, and TV. Available at kiosks and newsstands, 90ptas.

La Capital: Monthly artístico-cultural magazine focusing on Madrid, with essays, interviews, photography, and fiction. Available at kiosks and newsstands, 350ptas.

Accommodations

Demand for rooms rises dramatically in summer. *Habitaciones sencillas* (individual rooms) are particularly hard to find, because many are occupied by long-term residents. Reservations or early arrival reduce headache potential. Expect to pay between 1400ptas and 2100ptas per person for a typical *hostal* room, a bit more for a two-star *hostal*, and slightly less for a bed in a *pensión*.

Youth Hostels

Madrid's two HI youth hostels charge reasonable fees and serve meals for a modest price. They lack a central location and privacy, and with unlocked cubby holes often the only storage in the 8-person rooms, security can be dubious. Both hostels fill quickly, even in winter. An HI card is required and can be purchased for 1800ptas at either hostel. Both have a three-day maximum stay.

Albergue Juvenil Santa Cruz de Marcenado (HI), C. Santa Cruz de Marcenado, 28 (tel. 247 45 32), off C. Serrano Jover between Princesa and Alberto Aguilera. Metro: Argüelles. Modern, recently renovated facilities located near the student district. 75 firm beds in airy rooms. Locker use deters thieves. Message board. English spoken. Strict curfew 1:30am, midnight on Sun. 530ptas, over 26 650ptas. Tiny breakfast included. *Pensión completa* 1300ptas, over 26 1500ptas. *Pensión media* 900ptas, over 26 1100ptas. Reservations must be received at least 15 days in advance; otherwise show up 8-9:30am. 25% deposit required for groups.

Albergue Juvenil Richard Schirrman (HI), Casa de Campo (tel. 463 56 99). Metro: El Lago. Turn left immediately as you exit the Metro station, left again, and walk 1km on the unpaved rocky footpath along the Metro tracks. Cross over the small concrete footbridge and turn left at the Albergue Juvenil sign. On the outskirts of the city, in an enormous park, close to a lake and municipal swimming pool. Don't even contemplate walking alone through the unlit, densely wooded park at night. 130 bunk beds. Each 8-person room has a bath. No curfew. 550ptas, over 26 650ptas. Breakfast included. *Pensión completa* 1200ptas, over 26 1400ptas. *Pensión media* 900ptas, over 26 1100ptas. Same reservation requirements as above.

Hotels, Hostales, Pensiones

The actual differences between *hostales* of two stars, of one star, and *pensiones* in Madrid are often minimal. A room in a one- or two-star *hostal* will have at least these

Accommodations

basics: bed (small), closet space (too much), desk with chair (more like a stand and stool), sink and towel, window, light fixture (fluorescent), and a lock on the door. Winter heating is standard. As a rule in Madrid, especially in competitive central zones, *hostales* are well-kept and comfortable places to stay. You'll usually get your own set of keys, or the owner will be accustomed to opening the door, albeit groggily, at all hours. However, if you do plan to club-hop until the wee hours, make sure it's understood before taking the room: late-night lockouts or confrontations with irate owners are no fun.

Pensiones are like boarding houses, often dishing out home-cooked meals (*pensión completa* and *media*), as well as curfews. They usually lack winter heating. *Let's Go* doesn't include many in the following listings, as they tend to prefer longer-term guests (*estables*, as their signs say). The same goes for *casa de huéspedes* or simply *casas*. Unfortunately, Madrid is too large to have a network of *casas particulares* offering rooms to travelers.

In the listings below, exceptions to the basic features are noted, such as a shower or full bath in the room, the absence of winter heating, and unusual size, decor, or other amenities.

Between the Puerta del Sol and Palacio Real

Here you'll sleep in the oldest quarter of Madrid. Historic and atmospheric, with narrow streets, potted-flower balconies, and decaying façades, this centrally located zone is crawling with tourists. Stray several blocks from the Puerta del Sol to find better deals.

Hostal-Residencia Cruz-Sol, Pl. Santa Cruz, 6, 4th fl. (tel. 532 71 97), a stone's throw from the east side of Pl. Mayor. Metro: Sol. Sizeable rooms, some with balconies overlooking the Iglesia de Santa Cruz. Selvatic decor combines plants and hardwood floors with greenish wallpaper and crimson tiles. Doubles for single use 1800ptas. Doubles 2200ptas, with bath 3600ptas. Triples 3000ptas. Showers 200ptas.

Hostal-Residencia Paz, C. Flora, 4, 1st fl. (tel. 547 30 47), off C. Arenal by way of C. Donados. Metro: Opera or Sol. Cheery establishment with rooms off the street. Collegiate *Let's Go* users suck up the establishment's high cheer. Some English spoken. Singles 2000ptas. Doubles 3000ptas, with shower 3500ptas. Triples 4200ptas. Call ahead for reservations.

Hostal-Residencia Jeyma, C. Arenal 24, 3rd fl. (tel. 541 63 29). Metro: Opera. Quiet gloom and the venerable *dueña* soothe post-street bustle ailments. Singles 1100ptas. Doubles 2200ptas. Showers 300ptas.

Hostal-Residencia Malagueña, C. Preciados, 35, 4th fl. (tel. 559 52 23), between Pl. Santo Domingo and Pl. Callao. Metro: Callao. Spacious, airy rooms with high windows and now-decorative gas "hearths." Singles 1900ptas. Doubles 2800ptas. Triples 3600ptas.

Hostal-Residencia Callao, C. Preciados, 35, 3rd fl. (tel. 542 00 67). More beds (with newer mattresses) and higher water pressure than the Malagueña above and 1 less floor to climb. Singles 2200ptas, with shower 3200ptas. Doubles 3200ptas, with shower 3700ptas.

Hostal-Residencia Pinariega, C. Santiago, 1, 1st fl. (tel. 248 08 19). From Pl. Isabel II take the narrow C. Espejo (where C. Carlos III leaves the plaza) to its end and turn right. Metro: Opera. Springy beds; rooms not facing the street can be rather dim. Singles 2120ptas. Doubles 3000ptas, with shower 3500ptas, with bath 3800ptas. Triples 4800ptas.

Hostal Soledad, C. San Crístobal, 11, 2nd fl. (tel. 521 22 10), off C. Mayor near Puerta del Sol, east of the Pl. Mayor. All rooms face the street in this otherwise standard *hostal*. Basketball teams should look elsewhere; slightly sagging beds are designed for people under 6' tall. Hot water 7am-10pm. Doubles for single use 2400ptas. Doubles 3000ptas, with shower 3500ptas, with bath 4400ptas.

Hostal-Residencia María del Mar, C. Marqués Viudo de Pontejo, 7, 2nd and 3rd fl. (tel. 531 90 64), reached via C. Correo from the Puerta del Sol. Metro: Sol. Handy and ambitious manager of this large, 40-room establishment is renovating it himself. Finished rooms are immaculate. White tile floors and new furniture in box-like rooms. Singles 1300ptas. Doubles 2500 ptas, with bath (and larger room) 5000ptas.

Hostal-Residencia Encarnita, C. Marqués Viudo de Pontejo, 7, 4th fl. (tel. 531 90 55), above the María del Mar. Metro: Sol. Plenty of *hostal* charm: claustrophobic rooms, tired beds, dark halls. Hot water 8am-10:30pm. Singles 1400ptas. Doubles 2500ptas, with shower 2800ptas.

Hostal Montalvo, Zaragoza, 6, 3rd fl. (tel. 265 59 10), near Pl. Mayor. Metro: Sol. It doesn't get any closer to the Pl. Mayor than this. Old wooden furniture and plenty of sunlight. One floor up from a restaurant of Valladolid specialties (see Food listings). Singles 2200ptas, with bath 3500ptas. Doubles 3600ptas, with bath 4500ptas. Triples with bath 6200ptas.

Hostal-Residencia Rober, C. Arenal, 26, 5th fl. (tel. 541 91 75). Metro: Opera. Perhaps the only smoke-free *hostal* in all Spain. Elevator. All rooms include totally green baths. Singles 2900ptas. Doubles 4600ptas. Triples 6000ptas.

Hostal Alicante, C. Arenal, 16, 3rd fl. (tel. 531 51 78). Metrol: Opera or Sol. Quiet and dark rooms in a central location. Singles with shower 3500ptas. Doubles with shower 3600ptas, with bath 4000ptas. Triples with shower 5400ptas. Quads 6800ptas.

Hostal-Residencia Miño, C. Arenal, 16, 2nd fl. (tel. 531 50 79). Metro: Opera or Sol. Eerily similar to the Alicante overhead. A melting pot of rooms ranging from large with hardwood floors and balconies, to tight quarters with vinyl underfoot. Singles 2000ptas, with shower 2700ptas. Doubles with shower 3600ptas, with bath 4200ptas. Triples 5700ptas.

Hostal La Macarena, C. Cava de San Miguel, 8 (tel. 265 92 21), downhill from Pl. San Miguel which is on C. Mayor. Groups of 3 or 4 might consider this *hostal* before it evolves into a *hotel*. Immaculate rooms are spacious and bright, many with more than 1 window looking out on Puerta de Cachilleros of Pl. Mayor. All rooms with complete, comfortably-sized baths. Singles 3500ptas. Doubles 5500ptas. Triples 7000ptas. Quadruples 8000ptas.

Between Puerta del Sol and Museo del Prado

This area is just as historic as the neighborhood further west (see previous section), though not quite as noble. It's also very central and chock-a-block with bars and restaurants. Although once down-at-heel, increasing gentrification has made it relatively safe.

Hostal-Residencia Mondragón, Carrera San Jerónimo, 32, 4th floor (tel. 429 68 16). Metro: Sol. Glass-block and carved marble entry leads into a building full of *hostales* (the León, Centro, and Aguilar below)—over which Mondragón reigns supreme. Wide halls, clean rooms, and sun-splashed red-tiled terraces. Singles 1500ptas. Doubles 2200ptas, with shower 2400ptas. Triples with shower 3300ptas. Showers 100ptas. Open March-Dec.

Hostal-Residencia Sud-Americana, Po. del Prado, 12, 6th fl. (tel. 429 25 64). Metro: Antón Martín or Atocha. Conveniently located across from the Prado. High ceilings, chandeliers, hardwood floors, and antique furniture lend an air of pre-War elegance. Some rooms have spectacular views of the Paseo. Dress for success to humor the self-confessed "old-fashioned" (read: conservative) owners. Singles 1800ptas. Doubles 3200ptas. Showers 400ptas. Call ahead for availability in this 8-room *hostal*. No reservations by mail.

Hostal Carreras, C. Príncipe, 18, 3rd fl. (tel. 522 00 36), off Pl. Santa Ana. Metro: Antón Martín, Sol, or Sevilla. Recent renovation and expansion into the building down the street make for 2 worlds at Carreras: the old (wood floors, big rooms, obtrusive high-tech shower stalls) and the new (rooms off a long corridor, white tiled floors, new furniture). Singles 1900ptas. Doubles 2700ptas, with shower 3500ptas, with bath 4100ptas. Triples with shower 4500ptas.

Hostal-Residencia Regional, C. Príncipe, 18, 4th fl. (tel. 522 33 73), above the old Carreras. Metro: Antón Martín, Sol, or Sevilla. Rooms resemble its neighbor's: quality beds, some hardwood floors, elaborate molding, and views of the street. Singles 1900ptas. Doubles 2900ptas, with bath 3500ptas. Triples 4000ptas.

Hostal Lucense, C. Nuñez de Arce, 15 (tel. 522 48 88), off Pl. Santa Ana. Metro: Antón Martín; follow C. Atocha uphill and turn right on C. San Sebastián, which leads to C. Nuñez de Arce. Owners speak some English. Best for skinny people with lots of clothing—closely packed narrow singles have immense closets. Singles 1200-1500ptas. Doubles 2000-2400ptas. Triples 3000ptas. Showers 150ptas. If full, owners direct you down the street to their similar **Pensión Poza** (C. Nuñez de Arce, 11). Singles 1500ptas. Doubles 2000ptas. Showers 150ptas. No winter heating.

Pensión Apolo XI, C. Espoz y Mina, 6, 3rd fl. (tel. 532 14 09), off C. San Jerónimo near Puerta del Sol. Metro: Sol. Enormous, airy rooms with lofty ceilings and fresh blue or pink paint. Ultra-efficient interior design packs 3-4 beds per room; singles and pairs may wind up sharing. Flat rate of 1200ptas per person. No winter heating.

Hostal Coruña, Po. del Prado, 12, 3rd fl. (tel. 429 25 43). Metro: Antón Martín. Good sized rooms in well repair, though less spectacular than those at the Sud-Americana above. Singles 1800ptas. Doubles 3200ptas. Triples 4200ptas. Showers 200ptas, free for longer stays.

Hostal Lido, C. Echegaray, 5 (tel. 429 62 07), off C. San Jerónimo near Pl. Canalejus. Metro: Sol. One of 4 *hostales* in this building, which is surrounded by good restaurants and late-night activity. An excellent location, even if the rooms are cramped and dim. Breakfast offered. Singles 1700ptas. Doubles 3000ptas. Longer stays at reduced rates.

Hostal León, C. San Jerónimo, 32, 5th fl. (tel. 429 67 78). Metro: Sol or Sevilla. Pink walls and intricate molding attempt to distract the eye from the curiously lumpy beds. Singles 1200-1500ptas. Doubles 3000ptas. Triples 3600ptas. Quads 4800ptas.

Hostal Madrid Centro, C. San Jerónimo, 32, 5th fl. (tel. 429 68 13). Rooms vary from huge and bright with fireplace and sitting area, to miniscule, poorly-lit affairs. Wacky decor of green vinyl chairs and plastic "wood" panelling. Doubles with shower 3500ptas. Triples with shower 4200ptas.

Hostal Auilar, C. San Jerónimo, 32, 2nd fl. (tel. 429 59 26). Massive, clean, ugly rooms (all 30 of 'em), with phones and modern baths. Singles with shower 2400ptas, with bath 2700ptas. Doubles with shower 3800ptas, with bath 4200ptas, with bath and lounge 4700ptas. Triples 4200ptas. Quads 5600ptas.

The Gran Vía

The grand old buildings that tower imperially aloof above shops, *cafeterías,* hotels, and movie theaters at street level hide many *hostales* behind their imposing façades. Keep one eye on less ritzy building entries, the other on the upper floors. Rooms are typically more expensive, larger, higher of ceiling, and noisier than elsewhere. Some *hostales* in the area, especially the larger, more hotel-y ones, have adopted the high-low season system (unheard of among *hostales* elsewhere in Madrid). Summer travelers may find themselves priced out of this zone.

Hostal Alcázar Regis, Gran Vía, 61, 5th fl. (tel. 547 93 17). Metro: Pl. España or Santo Domingo. Rooms are spacious though simpler than their stained-glass doors and opulent reception halls suggest. Singles 2100ptas. Doubles 3900ptas. Triples 5700ptas. Fills up quickly; make reservations.

Hostal Margarita, Gran Vía, 50, 5th fl. (tel. 547 35 49). Metro: Pl. España. Spic-and-span, recently renovated rooms. English-speaking owners laugh, love, and cry with guests over the afternoon soaps. Singles 2700ptas, with shower 3200ptas. Doubles with shower 3900ptas, with bath 4100ptas. Triples 5700ptas. Prices not including 6% IVA. Large breakfast 375ptas. Laundry 1000ptas.

Hostal-Residencia Delfina, Gran Vía, 12, 4th fl. (tel. 522 64 23). Metro: Gran Vía or Sevilla. A bit of old-fashioned charm, with steel bedframes and oversized rooms. All rooms with cramped baths. Singles 2500ptas. Doubles 3400-3900ptas. Triples 4500ptas.

Hostal El Pinar, C. Isabel Católica, 19 (tel. 547 32 82), 2nd street to the right walking uphill on Gran Vía. Metro: Pl. España. Somewhat small but bright rooms, all on the street. Singles 2000ptas. Doubles 3300ptas. Triples 4500ptas. Showers 150ptas.

Hostal-Residencia Tanger, Gran Vía, 44, 9th fl. (tel. 521 75 85). Metro: Callao. Dizzying views of the street, savory views of old Madrid staples. No cooties here; rooms are scrubbed down to the hardwood floors. Singles 1600ptas, with shower 2000ptas. Doubles 2800ptas, with shower 3300ptas.

Hostal-Residencia Josefina, Gran Vía, 44, 7th fl. (tel. 531 04 66). General atmosphere of decay (peeling paint, old curtains, faded paintings, crepuscular lighting, slapdash showers) complements the *Blade Runner*-esque stairwell. Beds are decent and views tip-top. Singles 1300ptas, with shower 1500ptas. Doubles with shower 2400ptas. Triples with shower 3600ptas.

Hostal Luna, C. Luna, 6, 3rd fl. (tel. 532 45 85), a street parallel to Gran Vía reached via C. Silva or C. Tudescos, close to and opposite Pl. Callao. Metro: Callao. The manager gives the scoop on the scary-after-dark neighborhood. The rooms are brighter than the reception area. Singles 1500-2000ptas. Doubles 3000ptas, with shower 3500ptas.

Temporada Alta and Temporada Baja

The following *hostales* are on the high-low season system. High season generally begins sometime in May and ends at the end of October or beginning of November. Prices are given high season first, then low season.

Hostal Los Zamoranos, Gran Vía, 12, 6th fl. (tel. 532 90 26). Metro: Gran Vía or Sevilla. Uninspired rooms turn somewhat humid in summer. Showers hog a good bit of room space. Singles 1800ptas, with shower 2500ptas. Doubles 3000ptas, with shower 3500ptas. Triples with shower 4500ptas. Low season (ends April 30): 1600ptas; 2200ptas; 2600ptas, 2900ptas; 3900ptas.

Hostal Lauria, Gran Vía, 50, 4th fl. (tel. 541 91 82). Metro: Pl. España. In the same building as the Margarita, this *hostal* too offers large, well-lit rooms and a swish TV lounge. All rooms with full baths. Singles 3800ptas. Doubles 5500ptas. Triples 6800ptas. Low season (ends May 31): 3500ptas; 4600ptas; 6200ptas.

Hostal-Residencia Lamalonga, Gran Vía, 56, 2nd fl. (tel. 547 26 31). Metro: Callao or Santo Domingo. A superflux of amenities: prodigious bathrooms with rugs and tiles, TV lounge, and phones. All rooms with baths. Singles 4000ptas. Doubles 5200ptas. Triples 6500ptas. Low season: 3000ptas; 4600ptas; 6500ptas.

Calle Fuencarral

For all its narrowness, C. Fuencarral is the main traffic pipeline to the Gran Vía for buses, taxis, commercial vehicles, scooters, and pedestrians. Jam-packed with shops, bars, and *hostales,* its buildings are continually in renovation. It may be noisier and fumier than the Gran Vía, but it's less expensive and closer to the nightlife of Malasaña and Chueca.

Hostal Palacios-Ribadavia, C. Fuencarral, 25, 2nd fl. (tel. 531 10 58). Metro: Gran Vía. Owner fervently swears, "My job is the bed—you *will* have fresh sheets daily." No slacking in other departments either; other genres of furniture get their own fair share of attention. Singles 1800ptas, with shower 2000ptas. Doubles with shower 3200ptas. Triples with shower 4500ptas. 10% discount for bearers of *Let's Go.*

Hostal Medieval, C. Fuencarral, 46, 2nd fl. (tel. 522 25 49), on corner with C. Augusto Figueroa. Metro: Tribunal. Nothing remotely medieval about the immense and sunny rooms, the plant-ridden balconies, or the neon lobby sign. The rooms are quirkily decorated with miniature paintings, plants, picture-frame-ish molding, and fading paint. All rooms with showers. Singles 2800ptas. Doubles 4000ptas. Triples 5500ptas.

Hostal-Residencia Abril, C. Fuencarral, 39, 4th fl. (tel. 531 53 38). Metro: Tribunal. Cutesy prints and garish mirrors amongst furniture just out of the bag. Singles 1750ptas, with shower 2000ptas. Doubles with shower 3100ptas, with bath 3400ptas. Triples with shower 4100ptas, with bath 4400ptas.

Hostal Residencia Domínguez, C. Santa Brígida, 1 (tel. 532 15 47), off C. Fuencarral. Metro: Tribunal. Modern bathrooms have almost as much square footage as the spartan rooms. Dark, narrow hallways. Singles 1700ptas, with shower 2000ptas. Doubles with shower 3200ptas, with bath 3400ptas.

Elsewhere

The area behind the Gran Vía called **Chueca,** especially along and near C. Infantas, is about as rich in *hostales* (not to mention restaurants, bars, and nightlife) as any of the above districts. Less prestigious and touristy, it's a good place to search for lodging if you want to be near the nightlife of Chueca (see Entertainment). If you're hoping for a cheaper room, fewer tourists doesn't always mean lower prices in Madrid.

Other tourist-light zones include the mainly residential **Chamberí** (north of the boulevard formed by C. Alberto Aguilera, C. Carranza, C. Sugasta, and C. Genova) and **La Latina** (the area around the eponymous Metro stop stretching to Metro: Tirso de Molina and the Glorieta Puerta de Toledo). Near the **train station Atocha** are a handful of *hostales,* the closest down Paseo Santa María de la Cabeza. Near Chamartín train station budget lodgings are rare—it's wiser to call from the station to reserve something in town.

Hostal La Montaña, C. Juan Alvárez Mendizábal, 44, 4th fl. (tel. 547 10 88; Metro: Argüelles), is one of five *hostales* at this address in the residential neighborhood of **Argüelles.** Hilly Parque del Oeste, Pl. España, and Palacio Real are all within striking distance. Rooms are ample and sunny, quiet at night, and in much less demand. Singles 1800ptas. Doubles with shower 3400ptas, with bath 3700ptas. Triples 4800ptas.

Camping

Tourist offices can provide information about the 13 or so campsites within 50km of Madrid. The same information is in their **Guía Oficial de Campings, España '93**. For further camping information, contact the Consejería de Educación de Juventud, C. Caballero de Gracia, 32 (tel. 522 29 41 or 521 44 27). **Camping Madrid** (tel. 302 28 35) is on Ctra. N-1, Madrid-Burgos (11km). Take the Metro to Pl. Castilla, then bus #151, 154, or 155 to Iglesia de los Dominicos. (350ptas per person, per tent, and per car; 425ptas if tent holds over four people.) **Camping Osuna** (tel. 741 05 10) is located on the Ajalvir-Vicálvaro road (15.5km). Take the metro to Canillejas, then bus #105 to Av. Logroño. (350ptas per person, per tent, and per car.) Both campgrounds can pass as autonomous cities; each has phones, hot showers, washers and dryers, safes, currency exchange, medical care, a playground, a bar, and a restaurant. Camping Madrid has a swimming pool. Buses dash from Camping Osuna to El Escorial, Aranjuez, and Sierra de Madrid.

Food

Restaurants open for lunch at either 1:30 or 2pm and for dinner at 8 or 9pm, although most diners prefer to arrive after 10pm. Chefs prepare every regional Spanish cuisine and many international ones in this gastronomic capital. Madrid's delicacies include *caldereta de cordero* (lamb stewed with tomatoes and peppers), *cocido madrileño* (chickpea stew flavored with *chorizo* sausage), *callos a la madrileña* (tripe cooked with wine, sausage, and ham), *mojete* (mixed vegetables), and *pisto manchego* (a vegetable stew).

Excellent pastry shops and delis run riot in Madrid's streets. The sublime **Horno La Santiagüesa**, C. Mayor, 73, hawks everything from *roscones de reyes* (sweet bread for the Feast of the Epiphany) to *empanadas* (puff pastry pie with tuna, hake, apple, and other fillings) to chocolate and candy. You can't go wrong at the pastry shop **Niza**, near Palacio de Justicia. **Pastelería La Mallorquina**, on the corner of Puerta del Sol and C. Mayor, has the standard breakfast (*café* and *bollo* 150ptas) spiced up by just-baked *napolitanas* still warm from the oven. **Mallorca**, C. Velázquez 59 (and other branches), is a renowned deli. **Juncal**, on C. (not Po.) Recoletos, will satisfy the most exigent hankering for chocolate. Finally, **El Gourmet de Cuchilleros** is a gourmet store stocking all sorts of Spanish jams, honey, candy, and cheese, which make excellent gifts for that special someone. Walk through the Pl. Mayor's Arco de Cuchilleros; it's on the corner a few paces down the street facing you.

Guía del Ocio lists late night eateries under *Cenar a Última Hora*. The orange VIPS (pronounced veeps) and green BOBS signs that pop up all over Madrid signify a highly convenient restaurant chain. Each branch serves everything from sandwiches to full dinners to satisfy the late-night munchies. (Open Sun.-Thurs. 9am-3am, Fri-Sat. 9am-3:30am.) VIPS also carry English books and magazines, records, chocolate, and canned food.

> **Groceries:** **Mercado de San Miguel**, just off the northwest corner of Pl. Mayor (open Mon.-Sat. 9am-3pm and 5:30-7:30pm) and **Mercado de la Cebada**, at intersection of C. Toledo and Carrera de San Francisco, are two of the most convenient supermarkets. Every **El Corte Inglés** department store has a cheap, excellent food market, usually on the ground floor. You'll find lower prices only at an open market. (Open Mon.-Sat. 10am-9pm. See Practical Information: Other for addresses.)

In the following listings and Madrid in general, a *restaurante* or *casa* is open from 1 to 4:30pm and 8:30pm to midnight unless noted otherwise. Establishments such as *mesones, cafeterías, bares, cafés, terrazas,* and *tabernas* include a bar and serve drinks, *tapas, raciones, bocadillos,* etc., all day until midnight.

Around Puerta del Sol and Plaza Mayor

Choose carefully: this area is overrun by tourists. Restaurants outdo themselves in being *lo más típico;* more often than not they wind up *tópico*. The food *is* good, just overpriced.

Casa Ciriaco, C. Mayor, 84. Metro: Sol or Opera. *Castizo* (traditional, pure) Madrid fare without pretentions. Filling bean and ham or chicken plates 500-800ptas. Open Sept.-July Thurs.-Tues.

Mesón 1600, C. Cava de San Miguel. Metro: Sol. One of numerous "typical" restaurants on this street, this eensy stone-walled den has decent *cocido madrileño*. *Menú* 750ptas. Open 1-4pm and 8pm-midnight.

Museo del Jamón, C. San Jerónimo, 6 (tel. 521 03 46), off Puerta del Sol. Metro: Sol. Five other locations in the city. Ham lovers unite! The most overt expression of Spain's fascination with piggies. No hamless wall space. Lightly smoked Iberian ham sandwiches 150ptas (3 make a meal). *Menú del día* 850 or 1000ptas. Open Mon.-Sat. 9am-12:30am, Sun. 10am-12:30am. Restaurant upstairs, with same prices but a longer menu, opens at 1pm.

Lhardy, C. San Jerónimo, 8 (tel. 521 33 85), at C. Victoria. Metro: Sol. Easiest to spot by the blue-uniformed guards. One of Madrid's oldest restaurants, it doubles as a museum. Original 1839 decor in the upstairs dining rooms. A meal upstairs is a big investment; the house specialty, *cocido*, a stew of vegetables, chicken, sausage, and ham, is 3000ptas. Budget-hounds congregate in the first-floor store for cognac, sherry, and the best hors d'oeuvres in town. Open Mon.-Sat. 12:30-4:30pm and 8:30-11:30pm, Sun. 12:30-4:30pm.

Casa Paco, Puerta Cerrada, 11 (tel. 266 31 66), a couple of blocks south of the Pl. Mayor. A *madrileño* institution with a very expensive *menú* (2500ptas) but affordable entrées.

Restaurante-Cafeteria Sabatini, C. Bailén, 15 (tel. 247 92 40), opposite the Sabatini Gardens next to the Palacio Real. Come at sunset. Sidewalk tables face 2 of Madrid's most famous sights. Portly portions of *paella* (800ptas) or garlic chicken (700ptas). Open 9am-1am. Dinner served 8pm-midnight.

Near Plaza Santa Ana

By day, this area teems with gourmets seeking the right restaurant; at night the bar-hoppers take over. **Calles Echegaray** and **Manuel Fernández González** are the budget boulevards. Restaurants around here often prepare elaborate regional specialties. Overall quality is high and prices are reasonable.

Mesón La Caserola, C. Echegaray, off C. San Jerónimo. Metro: Sol. Bustling, crowded joint serving a solid *menú* (730ptas) to ravenous locals on lunch break. Cheap *raciones* and *tapas* during off-hours. Worth the short wait.

Restaurante Integral Artemisa, C. Ventura de la Vega, 4, off C. San Jerónimo. Metro: Sol. Perhaps the best veggie place in this book, despite slow service and long waits for a table. Quite flavorful *potaje* (stew), pizza, purees, and salads. *Menú* 950ptas. Main dishes 700-900ptas. Non-vegetarian entrees available. A/C.

South of Puerta del Sol

The neighborhoods south of Sol, bounded by C. Atocha and C. Toledo, are more residential and working class. No caviar or champagne here, but plenty of *menús* for 700-800ptas. A la carte is often a better bargain.

Casa Portal, C. Olivar, 3 (tel. 239 07 39). Metro: Sol. Dandy Asturian specialties such as salmon and *tortilla de angulas* (eel tortilla, 1200ptas), but come for the homemade *sidra* (300ptas) decanted in true Asturian style by pouring from a bottle held high above the shoulders into a glass on the floor. Open noon-midnight.

La Terraza, off C. Bailén just past the Viaducto, among the trees of a slope-side park (Las Vistillas) famed for the view of the sun setting over the Casa de Campo. This *café-terraza* serves excellent meals inside at the bar and, better yet, in its elegant *comedor* in the back. *Conejo al ajillo* (rabbit stewed in parsley and garlic) and *ensaladilla rusa* (potato salad with sweet red peppers, peas, and tuna) upstage the view.

El Granero de Lavapiés, C. Argumosa, 10 (tel. 467 76 11), on a lovely tree-lined street with balconied 19th-century façades in an old neighborhood rarely visited by tourists. Vegetarian. *Filetes de arroz con salsa de almendras* (rice fillets with almond sauce) and *empanadillas vegetales* (vegetable turnovers). *Menú* 900ptas.

La Biótica, Amor de Dios, 3 (tel. 429 07 80). Vegetarian. Varied salad and cereal entrees. Full à la carte meal around 1200ptas.

The Gran Vía

McDonald's (two on Gran Vía) is the cloth out of which many *cafeterías, hamburgueserías,* and *pizzarías* here have been cut. If you came to Spain to escape the Power of the Big Mac, prowl the small streets just behind the main thoroughfare.

Restaurante-Cafetería El Valle, C. Fuencarral, 8. Local shop attendants and businessfolk take refuge midday in the cozy back room. Specialties are *churrasco* (grilled steak) and *pulpo* (octopus). *Menú* 825ptas. Entrees 600-1300ptas.

Mesón Altamar, C. Luna, near bottom of the inclines and C. San Bernardo. Fried fish amidst high seas decor. Cramped back room really feels like a ship's mess. Try the "catch of the day." Entrees 400-700ptas.

Chueca

Here, it's mostly chic gourmet haunts (especially toward Po. Recoletos) or dim little holes-in-the-wall with cheap and unappetizing *menús.* Stick near **Calles Libertad** and **Marcos.**

Taberna Carmencita, C. San Marcos, 36, on the corner with C. Libertad. Metro: Chueca. Popular with tourists and businesspeople, this classic restaurant evokes pre-War Madrid: brass fixtures, black and white photos of *toreros,* polychrome *azulejos,* lace curtains, and iron and marble tables. The *menú* is a steal at 1100ptas for its unusually superb bread and wine, plus an appetizer.

Restaurante La Vaxcongada, Pl. Vázquez de Mella, 10, on the edge of Chueca toward Gran Vía. Yellow sign visible from C. Infantas near the ugly parking plaza. Typical dishes of Madrid and the País Vasco (Basque country). *Menú* 700ptas. Entrees 300-700ptas. High ceiling and A/C prevent smoke conglomeration. The lone waiter manages to keep everyone happy and retain his sanity.

Nabucco, C. Hortaleza, 108 (tel. 410 06 11), a couple of blocks off Pl. Santa Bárbara. A large pizza-pasta place. Much lower prices than the upscale clientèle and atmosphere suggest. Pizzas about 650ptas, pasta dishes 700ptas and up. Open 8pm-midnight.

Restaurante Zara, C. Infantas, 7. Metro: Gran Vía. Tropical food with a stained-glass sunset backdrop. *Carne asada* (roast beef) with black beans and white rice 800ptas.

La Chocolatería-Comedor Madrid, C. Barbieri, 15 (tel. 521 00 23), 4 blocks from Gran Vía. Metro: Chueca. Traditional Spanish cuisine in a restaurant which has gone increasingly upmarket. Entrees about 1200ptas. Open Sept.-July Mon.-Sat. 1:30-3:45pm and 9pm-1:45am, Sun. 9pm-1:45am. Bar open 6:30pm-1:45am. Closed during Semana Santa.

Malasaña

Streets radiating from Pl. Dos de Mayo drown in a sea of *cafeterías,* bars, restaurants, and pubs. **Calle San Andrés** is most densely populated, but **Calles San Bernardo** and **Manuela Malasaña,** on the fringes of this neighborhood, shouldn't be overlooked. Many spots here are more imaginative in their cuisine and setting than the "regional specialty" clones that are legion in Madrid.

La Gata Flora, C. 2 de Mayo, 1 (tel. 521 20 20), at C. San Vicente Ferrer. Metro: Noviciado or Tribunal. Tightly packed tables and a bohemian crowd in a marvelous Italian restaurant. There's a cat in every picture. Try the *cappelletti al pesto* (dumplings in a delicious basil sauce, 715ptas) or the great *ensalada Sabina* (500ptas). Wash your meal down with fabulous sangria (725ptas). Open Sun.-Thurs. 1-4pm and 9pm-12:30am, Fri.-Sat. 8:30pm-1am.

El Restaurante Vegetariano, C. Marqués de Santa Ana, 34, off Pl. Juan Pujol on the corner with C. Espíritu Santo. Metro: Tribunal. A small establishment that dishes out high quality vegetarian concoctions. Understanding waiter/cooks tell all about each dish. Chewy homemade bread. *Lasaña verde* is green. Main course 700-800ptas. Salad bar (small plate 550ptas, large 750ptas). A/C.

La Granja Restaurante Vegetariano, C. San Andrés, 11, off Pl. 2 de Mayo. Metro: Tribunal. Bigger, darker, warmer, dirtier, and cheaper than the above. The food is quite delicious, although not so carefully prepared (i.e., *menú* 700ptas). Basic salads with herb dressing 400-600ptas. Main courses 500-700ptas.

Beyond Bilbao

We're talking north of Glorieta de Bilbao (Metro: Bilbao) in the V formed by **Calle Fuencarral** and **Calle Luchana**, extending to the multiple bars, cafés, and *terrazas* in **Plaza Olavide**. Oh, so many bars, clubs, cafés, and restaurants. Most bars and *mesones* purvey splendid, cheap *tapas* to feed the vibrant crowd of strollers that fills the streets come evening. Lunch gets a tad pricey as you move north into more gentrified territory.

Cafetería-Marisquería Kenia, C. Fuencarral, 114. Metro: Bilbao. Not to be confused with the other Kenia down the street at #95. When the sun shines, tables sprout on the sidewalk. Perfect for people-watching on this busy avenue. No indoor seating. All they serve is a *menú* (700ptas)—make sure one of your choices is a seafood dish.

Peñasco Rodilla, C. Fuencarral, 119. Metro: Bilbao. One of several "Rodillas" in town, the Peñasco is a most popular spot for sandwiches (pronounced sán-wi; 65ptas) to go, and a marvelous bargain. Unusual fillings such as *sobresada* (red mystery meat paste), *espinacas* (spinach) *al roquefort*, and *queso con nueces* (cheese with nuts).

Bar Samara, C. Cardenal de Cisneros, 13, past Baskin-Robbins. Hardly the Egyptian food that the sign claims. Packed to the brim after sundown. *Bolsillo* (small pita pocket) of shwarma 475ptas. Kebabs too. You'll need plenty of beer to wash down the hot oil. Open Sun.-Thurs. until midnight, Fri.-Sat. until 1am.

Argüelles and Moncloa

Argüelles and Moncloa are middle-class *barrios* near the Ciudad Universitaria. You'll see at least two restaurants per block in the area around these two Metro stops. Prices are a bit higher here.

Restaurante El Parque, Fernando el Católico, 78 (tel. 243 31 27), down the street from the student travel office. Metro: Moncloa. Large and unpretentious, with simple food. Entrées about 600ptas. *Menú* 700ptas.

El Rey de las Tortillas, C. Andrés Mellado, 16. A bar-restaurant specializing in inexpensive tortillas with various toppings. Young and boisterous clientele put away whopping servings. "King of tortillas" with salsa, garlic oil, or tomato sauce 350ptas. *Patatas bravas* (baked potato slices in orange spicy sauce), 200ptas. 1 liter *sidra* (cider) 350ptas. Open Mon.-Sat. 11am-midnight, Sun. 5:30pm-midnight.

Tapas

A delightfully active alternative to a full sit-down meal is hopping from bar to bar gobbling *tapas* at the counter (see Spain: Life and Times: Food and Drink). Most *tapas* bars (a.k.a. *tascas* or *tabernas*) are open noon to 4pm and 8pm to midnight or later. Some, doubling as restaurants, flock about **Plaza Mayor** (tourist alert!) and **Plaza Santa Ana**.

La Toscana: C. Ventura de la Vega, 22 (tel. 429 60 31). A quiet *mesón* with old architectural implements dangling from the woodwork. *Raciones* are their strong suit. Open noon-4pm and 8pm-midnight.

La Trucha: C. Fernández y González, 3 (tel. 429 58 33). Cramped but cheap.

La Chuleta, C. Echegaray, 20 (tel. 429 37 29). Spacious and modern. Savory tortillas, *calamares* (squid), and peppers. Open Sun.-Thurs. 12:30pm-12:30am, Fri.-Sat. 12:30pm-2:30am.

La Dolores, C. Jesús de Medinaceli, 4 (tel. 468 59 30), on the corner of Calles Lope de Vega and Jesús. Beer cans from each and every corner of the globe adorn this brightly tiled, high-ceilinged *tasca*. Extensive and varied array of *tapas* and wine.

Viña P, Pl. Santa Ana, 3 (tel. 531 81 11), opposite Cervecería Alemana. This *mesón* with a curved bar specializes in fresh seafood and *jamón serrano* (mountain-cured ham). Foodies swoon over their *mejillones rellenos* (mussels stuffed with a cream-based seafood filling).

Barranco, C. San Isidro Labrador, 14. A classic *tasca* celebrated for its shellfish and *jamón de Guijuelo* (Guijuelo cured ham).

El Anciano Rey de los Vinos, C. Bailén, 19 (tel. 248 50 52), just over the Viaducto on the left corner. A bright bar with a curvy counter, lofty ceilings, hand-painted tiles, and reflecting surfaces aplenty. There's a wide selection of inexpensive house wines served by the glass, perfect for sampling.

Sights

Madrid has the cultural and architectural heritage you'd expect from a city that was once capital of the largest empire in the world. It is also somewhat of a garden oasis on the calcinated plain of Castile, with numerous tree-lined streets and a host of lush parks. The Prado isn't the only exhibition space in town: Madrid is one of Europe's great museum cities for number, variety, and quality. The municipal tourist office regularly updates its pamphlet *Madrid: Museums and Monuments,* with addresses, telephone numbers, public transport, opening hours, admission, and brief descriptions for Madrid's many museums (see Museums below). Spanish speakers can take one of City Hall's **Descurbre Madrid tours,** designed to acquaint Spaniards with Madrid (see Practical Information: Tours).

In the following pages, sights are arranged by geographical location. The grand scheme is roughly semicircular: we begin in the Medieval-Habsburg heart of the city, and then travel successively east, north, and west, concluding with El Pardo.

From Plaza Mayor to Puerta de Toledo

A good place to orient yourself for any walking expedition through Madrid is the elegant **Plaza Mayor.** The arcaded square is topped with the Habsburgs' elegant black slate roofs and spindly, pagoda-like towers. It was completed in 1620 for Felipe III; his statue is also from the 17th century, although it took the city until 1847 to get it up. The public executions and bullfights that took place here throughout the early modern period are now but ghosts haunting the lively cafés that line the plaza's edges. Every Sunday morning, hundreds of collectors assemble here at the **coin and stamp market.** For hundreds of years, Madrileños have celebrated San Isidro (the patron saint of Madrid) in this very plaza. The arcades and surrounding streets house highly specialized old shops, including a renowned **hat emporium.** (Metro: Sol. Bus #3, 53, M-1.)

When Felipe II made Madrid capital of his empire, most of the town huddled between Pl. Mayor and the Palacio Real, stretching north to today's Opera and south to Pl. Puerta de Moros. Only a handful of medieval buildings remain, but the labyrinthine layout is unmistakable. **Plaza de la Villa** marks the heart of what was medieval Madrid. Legend has it that François—Carlos V's archenemy—was held prisoner in the **Torre de los Lujanes,** a 15th-century building on the eastern side of the plaza. The tower is the sole remnant of the once lavish residence of the Lujanes family. Note the original horseshoe-shaped Gothic door on C. Codo. The characteristically Habsburg, 17th-century **Ayuntamiento** (or Casa de la Villa) on the plaza was both the mayor's home and the city jail. Its interior is elegant and sometimes gaudy. As Madrid grew (and so did bureaucracy), officials had to annex the neighboring **Casa de Cisneros,** a Plateresque house from the mid-16th century. Free guided tours (in Spanish) are offered every Monday at 5pm and start from the Oficina de Información, Pl. Villa, 5.

Southwest of Pl. Mayor on Pl. Santa Cruz, the **Palacio de Santa Cruz** exemplifies the Habsburg style with its alternation of red brick and granite corners and black-slate towers. Ask the guard to let you eye the splendid courtyard. One block south is **Plaza de la Paja,** the city's main square way back before Plaza Mayor existed. Here sits the imposing and highly elaborate Renaissance **Capilla del Obispo** (Bishop's Chapel), built in 1518 to hold the remains of San Isidro, Madrid's patron saint. The chapel eventually surrendered the saintly bones to its next-door neighbor, the Baroque, domed, red brick and granite **Iglesia de San Andrés** and **Capilla de San Isidro.** Inside the Iglesia de San Andrés is a magnificently carved polychrome altarpiece by Francisco Giralte, a disciple of Berruguete. An impressive set of his detailed alabaster sculptures adorns the tombs of the Vargas family. (Open for mass only.)

South of Pl. Mayor on C. Toledo looms **Catedral de San Isidro,** a 17th-century church designed by the famed Pedro Sánchez and Francisco Bautista. Inside, thin shafts of light squeeze their way through small stained-glass windows, and the walls drip with heavy gold leaf. The remains of San Isidro landed here after being tossed from church to church like a diseased hot potato. Little is known about him except for his status as a *labrador* (peasant). His lack of learning lent him prestige: Habsburg Madrid preferred the less cultivated *cristianos viejos* (old Christians), associating erudition with Jewish converts. The church was restored after the interior was burned by rioting workers in 1936. (Open for mass only. Metro: Latina; bus #17, 23, 35, 60.)

Carlos II's death ended Habsburg rule in Spain. Felipe V, the first Spanish Bourbon, ascended the throne faced with bankruptcy, industrial stagnation, military incompetence, and widespread moral disillusionment. Undaunted, Felipe V embarked on an urban renewal program continued with zest by successors Fernando VI and Carlos III during the 18th century. The majestic **Basílica de San Francisco el Grande** (St. Francis of Assisi) at Pl. San Francisco el Grande, down C. San Francisco (5min. walk from Pl. Mayor) is one of the most impressive results of this ambitious renewal. This Neoclassical temple wears a convex façade capped with a magnificent dome. In the somber interior Goya's *San Bernardino of Siena Preaching* hangs among many other paintings by Goya's contemporaries. St. Francis himself allegedly built a convent on this site in the 13th century. (Open in summer Tues.-Sat. 11am-1pm and 5-8pm. Optional brief tour in Spanish. Metro: Puerta de Toledo or Latina. Bus #3, 60, C.)

In Pl. Puerta de Toledo (down **Gran Vía de San Francisco,** the continuation of C. Bailén), the **biblioteca pública** is a library in the round. This and some of the buildings on Gran Vía de San Francisco are of the acclaimed Madrid School, featuring pastel hues, turrets, and glass-enclosed miradors.

The broad Baroque **Puente de Toledo** arches across Río Manzanares at the end of C. Toledo, beyond the Puerta de Toledo. Sandstone carvings on one side depict San Isidro rescuing his son from a well; on the other, it's saintly Santa María de la Cabeza, San Isidro's wife. Renaissance **Puente de Segovia,** which fords the river from C. Segovia, has an almost Roman grandeur in its unadorned masonry; not surprisingly, it was conceived by the talented designer of El Escorial.

Between Puerta del Sol and Paseo del Prado

In front of the 18th-century Casa de Correos (post office, now police headquarters) in **Puerta del Sol** is the zero-km marker. In the middle of the square a statue of a bear hugs an arbutus tree *(madroño),* the city's coat of arms. Folklore claims that a king chased a bear to an arbutus tree in a forest clearing, which became Madrid. Puerta del Sol was the scene of one of the most resonant moments in the country's history, when citizens fought Napoleon's army after learning that he planned to remove the Royal Infantas. Two of Goya's paintings in the Prado, *El Dos de Mayo* (May 2, 1808) and *Los Fusilamientos del tres de mayo* (The Execution of the Rioters: May 3, 1808), depict the gruesome episode. Every New Year's Eve citizens congregate here to swallow a dozen grapes as the clock strikes midnight.

The grand C. Alcalá leads from Sol to Po. Recoletos. Domed **Iglesia de las Calatravas,** C. Alcalá, 25, is all that remains of the huge Convento de la Concepción Real de Comendadoras. Pablo González Velázquez's Baroque altarpiece contrasts sharply with the building's stark Renaissance exterior. Artisans designed a unique ornamental cross motif now named after this church. (Open for mass only 7:30am-1pm and 6-8pm. Metro: Sevilla.) Also on C. Alcalá are the **Museo de la Real Academia de Bellas Artes de San Fernando** and **Calcografía Real** (see Museums).

A magnificent old library is somewhere inside the 18th-century austere **Real Academia de la Historia,** on the corner of C. Huertas and C. León. This area is Madrid's traditional literary quarter, where Cervantes, Góngora, Quevedo, Calderón, Moratín and others lived. Lope de Vega, the Golden Age playwright, and Miguel de Cervantes, author of *Don Quixote,* were bitter rivals; ironically, the 17th-century **Casa de Lope de**

Vega is at C. Cervantes, 11 (a few blocks south of C. San Jerónimo). Closed to the public, it should reopen soon as the Center for Studies on the Golden Age. Lope is buried in **Iglesia de San Sebastín,** C. San Sebastín, for centuries the church favored by Madrid's artists.

The **Paseo del Prado's** shady trees and pricey *terrazas* make it the strollers' favorite. Three aqueous masterpieces garnish the avenue. In **Fuente de Neptuno** at Pl. Cánovas del Castillo, dolphins spew torrents of water at the Roman sea god. **Fuente de Apolo** features Apollo and the four seasons. **Fuente de la Cibeles,** across from the post office, depicts the fertility goddesses' triumphant arrival in a lion-drawn carriage. Residents successfully protected this emblem of their city during Franco's Nationalist bomb raids by covering it with a pyramid made of sacks of sand. Near the southern end of Po. Prado, the **Centro de Arte Reina Sofía** preens its feathers (see Museums).

The Retiro and Jerónimos

Parque del Retiro, Madrid's top picnic and suntanning zone, was originally intended to be a *buen retiro* (nice retreat) for Felipe IV. The palace burned down in 1764, and all that remains are the **Casón del Buen Retiro** and **Museo del Ejército** (see Museums). Alfonso XII and his horse are glaring at the **Estanque Grande,** a rectangular lake in the middle of the park. You can row row row your boat here (10am-sunset, 400ptas for 2 people, 100ptas for each additional person). South of the lake the **Palacio de Cristal,** an airy greenhouse-like building, hosts a variety of art shows with subjects from Bugs Bunny to Spanish portraiture. There's a charming pond in front with a jet d'eau, swans, and geese. (Open Tues.-Sat. 11am-2pm and 5-8pm, Sun. 10am-2pm. Admission varies, but often free.) Many fountains punctuate the park's avenues, notably the **Fuente de la Alcachofa** (Artichoke Fountain). The northeast corner of the park swells with medieval monastery ruins and waterfalls. Carlos III moved the **Jardín Botánico** across Av. Alfonso XII onto Espalter (at the Parque del Retiro's southwestern corner). (Garden open 9am-9pm. Admission 100ptas.)

On a hill overlooking the Museo del Prado is **Iglesia de San Jerónimo,** built by Hieronymite monks and reendowed by the Catholic monarchs. The industrious monks built a new monastery in a meadow *(prado)* on the then-outskirts of town. This church has witnessed many a joyous milestone; Fernando and Isabel were crowned and King Alfonso XIII married here. (Open 6am-1pm and 6-8pm. Bus #10, 14, 15, 19, 34, 37, 45.)

Nearby on C. Montalbán sit the **Museo Naval** and **Museo de Artes Decorativas** (see Museums). Civil War bullets permanently scarred the eastern face of the imposing **Puerta de Alcalá** at Pl. Independencia. Revenue from an unpopular wine tax paid for the Neoclassical arch in 1778 honoring Carlos III.

Along Paseos Prado, Recoletos, and Castellana

Po. Recoletos-Prado from Estación Atocha to Pl. Colón is one of the great European ensembles of Neoclassical and revival architecture: the library, the **Palacio de Buenavista** atop a slope overlooking Pl. Cibeles (once the army ministry moves to the suburbs, the palace will be annexed by the Prado), the cathedral-like **Palacio de Comunicaciones,** Banco de España, Museo Thyssen Bornemizsa, the Bolsa, and the Prado. With most every major museum on or within a few blocks of this avenue, it's become a "museum mile," the cultural axis of Madrid.

Across the street from Estación Atocha sits the imposing 19th-century **Ministerio de Agricultura,** with ceramic tiles and stained glass. To its east, just outside Parque Retiro on Av. Alfonso XII, Villanueva's attractive 18th-century **Observatorio Astronómico** (Astronomical Observatory) reaches for the stars at the summit of a grassy slope. Between the Ministry and Observatory sits the **Museo Etnológico,** and south of Estación Atocha the **Museo del Ferrocarril** (see Museums). A short stroll farther south leads to the expansive Parque de Tierno Galván, which contains a popular new **Planetario** (tel. 467 34 61). (Admission 300ptas, children and retired people 190ptas. Metro: Méndez Alvaro.)

Just north of the Prado on Po. Prado, the **Obelisco a los Mártires del 2 de Mayo** stands in Pl. Lealtad stuffed with the ashes of those who died in the 1808 uprising against Napoleon. Across from the memorial, the elegantly curved, colonnaded **Bolsa de Madrid** (the city's stock exchange) generates income.

Opposite the post office on Pl. Cibeles is **Palacio de Linares,** a very 19th-century townhouse like many others built for the nobility all the way up the Po. Castellana to Pl. Gregorio Marañón. Long abandoned by its former residents and proved by a team of "scientists" to be inhabited by ghosts, it's now the Casa de América, with a library and lecture halls for the study of Latin American culture and politics. (Metro: Banco de España.) Up Po. Recoletos by Pl. Colón, the **Biblioteca Nacional** (entrance at #20) displays treasures from monarchs' private collections, including a copy of the first edition of *Don Quijote.* The **Museo Arqueológico Nacional** is also here (see Museums).

Jetlagged moles emerging from the ground in the **Jardines del Descubrimiento** (Gardens of Discovery) at Pl. Colón will discover a number of huge clay boulders inscribed with odd trivia about the New World, including Seneca's prediction of the discovery, the names of all the mariners on board the caravels, and quotes from Columbus's diary. Concerts, lectures, ballet, and plays entertain below the gardens in the **Centro Cultural de la Villa** (tel. 575 60 80). On its front, facing a noisy waterfall, a large map details the dicoverer's voyages to America. A more traditional monument to Columbus stands directly above the Centro Cultural. (Metro: Colón.)

On the way up **Po. Castellana** to Pl. Emilio Castelar, you can still admire some of the magnificent apartment buildings and mansions that made this boulevard the playground of the aristocracy until the war. While many of the buildings were pulled down in the 60s, the bank and insurance buildings that replaced them are often boldly imaginative, and the juxtaposition of new and old money is striking. Among others, note Moneo's Bankinter at #29, the first to integrate rather than demolish a townhouse; Banco Urquijo, known as "the coffeepot"; Banca Catalana, the delicate ice cube on a cracker near the American Embassy; and Adriática, on Pl. Emilio Castelar, whose architect Carvajal was influenced by the reverence for flowing water in the Hispano-Muslim tradition. The **Instituto de Valencia de Don Juan** and **Museo Sorolla** lurk on side streets (see Museums).

Up the street north of Pl. Emilio Castelar, exists the **Museo Nacional de Ciencias Naturales;** the **Museo Lázaro Galdiano** is nearby on C. Serrano (see Museums). Farther still, past Torres Picasso and Europa at Plaza de Lima, the lumpen **Estadio Santiago Bernabéu** squats (Metro: Nuevos Ministerios or Cuzco). From the stadium gates you can see all the way to Pl. Castilla and glimpse the leaning towers that form Madrid's modern colossus, the **Puerta de Europa.** Fans of modern skyscraper architecture may goosebump. Take the Metro—Pl. Castilla, near Estación Chamartín, is two or three hours away from Pl. Colón by foot. (Metro: Pl. Castilla. Bus #40 from C. Montera near Gran Vía stops at Pl. Cuzco.)

North of the Gran Vía

Calle Barquillo is the main throughfare of the Pl. Salesas district, along which noble carriages made their way to the *iglesia* (below). The long, narrow street is yet another microcosm of Madrid-style architecture. **Casa de las Siete Chimeneas** (House of Seven Chimneys, some say symbolic of the deadly sins), one of the oldest houses in the city, commands the corner of C. Barquillo and C. Infantas. Built in 1577, the old house is the eerie scene of many a ghost story. Its most famous resident was the Marqués de Esquilache, who provoked a riot in 1766 by unleashing an army of tailors on the city: they ran around pinning up men's wide-brimmed hats and trimming their ankle-length capes so that would-be royal assassins would have fewer places to conceal lethal little bodkins on their persons. (Metro: Banco de España.)

Near Pl. Colón on C. Bárbara de Braganza is **Iglesia de las Salesas Reales,** at Pl. Salesas. Commissioned by Bourbon King Fernando VI at the request of his wife Doña Bárbara in 1758, the Baroque-Neoclassical domed church is clad in granite, with façade sculptures by Alfonso Vergaza and dome painting by the brothers González Velázquez. The ostentatious façade and lavish interior prompted critics to pun on the queen's name: "Barbaric queen, barbaric tastes, barbaric building, barbarous expense." The royal couple are buried here. (Metro: Colón.)

If you think Barcelona has the monopoly on *Modernismo* (Gaudí et al.), stroll past Pl. Salesas up C. Fernando VI to the **Palacio de Longoria** ("Sociedad General Autores" on the map). Now housing the national writers' union, the former mansion's skew, grooves, and decorative ceramic and stained-glass whimsy make *Modernismo* fiends drool. The stained-glass windows and ornate staircase within justify gate-crashing. (Metro: Tribunal or Alonso Martinez.) **Museos Romántico, Municipal,** and **de la Ciudad** are in the district (see Museums).

Pedro de Ribera, the premier early 18th-century Spanish architect, designed many buildings in the area: **Palacio Miraflores,** C. San Jerónimo, 19; **Palacio del Marqués de Ugena,** C. Príncipe, 28; **Palacio del Marqués de Perales,** C. Magdalena, 12; and the delightful hermitage on the canal called **Ermita de la Virgen del Puerto** (Po. Virgen del Puerto).

Farther west, by Plaza de España, a row of olive trees surrounds a grandiose monument to Cervantes, author of *Don Quixote*. Next to the plaza are two of Madrid's tallest skyscrapers, the **Torre de Madrid** and the **Edificio de España,** both with superb views of the city. You must pay a 100ptas cover charge to enter the small café on the 26th floor. (Open noon to early evening. Metro: Pl. España.) Tucked between the two skyscrapers is crafty little **Iglesia de San Marcos,** a Neoclassical church composed of five intersecting ellipses; a Euclidean nightmare, there's not a single straight line in sight. The **Compañía Asturiana de Minas** building, **Depósito de Agua,** and **Museo de Cerralbo** linger near Pl. España, while **Palacio de Liria** is a bit north (see Museums).

The 19th century also witnessed the growth of several neighborhoods around the core of the city, north and northwest of the Palacio Real. Today, the area known as **Argüelles** and the zone surrounding **Calle San Bernardo** are a cluttered mixture of elegant middle-class and student housing, bohemian hangouts, and cultural activity. Heavily bombarded during the Civil War, Argüelles inspired Chilean poet Pablo Neruda, then a resident, to write his famous *España en el Corazón*. Be aware that the area around Pl. 2 de Mayo is Madrid's drug-dealing center; nevertheless, it is generally safe (because always busy).

The Palacio Real and Environs

With 20 square km of tapestry and the largest candelabra in Europe, the impossibly luxurious **Palacio Real** lounges at the western tip of central Madrid, overlooking the canal. Designed partly after Bernini's rejected designs for the Louvre, it was built for first Bourbon King Felipe V to replace the Alcázar, which burned down on Christmas Eve, 1734. His ambition was to build a palace to dwarf all others; only a fragment was completed, but it's still one of Europe's most grandiose piles. The shell of it took 40 years to build and interior decoration of its 2000 rooms dragged on for a century. Spanish monarchs abandoned it in the war-torn 1930s. To see the Palacio's Versailles-ish collection of porcelain, tapestries, furniture, armor, and art, you must take a guided tour (in Spanish or English, 40min.). (Metro: Opera. Buses #4, 15, 25, 33, 39.)

The palace's most impressive rooms include the raucously Rococo **Salón de Gasparini** and the **Salón del Trono** (Throne Room) with Tiepolo ceiling fresco. Nothing in the throne room has changed a bit since the 18th century, except for the current monarchs' two new thrones. Hundreds of ornate timepieces, collected mainly by Carlos IV, are strewn about the palace. Be sure to ask the tour guide about the massive sangria bowl, perhaps the largest in the world. The **Real Oficina de Farmacia** (Royal Pharmacy) features quaint crystal and china receptacles used to cut royal dope. The palace's **Biblioteca** shelves first editions of *Don Quijote* and a Bible in Romany (Gypsy language). The **Real Armería** (Armory) displays El Cid's swords, the armor of Carlos V and Felipe II, and other instruments of medieval warfare and torture. (Palace open, except during royal visits, Mon.-Sat. 9:30am-4pm, Sun. 9:30am-12:45pm. Admission 400ptas, students 325ptas; Wed. free for EEC citizens. Arrive early to avoid waiting.)

Beautiful gardens and parks swathe the Palacio Real. In the front across C. Bailén lies **Plaza de Oriente,** a semicircle square. On either side of the encircling geometric hedges, statues of Spanish monarchs rule two small plazas. The sculptures were originally intended for the palace roof, but it was feared they'd fall off.

To the west are the serene **Jardines de Sabatini,** the park of choice for romantics. Juan Carlos opened **Campo del Moro** (facing the canal) to the public only 12 years ago; the view of the palace rising majestically on a dark green slope is straight out of a fairy tale. The **Museo de Carruajes Reales** (see Museums) is on the grounds. (Enter the *campo* on Po. Virgen del Puerto. Open 10am-8pm.) Directly south of the palace across a square is the nearly-finished **Catedral de Almudena.** Madrid's two celebrated convents-turned-museums, **Conventos de las Descalzas** and **de la Encarnación,** are also in this vicinity (see Museums).

Parque del Oeste and Ciudad Universitaria

Parque del Oeste is a large slope-side park noteworthy for its **rosaleda** (rose garden), north of the Palacio Real. Nearby on C. Pintor Rosales stands the only Egyptian temple in Spain, with well-preserved hieroglyphs on the interior walls. The Egyptian government shipped the 4th-century BC **Templo de Debod** stone by stone in appreciation of Spanish archeologists who helped rescue a series of monuments from advancing waters near the Aswan Dam. (Open Tues.-Fri. 10am-1pm and 4-7pm, Sat.-Sun. 10am-1pm. Admission 10ptas. Metro: Ventura Rodríguez or Plaza de España. Bus #1, 25, 33, 39.)

The *terrazas* (outdoor cafés) along nearby **Paseo Rosales** are a perfect place to collapse in the shade of evenly spaced trees. In the vicinity you can catch the cable car *(Teleférico* 250ptas, round-trip 360ptas; noon-9pm) down to the city's largest park, the **Casa de Campo.** Woods, a municipal pool, a zoo, and an amusement park leave the city far behind. Don't attempt to explore the park on foot; it's so large it makes Madrid's center look like a clearing in the woods. Avoid straying beyond populated areas such as the zoo and amusement park after sunset. (Amusement park open Mon.-Wed. 6pm-1am, Thurs.-Sat. 6pm-4am, Sun. noon-1am. Metro: Lago or Batán. Bus #33 or 21.)

Ermita de San Antonio de la Florida is close to Parque del Oeste on Po. Florida, near the river. Goya's frescoed dome arches above his own buried corpse—but not his skull, which was missing when the remains arrived from France. Fishy. (Open Tues.-Fri. 10am-2pm and 5-9pm, Sat.-Sun. 10am-2pm; off-season Tues.-Fri. 10am-2pm and 5-8pm, Sat.-Sun. 10am-2pm. Free. Metro: Norte.)

Ciudad Universitaria (City University) is quite a distance northwest of the Parque and Pl. España. A battleground in the Civil War and resistance center during Franco's rule, Spain's largest university educates over 120,000 students per year, and is second in size in the Spanish-speaking world only to Mexico City's monstrosity. There are two mediocre museums hereabouts, the **Museo de Arte Contemporáneo** and the **Museo de América** (see Museums). The Prime Minister's official residence, the **Palacio de Moncloa,** can be seen—and not touched—from the road through these grounds. (Metro: Moncloa.)

Commanding the perspective on the other side of Arco de la Victoria is the grandiose, arcaded **Cuartel General del Aire,** a prime example of Fascist Neoclassicism. The complex was to form part of the "Fachada del Manzanares" urban axis linking Moncloa, the Palacio de Oriente and cathedral, and Iglesia de San Francisco. The building is clearly a ripoff of El Escorial (Franco's delusions of grandeur again).

El Pardo

An elegant Renaissance and Neoclassical country palace, painted butterscotch and white, **El Pardo** is a 15-minute bus ride from the city center. Set on the royal hunting grounds, it was a retreat of Castilian monarchs in the 16th century. The original hunting lodge was much enlarged and remodeled by the designer of the Palacio Real. Franco frequently chose to receive visitors here, and it still occasionally serves as the residence of visiting diplomats and heads of state. Inside there's a wealth of Flemish and Italian paintings and numerous tapestries designed by Goya. (Open Mon.-Sat. 9:30am-

12:15pm and 3-6pm, Sun. 9:30am-1:40pm. You must wait for a group to form for the compulsory guided tour. Admission 350ptas, 250ptas for students; Wed. free for EEC citizens. Bus #601 from Paseo de Moret, near Moncloa Metro stop; 95ptas.) Next door, there's an interesting 18th-century **Iglesia** and a lavish **Casita del Príncipe** by Villanueva, creator of the Prado.

Museums

The Prado

Spain's premier museum, and one of Europe's finest, is the Museo del Prado, on Po. Prado at Pl. Cánovas del Castillo (tel. 420 28 36). Metro: Banco de España or Atocha. The Neoclassical building sheltered the royal painting collection since the time of Fernando VII, who cared precious little for art and rather more about making an impression at home and abroad. Over 5000 paintings, many collected by Spanish monarchs between 1400 and 1700, include Spanish and foreign masterpieces, with particular strengths in the Flemish and Venetian Schools. The wonder of the Prado is that *every* work is a masterpiece.

The second floor presents Spanish works from the 16th and 17th centuries. The collection of works by **Diego Velázquez** (1599-1660), court painter and interior decorator to Felipe IV, is unmatched by any museum in the world. The ultimate masterpiece *Las Meninas* (The Maids of Honor), the fascinating *Las Hilanderas* (The Spinners), his exquisite portraits of the royal family, *The Forge of Vulcan*, and the rest of his major works—all are here.

Francisco de Goya (1746-1828) is represented by *La Maja vestida* (Clothed Maja) and *La Maja desnuda* (Nude Maja), thought to portray the Duchess of Alba although the face has been scrambled; the hilariously unflattering *La Familia de Carlos IV; Los Fusilamientos del tercero de mayo* (The Execution of the Rioters, May 3, 1808), which depicts the slaughter of Spaniards by Napoleon's army; and the "black paintings." The macabre black paintings were done in his late years when Goya retreated to a small country house outside Madrid, since nicknamed *la quinta del sordo* (deaf man's house). In sharp contrast, an early series of cartoons intended for tapestries in El Escorial depicts lazy afternoons and merry drinking games. Among the **El Grecos** (1541-1614) are *La Trinidad* and *La Adoración de los Pastore*. Works of Spanish painters from the same era fill the first floor, including **Murillo's** (1618-1682) *Familia con pájaro pequeño* (Family with Small Bird); **Ribera's** (1591-1652) *El Martirio de San Bartholomeo* (Martyrdom); and the austere mysticism of **Zurbarán** (1598-1664).

The Prado has a formidable stash of Italian works. The crown jewels are **Titian's** portraits of Carlos V and Felipe II. **Fra Angelico's** (1387-1455) *Annunciation* and **Mantegna's** (1431-1506) *Journey of the Virgin* inspire pilgrimages. **Raphael's** (1483-1520) *The Cardinal;* **Tintoretto's** (1518-1594) *Washing of the Feet;* and **Botticelli's** (1444-1510) series *The Story of Nastagio degli Honesti* live here too.

Because the Spanish Habsburgs long ruled the Netherlands, the Flemish holdings are also top-notch. At the top of the list is **Hieronymus Bosch** (1450-1516), called "El Bosco" by the Spanish, with the triptych *The Garden of Earthly Delights* and *The Seven Deadly Sins*. There's **Roger van der Weyden's** (1400-1464) *Descent from the Cross;* and **Albrecht Dürer's** (1471-1528) *Adam and Eve* and *Self-Portrait*. In **Peter Breughel the Elder's** (1525-1569) *Triumph of Death,* legions of skeletons torture the pitiable remnants of humanity. A number of famed **Rubenses** too.

Additionally, you'll find medieval and Renaissance Spanish works with gilt backgrounds à la Byzantine art, and two small chapels of 11th- and 12th-century paintings from the Mozarabic Church of San Baudelio de Berlanga and the Ermita de la Cruz de Maderuelo. The Spanish government swapped a monastery for some of these paintings with two New York art speculators. Open Tues.-Sat. 9am-7pm, Sun. 9am-2pm. Admission including the Casón del Buen Retiro (see below) 400ptas, students with ISIC free.

Others

Casón del Buen Retiro, C. Alfonso XII, 28 (tel. 420 28 02), facing the Parque del Retiro. Metro: Retiro or Banco de España (see Sights: The Retiro). Once part of Felipe IV's Palacio del Buen Retiro, then a porcelain factory, it was destroyed in the war against Napoleon. The rebuilt version has a superb collection of 19th-century Spanish paintings. Enter the *Sección de Arte Español del Siglo XIX,* a small collection of 19th-century Spanish masters, from the side. Plans for expansion and displaying overflow from the Prado's permanent collection are in the works. Open Tues.-Sat. 9am-6:45pm, Sun. 9am-1:45pm. Admission including the Prado 400ptas, students with ISIC free.

Compañía Asturiana de Minas building, corner of Pl. España and C. Bailén. Metro: Pl. España (see Sights: North of Gran Vía). This 19th-century building has been converted by the regional government into exhibition space for established 20th-century art. (Open Mon.-Sat. 9am-7pm, Sun. 9am-2pm).

Centro de Arte Reina Sofía, C. Santa Isabel, 52 (tel. 468 50 62), opposite Estación Atocha near the south end of Po. Prado. Metro: Atocha (see Sights: Between Puerta del Sol...). Suddenly Picasso's *Guernica* is part of (and the centerpiece in) its collection of 20th-century art. When Germans bombed the Basque town of Gernika for the Fascists in Spain's Civil War, Picasso painted this huge work of jumbled and distorted figures to denounce the bloodshed. When asked by Nationalist officials whether he was responsible for the picture, Picasso answered "No, you are." He gave the canvas to New York's Museum of Modern Art on condition that it return to Spain when democracy was restored. It finally arrived in Madrid's Buen Retiro in 1981, five years after Franco's death. The move to the Reina Sofia sparked an international controversy—Picasso's *other* stipulation was that the painting hang only in the Prado, to prove his equality with Titian and Velázquez. As if Picasso's masterpiece wasn't enough, this pink Neoclassical monolith of a museum contains a splendid art history library, bookstore, repertory cinema (art films in Spanish at noon and 4:30pm, 150ptas), and café. Open Mon.-Sat. 10am-9pm, Sun. 10am-2:30pm. Admission 400ptas, students free.

Convento de la Encarnación, off C. Bailen near and east of the Palacio Real. Metro: Opera (see Sights: Palacio Real). A poor cousin of the Descalzas Reales. The *Exchange of Princesses on the Bidasoa,* depicting the swap weddings of French King Louis XII's sister Isabel to Felipe IV and Felipe IV's sister Anne to Louis XII, hangs here. The austere Habsburgs—Europe's fashion trendsetters—contrast with the up-and-coming flashy French. The *relicuario* houses about 1500 relics of saints, including a vial of Saint Pantaleon's blood, which liquefies every year on July 27. Open same hours as Descalzas Reales (below). Admission with the same ticket.

Convento de las Descalzas Reales (Convent of the Royal Barefoot Ones), Pl. Descalzas (tel. 521 27 79, 248 74 04), between Pl. Callao and Sol. Metro: Callao or Sol (see Sights: Palacio Real). This convent founded in 1559 accepted only women of royal blood, thus acquiring an exceptional collection of religious artwork—tapestries, paintings, sculptures, and liturgical objects, not to mention discarded shoes. One the 33 chapels in the upper cloister is by La Roldana, one of the few known female artists of the 17th century. The Salón de Tapices contains 12 renowned tapestries woven from cartoons by Rubens. Other rooms hold paintings by Zurbarán, Titian, and Rubens. Very famous. Cloistered nuns have always hid themselves here, among them St. Teresa of Avila and Empress María of Austria. Open Tues.-Sun. 10am-1:30pm. Admission 300ptas, students 225ptas.

Depósito de Agua, C. Ferraz (tel. 409 61 65, 409 62 09), on Canal Isabel II, C. Santa Engracia. Metro: Pl. España (see Sights: North of Gran Vía). This Art Deco, neo-Egyptian temple now shows temporary exhibitions of contemporary art. Open Tues.-Fri. 10am-1pm and 4-7pm, Sat.-Sun. 10am-1pm. Admission free.

Museo Arqueológico Nacional, C. Serrano, 13 (tel. 577 79 12). Metro: Colón or Serrano. Bus #1, 9, 19, 51, 53, or M-2 (see Sights: Along Paseos...). Spain's distant past: astounding tile mosaics, mummies, crowns of Visigoth kings, ivories from Muslim Andalucía, the suspicious *Dama de Elche,* and the hollow *Dama de Baza* (ashes of cremated bodies were deposited in this 4th-century statue, found in a tomb in the province of Granada). Romanesque and Gothic sculpture, and Celtiberian silver and gold. Open Tues.-Sat. 9:30am-6:30pm, Sun. 9:30am-2pm. Admission 200ptas, students free.

Museo de América, Av. Reyes Católicos, 6, near Av. Puerta de Hierro and north of the C. Princesa junction. Metro: Moncloa (see Sights: Parque del Oeste...). Pre-Hispanic art of the Americas (mostly from Mexico and Peru). Open Tues.-Sun. 10am-2pm. Tues. free.

Museo de Arte Contemporáneo, Av. Juan de Herrera, 2 (tel. 549 71 50), by Pl. Cardenal Cisneros. Metro: Moncloa (see Sights: Parque del Oeste...). Looted for and inferior to the ascendant Reina Sofía, but still holds temporary exhibits. A sculpture garden and a fountain soften the entrance of the stark modern building. Inside, two important early Dalís, some Miró, and Catalan master Isidre Nonell still hang. Open Tues.-Sun. 10am-2pm. Admission 200ptas, students free.

Sights

Museo de Artes Decorativas, C. Montalbán, 12 (tel. 521 34 40). Metro: Banco de España (see Sights: The Retiro). Displays of old Spanish ceramics; leather, gold, and silverwork; tapestries and rugs; and its renowned Valencian kitchen. Open Tues.-Fri. 9:30am-3pm, Sat.-Sun. 10am-2pm. Admission 200ptas, students free.

Museo de Carruajes Reales, Po. Virgen del Puerto (tel. 248 74 04), in the Campo del Moro behind the Palacio Real. Metro: Opera (see Sights: Palacio Real). Carriage buffs' alert: this former greenhouse contains the royal family's 16th- to 20th-century horse-drawn carriages. Open 10am-1:30pm, Sun. 9am-3:30pm; winter 10am-1pm, Sun. 9am-2:30pm. Admission 300-500ptas.

Museo de Cerralbo, C. Ventura Rodríguez, 17 (tel. 247 36 46). Metro: Pl. España (see Sights: North of Gran Vía). A small palace with an eclectic assemblage of paintings, drawings, etchings, armor, coins, and rare books expressive of one man's very individual (and scandalous) taste. Closed for renovations.

Museo de la Ciudad, Av. Príncipe de Vergara (tel. 588 65 99), near the Auditorio Nacional (see Sights: North of Gran Vía). Ornate front doorway and bare remainder of building.

Museo de la Real Academia de Bellas Artes de San Fernando, C. Alcalá, 13 (tel. 522 14 91). Metro: Sol or Sevilla. Bus #3, 5, 20, 51, or 52 (see Sights: Between Puerta del Sol...). In Madrid, only the Prado surpasses this collection. Works by Velázquez, Rubens, and Zurbarán; El Greco's *Saint Hieronymus,* Ribera's *Ecce Homo,* and Goya's *Escena de Inquisición.* Open Mon.-Fri. 10am-7pm, Sat.-Sun. 10am-2pm. Admission 200ptas, students free. Next door the **Calcografía Real** (Royal Print and Drawing Collection) organizes excellent temporary exhibitions of works on paper.

Museo del Ejército, C. Méndez Núñez, 1 (tel. 531 46 24), just north of Casón del Buen Retiro. Metro: Retiro or Banco de España (see Sights: The Retiro). A cobbling together of military paraphernalia in a fragment of the Palacio del Buen Retiro. Amid the mess, a few intriguing exhibits—a sword of El Cid's, some darling baby cannons from the 18th century, an extraordinarily sumptuous tent used by Emperor Carlos I in a 1535 campaign in Tunisia. Plans to annex this to the Prado and recreate its original appearance as the Buen Retiro's Hall of Thrones (with painting cycles by Zurbarán and Velázquez) are in the works. Open Tues.-Sun. 10am-2pm. Admission 75ptas.

Museo del Ferrocarril, Po. Delicias, 61 (tel. 527 31 21), just south of Atocha. Metro: Delicias (see Sights: Along Paseos...). A small museum devoted to the early history of railroads in Spain in the old, beautiful iron-and-glass station. Open Tues.-Sat. 10am-5:30pm, Sun. 10am-2pm. Admission 200ptas.

Museo del Jamón, C. San Jerónimo, 6 (tel. 521 03 46), off Puerta del Sol. Metro: Sol. Five other locations in the city. Ham lovers unite! The most overt expression of Spain's fascination with piggies. No hamless wall space. Lightly smoked Iberian ham sandwiches 150ptas (3 make a meal). *Menú del día* 850 or 1000ptas. Open Mon.-Sat. 9am-12:30am, Sun. 10am-12:30am. Restaurant upstairs, with same prices but a longer menu, opens at 1pm.

Museo Etnológico, Av. Alfonso XII, 68 (tel. 530 64 18), across from Estación Atocha. Metro: Atocha-Renfe (see Sights: Along Paseos...). Excellent anthropological collection, mainly drawn from Philippine and African cultures. Open Tues.-Sat. 10am-6pm, Sun. 10am-2pm. Admission 300ptas.

Museo Iconos, C. Torrejón de Ardoz, 2 (tel. 675 39 00). Icons from the 12th-20th centuries. Open Sept.-July Tues.-Thurs. 11am-2pm and 3-7pm; Fri.-Sat. 11am-2pm, 3-7pm, and 9-10:30pm; Sun. 11am-2pm and 3-5pm. Admission 200ptas.

Museo Lázaro Galdiano, C. Serrano, 122 (tel. 261 60 84). Metro: Serrano or Av. América (see Sights: Along Paseos...). The Galdiano's collections are Madrid's best-kept secret. Among the riches are a 12th-century French ivory Virgin, ancient jewels, Celtic bronze objects, and a bronze head attributed to Leonardo da Vinci. Paintings by Bosch, Cranach, Murillo, Rembrandt, and Van Dyck plaster the walls. Some good English stuff too—Gainsborough, Reynolds, Hopper, Constable, and Turner. Open Sept.-July Tues.-Sun. 10am-2pm. Admission 300ptas.

Museo Municipal, C. Fuencarral, 78 (tel. 522 57 32). Metro: Tribunal (see Sights: North of Gran Vía). Works of art, documents, and scale models—including one of 1830 Madrid—trace the city's urban development. Open Sept.-July Tues.-Fri. 10am-2pm and 3-9pm, Sat.-Sun. 10am-2pm. Admission free.

Museo Nacional de Ciencias Naturales (Museum of Natural Sciences), C. José Gutiérrez Abascal, 2 (tel. 411 13 28), off Po. Castellana. Metro: Nuevos Ministerios (see Sights: Along the Paseos...). Open Tues.-Sat. 10am-6pm, Sun. 10am-2:pm. Admission free.

Museo Naval, C. Montalbán, 2 (tel. 524 04 19), across from the Palacio de Comunicaciones. Metro: Banco de España (see Sights: The Retiro). Maritime objects associated with the battle of Lepanto and the discovery of America. The map made by Juan de la Costa in 1500 was the first to chart North America. Open Sept.-July Tues.-Sun. 10:30am-1:30pm. Admission 75ptas.

Museo Romántico, C. San Mateo, 13 (tel. 448 10 45, 448 10 71). Metro: Alonso Martinez (see Sights: North of Gran Vía). Housed in a 19th-century mansion built by a disciple of avatar Ventura Rodríguez, the museum is a time capsule of Romantic period (early 19th-century) decorative arts and painting. Open Sept.-July Tues.-Sat. 10am-3pm, Sun. 10am-2pm. Admission 200ptas.

Museo Sorolla, Po. General Martínez Campos, 37 (tel. 410 15 84). Metro: Rubén Dario or Iglesia (see Sights: Along the Paseos...). Former home and studio of Joaquín Sorolla, the acclaimed 19th-century Valencian painter. Sorolla's seaside paintings and his garden make for a refreshing break from other crowded museums. Collection includes *Paseo a orillas del mar* (Seaside Promenade) and pre-World War I society portraits. Open Sept.-July Tues.-Sun. 10am-2pm. Admission 200ptas, students free.

Museo Taurino, C. Alcalá, 237 (tel. 255 18 57), at Pl. Monumental de Las Ventas. Metro: Ventas. In a corner of Madrid's largest bullring, a remarkable collection of *trajes de luces,* capes, and posters of famous *corridas.* Open Tues.-Fri. 9am-2:30pm, Sun. 10am-1pm. On bullfight days it opens 1 hr. before the *lidia.* Admission free.

Museo Thyssen Bornemizsa, corner of Po. Prado and C. San Jerónimo (tel. 420 39 44). Metro: Banco de España. This 18th-century palace has just been transformed into a museum to house the fabulous Thyssen-Bornemizsa collection for at least 9 years. Its collection of Old Masters (such as Holbein's *Henry VIII*) and 20th-century art complements the Prado's perfectly, filling out areas where the Prado is relatively weak. Scheduled to open in the winter of 1992.

Palacio de Liria, C. Princesa, 20. Metro: Ventura Rodriguez or Argüelles (see Sights: North of Gran Vía). A Neoclassical palace, the Duchess of Alba's estate is endowed with 15th- and 16th-century canvases by Titian, Rubens, and Rembrandt. The collection is open to the public by special arrangement.

Entertainment

Residents of Spain's first city like to say that no one goes to bed until they've killed the night. Lily-livered sleeping habits are scorned, so adjust your body clock accordingly. This is especially true in the summer, when the city sizzles by day and the stubborn sun refuses to set until at least 9pm. The only (relatively) quiet night of the week is Monday.

The weekly *Guía del Ocio* (75ptas at any kiosk) lists complete entertainment minutiae (including restaurants and clubs), as do the Friday supplement (*El Mundo's* "Metropoli," *El País'* "Guía," *Diario* 16's "Madrid") and the daily *cartelera* listings in any newspaper. The free municipal tourist office monthly *En Madrid* is slightly less comprehensive, but still helpful.

Pl. 2 de Mayo in Malasaña, Pl. Chueca, Pl. España, and the Gran Vía can be intimidating and sleazy. For a city of this size, however, Madrid is fairly safe, and the only places to avoid late at night are the parks.

Nightlife: Cafés, Bars, Clubs, and Discos

As the sun sets and bathes the streets in gold, **terrazas** (or **chiringuitos,** outdoor cafés) spill across sidewalks all over Madrid. In addition to our specific listings, the following neighborhoods are good places to explore.

Pl. Mayor. Handy for a glass of wine while digesting the tourist office's brochures.

C. Bailén, (by the Viaducto). Spectacular views of flaming sunsets (one thing urban pollution is good for).

Casa del Campo. A number of kiosks and open-air *cafeterías* sprinkled about.

Pos. Castellana, Recoletos, and Prado. Fashionable and hip, hence a bit pricey. La Castellana is the trendiest.

Parque del Retiro. Tranquil kiosks that close with the park at sundown.

Pl. 2 de Mayo (Malasaña) and **Pl. Olavide** (Bilbao). Drink-sippers in the shade of umbrellas and trees.

Po. Pintor Rosales. Many tree-shaded *chiringuitos* frequented by university students and park-goers.

El Viso, west of the Auditorio Nacional to Po. Castellana and south to C. María de Molina. A pre-war garden city within the city in which villas, walled gardens, and winding streets exude a charming village-like aura. Yet another popular *terraza* spot.

For **clubs and discos,** life begins at 1:30am. Many discos have "afternoon" sessions (usually 7-10pm, cover 250-1000ptas) for teens; but the "night" sessions (lasting until dawn) are when to really let your hair down. Don't be surprised if at 5:30am there's still a line of people waiting to get in. Really. Cover can get as high as 1500ptas, and men may be charged 200ptas more than women. The *entrada* (cover) often includes a drink.

In order to facilitate bar and club hopping, *Let's Go* lists bars, clubs, and discos by neighborhood (cafés are given their own special section).

Classic Cafés

Coffee at these places is expensive (200-250ptas)—but since that's all you're getting, and given that you're expected to linger, an hour or two spent at one of these historic cafés is a most economical way to soak up a little Madrid (and a lot of secondary smoke).

Café Comercial, Glorieta de Bilbao, 7 (tel. 531 34 72). Metro: Bilbao. The boulevards extending from Pl. Colón to C. Princesa in Argüelles make for elegant strolling (notice the many wrought-ironed, wainscoted, chandeliered foyers with cage elevators). Traditional café with high ceilings and huge mirrors. Frequented by artists and Republican aviators alike. Anti-Franco protests started here. Frequent *tertulias* (gatherings of literati and intellectuals). A/C. Sandwiches from 150ptas. Beer 100ptas. Open 11am-midnight.

Café Gijón, Po. Recoletos, 21. Metro: Colón. Choose between a breezy terrace and a smoky bar-restaurant. Long a favorite of the literati. Marmoreal tables, white-uniformed waiters. People bring their books to study and their friends to talk. Coffee 250ptas at the tables. Open noon-midnight.

Café de Oriente, Pl. Oriente, 2 (tel. 248 20 10). Metro: Opera. Beautiful old-fashioned café with a *terraza* across from the Palacio Real; lovely view at night when the palace is spotlighted. Rather expensive. Beer 300ptas outside. Desserts 300-400ptas. Open 9am-1am.

La Blanca Doble, C. Calatrava, 15, in the neighborhoods south of Sol. Specialty coffee drinks such as *jamaicano* (coffee, Tía María *licor,* brown sugar, and whipped cream) 250ptas. Open until midnight.

Plaza Santa Ana

Plaza Santa Ana's many bars and small *terrazas* are a jumping-off point for an evening of bar and club hopping. The area features a number of popular watering holes, packed with minglers, chatters, smokers, and drinkers. **Calle Huertas** is the main street, just off the plaza.

Cervecería Alemana, Pl. Santa Ana, 6 (tel. 429 70 33). A Hemingway hangout with a slightly upscale crowd. One of a row of three *cervecerías* (brasseries) that all deserve exploration. Open noon-2am.

No Se Lo Digas a Nadie, C. Ventura de la Vega, 7, next to Pl. Santa Ana. Metro: Antón Martín. Look for a black garage door; it's not marked on the street. Throbbing music and gyrating bodies downstairs; more sedate conversation, exhibits by local photographers, and beautifully preserved factory architecture upstairs. Live music starts around 11pm. Drinks 500-700ptas. Open Sun.-Wed. 7pm-1:30am, Thurs.-Sat. 7pm-2:30am.

La Fídula, C. Huertas, 57 (tel. 429 29 47), near Po. Prado. Metro: Antón Martín. A quiet place to listen to live classical music. Coffee 215ptas, wine 200ptas. Cover for musical performances (11:30pm) 200-300ptas. Open 7pm-1:30am.

Viva Madrid, C. Manuel Fernández González, 7 (tel. 467 46 45), next to Pl. Santa Ana. Metro: Antón Martín. U.S. expatriate hangout. Wonderful tiles and animals carved in wood. The poet Rafael Albertí drew an ink picture in honor of this place: look for it behind the bar. Beer and juice 400ptas, mixed drinks 700-800ptas. Open Sun-Fri. noon-2am, Sat. noon-3am.

Los Gabrieles, C. Echegaray, 17 (tel. 429 62 61). Metro: Antón Martín or Sol. The building's façade used to be covered with the same beautiful Andalusian tiles as the interior—until an American art dealer made off with them for a precious sum. A *caña* (beer) is 175ptas till 8pm, then rises to 300ptas. Open Mon.-Thurs. 1pm-2am, Fri.-Sat. 1pm-2:30am.

Café Central, Pl. Angel, 10 (tel. 468 08 44), off Pl. de Santa Ana. Metro: Antón Martín or Sol. Live jazz music 10pm-2am. Cover charge Mon.-Thurs. 300ptas, Fri.-Sun. 350ptas. Open Mon.-Thurs. 1pm-1:30am, Fri.-Sun. 1pm-2:30am.

El Oso y el Madroño, C. Bolsa, 4 (tel. 522 13 77). A hand organ and old photos of Madrid. Try the potent *Licor de Madroño,* an arbutus-flavored Spanish liqueur. Open 8pm-midnight.

Malasaña

Another perennial night hotspot, but with an entirely different feel. Darker, more bohemian, and a little more sedate(d) than the Plaza Santa Anna. Heaps of pubs. You won't find most of these places in the weekly entertainment guides, partly because they prefer word of mouth and partly because they're too small and ephemeral to spend money on advertising.

Hippies, intellectuals, bohemians, street musicians, and junkies check each other out in the **Plaza 2 de Mayo. C. San Vincente Ferrer,** with its tattoo parlors, secondhand clothing and leather stores, motorcycle repair shops, and countless pubs, is prime Malasaña. Unless you're particularly badass, be wary here alone at night.

Bar Las Maravillas, Pl. 2 de Mayo, 9. One of the few places to eat in Malasaña late at night. *Tapas, bocadillos, raciones.* Open Tues.-Sun. 8pm-2am.

El Puerto, C. Velarde, 13 (tel. 447 72 60). Laid-back rebels and wanna-bes drink here. Speak nicely to Antonio, *un buen tío.* Open 8am-2am.

Manuela, C. San Vicente Ferrer, 29 (tel. 531 70 37). Extremely elegant and mirrored café-bar. Live music (usually folky) begins at 11:30pm; cover for performances 300-400ptas. Open 6:30pm-3am.

La Tetera de la Abuela, C. Espíritu Santo, 37. "Granny's Teapot" brews together writers, actors, and students. Open Sun.-Thurs. 7:30pm-1am, Fri.-Sat. 7:30pm-2am.

El Sol de Mayo, Pl. 2 de Mayo, 4. A bar-café with a young crowd. Heavy bands play downstairs. Open Sun.-Thurs. 7pm-3am, Fri.-Sat. 7pm-4am.

Vía Láctea, C. Velarde, 18 (tel. 466 75 81). This club is jam-packed and deservedly famous. The "Milky Way's" loudspeakers and slightly expensive drinks will make you see stars all night. Open Tues.-Sun. 11pm-4am.

Ella's, C. San Dimas, 3, across and parallel to C. San Bernardo, on the corner of C. Palma. Just outside of Malasaña proper. A *terraza* popular with lesbians.

Bodegas el Maño, C. Jesús del Valle, 1. This enchanting place dates from 1890. Weird ancient wine casks. Stiff drinks 500-600ptas. Open 7pm-1:30am.

Bilbao

There are plenty of discos and bars around **Glorieta de Bilbao,** especially along and between **Calles Fuencarral and Luchana.** The *terrazas* on **Plaza Olavide** have a mellower, cold-drink sipping scene (drinks outside 150-250ptas).

The streets fill with young people, mostly high school and college students in groups or couples. You'll have no trouble finding inexpensive *tapas* and drinks. Bars and clubs tend to stay open later here than in any other neighborhood. Boisterous and packed year-round.

Cervecería Ratskeller's, corner of C. Luchana and C. Palafox (by the cinema Palafox). In the self-proclaimed House of Beer, on weekends there's barely enough room to raise glass to mouth. Expatriate (and native) students crowd into the 2 floors during the school year. Open noon-3am.

Entertainment

Club Andy Warhol's, C. Luchana, 20. Wait...Is that a Warhol print? or the person I'm dancing with? By the time you make it to this chic disco, you'll be seeing in multiples. Open 5am (yup, am)-10am, Sun. 5am-noon.

Archy, C. Marqués de Riscal, 11 (tel. 308 31 62). Dress to kill (no T-shirts) or the fashion police at the door might laugh. *Gente guapa* (beautiful people) only; at press time *the* in place to see and be seen. Also a fancy restaurant. No cover, but drinks cost 700-800ptas. Open from noon on.

Paseos Castellana, Recoletos, and Prado

The *terrazas* lining the broad avenue—some permanent, some seasonal—come alive every night around 11:30pm in summer (July and August). Drinks can be quite pricey, reaching 500ptas for beer, 1000ptas for mixed drinks. Fashionable *terrazas de verano* include:

Amnesia, Po. Castellana, 93. More sophisticated crowd **Nameless place,** Po. Castellana, 21. For the post-modern squad.

El Espejo, Po. Recoletos, 31. A petite orchestra and mixed-age clientele. Ornate and mirrored. The action usually starts around 10:30pm.

El Chiringuito de la Bolsa, in front of the Bolsa (stock exchange) at Pl. Lealtad, just north of the Prado.

Chueca

Several years ago the site of a trendy, wealthy series of pubs and clubs (their husks are still open on C. Costanilla Capuchinos), Chueca is now the home of a lively, albeit somewhat elusive, gay scene (mostly male). Clubs may come and go, but **C. Pelayo** is clearly the main drag.

For lesbian and gay club listings, *El Mundo's* Friday supplement "Metropoli" stands out from other papers' and from the *Guía del Ocio.* You should also look for the *Guía Gay Visado,* an annually-updated list of gay and lesbian entertainment throughout Spain. Lesbian and gay guides are sold at **Librería El Galeón,** C. Sagasta, 7 (Metro: Bilbao).

Argüelles and Moncloa

The nightlife here attracts students partying and socializing during the academic year until June (when exams hit) and July and August (when they leave town for vacation).

Oh! Madrid, C. Coruña, km 10. Metro: Moncloa. University hangout. Head-hurting rock. No cover. Drinks 600-800ptas. Open 8pm-5am.

Zarzuela Race-Track, Av. Coruña km 7800 (tel. 207 01 40). Buses leave from Metro: Moncloa. Hosts Nights at the Hippodrome: horseracing and betting, dancing, and a lively bar scene from dusk to dawn. Attracts a large crowd of university students. Cover charge 500ptas. Drinks 500-700ptas. July-Aug. Thurs. and Sat. 9pm-dawn; June. and Sept. Sat. 9pm-dawn.

Plaza Mayor and Puerta del Sol

An easy place to start, perhaps, but high prices, tourists galore, and limited options get old quickly.

Joy Eslava, C. Arenal, 11 (tel. 266 37 33). Metro: Sol or Opera. A 3-tiered theater turned disco; 3 bars, laser lights, videoscreen, live entertainment. Young crowd, disco music. Cover 1500ptas. Open Mon.-Thurs. 11:30 on, Fri.-Sat. 7-10:15pm and 11:30pm-5:30am.

La Coquette Blues Bar, C. Hileras on the corner with C. Arenal. Loud, live rock-blues at close quarters. The "no fumeis porros" sign (*porros* are hash-and-tobacco cigarettes) seems to be promptly ignored. Music starts around 10:30pm. Open Tues.-Thurs. 8pm-2am.

Gran Vía

Besides the luxurious movie theaters, this street doesn't offer much late-night entertainment. The crowd is older and wealthier on the south side of the street and on the Gran Vía itself (*salones de baile* and shows of cheesy comedians and topless female dancers). On the north side, in the tiny streets leading to and just behind the Gran Vía (Calles Luna, Tudescos, Desengaño, and Montera, for example), the rowdy crowd gets downright unsavory at night.

Film and Theater

In summer, the city sponsors free movies and plays. The *Guía del Ocio* (75ptas at kiosks), the *Villa de Madrid* (100ptas from bus-ticket kiosks), and the entertainment supplement in all the Friday papers list these activities; they often contain discounts for commercial events, too. In July and August, the **Plaza Mayor, Plaza de Lavapiés, Plaza Villa de París,** and other meeting places host frequent plays. The **Parque del Retiro** shows free movies nightly at 11pm.

Most *cinemas* have three showings per day: 4:30pm, 7:30pm and 10:30pm. In general, tickets are 500-700ptas. Wed. is usually *día del espectador:* tickets are 300-350ptas, so show up early. Spain's flawless dubbing industry is renowned throughout the world.

The state-subsidized *filmoteca* in the renovated Art Deco **Ciné Doré,** C. Santa Isabel, 3 (tel. 227 38 66; Metro: Antón Martín), is the best for repertory cinema. It also has a bar, restaurant, and bookstore. (Tickets 200-400ptas.) The **Centro Reina Sofía** has a repertory cinema of its own. The university's **colegios mayores** sponsor film series as well (not to speak of jazz concerts). Subtitled films are shown in many private theaters, such as **Alphaville** and **Renoir 1** and **2**—check the V.O. (for *versión original*) listings in entertainment guides. The **Gran Vía** is lined with plush cinemas replete with balconies, ushers, and huge screens.

Theatergoers may also want to consult the large-format, well-illustrated, beautifully-written magazines published by the state-sponsored theaters (which also sell fab posters of their productions for next to nothing), such as **Teatro Español, Teatro de la Comedia,** and the city's superb **Teatro María Guerrero.** A new Teatro Nacional will soon open; more than just a new stage, the organization will coordinate the resources of all the city's public theaters. Buy tickets at theater box offices or at agencies.

The theater district is bounded by Pl. Santa Ana and Pl. Colón (south to north) and Po. Prado-Recoletos and Puerta del Sol (east to west); this also happens to be the old banking district, so the larger streets are accordingly lined with majestic "bank palaces." The state-run theaters and many of the private theaters are sights in themselves.

Localidades Galicia, Pl. Carmen, 1 (tel. 531 27 32). Metro: Sol. Handles theater tickets, as well as those for soccer games and bullfights. Open Mon.-Fri. 10am-1pm and 4:30-7pm.

Teatro Español, C. Príncipe, 25 (tel. 429 03 18; tickets and information tel. 429 62 97). Metro: Sevilla. The 16th-century Teatro del Príncipe was on this site; the present theater dates from the 18th century. A new rehearsal studio, together with a video and theater library, are planned for the site next door. Established company run by city hall; mostly well-known Spanish plays. Regularly performs plays winning the prestigious Lope de Vega award. Tickets around 1300ptas, reduced prices Wed. Excellent, traditional **Café del Príncipe** within; classic *tarta de manzana* (apple pie), among other treats.

Teatro de la Comedia, C. Príncipe, 14 (tel. 521 49 31). Metro: Sevilla. The traveling *Companía Nacional Teatro Clásico* often performs classical Spanish theater here. Tickets 500-1000ptas, reduced prices Thurs. Ticket office open 11:30am-1:30pm and 5-9pm.

Teatro María Guerrero, C. Tamayo y Baus, 4 (tel. 319 47 69). Metro: Colón. Excellent state-supported repertory company that performs a wide variety of plays. Tickets 800-2500ptas. Reduced price Wed. Ticket office open 11:30am-1:30pm and 5-9pm.

Sala Olimpia (tel. 527 46 22), Pl. Lavapiés. National troupe produces avant-garde theatrical works. Tickets 750ptas.

Teatro Maravillas, C. Manuela Malasaña, 6 (tel. 447 41 35). Metro: Bilbao. Popular commercial theater; mostly musicals and comedies. Tickets 600-1300ptas.

Teatro Bellas Artes, C. Marqués de la Riera, 2 (tel. 532 44 37). Metro: Banco de España. Private theater devoted to staging new works.

Centro Cultural de la Villa, Pl. Colón (tel. 575 60 80). Metro: Colón or Serrano. A major performance center belonging to the city.

Music

In summer the city sponsors free concerts at **Plazas Mayor, de Lavapiés, and Villa de París.** Check the usual sources for information (see Entertainment: Introduction).

The finest classical performances happen at the **Auditorio Nacional,** C. Príncipe de Vergara, 136 (tel. 337 01 00). Home to the superb Orquesta Nacional, it's equipped with a magnificent hall for symphonic music and a smaller one for chamber recitals. The **Fundación Juan March,** C. Castelló, 77 (tel. 435 42 40; Metro: Núñez de Balboa), sponsors free weekly concerts in its own concert hall and hosts a university lecture series. The **Conservatorio Superior de Música,** recently moved into the 18th-century medical building next door to the Centro Reina Sofía, hosts free student performances, professional traveling orchestras, and celebrated soloists. **Teatro Monumental** is home to Madrid's Orquesta Sinfónica. Reinforced concrete—a Spanish invention—was first used in its construction in the 20s; the building's acoustics are unusual.

For opera and *zarzuela,* head for the ornate **Teatro de la Zarzuela,** C. Jovellanos, 4 (tel. 429 12 86; Metro: Banco de España), modeled on La Scala. In 1992 the grand, 19th-century granite **Teatro de la Opera,** on Pl. Opera, will reopen after years of reconditioning as the city's principal venue for classical ballet and the lyric genre.

For tangos, try **Cambalache,** C. San Lorenzo, 5 (tel. 410 07 01; Metro: Alonso Martínez or Tribunal). You'll find live tangos, Argentinian food, and drinks at the bar from 10pm to 5am for no cover charge.

Flamenco in Madrid is tourist-oriented and expensive. **Arco de Cuchilleros,** C. Cuchilleros, 7 (tel. 266 58 67; Metro: Sol), just off Pl. Mayor, features some emotive guitarists and stamping dancers. The small seating area makes for an intimate show. The 2000ptas cover includes the show and one drink; subsequent drinks, both alcoholic and non-alcoholic, are 800ptas. (Shows 10:30pm and 12:30am. No dining.) More down-to-earth is **Casa Patas,** C. Cañizares, 10 (tel. 228 50 70). The flamenco starts at midnight on Fri. and Sat. nights. The cover charge varies. (Open 7pm-2:30am.)

Shopping

Most stores in Madrid are open in the morning (approximately 9:30am-1:30 or 2pm) and early evening (approximately 5-8pm). The major department stores, such as **El Corte Inglés,** (see Practical Information: Other for details) and **Galerías Preciados** (Pl. Callao, 1), are open from around 10am to 9pm. Some shops now stay open on Saturday afternoons and a few, mainly department stores, stay open at lunch time. Many close in August, when practically everyone is on vacation.

Clothing

From Sol to the Gran Vía, and along C. Princesa, the main department stores—El Corte Inglés and Galerías Preciados—float in a sea of smaller discount stores. Gran Vía is now a little degraded (although easier on the purse); there's a scheme afoot to restore the avenue to its pre-war splendor. It still manages scope, from chichi leather goods to more middlebrow women's fashion (Cortefiel, Gran Vía, 27). Budgeters with weary spirits and scraped soles shop at Los Guerrilleros (a huge store with quite low prices), Puerta del Sol, 5, diagonally across from El Corte Inglés. (Metro: Sol or Gran Vía.)

In the lovely neighborhood west of Po. Recoletos, imaginative boutiques of young Spanish designers mingle with off-beat restaurants and pastry shops, cafés and bars, art galleries, and specialized bookstores (C. Almirante and streets north to C. Génova, south to C. Alcalá, and west to C. San Bernardo). (Metro: Chueca, Colón, or Banco d'España.)

The embassy quarter north of C. Génova is decidedly more haughty. Madrid's poshest shopping areas are Jerónimos and Salamanca. In the latter, couture and near-couture boutiques vogue on Calles Serrano, Principe de Vergara, Velázquez, Goya, Ortega y Gasset, Coello, and Alfonso XII. (Metro: Serrano or Velázquez.)

Books

Casa del Libro, Gran Vía, 29. Metro: Gran Vía or Callao. A 6-story department store of books. Open Mon.-Sat. 10am-9pm.

Librería Felipa, C. Libreros off Gran Vía. The entire street is books, but only Felipa gives a 20% discount off list price with a mischievous glint in her eye and a rant all her own. Generations of students have bought their textbooks here.

Librería Gaudí, C. Argensola, 17, and **Librería Argensola**, 20. Metro: Colón or Alonso Martínez. Two art and architecture bookstores in the arty neighborhood west of Po. Recoletos.

Librería Antonio Machado, C. Fernando VI. Metro: Colón or Alonso Martínez. A browser's store with an immense literature section.

Librería Crisol, C. Juan Bravo. A high-powered place with futuristic interior design; services and prices to match. Great hours. Open Mon.-Sat. 10am-10pm, Sun. 11am-6pm.

Cuesta de Moyano. Right by Metro: Atocha. Along the southern border of the Jardín Botánico, 30 open-air wood stalls hawk new and used paperbacks, reference books, comics, and rare books. Most open every day.

Librería Turner, C. Genova, 3 (tel. 319 09 26). Classics, guidebooks, and the very latest all in English.

Booksellers, C. José Abascal, 48 (tel. 442 79 59). Rather expensive, but a vast array of English-language books.

Librería de Mujeres (Women's Bookstore), C. San Cristóbal, 17 (tel. 521 70 43), near Pl. Mayor. International bookstore. Some English spoken.

Librería El Galeón, C. Sagasta, 7. Metro: Bilbao. A gay bookstore that carries *Guía Gay Visado*.

Other

On Sunday mornings the flea market **El Rastro** virtually explodes with second-hand goods and antiques (and pickpockets). Individual side streets specialize in pets, household items, and books. (Sun. and holidays 10am-2pm. Metro: Latina. From Pl. Mayor, take C. Toledo to Pl. Cascorro, where the market begins. It ends at the bottom of C. Ribera de Curtidores.) Antiquarians lend their peculiar mustiness to Calle (not Salón or Paseo) del Prado and adjacent streets.

For **cassettes and CDs, Discoplay** (several branches, including one on Pl. Callao) offers a dazzlingly extensive selection. **Turner**, on C. Génova (a block from Pl. Colón), next door to the eponymous English-language bookstore, sells classical recordings.

Down Gran Vía de San Francisco (the continuation of C. Bailén) in Pl. Puerta de Toledo, the city's oldest fish market has become a multi-level shopping complex. The **Mercado Puerta de Toledo**, Ronda de Toledo, 1, houses several bars, restaurants, and shops featuring Spanish fashion, ceramics, furniture, and handicrafts. The classic Spanish **cape store** Seseña has a branch here. (Gallery open Tues.-Sat. 11:30am-9pm, Sun. 11:30am-3pm. Metro: Puerta de Toledo. Buses #3, 60, C.)

Sports

Spanish sports-fans obsess on **fútbol** (soccer). Every Sunday, occasionally Saturday, between September and June one of two big local teams plays at home. "Real Madrid" plays at Estadio Santiago Bernebeu, Po. Castellana, 104 (tel. 457 11 12; Metro: Lima; buses #27, 40, 43). "Atlético Madrid" plays at Estadio Vicente Calderón, C. Virgen del Puerto, 67 (tel. 266 47 07; Metro: Pirámides or Marqués de Vadillos). Take care not to stand right behind the goal on either side, unless you enjoy neo-fascistic rallies. Tickets for seats 2500ptas, for standing 1000ptas. If tickets are sold out, shiftyish scalpers lurk by the stadium during the afternoon or evening a few days before the game. Their tickets only cost 25-50% more, whereas on game day their prices are astronomical. For the big games—Atlético vs. Real, either team vs. Barça, pennant races in April and May, summer Copas del Rey and de Europa—scalpers are the only option.

For **cycling** information and bicycle repair spin over to **Calmera Bicicletas**, C. Atocha, 98 (tel. 277 75 74; open Mon.-Fri. 9:30am-1:30pm and 4:30-8pm, Sat. 9:30am-1:30pm and 5-8pm). **Swimming** folk crawl in the outdoor **Casa de Campo** pool on Av. Angel (open summer 10am-8pm; admission 250ptas, ages 4-13 100ptas; Metro: El Lago); and the indoor **Municipal de La Latina** pool, Pl. Cebada, 2 (open

Sept.-July Mon.-Fri. 8am-6pm, Sat. 8am-8pm, Sun. 8am-2:30pm; admission 250ptas, ages 4-13 100ptas; Metro: La Latina).

Call the **Dirección General de Deportes** (tel. 409 49 04) for further sporting information (no English spoken).

La Lidia

Bullfighters are either loved or loathed. If the crowd thinks the matador is a man of mettle and style, they'll exalt him as an emperor. If they think him a coward or a butcher, they'll whistle cacophonously, chant "Vete" (Get out!), throw their seat cushions (40ptas to rent) at him, and wait outside the ring to stone his car. Critical reviews in next morning's paper rehash the event; a bloody killing of the bull, instead of the swift death-stab, can upset the career of even the most renowned matador. A top *matador* may earn over three million pesetas per bullfight.

Corridas (bullfights) are held during the Festival of San Isidro and every Sunday in summer, less frequently the rest of the year. The season lasts from March to October. If you can stomach the killing of six beautiful *toros bravos* (and occasionally a reckless matador), keep your eyes open for posters in bars and cafés (especially on C. Victoria, off C. San Jerónimo) or inquire at the ticket offices below. **Plaza de las Ventas,** C. Alcalá, 237 (tel. 356 22 00), east of central Madrid, is the biggest ring in Spain. (Metro: Ventas. Bus #21, 53, or 110.) Even if you leave by Metro or bus 1 1/2 hr. before the fight you'll have an asphyxiating trip. Tickets are usually available the Saturday before and Sunday of the bullfight. Typically, there are two bullfights, one in the afternoon and one in the early evening. Ticket outlets are at C. Victoria, 3, off C. San Jerónimo east of Puerta del Sol (Metro: Sol), Pl. Carmen, 1 (tel. 531 27 32), and Pl. Toros, C. Alcalá, 237 (Metro: Ventas). A seat is 1000-4500ptas, depending on whether you sit in the *sombra* (shade) or in the blistering *sol*.

From mid- to late May, the **Fiestas de San Isidro** bring a bullfight every day with top *toreros* (bullfighters) and fierce Miura bulls. The festival is nationally televised; if you don't have a ticket, slip into a bar. **Bar-Restaurante Plata,** C. Jardines, 11 (tel. 232 48 98; Metro: Sol) has cheap *tapas* and a *loud* television. Try **Bar El Pavón,** C. Victoria, 8, at C. Cruz (Metro: Sol); **El Abuelo,** C. Núñez de Arce, where aficionados brandish the restaurant's famous shrimp during arguments over bullfighters; and **Bar Torre del Oro,** Pl. Mayor, 26 (tel. 266 50 16; open 10am-2pm; Metro: Sol or Opera). The bar of ritzy **Hotel Wellington** on C. Velázquez is known to have its share of matadors and their groupies.

Festivals

The brochure *Las Fiestas de España* contains historical background and general information on Spain's festivals. Madrid's **Carnaval,** inaugurated in the Middle Ages and prohibited during Franco's dictatorship, has resurfaced as never before. The city bursts with street fiestas, dancing, and processions; the Fat Tuesday celebration culminates with the mystifying "Burial of the Sardine." In late April, the city bubbles with the excellent **Festival Internacional de Teatro.** The May **Fiestas de San Isidro,** in honor of Madrid's patron saint, bring concerts, parades, and Spain's best bullfights. Throughout the summer, the city sponsors the **Veranos de la Villa,** an outstanding variety of cultural activities, including free classical music concerts, movies in open-air settings, plays, art exhibits, an international film festival, opera and *zarzuela* (Spanish operetta), ballet, and sports. In August, the neighborhoods of **San Cayetano, San Lorenzo,** and **La Paloma** celebrate their own festivities in a flurry of *madrileñismo*. When the processions, street dancing, traditional games, food, and drink are combined with home-grown hard rock and political slogans, they're a microcosm of contemporary Madrid. October's **Festivales de Otoño** (Autumn Festivals) also conjure an impressive array of music, theater, and film. Tourist offices in Madrid will have information on all these festivals from two weeks in advance.

Near Madrid

The Comunidad de Madrid is a self-standing administrative region shaped like an arrowhead pointing right at the heart of Castilla y León. Historically Madrid and Castilla-La Mancha were known as Castilla La Nueva (New Castile), while the Castilla north of Madrid was called Castilla La Vieja (Old Castile, now part of Castilla y León).

El Escorial

They called it the eighth wonder of the world, and they were right. El Escorial is a fascinating, severe complex including a monastery, two palaces, a church, two pantheons, a magnificent library, and innumerable artistic treasures. Within easy striking distance of Madrid, you should arrive early in order to see it all. In the shadows of the colossus, the lively, charming small town **San Lorenzo** hosts those who need another day. Above all, *don't* come on Monday, when the whole complex and most of the town shuts down.

Orientation and Practical Information

Buses and trains run to El Escorial. From the train station, take the shuttle bus 2km to the town center to avoid a grueling uphill walk. This bus and the buses from Madrid stop right in **Plaza Virgen de Gracia**, the center of town. The tree-lined avenue leading up, up, and away from the plaza is **Calle Floridablanca,** where you'll find classier restaurants and the tourist office. To the left and slightly downhill from C. Floridablanca is the **Monasterio.**

Tourist Office: C. Floridablanca, 10 (tel. 890 15 54), near the beginning of the street on the right. The only town map. *La Semana de El Escorial* (free) is also useful. Open Mon.-Fri. 10am-2pm and 3-4:45pm, Sat. 10am-1:45pm.

Post Office: C. Juan de Toledo, 2 (tel. 890 26 90), on Pl. Virgen de Gracia. Open Mon.-Fri. 9am-2pm, Sat. 9am-1pm; for **telegrams** Mon.-Fri. 9am-8pm, Sat. 9am-1pm. **Postal Code:** 28200.

Telephone Code: 91.

Currency Exchange: Caja Madrid, C. del Rey, 26 (tel. 890 17 14). Open Mon.-Fri. 8:30am-2pm. After hours try **Hotel Victoria Palace,** C. Juan de Tòledo.

Trains: Ctra. Estación (tel. 890 04 13), 2km down from town where Ctra. Estación meets Pl. Virgen de Gracia. Herranz buses provide shuttle service (55ptas). To: Madrid's Atocha and Charmatín stations (28 per day, 1hr., 265ptas); Avila (11 per day; 1hr.; 340ptas, round-trip 600ptas); Segovia (same as for Avila).

Buses: Pl. Virgen de Gracia. **Autocares Herranz office,** C. Reina Victoria, 3 (tel. 890 41 22). Buy tickets at the Bar Casino, C. Rey, 3 (tel. 890 41 00). To: Madrid (15 per day; 1hr.; 315ptas, round-trip 600ptas); Valle de los Caídos (at 3:15pm, returning at 5:30pm; 15min.; 565ptas round-trip including admission); Guadarrama (7 per day, 20min., 100ptas).

Taxis: C. Floridablanca (tel. 890 17 17). Open 8am-10pm. Also on Pl. Constitución (tel. 890 40 01). Open 8:30am-10pm.

Lost Property: Cuartel de la Guardia Civil (tel. 890 26 11), 3km down the Ctra. de Guadarama.

General Store: C. Joaquin Costa, 4, under the black, yellow, and red CB Ahorro sign. Open Mon.-Sat. 9:30am-2pm and 6-9pm, Sun. 9:30am-2pm.

Swimming Pool: Club de Golf, Finca de Herreria (tel. 890 51 11), beyond the Monasterio.

Pharmacy: Fernández, C. del Rey (tel. 890 43 00). **Villar,** C. de la Reina Victoria (tel. 890 41 17).

Medical Services: Hospital de la Alcadesa, C. San Pedro Regalado, 1 (tel. 890 54 44). Call also for **ambulance.**

Emergency: tel. 091.

Police: C. Gobernador, 2 (tel. 890 52 23).

Accommodations and Camping

In summer, accommodations are neither cheap nor plentiful. Finding a room in July and August without reservations far in advance may be impossible. Call ahead to ensure a bed, or at least arrive early in the day. Plenty of vacancies in off-season.

Albergue Juvenil Campamiento Santa María del Buen Aire (HI) (tel. 890 36 40). Walk down Ctra. Estación just past the monastery, turn right and follow the road 1 1/2km. 92 beds with 4-8 people per room. Sometimes full of noisy school groups. No curfew, but packs of dogs bark at latecomers. Members only. 600ptas, over 26 700ptas. Breakfast and hot showers included. *Pensión completa* 1400ptas, over 26 1600ptas.

Hostal Vasco, Pl. Santiago, 11 (tel. 890 16 19). From the bus stop, head up C. Patriarca (at right-angles with C. Floridablanca) for 5 bl., then go left 2 bl. Charming 19th-century building with a terrace on the plaza and a lounge on each floor. Clean, spacious rooms, some with excellent views of the monastery. Popular with mobs of school kids. Singles 1800ptas. Doubles with shower 3600ptas, with bath 3800ptas. Triples 4500ptas. Tempting aromas seep from the eponymous restaurant next door. Breakfast 375ptas. Lunch or dinner 1500ptas. *Pensión completa* 3400ptas.

Hostal Malagón, C. San Francisco, 2, 2nd fl. (tel. 890 15 76), at C. Mariano Benavente. Comfortable rooms with high ceilings and saggy beds don't live up to the entryway. Singles 2000ptas. Doubles 2800ptas. Triples 4100ptas. Showers 200ptas.

Hostal Cristina, C. Juan de Toledo, 6 (tel. 890 19 61). Tranquil location, next to a park and overlooking the mountain range. Garden terrace. Clean rooms with modern wood furniture and tile floors. Doubles with bath 4500ptas. Nov. 1-April 30: 4000ptas. Breakfast 350ptas. Restaurant open 1-2:30pm and 9-10:30pm.

Caravaning El Escorial (tel. 890 24 12), 15km away on Ctra. de Guadarrama a El Escorial. 490ptas per person, per tent, per car. Ages 3-9 450ptas. Electricity 300ptas.

Food

If you don't like picnics, seriously consider fasting. The **Mercado Publico,** C. del Rey 9, 2 blocks off C. Floridablanca, sells a large selection of fresh produce, deli meats, cheeses, and other staples. (Open Mon.-Wed. and Fri.-Sat. 9am-2pm and 6-9pm, Thurs. 6-9pm.) Several good *panaderías* (bakeries) are on the same street. Shop at the general store farther down if you can't deal with fat dead pigs dangling from huge hooks. A number of inexpensive but nondescript bars and cafés lie at the end of C. Reina Victoria. The kiosks along C. Floridablanca offer lighter fare (*bocadillos* 200-300ptas, *raciones* 300-500ptas).

Cafetería-Restaurante del Arte, C. Floridablanca, 14 (tel. 890 15 20). One of the least expensive spots on this boulevard of pricey *cafeterías*. Eating outdoors in the pleasant shade ups prices about 50%. Sandwiches 335-375ptas. *Raciones* 700-1000ptas. *Platos combinados* 800ptas and up. *Café* outdoors 180ptas. Open 8am-midnight.

Taberna-Restaurante El Colmao, C. Rey, 26. Small and unpretentious, this *taberna* on the corner sells a substantial *menú* (1000ptas). For the truly famished, the *gran churrasco con ensalada* for two (3500ptas) really feeds three. Open 11am-midnight.

Mesón-Taberna La Cueva, C. San Antón, 3 (tel. 890 15 16). Built in 1768 by the same genius who designed the Prado. Stately interior, stately food. Mostly very expensive, but affordable tortillas (700ptas). Open 1-4pm and 9-10:30pm. For drinks and *tapas,* slip into the tavern on the 1st fl. (or around the side of the building). *Copa de vino* 100ptas. Open 10:30am-2am.

Sights

The entire complex of El Escorial is open Tues.-Sun. 10am-7pm. Last admission to palaces, pantheons, and museums one hour or 30 minutes before closing (depending on "zone"), 15 min. for the *casitas.* Admission to monastery is free; for the rest of the complex, admission is 350ptas, 325ptas for students, and free Wednesday for EEC citizens.

El Escorial—the Monastery

The **Monasterio de San Lorenzo de El Escorial** was a gift from Felipe II to God, himself, and the people, commemorating his victory over the French at the battle of San Quintín in 1557. Juan Bautista de Toledo was commissioned to design the complex in 1561; when he died in 1567, Juan de Herrera inherited his mantle. Save the Panteón Real and minor additional work, the monastery was finished in a speedy 21 years, accounting for its uncommon uniformity of style.

According to tradition, Felipe oversaw much of the work from a chair-shaped rock 7km from the construction site. That stone is now known as **Silla de Felipe II** (Felipe's Chair), and the view is still regal. For the carless, there's a worm's-eye view from the meadows near the Campamento Santa María del Buen Aire.

The floorplan of the monastery is a subdivided rectangle; a bird's eye view suggests a grill, the device on which St. Lawrence was martyred. Considering the resources Felipe II (son of Carlos V, who had ruled the most powerful empire in the world) commanded, the building is noteworthy for its austerity, symmetry, and simplicity of line—in his words, "majesty without ostentation." Four massive towers pin the corners in characteristic Spanish fashion. The towers of the basilica that rise from the center are surmounted by a great dome, giving the ensemble the shape of a pyramid. At Felipe II's behest, the steep slate roofs were introduced from Flanders—the first of their kind in Spain. The delicate slate spires lend a grace to the austere structure, further mellowed by the glowing *piedra de Colmenar,* a stone hewn from nearby quarries. The monastery is at once also a palace, a church, and a pantheon (again characteristically Spanish), prototype of what would later be called the *estilo herreriano*. Variations of this Habsburg style using unadorned alternating granite and red brick, the slate roofs, and corner towers would be influential throughout Spain—particularly in Madrid and Toledo—and abroad (for example, on Paris's Place des Vosges).

To avoid the worst of the crowds, enter the Escorial by the traditional gateway on the west side of the complex (the right-hand side from C. Floridablanca), and wander through the **Patio de los Reyes** into the **Basílica,** a cool and magnificent building. Marble steps lead to an altar graced by two groups of elegant sculpture by Pompeo Leoni. The figures on the left represent Carlos V and Isabel (parents of Felipe II), his daughter María, and his sisters María (Queen of Hungary) and Leonor (Queen of France). Those on the right depict Felipe II with three of his four wives and his son Carlos. The **Coro Alto** (High Choir) has a magnificent ceiling fresco of heaven filled with choirs of angels; the **cloister** shines with Titian's gigantic fresco of the Martyrdom of St. Lawrence.

The Palacio Real

The Palacio Real includes the **Salón del Trono** (Throne Room) and two **dwellings** in one—Felipe II's spartan 16th-century apartments and the more luxurious 18th-century rooms of Carlos III and Carlos IV. The Bourbon half is characterized by the sumptuousness of its furniture and beautiful **tapestries** (copies of works by Goya, El Greco, and Rubens worked in intricate detail and brilliant wool yarn cover every inch of wall). The Habsburg chambers are simple. A large collection of clocks and other *objets d'art* suffocate under condom-shaped glass covers.

The two parts of the palace are joined by the long **Sala de Batallas** (battle room). The huge fresco here depicts some of Castile's and Spain's greatest victories: Juan II's triumph over the Muslims in 1431 at Higueruela (note the fleeing townsfolk), Felipe II's two successful expeditions to the Azores, and the battle of San Quintín. Downstairs, in the royal chambers, observe Felipe II's very small bed, his terrible handwriting, and the view to which he woke every morning.

The Panteón Real

The astonishing **Panteón Real** (known affectionately as *el pudridero,* the rotting chamber) was another brainchild of Felipe II. Although he didn't live to see it finished, he's buried here with Carlos V and most of their royal descendants. Royal servants dumped bygone nobles in the small adjoining room so that they could dry before being stuffed into their permanent tombs (drying time varied based on climate conditions and fat content). The stairway leading to the **crypt** is elegantly adorned with black and red marble and jasper. Of the 26 gray marble sarcophagi, 23 contain the remains of Spanish monarchs, and three are still empty. A pathetic tradition discriminates against queens. All kings are buried here (except Felipe V and Fernando VI, who preferred to be interred elsewhere), but only those queens whose sons become monarchs are admitted.

The 19th-century **Panteón de las Infantas** is intended for the other queens and minor men of the royal household. The statue of studly Don Juan depicts him in uniform (even though he didn't die in battle); female visitors still slather him with kisses.

The Salas Capitulares and Biblioteca

The **Salas Capitulares** (chapter rooms), on the far side of the complex, now contain an outstanding exhibition on the construction of El Escorial, with some wooden models of 16th-century machinery and the buildings themselves. Also in the Salas Capitulares is the **Pinacoteca**, which holds a collection of masterpieces by Bosch, Dürer, El Greco, Titian, Tintoretto, Velázquez, Zurbarán, Van Dyck, and others.

Finally, if you haven't yet keeled over in cultural wonderment, walk up to the second-floor **Biblioteca** (library). Its holdings of books and manuscripts are priceless, despite several fires that have reduced the collection. Alfonso X's *Cántigas de Santa María,* the Book of Hours of the Catholic monarchs, Saint Teresa's manuscripts and diary, the *Aureus Codex* (by German Emperor Conrad III, 1039) written in pure gold, and an 11th-century *Commentary on the Apocalypse* by Beato de Liébana are just a small selection of the choice readings.

Outringers

Commissioned by Carlos, Prince of Asturias, who later became Carlos IV, the **Casita del Príncipe** has a splendid collection of *objets d'art,* including chandeliers, lamps, rugs, furniture, clocks, tapestries, china, and engraved oranges. The French roughed up the *casita* during the Napoleonic invasions, but many rooms were redecorated by Fernando VII in the then-popular Empire style. To get to the casita, follow the right side of the Carretera de la Estación as far as the corner of the monastic complex, turn the corner, and take the left-hand fork (15min.).

Three km down the road to Avila lurks the **Casita del Infante,** commissioned by Gabriel de Borbón, Carlos's brother, at around the same time. Though not as sumptuous as the Casita del Príncipe, it's tranquil and has a fine view.

Entertainment

San Lorenzo is not the fossilized tourist trap one might expect. Hiphopping youth frequent the bars and cafés beyond the walls of El Escorial. Older folks and parents stroll, sit, and sip in the plazas just off **Calles Floridablanca** and **Rey,** which overflow with *cervecerías* and *cafés.* Teens and twentysomes head a little further uphill.

> **Jandro's Bar**, Pl. de las Animas. A popular place for the young to build a buzz. Drinks are a tad expensive (beer 300ptas, whiskey 700ptas) and the music blares. Open 7:30pm-4am.
>
> **Café Cervecería la Jara,** C. Floridablanca, 34. Young, loyal clientele, but smaller and quieter than Jandro's. Open 6pm-3am.
>
> **El Gurniato,** C. Leandro Rubio, 3 (tel. 890 47 10), around the bend to the left at the end of C. Floridablanca. Although there's a TV and a miniature terrace, the place as a whole lacks oomph. Open noon-3pm and 6pm-3am.
>
> **Disco-Pub Que Maz Da,** C. Santiago, 11. More oomph: comfy seating plus cheap beer minus a cover charge. Open Sun.-Thurs. 8pm-midnight, Fri.-Sat. 8pm-4:30am.

During the **Festivals of San Lorenzo** (Aug. 10-20), parades of giant figures line the streets and fireworks fill the sky. Folk dancing contests and horse-drawn cart parades mark **Romería a la Ermita de la Virgen de Gracia,** the second Sunday in September. Ceremonies are also held in the forest of Herría.

Sierra de Guadarrama

The Sierra de Guadarrama, a pine-covered mountain range halfway between Madrid and Segovia, has the most spectacular scenery in the province of Madrid. Its dark geological shapes loom large in local imagination, as well as in the local economy. *La Mujer Muerta* (The Dead Woman) rots facing the West. The *Sierra de la Maliciosa* (The Evil Woman) schemes to the East. Between the two, the *Siete Picos* gnash their teeth silently at the skies. Yet none of these portents of doom can deter the influx of summer and winter visitors who come to hike and ski.

El Valle de los Caídos

In a previously untouched valley of the Sierra de Guadarrama, 8km from El Escorial, Franco built the overpowering monument of **Santa Cruz del Valle de los Caídos** (Valley of the Fallen) as a memorial to those who gave their lives in the Civil War. However, the massive granite cross (150m tall and 46m wide) memorializes only half of those "fallen"—those who died "serving *Dios* and *España*," the Nationalists/fascists.

Below the monument, engineers and political prisoners were forced to blast a hole in the mountain to make room for the **basilica,** begun in 1940 and not finished until the early 80s. The Generalísimo himself is buried at the top of the cross-shaped building. Intimidating, tunnel-like antechambers, vaguely medieval light fixtures and tapestries, and ornaments of angels holding swords make for an eerie, fitting monument to Franco and his particular brand of Catholic fascism. Mass is daily at 11am. (Open 10am-6pm. Admission 400ptas, free Wed. for EEC citizens.)

Autocares Herranz in El Escorial runs one **bus** here per day at 3:15pm (returns at 6:15pm, off-season 5:30pm; 15min.; round-trip including admission 365ptas).

Cercedilla

Cercedilla, a picturesque town of alpine chalets, is a hub for hiking and skiing in the Sierras. Those weary of busy cities will find it a relief that this town has no monuments; the most exciting event in its history is a passing mention in Quevedo's 17th-century novel *El Buscón*. Hiking trails leave straight out of Cercedilla, and many use the town as a base for daytrips to the nearby ski resorts (see Puerto de Navacerrada and Los Cotos below).

Cercedilla is the town in the Sierra most easily reached by **train** as a daytrip from Madrid (over 20 *cercanías* per day, 1 1/2 hr., 340ptas) or Segovia (10 *regional* per day en route to Madrid, 45min., 300ptas). To get to town from the train station, walk uphill, take the right-hand branch at the top, and carry straight on at the train track (15-20min.). Most of the hiking action begins up the **Carreterra las Dehesas,** beyond the intersection, uphill from the train station. One of the most strenuous hikes leads past the Hospital de Fuenfrías to the meadow of Navarrulaque.

During late summer, ski season, and weekends year-round, a steady flow of vacationers pours in from Madrid, vaporizing accommodations. At other times there's plenty for all. Near Cercedilla two capacious **HI youth hostels** offer the usual group sleeping, group meals, and 10am lockout. The **Villa Castora** (tel. 852 03 34) is closest to the train station, about 1 1/2km up Ctra. las Dehesas on the left; it's popular with school and community groups, so try to reserve at least two days in advance. (Reception open continuously July 1-Aug. 15; Oct.-June Tues.-Sun. after noon. 550ptas. *Pensión media* 900ptas. *Pensión completa* 1300ptas. Over 26: 650ptas; 1100ptas; 1500tpas.) **Las Dehesas** (tel. 852 01 35), is closer to the hiking trails and more removed from the highway, tucked back in among the trees just beyond the Agencia del Medio Ambiente on Ctra. las Dehesas. (Reception open same times and same prices as Villa Castora.) **Camping** is no longer allowed within Cercedilla's town limits; these extend surprisingly far beyond the town. Camping in general is pretty strictly controlled throughout the Sierra de Guadarrama; a list of campsites is available at the Agencia del Medio Ambiente (see below). Reaching most of these rather remote sites requires wheels (not necessarily motorized; see Bike Rental below).

Restaurant prices are middling. Scrounging at mini-supermarket **Maxcoop,** C. Docta Cañados, 2 (tel. 852 00 13), in the town center off Av. Generalísmo, is the most miserly thing to do. (Open Mon.-Sat. 9:30am-1:30pm and 5:30-9pm, Sun. 9:30am-1:30pm.) **Mesón-Restaurante Helio** (tel. 852 13 45) is close to the train station and just across the street from Hostal Longines. It's pricey. (*Menú* 1300ptas, entrees from 800ptas. Open 10am-11pm; off-season Mon.-Fri. noon-4pm, Sat.-Sun. 10am-11pm.) Hordes of cheaper bars peddle *bocadillos* and *raciones* in the town proper.

The **Agencia de Medio Ambiente,** Ctra las Dehesas, s/n (tel. 852 22 13), fills the function of a tourist office. About 3km up the road in a wooden chalet, they offer hiking information and sell several guidebooks and maps, including the excellent "Editorial Alpino" map of the Sierra. The free leaflet *Senderos Autoguiados* (self-guided tours) is stronger on ideas than geographical accuracy. From July 22 to Nov. 30 there are free guided tours of the valley, beginning from the shelter across the road from the chalet at 10am and 4pm. (Open June-Nov. 9 9am-9pm.) The **post office** is halfway between the train station and the town center on C. Marquesa Casa López, 9. (Open Mon.-Fri. 9am-1pm; Oct.-May Mon.-Sat. 9am-1pm; for **telegrams** Mon.-Fri. 10am-1pm.) Cercedilla's **telephone code** is 91. **Bike rental** occurs at Bicicletas Mariano, C. Marquesa Casa López, just past the train tracks. (Open 10am-2pm and 6-9pm.) For **medical assistance,** the Centro Médico (tel. 852 30 31, 852 31 59) is in a new and much-signposted building in the town center. In an **emergency,** dial 091. The **police** are in the Ayuntamiento, Pl. Mayor, 1 (tel. 852 02 00, 852 04 25); call them quick for an **ambulance.**

The **train station** (tel. 852 00 57) is at the base of the hill on C. Emilio Serrano. Frequent service to Madrid (over 20 per day, 1 1/2 hr., 340ptas); Segovia (10 per day, 45min., 300ptas); Los Cotos (11 per day; 45min.; 110ptas, round-trip 165ptas); Puerto de Navacerrada (11 per day; 1/2 hr.; 110ptas, round-trip 165ptas). The **bus station** Av. Jose Antonio, 2 (tel. 852 02 39), is across the street and to the left of the Ayuntamiento. To Guadarrama (15 per day, 20min., 85ptas) continuing to Madrid (1-1 1/2 hr. more, 350ptas).

Puerto de Navacerrada and Los Cotos

The strongest magnet for skiers and hikers is **Puerto de Navacerrada,** a bland ski resort frequented in winter by Madrid's residents and in summer by backpackers who use it as a starting point to climb the peaks. A little red train leaves for Puerto from a separate platform of the Cercedilla station (on the left). The train may pause for mountain cattle crossings. The skiing season lasts from December to April; there are special areas for beginners as well as competitions for the more accomplished. For hiking in summer, exit the station, turn left at the highway, and turn left again (off the road) at the large intersection marking the pass. The dirt path leads uphill. There are many hiking routes through the pine forests; the Vía de Schmidt (or Smit) to the left leads back to Cercedilla.

Los Cotos is another popular winter resort. Nearby **Rascafría** in Los Cotos has two ski stations that are well regarded by locals, **Valdesqui** (tel. 852 04 16) and **Valcotos.** (Both open in winter roughly 10am-5pm.) For detailed information on winter sports, call the Madrid office of the Dirección General de Deportes (tel. 409 49 04). After the skiers have packed and gone home, Los Cotos is completely desolate.

Alcalá de Henares

Alcalá is a demure city of erstwhile greatness: the seat of a university that enjoyed fame across Europe in the 16th century, and the birthplace of Cervantes, Juan Ruiz (author of the classic medieval celebration of earthly love, *El Libro de Buen Amor),* and Catherine of Aragón. Today it's primarily a commuter town whose population has grown astronomically in recent years. Frequent trains to and from Madrid make this the easiest of all excursions, but perhaps not the most rewarding.

Casa de Cervantes, on C. Mayor, is a reconstruction *in situ* of the house where the author was born. Within its 13 rooms, laid out on two floors around a peaceful whitewashed patio, is a collection of furniture, pottery, and other artifacts. Although they're all genuine period, none belonged to Cervantes or his father Rodrigo, who owned the original house. Cartophiles partake of the 16th-century maps downstairs. *Don Quixote* editions in each and every language live upstairs. (Open Tues.-Fri. 10am-2pm and 4-6pm, Sat.-Sun. 10am-2pm. Free.)

In Pl. San Diego, just east of Pl. Cervantes, sits the **Colegio Mayor de San Ildefonso,** the fulcrum of the once-illustrious university. Pioneering humanist and sharp dresser Cardinal Cisneros founded the college in 1495, thirteen years before he created the university itself. The Cardinal's printed heraldic symbol, a pair of swans, is carved on the mid-16th century façade. Inside, the highlights are a *Paraninfo* (Great Hall) with a colorful ceiling and the 17th-century Patio Santo Tomás de Villanueva, an elegant Baroque affair. Cisneros now decays in the altar of the adjoining **Capilla de San Ildefonso,** which has a marvelous coffered ceiling. Although the whole university was transferred to Madrid in 1836, the pitter-patter of student feet still echos through these halls; several academic departments have recently returned from Madrid. (8 tours per day 11am-7:15pm, 200ptas.) Those repulsed by academia visit the 16th-century **corral,** the oldest intact theater in Western Europe, currently under restoration.

Because very few tourists sleep over, there are always empty beds. One of the least expensive *hostales* is **Hostal El Torero,** Puerta de Madrid, 18 (tel. 889 03 73); (singles 2400ptas. doubles 4000ptas).

Topeca, Pl. Cervantes (tel. 888 45 25), is a very large air-conditioned bar-restaurant that does salmon justice *(menú* 700ptas). Don't expect refinement; waiters sprint up and down the aisles. In the plaza itself, drinks may be more expensive than you bargained for *(horchata* 200ptas, *cerveza* 300ptas).

The **tourist office**—still a little surprised to get visitors—is at the far left-hand corner of Pl. Cervantes on Callejón de Santa María, 1 (tel. 889 26 94; open Mon.-Fri. 11am-2pm and 4-6pm). All major sights are within three or four minutes' walk from here. **Taxis** can be called at 888 10 11. The **Centro de Salud** (health center) is at 888 50 64. The **police** are at 888 42 13 (091 or 092 in an **emergency**).

Trains pull into the RENFE station, Po. Estación, s/n (tel. 888 01 96), about once every 10 minutes from Madrid (220ptas), continuing to Guadalajara (220ptas). To reach the city center from the train station, walk up Paseo de la Estación (to the left as you leave the building), cross the next junction and continue for one block, then turn right on **Calle de Libreros,** which leads to the **Plaza de Cervantes,** the heart of things. The Continental-Auto **bus** station is on Av. Guadalajara, 2 blocks past C. Libreros, 36 (tel. 888 16 22). Buses runs every 15 minutes between Madrid and Alcalá (215ptas). To reach the city center from the bus station, turn right down Avenida Guadalajara and bear left onto C. Libreros at the fork.

Aranjuez

Centuries of Habsburg and Bourbon royalty fled to Aranjuez to escape Madrid's scorching heat. This is a town with peace and quiet, strawberries and cream, and impossibly tall elms and plane trees. Like other venerable royal retreats (such as La Granja), Aranjuez no longer hosts monarchs during the summer (it lost out to Mallorca a while back), but the decaying grandeur of its **Palacio Real** nonetheless warrants an excursion from Madrid.

In the 16th century, Felipe II hired Juan de Herrera, chief architect of El Escorial, to transform the dinky summer residence that stood on this spot into a real palace fit for a monarch. Bourbon Felipe V had the palace enlarged and embellished two centuries later to emulate Versailles (much like La Granja, his other palace near Segovia). Room after opulent room displays finely worked Vatican mosaic paintings in natural marble, chandeliers and mirrors from the La Granja crystal factory, Buen Retiro porcelain, Flemish tapestries, Chinese points, and ornate French clocks. The Oriental porcelain room with 3-D wallpaper has a dash of Rococo ceramic work; the Mozarabic smoking room has its own gaudy copy of the Alhambra. (Open Tues.-Sun. 10am-6:30pm; Oct.-May Tues.-Sun. 10am-6pm. Compulsory tour in Spanish. Admission 400ptas, students 275ptas. Free Wed. to EEC citizens.)

Aranjuez lies at the confluence of two rivers, the Tajo (which flows all the way to Lisboa) and its tributary the Jarama. The paths, sprinkled here and there by ornamental fountains, run from the smaller gardens outside the palace (the **Jardines de la Isla**—planted in the time of Isabel la Católica—with their banana trees and mythological statues) to the huge **Jardines del Príncipe,** sculpted for the youthful amusement of the future Carlos IV (Goya's patron). Inside the park the **Casa del Labrador,** a mock laborer's cottage, is a treasure trove of Neoclassical decorative arts destined for courtly galas. The queen's private quarters overflow with knickknacks such as Roman mosaics from Mérida and views of contemporary Madrid embroidered in silk. Also within Jardines del Príncipe, the **Casa de Marinos,** once the quarters of the Tajo's sailing squad, stores royal gondolas. (Gardens open 10am-sunset. Casas open Tues.-Sun. 10am-6:30pm; Oct.-May Tues.-Sun. 10am-6pm. Admission to Casa de Labrador and Casa de Marinos 300ptas, students 250ptas.) Nearby is the **embarcadero** (dock) from which the royal family set sail on the swampy river. If you wish to do the same, cross the precarious footbridge to the Arboleda Bar on the far side to rent **paddleboats** (350ptas per hr.).

The town's **strawberries** and **asparagus** have been famed for centuries. In fact, the very first Spanish locomotive, which ran from Madrid to Aranjuez on February 9, 1851, was dubbed the "strawberry train." The strawberry train continued to be all the rage in subsequent decades, carting Aranjuez strawberries to Madrid during the week and residents of the big city to Aranjuez on weekends. An exact replica of the steam train now takes tourists for a ride. (April-Oct. Sat.-Sun. at 9:35am from Estación Atocha in Madrid, return at 8:09pm; round-trip including admission to all sights 1800ptas, children 1200ptas.) *Fresón con nata* (strawberries and cream, 300ptas) are staples at the street cafés on **Calle Infantas,** across from the tourist office (300ptas).

On May 30, Aranjuez launches into its **Fiestas de Primavera** (Spring Festival) with arts and crafts shows and an agricultural-industrial fair. The **Ferias del Motín** on September 4 brings concerts, exhibitions, and a bull fair.

Hostal Infantas, C. Infantas, 6 (tel. 891 13 41), rents good clean rooms at convenient location just up the street from the tourist office. All rooms have phones. (Singles 1400ptas, with bath 1900ptas. Doubles 2500ptas, with shower 3100ptas.) **Hostal Rusiñol,** C. San Antonio, 76 (tel. 891 01 55), has an airy inner patio. (Singles 1800ptas. Doubles 3000ptas.) If a TV is what you want, dawdle around **Hostal Castilla,** C. Andalucía, 98 (tel. 891 26 27). All rooms have TVs and phones and are kept immaculate by exuberant cleaners. (Singles 3200ptas. Doubles with bath 4400ptas. Breakfast 350ptas.) **Camping Soto del Castillo** (tel. 891 13 95), complete with swimming pool and TV room, is within walking distance of the palace, just over the Tajo from Jardín del Príncipe. (400ptas per person, 300ptas per tent, 400ptas per car.)

Hungry much? **Bar-Kiosco El Brillante,** at the beginning of C. Infantas, serves *tapas, platos combinados* (450-850ptas), and *fresón con nata.* Across from the tourist office, renowned **Rana Verde** satisfies those who find relief in wanton indulgence (about 2500ptas per person). The opulent *tarta al licor* (brandy-flavored cake, 400ptas) is the corker. On the other hand, a regal picnic in the palace gardens costs less than any restaurant. The **mercado** hawks fresh produce, breads, and deli foods in a 19th-century building between C. Gobernador and C. Abastos.

The **tourist office** (tel. 891 04 27), temporarily housed in a kiosk opposite the construction in Pl. San Antonio and Pl. Rusiñol, has a small Spanish leaflet on Aranjuez and mounds of information on Madrid. English spoken. (Open Tues.-Sun. 10am-6:30pm; Oct.-May Tues.-Sun. 10am-6pm.) The **post office** (tel. 891 12 56) is at C. Peña Redonda (open Mon.-Fri. 9am-2pm). The **Red Cross** (tel. 891 02 52) is at C. Capitán, 10. To reach the **police,** dial 891 00 22.

To get to the **train station** (tel. 891 02 02), 1km out of town, take municipal bus N-Z from C. Stuart, about two blocks away from P. Rusiñol. Walking might be better (10min.); the bus has its own agenda. Take Ctra. Toledo away from the palace and follow the signs. Coming *from* the station into town, turn right out of the building, then left on the avenue that runs straight to the palace. Alternatively, catch the erratic shuttle bus and ask the driver to drop you off near the Palacio Real. Frequent trains run to Toledo (1/2 hr., 220ptas) and Madrid (50min., 265ptas). Direct service also to Andalucía, Cuenca, and Badajoz. **Buses** run to Madrid (7 per day, 480ptas) from C. Infantas, 8 (tel. 891 01 83).

Castilla-La Mancha

Cervantes deliberately chose this south-central tableland for Don Quixote's inspired adventures in order to evoke a cultural and material backwater. No need for the overworked fantasy of the Knight of the Sad Countenance to appreciate the austere beauty of this battered, windswept plateau punctuated by windmills, the occasional hilltop castle ruin, or the looming, black silhouette of the Osborne bull billboard. Scored by the Tajo and the Guadiana, two great Atlantic rivers, and the smaller Júcar, which eyes the Mediterranean, La Mancha's rolling flatness is broken by the hills of the Toledo and Cuenca *sierras* and interrupted here and there by lakes and great stands of game-rich primeval forest. This is the land that along with the Comunidad de Madrid was historically known as Castilla La Nueva.

La Mancha—*manxa* is Arabic for parched earth—is separated from the northern *meseta* (Castilla La Vieja and southern Aragón) by the Sierras de Gredos, Guadarrama, and the Montes Universales and from the southern Gualdalquivir basin by the towering Sierra Morena. Sandwiched between the mountains are rolling fields of golden-hued wheat, orderly rows of silvery sheened olive groves, deep green and mauve vineyards, and sprays of purple saffron.

It's futile to seek out isolated country houses here; long a military march between the Muslim south and the Christian north, these steppes were inhabited by hardy pioneers ever-ready to take up arms in the night. Residents congregated in whitewashed villages, on straight streets radiating from a central Plaza Mayor. As Christian forces barged into Muslim Spain (Toledo was captured in 1085), La Mancha became the domain of military orders (such as Santiago, Calatrava, Montesa, and San Juan) modeled on such crusading institutions as the Knights Templar, an order of powerful warrior-monks who cooked up elaborate schemes and synchronized their watches within the walls of their five and 12-sided castles. It's these castles, fortified churches, and monasteries that give Castilla its characteristic landmarks and name.

The region is Spain's largest wine-producing area (Valdepeñas and Manzanares are common table wines), renowned for its abundant olive groves and excellent hunting. Stews, pulses, roast meats, and game are *manchego* staples. *Gazpacho manchego* is a hearty stew of rabbit, lamb, chicken, and pork. *Perdices escabechadas* (marinated partridges) are a specialty of Toledo, while Cuenca is known for *monteruelo* (a pâté of pig's liver and game). A succulent sauté of red and green peppers, zucchini, onion, and garlic, *pisto manchego* has been compared by some to ratatouille. Perhaps Spain's most universal cheese is *manchego,* ranging from a young, creamy white to a sharp, friable *añejo* (aged).

Toledo

Toledo remains a treasury of Spanish culture, no matter how many armies of tourists and vendors of kitsch pass through. Cervantes called it that "rocky gravity, glory of Spain and light of her cities." Baroque poet Góngora called it a perpetual avalanche. To Surrealist filmmaker Luis Buñuel and his cohorts, Toledo was a temple of mystery and intrigue (their local headquarters, the *Posada de Sangre,* or Inn of Blood, was demolished during the Civil War). Successively a Roman settlement, capital of the Visigothic kingdom, stronghold of the Emirate of Córdoba, and imperial city under Carlos V, the city bears a rich history and heritage surpassed by few others in Spain.

In the 13th century, Alfonso X el Sabio (the Wise), King of Castilla, founded the renowned Escuela de Traductores de Toledo (Toledo School of Translators) and subsidized a vast scientific program of research. Local excellence in astronomy and medicine, as well as philosophy, universal history, legal codes, and even chess made Toledo the European capital for study of the natural sciences.

Trapped on three sides by the Tajo on a naturally moated promontory, the city's monuments press together in a madding crowd of periods and styles. Toledo was built like a rock on a rock; its steep, tortuous streets rendered it both easy to defend and cool in the summer. Numerous churches, synagogues, and mosques are proof of *convivencia* (peaceful co-existence of three religions), which lasted for centuries.

Toledo is famous for its swords and knives and for damascene, the ancient craft of inlaying gold filaments on a black steel background that now decorates everything from sabres to ashtrays. Many streets are cluttered with junky gift shops, and the city can feel like a noisy museum. Despite occasional crassness, Toledo (like Venice) exerts an irresistible pull.

Orientation and Practical Information

Getting here is a snap from Madrid; an almost unbearable number of buses and trains make the one and one-half hour journey every day. From a stop to the right of the train station, or from the inside the bus station, city buses #5 and 6 go directly to **Plaza de Zocodóver,** the center of town (60ptas). Only nuts walk to the plaza from the train or bus station (20min straight up). If you qualify, turn right from the RENFE station, take the left fork, cross the bridge, go through the arches, take the left-hand steps, and turn right at the top. From the bus station, turn right, follow the traffic uphill to the gateway, go through it, and continue all the way up and around to Pl. Zocodóver.

No Castilian city is as labyrinthine as Toledo, and to make things worse, many of the streets are unmarked. The detailed map handed out by Turismo is worth its weight in gold. Many major sights are near or atop the central hill, which is almost exactly circular. Pl. Zocodóver and the massive Alcázar are over to the east of the circle; the cathedral is roughly in the middle, and several other sights, including the Casa del Greco and the synagogues, are southwest in the *Judería.*

> **Tourist Office:** (tel. 22 08 43; fax 25 26 48), just outside the Puerta Nueva de Bisagra and Po. de Merchán, on the north side of town. From Pl. Zocodóver, take the main street leading downhill, C. Armas, through various name changes to the gate; pass under and cross the intersection. From the RENFE station, turn right and take the busy right-hand fork and continue past the bus station, skirting the city walls until you reach the huge gateway—the office is across the road, outside the walls. English spoken. Up-to-date maps and information. Open Mon.-Fri. 9am-2pm and 4-6pm, Sat. 9am-3pm and 4-7pm, Sun. 9am-3pm. For a map and rudimentary info without the walk, queue up at the gray **information booth,** Pl. Zocodóver (tel. 22 12 02). Open Mon.-Sat. 10am-6pm, Sun. and holidays 10am-3pm.
>
> **Budget Travel:** Oficina de Información Juvenil, C. Trinidad, 8 (tel. 21 20 62), by the cathedral. Student travel information, rail passes, bus and plane tickets. No English spoken. Open 9am-2pm and 5-6:30pm.
>
> **Post Office:** C. Plata, 1 (tel. 22 36 11). Open for Lista de Correos Mon.-Fri. 9am-2pm and 4-6pm; for **telegrams** (tel. 22 20 00) Mon.-Fri. 9am-2pm and 4-6pm, Sat. 9am-2pm. **Postal Code:** 45001.
>
> **Telephones:** C. Plata, 20. Open Mon.-Sat. 9am-1pm and 5-9pm. **Telephone Code:** 925.
>
> **Trains:** Po. Rosa (tel. 22 30 99), in a neo-Mudejar building opposite the Puente de Azarquiel. To Aranjuez (8 per day, 45min., 220ptas) and Madrid's Estación de Atocha (10 per day, 1 1/2 hr., 480ptas). No direct line to Avila (connection in Madrid) or Andalucía (connection in Algodor or Aranjuez, depending on destination).
>
> **Buses:** (tel. 21 58 50) in the Zona Safón, northeast of the old city walls. **Continental/Galiano** (tel. 22 29 61). To Madrid (12 per day, 1hr., 485ptas) and Cuenca (1 per day, 2 1/2 hr., 900ptas). Many other destinations.
>
> **Public Transportation:** Buses (60ptas). #5 and 6 stop to the right of the train station and inside the bus station and go to Pl. Zocodóver.
>
> **Taxis:** (tel. 22 23 96) C. Cuesta del Alcázar.

Car Rental: Avis, Po. Miradero (tel. 21 45 35), in an underground mall (Centro Comercial Miradero) downhill from Pl. Zocodóver.

Laundromat: Juan Pascual, C. Bolivia, 2 (tel. 22 16 03). Wash and dry 1000ptas per 5kg load. Open 9am-1:30pm and 4-8pm.

Red Cross: Ambulance, C. Moscardó, 6 (tel. 22 16 98).

Medical Services: Casa de Socorro (tel. 22 29 00), on C. General Moscardó, behind the Alcázar.

Emergency: tel. 091.

Police: Municipal, Ayuntamiento, 1 (tel. 23 34 07).

Accommodations and Camping

Finding a bed during summer weekends can be difficult. Arrive in the late morning or early afternoon when guests are checking out and rooms are more likely to be available. The tourist office provides a complete list of registered hotels and *hostales* with an address, phone number, capacity, and price for each establishment. Prices below, and basically across Toledo, include showers.

Residencia Juvenil "San Servando" (HI), Castillo San Servando (tel. 22 45 54), uphill on the left from the train station (15min.). A 14th-century castle. Pool, comfy TV room, and modern bathrooms. 96 rooms, each with 3 bunk beds, many with views. No toilet paper. Anyone returning alone at night should take a cab. Curfew around 12:30am. Reserve ahead; the hostel sometimes books large groups. 650 ptas. Breakfast included. *Pensión media* 950ptas. *Pensión completa* 1450ptas. Over 26: 750ptas; 1100ptas; 1600ptas.

Hostal Residencia Labrador, C. Juan Labrador, 16 (tel. 22 26 20). Almost a hotel, the three floors are rarely filled. Rooms are neat and whitewashed; some spacious, a few others with views of birds circling over south Toledo. Water somewhat rusty. 1992 brought construction to the surrounding area; if it's still going on you may be awakened bright and early. Singles 1590ptas, with shower 1860ptas. Doubles with shower 2650ptas, with bath 3180ptas. Triples with shower 3710ptas, with bath 4240ptas. Quadruples with bath 5300ptas.

Hostal Las Armas, C. Armas, 7 (tel. 22 16 68), just off the low end of Pl. Zocodóver. This two-hundred-year-old house, with low ceilings, narrow twisty steps, impossible angles, and flowering patio, is like an Escher print—or a mini Toledo. The rooms tend to be small and crepuscular, and those on the street can be noisy at night. Curfew 1am. Singles 1800ptas. Doubles 2800ptas. Open April 1-Oct. 31.

Posada del Estudiante, Callejón de San Pedro, 2 (tel. 21 47 34), just south of the cathedral. Not on the tourist office's list, which means they can't help you should you want to make a complaint—but it's unlikely that you would. The *posada* is in a repainted old building with a beer belly. Small rooms contain springy beds and baths. Singles with bath 1600ptas. Doubles with bath 2600ptas. Even neighborhood folks who aren't guests come for the *menú* (600ptas) served on the patio at high noon.

Pensión Descalzos, C. Descalzos, 30 (tel. 22 28 88), down the steps off Po. San Cristobal or down the Bajada Descalzos, in the southwest corner of town. One of the few places not near the cathedral or the Alcázar. Close to the Casa del Greco and Iglesia Santo Tomé (and bus lines #2 and #3). New and roomy, with luxe amenities such as soft toilet paper, liquid soap, and truly hot showers. Rooms at the back look out over San Marín's bridge. Singles 1875ptas. Doubles 3000ptas, with bath 4900ptas. Triples 6600ptas. Jan. 1-March 17: 1500ptas; 2500ptas, 4000ptas; 5400ptas.

Pensión Lumbreras, C. Juan Labrador, 9 (tel. 22 15 71), 2 bl. from Pl. Zocodóver, near Hostal-Residencia Labrador. Tired beds in unexceptional rooms, except for the ample triple. Singles 1300ptas. Doubles 2400ptas. Triples 3300ptas. Quadruples 4400ptas. Breakfast 175ptas.

Camping: Camping El Greco (tel. 22 00 90), 1 1/2 km from town on the road to Madrid (N-401). Wooded and shady 1st class site between the Tajo and an olive grove. 400ptas per person, per tent, and per car. **Circo Romano,** Av. Carlos III, 19 (tel. 22 04 42). 2nd class site. Closer but noisier, dirtier, and often in disrepair. 400ptas per person, per tent, and per car.

Food

Two-fork resaurants and not-so-cheap *cafeterías* abound; sleuth around. *Menús* may be pricey (1200-1600ptas or more) but supply well-prepared regional specialties such as *perdiz* (fowl), *cuchifritos* (a melange of sheep, eggs, tomato, and white wine), *vena-*

do (venison), and *carcamusas* (mystery dish). *Platos combinados* are the least expensive and the simplest, usually fried and salted.

> **Groceries: SPAR,** C. Sixto Ramon Parro, 5, opposite the rear southeast corner of the cathedral. This mini-supermarket sells fresh fruit and veggies, staples, and *bocadillos* at low prices. Open Mon.-Sat. 9am-2pm and 5-8pm. **Frutería-Pan,** C. Real Arrabal, inside the Puertas de Bisagra. Fresh fruit, basics, and water. Open same hours as SPAR.

> **Restaurante La Cubana,** Po. Rosa, 2 (tel. 22 00 88), across the river in front of Puente Viejo de Alcántara, down the road from the youth hostel. It's a coin-flipper—the wooded, tavern-like restaurant or the outdoor *terraza* with overhanging grapevines? *Gazpacho* (300ptas) and *pollo al ajillo* (garlic chicken, 550ptas). Open 1-4pm and 7:30-10:30pm.

> **Bar-Restaurante El Duende,** C. Descalzos, 10, on the intersection at the bottom of the stairs from Po. San Cristobal, near Pensión Descalzos. Settle into the small bright dining room decked out with brown and green wall tiles, El Greco prints, and expansive windows. There's also seating outside on the shady porch. *Menú* is high quality but expensive (2000ptas). Salads 400-500ptas. Meat and fish dishes 700-800ptas. Homemade *mazapán* (marzipan).

> **Restaurante-Bar Mariano,** Po. de Merchan (tel. 21 13 34), down the boulevard from Turismo. Indoor and outdoor seating. Scrumptious *platos combinados* 775-975ptas. Mountainous salad with eggs and tuna 650ptas. Open 1:30-3:45pm and 8:15-10:45pm.

> **Bar-Restaurante Bisagra,** C. Real del Arrabal, 14 (tel. 22 06 93), just within the Puerta de Bisagra, about 2 bl. from Turismo. A touch greasy, but way inexpensive. Privacy and tablecloths in the downstairs part. *Platos combinados* 375-750ptas. *Menú* 800ptas. Open Sun.-Fri. 1-4pm and 8-11:30pm.

Sights

Vestiges of circus, aqueduct, and sewer remain of the Roman settlement. Fortified walls, attributed to King Wamba (7th century), surround the city. There are seven gates: the **Puente de Alcántara** rebuilt in 1287 by Alfonso X; the Gothic **Puente de San Martín**; **Puerta del Sol,** a 14th-century Mudejar gate; **Puerta Vieja de Bisagra**; **Puerta Nueva de Bisagra,** rebuilt in 1550; **Puerta del Cambrón,** rebuilt in 1576; and **Puerta de Valmardón.** Within the walls, Toledo's major sights and attractions form a belt around its fat middle. An east to west tour, beginning in Pl. Zocodóver, is mostly downhill.

South and uphill from the plaza is the **Alcázar,** Toledo's most formidable landmark. Little remains of the original 13th-century structure; the building was largely reduced to rubble during the Civil War, as besieged Fascist troops held out against acute Republican bombardment. According to Falangist historians, the Republicans ordered Colonel Moscardó, the man in charge of the Alcázar, to surrender or lose his son. The Alcázar still exists and there's no evidence of Moscardó Jr. The alleged telephone conversation among the Republicans, Moscardó, and his son is posted in 19 languages in Moscardó's bullet-riddled office. You can visit the dark, windowless refuge where the five or six hundred civilians "lived" during the siege. The rooms above ground are now a slapdash, gung-ho, nationalistic military museum, dedicated to the arms, uniforms, and medals of the Spanish footsoldier. Another room contains a 19th-century English plant collection from Madeira. (Open Tues.-Sun. 9:30am-1:30pm and 4-6:30pm. Admission 125ptas.)

To the west, the grandiose **catedral,** with five naves, delicate stained glass, and endless ostentation throughout, soars from the city center. As the seat of the Primate of Spain, the opulent cathedral contains an embarrassment of riches. Noteworthy pieces are the 14th-century Gothic **Virgen Blanca** (White Virgin) by the entrance and, above all, Narciso Tomés' **Transparente** (1732), a fantastically flamboyant work of Spanish Baroque. Like Bernini's *St. Teresa,* this hybrid of architecture, sculpture, and painting uses much natural light. In the **Capilla Mayor** the enormous Gothic altarpiece stretches to the ceiling, slathered with whimsical carved decorations. Beneath the dome is the **Capilla Mozárabe,** the only venue where the ancient Visigothic mass (in Mozarabic) is still held. The **tesoro** flaunts the Church's worldly accoutrements, including a 400-

pound 16th-century gold monstrance lugged through the streets in the annual Corpus Christi procession. The **Sacristía** hoards El Grecos and two Van Dycks. In the **Sala Capitular** (chapter house), cool portraits of every archbishop of Toledo hang. (Cathedral open Mon.-Sat. 10:30am-1pm and 3:30-7pm, Sun. 10:30-1pm and 4-7pm; Sept.-June Mon.-Sat. 10:30am-1pm and 3:30-7:30pm, Sun. 10:30-1pm and 4-6pm. Admission to the Sala Capitular, Capilla del Rey, and Sacristía 300ptas.)

If you care, the Habsburg **Ayuntamiento** next door illustrates the High Spanish Renaissance style in alternating red brick and granite, slate roof, and elegant square corner towers.

Greek painter Domenico Theotocopuli, alias El Greco, was a *toledano* most of his life, painting wild skies and spindly saints in a warped version of Titian's palette. Many of his paintings never left Toledo. The **Casa del Greco** (House of El Greco), at C. Levi, 3, isn't really the house in which he lived. The museum has an okay group of paintings, including a copy of *Vista y Mapa de Toledo* (View and Map of Toledo) and many hagioportraits. (Open Tues.-Sat. 10am-2pm and 4-6pm, Sun. 10am-2pm. Admission 250ptas.) If you're hankering for some more, the nearby **Iglesia de Santo Tomeé** displays El Greco's *El Entierro del Conde de Orgaz* (The Burial of Count Orgaz). (Open Tues.-Sat. 10am-1:45pm and 3:30-6:45pm, Sun. 10am-1:45pm; off-season Tues.-Sat. 10am-2pm and 3:30-6pm, Sun. 10am-1:45pm. Admission 100ptas.)

Toledo fell to Alfonso VI in 1085; thereafter followed a brilliant flowering of Jewish culture known as its Golden Age, a period when Spain's Christian monarchs so graciously tolerated the religious practices of Muslim and Jewish subjects. Two synagogues are all that remain of what was once Spain's largest Jewish community, both in the Judería on the west side. Samuel Halevi, treasurer to Pedro el Cruel, built the **Sinagoga del Tránsito** (1366), a simple building with wonderful Mudejar plasterwork and an *artesonado* (coffered) ceiling. Manuscripts, lids of sarcophagi, inscriptions, and amulets stuff themselves into the **Museo Sefardí,** inside the synagogue. (Open Tues.-Sat. 10am-2pm and 4-6pm, Sun. 10am-2pm. Admission 200ptas.) **Sinagoga de Santa María la Blanca** (1180), down the street, was the city's principal synagogue, but was later converted to a church. Now the mosque-like building makes a calm antidote to the excess of the cathedral. (Open 10am-2pm and 3:30-7pm; off-season 10am-2pm and 3:30-6pm. Admission 100ptas.)

At the far western bulge of the city, with views of surrounding hills and the Río Tajo, Fernando and Isabel built the Plateresque **Monasterio de San Juan de los Reyes** to commemorate their victory over the Portuguese in 1476. Although they originally intended it as their burial place, the fickle monarchs changed their minds in 1492. Their initials adorn the *artesonado* ceiling of the delightful light-filled cloister. (Open 10am-2pm and 3:30-7pm; off-season 10am-2pm and 3:30-6pm. Admission 100ptas.)

Less touristed are the remnants of the city's Islamic past, near the Puerta del Sol off C. Real de Arrabal. Both a Muslim and a Christian house of worship at different points in its life, the **Mezquita del Cristo de la Luz** is Toledo's only extra-extra-old building (it's been around since the 10th century). The columns support arches inspired by the mosque at Córdoba. The Emirate was also responsible for the **hammams** (baths) on C. Angel.

Outside handsome Puerta Nueva de Bisagra on the road to Madrid is the 16th-century **Hospital de Tavera,** now a private museum with five El Grecos, including the marvelous *Sagrada Familia* (he married the woman who modeled the Virgin Mary). There are also some Titians—the *Portrait of Carlos V* rules the dining room. The museum was once the swish home of the Dukes of Lerma; a portrait of the last one (executed in the Civil War) eyes the gift shop. (Open 10:30am-1:30pm and 3:30-6pm. Admission 250ptas.)

One of the finest and least visited museums is the **Museo de Santa Cruz,** M. Cervantes, 3 (tel. 22 10 36), off Pl. Zocodóver. Its holdings are first-rate. The huge, 15th-century Flemish *Astrolabio* tapestry of the zodiac pleases practicing astrologers. The well-preserved patio is littered with sarcophagi lids and fragments of carved stone. Down below, the basement collects the remains from archaeological digs throughout Toledo province, including elephant tusks. (Open Tues.-Sat. 10am-6:30pm, Sun. 10am-2pm, Mon. 10am-2pm and 4:30-6:30pm. Admission 200ptas, students free.)

Toledo was the seat of Visigothic rule and culture for three centuries prior to the Muslim invasion of 711. The **Museo de los Concilios y de la Cultura Visigótica,** C. San Clemente, 3, is set in a 13th-century Mudejar church where the exhibits can't possibly compete with the surrounding architecture and frescoes. The delicious votive crowns of the Visigoths give lovers of finery a buzz. (Open Tues.-Sat. 10am-2pm and 4-6:30pm, Sun. 10am-2pm. Admission 100ptas includes **Museo del Taller del Moro** (carved woodwork and *azulejos*) on street of same name, by Iglesia de Santo Tomé, and **Museo de Arte Contemporáneo,** on C. Bulas.) All three museums are in the relatively serene southwestern quarter of the city.

Entertainment

El Martes, the outdoor market, shakes every Tuesday (9am-1:30pm) in the shaded area behind the Convento de los Concepcionistas, east of Pl. Zocodóver. You can buy cheap clothing and food to go here, but no fruits or vegetables. The best area for the city's trademark gold-and-black **damascene** trinkets is C. San Juan de Dios, by the Iglesia de Santo Tomé. The owners of the small shops lining this street are aggressive but willing to haggle. Quality varies. Since most nightspots cater to tourists, local nightlife tends to wander down side streets and get lost.

Calle de Santa Fe, east of Pl. Zocodóver, through the arch. Congregations of young people scarf *tapas* and gulp beer along this street; try **Café-Bar Trebol.**

Calle de la Sillería, west of Pl. Zocodóver. Another popular area for hedonizers. **T Beo,** Callejón de la Sillería (just off C. Sillería), is popular for dancing.

Calle de los Alfileritos, the continuation of C. Sillería. Several upscale bars and clubs here, such as the new double-decker **Kaya Bar.**

Calle de la Sinagoga, north of the cathedral. Some nightlife here. For bowling and beer, try the **Pub-Bolera.**

Zaida, in the Centro Comercial Miradero downhill on C. Armas from Pl. Zocodóver. A perennial hotspot with dancing.

Corpus Christi, celebrated the eighth Sunday after Easter, is an excuse to feast. Looking like they just stepped out of an El Greco, citizens parade through the streets alongside the cathedral's weighty gold monstrance. In the middle of August, the **Fiestas de Agosto** honor of the Virgen del Sagrario.

Near Toledo

Most towns in La Mancha are accessible by bus from Toledo, but schedules tend to cater to people travelling into Toledo rather than tourists visiting smaller towns in the region. Inconvenient bus departure times may force you to spend a night where you only want to stay several hours. For greater flexibility, rent a car and use Toledo as a base for excursions into this region.

Cervantes freaks come to La Mancha to follow his footsteps and those of his most famous creations, Don Quijote and the faithful Sancho Panza. Cervantes met and married Catalina de Palacios in the main church in **Esquivias** in 1584. Legend has it that he began writing his masterpiece while imprisoned in the Cueva del Medrano, in the town of **Argamasilla de Alba.** It was in **El Toboso,** 100km southeast of Toledo, that the noble Quijote fell in love with Dulcinea. A dementia worthy of the Don himself has led to the establishment of a house, the **Museo de Amor,** C. José Antonio (tel. 19 72 88), which pretends to mark the spot where Cervantes first glimpsed Dulcinea. All it contains is a bunch of old housewares. (Open Tues.-Sun. 10am-2pm and 4-6:30pm. Admission 100ptas.)

Of all Manchegan villages, tiny **Consuegra** has perhaps the most raw material for an evocation of Quijote's world. The **castle** is called the "Crestería Manchega" by locals. Now partly in ruins, it was a Roman, then Arab, then Christian fortress. El Cid's only son, Diego, died in the stable. The castle keeps erratic hours, but the view of the surrounding plains justifies a climb anytime. Consuegra's **post office** is at C. Florinda, 5, in the town center. (Open Mon.-Fri. 9am-2pm; in winter Mon.-Fri. 9am-2pm, Sat. 9am-1pm.) In case of **medical emergency,** dial 48 13 12. The municipal **police** station is at Pl. España, 1 (tel. 48 10 05, 48 09 11).

Consuegra is an easy daytrip from Toledo. Samar **buses** (tel. 22 39 15) depart from Toledo's Zona Safón (4 per day, 410ptas, just across the Puente de Azarquiel near the train station). Returning to Toledo, buses take off from C. Castilla de la Mancha (4 per day). Purchase tickets from the driver. Alcázar de San Juan is the primary junction for southbound trains from Madrid.

Almagro

A walking tour of Almagro takes under an hour, but its blend of blinding whitewashed walls, once-great churches, and a major theater festival makes for a pungent brew. In the 13th century, this tiny Castilian town became the seat of the vast and powerful **Orden de Calatrava,** the oldest of the fraternities of monks-turned-soldiers (see Tomar: Knights Templar) that fueled the Reconquista. Built in 1519, the **Convento de la Asunción de Calatrava** testifies to the order's immense power, wealth, and cabalistic machinations. (Cloister open Mon.-Sat. 9am-1:30pm and 3:30-7pm, Sun. 8am-12:30pm. Church open Sun. for mass and unofficially some evenings after 6pm.)

More striking is the **Plaza Mayor,** whose unusual dark trim, streamlined balconies and windows, and squat proportions are due to German influence transmitted by the Fuggers, Emperor Carlos V's bankers, who made Almagro one of their bases of operation in the early 16th century.

On the plaza stands Almagro's biggest deal, the **Corral de Comedias,** a miraculous open-air multilevel theater, one of only two left from the Golden Age of Spanish drama (see Alcalá de Henares). Every July the city celebrates its heritage with the **Festival Internacional de Teatro Clasico de Almagro,** in which Spain's most prestigious theater companies and players from around the globe perform Calderón de la Barca, Lope de Vega, Alarcón, Tirso de Molino, et al. The box office is a few doors away at Pl. Mayor, 22 (tel. 86 07 17). (Theater open during the festival 10am-2pm and 5-10:30pm. Shows at 10:45pm. Admission 1000ptas.) For the academic in you, the festival also sponsors a series of conferences and lectures on Spanish classical theater.

Directly across the plaza from the Corral and through the arches, the new **Museo del Teatro** acts out the story of Spanish drama, including the famous rivalry between Cervantes and Lope de Vega. It focuses on costume design, stage design and technology, other theatrical arts, original manuscripts, and scores for incidental music. (Open Tues.-Sat. 10am-2pm and 6-9pm, Sun. 11am-2pm. Free.)

Most spendthrifts stay at the ever-pricey **Parador Nacional,** C. San Francisco, inside 16th-century Iglesia de Santa Catalina. For poor people, small, clean rooms are available at **Fonda San Bartolomé,** to the right of the plaza's open end and under the blue "F" sign. (850ptas per person. Showers included. Meals 650ptas.) **Bar-Restaurante Ches,** Pl. Mayor, 41, serves hefty *platos combinados* (450-950ptas; open noon-4pm and 8:30pm-midnight). Most restaurants lie around Pl. Mayor or on the Ronda.

The **tourist office** is at C. Mayor de Carnicerías (tel. 86 07 17); the **Ayuntamiento** (tel. 86 00 46) also helps on Pl. Mayor opposite the statue. The **post office** sends letters from C. José Antonio, 2 blocks from Pl. Mayor. (Open Mon.-Fri. 9am-1pm.) The **telephone code** is 926. The **police** (tel. 86 00 33) are in the same building. In an **emergency,** call 091.

The RENFE **train station** (tel. 86 02 76) lies about 1km from the center, on the tree-lined walkway off C. Caudillo Franco. Trains to Madrid (8 per day, 2 3/4 hr., 1250ptas) and Alicant (1 per day, 2070ptas). Bar El Pescador (tel. 86 08 96) sells **bus** tickets. Two per day travel to Madrid and four per day to Ciudad Real.

Cuenca

Cuenca's vertical landscape assaults the eye. Dramatic cliffs drop to swift-flowing rivers on three sides, and mountains protect the fourth. To compensate for the lack of space, buildings crowd close, expand upward, and actually hang over the clifftops. More concerned with safety than security, modern-day Cuenca has overflowed its hill to trickle, like the Río Huécar, into the valley below. The new city is the site of cheap accommodations and food, but the old city remains the stronghold of Cuenca's charm; its narrow alleyways, still uncluttered by giftshops, are home to fabulous museums.

Orientation and Practical Information

To reach the center of the **ciudad nueva** from the RENFE station, or from the nearby bus station, turn left and follow the signs a few blocks to the Plaza del Generalísimo. From here you have a choice. 1) Carry on down Avenida de José Antonio and bear right at the next plaza (but don't take the street at right angles) to begin a grueling uphill walk to the **ciudad vieja.** 2) Leap on bus #1 to **Plaza Mayor** (every 1/2 hr., 75ptas). All bus stops post clearly marked signs and maps of Cuenca.

Tourist Office: C. Dalmacio García Izcara, 8 (tel. 22 22 31), 2 bl. to the left of the train station exit. No English spoken. They give out a glossy *Castilla-La Mancha* book. Open Mon.-Fri. 9am-2pm and 4:30-6:30pm, Sat. 10am-1pm.

Post Office: Parque de San Julián, 18 (tel. 22 40 16; telegrams 22 20 00). Open for stamps Mon.-Fri. 9am-2pm and 4-6pm, Sat. 9am-2pm; for **telegrams** Mon.-Fri. 8am-10pm, Sat.-Sun. 8am-8pm. **Postal Code:** 16000.

Telephones: C. Cervantes, 2, near Pl. Generalísimo. Open Mon.-Sat. 9am-1pm and 5-10:30pm. **Telephone Code:** 966.

Trains: Av. Estación, in the new city. To: Madrid (8 per day, 2 1/2 -3hr., 1230ptas); València (5 per day, 2 3/4 -3 3/4 hr., 850ptas); Toledo (1 per day, 3hr., 955ptas); Aranjuez (760ptas).

Buses: C.Fermín Caballero, s/n (tel. 22 11 84). Look for the orange canopy. To: Madrid (4 per day, 2 1/2 hr., 1135ptas); València (4 per day, 4 1/2 hr., 1400ptas); Barcelona (2 per day, 7hr., 3560ptas).

Car Rental: Avis (tel. 22 51 39), 2km from the train station away from the city center.

Hospital: Residencia Sanitaria Virgen de la Luz, Ctra. de Madrid, km 81 (tel. 22 42 11.)

Emergency: tel. 091.

Police: C. Martínez Kleiser, 4 (tel. 22 48 59).

Accommodations

Rooms in the new city are inexpensive, but not particularly memorable. It might be worth it to spend more money for a night on the hill, where views of the old town and the gorge are spectacular.

Hostal Residencia Posada de San José, C. Julián Romero, 4 (tel. 21 13 00), just up the street from the cathedral. The cheapest lodging on the hill in a lovely 17th-century house that looks out over the cliff. Spotless rooms with charming old furniture. Those with bath flaunt sunny terraces and views of the Puente de San Pablo. Cozy bar hosts literary *tertulias* (salons) every 2nd and last Fri. of the month. Anybody can participate (6-10:30pm). Singles 1900ptas, with shower 3300ptas. Doubles 3300ptas, with shower 5500ptas, with bath 6250ptas. Triples 4650ptas, with bath 7450ptas. One quad with bath 8800ptas. Nov. 1-April 30: 1600ptas, 3000ptas; 3000ptas, 5000ptas, 5350ptas; 4150ptas, 6800ptas; 8200ptas. Make reservations by phone at least 3 wks. in advance.

Fonda La Mota, Pl. Calvo Sotelo, 7 (tel. 22 55 67), the next plaza after Pl. Generalísimo coming from the train station. Clean but plain rooms in a modern office building. Singles 1100ptas. Doubles 1900ptas. Showers 100ptas. Generous *menú* on weekdays 650ptas.

Pensión Cuenca, Av. República Argentina, 8 (tel. 21 25 74). Take Hurtado de Mendoza from the train or bus station. One of several cheap *hostales* and *pensiones* in the area. Two-star *pensión* with countless rooms. New furniture, mattresses, and tile floors. Singles 1200ptas, with shower 1650ptas. Doubles 2100ptas, with shower 3200ptas. Showers 300ptas.

Food

Cuenca's budget restaurants are mediocre. A few places still dish out *zorajo* (lamb tripe), a rare regional specialty. Budget food lines **Calle Cervantes** and **Calle República Argentina**. Some of the *terrazas* on **Plaza Mayor** are reasonable for drinks (beer 150ptas) and *tapas* (100-250ptas). The morning **market** is held in Pl. Carros, behind the post office.

> **Groceries: Día,** C. División Azul, on the corner with Hurtado de Mendoza. Open Mon.-Sat. 9:30am-2pm and 5:30-8:30pm.
>
> **Mesón-Bar Tabanqueta,** Pl. Trabuco, 13, at the end of C. San Pedro coming from Pl. Mayor. The hidden entrance keeps this place from getting too crowded. Classy little *mesón* offers diners and snackers a terrific view of the Río Júcar gorge. Avoid the *menú del día* (1900ptas) in favor of the simply-prepared entrees (350-600ptas). *Ensalada manchega* means chunks of tomato, egg, and tuna with olives. Open noon-1am.
>
> **Restaurante Cueva del Tío Serafín,** in a cave across from Hoz de Huécar and Posada Huécar, with a lair-like interior to match.
>
> **Bar-Restaurante San Miguel,** at the foot of the stairs leading down toward Río Júcar from Pl. Mayor opposite the cathedral; next to Iglesia de San Pablo. Crepuscular and cramped inside, delightful terrace outside. Eye the Júcar, the town below, and the ridge across while snarfing a tortilla (300ptas) or two. Fish and meat entrees 400-700ptas. Open noon-late. (See Entertainment below.)

Sights and Entertainment

The **ciudad vieja** dodders beneath covered arcades set back from the steep cliffs. The 18th-century **Ayuntamiento** is built into a Baroque arch at the plaza's southern end, while the recently abluted **catedral** dominates the other side. Alfonso VIII of Castille ordered the cathedral six years after he conquered Castille (1183). Under the spell of the king's English wife, Eleanor of Aquitaine, the architects built what would become the only Anglo-Norman Gothic cathedral in Spain. A Spanish Renaissance façade and tower were added in the 16th and 17th centuries, only to be torn down once deemed inappropriate. In 1724, fire cut short the latest attempt to build a front, leaving the current exterior incomplete, though still attractive. (Open 9am-1:30pm and 4:30-7:30pm. Free.)

Inside the **Museo del tesoro** are some late medieval psalters and a great deal of gold jewelry, but more impressive is the Sala Capitular and its positively edible ceiling, through which you pass en route. (Open 11am-2pm and 4-6pm. 150ptas.)

Down C. Obispo, the **casas colgadas** (hanging houses)—possibly summer retreats for royalty—dangle over the riverbanks as precariously today as they did six centuries ago. In his memoirs Buñuel recalls a pre-war visit to Cuenca in which he spied wheeling birds beneath his toilet seat in one of these houses. The footbridge 60m above the river affords a grand view of the old houses huddling high on the cliffs, the new city spreading into the green fields beyond, and the waters rushing beneath. Many good hiking trails etch the hill and stone cliffs opposite the old city and footbridge. Bring sturdy shoes and food unless you want to fall or starve.

Inside one of the *casas* at Pl. Ciudad de Ronda, the award-winning **Museo de Arte Abstracto Español** displays important works by the weird and internationally known "Abstract Generation" of Spanish painters. Artist Fernando Zóbel donated his own house to the project, which now hoards canvases by himself, Canogar, Tápies (of Poliscar patronage fame), and Chillida. The museum is exceptionally attractive, with small and rambling whitewashed rooms and some bare rafters. (Open Tues.-Fri. 11am-2pm and 4-6pm, Sat. 11am-2pm and 4-8pm, Sun. 11am-2pm. Admission 200ptas, students 100ptas.)

Nearby on C. Obispo Valero, the **Museo Municipal** has a wide range of Roman mosaics, ceramics, coins, and other finds from local excavations, such as some excellent Visigoths' jewelry. (Open Tues.-Sat. 10am-2pm and 5-7pm, Sun. 10am-2pm. Admission 200ptas, EEC citizens free.) Perhaps the most beautiful of the museums along this short street is the **Museo Diocesano.** Its exhibits are imaginatively displayed and include Juan de Borgoña's *retablo* from local Convento de San Pablo; many colossal Flemish tapestries; and two El Grecos, the *Oración del Huerto* and *Cristo con la Cruz.*

Walking along either of the two roads that surround the old part of Cuenca (**Hoz del Júcar** or preferably **Hoz del Huécar**) is so much fun! The best view of the valley is from the side of Hoz del Huecar opposite the *casas colgadas.* To get there, dash across the terrifying Puente de San Pablo, whose wooden beams are beginning to wobble just a little too much. Be careful if you cross.

Nightlife in new Cuenca centers on bars and extends into the wee hours. Several progressive bars with loud music and a young, snazzily dressed crowd line small **Calle Galindez,** off C. Fray Luís de León. For nightclubs, just off Pl. Mayor across from the cathedral, take the winding street/staircase down toward the Río Júcar. Three new spectacularly situated clubs (**El Tunéz, Vay Vaya, Rothus Sala-Bar**) line the descent.

Cuenca rings with song during the **Festival de Música Sagrada.** This famous celebration takes place during Holy Week and has hosted the world premieres of several Spanish and international groups.

Guadalajara

The provincial capital of Guadalajara takes a drag of its industrial neighbor, inhales *madrileños* for the weekend, exhales, and sends them shuffling back with its own residents for the business week. Over the past 10 years, a constant traffic cycle has developed between the two cities. Tourists usually join the 55km trek to partake of the Castilian town's relaxed atmosphere. Although the outskirts are heavily industrialized and ugly, the old city center and monuments breathe crisp air on a hill above.

From the RENFE train station, 1 1/2 mi. from the action, take buses #1, 2, or 4. Alternatively, walk for 20 uninteresting minutes down the Paseo de la Estación, over the river, and straight uphill; Po. Estación becomes Calle de Madrid, and then Calle Miguel Fluiters, which runs into the **Plaza de los Caídos en la Guerra Civil.**

Here in the plaza is Guadalajara's central sight, the **Palacio del Infantado,** built in 1480 by Flemish architect Juan Guas. Somber, fat-lipped Felipe II married his third of four wives, Elizabeth Valois, in the palace. The building was seriously damaged by Civil War bombing, but the filigree masonry of the principal door survives (note the rampant griffins and the coats of arms of two great Castilian families, the Mendoza and the Luna, left and right respectively) as does the ornate Patio de los Leones. Inside, the **Museo Provincial de Guadalajara** has a collection of largely anonymous paintings from the 15th-17th centuries. The ethnographic section of the museum has been and will be closed for several years due to flooding. (Open Tues.-Sat. 10:15am-2pm and 4-7pm, Sun. 10:15am-2pm. Admission 100ptas, free with ISIC.)

Iglesia de San Nicolás el Real, in Pl. Jardinillo, is embellished with a magnificent Rococo altar. **Iglesia de San Ginés,** on C. Virgen del Amparo, has a Gothic pantheon, where Guadalajara's once-dominant Infantado and Mendoza families mingle in postmortem subterranean harmony. The solitary **Panteón de La Duquesa** haunts a field above the town, on Po. Francisco Aritmendi by **Parque del San Roque.** To enter this Byzantine-style rotunda, ask the nuns at the *portería* reception of the adjacent Convento de San Francisco; the door is in the far corner of the yard opposite the locked gate. Inside the pantheon are a great many vast blocks of marble (crafted, as the nuns will tell you several times, by men's hands, not by machines). The **tombs of the duchess** and her family, are in the cavernous space below. (Open 10am-12:30pm and 4-6pm. Admission 100ptas.)

Inexpensive accommodations are plentiful even on weekends. **Pensión Galicia,** C. San Roque, 16 (tel. 20 00 59) has decent bathrooms and antiseptic rooms. (Doubles 2100ptas, with bath 3000ptas.) In **Hostal España,** C. Teniente Figueroa, 3 (tel. 21 13 03), small beds squeal; but the rooms are large and clean, some have nice views, and all have toilets. (Singles 1700ptas, with bath 2700ptas. Doubles 3000ptas, with shower 3800ptas. Breakfast 300ptas.)

The bars here are masters of budget cuisine. **Bar Soria**, on the corner of C. Miguel Fluiters and C. Teniente Figueroa, serves *tapas*. *Patatas bravas* (baked potato slices in a spicy orange sauce) 225ptas. *Boquerones fritos* (fried smelts) 450ptas. **Terraza San Roque,** bordering Parque de San Roque, is an ideal spot for an *al fresco* drink (beer 150ptas).

The **tourist office** (tel. 22 06 98) occupies the Ayuntamiento in Pl. Mayor, one block up from Pl. Caídos. (Open Mon.-Fri. 9am-3pm and 4-6pm, Sat. 10am-1pm.) The **post office** is at C. Teniente Figueroa, 5 (tel. 21 14 93), and the **telephone code** is 911. For medical oddities contact the **Red Cross,** Av. de Venezuela, 1 (tel. 22 62 12, 22 11 84). In **emergency** dial 091 or 092. For **police**, dial 21 51 11.

The **train station** (tel. 21 13 42) is on C. Francisco Aritio. Frequent service to Madrid (340ptas). The Continental-Auto **bus station** is at C. 2 de Mayo, 1 (tel. 21 14 21). Buses leave every hour for Madrid (410ptas).

Sigüenza

Sleepy Sigüenza tumbles down a gentle slope halfway between Madrid and Zaragoza; its pink stone buildings cluster around a cathedral with the attitude of a hilltop citadel. Sigüenza's role as a rail junction hasn't spoilt the wonderful harmony of its architecture, and the damage inflicted on it during the Civil War has been painstakingly reversed.

Work on the **catedral** began in the mid-12th century and continued until 1495; the building ranges through Romanesque, Mudejar, and Plateresque styles. Its most renowned possession is the 15th-century **Tumba del Donzel,** commissioned by Isabel la Católica in memory of a favorite page who died fighting the Muslims in Granada; the young man lies, immortalized, happily reading a book. Across the nave in the Capilla Mayor, is the tomb of Archbishop Bernardo of Toledo, the first bishop of Sigüenza. Three hundred and four stone heads, each supposedly a real-life portrait from life, jut out of the **sacristy's** bizarre Renaissance ceiling. The staring faces include pious bishops, uppity soldiers, and local women. Nearby there's an El Greco *Anunciación.* Just off the **cloister,** one room is hung with Flemish tapestries and houses an assortment of documents from the cathedral archives, including a 13th-century codex. Free spirits and loners are frowned upon here; the people who control the place restrict visits to the Donzel tomb, sacristy, and cloister to small guided groups. (Cathedral open 11:30am-1:30pm and 4-7pm. Tour in Spanish 200ptas.)

Opposite the cathedral, the small **Museo de Arte Antiguo** exhibits medieval and early modern religious works, most of them unmemorable. The highlight is Zurbarán's rather weak *Inmaculada.* There are also some 16th-century *retablos* and a couple of charming Mudejar boxes. (Open 11am-2pm and 5-7:30pm; Sept.-May 11am-2pm and 4-6:30pm. Admission 200ptas.) From the lovely Plaza Mayor, a cobblestoned street with most photogenic views of the town leads up towards the **castillo.** This castle is a reconstruction of a 12th-century castle, now a *parador* not open to the public.

In town, the **Hostal San Verancio,** Barrio San Roque, is reasonably clean, if a bit shopworn. There's no hot water in the rooms. (Singles 1500ptas. Doubles 2800ptas.) For a basic *menú* (850ptas) and a mouthwatering variety of ice cream, try the **Restaurante El Motor,** C. Calvo Sotelo, 2 (tel. 39 00 88), on the street marked as C. Humilladero on the tourist map.

The **tourist office,** Pl. Obispo San Bernardo, s/n (tel. 39 12 62), is just down the street to the right when facing the Museo de Arte Antiguo. The **Red Cross** is on Ctra. Madrid (tel. 39 13 33). The **police** (tel. 39 01 95), on the Carreterra de Alcolea-Aranda de Duero, can be reached at 091 in an **emergency**. The town center is an uphill walk from the **train station**. Follow Av. Alfonso VI, then take the first left (C. Cardenal Mendoza).

Castilla y León

In the High Middle Ages, this Christian kingdom emerged from obscurity to lead the battle charge against Islam. The nobility grew immensely wealthy as it seized more and more land; and well before the famous union with Aragón in 1492, it was clear that Castilla had the whip in hand. The concept of a unified Spain—under Castilian command—took root here, and *castellano* (called simply "Spanish" by foreigners) became the dominant language throughout Spain. At the turn of this century, the "Generation of '98," a group of writers and intellectuals discouraged by defeat in the Spanish-American War, turned to Castilla's landscape and rich traditions for inspiration. Between the imperial hauteur of Castilla and the provincial pride of León, the region overflows with ego.

Green and rolling León (the provinces of León, Zamora, and Salamanca) still crows that it had 24 kings before Castilla even had laws. When Spain's provinces were reorganized earlier in this century, León was lumped with Castilla, an act that still upsets many *leoneses*. The vast rippled plateau of Castilla possesses its own landlocked beauty, rough and intense. The plateau is broken only by a few mountain ranges, of which the most striking is the Sierra de Guadarrama. This area of Castilla was historically known as Castilla La Vieja, counterpart to Castilla La Nueva to the south. (see Castilla-La Mancha). Farmland, acres of primeval woods rich in game, and even more of it sheer wilderness, this region's landscape is studded with splendid cathedrals, sumptuous palaces, and well-defined urban personalities. The majestic Gothic cathedrals of Burgos and León; the slender Romanesque belfries along the Camino de Santiago in León; the warm, intricately chased sandstone of Salamanca; and the proud city walls of Avila emblazon themselves as images not only of Castilla and León but also of all Spain.

Sopa castellana is a soup made with garlic bread, ham, and eggs. Castilian-style *gazpacho* has more of a tomato base, is thicker, and is stocked more heavily with vegetables than the *andaluz* original. Beef, ham, potatoes, chorizo, carrots, and garlic stewed together is called *Cocido castellano*. Both pork and mutton are popular in Castilla and are prepared in various succulent dishes, while potatoes form the base of many a home-cooked meal. Belgian waffles (*gofres belgas*) have inexplicably taken the entire region by storm.

Segovia

Rising majestically above the Castilian countryside, the old city of Segovia proffers beautiful golden churches, twisting alleyways, and a people fiercely proud of their city and province. The city was such a prominent a part of the Roman Empire that it had its very own aqueduct and city mint. Things looked even brighter with the Reconquista; in the early 15th century, Juan II and Enrique IV, kings of the House of Trastámara, established courts here and littered the town with new monuments.

Segovia's overweening pride proved its Achilles heel. After headstrong local nobles and merchants clashed with Emperor Carlos V during the Revolt of the Comuneros (1520), it fell into decline until the Bourbons built the Palacio de La Granja nearby. Today its tourist appeal is slightly sterilized by self-satisfaction and commercialization.

Orientation and Practical Information

On the far side of the Sierra de Guadarrama, 88km northwest of Madrid, Segovia is close enough for a daytrip. Most people stay more than a day; it's not possible to do justice to the sights and the Palacio de la Granja in a lightning visit.

To get to the tourist office from the bus or train station, take bus #3 (every 15min., 85ptas) to **Plaza Mayor** (Plaza de Franco on maps), next to the cathedral. Only masochists would contemplate the mountainous walk from the train station. If you're one of the privileged berserk, follow Po. Conde de Sepúlveda and turn right onto Av.

Fernández Ladreda once you see the bus station. This avenue leads past the Iglesia San Millán to **Plaza Azoquejo,** where you'll see the aqueduct. Take a sharp left and follow the street to the top of the hill, the Plaza Mayor (30min.). From the bus station, cross the road onto Av. Fernández Ladreda and follow the directions above (15min.).

The city is nearly impossible to navigate without a map. The old city, high up above the newer *barrios,* is loosely triangular in shape, with the Alcázar at its northern tip and the Pl. Mayor dead center. Running between here and Pl. Azoquejo is the busy pedestrian thoroughfare, **Calle Isabel la Católica—Calle Juan Bravo—Calle Cervantes,** where all the world and its dog promenades.

Tourist Office: Pl. Mayor, 10 (tel. 43 03 28), in front of the bus stop, on the south side of the plaza. Complete information on accommodations, bus, train, and sights posted in the windows. Helpful staff. Open Mon.-Fri. 9am-2pm and 4:30-7:30pm, Sat. 10am-2pm; Oct. to mid-June Mon.-Fri. 9am-2pm, Sat. 10am-2pm. If still closed for repairs, go to the **temporary office**, C. Infanta Isabel, 16, around the corner and to the right. Same services.

Post Office: Pl. Dr. Laguna, 5 (tel. 43 16 11), up C. Lecea from Pl. Mayor. Open Mon.-Fri. 9am-2pm and 4-6pm, Sat. 9am-2pm; for Lista de Correos Mon.-Sat. 9am-2pm; for **telegrams** Mon.-Fri. 8am-9pm. **Postal Code:** 40006.

Telephones: C. Juan Bravo, 6. Three deluxe booths in an office within the shopping mall. **Telephone Code:** 911.

Trains: Po. Obispo Quesada (tel. 42 07 74). To Valladolid (2 per day, 2hr., 660ptas) and Madrid (10 per day, 2hr., 515ptas). For Salamanca, change at Medina del Campo, on line to Valladolid. For El Escorial or Avila, change at Villalba, on line to Madrid.

Buses: Estacionamiento Municipal de Autobuses, Po. Ezequile González, 10 (tel. 42 77 25), on Po. Conde de Sepúlveda at Av. Fernández Ladreda. To: La Granja (11 per day, 20min., 90ptas); Avila (3 per day, 1 1/2 hr., 485ptas); Madrid (9 per day, 1 3/4 hr., 655ptas); Valladolid (4 per day, 2 1/2 hr., 670ptas).

Public Transportation: Buses 85ptas. #3 from train and bus stations to Pl. Mayor (every 15min.).

Taxis: Pl. Mayor (tel. 43 66 81), Pl. Azoquejo (tel. 43 66 81), and train station (tel. 43 66 66).

Luggage Storage: At the **train station** (300ptas per checked bag). Open 5:45am-11:30pm.

Skiing: La Pinilla (winter tel. 55 03 04), accessible via the Madrid-Burgos RENFE train (stop at Riaza) or La Castellana buses (4 per day, 380ptas). Segovia province's ski station. Ski rentals, lift tickets, tennis courts, and low-priced *hostales.*

Red Cross: Casa de Socorro, C. Arias Dávila, 3 (tel. 43 41 41).

Medical Services: Hospital de la Misericordia, Dr. Velasco, 3 (tel. 43 08 12). **Ambulance** (tel. 43 01 00).

Police: Municipal (day tel. 42 12 12; night tel. 43 12 12).

Accommodations and Camping

During the summer finding a *hostal* room may be a nightmare; reservations are vitally important. You may want to consider visiting Segovia as a daytrip. The tourist office posts a list of accommodations in its window, some of which are expensive.

Hostal Juan Bravo, C. Juan Bravo, 12 (tel. 43 55 21), right on the main thoroughfare in the old town, near Iglesia de San Martín. Large rooms serve as spacious doubles or decent triples. Balconied street front-rooms perfect for water balloon enthusiasts. Clean sheets and sparkling bathrooms. Doubles 3000ptas, with bath 3900ptas. Triples 4050ptas, with bath 5245ptas. Quadruples possible if you say pretty please.

Hostal-Residencia El Postigo, Pl. Seminario, 2 (tel. 43 66 33), the stark modern building next to the police station. May be completely booked for days in summer. Singles with shower 1800ptas. Doubles with bath 2500ptas. Breakfast 250ptas. Dinner 680ptas. *Pensión completa* 1480ptas.

Casa de Huéspedes Cubo, Pl. Mayor, 4, 2nd fl. (tel. 43 63 86). Terrific location. Two windowless doubles the size of a raisin. 900ptas per person. Hot showers 150ptas.

Casa de Huéspedes Aragón, Pl. Mayor, 4, 1st fl. (tel. 43 35 27). Remarkably akin to the place upstairs. One single 1000ptas. One double 1700ptas. One triple 2000ptas. Hot showers (and hot water) 200ptas. No reservations accepted.

Hostal Sol Cristina, C. Obispo Quesada, 40 (tel. 42 75 13), opposite the train station. Convenient. Don't expect a warm welcome or peace and quiet (the *hostal* is connected to a bar-restaurant). Plain and cramped rooms barely hold a bed. Singles 2000ptas. Doubles 3000ptas, with bath 4000ptas. Triples with bath 5000ptas. Showers 350ptas. Breakfast 250ptas. *Pensión completa* 1742ptas.

Camping Acueducto, Ctra. Nacional, 601 (tel. 42 50 00), 2km from Segovia toward La Granja. 2nd-class site in the shadow of the Sierra de Guadarrama. 360ptas per person and per tent. Children 320ptas. Open June-Sept.

Food

Culinary ecstasy comes at a price. Basically, steer clear of Pl. Mayor and Pl: Azoquejo and of signs that simulate ancient, worn parchment. Segovia is famed for sublimely tender roast suckling pig (*cochinillo*) and lamb.

Groceries: At the end of C. Isabel la Católica. Open Mon.-Fri. 10am-2pm and 4-7pm, Sat.-Sun. 10am-2pm.

Mesón del Campesino, C. Infanta Isabel, 12 (tel. 43 58 99), opposite Vogue 2. Tall tables, young crowds, filling portions. *Platos combinados* 300-700ptas. *Menú* 800-1000ptas. *Gazpacho* 325ptas. Open Fri-Wed. 11am-4pm and 8:30pm-12:30am.

Bar-Mesón Cueva de San Estéban, C. Valdelaguila, 15, off Pl. San Estéban. Downright plush for a cave; the space in back on the patio is even bright. Stone and mortar walls, wooden pygmy footstools for seats, and reasonable *platos combinados* (375-825ptas). Entrees 500ptas and up. Cold beer from the font at the rear of the cave 125ptas.

Restaurante La Oficina, C. Cronista Lecea, 10 (tel. 43 16 43), off Pl. Mayor. Almost a centurian. Full of Castilian cookware and pictures of suckling pigs past. Caters to transient money-spenders. Ask specifically for the complete *menú* (1300ptas, not including wine). Open 12:30-4:30pm and 7:30-11:30pm.

Mesón Cándido, Pl. Azoguejo, 5 (tel. 42 81 03), on the far side coming from the Pl. Mayor. Go only if a rich great aunt happened to die this very morning, leaving you her entire fortune. A steal considering it's a Segovian institution. Authentic *menú* (2600ptas) begins with soup made from pigs' ears and feet. Succulent *cochinillo asado* (roast suckling pig) 1700ptas. In summer, reserve a few hours in advance. Open 12:30-4:30pm and 8-11:30pm.

Bar El Túnel, C. Santa Columba, 3, off Pl. Azoquejo and up the stone steps by the bank. Add your keychain to the hundreds above the bar. Savory *platos combinados* 400-800ptas. Meals served 11am-3:30pm and 7-10:30pm.

Sights

The Alcázar

The Alcázar juts audaciously into space at the far northern end of the old quarter, an archetypal late-medieval castle. Much of its dramatic effect actually derives from an inspired reconstruction after a devastating fire in 1862. The original 11th-century fortress was fattened up by Alfonso X and gussied up by successive monarchs, becoming ever more sumptuous. Isabel was crowned Queen of Castile in the Alcázar in 1474 (hence the two streets named in her honor).

Inside, instruments of destruction and mounted knights in armor terrorize from every side. The fanciful **Sala de las Piñas** (Pineapple Room) has a stained-glass window and a wacky ceiling decorated with small gold pineapples. The **Sala de Armas** houses cannons, bows, and barbed weapons from Carlos III's 18th-century artillery academy, plus an old coin press. Wooden sculptures of all the Queens and Kings of Castile stand in the **Sala del Solio** (Throne Room).

The fortress-palace's **torre** commands a stellar view of Segovia and the surrounding plain. Prince Pedro, son of King Enrique IV, slipped from his nurse's arms on the balcony and fell over the ramparts to his bloody death; out of desperation the nurse leapt after him and ended her own life. The *torre* was used as a dungeon in the 16th century, but even today the dark, steep staircase is enough of a torture to separate the smokers from the non-smokers. (Alcázar open 10am-7pm; Oct.-March 10am-6pm. Admission 250ptas.)

The Aqueduct, Cathedral, and all the Little Churches

The Romans built Segovia's elegant **Acueducto Romano** around 50 BC to pipe in water from the Río Frío, 18km away. Supported by 128 pillars that span 813m, the two tiers of 163 arches are constructed of great blocks of granite—without any mortar. Frighteningly, the Romans' feat of engineering was used, once the Catholic Monarchs had restored it in the 15th century, until 5 years ago. The most impressive view of the aqueduct is from Pl. Azoquejo (in front and to the right), where the grand structure reaches its maximum height of 28.9m. The steps on the left side of the plaza allow a diagonal view; to see the inside continue to the top and climb over the small wooden fence.

Commissioned by Carlos V in 1525, the **catedral** towers above Pl. Mayor in the center of town. The late Gothic naves are impressively high, with a striking ceiling pattern of rib vaulting, and the stained glass windows are ethereal. Skip the snoozy taped tour (50ptas) and luxuriate in the tranquillity of the cloisters. The **museo** contains a fine assortment of Flemish tapestries and paintings. (Open 9am-7pm; Oct.-March Mon.-Fri. 9:30am-1pm and 3-6pm, Sat.-Sun. 9:30am-6pm. Admission 200ptas.)

Segovia is blessed with an exceptional number of Romanesque churches of the 12th and 13th centuries, used by guilds and brotherhoods for their (sometimes clandestine) meetings. These modest, plain structures are garnished with grotesque little stone creatures that pop up among the arches and columns: glaring faces, sphinxes, birds, cats, people, and various leafy growths. **San Justo,** not far from the aqueduct outside the wall, displays a powerful collection of frescoes in its main apse. To the west, 10th-century **San Martín,** on Pl. San Martín off C. Juan Bravo, is spiced with Mozarabic touches. Thirteenth-century **San Esteban,** in the north of the city, houses a calvary from the same period. It was restored in the early 20th century. There's a splendid view of **San Andrés** from small Pl. Merced. **San Nicolás** and **San Sebastián** round out the roster of outstanding churches. The churches are open only for services (Mon.-Sat. 8am, 9am, 7pm, and 8pm; Sun. 9am-1pm, 7pm, and 8pm.)

Segovia also has palaces. There's a series of 14th and 15th-century ones, such as the **Lozoya** and **Dávila.** Perhaps the most remarkable is 16th-century **Casa de los Picos,** in the southeast of the city, whose façade is studded with rows of diamond-shaped stones.

Just Outside the Walls

Follow the road down to the left away from the Alcázar to reach three buildings across the Eresma river. The divine numerological Knights Templar were at it again in 1208 when they built Romanesque **Iglesia de la Vera Cruz,** a suspiciously 12-sided basilica. Among its lofty vaults are two hidden chambers where clergymen secreted themselves and their valuables from robbers and highwaymen. In the same concealed rooms, the crafty Templars gathered to perform their enigmatic initiation ceremonies. Walk 90° around to the right, and look up into the central space. The nave is circular too. (Open Tues.-Sun. 10:30am-1:30pm and 3:30-7pm; Oct.-March Tues.-Sun. 10:30am-1:30pm and 3:30-6pm. Admission 100ptas.)

The **Iglesia del Convento de las Carmelitas Descalzas,** whose pretty façade is flanked by cypresses, is downhill from the Vera Cruz and to the right. St. John of the Cross—the great mystic, poet, and confessor to St. Teresa—is buried here in the most grandiose of **mausoleums.** The most valuable exhibit in the petite museum is his manuscript of *cántico espiritual.* (Open 10am-1:30pm and 4-7pm. Free.) Finally, the **Monasterio del Parral,** to the east of the Vera Cruz, looks most impressive from afar, but its polychrome altarpiece calls for a close-up. (Open Mon.-Fri. 9am-1pm and 3-6:30pm. Free.)

Entertainment

Nighttime activity calls for the Pl. Mayor and its tributaries. Pubs crowd **Calles Infanta Isabel** and **Isabel la Católica** (nicknamed "the streets of the bars").

> **Café Jeyma,** Pl. Mayor, 12. Extremely welcoming and popular with middle-aged and elderly locals.
>
> **Pub Oja Blanca,** Pl. Mayor, 6, next to the Hotel Victoria. Slightly more expensive and attracts a more uptown crowd. Open 9 or 10am-3am.
>
> **La Planta Baja Bar,** C. Infanta Isabel, 8. A favorite haunt of teens. Loud music, billiards, and rather young company. Open 6pm-1 or 2am.
>
> **Vogue 2,** C. Infanta Isabel, 13. More chic, swish, and caters to college students. Open 6pm-3am.
>
> **Bar Basílio** on C. Herrería off C. Cronista Lecea, next to Restaurante la Oficina. A laid-back place to drink. Open 10am-2am.

Near Segovia, **Zamarramala** hosts the **Fiestas de Santa Agueda** (St. Agatha) on the second Saturday and Sunday in February. For a day, women symbolically take over the town's administration, dress up in beautiful, old-fashioned costumes, and parade through the streets. The mayor's wife carries the scepter of authority and leads the married women; later women feast at a banquet for their sex only. Origins of this festival date back to an attempted sneak attack on the Alcázar based in Zamarramala in which the town's women tried to lull the castle guards with wine and song. Zamarramala, visible from the Alcázar, is 3km to the northwest.

Near Segovia

La Granja de San Ildefonso

The royal palace and grounds of La Granja, 11km southeast from Segovia, are frequently called the Versailles of Spain. One of four royal summer retreats (with El Pardo, El Escorial, and Aranjuez), it's far and away the most extravagant. Marble everywhere, windows framed by original 250-year-old lace curtains, ceilings painted in false perspective, and lavish crystal chandeliers (made in San Ildefonso's renowned crystal factory) are just the tip of the iceberg.

In the early 18th century, the first Bourbon King Felipe V, grandson of Louis XIV, detested the Habsburgs' austere El Escorial and commissioned La Granja out of nostalgia for Versailles. The imitation never matched the original in conspicuous consumption, but its setting in dramatic mountains is out of this world. Although parts of the gardens and buildings suffer from lack of care, this daytrip will quench that thirst for over-the-top palatial splendor.

The guided tour is mandatory but worth enduring, as the best exhibit comes last. In 1918 a fire destroyed the living quarters of the royals and their servants. The rubble was rebuilt to house one of the world's finest collections of **tapices flamencos** (Flemish tapestries). Habsburg Kings Carlos I and Felipe II collected these tapestries made by artisans from the Low Countries in the 16th and 17th centuries, which now cover entire walls. The domed **iglesia** flanking the palace has a red marble face and elaborate gilded woodwork. In a side chapel, bones of various saints and martyrs make a kick-ass display.

Wipe your fevered brow in the cool and expansive **jardines,** with their intricate, playful fountains. The surrounding forest conceals statues of children and animals. The **Cascadas Nuevas** (New Cascades) are an ensemble of sometimes illuminated pools representing the continents and the four seasons. (Palace open Tues.-Fri. 10am-1pm and 3-5pm, Sat.-Sun. and holidays 10am-2pm. Admission 300ptas, students and professors 100ptas, Wed. free for EEC citizens. Pools turned on Thurs. and Sat.-Sun. at 5:30pm.)

Frequent **buses** leave Segovia for La Granja (11 per day, 20min.). Travellers with a car might want to make for the **Palacio de Riofrío,** 11km from Segovia in a different direction, commissioned by Queen Isabel Farnese. The queen's failed intention was to top the grandeur of La Granja, which she had to leave when her husband (Felipe V) died. It was always a glorified hunting lodge, and game still roams the surrounding parkland. Inside is a **Museo de la Caza** (Museum of Hunting) and some ritzy royal apartments. No public transport serves the palace. (Open Mon. and Wed.-Sat. 10am-1:30pm and 3-5pm, Sun. 10am-2pm. Admission 300ptas, students and professors 100ptas, Wed. free for EEC citizens.)

Coca and Pedraza

Coca and Pedraza, slices of life in a Castilian hamlet, have splendid castles. **Coca Castle** is flamboyant to the max, a Gothic monument to the power of the Fonseca family in the 15th century. Two trains (45min., 240ptas) and two buses (300ptas) run to Coca from Segovia; return buses are few.

Pedraza, thought to be the birthplace of Roman Emperor Trajan, is a charming mountain village dominated by its **castle** on an enormous crag nearby. Restored in 1430 by Don Pedro Fernández de Velasco, the walls are still in perfect shape. 37km northeast of Segovia, Pedraza is accessible by bus (230ptas).

Avila

Avila's fame is forever ensured by St. Teresa of Avila (1515-1582)—mystic, writer, reformer of monastic life, the nun who founded the Order of the Discalced Carmelites and whose raptures were immortalized in marble by Bernini. Her landmark autobiography recounted the near-sexual bliss she experienced through asceticism and contributed to the Counter-Reformation's insistence on a sensuous experience of Christ. The *Libro de las Fundaciones* (Book of the Foundations) recounts the perils and misadventures she encountered as she founded convents across the country. The people of Avila refer to her simply as *La Santa,* and have named everything from pastries to driving schools after her.

Because the city sits on a rocky escarpment high above the Río Adaja valley, Avila keeps its cool in the summer while the plain swelters below. Within the classic medieval walls, carved images of bulls and hogs are mute reminders of a Celtiberian culture much older than the ancient fortifications. King Alfonso VI entrusted Raimundo de Borgoña with fortifying and repopulating Avila in 1090 in order to consolidate the kingdom of Castilla; from that moment it became one of Castilla's most important cities.

Orientation and Practical Information

Just west of Segovia and northwest of Madrid, Avila is a reasonable daytrip from either city. The city has two central squares; **Plaza de la Victoria,** inside the city walls, and **Plaza de Santa Teresa,** just outside them. The cathedral and most of Avila's other monuments cluster between the two plazas, in the eastern half of the old city. To get to the city center from the bus station (east of the center), cross the intersection, walk down Calle del Duque de Alba (keeping the small park to your right), and follow the street to café-filled Pl. de Santa Teresa. To reach Pl. Santa Teresa from the train station (northeast of the center), follow Avenida José António to Calle de Isaac Peral, bear right, and turn left on C. Duque de Alba. From C. Duque de Alba, follow the directions above (15min.). Municipal buses run from nearby the train station (1 block in) to the Pl. de la Victoria.

> **Tourist Office:** Pl. Catedral, 4 (tel. 21 13 87). From Pl. Santa Teresa, walk through the main gate and turn right up winding C. Cruz Vieja; the office is directly opposite the entrance to the cathedral. Open July-Sept. Mon.-Fri. 9am-8pm, Sat. 9am-3pm, Sun. 11am-3pm; Oct.-May Mon.-Fri. 9am-2pm and 4-6pm, Sat. 9am-2pm.
>
> **Post Office:** Pl. Catedral, 2 (tel. 21 13 54; telegrams tel. 22 20 00), to left side of cathedral when facing main entrance. Open for stamps Mon.-Sat. 9am-2pm and 4-6pm; for **telegrams** Mon.-Fri. 8am-9pm, Sat. 8am-7pm. **Postal Code:** 05001.
>
> **Telephones:** Pl. Catedral (tel. 003), next to the post office. Open Mon.-Sat. 9am-2pm and 5-11pm. **Telephone Code:** 918.

Trains: Av. Portugal, 17 (tel. 22 01 88; information tel. 22 65 79; office tel. 22 07 81), at the end of Av. José António on the northeast side of town. To: Medina del Campo (16 per day, 1hr., 465ptas; change here for Segovia); Valladolid (14 per day, 1 3/4 hr., 625-1050ptas); Salamanca (13 per day, 2hr., 565ptas); Madrid (28 per day, 2hr., 575-1000ptas).

Buses: Av. Madrid at Av. Portugal (tel. 22 01 54), on the northeast side of town. To: Segovia (1-5 per day, 45min., 475ptas); Salamanca (5-9 per day, 1 1/2 hr., 705ptas); Madrid (3 per day, 2hr., 650ptas).

Taxis: Pl. Santa Teresa (tel. 21 19 59). Open 8am-10:30pm. Also at the train station (tel. 22 01 49). Open 6am-2am. From train station to Pl. Santa Teresa 300ptas plus 20ptas per piece of luggage.

Luggage Storage: At the **train station** (300ptas).

Medical Services: Emergency Clinic (Seguridad Social) (tel. 22 24 00). **Ambulance** (tel. 21 12 20).

Emergency: tel. 091.

Police: Av. José António, 3 (tel. 21 11 88).

Accommodations

Accommodations are expensive. Many visitors make this a (somewhat rushed) daytrip from Madrid.

Residencia Juvenil "Duperier" (HI), Av. Juventud (tel. 22 17 16), Ciudad Polideportiva, past the Convento de Santo Tomás and the cinema next to the municipal swimming pool. Only 10 beds—call before leaving the train station. Doubles have bunkbed, desk, and small wooden closet. Clean and bright. Curfew 11pm. 650ptas per person. With 1 meal 1000ptas.

Hostal Santa Ana, C. Alfonso Montalvo, 2 (tel. 22 00 63), off Pl. Santa Ana, down Av. José Antonio from train station. Efficiently run well-kept *hostal*: sheets are snow-white, baths spic and span. Doubles 2600ptas. Triples 3600ptas. Sept. 16-June 14: 2400ptas; 3400ptas. Showers 200ptas.

Hostal Continental, Pl. Catedral, 6 (tel. 21 15 02), next to the tourist office. Superb location. An ancient, once-grand hotel beginning to show its age. Some of the 60 rooms have fabulous views of the cathedral; all are large and have phones. Singles 1950ptas. Doubles 3080ptas, with bath 3550ptas. Triples 3900ptas. Nov. 1-June 30: 1730ptas; 2640ptas, 3030ptas; 3900ptas.

Fonda San Francisco, Trav. José Antonio, 2 (tel. 22 02 98), off Av. José António. Fairly large rooms almost filled completely by wide, low-slung beds. Religious *retratos* and simple decor. Singles 1700ptas. Doubles 2400-2500ptas. Showers 200ptas.

Food

The city won fame for its *ternera de Avila* (veal) and *mollejas* (sweetbread). The *yemas de Santa Teresa* or *yemas de Avila,* local confections made of egg yolks and honey, and *vino de Cebreros,* the smooth regional wine, are delectable.

Plaza de la Victoria is capital of budgetism, even though the atmosphere and prices are tourist-inspired. Every Friday (9am-2pm) a **mercado típico** in Pl. Victoria sells local food, flowers, and crafts.

Groceries: Mercado de Abastos, C. Comuneros de Castilla near Pl. Victoria. **Mercado Gimeco,** C. Jardín de San Roque. Both open 9:30am-1:30pm and 4-7:30pm.

Mesón El Rastro, Pl. Rastro, 4, at C. Cepadas and C. Caballeros at the southern wall. Convenient location for a post-meal stroll. Large, noisy dining hall decked out like a hunting lodge. Expect to wait; it's popular with locals and tourists. Choose from the two *menús del día* (1300ptas), both of which feature regional specialties in hearty portions. Entrees 600-1500ptas. Open 1-4pm and 9:30-11pm.

Bar/Restaurante Palomar, C. Vara del Rey (tel. 21 31 04), at C. Tomás L. de Victorias, a street to the right of the tourist office (as you face it). Pig out on *cochinillo asado* (roast suckling pig, 1500ptas). *Menú semanal* 1100ptas. *Menú del día* 1950ptas. Open 1:30-4:30pm and 8:30-10pm; off-season 1:30-4pm. Bar open 7:30pm-midnight.

Restaurante El Ruedo, C. Enrique Larreta, 7 (tel. 21 31 98). Unpretentious. Regional specialties. *Menú* 1100ptas. Open Wed.-Mon. 1:30-5pm and 9pm-midnight.

El Molino de la Losa, Bajada de La Losa, 12 (tel. 21 11 01), outside the western walls. Cross the Puente del Adaja and turn right. A water mill/restaurant specializing in rummy *ò* (sangria, 9-glass pitcher 650ptas). Yuppies talk too much on the outdoor terrace above the river. Open for meals 1-4pm and 9-11pm. Bar open 10:30am-1am, weekends later.

Sights and Entertainment

Avila proudly wears the oldest, most complete fortified medieval belt of any Spanish city. Construction of the **murallas medievales** began in 1090, but most were realized in the next century; the concentrated burst of activity leant the walls their unusual uniformity. Mudejar features suggest *morisco* citizens helped fortify Christian Avila. Eighty-two massive towers reinforce walls whose thickness averages 3m. The most imposing of the towers, called **Cimorro,** is actually the cathedral's bold apse. Nine gates allow access; the two oldest are **Puerta del Alcázar** and **Puerta de San Vicente,** at the end of C. López Núñez.

The best view of the walls and of Avila itself is from the **Cuatro Postes,** a tiny four-pillared structure past the Río Adaja on the highway to Salamanca, 11/2km to the northwest of the city. This is the spot where the precociously religious child-Teresa was nabbed by her uncle while she and her brother were trying to flee to the Islamic South to be martyred. The walls can be climbed along the Parador Nacional in Pl. Concepción Arenal; enter through the garden. Avila's walls are illuminated most summer nights from 10:30pm to midnight; Saturdays, Sundays, and holidays in off-season from 8pm to midnight; and daily from 8pm to midnight during *Las Fiestas de Santa Teresa* (Oct. 7-15) and Christmas time (Dec. 22-Jan. 7).

Inside the Walls

Some believe that the profile of the **catedral** looming over the watchtowers inspired St. Teresa's metaphor of the soul as a diamond castle. Begun in the second half of the 12th century, the oldest Spanish cathedral in the transitional Romanesque-to-Gothic style recalls the long, turbulent centuries of the Reconquista, when war and religion went hand in hand. The cathedral's originality lies in its being embedded in the city's walls, thereby participating in its system of defense. Just inside the entrance, pale stained glass renders a well-rubbed bronze of San Pedro exceptionally bright. Behind the chancel is the alabaster **tomb** of Cardinal Alonso de Madrigal, an Avila bishop known as El Tostado (the Toasted) because of his dark complexion; he was a prolific writer whose nickname was applied in the Golden Age to all literary windbags. The small **museo** has a fine collection of gold and silver work, sculptures, and paintings from the 12th to 18th centuries, including a small El Greco. (Cathedral open 8am-1pm and 3-7pm; Oct.-April 8am-1pm and 3-5pm. Free. Museum open 10am-1:30pm and 3-7pm; Oct.-April 10am-1:30pm and 3-6pm. Admission 100ptas.) So much more religious architecture! Innumerable convents pray within the city walls, many, such as Convento de la Encarnación and Convento de San José, associated with St. Teresa. Most of her mystical experiences took place during the 30 years she spent in the **Convento de la Encarnación.** The tiny cell where she lived is through the farthest door in the farthest chapel. Upstairs from the cloister, a museum features a collection of furnishings, letters, and other personal effects, plus musical instruments and elaborate trunks that wealthier nuns gave to the convent as bribes to procure entrance. Teresa's reforms did away with this system of preference and imposed norms of collective poverty and simplicity for all nuns, as exemplified by her own *celda*. (Open 9:30am-1:30pm and 3:30-6pm; winter 9:30am-1pm and 4-7pm. Obligatory tour in Spanish 75ptas.)

Locals built the **Convento de Santa Teresa** in the 17th century on the site of her parents' home. The church's restrained façade offers no hint of the extravagance of the chapel built over Teresa's birth spot. Among other treasures, the convent supposedly holds one of Teresa's severed fingers; the other nine are somewhere else. (For more of her body parts, see Alba de Tormes.) (Open 9:30am-1:30pm and 3:30-7pm. Free.)

Secular architecture is also well-represented within the walled town. Spare, elegant Renaissance **palacios,** such as those of the Velada, Aguilar y Torre Arias, Verdugo, and Bracamonte, and seignorial mansions, such as those built for the Oñate and the Marqués de las Navas, stand out. The **Palacio de los Polentinos,** on C. Vallespín, is fronted with a beautiful Renaissance façade. Inside, there's a majestic blue-and-white tiled courtyard with seemingly weightless pillars supporting the upper story.

Casa de los Deanes, a mansion in Pl. Nalvillos with a Renaissance façade, houses Avila's splendid **Museo Provincial.** Labels are in Spanish only, but the collections are impressive just visually. Its holdings include some lovingly restored agricultural implements, an old loom, some fancy local straw hats called *gorras* and a bed artistically strewn with traditional costumes. Upstairs are a few outstanding medieval paintings and two Baroque desks. (Open Tues.-Sat. 10am-2pm and 7-8pm, Sun. 10am-2pm. Free while upper floor is closed for renovations. When reopened, admission 200ptas, students free.)

Outside the Walls

As if unable to contain so much art within its walls, Avila has a number of remarkable convents and Romanesque churches just outside. The first convent Teresa founded was the **Convento de San José,** also known as the Convento de las Madres, at C. Madres, 3, off C. Duque de Alba. Although the 1608 building is closed to visitors, the small **Museo Teresiano** exhibits the saddle she used while roaming around establishing convents, the drum she played at Christmas, and a letter written in her elegant, educated hand—not to mention one of her bones and a wonderful Zurbarán. (Open 10am-1pm and 3:30-6pm. Admission 25ptas.)

Basílica de San Vicente is a large 12th-century Romanesque and Gothic building dedicated to Vicente, Sabina, and Cristeta, three martyred saints buried beneath the church. Near the east end is Vicente's unbelievably ornate tomb and some very odd tile artwork. The convent has a magnificent ensemble of Romanesque sculpture, including depictions of Jesus and 10 of his apostles. (Open 10am-1pm and 4-7pm; winter 10am-1pm and 4-6pm.)

Monasterio de Santo Tomás, some way from the city walls, at the end of C. Jesús del Gran Poder, was the summer palace of the Catholic monarchs (commissioned by Fernando and Isabel) and a frightening seat of the Inquisition. *Granada* (pomegranate) motifs recall the monarchs' triumphant 1492 capture of Granada, the last Moorish kingdom in Spain. (Open Mon.-Sat. 10am-1pm and 4-7pm, Sun. 4-6pm. Admission to museum 50ptas, to the cloister 50ptas.)

Every year from October 7 to 15, the city gets a little crazy in honor of Teresa, with fairs and parades of *gigantes y cabezudos* (giant effigies). From July 16-26, the **Fiestas de Verano** (Summer Celebrations) bring exhibits, folksinging, dancing, pop groups, fireworks, and a bullfight. The tourist office puts out a calendar of events.

Salamanca

For centuries the "hand of Salamanca," the brass knocker traditionally found on the doors of this city, has welcomed students, scholars, rogues, royals, and saints. In the old city, golden sandstone has lent itself to every major architectural style from Romanesque to Baroque; even the modern quarters are built largely in this stone.

The university here is Spain's oldest (founded in 1218). It was one of the four great medieval centers of learning along with Bologna, Paris, and Oxford. Many outstanding Spanish intellectuals were weaned in its halls. Nebrija, responsible for the first grammar of a modern language (1492), taught here until, disgusted by its stodgy ways, he was invited to join the faculty of the new humanistic university in Alcalá. Miguel de Unamuno was Professor of Greek and University Rector for many years in the early 20th century; he wrote the bulk of his philosophical and literary *obras* here. After almost two centuries of decline, the school is striving to be worthy of the prestige it enjoyed in medieval times, and is catching up to Madrid and Barcelona.

The perfect balance of the active and the contemplative life is the hallmark of the Salmantine way. In summer, a huge influx of foreign students adds a certain tang to the atmosphere, but the city in winter, with a thin layer of snow on the cathedrals, is hauntingly attractive.

Orientation and Practical Information

Most sights and a great deal of cheap food and accommodation lie south of the **Plaza Mayor.** The farther north of the plaza, the newer and more expensive the area. The **Universidad** (university) is south of the Plaza Mayor, near the **Pl. de Anaya.**

Whether you arrive by bus or train, you'll be 20 minutes from the town center. From the train station (northeast from the center), either catch the bus that goes to **Plaza Mercado** (next to Pl. Mayor), or, with your back to the station, turn left down Paseo de la Estación to Plaza de España, and walk down Calle Azafranal or Calle Toro to Pl. Mayor. From the bus station, either catch bus #4 to Pl. Mercado or walk all the way down Calle de Filiberto Villalobos, cross the busy main road, and plummet down Calle Ramón y Cajal; then turn left and immediately right up Calle Prior, which runs directly to Pl. Mayor.

Tourist Office: Municipal, Pl. Mayor (tel. 21 83 42). More of an information booth, but good for quickfire questions. Open Mon.-Fri. 10am-1:30pm and 5-7pm, Sat. 10am-2pm, Sun. 11am-2pm. **Provincial,** Gran Vía, 39-41 (tel. 26 85 71). Informative English-speaking staff. Excellent pamphlet (with map) on accommodations. Open Mon.-Fri. 9:30am-2pm and 4:30-7pm, Sat. 10am-2pm, Sun. 11am-2pm.

Budget Travel: TIVE, C. Reyes Católicos, 11-19 (tel. 26 77 31). Long lines; go early. Open Mon.-Fri. 9am-2pm. **Viajes Juventus,** Pl. Libertad, 14 (tel. 21 74 07). **Viajes Zarco,** Cuesta del Carmen, 27 (tel. 26 94 61).

Currency Exchange: Oficina de Cambio, Pl. Mayor, next to municipal tourist office. Open Mon.-Fri. until midnight. **Banco Exterior de España,** C. Toro, 40 (tel. 21 71 02) and Gran Vía, 28 (tel. 21 71 02). Open Mon.-Fri. 8:30-11:45am and 1-2:45pm, Sat. 9am-noon; winter Mon.-Fri. 8:30-11:45am and 1-2:45pm.

Post Office: Gran Vía, 25 (tel. 24 30 11), 2 bl. from the national tourist office toward Pl. España. Open for stamps and information Mon.-Fri. 9am-2pm and 4-6pm, Sat. 9am-2pm; for Lista de Correos Mon.-Fri. 9am-2pm; for **telegrams** Mon.-Sat. 9am-9pm. **Postal Code:** 37008.

Telephones: Pl. Peña Primera, 1, off Pl. Bandos. Open Mon.-Sat. 9am-3pm and 4-10pm. **Telephone Code:** 923.

Trains: Po. Estación Ferrocarril (tel. 22 57 42), northeast of town. **RENFE office**, Pl. Libertad, 10 (tel. 21 24 54). Open Mon.-Fri. 9am-2pm and 5-7pm. To: Avila (3 per day, 1hr., 320ptas); Valladolid (9 per day, 1 1/2 hr., 645ptas); Ciudad Rodrigo (5 per day, 1 3/4 hr., 515ptas); León (at 6:35am, 3 1/2 hr., 1490ptas); Madrid (4 per day, 3 1/2 hr., 1235ptas); Barcelona (at 10:15pm, 14hr., 5700ptas); Porto, Portugal (at 2:05am, 8 1/2 hr., 2725ptas).

Buses: Av. Filiberto Villalobos, 71 (tel. 23 67 17, 23 22 66). To: Avila (1-5 per day, 1-2hr., 639ptas); Ciudad Rodrigo (3-7 per day, 1hr., 630ptas); Zamora (8-14 per day, 1hr., 430ptas); Valladolid (1-8 per day, 2hr., 795ptas); Segovia (2-4 per day, 2hr., 1180ptas); Madrid (very frequent, 2 1/2 -3hr., 1300-1800ptas); Cáceres (1-5 per day, 4hr., 1455ptas); León (4-6 per day, 3hr., 1410ptas); Barcelona (1-3 per day, 11 1/2 hr., 4965ptas).

Taxis: tel. 26 44 44, 25 00 00.

Car Rental: Hertz, Av. Portugal, 131 (tel. 24 31 34). **Avis,** Po. Canalejos, 49 (tel. 26 97 53). **Europcar,** C. Torres Villarroel (tel. 23 35 26).

Lost Property: Policía Municipal keeps objects a few days, then turns them over to **Edificio Lasalle** (tel. 26 25 95), Av. Lasalle.

English Bookstore: Cervantes, Pl. Hermanos Jerez (tel. 21 86 02). Just opened an annex nearby on Pl. Santa Eulalia to expand its already large collection of English books. **Portonaris,** R. Mayor, 33, opposite the Casa de Conchas. Salamanca's most renowned bookstore. Penguin Classics. Open Mon.-Fri. 9:45am-1:30pm and 4:30-8pm, Sat. 9:45am-1:30pm.

Laundromat: Lavandería la Glorieta, C. Torres Villarroel, 61 (tel. 23 57 27), on the north side of town. Walk north from Pl. Mayor on C. Zamora to Pl. Ejército, then continue in the same direction on C. Torres Villarroel (15min.). Wash, dry, and fold 500ptas per 5kg load. **Lavandería**

Soap, Av. Italia, 29 (tel. 25 32 57), slightly closer to the city center. Wash and dry 720ptas per 5kg load. Open Mon.-Sat. 10am-9pm, Sun. 10am-2pm.

Swimming Pool: Las Torres, Ctra. Madrid (tel. 21 90 97), across railroad bridge (bus from Pl. España 20min.). The cleanest and nicest of the city's 10 pools. Large afternoon crowds. Open summer 11am-8pm. Admission 400ptas, Sat.-Sun. 800ptas. **Regio,** Ctra. Madrid (tel. 20 02 50), 4km away. Smaller, grassier, less crowded. Admission 425ptas.

Medical Services: Hospital Clínico, Po. San Vicente, 23 (tel. 29 11 00). **Prusa España,** Edificio España, Pl. España, 4th fl. (tel. 22 20 29, 24 91 76; weekends 20 09 07). Pricey private medical clinic. Fluent English, French, German, and Japanese staff. Foreign medical insurance accepted. **Ambulance** (tel. 24 09 16, 25 54 64, or 24 37 87).

Emergency: tel. 092. **National Police** (tel. 091).

Police: Municipal (tel. 21 96 00), in Ayuntamiento.

Accommodations and Camping

Between Plaza Mayor and the University

Many students, many rooms. Plenty of cheap *pensiones* off the side streets from Pl. Mayor, especially on **Calle Meléndez,** just south of the plaza.

Pensión Marina, C. Doctrinos, 4, 3rd fl. (tel. 21 65 69), between C. Compania and C. Prado. Gigantic bathroom, plush TV lounge, and beautiful rooms. The lone single 1600ptas. Doubles 2200ptas.

Pensión Barez, C. Meléndez, 19 (tel. 21 74 95). Owners treat you like one of the family. Sparkling clean. Balcony rooms with a view of San Benito. TV lounge with table. Windowless singles 1000ptas. Doubles 2000ptas. Showers 125ptas.

Fonda Lisboa, C. Meléndez, 1 (tel. 21 43 33). Small but comfortable newly renovated rooms. Singles 1400-1800ptas, with bath 2400ptas. Doubles 2100ptas, with bath 2900ptas. Breakfast 200ptas. Lunch or dinner 900ptas.

Hostal Tormes, R. Mayor, 20 (tel. 21 96 83). Heavy doors opening off long white halls. Airy rooms. TV lounge. Singles 1500ptas, with bath 2400ptas. Doubles 2800ptas, with shower 3000ptas. Nov. 1 to eve of Semana Santa: 1100ptas, 2000ptas; 2400ptas, 2500ptas.

Pensión Las Vegas, C. Meléndez, 13 (tel. 21 87 49). Clean but bare rooms with sunken beds. Singles 1000ptas. Doubles 2000ptas.

North of Plaza Mayor

Prices escalate north of the Plaza Mayor. The density of *pensiones* decreases and gives way to more expensive *hostal residencias* near Pl. España.

Hostal Oriental, C. Azafranal, 13 (tel. 21 21 15), halfway between Pl. Mayor and Pl. España. Comfortable rooms jazzed up with colorful floor tiles and tiny tables. Singles 1600ptas. Doubles 3000ptas. Showers 200ptas.

Hostal Carabela, Po. Canalejas, 10-12 (tel. 26 07 08), off Pl. España. Like Hostal Los Hidalgos (see below), it tends to be noisy, but rooms are impeccable if uninspired. Tight baths. Singles 1800ptas, with shower or bath 2500ptas. Doubles 2400ptas, with shower or bath 2500ptas. Nov.-Feb.: 1500ptas, 2200ptas; 2100ptas, 2200ptas. Showers 200ptas.

Hostal Los Hidalgos, Po. Canalejas, 14-16, 2nd fl. (tel. 26 10 36), next to the above. Noisy since it's off a major intersection. Rooms are more tasteful than those of its neighbor, but the same cramped baths. Parking garage for guests. Doubles with shower 2400ptas, with bath 2900ptas. Oct. 1-June 30 except Semana Santa: 2200ptas, 2600ptas.

Camping: Regio (tel. 20 02 50), 4km toward Madrid, has the nicest sites. Part of a complex that includes a four-star hotel and pool. 400ptas per person and per car, 350ptas per tent. **Don Quijote** (tel. 25 75 04), 4km toward Aldealengua. 300ptas per person, 250ptas per tent. Open July-Sept.

Food

Every clique has its favorite café in **Plaza Mayor;** all serve the same moderately good food at a standard, slightly inflated price—you'll pay for the atmosphere. A slew of bar-restaurants line streets between the plaza and the university, where a full meal costs no more than 800ptas. Lots of students hang out at these little places. During the academic year, drop in on the **Comedor Universitario,** the university dining hall open to the public. (Meals 600ptas or less. Open Oct.-May.)

Don't miss *jeta,* a local *tapas* specialty (fried pig lips). You don't have to be a Catholic or a heretic to munch *obleas,* overgrown sweetened communion wafers. The daily **market** (8:30am-2pm) peddles on Pl. Mercado to the east of Pl. Mayor.

> **Groceries: Supermercado,** C. Iscar Peyra, two bl. from Pl. Mayor. Open Mon.-Fri. 9:45am-1:45pm and 5:30-8:30pm, Sat. 10am-2pm.
>
> **Restaurante El Bardo,** C. Compania, 8 (tel. 21 90 89), between the Casa de Conchas and the Clerecía. Three tiers serve excellent 3-course vegetarian and classic 2-course *menús* at lunch. Lively at mid-day; more sedate at night. Á la carte meal 1500ptas. Open Nov.-Sept. Tues.-Sun. 11am-4pm and 7pm-midnight.
>
> **Bar Restaurante La Luna,** C. Libreros, 4, down the street from the university façade. Wood and plaster interior, nostalgic photos, and mood music. Salamanca's largest *menú* (850ptas). Á la carte meal 1000ptas. Open Mon.-Thurs. 10:30am-1:30pm, Fri.-Sun. 10:30am-3am.
>
> **Restaurante Vegetariano El Trigal,** C. Libreros, 20 (tel. 21 56 99), near the cathedral and the Patio de las Escuelas. An intimate setting. Although you wouldn't think a place serving non-alcoholic wine could be cool, it's a popular hangout. *Platos combinados* 575-750ptas. Filling 4-course *menú* 750ptas. Open 1-4pm and 8:30-11pm.
>
> **Bar Palafox,** under the clock in the Pl. Mayor. TV and sandwiches (about 100ptas). *Bocadillos* 250ptas. Open 9am-2am.
>
> **Imbis,** R. Mayor, 31. Rather lifeless, but a good selection of *tapas. Platos combinados* about 700ptas. *Menú* 1000-1100ptas. Open 8am-midnight.

Sights

Near the Plaza Mayor

Here there are splendid examples of Roman, Romanesque, Gothic, Renaissance, and Baroque structures, all in sandstone. Nowhere is the golden glow more apparent than in the **Plaza Mayor,** a trapezoid begun in 1729 during the reign of Felipe V. Between the arches—almost 100 of them—hang medallions with bas-reliefs of famous Spaniards, from El Cid to Franco. The façade of the **Ayuntamiento** was designed by Andrés García de Quiñones. The Churrigueresque **Pabellón Real** by the man himself is to its left.

One of the city's most famous landmarks, the 15th-century **Casa de las Conchas** (House of Shells), is adorned by rows of scallop shells chiseled in sandstone. The owner of the house, a knight of the Order of Santiago, wanted to create a monument to Santiago de Compostela, the renowned pilgrimage site. Pilgrims who journeyed to Santiago wore shells like these as a token of their visit to St. James the Apostle's tomb. (Closed while under renovations. Future home of a public library.)

Across the street, the **Clerecía** (a.k.a. Real Colegio del Espíritu Santo) is a Baroque complex that until recently was used by a major Jesuit community. It consists of a church, a *colegio* (school), and what used to be the community's living quarters: in all, 300 rooms, with 520 doors and 906 windows. Now owned by the Universidad, parts of the complex were under restoration for 13 years. Its wonderful façade can't be appreciated properly because of the narrowness of the street. In fact, a few wealthy believers once offered a large sum of money to have the Casa demolished to clear the way for admiring viewers. (Closed to the public.)

The University

The focal point of Salamanca, the **Universidad,** is entered from the **Patio de las Escuelas,** off C. Libreros. The statue here represents Fray Luís de León, one of the most respected literati of the Golden Age. A Hebrew scholar and a classical Spanish stylist to boot, Fray Luís was condemned for heresy by the Inquisition for translating Solomon's *Song of Songs* into Castilian. After five years in prison, he returned to his chair at the university and started his first lecture with the words: *"Decíamos ayer..."* ("As we were saying yesterday..."), and resumed where his last lecture had ended.

The university's **entryway** is one of the best examples of Spanish Plateresque, a style named for the filigree work of *plateros* (silversmiths). The central medallion represents King Fernando and Queen Isabel. Some bystanders may well be seeking out Salamanca's gray eminence: a smallish frog carved on a skull on the right side of the façade. It's said to represent the dankness of prison life, but those wacky students allege it brings them good luck on exams. Another bizarre tradition holds that if you spot it without help you'll be married within the year. The walls are marked here and there by students' initials in bold red, painted upon graduation in an ink of bull's blood, olive oil, and herbs.

The old lecture halls inside are open to the public. **Aula Fray Luís de León** has its original benches and Fray's pulpit, with a plaque that bears Unamuno's poem on love and the students of Salamanca. The extraordinarily sumptuous (and quiet) **Paraninfo** contains Baroque tapestries and a portrait of Carlos IV attributed to Goya. Fray Luís is buried in the 18th-century chapel. (Open Mon.-Sat. 9:30am-1:30pm and 4:30-6:30pm, Sun. 10am-1pm. Admission 125ptas, students free.)

The **Escuelas Menores,** also on the Patio de las Escuelas, is yet another university building with a Plateresque façade and an arcaded patio. The ceiling of the **Sala Calderón de la Barca,** depicts the famous *Cielo de Salamanca* (Sky of Salamanca), a 15th-century fresco of the zodiac. (Open same hours as the university. Admission with the same ticket.)

Casa de Alvarez Abarca belonged to Fernando Alvarez Abarca, physician to Queen Isabel. This beautiful 15th-century building now houses the **Museo Provincial de Bellas Artes.** In Room II, the handsome lid of a sarcophagus portrays a reclining Knight of Malta (not a Knight Templar). Spanish paintings predominate, but the Italian, French, and Dutch schools show up; also modern and regional art. (Open Mon.-Tues. 8am-3pm, Wed.-Fri. 8am-3pm and 6-9pm, Sat. and Sun. 10am-2pm. Admission 200ptas.)

To the right of the principal entrance to the university is the absorbing **Casa-Museo de Unamuno.** If it seems closed, ring the bell and wait for the caretaker to show up. Another interrupted lecture: a Fascist general in 1936 ran in on Unamuno's lecture and shouted *"Muera la inteligencia"* ("Death to intelligence"); Miguel de Unamuro is reported to have answered: *"Vencerá pero no convencerá"* ("You may conquer but you will not convince"). Among the more charming exhibits in the philosopher-poet's house are his scatterbrained ruminations on his birth in the first window of manuscripts, and his dexterous origami in the study. The library is dauntingly polylingual. (Open Tues.-Fri. 11am-1:30pm and 4:30-6:30pm, Sat.-Sun. 10am-2pm. Free.)

Cathedrals and Convents

Begun in 1513 to accommodate the growing tide of Catholics, the spindly spires of the **catedral nueva** weren't finished until 1733. The basic structure is late Gothic, built from elegant pale stone and pierced by colorful flashes of stained glass. On the vaulting, the giltwork is luxuriant. Churriguera fashioned the lovely cloister with its Renaissance and Baroque flourishes. The *Cristo de las Batallas,* carried by El Cid in his campaigns, is in the **Capilla de Sagrario.** At night, dozens of storks and buzzards perch eerily on the church's spires.

The Romanesque **catedral vieja** (1140) features heavy lines that are a relief from the Goth next door. The central altarpiece narrates the story of the Virgin Mary in 53 scenes. Inside the cupola, apocalyptic angels separate the sinners from the saved. The oldest part is the **Capilla de San Martín,** with brilliantly-colored frescoes from 1242. Off to one side is the 12th-century cloister, rebuilt after the earthquake of 1755. Here, the **Capilla de Santa Barbara,** also called the "Capillades Título," was once the site of final exams. Prior to taking the tests, students placed their feet on the soles of a particularly wise bishop's sarcophagus, hoping to absorb his intelligence. The **Capilla de Santa Catalina** has the best gargoyles.

The **cathedral museum** features a paneled ceiling by Fernando Gallegos, Salamanca's most famous painter, and houses the Salinas organ, named for the blind musician to whom Fray Luís dedicated an ode. (Both cathedrals open 10am-2pm and 4-8pm; Oct.-March 10am-1pm and 4-6pm. Box office closes 1/2 hr. before closing. Admission to old cathedral, cloister, and museum via new cathedral 200ptas. New cathedral free.)

The **Convento de San Esteban,** downhill from the cathedrals, is one of Salamanca's most dramatic monasteries. In the afternoon, its monumental façade becomes a solid mass of light depicting the stoning of St. Stephen and the crucifixion of Jesus. The beautiful **Claustro de los Reyes** (Kings' Cloister) is both Gothic and Plateresque. In the church, the huge central altarpiece, crafted in 1693 by Churriguera, is a Baroque masterpiece with intricate golden columns entwined with grapevines. The chancel contains unadorned stalls and a large allegorical fresco representing the victory of the church over vice and sin through the Dominican order. (Open 9am-1pm and 4-8pm; Oct.-May 9am-1pm and 4-7pm. Admission 100ptas.)

The nearby **Convento de las Dueñas** was formerly the Mudejar palace of a court official. The elegant cloister was a later addition, explaining why its five sides are of unequal length. The cloister, with its elegant medallions, is perhaps the most beautiful in Salamanca. (Open 10am-1pm and 4-7pm; Oct.-May 10:30am-1pm and 4-5:30pm. Admission 75ptas. A good candy shop sits inside the 1st floor.)

Elsewhere

In the center of the **Puente Romano,** a 2000-year-old Roman bridge spanning the Tormes, stands the **Toro Ibérico,** a huge headless granite bull. The bridge was part of an ancient Roman road called the Camino de la Plata (Silver Way) that went from Mérida, in Extremadura, to Astorga, near León. The old bull made it into literature in one of the most famous episodes of *Lazarillo de Tormes,* the classic 16th-century picaresque novel, when our diminutive hero finds his head unexpectedly slammed into the bull's stone ear and decides he needs to wise up.

Entertainment

The **Plaza Mayor** is the social as well as geographic center of town. Locals, students, and tourists come at all hours to sit in its cafés, *dar una vuelta* (take a stroll), or generally lay about. At night, members of various local college or graduate school **tunas,** medieval-style student troubador groups, often finish their *rondas* (rounds) here, serenading women. Dressed in traditional beribboned black capes, these studly men strut around the plaza carrying guitars, mandolins, *bandurrías,* and tambourines. When the show's over, they make excellent drinking partners and do their best to aggressively emulate Don Juan.

Many people overflow from the plaza as far west as **San Vicente.** A lot of the student nightlife also concentrates on the **Gran Vía** and side streets. Bars blast music ranging from reggae to vintage hard rock to annoying *nueva canción* (modern ballads).

Avoid the poor southwest section of town after dark unless you're accompanied by a friend or bodyguard.

>**Café Novelty,** on the northeast corner of Pl. Mayor, The oldest café in town and a meeting place for students and professors. Miguel de Unamuno was a regular.
>
>**Café El Corrillo,** Pl. Mayor by C. Juan del Rey. Proud possessor of a video jukebox and mellow clientele.
>
>**Pub Rojo y Negro,** C. Espoz y Mina. Scrumptious coffee, liquor, and ice cream concoctions (250-600ptas) in an old-fashioned red and black setting. A dance floor down below. Open until 12:30am.
>
>**El Puerto de Chus,** Pl. San Julián. One of the best late-night spots away from the Pl. Mayor.
>
>**El Gran Café Moderno,** Gran Vía. A rockin' good time.
>
>**Metro,** Gran Vía. Reggae.

The city's discos range from the expensive Euro variety (600-1000ptas cover) to bars with dance floors and no cover charge. All discos have evening (7-10pm) and late night (11:30pm-4am) sessions.

Limón y Menta, C. Bermejeros, 18-20. A popular Euro style club. Pricey.

Camelot, C. Bordadores, near several other clubs/pubs. A medieval-chapel-turned-disco is a cheesy example of the latter. If you've got to go, go now, because the nuns who own the chapel are trying to stop the party.

De Laval Genoves, C. San Justo (off Gran Vía). Built in an old submarine, a straight and gay clientele grooves under black lights.

Mezcal, Cuesta del Carmen. Live jazz nightly (at midnight and 1:30am, except in summer) in a laid-back basement.

Ambiente, an inexpensive pamphlet sold at kiosks, lists movies and special events. Posters at the **Colegio Mayor** (Palacio de Anaya) advertise university events, free films, and student theater.

In summer, the city sponsors the **Verano Cultural de Salamanca,** silent movies, contemporary Spanish cinema, pop singers, and theater groups from Spain and abroad. On July 12, in celebration of San Juan de Sahagún, is a **corrida de toros** charity event. From September 8 to 21, the town indulges in **festivals** and **exhibitions.**

Near Salamanca

Ciudad Rodrigo

A medieval town characterized by its fabulous masonry and its honey-colored stone (a little more golden than even Salamanca's), Ciudad Rodrigo rises from the plains near the Portuguese border. After Count Rodrigo González Girón defeated the Moors nearby in 1100, King Alfonso VI ordered him to repopulate the town.

The **catedral** is the town's greatest masterpiece. Originally Romanesque, the church was commissioned by Fernando II of León, who was also responsible for the city walls; it was substantially modified, in Gothic style, in the 16th century. The **coro** was the master work of Rodrigo Alemán from 1498-1504, and includes the sculptor's signature—a carving of his head in the lower right corner. The two 16th-century organs star in a series of concerts every August.

It's the **claustro,** though, that perhaps merits a trip to Ciudad Rodrigo in itself. The left-hand triangle, as you enter, is medieval, and the right-hand triangle is early modern. At one corner, monsters devour Muslims; halfway around, at the beginning of the second side, two demons smirk as Adam and Eve receive their punishment; at the far end, two birds kiss. There's a hidden well and carvings created by the artist at the space missing a column. (Open 8am-7pm. Admission to cloister 50ptas.)

Few structures have appeared in Rodrigo since the days when many of the more ornate buildings served as palaces for noble families. The **Castillo de Enrique de Trastámara,** built in the 14th and 15th centuries by Gonzalo Arias de Genízaro, crowns the battlements. It has now been converted into a leading *parador.*

Pensión Madrid, C. Madrid, 20, has large, clean rooms and a selfless owner. (Doubles 1600ptas, with bath 3200ptas.) Cafés on the Plaza Mayor serve inexpensive *combinados.* As a daytrip from Salamanca, there's enough time to see the whole city (**buses,** 7 per day, 1hr., 630ptas; **trains,** 3 per day, 1 3/4 hr., 515ptas)**.**

La Alberca and Alba de Tormes

Three mountain ranges to the south conceal a number of delightful small towns between the plains of Castilla y León and Extremadura. Above **La Alberca** in the Sierra de Francia rises the province's highest peak, the **Peña de Francia** (1723m). **Buses** are very scarce; only in July and August, an organized excursion to La Alberca and the Peña de Francia leaves at 9am from the street outside the Convento de San Esteban in Salamanca. Buy a ticket in advance, if possible, at the desk inside the Convento (650ptas).

If Santa Teresa hadn't died in **Alba de Tormes,** 19km south of Salamanca, people would've forgotten about it by now. The Saint's coffin forms part of the *retablo* in **Ig-**

lesia de Santa Teresa. If you ask the nuns, they'll show you two parts of her body not in the coffin: her left arm, cut off three years after her death that it might lead Christians into battle; and her heart, removed nine years after her death by doctors who wanted to see what an uncorrupted heart looked like, now beats in a jar.

Zamora

Sancho II died in Zamora during his attempt to subdue his errant sister Doña Urraca and consolidate his hold on the House of Castile. Although Urraca was at first excluded from her father's will in favor of her two brothers, she managed to weasel the city out of the king by threatening to sleep with every man in the kingdom.

The iron-willed princess is in fact the perfect symbol of the walled city, which tenaciously clung to its early glory. In Zamora's shocking past, fierce warriors blazoned the city's name far and wide. Viriatus, the "Terror of the Romans," wore eight red streamers, one for each of his consular victories, and King Fernando added an emerald one to the town's shield for the citizens' display of bravery in the Battle of Toro, 1476. Although this pomp was a noble effort to promote the city, the Zamora of the 1990s is hardly known from afar. Yet the soothing, whitewashed haven welcomes guests with perhaps the greatest concentration of Romanesque architecture in Spain. Its tranquility is unexpected in a town with so many tourist attractions. The graceful arches, bleached stone structures and tile roofs offer a calming, blue-skied, almost spiritual antidote to the congestion, pollution, and tourist traffic of Spain's larger cities.

Orientation and Practical Information

The modern, elegant **train** and **bus stations** lounge in the northeast corner of the city. From the bus station, exit and turn left onto C. Alfonso Peña; from the train station, exit and C. Alfonso Peña is straight ahead. Walk down C. Alfonso Peña to **Plaza Alemania**, turn left onto C. Alfonso IX, and continue on two blocks to **C. Santa Clara**. This major pedestrian street leads to the **Plaza Mayor.** Many churches lie on the streets off C. Santa Clara, which becomes **C. Ramos Carrión**, then **Rua de los Francos,** and finally **Rua de los Notarios.** It all ends at **Plaza de la Catedral**, the setting for Zamora's beauteous **catedral.**

> **Tourist Office:** C. Santa Clara, 20 (tel. 53 18 45, fax 53 38 13). Gives away totally adorable and clear maps. Posters too. Open Mon.-Fri. 8am-3pm, Sat. 8am-2pm.
>
> **Post Office:** C. Santa Clara, 15 (tel. 51 33 71, 51 07 67; fax 53 03 35), just past C. Benquente. Open for stamps, Lista de Correos, and **telegrams** Mon.-Sat. 8am-9pm. Also, **faxes** sent and received. **Postal Code:** 49070.
>
> **Telephones:** Down Av. Requejo (an outward-bound continuation of C. Santa Clara) in a circular stone building in the small park on the left. Open Mon.-Sat. 10am-1:30pm and 5-9pm. **Telephone Code:** 988.
>
> **Trains:** The station (tel. 52 19 56) is at the end of C. Alfonso Peña, 100m behind the bus station. Information open 24 hrs. To: Madrid (3 per day, 3hr., 1470ptas); Santander (2 per day, 4hr., 1955ptas); Santiago de Compostela (2 per day; 4 1/2 hr.; *talgo* 3560ptas, *estrella* 2525ptas); Valladolid (2 per day, 1 1/2 hr., 650ptas).
>
> **Buses:** C. Alfonso Peña, 3 (tel. 52 12 81). Enter from C. Donantes de Sangre on the right when coming from Pl. Alemania. Spankin' new station. To: Salamanca (14 per day, 1hr., 440ptas); Valladolid (6 per day, 1 1/2 hr., 2670ptas); León (6 per day, 2hr., 905ptas); A Coruña (3 per day, 5hr., 2605ptas); Bilbao (1 per day, 2hr., 2565ptas); Madrid (7 per day, 3 1/2 hr., 1678ptas); Barcelona (3 per day, 12hr., 5320ptas); Sevilla (2 per day, 9hr., 5410ptas).
>
> **Taxis:** Radio Taxi (tel. 52 10 56). Tele Taxi (tel. 54 44 44).
>
> **Car Rental: Europcar,** C. Fray Toribio de Motolinia, 20 (tel. 51 24 25). Must be over 21 and have had license 1 yr.
>
> **Luggage Storage:** The **bus station** has lockers (57ptas per bag). Open 7am-10pm. The **train station** also has lockers (200ptas). Open 24 hrs.

English Bookstore: Librería Religiosa, C. Ramos Carrión, 13 (tel. 53 34 24), about 2 bl. past Pl. Mayor. Petite sampling of Penguin Classics and guidebooks in English. Open Mon.-Fri. 10am-2pm and 4-8pm.

Red Cross: C. Hernán Cortés, s/n (tel. 52 33 00).

Medical Services: Hospital Provincial, C. Hernán Cortés (tel. 52 02 00). **Casa de Socorro,** Pl. San Esteban (tel. 53 21 98). **Ambulance:** tel. 52 73 51, 51 69 69.

Police: tel. 53 04 62 or 092.

Accommodations

For simple rooms at reasonable prices, investigate the streets off C. Alfonso Peña by the train station, or off C. Santa Clara near Pl. Mayor.

Hostal de la Reina, C. de la Reina, 1, 1st fl. (tel. 53 39 39), behind Iglesia San Juan off C. Santa Clara. The building bears a *hostal* sign, but the door inside is unmarked. Mammoth chambers fit for a queen; some have a view of the *iglesia*. Singles 1600ptas, with bath 2100ptas. Doubles 2300ptas, with bath 2900ptas. Winter: 1300ptas, 1800ptas; 1800ptas, 2400ptas. Breakfast 200ptas.

Pensión Gemi, Pl. Mayor, 2nd fl. (tel. 53 04 60), right in front of the church. High windows, dark green walls, and a sign that entreats *"se ruega silencio"* (silence please). 800ptas per person. Showers 200ptas.

Pensión Gemi, C. Alfonso Peña, 3, 3rd fl. (tel. 51 71 75), across from the bus station. Aromas drift from the kitchen into the clean rooms. Quaint flowered bedspreads and snazzy brown tiled bathrooms. Singles 800ptas. Doubles 1600ptas.

Pensión Mari Trini, C. los Herreros, 8, 2nd fl. (tel. 53 10 19). Take a left off C. Santa Clara at Pl. Mayor. Plain, clean rooms above a bar. Singles 1000ptas. Doubles 1300ptas.

Food

Restaurants and *mesones* rub elbows around Pl. Mayor, off C. Santa Clara, and on C. los Herreros. The **Mercado de Abastos,** in a domed building with wrought iron gates, purveys basics. (Open Mon.-Sat. 9am-2pm.)

Groceries: Autoservicio Samba, C. Alfonso Peña, 15, across from the bus station. Open Mon.-Fri. 9am-2pm and 5-8pm, Sat. 9am-3pm. Other supermarkets line C. Tres Cruces and C. Víctor Gallego.

Mesón Los Abuelos, C. los Herreros, 30. Spanish hams dangle over the heads of a helpful staff. *Setas* and *pulpo* (mushrooms and octopus) are specialties. *Bocadillos* 275-400ptas. Open noon-2am.

Restaurante Pozo, C. Ramón Alvarez, 10 (tel. 51 20 94), off the northern edge of Pl. Mayor. A popular old-fashioned restaurant of plain, filling fare. *Merluza* (hake) is a specialty. Green-walled, cavernous dining room. *Menú* 900ptas. Open Mon.-Sat. 2-4:30pm and 8:30pm-midnight, Sun. 2-4:30pm.

Restaurante-Bar La Cooperativa, C. los Herreros, 18. Eclectic decor: an antique cigarette machine beneath a deer head on the wall. Spicy *morilla* 500ptas per *ración*. Why not have a nibble of *bacalao con pimiento y cebella?* Open Tues.-Sun. noon-1:30am.

Restaurante "España", C. Ramón Alvarez, 3, next door to the Pozo. The "dining room" is resplendent in lace curtains and wood-and-mirror columns. Huge "bar." Ample variety of vegetable dishes. *Menú* of *sopa de pescado* (clear "fish" soup) and *lomo de cerdo* (loin "of" pork) 900ptas. Open Mon.-Sat. 1:30-4:30pm and 8:30pm-2am, Sun. 1:30-4:30pm.

Sights

Zamora's foremost monument is its **catedral,** begun in 1135, whose cool Serbian-Byzantine dome sits like a bulb waiting to burst. Inside the cloister, the **Museo de la Catedral** holds a collection of art, documents, and the priceless 15th-century "Black Tapestries. Keep an eye out for those once-trendy oversized hymnals. (Open May-Sept. 11am-2pm and 5-8pm; Oct.-April 11am-2pm and 4-6pm.)

Remarkably, eight handsome **Romanesque churches** remain within the walls of the old city: San Ildefonso, Santa María de la Horta, Santo Tomé, La Magdalena, San Cipriano, San Juan, San Vicente, and Santiago del Burgo. All except San Ildefonso and

San Vicente have a summer visiting schedule. (Open June-Oct. Mon.-Sat. 10am-1pm and 5-8pm, Sun. 10am-1pm; Nov.-May only during mass.) Each one gleams (inside and out) in the wake of recent restoration. If pressed for time, at least drop by the intricately carved porch of **La Magdalena**. In **Santiago de Burgo**, 12th-century masons left their signature marks on the columns of the nave.

Scattered about like crumbs are ruins of the mostly Roman **walls**, the most famous being the "Puerta del Traidor" (Traitor's Gate) near the castle. This is the actual site where Sancho tried to do in poor Urraca, yet another victim of the evil patriarchy all women put up with. In the **Casa del Cid**, Governor Arias tutored the young siblings. Sancho II was knighted in **Iglesia de Santiago de Caballeros**; Urraca wasn't.

León

The medieval *Codex Calixtinus* heaps a whole pile of praise on León, calling it "the court and royal city...brimming with all kinds of felicity." Happily, this city at the juncture of the Ríos Torío and Bernesga is still grand—and not due to the lofty stained glass of its Gothic monuments alone. In Spain the city is called *la ciudad azul* (the blue city) after the dominant hue of the cathedral's sheets of stained glass, but the epithet suits the fountains, parks, and elegant broad avenues as well.

Founded by camping Roman legionnaires, León's name is a demotic corruption of *legio* (legion); the lion emblazoned everywhere postdates the naming of the city and is simply an inspired misreading. Once a springboard for the Reconquista, León owes its continuing material comfort to the fertile agricultural hinterland—chiefly cereal country—and the deposits of iron and cobalt mined throughout the province.

Orientation and Practical Information

Most of León puts the Río Bernesga between it and the bus and train stations. Heading east across the river from the stations, the new commercial district is followed by the old city. Take Avenida de Palencia over the bridge (left out of the bus station and right out of the train station). After crossing the river, you pass through **Plaza Guzmán el Bueno**. Av. Palencia then becomes **Avenida de Ordoño II**, which leads into and bisects the new city. It becomes **Avenida del Generalísimo Franco** in the old town, on the other side of **Plaza de Santo Domingo**. Av. del Generalísimo Franco splits the old town in two, with the **cathedral** in Plaza de Regla and the Basílica de San Isidoro to one side, the Ayuntamiento and **Plaza Mayor** on the other.

Tourist Office: Pl. Regla, 3 (tel. 23 70 82, fax 26 33 91), in front of the cathedral. Free city map and poster. Open Mon.-Fri. 9am-2pm and 4-6pm, Sat. 10am-1pm.

Budget Travel: TIVE, C. Conde de Guillén, 2 (tel. 20 09 51). ISIC 500ptas. IHYF card 500ptas. Some English spoken. Open Mon.-Fri. 9am-2pm.

Post Office: Jardín San Francisco (tel. 23 42 90, fax (987) 23 47 01). From Pl. Santo Domingo, down Av. Independencia and opposite Parque San Francisco. It's the ugly modern building. Open for stamps Mon.-Fri. 8am-9pm, Sat. 9am-2pm; for Lista de Correos Mon.-Fri. 9am-9pm, Sat. 9am-2pm; for **faxes** Mon.-Fri. 8am-9pm, Sat. 9am-7pm. **Postal Code:** 24071.

Telephones: Telefónica, C. Burgo Nuevo, 15. From Pl. Santo Domingo, take Av. Independencia and turn right onto C. Burgo Nuevo. Open Mon.-Fri. 9am-2:30pm and 4-10:30pm, Sat. 9am-2pm and 4-9pm. Also, **faxes** sent but not received. **Telephone Code:** 987.

Trains: RENFE, Av. Astorga, 2 (tel. 27 02 02), across the river from Pl. Guzmán el Bueno and a right turn off Av. Palencia. Far away. Information open 24 hrs. Ticket office at C. Carmen, 4 (tel. 22 05 25). Open Mon.-Fri. 9:30am-2pm and 5-8pm, Sat. 10am-1:30pm. To: Astorga (13 per day, 45min., 565ptas); Zamora (7 per day, 1 1/4 hr., 1515ptas); Palencia (20 per day, 1 1/2 hr., 575ptas); Valladolid (1 per day, 2 1/2 hr., 855ptas); Oviedo (8 per day, 2hr., 685ptas); Santander (3 per day, 5hr., 1710ptas); Salamanca (1 per day, 3 1/2 hr., 1330ptas); A Coruña (3 per day, 7-8hr., 2395ptas); Madrid (5 per day, 4-5 1/2 hr., 2055ptas); Barcelona (3 per day, 9 1/2 -11hr., 5105ptas). **FEVE,** Estación de Matallana, Av. Padre Isla, 48 (tel. 22 59 19), north of Pl. Santo Domingo.

Buses: Estación de Autobuses, Po. Ingeniero Saenz de Miera (tel. 21 10 00), along the river. Information open Mon.-Sat. 7:30am-9pm. To: Astorga (15 per day, 45min., 355ptas); Valladolid (5 per day, 2hr., 875ptas); Santander (1 per day, 5hr., 1930ptas); Bilbao (1 per day, 6hr., 2500ptas); Cáceres (3 per day, 6hr., 2400ptas); Oviedo (8 per day, 2hr., 845ptas); Zamora (5 per day, 1 3/4 hr., 905ptas); Madrid (15 per day, 6hr., 2125ptas); Sevilla (3 per day, 11hr., 6000ptas).

Taxis: tel. 24 24 51, 24 12 11.

Car Rental: Hertz, Av. Sanjurjo, 23 (tel. 23 25 54). Must be over 21 and have had license 1 yr. Open Mon.-Fri. 9am-2pm and 4-7pm, Sat. 9am-1pm.

Luggage Storage: At the **train station** (lockers 200ptas). Open 24 hrs. At the **bus station** (6ptas per bag). Open Mon.-Fri. 9-11am and 6-8pm, Sat. 9-11am.

Lost Property: At the police station.

English Bookstore: Pastor, Pl. Santo Domingo, 4 (tel. 22 58 56). Rather good array of Oxford and Penguin Classics. Open Mon.-Fri. 10am-1:30pm and 4:15-8pm, Sat. 10am-1:45pm.

Library: Biblioteca Pública del Estado, C. Santa Nonia, 5 (tel. 20 67 10). Open July-Aug. Mon.- Fri. 9am-2:30pm, Sat. 9am-1:30pm; Sept.-June Mon.-Fri. 9am-2pm and 4-9pm, Sat. 9am-1:30pm.

Laundromat: Lavasec, C. Pérez Galdós, 1, off Av. Quevedo, 3 bl. from Puente San Marcos. Wash 290ptas per load, dry 100ptas. Open Mon.-Sat. 9:30am-2pm and 4-8pm.

Athletic Facilities: Polideportivo, Po. Ingeniero Saenz de Miera (tel. 20 05 19), just past the bus station. Squash courts and a track. Pool 140ptas (open 10am-9pm). Sauna 315ptas.

Red Cross: tel. 27 00 33.

Medical Services: Hospital Provincial, C. Alvaro López Núñez, 26 (tel. 22 71 00). **Hospital General,** C. San Antonio, s/n (tel. 23 49 00). **Casa de Socorro** (tel. 25 12 10). **Ambulance** (tel. 27 00 33).

Emergency: tel. 091, 092.

Police: Villa Benavente, 6 (tel. 20 73 12).

Accommodations

Budget beds aren't scarce in León, although soldiers on leave in late spring snap up the *fondas* and *casas de huéspedes* during holidays and weekends. For a start, look on **Avenida de Roma, Avenida de Ordoño II,** and the side streets surrounding them, which lead into the new town from Pl. Guzmán el Bueno. *Pensiones* also clump on the streets by the train and bus stations, but they're less convenient to the sights. This neighborhood is also somewhat forbidding at night.

Residencia Juvenil Infanta Doña Sancha (HI), C. Corredera, 2 (tel. 20 22 01, 20 38 11), 2 bl. past the Jardín San Francisco. A clean university dorm during the school year. Singles, doubles, and triples available. 700ptas per person. Groups larger than 8, 650ptas. *Pensión media* 1200ptas. *Pensión completa* 1550ptas. Over 26: 900ptas; 800ptas; 1600ptas; 2100ptas. Showers included. Breakfast 100ptas. Sheets included. Winter heating. Often booked solid; call ahead. Open July-Aug.

Consejo de Europa (HI), Po. Parque, 2 (tel. 20 02 06), off Pl. Toros. Fully renovated accommodations. 700ptas, over 26 900ptas. Breakfast 250ptas. Winter heating. Often booked solid; call ahead. Open July-Aug.

Fonda Condado, Av. República Argentina, 28 (tel. 20 61 60), the right branch of the fork at Pl. Guzmán el Bueno. Medievalish waiting room with framed *arras* and stained glass windows. Mammoth rooms and a TV room. Singles with bath 1500ptas. Doubles with bath 2000ptas.

Hostal Residencia Londres, Av. Roma, 1 (tel. 22 22 74), at the end of Av. Roma off Pl. Calvo Sotelo. The oil painting in the hallway is only the tip of the swish iceberg: terraced rooms have comfy beds, and the bathroom is *luxe* gray and pink marble. Leona Helmsley would be proud. Singles 1500ptas. Doubles 2500ptas. Oct.-March: 1100ptas; 1700ptas. Showers 200ptas.

Hostal Europa, Av. Roma, 26 (tel. 22 22 38), near Pl. Guzmán el Bueno. Swoon over the dreamy beds, plushy olive bedspreads, and Scarlett O'Hara curtains in the hallway. The brown tiled bathroom is spotless. Singles 1500ptas. Doubles 2500ptas.

Hostal Residencia Guzmán el Bueno, C. López Castrillón, 6 (tel. 23 64 12). Walk up C. Generalísimo Franco from Pl. Santo Domingo, and turn left on C. Cid; López Castrillón is the street on the right. Complicated, but right there in the old city. Dull rooms are at least white and bright. Huge sitting room adorned by brown couches and a gold shoe with flowers growing in it. Very clean. Singles 1900ptas, with bath 2400ptas. Doubles 3000ptas, with bath 3800ptas. Breakfast (8-11am) 250ptas.

Hostal Central, Av. Ordoño II, 27 (tel. 25 18 06). Look for the sign. Vaguely Art Deco headboards on the beds. Beware the paper-walled windowless single right on the hallway. Singles 1000ptas. Doubles 2000ptas. Showers 200ptas.

Hostal Oviedo, Av. Roma, 26, 2nd fl. (tel. 22 22 36), upstairs from the Europa. Pristine establishment run by archetypical grandparents. Many rooms have terraces; all have rosebudded tan and pink bedspreads. Singles with sink 1400ptas. Doubles 2500ptas. Showers 250ptas.

Hostal Orejas, C. Villafranca, 8, 2nd fl. (tel. 25 29 09), above the Condado. Clean rooms with blue flowered bedspreads. Slightly upscale, but the extra *pesetas* fetch nice tiled bathrooms and a TV room. Singles 1800ptas, with bath 2250ptas. Doubles with bath 4000ptas, with TV 4200ptas. Triples 5000ptas. *Pensión completa* 1800ptas. Breakfast 250ptas. Lunch or dinner 1000ptas.

Food

The rich countryside around León is a veritable Cockaigne. Although not near any coast, the town hosts the annual International Trout Festival in June. Food in the buff is sold at **Mercado Municipal del Conde,** Pl. Conde off C. General Mola. (Open Mon.-Sat. 9am-2pm.) Vegetable **markets** invade Pl. Mayor Wednesdays and Saturdays. Inexpensive places cluster by the cathedral, on **C. Cid,** and on nearby streets. Also seek around **Plazas Mayor and San Martín.**

Groceries: Super Ama, C. Santa Nonia. Turn right off Av. Ordoño II onto Av. Independencia; Santa Nonia is the 2nd right. Open Mon.-Sat. 9:30am-2pm and 5-8pm.

Bar-Restaurante Cortijo Susi, C. López Castillón, 8 (tel. 23 60 46), on the same street as Hostal Guzmán. Friendly, family-run place with an adjoining lively bar. *Fabada* 375ptas. The 700ptas *menú del día* of *sopa de pescado* and *chuletillas de cordero* is served quickly and affectionately. You'll leave satisfied, thank Jesus. Open Mon.-Sat. 1-4:30pm and 9-11:30pm.

Restaurante La Esponja, C. Cid, 18 (tel. 23 60 26). Inauspicious exterior, standard formal decor within. 650ptas *menú* changes daily. Open 1:30-4:30pm and 8-11:30pm.

Restaurante Buenos Aires, Av. Roma, 12. Av. Roma starts at Pl. Guzmán el Bueno. Argentine-by-way-of-Italy cuisine. 850ptas *menú* includes *sopa de cocido* and *pimientos rellenos*. Also pizza (try the *picola* with anchovies, tomato, and oregano, 400ptas) and miscellaneous Italian food. Bar leads to a *comedor* with heartwarming light blue tablecloths and a TV. Open Mon.-Sat. 9am-midnight.

Mesón San Martín, Pl. San Martín, 8 (tel. 25 60 55), a winding block from Pl. Mayor. Quite classy, and right in the middle of the action. Like no bargain basement you've ever seen. Assorted daily specials include *menestra* (mushroom, artichoke, pea, and ham soup, 400ptas) and *cocido* (stew with boiled sausage, carrots, lettuce, and chickpeas, 875ptas). Open Mon. and Thurs. 1-4pm, Tues.-Wed. and Fri.-Sun. 1-4pm and 8-11:30pm. Closed part of July.

Cafetería-Pizzeria Santa Rita, C. Juan Lorenzo Segura, 4, a left turn off Av. Ordoño II. Neon sign. Dining room upstairs, bar below. *Platos combinados* from 300ptas (eggs, bacon, and fries). Savory individual pizzas 425-600ptas. The *copa Santa Rita* is their prize dessert (325ptas). Open 8am-midnight.

Bar-Restaurante Gijón, C. Alcázar Toledo, 15 (tel. 22 22 83), a left off Av. Ordóno II from Pl. Santo Domingo. Diverse stewed animal parts keep locals salivating and licking their chops. *Carne guisada* (stewed meat, 500ptas), *callos* (tripe), and *lomo* (loin of pork). *Menú* 900ptas. Open Mon.-Sat. 10am-5pm and 8-12pm.

Sights

The Gothic **catedral** is undoubtedly one of the most beautiful in the land. Its exceptionally well-preserved façade depicts everything from a smiling *Santa María la Blanca* to bug-eyed monsters munching on the damned, but the stained-glass interior is the real knock-out. The windows occupy so much of the wall area that the building suffers from a lack of solid rock support. Every imaginable hue is represented. If you're into plot, the cathedral guidebook is worth 700ptas, as it deciphers the complicated narrative depicted in stained glass. A splendid **museo** on the evolution of Romanesque sculpture hides beyond the vast cloister and strange twisting sculptures. (Museum open 10am-1:30pm and 4-6pm. Admission to cloister and museum 200ptas, cloister only 100ptas.)

Basílica de San Isidoro was dedicated in the 11th century to San Isidoro of Sevilla, whose remains were brought to León while Muslims ruled the South. The distinctly Muslim arches are characterized by small lobes that form a larger arch. The corpses of León's royal family rest in the impressive **Panteón Real**. Yet some argue that the real treasures here are not underground, but overhead: remarkably vibrant tempera frescoes cover two crypt ceilings. The frescoes were something of a religious coup in their day; they portray scenes of the New Testament, if you can believe it. Specialists have been trying to preserve the 800-year-old paintings; they've also taken protective steps against the sun's harmful intrusion into the vault. Admission to the pantheon allows entrance to the treasury and library of rare books. Doña Urraca's famous chalices, two Roman cups set in gold and jewels, outshine the rest of the treasury room. A 10th-century handwritten Bible is the library's highlight. (Museum open Mon.-Sat. 10am-1:30pm and 4-6:30pm, Sun. 10am-1:30pm. Admission and interminable tour 200ptas.) The city's **murallas romanas** are well preserved around the cathedral and San Isidoro.

Once a resting place for pilgrims en route to Santiago de Compostela, the **Monasterio San Marcos** is León's only five-star hotel with a Plateresque façade. The **museo** in the adjacent Gothic church houses objects from Roman and medieval times. Among its treasures are the 11th-century Byzantine *Carrizo Crucifix* and a Mozarabic cross encrusted with jewels. (Museum open Tues.-Sat. 10am-2pm and 5-7pm, Sun. 10am-1:30pm. Admission 200ptas.)

The **Casa de los Botines**, near Pl. Santo Domingo, is one of the few buildings Antoni Gaudí designed outside his native Catalunya. This one's relatively restrained yet still whimsical.

Entertainment

Once the afternoon drags to a close, the university students go out. For the early part of the night (around 11pm-2am), the **barrio húmedo** around Pl. San Martín is crawling with bars, discos, techno-pop, and revelers—slightly teenybopping, but not unduly so. After 2am, the crowd weaves to **C. Lancia** and **C. Conde de Guillén**, where discos and bars take over.

Fiestas commemorating St. John and St. Peter run together for a week-long celebration (June 20-29) including ritual taurean blood-letting. The highlights are the feast days of San Juan on the 24th and San Pedro on the 29th. Concerts and theatrical performances enliven the celebration (schedules available shortly beforehand). Book stalls and jewelry stands line the Po. Papalaguinda, and an amusement park is erected for the week. On opening day, catch the parade of bright costumes, music, and *churrería* stands galore. Such notables as the King of Spain and his wife Sofía come on a yearly basis and often participate in the **International Organ Festival** at the cathedral.

Near León

Astorga

Antoni Gaudí fans might finally make it out of Catalunya to visit one of his quirkiest neo-Gothic fantasies in Astorga, a breeze of a daytrip from León. The fairy-tale **Palacio Episcopal** (Bishop's Palace) is one of his most fanciful creations. After the original residence of Astorga's bishop burned down in 1886, the bishop commissioned his friend Gaudí to design the new one. The architect drew up curving pillars, elaborate stained glass, jutting turrets, enormous halls, and tiled ceilings, and surrounded the entire castle with a deep moat. The expense proved enormous for the poor parish; after its bishop's death, the construction dragged on for 20 more years and even then, no bishop dared occupy it.

Today the palace houses the **Museo de los Caminos**. The museum's ostensible purpose is to illustrate the various *caminos* (roads) that have passed through Astorga.

Among the extremely miscellaneous exhibits are elaborate Gothic tombs for the Counts of Benavente in the basement. On the first floor, in the room dedicated to the Camino de Santiago, don't miss the bewitching handwritten pilgrimage guides, dating from the 17th and 18th centuries. The second floor includes such highlights as Gaudí's effervescent chapel and a delightful light-filled dining room to swoon over. (Open May-Sept. 10am-2pm and 4-8pm; Oct.-April 11am-2pm. Admission 200ptas; to palace and Museo Diocesano below 325ptas.) To get to Gaudí's palace from the train station, follow C. José Antonio Primo de Rivera; it becomes tree-lined C. Pedro de Castro, passing Pl. Porfirio López. Then turn right at the newsstands and follow the signs. From the bus station, exit and cross the street to the huge stone walls; climb the stairs and the palace is on the left.

While in Astorga, glance at its **catedral,** conveniently opposite Gaudí's *palacio*. Though weak in comparison with León's, it does have a insanely ornate 18th-century façade and beautiful *coro*. Whip through the **Museo Diocesano,** whose most intriguing possession is Alfonso III's glamorous golden casket. (Cathedral open June-Sept. 9am-noon and 5-6:30pm, Oct.-May 9am-noon and 4:30-6pm; free. At other times enter through the museum for 200ptas; open June-Sept. 10am-2pm and 4-8pm, Oct.-May 11am-2pm and 3:30-6:30pm.)

Turismo operates out of a wooden box in the square between the cathedral and Gaudí's palace. (Open mid-June to mid-Sept. Mon.-Sat. 10am-1:30pm and 4-7:30pm, Sun. 10am-1:30pm.) Astorga is an easy **train** ride from León on the line running northwest to Galicia (13 per day, 40min., 265ptas). The **train station** (tel. 61 51 63) is at Pl. Estación. Empresa Fernandez (tel. 61 66 01) runs 14 **buses** per day from León (45min., 355ptas). The bus station leaves you much closer to the cathedral and Palacio Gaudí.

Sahagún

Southeast of León, otherwise unremarkable Sahagún has some superb samples of Mudejar architecture. Horseshoe arches frame the three altars inside the 12th-century **Iglesia de San Tirso,** a church with a famous tower. Up a small hill near San Tirso sits the **Iglesia de la Peregrina.** Muslim stonework covers the exterior of this 12th- and 13th-century building. The building's glory hides in a small chapel lined with delicate geometrical reliefs. The eye-straining patterns of the molded weaves appear repetitive, but in fact, each design is unique. If the door of either is locked, walk over to the other; one *señor* holds all the keys. (Both churches open Tues.-Sat. 10:30am-2pm and 5-8pm, Sun. 10am-3pm; Oct.-May Tues.-Sat. 10:30am-2pm and 4-7pm, Sun. 10am-3pm.) To get here from the train station, go right and walk to Pl. Gen. Franco, about 10 minutes away; walk out C. Flora Flórez and turn right on C. de San Benito. San Tirso is to the left.

The **town hall** (tel. 78 00 01) is on Pl. Mayor. The **Red Cross** (tel. 78 01 45) is on the far side of the Roman bridge. The **consultorio médico** (tel. 78 01 00) is a block from the police. **Buses** leave from and for León twice per day (tel. 21 10 00 for schedule).

Valladolid

The splendid and the commonplace interweave in Valladolid as in no other Spanish town. An industrial boom and the consequent influx of workers from the countryside, combined with unchecked construction in the 70s, accelerated the old quarter's deterioration and brought a fair crop of urban problems. Nevertheless, individual sights still evoke Valladolid's Renaissance magnificence.

A favorite seat of Castilian kings since the 12th century, Valladolid supplanted Burgos as capital of Castile (and newly unified Spain) after the conquest of Granada; Fernando and Isabel had been married here in 1469. Save for a brief spell under Felipe III (1601-1607), owing to a whopping bribe palmed by his infamous prime minister Conde-Duque de Lerma, Valladolid lost out as capital definitively to Madrid in 1561. Miguel de Cervantes lived here during Valladolid's second coming, and it has been suggested that Shakespeare might have been in the English ambassador's retinue.

Though its heyday as the hotseat of monarchical intrigue is past, the sheer number of young people infuse Valladolid with a vigor that adds to its already bustling commercial activity. Most citizens welcome the escape from the city's former dreary provincialism to a genuine big-city ambience. The city's nickname "Facha-dolid" (that is, Fascist-dolid) has long since been outgrown.

Orientation and Practical Information

The keystone in Castilla y León's arch, Valladolid occupies a central position halfway between León (133km) and Segovia (110km), and, at the same time, halfway between Burgos (122km) and Salamanca (114km). The bus and train stations sit on the southern edge of town. From the bus station, turn left to reach the train station. From the train station, walk straight down Calle Estación del Norte to Plaza de Colón (200m) and follow the signs to **Plaza de Zorrilla** (and the tourist office) or **Plaza de España** at the center of town. Beyond Pl. Zorrilla and Pl. España, **Pl. Mayor,** the cathedral, and the centers of nightlife radiate in a semicircle.

Tourist Office: Pl. Zorrilla, 3 (tel. 35 18 01). Maps, the lowdown on museums, the hotel listings. English spoken. Open Mon.-Fri. 9am-2pm and 4-6pm, Sat. 9am-2pm.

El Corte Inglés: Paseo Zorrilla, 130-32 (tel. 27 23 04, 47 83 00). Po. Zorrilla starts at Pl. Zorrilla; just walk down past the *plaza de toros* (bullring). Their **map** beats the one from the tourist office. **Currency exchange:** 1% commission (250ptas min. charge). They also offer novels and guidebooks in English; haircutting; both cafeteria and restaurant; and **telephones.** Open Mon.-Sat. 10am-9pm.

Budget Travel: TIVE (tel. 35 45 63), on the 3rd floor of the Edificio Administrativo de Use Múltiple. From Pl. Zorrilla, take C. María de Molina to C. Doctrinos, follow Doctrinos across puente Isabel la Católica, and then pass the parking lot. Open Mon.-Fri. 9am-2pm.

Currency Exchange: Caja Postal, in the post office on Pl. Rinconada. 1% commission (250ptas min. charge). Open Mon.-Fri. 8:30am-2pm, Sat. 8:30am-1pm.

Post Office: Pl. Rinconada (tel. 33 06 60, fax (983) 35 19 87), just past Pl. Mayor. Information open Mon.-Fri. 9am-2pm. Open for stamps Mon.-Fri. 8am-9pm, Sat. 9am-2pm; for Lista de Correos Mon.-Fri. 8am-9pm. Open for **telegrams** Mon.-Fri. 8am-9pm, Sat. 9am-7pm. **Faxes** sent and received Mon.-Fri. 8am-8pm. **Postal Code:** 47071.

Telephones: Telefónica, Pl. Mayor, 7. You can send but not receive **faxes**. Open Mon.-Sat. 9:30am-2pm and 4:30-10pm. **Telephone Code:** 983.

Flights: Villanubla Airport (tel. 56 01 62). The taxi ride is 1500ptas. Daily service to Barcelona all year; service to the islands in the summer. Information open 12:30-7:30pm. **Iberia,** C. Gamazo, 17 (tel. 30 26 39). Open Mon.-Fri. 9:30am-1:30pm and 4-7pm, Sat. 9:30am-1:30pm.

Trains: Estación del Norte, C. Recondo, s/n (tel. 30 34 00), at the end of Campo Grande. To: Medina del Campo (24 per day, 1/2 hr., 220ptas); Zamora (2 per day, 4hr., 600ptas); Burgos (11 per day, 2hr., 615ptas); Salamanca (8 per day, 1 3/4 hr., 590ptas); León (12 per day, 1 1/2 hr., 855ptas); Madrid (22 per day, 4hr., 1225ptas); Santander (4 per day, 4 3/4 hr., 1400ptas); Irún (2 per day, 4 1/2 hr., 1905ptas). Information (tel. 20 02 02, 30 12 17) open 7am-11pm.

Buses: Puente Colgante, 2 (tel. 23 63 08). From the train station, turn left and stick close to the train tracks for the 5min. walk. To: Medina del Campo (8 per day, 1/2 hr., 335ptas); Zamora (7 per day, 4hr., 640ptas); Burgos (3 per day, 2hr., 800ptas); León (4 per day, 2hr., 875ptas); Segovia (5 per day, 2hr., 745ptas); Oviedo (4 per day, 4hr., 1775ptas); Donostia/San Sebastián (2 per day, 6hr., 2750ptas); Bilbo (2 per day, 5hr., 1930ptas); Barcelona (3 per day, 9hr., 4680ptas); Madrid (12 per day, 2 1/2 hr., 1265ptas). Information open 8:30am-8:30pm.

Taxis: Radio Taxi (tel. 29 14 11). **Agrupación de Taxis** (tel. 20 77 55).

Car Rental: Autos Castilla, C. Muro, 16 (tel. 30 18 78). Must be over 22 and have had a license for at least 1 yr. Open Mon.-Fri. 9am-2pm and 4-8pm, Sat. 9am-2pm.

Luggage Storage: Estación del Norte has lockers. Counters are available at the ticket window (200ptas). Baggage check at the **bus station** (200ptas per bag). Open 8am-8pm.

Lost Property: in the Ayuntamiento in Pl. Mayor (tel. 35 04 99). Open Mon.-Fri. 9am-2pm.

Bookstore: Librería Lara, C. Fuente Dorada, 17 (tel. 30 03 66). About 40 Penguin titles and 40 Grafton and Oxford titles. Open Mon.-Fri. 10am-1:30pm and 5-8pm, Sat. 10am-2pm.

Library: Biblioteca Pública de Chancilleriá, C. Chancilleriá (tel. 35 85 99), between Av. Ramón y Cajal and C. Real de Burgos. Open Mon.-Fri. 9am-2pm and 4-9pm, Sat. 9am-2pm.

Swimming Pool: Piscinas Deportivas, next to the river off Po. Isabel la Católica near Puente del Poniente. Outdoors. Admission 260ptas. Open June-Sept. 11am-8:30pm.

Crisis Lines: AIDS hotline (tel. 33 93 35). **Women's information line** (tel. 30 08 93). **Drug abuse hotline** (tel. 35 33 18). **De la Esperanza** (tel. 30 70 77) and **Voces Amigas** (tel. 33 46 35, 33 19 13) for depression.

Red Cross: tel. 22 22 22.

Late-Night Pharmacy: Check *El Norte de Castilla* or *El Mundo de Valladolid* (local papers, 90ptas) for listing.

Hospitals: Hospital Clínico Universitario, Av. Ramón y Cajal, s/n (tel. 42 00 00). **Hospital Pío del Río Hortega,** C. Santa Teresa, s/n (tel. 42 04 00, 35 76 00). Some doctors speak English.

Emergency: tel. 092 (local) or 091 (national).

Accommodations

Since the youth hostel is a student dorm, it's only open during summer vacation. Luckily, Valladolid offers plenty of other good lodgings; all have winter heating. Fertile ground includes the streets near the cathedral, Plaza del Val, and the triangular area formed by **Avenida Recoletos, Calle Miguel Iscar,** and **Calle Gamazo** just East of the Pl. Colón (but do not wander alone here after dark).

Río Esqueva Albergue Juvenil (HI), Ctra. Cementerio (tel. 25 15 50). Take bus #1 or 8. A 5-minute ride from the Pl. Mayor (every 20min., 50ptas). Get off the #1 at Río Esqueva and walk across the park on your right. Get off the #8 at the river, then proceed down C. Chancillería, which turns into C. Madre de Diós and finally into C. Cementerio. 3-day max. stay. No curfew. 600ptas, over 26 700ptas, *pensión completa* 1300ptas. Open July-Aug.

Pensión Dos Rosas, C. Perú, 11 (tel. 20 74 39). From the train station, walk up Av. Acera Recoletos and turn right on C. Perú. The management bends over backward to scrub and care for the place. A fantastic bargain only 2 blocks from Pl. Zorrilla. Singles 950ptas. Doubles 1750ptas. Showers 150ptas.

Pensión Asturiana, C. Zapico, 1 (tel. 33 01 15), up the street from Pl. del Val. Slinky peach bedspreads. Singles 1000ptas. Doubles 2000ptas. Triples 3500ptas. Showers 100ptas.

Hostal Val VI, Pl. Val 6 (tel. 35 25 12), a short distance beyond the right-hand corner of Pl. Mayor as you face the Ayuntamiento. Clean rooms with basin or bath. TV rooms with Ponti-pleasing couches. Singles with basin 1500ptas. Doubles with basin 2500ptas, with bath fit for a queen 3500ptas. Prices slightly higher for *Semana Santa.*

Pensión Segoviano, C. Perú, 11 (tel. 30 02 49), off Av. Acera Recoletos. Reasonably clean, reasonably large rooms with reasonably cute flowered bedspreads. The manager gives the scoop on the scary-after-dark neighborhood. Singles 1500ptas. Doubles 2500ptas. Triples 3000ptas.

Hostal Vuelta, C. Val, 2 (tel. 35 60 66), between Pl. Mayor and Mercado del Val. The yellow sign is visible from the right-hand corner of Pl. Mayor as you face the Ayuntamiento. Jovial family rents large, spotless rooms, some with balconies. Singles with sink 1400ptas. Doubles with sink 2600ptas.

Pensión Benavente, C. Val, 1 (tel. 35 56 92). Follow C. Santiago to Pl. Mayor, then keep to the right and pass Pl. Corrillo. Rooms just big enough for one-on-one basketball. Singles 1600ptas. Doubles 1600ptas. Showers 150ptas.

Food

In Valladolid, as in every university town, cheap food is never far away. Explore **Plaza de la Universidad,** near the cathedral, for *tapas.* The **Mercado del Val** on C. Sandoval, in Pl. Val, handles vegetable, meat, and fruit. (Open Mon.-Sat. 9am-3pm.) **Feri,** C. Santiago, 14, is a candy store-*cum-herbolario,* with sweets in front and a small selection of health foods in back (open 10:30am-2pm and 5-9pm; open Mon.-Sat. in July). Similar goods at **Alimentación Natural Flor,** C. Vega, near Pl. España.

Groceries: Supermercados Max Coop, C. Estación del Norte (tel. 39 26 04), on the right as you walk up from the train station and through the gate. Open Mon.-Fri. 9am-2pm and 5-8pm, Sat. 9am-2pm. **Simago,** C. Santiago, 3 blocks from Pl. Zorrilla. Open Mon.-Sat. 9:30am-8:30pm.

Restaurante Covadonga, C. Zapico, 1, up the street from Pl. del Val. Busy yet surprisingly elegant atmosphere, at equally surprising prices. *Menú del día* includes bread, wine, and dessert (795ptas). *Sopa de mariscos* (soup with shellfish) 295ptas. *Escalope de ternera* 380ptas. Open Tues.-Sat. 1-4pm and 9-11pm, Sun.-Mon. 1-4pm.

Restaurante Dover, C. Francisco Zarandona, 8, around the corner from Mercado del Val. Serves up a generous *ensalada rusa* and *pollo al ajillo* as their *menú de la casa* (700ptas). *Bocadillo de ternera* 375ptas. Open 1-4:30pm.

Restaurant El Val, Pl. de la Rinconada, 10. From Pl. Mayor, up C. Jesús and keep to the right. On the 1st floor of building with huge wood doors. Gray door on the right that says "Entren sin llamar." Warm *comedor* resembles a bar mitzvah reception room. *Menú* 725ptas. *Lentejas* 240ptas. Roasty good 1/2-chicken 325ptas. 1/2-portions of other items too. Open Sept.-July Tues.Sun. 10-4pm and 9-11pm.

Cafetería Beatriz, C. Tarandona, 4 (tel. 33 00 63), near the market. Fab decor (bright orange counter and blue vinyl seating). 1/2-chicken, french fries, and salad 475ptas. *Filete* (steak) and eggs 575ptas. Open Tues.-Sun. 7am-4pm and 7pm-midnight.

Tele Pizza, C. Puente Colgante, 49. Follow Po. Zorrilla 2 blocks past the park. Spain's answer to Domino's. They deliver, or you can eat there. Pizza 650ptas, 80ptas per each additional topping. 900ptas min. for delivery. Open Sun.-Thurs. 1-4pm and 6:30pm-midnight, Fri.-Sat. 1-4pm and 6:30pm-1am.

Cerveceria Vavi, C. Arzobispo Gondásegui, 2, on the left corner of Pl. Portugalete as you face cathedral. Strange hybrid of American and Spanish quick eats. *Bocadillos* 200-250ptas. *Sandwich vegetal* 225ptas. French fries 120ptas. Crown jewel of the bunch is *hamburguesa vavi* (bacon cheeseburger, 225ptas). Big buns. Open Tues.-Sun. 6pm-midnight, later on weekends.

Café Bar Yoalmar, C. San Blas, 17. From Pl. Val, take C. Platerias to C. Felipe II, then right onto San Blas. Sandwiched between 2 sex shops, Yoalmar has you panting after a *pincho* of *tortilla de bonito, champiñón y patata,* their specialty, 125ptas. Open Mon.-Fri. 8am-11:30pm, Sat.-Sun. noon-12:30am.

Café El Norte, Pl. Mayor, 12. From C. Santiago turn right. The *terraza*'s bird's-eye view of Pl. Mayor ups prices. *Pinchos* 100-300ptas. Pastries 90-300ptas. *Bocadillos* 250-350ptas. Open 9am-1am.

Sights

Glory slipped through the fingers of Valladolid. The **catedral,** in Pl. Universidad, should have been four times larger, and there is something poignant about this monumental fragment. Designed by Juan de Herrera (responsible for El Escorial), its interior is cold and severe, with light streaming through the windows set in colossal white stone arches. (100ptas to illuminate the main altar for 15 seconds; side altar 25ptas.) The **Museo Diocesano** inside is worth a look for its jewelry, wooden polychrome statues of John the Baptist, and a model of the basilica's original design. (Open Tues.-Fri. 10am-1:30pm and 4:30-7pm, Sat.-Sun. 10am-2pm. Cathedral free, museum 200ptas. Cathedral often closes early afternoon.) Behind the cathedral, the Romanesque tower of **Santa María la Antigua** caps a mainly Gothic underpinning. Up C. San Blas and C. Héroes de Teruel, **Iglesia de San Benito el Real** flaunts a portico big enough to shelter a whole team of monks.

Expressionistic gilt wood fans are sated at the **Museo Nacional de Escultura Policromática** in the **Colegio de San Gregorio** (tel. 25 03 75). The *colegio* is some minutes beyond the cathedral and Iglesia de Santa María. (Open Tues.-Sat. 10am-2pm and 4-6pm, Sun. 10am-2pm. Admission 200ptas.) The **patio's** interwoven masonry is hypnotizing—the stone looks like it's dripping off the building.

Spain's best collection of Asian art is tucked away in the **Museo Oriental,** in the basement of the **Real Colegio Padres Agustinos Filipinos,** Po. Filipinos, 7 (tel. 30 68 00). During four centuries of missionary work, Jesuits accumulated the collection of largely Chinese and Philippine works. The highlight is a 15-inch ship crafted from cloves. (Open Mon.-Sat. 4-7pm, Sun. 10am-1pm. Admission 200ptas, groups of students and seniors 150ptas. Located near the train station, on the south side of Campo Grande.)

The discoverer of America and the creator of Don Quixote both came here to die. Plush **Casa de Colón**, on C. Colón (tel. 29 13 53), is now part research library and part museum. (Open Tues.-Sat. 10am-2pm and 4-6pm, Sun. 10am-2pm. Free.) From the looks of the **Casa de Cervantes**, off C. Castro, you might conclude that he died of boredom. There's an amusing collection of old books and furniture, but the medieval bed-warmer is the real highlight. His secluded garden, protected by a stone wall, is snipped to pristine perfection. (Open Tues.-Sat. 10am-3:30pm, Sun. 10am-3pm. Admission 200ptas.)

The **Campo Grande** is a fave of afternoon strollers. Lush trees blend with waterfalls and babbling brooks, geese, swans, and the occasional peacock. During the *paseo* (roughly 7-9pm), residents browse in the shops on the pedestrian walks between here and **Pl. Mayor**. However, the Campo Grande turns sleazier after nightfall.

Entertainment

Although Valladolid's nightlife wins no points for variety, its cafés and bars are vibrant. In the early evening after classes, many dally in the pasture near the cathedral (a liter bottle of San Miguel beer is the standard accessory). Later, the herds migrate from bars near the university to **Plaza Cantarranas**, two blocks east. En route they pass by a Valladolid institution, **El Penicilino** (tel. 30 50 32), on Pl. Libertad. Cristina, the proprietor, will tell you about the medical student who used to request a special concoction that others found so delicious the bar now bottles the mixture (50ptas a glass). "Penicilino" was named in honor of the antibiotic discovered at the same time. The sign in front reads "Juan Martín Calvo." (Open Thurs.-Tues. 11:30am-2:30pm and 6-11pm.) In summer, ubiquitous *terrazas* can be found on Po. Zorrilla, C. de Santiago, and in the plazas of most of the city's museums and monuments.

Cine Casablanca, C. Platerías, 1, shows movies with English subtitles (*voz original subtitulada*). From Pl. Mayor, turn right on C. Ferrari, follow C. Quiñones and its continuation, C. de la Lonja, to Pl. Ochavo. Cross the street to C. Platerías. Movies screen at 5:30, 8, and 10pm (admission with ISIC 350ptas). The city holds a highly regarded **Festival Internacional de Cine** at the end of October and the beginning of November. Schedules are not available until shortly beforehand.

Semana Santa (Holy Week) in Valladolid ranks with Sevilla's as one of Spain's most fascinating religious festivals. It is distinguished by its solemnity and austerity, enriched by the rituals of *cofradías* (brotherhoods) and religious orders. Veiled women dressed in white carry palm fronds through the city on Palm Sunday. High masses are held on Holy Wednesday, and multicolored floats from the 17th century are borne through the streets on Holy Thursday. On Good Friday, all the orders march in total silence except for the beating of a lone, mournful drum. September 16-23 marks the **Fiesta Mayor** celebrations, featuring bullfights, carnival rides, and parades.

Palencia

Palencia is not València. Without a Mediterranean beach, raging nightlife, or fertile orange groves, the city distinguished itself in 1208 by establishing Spain's first university (moved to Salamanca in 1239). This ambitious streak lasted a full century; in 1321 the city built its crowning glory, the Santa Iglesia Catedral de San Antolín, called *la bella desconocida* (the unknown beauty).

Although some parts of Palencia are in fact dismal and dull, sights here and in nearby towns offer refreshing calm compared to Spain's more popular tourist sites. For those who wish to take in a concentration of Spanish architecture without the hype of heavy tourism, Palencia and its satellite *pueblos* placidly guard some of the country's most important Romanesque and Visigothic monuments.

Orientation and Practical Information

You'll be seeing a lot of **Calle Mayor,** the main pedestrian artery and shopping zone that runs through the heart of the old city. The train and bus stations are just across **Los Jardinillos,** a park at the north end of C. Mayor. **Plaza León,** on the other side of the park, is where C. Mayor starts. The **tourist office** is 5 minutes away at the south end of C. Mayor, on the left before Av. José Antonio Primo de Rivera. To get to the **cathedral,** follow C. Mayor from Pl. León and turn right on Calle Barrio y Mier. The cathedral is three blocks down. To reach the **Plaza Mayor,** take C. Mayor and turn left at the fifth cross street, called Boca Plaza. It opens onto Pl. Mayor after a half-block.

Tourist Office: C. Mayor, 105 (tel. 74 00 68, fax 70 08 22). Free maps, posters, and all sorts of nifty information on Palencia and its environs. Some English spoken. Open July-Aug. Mon.-Fri. 9am-2pm and 5-7pm, Sat. 10am-1pm; Sept.-June Mon.-Fri. 9am-2pm and 4-6pm, Sat. 10am-1pm.

Currency Exchange: Banco Central Hispanoamericano, C. Mayor, 21 (tel. 74 98 22), on the corner with Boca Plaza. 1% commission (min. charge 250ptas). July-Aug. Mon.-Fri. 8:30am-2pm; Sept.-June Mon.-Fri. 8:30am-4:30pm.

Post Office: Pl. León, 1 (tel. 74 21 80). Open for stamps Mon.-Fri. 9am-9pm, Sat. 9am-7pm; for Lista de Correos Mon.-Fri. 9am-7pm, Sat. 9am-2pm. Open for **telegrams** Mon.-Fri. 8am-9pm, Sat. 8am-7pm. **Postal Code:** 34070.

Telephones: Telefónica, Patio de Castaño, off C. Mayor. You can send, but not receive, **faxes.** Open Mon.-Sat. 10am-2pm and 4-9pm. **Telephone Code:** 988.

Trains: at Jardinillos (tel. 74 30 19). Information open 24 hrs. To: Madrid (13 per day, 4 1/4 hr., 1470ptas); Barcelona (3 per day, 8hr., 4690ptas); Santander (6 per day, 4hr., 1075ptas); Valladolid (18 per day, 45min., 265ptas); Burgos (4 per day, 45min., 455ptas); León (14 per day, 1 1/4 hr., 115ptas).

Buses: (tel. 74 32 22), around the block to the right of the train station. To get to Pl. León and C. Mayor, exit the station and turn right; then turn left on Av. Dr. Simón Nieto, which hits Pl. León. Information open 9:30am-8pm. To: Madrid (4 per day, 3 1/2 hr., 1660ptas); Barcelona (2 per day, 8hr., 3985ptas); Vitoria (1 per day, 4hr., 1395ptas); Valladolid (12 per day, 45min., 270ptas); Burgos (3 per day, 1 1/2 hr., 640ptas); León (1 per day, 2hr., 930ptas).

Taxis: tel. 74 39 19, 74 21 26.

Car Rental: Avis, Av. Casado del Alisal, 43 (tel. 74 11 76). From the train station it's straight up Casado del Alisal on the left. Must be over 22 and have had a license for at least 1 yr. Open Mon.-Fri. 9am-1:30pm and 4-8pm, Sat. 9am-1:30pm.

Luggage Storage: The **train station** has lockers (200ptas per day). At the **bus station,** check bags with the attendant behind the information desk (50ptas per bag). Open Mon.-Fri. 9:30am-7pm, Sat. 9:30am-2pm.

English Bookstore: Librería Iglesias, C. Mayor, 80 (tel. 74 11 10). Some novels in English. Open Mon.-Fri. 10am-2pm and 4:30-8pm, Sat. 10am-2pm.

Library: Biblioteco Pública de Palencia, C. Eduardo Dato, 4 (tel. 75 11 00). Open July-Aug. Mon.-Fri. 9am-3pm, Sat. 9am-2pm; Sept.-June Mon.-Fri. 9am-9pm, Sat. 9am-2pm.

Athletic Facilities: Campo de la Juventud, C. Cardenal Cisneros, 12 (tel. 72 20 56). From Pl. España, turn right on C. Casañe and left on Cisneros. Huge and luxurious with a **pool** (open June 20-Sept. 15 11am-8pm), indoor and outdoor basketball courts, squash courts, and track. Open 8am-2pm and 4-10pm.

Red Cross: tel. 72 41 00. Red Cross **ambulance** (tel. 72 22 22).

Late-Night Pharmacy: check *El Norte de Castilla* (local paper, 150ptas) under *de guardia* listings.

Hospital: Hospital Provincial "San Telmo," Av. San Telmo (tel. 72 82 00). **Hospital Rio Carrión,** Carretera de Villamuriel, s/n (tel. 72 29 00, 72 29 84). **Ambulance:** tel. 72 22 40.

Emergency: tel. 092 (local) or 091 (national).

Police: tel. 74 76 77 or 092.

Accommodations

Albergue Juvenil: Victorio Macho (HI), C. Cardenal Cisneros (tel. 72 04 62, 71 16 76). From Pl. España, go straight up C. Casañe; C. Cardenal Cisneros is the 1st cross street. Next to the *polideportivo* in Campo de la Juventud. A student dorm, 10% of which is allocated to travelers; call to check availability. The TV room is a couch potato's fantasy. Curfew midnight. Worth a hike at 700ptas; over 26 900ptas. Breakfast 800ptas. Open July-Aug.

Escuela Castilla (HI), Ctra. Burgos (tel. 72 14 75). After Pl. España, the left fork in the main road: the hostel is on the right. Same prices and restrictions as Victorio Macho, but with more rooms.

El Salón, Av. República Argentina, 10 (tel. 72 64 42). C. Mayor becomes Av. República Argentina 9 blocks from both stations, but few rue the walk when they see the very large and popular El Salón. Chandeliers and an endearing bathroom floral motif embellish the spotless white interior and spacious rooms. July 10-Sept. 30: Singles 2000ptas. Doubles 3000ptas. Oct. 1-July 9: 1500ptas; 2500ptas.

Pensión el Hotelito, C. General Amor, 5 (tel. 74 69 13). From Pl. León take C. Mayor to C. General Granco, turn right, then left onto General Amor. A mirage in the desert of budget lodgings. Elegant, with plaid bedspreads and curtains and wooden beds. July-Sept.: Singles 2000ptas. Doubles 4000ptas. Oct.-June: 1800ptas; 3500ptas.

Pensión Comercio, C. Mayor, 26 (tel. 74 50 74), near both stations. Entertaining owner sets up guests in front of the TV with the family. Squeaky-clean linoleum floors like to masquerade as wood. Singles 1800ptas. Doubles 2200ptas. Cold showers free, hot showers 150ptas. Breakfast 175ptas.

El Edén Camping (tel. 88 01 85). Two blocks from the Ayuntamiento in Carrión de los Condes, hugging the river. Follow the signs. Three buses per day connect Palencia to Carrión (45min., 225ptas). 300ptas per person, 250-300ptas per tent, 300ptas per car. Children 250ptas. Electricity 300ptas.

Food

Hungry misers can pennypinch at the **market** off Pl. Mayor (open 9am-2pm).

Groceries: Simago, C. Menéndez y Pelayo at the corner of C. Pedro Moreno across the street from Telefónica. Down C. Mayor from Pl. León and right on C. Patio de Castaño. Basics and household products. Open Mon.-Sat. 9:30am-9pm.

Bar-Restaurante Granada, C. Mancornador, 10. From C. Mayor turn right on Martínez Baladrón, then right again on Mancornador. Soothing tiled walls and cushiony chairs. *Menú* of *judías verdes* (green beans with ham and potato), *filete de cerdo* (pork cutlet), and *patatas fritas* drenched in olive oil (750ptas). Open Wed.-Mon. noon-2:30am.

Taberna Sallana, Av. Miguel Primo de Rivera, 3. On the far side of Jardinillos, across from the bus station. SoHo-ish decor of green tiles and blond wood furnishings. The food is reassuringly traditional. Try *gambas a la plancha* (600ptas) after light *sopa de cocido* (consommé with peas and thin noodles, 350ptas). *Bocadillos* 175-300ptas. Open Sept.-July Tues.-Sun. 7am-12:30am, Mon. 7am-4pm.

Cafetería Palentino, C. Mayor, 21 (tel. 74 30 60). Look for the big green "cafeteria" sign. Its elegance—marble floor and high ceiling—belies the name. Perfect for a sweet snack of *tortitas* (250ptas) or for a *pincho* of tortilla (75ptas). The dining room in back gazes at Pl. Mayor. Open 8am-midnight.

Taberna Plaza Mayor, Pl. Mayor, s/n. Sign outside touts the *menú del día* (1000ptas); inside specialties are written on the tiled wall behind the bar. *Canapés* of *pan tostado* with *bonito* (tuna), *jamón* (ham), or salmon 125-175ptas. Hot *bocadillo* (200ptas). Open 7:30am-1am.

El Charval de Lorenzo, C. José Antonio Primo de Rivera, 3. Turn left at the south end of C. Mayor past the tourist office. Students come to play pool and cards or watch TV on the big screen. Choice array of *tapas: champiñones al ajillo* (mushrooms in garlic sauce) and tortilla are among the staples, along with *bocadillos*. *Gofres belgas* (belgian waffles) with assorted toppings 145-225ptas. Open 10am-1am.

Sights

The big attraction to Palencia is clearly the **catedral, Santa Iglesia de San Antolín** (tel. 70 13 47), in which 14-year-old Catherine of Lancaster married 10-year-old Enrique III in 1388. Both the cathedral and its corresponding **Plaza de la Inmaculada Concepción** are currently undergoing facelifts to restore their virgin glow. A statue of the virgin under a gravity-defying halo greets penitents in the plaza. The outstanding **museum** is open only if you're accompanied by an attendant, usually the postcard seller in the sacristy. 200ptas goes a long way as you're led through the anteroom of the **sala capitular,** where El Greco's famed *San Sebastián* is tacked up. Inside the *sala capitular* hang four huge 16th-century Flemish tapestries. In the glass cases beneath the tapestries, medieval hymnals are bound in the skin of unborn calves. The orgy of medieval religiosity ends down a stone staircase at the **Cripta de San Antolín,** a 7th-century sepulchre. Dank, musty, and far beneath the cathedral, it sends a shiver up the spine as the guide's keys clank away in the silent tomb. (Cathedral and museum open Mon.-Sat. 9:30am-1pm and 4-6:30pm, Sun. 9:30am-2pm. Open for mass Mon.-Sat. 9am and 6pm, Sun. and holidays 9am, 10:30am, noon, and 1pm.)

More religious stuff reposes in the **Iglesia de Santa Clara**, the resting place for a singularly odd Jesus with a mummy-like corpus, blackened fingernails, decomposed toes, and gaping mouth. The church is two blocks from Pl. San Lázaro. (Open 8:30am-8pm.)

El Cristo del Otero is an ostentatious monument towering over the plain around Palencia. An Art Deco Jesus models a streamlined gown and appears hands-up, as if to say "Don't shoot!" The statue is a 35-minute walk from town on the highway to Santander.

Near Palencia

Palencia is close to some of the oldest examples of Romanesque architecture in Spain. It takes effort to reach these outlying towns by train and bus.

Carrión de los Condes

Forty km north of Palencia on the **Camino de Santiago** (Road to Compostela), Carrión offers a few incredible sights and its own riverside beauty. The **Iglesia de Santa María** (tel. 88 00 72), is a 12th-century temple with a decidedly morbid portal. The doorway on the south side allegedly depicts the tribute of 100 Carrión maidens demanded by Moorish conquerors, who were stampeded by bulls on their way to collect. (Open 8am-2pm and 5-8pm. Open for mass 8:30am, holidays 10:30am and noon.) Since the town is on the road to Santiago de Compostela, tourists mingle with present-day *peregrinos* (pilgrims) making their way north to The Great City. (The church offers them lodging in a back room.)

On the far side of the Rió Carrión looms the secularized **Monasterio de San Zoilo.** Faces of saints and popes stare down their flock from the ornate arches of the Renaissance cloister, which is only partially open to the public. The recently abandoned seminary garden still has blooming rose bushes. On the way out the guard will point at tombs of the unfortunate evil-doers of the *Cantar del Mio Cid,* who married El Cid's daughters and then abandoned them in the middle of nowhere. (Open Wed.-Sun. 10am-1pm and 4-7pm.)

Carrión's hidden treasure is the **Convento de Santa Clara** (whose aliases include Las Clarisas and Café España). The *repostería* (pastry shop) bakes delicious cookies. Since the nuns are cloistered, all food-money exchanges are expedited by a revolving cabinet while they peer out from behind two iron gratings. The convent has recently inaugurated a **museo.** Ring the bell and ask for Sr. Antonio (50ptas). The whimsically eclectic collection includes shepherds' nutcrackers, a statue of baby Jesus with a toothache, and 14th-century fabric from bishops' frocks. (Open Tues.-Sun. 10:30am-2pm and 5-8pm; off-season Tues.-Sun. 11am-2pm and 4-7pm.)

Hostal La Corte, C. Santa María, 34 (tel. 88 01 38), provides downright luxurious, spotless, and spacious singles (1500ptas). For 3000ptas, you can revel on your pastel bed and throw a party in your private bathroom. For **camping**, see Palencia: Accommodations. Carrión's **tourist office** (not a government office; hours vary) is in a woodframe hut across the street from Café-Bar España, where the bus drops folk off. Only three **buses** per day (tel. 74 32 22 for information) travel from Palencia to Carrión.

Paredes de Nava

Twenty km northwest of Palencia on the Castilian plain, Paredes exists without fanfare: a small cathedral, three identical-looking churches, a plaza, two *fondas,* four bars, and under 3000 people. Painter Pedro Berruguete, sculptor Alonso Berruguete, and poet Jorge Manrique were born here.

The town's *raison d'être* is the **Catedral de Santa Eulalia** and the enclosed **Museo Parroquial**. Only the 12th-century Romanesque tower was spared when the church was enlarged in the 15th century. Pedro Berruguete painted the scenes of *La Restauración de la Virgen* for the main retable in 1485, while Esteban Jordán, married to one of the master's daughters, designed the architecture. In addition to more Berruguete paintings, Mudejar relics, some vestal garments, and a collection of retables in the Berruguete style (bound in the skin of unborn lambs), the museum enshrines St. James' rib. (Museum open Tues.-Sun. 11am-1pm and 4-6pm. Admission 100ptas. If locked, ask around for the priest or call 83 04 69 for a personal tour.)

Only six **trains** (225ptas) and three **buses** (230ptas) per day connect Palencia with Paredes de Nava (20min). Check the schedule; departures are erratic.

Banós de Cerrato

Time-warp from Palencia to Baños de Cerrato for the perfectly preserved Visigothic **Basílica de San Juan de Baños.** Built in 661, it's the oldest Christian temple still standing in Spain. Visigothic King Recesvinto twice had a hand in it: the inscription above the altar is his, as is the impression of his royal extremity on the floor. Reaching the basilica is at least half the fun, especially if you enjoy dodging cowchips and lunatic tractor drivers. Take the train 9km from Palencia to **Ventas de Baños** (17 per day, 10min., 90ptas), an ugly industrial town. Turn left at the station entrance and keep walking; Baños de Cerrato is visible 2km down the road. The basilica is on the far side of this farming community. The caretaker and his impossibly large keys reside at C. San Juan de Baños, just up from the basilica. Sr. Patricio unlocks the doors, sells postcards, and reveals all the basilica's deep, dark secrets. It's more impressive from the inside, where six cool marble columns stretch up to the ceiling. The basilica is now functional only for special festivals or parish groups with priest. (Basilica open Tues.-Sun. 9am-1pm and 5-7pm.)

Burgos

Conservative Burgos is one of Spain's finest repositories of Gothic art and architecture, with well-trimmed roses everywhere and gracious riverside promenades. Everything in Burgos stands tall, from its starched citizens to its stone architecture. The *Cabeza de Castilla* (Head of Castile), Burgos rose to prominence as capital of the county, then of the kingdom of Castile, claiming the purest form of Castilian. Although Burgos lost to Valladolid in 1492 as permanent court of newly unified Spain, the city retained some clout as headquarters for the powerful *Mesta* guild of shepherds, center of the international merino wool trade, and crossroads for several important routes, including the *Camino de Santiago.* Burgos' associations with Spanish unification were revived when Franco made Burgos his wartime capital. In 1970 Burgos hit the network news when Franco sentenced a handful of Basque nationalists to death in what became known as the "Burgos Trials." He repealed this sentence only after widespread local and international condemnation.

The town's other claim to fame is Rodrigo Díaz de Vivar, a.k.a. El Cid, Spain's real-life epic hero. Although not born here, his more memorable exploits took place in this suave, graceful city.

Burgos

Orientation and Practical Information

Burgos lies about 240km north of Madrid on the main route between Madrid and the French border. About 160,000 people live here in the valley of the Río Arlanzón, which divides the city into north and south sides. The **cathedral** and most other monuments are located to the north in the old city of plazas and curving streets. In the south, across the river, hulk the train and bus stations. To reach the cathedral and city center from the south side, follow **Av. Conde de Guadalhorce** across the river and take the first right onto **Avenida del Generalismo Franco** which turns into **Paseo del Espolón** farther down. The cathedral is just beyond this tree-lined street. The **Plaza Mayor** (or **Plaza José Antonio**) is just east of the cathedral.

Tourist Office: Pl. Alonso Martínez, 7 (tel. 20 31 25, 20 18 46). From Pl. Mayor take Laín Calvo for 3 blocks. The office, which could double as a slick art gallery, is between Calles San Juan and 18 de Julio. Multilingual brochures and maps. Some English spoken. Open Mon.-Fri. 9am-2pm and 4:30-6:30pm, Sat. 10am-1:30pm.

Budget Travel: Viajes TIVE (tel. 20 98 81), in the Casa de Cultura on Pl. San Juan. Unmarked door; hang a left after entering. Helpful tips and brochures on discount travel, lodging, and museum prices. Student IDs (500ptas) and HI card (1800ptas). Some English spoken. Open Mon.-Fri. 9am-2pm.

Currency Exchange: Caja de Ahorros del Círculo Católico, Av. Reyes Católicos I (tel. 28 82 00), just off Pl. España. Better exchange rate than most banks.

Post Office: Pl. Conde de Castro, 1 (tel. 26 27 50), across the river from Pl. Primo de Rivera where El Cid points the way. Open for stamps, Lista de Correos, and **telegrams** Mon.-Fri. 8am-9pm, Sat. 9am-2pm. **Postal Code:** 09000.

Telephones: Telefónica, C. San Lesmes, 18, off Pl. España. Entrance on the side (on C. Hortelanos). You can also send but not receive **faxes** here. Open Mon.-Sat. 9am-1pm and 5-9pm. **Telephone Code:** 947.

Trains: at the end of Av. Conde Guadalhorce across the river from Pl. Castilla (tel. 20 35 60). It's a 10-min. walk southwest of the city center. Information open 7am-11pm. **RENFE,** C. Moneda, 21 (tel. 20 91 31). Open Mon.-Fri. 9am-1pm and 4-7pm, Sat. 9am-1pm. To: Palencia (5 per day, 1hr., 430ptas); Valladolid (8 per day, 1 1/2 hr., 615ptas); Donostia/San Sebastián (11 per day, 3hr., 1270ptas); Logroño (3 per day, 2hr., 980ptas); León (5 per day, 2hr., 1285ptas); Bilbo (8 per day, 3hr., 1195ptas); Madrid (8 per day, 3 1/2 hr., 1665-2105ptas); Barcelona (3 per day, 6hr., 4215ptas); Santiago (1 per day, 8hr., 5855ptas).

Buses: C. Miranda, s/n (tel. 20 55 65), just off Pl. Vega and snuggled between Calles Miranda and Madrid. (To reach Av. Conde Guadalhorce from Pl. Vega, find C. Merced on the north boundary of the plaza. Turn left onto C. Merced, which runs along the river, and continue until C. Merced hits Av. Conde Guadalhorce. Turn right for the cathedral, left for the train station.) Each bus company has its own window, its own routes, and alas! its own schedule. To: Madrid (10 per day, 3 1/4 hr., 1600ptas); Barcelona (4 per day, 7hr., 3880ptas); Bilbo (4 per day, 2hr., 1175ptas); Palencia (3 per day, 1 1/2 hr., 640ptas); Valladolid (2 per day, 1 1/2 hr., 815ptas); Santander (4 per day, 3hr., 1195ptas); León (1 per day, 2hr., 1465ptas); Vitoria (3 per day, 1 1/2 hr., 770ptas).

Taxis: Radio Taxi (tel. 27 77 77, 48 10 10).

Car Rentals: Hertz, C. Madrid, 10 (tel. 20 16 75), around the corner from bus station. Must be over 21 and have had a license for at least 1 yr. Open Mon.-Fri. 9am-2pm and 4-7pm, Sat. 9am-1pm.

Hitchhiking: To Madrid, walk south along C. Madrid from Pl. Vega until highway N-1. To Santander, walk north on Av. General Vigón.

Luggage Storage: At the **train station** (tel. 20 33 60; lockers 200ptas). At the **bus station** you can check your bag (65ptas per bag). Open Mon.-Sat. 9am-8pm, Sat. 9am-6pm.

Bookstore: Librería Hijos de Santiago Rodríguez, Pl. José Antonio, 22 (tel. 20 15 88). A fair selection of fiction in English upstairs; paper and office supplies sold downstairs. Open Mon.-Fri. 10am-2pm and 5-8pm, Sat. 10am-2pm.

Library: Biblioteca pública de Burgos, Pl. San Juan, in the Casa de Cultura on the 2nd floor. Open Mon.-Fri. 10am-1pm and 5-8:30pm, Sat. 10am-1pm.

Swimming Pool: El Plantío (tel. 22 00 01), to the east along the river, by the *plaza de toros* (bullring). Open in summer 11am-9pm.

Athletic Facilities: Gimnasio Sport Tres, C. San Agustín, 9 (tel. 27 62 63). Walk up C. Madrid, cross the train tracks, and turn right at the bunch of trees. Membership (500ptas) includes tae kwon do, karate, and aerobics classes and use of the weight room. Open Mon.-Fri. 9am-2pm and 4-10pm, Sat. 10am-1pm and 5:30-8:30pm.

Crisis Hotlines: Don't count on English being spoken. **SOS Droga** (tel. 26 36 00) for drug addiction. **Alcoholics Anonymous** (tel. 23 65 52). **Teléfono de Esperanza** (tel. 20 42 22) for depression and suicidal thoughts.

Red Cross: tel. 22 15 00.

Late-Night Pharmacy: Check the listings in *El Diario de Burgos* (local paper, 90ptas).

Medical Services: Casa de Socorro, Conde de Vallellano, 4 (tel. 26 14 10), at C. Ramón y Cajal near the post office.

Ambulance: tel. 24 12 12.

Emergency: tel. 091 or 092.

Police: tel. 28 88 34, 28 88 39.

Accommodations and Camping

Head either to the streets radiating from the far side of Pl. Mayor or the neighborhood around Pl. Vega. In general, cheaper accommodations are on the south side of the river. The area stretching from Pl. San Juan west to Pl. Mayor is dotted with reasonably priced *hostales*. Reservations are crucial for the last week of June and the first week of July (when the city celebrates the feast days of St. Paul and St. Peter) and are advisable through August.

Hostal Niza, C. General Mola, 12 (tel. 26 19 17). From Pl. Vega, follow C. Madrid and take the 2nd left onto General Mola; it's where C. San Pablo meets General Mola. Meticulously color-coordinated rooms, each with 2 endearing little puffy chairs. Some rooms have a balcony. Singles 1900ptas. Doubles 2700ptas. Showers 250ptas. Open Nov.-Sept.

Hostal Joma, C. San Juan, 26 (tel. 20 33 50). From El Cid's statue, walk up C. Santander past Pl. Calvo Sotelo and turn right on San Juan. 60s-style chandeliers in the rooms and classic red-checked tablecloths in the small dining room. Singles 1200ptas. Doubles 1600ptas. Triples 3000ptas. Showers 200ptas. Owner serves up *café* and *galletas* for breakfast (150ptas).

Hostal Hidalgo, C. Almirante Bonifaz, 14 (tel. 20 34 81). From northeast corner of Pl. Mayor, just past Galerías Preciados; a dusty staircase leads up to the 2nd floor. Some rooms with a balcony. All have high ceilings and hardwood floors. Dam-busting shower water pressure. Singles 1400ptas. Doubles 2500ptas. Triples 3200ptas. Winter: 1200ptas; 2200ptas; 3000ptas.

Hostal Victoria, C. San Juan, 3 (tel. 20 15 42). C. San Juan is at the end of the streets radiating north from Pl. Mayor (see listing for Hostal Joma). High ceilinged, bare rooms with bright red doors like gaping mouths. Clean bathrooms. Winter heating. Singles 1400ptas. Doubles 2400ptas. Showers 200ptas.

Pensión Angelita, C. Agustín, 9 (tel. 20 63 95). Walking away from Pl. Vega, follow C. Madrid across the train tracks and turn right on Agustín. Wood floors and spanking new common bathroom. Singles 1100ptas. Doubles 1900ptas. Showers 200ptas.

Pensión Peña, C. La Puebla, 18 (tel. 20 63 23). From Pl. España, take C. San Lesmes; C. La Puebla is the 3rd right. Soft beds wrapped in paisley bedspreads. Teensy rooms with eye-boggling wallpaper. Singles 800ptas. Doubles 1700ptas. Showers 175ptas.

Hostal-Restaurante Castellano, C. Laín Calvo, 48 (tel. 20 50 40), between Pl. Mayor and Pl. Alonso Martinez. The restaurant is no more. Singles lack windows. Singles 1500ptas. Doubles 3000ptas. Triples 4500ptas. Open late Feb.-early Dec.

Camping: Camping Fuentes Blancas (tel. 22 10 16), 3 1/2km outside Burgos, near the Cartuja de Miraflores, has all the facilities you could ever need. 400ptas per person, per tent, and per car. Capacity 1200. Open April-Sept. 30. The "Fuentes Blancas" bus leaves from Pl. Primo de Rivera (every hr., July-Aug. 11am-9pm, 55ptas). During the rest of the year, take the Eladio Perlado bus

(#10), ask the driver to stop at the pedestrian bridge near Fuentes Blancas, cross the river, and walk 1km east.

Food

Landlocked Burgos means meat, meat, and more meat. Pork and lamb in a variety of guises show up on nearly every *menú*. Try *picadillo de cerdo* (minced pork), *cordero asado* (roast lamb), or, for a taste of everything, *olla podrida,* a stew in which sausage, beans, pork, cured beef, and bacon mingle as one. Sausage straight up is another specialty, especially *morcilla* (translated as "black pudding," but don't be fooled—it's blood sausage). Locals also covet *sopa burgales,* prepared with lamb and crawfish tails. Burgos lends its name to *queso de Burgos,* delicious by itself or with honey. Polish off a meal with *yemas de Burgos,* the unique sickly-sweet sugared egg yolks.

Burgos has two markets, **Mercado Norte** near Pl. España and the smaller **Mercado de Miranda,** on Miranda opposite the Museo Arqueológico. Fresh fish is brought in from the northern coast. (Markets open Mon.-Sat. 7am-3pm. Mercado Norte has late hours Fri. 5:30-8pm.) Numerous **health food stores** sprouted over the past decade. **Los Tilos** is closest to the town center at C. General Yagüe, 6, one block from Pl. España. (Open Mon.-Fri. 10am-2pm and 5-8pm, Sat. 10am-2pm.)

Restaurante La Flor, C. Avellanos, 9 (tel. 26 60 52), off Pl. Alonjo Martínez. The light, airy *comedor* is just past the bar. Light blue walls and TV humming overhead. A feast. *Platos combinados,* 575-725ptas. *Menú* with *pollo asado* prepared with garlic (a house specialty), bread, wine, and dessert (1400ptas). Open 1-4pm and 8-11pm; winter Fri.-Wed. 1-4pm and 8-11pm.

Restaurante de Angel, C. Fernán González, 36, uphill from the cathedral. 900ptas buys the *menú del día, lechazo* (milk-fed lamb), and entrance to the heavenly dining room, decked out with artful paintings and tabletop flowers. Open March to mid-Sept. and Oct. to mid-Feb. Thurs.-Tues. 1-3:30pm and 8-11:30pm.

Mesón Arlanza, C. Fernán González, 44, uphill behind the cathedral. *Pinchos* (canapé-sized niblets) 100-150ptas. *Bocadillos* 200-250ptas. *Menú* of *sopa de pescado* (fish soup) and *filetes de lomo con patatas fritas* 800ptas. Tetris addicts fix next to the bar. Open Sun.-Thurs. 10am-midnight, Fri.-Sat. 10am-2:30am; winter Sun.-Mon. and Wed.-Sat.

Bodega Riojana, Pl. Alonso Martínez, 9 (tel. 26 07 19), on the corner of C. San Juan. *Cerveza*-induced exuberance but weak decor. Blue and white checkered curtains. *Tapas* with a twist—*calamares* (squid) and *picadillo* (minced pork) in mini casseroles. Hint: ask for *cazuelitas* (225ptas) not *cazuelas,* which are only slightly bigger servings at much bigger prices. Open 9am-3pm and 7-10:30pm.

Cafeteria Canarias, C. San Lesmes, 18, between Pl. San Juan and Pl. España and off the latter. *Bocadillos* from 175ptas at the bar, but more expensive banquette seating facilitates people-watching out the window. *Calamares fritos* (fried squid) 425ptas. Open Mon.-Sat. 8am-midnight.

Mesón de los Herreros, C. San Lorenzo, 20, between Pl. Mayor and Pl. Alonso Martínez. *Tapas*-a-rama. The *cojonudo* (spicy sausage with egg and pimiento) is a specialty. *Patatas bravas* (cubed french fries in spicy orange sauce) 100ptas. *Raciones* 300-800ptas. Only diehards eat the *morritos* (pig nose), *sesos* (lamb brains), and *patas de cordero* (lamb feet). Open Mon.-Sat. 9:30am-3:30pm and 6pm-12:30am, Sun. 11am-3:30pm and 6pm-midnight.

Restaurante La Riojana, C. Avellanos, 10 (tel. 20 61 32), off Pl. Alonso Martinéz. The sort of place where a girl might roll her hoop up and down the room while patrons watch TV. Dandy *menú,* including *pollo asado* and *ensalada,* 690ptas. *Queso de Burgos* 300ptas. Euphorically savory *judías verdes* with *jamon serrano* 475ptas. Open Tues.-Sat. 1-4pm and 7-11pm, Sun. 10am-4pm.

Sights

The slender, lacy spires of the **cathedral** (tel. 20 47 12) soar above the city. A powerful group of 13th-century gentlemen sheep farmers (the Mesta) paid for this Gothic masterpiece as testimony to the wealth they brought to Burgos with their extraordinary merino wool. Two towers flank the main **fachada,** a fantastic concoction of intricately detailed windows and quirky sculpture crowned by openwork spires from the 15th century. The north facade and the Puerta del Sacramental are 13th-century Gothic; the Puerta de la Pellejería was added in the 16th century. Even those sick of cathedrals should really muster up the energy to visit the church's breathtaking bronze interior. In the **Capilla Mayor,** at the east end, El Cid's bones and those of his wife Jimena commingle in marmoreal serenity. Meanwhile, the late 15th-century Constable of Castilla and his wife rest in a richly carved tomb behind the altar of the late Gothic **Capilla del Condestable,** four-sided at its base and octagonal in the upper part. It projects outside the body of the cathedral as if a monument apart. Sunlight pours through an eight-point glass skylight set into the **cimborrio** (dome) above. More glass than stone, the main Gothic crossing is strikingly impressive with a rapturous dome; as is the early 16th-century **Escalera Dorada** (Gilded Staircase) in the northern transept. Before leaving the cathedral, look for the fly catcher high up near the main door in the central aisle. As it strikes the hours, the strange creature opens its mouth in imitation of the crowds gawking below. (Cathedral open 9:30am-1pm and 4-7pm. Free. Admission to chapels or museum 300ptas, students 100ptas.

The cathedral's dwarfish neighbor, the **Iglesia de San Nicolás,** cowers across the Plaza de Santa María and up the steps. The elaborately carved *retablo* is the highlight of the unfinished interior. (Open Mon.-Fri. 9am-2pm and 5-9pm, Sun. 9am-2pm and 5-6pm. Free.)

After the cathedral, the **Estatua de El Cid** in Pl. General Primo de Rivera is Burgos' most venerated landmark. Rodrigo Díaz de Vivar (Cid comes from the Arabic for Lord) won his fame through bold exploits at home and in battle against Moors and Christians. Despite the statue's inscriptions and the orthodox nonsense spun about him, El Cid was no Christian hero. He was a particularly successful mercenary who spent much of his life exiled from various Christian states whose nobles he had outraged. He had no qualms about befriending Muslims.) The medieval poem celebrating his life, *El Cantar de Mío Cid,* is considered the first great work of Castilian literature. Burgos tradition compels its youth to climb the statue and fondle the testicles of El Cid's horse.

Just up C. Santander on the other side of the statue, the restored **Casa del Cordón** glows in the sunshine. Here Columbus met with Fernando and Isabel after his second trip to America; and Felipe el Hermoso (the Handsome) died after a trying game of *pelota,* driving his wife Juana la Loca (the Mad), daughter of the Catholic Monarchs, insane.

Renovations of the **Monasterio de San Juan** (now called **Museo de Pintura Marceliano Santa Maria**) left the remaining walls of a destroyed church untouched while fully recovering and enclosing the cloister. Rich landscape scenes and portraits by Marceliano Santa María, a 20th-century local artist, hang within. To reach the monastery, follow C. Vitoria away from the statue of El Cid and take the second left. (Open Tues.-Sat. 10am-2pm and 5-8pm, Sun. 10am-2pm. Admission 200ptas.) The **Museo Arqueológico** (tel. 26 58 75) displays prehistoric and Roman artifacts from the nearby town of **Clunia** in Casa de Miranda, a Spanish Renaissance building across the river on C. Miranda. The museum has a stunning medieval collection, including the Gothic tomb of Juan de Padilla and an 11th-century Moorish ivory casket. (Open Mon.-Fri. 10am-1:30pm and 4:30-7:15pm, Sat. 11:15am-1:45pm, Sun. 10:15am-1:45pm. Admission 200ptas, students free.) One km west of Burgos, the **Museo-Monasterio de las Huelgas Reales** (tel. 20 16 30) was a summer palace of Castilian kings and later a convent for Cistercian nuns. The convent only accepted the elite of the elite, led by an abbess who was rumored to be only slightly less regal than the queen herself. A small band of nuns still camps out here; their convent is separate from the church and museum, across the courtyard from the entrance and ticket office. The church, in which several Castilian kings were knighted, takes the form of a Latin cross. Some classic Islamic motifs such as the peacock tail and stars are still visible in the Gothic cloister's badly damaged ceiling. The contents of the one unsacked tomb, that of Fernando de la Cerda (1225-1275), oldest son of Alfonso el Sabio (the Wise), are in the **Museo de Telas** (Textile Museum). The museum keeps his entire wardrobe, including billowing silver-threaded smocks and elaborately embroidered shirts. The only way to visit the museum and the monastery is with a tour in Spanish, worth it even if you don't understand a word. (Open Tues.-Sat. 11:15am-1:15pm and 4:15-5:15pm, Sun. and holidays 11:15am-1:15pm. Admission 400ptas, free Wed.) To get here, take Av. Palencia west and upriver, away from the city center. After a half-mile, bear left at the gas station, then follow the signs leading you through the residential area beyond. The monastery will be on the left. Or simply take the "Barrio del Pilar" bus from El Cid's statue in Pl. Primo de Rivera (55ptas).

The **Cartuja de Miraflores** is a Carthusian monastery that houses the ornate tombs of King Juan II of Castile, Queen Isabel of Portugal, and their son Don Alfonso. Debate rages as to whether Alfonso's early death was caused by evil scheming noblemen or a bad cold. His sister Isabel benefited from his demise: she eventually ascended the throne and married Fernando. (Open Mon.-Sat. 10:15am-3pm and 4-6pm, Sun. and holidays 11:20am-12:30pm, 1-3pm, and 4-6pm. Open for mass Mon.-Sat. 9am, Sun. and holidays 7:30am and 10:15am. Free.) To get here, take the "Fuentes Blancas" bus (July-Aug., 55ptas) or walk 3km east along the Paseo de La Quinta.

Entertainment

Some say the nightlife in Burgos rivals that of Spain's larger cities. Believe it. Even on a slow weekend, people find themselves stumbling home at dawn. The zone next to the cathedral, known as **Las Llanas,** is a fervent intoxication site catering largely to adolescents and college students. The bars in **Pl. Huerto del Rey** (at the center of the zone) often overflow every night of the week. Around 10pm the plaza starts to fill up with imbibers bearing plastic beer cups. As an alternative, head a few blocks east to **Las Bernardas**. The popular pubs and clubs hereabouts are more modern than those in Las Llanas, although they're deserted on weeknights. The elegant and relatively tranquil cafés along **Paseo del Espolón** draw a slightly more mature crowd. Those in search of a boppy disco or kisses galore could try the neon and mirrors of **Bésame Mucho,** at Pl. Bernardas, 5, and its neighbors **La Farándula** and **Rock Cola.**

Nightlife switches into high gear from June 23 to July 8, when Burgos honors its patron saints Peter and Paul with concerts, parades, fireworks, bullfights, and dances. The day after Corpus Christi, citizens parade through town with the *Pendón de las Navas,* a banner captured from the Moors in 1212.

Near Burgos

San Pedro de Cardeña

El Cid left Jimena in the Cistercian monastery of **San Pedro de Cardeña** (tel. 29 00 33), 10km east of Burgos, when he went into exile. He was buried here until 1921. No one knows what happened then. The 11th-century building was built from earlier ruins. (Open Mon.-Sat. 10am-1pm and 4-6:30pm, Sun. and holidays noon-2pm and 4-6:30pm. Admission 100ptas.)

Abadía de Santo Domingo de Silos

. 59km from Burgos is the village and Benedictine **Abadía de Santo Domingo de Silos** (tel. (947) 38 07 68), renowned for its Romanesque **cloister,** and for being one of two monastic establishments that allegedly produced the first written Castilian. Construction began in the 11th century to honor monastic leader Domingo. The trapezoidal cloister, one of the most extraordinary ensembles of Romanesque sculpture in Europe, contains elaborately decorated columns and capitals. A parade of stylized, hieratic, symmetrically paired harpies, monster gazelles, and other quadrupeds files past on the capitals of the east gallery. In the 18th century the original Romanesque basilica was replaced by a grand, restrained Baroque church. The monastic choir reputedly sings the most tuneful Gregorian chants. A **bus** leaves Burgos (Mon.-Thurs. at 5:30pm, Fri. at 6:30pm, Sat. at 2pm) for the monastery and returns at 8:30am the following day. Perfect for a daytrip. (Monastery open Mon.-Sat. 10am-1pm and 4:30-6pm, Sun. and holidays 4:30-6pm. Open for Gregorian mass 9am, holidays noon. Admission 150ptas.)

Soria

The compact capital of the homonymous agricultural province rests in the lap of a green and yellow hilled landscape. Modern development hasn't bypassed Soria, but the pace of the city is still slow and healthy. Black-bereted men wield loaves of bread past reddish Romanesque churches, and Soria's inhabitants still rigorously observe the *paseo,* strolling and chatting with neighbors and friends every evening before dinner. In contrast to other Castilian towns, Soria receives few foreign visitors.

Orientation and Practical Information

The bus station is northwest of the city center. From the traffic circle outside the station, signs on Avenida Valladolid point the way to the *centro ciudad.* Persist for about five blocks, then bear right at the traffic light onto **Paseo Espolón.** Where the park comes to a halt you'll see the central **Plaza Mariano Granados** on the right. To get here from the train station (south of the center), turn left onto Carretera de Madrid and follow the signs to *centro ciudad.* Follow C. Almazán until it forks; take Av. Mariano Vicen on the left for four blocks and stay left on C. Alfonso VIII at the next fork for two blocks until you reach Pl. Mariano Granados.

Tourist Office: Pl. Ramón y Cajal, s/n (tel. 21 20 52). Cross Pl. Mariano Granados from the entrance past the sculpted column; a small booth set back from the street. Open Mon.-Sat. 9:30am-2pm and 4:30-8:30pm, Sun. 10am-2pm; Nov.-May Mon.-Fri. 9:30am-2pm and 5-7pm.

Budget Travel: TIVE, C. Campo, 5 (tel. 22 79 50), up the hill from Pl. Mariano Granados at the corner of C. Mesta. ISIC 500ptas. HI cards 1600ptas. Open Mon. 8am-3pm and 5-8pm, Tues.-Fri. 8am-3pm.

Post Office: Po. Espolón, 6 (tel. 22 13 99), on the left from the bus station near Pl. Mariano Granados. Open Mon.-Fri. 8am-9pm, Sat. 9am-7pm; for **telegrams** (tel. 22 20 00) Mon.-Sat. 8am-8pm. **Postal Code:** 42001.

Telephones: C. Aduana Vieja, 2, off C. Collado en route to Pl. Mayor. Open June 15-Sept. 15 Mon.-Fri. 9am-2pm and 4:30-9pm, Sat. 9am-2pm; Sept. 16-June 14 Mon.-Fri. 9am-1:30pm and 4-9pm, Sat. 9am-2pm. **Telephone Code:** 975.

Trains: Estación El Cañuelo (tel. 23 02 02). Bus shuttles to and from the station 7:15am-7:15pm 3-6 times per day from the tourist office. Information booth open 7am-8:30pm. To: Tudela (2 per day, 2hr., 850ptas); Zaragoza (2 per day, 2 3/4 hr., 995ptas); Alcalá de Henares (3 per day, 2 3/4 hr., 1075ptas); Madrid (4 per day, 3hr., 1225ptas).

Buses: Av. Valladolid, s/n (tel. 22 51 60), at C. Eduardo Saavedra. Information open 6:30am-9pm. Where bus companies are listed without a phone number, call the station for information. **Therpresa** (tel. 22 20 60). To Tarazona (4-7 per day, 1hr., 405ptas) and Zaragoza (4-7 per day, 2hr., 925ptas). **Gonzalo Ruiz Ruiz** (tel. 22 43 55). To El Burgo de Osma (Mon.-Sat. 2 per day, 50min., 375ptas). **La Serrana**. To Burgos (3-4 per day, 3hr., 935ptas). **Linecar** (tel. 22 51 55). To Zaragoza (3-5 per day, 2hr., 850ptas) and Valladolid (3-6 per day, 3hr., 1140ptas). **CONDA** (tel. 22 44 01). To Pamplona (1 per day at 3:15pm, 2hr., 1190ptas). **Continental Auto** (tel 22 44 01). To Madrid (4 per day, 3 3/4 hr., 1435ptas). **Martínez**. To Logroño (3 per day, 1 3/4 hr., 710ptas). **RENFE-Iñigo**. To Salamanca (2 per day, 5hr., 2200ptas) and Barcelona (1-3 per day, 3170ptas).

Car Rental: Avis, Av. Mariano Vicente, 1 (tel. 22 84 61). Left from tourist office into Pl. Los Jurados, then follow Av. Navarra until it meets Av. Mariano Vicen.

Moped Rental: Petreñas, C. Angel Terrel, 3 (tel. 22 05 05). From the the bus station on Av. Valladolid, bear left at the intersection onto C. San Benito and take the first left after 1 bl.

Hitchhiking: *Let's Go* does not recommend hitchhiking as a means of travel. Those who choose to hitch to Madrid walk south along C. Alfonso VIII and continue on Av. Mariano Vicente to the highway. Those going north walk up C. Numancia to C. Casas. People going east tend to cross the Duero and find a nice, shady spot to wait (and wait, and wait).

Luggage Storage: At the **bus station,** bags checked (50ptas). Open 6:30am-9pm.

Library: Biblioteca Pública, on corner of C. San Benito and C. Mesta. From the TIVE office turn right and follow C. Mesta. Open July-Aug. Mon.-Fri. 8:30am-2:30pm, Sat. 10am-2pm.

Swimming Pool: Pabellón Polideportivo San Andrés, E. C. Geólogo Palacios, s/n. From Residencia Juvenil Antonio Machado onto Po. San Andrés and left after 1 bl. Open June-Sept. 11am-8:30pm. Admission 200ptas.

Red Cross: tel. 22 22 22.

Medical Services: Casa de Socorro, C. Medinacelli, 1 (tel. 21 20 30), off Pl. Mayor. **Hospital General,** Po. Santa Bárbara. **Ambulatorio (National Health Clinic)** (tel. 22 15 50). **Ambulance** (tel. 22 61 54).

Emergency: tel. 22 15 29, 091, or 092.

Police: National Police, C. Nicolás Rabal, 11 (tel. 21 12 89). **Municipal Police** (tel. 21 18 62). **Guardia Civil** (tel. 22 11 00).

Accommodations and Camping

Don't expect any bargains. Residents treat guests with reserved friendliness. Because of *fiestas,* reservations are necessary in the last week of June.

Residencia Juvenil Juan Antonio Gaya Nuño (HI), Po. San Francisco, 1 (tel. 22 14 66). From Pl. Mariano Granados take C. Nicolás Rabal, the 2nd left on C. Luisa de Marillas, then the next right. A modern college dorm disguised as a hostel July 4-Sept. 15. Mostly doubles and quads. Swimming pool. Alternates as active hostel with **Residencia Juvenil Antonio Machado (HI),** Pl. José Antonio, 1 (tel. 22 17 89). Continue down Po. San Francisco, turn right on C. Diego Laínez, left on C. Nicolás Rabal, and then left again on reaching Pl. José Antonio. 11pm curfew. 700ptas, over 25 900ptas. Open July 4-Sept 15.

Casa Diocesana Pío XII, C. San Juan, 5 (tel. 21 21 76). From Pl. San Estéban bear right onto C. El Collado, then take the first right; enter through iron gates under "Residencias" sign. Pious indeed. Popular, modern summer retreat for local seniors and travelers; winter quarters for students and travelers. Singles 1300ptas, with bath 1950ptas. Doubles 1900ptas, with bath 2550ptas. Sept.-June: 1000ptas, 1650ptas; 1600ptas, 2250ptas.

Camping: Camping Fuente de la Teja (tel. 22 29 67), 1 1/2 km from town on Ctra. Madrid (223km). Swimming pool. 300ptas per person, per tent, and per car. No bus, so walk it. Open June-Sept.

Food

Such specialties as *sopa castellana* (soup of bread, garlic, *chorizo,* and ham) and *migas pastoriles* (shepherds' bread crumbs, i.e., bread with garlic and *chorizo*) are especially delectable here. The region's bread and butter are celebrated throughout Spain. **Calle D.M. Vincente y Tutor** can hardly breathe, it's so congested with restaurants. Merchants sell fresh produce, meat, and fish at the **market** on C. Los Estudios, a left from C. Collado. (Open 9am-3pm.)

Bar Restaurante Palafox, C. Manuel Vicente Tutor, 4 (tel. 22 00 76), 1st left up the hill after skirting Pensión Ferial. Relaxed. Functional decor spiced up by a TV. Decent 2-course *menú* 750ptas. Entrees 400-950ptas. Open 1-4:30pm and 9-11:30pm.

Cafetería Restaurante Josán, Pl. Ramón Benito Aceña, 2, left on the way to the phone center from Pl. Mariano Granados. Brightly lit dining room. *Menú* 950ptas. Open 1-4pm and 9pm-midnight.

Bar Restaurante David, C. Campo, 6. From Pl. Mariano Granados, skirt the left side of Pensión Ferial and walk uphill. 1100ptas *menú* includes heartwarming chicken. Open 1:30-4pm and 9:30pm-midnight.

Nueva York, C. Collado, 14 (tel. 22 68 84). From Pl. San Estéban walk past the road to the phone center. Breakfast (served until 12:30pm) of coffee, fresh orange juice, and choice of *tapa* 185-200ptas. Open 9am-10pm.

Sights and Entertainment

Coursing in a lazy arc round Soria—compared to a drawn bow by Antonio Machado—the **Río Duero** has captivated many a Spanish writer. The melancholy elms, poplars, and oaks bordering the river inspired Machado, one of Spain's greatest 20th-century poets, to compose a collection of poetic meditations on Castile's landscape. Gustavo Adolfo Bécquer made Soria his home for a time (a plaque on Pl. Ramón Benito Aceña marks the spot), and many of his 19th-century prose classics, the *Leyendas,* are set in the hills bordering the Duero. To find the river, from Pl. Mariano Granados walk past Nueva York and bear left onto C. Aguirre. Continue downhill to Pl. Aguirre, which becomes Pl. Ramón Ayllón. Turn left from the plaza onto Travesía Cinco Villas and head downhill from Pl. Cinco Villas on unmarked C. Obispo. The **Concatedral de San Pedro** will be on the left; the bridge lies just ahead. The far side of the river is the place to take in Soria's becoming profile of churches, convents, and monasteries:

> **Iglesia de Santo Domingo** has a 12th-century Romanesque façade and remarkable sculpture.
>
> **San Juan de Rabanera** is smaller and perhaps more beautiful than the Santo Domingo. A typical Romanesque church with Byzantine touches. Its tympanum was salvaged from the ruins of the Iglesia de San Nicolás.
>
> **Convento de las Carmelitas,** Pl. Fuente de Cabrejos, off C. Zapatería, was founded by St. Teresa of Avila in the 16th century. The square is a favorite hangout for Soria's elderly.
>
> **Catedral de San Pedro,** with a fine Plateresque door, is a late Gothic church built over a Romanesque structure.
>
> **Monasterio San Juan de Duero,** in a peaceful setting across the river, is more original than any of the above. Its beautiful cloister is partially in ruins, but the fanciful colonnades (a mixture of the Romanesque and Moorish) are still here. To reach the monastery, follow the signs after crossing the bridge. Open Tues.-Sat. 10am-2pm and 5-9pm, Sun. 10am-2pm. Admission 200ptas.
>
> **Ermita de San Saturio,** downstream, clings dangerously to rocky riverside slopes riddled with caves. The monks who built it decided to integrate the caves into their *ermita*; hence rooms and chambers are partly monk-made, partly geological givens. To reach the frescoed chapel at the top, follow a series of climbing passages that wind in and out of the limestone caves. Note the window from which a young child fell in 1772, landing on his knees unharmed thanks to the intervention of the *Santo.* (So the monks claim.) Open May-Sept. 10am-2pm and 4:30-1pm; Oct.-April 10:30am-6:30pm. Free.

Regarding secular architecture, the **Palacio de los Condes de Gómara** houses government offices behind a 16th-century Renaissance façade and a handsome tower. Seven statues out front honor Soria's greats, plus one statue of a visionary nun (fast gaining attention in the academic world) killed in the Inquisition for heresy. The **Museo Numantino,** Po. Espolón, 8, displays an excellent collection of elephant pelvises, not to mention Stone, Bronze, and Iron Age artifacts and Roman relics. The third floor is reserved for an excellent exhibit (labeled in Spanish) on the ruins of nearby Numancia, along with others illustrating the history of the region. (Open Tues.-Sat. 10am-2pm and 5-9pm, Sun. 10am-2pm; Oct.-April Tues.-Sat. 9:30am-7:30pm, Sun. 9:30am-2pm. Admission 200ptas.)

In evening, dawdlers and bar-hoppers crowd the area around C. El Collado and Pl. Postigo, affectionately known as **El Tubo Estrecho** (the narrow tube). Late-night hedonism takes place at the disco/bars grouped around the intersection of **Rota de Calatañazer** and **C. Cardenal Frías.**

The **Festival de San Juan** starts in late June and ends in early July. Celebrations include bullfights, regional costume displays, and dancing in the streets. The highlights are saved for Sunday.

Near Soria

Ruins of Numancia

A series of 19th-century archeological digs uncovered the ruins of Numancia, a settlement on the hilltop 8km north of Soria that dates back more than 400 years. The two most important periods represented at the site are Celtiberian and Romans. The former settled by the 3rd century BC and tenaciously resisted the Roman. It took 10 years of the *Guerras Numantinas* (Numantian Wars) and the direction of General P. Cornelio Escipión (Scipio Africanus), called in after his victory at Carthage, to dislodge the stubborn Celtiberians. Escipión erected an elaborate system of walls 9km long, 3m wide, and 2 1/2m thick to encircle the town and cut it off from all sources of supply. High on his victory, he also saved 50 surviving residents as living trophies, sold the rest into slavery, burned the city, and divided its lands among the tribes that had collaborated with him. Numancia, however, lived on as a metaphor for patriotic heroism in Golden Age and Neoclassical tragedies.

The ruins are rather battered but still worth a visit. The information booth has no English-language brochures, but even if you don't read Spanish you can probably figure out the 12-point itinerary through the ancient city. Most interesting are the foundations of the Roman houses and the underground wells (itinerary points 5, 8-10, and 12). (Ruins open June-Aug. Tues.-Sat 10am-2pm and 5-9pm, Sun. 10am-2pm; Sept.-Oct. and April-May Tues.-Sat. 10am-2pm and 4-7pm, Sun. 10am-2pm; Nov.-March Tues.-Sat. 10am-2pm and 3:30-6pm, Sun. 10am-2pm. Admission paid at information booth 200ptas, EEC citizens under 21 free.)

Getting to the ruins is a problem for the carless. A **bus** runs to Garray (1km from ruins) from Soria (Mon.-Sat., 10min., 60ptas). Unfortunately it leaves at 2pm, so you'll arrive minutes after morning closing time and several hours before evening opening time. The 10-minute walk up to the ruins starts just out of Garray on the road to Logroño; signs mark it clearly. Getting back from Numancia is even more problematic; the bus doesn't return until the next day. The trek along the highway back to Soria takes two hours.

El Burgo de Osma

El Burgo de Osma is a largely 18th-century Baroque town with arcaded streets and squares and numerous monumental buildings such as **Hospital San Agustín** and the **Casas Consistoriales** on Plaza Mayor. In fulfillment of a vow, the Cluniac monk Don Pedro de Osma erected the magnificent 13th-century Gothic **catedral** on the site of an earlier cathedral. Most of the work is Gothic, save for Renaissance elements within (16th-century wrought-iron screens, a white marble pulpit, and a notable retable) and the Baroque belfry and chapels. The **museo** has an important collection of codices, including a richly illuminated Beato de Liébana commentary on the Apocalypse and a 12th-century charter thought to be one of the earliest examples of usage of the written Castilian vernacular. (Open 10am-1pm and 4-7pm; Oct.-May 10am-1pm and 3:30-6pm. Admission 100ptas.)

If you're pooped, there's the **Hostal Residencia La Perdiz**, C. Universidad, 33 (tel. 34 03 09; singles 1250ptas, with bath 2000ptas; doubles 2500ptas, with bath 3000ptas). From June to September, **Camping La Pedriza** on Ctra. El Burgo-Retortillo (tel. 34 08 06) is open for campers (300ptas per person, per tent, and per car).

A **tourist office** operates from July to September in the Ayuntamiento building, C. Universidad, 29 (tel. 34 08 83; open Mon.-Sat. 10am-2pm and 4-8pm). The **post office** is at 34 00 25; the **postal code** is 42300. The **telephone code** is 975. The **Red Cross** respond at 34 01 51, the **ambulatorio** at 34 12 11, the **municipal police** at 34 01 07, and the **Guardia Civil** at 34 00 74. **Buses** (tel. 34 10 24) run to and from Soria (Mon.-Sat. 2 per day, 50min., 375ptas).

Galiza (Galicia)

A rest stop on the Celts' journey to Ireland, this region in the far northwestern corner of Spain has always been an outsider. Galiza looks like no other region in the country: it's frequently veiled by a misty drizzle, and dense woods, plunging valleys, and slate-roofed fishing villages sit beside long white beaches. Rivers wind through the hills, gradually widening into the famous *rías* (inlets or firths) that empty into the Cantabrian Sea and Atlantic Ocean. Ancient Celtic *castros* (fortress-villages) and *dólmenes* (funerary chambers) testify to Galiza's ancient past, as does lingering lore about witches, fountain fairies, and buried treasure beneath the *castros*.

Yet the region also cradles that most Spanish of holy cities, Santiago de Compostela. Great stone *cruzeiros* (crosses planted at crossroads) pointed the way for hundreds of thousands of Catholic faithful as they tramped *El Camino de Santiago* (the road to Santiago). In recent years the pilgrims' destination has become an idiosyncratic regional center of fashion—native son Adolfo Domínguez popularized the slogan *la arruga es bella* (the wrinkle is beautiful).

Near-impenetrable mountain barriers kept the region historically isolated from the rest of Spain. Until Columbus's voyage, Cabo Fisterra was widely regarded as the end of the world. The Romans halfheartedly tossed off an occasional settlement here long after they had colonized the Iberian coast. The Moors could barely pay attention to Galiza long enough to destroy Santiago.

Galizans speak a unique tongue, *galego,* a language vaguely related to Portuguese and Castilian. It differs from Castilian mainly by replacing "La" and "El" with "A" and "O." We give place names in *galego,* followed by Castilian in parentheses.

The net and the plow remain Galiza's economic mainstays, bolstered by tourism. National and regional governments are trying to upgrade Galiza's roads, which aren't always adequate. Bus connections are infrequent and hitchhiking difficult. Rail service by RENFE is reliable but limited to the major cities, while clanking FEVE does its erratic thing in the rural areas.

Regional cuisine features *caldo gallego* (a vegetable broth), *pulpo a la gallega* (marinated octopus), *vieiras* (scallops, the pilgrim's trophy), and the *empanada* (turnover/pasty stuffed with tomato and tuna, among other fillings). *Tetilla* is a creamy, tangy cheese shaped like a large Hershey's kiss. A sublimely dense almond pie named for Santiago, *torta compostelana* has escaped to conquer dessert menus all over Spain. The area's Ribeiro wine, served in white ceramic cups, is a tart, slightly cloudy, young white wine that perfectly washes down *tapas.*

Santiago de Compostela

Embraced by the Ríos Tambre and Ulla, Santiago was founded in 813, according to legend, when Bishop Teodomiro informed Asturian King Alfonso II of the miraculous discovery of a tomb containing the remains of the Apostle St. James. In his Spanish incarnation, the gruesomely named St. James the Moorslayer (Santiago Matamoros) rallied the peninsula's Christians and occasionally appeared on a white charger to lead them into battle. The Christians attributed their victory at Clavijo (844) to the convenient intervention of the saint. Cordoban dictator Almanzor razed the city in 997; it was entirely rebuilt two centuries later. The town's name derives from *campo stellae,* Latin for field of the star—the star which guided Alfonso to discover the tomb.

Santiago thus became one of Christianity's three holy cities, and, like Rome and Jerusalem, the destination of pilgrimages. The clever Benedictine monks built moasteries to host the pilgrims on the way, giving rise for the first time in European history to a large-scale tourist industry. By the 12th century, the pilgrims' route became one of the most traveled in Europe. Many came as true believers, but an equal number followed the Camino as a stipulation to inheritance, an alternative to prison, or a lucrative adventure, hoping to make money from all that faith, hope, and charity.

Pilgrims of every category still follow the superhighway (Ctra. 120) to Santiago, and in 1993 they're likely to be out in record numbers because it's a holy year (the Feast of St. James, July 25, falls on a Sunday). An international center for pilgrims and tourists, Santiago's population is rounded out by over 30,000 university students. All members of this unholy trinity enjoy the cathedral, the all-granite old town, and the local delicacy (a mild cheese packaged in the shape of a woman's breast).

Orientation and Practical Information

Street names in Santiago are a mess. The signs on the street are in both *galego* and Castilian, but the map uses Castilian. Since the two languages are similar, it's not a total nightmare: *del* in Castilian becomes *do* in *galego,* and *Calle* becomes *Rúa.* The **ca-**

Santiago de Compostela

thedral marks the center of the old city. The old city is corralled in by **R. Fonte Santo Antonio (C. Calvo Sotelo)**, and sits higher than the new city. Three streets lead directly to the cathedral from the south side of town (train station side): **Rúa do Franco** (Calle del Franco), **Rúa do Vilar** (Rúa del Villar), and **Rúa Nova** (Calle Nueva).

From the train station, turn right at the top of the stairs and take C. Hórreo to **Praza de Galiza** (do *not* take Avenida de Lugo). From here, it's one more block to **Entrecalles,** from which the three cathedral-bound streets spring. From the bus station, take bus #10 to Pr. Galiza (every 10-15min., 60ptas). The worst part is that two streets are currently undergoing a **name change** (on street signs): Rúa Senra is also known as Calle General Mola; its continuation, Rúa da Fonte de Santo Antonio, is now Calvo Sotelo. N.B.—don't confuse C. General Franco (runs from the train station into town) with R. Franco (near the cathedral, right in the center).

Tourist Office: R. Villar, 43 (tel. 58 40 81), in the old town under the arches of a colonnade. English and French spoken. Useful pamphlets with maps of Santiago (woefully not indexed) and all of Galiza. Bus schedules and accommodations information. Guided tours. Open Mon.-Fri. 9am-2pm and 4-7pm, Sat. 10am-1:30pm.

Budget Travel: TIVE, Plazuela del Matadero, s/n (tel. 57 24 26), up R. Fonte Santo Antonio (Calvo Sotelo) from Pr. Galiza. Train, bus, and plane tickets for international destinations. ISIC 500ptas. HI card 1800ptas. Open Mon.-Fri. 9am-2pm.

Currency Exchange: Banco Hispano Americano, R. Vilar, 30 (tel. 58 16 12). 1% commission (500ptas min. charge). Open Mon.-Fri. 9am-2pm. Many banks on Pr. Galiza.

Post Office: R. Franco (tel. 58 12 52; fax 56 32 88), on the corner of Trav. Fonseca. Open for stamps and Lista de Correos Mon.-Fri. 8am-9pm, Sat. 9am-2pm; for **telegrams** Mon.-Fri. 8am-9pm, Sat. 9am-7pm; for **faxes** Mon.-Fri 8am-9pm, Sat. 9am-9pm. **Postal Code:** 15080.

Telephones: C. Bautizados, 13, in the old town off Pl. Toral. Open Mon.-Fri. 10am-11:30pm, Sat. 10am-8pm, Sun. 11am-3pm and 5-9:30pm. **Telephone Code:** 981.

Flights: Aeropuerto Lavacolla (tel. 59 74 00), 11km away on road to Lugo. A bus connects it to Santiago (8 per day, 100ptas). Good national connections and direct flights to London, Paris, Zürich, Amsterdam, and Frankfurt. Information open 24 hrs. **Iberia office,** R. Fonte Santo Antonio (Calvo Sotelo), 25 (tel. 57 20 28). Open Mon.-Fri. 9:45am-2pm and 4-7pm, Sat. 9am-1:30pm.

Trains: C. Hórreo (tel. 59 18 59, 52 02 02). Information open Mon.-Sat. 7am-11pm, Sun. 7am-1pm. To: Madrid (2 per day, 7hr., 4325-6125ptas); Pontevedra (10 per day, 1 1/4 hr., 340ptas); A Coruña (14 per day; 1hr.; 340-640ptas, *talgo* 800ptas); Barcelona (2 per day, 7hr., 6870ptas).

Buses: Estación Central de Autobuses (tel. 58 77 00), C. San Cayetano. Nothing central about it: 1/2 hr. west of downtown. Information open 6am-10pm. **ALSA** (tel. 58 64 53). To: Madrid (2 per day, 8-9hr., 4970ptas); Donostia/San Sebastián (1 per day, 6hr., 1610ptas); Ferrol (5 per day, 1 1/2 hr., 765ptas); Bilbo (2 per day, 4hr., 5260ptas). **Castromil** (tel. 58 97 00). To: A Coruña (frequent, 1 1/2 hr., 645ptas); Pontevedra (frequent, 1 1/2 hr., 490ptas); Noia (every hr., 1hr., 285ptas); Muros (every hr., 2hr., 570ptas). **Finisterre** (tel. 58 73 16). To: Muxía, Cabo Fisterra, and Camariñas. Call first; service is infrequent.

Taxis: tel. 59 84 88 or 58 59 73.

Car Rental: Autotur, C. General Pardiñas, 3 (tel. 58 64 96), in the new town. Must be at least 21 and have had license 1 yr. Open Mon.-Fri. 9am-2pm and 4-8pm, Sat. 10am-1:30pm.

Luggage Storage: At the **train station** (lockers 200ptas). Open 7:30am-11pm. At the **bus station** (70ptas per bag). Open 6am-10pm.

English Bookstore: Librería Econtros, R. Vilar, 68 (tel. 57 25 47). Guidebooks, Agatha Christie, and Tom Clancy. Open Mon.-Fri. 9am-1:30pm and 4-8pm, Sat. 9:30am-2pm.

Library: Biblioteca Xeral Universitaria, Trav. Fonseca, s/n (tel. 56 38 33), off R. Franco. Open Mon.-Fri. 9am-2pm; Sept.-June Mon.-Fri. 9:30am-9:30pm, Sat. 9am-2pm.

Laundromat: Lava-Express, C. República El Salvador, 21 (tel. 59 00 95), in the new town at the corner with C. Alfredo Brañas. Self-service wash and dry 550ptas per 4kg load. Full same-day service 750ptas per load. Open Mon.-Fri. 9:30am-2pm and 4-8:30pm, Sat. 10am-2pm.

Swimming Pool: Piscina Municipal, Tras de Santa Isabel, s/n (tel. 58 67 20), to the left off C. Galeras, west of the old town. Adults 350ptas, children 200ptas. Open late Sept.-July Mon.-Fri. 4-10pm, Sat. 5-8pm.

Crisis Lines: UMA Drogodependencia (tel. 58 86 56).

Red Cross: C. San Cayetano (tel. 58 69 69).

Medical Assistance: Hospital Xeral, C. Galeras (tel. 54 00 00). **Ambulance:** tel. 59 36 56.

Late-Night Pharmacy: Check listings in *El Correo Gallego* (local paper, 200ptas).

Emergency: Policía municipal (tel. 092 or tel. 58 16 78).

Guardia Civil: 58 15 11.

Accommodations and Camping

To accommodate millions of pilgrims and tourists, Santiago has a seemingly endless supply of rooms. **Rúa do Vilar** and **Calle Raiña** spill over with *fondas* and *pensiones,* and every other building in town has a hand-drawn *"habitaciones"* sign. Some citizens linger about the stations and offer rooms in their homes, but these lodgings vary vastly in quality and price.

Hospedaje Ramos, C. Raiña, 18, 2nd fl. (tel. 58 18 59), above Restaurante O Papa Upa. Simple but comfortable. Rooms with private baths are nicer and a far better deal. Try to get one with a view of the cathedral. Some rooms even have balconies. Heavenly beds—firm, thick mattresses upon which to rest your pilgrim's bones. Singles 1100ptas, with bath 1250ptas. Doubles 2000ptas, with bath 2200ptas.

Hostal La Senra, R. Senra (a.k.a. C. General Mola), 13, 3rd fl. (tel. 50 04 48). Turn left at the far end of Pr. Galiza when coming from the train station. Pastel bedspreads and enormous billowing curtains. The rooms rival some of the cathedral's chapels in size. Doubles with sink 3000ptas. Triples with sink 4000ptas, with bath 5000ptas.

Hospedaje Francis, C. Cardenal Paya, 2, 3rd fl. (tel. 58 03 63), 100 yds. north of Pr. Galiza in a quiet corner of the old city. Large rooms with glass-enclosed terraces overlooking the street. TV hums in the yellow-and-brown, 60s-motif-wallpapered waiting room. Almost all doubles. 1000ptas per person.

Hospedaje Sofía, C. Cardenal Paya, 16 (tel. 58 51 50), just past Hospedaje Francis. See the sign? Super shiny wood floors and spic 'n' span rooms. Son's track trophies lounge around the sitting room; you can too, in front of the huge TV. Mother-daughter duo run the show. Singles with sink 1500ptas. Doubles with sink 2500ptas.

Hospedaje Viño, Pl. Mazarelos, 7 (tel. 58 51 85). After Pr. Galiza, take a right onto R. Fonte San Antonio and turn left through purple-flowered archway. Spotless rooms overlook a peaceful plaza, with exposed stone in the bay windows. It doesn't get quainter than this. Above an eponymous bar. Singles 1000ptas. Doubles 1500ptas. Breakfast 150ptas.

Hospedaje Recarey, Patio de Madres, 15, 3rd fl. (tel. 58 81 94). Up R. Fonte Santo Antonio (Calvo Sotelo) and to the right after 2 bl. On a quiet street. Flower power bedspreads on soft beds. Singles with sink 1200ptas. Doubles with sink 2000ptas, with bath 3500ptas.

Camping: Camping As Cancelas, R. 25 de Xullo, 35 (tel. 58 02 66), 2km from the cathedral on the northern edge of town. Take bus #6 or 9. Souvenirs, laundry, supermarket, and pool make this the Club Med of camping. 445ptas per person, 465ptas per car, 465ptas per tent. **Camping Santiago** (tel. 88 80 02), about 6km from town on the road to A Coruña, next door to the Guardia Civil. 415ptas per person, 420ptas per car. Electricity 350ptas. Open June 25-Sept. 25.

Food

Pilgrims need to eat too; Santiago is a budget diner's dream. Bars and cafeterias line the streets of the old town, proffering a shocking variety of fishy and meaty *menús*. *Empanadas* galore satisfy even the most finicky eaters. Most restaurants are in the old town east of the cathedral, notably on **Rúa del Villar, C. General Franco,** and **Calle de la Raíña.**

Produce carts, meat stalls, and everything else from flowers to baby clothes for pilgrim tots line the streets of the open **market,** which stretches from Pl. San Felix to Convento de San Augustín, north of the cathedral. (Open Mon.-Sat. 7:30am-2pm.)

Supermarket: Supermercados La Concha, C. Montero Ríos, 32, between C. General Pardiñas and C. Alfredo Brañas. Open Mon.-Sat. 9am-9pm.

O' Sotano, C. General Franco, 8 (tel. 56 50 24). Follow the sign down to a deep subterranean restaurant with inviting wood tables and a TV. Hearty *menú* of *merluza* 800ptas. *Vieiras* (scallops) 650ptas. Open noon-4:30pm and 7:30-midnight.

Café-Bar El Metro, R. Nova, 12. Pro-choice *menú* (700ptas). Entrees 300-450ptas. *Tortilla de queso* and a belly-swelling *salmón a la plancha.* Snag one of the tables beneath the archway outside. Open 1-5pm and 8pm-midnight. Closed Christmas week and Semana Santa.

Restaurante Abella, R. Franco, 28 (tel. 58 29 81). Dining room in back with light, lip-smacking *menús* (500ptas) with *merluza* or *churrasco* (roast beef). Bargain basement *empanadas* (turnovers) 200ptas. Woody walls and a keg full of *vino de Ribeiro,* tapped right before your booze-starved eyes. Open 9:30am-4pm and 6-11:30pm.

Bar Coruña, C. Raíña, 17. Spazzy *jamoñes* dangle from the ceiling. The Coruña is known as *"el rey del bocadillo"* —that is, just about anything slapped between two slices of bread, from anchovies (185ptas) to tortillas (140ptas). Open Sun.-Fri. 9:30am-midnight.

Bar Rois, C. Raíña, 12 (tel. 58 24 44). Satisfying 600ptas *menú* of *pollo* or *merluza.*

Mesón-Restaurant O Papa Upa, C. Raíña, 18 (tel. 56 65 98). Two octopi hang out behind the long bar's dizzy array of *vinos.* Bright dining room in back. *Menú* (850ptas) offers *caldo gallego* and *cordero.* Open 1-4pm and 7pm-midnight.

Restaurante la Carrileña, R. Franco, 48. Cozy, with a Zurbarán still life on the wall. *Menú del día* of *caldo gallego* and *callos* (spicy grilled green peppers) only 500ptas. Even St. James would have gobbled *pimientos de Padrón* at 250ptas. Open Mon.-Sat. 2-4:30pm and 7:30-10:30pm.

Café-Bar O'Bigotes, C. Raíña, 7. Garlic, not pig, hangs in front of the wine rack. Standing room only in this bar. Simple, but what value! *Empanadas* 160ptas. *Bocadillos* 130-175ptas. *Mejillones,* the city's least expensive, 275ptas. Open Wed.-Mon. 9am-1am.

Cervecería Dakar, R. Franco, 13. An amiable and active bar. Elegant and spacious with wood panelling. Rich *batidos* (milkshakes, 200ptas) of nutmeg and delicious liqueurs. Five flavors. Students spread their papers all over tables. Delightful breakfast of *café y curasán* (coffee and croissant) 225ptas. Open Oct. to mid-Sept. Fri.-Wed. 8am-midnight.

Sights

The entire old town has been designated a national monument; feast your art-historical heart out on every door and square. The **catedral's** kernel is an admirable Romanesque Latin cross with ambulatory and radiating chapels. The cathedral has four façades, each a masterpiece from a different period. There are also four separate entrances, each opening onto a different **plaza:** Pr. Platerías, Quintana, Obradoiro, or Azabaxería. From the southern **Praza de Platerías,** enter the cathedral by way of a Romanesque-arched set of double doors, crusted over with columns and an assortment of icons in various stages of undress. This is the oldest façade, its portico is adorned with robust granite figures and includes a profusion of rounded arches, statues, and bas relief details.

The **Torro do Reloxio** (clock tower), which faithfully tolls away the hours, has a Gothic, craggy touch. The clock tower, Pórtico Real, and Porta Santa face onto the **Praza da Quintana,** to the west of the cathedral. Because 1993 is one of the rare *Años Jacobeo* (holy years when the Feast of St. James falls on a Sunday), the locked doors of the Porta Santa will be open for lucky pilgrims to pass through. Crowning the door is a 17th-century rendering of Santiago in *mufti;* his stylish pilgrim's cloak, broad-brimmed felt hat, mod cockle-shells, and staff with gourd for water (no canteens then) were standard attire for pilgrims. To the north, the **Azabaxería** façade blends Romanesque and Neoclassical styles in a headache-inducing blend of Doric columns, Ionic columns and a smattering of those ubiquitous religious icons. Consecrated in 1211, the cathedral later acquired Gothic chapels in the apse and transept, a 15th-century dome, a 16th-century cloister, and the Baroque façade called the **Obradoiro,** whose two exquisitely ornate towers soar above the city. The shrine's international clout is made manifest by the 18th-century stone flowers representing the world over. The Obradoiro façade faces (duh) **Praza da Obradoiro** (to the west), a plaza that sees camera-snappers, souvenir hawkers and (watch out!) *tunas* coexist in a Baroque frenzy of travel and tourism. Encased in this facade, the **Pórtico de la Gloria,** by Maestro Mateo, is oft considered the crowning achievement of Spanish Romanesque sculpture. It includes a life-like bust of the Mateo; some believe that by knocking one's head against his, some of his talent will rub off.

Inside the cathedral, the organ pipes protruding from stone arches along the central aisle are designed to resemble trumpet horns over the heads of the congregation. Santiagos' revered remains (read: putrefying body parts) lie beneath the high altar in a silver coffer, while his more savory bejewelled bust sits above. Santiago's bones were misplaced in the 16th century when they were hidden from the English. Somebody finally dug up his holy remains three centuries later; the identity was confirmed when a shard of skull, brought from Italy, fit perfectly into the hole in the skeleton's head. The **bota fumeiro** is an enormous silver incense burner swung from end to end in the transept during high mass and major liturgical ceremonies. The **museo** and **claustros** impress some people with gorgeous 16th-century tapestries, so detailed that they threaten to leave your eyes permanently crossed if you look too closely. The museum also houses manuscripts from the *Códice Calixtino* and Romanesque remains dug up during one of the many archeological excavations here. (Cathedral open 10:30am-1:30pm and 4-6:30pm, holidays 10:30am-1:30pm. Admission to museum and cloisters 200ptas.) Across Pr. Obradoiro, facing the cathedral, the long, majestic façade of the former **Pazo de Raxoi** (Royal Palace) extrudes gold-accented balconies and monumental columns in vigorous Neoclassical style. The bas-relief within of the Battle of Clavijo is a remarkable work in the same style. It's now home to the Ayuntamiento and the office of the president of the Xunta de Galiza. Also in Pr. Obradoiro, in all its glory, stands the 15th-century Renaissance **Hospital Real,** now the ritzy *parador* Hostal dos Reies Católicos. The *parador* still upholds the building's ancient traditon of feeding 10 pilgrims per day—not, however, in the hotel's restaurant, but in the employees' dining hall. The *hostal's* doorway is a carved masterpiece; ask the concierge for permission to see its four courtyards, the chapel, and sculpture. (Open 10am-10pm and 4-7pm.)

Back on the other side of the cathedral in Pr. Quintana, the **Mosteiro de San Pelayo** surpasses the usual supply of relics with a bizarre statue of Mary holding Jesus and clubbing a demon. (Open Mon.-Sat. 10am-1pm and 4-7pm, Sun. 10am-2pm. Admission 100ptas.)

Off Pr. Platerias, residential architecture holds its own in Baroque **Casa del Deán** and **Casa del Cabildo.** Farther from the cathedral area near Pr. Camino, both the **Museo do Pobo Galego** (tel. 58 36 20) and the **Museo Municipal** exhibit interesting tidbits of Galician culture in the Gothic **Igrexa de Santo Domingo**. (Open Mon.-Sat. 10am-1pm and 4-7pm. Free.) The city was not oblivious to the renovating airs of Enlightenment and wove a Neoclassical **Universidad** into its predominantly Romanesque and Baroque warp. The University is west of the old town. Located one km from the cathedral, the 15th-century **Colexiata de Santa María do Sar** has a disintegrating Romanesque cloister that started crumbling in the 12th century and just never stopped. Inside, pillars leaning at frighteningly unlikely angles give the impression that the whole is about to collapse into a picturesque pile of rubble. (Open Mon.-Sat. 10am-1pm and 4-6:30pm. Admission 50ptas.)

Entertainment

The city has proudly unveiled an airy new **auditorio** (concert hall), which schedules a full program of instrumental and lyric music (check at the tourist office and in the entertainment sections of the dailies).

At night a singing student troupe, the **tuna,** bothers females in the old town with ribald songs and an occasional serenade. Traditionally the singers serenaded women, hoping that they would swoon and trade their prized long school ribbons for a rotten *tuna* cape. If a woman doesn't like the song, she can pour water on the singer's head. Nowadays the *tuna*-ers focus their energy on collecting tips from gawking tourists.

Crowds of all ages flood the city's cellars for mix-and-match nightlife. (All clubs open roughly 11pm-4am, with action starting well after midnight; women free, men 400-600ptas.)

Modus Vivendi, Pr. Feixoo. An eclectic dungeon whose heartbeat alternates between Galician bagpipes and David Bowie.

Poison, near Pr. Cervantes. Serves refreshing local wines in large glasses to a student crowd.

Araguaney, C. Montero Rios, in the new town. A disco where a copy of the Venus de Milo cohabits uneasily with a slick neon interior.

Discoteca Black, C. Rosalia de Castro, inside Hotel Peregrino. Popular club for all age groups.

Clangor, in Puente la Rocha, near town. Students kick up their heels during the Oct.-May academic year.

Santiago's **fiestas** occur July 18 to 31. The climax is the bacchanalian **Féstival del Apóstol;** tension and parties mount for a week or more beforehand. Street musicians and performers set up shop in Pr. Inmaculada, while costumed stilt-walkers teeter through the streets. A witch with a broom sweeps pedestrians aside, clearing a path for an old hat-snatcher who keeps people at bay with loud fireworks. On July 25, the cathedral's façade is rigged with hundreds of fireworks.

Rías Baixas (Bajas)

Protected coves lure *galegos* to the Rías Baixas for weekend visits. Tourism is gradually eclipsing fishing as the main local industry, since foreigners as well as Spaniards realized there are reasons to travel to the Rías other than the surf. Quaint stone villages and Celtic ruins speckle the countryside. Public transportation between towns in this area is sparse; either rent a car or plan your itinerary carefully.

Ría de Vigo: Vigo

Chiefly a port city, hilly Vigo's biggest virtue is its well developed service economy. The city's efficient ferries and buses shuttle visitors to the nearby Ría de Vigo and Río Mino, while its hotels, shopping, and communications network pamper them between excursions.

Orientation and Practical Information

The **Gran Vía** is the main thoroughfare, stretching south to north from **Praza de América,** through Praza de España, ending at the perpendicular **Calle Príncipe Urzáiz.** The train station lies just off C. Urzáiz in Praza de la Estación. C. Urzáiz runs all the way to near the port. **As Avenidas** is the main street along the water, just north of **Praza de Compostela.**

Tourist Office: As Avenidas, s/n (tel. 43 05 77). C. Urzáiz is up the hill from the train station. Take a right onto it, then right again at C. Colón. Follow C. Colón to its port end; As Avenidas is to the left. From the bus station, turn right onto Alcalde Gregorio Espino; then left onto C. Urzáiz (5min.). From there, follow the directions above. Alternatively, catch a red Vitrasa bus at the bus station (#L27, L23, or R7 to the city center; 85ptas). The office is in the gray circular building. Open Mon.-Fri. 9am-2pm and 4:30-6:30pm, Sat. 10am-12:30pm.

El Corte Inglés: Gran Vía 25-27 (tel. 41 51 11, 41 61 11). From C. Urzáiz, turn left onto Gran Vía. As always, they have the best **map. Currency exchange:** 250ptas min. charge for cash, 500ptas for traveler's checks—same as the banks. They also offer novels and guidebooks in English; haircutting; both cafeteria and restaurant; and **telephones.** Open Mon.-Sat. 10am-9pm.

Budget Travel: Viajes TIVE, C. Uruguay, 15, 2nd fl. (tel. 22 61 17, 43 59 44). From C. Urzáiz, turn right onto C. Cervantes; C. Uruguay is the 3rd left. ISIC 500ptas. HI card 1800ptas. Some English spoken. Mon.-Fri. 9am-2pm.

Currency Exchange: see **El Corte Inglés** above.

Post Office: Pr. Compostela, 3 (tel. 21 70 09, 43 40 09; fax (986) 37 47 26). From C. Colón, turn left onto Pr. Compostela. Open for stamps, Lista de Correos, and **telegrams** Mon.-Fri. 8am-9pm, Sat. 9am-2pm; for **faxes** Mon.-Fri. 9am-9pm. **Postal Code:** 36200.

Telephones: Telefónica, C. Urzáiz, 3, near the intersection with C. Colón. Also, **faxes** sent but not received. Open Mon.-Sat. 9am-9pm. **Telephone Code:** 986.

Galiza (Galicia)

Flights: Aeropuerto de Peinador, Av. do Aeroporto, s/n (tel. 48 74 12). Daily flights to Madrid, Barcelona, Bilbao, Valencia, and Valladolid. **Iberia's** office is at Marqués de Valladares, 17 (tel. 22 70 05).

Trains: RENFE, Pl. de la Estación, s/n (tel. 43 11 14), down the stairs from C. Urzáiz. Information open 7am-11pm. To: Pontevedra (14 per day, 40min., 165ptas); Túi (4 per day, 45min., 220ptas); Santiago de Compostela (11 per day, 2hr., 515ptas); A Coruña (9 per day, 3hr., 880ptas); Valladolid (1 per day, change at Medina del Campo, 3135ptas); Madrid (2 per day, 9-10hr., 4355ptas); Valença do Minho in Portugal (6 per day, 1 1/4 hr.).

Buses: Estación de Autobuses, Av. Madrid, s/n (tel. 37 34 11). On the corner with Rua do Alcalde Gregorio Espino, it's a red version of the Sydney Opera House. **Gastromil** (tel. 27 81 12). To: Santiago de Compostela (17 per day, 2hr., 795ptas); A Coruña (8 per day, 2 1/2 hr., 1400ptas); Madrid (8 per day, 9hr., 2910ptas); Santander (2 per day, 14hr., 5505ptas). **ATSA** (tel. 60 00 22, 61 02 55). To: Túi (every 1/2 hr., 45min., 245ptas); A Garda (every 1/2 hr., 1hr., 450ptas); Baiona (every 1/2 hr., 1/2 hr., 180ptas); Pontevedra (16 per day, 40min., 240ptas). For ATSA buses, go straight downstairs to the gates and buy ticket on board. **Viba** (tel. 26 13 23) travels to Barcelona (1 per day, 14hr., 6015ptas).

Public Transportation: Red *Vitrasa* buses (tel. 19 16 00) run to every corner of the city (85ptas). For schedules and routes, check *Faro de Vigo* (local paper, 90ptas).

Ferries: Estación Marítima de Ría, As Avenidas, s/n (tel. 43 77 77). From Pr. de Compostela, follow C. Garcia Olloqui to its end at As Avenidas. Ferries to Cangas (every hr., 20min., round-trip 200ptas) and Moaña (every hr., 30min., round-trip 200ptas). Service June-Sept. only to Islas Cíes (5 per day, round-trip 1250ptas).

Taxis: Radio Taxi (tel. 47 00 00).

Car Rental: Atesa, C. Urzáiz, 84 (tel. 41 80 76). Must be 21 and have had license 1 yr. Open Mon.-Fri. 8:30am-1:30pm and 4-8pm, Sat. 9am-1pm. **Avis,** C. Uruguay, 12 (tel. 43 59 11). Must be 23 and have had license 1 yr. Open Mon.-Fri. 9am-1:15pm and 4-7pm, Sat. 9am-noon.

Luggage Storage: At the **train station** (lockers 200ptas). Open 7am-9:45pm. At the **bus station** (50ptas per bag checked). Open Mon.-Fri. 9:30am-1:30pm and 3-7pm, Sat. 9am-2pm.

English Bookstore: Librería Cervantes, C. Policarpio Sanz, 27 (tel. 43 94 08), off C. Colón. Small miscellany of novels in English. Open Mon.-Fri. 9:30am-1:30pm and 4:30-8pm, Sat. 9:30am-1:30pm.

Laundromat: Don Coche, C. Urzáiz, 97 (tel. 47 39 09). Not self-service. Wash and dry 800ptas per load; wash only 500ptas. Open Mon.-Sat. 9am-1:30pm and 4-8pm.

Red Cross: C. Ecuador, 16 (tel. 42 36 66, 43 89 00).

24-Hour Pharmacy: Check *Farmacias de Guardia* listings in *Faro de Vigo* or *La Voz de Galicia* (local papers, 90ptas).

Medical Services: Hospital Meixoeiro, C. Meixoeiro, s/n (tel. 81 11 11). **Hospital Xeral,** C. Pizarro, s/n (tel. 81 60 00). **Ambulance** (tel. 41 64 29, 22 60 31).

Emergency: tel. 092. **Casa de Socorro** (tel. 43 25 09).

Police: Municipal Police, Pr. do Rey (tel. 43 22 11). **Guardia Civil** (tel. 22 45 44).

Accommodations

Budgeters come from far and wide for Vigo's inexpensive rooms. The hill from the train station may cripple you, the city's ugliness may blind you, but the *hostales* on **Calle Alfonso XIII** (to the right from the train station) win the nationally coveted best-budget-*hostales*-on-a-single-street award. The accommodations around the train station and around **Calles Carral and García Olloqui** are close contenders.

Hostal Gran Peña, C. Alfonso XIII, 52 (tel. 43 35 09). Green reception room and ecologically-minded posters. Singles 1000ptas. Doubles 2000ptas. Shower included.

Hostal Ría de Vigo, C. Cervantes, 14 (tel. 43 72 40), a left off C. Alfonso XIII. Look for the sign. Simple, spacious, and squeaky-clean. Soft beds work better than Halcion. Single with bath 1500ptas. Doubles with bath 3000ptas.

Hostal-Residencia Madrid, C. Alfonso XIII, 63 (tel. 22 55 23). Singles 1300ptas. Try for the 2-bed double with sitting room! 1800ptas.

Hostal Noso-Lar, C. Urzáiz, 53 (tel. 22 42 59), at the corner with Gran Vía. Marble stairs soar up to the reception desk. Some rooms have terraces. Late July-late Aug.: Singles 2800ptas. Doubles with bath and TV 4200ptas. June to mid-July and late Aug.-early Sept.: 2000ptas; 3000ptas. Open June-Sept.

Camping: Camping Samil, Av. Samil, 163 (tel. 20 43 54), 6km from the city. Take the "Playa-Samil" red Vitrasa bus. Adults 400ptas; 2-person tent 400ptas, 4-person tent 600ptas; 500ptas per car. Open April 1-Sept. 30 and Oct. 1-Dec. 30.

Food

The **Gran Vía** and **C. Venezuela** are clotted with outdoor *terrazas* and shiny, bright *cafeterías* that aren't overly expensive. Side streets off **C. Urzáiz** tend to be cheaper, and the bars and cafés just don't stop.

Groceries: Exo-Ama, Av. Alcalde Vásquez Varela, 31, a left turn immediately after exiting the train station (it's perpendicular to C. Urzáiz). Open Mon.-Fri. 9am-2pm and 5-8:30pm, Sat. 9am-2pm.

Cafetería Lido, Gran Vía, 3. Elegant, long wood bar with tables in back. A glass case of rich desserts. Sandwiches 200-250ptas. *Pinchos morunos* 500ptas. *Tarta de queso* (cheesecake) 300ptas. Open Tues.-Sun. 7:30am-2am.

Cafetería Cariba, C. Ecuador, 73, right behind El Corte Inglés. Cavernous pink and green interior and tranquilizing music soothes the harrowing infirmity many call "traveler's nerves." *Terraza* outside, A/C inside. *Platos combinados* with bread 500-700ptas; #3 is chicken, *pimientos,* and monster portion of *ensalada rusa.* Diverse *bocadillos* and *raciones.* Open July-Aug. Mon.-Sat. 7am-1am; Sept.-June 7am-1am.

Cafetería la Flor de Vigo, Gran Vía, 19, near El Corte Inglés. Electronic paradise: slot machine, video game, and TV. Huge dining room and terrace outside. *Merluza a la plancha* 600ptas. *Gambas a la plancha* 400ptas. *Chocolate con churros,* 275ptas. Open Mon.-Sat. 6:30am-midnight.

Excursions

The Vigo estuary has a particularly wide entrance—as if, the tourist brochure so eloquently states, "it were about to swallow up a big piece of ocean." The big fat mouth and its lively port explain why the cities of this *ría* have grown like mad in the past half century. Although it's all very hush-hush, rumor has it that maybe not so long ago witches (nice ones and evil ones) were the last word on the banks of this *ría*.

Cangas

It's only a ferry ride across the Ría de Vigo from urban decay to Club Paradise. Cangas does manage to get a fair amount of tourism due to its proximity to Vigo but the overabundance of thriving palms and unsullied hills show that this small town hasn't yet lost its looks. Turn right from the ferry onto a cobblestoned walk and pass a green park to get to the beach. Cangas is best as a day trip. **Rodeiramar 2-A,** C. Orense, 76 (tel. 30 17 49), right behind the more expensive hotel (a 5min. walk down the beach), has apartments for two (5380ptas), three (6410ptas), and four (7441ptas) people. There's also **Camping Cangas** on Playa de Limens-Darbo (tel. 30 47 26; open June 3-Sept. 9). Restaurants and cafés along the beach on C. Montero Ríos vend *bocadillos* and some *raciones,* but beware the tourist prices. **Cafetería Airínos do Mar,** Av. Eugenio Sequeiros, 30, hawks *platos combinados* (450-600ptas) and *bocadillos* (250-370ptas). Where the ferry dumps visitors, the **Turismo** welcomes them in a small, light blue shack behind the ticket office/bar in front. **Ferries** go from Vigo to Cangas every half hour (20min., 120ptas).

Baiona (Bayona)

21km southwest of Vigo, snug in its own mini estuary, lies Baiona (Bayona), a hotbed of trading until the late 19th century when Vigo took over as the Galician industrial monster. Now Baiona is a beach town with one *parador nacional* and a handful of churches to its credit. The most imposing edifice in town is certainly the 16th-century **castillo-***cum*-hotel, a *parador nacional* that was once the castle of the Condes de Gondomar. From where the bus stops on C. Angel Eldouayan, it's a short walk up the street (the water to the right). The huge stone walls, intricate walkways, and nausea-inducing ledges are surrounded by perfectly clipped hedges and a rainbow of flowers. For your own accommodations you may have to settle for slightly less. **Hospedaje King,** C. Ventura Misa, 27 (tel. 35 72 15), offers singles with sinks for 1300ptas. (Doubles 2500ptas, with bath 3500ptas.) **Camping Bayona Playa** (tel. 35 00 35) is 485ptas per person, 400-495ptas per tent, and 495ptas per car (open June-Sept.). Up and down C. Ventura Misa are *mesones* and *cafeterías*. **La Farda,** C. Ventura Misa, 36, promotes its lightly fried *calamares* (*raciones* 400ptas). **Turismo,** on Plaza Pedro de Castro, to the left as the bus pulls in, is open Mon.-Sat. 9:30am-1:30pm. **Buses** leave Vigo for Baiona every half-hour during the summer (last bus returns at 10:15pm, 1/2 hr., 180ptas).

Río Miño

The slow Río Miño marks a quiet and, after Maastricht, altogether porous national border. Running southwest from Lugo, the Río Miño empties into the Atlantic Ocean, about 25km further west. One lone bridge carrying trains, automobiles, and pedestrians spans the river between Túi in Galiza (Galicia) and Valença do Minho in Portugal.

Túi

The most clumsy, over-equipped backpacker in the whole wide world could easily walk to Portugal from Túi, a mere km north of the border. The metal planked walkway (a.k.a. bridge) to Portugal, while slightly nerve-wracking to 'fraidy cats, may turn even non-shutterbugs into aspiring photojournalists. This is the stuff that *National Geographic* is made of. Rolling hills, farmlands, and trees dripping with chlorophyll cover the banks of the Río Mino. The walk alone is well worth a daytrip from Vigo.

A charming town, that Túi. Tough and hardy, it has seen wars with Portugal and invasions from France. The impressive **catedral** is a mix of Gothic and Romanesque, reflecting Túi's Portuguese, Spanish, and Galician roots. (Open 9am-1pm and 4-8pm.) The center city, above the new town, is a beautifully preserved medieval stone fortress, surrounded by graceful parks, a river, and paths that snake into the hills.

To round your day off with a little sleep, **Habitaciones Otilia,** Generalísimo, 8, 2nd fl. (tel. 60 10 62), behind C. Calvo Sotelo en route to the cathedral, has snuggly beds topped by quilted bedspreads. (Doubles 1800ptas. Triples 2700ptas.) **Bar Nuevo** on C. Calvo Sotelo, as well as a few bar-cafeterias in the surrounding blocks, serve quick vittles. If it happens to be Thursday, stroll down the Paseo Calvo Sotelo to the weekly **market,** which has been around (uninterrupted, some claim) since 1679. **Turismo** (400m from the border) supplies national and regional information. (Open 9:30am-1pm and 4-6pm.) For the **Red Cross,** call 60 16 84. In **emergency,** call Servicio de Urgencias, Pr. Galicia (tel. 60 09 08). **Policia Municipal** (tel. 60 08 10) is at Pl. Inmaculada.

The **bus** from Vigo (every 1/2 hr., 45min., 350ptas) stops on C. Calvo Sotelo opposite the Iglesia de San Francisco, and leaves for the return trip from the bus shelter outside the church. Only three **trains** (tel. 60 08 13) per day cross the border (to Vigo, 45min., 200ptas; to Viana do Castelo in Portugal, 11/2hr., 330ptas). They stop for 15 minutes on both sides for customs and passport control. The train stations in each town are nowhere near the border; taking the bus or walking makes more sense.

A Garda

At the mouth of the Miño, this well-proportioned town guards Spain and a small, sheltered beach. The bus stops at the corner of Calle Dominguez Fontela and Calle Concepción Arenal. Take C. Dominguez Fontela to the central Calle José Antonio and turn right to climb the majestic **Monte Santa Tecla.** Bear right onto Calle Rosalía de Castro to start the 6km ascent up the mountain. At the checkpoint 300m from the end of C. Rosalía de Castro, hikers pay 50ptas to sweat their way to the peak. Near the top is a chapel dedicated to Saint Tecla, the patron saint of headaches and heart disease. From the summit, you can see the entire Iberian peninsula. There's only one hotel on the mountain, **Hotel Pazo Santa Tecla** (tel. 61 00 02). It's downright elegant; almost all rooms have terraces overlooking the valley. (Singles with bath 3100ptas. Doubles 4200ptas. Sept. 2-June 30: 2650ptas; 3850ptas. Breakfast 300ptas. Open Semana Santa-Oct.) In A Garda proper, **Casa Arturo,** C. Pontevedra, 12 (tel. 61 03 08), has singles (1200ptas) and doubles (2000ptas). Check at the restaurant across the street; they own the Arturo. Sustenance-wise, the **supermarket** on the corner of C. Concepción Arenal and Brasilino Alvarez Sobrino is plump with basic staples. **Buses** leave for A Garda from the center of Túi (every 1/2 hr., 45min., 250ptas).

The **Islas Cíes** have the whitest sands and the bluest water (ferries run every hr., 45min., 1250ptas). The only sleeping option is **Camping Islas Cíes** (tel. 43 46 55, 27 85 01), a third-class site. Clandestine camping is a no-no. (375ptas per person. Open June-Sept.)

Ría de Pontevedra: Pontevedra

A granite, arcaded city of seignorial houses, Pontevedra makes an excellent jumping-off point for tours of the Rías Bajas. Although Vigo has more *hostales*, Pontevedra is more convenient for excursions along the Ría de Pontevedra and the Ría de Arousa. The train and bus station are a hike from the city center, however, and sometimes druggies crawl the *casco viejo* at night. The old town is nothing special, but merits a walking tour. The **Basílica Menor de Santa María,** has golden Plateresque portico that's spectacularly floodlit at night. Eighteenth-century **Basílica de la Peregrina** houses the city's patron saint, the Virgin Mary, disguised as a pilgrim. The **museo** has exhibits on Galician life and a collection of statuary in a typical 18th-century Galician residence. (Open Tues.-Sat. 11:30am-1pm and 4-8pm, Sun. 11am-1pm.) The broad **Alameda,** with its illuminated fountains, is choice *paseo*. Locals head to beaches nearby on the peninsula. **Sanxenxo, Porto Novo,** and **La Lanzada** are favorites among boogie boarders and windsurfers. To reach the center of town, follow Av. Vigo (straight ahead after exiting the train station, or a left after exiting the bus station) until it becomes major **Calle de la Peregrina.** The center of town is **Plaza Peregrina,** at the end of Calle de la Peregrina. Both transport stations are approximately 1km out of town, requiring a hike on a desolate road (absolutely not to be done alone at night). Rooms are not terribly easy to come by; C. Michelina and C. Peregrina are lightly dotted with *fondas* and *pensiones*. **Casa Fortes,** C. Sagasta, 13 (tel. 85 12 62), has beautiful wooden fixtures and friendly grandparent-like owners. To get here, take a right onto C. Navarrete from C. Peregrina, then a left onto C. Sagasta. (Singles 1000ptas. Doubles 2000ptas. Shower included. Oct.-June: 1650ptas; 2800ptas.) If they're full, try **Casa Florida,** C. García Cambas, 11 (tel. 85 19 79), on the corner with C. Peregrina; the owner hangs out in the candy store downstairs. Prepare to sweat your way up to her 4th-floor terraced rooms. (Singles 1500ptas. Doubles 2500ptas. Triples 3000ptas.)

Bar As 5 Calles, on the corner of C. Charino and C. Isabel II, has endorphin-inducing food. Lots of big windows make it feel like the outdoors. Á la carte meals cost about 500ptas. *Raciones* of *jamón asado* (baked ham) run 350ptas. (Open Fri.-Wed. 10:30am-midnight.) At **Bar Estrella,** one of many on C. Figueroa just off Pl. España, an *empanada* costs 250ptas. *Gambas al ajillo* are a treat and a steal at 500ptas. (Open Fri.-Wed. 11am-3pm and 7pm-midnight.)

One block from Pl. Peregrina via C. Michelina lands you at the very helpful **tourist office,** to the left on C. General Mola, 1 (tel. 85 08 14). Swipe their list of accommodations. (Open Mon.-Fri. 9am-2pm and 4:30-6:30pm, Sat. 10am-12:30pm). The **post office** is on the corner of C. Oliva (a pedestrian street off Pl. Peregrina) and C. García Cambas (open Mon.-Fri. 8am-9pm, Sat. 9am-2pm). The **postal code** is 36001. **Telephones** are on C. Alóndiga, 1, just off Pl. España (open Mon.-Sat. 9am-9pm). You can **rent a car** at Avis, C. Peregrina, 49 (tel. 85 20 25), a wise plan if you plan to do much traveling around the Rías. You must be at least 23 and have had a license for one year (open Mon.-Fri. 9am-1:15pm and 4-7pm, Sat. 9am-12:45pm.) **Red Cross** answers at 85 20 77. And the **hospital Sanatorio Santa Rita** is on C. Peregrina at #54 (tel. 85 44 00).

The **train station** (tel. 85 70 02), an old building at the end of C. Alféreces Provisionales, has information (open 7:30am-1:30pm and 3:30-9:30pm). To Madrid (1 per day, 11hr., 4450ptas) and Santiago (10 per day, 1hr., 340ptas). Just across the street, the **bus station** (tel. 85 24 08) has information (open Mon.-Sat. 8:30am-9pm) and a guard on duty Sundays. Service is more frequent than by rail, with buses to larger cities as well as to the tiny Ría de Arousa and Ría de Pontevedra. To: Madrid (8 per day, 8hr., 2800ptas); Santiago (15 per day, 1 1/4 hr., 490ptas); A Coruña (10 per day, 2 1/4 hr., 1120ptas); Lugo (6 per day, 3hr., 1000ptas). For the Rías, buses wheel and bump to: Cambados (9 per day, 1hr., 400ptas); Porto Novo (frequent, 45min., 200ptas); Sanxenxo (frequent, 1/2 hr., 180ptas); A Toxa and O Grove (frequent, 1hr., 340ptas); and Combarro (frequent, 1/2 hr., 100ptas).

Ría de Arousa

Frequent bus service runs through this area between Pontevedra and **Vilagarcía de Arousa** (halfway between Catoira and Cambados), the commercial center of central Galiza. (45min., 265ptas).

O Grove (El Grove) and A Toxa (La Toja)

Many Spaniards and other Europeans pass their holidays at rocky-shored **O Grove (El Grove)**, 32km west of Pontevedra, and the nearby island of **A Toxa (La Toja)**. Sunbathers should spend all of their time on the island, with its tall trees, palm fronds, and seashell-covered church. It's also home to reputedly the best casino in Galiza. Unlike O Grove, there are no rocks in A Toxa, except for on the fingers of the women in the island's casino. This tiny isle somehow produces the world-famous lathery black soap used all over Spain (Magno). The soap is jet black not from dye but from the iron oxide in it, which makes it strangely semi-transparent and thus creates an optical illusion of utter ebon. When the **bus** from Pontevedra (1hr., 340ptas) drops you off in O Grove (on C. Teniente Domínguez), the stony beach is straight ahead, as is the bridge to A Toxa. The island is home to luxury hotels and a posh housing development; you'll save money sleeping in O Grove. On C. Teniente Domínguez, **Hostal-Restaurante Miramar**, #15 (tel. 73 01 11), has only white and spotless doubles with baths (4000ptas; Oct.-June 3000ptas). The restaurant below has some decently priced *raciones*. **Hostal Otero**, on R. Castelao, 133 (tel. 73 01 10), is to the left at the bridge to A Toxa. Rooms with water views are ample and airy. (Singles 1800ptas. Doubles 3000ptas. Oct.-June: 1500ptas; 2500ptas.) Camp near San Vicente do Mar at **Camping Moreiras** (tel. 73 16 91; 450ptas per person, 450ptas per tent, 475 ptas per car). Just up R. Castelao from Hostal Otero at #157, **Cafeteria Mareira** serves *bocadillos* for 200ptas in a lofty dining room. Hamburgers 255-275ptas.

Cambados

Twenty km away, the Cambados needs only one thing—a beach. Perhaps to celebrate the absent crowds, the town throws a **fiesta** in the streets virtually every night in midsummer, culminating on the first Friday in August with the official tasting of the previous year's local Albariño wine. The **Pazo de Fefiñanes** is an attractive 16th-century palace turned *bodega*.

Rooms couldn't be any easier to find. Try **Hostal Pazos**, C. Aseo, 1 (tel. 54 28 10), with marble-floored shiny rooms (doubles 4000ptas).

Catoira

Across the train tracks are the ruins of several **torres** which originally guarded the mouth of the Río Ulla. The towers, variously rebuilt since pre-Roman peoples first constructed them, have finally been left to crumble. The ship returning Santiago's body to Spain docked farther inland at **Padrón**. The rock it was tied to lies under the altar of the **Igrexia de Santiago**. Many people camp illicitly in Catoira, a sleepy town at the top of the *ría*.

Ría de Muros e Noia

The northernmost of the Rías Baixas, this *ría* isn't much touristed.

Rías Baixas (Bajas)

O Castro de Baroña

One of the coast's hidden treasures, **O Castro de Baroña** was originally an ancient Celtic fortress (inhabited until the 5th century). The circular foundations of the houses remain here, protected by defensive walls on the narrow isthmus. Thank the Romans for the lighthouse, from which you can luxuriate in glorious viewing. Today only a handful of daytrippers and illegal campers visit the long expanse of soft sandy beach.

Café-Bar O'Castro (tel. 85 30 76), through the woods on the main road, has spotless rooms upstairs. (Singles 1500ptas. Doubles 2000ptas. Bargain for stays longer than one night. *Menú* 750ptas. *Ración* of *empanada* 300ptas.) The nearest town is **Porto do Son,** which itself has a virtually empty beach.

Noia (Noya)

Noia may be best known for its braided straw hats with black bands, but some have called it "the little Compostela" for the density of its monuments. Its greatest virtue, however, may be that it marks the halfway point on the bus ride from Santiago to Muros—a 16km hair-raising, gut-wrenching, treacherous roller-coaster ride on gusty coastal mountain roads.

For the death-obsessed, an interesting assortment of tombstones dating to the 10th century surrounds the 14th-century **Igrexa de Santa María.** Nearby are the 16th-century **Igrexa de San Francisco** and the **Ayuntamiento.** Odd statues stand around on the façade of the **Igrexa de San Martín.**

Even the toughest of stomachs won't like the Castromil **bus** (tel. 58 97 00) from Santiago to Muros (every hr., 2hr., 570ptas). If driving, the trip takes half as long.

Muros

The extra 200ptas you spent on Spanish Dramamine for the bus ride proves worth it once you arrrive in Muros. Sitting pretty 65km west of Santiago (on the north side of the *ría,* the town combines exquisite mountain and *ría* views with the warmth and friendliness of a fishing village. Stone houses, winding, hilly streets with eccentric names (ie. street of anguish), and a collection of chapels tell the story of a lively little town high in the mountains of Galiza.

On the approach from Santiago, the **Virgen del Camino** welcomes visitors much as it did in times past, when the town was a leper hospital. Later it became a pit stop for pilgrims en route to Cabo Finesterre. Indeed, the town's church, the **Colexiata do Santa María,** is of interest to pilgrims and the unfaithful both. The church sports Romanesque and Gothic vestiges, thanks to Lope de Mendoza's refurbishing of it in 1400. The town itself, founded by Sancho IV the Crass in the 10th century, rose to fame as an important port. Shellfish continue to be the lifeblood of its economy. The **Paseo Maritimo,** along the port where the bus stops, crackles with action in summer. Further down this street is the be-clocked **Ayuntamiento**, which stocks maps and brochures.

Another great attraction in Muros is little **Louro,** 4km away. Isolated beaches hug an untamed forest, and some say these are the most virgin of beaches in the Rías Baixas. **Camping A Bouga** (tel. 82 60 25, 82 71 78) makes the trip a great wilderness escapade. (385ptas per adult, per tent, and per car. Electricity 330ptas. Open May 15-Sept. 30.)

Back in Muros, **Hostal Ría de Muros,** just behind the bus stop on R. Castelao, 53 (tel. 82 60 56), offers huge rooms with baths, ceilings with wood beams, and spectacular views of the port and the *ría*. (Doubles 3000ptas; Sept.-June 2000ptas.) Up the street at **Candilexas Pizzeria Restaurante,** gluttonize yourself on personal pizzas (650-725ptas) or the local specialty, *vieiras* (scallops). The only **tourist office** of sorts is in the Ayuntamiento (see above). For **taxis,** call 82 62 27. The **municipal police** hide out in the Casa do Concello building with the Ayuntamiento (tel. 82 72 76). For **medical assistance,** call 82 72 50, and for **ambulances** call 82 68 91 or 76 33 89. Aside from Castromil, Transportes Finisterre **buses** (tel. 82 69 83) provide service between Muros and nearby towns.

Rías da Costa da Morte (Rías de la Costa de la Muerte)

If Galiza is the forgotten corner of Spain, then the Costa da Morte is the forgotten corner of Galiza. Shipwrecks along this rocky shoreline have earned it the title "Coast of Death." Although they possess Spain's cleanest, emptiest, and loveliest beaches, the towns here are dead to tourism.

The greatest challenge is finding quick transportation to these remote Elysian fields. Trains dodder through the region, stopping for mail at each tiny town and spending half the trip in dark tunnels. Bus service to the smaller towns and isolated beaches is infrequent or nonexistent. The roads are tortuous and sometimes poorly paved. Road signs are vague, and soupy mists tend to settle in during the morning.

The local population enjoys its isolation; here, more than anywhere else in Spain, people are able to preserve tradition. Guests are so rare that some towns have only one official *hostal*. There are many campgrounds along the coast, but most are overpriced and dirty; some fail to offer even the basic amenities. Many people believe that it's quieter and more fun to camp illegally in the forests.

Cabo Fisterra (Cabo Finisterre)

It's the end of the world as the ancients knew it. When you hike 4km (45min) up to the **faro** (lighthouse) on Cabo Fisterra (Cape Fisterra), the view might convince you that you've indeed reached *finis terrae*—the end of the earth. The road from the town of **Fisterra** (Finisterre) to the end of the cape is literally carved out of the mountain. To the left spreads the Ría de Corcubión, across which you can see to Muros, and the attractive beaches of Sardineiro and Langosteira. To the right shimmers the unforgiving landscape of the open sea, where rocky, craggy mountains meet the crashing waves of the Atlantic at the westernmost point of the Costa da Morte. Straight ahead looms the lighthouse that beaconed doomed ships to their *finis* on the rocks. The whirlpools and fatally strong currents along the coast prevent the region from becoming another Club Med. Hidden beaches built for two, such as the **Praia de Corbeiro**, its aqua-green water lapping the shore, seduce the more intrepid traveler.

Fisterra itself is an unassuming fishing village better known for its geographical location than for anything else. Still, its gorgeous beaches and out-of-this-world views attract thousands of tourists—including Spain's Nobel Prizewinning novelist Camilo José Cela—every summer. The rocky promontory over Fisterra's harbor was once a sacred hill for Roman legionnaires and then for Celtic settlers. Locals hid in the cliff's cool caves to escape the Viking raids. Nearby, **Ezaro** is a typical beach town with the added allure of magnificent waterfalls and a picturesque lagoon 1km up the river behind Fisterra.

If you ever manage to get to Fisterra, **Hospedaje López,** C. Carrasqueira, 4 (tel. 74 04 49 or 74 03 68), has immaculate, light-filled rooms, firm beds, and views of the ocean. From the bus stop, follow C. Santa Catalina until the Casa do Concello, then follow the signs that point left. (Singles 1500ptas. Doubles 2500tpas. Triples 3000ptas. Call first in winter.) In the opposite direction, **Casa Velay,** C. Cerca (tel. 74 01 27 or 74 03 50) also has shiny clean rooms with views and quilted bedspreads. From the bus stop, turn right and walk along the water until the palm trees—Casa Velay hides behind them on the Playa de la Ribeira. (Singles 2000ptas. Doubles 2500ptas, with bath 3300ptas. Oct.-May: 1500ptas; 2000ptas, 2500ptas. Call first.) For organized camping and more temperate water, head to the opposite side of the isthmus connecting Fisterra with the mainland. **Camping Ruta Finisterre** (tel. 74 63 02) is on Ctra. Coruña, east of Fisterra on the Playa del Estorde in Cee. (425ptas per person, per tent, and per car. Call first.)

Downstairs, the owner of Casa Velay serves a *menú* (1000ptas) and a choice of à la carte dishes. The restaurants on the dock are rather overpriced. **Supermercados El Cruce,** C. Coruña (the continuation of C. Santa Catalina), stocks the basics. (Open Mon.-Sat. 8:30am-3pm and 5-9:30pm.) It's rivaled by **Alimentación Santos,** in the other direction on C. General Franco, to the right from the bus stop. (Open Mon.-Sat. 9am-2:30pm and 5-10pm, Sun. 9am-2:30pm.)

Half tourist office, half Ayuntamiento, the **Casa do Concello,** C. Santa Catalina (tel. 74 00 01), may be some help. (Open Mon.-Fri. 8:30am-2:30pm, Sat. 9am-1pm; Oct.-May Mon.-Fri. 9am-2pm and 5-7pm, Sat. 9am-2pm.) Next door the Casa del Mar Clínica (tel. 74 02 52) offers **medical assistance.** In medical **emergency,** call 74 52 83.

Three **buses** per day head for Fisterra from Santiago (3hr., 1050ptas), many of which pass through commercial center **Cee** (north and west from the cape) along the drive. It is possible to hitch (although *Let's Go* doesn't recommend hitching) or walk to the *faro*.

Camariñas

The thing to do in Camariñas, north of Cabo Fisterra on the other side of the *ría,* is to watch the women make lace on their doorsteps. Indeed, these *palilleiras* are the town's secret weapon: a statue of one has an honored position in the town square. A long, sandy beach is there for the taking, but the townsfolk prefer to stay in their white-washed houses.

There's also a tranquil harbor with scores of fishing boats, many of which do their work in the middle of the night. Towards the main highway, the Ctra. General, rest **Area da Vila** and **Lingunde,** two small beaches. In the other direction, (with the port to the left), the **faro** (lighthouse) looms about 4km up a mountain road adorned with shepherds, roosters, and the odd farmer. At the top, you can barely see little Muxía and the untouched white sand beaches beyond. The reason these beaches remain untouched is because the only way to touch them at all is via a sandy, rocky cliffhanger of a path (off the road to the lighthouse). If you value your car and/or your life, stick to the view from above. Many a watery tragedy has struck here; the wreck of *The Serpent* is remembered by a mass grave and **tombstone** for the sailors who died when the ship approached Camariñas one cold, rainy night in 1890. Only three men survived, over 100 died. The town, apparently suffering from an excessive guilt complex, rebuilt the stone monument in 1990. Surrounded by flowers and an iron gate, it sheds its eerie shadow over the Coast of Death.

Across the *ría* from Camariñas, on one rocky point in **Muxía** a collection of historical model ships hangs from the ceiling of **Igrexa de Nossa Señora da Barca** (Our Lady of the Ship). The rocks in front of the church supposedly hum when innocent people walk by.

Hostal Plaza, C. Real, 12 (tel. 73 61 03), toward the dock and turn right onto C. Real, hosts overnight visitors. It has ridiculously clean rooms, a sitting room with a TV, and pink wonderland bathrooms that are big enough for a game of one-on-one. (Singles with sink 2000ptas. Doubles with sink 3500ptas, with bath 4000ptas. Oct.-May: 1500ptas; 3000ptas, 3500ptas.) On the way there, equally lovely **Hostal La Marina,** on Cantón Miguel Freijo, 4 (tel. 73 60 30), rents singles for 1750ptas and doubles for 3100ptas.

The *hostal's* restaurant downstairs serves a filling *menú* (700ptas) of *caldo gallego* and *chuletas.* On the same street, **Cafetería Portomar** minces fresh-caught *pulpo* (octopus) for 500ptas per *ración.* (Open Thurs.-Tues. 11am-3pm.) **Supermercados Más y Más,** on Pl. Insuela by the statue of the *palilleira,* sells picnic fixings. (Open Mon.-Fri. 9am-2pm and 4:30-8:30pm.)

Behind the statue of the *palilleira* stands the **Casa Consistorial** (tel. 73 60 00, 73 60 25), purveyor of tourist tips. (Open Mon.-Fri. 8am-2:30pm, Sat. 9am-2pm.) Right on C. Miguel Freijo on the water is Caixa Galicia for **currency exchange.** (Open Mon.-Fri. 8:30am-2pm.) Up on C. Generalísimo Franco, 5, sits the **Guardia Civil** (tel. 73 62 62; if closed 66 86 01 or 062; open 9am-2pm and 5-8pm).

Buses run two times per day from Cee to Camariñas (45min., 340ptas) and twice daily from Camariñas to A Coruña (2 1/2 hr., 890ptas). Buses from Fisterra change in Cee or Vimianzo. Transportes Finisterre (tel. 74 51 71) is the only company that covers routes to the Costa da Morte from Santiago and A Coruña.

Elsewhere

The minor coastal road passes isolated beaches such as **Praia Traba** on its way to the Ría de Laxe-Corme. At **Laxe** on the western side of the *ría,* a vast, open stretch of sand separates a Geological Institute at one end from the fishing fleet at the other.

On the other side of the *ría,* **Corme** is famous for its delicious *percebes* (barnacles) and its mermaid offspring. Skilled *percebes-*pluckers pry them off of rocks in the treacherous waters of the Coast of Death. Try them or whatever else is swimming in the tanks at **O'Biscoiteiro** (tel. 73 83 76), C. Remedios. They bake their own tart bread and cook fresh, bountiful entrees (600-800ptas). Locals insist that many citizens of Corme descend from mermaids.

The pleasant town of **Malpica** has its own small peninsula further north. The town's **Concello**, R. Emilio González, 1 (tel. 72 00 01), has brochures on the area. Any beach here will do, but the mayor prefers **Praia de Barizo,** 7km away. Join the seagulls on the **Illas Sisargas,** three green rocks off the cape. No boats head that way, but fishers sometimes schlepp tourists there. At **Restaurante San Francisco,** on R. Eduardo Podal and overlooking the rocks, the beaming owner serves fresh fish cooked to order.

A Coruña (La Coruña)

A Coruña is a rosy-cheeked city grown too big for its peninsula. Afternoon sun shines through a forest of masts in the harbor and glints off warehouse windows and glass-enclosed residential *galerías* locked in a white wooden grid. A lovely base for seeing the Rías Altas, the city itself has a stellar nightlife, an historic old town, plenty of waterfront restaurants, and beaches galore. A Coruña is the primary transportation center for the Rías Altas.

Orientation and Practical Information

The loveliest quarter is the *ciudad vieja* (old city), whose shaded streets and old stone buildings fill the southern tip of the peninsula overlooking the port. The **Avenida de la Marina** leads past the tourist office into this section of town. The **Praia del Orzán** (municipal beach; boogie and surfboard heaven) and **Praia de Riazor** are about a 10-minute walk northwest from the tourist office at the other extreme of the peninsula's neck. The bus and train stations are 20 minutes south of the port. From the stations, find Avenida Primo de Rivera and follow it around way, way down through five or so name changes to Turismo, on **Dársena de la Marina.** The street follows the curve of the port (to the left facing the water). Alternatively, bus #1 runs straight to the tourist office (85ptas).

> **Tourist Office:** Dársena de la Marina (tel. 22 18 22), on the south side of the isthmus connecting the peninsula and the mainland, near the waterfront. Very helpful and full of tips on trips to the Rías Altas. Slick brochures on Galiza and the rest of Spain. Open Mon.-Fri. 9am-2pm and 4-6pm, Sat. 10:30am-1pm.
>
> **El Corte Inglés:** C. Ramón y Cajal, 57-59 (tel. 29 00 11). A sharp right from the bus station exit. **Map** and **Currency exchange:** 1% commission (500ptas min. charge on cash, 250ptas on traveler's checks). They also offer novels and guidebooks in English, haircutting, both cafeteria and restaurant, and **telephones.** Open Mon.-Sat. 10am-9pm.
>
> **Consulate: U.S.,** Cantón Grande, 16-17, 8th fl. (tel. 21 32 33). Opposite the Hotel Atlántico. Open Mon.-Fri. 10am-1pm.
>
> **Currency Exchange: El Corte Inglés** (see above). Where else can you exchange money, eat lunch, and buy a bathing suit under the same roof?
>
> **American Express Travel: Viajes Amado,** C. Compostela, 1 (tel. 22 99 72). Open Mon.-Fri. 9:30am-1:30pm and 4:30-7:30pm, Sat. 9:45am-1:30pm. Just like a real AmEx office—all the usual services.
>
> **Post Office:** C. Alcalde Manuel Casas (tel. 22 19 56; fax 29 51 63), just past Teatro Colón on Av. Marina. Open for stamps and Lista de Correos Mon.-Fri. 8am-9pm, Sat. 9am-2pm; for **telegrams** and **faxes** Mon.-Fri. 8am-9pm, Sat. 9am-7pm. **Postal Code:** 15080.

Telephones: C. Alcalde Canuto Berea, 4, off C. Real. Open Mon.-Sat. 9am-11pm. Also at C. San Andrés, 90. Open Mon.-Sat. 9am-3pm and 4:30-10:30pm. Phone banks all over the city. **Telephone Code:** 981.

Flights: Aeropuerto de Alvedro (tel. 23 22 40), 9km south of the city. Served only by Aviaco. **Iberia,** Pl. Galicia, 6 (tel. 22 87 20). Open Mon.-Fri. 9:30am-2pm and 4-7pm, Sat. 10am-1pm.

Trains: C. Joaquín Planelles, s/n (tel. 23 03 09). Bus #1 (85ptas) runs from here to Turismo and the post office. Information (tel. 15 02 02) open 7am-11pm. To: Madrid (3 per day, *talgo* 8 1/2 hr., 6835ptas; *expreso* 11hr., 4820ptas); Barcelona (1 per day, 17hr., 6485ptas); Santiago (13 per day, 1 1/4 hr., 340ptas); Vigo (8 per day, 3hr., 880ptas); Ferrol (3 per day, 1 3/4 hr., 340ptas); Betanzos (3 per day, 1/2 hr., 160ptas). **RENFE,** C. Fonseca, 3 (tel. 22 19 48), just up from Pl. Lugo.

Buses: C. Caballeros (tel. 23 96 44), across Av. Alcalde Molina from the train station. Bus #1 (85ptas) runs from here to Turismo. Buses from here serve the Rías Altas and surrounding area. **ALSA-Intercar** (tel. 23 70 44). To: Madrid (4 per day, 8-8 1/2 hr., 4410ptas); Santiago (every hr., 1hr., 645ptas); Vigo (9 per day, 3 hr., 1400ptas); Oviedo (3 per day, 5hr., 2555ptas); Donostia/San Sebastián (1 per day, 14hr., 5750ptas). **IASA** (tel. 23 90 01). To: Betanzos (frequent, 40min., 185ptas); Camariñas (2 per day, 1 1/2 hr., 890ptas); Malpica (2 direct per day, 1hr., 535ptas); Viveiro (with stops at O Barqueiro, Ortigueira, Ferrol, Vicedo, Betanzos; 4 per day, 4hr., 1240ptas); Ribadeo (2 per day, 3hr., 1070ptas).

Public Transportation: Red buses run by **Compañía de Tranvías de la Coruña** (tel. 25 01 00; about 7am-11:30pm; 85ptas). Each bus stop posts the full itineraries of the buses that stop there. #1 from train and bus stations down Av. Linares Rivas to Turismo.

Taxis: Radio Taxi (tel. 24 33 33, 24 33 77). **Tele Taxi** (tel. 28 77 77).

Car Rental: Useful for exploring the Rías Altas. **Autos Brea,** Av. Fernández Latorre, 110 (tel. 22 83 74). From the bus station turn right, then a sharp left before El Corte Inglés. Must be at least 21 and have had license 1 yr. Open Mon.-Fri. 9am-1pm and 4-7pm, Sat. 9am-2pm. **Avis,** Pl. Vigo (tel. 22 69 55), under the awnings. From Av. Linares Rivas, turn left onto Marcial de Adalid. Must be at least 23 and have had license 1 yr. Open Mon.-Fri. 9am-1:15pm and 4-7pm, Sat. 9am-12:45pm.

Luggage Storage: At the **train station** (lockers 300ptas). Open 6:30am-1:30am. At the **bus station** (60ptas per checked bag). Open 8am-10pm.

Lost Property: At the **guardia municipal** (see below).

English Bookstore: Librería Colón, C. Real, 24 (tel. 22 22 06), a few bl. from the tourist office. Shakespeare rubs covers with Tom Clancy and Danielle Steele. Classics and the ever-elusive *Let's Go.* Open Mon.-Fri. 10am-1:30pm and 5-8:30pm, Sat. 10:30am-2pm.

Library: Archivo del Reino de Galicia, Casa de Cultura (tel. 20 92 51), in the Jardin de San Carlos.

Laundromat: Lavandería Glu Glu, C. Alcalde Marchesi, 4 (tel. 28 28 04), off Pr. Cuatro Caminos. Wash and dry self-serve 700ptas per 5kg load. Full service 800ptas per load. Open Mon.-Sat. 9:30am-9pm.

Red Cross: C. Curros Enríquez, s/n (**ambulance** tel. 20 59 75; urgent care 22 22 22).

Late-Night Pharmacy: Check listings in *La Voz de Galicia* (local paper, 90ptas).

Medical Services: Casa de Socorro, C. Miguel Servet, s/n (tel. 18 42 06). **Ambulatorio San José,** C. Comandante Fontanes, 8 (tel. 22 60 74; urgent care 28 61 44).

Police: Av. Alférez Provisional, s/n (tel. 22 61 00). **Guardia Civil,** C. Lonzas, s/n (tel. 25 11 00 or 062). **Guardia Municipal,** C. Miguel Servet, s/n (tel. 18 42 25).

Accommodations

You'd hardly expect a town with so much late-night life and so many all-night discos to bother with sleep. People who need beauty rest should scour **Calle Riego de Agua** and the entire area from Pl. Maria Pita down to Pl. San Agustín and C. San Andrés. *Pensiones* load the streets near the bus and train stations, but they're a looong walk from the *ciudad vieja.*

Marina Española (HI) (tel. 62 01 18), in the town Sada, about 20km east of A Coruña. The Empresa Calpita bus (tel. 23 90 72) runs to Sada (1/2 hr., 165ptas). 3-day max. stay. 625ptas, over 26 900ptas. Meals available. Call first, as they fill with student groups in summer.

Albergue Xuvenil "Gandario" (HI) (tel. 79 10 05), in the town Gandario, 19km outside A Coruña. Take the bus to Gandario (1/2 hr., 165ptas). Marina Española's identical twin.

Fonda María Pita, C. Riego de Agua, 38, 3rd fl. (tel. 22 11 87). Pristine, with white lace curtains. Cheery rooms, some huge, some with balcony, always clean. Singles 1200ptas. Doubles 2500ptas. Showers 100ptas. There are 3 other attractive *hostales* in this building.

Hospedaje Varela, C. Riego de Agua, 28 (tel. 22 19 79). Spanish interior decorating at its best. Marbleized wallpaper and oil painting in the foyer welcome guests into clean, airy rooms, themselves papered in a floral print. *Comedor* with TV. Singles with sink 1000ptas. Doubles with sink 2200ptas. Breakfast 200ptas.

Pensión la Alianza, C. Riego de Agua, 8, 1st fl. (tel. 22 81 14). Clean and likely to be full. Appealing beach pictures. Gigantic beds and spotless gray-tiled bathroom down the hall. Singles 1700ptas. Doubles 2800ptas.

Hostal Oriental, C. Juana de Vega, 21 (tel. 22 36 05), left off Av. Linares Rivas. Large rooms, high windows. Singles with bath 1800ptas. Doubles 3800ptas.

Food

Sustenance for scrooges comes easy. **Calle Estrella, Calle de la Franja,** and the surrounding streets are fraught with possibilities. Fresh fruit and vegetables huddle in the big **market** in the oval building on Pr. San Agustín, near the old town. (Open Mon.-Sat. 8am-12:30pm.) If you roll out of bed post-closing time, buy your groceries in the supermarket downstairs.

Groceries: Supermercados Claudio, C. Menéndez Pelayo, 4-6, just off Av. Linares Rivas. Huge and open late. Open Mon.-Fri. 9am-2pm and 5-8pm, Sat. 9am-2pm and 5:30-8:30pm.

Casa Santiso, C. Franja, 26 (tel. 22 86 34). TV and flowery tablecloths. *Menú del día* of *caldo gallego* and *ternera* 800ptas. *Paella de carne* 675ptas. A miscellany of meats make a spectacle of themselves in the window. Open 10am-midnight.

Mesón Laporte, C. Franja, 23, on the corner with C. Trompeta. Tortilla made with eggs from the owner's nearby farm. *Tapas* galore (80-200ptas), including *pulpo* (*ración* 690ptas). Open 6am-2am.

Cafetería Delfos, C. Marina, 7 (tel. 22 08 35). Pink and gray decor. Hulking, flavorful *platos combinados* cost 650-750ptas outside; even cheaper at the bar. *Menú* 1200ptas. Open 11am-1:30am.

Café-Bar Pizzeria Star, C. Estrella, 6 (tel. 22 90 27), on the corner with C. Mantelería. Individual pizzas in a cozy tavern 475-550ptas. Assorted fresh seafood *raciones,* such as *chipirones en su tinta.* Open Mon.-Sat. 7:30am-2am.

Cafetería Piscis, C. Franja, 19-21 (tel. 22 61 07). Best and freshest-looking seafood in this stretch. Startling range of seafood *raciones* (350-500ptas). *Fanta Naranja* tall boys in window. Open 11am-11pm.

Cafetería-Restaurante Gasthof, Av. Marina, 6 (tel. 22 10 27). in the middle of the action near the port. Huge, neon, and busy; the VIPS of A Coruña. Croissant sandwiches (225-265ptas) and generous *platos combinados* (650-975ptas). Fast food nirvana. Open 7am-2am.

Sights and Entertainment

Simple arches and windows surround the cobbled **Praza de María Pita.** The three red tile domes of the **Pazo Municipal** rise majestically from the north side. Close by, **Plazuela Santa Bárbara** borders a 15th-century convent of the same name. A small Gothic doorway opens to **Igrexa de Santa María del Campo,** with granite columns in the central aisles and a bright rose window. All were built between the 12th and 15th centuries.

The 16th-century **Castelo de San Antón,** now the home of the **Museu Arqueolóxico** (tel. 20 59 94), juts out into the bay on the southeast side of the peninsula. There's a bizarre 14th-century stone pig running loose bearing a large cross on its back. There are also Bronze Age artifacts, bones from the local Roman necropolis, and a reconstruction of a 4th-century wicker and skin boat. The ramparts look over the sprawling city beyond the port and the Galician greenery that rolls abruptly into the Atlantic. (Open 10am-2pm and 4:30-7:30pm. Admission 100ptas.)

Sandwiched between Av. Marina and the dock, elegant **Jardín Méndez Núñez** is of interest to experts in the fine art of topiary. Green, lush, and meticulously manicured, the park has a clock snipped to botanical perfection, whose arms really work and tell the correct time.

A Coruña's other famous tourist magnet, the **Torre de Hércules,** towers over the western end of the peninsula. Although the original Roman part is visible only from within, this 2nd-century structure is the only Roman lighthouse that still actually throws out a nightly signal to lost ships. Legend has it that Hercules himself erected the tower upon the remains of his defeated enemy Gerión. The *Armada Invencible* departed from here on its way to Britain, where most of it sank in a storm. Rising more than 100m, the tower provides a fine view of the sea and city. (Open Tues.-Sun. 11am-2pm and 4-7pm; Oct.-June Tues.-Sun. 11am-3pm. Free.) The lighthouse is 2km down the Ctra. Torre; walk or take bus #9 or 13 (85ptas).

The **Real Academia Gallega** (Royal Galician Academy; tel. 20 73 08) made the family seat of 19th-century novelist **Condesa Emilia Pardo Bazán** its headquarters. The library contains 25,000 volumes on Galician literature, history, and culture. Next door, at C. Tabernas, 11, the academy devotes part of a museum to Emilia's work, and part to a rotating exhibition of modern and 19th-century Galician art. (Open Mon.-Fri. 10am-noon. Free.)

Soothing **Jardín de San Carlos,** in the old part of the city, was originally planted in 1843 on the site of old Forte San Carlos. It shelters the tomb of Sir John Moore. Locals say killing this incompetent general cost Napoleon his crown, since Wellington took over Moore's command.

The **Orzán** and **Riazor** beaches within easy walking distance on the northwest side of the isthmus, pack in tanners, boogie boarders, and surfers. The city plans to inaugurate a brand new esplanade connecting the two in 1993.

Summer nightlife in A Coruña is perhaps the liveliest in all Galiza. Use the afternoon as nap time because most of the action doesn't start until 2am. Residents bar hop around C. Franja, C. La Florida, and the surrounding side streets. When bars die at around 2am, the discos along the two beaches start making a ruckus. Also try the discos and cafés on C. Juan Florez. **Pirámide,** at #50 (tel. 27 61 57), plays dance music to rouse the dead.

Near A Coruña: Betanzos, Miño, and Pontedeume

Betanzos charms visitors into believing it's isolated, despite its position at a crucial highway and train intersection 23km east of A Coruña and 38km south of Ferrol and its possession of the world's largest paper ball. Founded in 1219 as a center of navigation, the town's citizens were referred to as the "Genovese of Spain," although today the feeling in town is entirely *gallego*. Betanzos's economic mainstays are fishing and farming, yet upon entering the town, mooing cows and undulating octopi don't really spring to mind. For the 12,000 citizens, no business is so important that it can't be postponed for a drink, an afternoon snooze, or a walk through the town's compact, hilly center. There's only one *hostal* in Betanzos, but the town makes a good daytrip, thanks to frequent bus service.

Plaza Garcia Hermanos, a.k.a. O Campo, is home to a statue of the *hermanos* Garcia, two brothers who were great benefactors of the city. Cafés with *terrazas* line this central plaza, and a fountain with a statue of Diana (an imitation of the real thing at Versailles) sits in the middle. The **Plaza de la Constitución** and the the elegant 18th-century **Ayuntamiento** are just up the street. Here's the *casco antiguo,* filled with medieval churches, a palace or two, and some eye-popping views of the lush countryside. Curving, hilly streets wind to stone arches, walkways, and the two rivers, which weirdly seem to turn up around every street corner.

Betanzos's great festival involves the launching of the world's largest paper ball (about 25m high) on the night of San Roque. The tradition began in 1814 as a celebration for Fernando VII, and is kept alive as the town parties for two weeks in mid-August, celebrating a saint who seems to have become the patron of paper balloons.

Please enjoy your night at the lone **Hostal Barreiros**, R. del Rollo, 6 (tel. 77 22 59). Solo travelers are difficult to accommodate. (Doubles 2000ptas, with bath 2500ptas; Oct.-May 1600ptas, with bath 1800ptas.) The owner, Manuel, also owns the restaurant below, where you can get a meal for 700ptas or just munch on *tapas* and gawk at the huge kegs from which the local wine is tapped. *Tabernas* galore line the side streets off the stone arches in Pl. Garcia Hermanos. The *calamares* are particularly good at **Café-Bar Las Vegas,** Trav. Progreso, 77 (open 10am-1am).

The **tourist office** operates from a clandestine little hut near the bus stop (open July-Sept. 15 Mon.-Fri. 10am-2pm and 4-8pm, Sat.-Sun. 10am-2pm). If they're out, try the Ayuntamiento, **Casa do Concello** (tel. 77 00 11), straight ahead in Pl. Constitución, and they'll probably offer you some flashy pamphlets. The **post office** (tel. 77 18 88) is on Pl. Alfonso IX (open Mon.-Fri. 8am-2pm and Sat. 9am-1pm). For **currency exchange,** try Banco Bilbao Vizcaya (open June-Sept. Mon.-Fri. 8:30am-2pm; Oct.-May Mon.-Fri. 8:30am-2pm, Sat. 8:30am-1pm. For medical help, call the **Red Cross** at 77 15 15. The **police** are at 77 06 02, the **Guardia Civil** at 77 00 53.

Buses run to Betanzos from both A Coruña and Ferrol (every 1/2 hr., Sun. every hr.; 1/2 hr.; 185ptas). IASA (tel. 23 90 01) also runs to points farther out along the *riás*. The **train station,** Betanzos-Cidade, sits across the river. To reach the city center, go left as you exit and cut through the park; cross the bridge, pass through the arch, and head straight uphill to Pl. Garcia Hermanos. About six trains per day run between A Coruña and Ferrol, stopping en route in Betanzos.

Miño, 2km north of Betanzos, is said to have the nicest beach in the Rías Altas. Judging by the fact that there are any people on it at all, it's certainly the most popular. On Saturday afternoons in **Pontedeume,** workers at the town market cook *pulpo* (octopus) in huge copper urns and mock the citizens of Betanzos for saving that huge ball of paper.

Rías Altas

Not so isolated as the Costa da Morte (Costa de la Muerte), these smooth *rías* have an urbane sophistication that the Rías Baixas lack. Fishing towns predominate here as they do in all the *rías,* and many towns have roots deep in the Middle Ages. Old lighthouses, churches, and the remains of a wall or two dot the luscious green countryside. In the misty mountains of Galiza the weather is anything but predictable (even in summer), but views are spectacular year-round. Thanks to a healthy burst of summer tourism from landlocked Spaniards, the Rías Altas have the resources to augment a relatively unspoiled coastline with a transportation system slightly more viable than the Dead Coast's (for details, see A Coruña: Practical Information: Buses). *Hostales* remain scarce, so *casas particulares* (800-900ptas per person) are the way to go.

Rías de Cedeira, Ortigueira, and Viveiro

In A Coruña's northern coast, where buses and trains seldom run and where hitchhiking is useless, ferny rain forests give way to soft, empty beaches. These are the northernmost of the *rías,* where thick mists veil and isolate the valleys. Buses and the occasional FEVE train run inland to Ortigueira from Ferrol, but the sporadic coastal bus is preferable—you can always hop off if you see a place you like.

Valdoviño

Only 17km from industrial Ferrol and not on a *ría* at all, Valdoviño is a town of old flagstone farmhouses among eucalyptus trees. The enormous **Praia de Frouxeira** is a hike across the fields from town. Camping is allowed on a nearby beach at **Camping**

Fontesín (tel. 48 50 28), off the highway between Valdoviña and Meirás. (Open June 15-Sept. 15. 250ptas per person, per tent, and per car.)

Cedeira

If you don't give a damn about monuments (and many people don't), you might appreciate the calm beauty of Cedeira. The small town hangs out on its very own *ría* 32km northeast of Ferrol and 84km northeast of A Coruña. Straddling the petite Río Condomiñas, Cedeira town is a melange of farmers, summer residents, locals, and fish. The river Condomiñas recedes entirely and fills again every twelve hours, like clockwork. Of course, if you get a monument attack, you can hike to both ancient monuments in the nearby woods as well as to secluded beaches.

The **Santuario de San Andrés de Teixido** looks out over the sea from 620m in the air: the highest coastline in all of Europe. Legend has it that if you haven't visited this chapel and converted to Christianity during your mortal existence, you'll be converted in your next life into some base animal. Nevertheless, think twice before making the 12km hike up from town.

Closer to town lies the hermitage **San Antonio de Corbeiro,** an easy 2km walk up a gentle slope. Cross either of the town's two bridges and turn right; follow the signs to the turnoff (1/2km farther on the left), then it's up, up, and away. The hermitage is a plain white structure high above the *ría*, high enough to send any weak-stomached acrophobe into a cold sweat. If that isn't enough, 6km past the turnoff for San Antonio is a lighthouse, **Faro de Punta Candieira.** The walk up calls for more exertion on a steep, curving, narrow mountain road. It's very quiet here.

Back down below in civilization, settle into the very civilized **Hostal Chelsea,** Pl. Sagrado Corazón, 15 (tel. 48 11 11), around the corner from the bus stop. Guests spy on the plaza from windows of their spotless rooms. (Singles 1800ptas. Doubles 2300ptas, with bath 2800ptas.) Across the bridge to the right, en route to the lighthouse, sits **Hostal Brisa,** Arriba da Ponte, 19 (tel. 48 10 54). Huge rooms with flowered curtains give onto the sometimes wet, sometimes dry river. (Doubles with shower 2600tpas, with bath 2800ptas.)

Commendable *tapas* bars line both sides of the river. **Restaurante Aldebaran,** Av. López Cortón, 11, serves *chipirones a la plancha* (squid, 300ptas) with fries and a bulging basket of bread. (Open Tues.-Sun. 11am-1am.) Around the corner of Av. del Generalísimo is the supermarket **Aldi** (open Mon.-Sat. 9am-1:30pm and 6-9pm).

The **tourist office** (tel. 48 21 87) helps tourists across the river. From the bus stop, walk straight and turn left onto C. Ezequiel López, stopping at #22. They'll slap you one of their glossy brochures. (Open Semana Santa to mid-Oct. Mon.-Sat. 11am-2pm and 6-9pm, Sun. noon-2pm.) Up the street from the bus stop is a **telephone** bank, on Av. Suevos (open 9:30am-2pm and 4:30-11pm). Also on this side of the river is the **post office,** Av. Zumalacarregui (open Mon.-Fri. 8am-3pm, Sat. 9am-2pm).

Bus service is sparse. IASA's A Coruña-to-Ferrol route requires a transfer in Ferrol or Campo del Hospital to get to Cedeira (505ptas). RIALSA, up C. Ezequiel López from Turismo at #28, runs frequently between Cedeira and Ferrol (315ptas). There's not a train in sight.

Ortigueira

Ortigueira is an overgrown fishing village and transportation center. If trapped here by the vagaries of IASA, try the much-polished **Hostal Monterrey,** Av. Franco, 105 (tel. 40 01 35). (Singles 1500ptas. Doubles 2400ptas.) Ortigueira is home to several Celtic music festivals, as well as to the sandy **Praia de Morouzos.**

Viveiro (Vivero) and Covas

Emblazoned on the tourist office's pamphlet is the bold motto *"No es un sueño. Existe."* ("It's not a dream. It really exists.") The only way to confuse this town with a dream is if you come by bus, in which case you're likely to have fallen into a deep sleep (four hours from A Coruña, five from Oviedo). Viveiro is an active little mother of a city, light on the monuments and heavy on the nearby beaches. Most of the tourists here are Spanish.

The town center preserves bits of its ancient walls, notably the **Porta da Vila** (at the far end of town) and the **Puerta de Carlos V** (just up from the bridge to Covas). Up the street from Carlos's *puerta* is sunny **Praza Maior** and the *casco antiguo*. In the old town presides the church and convent of **San Francisco** and a collection of winding, hilly streets laden with shops and restaurants.

If esplanaded beach is your opiate, de-bus one stop before Viveiro in **Covas**. There, **Hostal La Terraza,** C. Granxas, 8 (tel. 56 06 06), puts up visitors for the night in its beachfront pleasure palace. Past the rose gardens, past the TV room, and up the stairs, are the capacious, airy rooms. (Singles 2000ptas. Doubles 3000ptas, with bath 4000ptas.) On the same road, just across the bridge (500m from Viveiro), is **Camping Viveiro.** Follow the signs to the be-flagged reception hut. A café and the broad beach are just steps away from the slightly dingy 2nd-class campsite. (Reception open 9am-11pm. 290ptas per person, per tent, and per car. Electricity 325ptas. Open June-Sept.)

In Viveiro proper, **Hospedaje García,** Pr. Maior, 18 (tel. 56 06 75), offers bare, impossibly immaculate rooms, most of which overlook the plaza. (Singles 1700ptas. Doubles 3000ptas. Oct.-May: 1400ptas; 2500ptas.) **Fonda Bossanova,** Av. Galicia, 11 (tel. 56 01 50), also has rooms (1000ptas per person; showers 200ptas). The friendly eating place below cooks up a substantial *menú* (800ptas) of local fish. Its kitchen lures diners with inviting smells and the crackle of grilling flesh. (Open 7am-midnight.)

All about the Pr. Maior area, especially on **Calle Almirante Chicarro,** budget *menús* and *raciones* proliferate. **Supermercado Vivero** twinkles on C. Navia Castrillón, just up from Pl. Lugo. (Open Mon.-Sat. 9:30am-1:30pm and 4:30-8:30pm.)

The **tourist office** (tel. 56 04 86) is a snap to find; pass through Puerta de Carlos V and it's on the right. (Open Mon.-Sat. 10:30am-1:30pm and 4:30-7:30pm.) If it's closed, see the **Ayuntamiento** (tel. 56 01 28) in Casa Consistorial, Pr. Maior (open Mon.-Sat. 9am-2pm). By the water, the **post office** (tel. 56 09 27) is down C. Benito Galera, which becomes C. Ramón Canosa. (Open Mon.-Fri. 8am-3pm, Sat. 9am-1pm.) **Telephones, faxes,** and photocopies are up the street from Turismo at C. Teodoro de Quirós, 6 (tel. 55 12 02). The **telephone code** is 982. To call a **taxi,** ring 56 18 50 or 56 00 26. This is the only town in the Rías Altas with **motorcycle rentals.** They **rent cars** and **bikes** as well at Viajes Arifran, C. Rosalía de Castro, 54 (tel. 56 04 97 or 56 06 89; open Mon.-Fri. 9:30am-1pm and 4-7:30pm, Sat. 9:30am-1pm). **Municipal police** (tel. 56 01 28) are in the Ayuntamiento's Casa Consistorial, Pr. Maior.

IASA (tel. 56 01 03) at Trav. Marina and ERSA, Pl. Lugo, 2 (tel. 56 03 90) are two **bus** companies that recently merged. They serve A Coruña (2 per day, 4hr., 1240ptas); Ferrol (2 per day, 2hr., 735ptas); Lugo (2 per day, 875ptas); Oviedo (2 per day, 5hr., 1440ptas); and Ribadeo (3 per day, 1 1/2 hr., 375ptas). If you insist on taking a FEVE **train** (tel. 55 07 22; down Trav. Marina past Pl. Lugo), know that they chug two times per day to points in the Rías Altas (Ortigueira, Barqueiro, Vicedo, Ribadeo) and four times per day to Ferrol.

Rías de Foz and Ribadeo

East of Viveiro and inland from Ría de Foz, **Mondoñedo** is about 50km from Lugo on the FEVE line. The picturesque town is smack on the river Masma. The place to stay is **Hostal Padornela** at C. Buenos Aires, 1 (tel. 52 18 92). There are 10 rooms with baths (singles 1800ptas; doubles 2500ptas).

Ribadeo

Stunning Galician scenery is the reason to stay in Ribadeo, a town that's haunted by many summer residents 25km farther east on the *ría* of Río Eo. Choose your view or enjoy more than one:

> **Igrexa de Santa Cruz,** 3km from the town on a hill overlooking the *ría*. If the climb doesn't take your breath away, the view of the countryside and ocean will.
>
> **Praia de Rocas Blancas,** 3km in another direction. Here is a *faro* (lighthouse) near a small, sweet beach. Both the dock's Paseo Marítimo and the **Praia Os Bloques,** just past the dock, offer more swell views of the *ría*.

R. Buenos Aires, off Pr. España in town. More thrilling views for *ría* buffs.

Otherwise, the town does precious little to appeal to the average tourist. In Pr. España, the building containing the **Concello** (Ayuntamiento) is strange, white, and stuck to a bulbous orange copper tower. Pleasant for a stroll or afternoon picnic, the **park** boasts another fine sample of that little-known Galician passion: topiary. Painstakingly carved from a hedge at the far end are the words "Parque Municipal." Outdoor *terrazas* surround the park on sunny days (and on other days too). Alas, the town doesn't hold a candle to the majesty of its setting: the mountain, the *ría,* and the Cantabrian Sea.

Right off Pr. España, **Hostal Costa Verde**, #7 (tel. 11 01 13), has clean rooms with sag-free mattresses and skin-splitting water pressure. (Singles 1200ptas. Doubles 2500ptas.) Down the street is the grand **Hostal Ribanova**, C. San Roque, 8-10 (tel. 11 06 25), with high ceilings, carpeted stairs, and lacy bedspreads. (Singles 2000ptas. Doubles with bath 4500ptas. Sept. 16-June 14: 1500ptas; 3800ptas.) Westward ho 14km, **Camping Gaivota** (tel. 12 44 50), in the town of Benquerencia, has a ground. (325ptas per person and per car, 275-325ptas per tent. Open June-Sept.)

A miscellany of low-priced *cafeterías* surround Pr. España. **Restaurante Ros Mary**, C. San Francisco, 3, has *tapas* (300-450ptas), *platos combinados* (675-850ptas), and a *menú* (875ptas). (Open 8am-2am.) **Supermercado El Arbol** on Av. Galicia is well-stocked. (Open Tues.-Sat. 9:30am-2pm and 5-8pm, Mon. 9:30am-2pm.)

The **tourist office** (tel. 11 06 89) is in central Pl. España. Grab the decent map, as the staff isn't much help. (Open Mon.-Fri. 9:30am-2pm and 4-7pm, Sat. 9:30am-2pm; Oct.-June Mon.-Fri. 4-7pm.) The **post office** (tel. 11 02 48) is on Av. Asturias, 17 (open Mon.-Fri. 8am-3pm, Sat. 9am-1pm). For a **taxi,** call 11 01 11. **Rent a car** at Autos Eo, Pasarón Ilasta, s/n (tel. 11 04 89).

Getting in and out of here isn't all that bad. The FEVE **train station** (tel. 13 01 39) is ten minutes away; from Pr. España follow C. Villafranco Bierzo through four name changes. The road ends at the station. Two trains per day crawl eastwards on the coastal route from Ferrol to Ribadeo to Oviedo (Ribadeo to Oviedo 4hr., 1030ptas; to Ferrol 905ptas). This train stops at Ortigueira and Viveiro too. (Information open Mon.-Fri. 8:20am-3:30pm and 4:30-8:15pm, Sat.-Sun. 9am-2:30pm and 4-8:30pm.) IASA **buses** (tel. 22 17 60) run to Oviedo (6 per day, 4hr., 1050ptas), A Coruña (3 per day, 3hr., 1060ptas), and Ferrol (1 per day, 1060ptas). The bus stops in Pr. España across from Viajes Proa, a **travel agency** (tel. 11 09 10) at Pr. España #9. They give out complete bus and train information (open Mon.-Fri. 10am-2:30pm and 4:30-8pm, Sat. 10:30am-1:30pm).

Asturias and Cantabria

Rugged, rocky, and leafy regions, Asturias and Cantabria are wedged between Euskadi in the east and Galiza in the west. They live with their backs to the towering peaks of the Cordillera Cantábrica—ideal for hunting, fishing, and hiking and repository of Europe's best-preserved prehistoric art—pushed right up against the broad Atlantic. Administratively, the coast is divided into two autonomous regions, the Principado de Asturias (the province of Oviedo) and Cantabria (the province of Santander).

Possessing numerous industrial centers and prosperous dairy farms, Cantabria has grown rich as a summer getaway for the Spanish elite. Meanwhile, the decline of the mining, steel, and shipping industries has crippled Asturias. Authorities have mobilized to turn the region into a center for scientific research and "green" tourism, promoting an extensive network of country inns in old mansions, *casas de indianos* (rambling Victorian houses built around the turn of the century by Asturians who'd made their fortune in the Americas), and cottages.

After the Moors invaded in 711, Asturias became the mountain stronghold of the Christian resistance, chiefly because the Moors couldn't care less about these harsh lands. Since the Middle Ages the region has been titular fiefdom of the crown prince, the *Príncipe de Asturias* (Prince of Asturias). As the Christian kingdoms expanded southward, Asturias was gradually absorbed into the Kingdoms of León and then Castilla.

Split from the rest of Spain by the Picos de Europa, Asturians maintained their dialect, *bable,* linguistically somewhere between *castellano* and *gallego.* Culturally Asturias is closer to Galiza than to Cantabria. Politically, the Cantabrians for their part often collaborated with their Basque neighbors, although they're ethnically distinct. Indeed, Cantabria is ethnically Castilian, having been Castile's medieval outlet to the sea.

Because of the abrupt terrain, public transport in these regions can be erratic. The roads, however, are striking, winding through deciduous and alpine forests or green valleys now quilted with cornfields and lush pastures. The Atlantic currents might be cool and the weather unpredictable, but Asturias and Cantabria are an idyllic land of flowering valleys, snowy mountains, and spectacular seascapes, without the ravages mass tourism inflicts elsewhere.

Oviedo

The mainstay of the Asturian industrial nexus, Oviedo is a charming city of distinctly modern appearance at the foot of spectacular mountains. Founded as a monastery on the site of the ancient Roman town of Ovetum, Oviedo was later capital of the Kingdom of Asturias for over a century. A General Miners' Strike in 1934 and the workers' uprising of 1936 led to widespread destruction and prompted the building of the new town.

Some might see Oviedo as merely a rest stop en route to the mountaineer's paradise, the Picos de Europa. Yet the capital of Asturias is good for more than just that. The city has preserved a handful of seignorial mansions, and high up on a hill outside the city, you'll find a couple of marvelous 9th-century Pre-Romanesque churches. Oviedo is a transportation hub for northern Spain due to its choice location smack in the center of Asturias, between Galiza to the west, León to the south and Cantabria to the east.

Orientation and Practical Information

Two-way **Calle de Uría** is the city's main artery, running north-south from its origin at the RENFE train station. On the west side of C. Uría is the leafy, luscious **Campo de San Francisco;** and on the east side, the old city, where you'll find the cathedral, **Plaza Mayor,** and the tourist office in **Plaza de Alfonso II.**

The first FEVE station (serving Cantabria and Pais Vasco) is a stone's throw from RENFE on **Avenida Santander.** To reach the bus stations from here, take **Calle Jerónimo Ibrán,** on which Económicos (EASA) and Turytrans buses make their stops, to **Plaza General Primo de Rivera,** which is where the bus biggie, ALSA, has its station underneath the shopping arcade. To reach C. Uría from Pl. General Primo de Rivera, take a right onto C. Fray Ceferino, which ends at C. Uría.

The second FEVE station (serving the Galiza-Asturias route) is a good deal east of the other bus stations on **Calle Victor Chávarri.** To reach C. Uría from here, take C. Victor Chávarri, which becomes Alcalde Garcia Conde and ends at Pl. Carbayón. On the far side of the plaza, pick up Calle Argüelles and you'll hit C. Uría.

Tourist Office: Pl. Alfonso II (tel. 521 33 85). English spoken by helpful staff who give out bus and hostel information and advice on travel in the Picos de Europa. Their computer spits out chunks of useful information. Open June-Sept. Mon.-Fri. 9:30am-1:30pm and 4:30-6:30pm, Sat. 9am-2pm; Oct.-May Mon.-Fri. 9am-2pm and 4-6:30pm.

Youth Center: Dirección Regional de la Juventud, C. Calvo Sotelo, 5 (tel. 523 11 12), in the same building as TIVE (see below). Travel information, including a comprehensive pamphlet on camping, youth hostels, and hiking. Information on cultural activities too.

Hiking Information: Federacíon Asturiana de Montañismo, Av. Juliàn Clavería, s/n (tel. 525 23 62), in front of the sport complex. Take bus #2 from C. Uría. Good collection of trail maps and mountain guides. Information about the best hiking routes and weather conditions. They also organize excursions. Open Mon.-Fri. 6:30-8:30pm.

Budget Travel: TIVE, C. Calvo Sotelo, 5 (tel. 523 60 58), past the Campo San Francisco, up from C. Marqués de Santa Cruz. Information on traveling and hiking nearby. They also organize excursions. ISIC 500ptas. HI card 1800ptas. Open Mon.-Fri. 10am-1pm.

Currency Exchange: Centro Comerical Salesas, between C. Nueve de Mayo and C. General Elorza. The basement has a supermarket **Hipercor** that does it. 1% commission on traveler's checks (500ptas min. charge). Open Mon.-Sat. 10am-10pm.

American Express: Viajes Cafranga, C. Uría, 26 (tel. 522 25 17, 522 25 18). The usual cardholder services. Open Mon.-Fri. 9am-1:30pm and 4:30-7pm, Sat. 9am-1pm.

Post Office: C. Alonso Quíntanilla, 1 (tel. 521 41 86). From C. Uría, turn left onto C. Argüelles and left again. Open for information Mon.-Fri. 9am-2pm; for stamps Mon.-Fri. 8am-9pm, Sat. 9am-7pm; for Lista de Correos Mon.-Fri. 8am-9pm, Sat. 9am-2pm; for **telegrams** Mon.-Fri 9am-8pm, Sat. 9am-7pm. **Postal Code:** 33080.

Telephones: Telefónica, C. Foncalada, 6. Open Mon.-Sat. 10am-2pm and 5-10pm. **Faxes** sent. **Telephone Code:** 98. The telephone company recently added a five (as the first digit) to all city phone numbers. If you see a phone number without a five in an old publication, tack one on.

Flights: Aeropuerto de Ranón (Aeropuerto Nacional de Asturias), (tel. 555 18 33). In Avilés, a town northwest of Oviedo. **Aviaco,** C. Uría, 21 (tel. 524 02 50) runs flights to Madrid, Barcelona, Bilbao, and A Coruña. **Pravia,** C. Marqués de Pidal, 20 (tel. 582 01 09) runs frequent buses to the airport.

Trains: RENFE, C. Uría (tel. 524 33 64), at the junction with Av. Santander. Serves points south of León. Pay attention to the kind of train you take; a slow local through the mountains can double your travel time. Information open 7:45am-11:15pm. To: Gijón (frequent, 1/2 hr., 220ptas); León (9 per day, 2-3hr., 650ptas); Madrid (3 per day, 6 1/2 -8 1/2 hr., 2940-5515ptas); Barcelona (2 per day, 13hr., 5880ptas). **FEVE,** Av. Santander, s/n (tel. 528 40 96), 2min. from RENFE; turn left as you exit. To: Llanes (3 per day, 3hr., 695ptas); Santander (3 per day, 4 3/4 hr., 1315ptas); Bilbo (2 per day, 7hr., 1315ptas). Another **FEVE,** C. Jovellanos, 19 (tel. 521 90 26). Enter from C. Víctor Chávarri. It's hard to get to Galiza from here; the trains run only as far west as Ferrol. To: Ferrol (2 per day, 7 1/4 hr., 925 ptas); Viveiro (2 per day, 5 1/4 hr., 1440ptas); Ribadeo (2 per day, 4hr., 1030ptas).

Buses: ALSA, Pl. General Primo de Rivera, 1 (tel. 528 12 00), on the lower level of a shopping arcade. To: León (12 per day, 2hr., 850ptas); A Coruña (3 per day, 6hr., 2555ptas); Madrid (7 per day, 6hr., 3080ptas); Sevilla (2 per day, 13hr., 4765ptas). **Econòmicos (EASA),** C. Jerónimo Ibrán, 1 (tel. 529 00 39). To Cangas de Onís (12 per day, 1 1/4 hr., 550ptas) and Covodonga (5 per day, 1 3/4 hr., 630ptas). **Turytrans,** C. Jerónimo Ibrán, 1 (tel. 528 50 69), next to EASA. To Llanes (9 per day, 2hr., 795ptas).

Public Transportation: TVA (tel. 524 12 88) runs **buses** (55ptas). The tourist office has a list of the routes.

Taxis: Radio Taxi (tel. 525 00 00, 525 25 00).

Car Rental: Avis, C. Ventura Rodríguez, 12 (tel. 524 13 83). Must be 21 and have had license 1 yr. Open Mon.-Fri. 9am-1pm and 4-7:30pm, Sat. 9am-1pm. **Europcar,** C. Independencia, 24 (tel. 524 44 16). Must be 21 and have had license 1 yr. Open Mon.-Fri. 9am-1:30pm and 4-7:30pm, Sat. 9am-1:30pm.

Luggage Storage: At the **RENFE station** (lockers 200ptas). Open 8am-11pm. At the **ALSA** bus station (small locker 200ptas, large locker 300ptas). Open 7am-11pm.

Lost Property: tel. 524 03 00.

English Bookstore: Librería Cervantes, C. Doctor Casal, 3 and 9 (tel. 521 24 55). Penguin Classics at #9; guidebooks at #3. Open Mon.-Fri. 9:30am-1:30pm and 4-7:30pm, Sat. 9:30am-1:30pm.

Public Library: Pl. Fontán (tel. 521 80 95), near Pl. Mayor. Some books and magazines in English. Open July-Aug. Mon.-Fri. 9am-3pm; Sept.-June Mon.-Fri. 9am-8:45pm, Sat. 9am-2pm.

Laundromat: El Lavadero, C. Marqués de Pidal (tel. 523 95 56), between C. González del Valle and C. Gilde Jaz in the mini-mall Galerías Pidal. Wash and dry 500ptas. Wash alone 350ptas. Dry alone 200ptas. Get tokens at the copy center Folgueras across the way. Open Mon.-Fri. 9:30am-2pm and 4-9pm.

Athletic Facilities: Instalaciones Deportivas de El Cristo, C. Julián Clavería, s/n (tel. 523 24 30), behind the youth hostel. Take bus #2 from C. Uría. Pool (275ptas), tennis courts (450ptas per hr.), track (175ptas), weight room (175ptas), and there's even a sauna. Open Mon.-Fri. 9am-10pm, Sat.-Sun. and holidays 9am-9pm. Call to check for each specific activity.

Late-Night Pharmacy: Check the listings in *La Voz de Asturias* (local paper, 90ptas).

Red Cross: tel. 521 60 93, 521 84 85.

Hospital: Hospital General de Asturias, J. Clavería (tel. 523 00 50).

Emergency: tel. 091.

Police: Comisaría de Policía, C. General Yagüe, 5-7 (tel. 524 03 00). **Policía Municipal,** C. Quintana, s/n (tel. 521 32 05).

Accommodations and Camping

A superflux of *hostales* crowds the new city near the transport stations, generally much cleaner inside than their discolored facades suggest. Even at the height of summer they rarely fill. Try **C. Uría** (straight ahead from the RENFE station), **C. Campoamor** (1 block to the left, i.e. east), and **C. Nueve de Mayo** (a continuation of C. Manuel Pedregal, 1 more block more to the left, i.e. east).

Residencia Juvenil "Asturias," C. Hermanos Pidal, 7-9 (tel. 524 27 87, 524 27 54), near Pl. América; and **Residencia Juvenil "Ramón Menéndez Pidal,"** C. Julián Clavería, 14 (tel. 23 20 54), across from the hospital. Take bus #2 from C. Uría. Welcome, clean alternatives to a rather touch-and-go hostel and *pensión* network. There's a TV room, library, and dining room. Call first; in summer they have only 12 beds. 650ptas per person; over 26 850ptas. Closed in summer 1992, to open in 1993.

Pensión Riesgo, C. Nueve de Mayo, 16 (tel. 521 89 45), 1 bl. from the ALSA station, 2 bl. from C. Uría. No *reisgo* here. Smallish but clean rooms with basins and colorful bedspreads. A light green kind of place; parquet floors. Singles with sink 2000ptas. Doubles with sink 4000ptas. Oct.-May: 1700ptas; 3800ptas.

Pensión Fidalgo, C. Jovellanos, 5, 4th fl. (tel. 521 32 87), just off Pl. Juan XXII. Sunny rooms with frosted glass chandeliers and geraniums on the windowsills. Singles with sink 2000ptas. Doubles with bath 4000ptas.

Pensión Rubio, C. Covadonga, 8, 3rd fl. (tel. 521 56 01), just off C. Alonso de Quintanilla. High ceilings, brand-new wooden desks, bedframes, and dresser. Singles 2000ptas. Doubles 3600ptas.

Pensión La Armonía, C. Nueve de Mayo, 14, 3rd fl. (tel. 522 03 01), next door to the Riesgo. Tile floors (you'll like them) and clean bathrooms. No locks on some doors of this *pensión*. Singles 2000ptas. Doubles 2500ptas.

Food

Oviedo's proximity to the seashore and the mountains makes for both fresh seafood and hearty country dishes. The specialty is *fabada,* a filling stew of *fabes* (beans) and a tomato base served *a la asturiana* (with chunks of sausage). The *sidra* (hard cider) of Asturias is also celebrated, and Oviedo has plenty of *sidrerías* (cider bars). Usually you must order by the bottle, but it shouldn't cost more than 150ptas and even featherweights can polish one off. The **market** is on C. Fontán, near Pl. Mayor. (Open Mon.-Fri. 7am-7pm, Sat. 7am-3pm.)

Mesón la Caleya, C. Lila, 7 (tel. 22 01 15). Cool woodcut of Asturias on the wall. Try the toothsome specialty *cebollas rellenas* (onions stuffed with ham and eggs). *Menú* 700ptas at the tile bar or in the wicker seats at green tables. Open 9am-1am.

Mesón de Paco, C. Foncalada, 8, up the street from Telefónica underneath a diet center. Next door to a snazzier, pricier café; go downstairs. Long benches and tables like a monks' refectory, Spanish music, and stuffing *menú* that changes daily (500ptas). *Platos combinados* (try *albóndigas* with *huevos fritos* and *cħampiñones*, 500ptas) 475-525ptas. Open Tues.-Sun. 9:30am-midnight.

El Café de Vetusta, C. Pozos, 17 (tel. 521 75 05). After C. Uría turns into C. Fruela, turn left onto C. Pozos. Mirrors line this slender elegant restaurant, with adorable lanterns and paintings of Oviedo on the wall. Generous 800ptas *menú* of *paella* and *jamón asado.* Pizza too. Open Mon.-Sat. 7:30am-2am. Closed 15 days in August.

Casa Albino, C. Gascona, 15 (tel. 21 04 45). Hams dangle from the ceiling in this busy restaurant. Walls littered with Real Oviedo Fútbol Club photos. 790ptas *menú* varies. Open 9:30am-5pm and 7pm-1am.

Casa Muñiz, C. Lila, 16 (tel. 522 30 77). High ceilings and busy, no-frills atmosphere crowded with locals. Their *jamón asado* (baked ham, 650ptas) is superb. When they say *ensalada,* they mean a mammoth metal bowlful. Three choices of *menú* 550-700ptas. *Bocadillo de tortilla* (180ptas) could feed one side of the family. Open Mon.-Sat. 10:30am-12:30am; winter Mon.-Tues. and Thurs.-Sat. 10:30am-12:30am. Closed in November.

Sights

In Clarín's 19th-century novel *La Regenta,* Ana Osorio throws herself at the feet of her ecclesiastical lover in Oviedo's **catedral,** Pl. Alfonso II (tel. 522 10 33). No need to be so dramatic; don't throw yourself off its 80m **tower** while you're enjoying the view of the city far below. Some breathtaking **stained glass** windows hang high above its stone walls, and the brilliantly blue ceiling above the **altar** was painted with crushed lapis lazuli stone.

In the north transept, the **Capilla del Rey Castro** houses the royal pantheon, designated by Alfonso II as resting place of Asturian monarchs. The more unusual **Capilla de San Pedro** houses a demented sculpture in metal relief depicting Simon Magnus being dropped from the sky by hideous demons. While the event was instrumental in the conversion of Rome to the Christian faith, records do not indicate whether poor Simon survived his fall. The elaborate masonry of the **Capilla de Santa Eulalia** (the province's *patrona*) is in fine repair.

The cathedral also has countless peculiar details that its curator, Sr. António, can spend all your time pointing out. He'll dwell on the Berruguete sculpture of a naked crucified Jesus that had the bishops painting loincloths, and the sexual acrobatics (carvings called *misericordias*) on the old choir stalls. (Cathedral open 10am-1pm and 4-6pm. Free.)

The Cruz de Los Angeles and the Cruz de la Victoria are in a shrine to medieval pilgrims in the **Cámara Santa.** The **Claustro de San Vicente** adjoins the south transept. The cloister mourns over a graveyard of pilgrims who never made it to Santiago and back. The **museo** here contains ho-hum pre-Romanesque art. (Open Tues.-Sat. 10am-1pm and 4-7pm. Admission to the Cámara Santa, *claustro,* museum, and *sala capitular* 250ptas.)

Also in Pl. Alfonso II are the **Casa Palacio de la Rúa,** whose 15th-century façade is the oldest in town, and the **Palacio de Campo Sagrado,** now the provincial courthouse. Just up C. Santa Ana from the plaza is the **Museo de Bellas Artes,** at C. Santa Ana, 1 and C. Rúa, 8 (tel. 521 30 61). The two-building, three-story complex has an ample collection of Asturian artists and a small collection of 16th- to 20th-century (mainly Spanish) art, including Murillos, school-of- Rubenses, and a chilling depiction of *Stigmatización de San Francisco.* (Open Tues.-Sat. 11am-1:30pm and 4-7pm, Sun. 11am-1:30pm. Free.)

Asturian Pre-Romanesque was the first European attempt to blend architecture, sculpture (including representations of humans), and mural painting since the fall of the Roman Empire. It was developed under Alfonso II (789-842) and perfected under his son Ramiro I (842-859), for whom the style is called *Ramirense.* High above Oviedo, strategically placed on **Monte Naranco,** are two beautiful examples of this style: **Santa María del Naranco** (tel. 529 67 55) and **San Miguel de Lillo** (tel. 529 56 85). (Both open Mon.-Sat. 10am-1pm and 3-7pm, Sun. 10am-1pm; Oct.-April Mon.-Sat. 10am-1pm and 3-5pm, Sun. 10am-1pm. Admission 150ptas, Mon. free.) Ask the tourist office for directions to Monte Naranco.

Picos de Europa

Just an inch from the ocean on the map, these immense corkscrews of rock and snow rise sharply to heights of over 2600m. While other mountains in Europe may surpass the Picos in altitude, few can match the savage beauty of the *sierra's* jagged profile. The range doesn't enjoy the prestige of the Pyrenees or the Alps, which is precisely why you'll find peace and quiet here amid untamed nature. If you're not interested in hiking, mountain climbing, spelunking, horse riding, or biking, get out of the Picos, where even the word *hostal* is uttered by local mountaineers with disdain. Real mountaineers camp. Yet even those willing to go out on a limb (literally), especially novices, will find that there are resources here to guide them. Numerous companies, organizations, and associations devoted to mountain sports flourish in this area. One place to start is Oviedo, where many *federaciones* have their home base:

> **Federación Asturiana de Montañismo, Dirección Regional de la Juventud**, and **TIVE** travel agency. Referral to mountain guides, organized tour groups, and instructors in anything from paragliding to kayaking and spelunking. See Oviedo: Practical Information for addresses and phone numbers.
>
> **ICONA**, C. Arquitecto Reguera, 13, 2nd fl. (tel. 524 14 12). Good for general information. They offer free excursions, camping info, information on routes (including difficulty levels), and a 1/2-hour video presentation on the flora, fauna, and cheese indigenous to the Asturian mountainside. Another office in Cangas de Onís (Av. Covadonga, 35; tel. 584 91 54).

Generally, short (less than 1/2-day) excursions shouldn't cost more than 4000ptas. Some companies (based in various towns throughout the Picos) that offer guided tours are listed below.

> **Alfredo Fernandez**, in the town of Arenas de Cabrales (central Picos), Plaza de Castñeu (tel. 584 55 45). He organizes a wide variety of excursions—from hardcore mountain climbing to a less strenuous tour (complete with a rest stop at a local *sidrería* and farm where you can witness the mysteries of the local *queso de cabrales*).
>
> **Companía de Guías de Montaña**, in the town of Cangas de Onís (west Picos), C. Emilio Laria, 2 (tel. 584 87 16).
>
> **Spantrek Ltd.**, in the town of Carreña de Cabrales (central Picos), Casa Corro (tel. 584 55 41). They guide in style, often including a box lunch on a tour led by English-speaking guides. Full-day excursions 3500-5000ptas.
>
> **Casa Cipriano**, in the town of Sotres (bordering the eastern Picos) (tel. 584 55 24). Tours, including one leading to the **teleférico** in Fuente Dé.
>
> **Senda**, in the town of Llanes (close to the coast), Av. Las Llamas (Ctra Llanes-Cué) (tel. 540 24 30). Bike tours, minivan tours, and plump horse tours.

Often only campers can find beds during the busy months of July and August. When camping in this area, pack warm clothes and raingear for temperature drops and rainstorms. Contact *hostales* or *pensiones* in June or earlier to make reservations. In a jam, tourist offices can help find a bed in a private residence. Also, if you set off independent of a tour, leave a copy of your planned route so a rescue squad can be alerted if you don't return or call by a certain time.

Getting from the cities to the Picos is relatively easy. The bus company **ALSA** and its subsidiary, **Econòmicos,** are the best way to get around. For details contact their Oviedo office (see Oviedo: Practical Information).

Cangas de Onís

Cangas de Onís is the gateway to the National Park that spreads across the Western Picos. Cangas was the first capital of the Asturian monarchy and a launch-pad for the Reconquista, having been founded after the Castilian victory over the Moors at Covadonga in 722. For the budget traveler, it's a place to eat and sleep between excursions.

The **Puente Romano** is a misnamed Romanesque bridge that gracefully spans the Río Sella. The bus from Oviedo passes it by on the way into town; it's worth backtracking from the bus stop to check it out.

Walking back into Cangas, turn left opposite the park and cross a modern bridge to **Capilla de Santa Cruz.** This reconstruction of a Romanesque chapel was built above the town's oldest monument, a Celtic *dolmen* (monolith). The chapel is almost completely bare, although its exterior is shapely. In summer, students at the school next door guard the place and give the full 10-minute lowdown on the cave underneath the chapel, where priests hid from invading Moors.

Other sights in the area include **Iglesia de Santa Eulalia** in **Abamia** (11km away), a Romanesque church where King Pelayo and his wife were buried, and the **Cueva del Buxu** (BOO-shoo; 5km away), whose walls bear 15,000-year-old paintings. Only 25 people are admitted to the cave each day; arrive early. (Open Tues.-Sun. 10am-noon. Admission 125ptas, Tues. free.) Both attractions are less than a two-hour walk from Cangas. The **bus** to Covadonga runs nearby the Cueva del Buxu (ask to be dropped off at the Cruce de Susierra).

A few clean *pensiones* welcome guests on Av. Covadonga, the main street. **Pensión Audelina,** Av. Covadonga 6, 4th fl. (tel. 584 83 50), has such firm mattresses. (2000ptas per person.) Down the same street, but with an entrance on Av. Castilla, is **Pensión María Teresa,** Av. Castilla 1, 2nd fl. B (tel. 584 90 78). Soft shiny bedspreads and a new brown tiled bathroom belie the reasonable prices. (Singles 1500ptas. Doubles with 1 bed 2500ptas, with 2 beds 3000ptas.) Stay at **Fonda El Chofer,** C. Emilio Laria, 10 (tel. 584 83 05), on the street opposite the little park by the Ayuntamiento, if you're thin enough to squeeze into one of their rooms. Great showers. (Singles 2000ptas. Doubles 3500ptas.) Campers frequent the second-class **Camping Covadonga** (tel. 594 00 97), on Soto de Cangas about 5km up the road toward Covadonga (5 buses per day). Amenities everywhere: cafeteria, bar, and showers. (425ptas per person, 375ptas per car, 375-425ptas per tent. Open April 11-16 and June-Sept.) Some people camp illegally in a secluded meadow by the river.

After a rousing hike, few pleasures surpass a substantial meal in the land of *fabes* and *sidra*. **Restaurante El Casín,** Av. Castilla, 2 (tel. 84 83 31), serves *fabada, calamares en su tinta* (squid in its own ink), or veal stew on its 900ptas *menú*. Down the street and left into the park, **Supermercados El Arbol,** El Parque, s/n, sells preparations for a do-it-yourself meal. (Open Mon.-Fri. 9am-2pm and 5-8pm, Sat.-Sun. and holidays 9am-2pm.)

The **tourist office** (tel. 584 80 05) has a cabin in the small park by the Ayuntamiento. (Open 10am-2pm and 4-10pm; Sept.-June Mon.-Sat. 10am-2pm and 4-7pm.) Hikers and mountaineers generally prefer the **Compañia de Guías de Montaña,** C. Emilio Laria, 2 (tel. 584 87 16). The staff has a list of mountain refuges and a collection of maps. (Hours variable.) The **ICONA** office, Av. Covadonga, 35 (tel. 584 91 54), down the street from Turismo, has its own share of hiking and nature information. (Open Mon.-Fri. 8am-8pm, Sat.-Sun. 8am-2pm.) Up the street from Turismo, **Librería Imagen** stocks guides, and maps. (Open 8:30am-9pm; Oct.-June Tues.-Sat. 8am-1:30pm and 3:30-7:30pm, Sun. 8am-3pm). The **post office** (tel. 584 81 96) is down Av. Covadonga from Turismo. Take a right after 2 blocks onto Av. Constantino González; it's on the left. (Open Mon.-Fri. 8am-3pm, Sat. 9am-1pm.) **Telephones** are in a little Telefónica stand behind Turismo (open July-Sept. 10am-2pm and 5-11pm). For police, call the **Guardia Civil** at 584 80 56.

EASA (tel. 522 28 44) runs frequent **buses** from Oviedo to Cangas (1 1/2 hr., 630ptas). Several others skirt the northern Picos from Panes (2hr., 320ptas), connecting or continuing to Santander. In Cangas de Onís, the Económicos (EASA) office is across from Turismo, down a few stairs next door to a bar (tel. 584 81 33).

Covadonga

"This little mountain you see will be the salvation of Spain." So prophesied Don Pelayo to his Christian army, gesturing maniacally to Covadonga, the rocky promontory that was to be the site of the first successful rebellion against the Moors. It was here that nationalistic legend claims the Virgin interceded with God on behalf of Don Pelayo's forces, creating an invisible shield and ensuring them a victory against the Muslims.

The **Santa Cueva** (Holy Cave) where Don Pelayo prayed to the Virgin is the most important religious and historical site in Covadonga. The virgin owns a number of lovely cloaks; she changes her outfit every few days in the summer. Pilgrims and tourists crowd the sanctuary at all hours. (Open 8am-10pm. Free.)

Right beneath the Santa Cueva and next to its giant waterfall is the **Fuente de los Siete Caños,** also known as the **Fuente del Matrimonio.** Legend says that anyone who drinks from each of the 7 spouts will marry in the next year.

The Santuario de Covadonga, a pale pink neo-Gothic **basílica,** towers above the town. (Open 8am-10pm.) The priceless *Corona de la Virgen,* a crown of gold and silver studded with no less than 1109 diamonds and 2046 rubies, lives in the **Museo del Tesoro,** directly across the square from the basilica. Right underneath mama's crown is baby Jesus's, also encrusted with sparklers. (Open 11am-2pm and 4-7pm. Admission 50ptas.)

On July 25 the shepherds of Covadonga whoop it up at their annual **festival** with tree-climbing competitions and folksy song and dance.

Covadonga makes a fine half-day trip. If you decide to stay the night, the **Hospedería del Peregrino,** the only official lodging in town, has a bar and dining room on the floor below the bedrooms. *Fabada* costs 500ptas. (Singles 3300ptas. Doubles 3800ptas.) For a more rustic approach, try the nuns' places: **El Mesón** (July-Sept. tel. 584 60 33; Oct.-June tel. 584 60 68; 375ptas per person), **Casa Rosa** (tel. 584 60 68; 375ptas per person), and the **Albergue de Covadonga** (tel. 584 60 68; 200ptas per person). All three are within walking distance from the basilica. The trio offer spartan accommodations in ancient buildings with (some working) wood-burning stoves.

Mountain climbers in the **information office** (tel. 584 60 35) across from the basilica can inform on local accommodations and sights. **Buses** traveling from Oviedo to Cangas grace Covadonga with two stops: one at the Hospedería and one uphill at the basilica (5 per day, 1 3/4 hr., 630ptas).

Near Covadonga: Los Lagos de Enol y Ercina

One bus per day from Oviedo to Cangas continues 12km higher past Covadonga to **Los Lagos de Enol y Ercina** (the lakes of Enol and Ercina), 1500m above the **Parque Nacional de Covadonga.** The ride into the mountains is itself spectacular, and during the summer you can swim in the warm lake.

There are three mountain *refugios* on the paths leading from the lakes. In summer reserve in advance. The **Refugio de Vega de Enol** (tel. 584 82 05, 584 85 76), close by the lakes, has merely 30 spots, but is open all year and provides meals and guides. To get there, take highway C6312 (Cangas de Onís-Panes, desvío hacia Covadongas y Lagos). Take a right at Lago Enol and keep going until the *refugio* (400ptas per person, *pensión completa* 2500ptas). For solitude, take the 2-hr. hike to the **Refugio de Villaviciosa-Vega de Ario** (contact the Federación Asturiana de Montañismo in Oviedo for information; tel. 584 41 19 or 584 85 16). Take road A-7 from the Lago Ercina; it's on the left, facing the lake. (Open May 15-Oct. 15.) The **Refugio de Vegarredonda** (contact Refugios de Montaña de Asturias, tel. 584 89 16) is also two hours away and open all year with supervision, meals, guides, hot showers, and kitchens (600ptas per night, breakfast 350ptas). To get there from Lago Enol, take highway A-6.

Arenas de Cabrales

This small town between Cangas and Panes is a strictly one-street, no-nonsense affair. The surrounding countryside is stunning. Rocky green mountains loom and small rivers and creeks gurgle with fresh, cold water. Moreover, *queso de cabrales,* a reekingly pungent blue cheese coveted by gourmets worldwide, is made here. Nineteenth-century novelist Benito Pérez Galdós described the cheese (an ancestor of Roquefort) as a "pestiferous fragrance." Made from goat, cow, and sheep milks, the mush is wrapped in leaves and aged in local caves.

Smack in the Central Picos and east of the Parque Nacional de Covadonga, Arenas makes the ideal place to dump your stuff while you explore the area. **Senda del Cares** (Cares Gorge), near the town of **Poncebos,** is a 5km walk from Arenas. Hewn and blasted out of mountain and sheer rock faces, the 12km trail was built by the government to monitor an artificially-made channel of water. At points, the Río Cares gurgles 500ft. below the trail; the walls of the gorge often become vertical, allowing you to see your shoes, the trail, and a tiny stream far beneath you. The trail crosses the gorge twice, ending in **Caín,** a town recently hooked to civilization by a paved road. The walk takes about five hours, and the only way back is by foot.

Another shorter and less taken path leads south along the Río Tejo to **Bulnes,** a microscopic, roadless village. (In fact, as there aren't any cars in the town, a helicopter must fly in for emergencies.) The blistering hike takes one-and-a-half hours out and one hour back, but is actually more difficult than the Senda del Cares. If Bulnes seduces you, consider tucking in at **Albergue de Bulnes** (tel. 536 69 32). There are 20 beds in 3 rooms, a bar, a library, games, showers, and guides; meals are served. Reservations are suggested (800ptas per night, 350ptas breakfast, *menú* 1200ptas).

A third path with terrific views leads straight up a cliff from Poncebos to **Camarmeña.** For a longer, killer hike (10-12hr.), try the 17km route from Poncebos to **Invernales de Cabao,** then 9km more to the Picos' most famous mountain, **Naranjo de Bulnes.** From here you can see all of the major *picos* in the area and the blue waves of the Cantabrian Sea in the distance.

Arenas abounds with exceptional (clean, new, and reasonable) *hostales*. At the recently renovated **Hostal Naranjo de Bulnes,** Ctra. General, s/n (tel. 584 51 19), enormous rooms with *terrazas*, panoramic views, and Guatemalan bedspreads are surprisingly inexpensive—as is the *menú* (900ptas) served in the airy, elegant dining room. Signs in the reception area advertise excursions. The owner can fill in the details. (Singles 2000ptas, with bath 3000ptas. Doubles 3500ptas, with bath 5000ptas. Breakfast 350ptas.) **Hostal Torrecerredo,** up a long driveway from the main road (look for the sign) at Los Llambriosos, s/n (tel. 584 52 40), is a budget hotel/health spa. Aside from rooms with splendid views, they offer a huge dining room, vegetarian dishes, excursions on mountain bikes (1500-2800ptas), Land Rover excursions (1 day including lunch 3000ptas), and horse rides with the owner's cowboy son Monchu and Lucita, his sexy long-haired lover. (Singles 1300ptas. Doubles with 1 bed 2500ptas, with bath 3500ptas. Doubles with 2 beds and bath 4500ptas. Triples 6500ptas.) At **Pensión El Castañeu,** Pl. Castañeu (tel. 584 52 03), up the street to the right from the bus stop, the *menú del dia* will make you a butterball (650ptas). (Singles 1500ptas. Doubles 2500ptas. Oct.-May: 1100-1200ptas; 2000-2200ptas.) One km up the highway heading east toward Panes, the spectacular **Camping Naranjo de Bulnes** (tel. 584 51 78) has a cozy TV room, cafeteria, bar, shower facilities, and plenteous info on hiking and assorted mountain sports. A **message board** lists excursions and local guides. **Bike rental** also available. (300ptas per person, 390-430ptas per tent, 390ptas per car.) Numerous **refugios** speckle the Picos; check with Turismo first.

A **tourist office** (tel. 584 52 84) in Arenas is small but helpful; some English spoken. (Open 9am-2pm and 6-9pm; Oct.-May Tues.-Sat. 9am-2pm and 6-9pm.) If they're not home, it's a 3km walk west to nearby Carreña de Cabrales, where the regional **ayuntamiento** reigns (maps and a list of accommodations; open Mon.-Sat. 9am-3pm). Arenas' **post office** is up the street from the bus stop (open Mon.-Fri. 10am-1pm, Sat. 10am-noon). In the other direction from the bus stop are **telephones**, inside the photo shop Foto J. Tomás (open 10am-9:30pm). For police, call the **Guardia Civil** in Carreña de Cabrales (tel. 584 50 16).

Transportation to Arenas is annoying. Económicos (EASA) **buses** service this part of the Picos. Two per day connect to Cangas de Onís. Two per day go to Unquera (1 1/4 hr., 275ptas), whence you can catch a Turytrans bus to Santander (1 1/2 hr., 530ptas).

Potes

The most convenient base for exploring the southeastern and central Picos is Potes, on the Río Deva. Quiet and snow-bound in winter, the town's squares and cafés shimmy in summer with cosmopolitan climbers. Luckily this way-station is also quite beautiful, sheltered by immense white peaks and watered by a burbling stream. The rugged terrain formed the front-line early in the Reconquista. The **Torre del Infantado** stands guard over the main square; across the river is the **Convento de San Raimundo,** a quaint 17th-century Dominican monastery.

Several *hostales* and *pensiones* line the road through town. **Casa Cayo** (tel. 73 01 50), on the nameless cobblestoned street on the left off the main square, rents spotless, spacious rooms, some overlooking the mountains and river. (Singles 2000ptas. Doubles 4500ptas, with bath 5000ptas.) Sating *menús* in their bright dining room cost 950ptas. **Hostal Rubio,** C. San Roque, 17 (tel. 73 00 15), is most conveniently located next to the bus stop. English spoken. The adequate rooms have basins and street balconies. (Singles 2500ptas. Doubles 3200ptas, with bath 4300ptas.) Restaurant **Casa Gómez** (tel. 573 02 81) serves a refreshing 1200ptas *menú*.

There's no official camping in the town of Potes, only at three rather distant second-class sites. The closest is **La Isla Picos de Europa** (tel. 73 08 96), 3km down the road to Fuente Dé. (325ptas per person, 350ptas per tent, 325ptas per car. Open April-Oct.) Two km farther down this road waits **San Pelayo** (tel. 73 05 97; 325ptas per person, 250-325ptas per tent, 325ptas per car; open April-Oct.) Walk to these or ask the driver of the bus to Fuente Dé to drop you off. The third campsite, **El Molino** (tel. 73 04 89), is 8km down the road to León (325ptas per person, 300ptas per tent, 325ptas per car. Open June 15-Sept. 15.)

The **tourist office** on Pl. Jesús del Monasterio (tel. 73 08 20), across the bridge and near the church, has general information about the region, though very little about Potes itself. Ask here about mountain *refugios*. (Open Holy Week and June-Sept. Mon.-Fri. 10am-1pm and 4-8pm, Sat. 10am-1pm.) **Bustamante,** a photo shop in the main square, sells detailed maps and guidebooks to the region. The **maps** published by the *Instituto Geográfico Nacional* and the *Federación Española de Montañismo* are the best, although serious mountaineers may find them a bit vague (500ptas). Picos is linked by **bus** to León in the southwest and to Santander in the northeast (3 per day, 2 1/2 hr., 705ptas),

Excursions

Fuente Dé. A mind-blowing 800m *teleférico* glides up the sheer mountain face to reach a fancy *parador*. There are usually huge lines for the lift in the middle of summer. (Open 10am-8pm; Sept.-June 10am-6pm. Round-trip 800ptas.) From the top, it's a 4km walk to the **Refugio de Aliva** for a meal or bed. The rooms in their modern buildings are usually full; ask about vacancies at the lift in Fuente Dé or at the Ayuntamiento in Potes. (500ptas per person.) The peculiar rock faces near Aliva have earned this area the nickname "La Luna" (the moon). To return, either retrace your steps to the *teleférico* or walk three hours to **Espinama.** On July 10, a rowdy **festival** brings horse racing and dancing to Aliva. Two **buses** per day run from Potes to Fuente Dé (205ptas).

Monasterio de Santo Toribio de Liébana, 3km west of Potes, claims to hold part of the true (original) cross.

Mogrovejo, 10km west of Potes, is the start of a back-breaking hike. The trail winds down to **Pembes** and then back to the road near Espinama: about 15km, or 4hours.

Peña Sagra is about 13km east and two hours from the towns of **Luriezo** or **Aniezo**; from the summit you can survey all the Picos and the sea 51km away. On your way down, visit **Iglesia de Nuestra Señora de la Luz,** where the beautifully carved patron saint of the Picos lives 364 days a year. Known affectionately as *Santuca* (tiny saint), the Virgin is honored on May 2.

Panes, on the routes to Santander and Cabrales, is near some spectacular scenery. The Río Deva has carved a sharp gorge, the **Desfiladero de Hermida.**

Santander

In 1941, an enormous fire gutted the entire city of Santander. Miraculously, the capital of Cantabria has managed to rebuild itself along modern lines, packing delightful beaches, tree-lined promenades, a swish casino, and a trendy shopping district all into its mini peninsula. It's a favorite seaside resort among the Spanish, while the presence of the Universidad Internacional Menéndez Pelayo attracts renowned artists and scholars to town.

Orientation and Practical Information

This slender, elongated city sits on the northwestern side of a bay. The small **Plaza Porticada** is its heart. **Avenida Calvo Sotelo,** which becomes **Paseo de Pereda** to the east, runs along the waterfront. Buses and trains arrive at **Plaza de Estaciones,** about six blocks west of Pl. Porticada.

Beach activity centers on the neighborhood of **El Sardinero,** in the eastern part of town. Buses #1, 2, 3, 4, and 7 connect the two parts of the city (frequent service until midnight, Sept.-June 10:30pm; 70ptas). The beach is bordered by lengthy **Avenida Reina Victoria** and **Avenida de Castaneda.** Between the two beaches (El Sardinero and Playa de la Magdalena) lies the swanky casino in **Plaza de Italia.**

Tourist Office: Pl. Porticada, 1 (tel. 31 07 08). From the train and bus stations, take C. Calderón de la Barca and turn left on Av. Alfonso XIII (at Banco de España), which ends at the plaza. Maps, some info on Cantabria, and a space-age computer that spits out listings. Open Mon.-Fri. 9am-1:30pm and 4-7pm, Sat. 9-1:30pm.

Budget Travel: Viajes TIVE, C. Canarias, 2 (tel. 33 22 15), a 20-min. walk northwest from the center. Take bus #5 just off Av. General Camilo Alonso Cela. Travel discounts and flights; English spoken. ISIC 500ptas. HI card 1800ptas. Open Mon.-Fri. 9am-2pm, Sat. 9am-1pm.

Consulate: U.K., Po. Pereda, 27 (tel. 22 00 00). Open mid-Sept. to mid-June Mon.-Fri. 9am-12:30pm and 4-6:30pm; mid-June to mid-Sept. Mon.-Fri. 8:30am-1:30pm.

Currency Exchange: When banks close, there's always **Bar Machichaco,** C. Calderón de la Barca, just past C. Isabel II. Open 1pm-midnight.

American Express: Viajes Altair, C. Lealtad, 24 (tel. 31 17 00, fax 22 57 21), at the corner with C. Calderón de la Barca. Cardholder mail held, and the standard services. Open Mon.-Fri. 9:30am-1:30pm and 4:30-8pm, Sat. 10am-1:30pm.

Post Office: Av. Alfonso XIII (tel. 36 19 42, fax 31 02 99), overlooking the Jardines de Pereda on the waterfront. Open for stamps and Lista de Correos Mon.-Fri. 8am-9pm, Sat. 9am-2pm; for **fax** and **telegrams** Mon.-Fri. 8am-9pm, Sat. 9am-7pm. **Postal Code:** 39080.

Telephones: Telefónica, C. Hernán Cortés, 37, up the street from Pl. José Antonio. **Faxes** also sent. Open Mon.-Fri. 9am-3pm and 4-11pm, Sat. 9am-3pm and 4-10pm. Another office is alongside the casino, Pl. Italia. **Telephone Code:** 942.

Flights: Aeropuerto de Santander (tel. 25 10 07, 25 10 04), 4km away. Daily to Madrid and Barcelona. Accessible only by taxi (1000-1200ptas). **Iberia,** Po. Pereda, 18 (tel. 22 97 00). Open Mon.-Fri. 9am-1:30pm and 4-7:15pm.

Trains: Pl. Estaciones, on C. Rodríguez. **RENFE station** (tel. 28 02 02). Information open 7:15am-10:30pm. Santander is the northern terminus of one RENFE line, so for service to points north, take FEVE to Bilbo and then pick up RENFE again. To: Madrid (4 per day, 5hr., 3380-4740ptas); Salamanca (7 per day; 7hr.; *regional* 1900ptas, *talgo* 3700ptas); Valladolid (5 per day, 5hr., 1320ptas). **RENFE ticket office,** Po. Pereda, 25 (tel. 21 23 87). Open Mon.-Fri. 9am-1pm and 4-7pm, Sat. 9am-1pm. **FEVE station** (tel. 21 16 87). Information open 9am-2pm and 4-7pm. To: Bilbo (4 per day, 2 1/2 hr., 725ptas); Oviedo (2 per day, 4hr., 1325ptas).

Buses: Pl. Estaciones (tel. 21 19 95), on C. Rodríguez. Information open 9am-9pm. To: Santillana (7 per day, 45min., 180ptas); Potes (3 per day, 2 1/2 hr.,705ptas); Bilbo (14 per day, 3hr., 755ptas); Oviedo (2 per day, 4hr., 1390ptas); A Coruña (2 per day, 12hr., 4330ptas); Madrid (4 per day, 6hr., 2805ptas); Llanes (7 per day, 2hr., 690ptas); San Vincente de la Barquera (7 per day, 1 1/2 hr., 455ptas); Logroño (3 per day, 4hr., 1760ptas).

Public Transportation: Buses #1, 2, 3, 4, and 7 run between the city center and El Sardinero (frequently until midnight, Sept.-June 10:30pm; 70ptas).

Ferries: Brittany Ferries, Muelle del Ferrys, near the Jardines de Pereda. All the way to Plymouth, England (2 per week, 13,100-15,600ptas plus 700-1100ptas for seat reservation). Tickets sold by Modesto Piñeiro, S.A. (tel. 21 45 00), at the ferry station. Information open Mon.-Fri. 7:30am-7pm. In summer reserve 2 weeks in advance, although seventh sons of seventh sons sometimes get tickets just before departure. **Las Reginas** (tel. 21 66 19), from Embarcadero by the Jardines de Pereda. To Pedreña (summer every 1/2 hr., round-trip 200ptas). They also do tours around the bay (summer 2-6 per day, 80min., 400ptas).

Taxis: Radio Taxi (tel. 33 33 33, 33 10 37, or 22 20 46).

Car Rental: Avis, C. Nicolás Salmerón, 3 (tel. 22 70 25). Must be 23 and have had license 1 yr. Renault 7000ptas per day. Open Mon.-Fri. 9am-1pm and 4-7:30pm, Sat. 9-11:30am. **Europcar,** C. Rodríguez, 9 (tel. 21 47 06). Must be 21 and have had license 1 yr. Opel Corsa 4000ptas per day, 40ptas per km. Open Mon.-Fri. 9am-1pm and 4-8pm.

Luggage Storage: At the **train station** (lockers 300ptas), by the counter at the ticket window. Open daily 7am-11pm. At the **bus station** (lockers 200ptas). Open 7:30am-10:30pm.

Lost Property: Ayuntamiento building, Pl. Generalísimo Franco (tel. 22 04 64).

English Bookstore: El Estudio, C. Calvo Sotelo, 21 (tel. 37 49 50). Penguin Classics, bestsellers, and guidebooks in English. Open Mon.-Fri. 9:15am-1pm and 4:30-8pm, Sat. 10am-1:30pm. **La Estilográfica,** C. Hernán Cortés, 1 (tel. 21 19 05). A cramped stationery store with a small but farflung choice of books in English. Bestselling Book-of-the-Month Club authors. Open Mon.-Fri. 9:45am-3:30pm and 4:30-8pm, Sat. 9:45am-1:30pm.

Library: Biblioteca Menéndez Pelayo, C. Gravina, 4, on the corner with C. Rubio, connected to the museum. Open Mon.-Fri. 9am-2pm and 4-9:30pm.

Women's Center: Instituto de la Mujer, Pasaje de la Puntida, 1 (tel. 31 36 12). Information on gatherings, exhibitions, and talks.

Laundromat: Lavomatique, C. Cuesta de la Atalaya, 18 (tel. 37 41 78), on the corner of San Celedonio. Wash 600ptas per load. Dry 100ptas per 15min. Soap 75ptas. Open Mon.-Fri. 9am-1:30pm and 4-8pm, Sat. 9am-1:30pm. **El Lavadero,** C. Mies del Valle, 10 (tel. 23 06 07), just off C. Floranes west of the train station. Wash 600ptas per 6kg load. Dry 200ptas per 6kg load. Soap 40ptas. Open Mon.-Fri. 9:30am-2pm, Sat. 10am-1:30pm.

Swimming Pool: Piscinas Municipales, in sports complex Albericias (tel. 33 75 06). Take bus #6 to the end of the line.

Rape Crisis Line: Asociación de Asistencia a Mujeres Violadas, Comisiones Obreras Building, C. Santa Clara, 5, 3rd fl. (tel. 21 95 00). English spoken. Open Mon.-Fri. noon-2pm.

Red Cross: Ambulance (tel. 27 30 58).

Late-Night Pharmacy: Check listings in *El Diario Monañés* (local paper, 80ptas).

Medical Services: Casa de Socorro, C. Escalantes (tel. 21 12 14). **Medical Center,** Av. Valdecilla (tel. 33 00 00).

Emergency: tel. 091.

Police: Travesía de los Escalantes, s/n (tel. 22 04 64), behind the Ayuntamiento. **Guardia Civil,** C. Alta, 81 (tel. 22 11 00, 23 20 04).

Accommodations and Camping

It's not easy to find affordable rooms in July and August, especially if you arrive late in the day. Singles cost around 2000ptas, doubles over 3000ptas. Highest hotel density is near the market, around **Calle Isabel II,** and along elegant **Avenida de los Castros** in El Sardinero. El Sardinero, the modern residential beach neighborhood, is a bus ride (see Practical Information: Public Transportation) and worlds away from the hyperactive city center.

Pensión Puerto Rico, C. Isabel II, 1, 4th fl. (tel. 22 57 07). Enough room space to cut a dress from Scarlett's green brocade curtains in the foyer. Some windows look out onto the market across the street. Try for the double with the sofa. Plants galore. Doubles 3700ptas. Triples 4500ptas. Quads 6000ptas.

Hostal Real, Pl. Esperanza, 1, 4th fl. (tel. 22 57 87), at end of C. Isabel II. Bright flower-filled rooms, many with terraces. Singles 3200ptas. Doubles 3500ptas. July-Sept: 3800ptas; 4000ptas. Oct.-May: 2700ptas; 3000ptas.

Hostal Botín, C. Isabel II, 1, 2nd fl. (tel. 21 00 94), downstairs from the Puerto Rico. Just 1 single. Doubles large enough for a gymnastics competition. Wicker chairs and Japanese lanterns in waiting room. Singles 2400ptas. Doubles 4000ptas. Triples 5400ptas. Quads 6400ptas. Mid-Aug. to mid-June: 2000ptas; 3400ptas; 4590ptas; 5400ptas.

Pensión Angelina, C. Rodríguez, 9, 2nd fl. (tel. 31 25 84), around the corner from the train station. Quilted bedspreads and a whole hall of snazzy tiled baths. Pray to the gods for the double with the easy chair. Singles 1000ptas. Doubles 2000ptas. Triples 3000ptas.

Pensión Fernando, C. Rodríguez, 9, 4th fl. (tel. 31 36 96), above the above. (Two more *pensiones* in the same building.) Mounted boar head eyes guests suspiciously. Sometimes flowers adorn the windowsills. Singles 1500ptas. Doubles 3000ptas.

Fonda Perla de Cuba, C. Hernán Cortés, 8 (tel. 21 00 41), across from the Banesto building past C. Bailén. Terraced rooms, some with flowered bedspreads. Vaguely odorous and only one bathroom for everyone. Singles 850ptas! Doubles 1625ptas. Showers 100ptas. Breakfast 130ptas. *Pensión media* 1575ptas.

Hostal-Residencia Luisito, Av. de los Castros, 11 (tel. 27 19 71), 1 bl. from beach. Take bus #4 to Hotel Colón (Pl. Brisas). Beach heaven (but far from downtown). Exceptionally huge rooms, many with exceptionally huge balconies looking over flowery gardens and fruit-bearing trees. Prices don't include IVA. Singles 1785ptas. Doubles 3175ptas. Breakfast 180ptas. Open July-Sept.

Pensión Picos de Europa, C. Calderón de la Barca, 5, 4th fl. D (tel. 22 53 74). Chandeliers and pillars embellish majestic rooms with flowery pastel walls and views of the water. Call first. Singles 2500ptas. Doubles 3200ptas. Triples 4220ptas. Showers 125ptas.

Camping: On the scenic bluff called Cabo Mayor, 3km up the coast from Playa de la Magdalena, there are two back-to-back sites. Both are *enorme*. Take the "Cueto-Santander" bus from in front of the Jardines de Pereda. **Camping Bellavista** (tel. 27 48 43), a 1st-class site on the beach. 325ptas per person, 300-350ptas per tent. *Parcela* (parking spot) 1500ptas. **Camping Cabo Mayor** (tel. 27 35 66), with pool and tennis courts. 450ptas per person, 350-450ptas per tent. *Parcela* 1400ptas. Open mid-June to Sept.

Food

Interesting eateries crowd the **Puerto Pesquero** (fishing port), serving up the day's catch on a small stretch at the end of **Calle Marqués de la Ensenada**. From the train station, walk eight blocks down C. Castilla and turn left on C. Héroes de la Armada; cross the tracks and turn right after about 100m (20min.). Closer to the city center, reasonable *mesones* and bars line **Calle Daoiz y Velarde** and **Plaza Cañadío**. The **Mercado Plaza Esperanza,** C. Isabel II, sells produce near Pl. Generalísimo behind the police station. (Open Mon.-Fri. 8am-2pm and 5-7:30pm, Sat. 8am-2pm.)

Groceries: Supermercados Más y Más, C. Hernán Cortés, 42, 3 bl. past Pl. José Antonio. Open Mon.-Sat. 9:30am-1:30pm and 5-8pm.

La Cueva, C. Marqués de la Ensenada (tel. 22 20 87), in the *barrio pesquero.* Serves *chipirrones encebollados* (baby squid fried in onions) and *pulpo* (octopus). Little plants on each table, barbeque outside. Intriguing dishes on its 900ptas *menú*. Open noon-4pm and 7:30-11:30pm.

Bar Restaurante La Gaviota, C. Marqués de la Ensenada, at the corner of C. Mocejón. The kitchen is smack in the middle of the cavernous curtained dining room. *Menú* offers *sopa de pescado* and *chipírones* (800ptas). Paella a specialty. Open 1-4pm and 7:30-midnight.

Restaurante-Bar Fradejas, Pl. Cañadío, 1. A glorified cafeteria. Exports meals outside. *Menú* 850ptas, 950ptas on the *terraza*. Hamburger 225-325ptas. Open Tues.-Sun. 9am-2:30am.

Cervecería Santander, C. Lope de Vega, 5, off Po. Pereda near the ferry station. Plaid tablecloths and cloth napkins. Outside tables front the water. Broad 800ptas *menú* includes *fabada* and *albóndigas*. Open 7:30am-midnight.

Bierhaus, C. Daoizy Velarde, 23, near Pl. Cañario. Young crowd and pop music. Mouthwatering *tapas* knock knees with German specialties such as *salchicha bratwurst* (400 ptas). Chef's salad 450ptas. Open 12:30-4pm and 6:30pm-2am.

Cervecería Aspy, C. Hernán Cortés, 32, just off C. Lope de Vega. Elegant dining room has it all: wine rack, sprigged banquettes, and a signed photo of golf star Seve Ballesteros. *Gambas a la plancha* 475ptas. *Platos combinados* 475-600ptas. Open 8am-1am; winter Thurs.-Tues. 8am-1am.

Restaurante Cormorán, Segunda Playa del Sardinero (tel. 27 24 92), light years away down the boardwalk in a nondescript gray building hung with flags. Sprawling. Views of the beach accompany good food. *Menú* includes *pan* and *vino* (600-750ptas). Desserts 200ptas. Open noon-4pm and 8-11:30pm.

Sights

The **Museo Marítimo,** C. San Martín de Bajamar (tel. 27 49 62), stands beyond the *puerto chico* (little port). In addition to the nifty aquarium, there are traditional fishing boats and salvaged remains from marine disasters (no buried treasure). (Open Tues.-Sat. 11am-1pm and 4-7pm, Sun. 11am-2pm; mid-Sept. to mid-June Mon.-Sat. 10am-1pm and 4-6pm, Sun. and holidays 11am-2pm. Free.) Near the Ayuntamiento the **Museo de Bellas Artes,** C. Rubio, 6 (tel. 23 94 85), exhibits a congregation of 16th-through 18th-century paintings. The prize is Goya's portrait of Fernando VII commissioned by Santander's Ayuntamiento. (Open Mon.-Fri. 10am-1pm and 5-8pm, Sat. 10am-1pm. Free.)

Paleolithic skulls and tools at the **Museo de Prehistoria y Arqueología,** C. Casimiro Sainz, 4 (tel. 21 50 00), remind you that humans are the children of more apelike peoples. Artifacts from and photographs of the Cuevas de Altamira console the many who won't get to see the real thing. (Open Mon.-Sat. 9am-1pm and 4-7pm, Sun. and holidays 11am-2pm. Free.)

While the 1941 fire scorched the façade of the **catedral,** the downstairs chapel retains an unusually low Romanesque vaulting. Here you can examine the remains of the earlier church through a glass floor. Crypt, too. (Open 9:30am-1:30pm and 5:30-8:30pm. Free.)

Jutting into the sea between El Sardinero and Playa de la Magdalena, the **Península de la Magdalena** is crowned by an early 20th-century neo-Gothic fantasy **palacio.** Originally Alfonso XIII's summer house, the clifftop palace is a classroom building and dorm for the university. In summer, renowned cultural figures from around the globe arrive for a term of seminars, master classes, and lectures. (Peninsula open 7am-10pm. The *palacio* doesn't have visiting hours.)

The beaches are truly spectacular. **El Sardinero,** at the end of town, is the old standby. Some fine, less crowded beaches—**Playas Puntal, Somo,** and **Loredo**—fringe the other side of the bay. In summer, Las Reginas **boats** (tel. 21 66 19) run across to Pedreña and sail on 80-minute tours around the bay (see Practical Information: Ferries).

Entertainment

A trendy **shopping** district centers around Av. Calvo Sotelo. **Outdoor cafés** overlooking the bay hum on Po. Pereda. A 10-minute walk along the water leads to the **barrio pesquero,** hopping with busy restaurants and their outdoor barbeques. As night falls, Santander starts to drink. Students frequent the area around **Pl. Cañadío, C. Pedrueca,** and **C. Daoíz y Velarde,** and up the hill from Pl. Cañadío on **Pasadillo de Zorilla.**

> **Blues,** Pl. Cañadío. Thirtysomething jazz fans mingle under huge plastic statues of jazz greats.
>
> **Zeppelin,** Po. Menéndez Pelayo, near C. Santa Lucía. A popular spot on a chic street that rages after 1am.

In the **El Sardinero** district, tourists and students mix all night long. **Pl. Italia** and nearby **C. Panamá** are the hotspots in this neighborhood.

> **Gran Casino,** Pl. Italia. An imposing white elephant perfect for an evening of *Belle Époque* gambling. Passport and proper dress required. Open 7pm-4am. Admission 400ptas.
>
> **Rebeca** and **Albatros,** C. Panamá. Innumerable students.
>
> **Amarras,** behind the Casino. Packed with the thirtyish crowd.

The **Festival Internacional de Santander** follows immediately after Donostia/San Sebastián's famous fest at the end of July. So during August, Santander's citizens (and people from Donostia who aren't done partying) enjoy a myriad of music and dance recitals. The events culminate in the **Concurso Internacional de Piano de Santander.** Daily classical concerts ring through Pl. Porticada; recent festivals have featured the London Symphony Orchestra and the Bolshoi Ballet. Fabulously high-priced tickets are sold in booths on Po. Pereda and Pl. Porticada; a few are under 1000ptas. (Consult the Oficina del Festival, Av. Calvo Sotelo, 15, 6th fl.; tel. 21 05 08, 21 03 45; fax 31 47 67.) The new **Auditorio,** a grand venue of controversial design for classical music and ballet, has just opened.

Near Santander

Since only a handful of people each day get into the Cuevas de Altamira (see Cantabrian and Asturian Coast), many spelunk in the lesser-known town of **Puente Viesgo,** about 30km south of Santander. The **Cuevas del Castillo** (tel. 59 84 25) display paintings nearly as well-preserved as those in Altamira. (Open Tues.-Sun. 10am-12:15pm and 3-6:15pm. Admission 250ptas.) Continental **buses** stop in Puente Viesgo en route from Santander to Burgos (2 per day, 45min., 425ptas).

Cantabrian and Asturian Coast

Perfect daytrip material, fishing villages and beach towns dot the soft and sandy shore of Cantabria and Asturias. La Cantabríca buses follow the coast and link most of these towns with each other and with Santander.

Santillana del Mar

This town-of-three-lies is neither *Santa* (holy), *llana* (flat), nor *del Mar* (on the sea). The Spanish government declared the village a national monument for good reason: some of its adorable stone houses and cobblestoned streets date from as far back as the 9th century. In fact, it's possible to trace the evolution of Spanish architecture from the 13th to the 18th century in the very streets of this village.

Emblazoned above the door of virtually every house is a heraldic shield proclaiming the rank and honor of former noble residents. The shield at **La Casa de los Villa,** near the bus stop, proudly proclaims the glory of honorable death. The current inhabitants don't seem to mind the gawkers and photographers; many residents have converted their doorways into stands selling the local, delectable (if overpriced) sweet milk, *bizcocho* (sponge cake), and ceramics.

The **Colegiata de Santa Juliana,** a 12th-century Romanesque church, occupies one end of C. Santo Domingo. The charming, ivy-covered **claustro** has some fragmented capitals of Jesus and his disciples. The 12th-century reform of the Cistercian Order prohibited the representation of any human form on pillars—hence the vegetable patterns. (Open daily 10am-1pm and 4-7:30pm. Admission 100ptas.)

In a town that's a museum itself, the **Museo Diocesano** is the only official one. Religious art and artifacts spread throughout the harmonious Romanesque cloister and corridors of the Monasterio Regina Coeli. One display, put together by Benedictine monks from Burgos, explains how polychromed wood sculptures are enameled. Another room is devoted to the process of wood carving. (Museo open 10am-1pm and 4-7pm. Admission 100ptas.)

Don't be lured by the *hostales* on the highway near the bus stop; *casa particulares* right in town are sure to be cheaper. The tourist office can help find one. **Pensión Angélica** (tel. 81 82 38), on C. Hornos off Pl. Ramón Pelayo (look for the *habitaciones* sign), is as beautiful inside as it looks from the outside, with a black iron gate and flowers. Flowered bedspreads and wooden fixtures make it feel like Bob Newhart's inn. (Singles 2000ptas. Doubles 2500ptas.) Nearby **Posada Santa Juliana,** on C. Carrera, 19 (tel. 84 01 06) is equally sweet. Some rooms have exposed wood beams, and all have TV, quilts, and downy pillows. (Doubles 4500ptas-6000ptas; Sept.-June 3500ptas.) Less than 1km away on the road to Comillas is **Camping Santillana** (tel. 81 82 50). Don't mistake the deluxe 1st-class site for a *parador*: Not only does it boast a panoramic view of the town, it also has a supermarket, shiny cafeteria, pool, miniature golf, and tennis courts. (Reception open 8:30am-10pm. 475ptas per person, 400-425ptas per tent, 425ptas per car. Golf and tennis 200ptas per person and per hr.)

The closest thing to budget fare is a 950ptas *menú* at the stone-walled and wooden-columned **Casa Cossío**, C. El Río and Pl. Francisco Navarro (tel. 81 83 55; open 10:30am-11:30pm). **Asador la Huerta**, between C. del Escultor Jesús Otero and C. Cantón, is a large outdoor cafetería with a cheery orange and yellow tent to fend off rain and depression. *Platos combinados* 650-725ptas.

Ana runs the show at the **tourist office** in the Casa del Águila y la Parra, across from the *parador de turismo* in Pl. Ramón Pelayo. She'll help find lodgings, describe the town's sights, and might even kiss you goodbye. (Open Mon.-Sat. 9:30am-1pm and 4-7pm, Sun. 10:30am-1:30pm and 4-7:30pm.) Exiting Turismo and turning left leads to the **post office** (open Mon.-Fri. 8am-3pm, Sat. 9am-1pm). The **postal code** is 39330. **Telephones** neighbor the post office, and from June to September a phone stand operates down by the municipal parking lot. (Open 11am-10pm.)

Santillana makes a fine daytrip from Santander (26km away) by **bus.** La Cantábrica (tel. 72 08 22) sends six buses per day (Sept.-June 3 per day, 45min., 235ptas) from Pl. Estaciones in Santander. Ask the tourist office for an exact schedule.

Cuevas de Altamira

Bisons roam and horses graze on the ceilings of the limestone **Cuevas de Altamira** (2km from Santillana del Mar), sometimes called the "Sistine Chapel of Primitive Art" by gushing art historians and archeologists. The large-scale polychrome paintings are known for scrupulous attention to naturalistic detail (such as genitalia and the texture of hides) and resourceful use of the caves' natural texture. To see what are probably the most famous anthropomorphic figures with animal heads on earth, you must obtain written permission from the Centro de Investigación de Altamira, Santillana del Mar, Cantabria, Spain 39330 (tel. 81 80 05). Send a photocopy of your passport. You must write 10 months in advance. Only 10 people per day get to make the 15-minute tour. If you can't get in, snivel and wander through the **museum** of prehistory. (Open Mon.-Sat. 10am-1pm and 4-6pm, Sun. 10am-1pm. Free.)

To walk here, follow the signs from Santillana past the abandoned **Iglesia de San Sebastián**, now a hot spot for picnickers. Make a detour through the streets of Herrán, and turn right into the corn field at the wooden barrier on the other side of town.

Comillas

Comillas is an understated resort favored by Spain's noble families, who retain their modest palaces along with their anachronistic titles. One of the only places in historically leftist northern Spain where people can refer to themselves as count or duchess with a straight face, the town reeks of conservativism that is diluted only by the thousands of young people tracking sand through the streets each summer.

Broad **Playa Comillas**, haunt of the titled, ends in a small port. Quieter **Oyambre**, 2km away, stretches twice the length and has half the tourists. Many petite palaces and an enormous Jesuit **colegio** rise in Gothic splendor between the sea and Picos de Europa. A looming neo-Gothic **palacio** outside of town has gardens open to the public. (Open 10am-1pm and 3-8pm.) Nearby, **El Capricho**, a small stone palace by Gaudí, has become a very good, very expensive restaurant. It's one of only three Gaudís outside of Catalunya; the other two are in León and Astorga.

In the **Convento de Ruiloba**, a 30-minute walk down the road (the apparent shortcut through the fields isn't), cloistered nuns sell hand-painted ceramics. Ring the bell and the merchandise magically appears on a lazy susan in the rock wall.

Comillas is an active little town thanks to summer residents and a disproportionate number of clothing stores. It comes to life during the weekend of July 15 when the **fiestas** go up in a blaze of fireworks. Have a go at greased pole-walking, goose-chasing, and dancing in the plaza. Dance the rest of the summer away at **El Bote**, on the sand at the end of the parking lot.

Plan on camping or paying extra for a decent bed. **Hostal Esmeralda,** C. Antonio López, 7 (tel. 72 00 97), has antique-furnished rooms with windows that stretch from the wood floors to the ceiling moldings. (Singles 3000ptas, with bath 3500ptas. Doubles 5000ptas, with bath 6000ptas.) **Pensión la Aldea,** C. Aldea, 5 (tel. 72 03 00), has a bar downstairs with kegs aching to be tapped. (Doubles 3500ptas.) Frills at **Pensión Tuco,** C. Antonio López, 4 (tel. 72 10 30), by Hostal Esmeralda, include wood armoires, quilted bedspreads, and lots of plants. (Singles 3000ptas. Doubles 3500ptas, with bath 4500ptas. Sept. 16-May: 2500ptas; 2500ptas, 3500ptas.) **Camping de Comillas** (tel. 72 00 74) is a first-class site on the water. There's a supermarket, cafeteria, laundromat, and beautiful views. (400ptas per person, 1590ptas per *parcela*. Open June-Sept.) Nearby **Camping El Helguero** (tel. 72 21 24), 3km from Santillana in **Ruiloba,** rivals the Comillas site. In addition to a supermarket, restaurant, café, and laundromat, they've a swimming pool. Buses from Santander's bus station wheel here about 5 times per day. (325ptas per person, 325-450ptas per tent, 325ptas per car.)

As the name suggests, **Restaurante los Mellizos,** on C. Constanillo de la Cruz, is run by twins. One makes an inspired rum *sangría,* while together they whip up the spiciest *mariscadas* (shellfish) in town. **Cafetería el Artico,** next to the post office, has a 1000ptas *menú* and tempting ice cream in the front of the bar. *Platos combinados* 450-640ptas. (Open 10am-midnight.) In Plaza Generalisimo Franco, **Bodega el Siglo** has yummy *costillas* (ribs) for 500ptas. *Bocadillos* run 275-400ptas, and *tapas* slightly more (open 9am-2am). The supermarket **SPAR** is on the corner of Po. Infantas and C. Solatorre, back from the bus stop. (Open Mon.-Sat. 9am-2pm and 4:30-9pm.)

The **tourist office,** C. Aldea, 2 (tel. 72 07 68), stocks bus and excursion information and a list of *casas particulares.* The only map costs 100ptas and is useless. (Open 10am-1pm and 4-7pm.) The **post office** is on C. Antonio Lopez, 6. (Open Mon.-Fri. 8am-3pm, Sat. 9am-1pm.) **Telephones** ring up the street from Turismo; take a sharp left up the little hill. (Open 10:30am-2pm and 5-11pm.)

At 18km from Santillana del Mar and 49km from Santander, Comillas is an easy daytrip from either. La Cantábrica (tel. 72 08 22) **buses** run from Santander (6 per day, Sept.-June 3 per day; 305 ptas). Alternatively, the **train** goes as far as **Torrelavega,** from whence a bus runs to Comillas.

San Vicente de la Barquera

San Vicente is a rapidly growing jigsaw puzzle of modern hotels and older houses just west of Comillas. The 12th-century church-fortress **Santa María de los Angeles** has a handsome Romanesque portico and the delightful Renaissance tomb of Antonio Corro, the infamous 16th-century Grand Inquisitor. His effigy lounges jauntily, reading about a nun from Soria whom he ordered burned for heresy.

From the expansive sands of **Playa Merón,** 15 minutes' walk away on the other side of the river, there are fabulous views of the Picos de Europa. Nearby beaches of **Merón** and **El Rosal** may entertain. San Vicente does manage to rally for **La Folia,** held the first Sunday after Easter. The torchlit seaside procession coincides with high tide, while a costumed Virgen de la Barquera parades through the streets. The madness is followed by dancing in the plaza that night.

The most convenient hotel is **Hostal La Paz,** C. Mercado, 2 (tel. 71 01 80), in the plaza where the bus stops. A yellow sign points the way. (Singles 2600ptas. Doubles 3800ptas. June: 2000ptas; 3200ptas. Oct.-May: 1600ptas; 2700ptas.) Around the corner, the agreeable **Fonda Liébana** on C. Ronda (tel. 71 02 11), at the top of the stairs off Pl. Canton, is quite popular with the locals. Deluxe rooms (at deluxe prices) have TV and full bath. (Singles 3000ptas. Doubles 3500ptas, with 2 beds 4500ptas.) To find **Camping El Rosal** (tel. 71 01 65), cross the bridge by the bus stop and Red Cross stand and keep going (20min.). An area with stores, like a little town, surrounds the 2nd-class site near the beach: lively *cafetería* and bar, supermarket, laundry, currency exchange, and camping equipment rental. They also provide some information on excursions to towns in the vicinity. (Reception open daily 9am-10pm. 375ptas per person, 330ptas per tent, 375ptas per car. Open Semana Santa-Sept.)

Most restaurants on Av. Generalísimo are generic and overpriced, but their seafood is fresh. **Bodega Marinera,** C. Arena, 10, serves *paella* (800ptas) outdoors until midnight. Under the stone arch at the other end of town, **Restaurante El Puerto** on Av. Generalísimo cooks up a 900ptas *menú*.

The **tourist office** (tel. 71 07 97), on main street Av. Generalísimo, helps with accommodations. (Open Semana Santa and July-Sept. Mon.-Sat. 9am-9pm.) The **post office** is at C. Miramar, 9 (tel. 71 02 19), on the busy street that runs down the waterfront at right angles to Av. Generalísimo. (Open Mon.-Fri. 8am-3pm, Sat. 9am-1pm.) **Telephones** are in front of the Red Cross stand at the bus stop, by the water. (Open Mon.-Fri. 10am-2pm and 5-11pm, Sat.-Sun. and holidays 10am-2pm.) **Taxis** answer at tel. 71 08 80. Tend to hygiene at the **public showers** and **toilets** (end of Av. Generalísimo, to the right exiting Turismo; showers 200ptas, toilets 50ptas). The **Red Cross** (tel. 71 09 20) is at the bus stop on Av. Generalísimo. The **Guardia Civil** (tel. 71 00 07) is at C. Padre Antonio, 8, behind the *murallas*.

Six **buses** per day run from Santander to San Vicente in July and August (1 1/2 hr.). Call **La Cantábrica** (tel. 72 08 22) for schedules. **Turytrans** (tel. 21 56 50) also covers the same dirt (1 1/2 hr., 560ptas).

Llanes

The most popular and major **beach** on the Asturian coast is Llanes. Its bit of coast is not yet overdeveloped, and it draws Asturians by the gross. The breezy promontory hangs over a blue horizon, the dramatic remnants of the 13th-century walls, and the ruined palace of the Dukes of Estrada. Monument fans should peek at the **Iglesia de Santa María del Conceyu's** early 16th-century Plateresque altar and ornately detailed (but badly worn) portal. Violets creep across the walls of the white church in summer; inside, high stained-glass windows spill colorful light across the pews. (Open for mass Mon.-Fri. 11am and 8pm; Sat. 11am, 8pm, and 9pm; Sun. 9:30am, 11:30am, 1pm, and 7pm.)

Far and away the best place to sleep, **Casa del Río** at Av. San Pedro, 3 (tel. 540 11 91) is in a red house behind light blue iron gates. Facing Turismo, hang a left to the first real street. It has excellent rooms, some with *two* balconies, very close to the beach. (Singles 2000ptas. Doubles 4000ptas. Sept.-June 14: 1500-1800ptas; 3000-3500ptas.) Centrally located **Pensión La Guía** (tel. 540 25 77), Pl. Parres Sobrino, 1, is beneath the stone archway in the thick of the action. (Singles 1800ptas. Doubles 2500ptas. Triples 3750ptas. Open May-Sept.) Campers may have to eeny-meeny-miny-moe over nearby sites. First-class **Las Barcenas** (tel. 540 15 70), with showers, medical facilities, and currency exchange, sits right past the bus station. (Reception open 8am-11pm. 375ptas per person, 550ptas per tent. Open June-Sept.) **El Brao** (tel. 540 00 14), a large site with showers, currency exchange, cafeteria, and supermarket, is a mere 15m outside town. (Reception open 8:30am-midnight. 360ptas per person and per tent, 330 ptas per car. Open June-Sept.)

Bar El Muelle, C. Las Barqueras, across the river over the bridge from the old quarter, has its menu posted on a tree. Sounds of the terrace café below waft through the windows. A wise splurge is **Restaurante La Villa** at C. Jenaro Riestra, 2 (tel. 540 23 84), near the beach. The *menú* costs 1200ptas, but satisfies utterly. Anything else will send you to the poorhouse. Wear your best jeans; the check is presented in a silver box. (Open July 15-Sept. 15 1:30-5pm and 8pm-midnight.) Supermarket **Autoservicio Briñasoles,** near Bar El Muelle on C. Las Barqueras, sells groceries opposite Banco Central across the river from the old quarter. (Open Mon.-Sat. 9am-1:30pm and 4-8pm.)

Busy **Turismo** (tel. 540 01 64) shares its space with the Ayuntamiento. Their adorable map has a representation of every building in town, but many streets lack names. (Open Mon.-Sat. 10am-1:30pm and 4-6:30pm, Sun. 10am-1:30pm.) The **post office** (tel. 540 11 14) is on C. Pidal. From Turismo, head left in the direction of the bus station. (Open Mon.-Fri. 8am-3pm, Sat. 9am-1pm.) The **postal code** is 33500. **Telephones** are in Pl. Parres Sobrino from June to September only. (Open 10am-2pm and 5-11pm.) For medical services, call the **Red Cross** (tel. 540 10 60) or **Ambulatorio de** la **Seguridad Social** (tel. 540 02 20) at C. Nemesio Sobrino, 25 (emergency room of public hospital). For an **ambulance,** call tel. 540 10 60. The **Policía Municipal** (tel. 540 18 87) is on C. Nemesio Sobrino (near Turismo). For the **Guardia Civil,** C. La Galea, call 540 00 70.

The **bus** and train stations are at opposite ends of town. **ALSA-Turytrans** (tel. 540 24 85) runs buses from Santander to Llanes (5 per day, 2hr., 690ptas). From Oviedo, **Económicos (EASA)** will also get you there (6 per day, 2hr., 795ptas). To reach the center from the bus station exit, take a left and go down C. Cueto Bajo until Correos, then turn left and keep going.

The quirky, capricious FEVE **train station** lives at the end of Av. Estación. To find Turismo, exit the station and turn right at the first cross street, C. Egidio Gavito. Trains limp to Santander (2 per day, 2 1/2 hr., 630ptas) and Oviedo (3 per day, 2 1/2 hr., 695ptas).

Euskadi (País Vasco, Basque Country)

Hilly, forested Euskadi remains for the most part unsullied, despite heavy industrialization in Bilbo's estuary. The rain in Spain falls mainly on the beaches of the northern coast, a relief from the summer sizzle of the central plains. Euskadi is made up of three provinces: Gipuzkoa (Guipozcoa in Castilian), with its capital in Donostia/San Sebastián; Bizkaia (Vizcaya), centered about Bilbo (Bilbao); and Araba (Alava), whose capital Vitoria-Gasteiz is also administrative capital of the whole.

Culturally the Basques are a people apart. Outside of Euskadi, Basques live in sizable concentrations in southwestern France, northern Navarra, Idaho, Texas, and Nevada. Linguists still disagree on the origin of *euskera,* an agglomerate non-Indoeuropean language that has similarities to both Caucasian and African tongues, suggesting the prehistoric Basques may have migrated from the Caucasus through Africa. Historically referred to by other Spaniards as *la lengua del diablo* (the devil's tongue), *euskera* has become a symbol of cultural self-determination. It's spoken chiefly in Gipuzkoa, Bizkaia, and northern Navarra by perhaps half a million native speakers, a minority in every region. Vigorous regional television channels, a press, an innovative film industry, and primary and adult instruction have arrested the erosion of the language. As recently-won autonomy depoliticizes the linguistic question, some of the Basque intelligentsia are beginning to question the wisdom of a tongue that cuts them off from the rest of Spanish and Latin American culture.

Written *euskera* is phonetic, often in a stylized alphabet. Basque-language signs have replaced some Castilian ones altogether, particularly in the smaller towns. We provide both names if there's any potential confusion, with the Castilian in parentheses in primarily *euskera*-ed towns.

Iberians, Celts, Romans, Visigoths, Moors, and others have tried—and failed—to conquer the Basques. The medieval preeminence of Castilla can at least partly be ascribed to their alliance with the hardy Basques. Like the Navarrese, Basque medieval *fueros* (laws) were largely honored by Castilian monarchs until the 19th-century Carlist Wars. The administrative autonomy recovered in 1979 puts Basques at the helm once again of all but their foreign affairs.

Although the region is officially autonomous, a minority of Basques seek full independence. Under the Franco regime, Euskadi Ta Askatasuna (ETA) began an anti-Madrid terrorist movement that has lasted over 30 years. The radical ETA-affiliated party, Herri Batasuna, draws insignificant popular support, and ETA's violent tactics are roundly eschewed. Since autonomy it's been fighting a losing war for popular sympathy. In any event, save for some increasingly desperate recent hits, targets are almost exclusively military, usually young Guardia Civil recruits from other regions stationed on rotation in Euskadi.

Few traditions can match the depth and sophistication of Basque cuisine. Gastronomic clubs (until recently all male) are a tradition in Donostia, where members vie with each other in the invention of new dishes. Spaniards throughout the peninsula prize *bacalao a la vizcaina* (salted cod in a tomato sauce), preparations *a la vasca* (in a delicate parsley-steeped white wine sauce), and *chipirones en su tinta* (cuttlefish in their own ink).

All regional tourist offices stock a guide for Compostelan pilgrims and art lovers called *Los Caminos de Santiago* (The Roads to Saint James) and the comprehensive booklet *Los Museos de Euskadi* (The Museums of the Basque Country). Rural tourism is being heavily promoted by the regional authorities (lodgings in renovated farmhouses and cottages 1000-2000ptas), here as elsewhere in Spain; tourist offices in major Basque cities are stocked with brochures on this *agroturismo*.

Bilbo (Bilbao)

Bilbo is capital of Bizkaia and the commercial, financial, and industrial engine of Euskadi. Few visitors come, scared off by the city's reputation as the Pittsburgh or Manchester of Spain. But even before the current spree of renovations got underway, those who could see past the industrial suburbs, smokestacks, abandoned warehouses, and sooty facades delighted in the city's almost comically picturesque site on steep hills, medieval quarter tucked in the crook of a great river estuary, and the grandiose remains of its 19th-century economic and cultural ambitions.

Historically, the port of Bilbo served as the key sea link between Castilla and Flanders, and the city was the birthplace of mercantile and commercial law emulated worldwide in the 16th century. Bilbo has also given its share of nationalists: Sabino Arana, founder of the Basque nationalist party Herri Batasuna, and José Antonio Agirre, the first *Lehendakari* (president) of the Basque government.

Meanwhile, Bilbo chugs along like an old train. Hard at work as usual, the city forgot to participate in the national wave of primping and preening for the now-legendary 1992. But Bilbo's work will pay off in good time—look out 1997. The Metro (already underway) is scheduled to be ready by then, and plans for a central bus station are also shooting for the millenium. Don't judge the city by the dirt under its nails—with an outstanding art museum, several parks, and orgiastic nightlife, Bilbo rewards the persistent.

Orientation and Practical Information

Bilbo has two quarters, the modern quarter and the *casco viejo*, across the Ría de Bilbao. In the new quarter and two blocks from the river, the main artery **Gran Vía de Don Diego López de Haro** sprouts from one side of **Plaza de España**. Nearly all important transport terminals, stops, and stations cluster around Pl. España and its offshoots, whereas the city's parks and scenic plazas spread out from the Gran Vía.

Puente del Arenal, only two blocks from Pl. España, bridges the river to link the new town with the so-called "seven streets" of the **casco viejo. Plaza de Arriaga,** at the foot of Puente del Arenal, is the *casco viejo*'s main plaza.

From any one of the sixteen bus stations, navigate toward the Gran Vía, which leads to Pl. España, Puente del Arenal, and the *casco viejo*.

> **Tourist Office: Oficina de Turismo de Bilbao,** Bajas del Teatro Arriaga (tel. 424 48 19). From Pl. España, take C. Navarra to the Puente del Arenal. Pl. Arriaga is just across the river, the theater to the right. Eager beaver staff speaks English. Their booklet about Bilbo practically puts us out of business. Publishes a monthly bulletin on city events. Open Mon.-Fri. 9am-1:30pm and 3:30-7:30pm.
>
> **El Corte Inglés:** Gran Vía, 7-9 (tel. 424 22 11), on the east side of the Pl. España. They have a **map. Currency exchange:** 1% commission (250ptas min. charge). They also offer novels and guidebooks in English; haircutting; both cafeteria and restaurant; and **telephones.** Open Mon.-Sat. 10am-9pm.

Bilbo (Bilbao)   191

Budget Student Travel Office: TIVE, Gran Vía, 50 (tel. 441 42 77), 8 bl. east of Pl. España. Open Mon.-Fri. 9am-2pm.

Consulate: U.K., Alameda Urquijo, 2, 7th fl. (tel. 415 76 00), from Pl. España down Gran Vía and left at El Corte Inglés. Open Mon.-Fri. 9am-1:30pm.

Currency Exchange: Hotel Ercilla, C. Ercilla, 37 (tel. 443 88 00, 410 20 00), from Pl. España down Gran Vía to Pl. Federico Moyúa, then left on C. Ercilla. 1% commission (250ptas min. charge). Open 24 hrs. **El Corte Inglés** (see above). Open for exchange Mon.-Sat. 10am-8pm.

American Express: Viajes Cafranga, Alameda de Recalde, 68 (tel. 444 48 58), off Autonomía. Open Mon.-Fri. 9am-1:30pm and 4:30-7:30pm, Sat. 10am-1pm.

Post Office: Main office, Alameda Urquijo, 19 (tel. 422 05 48, fax 443 00 24). Walk 1 bl. down Gran Vía from Pl. España and turn left after El Corte Inglés; it's on the corner with C. Bertendona. Open for information Mon.-Fri. 8am-10pm; for stamps 8am-10pm; for Lista de Correos Mon.-Fri. 8am-10pm, Sat. 9am-2pm; for **telegrams** and **fax** Mon.-Fri. 8am-midnight, Sat.-Sun. 8am-10pm. **Postal Code:** 48071.

Telephones: C. Barroeta Aldámar, 7. From Pl. España walk 2 bl. down C. Buenos Aires, turn left on C. Colón de Larreategui, then an immediate right. Open Mon.-Sat. 9am-9pm. **Telephone Code:** 94.

Flights: (tel. 453 13 50), 10km from Bilbo in Sondika (Sondica). To get there take Bizkai Bus A-3821 (Transportes Colectivos tel. 475 82 00) from Pl. España (75ptas). Served by all major European airlines. **Iberia** office, C. Ercilla, 20 (tel. 424 43 00; at airport 471 12 10), at the corner of C. Colón de Larreátegui. Open Mon.-Fri. 9am-1:15pm and 3:30-6:45pm.

Trains: Bilbo has at least 6 train stations, each with at least two names; the 4 major ones cleave to the old town and the river.

RENFE: Estación de Abando/del Norte, Pl. España, 2 (tel. 423 96 36, 423 86 23). Ticket booth open 7am-11pm. To: Madrid (4 per day; 5 3/4 -8 1/2 hr.; *talgo* 3960ptas, *expreso* 3680ptas); Barcelona (2 per day, 9 1/2 -11 1/2 hr., 3765-4780ptas); A Coruña (1 per day, 11 1/2 hr., 4130-5365ptas); Sevilla (3 days per wk. 1 per day, 13 1/2 hr., 6135ptas).

FEVE: Estación de Portugalete/de Ferrocarriles de Vía Estrecha, C. Bailen, 2 (tel. 423 22 66). From Pl. España walk down C. Navarra towards the river and take a right just before the bridge. A huge tiled building on the water. Information open Mon.-Fri. 7am-10pm. To: Santander (5 per day, 2 1/2 hr., 725ptas); Oviedo (2 per day, 5hr., 2050ptas); Ferrol (2 per day, 7hr., 3975ptas).

Ferrocarriles Vascongados (FFVV)/Eusko Trenbideak (ET): Has two train stations. **Estación Las Arenas/de San Nicolás/del Arenal,** Plazuela de San Nicolás (tel. 433 80 07). From Pl. España, walk down C. Navarra across the bridge and take a left on C. Arenal to the *plazuela*; enter under the clock. To the beach at Plentzia (at 6am and 11pm, 45min., 145ptas). **Estación de Atxuri** (tel. 433 80 07, 433 80 08). From Pl. España walk down C. Navarra, cross the river, and take a right through Pl. Arriaga and down C. Ribera for a fair stretch. To Gernika (every hr., 50min., 220ptas) and Donostia/San Sebastián (4-7 per day, 2 1/2 hr., 580ptas).

Buses: Bilbo's bus system is even harder to figure out than the train system. Sixteen lines with departure points throughout the city; 6 stand out.

ANSA (GETSA, VIACAR), C. Autonomía, 17 (tel. 444 31 00). From Pl. España down C. Hurtado de Amézaga to Pl. Zabálburu, bearing right on C. Autonomía for 2 bl.; enter through Bar Ansa. To: Burgos (7 per day, 3hr., 1175ptas); Madrid (9 per day, 5hr., 2810ptas); Barcelona (4 per day, 6-7hr., 4760ptas); León (2 per day, 7hr., 2330ptas).

Compañía Automóviles Vascongados (CAV), Pl. Encarnación, 7 (tel. 433 12 79 or 433 35 93), to the left after exiting Estación de Abando. Go to the tunnel for info and departures. To Gernika (7-10 per day, 45min., 245ptas) and Lekeitio (Mon.-Sat. 6 per day, Sun. 2 per day; 45min.; 455ptas).

ENATCAR, C. Pedro Martinez Artola (te. 444 00 25), off Pl. Zabálburu. Ticket booth open Mon.-Sat. 9am-1pm and 4-8pm, Sun. 9am-noon. Buses depart from adjacent Pl. Zabálburu. To: Zaragoza (6 per day, 4hr., 1250ptas); Valladolid (4 per day, 5hr., 1930ptas); Badajoz (1 per day, 12hr., 4990ptas).

PESA, C. Hurtado de Amézaga (tel. 416 94 79, 424 88 99), in the RENFE building. Buses depart from C. Luchana. From Pl. España walk 3 bl. on C. Hurtado de Amézaga, cross the bridge, and take the next right. To Donostia/San Sebastián (12 per day, 1 1/4 hr., 880ptas) and Hendaya (4 per day, 2 1/4 hr., 1000ptas).

La Unión, C. Henao, 29 (tel. 424 08 36). From Pl. España walk down Gran Vía, turn right onto Alameda Mazarredo, follow for 4 bl., then take the next left on C. Henao. To: Vitoria (9 per day, 1 1/2 hr., 530ptas); Logroño (3 per day, 4hr., 1200ptas); Pamplona (4 per day, 2 1/2 hr., 1225ptas); Zaragoza (Sat.-Mon. 3 per day, 3 1/2 hr., 1885ptas).

ALSA-Intercar, Alameda de Recalde, 68 (tel. 444 48 58), near Pl. Amézola. To: Santander (12 per day, 2 1/4 hr., 755ptas); Irún (6 per day, 1 3/4 hr., 930ptas); A Coruña (1 per day, 14hr., 5055ptas).

Public Transportation: Bilbobús (tel. 435 82 00) runs 26 lines across the city (6am-11:30pm, 80ptas). The tourist office has a detailed map. **Bizkai Bus** connects Bilbo to suburbs and the airport in Sondika (55-160ptas). (A **subway** running through the center of the new city and the *casco viejo* is scheduled to begin operation by the time your children visit in 1997.)

Taxis: Radio Taxi Bizkaia (tel. 416 23 00). **Radio Taxi Bilbao** (tel. 443 52 00, 444 88 88). **Teletaxi** (tel. 444 23 33). The tourist office map marks taxi queues. To airport 1100ptas.

Car Rental: Avis, Alameda Dr. Areilza, 34 (tel. 427 57 60). From Pl. España walk 9 bl. down Gran Vía (away from the river) and turn left; on the corner of C. Simón Bolívar. Must be 23. Renault V *tarifa amiga* 3990ptas. Open Mon.-Fri. 8am-1:30pm and 4-7pm, Sat. 8am-1pm. **Europcar,** C. Rodríguez Arias, 49 (442 22 26), 3 bl. past AmEx office at the corner of C. Máximo Aguirre. Must be 21. Renault V Oasis 4000ptas per day, 40ptas per km. Open Mon.-Fri. 9am-1pm and 4-7:30pm, Sat. 9am-1pm. **Hertz,** C. Dr. Nicolás Achúcarro, 10 (tel. 415 36 77). From Pl. España walk about 7 bl. down Gran Vía, turn left on C. Iparraguirre, and left again. Must be 21. Ford Fiesta 4710ptas per day, 36ptas per km. Open Mon.-Fri. 9am-1pm and 4-7:30pm, Sat. 9-11:30am.

Luggage Storage: In the **Estación de Abando** (lockers 300ptas). Open 7am-11pm.

Lost Property: tel. 420 50 00.

English Bookstores: El Corte Inglés (see above). Always dependable, always convenient. **Casa del Libro,** C. Colón de Larreátegui, 44 (tel. 424 07 04), off Alameda de Recalde. Guidebooks in English, literature, poetry, trashy novels, and a fair-to-good selection of CliffNotes.

Library: Biblioteca Municipal, C. Bidebarrieta, 4 (tel. 415 69 30), in the *casco viejo*. From Pl. España take C. Navarra across the bridge, hang a right through Pl. Arriaga, and walk straight across C. Ribera. Open Mon.-Fri. 9am-1:30pm and 4-7:30pm.

Red Cross: For emergencies (tel. 422 22 22).

24-Hour Pharmacy: Check listing on the door of any pharmacy, or ask the municipal police.

Medical Services: Hospital Civil de Basurto, Av. de Montevideo, s/n (tel. 441 88 00, 442 40 51). **Ambulance** (tel. 410 06 03).

Police: Municipal, C. Luís Briñas (tel. 420 50 00, in emergency 092). **National** (tel. 421 00 00, in emergency 091).

Accommodations

Other than the August festival season, most areas have never heard the words *temporada alta* (high season). The tourist office has a list of recommended budget *pensiones,* most of which are in the *casco viejo*. The **Plaza Arriaga** is at the base of the bridge, down the stairs to the right; **Calle Arenal** runs up to the left.

Pensión Ladero, C. Lotería, 1, 5th fl. (tel. 415 09 32). From Pl. Arriaga, take C. Bidebarrieta and turn left on C. Lotería. Every huge room has a chandelier and most have terraces. Since a painter lives here, many rooms have oil paintings. Spotless bathrooms. Singles 1500ptas. Doubles 2400ptas. Triples 3600ptas.

Pensión Mardones, C. Jardines, 4, 3rd fl. (tel. 415 31 05). From the bridge, take C. Bidebarrieta and turn right. Brand spanking new, down to the light blue blankets and sheets on the firm mattresses. Some balconied rooms with geraniums. Singles 1500ptas. Doubles 2200ptas.

Pensión Mendez, C. Santa María, 13 (tel. 416 03 64). From the bridge, turn right on C. Ribera; C. Santa María is on the left, at the end of the street on the left. Two somber stone dogs greet visitors in the downstairs hall, but there's nothing forbidding about this *pensión*. Five floors insulate the pensión from the raging nightlife below. Glossy bedspreads and firm mattresses. Gossip mags in the waiting room. Singles 1500ptas. Doubles 2500ptas. Triples 3000ptas.

Pensión de la Fuente, C. Sombrería, 2 (tel. 416 99 89). From mid-C. Arenal, turn left on C. Correo, follow 1 bl., then left again. Clean carpeted halls and large tiled bathrooms. Small, well-furnished singles. Try for the double with the couch, or else loiter in the airy TV room. Singles 1000-1500ptas. Doubles 2000-2500ptas, with bath 3500ptas.

Hostal Arana, C. Bidebarrieta, 2 (tel. 415 64 11), amid all the trendy shops off Pl. Arriaga. Pink arched halls and a nautical style reception area. Very luxe and pricey. There are phones in each room, and there's even an elevator. Prices don't include IVA. Singles 3000ptas. Doubles 2800ptas, with bath 4800ptas. Triples 4700ptas, with bath 6000ptas. Breakfast 275ptas. Open Jan. 7-Dec. 23.

Pensión Jofra, C. Elcano, 34, 2nd fl. (tel. 421 29 49), our only listing in the new city. From Pl. España, walk 5 bl. down C. Hurtado de Amézaga past Estación de Abando and turn left. Elegant wallpaper. Singles 1350ptas. Doubles 2400ptas. Open Sept.-July.

Hospedaje Ulloa, C. Somera, 6, 2nd fl. (tel. 412 44 03), in the old city south of the other pensions. From the bridge, take C. Ribera past the market and turn left onto C. Somera. Microscopic rooms. No intercom—the manager will probably throw you a key. Singles 1000ptas. Doubles 2000ptas. Hot showers 100ptas.

Food

Restaurants and bars on the "seven streets" are as cramped as the medieval *casco viejo* itself, but are convenient to most of the sights. Dining spots in the more expansive, modern quarter of the city offer more variety and amenities. Most establishments serve their *menú del día* only at lunch.

Mercado de Atxuri, riverside en route to Estación de Atxuri, has fish downstairs and meat, produce, and bread on the main level. (Open Mon.-Thurs. and Sat. 7:45am-2pm, Fri. 7:45am-2pm and 5-8pm.)

Groceries: Eroski, C. Licenciado Poza, between Alameda del Dr. Areilza and C. Gregorio Revilla. Open Mon.-Fri. 9am-1:45pm and 5:45-7:45pm, Sat. 9am-1:30pm.

Charcutería Claudio, C. Esperanza, 11, past the train station on the left. *"La feria del jamón"* is their motto. Go ham go! Hams and cloves of garlic hang from *every* inch of the ceiling. *Vive le jambon!* Ham in every conceivable permutation. *Jamón serrano* (mountain-cured ham), cheese, and hearty bread with a beverage under 500ptas. *Mi piace la porchetta!* Sandwiches 125-175ptas. *¡Te amo, jamonita!* Open 10:30am-2pm and 6-11pm.

Restaurante Juanak, C. Somera, 10. Cute menu, cute canapés, cute waiters. Choice array of salads 400-525ptas. *Tabla de quesos* 900ptas. Open 10:30am-12:30am, later on weekends.

Bar-Restaurante Bizkaia II, C. Jardines, 2. From the river turn left onto C. Santa Maria, then right on C. Jardines. You want authentic? Sawdust on the floor, kegs and wine cartons all around, and *fútbol* team photos on the wall. Hometown fave. *Menú* with *paella* and *merluza* 700ptas, Sun. 900ptas. Fawning service. Open 1-4pm and 7-11pm.

Café La Granja, Pl. España, 3, opposite Estación de Abando. Shiny, slinky place where you can lunch with bankers. Red velvet banquettes and wood paneling make for good flirting. *Menú* (850ptas) includes salmon. Open 1-4pm.

Fük, C. General Concha, 2, just off Pl. Pedro Equillor behind Hotel Carlton. Our agent in Spain likes the name. Spanish fast food with a whisper of German zing. Hamburgers and sandwiches 250-350ptas. Try the *zipi-zape* (meatballs, 200ptas). Breakfast of *café* and a *bocadillo* 250ptas. Open Mon.-Fri. 9am-midnight, Sat.-Sun. 6:30pm-1:30am.

Vegetariano, Alameda de Urquijo, 33. *Ensalada de Hawaii* (salad with pineapple), *crema de champiñón* (cream of mushroom soup), and *tarta de acelgas* (beet pie). A la carte meal about 800ptas. Open Mon.-Sat. 1-4pm.

Sights

Bilbo's **Museo de Bellas Artes,** ranked among Europe's best, is a treat in such an unaesthetic city. Among its delicious Spanish and Flemish (12th-19th century) holdings are versions of *St. Francis Praying* by El Greco and Zurbarán, Goya's *Carlos IV* and *María Luisa,* a Gauguin, and numerous canvases by Basque painters. The substantial contemporary art collection consists mainly of international abstract art. Of course, the highlight is one of Velázquez's red-nosed *Portrait of Felipe IV*s. The ivy-covered building sits on the edge of **Parque de Doña Casilda de Iturriza,** in the west of the city. From Pl. de España take the Gran Vía for five blocks, turn right on C. Elcano and follow it to Pl. Museo. (Open Tues.-Sat. 10am-1:30pm and 4-7:30pm, Sun. 10am-noon. Free.)

The **Museo Arqueológico, Etnográfico, e Histórico de Vizcaya,** C. Cruz, 4 (tel. 415 54 23), housed in a beautiful old stone cloister, does Basque culture. The upstairs galleries have displays on hand-weaving, blacksmithing, armaments, and a few rooms devoted to the sea, with a couple of amazingly large preserved boats. Other parts of the exhibit highlight clothing, ceramics, and furniture. The museum is in the old city; walk past Pensión de la Fuente away from C. Correo to Pl. Miguel de Unamuno, whence C. Cruz springs. (Open Tues.-Sat. 10:30-1:30pm and 4-7pm, Sun. 10:30am-1:30pm. Free.)

Surrounded by a bodyguard of tower blocks, the **Basílica de Nuestra Señora de Begoña** sits atop a hill overlooking the old quarter. Legend holds that a man found an image of the patron Virgin in an oak on the hill while he was scrounging up materials for a hermitage outside of town. The vision supposedly said "don't move" (or words to that effect), meaning build me a basilica here; the current church was built on the site in 1907. Inside, on the strangely sloping floor, you'll have the curious sensation of being about to tumble backwards all the way down again. The *patrona* of the province shines brightly in a long flowing robe over the altar in an otherwise gloomy edifice. From Pl. Unamuno, a long-distance flight of stairs makes the ascent to heaven. Take the first right at the top on C. Virgen de Begoña, which leads to the church. (Open for mass at 7, 9, and 11am and 6 and 8pm.)

Beaches are within easy reach by train, north of the city at **Plentzia** (Plencia) or at **Sopelana** along the way. Plentzia in particular has cobblestone character, except on Sunday afternoons when the town goes belly up. **Getxo** also lies just a little nearer the surf; its illuminated **Puente Colgante** (suspension bridge) fords the river, leading to a huge proliferation of all-night bars. The city makes money off late-night partiers; the bridge carriage costs 15ptas before midnight and 65ptas after. You can also take a **bus** here from Pl. Ensanche in Bilbo (110-115ptas), near the market. Past midnight, revelers will miss the last train and find themselves obliged to taxi home (1500-2000ptas).

Entertainment

A city with so many comfortable bars can be expected to have a thriving after-dark scene, especially on weekends. In the **casco viejo** people spill out into the streets to tipple *chiquitos,* small glasses of beer or wine characteristic of the region (the sport is called *chiquiteo*). The young jam C. Licenciado Poza, inflicting their teeny-bopperness on everyone in sight. With 200 bars within 200m, **Calle Ledesma** exerts a similar pull on students and professionals. Upscale Bilbo retires to the Jardines de Albia to get its *copas.* The coolest, most radical bar in town is **Herriko Taberna,** C. Somera, 20. Unmarked save for an outer wall splattered with militant graffiti, its interior is papered with political posters and photos of Basque detainees.

The massive blowout *fiesta* takes place during **Semana Grande** in August, held in honor of *Nuestra Señora de Begoña.* Music, theater, and bullfights climax in a fireworks display. Documentary filmmakers from the world over gather here in November for the **Festival Internacional de Cine Documental de Bilbao.**

Gernika (Guernica)

"If the cities are destroyed by flames, if women and children are victims of asphyxiating gases, if the populations of open cities, situated at long distances from the front, fall victim to the bombs and torpedoes launched by airplanes, then the immediate end to hostilities is possible and a government where nerves resist all tests will not be able to resist such for long."

Such was the philosophy, outlined by M. K. L. Dertzen in 1935, behind the massive aerial bombing that destroyed 70% of Gernika on April 26, 1937. At the request of

Franco's forces, the Nazi "Condor Legion" dumped an estimated 29,000kg of bombs on market day, just as citizens and large numbers of farmers from outlying areas gathered for the weekly exchange of goods and traditional *pelota* games. The incendiary and shrapnel bombs killed between 200 and 1600 civilians and demolished the town. In the course of the three-hour raid neither the strategic bridge or arms factory was scratched. Mass aerial bombing of undefended civilian populations had made its European debut.

Gernika was etched into world consciousness as the scene of one of the most gratuitously brutal acts of the Civil War; it moved Pablo Picasso to paint *Guernica*, now exhibited behind bullet-proof glass in Madrid (see Madrid: Museums). In 1991, the town sponsored an *exposición* about the bombing. Chillingly serene music accompanied the exhibition of photographs, maps, and the occasional recovered bone fragment. An guidebook to the exhibition, an excellent historical resource, is still available in *castellano* and *euskera* (300ptas). Eduardo Chillida's **escultura** is a monument to peace, plurality, and understanding erected on the 50th anniversary of the bombing. From the RENFE station, follow C. Urioste as far as it goes. Turn right at the top and cross the little wooden bridge. Farther on is a Henry Moore sculpture called *Large Figure in a Shelter;* Moore was both a pacifist and a great fan of Picasso's *Guernica*.

The emotional focus of the town is the **Arbola Zaharra** and its decendants. The remains of this 2000-year-old oak tree stand beneath an eight-pillared dome next to the **Juntetxea,** the Basque Parliament. Medieval Basques gathered to debate community issues under the oak. Later, Gernika became the political center of Bizcaia. When the area passed into Castilian hands, *castellano* monarchs were expected to make a ritual voyage to Gernika and its oak and swear to respect the autonomy of the *juntas* (local governments) and local *fueros* (laws). The oak's offspring, an august tree of 130 years, grows next to the building behind the grillwork fence. A grandchild oak, now just entering puberty, was planted in 1979 to celebrate the return of regional autonomy. (Open July-Aug. 10am-2pm and 4-7pm; Sept.-June 10am-2pm and 4-6pm. Free.) Paintings and artifacts on display in the **Museo de Euskalerria** help with Basque history. (Open Tues.-Sat. 10am-2pm and 4-7pm, Sun. 10am-2pm. Free.)

To reach the area from the train station, walk one block up C. Adolfo Urioste and across the tidy flower beds on the hillside to the town's central plaza. Turn left on C. Señorió de Vizcaya, then ascend the stone staircase on the right to the auditorium. From the top of the stairs, the Juntetxea is directly ahead; the Museo de Euskalerria and the *escultura* are to the right.

If you wish to dally, consider staying in a *hostal* or *casa particular*. **Hostal Iratxe,** C. San Juan Tomás Gandarias (C. Industria on the map), 4 (tel. 625 58 17), has new, big rooms that come with TV. If nobody's home, try Bar Fronton, down the street; the bartender owns the *hostal*. (Singles 3000ptas. Doubles 4000ptas.) From the main square, turn left on C. Pablo Picasso and follow it to C. San Juan Tomás Gandarias.

Restaurante Julen, #14 on C. San Juan Tomás Gandarias, has unvarnished wood tables and a fine selection of *pinchos*. *Platos combinados* 400-700ptas. **Bar-Restaurante Pospolin,** on central C. Artecalle, 4 (underneath the archway on the right), fixes sandwiches (225-350ptas) and multiple *platos combinados* (600-750ptas; open 8:30am-1am). Market-goers go to the huge round building on the pedestrian street next to Turismo. (Open Mon.-Fri. 9am-1:30pm and 4:30-8:30pm, Sat. 9am-1:30pm.)

To reach the **tourist office,** C. Artecalle, 8 (tel. 625 58 92), from the train station, turn right at the town's main plaza and go through the arches. The office is below the green and yellow "i" on the right. It stocks a list of hotels, *casas particulares*, and restaurants and a decent map. You might be able to **store luggage** here. (Open Mon.-Sat. 10am-2pm and 4-8pm, Sun. 10am-2pm.) The **post office** at Pl. Foruen, s/n (tel. 625 03 87), is across the street from the tourist office. (Open Mon.-Fri. 8am-3pm, Sat. 9am-1pm.) The **postal code** is 48300, the **telephone code** 94. For a **taxi,** call 625 10 02. For a **24-hr. pharmacy,** check the listing on the door at C. Artecalle, 1. **Medical services** are available at the *ambulatorio*, C. San Juan, 1 (tel. 685 19 88). An **ambulance** can be summoned at 685 05 54. The **municipal police** are on C. Artecalle (tel. 625 05 54).

Trains (tel. 625 11 82) journey to Bilbo (every hr., 50min., 220ptas). Compañía de Automóviles Vascongados (tel. 433 12 79) sends **buses,** from a spot one block left of the train station exit. To Bilbo (7-10 per day, 45min., 230ptas) and Lekeitio (6 per day, Sun. 2 per day; 45min.; 206ptas).

Near Gernika: Cueva de Santimamiñe

Settlement in the area goes back at least 17,000 years, and at the **Cueva de Santimamiñe,** 5km north of Gernika, you can ogle a well-preserved set of prehistoric paintings on cave walls. Some (mainly nationalists) argue that the Basque language originated here when the population abandoned the caves during the Neolithic period, spreading their tongue to the rest of the area. (Admission by free guided tour only. Tues.-Fri. 5 per day, Sun. at 11am and 12:30pm.) No **buses** come near the cave; try to cajole the driver of the bus from Gernika to Lekeitio or Elantxoba (2-3 per day) to stop at **Kortezubi,** 2km away.

Lekeitio (Lequeitio)

There is a place on the highway, somewhere deep in the hills of Euskadi, where the highway signs flip from *castellano/euskera* to *euskera/castellano*. You're whipping down the highway, cruising along, and you suddenly notice; don't have a hissy fit—you're heading into real Basque country. Welcome to Lekeito. Graffiti in *euskera* covers most available surfaces and quite a few *castellano* road signs, the most common theme being "AMNISTIA" for ETA prisoners. In the town proper, older men wear the traditional black berets.

Street signs are in *euskera* only, and you'll hear *euskera* in the streets of this small fishing town. *Castellano* is universally spoken though, which comes in handy when you have to ask people for directions (because the map in the "Lekeitio" brochure is so godawful).

Squeezed between steep pine-covered hillsides and the stony undulations of the coast, Lekeitio remains reasonably undeveloped, although its **beach** and harbor are popular daytrip destinations from Donostia/San Sebastián and Bilbo. The public beach suffers from brown waters, especially around the town center. A sign warns potential swimmers against bathing in these fishy waters.

The town's biggest problem has been overfishing. The number of boats has diminished greatly, and fishers must traverse the deep seas for up to a fortnight to pull in a few measly *bonito* (tuna) and anchovies. The *bonito* fishers operate out of the port area, next to the beaches. There's only an hour of low tide when it's possible to walk out to the evergreen **Isla San Nicolás** and rummage around the ruins of the old Franciscan **convent**.

Lekeitio revels in a series of summertime fairs and fiestas. The town shows off its slapstick sense of humor with cartoon-colored trawlers in the harbor and the low burlesque of its **Antzar Joku** (Goose Festival) on September 4. As tribute during the **Jaiak San Antolín** (Sept. 1-8), seven to nine dead geese get their necks greased and are strung up across the harbor. Young men standing in rowboats try to yank the geese off while the feathery ones are raised and lowered. Many contestants fall in—hence much hilarity. The winner gets a prize and his picture in the paper. On the final night, an impressive candlelight march winds through the streets. Paraders dress in white to mourn not the martyred fowl but the end of the fiesta.

For the **Fiesta de San Pedro** (June 28-July 1), fishers take the statue of St. Peter from its niche and parade it down to the wharf. The bearers wave the statue menacingly toward the water in an attempt to cow the sea with the wrath of the fishers' patron apostle. The statue fell in the water a few years ago and lost its golden crown (the present one is made of tinfoil).

Film, videotape, and Super8 are the media of choice for the **Euskal Zinema Bilera** (Basque Amateur Film Festival, late June to early July), which screens a variety of political, humorous, and experimental films for little or no cost. Mid-July brings the four-day **Festival Internacional de Teatro Callejero** (International Festival of Street Theater), with performers from all over Europe. Top-of-the-line Spanish performers crash town the first week of August for the **Itxas Soinua** music festival in Iglesia Santa María (admission 800-1000ptas).

The two hotels have a monopoly on official accommodations. The tourist office can help find *casas particulares*, which are altogether a better option. **Bar-Restaurante Mantxúa,** C. Beasko Kalea, 24 (tel. 624 30 72) has a few rooms. (Doubles with bath 3500ptas.) **Camping Leagi** (tel. 684 23 52) is one km down the road to Mendexa and open all year. (Reception open 8am-10pm; 350ptas per person, 300ptas per tent, 375ptas per car.) **Camping Endai** (tel. 684 24 69), open mid-June to mid-Sept., is 3km away from Lekeitio on the road toward Ondarroa. Although it's ranked as a third-class site, it has a bar, supermarket, dining area, and washing machines. (Reception open 9am-midnight. 250ptas per person, 210-275ptas per tent, 150ptas per car.)

The bereted crowd gathers at **Restaurante Egaña,** Santa Katalina Ibilpedea, 4 (tel. 684 01 03), where waiters serve a *menú* (795ptas) that may include *chipirones en su tinta* (cuttlefish in its own ink). From the main bus stop, head for the crossroads, cross the intersection, and turn left. (Open 1-4pm and 8-11pm.) The food at **Restaurante Txalapartá,** Paskual Abaroa Etorbidea, 22 (tel. 784 23 66), just past the crossroads, is less rich than Egaña's but there's more of it. A lively crowd debauches at the bar. The *menú* (600ptas) usually includes fish (entrees 400-600ptas). The owners may help locate *casas particulares* in summer; half the town drinks here. (Open Nov.-Sept. 1-4:30pm and 8pm-midnight.)

To reach the **tourist office,** C. Gamarra, 1 (tel. 624 33 65), turn right at the crossroads onto San Kristobal Emparantza and follow the paved road past the church; it's just beyond the gas station under the Ayuntamiento. The staff speaks some English, and they'll give you a hand-drawn, indexed map. For help finding a *casa particular,* arrive around 6-7pm. (Open June-Sept. Tues. 5-8pm, Wed.-Sun. 11am-2pm, 5-8pm.) If the tourist office is closed, try the 2nd floor of the **Ayuntamiento** (tel. 684 00 01) for a map and bizarrely translated brochure. (Open Mon.-Fri. 8am-3pm.) At the exit of the Ayuntamiento, head up to the left past the gas station to find the **post office** on C. Eliz Atea, 10 (tel. 684 06 10; open Mon.-Fri. 8am-3pm, Sat. 9am-1pm). The **postal code** is 48280. To hail a **taxi,** call 684 08 59. The **Red Cross** (tel. 684 18 88) is on the opposite side of the harbor from the tourist office. The **ambulatorio** (tel. 684 20 06) provides **medical services** on the waterfront, just past the tourist office. For the **24-hr. pharmacy,** ask the **municipal police** (tel. 684 14 69) on the harbor.

Compañía de Automóviles Vascongados (CAV) runs **buses** from beside the Hotel Piñupe to Gernika (3-6 per day, 45min., 205ptas), Bilbo (3-6 per day, 1 1/2 hr., 475ptas), and Donostia/San Sebastián (3-4 per day, 1 1/2 hr., 570ptas).

Donostia (San Sebastián)

This provincial capital is a blue-blood resort in a come-here-to-die setting. Wide boulevards, garden avenues, and stately, ornate buildings give the town a regal air. By day, people come to La Concha—the half-moon beach—for a taste of Brighton Beach. On either side of this giant playground, two steep hills elbow their way into the sea. They call Donostia "the seashell with the pearl" because La Concha curves like an oyster round a pearl-like islet in the bay.

While Gernika is the political and emotional center of Euskadi, Donostia has in the past been the region's trouble spot. Tranquil Alameda del Boulevard marks the spot where two men on a motorcycle dropped a bomb on the roof of a general's car. With the granting of regional autonomy for the *País Vasco* and the dissipation of support for the ETA, the separatist tensions that marred this pleasure-loving town have eased considerably. Residents seem eager to ignore the political graffiti lingering on walls, preferring to promote the enjoyment of sun and surf.

Though traditionally an elite resort of the very wealthy (Spanish nobility sniffed out the pleasures of this seaside resort over 150 years ago), Donostia's annual jazz, dance, and film festivals, its powerful nightlife, and its proximity to the French border appeal to visitors of every sort. Enjoy Donostia's commodities, but don't expect to cut corners; over a century and a half of exclusivity are still reflected in the prices.

Orientation and Practical Information

Street and place names on signs are in either *castellano* or *euskera*. The difference can cause slight letter changes (Castilian V becomes B, CH becomes TX). Don't panic: usually both names are present; the street guide on the tourist office map gives both versions in its index. Practically no one speaks *euskera* in the street.

The Río Urumea splits Donostia in two. The city center and most of the monuments are on the west side of the river, in a peninsula that juts into the sea. In the north or the peninsula is the **parte vieja** (old city), where the nightlife rages and budget accommodations and restaurants cluster. To the south, the **Cathedral de San Pastor** sits on the edge of Calle de San Martín, in the heart of the commercial district. Three bridges span the river: **Puente María Christina** to the south, **Puente Santa Catalina** in the middle, and **Puente Zurriola** to the north. Puente Santa Catalina turns into **Avenida de la Libertad** on the west side of the river, and runs from the bridge to the **Playa de la Concha**, which fronts a large bay. To the left, past the tunnel, is **Playa de Ondarreta;** to right is **Monte Igüeldo.**

The east side of the river is home to the RENFE station and the **Barrio de Gros.** To get to *parte vieja* from the station, head straight to Puente María Christina, cross the bridge, then turn right along the river and walk four blocks north to Avenida de la Libertad. Turn left and follow it to the **puerto** (port); the *parte vieja* fans out to the right. To get to the tourist office from the station, turn right after crossing Puente María Cristina and continue past Puente Santa Catalina and Puente Zurriola; Calle Reina Regente will be on the left.

The bus station is in the south of the city in Plaza de Pío XII. **Avenida de Sancho El Sabio** runs to the right (north) straight toward the ocean and the center of the city. To get to the tourist office, head down Av. Sancho El Sabio for about four blocks; after Plaza Centenario, bear right onto Calle de Prim, and follow it to Puente María Cristina. From here, follow the directions above.

Tourist Office: Municipal: Centro de Atracción y Turismo (tel. 48 11 16), C. Reina Regente s/n, in the vast Teatro Victoria Eugenia. Glossy office, slinky brochures, and a dedicated staff. Gorgeous, detailed, utilitarian map. Transit and accommodations information available. The *Guia práctica* (500ptas in bookstores) is a gold mine of local information. Open Mon.-Sat. 8am-8pm, Sun. 10am-1pm; Oct.-May Mon.-Fri. 9am-1:30pm and 3:30-6:30pm, Sat. 9am-1pm. **Regional Office:** Po. Fueros, 1 (tel. 42 62 82), at Av. Libertad and Puente Santa Catalina. Open Mon.-Fri. 9am-1:30pm and 3:30-6:30pm, Sat. 9am-1pm. Tourist information booth at **RENFE station** station (tel. 28 37 67) has a good enough map to get you to luggage storage and the real tourist office. Open Mon.-Sat. 8am-noon and 4-8pm, Sun. 8am-noon.

Budget Travel: TIVE, C. Tomás Gros, 3 (tel. 27 69 34), 1 bl. off Pl. Euskadi down C. Miracruz and then right; below street level. ISIC 500ptas. HI card 1800ptas. They process train, bus, and plane tickets only to international destinations. Message board with some travel info. Open Mon.-Fri. 9am-2pm.

Currency Exchange: Banca Besné, C. Fuenterrabía, 4 (tel. 42 04 41), fourth left off Av. Libertad heading toward the water (west). Open Mon.-Sat. 9am-7:30pm, Sun. and holidays 9am-1pm; Oct.-June Mon.-Sat. 9am-1pm and 3:30-7pm. **Agencia de Cambio,** C. San Martín, 35 (tel. 43 03 47), at the corner of C. Easo. Open 9am-9pm; Oct.-May Mon.-Sat. 9am-1pm and 4-8pm.

Post Office: C. Urdaneta, 11 (tel. 46 49 14; fax 45 07 94), the street just south of the cathedral. Heading toward the water on Av. Libertad (west), take a left on C. Fuenterrabía and walk 5 bl. Open for information Mon.-Fri. 8am-9pm, Sat. 9am-noon; for Lista de Correos Mon.-Fri. 8am-9pm, Sat. 9am-2pm; for stamps, **telegrams,** and **fax** Mon.-Fri. 8am-9pm, Sat. 9am-7pm. **Postal Code:** 20007.

Telephones: C. San Marcial, 29, one street south of Av. Libertad. Open Mon.-Sat. 9:30am-11pm. **Branch office** off Pl. Zaragoza, between Playa de la Concha and C. Zubieta. Take Av. Libertad to the waterfront, turn left on Po. Concha along the beach. Open June-July 9:30am-10pm; Aug. 9:30am-midnight. **Telephone Code:** 943.

Flights: tel. 64 22 40, 64 12 67. In Hondarribía (Fuenterrabía), 18km east of the city. Interurbanos buses to Fuenterrabía (every 12min. 7:48am-10pm). Information open 8am-1pm and 4-8pm. To Madrid (3 per day, 12,000ptas) and Barcelona (1 per day, 12,500ptas).

Donostia (San Sebastián) 199

Trains: Two stations make everything just a bit more fun. Fares and travel times vary for each type of service. **RENFE, Estación del Norte,** Av. Francia, s/n (tel. 27 92 56), on the east side of Puente María Cristina. Information (tel. 28 30 29) open 7am-11pm. To: Irún (14 per day, 25min., 160ptas); Vitoria (16 per day, 1 1/2 -2hr., 835-1275ptas); Pamplona (3 per day, 1 3/4 hr., 720-900ptas); Burgos (11 per day, 3 1/2 -4 1/2 hr., 1545ptas); Zaragoza (2 per day, 4hr., 2055ptas); Logroño (5 per day, 5 1/2 hr., 1185-1475ptas); Madrid (5 per day, 7 1/2 hr., 4240-5685ptas); Barcelona (2 per day, 8-9hr., 3845ptas); Santiago de Compostela (2 per day, 11hr., 5300ptas); Sevilla (on Mon., Wed., and Fri., 15 1/2 hr., 6235ptas; change at Bilbo); València (1 per day, 15hr., 6120ptas); Lisboa (1 per day, 16hr., 6500ptas); Paris (6 per day, 7000ptas; change at Hendaya).
RENFE office, C. Camino 1, on the corner with C. Oquendo, one block north of the Puente Santa Catalina and one block west of the river. Open Mon.-Fri. 9am-1pm and 4-7pm, Sat. 9am-1pm.
ET/FFVV, Estación de Amara (tel. 45 01 31). Where Av. Libertad hits the Playa de la Concha, turn left on C. Easo and follow for 8 blocks. Information open 6am-10:45pm. Mostly for destinations within Donostia. To Hendaya (every 1/2.hr., 45min., 150ptas) and Bilbo (8-11 per day, 3hr., 550ptas).

Buses: Several private companies run from different points in the city. Most companies pass through the central station. The booklet from the tourist office covers all companies, with phone numbers and routes. Most leave from Pl. Pío XII (buy tickets at ticket booths along river).

PESA (tel 45 05 45, 46 39 74). To: Bilbo (9-16 per day, 1hr., 880ptas); Lekeitio (4 per day, 1 1/2 hr., 565ptas); Vitoria (5-8 per day, 1 3/4 hr., 765ptas).

Continental Auto, Av. Sancho el Sabio, 31 (tel 46 90 74). To Madrid (6 per day, 6hr., 3080ptas) and Burgos (6 per day, 4hr., 1520ptas).

La Roncalesa (tel. 46 10 64). To Pamplona (5 per day, 3hr., 625ptas) and Barcelona (1 per day, 7hr., 3400ptas).

Turytans (tel. 46 23 60). To Paris (1 per day, 14hr., 6275ptas).

Enatcar (tel. 46 80 87). To London (4 per wk., 22hr., 10,250ptas).

Interurbanos, from C. Oquendo, 16, behind the city tourist office. To Fuenterrabía (160ptas) and Irún (130ptas) Mon.-Fri. every 12min. 7:48am-10pm.

Public Transportation: 20 bus routes throughout the city (75ptas). List of routes available at tourist office.

Taxis: Radio Taxi Easo (tel. 46 76 66). **A.D.** (tel. 42 66 42). **Coop. Suital** (tel. 39 80 18). **Santa Clara** (tel. 46 64 55).

Car Rental: All agencies on C. San Martín or its side streets; take Av. Libertad toward the beach (west), turn left at C. Urbieta, then right after 3 blocks. **Avis,** C. Triunfo, 2 (tel. 46 15 27, 26 15 56), off Pl. Zaragoza. Must be 23 or over. Open Mon.-Fri. 8am-1pm and 4-7pm, Sat. 9am-1pm. **Europcar,** C. San Martín, 60 (tel. 46 17 17; fax 46 09 72). Must be 21 or over. Open Mon.-Fri. 9am-1pm and 4-7:30pm, Sat. 9am-1pm. **Hertz,** C. Marina, 2 (tel. 46 10 84). Open Mon.-Fri. 9am-1pm and 4-7pm, Sat. 9am-1pm.

Automobile Club: Real Automóbil Club, C. Echaide, 12 (tel. 43 08 00).

Bike Rental: Mini, C. Escolta Real, 10 (tel. 21 17 58), in the old quarter. Mountain bikes 1500ptas per day. 10-speed bikes 1200ptas per day. Sat.-Sun.: 2200ptas; 1900ptas.

Luggage Storage: From the RENFE station, cross Puente María Cristina, turn right, walk 1 bl., then take C. San Martín to the left; after 5 bl., left on C. Easo (en route to Estación Amara, next to the firefighters). 125ptas per day, 250ptas overnight. Bikes 250ptas per day. Open summer 8:30am-9pm. **Bar Self-Service,** Po. Duque de Mandas, 49 (tel. 29 14 52), below street level behind RENFE station. Small bags 100ptas, large bags 200ptas. Open winter Sun.-Fri. 9am-10:30pm, Sat. 9am-4:30pm.

Lost Property: Maybe the **municipal police** are hoarding your possessions.

English Bookstore: Donosti, Pl. Bilbo, 2 (tel. 42 21 38), 1 bl. west of Puente María Christina, near the cathedral. Open Mon.-Fri. 9am-1pm and 4:30-8pm, Sat. 9am-1pm. **Azoka,** C. Fuenterrabía, 19 (tel. 42 17 45), off Av. Libertad. Penguin Classics, Agatha Christie, and bestsellers. Open Mon.-Sat. 10am-1:30pm and 4-8pm. **La Internacional,** C. Churruca, 6 (tel. 42 02 39, 42 57 16), the 4th right off Av. Libertad, heading toward the beach (west). Some guidebooks and novels in English. Open Mon.-Fri. 9:30am-1pm and 3:30-7:30pm, Sat. 9:30am-1pm.

Libraries: Biblioteca Municipal, Pl. Constitución (tel. 42 54 53). Open Mon.-Fri. 8am-8:30pm, Sat. 8am-1:30pm. **Biblioteca Provincial,** Pl. Gipuzkoa. Xerox machine. Open Mon.-Fri. 8:30am-8:30pm, Sat. 8:30-2pm.

Laundromat: Lavomatique, C. San Juan, 13. Enter from C. Iñigo in the old quarter. Wash 400ptas per 4kg load. Dry 25ptas per 7min., 200ptas per 1/2 hr. Soap 25ptas. Ironing 50ptas. Open Mon.-Fri. 10am-1pm and 4-8pm, Sat.-Sun. and holidays 10am-1pm.

Public Toilets: Alameda del Boulevard, the pedestrian walk that runs towards the beach (west) from Puente Zurriola; also some near the Puente Santa Catalina (5ptas). Open 9am-1:30pm and 3:30-7:30pm.

Public Showers: Pl. Easo, on C. Easo en route to Estación Amara. Showers 15ptas. Soap and towel 5ptas each. Open Wed.-Mon. 8am-1:15pm and 3-8:15pm.

Swimming Pool: Polideportivo de Anoeta (tel. 45 87 97). Open-air pool, track, tennis courts, gym. Call for address and prices.

Hiking Information: Club Vasco de Camping, San Marcial, 19 (tel. 42 84 79), 1 bl. south of Av. Libertad. Below street level. Organizes excursions too. Open Mon.-Fri. 6:30-8:30pm. **Club de Montaña Kresala,** C. Euskalerría, 9 (tel. 42 09 05). **Noresta,** Po. Ramón (tel. 29 35 20). Bookstore of travel guides, hiking guides, and maps, many in English. Organizes tours and rents skis, wetsuits, and hiking equipment. Open Mon.-Sat. 10am-1pm and 4-8pm.

Early Closing Day: Clothing and shoe stores close Mon. morning. Food stores close Sat. afternoon.

Red Cross: C. Matías, 7. **Ambulance** (tel. 22 22 22, 21 46 00, or 21 51 64).

24-Hour Pharmacy: Ask **municipal police.**

Medical Services: Casa de Socorro, C. Pedro Egaño, 8 (tel. 46 63 19, 46 41 20).

Police: Municipal (tel. 46 40 20; **emergency** tel. 092).

Accommodations and Camping

Desperate backpackers are always forced to scrounge and grovel for rooms in August. If you get away with 2000ptas per night, consider yourself lucky. But Donostia's *hostales* and *pensiones* live up to their price. Budget options congregate both in the *parte vieja* and around the **cathedral;** they're often two or more per stairway, so look for signs one or two floors up. Many places don't take reservations during the busy summer months. Almost all have winter heating.

Some people choose to sleep on the beach, but this is illegal and potentially dangerous. The police won't protect beach-sleepers, and the area is reputed to be full of crazed dope fiends. Others try sleeping in the park near the RENFE station. Those who choose to do so often sleep in groups to discourage thieves.

Albergue Juvenil la Sirena (HI), Po. Igueldo, 25 (group reservations tel. 47 15 46; fax 45 30 65), near Playa de Ondarreta, in the far west end of the city. Bus #16 (direction: Igueldo) or 27 (direction: *antiguo*) runs there. Like an answered prayer: brand-new facilities to be open by Dec. 1992. Rooms for 4, 6, or 8 all have bathrooms. Must be under 26. 1000ptas per person. Breakfast included. Lunch or dinner 550ptas. Sheets 300ptas. Luggage stored and laundry service included. Handicapped accessible.

In the Parte Vieja

A lengthy walk from the train and bus stations, the *parte vieja* burgeons with reasonably priced and pleasing *pensiones*. This is where the action is at night; scores of *pensiones* sleep (or try to) above loud *tapas* bars. A prime location because of its proximity to Playa de la Concha and the port; the wise call before hiking over here. **Alameda del Boulevard,** just west of the Puente Zurriola, is the major artery.

> **Pensión Amaiur,** C. 31 de Agosto, 44, 3rd fl. (tel. 42 96 54). From Alameda del Boulevard go up C. San Jerónimo to the end and turn left. Recently renovated and scrupulously tended, with floral wallpaper, a gardened balcony, and glowing tile bathrooms. Dreamy mattresses. Semana Santa and June 21-Sept. 21: Singles 2500ptas. Doubles 4500ptas. Triples 6000ptas. After Semana Santa-June 2: 2000ptas; 3000ptas; 4200ptas. Sept. 21-before Semana Santa: 1500ptas; 2500ptas; 3300ptas. Bring *Let's Go* and get 500ptas knocked off the price.

Donostia (San Sebastián)

Pensión San Lorenzo, C. San Lorenzo, 2 (tel. 42 55 16), a right off C. Narrica from Alameda del Boulevard, on the corner of C. San Juan. Geometric bedspreads match the lampshades. Owner stores backpacks and keeps guests' food in her fridge. Doubles 4000ptas. Triples 4500ptas. Sept.-June: 2500ptas; 3000ptas. Laundry 300ptas per load.

Pensión Boulevard, Alameda del Boulevard, 24 (tel. 42 94 05). Latest business venture of San Lorenzo's owner. Shiny and new, with firm mattresses and Fred Flintstone bedspreads. Spic 'n span bathrooms touched for the very first time. Swoony view of Alameda del Boulevard. Doubles 5000ptas, with bath 6000ptas. Triples 6000ptas. Winter: 1500ptas per person.

Pensión Arsuaga, C. Narrica, 3, 4th fl. (tel. 42 06 81), off the middle of Alameda del Boulevard. Fancy rooms, most with balconies. Intermittent oil paintings and a lovely sitting room. Jovial owner runs a cheery *comedor*. Singles 2000ptas. Doubles 3500-3700ptas. Breakfast 250ptas. Lunch or dinner 900ptas.

Pensión Urgull, C. Esterlines, 10, 4th fl. (tel 43 00 47). From Alameda del Boulevard, right onto C. San Jerónimo, then the 2nd right from there. A hike upstairs. Attractive, well-lit rooms with pastel walls and bedspreads. Fantastic water pressure in the shower. Singles 2000ptas. Doubles 4000ptas. Triples 5000ptas. Oct.-June except Semana Santa: 1500ptas; 3000ptas; 4000ptas.

Pensión Lizaso, C. San Vicente, 7 (tel. 42 29 77), near Monte Urgull and next to Iglesia San Vicente. Some closets—oops, those are rooms—have makeshift doors; others are larger, brighter, and balconied. Doubles only, 3000ptas.

Near the Cathedral

These *hostales* are in the heart of the commercial zone, but farther away from the port, the buses, the trains, and the beach.

Pensión La Perla, C. Loyola, 10, 2nd fl. (tel. 42 81 23), the street directly ahead of the cathedral. Handsome wood floors and doorframes. All rooms with balconies and showers. English-speaking owner. Winter heating. Singles 3000ptas. Doubles 4000ptas. Oct.-June: 2500ptas; 3000ptas.

Pensión Urkia, C. Urbieta, 12 (tel. 42 44 36), 1 bl. north (left) of the cathedral at C. Arrasate. Quaint, dusty antique furniture, some big old armoires. Some rooms look out onto the plaza. Blue tiled bathrooms. Prices not including IVA. Singles 2000ptas. Doubles 3000ptas. Triples 4500ptas. Quads 6000ptas. Larger groups easily accommodated.

Hostal Comercio, C. Urdaneta, 24 (tel. 46 44 14), at C. Easo. From C. San Martín, C. Urdaneta runs behind the church. Proprietors hard at work in the afternoons; arrive early. Some rooms small, but all clean. 3 floors and multiple beds, yet likely to be full by midday in peak season. Winter heating. Singles 3600ptas. Doubles 4300ptas. Oct.-June: 3300ptas; 3900ptas.

Hostal Residencia Easo, C. San Bartolomé, 24 (tel. 46 68 92), to the west of the cathedral. Turn left from cathedral, and left again on C. Triunfo—so easyo. Big, modern rooms, tastefully adorned. Owner can help find *casas particulares* if the Easo is full. Winter heating. Singles 2800ptas. Doubles 3600ptas, with shower 3800ptas. Nov.-April: 2800ptas; 3200ptas, 3400ptas.

Hostal Ozcariz, C. Fuenterrabía, 8 (tel. 42 53 06). Exit cathedral, turn right, then left. Luxe wood floors and high ceilings. Clean bathrooms. Winter heating. Singles 3200ptas. Doubles 4400ptas. Triples 5500ptas. Reservations not accepted in summer; book 1 week in advance in winter.

Elsewhere

Hostel La Concha, C. San Martín, 51 (tel. 45 03 89, 46 08 93), up the street from Pl. Zaragoza, near the beach. Pleasant waiting room with fluffy chairs. Carpeted stairs rise to all-white rooms. All are doubles with bath. Semana Santa and July-Sept. 5000ptas; Oct.-Semana Santa 4500ptas.

Fonda Vicandi, C. Iparraguirre, 3F (tel. 27 07 95), in Barrio de Gros, on the east side of the river. Take C. Miracruz east from Pl. Euskadi and turn right after 2 bl. Quiet, old-fashioned rooms. Sunnier inside than you'd expect; less crowded in summer than elsewhere. Immaculate linens. Watch TV or the Goya print above it. Doubles 3500ptas. Showers 200ptas, winter 150ptas.

Hostal Fernando, Pl. Cruipuzcoa, 2 (tel. 42 55 75), under the arches, 2 bl. from Alameda del Boulevard. Light and airy, with high ceilings and quilted flower bedspreads. Singles 2700ptas. Doubles 4700ptas. Oct.-Mar.: 2200ptas; 3250ptas. Apr.-May: 2400ptas; 3500ptas.

Camping: Camping Igueldo (tel. 21 45 02), 5km west of town. 268 *parcelas* fill in the blink of an eye. Bus #16 "Barrio de Igueldo-Camping" runs between the site and Alameda del Boulevard (roughly every hr. 6:50am-10:30pm, 75ptas.) Bear in mind Donostia's unpredictable weather; hammer in the rain fly. Bar-restaurant and supermarket. Reception open 8am-midnight. *Parcela* 2700ptas plus IVA (includes car, tent and up to 4 people).

Food

Tapas are a religion here. The standard chaser is the strong regional wine *Txacoli*. The bars in the old city spread an array of enticing tidbits on a toothpick (10 *pinchos* and a drink, 1000ptas). Graze on *pinchos* and *bocadillos* here; it's livelier and easier on the wallet than any other area. Thirty-nine restaurants and bars breathe cheaply on **Calle Fermín Calbetón.** The least expensive hunting ground for a full meal at a *jatetxea* (restaurant in *euskera*) is the **Gros** neighborhood. The majority of restaurants offer their best deals on lunchtime *menús del día*.

Many small places in the harbor serve tangy sardines with cider. Vendors sell small portions of *gambas* (shrimp) in eggcups and *caracolillos* (periwinkles) in paper cones (100-200ptas). Otherwise, you can't afford Donostia's tasty seafood (see the notable exception below).

Mercado de la Bretxa inhabits imposing buildings on Alameda del Boulevard at Narrika Kalea. (Open Mon.-Sat. 8am-2pm and 5-7:30pm.) **Mercado de San Martín** is on C. San Marcial, 1 block south (left) of Av. Libertad heading to the beach, between C. Loyola and Urbieta a block north of the cathedral and near the tourist office. (Open Mon.-Thurs. 7:30am-2pm and 4:30-7:30pm, Fri.-Sat. 6:30am-2pm and 4:30-7:30pm.)

A visit to Donostia wouldn't be complete without sampling the strong, slightly bitter **sidra.** Once the most common drink in the *País Vasco,* it's back in style again. The best *sidra* is quaffed between January and March, when the *kupelas* (kegs) are tapped and you drink directly from the source; during the rest of the year you'll have to settle for the bottled variety. Custom insists on pouring it with arm extended, so that the force of the stream hitting the glass will release the *sidra*'s bouquet. It's stronger than the *sidras* of other regions (e.g., Asturias), and while not purple-haze-inducing, it'll get you drunk quicker than beer. (See Entertainment: Bars below.)

In the Parte Vieja

Groceries: Iñigo Saski, C. Iñigo, 7, in the old city. Open Mon.-Fri. 9am-1:30pm and 4:45-7:15pm, Sat. 9am-1:30pm.

Mariscos Kaia el Puerto (tel. 42 71 44), beneath the stone wall on your right past the marina in the old quarter. The exception to the no-affordable-seafood-in-town rule. They sell cooked and dressed seafood, especially shellfish, by the kilo (1400-3000ptas per kg; open 10am-2pm and 5-9:30pm).

Bar la Cepa, C. 31 de Agosto, 7, up C. Narrica from Alameda del Boulevard and to the left (the 7th street). There are hams and inverted wine bottles hanging from the ceiling, pictures of *matadores* on the walls, and a wagon-size wheel of Swiss cheese on the bar. *Tapas* city. *Bocadillos* 325-625ptas. *Bacalao a la vizcaina* 875ptas.

Bar Extaniz, C. Fermín Calbetón, 24, up C. San Jerónimo from Alameda del Boulevard; the 3rd right. Light-tiled, refreshingly modern interior. 15 different tortillas. *Bocadillos* 250-350ptas. Open Thurs.-Tues. 10:30am-4pm and 6:30pm-midnight.

Bar Juantxo, C. Embeltrán, 6, where it meets C. Esterlines in the *parte vieja*. Small and crammed with locals who know a good deal when they see one. *The* place for *bocadillos*—unbelievable array, and they're delivered by a dumbwaiter behind the bar! Weighty *bocadillos* 300-400ptas. *Ración* of *champiñones* (mushrooms) 290ptas. Open 9am-midnight, later on weekends.

Bar-Restaurante Txalupa, C. Fermín Calbetón, 3, up C. San Jerónimo and the 3rd right. Lobster tank and a dazzling selection of *pinchos* (100-150ptas). The *menú* (1600ptas) served in a tranquil plant-filled room downstairs. Open Wed.-Mon. 1-3:30pm and 8-11:30pm.

Bar-Restaurante Alotza, C. Fermin Calbetón, 7 (tel. 42 07 82), off C. Narrica. Beaming proprietor presides over alotsa *pinchos* and *banderillas. Menú* 500ptas. Nautical theme in back; cavernous stone walls. Open Tues.-Sun. 10am-4:30pm and 6pm-12:30am.

Near the Cathedral

La Barranquesa, C. Larramendi, 21 (tel. 45 47 47), 3 bl. behind (south of) the cathedral. It's in the basement, but the soothing pink walls and elegant decor are a break from the madness of the *parte vieja. Menú* with *paella* and chicken 750ptas. Open Mon.-Sat. 1:15-3:30pm and 8:15-11:30pm.

Bar Etxadi, Errenge Katolikoen Kalea (C. Reyes Católicos), 9 (tel. 46 07 85), the street running perpendicular to the cathedral's east end. Swish as hell. House specialties are *anchoas* or *gambas al ajillo* (anchovies or shrimp with garlic). Entrees 400-800ptas. *Bocadillos* 350-475ptas. *Menú* of *alubias* and *lomo* 1100ptas. Open Tues.-Sat. 11am-1am.

O Mamma Mia, C. San Bartolomé, 18 (tel. 46 52 93), on the corner of C. Triunfo. Italian, for a change. Wine caskets swing from ceiling, checkered tablecloths, etc. Individual pizzas 495-795ptas. Enormous amounts of pasta 595-895ptas. Open 1:30-4pm and 8:30-12:30am.

Self-Service la Oka, C. San Martín, 43 (tel. 42 31 82), between C. Triunfo and C. Lezo. Cafeteria-style atmosphere recalls the dreaded dining hall, except this food is good. From basics (1/2 *pollo asado* 515ptas) to the more unusual (*conejo*—rabbit—750ptas). Antiseptic white benches and tables. Open Sun.-Thurs. 1-3:30pm, Fri.-Sat. 1-3:30pm and 8:30-11pm. Closed for Christmas season and part of June.

Sights

The top of **Monte Igüeldo** at the far side of the bay, provides the best view. From here you can see the hilly Basque countryside meet the Atlantic in a long line of white and azure. The city spreads in a solid wall of buildings around the fan-shaped bay. The view of the bay—from anywhere—is especially spectacular on weekends after dark, when the base of Isla Santa Clara is lit by banks of floodlights so that it seems to float on a ring of light. The summit of Monte **Igüeldo,** also floodlit on weekends, vibrates to an **amusement park** with bumper cars, mini trains, and donkeys for hire. For the **funicular** that climbs to the top, take the #16 "Igueldo" bus from Alameda del Boulevard or walk along the beach and turn left just before the tennis courts. (Funicular every 15min. June 15-Sept. 15 10am-10pm, April-May 11am-8pm; 65ptas.)

At the other end of the curved beach, gravel paths wind through the cool, shady woods of **Monte Urgull.** The ruins of the **Castillo de Santa Cruz de la Mota** crown the summit with several cannon and an indoor chapel. Other reminders of a tumultuous past litter the mountainside: halfway up, the **Cementerio Británico** faces the sea. The huge monument and tomb commemorates the unknown British soldiers who died in 1833 defending the Spanish monarchy from the French during the Peninsular War. A more jarring "monument" to a fallen hero is the unmarked, white-plaster **smear on a rock** near the *paseo* as it rises above the aquarium. A member of ETA (Basque terrorist organization) accidentally blew himself up here trying to plant a bomb.

Circling the base of Monte Urgull, **Paseo Nuevo** lets you get close enough to the untamed waves for a gentle saltwater shower. At one end, the **acuario** (tel. 42 49 77) maintains only a few live fish, but has thorough displays on seafaring history. (Open 10am-1:30pm and 3:30-8:30pm; winter 10am-1:30pm amd 3:30-7:30pm. Admission 250ptas.)

At the other end of Paseo Nuevo (cut through the *parte vieja* by Pl. Trinidad if you don't want to walk around the whole *monte*), the **Museo de San Telmo** (tel. 48 12 46) waits in a former Dominican monastery. The serene, overgrown cloister is strewn with Basque funerary monuments. The main museum is beyond the cloister, comprised of a fascinating array of Basque artifacts dating to prehistory, a couple of **dinosaur skeletons,** some El Grecos, and exhibitions of contemporary art. The graceful stone arcade leads to the old church, now a *sala de actos* (conference room) ablaze with the gold and sepia epic mural depictions of Basque life and culture painted in 1931 by Catalan Josep María Sert. (Open Mon.-Sat. 9:30am-1:30pm and 3:30-7pm, Sun. 10:30am-2pm. Free.)

Isabel II started vacationing here in 1846; members of the court followed her, and the usual slew of fancy buildings followed them. To this day the Spanish government moves north in August. Even the railings on the boardwalk and the grandiose street lamps hark back to the time when the city was a stage set for the languid elite. **El Palacio de Miramar,** built on the land that splits Playa de la Concha and Playa de Ondarreta, was home-sweet-home at various times to the Spanish court, Napoleon III, and Bismarck. Now it's mainly used for conferences and art exhibitions and isn't otherwise open to the public, but visitors can stroll through the grounds. (Open 8am-8:30pm; winter 8am-5pm.) A 30-minute walk from the cathedral up Cuesta de Aldapeta (or a 75ptas bus ride on #19) heads to another regal love shack, the **Palacio de Ayete.** Again, the residence is closed to the public, but the lush forest trails of the summer house aren't.

Few traces remain of Donostia's past, largely because the city has been repeatedly destroyed by fires (Napoleon's troops set a doozy in 1813). The rebuilt old quarter, *parte vieja* (*alde zaharrean* in *euskera*), centers on **Plaza de la Constitución,** an arcaded square faced with balconies. The square has been a focal point for Basque nationalism; at one end the government buildings are plastered with Basque slogans. Nearby is the 18th-century Baroque **Iglesia de Santa María,** with its intricate concave portal and unsavory statue of San Sebastián shot through with arrows. The plain-jane 16th-century Romanesque **Iglesia de San Vicente** is festooned with political slogans. (Both churches open only for mass.)

Madrid School architect Rafael Moneo has been commissioned to design a **Palacio de Congresos** here that will double as convention and cultural center. To redeem the crying of *Solar K* (Lot K)—site of the *belle époque* casino, lamentably torn down in the 70s—Moneo has planned an abstract structure designed to ape the rocks strewn along the city's shore.

Entertainment

Bars

The **parte vieja** pulls out all the stops after dark.

> **Bar Uraitz** and **Bar Eibartarra,** Calbetón Kalea, 26 (Calle Mayor). These are the two most packed bars on the street virtually impassable after dark. A human zoo.
>
> **Bar Sariketa** and **Bar Txalupa,** near Calbetón Kalea (Calle Mayor). Where the music is eardrum-threatening and the climate sweltering.
>
> **Bar Colchonería,** Sant Vicente Kalea, 9. More tranquil. Bright modern art and small tables make for intimate conversation.
>
> **Akerbeltz,** Koroko Andra Mari, 10, near the port. Shafts of light and a sleek black bar inside a cave-like *bodega* (wine-cellar). Most patrons hang out on the stairs outside the bar.

The twentysomething crowd packs the streets around the **cathedral.**

> **Bar Udaberri-Beri,** C. Reyes Católicos (or Errege Katolikoen Kalea), 8, and **Splash,** #4, south of the cathedral. Drinks are handed through a window to the crowds on the sidewalks and blocked-off streets.
>
> **El Cine,** C. San Bartolomé, 21, on the other side (west) of C. Easo. This whole street and the area called *"la zona"* jump on weekends with spoiled, over-dressed *90210* teenyboppers on their precious motorscooters. Mod music.
>
> **Komplot,** C. Pedro Egaña, 7, off C. Easo, south of the cathedral. A popular after-hours drinking den. Open until 5am.
>
> **El Muro,** not near the cathedral. On the east side of the river. Down the *paseo,* past Playa de Gros, the eclectic and hip trudge through a muddy parking lot to listen to the Smiths and the Cure and to sip a large variety of British ales.

Discos

At about 2am, Donostia's small but mighty disco scene starts thumping.

> **La Perla,** Po. Concha, bordering the beach. Mobs jam a huge floorspace. Neon and strobes. Cover charge 600ptas. Open 1-5:30am.
>
> **Bataplán,** beneath the boardwalk near La Perla. The small, steamy dance floor overlooks the beach. Cover charge 1000ptas. Open 1-6am.
>
> **Boga Boga,** C. Esterlines, in the *parte vieja.* The town's punk club.
>
> **Iguana,** C. San Jerónimo, in the *parte vieja.* Modern music for those who like a mix.
>
> **Keops,** C. Anoeta, s/n, by the stadium. The disco of choice for many suntanned beachcombers.
>
> **Ku,** atop Monte Igüeldo. See Keops.

Beaches and Sports

Playa de la Concha curves from the port to the **Pico del Loro,** the beak-shaped promontory on which Palacio de Miramar dwells. Unfortunately, the virtually flat beach disappears during high tide. The Atlético San Sebastián **windsurfing school** is here (July-Aug. 10-day courses; four 1/2hr. sessions per day 11am-6pm). Crowds jam onto the shorter but steeper **Playa de Ondarreta,** beyond Miramar.

Both beaches face **Isla de Santa Clara,** in the center of the bay—a delectable spot for picnics. A **motorboat** leaves from the port (tel. 42 23 36; every 1/2hr. until 8:30pm; round-trip 190ptas, seniors 100ptas, ages 4-8 50ptas; 25-trip ticket 3800ptas, children 1100ptas). Oarspeople rent **rowboats** (tel. 42 23 36; June 1-Sept. 30 875ptas per hr.; 2hr. minimum, each additional hr. 350ptas). Both services operate from the kiosk by the port, the Oficina de Servicios del Puerto (tel. 42 23 36; June-Sept. only).

The **information** number for all summer sports is 48 11 39. Consult the *UDA Verano* brochure, available at the tourist office, for further information.

Festivals

Donostia's four-day **Festival de Jazz** is one of Europe's most ambitious; such giants as Art Blakey, Wynton Marsalis, Dizzy Gillespie, and Gerry Mulligan have played here. Local jazz artists perform once or twice a week at the **Be Bop Bar,** Po. Salamanca, 3. Lesser-known artists play at Pl. Trinidad in the *parte vieja*; the *terraza del Ayuntamiento* by the water is used for larger concerts. For **information** on the 1993 festival, contact the Oficina del Festival de Jazz at C. Reina Regente, s/n, 20003 San Sebastián (beneath the tourist office). The tourist office also has the scoop on concerts, schedules, and ticket information.

There are so many festivals in Donostia that the tourist office prints a little (53-page) booklet with the year's schedule: everything from music to horseracing to regattas to sculpture exhibitions. They host a marathon in mid-October; **El Día de San Sebastián** (Jan. 20) with local dances; a **carnival;** an **Underwater Film Festival** in April (for information contact Federación Guipuzcoana de Actividades Subacuáticas, C. Virgen del Carmen, 25; tel 28 63 88); and a **Festival Internacional de Danza** in May (contact Diputación Foral de Guipuzcoa at 42 35 11).

The week of August 15, **Aste Nagustia** (Big Week), is ablaze with fun. Sports events, concerts, movies, and an international fireworks display outdo each other for six blessed nights. On August 31, a candlelit procession makes its way down C. 31 de Agosto as a reminder of the 1813 fire that consumed the city. Movie stars and directors own the streets in the second fortnight of September during the **Festival Internacional de Cine,** classified among the four most important in the world (along with Venice, Cannes, and Berlin). Luminaries parade for the stargazers at Edwardian Hotel María Cristina. For information about the film festival, call 48 12 12 or write to Apartados de Correos 397, 20080 Donostia/San Sebastián, Spain; the office shares the same building as the tourist office.

For more specific information on any of Donostia's festivals call or write to the tourist office, **Centro de Atracción y Turismo**, C. Reina Regente, s/n, 20008 San Sebastián—it's a hyperinformed conduit for such information.

Near Donostia

Hondarribia (Fuenterrabía)

This beach town on the French border used to be popular with smugglers and fugitives, but now is popular with anyone whose heart is still beating. The **playa** itself, distinctly a family affair, is unutterably crowded in summer with vacationing *madrileños* and other city folk.

Concrete hotels encroach upon the new town, but up in the **barrio viejo** cobbled streets twist between colorfully painted and elaborately carved buildings. The city itself is an excuse for a visit. The **Portuko Eliza** is the oft-remodeled Gothic church where Louis XIV of France was married by proxy to Spanish Habsburg Infanta María Teresa. (Open for mass only.) The cold stone box of the **Karlos V Gaztelua** has been converted from a castle into an expensive *parador,* which means paupers won't be tolerated. The **museo** on C. Mayor mounts good exhibitions, usually with labels in *castellano* and *euskera* and sometimes in English and French. (Open Mon.-Sat. 10am-1pm and 5-9pm. Free.)

Budget rooms mean a scramble. Modern, attractive **Albergue Juan Sebastián Elcano (HI),** Ctra. Faro (tel. 64 15 50; fax 64 00 28) perches on a hillside overlooking the sea. From the town center, head to the beach or take the "Playa" bus. Turn left where the road forks right near the beach entrance (also where the bus swivels) and follow the signs to the hostel. If lucky or you've called ahead, you may find space in this four-bedroom house holding 200. (3-day max. stay when full. Flexible curfew 11pm. 825ptas per person, over 26 1200ptas. Breakfast included. Sheets 200ptas.) When the hostel's full, the owner will let you camp (400ptas per person).

Closer to the center is **Hostal-Residencia Alvarez Quintero,** C. Miramar, 7 (tel. 64 22 99), behind a light green garage door. Airy rooms, many with huge windows (some bay windows). (Singles with bath 3700ptas. Doubles with bath 4700-5700ptas. Breakfast 450ptas.) **Camping Jaizkebel** (tel. 64 16 79) spreads 2km from town on the Ctra. a Guadelupe towards Monte Jaizkebel. They've got a bar-restaurant, laundry, supermarket and hot showers. (Reception open 24 hrs. 390ptas per person, 370ptas per tent and per car.)

Like the accommodations, nearly every restaurant takes plastic. **Restaurante Kai-Alde** (tel. 64 46 22), on Itxasargi Kalea (an eastward metamorphosis of San Pedro Kalea), has a 900ptas *menú.* (Open 12:30-3:30pm and 8:30-11pm.)

The closest thing to a tourist office in Hondarribia is the *euskera/castellano* map handed out by the guard in the **Ayuntamiento** building. It's located on C. Mayor, a.k.a. Kalea Nagusia on the street signs. At the other end of town, the **post office** (tel. 64 12 04) lies on Pl. San Cristobal at the intersection with the traffic circle. (Open Mon.-Fri. 8am-3pm, Sat. 9am-1pm.) The **postal code** is 20280. For a **taxi,** call 64 12 56. The **Red Cross** at El Puntal can be reached at 64 40 39. If you need an **ambulance,** call 22 22 22. The **police** come running when you dial 64 23 40. Interurbanos **buses** (tel. 64 13 02) run to Donostia (every 12min., 1hr., 160ptas) via Irún (every 15min., 70ptas). The bus stop is at Zuloaga Kalea.

Irún

Irún is Basque for "I run," which is probably what you'll want to do when you land in this frontier town before hopping on a connection to Madrid or Paris. Urban sprawl fills the 5km that officially separates the town from Fuenterrabía. The town itself has little to see, and it has ugly shoe stores. There's a **monasterio** on Mt. San Marcial where—in a reenactment of *La Chanson de Roland*—citizens defeated the entire French army on June 30, 1522. Residents commemorate the victory each year by dressing in red, white, and black and carrying rifles through the streets.

There are quite a few *hostales* in the area round the crossroads just up from the train station, but in summer they fill quickly. Some people who manage to secure rooms use Irún as a base for visiting Donostia, where the *hostal* climate is even rougher (and pricier). Bear in mind, however, that Irún is much less convenient and public transport back to Irún is scarce after 9pm. Just up the street from RENFE is **Hostal Residencia Lizaso,** C. Aduana, 5 (tel. 61 16 00), with a TV room and clean, unremarkable rooms. (Prices not including IVA. Singles 1800ptas, with bath 300ptas. Doubles 3100ptas, with shower 3600ptas, with bath 4500ptas.) **Restaurant Itxaso** next door serves a decent 700ptas *menú. Platos combinados* 540-740ptas. (Open Sat.-Thurs. 9:30am-10:30pm). The **mercado** is up Argentinas Errepublika, 12. (Open 8:30am-1:30pm.)

Another town without a tourist office, Irún's **Ayuntamiento** (tel. 62 55 00) at Pl. San Juan Harria dispenses eye-crossing maps. (Open Mon.-Fri. 8:30am-2pm, Sat. 8am-noon.) The **post office** is down the street at Argentinas Errepublika, 6 (open Mon.-Fri. 8am-9pm, Sat. 9am-2pm). For **taxis,** call 61 22 29 or 62 29 71. The **Red Cross** can be reached at 61 12 03, the **ambulance** at 22 22 22. The **police** (tel. 62 03 00; in **emergency** 091) are stationed in Pl. Ensanche, s/n. For other services, call Fuenterrabía (see above).

RENFE **trains** (tel. 61 22 36) flounce out to all of Spain; connections to Donostia are frequent (20min., 115ptas). Information (tel. 61 67 08) open 7am-11pm. The station has **currency exchange,** a **post office,** and some stores.

Vitoria-Gasteiz

Maybe it's not on the water, and maybe it's not famous for anything more than the production of chocolate truffles and playing cards—so what? There are more square meters of *zona verde* per inhabitant in Vitoria than any other European city (more than 1.5 square kilometers in total of parks, trees and general greenness) and there are airy plazas, broad avenues, and first-class museums. Vitoria has all the charm of an old city packaged in a sleek, modern cosmopolis.

The city's so old that no one's sure when it was founded as the town of Gasteiz. In 1181 the Navarrese king Sancho el Sabio (Sancho the Wise) changed the Gasteiz's name to Villa de Nueva Vitoria, promoting the town to the status of a city in a single stroke. Vitoria's strategic position on the plain between the Kingdom of Navarra and increasingly dynamic Castille made it a territorial hot potato, juggled back and forth between the two crowns during the 12th and 13th centuries. The critical Battle of Vitoria was fought in 1813 by the Duke of Wellington and the Spanish General Alava, who drove out Bonaparte's troops from their positions just north of the town and secured the Basque provinces.

As Castilla's commercial routes took on increasing importance, *castellano* came to displace *euskera* in everyday discourse; so that the province of Araba ("Alava" in *euskera*) speaks almost entirely Castilian. But on recovering administrative autonomy in 1979, the Basques declared Vitoria the seat of their regional government.

Orientation and Practical Information

Vitoria is the orientation dream come true: signs to all major sights are clear and accurate, and street names are actually posted on clearly visible signs. For motorists, street signs face you instead of lining up flush with the direction of traffic.

The medieval **casco viejo** (old city) is the egg-shaped epicenter of the city. **Plaza de la Virgen Blanca,** at the base of the old city, marks the center of town. Around the old city lies an expansive quarter built according to the Enlightenment urban planning recipe, with wide tree-lined pedestrian streets. From the train station, follow **Calle Eduardo Dato** straight to the plaza.

The bus station is on **Calle Francia,** just north of where it changes name to Calle de la Paz. These modern thoroughfares skirt the eastern edge of the *casco viejo*. To get to Pl. Virgen Blanca, turn left on C. Francia and follow it four blocks, then hang a right C. Postas; it leads to the plaza.

> **Tourist Office:** Parque de la Florida, s/n (tel. 13 13 21), southwest of the old city. From the train station, take the 2nd left on C. Florida and follow it to the edge of the Parque. From the bus station, turn left onto C. Francia, follow it through its metamorphosis into C. Paz, then bear right on C. Ortiz de Zárate to C. Florida. The tourist office is past the gazebo on the corner of C. Ramón y Cajal and C. Cadena y Eleta. The map is slick and beauteous, but falls short in the *casco viejo*. Don't let them convince you a youth hostel exists. Open June 15-Sept. 15 Mon.-Fri. 8am-2pm and 4-8pm, Sun. 8am-2pm; Sept. 16-June 14 Mon.-Fri. 9am-1:30pm and 3-6pm.
>
> **Budget Student Travel: TIVE,** Instituto Provincial de Sanidad building, C. Santiago, 11, 2nd fl. (tel. 26 35 11), behind the hospital. All the way to the left in an office marked "Ministerio de Asuntos Sociales." The staff emphasizes that it's a branch office, which means they don't have jack. Good for ISIC (500ptas) and HI card (1800ptas). Open Mon.-Fri. 9am-2pm.
>
> **Post Office:** C. Postas, 9 (tel. 23 05 75; fax 23 37 80), a pedestrian street just south of Pl. Virgen Blanca. From the bus station, turn right off C. Paz. From the train station, take C. Dato to the end and turn right. Open for info Mon.-Fri. 8am-9pm; for stamps, **telegrams,** and **fax** Mon.-Fri. 8am-9pm, Sat. 9am-7pm. For Lista de Correos walk around the corner to the C. Nuestra Señora del Cabello side of the building. It's the unmarked door open Mon.-Fri. 8am-9pm, Sat. 9am-2pm. **Postal Code:** 01080.

Telephones: Telefónica, Av. Gasteiz, 69. From the tourist office bear right on C. Luis Heinz, walk through Pl. Lovaína and onto C. Sancho el Sabio until Av. Gasteiz; it's on the corner of C. Beato Tomás de Zumárraga. Open Mon.-Sat. 9am-2pm and 4-10pm. **Telephone Code**: 945.

Flights: Aeropuerto Vitoria-Foronda (tel. 27 40 00), 9km away from town. **Iberia**. Information open 6am-11pm. To: Madrid (Mon.-Sat. 1 per day, 50min., 10,625ptas); Palma de Mallorca (3 per wk., 1hr., 12,650ptas); Sevilla (3 per wk., 1hr., 16,000ptas). Check p. 2 of *El Correo Espanol* (local paper) for current flights. Charter flights to international destinations. Accessible only by car or taxi (1200-1400ptas).

Trains: RENFE, C. Eduardo Dato, 46 (tel. 23 02 02, 14 12 07), at the end of the road, south of the old city. Information open 8am-10pm. To: Pamplona (3 per day, 11/2hr., 500ptas); Donostia/ San Sebastián (14 per day, 11/2-21/2hr., 650-950ptas); Burgos (15 per day, 2hr., 675ptas); Zaragoza (1 per day, 3hr., 1990ptas); Madrid (7 per day, *talgo* 5hr., 3500ptas); A Coruña (2 per day, 11hr., 4300ptas); Lisboa (2 per day, 14hr., 5895ptas); Paris (2 per day via Hendaya, 8500ptas).

Buses: C. Francia, 24, in a big ol' building east of the old city. Tons of different companies. **La Burundesa** (tel. 25 55 09). To: Donostia/San Sebastián (4 per day, 11/2hr., 765ptas); Pamplona (9-11 per day, 13/4hr., 725ptas); Zaragoza (6 per day, 3hr., 1020ptas). **La Unión** (tel. 26 46 26). To Bilbo (6 per day, 1hr., 530ptas). **Compañía Automóviles Alava** (tel. 24 06 50). To: Logroño (7 per day, 1-2hr., 805ptas). **Turytrans** (tel. 28 32 74). To: Santander (3 per day, 3hr., 1195ptas). **Viajes Bascotour** (tel. 25 02 49). To: Barcelona (2 per day, 71/2hr., 3500ptas); Málaga (1 per day, 12hr., 5600ptas); València (1 per day, 9hr., 5300ptas including meal). **Continental Auto** (tel. 28 64 66). To: Burgos (6 per day, 11/2hr., 730ptas); Donostia/San Sebastián (4 per day, 13/4hr., 765ptas); Madrid (8 per day, 4-5 hr., 2330ptas). **Line-bus** (tel. 28 67 45). To London (2-3 per wk., 23hr., 12,200ptas).

Public Transportation: Buses cover the entire metropolitan area, including suburbs (65ptas). Tourist office has a vague pamphlet on routes.

Taxis: Radio-Taxis (tel. 27 35 00, 23 00 60).

Car Rental: Avis, Av. Gasteiz, 53 (tel. 24 46 12), just past C. Adriano VI. Opel Corsa Swing 3990ptas with *tarifa amiga* (plus insurance and IVA). Must be 21 years old and have had driver's license 1 yr. Open Mon.-Fri. 9am-1:30pm and 4-7pm, Sat. 9am-1pm. **Hertz,** C. Nicaragua, 10 (tel. 24 77 83), bear right off the right side of Pl. Constitución coming from Av. Gasteiz. Ford Fiesta 4510ptas plus 36ptas per km. Must be 21 or over. Open Mon.-Fri. 9am-1pm and 4-8pm, Sat. 9am-1pm.

English Bookstore: Linacero, C. Fueros, 17-19 (tel. 25 06 88). From the bus station, turn right onto C. Postas from C. Paz, then left on C. de los Fueros. Novels everywhere (basic classics) and travel guides. Open Mon.-Fri. 9:45am-1:30pm and 4:30-8pm, Sat. 9:45am-1:30pm.

Library: Biblioteca Pública-Casa de Cultura, Po. Florida, 9 (tel. 13 44 05). From the tourist office, turn left; the library borders Parque de la Florida in an ugly modern building. Open Mon.-Fri. 9am-3pm and 4-8:30pm.

Youth Center: Instituto Foral de la Juventud, Pl. Provincia, 13 (tel. 26 69 86). From Pl. Virgen Blanca, turn left onto C. Diputación, which ends at Pl. Provincia. Information on trips, camping, travel. Open July-Aug. Mon.-Fri. 11am-2pm; Sept.-June Mon.-Fri. 11am-2pm and 5-7pm.

Laundromat: Lavomatique, C. Torno, 2 (tel. 27 65 30). From the bus station turn left on C. Francia, then right on C. Abrevadero, then right again. Wash and dry 1000ptas per load. Open Mon.-Fri. 8am-8pm, Sat. 8am-1pm.

Swimming Pool: Complejo Polideportivo Mendizorroza, Pl. Amadeo García Salazar, s/n (tel. 16 10 69), off Portal de LaSarte behind the train station. "Circunvalación" bus runs here (65ptas). Admission to the sports complex 500ptas.

Red Cross: Portal de Castilla (tel. 13 26 30, **emergency** (tel. 22 22 22).

24-Hour Pharmacy: tel. 23 07 21. Check pharmacy doors for the listing or p. 2 of *El Correo Español*, which also lists other useful telephone numbers.

Medical Services: Hospital General de Santiago, C. Olaguíbel (tel. 25 36 00). From the bus station turn left where C. Francia becomes C. Paz. **Ambulance** (tel. 16 11 61, 27 98 97).

Emergency: Medical or otherwise (tel. 088).

Police: Municipal (tel. 16 11 11 or 092). **National** (tel. 091).

Accommodations and Camping

As usual, singles are rare, and solo travelers will most likely find themselves in uselessly large beds for the full double rate. If that doesn't appeal to you, the tourist office compiles a list of the very few budget *pensiones* and *casas de huéspedes*. Early risers should bear in mind that some establishments don't usually turn their hot water on before 9am.

Pensión Zurine, C. Florida, 24 (tel. 14 22 40). Turn left from the tourist office; it's on the far side of C. Eduardo Dato. Nice bedspreads, new furniture, and *miradores* with ice-blue bathrooms. Some terraces with geraniums. Singles 2000ptas. Doubles 3000ptas.

Pensión Araba, C. Florida, 21, 2nd and 4th fl. (tel. 23 25 88). From the tourist office turn left and walk down C. Florida. Old but well-maintained blue-trimmed rooms. Sturdy beds with half-moon headboards. Singles 1400ptas. Doubles 2500ptas.

Hostal-Residencia Nuvilla, C. Fueros, 29, 4th fl. (tel. 25 91 51). Turn left on C. Francia from the bus station, then right onto C. Postas, then left; it's past the pink granite *pelota* court and sculpture. Coin-motif brown wallpaper will have you seeing double. Rooms on the street side look upon evening *paseo*. Rare singles 1350ptas. Doubles 2550ptas. Showers 250ptas.

Hostal Florida, C. Manuel Iradies, 33 (tel. 26 06 75). From the train station, the 1st right. Resplendent *hostal* in a resplendent building with cushiony hall chairs and classy flower-tiled bathrooms. Singles 2400ptas, with bath 3200ptas. Doubles 4000ptas, with bath 4800ptas.

Hostal Savoy, C. Prudencia María de Verástegui, 4 (tel. 25 00 56). Turn left from the bus station then curve around the corner to the left. Modern rooms with phones in a new building. Verging on *hotel*, with prices to match. Breakfast 250ptas. Singles with bath 2800ptas. Doubles with bath 4100ptas. *Menú* 950ptas.

Hotel la Bilbaina, C. Prudencio María de Verástegui, 2 (tel. 25 44 00), next door to Savoy. Swanky, with phones and TVs in rooms. Marbleish floors in spotless bathrooms. Singles with bath 3500ptas. Doubles with bath 4200ptas, with bath and 2 beds 5700ptas.

Camping Ibaya (tel. 13 04 94), 5km from town toward Madrid. Follow Portal de Castilla out west from the tourist office intersection. Supermarket, café-restaurant, hot showers. Reception open 8am-2pm and 4-10pm. 325ptas per person, per tent and per car. Open June-Sept.

Food

Flee from boring old C. Eduardo Dato and its pedestrian sidestreets. **Calle Cuchillería** in the *casco viejo* is lined with budget bar-restaurants—and you'll find a young SoHo-esque crowd. To get there from the train station, take C. Eduardo Dato, turn right on C. Postas, and then left past the post office and uphill, where C. Cuchillería and other old-town streets radiate from C. San Francisco. Most restaurants serve their *menú* only at lunch.

Fresh produce and food are traded at the 2-level market, **Mercado de Abastos,** on Pl. Santa Bárbara. From the bus station, take C. Francia to C. Paz and turn left on C. Postas. (Open Mon.-Thurs. 9am-2pm and 5-8pm, Fri. 9am-2pm and 5-8:30pm, Sat. 8am-1pm.)

Groceries: Simago, C. General Alava, 10, between C. Eduardo Dato and C. San Antonio. Open Mon.-Sat. 9am-8pm. **Eroski,** C. Florida, 56, a right off C. Eduardo Dato. Open Mon.-Fri. 9am-1:30pm and 5-8pm, Sat. 9am-2pm.

Restaurante Casa Paco, C. Mateo Moraza, 17, under the arches near C. San Francisco. Elegant arches and lace curtains. Wall-bound woodcuts. *Merluza a la vasca* a specialty. Entrees 800-1200ptas. Lunch *menú* 700ptas. Open Aug. 15-July 31 1:30-3:30pm and 9-11pm.

Museo del Organo, C. Manuel Iradier, 80. Take C. Florida east from the Parque to the Pl. Toros, then turn right. Veggie food, modern music and thirtysomething crowd in a plant-filled haven. Really savory *tarta de cebolla* (onion pie) and generous salad in a 3-course *menú* (800ptas). Open Mon.-Sat. 1-4pm.

Restaurant Hirurak, C. Cuchillería, 26, off C. San Francisco on the right. Old stone walls bedecked with modern art. Relaxed, young clientele be-bops to reggae. Staff has their hands full. Decent quiche. *Menú* 800ptas. Open Tues.-Fri. 1-3:30pm and 9-11pm, Sat.-Sun. 2-3:30pm and 9-11:30pm.

Bar La Bodega, C. Florida, 36. From the park, walk past Pensión Zurine (see above). Medieval interior of stone walls and a frightening, spiky chandelier (what if it fell?). *Cazuelitas* and *bacalao a la vizcaina* (600ptas) are specialties. *Menú* 900ptas. Open 9am-11pm.

Amboto Oleagarena, C. Cuchillería, 29. Small dining room with benches that come out of the wall, Murphy-bed style. A stone tavern with modern music and traditional food. *Alubias rojas, anchoas cantábricos,* and *pimientos rellenos* might crop up on the 700ptas *menú*. *Bocadillos* and *raciones* too. Open Tues.-Sun. 1:30-3:30pm, Fri.-Sat. 9:30-11:30pm.

Restaurante Los Guaranís, Portal de Castilla, 42. *Menú* 900ptas. Outdoor tables that look onto a slightly out of the way park. Inside, it's a pink, swish dining room. *Pulpo a la gallega* (octopus) recommended. A la carte drains wallets. Open Tues.-Sat. 8am-midnight, Sun. 2pm-midnight.

Sights and Entertainment

Vitoria is a city to be taken in slowly, on a walk, stopping every so often for a few *copas*. The action, if there were any, would be at central **Plaza de la Virgen Blanca,** the focal point of Vitoria's *fiestas*. At its side sits sprawling, arcaded **Plaza de España**. Architecturally and geographically it divides the old town of concentric streets, balconied seignorial houses, and palaces on the hill from the new town of broad avenues (beginning with C. Eduardo Dato) and grid streets.

When Gasteiz became Vitoria-Gasteiz, it was necessary to join the hill to the rest of the town below; architects Sefurola and Olaguíbel pulled this off in virtuosic fashion. C. Mateo de Moraza is the first of three levels of **Los Arquillos,** a set of arches that merge old and new Vitoria through stairs and streets arrayed like terraces. The *casco viejo* begins uphill through the arches. Down C. Cuchillería is the 17th-century **Casa del Cordón,** so-called because of the stone *cordón* (rope) that embellishes its central arch; it now houses a museum. Skirting the left side of the cathedral and downhill is the **Museo Provincial de Arqueología,** with artifacts from the Paleolithic Era. A loop-de-loop left through the plaza next to the archeology museum onto C. Siervas de Jesús deposits the looper at the **Museo de Ciencias Naturales,** where there are some geological, botanical, and zoological exhibits.

The **Museo Provincial de Armería** has a weapon collection that features battle plans and uniforms from the Battle of Vitoria. Opposite the museum, the gorgeous stained-glass Casa de Araba houses the **Museo de Bellas Artes,** with sculptures in the garden and a collection of Romanesque and polychrome sculptures and paintings by Ribera, Miró, and Picasso. Pending its eventual transfer to the *casco viejo,* you may also inspect one of the best playing-card collections in the world. There's even a nifty video explaining the history of the playing card and how they were once hand-painted. To get to the museum from the tourist office, walk past the gazebo and follow Po. Senda to Po. Fray Francisco de Vitoria; the museum is ahead on the left. (Museums open Tues.-Fri. 11am-2pm and 5-7pm, Sat.-Sun. 11am-2pm. Free.)

Any evening of the year sees all of Vitoria out on **Calle Eduardo Dato** or in the *casco viejo* getting pissed. On weekdays the action settles down by midnight, but the thrashing weekend scene lasts till dawn. **Calle Cuchillería** draws an older, upscale crowd. **Calle Zapatería,** also in the *casco viejo,* teems with teens at dance bars and discos.

World-class jazz comes to Vitoria the third week of July for the **Festival de Jazz de Vitoria-Gasteiz.** (Tickets 500-1700ptas; for information call 14 19 19 or write to C. San Antonio, 16, 01005 Vitoria. Box office open 8:30am-2pm prior to and during the festival. English spoken.) The other major festival is the traditional **Fiesta de la Virgen Blanca** (Aug. 4-9). Dancing and revelry is launched in Pl. Virgen Blanca with a rocket; highlights are the demented people hanging from umbrellas in the middle of the plaza and roving musical bands of young, male *Blusas* (sort of like *tunas*).

La Rioja and Navarra

Tucked away between Castilla and Navarra, La Rioja is synonymous with great wine, produced here since the 12th century. While the western section of the region benefits from its proximity to the rainy hills of Euskadi, irrigation ensures that even the dry regions near Aragón produce bumper crops. The name "La Rioja" derives from the Ebro tributary Río Oja, whose muddy red waters trickle through the vineyards.

Logroño, capital of La Rioja, lies in the center of the region. Oenophiles may prefer Haro, in the western Rioja Alta, where most of the best *bodegas* (wine cellars) live. The Camino de Santiago traverses this region; all the tourist offices stock a pamphlet called *El Camino de Santiago por La Rioja* (The Way of St. James through La Rioja), available in many languages. The monasteries in Santo Domingo de la Calzada and San Millán de la Cogolla, both accessible by bus from Logroño, are two of the most important historic and artistic stops on the road. For tranquil fields beneath the strange moonscapes of the mountainous Sierra, ask at any tourist office about the *zonas de acampada*, three scenic zones along the southern border of La Rioja in which the government has provided basic facilities for camping in otherwise unspoiled land.

Navarra lies just north of La Rioja, extending the tawny plains of the *meseta* above Pamplona to the lush Pyrenean valleys which border France. Although the majority of the region is of non-Basque origin, a small group of towns in the north cling to their Basque roots. The *euskarra* language appears on street signs and in graffiti from Pamplona onward. An occasional "Gora Euskadi!" ("Long live Euskadi!") rings through the streets. The Navarrese have always shown a feisty self-reliance. After demolishing Charlemagne's rear guard at Roncesvalles in revenge for their tearing down a segment of Pamplona's walls, Navarra came into its own as a kingdom in the 9th century. In the early 10th century under King Sancho the Great (1000-1035) it was the most powerful Christian kingdom in Iberia. Fernando el Católico annexed it to recently unified Spain in 1512. Traditional Navarrese privileges embodied in the *fueros* (medieval laws)—including exemption from military service—weren't fully revoked until 1876, as a result of Navarra's persistent support for the conservative cause in the Carlist Wars.

Logroño

Logroño, the capital of La Rioja and wine country, is fighting its overindustrialized image. While some areas of the city have become derelict, gentrification and government intervention have restored much of the *casco antiguo* (old quarter) and many of the 17th- and 18th-century homes which line the river. Some feel that the government-sponsored renovation of the traditionally *gitano* (gypsy) neighborhood is a pretext for removing an undesirable group. Nevertheless, some of the neighborhood's *gitano* character remains. Residents emphasize the city's history as a stopover for Compostela-bound pilgrims and the area's *bodega* tradition; the city's rail and bus connections make it the best entry point to the small wine and monastery towns of the region.

Orientation and Practial Information

The town radiates out from the **Parque del Espolón**, a tree-lined set of gravel paths with a large, splashing fountain at its center. The **casco antiguo** runs between the park and the **Río Eloro**, on the far side of the city from the bus and train terminals.

To reach the park from the train station, cross the major traffic artery of **Avenida de Lobete** and head straight on **Avenida de España**. The bus station is at the next major intersection; its doors face diagonally towards **Calle del General Vara del Rey**. A right turn on C. General Vara leads to the park. To reach the river from the park, turn left from C. General Vara at the end of the park and follow the arcaded storefronts until you reach **Calle de Sagasta** on the far side. Turn right and follow this as it slopes downhill to the river.

Tourist Office: C. San Miguel Villanueva, 10 (tel. 29 12 60), the 1st left off C. General Vara before Parque del Espolón. In summer, another tent is set up on the Espolón itself. Basic information on the wine and monastery routes and a weak map of Logroño. Open July-Sept. 10am-2pm and 5-9pm; Oct.-June 10am-2pm.

Budget Travel: Dirrecíon de la Juventud, C. Portales, 1 (tel. 29 11 12). Information about youth discounts and special events in the city. Open Mon.-Fri. 9am-3pm.

Post Office: Pl. San Agustin (tel. 22 00 66, 22 89 06), next to the *museo*. Open for stamps and Lista de Correos Mon.-Fri. 8am-9pm, Sat. 9am-7pm. **Postal Code:** 26006.

Telephones: C. Portales, 75, just past the post office. Open Mon.-Sat. 9am-1pm and 5-9pm. **Telephone Code:** 941.

Trains: RENFE, Pl. Europa (tel. 24 02 02), off Av. España. Information open 7am-11pm. To: Haro (5 per day, 50min., 265ptas); Tudela (12 per day, 13/4hr., 455ptas); Burgos (3 per day, 21/4hr., 786-980ptas); Zaragoza (11 per day, 3hr., 835-1040ptas); Bilbo (3 per day, 31/2hr., 855-1070ptas); León (3 per day, 41/4hr., 2260ptas); Madrid (2 per day, 5hr., 3010ptas); Barcelona (5 per day, 71/2hr., 2940-3620ptas); València (2 per day, 91/2hr., 5745ptas); A Coruña (1 per day, 111/2hr., 4965ptas).

Buses: Av. España (tel. 23 59 83), on the corner of C. General Vara and Av. Pío XII. Several companies; check the information board for the appropriate counter. Information open 6:30am-10:30pm. To: Haro (3-4 per day, 45min., 305ptas); Santo Domingo de la Calzada (8-9 per day, 1hr., 285ptas); San Millán de la Cogolla (1-2 per day, 1hr., 250ptas); Vitoria (5-7 per day, 1-2hr., 875ptas); Soria (2 per day, 2hr., 710ptas); Pamplona (3-5 per day, 2hr., 745ptas); Zaragoza (8 per day, 2hr., 1100ptas); Bilbo (4-6 per day, 2 1/4 hr., 1115ptas); Burgos (4-5 per day, 3-5hr., 730ptas); Santander (3-4 per day, 4-5hr., 1685ptas); Madrid (2 per day, 4 3/4 hr., 2075ptas); Barcelona (3-4 per day, 6hr., 3140ptas).

Public Transportation: City buses (45ptas) are generally unnecessary for tourists.

Car Rental: Avis, Gran Vía del Rey Don Juan Carlos I, 67 (tel. 20 23 54), left from C. General Vara. Open Mon.-Fri. 9am-1pm and 4pm-6pm, Sat. 10am-1pm. **Hertz,** C. General Vara, 67 (tel. 25 80 26), left from Av. España with the stations behind you. Open Mon.-Fri. 9am-2pm and 4pm-6pm, Sat. 9am-1pm.

Luggage Storage: Paquete Express at the train station. Go left, out the station doors, and through the gate in the brick wall.

English Bookstore: Libreria Gumersindo Cerezo, C. Portales, 23 (tel. 25 17 62). A small number of novels in English. Open Mon.-Fri. 10am-2pm and 4-8pm, Sat. 10am-1pm.

Public Toilets: In Parque del Espolón. Open 9:30am-8pm.

Red Cross: C. Saturnina Ulargui, s/n (tel. 22 22 22; information 22 53 08).

Medical Services: Hospital San Millán (tel. 29 45 00), on the edge of town in the direction of Zaragoza. **Ambulance** (tel. 22 52 12).

Police: tel. 091. **Municipal police** (tel. 092). **Guardia Civil** (tel. 062, 22 11 00).

Accommodations and Camping

The area around the *casco antiguo* is brimful with pensions and hostels. **Calle San Juan,** the first left past the Espolón from the stations, and **Calles San Agustín** and **Laurel,** a little deeper into the old quarter past the far corner of the Espolón, offer particularly good hunting. Although some lodgings look a bit shabby, most are family-run and very clean. Reservations are crucial for the *fiesta* week of June 11.

Fonda Bilbaína, C. Capitán Eduardo Gallarza, 10 (tel. 25 42 26). The façade is the only part that hasn't been renovated—you don't have to look at it once you're inside. Freshly painted white walls and high ceilings. Room size varies; some have glassed-in balconies. Singles 1500-2000ptas. Doubles 2500ptas, with shower 3000 ptas.

Hotel Sebastián, C. San Juan, 21 (tel. 24 28 00). Reception has a doorbell on the 2nd floor. Decent sized rooms and sparkling bathrooms. Front rooms have balconies. Singles 2000ptas. Doubles 3000ptas.

- **Camping La Playa,** Av. Playa, s/n (tel. 25 22 53), off the main highway across the river from the *casco antiguo*. A riverbank site with a sandy beach. Municipal swimming pools next door are free. 350ptas per person, per tent, and per car. Open June-Sept.

Food

Scads of bars will happily uncork a bottle of the region's wine. Restaurants in the *casco antiguo* stock La Rioja's gastronomical delights. One such specialty is *patatas en salsa picante*, potatoes with melted cheese in a slightly spicy sauce. The local **market** is in the large concrete building on C. Capitán Eduardo Gallarza, left off C. de Sagasta en route to the river. (Open Mon.-Sat. 9am-2pm and 5-8pm; winter Mon.-Sat. 9am-2pm.)

> **Restaurante La Cuera,** C. San Juan, 13 (tel. 24 27 48). Special effects of the concrete roof make this small diner look like a cave; assorted wild mushrooms adorn the walls and are cooked up for patrons. Entrees 550-1300ptas. Open Fri.-Tues. 1:30-3pm and 8:30-11pm.
>
> **El Arca de Noé,** C. Oviedo, 6. From the bus station, turn right and walk across the street. The animal kingdom is eternally grateful for this vegetarian salvation. *Menú* 850 ptas. Open Sun.-Thurs. 1:30-3:45pm, Fri.-Sat. 1:30-3:45pm and 9:30-11:30pm.
>
> **Bar Soriano,** Trav. Laurel, 2 (tel. 22 88 07), in the *casco antiguo*. A hole-in-the-wall which has an entire town jumping for its 'shroomy specialty: *champignons con gambas* (mushrooms with shrimp). Open all day.

Sights and Entertainment

Catedral de Santa María de la Redonda, on Pl. Mercado, wears a nondescript 18th-century façade and an engraved tribute to Franco's "crusade against communism." Poor lighting and narrow windows leave the upper reaches of the vaulting in almost complete darkness. More alive than the supposed-Michelangelo etching of Calvary behind the main altar are the enormous birds that nest atop the belfry. From C. General Vara turn left on C. Portales; the cathedral is two blocks away on the right. (Open 8am-1pm and 6-8:30pm. Free.)

Another three blocks along C. Portales in Pl. San Agustín is the **Museo de La Rioja,** C. Agustín, 23, which exists thanks to the rifling of the area's monasteries and convents under the Disentailment Law of 1835. (Open Mon.-Sat. 10am-2pm. Admission 200ptas, EEC citizens under 21 free.) The grassy lawns by the **Río Eloro** provide good strolling; two bridges, the **Puente de Hierro** and the **Puente de Piedra,** and a brand-new pedestrian path allow access to the other side.

At night the partying begins in the *casco antiguo*, moving later to C. Argentina (across Gran Vía del Rey Don Juan Carlos I). The **Ferias de San Bernabé** take place the week of June 11. During this festival, the Pez brotherhood distributes fish, bread, and local wine from the Revellín gate in memory of the passing of the Jacobean pilgrims. The **Ferias de la Vendimia,** complete with bulls and folkloric festivity, happen in mid-September.

Near Logroño

Santo Domingo de la Calzada

When the hermit namesake of this small village retired to the woods southwest of Logroño in the 11th century, he certainly didn't renounce his entrepreneurial spirit. Seeing first-hand from his hermitage the trials and travails of the pilgrims crossing the river, he built a bridge for them. He followed this up by driving a road (the *calzada,* or causeway) through the woods and converting his hermitage into a hospice for the pilgrims. Soon business in the town of Santo Domingo de la Calzada was booming. Domingo proved an able administrator to the end of his 90 years, successfully playing off the rival crowns of Navarra and Castilla against each other to win bigger donations for his charitable services.

King Alfonso VI noticed the work of this monastic reject, and donated resources for the construction of a grand church. The king himself lay the first stone for the construction of the **Catedral de San Domingo,** which stands on the site of the original temple. With some Romanesque features, the current form dates from the 12th and 13th centuries. The *retablo mayor* depicts the miracle of Santo Domingo, known as "the cock that crows after it has been roasted."

As the legend goes, there once was a married couple and their son who stopped in Santo Domingo on their way to Santiago de Compstela. Upon seeing Hugonell, the couple's son, the innkeeper's young daughter fell madly in love with him, and swore that one day they would marry. The attraction wasn't mutual. In a spasm of frustrated lust, the heartbroken girl slipped a silver cup into the young pilgrim's bag and snuck out unnoticed to report the "robbery" to the mayor. Poor innocent Hugonell was hanged. Curiously, when his distraught parents visited the site of execution, they heard their son's voice insisting that he was in fact alive, that Santo Domingo had saved him. Elated, but still skeptical, Hugo's parents rushed to the mayor's house and related the bizarre series of events. Just as soon as the mayor finished scoffing that Hugonell was as dead as the roast cock on his plate, the cooked cock suddenly sprouted feathers and crowed the young pilgrim's innocence. In memory of this occurrence, a live white hen and rooster are kept in a cage in the cathedral near the main altar (they are changed monthly). There is a piece of wood from the gallows on which Hugonell was hanged opposite the fowl. On the right past the entrance are stairs into the cobwebbed *muralla* (wall) of the cathedral that lead past slit windows to the roof (with views of the streets below).

From the bus stop at Pl. Beato Hermosilla, cross Av. Rey Don Juan Carlos I and follow C. Alcalde Rodolfo Varona. Take the next left—unmarked C. Pinar—for one block, then turn right on C. Hilario Pérez, which ends at the cathedral square. Entrance to the cathedral is from C. Cristo, the second door from the left corner of the west façade. (Guided tours 10am-noon and 3:30-6pm. Cathedral open Mon.-Sat. 10am-2pm and 3:30-7pm. Admission 150ptas, children 50ptas.) **Hospedelario del Santo,** the still-functioning refuge for pilgrims, also stands on the cathedral square. Seventy free beds are granted to the journeying, along with free potatoes, cooking oil, and use of a kitchen.

The town honors its founding entrepreneur the first 12 days of May in a series of rituals that symbolically reenact episodes from his life. The **festival** culminates May 12 when thousands of inhabitants line up for their share of the *Carneros del Santo,* special rams sacrificed as symbols of Santo Domingo's hospitality. At noon a procession bearing the saint's image parades through the streets.

Hostal Río, C. Alberto Etchegoyen, 2 (tel. 34 02 77), has rooms for 1500ptas per person. Turn left on Av. Rey Don Juan Carlos I, follow it for a block, and turn right. Farther down on the left at #23, **Casa de Huéspedes Miguel** (tel. 34 03 52) has newly renovated rooms. (Tiny singles 1500ptas. Doubles 3000ptas. Triples 4000ptas.) More worldly pilgrims can afford **Hospedería Santa Teresita,** C. Pinar, 2 (tel. 36 07 00), staffed by nuns. It lies at the end of C. Pinar, a right turn from C. Alcalde Rodolfo Varona. (Singles 1775ptas, with shower 2435ptas. Doubles 3330ptas, with shower 4530ptas.) The nearest camping is 5km away towards Logroño at **Camping Bañares** (tel. 34 28 04; 400ptas per person, per tent, and per car).

The local specialty foods are *pimientos* (peppers) and *patatas* (potatoes). **Restaurante Conde,** C. Navarra, 2, serves a 950ptas *menú* on red-checked tablecloths. From the cathedral walk towards the bus stop and take a right on C. Pinar, then a left onto C. Navarra. The town **market** is held near Pl. Beato Hermosilla (Sat. 9am-2pm).

The **tourist office** lodges in Casa de Trastámara, C. Zumalacorregui, s/n (tel. 34 33 34), under the long stone arch a half-block from the cathedral square. Totally lame maps, but a detailed brochure in English with information about the city's monuments. (Open June-Sept. Mon.-Sat. 10am-2pm and 5-9pm, Sun. 10am-2pm.) The **post office** is across the street from Hostal Río at C. Alberto Etchegoyen, 1 (tel. 34 14 93), at the corner of C. Pinar. (Open Mon.-Fri. 9am-2pm, Sat. 9am-1pm.) The **postal code** is 26250 and the **telephone code** 941. The **Red Cross** answers at 34 03 34; the **Centro de Salud** at 34 21 79. In an **emergency,** call the local **police** at 34 00 05. The **Guardia Civil** are at 34 03 91.

Buses run to and from Logroño (8-9 per day, 1hr., 315ptas). The bus stop is in Pl. Beato Hermosilla.

San Millán de la Cogolla

The enshrined remains of another hermit, the shepherd *de la cogolla* (hooded) Millán, became the seed of San Millán. Two nationally registered monasteries now grace the town. **Monasterio de Suso** is a Mozarabic structure dating from the 10th century, although the chapel is thought to be of Visigothic origin. The library contains a Codex with 12 lines scrawled in the lower right hand margin—today known to be one of the first ever Castilian texts. (Open Tues.-Sun. 10am-2pm and 4-7pm. Free.) Erected in the 16th and 18th centuries, **Monasterio de Yuso**, also known as **El Escorial de La Rioja** (after Felipe II's severe palace), features several Romanesque and Byzantine ivory plaques of San Millán and San Felices. (Open Tues.-Sun. 10:30am-1pm and 4-7pm. Guided tours 200ptas.) The monasteries have a **tourist office** (tel. 37 30 49; open June-Sept. Tues.-Sat. 10am-2pm and 5-9pm, Sun. 10am-2pm). The **telephone code** is 941. **Buses** (tel. 22 42 78) shuttle to and from Logroño (2 per day, Sat.-Sun. 1 per day; 1hr.; 260ptas).

Haro

Clustered like plump grapes on a vine, 96 wine-makers overwhelm the tiny town of Haro, drawing international merchants and acclaim. At least half a dozen of these *bodegas* give **tours** of their facilities, in large warehouses grouped around the RENFE station (across the river from the town center). The wine ferments in 15-ft. barrels, is aged for at least two years, and then is returned to the oversize barrels, where egg whites speed the clarification process. A month later, the final product is bottled. Some companies still use traditional oak barrels (the guide will show where they're made by hand)—which recognizably flavor Rioja reds—but many now use stainless steel tanks. Tours are generally held between 9am and 2pm; schedules change frequently, so it's advisable to have the tourist office call ahead to arrange a visit. Many tours are in Spanish only; Bodegas Rioja Alta and Bodegas Bilbaínas are among those with English-speaking guides.

While the rest of Spain goes on *paseo*, citizens of Haro prefer to spend 7 to 10pm in *chiquiteo*—drinking wine in the **bars** on the streets between Pl. Paz and Pl. Iglesia. The custom is cheap (around 30-40ptas a glass), but it sometimes tastes cheap too. The tourist office distributes an official classification of vintages (the *Vinícola Riojana Comercial* booklet).

From June 24 to 29, the wine flows continually for the town's **Fiesta Mayor.** On the last day, the townspeople migrate to a nearby hermitage where **La Batalla del Vino** (The Battle of the Wine) is waged at precisely 10 in the morning. Everyone douses everyone else with wine in this ritual apparently rooted in a historic dispute over property with neighboring Miranda de Ebro.

Although wine-making so pervades the town that some streets actually smell of wine, it's possible to amuse yourself without so much as sniffing a cork. A beautiful stained-glass window radiates through the *retablo* of the **Basílica de Nuestra Señora de La Vega**. The church gardens command a view of the surrounding valley and wine-plant covered hills. To get to the church from the tourist office, turn left and follow C. La Vega for about three blocks. (Church open for services only. Free.) An appealing Plateresque exterior that has nothing to do with wine is the outside of the **Iglesia Parroquial de Santo Tomás,** on Pl. Iglesia. The church is on C. Santo Tomás, a left from Pl. Paz as you face the non-winey Ayuntamiento.

Hostal Aragón, C. La Vega, 9 (tel. 31 00 04), has comfy rooms. (Singles 1100ptas. Doubles 1800ptas. Showers 200ptas, up a spiral staircase.) It's a right from the tourist office. **Camping de Haro,** Av. Miranda, s/n (tel. 31 27 37), has staked out a plot on the same riverbank as the train station, only to the left of the bridge coming from town. (360ptas per person, per tent, and per car; Sept.-June 270ptas.)

Restaurante La Parra, Pl. Juan García Gato (tel. 31 08 72), off Pl. Paz, throws in an entire bottle of wine to ensure customers are satisfied with the 700ptas *menú*. From Pl. Paz, follow the RENFE station sign down C. Navarra and turn left. (Open 1-4pm and 9pm-midnight.) Near the swimming pool down C. Navarra from Pl. Paz and left on the road to Bilbo is the self-service **Asador Tirondoa** (tel. 31 17 97), highly popular with locals, where you can feast on half a roast chicken and an intimidating salad for 600ptas. (Open 1-10:30pm.) The bars in the **Herradura** quarter round the Iglesia Parroquial de Santo Tomás serve more modest meals and excellent *tapas*. Also on C. Santo Tomás, many **wine shops** sell the region's fruit of the vine; the best vintages list for around 6500ptas per bottle, but others cost as little as 200-500ptas.

The **Centro de Iniciativas Turísticas** dispenses knowledge at Pl. Monseñor Florentino Rodríguez, s/n (tel. 31 27 26). With your back to the Ayuntamiento, take C. Vega out of the far left corner of Pl. Paz. The office is in the plaza on your left after you round the bend. (Open Holy Week, Christmas, and June-Sept. Tues.-Sun. 10am-2pm and 5-8pm. If closed, get a map and brochures from the Ayuntamiento.) The **post office** (tel. 31 18 69) is at the corner of Av. Rioja and C. Alemania, a left from C. Ventilla. (Open for stamps and Lista de Correos Mon.-Fri. 9am-2pm, Sat. 9am-1pm.) The **postal code** is 26200 and the **telephone code** is 941. **Public toilets** squat beneath the gazebo in Pl. Paz. The **Red Cross** is at C. Siervas de Jesús, 2 (tel. 31 18 38); the **Centro de Salud** on C. Manuel Bartolomé Cossío (**emergency** tel. 31 05 39). The **municipal police** are at C. Sánchez del Río, 11 (tel. 31 01 25).

RENFE **trains** run to Miranda de Ebro (5 per day, 20min., 105ptas); Logroño (5 per day, 1hr., 265ptas); Bilbo (3 per day, 615ptas); Donostia/San Sebastián via Miranda de Ebro (2 *talgos* and 2 others per day, *talgo* 880ptas). To reach Pl. Paz from the train station, take the road downhill, turn right and then left across the river, and let C. Navarra lead you uphill to the plaza. **Luggage storage** is at the train station (bags checked). The last **bus** to Logroño leaves Haro around 8pm (5 per day, 45min., 305ptas). The bus stops once before reaching the station. To get to Pl. Paz from the bus station, follow the signs to *centro ciudad* along C. Ventilla and bear left from Pl. Cruz. Haro is 43km from Logroño.

Pamplona

Forget Hemingway, impotence, and Lady Brett Ashley. The real Pamplona is all elegance, with its broad and airy Enlightenment streets and the historic alleyways of the old Jewish quarter. Watered on two sides by the Río Arga and flanked by decorative parks, Pamplona (pop. 183,000) is known to Spaniards for its high-powered university, one of the premier medical institutions in Europe. Tourists know the city, of course, for its Running of the Bulls (the *encierro*) each July.

Orientation and Practical Information

Everything liable to interest most visitors is concentrated in the narrow, meandering streets of the **casco antiguo,** the northeastern quarter of this provincial capital. **Plaza del Castillo,** marked by a bandstand, lies in this neighborhood's center. To get there from the bus station, turn left onto Avenida del Conde Oliveto. At the traffic island on Plaza Príncipe de Viana, take the second left onto Avenida San Ignacio, follow it four blocks past a statue on the left, and bear right. To reach Pl. Castillo from the train station: take the #9 bus from the station exit and debark at the head of **Paseo Sarasate,** an important pedestrian street. Walk diagonally left of the statue to Pl. Castillo. To the north of Pl. Castillo, the Baroque red and gold **Casa Consistorial** (a.k.a. Ayuntamiento) makes a handsome marker amid the swirl of medieval streets in the old quarter. From Pl. Castillo walk downhill on C. Chapitela and turn left on the second street, C. Mercaderes.

A right onto Av. Conde Oliveto from the bus station leads to the **Ciudadela,** a sprawling fort in park grounds that guards the southeastern border of the *casco antiguo*. Incidentally, the *encierro* route begins in the **Calle Hilarión Eslava** neighborhood, a couple blocks west of Casa Consistorial, passing near Pl. Castillo and winding up in the Plaza de Toros.

The city on the whole is safe, but still take precautions. Theft multiplies during *Los Sanfermines*. Parks and streets shadowed by the city's old walls in the *casco antiguo* are to be avoided at night.

Tourist Office: C. Duque de Ahumada, 3 (tel. 22 07 41). From Pl. Castillo, take Av. Carlos III 1 block, turn left on C. Duque de Ahumada, and cross C. Espoz y Mina. Indispensible street-indexed map cut short at S streets. Not too well-informed on budget accommodations. Ridiculous during the *Sanfermines*—the line forms by 9:30am. Currency exchange, public baths, and buses to campsite are posted on a bulletin board outside. Open July-Sept. 10am-7pm; Oct.-June Mon.-Sat. 10am-2pm and 4-7pm, Sun. 10am-3pm. **City Information Office,** in the rear of the Ayuntamiento (tel. 22 12 00), off the plaza by the market, can offer a good map and the helpful publication **BIM,** which lists many town services. Open Mon.-Sat. 8am-3pm.

Budget Travel: TIVE, C. Paulino Caballero, 4, 5th fl. right (tel. 21 24 04). In the direction of Pl. Castillo, take Av. San Ignacio, turn right on C. Roncesvalles and follow for 2 bl., then turn right on C. Paulino Caballero. Discount travel tickets, ISIC cards (500ptas), and HI coupon cards (1500ptas). Open Mon.-Fri. 9am-1:30pm.

Currency Exchange: Reception desk at **Hotel Tres Reyes** changes money 24 hrs. Ten percent discounts from the market rate. From the bus station turn right, then right again on Av. Taconera at the traffic circle for 5 blocks and bend left; it's the beflagged hotel to the left where the road forks. Better rates during the *Sanfermines* at **Caja de Ahorros de Navarra** central branch, with special extended weekday hours. July 8-12 open Mon.-Fri. 9:30am-12:30pm and 4-6pm. From Pl. Castillo take Av. Carlos III; the bank is at C. Roncesvalles on the right. Otherwise during *fiesta,* banks open 9:30-1pm only.

Post Office: Central office at Po. Sarasate, 9 (tel. 22 12 63, after hours (944) 24 20 00), at corner of C. Vínculo. Lista de Correos. Open Mon.-Fri. 8am-9pm, Sat. 9am-7pm. **Postal Code:** 31001.

Telephones: C. Amaya, 2, across from Pl. Toros. From the tourist office, turn left, then bear right at Pl. Toros. Open Mon.-Fri. 9am-1pm and 5-9pm, Sat. 9am-1pm. **Telephone Code:** 948.

Flights: Aeropuerto de Noaín (tel. 31 75 12), 6km away and accessible only by taxi. To Madrid and Barcelona (2 per day, 30min., about 12,000ptas).

Trains: Estación RENFE, off Av. San Jorge, 20min. from the *casco antiguo* by bus (#9 from Po. Sarasate). Information (tel. 13 02 02) open Mon.-Fri. 8:30am-1:30pm and 4-7pm. Another ticket/ information office (tel. 22 72 82) behind the bus station. Exit the bus station and go around the left corner; office is across C. García Ximinez to the left. (Open Mon.-Fri. 9am-1:30pm and 4-7pm, Sat. 9am-1pm.) Pamplona is miserably connected by rail. No *talgo* service; much faster and easier to take the bus. To: Olite (3 per day, 1 1/2 hr., 265ptas); Tudela (7 per day, 1 1/2 hr., 970ptas); Vitoria (5 per day, 1 3/4 hr., 800ptas); Zaragoza (8 per day, 2hr., 1200ptas); Donostia/ San Sebastián (1 per day at 6:05am!, 2 1/2 hr., 685ptas); Madrid (3 per day, 5hr., 2200-3650ptas); Barcelona (3 per day, 6hr., 3785ptas). For Logroño you must go first to Castejon de Ebro (8 per day, 1hr., 680ptas).

Buses: Estación de Autobuses, C. Conde Oliveto at the corner with C. Yanguas y Miranda. Nearly 20 companies. Consult the bulletin board's alphabetized list of destinations for the appropriate ticket window. To: Sangüesa (3-4 per day, 45min., 345ptas); Javier (2 per day, 1hr., 400ptas); Yesa (1 per day, 1hr., 425ptas); Estella (7 per day, 1 1/4 hr., 345ptas); Tudela (7 per day, 1 1/2 hr., 660ptas); Roncal (1 per day at 5pm, 2hr., 780ptas); Isaba (1 per day at 5pm, just over 2hr., 780ptas); Vitoria (4 per day, 2 1/4 hr., 725ptas); Burguete (1 per day at 6pm, 2 1/2 hr., 330ptas); Ochogavía (1 per day at 6pm, 2 1/2 hr., 630ptas); Logroño (5 per day, 2 1/2 hr., 745ptas); Donostia/ San Sebastián (6 per day, 2 3/4 hr., 625ptas); Zaragoza (9 per day, 3 1/2 hr., 1225ptas); Bilbo (4 per day, 1825ptas); Madrid (6 per day, 5 1/2 hr., 3175ptas); Barcelona (1 per day at 4:30pm, 2675ptas).

Public Transportation: 14 intercity bus lines dodge between the *casco antiguo* and all corners of the city. Foreign-user-friendly. #9 from Po. Sarasate to train station (6:30am-10:30pm every 10-12min., 20min., 70ptas). Route map available at the tourist office.

Taxis: Radio-dispatched at 23 21 00, 23 23 00.

Hitchhiking: Tourist office claims that hitching to Logroño and France is more feasible here than elsewhere. Due to the risks involved, *Let's Go* does not recommend hitchhiking; solo women should not hitchhike.

Car Rental: Europcar, Hotel Blanca Navarra, Av. Pío XII, 43 (tel. 17 66 80). Bus lines #1, 2, and 4 go here; get off after the traffic circle on the way out of town. Must be 21. Renaults 4000ptas per day, 40ptas per km. **Hertz** is in Hotel Tres Reyes and the train station (for either, tel. 22 35 69, 22 66 00). **Avis** (tel. 17 00 98) rents from the airport. Ask for promotional rates.

Luggage Storage: July 5-14 there's a 24-hr. storage room at the **bus station** (150ptas per day). On other days, in the bus station loading area (tel. 22 38 54). 115ptas per bag per day, large packs 170ptas per day. Open Mon.-Sat. 6:15am-9:30pm, Sun. 7am-9:30pm.

Lost Property: Objetos perdidos, C. Mo. de Iratxe, 2 (tel. 25 51 50).

English Bookstore: Librería Gómez, Pl. Castillo, 28 (tel. 22 67 02). Small selection of novels. Open Mon.-Sat. 9am-1:30pm and 4:30-8pm.

Library: Biblioteca General, opposite the Escuelas Municipales on Pl. San Francisco, at C. Nueva.

Laundromat: Lavomatique, C. Descalzos, 28-30 (tel. 22 19 22). From Pl. San Francisco follow C. Hilarión Eslava to the end, then turn right. Harried staff during *Sanfermines* can even get the bull blood out. Wash, dry, and soap for 700ptas. Open Mon.-Sat. noon-5pm. At other times wash 350ptas, dry 25ptas per 5min., soap 50ptas; open Mon.-Fri. 10am-2pm and 4-8pm. Washing machines also at **Public Baths,** C. Eslava, just beyond Pl. San Francisco. Wash and dry 4 1/2kg 375ptas. Open Tues.-Sat. 8am-8:30pm.

Public Toilets and Baths: C. Conde Oliveto, 4 (tel. 22 88 26), in the bus station. Squat variety. Also on C. Jarauta. Open 8am-9pm; during *Sanfermines* 24 hrs. Showers at **Casa de Baños,** C. Hilarión Eslava, 9 (tel. 22 17 38), up from Pl. San Francisco on the left past C. Mayor near corner of C. Jarauta. 80ptas, with towel and soap 140ptas. Open Tues.-Sun. 8am-9pm.

Swimming Pool: Piscinas de Aranzadi, 15min. from Pl. Castillo on Vuelta de Aranzadi (tel. 22 30 02). From the tourist office walk round the left corner, take C. Estafeta to Pl. Mercaderes, turn right, then turn left on C. Carmen, following it out of the city. Open 10:30am-9pm. During *Sanfermines* 430ptas, under 14 215ptas; rest of year 200ptas; 50ptas.

Red Cross: C. Yanguas y Miranda, 3 (tel. 22 64 04, 22 92 91). Also sets up stands at the bus station and the *corrida* during the *Sanfermines.*

Medical Services/Emergency: Any emergency call 088, 006, or 091. Call these also for **24-hr. pharmacy** and **ambulance. Hospital de Navarra,** C. Irunlarrea, s/n (tel. 10 21 00).

Police: C. General Chinchilla (tel. 091), to the right on Av. Taconera with your back to the statue on Po. Sarasate. **Municipal Police,** C. Monasterio de Irache, 12 (tel. 25 51 50).

Accommodations and Camping

Only when your moon is in its 7th house and Jupiter aligns with Mars will you get a bed in Pamplona during the first few days of the *encierro*. Diehard *sanferministas* book their rooms for next year before going home. In most cases, you must reserve about two months ahead and pay rates two to three times higher than those listed below. Check newspapers *(Diario de Navarra)* for **casas particulares** (from 2000ptas per person, showers 150ptas). Many who can't find rooms sleep outside on the lawns of the Ciudadela and the Pl. Fueros traffic circle (from the bus station turn left, then left again at the traffic circle). Park-sleepers recommend extreme caution: if you can't leave your belongings at the *Consigna* in the bus station (it fills fast), they urge you to sleep on top of them. When the bulls stop running, any old moon rising will do. Rooms line **C. San Gregorio** and its continuation, **C. San Nicolás.**

Casa Marceliano, C. Mercado, 7-9 (tel. 22 14 26). From the tourist office turn left, then left again on C. Estafeta, through Pl. Mercaderes; C. Mercado runs behind the Ayuntamiento. A distinctive silver-gray building with low beds, old bathrooms, and balconies. At night, Pavarotti wannabes belt it out from the bar downstairs until the wee hours. Try for a higher room unless opera gives you goose bumps. 2000ptas per person. Sept.-June 1500ptas.

Hostal Bearán, C. San Nicolás, 25 (tel. 22 34 28). Comfortable, clean white rooms with pink trim. If you've run the *encierro* before, you may find yourself in the standard action photos on the walls. Doubles with bath 4500ptas; Nov.-May 3500ptas. Friendly proprietor rents rooms without baths across the street at **Fonda La Aragonesa;** the narrow, decrepit entrance (soon to be renovated) belies the new, big rooms inside. Singles 2000ptas. Doubles 3000ptas, with bath 3500ptas.

Hostal Otano, C. San Nicolás, 5 (tel. 22 50 95). Enact your favorite jailbird fantasy in this former prison. The caged black stairwell and wood floors discipline and punish—no, really, it's a nice place now. 1500ptas per person, with bath 2000ptas. You must pay up front.

Casa García, C. San Gregorio, 12 (tel. 22 38 93). Kitchen smells waft through the halls. Decent bathrooms. Singles 2000ptas. Doubles 3500ptas. Sept.-June 1600ptas; 3100ptas.

Camping: Camping Ezcaba (tel. 33 03 15), in Oricaín, 7km outside of Pamplona on the road to Irún. From town bus station there's a private bus (4 per day, 9:10am-8:30pm). Capacity for 480. Fills as fast as other accommodations during you know what. 355ptas per person, per tent, and per car. Open June-Sept. No reservations accepted.

Food

Pamplona vends unremarkable cuisine at high prices. Skip the *fiesta*-priced restaurants around Pl. Castillo in favor of the side streets in the neighborhood of Casa de Huéspedes Santa Cecilia, the cathedral area above Pl. San Francisco, and off Po. Sarasate opposite the post office. **Calle Navarrería,** near the cathedral, overflows with small bars and restaurants. Food and sandwich stands sprout fungus-like everywhere for the week of celebrations. More restaurants crank away on **Calle Estafeta, Calle Mayor,** and **Calle San Nicolás;** the last is longer on crowds and alcohol than solid food. A fine Navarrese finish is the dessert liqueur *Patxaran (Pacharán)*.

The **market** on C. Mercado, to the right of Casa Consistorial's facade and down the stairs, has been recently renovated. Most fruit downstairs, all else above. Open Mon.-Thurs. and Sat. 8am-2:30pm, Fri. 8am-2:30pm and 4-7:30pm.

Restaurante Sarasate, C. San Nicolás, 19-21, above the seafood store. Indian tapestries and Dylan tunes for vegetarian beatniks wishing that Dean and Sal had hit Spain. Boho crowd settles in early. Nutritious *menú* 750ptas. Open Mon.-Thurs. 1:30-4pm, Fri.-Sat. 1:30-4pm and 9-11pm.

Café Niza, C. Duque de Ahumada, s/n, across from the tourist office. Stained-glass windows and reggae music set off a young, fashionably artistic crowd. *Bocadillos* served at the bar. Open Mon.-Sat. 8am-1pm.

Bar-Restaurante Lanzale, C. San Lorenzo, 31 (tel. 22 10 71), between C. Mayor and C. Jarauta in the district above Pl. San Francisco. Good-natured service of better-than-average food. *Menú* 700ptas. Open Sept. 11-Aug. 19 Mon.-Sat. 1:30-3:30pm and 9-11pm.

Casa García, C. San Gregorio, 12 (tel. 22 38 93). Praiseworthy food in a bright, modern dining room. *Menú* 600ptas. Encyclopedic range of entrees 600-1000ptas. Open Mon.-Sat. 1-4pm and 9-11pm.

Self-Service Estafeta, C. Estafeta, 57 (tel. 22 16 05). *Platos combinados* 375-750ptas, roasted 1/2-chicken 375ptas. Open Mon.-Tues. and Thurs.-Sat. 1-4pm and 8:30-11pm, Wed. and Sun. 1-4pm.

Sights and Entertainment

Pity the city its *Sanfermines*. The clatter of cranky cloven-hoofed bovines somehow obscures Pamplona's varied architectural legacy. In the late 14th century Carlos III el Noble endowed the city with a proper Gothic **catedral;** his tomb and Queen Leonor's rest within. The Gothic nave, *refectorio,* and *claustro* stand in odd juxtaposition to the Neoclassical west facade. Neighboring streets are dense with palaces, Baroque mansions, and artisan houses from different periods. Aside from the cathedral, there are the Gothic 13th-century **Iglesia de San Cernín** and 16th-century **Santo Domingo**, with its sumptuous *retablo* and brick cloister. Near this basilica, soldier Ignacio de Loyola (later founder of the Jesuit Order) fell wounded in a war; this brush with mortality convinced him to devote his life to God, radically changing his life and Church history. Expansion in the 17th century deposited the Baroque **Palacio Arzobispal** and **Casa Consistorial** and the Neoclassical **Palacio de la Diputación,** which is at the east end of the Pl. Castillo. Navarra's ancient laws--along with other manuscripts and artifacts related to the history of the kingdom—are exhibited in the Diputación's annex, the **Archivo de Navarra.**

The **Museo de Navarra,** up C. Santo Domingo from Casa Consistorial, shelters Romany funerary steles and mosaics, architectural fragments (such as brilliantly carved capitals) from the cathedral, mural paintings from all over the region, and a collection of 14th- to 18th-century paintings, including Goya's portrait of the Marqués de San Adrián. (Open Tues.-Sat. 10am-2pm and 5-7pm, Sun. 10am-2pm. Admission 200ptas, students free.)

The pentagonal **Ciudadela** built by Felipe II sprawls next to the city's largest botanical attraction, the delicious **Jardines de la Taconera.** The most scenic route to the Ciudadela from the old quarter follows the city's third set of **walls,** built between the 16th and 18th centuries. When Charlemagne dismantled the walls in the 9th century, the Navarres and Basques joined at the pass of Roncesvalles to massacre his rear guard (and his nephew Roland). This violence was the basis of the French medieval epic *La Chanson de Roland.* The most spectacular view from the walls is behind the cathedral. At the far end of the cathedral plaza, pick up C. Redín, which runs to the walls. A left turn follows the picturesque walls until they meet the Ciudadela, where there's an open *pelota* pitch, a pond for ducks, a recreational area stocked with deer, and gravel paths for strollers.

For another view of the fortress, exit the old city by one of two gateways, **Portal de Francia** or **Portal de Guipúzcoa** and stroll along the **Río Arga,** following the curve of the walls. These awesome structures scared off Napoleon himself, who refused to attack frontally and staged a trick snowball fight instead. When Spanish sentries came to join them, the French entered the city through the gates.

On weekends youth activity concentrates on **bars** in the *casco antiguo.* **Herriko Taberna,** C. Carmen, 34, mixes hardcore music with posters demanding "amnisty" for ETA prisoners. Those who feel trapped by the narrow streets of San Gregorio and San Nicolás escape to bars in **Barrio San Juan,** beyond Hotel Tres Reyes on Av. Bayona.

Los Sanfermines (The Running of the Bulls, July 6-14)

La Fiesta de San Fermín—known to locals as **Los Sanfermines**—is such an institution that it's become one word. The week-long orgy of bull worship celebrates Pamplona's patron saint San Fermín, who was martyred when bulls dragged him through the streets. In an historical simulation, each morning thousands of fools in white shirts and red sashes flee from bulls, and barricades go up along Calles Santo Domingo, Mercaderes, and Estafeta. The non-stop action is punctuated by brief cat-naps and even briefer heroic moments spent hightailing away from the violent beasts.

The frenzy lasts eight days, with enough parades, wine, bullfights, wine, parties, wine, fireworks, wine, rock concerts, and wine to annihilate even the most robust. The mayor kicks off the festivities at noon on July 6 by lighting the first *cohete* (rocket) of the festival from the Ayuntamiento's balcony. Then the fantastical **Raui Raui procession** winds through the streets. Since the 13th century, towering *gigantes* (giant monarchs), *cabezudos* (swollen-headed courtiers), *kilikis* (court buffoons), and *zaldikos* (more court buffoons) hold court and dance minuets in Pamplona's streets in a traditional charivari. The city's present wood, aluminum, and cardboard effigies were cloned in the 19th century.

The **encierro** takes place at 8am every morning as bystanders cheer, provoke, and make mischief from windows, balconies, doors, and TV sets. Crazed with their own blood-lust, macho runners throw method overboard and dart in front of the bulls charging down to the *encierro.* These guys actually run down the street with a bunch of very large and very angry cowflesh: six steers accompany the six bulls, and they have horns too. Witness the madness from the Santo Domingo stairs and inside the Plaza de Toros itself. Be there by 7am.

Rockets mark the bulls' progress on their 825m dash down Cuesta de Santo Domingo through Pl. Consistorial, C. Mercaderes, and C. Estafeta to the Pl. Toros. It lasts about two minutes when the bulls stay packed. Isolated bulls are far more dangerous, since they run into the crowds in search of company. Try not to cower in a doorway; three people were trapped and killed by bulls this way. Many people are injured at the end of the course, where the river of adrenaline (bearing the occasional chunk of flesh with it) cascades through a terribly narrow opening. If you decide to participate, watch an *encierro* first. Avoid running in the dangerous weekend traffic jams at all costs: there's usually a lot of pushing, shoving, and pain.

The scene in the **bullring** is exciting enough for those who would rather not be mauled, but seats (1500ptas or more) sell out fast. Two free sections are reserved in the stands for women and children. Another kind of running takes place in the stands: some fans bring large vats of sangria and canisters of flour to the stadium to pour then dump on their neighbors. Heifers with sawed-off horns are periodically released on the crowd.

After the taurine track-and-field event, the hoopla moves into the streets, gathering steam until it explodes at nightfall. Come darkness the veneer of civilization dissolves in waves of alcohol. Singing in the bars, dancing in the alleyways, spontaneous parades, and a no-holds-barred party in Pl. Castillo, southern Europe's biggest open-air dance floor. The *Mardi Gras*-type chaos (which beats Times Square on New Year's Eve hands down) kicks off the evening of the sixth with a mass for purists and merry mayhem for everyone else. The truly inspired carousing takes place the first few days. After that, the crowds begin to thin. It's best to leave before the giddy delirium dwindles to mere decadence and the locals get impatient with tourists sleeping in their gardens.

The *encierro* has become highly politicized. In the 60s, Franco's Minister of Tourism, Manual Fraga (now President of Galiza's regional government), made it one of the centerpieces of his *Spain is Different* campaign, an aggressive international promotion of canned folklore and concrete beaches. Locals complain that the influx of newcomers and rampant commercialism have ruined their festival. In 1991, the 400th anniversary of the event, city police and youth clashed over unlicensed stands set up for the festival by leftist political parties.

Nearby towns sponsor *encierros* with fewer political overtones. Tudela holds its festival during the last week of July, Estella for a week from the first Sunday in August, Tafalla during the week of August 15, and Sangüesa for a week beginning September 12.

Near Pamplona

Olite

In Olite, the Río Cidacos—a trickle given the benefit of the doubt—drips by the slender walls of the **Palacio Real**, which rises proudly out of the flatlands 42km south of Pamplona. The palace stands in the very center of **Plaza Carlos III el Noble**. Intrigue and sabotage have lurked about the palace of the kings of Navarra for centuries. King Carlos III made the Palacio Real the center of Navarrese courtly life in the early 15th century by creating a sumptuous palace of pointed turrets, arched windows, soaring stone walls, and flowery courtyards. Ramparts, spiral staircases, guard towers, lookout perches, moats, and alligators and court princesses and dragons, and armored attackers and poison-dipped arrows, and court jesters: the medieval palace of your dreams.

The metal cages in the middle of Plaza Carlos III lead to a series of **tunnels** kept padlocked most of the year. Some think they were an escape route from the palace in case of siege; others insist they were the breeding ground for the palace's pet trolls. Now they're opened occasionally for exhibitions. The palace becomes a cultural center for the **Festivales de Navarra** every August. (Palace open April-Sept. Mon.-Sat. 10am-2pm and 6-8pm, Sun. 10am-2pm; Oct.-March Mon.-Sat. 10am-2pm and 4-5pm, Sun. 10am-2pm. Admission 100ptas.)

The palace chapel, **Iglesia de Santa María**, is noted for its 14th-century Gothic facade and its belfry. **Iglesia de San Pedro** is fitted with an octagonal tower; for San Pedro turn right on Rúa Villavieja and follow it to its end. (Both always open and free. Services at 10am and 8pm.)

For the most part, the luxurious and rarefied air of the court lingers in Olite's restaurants and accommodations. The exception is the budget-minded **Fonda Gambarte**, Rúa del Seca, 13, 2nd floor (tel. 74 01 39), off Pl. Carlos III. They don't have many rooms here, however, and like the bigger hotels in town they fill during *Los Sanfermines.* (1250ptas per person.) Downstairs from the *fonda,* **Restaurante Gambarte** serves a royal three-course *menú* for a less-than-extravagant 900ptas (open 1-3:30pm and 8:30-10:30pm).

The bus unloads on the main highway to Pamplona, which runs through Olite. From there, turn left to reach the palace on Pl. Carlos III. The **tourist office** (tel. 74 00 35) galumphs in the first turret. While helpful, the staff is rather clueless about budget accommodations. (Open same hours as palace.) The **post office** (tel. 74 05 82) is on the left side of the plaza as you face the palace (open Mon.-Sat. 9-11:30am). **Telephone booths** are located on Pl. Teobaldos. The **telephone code** is 948. There are **public bathrooms** next to the post office. **Emergencies** in all of Navarra are directed to 088 or 091 for assistance. For medical attention, call the **pharmacy** at 74 00 36; it will open after hours if you call. The **Centro de Salud** (medical center; tel. 71 23 64) is on the outskirts of the city on the road to Zaragoza. The three **municipal police** have no permanent office, so call the **Guardia Civil** at 70 32 44.

Trains run between here and Pamplona (3 per day, 35min., 265ptas). To get from the RENFE station to Pl. Carlos III, take C. Estación and turn left, following the sign to Zaragoza. The next left is C. El Portillo, which leads to the plaza. La Tafallesa (tel. 22 28 86) runs **buses** to Pamplona and back (7 per day, 50min., 280ptas), depositing you just short of C. El Portillo on the road to Zaragoza. Note that the return bus stops a little farther down the road on the way to Pamplona, in front of Bar Orly.

Near Olite

Ujué crowns a hill 20km from Olite. Perched at the top is **Iglesia Fortaleza de Santa María,** a Romanesque fortress-basilica of the 11th century. The church guards the two silent atria and two silent ventricles of Charles's II's unbeating heart. The splendid view from here encompasses all of southern Navarra. At the close of April, a solemn procession of the faithful, shoeless and dressed in tunics, some bearing crosses, climbs silently to the top to worship the **Imágen románica de la Virgen** (Romanesque Image of the Virgin) inside. The Tafallesa **bus** from Pamplona to Olite (see Olite for details) pauses in Tafalla, from which there's a bus to Ujué (Mon., Wed., Fri. 7pm; 125ptas; return to Tafalla Mon., Wed., Fri. 8:45am).

The poor **Monasterio de la Oliva,** also near Olite, has survived numerous sackings and years of neglect since it was built in 1164. The result is an architectural palimpsest of Romanesque, Gothic, and Baroque. It's now a functioning monastery. Three buses run from Pamplona to Olite and continue on to **Carcastillo,** a town 2km from the monastery (1 1/2 hr., 550ptas).

Tudela

The second-largest city in Navarra, **Tudela** emerged as a force under 9th-century Muslim rule in Spain. The Christians expelled the Moors in 1119, but Muslim and Jewish culture continued to flourish, furnishing such figures as poet and philosopher Jehuda Haleví and Benjamín de Tudela. The 12th- and 13th-century **catedral** in the *casco antiguo* harbors the elaborately ornate **Capilla de Santa Ana,** topped by an intricate Baroque cupola. **Festivals** to honor Santa Ana start July 24 in Pl. Fueros, and consist of a week of scaled-down *encierros, gigantes,* and the Navarrese version of *la jota.* Tudela is 94km from Pamplona and linked by Conda **buses** (tel. 22 10 26; 6 per day, 1 1/2 hr., 660ptas). The **tourist office** (tel. 82 15 39) is open Mon.-Sat. 10am-2pm and 4-7pm, Sun. 10am-2:30pm.

Estella

Although dwarfed by its robust neighbors to the northeast, Estella is the hostess with the mostest on the Camino de Santiago. Pilgrims, whether the religious or *sanfermines* sort, pass through without affecting the small-town quality. A number of monuments to Estella's medieval dynamism remind visitors it was once the second largest market town in Europe (c. 13th century). The city still bears traces of its days as a segregated, multi-ethnic metropolis with Jewish, Frankish, and Navarrese quarters. In the 17th century, this city faced its most embarrassing moment; the Ayuntamiento went bankrupt properly attiring every citizen for a visit by Felipe III at which the elaborate fireworks refused to go off.

The front exit of the bus station on Pl. Coronación faces the center of town. Directly ahead, C. San Andrés runs for two blocks before crossing **Paseo de la Inmaculada.** One black past the *paseo* is **Calle Mayor;** yet another block delivers you to **Plaza de los Fueros,** the *Autobahn* of the evening *paseo.*

The area along C. Mayor sprang up in the 12th century to compete with Frankish merchants across the Río Ega. At its center, **Iglesia de San Miguel's** five-arch doorway with capitals of the baby Jesus is certainly out of the ordinary. *Le tout Estella* meets at the arcades on Pl Fueros.

Iglesia de San Pedro de la Rúa towers above **Calle de la Rúa,** the main street of the original mercantile center. This elderly Gothic church flaunts a Romanesque baptismal font. Behind the building, a 100-ft. cliff rises above the Romanesque cloister, whose capitals allegedly represent scenes from the New Testament and the lives of saints. The church is up the stairs opposite the tourist office. (Open Mon.-Sat. 10am-2pm and 4-7pm, Sun. 10am-2:30pm. Admission 100ptas.)

Across from San Pedro, next to the tourist office, the oldest stone Roland in the world jousts with Farragut the Moor on the capitals of the 12th-century **Palacio de los Reyes de Navarra.** The *palacio* houses the **Museo Gustavo de Maetzu** and displays a rather lame collection of the Basque artist's work. (Open Tues.-Sat. 11am-1pm and 5-7pm, Sun. 11am-1pm. Admission 100ptas.) Left from the tourist office at the end of C. Rúa lurks the street's crowning glory, the restoration-hungry **Iglesia del Santo Sepulcro,** whose 14th-century facade features a monstrous Satan swallowing the damned by the mouthful. Many other odd characters wave from the arches. As interest in the Camino de Santiago revived in the 80s, a record number of pilgrims traipsed through, increasing revenue and curiosity about the town's past. A **crafts artist** at C. Rúa, 19, recreates medieval Navarrese carved-wood furniture and knick-knacks, including *templetas* (wooden knockers used to clack the hours of Mass during Lent) and *argisaiolas* (human-shaped sculptures used by Navarrese witches and the Catholic clergy).

Spanning the Ega, the largely useless **Puente de la Cárcel** was blown up in 1873 during one of Estella's frequent rebellions. In a architectural nightmare over a century later, builders raised the pointed arch in the middle of the bridge twice as high as before; hence, no car could pass over it. The slippery cobblestones make even walking hazardous.

Las Fiestas de la Virgen del Puy y San Andrés last for one week from the Friday before the first Sunday in August, when Estella has its own *encierro* with heifers, smaller and less ferocious than Pamplona's *toros*. Women are officially permitted to run here (oh, thank you). The usual kiddie entertainment, a fair, and Navarrese *aubades* (bagpipe music) in the streets round out the *fiestas.*

During these *fiestas,* most lodgings fill up; make reservations a couple of lightyears in advance. Estella's proximity to Pamplona makes it an excellent source of lodgings during *Los Sanfermines*—the somewhat tougher room scene here doesn't even compare to the total blockout in Pamplona. Classical Spanish guitar players favor **Pensión San Andrés,** Pl. Santiago, 1 (tel. 55 04 48, 55 41 58). C. Mayor runs to the plaza. (July to mid-Sept. doubles 2800ptas, with bath 4000ptas. Triples 5000ptas. Quads 6000ptas. Oct.-June: 2800ptas, 3700ptas; 4000ptas; 5000ptas.) **Fonda Viuda de Joaquín,** Po. Inmaculada, 15 (tel. 55 06 80), offers pleasant if dingy rooms. (Singles 1500ptas. Doubles 2500ptas. Reservations accepted only for lengthy stays or in winter.) The tourist office keeps a full list of accommodations and prices.

Pl. Fueros is best for strolling; the dining deals are off C. Estrella, leading out of the corner diagonally to the right as you enter the plaza from C. Baja Navarra. The hearty two-course *menú* at **Casa Cachetas,** C. Estudio de Gramática, 2 (tel. 55 00 10), at the very end of C. Estrella, costs 850ptas; the *alubias rosas* (beans in heavy broth) are savory and filling. (Open 1:30-3:30pm and 8-11pm.) The town **market** is held in Pl. Fueros and Pl. San Miguel (Thurs. 8am-2pm).

The **tourist office,** C. Rúa, 3 (tel. 55 40 11), is on the ground floor of the Palacio de los Reyes de Navarra. From the bus station, turn right off C. San Andrés and follow Po. Inmaculada until it curves over a bridge. Turn left from the bridge into Pl. San Martín and walk right around the corner, past the museum gates. (Open Mon.-Sat. 10am-2pm and 4-7pm, Sun. 10am-2:30pm.) The **post office** is at Po. Inmaculada, 5 (tel. 55 17 92; open Mon.-Fri. 8am-3pm, Sat. 9am-1pm). The **postal code** is 31200. The **telephone code** is 948. **Medical services** are available in the *ambulatorio* (tel. 55 07 37). For an **ambulance,** call the **Red Cross** at 55 10 11. The **24-hr. pharmacy** listing is posted on the door of any pharmacy, or call the **municipal police** (tel. 55 08 13) in the Ayuntamiento, on Po. Inmaculada.

A 1920s ex-RENFE building is now the **bus station,** Pl. Coronación, off Po. Inmaculada. La Estellesa runs buses 44km to Pamplona (10-11 per day, 1hr., 345ptas) and to Logroño (5-7 per day, 1hr., 415ptas), Donostia/San Sebastián (3-4 per day, 2 1/4 hr., 830ptas), and Zaragoza (1 per day, 3hr., 1220ptas). Automoviles Pinedo runs buses to Vitoria (3-5 per day, 1 1/2 hr., 515ptas).

Navarrese Pyrenees

The rugged mountainous landscape northeast of Pamplona covers the most diverse part of the Pyrenees. Although truly jagged peaks reach as far as Valle de Roncal, farther west the mountain slopes lose their ferocity, allowing greater access to the streams, waterfalls, and windy meadows which mark the area. Comparison shoppers find that these steep slopes are lusher and greener than their Aragonese or Catalan neighbors. The valleys of this part of the Pyrenees fill with mist and fog even on summer mornings, obscuring visibility on winding roads straight out of luxury car commercials. The villages in this area remain largely isolated; their main industries are cattle and logging.

Tourism too is a booming business. **El Camino de Santiago** is fast regaining popularity. El Camino, or St. James's Road, is the celebrated cross-kingdom supertrek of daring pilgrims who clambered over these peaks from France. The pilgrimage route crosses the French border at Roncesvalles or Somport and continues to Santiago de Compostela in Galiza. Many free or cheap *refugios* pamper footsore pilgrims along the way. To follow the route, get the best available guide (in Spanish), the *Guía de peregrinos,* published by Ediciones Everest. For a list of *casas rurales,* or farmhouses who lodge travelers, ask for the *Guía,* free in Navarra's tourist offices. For reservations, call the central office at (948) 22 07 41.

From Pamplona, you can head east toward Valle de Roncal (via Sangüesa), or north toward Roncesvalles. Buses are one-a-day affairs (if at all) through most of the area; Pamplona is the only sensible base, and you should bring your raincoat and sweater if you plan to get up before noon.

Sangüesa

Set in the arid foothills 40km east of Pamplona, Sangüesa is really a preface to the Pyrenees. During the Middle Ages, the city was an important pitstop on the Camino de Santiago, a heritage which gives the small city artistic and architectural depth. Sangüesa attracts vacationing Spaniards and hikers exploring the nearby Lumbier and Arbayrín gorges, which have made Navarra's monumental landscape famous. Although the city's economy is traditionally agricultural, on bad days it sniffs of its newer industrial side. When the wind blows the wrong way, an onion-like stench from nearby paper and textile factories fills the town.

The legacy of the Camino de Santiago appears first and foremost in the main entrance to the **Iglesia de Santa María,** an extraordinary triumph of Romanesque sculpture. The central relief depicts the Day of Judgment with fanged devils casting the damned into the cavernous mouth of Lucifer. The woman nursing a toad on one breast and a snake on the other is, of course, a conventional iconographic rendering of Lust. Inside is a wackily hairy Baroque Madonna whose human locks are changed every 10 to 15 years. To get to the church from the bus stop, go left on C. Mayor off C. Alfonso El Batallador and continue to the river.

On the way you'll pass the facade of the **Palacio de Vallesantoro**, the Baroque palace which houses the tourist office and a small number of regional artifacts. Finally, the Gothic stone St. James straddles a large conch before the **Iglesia de Santiago**. On the wall behind him, two giggling cloaked pilgrims hold staffs and cockleshells in homage to him. St. Francis himself is supposed to have sojourned in Sangüesa during his pilgrimage to Compostela, home of the first Franciscan hermitage outside of Italy.

The town's **Fiesta Mayor** falls September 11-17 and includes a communal dance to the C. Mayor at midnight every night and an even more communal boogie back up at 1:30am.

The only reasonably priced lodgings are at **Pensión Las Navas,** C. Alfonso el Batallador, 7 (tel. 87 00 77). Flamboyant pink curtains and bedspreads simper in the clean and comfortable rooms (1500ptas per person, with bath 1750ptas). Ask at the tourist office for a guide to *casas particulares*; some have luck with the houses on C. Mayor. If all else fails, check with the tourist office and the municipal police about free open-air camping at the **Ciudad Deportiva** outside town. **Restaurant Acuario,** C. Santiago, 9, off C. Mayor, serves a *menú* for 750ptas. The town's **market** is held on Pl. Toros (Fri. 9am-2pm), at the end of C. Alfonso el Ballatador away from C. Mayor.

The slick new yellow and blue **tourist office,** C. Alfonso el Batallador (tel. 87 03 39), is on the right as you enter the Palacio de Vallesantoro. The staff is fluent in English. (Open mid-March to Sept. Mon.-Sat. 10am-2pm and 4-7pm, Sun. 10am-3pm.) The **post office** is at Fermín de Lubián, 17, past the tourist office on Pl. Fueros. The **postal code** is 31400. The **telephone code** is 948. The **Red Cross** (tel. 87 05 27) is on C. Mercado, s/n, past the tourist office. For **medical services** there is a Centro de Salud (tel. 87 03 38) on the road to Cantolagua. The **municipal police** can be called at 87 03 10 and the **Guardia Civil** (tel. 87 00 55) are posted at Benabé Armendaríz, 17. **Emergencies** of any kind may be called in to 088 and 091 in all of Navarra.

Veloz Sangüesina **buses** (tel. 22 69 95) go to and from Pamplona (2-3 per day, 45min., 345ptas) and deposit passengers on C. Alfonso el Batallador near the corner with C. Gil de Jaz.

Near Sangüesa

Hoz de Lumbier and Hoz de Arbayún

Two fantastic gorges lie within 12km of Sangüesa. The **Hoz de Lumbier** (Lumbier gorge) is 2km outside of the little town of **Liédana,** on the bus route from Sangüesa to Pamplona. Hundred-and-fifty-foot walls, home to a large flock of griffin vultures, surround one side of this yawning gorge on the Río Irati. About 2km from the opposite edge of the gorge sits the town of **Lumbier.** A 12km ride from here brings you to **Iso** and to the mouth of an even more impressive gorge, the **Hoz de Arbayún** (Arbayún Gorge). If the Río Salazar is low enough in the late summer, you can swim, hack, or just hike your way through this 4km chasm, but at other times of year, the petrifyingly cold water forces hikers to raft or canoe it. There is no pre-blazed trail here, so watch out. Ask locals in Iso about conditions before setting up the TNT, sharpening the machete, or attempting any kind of expedition. The tourist office in Sangüesa provides more detailed information on how to reach these gorges. If you're lucky enough to have a car, look for the signs off N-240 in the direction of Pamplona.

Castillo Javier

Near the small village of **Yesa,** 8km from Sangüesa, is the restored **Castillo Javier.** The castle now belongs to the Jesuit order, who have made it a monument to St. Francis Xavier, the Spanish Church's missionary who was born here in 1506. A giggling Jesuit priest conducts a tour of the Disneyesque castle in Spanish only. It seems as if you'll stumble upon Sleeping Beauty in the very next room. The Tower of the Holy Christ houses a 14th-century effigy which allegedly has spontaneous blood-sweating fits. At the very least the castle provides the very best in moat crossing and boiling oil pouring practice. (Open 9am-1pm and 4-7pm. The light and sound *espectáculo* depicting the life of St. Francis will, barring catastrophe, be fixed soon. Free.) The former Hostal Xavier next to the castle is now the multistar **Hotel Xavier.** La Tafallesa (tel. (948) 22 28 86) runs two **buses** per day to Castillo Javier from Pamplona, one of which continues on to Yesa (to Javier, 1hr., 400ptas; to Yesa, just over 1hr., 425ptas).

Monasterio de Leyre

Windswept and austere, miles from any other settlement (16km from Sangüesa), the Monasterio de Leyre silently surveys the foothills of the Pyrenees and the fabricated Lago de Yesa. Hang-gliders launch themselves off the very same hills where great wealth and power once presided. Several centuries back, medieval Navarrese kings took up residence in the **monasterio medieval.** Because monks still live at Leyre, you cannot enter this part of the complex, nor the 20th-century **monasterio nuevo.** However, the **cripta** eagerly welcomes the public (admission 100ptas). The architectural highlight of the monastic complex is the **Portal de la Iglesia.** Ghouls and snakes sculpted above the exit scare away evil spirits. The plain church interior drips with spirituality. Outside the monastery, there is a path to the **Fuente de San Virila.** The fountain occupies the site where the abbot of San Virila, attempting to determine the nature of heaven, swung into a 300-year trance induced by the singing of a little bird.

The only likely option for a room in Yesa is **Hostal El Jabalí** (tel. 88 40 42), just off the road from Huesca at the edge of town, with warring shades of red within and a soothing pool without. (Singles 2800ptas. Doubles 4000ptas, with bath 4800ptas. Sept.-June: 2400ptas; 3500ptas, 4300ptas.) The monks themselves sometimes will put men up for next to nothing (though just for one night). You need not be a pilgrim, but you're expected to respect the code of silence. (You can speak to their voice-lackey at tel. (948) 88 40 11. Singles only.) Eating choices are equally limited. **Bar Restaurant Yamaguchy 2,** at the intersection of the roads to Pamplona and Sangüesa, has a 900ptas *menú*. The Navarrese government runs a **tourist office** across the same intersection (tel. 88 40 40). The **Red Cross** (tel. 88 41 52) is back a bit towards Huesca. The **telephone code** is 948.

The monastery lies about one hour away from Pamplona, off the highway to Huesca. To get to it, take the La Tafallesa **bus** (tel. (948) 22 28 86) from Pamplona to Yesa (1 1/4 hr., 425ptas). From Yesa, follow the road back to Pamplona for about 1km and turn right at the clearly marked sign. From there, it's about 4km uphill, not too strenuous in fine weather but a real grind in one of the frequent gales that wrack the region.

Roncal and Isaba

Roncal, at the heart of Navarre's easternmost valley, is famous for two products: *Queso Roncal* and the world-renowned tenor Julián Gayarre. Every grocery store in the valley sells the former, a sharp cheese made from sheep's milk. Numerous sculptures and monuments scattered about town commemorate the latter. Gayarre's tomb, an ornate flourish of mourning cherubs and weeping muses, was in the Paris Expo of 1900 and now blooms in the town cemetery, 800m along C. Castillo, which runs behind the *pelota* court from Pl. Julián Gayarre at the main bridge over the river. Somehow Roncal won out over Queen Maria Cristina, who would have just died to have the fab mausoleum in front of the Teatro Real in Madrid. Perhaps it was for the best, as the grand tomb seems strangely out of place in this little mountain village. Along the way to the cemetery, you'll pass the **Casa de Junta de Valle,** which displays the town's traditional festival clothing. If its wrought-iron door won't open, schlep to the Casa Consistorial on the main road and ask for a key.

Across the river from the *pelota* court over Bar Zaltua is **Hostal Zaltua** (tel. (948) 47 50 08), with swept wood floors and full-size shower stalls. (Singles with bath 1750ptas. Doubles with bath 4400ptas.) You can also stay in a family's house by requesting the *casa particular* brochure at the **tourist office** (tel. 89 32 34) in the Ayuntamiento building on Pl. Julian de Gayarre (open July-Sept.). Free camping is permitted in the valley, but check with the tourist office or **Guardia Civil** (tel. 89 50 05) before you head out.

The **post office** is uphill from Pl. Julián Gayarre near the smaller bridge across the river (open Mon.-Sat. 10am-2pm). The **postal code** is 31415. The **telephone code** is 948. Across the street, **Banco Central** doles out pesetas (open Mon.-Fri. 8:30am-2pm). There is a **pharmacy** downhill from the post office. La Tallafesa **buses** from Javier continue to Roncal (2 hr., 780ptas from Pamplona).

The more populous village of **Isaba** (pop. 300) straddles the highway 7km north of Roncal. Isaba's history consists of border disputes (fueled by wandering French livestock) that gripped the valley from 125 BC through the Middle Ages. These ancient squabbles are commemorated once a year with the **Tributo de las Tres Vacas (Tribute of the Three Cows).** Nearly every year since 1375, the French have donated three cows to the town on July 13 (approximately 1851 cows to date). French and Spanish officials, dressed in traditional costume, place their hands on top of each other and solemnly pray for peace as the bovine harbingers of harmony switch nationalities. On any other boring cowless day, Isaba's big attraction is the large, 16th-century **Iglesia de Santa Engracia** with a large, 18th-century organ.

Albergue Oxanea, C. Bormapea, 47 (tel. 89 31 53), left up the stone staircase uphill past the Centro de Salud, is run by a group of young, friendly locals. Neat wooden *literas* (bunks) fit 8 and 14 to a room, and there's a VCR in the TV room. (700ptas per night with your own locker, 600ptas if you bring your own sleeping bag. Hot showers and sheets included.) Downhill from the Centro de Salud on the main road, **Fonda Tapia** (tel. 89 30 13) has large rooms. Enter through the gate to the right, not through the front, and go in the door to the dining room. (1300ptas per person, with bath 1500ptas. Triples 2800ptas, with bath 3500ptas.) **Camping Asolaze** (tel. 89 31 68), 6km towards the French border, houses a restaurant and a store. (Open June-Sept. 375ptas per person, per tent, and per car.) Eight km north, the earth opens up into the **Valle de Belagua.** A refuge/shelter operates near the valley. (Open June-Sept.) Check also in the guide to *Casas Rurales,* at any Navarrese tourist office, for local houses offering lodging.

To reach the **Centro de Salud** on the main road at the bottom of town, call 89 32 52 (**emergency** tel. 061). The **Guardia Civil** answer at 89 30 06. The **post office** is next to Hostal Lola. The **telephone code** is 948. A La Tafallesa **bus** churns this far from Roncal (2hr., from Pamplona 780ptas).

Ochagavía

Set on the banks of the Río Andena, Ochagavía is 40km (but a draining 90km bus ride) from Pamplona, and the biggest town in the **Valle de Salazar.** Cobblestoned streets and bleached stone buildings with pastel roofs make Ochagavía most picturesque. The annual pilgrimage to the **Hermita de Musquilda** on September 8 revives some of the valley's ancient customs. In one event, the local dance group reenacts a warlike stick dance in which groups of four men bang wooden cudgels. Although the village's trek happens only at this time, you can make the 30-minute hike to the rebuilt 16th-century hermitage year-round.

Over the river and through the woods, the **Pensión Auñamendi** (tel. 89 01 89) is beyond the tourist office and to the left. (Doubles 3200ptas, with extra bed 4200ptas. Breakfast 300ptas.) **Hostal Orialde** (tel. 89 00 27), across the last bridge from the main street in the direction of Pamplona, usually hangs its *completo* shingle in July and August. (Singles 2400ptas. Doubles 2600ptas, with bath 3200ptas. Closed on holidays.) **Camping Osate** (tel. 89 01 84), at the entrance to town, provides a modern campsite on the river (350ptas per person, 375ptas per tent, 350tpas per car). They also happen to rent **mountain bikes** (1500ptas per 1/2-day, 2500ptas per full day).

The **tourist office** (tel. 89 00 04) on the main road opens during Holy Week and from July 1 to September 20 (Tues.-Sat. 10am-2pm and 4-7pm, Sun. 10am-3pm). The **post office** is open Mon.-Fri. 10-11:45am and Sat. 11-11:45am for urgent telegrams only. The **postal code** is 31680. The **telephone code** is 948. Río Irati (tel. 22 17 40) runs **buses** to and from Pamplona (from Ochogavía Mon.-Sat. 1 per day at 7am; from Pamplona Mon.-Fri. 1 per day at 6pm, Sat. 2 per day at noon and 6pm; 600ptas).

Roncesvalles

No bus, no train: nothing but a cold stone monastery and thick mountain forests in the mist and fog. The Valley of Thorns is 48km from Pamplona, 20km from the French border, and centuries from reality. The whole area feels more like Narnia than like France or Spain. For more than a thousand years, pilgrims, poets, and romantics have been drawn by the legend and spiritual shrine planted in the rugged slopes of **Puerto Ibañeta.** Supposedly the sword of the Moor Marsillo crushed Roland here in 778; a 14th-century cross at the south entrance to the village marks the spot of his defeat. Charlemagne's nephew actually fell at the hands of the Navarrese, who were pissed at the emperor's razing the walls of Pamplona, but no resident seems to care that the battle didn't take place here. Roncesvalles remains the mythical site of Roland's last hours, and the town is filled with remembrances of the legendary warrior. The heavily restored **Capilla de Sancti Spiritus** stands over the remains of a bone-heap (supplied by dead soldiers and pilgrims), marking the spot of Roland's unanswered plea for help. The gates are always closed, as is the entrance to the tiny 12th-century **Capilla de Santiago** next door to the left. The light switch will illuminate all you can see from the window in the door: a religious statue silhouetted against an alabaster window.

Inside the **Colegiata,** just up the driveway from the *capilla,* tombs of King Sancho El Fuerte (the Strong) and his bride rest in solitary splendor, lit by huge stained-glass windows. The monastery's Gothic church, endowed by the dead king and consecrated in 1219, is its main attraction; the elegant vaulting and luminous stained glass were ahead of their 13th-century time. Beneath a soaring canopy weeps the golden and silvery **Virgen de las Lágrimas** (Virgin of Tears). (The few monks who live in the monastery hold mass Mon.-Fri. at 8pm, Sat. at 6pm, Sun. at 8:30am, noon, and 6pm.) The deep organ and rhythmic chanting do draw tears. To the left after the first arch on the monastery is a small **museo** that houses religious artifacts. (Open July 3-19 11am-1:30pm and 4-6:30pm, Sat.-Sun. May 1-July 19. Admission 100ptas.)

Those undertaking the Camino de Santiago love to start from Roncevalles. The **monastery** has free lodging for pilgrims. To take advantage of these accommodations, go in the door to the right as you face the monastery. Unwieldy youth groups crowd the **Albergue Juvenil Roncesvalles (HI)** (tel. 76 00 15), at the back of the monastery and to the right. (Members only. 750ptas per person. *Pensión completa* 1750ptas. Breakfast 225ptas.) The newly redone **Posada** at the entrance to Roncesvalles provides doubles (4000ptas) and a pricey restaurant (entrees 900-1800ptas). **Camping Urrobi** (tel. 76 02 00) is 3km downhill from the town in Espinal. (Open April-Oct. 275ptas per person, per tent, and per car.) The **Casa Sabina Hostería** (tel. 76 00 12), a bit uphill of the monastery on the main road, feeds guests in the restaurant downstairs.

An **information office** (tel. 76 01 93) lurks in the old domed mill behind Casa Sabina Hostería. (Open mid-March to Oct. Tues.-Sat. 10am-2pm and 4-7pm, Sun. 10am-2:30pm.) The **telephone code** is 948.

About 1km up the road from the monastery the **Puerto Ibañeta** (1057m), marked by a small church and a stone decorated with a sword and two mules, stands in honor of Roland. When not shrouded in a fog, the view of both valleys is bowel-loosening.

It's a pleasant 3km walk to **Burguete,** the nearest town braved by public transportation. If you catch the early morning bus to Pamplona, accommodations in Burguete are easy to find. Forget the *menú* at **Hostal Burguete** (tel. 76 00 05) and get a room: full-length mirrors and high, plump beds. (1500ptas per person. Breakfast 300ptas.) Downhill, **Hostal Juandeaburre** (tel. 76 00 78) has cheaper rooms. (Singles 1600ptas. Doubles 2800ptas. Mid-Sept. to mid-July 1400ptas; 2400ptas.) La Montañesa's **bus** from Pamplona to Burguete leaves Monday through Saturday at 6pm (2 1/2 hr., 330ptas) and returns at 7:30am.

Valcarlos

"Caution: Cattle on the loose" reads the sign welcoming visitors to Valcarlos, a mere 3km south of the French border and 17km north of Roncesvalles. Curiously, the town is home to an inordinate number of former Californians—Basques who took refuge in Bakersfield when they fled Franco's Spain en masse. Now back in their homeland, these one-time autonomists are more vocal than their stay-at-home cousins on the subject of Basque independence. And they're happy to show off their English to boot. Most residents also speak French.

The relatively modern **iglesia** is notable for its fascinating *retablo,* which depicts St. James in his popular incarnation as Santiago el Matamoro (the Moorslayer). El Matamoro sits on a white horse aiming a saber at a falling *moro* who bears a crescent moon.

Hostal Maitena is on C. Elizaldea, the only street in town (tel. 76 20 10). There's much wainscoting and a big common bathtub with shower. (Doubles 2900ptas, with bath 4000ptas.) Below, the restaurant-on-stilts wobbles directly on the face of the mountain. In a gorgeous setting, the restaurant serves scrumptious dishes at decent prices. (Breakfast 260ptas. Lunch or dinner 925ptas.) The tourist office's guide lists *casas particulares* and the bar with the "Ene Sort Lekua" sign next to the *pelota* court is usually in the know.

Upstairs in the stone-arched **Ayuntamiento** building and behind the door on the right, the secretary (tel. 79 01 17) can give you some touristy **information** (open Mon.-Fri. 8am-3pm, Sat. 9am-noon). The **post office** (tel. 79 00 90) is in a little white house with a yellow mailbox uphill past the Ayuntamiento (open Mon.-Fri. 9am-noon and Sat. 9-11:30am). The **postal code** is 31660. The **telephone code** is 948. **Emergency** numbers for all of Navarra are 088 or 091. You may also call the **Guardia Civil** at 79 00 65 or 79 00 76. Shops in Valcarlos accept French francs; the **Caja de Ahorros de Navarra** on the main road has the best **exchange** rates.

If you're coming from **France,** you'll have to hike across the border from St.-Jean-Pied-de-Port, 10km away. The last Spanish town accessible by **bus** is Burguete, 20km downhill.

Aragón

Comprising the provinces of Huesca, Zaragoza, and Teruel, the kingdom embraces the towering central Pyrenees, the deeply ravined terraces of the Ebro basin, and the tawny, windswept plateaus of the south. Sheltered in green valleys below the snow-capped peaks, 12th-century Romanesque churches and monasteries mark the pilgrims' progress toward Santiago de Compostela. Hydroelectric and irrigation schemes harnessing the mountain streams and the Río Ebro transformed large areas of the reddish desert into a vast green *huerta* (orchard). Both the names of towns and regional artwork reflect the Muslim influence here; from the fusion of Christian and Muslim cultures in this region, the Mudejar style of brick architecture developed.

The harsh terrain and climate coupled with the region's strategic location engendered a martial culture, known among Spaniards for its obstinacy. Established as a kingdom in 1035 and united with the commercially enterprising Catalans in 1137, Aragón forged a far-flung Mediterranean empire that brought Roussillon, València, Murcia, the Baleares, Naples, and Sicily, and even the Duchy of Athens under its sway. Aragonese kings were held in check by the nobility, *cortes* (parliaments), and cities with restrictive *fueros* (laws). From the 12th century an elected Justicia (magistrate) defended commoners' rights against overbearing royal or seignorial fiat. Aragón retained these privileges even after union with Castile in 1492, until Felipe II marched into Zaragoza in 1591 and seized the Justicia Juan de Lanuza for giving sanctuary to his fallen minister Antonio Pérez.

Regional specialties take advantage of the abundant fresh-water fish from northern rivers and produce from the Ebro basin's orchards. *Ternasco* (roast lamb) and preparations with *chilindrón* (pepper and tomato) sauce are especially good here. Possibly the most famous local products are the strong, full-bodied reds and whites from the Cariñena-Daroca vineyards. *Frutas de Aragón* are dried fruit (not candied) dipped in semi-sweet chocolate.

Zaragoza

The pulse of this major transport hub has quickened dizzyingly since Augustus founded it in 24 BC as a retirement home for war veterans. Despite its illustrious heritage, modern Zaragoza hasn't quite hit its cultural stride: it's a kind of Miami with a flourishing nouveau riche culture.

Orientation and Practical Information

Zaragoza is laid out like a bicycle wheel. The center of the wheel is **Plaza Basilio Paraíso,** from which five spokes radiate outward. Facing the fountain in the middle of the plaza with the IberCaja bank building at your back, the spokes going clockwise are: **Paseo de Sagasta; Gran Vía** which turns into Paseo Fernando el Católico; **Paseo de Pamplona** which leads to Paseo Marí Agustin and the train station; **Paseo de Independencia** which ends at **Plaza de España** (the entrance to the *casco antiguo*); and **Paseo Constitución.**

The *casco antiguo,* or the old quarter, lies at the end of Po. Independencia between Pl. España and Plaza de Nuestra Señora del Pilar (commonly known as **Plaza del Pilar).** Most of the city's museums and sights frame this plaza's borders, the most central and important being the grandiose **Basilica de Nuestra Señora del Pilar.** The cathedral's blue-and-yellow tiled domes are a good landmark.

To reach Pl. Pilar from Pl. Paraíso, walk down Po. Independencia to Pl. España, then take C. Don Jaime I (on the right) which runs straight to the plaza. The user-friendly public bus system, plus city map blow-ups at major intersections, make touring easy.

Take care at night around the red-light and drug-dealing districts of Plaza Magdalena, five or six blocks to the right of Pl. Pilar; and the dim, narrow streets of the more decrepit neighborhood of Iglesia San Pablo, across Av. César Augusto, which borders the left side of Pl. Pilar as you face the basilica. Women travelers, especially solo, should be wary.

Tourist Office: City: Pl. Pilar, directly in front of the basilica. Open Mon.-Sat. 9:30am-2pm and 4:30-7:30pm, Sun. 10am-2pm. Request the *plano callejero* (indexed street map), as well as the tourist map. Several useful guides to the city. Plans are afoot to open a second office at the train station to replace the office currently at C. Don Jaime I, 5 (tel. 29 75 82), 1 bl. from the train station on the right in the direction of Pl. Pilar. Open Mon.-Sat. 9am-2pm and 4-6pm. **Regional: Torreón de la Zuda,** Glorieta de Pío XII (tel. 39 35 37), imprisoned in the tower to your right as you face Pl. Pilar's fountain at the end farthest from C. Don Jaime I. Covers all of Aragón. Open June-Aug. Mon.-Sat. 8:30am-2:30pm and 5-7:30pm, Sun. 10-11am; Sept.-May Mon.-Fri. 8:30am-2:30pm and 4-6pm, Sat. 9am-1:30pm.

El Corte Inglés: Po. Sagasta, 3 (tel. 21 11 21), near Pl. Paraíso. They have a **map. Currency exchange:** 1% commission (250ptas min. charge). They also offer novels and guidebooks in English, haircutting, both cafeteria and restaurant, and **telephones.** Open Mon.-Sat. 10am-9pm.

Budget Travel: TIVE, Residencial Paraíso, building 4, local 40 (tel. 21 83 15, 22 98 46). From behind El Corte Inglés (see above), through the courtyard, up the stairs, and left; office on left. ISIC 500ptas. HI card 1800ptas. Usually deals only with foreign travel destinations, along with the Baleares. Open June-Sept. Mon.-Fri. 9am-1:30pm; Oct.-May Mon.-Fri. 9am-2pm.

Currency Exchange: El Corte Inglés (see above). Some luxury hotels will change currency in emergencies.

American Express: Viajes Turopa, Po. Sagasta, 47 (tel. 38 39 11), 6 bl. from Pl. Paraíso; entrance around the corner on Camino de las Torres. Full services. Cardholder mail held. Slightly better exchange rates than banks. Open Mon.-Fri. 9am-1:30pm and 4-8pm, Sat. 9am-1pm.

Post Office: Po. Independencia, 33 (tel. 22 26 50), 1 bl. from Pl. Aragón on the right. Information booth open Mon.-Fri. 9am-2pm. Lista de Correos downstairs at window 4. Open for stamps, Lista de Correos, and **telegrams** Mon.-Fri. 8am-9pm, Sat. 9am-7pm, Sun. 9am-2pm. **Postal Code:** 50001.

Telephones: C. Castellano Tomás, 4, behind the post office. From Pl. Aragón take Po. Independencia 1 bl., turn right on C. Bruíl, continue for a block, then turn left. Open Mon.-Sat. 9am-1:30pm and 6-10pm. **Telephone Code:** 976.

Zaragoza 231

Flights: tel. 34 90 50. The Ebrobus (tel. 32 40 09) shuttles between the airport and Pl. San Francisco (7-8 per day about every hr. 7:15am-8:30pm, 75ptas). For Pl. San Francisco, take Gran Vía until it turns into Po. Fernando El Católico; the square is 3 bl. away. A taxi (see Taxis below) to the airport costs about 1000ptas. About 1-2 flights per day to Barcelona, València, Madrid, Jerez, and Paris. Check p. 2 of local paper *El Heraldo de Aragón* for current flight schedules. **Iberia,** C. Canfranc, 22-24 (tel. 21 82 59; reservations tel. 21 82 50). From Pl. Paraíso, 3 bl. down Po. Pamplona on the right near Puerta del Carmen arch. Open Mon.-Fri. 9:30am-2pm and 4-7pm, Sat. 9:30am-1:30pm.

Trains: Estacíon Portillo, Av. Anselmo Clavé (tel. 21 11 66). To find Pl. Paraíso from here, start upstairs, bear right down the ramp and walk across Av. Anselmo Clavé. Head 1 bl. down C. General Mayandía and turn right on Po. María Agustín; continue 7 bl. as the street becomes Po. Pamplona ending at Pl. Paraíso. (Bus #21 from Po. María Agustín.) Information booth open 6am-10pm. **RENFE** information and ticket office, C. San Clemente, 13 (tel. 22 65 98). From the post office, turn right and follow Po. Independencia 2 bl., then turn right again. Open Mon.-Fri. 9am-2pm and 5-7pm, Sat. 9am-2pm. To: Tudela (16 per day, 1 1/4 hr., 340ptas); Huesca (4 per day, 1 1/4 hr., 410-600ptas); Jaca (3 per day, 21/4hr., 955-1100ptas); Logroño (12 per day, 3hr., 835-1240ptas); Soria (3 per day, 3hr., 975ptas); Pamplona (9 per day, 3hr., 880-1620ptas); Teruel (Sat.-Sun. 3 3/4 hr., 905-1130ptas); Madrid (14 per day, 3-4hr., 2280-3190ptas); Vitoria (1 per day, 4hr., 1370-1910ptas); Barcelona (5-16 per day, 4 1/2 hr., 1710-3625ptas); Donostia/San Sebastián (1 per day, 4 1/2 hr., 1765-3020ptas); València (2 per day, 6 1/2 hr., 1760-2400ptas); Bilbo (3 per day, 5hr., 1910-2340ptas); A Coruña (1 per day, 13hr., 5625ptas); Algeciras (1 per day, 17hr., 4860).

Buses: Various bus companies each have their own terminals. The tourist offices stock schedules for all companies. The most important lines are accessible by city bus from Pl. Paraíso.

Agreda Automóvil, Po. María Augustín, 7 (tel. 22 93 43). (Bus #21 in direction of Pl. Paraíso, which stops directly in front.) To: Muel (2 per day, 1/2 hr., 225ptas); Cariñena (2 per day, 1hr., 335ptas); Daroca (3 per day, 2hr., 640ptas); Soria (1-3 per day, 2hr., 850ptas); El Burgo de Osma (1-3 per day, 3hr., 1160ptas); Barcelona (4-6 per day, 3 1/2 hr., 1895ptas).

Arión Express, C. Asalto, 53 (tel. 20 05 23). From Pl. Paraíso down Po. Constitución 6-7 bl., then left on Po. Mina, which becomes C. Asalto. To València (6 per day, 5 1/4 hr., 1160ptas).

CONDA, Av. Navarra, 77-81 (tel. 33 33 72). From Pl. Paraíso follow Po. Pamplona to Po. María Agustín; turn left at 2nd major intersection onto Av. Madrid. Cross the highway and railbed on the blue pedestrian bridge; hang a right on Av. Navarra, then left after a long stretch. (Bus #25 from Po. Pamplona; watch for the station on the left.) To: Tudela (1 per day, 1hr., 575ptas); Pamplona (9 per day, 2 1/2 hr., 1375ptas); Donostia/San Sebastián (3 per day, 4hr., 1845ptas).

La Oscense, Po. María Agustín, 84 (tel. 43 97 82). By the traffic circle at the river's edge. (Bus #34 from Po. Pamplona to Pl. San Domingo, then left from Pl. San Domingo onto C. Santa Lucia.) To: Huesca (4-5 per day, 1hr., 545ptas); Jaca (2-3 per day, 2 1/2 hr., 1130ptas).

Samar Buil, C. Borao, 13 (tel. 27 61 79). From Pl. Paraíso down Po. Pamplona, the 1st left after 1st major traffic intersection. (Bus #21 from Po. Pamplona to the stop in front of the Jefatura Superior building, then walk.) Office is mid-block on the left. Tickets must be purchased 1/2hr. before departure. To Fuendetodos (2 per day, 30-45min., 310ptas).

Therpasa, C. General Sueiro, 22 (tel. 22 57 23). From Pl. Paraíso 1/2-bl. down Po. Constitución, then right for 2 bl. Open Mon.-Fri. 9am-1pm and 4:15-7:30pm, Sat. 9am-1pm. To: Empalme de Vera (5 per day, 1 1/4 hr., 485ptas); Vera de Moncayo (1 per day, 1 1/2 hr., 525ptas); Tarazona (5-6 per day, 1 1/2 hr., 550ptas); Soria (3-5 per day, 2 1/2 hr., 875ptas).

Zuriaga, C. San Juan Pablo Bonet, 13-15 (tel. 27 61 79, 27 51 33). From Pl. Paraíso 7 bl. down Po. Sagasta, then right. (Bus #34 from Po. Pamplona; seek out road sign for C. San Juan Pablo Bonet after 3 stops on Po. Sagasta; stop is in front of a white apartment complex.) To: Logroño (3-5 per day, 1 3/4 hr., 1230ptas); Teruel (3-4 per day, 2 3/4 hr., 1025ptas); Vitoria (1-3 per day, 2000ptas); Bilbo (2 per day, 3 1/2 hr., 1885ptas); Burgos (2-3 per day, 4hr., 1885ptas); València (1-3 per day, 5hr., 2015ptas); Santander (Mon.-Sat. 1 per day, 6hr., 3000ptas).

Public Transportation: Red **TUZSA** buses (tel. 22 64 71) cover the city (35ptas, 10-ride ticket 300ptas from booth in Pl. España). Route information in *Guía Tuz* at tourist offices. Bus #21 is most useful, running from near the train station up Po. María Agustín to Po. Pamplona, Pl. Paraíso, Pl. Aragón, Po. Independencia, and Pl. España, then back. For the train station use the stop near the intersection of Po. María Agustín and C. General Mayandía, by the Jefatura Superior police station.

Taxis: Pretty: white with red and yellow stripes. They love to hang out near the train station. **Radio-Taxi Aragón** (tel. 38 38 38). **Radio-Taxi Zaragoza** (tel. 42 42 42). **Radio-Taxi Cooperativa** (tel. 37 37 37).

Car Rental: Hertz, at train station and C. Luís del Valle, 26 (tel. 35 34 62). From Pl. Paraíso take Gran Vía, follow Po. Fernando El Católico 2 bl., turn right on Corona de Aragón, then take 3rd right. **Avis,** Po. Fernando El Católico, 9 (tel. 35 78 63). From Pl. Paraíso take Gran Vía, which becomes Po. Fernando El Católico. **Atesa,** Av. Valencia, 3 (tel. 35 28 06, 35 28 05). Take Gran Vía to Av. Goya, turn right, then left. Citroën Ax, 3 days with A/C, unlimited mileage, insurance, and tax included 20,000ptas. Must be 21 and have had license 1 yr.

Luggage Storage: At the **train station.** *Equipaje* office sells locker tokens (200ptas). Open 24 hrs. At **Agreda Automóvil** bus station, 75ptas per piece. At **Therpasa** bus station, 100ptas per piece (open Mon.-Fri. 9am-1pm and 4:15-7:30pm, Sat. 9am-1pm).

English Bookstore: Librería General, Po. Independencia, 22. Select literature section downstairs. Open Mon.-Fri. 9:30am-1:30pm and 4:30-8:30pm, Sat. 9:30am-1:30pm. **El Corte Inglés** (see above).

Library: Biblioteca Pública de Aragón, C. Dr. Cerrada, 22. As you face IberCaja in Pl. Paraíso just past the university building off Po. Pamplona on right. Open Mon.-Fri. 9am-8pm, Sat. 9am-2pm; Sept.-June Mon.-Fri. 9am-8pm, Sat. 9am-1:30pm.

Youth Center: CIPAJ (Centro de Información de Actividades Juveniles), C. Bilbao, 1 (tel. 21 39 60). From Po. Independencia turn left on C. Casa Jiménez 2 bl. past Pl. Aragón, then left. Clearinghouse for sundry youth information. Great monthly bulletin of city happenings. Some English spoken. Open Mon.-Fri. 10am-2pm.

Laundromat: Lavandería Rossell, C. San Vicente de Paúl, 27 (tel. 29 90 34). A right on C. Coso, 4 bl., then left 4 1/2 bl. Wash and dry 870-1470ptas per load, depending on size. Open July 31-July 14 Mon.-Fri. 9am-1pm and 4-8pm, Sat. 9am-1pm; July 15-30 9am-1pm and 5-8pm, Sat. 9am-1pm.

Swimming Pool: Sixteen of them. *Piscinas municipales* is a comprehensive guide to the city's pools available at tourist offices. **C.D.M. Salduba,** Parque Primo de Rivera, s/n (tel. 55 36 36), at the very end of Po. Fernando El Católico. (Buses #29, 30, 35, 40, 42, and 45.) Open June 15-Sept. 15 10:30am-10pm. Admission 180ptas, over 60 80ptas, ages 6-18 105ptas.

Late-Night Pharmacy: Check listings in *El Heraldo de Aragón* (local paper), or posted notices on pharmacy doors.

Medical Services: Hospital Miguel Servet, Po. Isabel La Católica, 1 (tel. 35 57 00). In **emergencies,** turn to Ambulatorio Ramón y Cajal, Po. María Agustín, 12 (tel. 43 41 11). **Casa de Socorro,** C. Canelejas, 5 (tel. 23 02 91). **Ambulance** (tel. 35 85 00).

Police: Jefatura Superior, Po. María Agustín, 34 (tel. 43 67 11). **Municipal Police,** C. Domingo Miral, s/n (tel. 49 91 76). **National Police,** Po. María Agustín, 36 (tel. 091).

Accommodations and Camping

Be wary the week of October 12, when Zaragoza celebrates the *Fiesta de la Virgen del Pilar;* make reservations as early as possible. Also know that *ferias* (trade shows) go on February through April. The biggest is the agricultural machinery show FIMA, usually in late March or early April, during which the tourist office has to scour everything within a 100km radius to find rooms.

Hostals and *pensiones* cram the narrow streets of the *casco antiguo,* especially within the rectangle bound by **Calle Alfonso I, Calle Don Jaime, Plaza España,** and **Plaza del Pilar.** Hunting can be depressing, as many *pensiones* prefer long-term residents. *Casas particulares,* too, are scarce. Worst of all, **Residencia Juvenil Gracián Baltázar (HI)** is still under renovations. Call 55 15 04 to check on progress or ask at the tourist office.

Fonda Satué, C. Espoz y Mina, 4, 3rd fl. (tel. 39 07 09), from Pl. España 4 bl. down C. Don Jaime I, then left. The double stairway twists upward through the gloom. Well-kept rooms + low price = way popular. Make reservations. Singles 750ptas. Doubles 1460ptas. Showers 150ptas.

Casa de Huéspedes Elena, C. San Vicente de Paúl, 30 (tel. 39 65 80), across the street from Lavandería Rossell. Capacious, modern rooms with superior new hall bathroom. Singles 1400ptas. Doubles 1800ptas.

Pension Rex, C. Méndez Nuñez, 31 (tel. 39 26 33), on the corner of C. Don Jaime I. Roomy rooms with balconies in the heart of the *casco antiguo*. Easy access to nightlife. Bathrooms are slightly moldy. Singles 1500ptas. Doubles 2500ptas. Showers 350ptas.

Hostal Residencia Montaña, C. Castillo, 10 (tel. 43 57 02). From the train station, turn left on Av. José Anselmo Clavé, which becomes Po. María Agustín; after crossing Av. Madrid, it's the next left. Clean rooms with walls the color of Easter-flavor M&Ms. Loose tiles and worn bathrooms. Singles 1400ptas. Doubles 1800ptas. Breakfast 250ptas.

Camping: Casablanca, Po. Canal, 175 (tel. 33 03 22), down Ctra. Nacional 2. (Bus #36 from Pl. Pilar or Pl. España to the suburb of Valdefierro.) Ask the driver to let you know when you've arrived, as it's notoriously difficult to find. Camping site with good facilities, including pool. 420ptas per person, per tent, and per car; July-Aug. 475ptas. Open May-Nov.

Food

Plaza de la Magdalena is a likely area for a meal, but take the evening *paseo* elsewhere. For the scoop on Zaragoza's restaurants, lay your hands on *Places to Eat* brochure (200ptas), available at the city tourist office. The **market** thrives in the long green building on Av. César Augusto off Pl. Pilar. Fresh fruit and veggies, cow's tongue, and live squid go to the buyer. (Open Mon.-Sat. 9am-2pm and 5-8pm.)

Restaurante Alcarabea, C. Zumalacárregui, 33. From Pl. Paraíso take Po. Sagasta 3 bl. and turn right. Serve yourself exquisite vegetarian food. Substantial 675ptas *menú*. *Platos combinados* 450ptas. Open Sept.-July 1-4pm, Aug. Mon.-Fri. 1-4pm.

La Zanahoria, C. Tarragona, 4 (tel. 35 87 94). From Pl. Paraíso take Gran Vía, turn right on Av. Goya, then the 1st left after crossing Av. Valencia. Elegant yuppie vegetarians. Excellent salads and *spaghetti al pesto*. Lunch *menú* 900ptas. *Platos combinados* 750ptas. Two-course dinner with beverage under 1200ptas. Open 1:30-4pm and 9-11:30pm. For dinner, arrive before 10pm or call for reservations.

Tres Hermanos, C. San Pablo, 45 (tel. 44 10 85), from Pl. Pilar turn right from C. César Augusto 1 bl. past the market. Tables downstairs from bar. Vapid atmosphere, good *menú* (600ptas). Open mid-Aug. to mid-July Wed.-Mon. 1-4pm and 8:30-11pm.

La Creperie, C. Don Jaime I, 34 (tel. 29 07 65). Yuppie atmosphere, yummy crepes. Dinner crêpes 800ptas. Dessert crêpes 600ptas. Open 8am-midnight.

Sights

The towers and brightly colored tile domes of the **Basílica del Pilar** in Pl. Pilar pierce the skyline. The domes, decorated with frescoes by Goya, González Velázquez (a contemporary of Goya's), and Bayeu, cap a creamy interior. The pillar in the central chapel is "proof" that the Virgin stopped by in 40 AD. Where it isn't covered, the pillar has been eroded by the kissies of pilgrims in homage to the Virgin's continued protection of the city. Beside the chapel are two of the three bombs dropped on the basilica during the Civil War and defused by the Virgin. The **Museo del Pilar** displays the glittering *joyero de la Virgen* (Virgin's jewels) and a collection of original sketches of the ceiling frescoes. The Gothic-Renaissance altar of polychrome alabaster is geniusy. (Museum open 9am-2pm and 4-6pm. Admission 50ptas. Basilica open 5:45am-8:30pm. Children can pass through the Madonna's mantle 8-10am, 1:30-2pm, and 5:30-7:30pm.) An elevator to the top allows a giraffe's-eye view of the city and surrounding plains. (Open Aug. 1-July 14 Sat.-Thurs. 9:30am-2pm and 4-7pm. Admission 75ptas.)

Catedral de la Seo has been tinkered with a few times since it was erected as a mosque. The first changes brought the Gothic style, with important Mudejar elements such as the east end wall (visible from C. Sepulcro) of brick and *azulejo* tiles. Later alterations introduced the Plateresque, Renaissance (interior), and Baroque (façade, belfry). Its chapels are opulently decorated; the chapter house is hung with Riberas and Zurbaráns. Under restoration, the building, which sits across C. Don Jaime I from the basilica, is closed to the public.

Between the cathedral and the Ayuntamiento, Zaragoza's 16th-century Gothic and Plateresque **Lonja** (stock exchange) is distinguished by star vaulting and its forest of soaring Ionic columns that rise to a ceiling of gilt crests. Mudejar art shows in the **torres** of the Iglesias de San Pablo and de la Magdalena. Numerous seignorial mansions, the medieval baths, and several old university buildings embellish **Calle del Coso,** the southern boundary of the old city.

In addition to an extensive collection of medieval Aragonese paintings, the **Museo Provincial de Bellas Artes** hangs works by Ribera, Lucas van Leyden, and Claudio Coello, along with a Goya self-portrait and likeness of Carlos IV and María Luisa. From the post office, turn right and walk around the corner; the museum is five blocks away to the left. (Open Tues.-Sat. 9am-2pm, Sat. 10am-2pm. Admission 200ptas.)

The charming **Museo Pablo Gargallo** is dedicated to Pablo, one of the most innovative artists of the 1920s. The small but marvelous collection of his works—including a gallery of copper and iron *faunos* and an inner courtyard of amusing bronze figures—shines in the graceful Palacio de Arguillo, a national monument. From C. Don Jaime I in the direction of Pl. Pilar, turn left on C. Casto Méndez Núñez; the museum is on Pl. San Felipe, which is on the left five blocks down. (Open Tues.-Sat. 10am-1pm and 5-9pm, Sun. 11am-2pm. Free.)

Following the Muslim conquest of the Iberian Peninsula in the 8th century, a fuss over succession smashed the kingdom into petty tributary states called *taifas*. The **Palacio de la Aljafería,** on C. Castillo between the train station and the river, remains the principal relic of Aragón's *taifa*. The ground floor has a distinctly Moorish flavor with its intricately carved capitals and its *musallah* (private mosque) of multi-lobed, scalloped arches and geometric and floral tracery. In contrast, the second floor is flamboyant Gothic, dating from the time of the Catholic monarchs. The fortified tower imprisoned *El Trovador* in García Gutierrez's drama, source of Verdi's opera. (Open Tues.-Sat. 10am-2pm and 4-8pm, Sun. 10am-2pm. Free.)

Entertainment

Young citizens brag that their city has *mucha marcha* (a lot of action). The *marcha* (nightlife) is well described in *Night Spots,* one of the slick tourist office brochures that covers the scene, both gay and straight. The scene centers around the market, on **Calles Predicadores, El Olmo, El Temple, Contamina,** and **Manifestación.** The 20ish bunch favors **C. Dr. Cerrada,** off Po. Pamplona, while the more mature patronize **Residencial Paraíso** and Calles Doctor Casas, Bolonia and La Paz. University students storm **Po. Sagasta** and its offshoot C. Zumalacárregui. Gulping beer from *litros* (literally liters—about 250ptas a pop) is the primary sport around **El Rollo,** the zone bounded by C. Moncasi, C. Bonet, and C. Maestro Marquina at the southern end of Po. Sagasta. **Torreluna,** C. Miguel Servet, 193, is the only one of Zaragoza's many discos that has dancing *al aire libre* all night long. The most popular of the indoor versions include **Atuaire,** C. Contamina, 13 (tel. 21 37 34), and **Sirenas,** on Pl. Verónica.

The city erupts for a week of unbridled hoopla around October 12 in honor of La Virgen. **Festivities** include sporting events, performances of the regional dance, *la jota,* and the final *Rosario de Cristal* procession that wheels through town illuminated by 350 carriage-borne lanterns. City patrons San Valero (Jan. 29) and San Jorge (April 23) are also feted.

The city tourist office distributes information on party days, including the **Conciertos para una Noche de Verano** festival (Sat. in July and Aug.), which brings concerts to the Rincón de Goya amphitheater in Parque Primo de Rivera. In May, Zaragoza hosts a national exhibition of painting and sculpture.

Near Zaragoza

Sos del Rey Católico

A medieval knot of winding alleys overshadowed by noble mansions, this hamlet north of Zaragoza takes its name from King Fernando El Católico, begat in the town's **Palacio de Sada** in 1452. Sos now numbers about 1100 inhabitants who live in and around a **casco urbano** that is old.

The **tourist office** at C. Arquitecto Sainz Vicuña, 1 (tel. 88 84 31), will surely tell you more than we do. If you want postal information, please call the **post office** at 88 81 96. The **postal code** is 50680, the **telephone code** 948. If you need protection, the **Guardia Civil** are at Av. Zaragoza, s/n (tel. 88 80 94). You'll have to spend the night in Sos thanks to erratic public transport; ATCAR runs one **bus** per day from Zaragoza (Mon.-Sat. at 7pm). Departures are from the parking lot on the lower floor of the train station (21/4hr., 790ptas).

Fuendetodos

The Goya route begins at the painter's birthplace, Fuendetodos, 50km south of Zaragoza. Unlike most 19th-century house museums, Goya's is actually sort of a hoax; the house is not his real birthplace, but was chosen after his death to be the **museum**. This impostor recreates Goya's life and times by dressing itself up with period furnishings and curiosities. (Open March-Oct. Tues.-Sun. 11am-2pm and 4-7pm; Nov.-Feb. Tues.-Sun. 11am-2pm and 3:30-6:30pm. Admission 150ptas.) The village itself is a authentic, unremarkable, and Aragonese. Samar Buil **buses** make the run (see Zaragoza: Practical Information).

Cartuja de Aula Dei

Woefully, only men are allowed to enter the Cartuja de Aula Dei, a 16th-century Carthusian monastery which lies 12km from Zaragoza. Here the young Goya completed one of his first major works, a series of 11 tableaux depicting the life of Mary. The monastery is under renovations, so call ahead (if you're a man, that is; tel. 57 54 67) or check with a tourist office. Women can twiddle their thumbs back in the hotel or start out on dinner. Take **bus** #28 from the stop alongside the Roman walls (near Zaragoza's regional tourist office) to the leafy entrance of *la cartuja* (every 1/2 hr., 20min., 35ptas). Look for the large complex in the open on the left after passing the Universidad de la Cartuja de Aula Dei sign. It's a bit of a wait for the return bus.

Monasterio de Veruela

West of Zaragoza rise the purple crests of the Sierra de Moncayo. Romantic, sickly poet and painter Gustavo Adolfo Bécquer sought the mountain air in Monasterio de Veruela and penned his *Cartas desde mi celda* (Letters from my cell) within these walls. Founded in 1146, the Cistercian **monastery** (tel. 64 90 25) centers about a church with an ornate Gothic cloister. Also on the grounds is a museum displaying contemporary Aragonese art. (Grounds open Tues.-Sat. 10am-2pm and 4-7pm; Nov.-March Tues.-Sat. 10am-1pm and 3-6pm. Admission 200ptas.) Public transportation only goes as near as **Vera de Moncayo** (2-4km; see Tarazona) and **Empalme de Vera** (8-10km). Therpasa **buses** serve both towns (see Zaragoza: Practical Information).

Tarazona

People call Tarazona "La Ciudad Mudéjar" (The Mudejar City) after they eye the distinctive cathedral towers on the Río Queiles. In fact, buildings everywhere in this town of 11,000 show the typical Arabic-influenced brickwork style of the 16th century. If this toots your horn, Tarazona is a great daytrip from either Soria and Zaragoza.

Like so many monuments here, the splendid Gothic 15th- to 16th-century **catedral** is being painstakingly restored. The belfry and lantern are particularly fine examples of Mudejar work, not to mention the 16th-century Moorish plasterwork tracery in the inner cloister. From the bus station, turn right onto Av. Navarra and follow to Pl. San Francisco, then head right (following signs to Soria and Zaragoza); the first left leads up a flight of stairs to the cathedral. Skirt the right side of the cathedral and follow C. San Antón for half a block or so. The 18th-century, octagonal **Plaza de Toros Vieja** has balconied and arcaded upper tiers; its outer ring now houses 32 families. From the cathedral, take a left at the sign for Soria, then turn right and pursue for a block.

Tarazona was a seasonal residence of medieval Aragonese kings until the 15th century; their Alcázar has since served as **Palacio Episcopal.** The bishop's home lies across the bridge, left one block, and then up the twisting stairs of the Recodos. The former dungeons of the palace lie downhill on Rúa Alta de Bécquer; they've since been gentrified by the **Centro de Estudios Turiasonenses** (Center for Tarazona Studies) and its temporary exhibitions. (Open Mon.-Sat. 11am-1pm and 6-9pm, Sun. 11am-2pm. Free.)

Opposite the Palacio Episcopal in the heart of the medieval quarter, "El Cinto," rises **Iglesia de la Magdalena,** with a Romanesque east end and a Mudejar tower that dominates the old town. The entrance is a left up Cuesta de Palacio and another left. **Murallas** (walls) surround the quarter's heart; push up the hill from La Magdalena past the remarkable Renaissance façade of Iglesia San Atilano until you hit Pl. Castelar, where you should exit left on C. Puerto. Your reward for the effort is the sweep-o-ramic pan of the broad Valle del Moncayo, which even takes in the distant Aragonese Pyrenees.

Budgeters struggle to lodge here. **Hostal Residencia María Cristina,** Carrera de Castilla, 3 (tel. 64 00 84), is on the highway to Soria from Pl. San Francisco. Hardly sumptuous, but surprisingly quiet for a roadside inn. (Curfew 11:30pm. Doubles 1800ptas; Oct.-Feb. 1440ptas; March-May 1560ptas. Solo travelers pay about 80% of the double rate.)

Bar Avenida, on Av. Navarra just down the street from the bus depot toward Pl. San Francisco, serves zesty *tapas* (30-40ptas). **Restaurante Marisquería Galeón,** Av. La Paz, 1 (left from Pl. San Francisco), nets seafood and its generous 750ptas *menú*. (Open 1:30-4pm and 9pm-midnight.)

The **tourist office** has cornered the left side of the cathedral at C. Iglesias, 5 (tel. 64 00 74). Their paraphernalia is useful. A signboard outside provides a rudimentary orientation to monuments. (Open Tues.-Fri. 9am-1:15pm and 4-7:30pm, Sat. 9am-1:15pm, Sun. 11am-1pm.) The **post office** is at Av. Navarra, 17 (tel. 64 13 17), two storefronts to the left from the bus station. (Open Mon.-Fri. 9am-2pm, Sat. 9am-2:30pm.) The **postal code** is 50500, the **telephone code** 976. The **Red Cross** is outside town on Ctra. Zaragoza (tel. 64 09 26). In **emergencies** also turn to **Ambulatorio San Atilano,** Av. Paz, 29 (tel. 64 12 85), past Restaurante-Marisquería Galeón. The **municipal police** are next to the library on Pl. San Francisco (tel. 64 16 91, **emergency** tel. 092). They provide maps when the tourist office is dead.

Therpasa **buses** (tel. 64 11 00) operate from the station on Av. Navarra. To Soria (5-6 per day, 1hr., 445ptas) and Zaragoza (4 per day, 1hr., 550ptas). The 7am bus to Zaragoza stops in Vera de Moncayo (15min., 95ptas) (see Near Zaragoza: Monasterio de Veruela). Other buses to Zaragoza pause at **Empalme de Vera** (10min., 60ptas), 6km from Vera de Moncayo. If you ask nicely in Spanish, you'll probably be allowed to leave your **luggage** for a few hours at the ticket window at the bus station, although it's not an official storage area.

La Ruta del Vino: Muel, Cariñena, Daroca

No need to sniff for a bouquet to follow the **wine route,** running about 100km to the south of Zaragoza through the towns of Muel, Cariñena, and Daroca. In this ideal grape-growing climate where nights are cool and the days scorching, wine is more common than water. The regional tourist office in Zaragoza has a little book that has all the answers to the two most commonly asked questions: 1) What is the history of winemaking in this region? and 2) Can you tell me vintage details of these wines?

Muel is also noteworthy as home to a renowned school of ceramics and to a fountain painted by Goya. **Cariñena's** church is a fragment of a fortress built by the **Orden de los Caballeros de San Juan** (Order of the Knights of St. John); its Capilla de Santiago did duty as a mosque. Agreda Automóvil **buses** cover all three towns from Zaragoza; Zuriaga's bus service to Teruel from Zaragoza is faster, but doesn't always include all three towns (see Zaragoza: Practical Information).

Last stop on the line, **Daroca** is a fantastic town founded by Muslims and surrounded by ruins of a 4km wall punctuated by 114 towers. The two main gates in the wall, **Puerta Alta** and **Puerta Baja**, still provide the only access to the main part of town, and the glazed red-tile towers of the latter have been declared a national monument. The rest of the wall is less well-preserved, running in fits and starts along the ridges of the hills around town. Footpaths shadow the wall, so hikers can get a sentry's view of the town and the whole valley from the towers. Calle Arrabal is one approach to the wall; exit the Puerta Baja and turn right. Go up, then right, then up (and up and up).

Daroca is a one-street town. **Calle Mayor** is the backbone from Puerta Alta to Puerta Baja, and everything within the walls are like so many ribs. Within the walls spill the **Sagrados Corporales,** evidence of a miracle that occured in 1239 during the Moorish conquest of València. Spanish soldiers were taking communion at Mass when the Muslims attacked, so a priest hid the wafers under some rocks; when he returned for them they had liquefied into blood. The stains are preserved today amid other less red religious art in the museum of **Iglesia de Santa María,** a Renaissance church. The church is being restored and, along with the museum, is closed to the public; check the tourist office for an opening date. To reach the church, take either of the two Calles Juan de la Huerta from C. Mayor.

The town transubstantiates most feverishly on the **Fiesta de Corpus Christi,** held every year in late May or early June, when a cortège bearing the *Corporales* processes through the streets. On a secular note, Daroca also hosts the annual **Curso Internacional de Música Antigua** (International Course of Ancient Music) the first week of August, when musicians the world over gather in Daroca to teach, learn, and give free concerts on Baroque instruments.

To bed down, try **Pensión El Ruejo,** C. Mayor, 88 (tel. 80 11 90), complete with a disco. (Singles 1900ptas, with bath 2400ptas. Doubles 3800ptas, with bath 4800ptas.) **Hostal Agiria,** Ctra. Sagunto-Burgos km 218 (tel. 80 07 31, 80 07 39), is outside the city on the highway to Zaragoza, past the gas station. (Indifferent rooms. June 15-Nov. 20 and Christmas: Singles 1600ptas. Doubles 2600ptas, with bath 3300ptas. Nov. 21-June 14: 1400ptas; 2100ptas, 2800ptas.)

The *roca* of the **Bar Restaurante La Roca,** C. Mayor, 107, juts defiantly into the dining room. The 800ptas *menú* embraces a scrumptious *trucha con champiñones* (trout with mushroom sauce). (Open 1:15-3:15pm and 9-10:30pm.) The town **market** vends in Pl. Santiago, off C. Mayor (Thurs. 9am-2pm).

The **tourist office** is at Pl. España, 4 (tel. 80 01 29), opposite Iglesia Santa María. To get here from Puerta Alta, pursue C. Mayor for four or five blocks, and hang a right on C. San Juan de la Huerta. The map (100ptas) is superfluous. (Open Tues.-Sat. 11am-2pm, Sun. noon-2pm.) The **post office,** C. Mayor, 157 (tel. 80 02 15), is near Puerta Baja. (Open Mon.-Fri. 9am-2pm, Sat. 9am-1pm.) The **postal code** is 50360. **Telephone booths** are located at various points along C. Mayor and near Hostal Legido on Av. Escuelas Pías. The **telephone code** is 976. The **Red Cross** (tel. 80 03 36) is outside Puerta Alta and across the highway. The **Guardia Civil** (tel. 80 01 13) has headquarters on the highway next to the swimming pool.

Buses back to Zaragoza or on to Teruel depart from C. Mayor near Puerta Baja. Buses arriving in Daroca stop at Puerta Baja or on the highway by Hostal Legido. To reach C. Mayor from the highway stop, walk past the *hostal* to Av. Escuelas Pías, turn left, and continue downhill. Bear right at the traffic circle on Av. Libertad to pass through Puerta Alta and onto C. Mayor.

Teruel

All dressed up with no place to go, Teruel captivates visitors with Mudejar, *Modernista* (the movement led by Gaudí), and Fascist Neoclassical attire. The merit of the Mudejar churches and cathedral make Teruel one of the most distinguished cities in Spain for this prolific Hispano-Islamic style. The city is also known as the *Ciudad de los Amantes* (City of Lovers) for Diego and Isabel, 13th-century lovers who died of

Aragón

thwarted love. Young lovers still visit their tombs to assure themselves of more auspicious outcomes.

Orientation and Practical Information

Rising 920m above sea-level, isolated, hilltop Teruel is still most accessible. Located 165km northeast of Valencia and 190km south of Zaragoza, the town is linked by train and bus to both.

The map of the city available at tourist offices is ugly and lame and covers only the historic center of town. Most street signs, where they exist at all, are in illegible script. Worse yet, some major streets and plazas go by two names. On the other hand, street maps are posted at the train station and on the major streets in the old quarter.

The *casco histórico* perches on a roughly circular hilltop linked to modern Teruel by bridges. The center of the *casco* is **Plaza de Carlos Castell,** affectionately (to judge by the typical Aragonese *-ico* suffix of endearment) known as **Plaza Torico** for the fountain with a stone bull calf lowering atop it. **Ronda Ambeles** (home of bus terminal) and **Paseo del Ovalo** (home of train station) are the most salient of the series of *rondas* that girdle the town's circumference.

Until Teruel finishes renovating its bus station (summer 1993), the RENFE platform will remain by far the more convenient access to the *casco antiguo*. To reach Pl. Carlos Castell/Torico from the train station, take the flight of stairs leading out of the park. Bear left across Po. Ovalo and follow the signs to *centro histórico* and *oficina de turismo* all the way up C. Nueva. Once the bus station is finished, buses will arrive on Ronda Ambeles, near the *casco*. For Pl. Carlos Castell/Torico, hone in on the stone tower at the edge of the station lot and turn left at the traffic light; then turn right on C. Abadía and follow the road downhill to its end. A right on C. Ramón y Cajal/San Juan leads to the square.

Until the new bus station is done, arrivals are in the modern quarter at a provisional station. For Pl. Carlos Castell/Torico, make your way past the small gas station to C. Castellón, follow it for one block to unmarked Av. José Torán, turn right and continue for three to four blocks to the **viaducto** (10min.). Once in the *casco histórico,* bear a right up C. General Pizarro past the park with the fountain on your left, walk across Pl. San Juan to the pyramid, and follow C. Ramón y Cajal/San Juan until you arrive at the plaza. The city bus also makes the trek to Pl. Carlos Castell/Torico (every 1/2 hr. Mon.-Sat. 10:30am-2pm and 5:30-8pm, Sun. 11am-2pm and 5-10pm, 35ptas); from the station, walk past the athletic fields on the right up one block to the bus stop awning on unmarked Av. Aragón. A new bridge is being built parallel to the *viaducto*.

Tourist Office: C. Tomás Nogues, 1 (tel. 60 22 79), at the corner of C. Comandante Fortea/del Pozo. From Pl. Carlos Castell/Torico, follow C. Ramón y Cajal/San Juan and take the first left; the office is a block away on your right. English spoken. Free guided tours of the city when there's a quorum in July and Aug. Open July 15-Sept. 15 Mon. 10am-2pm, Tues.-Sat. 9am-2pm and 5-8pm; Sept. 16-July 14 Mon.-Sat. 8am-2:30pm and 5-7:30pm.

Post Office: Pl. Pérez Prado, 2 (tel. 60 11 92), in the Seminario Conciliar building to the left of the Casa de Cultura. From Pl. Carlos Castell/Torico, take C. Los Amantes for 2 blocks. Open Mon.-Fri. 8am-9pm, Sat. 9am-2pm. **Postal Code:** 44001.

Telephones: Center at C. San Andrés, 13. Left from the tourist office down C. Tomás Nogues, left on C. Barón, then right on C. San Andrés. Open Mon.-Fri. 9am-1:30pm and 5-9:30pm, Sat. 9am-1:30pm. **Telephone Code:** 974.

Trains: Camino Estación, 1 (tel. 60 26 49), beneath Po. del Ovalo near the river. To: Mora de Rubielos (2-4 per day, 50min., 265ptas); Rubielos de Mora (1-3 per day, 55min., 275ptas); Cariñena (3 per day, 2-3hr., 660ptas); Muel (2 per day, 3 1/2 hr., 785ptas); València (3-5 per day, 3 1/2 hr., 835ptas); Zaragoza (3-4 per day, 3 1/2 -4hr., 905ptas).

Buses: at Ronda Ambeles or across the Viaducto as described above. See Orientation. **La Rápida** (tel. 60 20 04). To: Barcelona (Mon.-Sat. 2 per day, Sun. 1 per day; winter Mon.-Sat. 1 per day; 5 1/2 -6 1/2 hr.; 2550ptas) and Cuenca (Mon.-Sat. 2 per day, Sun. 1 per day; summer 1 per day; 2-3hr.; 930ptas). **Samar** (tel. 60 10 14 or 60 34 50). To València (2-5 per day, 2-3hr., 1080ptas) and Madrid (1-3 per day, 5hr., 2030ptas). **Zuriaga** (tel. 60 28 28 or 60 10 14). To Zaragoza (4 per day, 3 1/2 hr., 960ptas). **Autotransportes Teruel** (tel. 60 47 14 or 60 26 80). To Albarracín (Mon.-Fri.

1 per day at 3:30pm, 1 1/2 hr., 250ptas). **Furio** (tel. (964) 60 01 00). To: Mora de Rubielos (1hr., 214ptas); Rubielos de Mora (1 per day Mon.-Fri. at 2:30pm, 1 1/2 hr., 285ptas); Daroca (3 per day, 2hrs, 550ptas).

Luggage Storage: Lockers (200ptas) at train station. Bus station luggage check open Mon.-Fri. 8:30am-7pm, Sat. 8:30am-3:30pm (125ptas per piece).

English Bookstore: Librería Senda, Pl. Carlos Castell/Torico, 17. Good literature section. Open Mon.-Fri. 10am-2pm and 5-8pm, Sat. 10am-2pm.

Library: Casa de Cultura, Pl. Pérez Prado, 3, 1st floor, to the right of the post office building. Open July-Aug. Mon.-Fri. 9am-2pm; Sept.-June Mon.-Fri. 9am-2pm and 4-9pm, Sat. 9am-2pm.

Public Toilets: Paseo de la Glorieta, a park between the provisional bus station and Pl. Carlos Castell/Torico. With the *viaducto* behind you, take the left side of the *paseo* downstairs.

Swimming Pool: Piscina San Fernando, C. Barbastro, in the modern quarter near the provisional bus station. Cross the *viaducto*, walk down Av. José Torán to the traffic circle, turn left, and then right after 1 bl. Overrun. Open June 17-Sept. 15 11am-8pm. Admission 295ptas.

Medical Services: 24-hr. Pharmacy, consult p. 2 of *El Heraldo de Aragón,* which also lists other emergency numbers. **Red Cross,** C. San Miguel, 3 (tel. 60 22 22 or 60 26 09), past the Museo Provincial (see Sights below). **Hospital Provincial:** tel. 60 53 17 or 60 53 68. **Casa de Socorro:** tel. 60 53 68.

Police: National Police: tel. 60 12 52. **Municipal Police:** tel. 60 21 78 or **emergency:** tel. 092. **Guardia Civil,** C. San Francisco, 1 (tel. 60 11 00 or 60 12 02; **emergency** tel. 062).

Emergency: tel. 091.

Accommodations and Camping

The only remotely difficult time to find space is during the *fiestas* in early July. Even then, a call a week ahead of time should suffice. Teruel winters can be harsh—Nationalist and Republican forces battled it out here in December of 1937 with temperatures that fell to 18° C below 0 (0° F). The worst months are November to January, but the cold persists until April or May. The only decent weather is between May and September. Unless otherwise noted, all of the establishments below have winter heating.

Habitaciones Santa María, C. Santa María, 4 (tel. 60 35 45 or 60 93 37). From Pl. Carlos Castell/Torico, find C. Joaquín Costa/del Tozal and make the first left. Smallish but clean rooms with hexagonal tile floors. Singles 1100ptas. Doubles 2200ptas, with bath 3000ptas. Oct.-June 1000ptas; 1900ptas, 3000ptas.

Fonda/Posada del Tozal, C. Rincón, 5 (tel. 60 10 22), 3 bl. up C. Joaquín Costa/del Tozal and left. Old and cold. Compulsive owner loves to sand, stain, and varnish the antique furniture. 300-year-old sloping stone floors mess with your balance. No winter heating. Singles 1000ptas. Doubles 1500-2000ptas. Clean showers, but often cold water.

Pensión García, C. Rosario, 10 (tel. 60 10 62), off the hill. Bummer of a location. From the train station, turn left on Po. Ovalo and bear right downhill; C. Rosario is the first left after the *viaducto*. Clean, modern rooms above a popular bar. Excellent bathrooms. Compact singles 1000ptas. Large doubles 2100ptas. Ample triples 3000ptas.

Fonda Pilar, C. Huesca/Tremedal, 2 (tel. 60 26 32). From the corner of Pl. San Juan nearest the viaduct, to the left. Slightly old rooms in a central location. Owners take off for vacation in July. Singles 900ptas, doubles 1700ptas.

Camping: The nearest **campground** is in Mora de Rubielos, 42km away (see Near Teruel below). If you clear it first with the Ayuntamiento, next to the cathedral (see Sights below) in Pl. Catedral, and with the Guardia Civil, you are allowed to pitch a tent for free at Parque de la Fuente Cenada, about 3km down the road to the coast.

Food

Teruel wreaks sweet havoc on the food budget. The standard of restaurants is high, as are prices. Teruel is famous for its locally cured ham, *jamón de Teruel*. The specialty is worth at least one heart-stopping check at any restaurant. Misers can *tapas*-it at a bar on Pl. Carlos Castell/Torico. A **market** is on Pl. Domingo Gascón. From Pl. Carlos Casett/Rorico take C. Joaquín Costa/del Tozal. (Open Mon.-Sat. 8am-1:30pm.)

> **La Parilla,** C. San Estéban, 2. From the tourist office, turn right and walk uphill 2 bl., then right again. Fresh meat grilled in dining room fireplace. Excellent *menú* 1300ptas, entrees 700-1000ptas. *Longaniza* (salami *tapas,* 400ptas). Open 1-4pm and 8:30-11:30pm.
>
> **Cafetería Restaurante Mercantil,** C. Nueva, 22, on the left off Po. Ovalo from the train station. 900ptas *menú* engages the maw in prolonged conversation. Open Wed.-Mon. 10:30am-5:30pm and 7:30pm-12:30am.
>
> **Torre del Salvador,** C. El Salvador, 20. Take the street to the right out of Pl. Carlos Castell/Torico. Elegant dining room. 900ptas lunch *menú,* 1400ptas dinner *menú.* Good *riñones* (kidneys in garlic sauce). Open 1:30-3:30pm and 9-11:30pm. Closed Jan. or Feb.
>
> **Mesón Ovalo,** Po. Ovalo, 2, opposite the stairs from the train station. Oh what a source for local ham! Ovations for succulent *jamón al horno* (roast ham, 1250ptas). *Menú* 1300ptas. Open Tues.-Sun.

Sights and Entertainment

Aragonese King Fernando II el Sabio conquered Teruel in 1171; it was still royal policy for Christian kings to respect the Muslims' religious customs. Teruel's last mosque did not close until 1502 and the Jewish community remained until 1486. Mudejar is the fruit of a symbiosis between the Hispano-Muslim and Christian aesthetic traditions; the *morisco* artisans of Teruel gave the city its greatest asset, the three brick-and-glazed-tile **Torres Mudéjares** (Mudejar Towers) built between the 12th and the 15th centuries. The Christian churches adapted the structure and decorative schemes of the Almohad minarets to their own purposes. The towers as a rule divide into three sections: the simple base with a pointed arch providing access to the street, the elaborate shaft pierced by Romanesque lancets and decorated with intricate brick and *azulejo* work, and the crown with Roman columns and a bell-tower pierced by bays.

The two more intricately designed of the three towers are the richly tiled, 14th-century **Torre de San Martín,** in Pl. Pérez Prado near the post office; and the **Torre de San Salvador,** on C. El Salvador, built around 1277. Torre San Martín rises from the west side of the church and includes a vaulted corridor. A third tower, **Torre de San Pedro,** is not so tall or ornate and was completed by 1258. Inside the adjacent **Mausoleo de Los Amantes** are the tombs of young 13th-century lovers, Diego de Marcilla and Isabel de Segura. To prove himself worthy to Isabel's wealthy family, Diego set out to win fame and fortune. He returned five years later, the very day Isabel was to marry his slimy rival. Diego desperately requested one last kiss and when she refused, he fell to the floor, definitely dead. At Diego's funeral, Isabel rushed through the crowd of mourners, kissed the corpse, and—overcome with grief—expired herself. Life-size alabaster statues of the lovers reach out to touch hands; beneath the frozen pas de deux, skeletons of the actual lovers commingle in eternal passion beneath the glass tombs. Back to back with *torico* in Pl. Carlos Castell/Torico, bear left; take the left on the alleyway mid-block. Stairs there lead directly to the *mausoleo.* Iglesia de San Pedro is under the tower and then right. *(Mausoleo* open Tues.-Sun. 10am-1pm and 4:30-8pm. Admission 50ptas.)

Perhaps Teruel's greatest Mudejar building is the 13th-century **catedral** in Pl. Catedral. The cathedral's Capilla Mayor is polygonal, its ambulatory rectangular. The spectacle of the magnificently decorated square brick tower is mere preface to the wonderment of the see's celebrated 14th-century stylized *Artesonado Mudéjar* (Mudejar coffered ceiling) roofing the central of three naves, considered the summa of Teruel's Mudejar. Cheek to cheek with *torico,* all roads left of Pl. Carlos Castell/Torico lead one block away to Pl. Catedral. (Cathedral open 8am-9pm.)

The **Palacio Episcopal,** Pl. Cristo Rey/Monjas, a block in the direction of Pl. Carlos Castell/Torico from Pl. Pérez Prado, has a Renaissance entrance and patio. Three **casas modernistas** (Art Nouveau houses) in Pl. Carlos Castell/Torico were and remain symbols of Teruel's receptiveness to avant-garde art. Built around the turn of the century and reminiscent of contemporary work in Barcelona, the wavy lines and protruding balconies make architecture look like so much fun. All three houses are being restored.

The **Museo Provincial,** Pl. Fray Anselmo Polanco (tel. 60 11 04), is housed in the 16th-century porticoed **Casa de la Comunidad.** From Pl. Carlos Castell/Torico walk up C. Joaquín Costa/del Tozal and turn left on C. Rubio. Several floors of exhibition space are given over to municipal history and folklore, ceramics and pharmaceuticals, and off-the-wall modern art. (Museum open July-Aug. Tues.-Fri. 10am-2pm and 5-7pm, Sat.-Sun. 10am-2pm; Sept.-June Tues.-Sat. 10am-2pm and 4-7pm, Sun. 10am-2pm. Free.)

The clubs and bars on Pl. Botamar (known as **La Zona)** cater to the evening crowd. But the hip and the cocky spin out of the twilight Zona to **Vertigo,** C. Ainses, 4 (tel. 60 92 09), off Pl. Judería, an old stone house with high ceilings, video music, and an outdoor terrace. (Beer 175ptas. Open nightly 7pm-4am.)

The main event here, the yearly **Fiestas del Angel,** explodes on the week following the first Monday in July. Parades cross the city, fireworks light the sky, and the town salutes *the* lovers. The **Fiesta de Jamón** (Ham Holiday) in September is also festive, drawing motorcycled men and women from all over Spain.

Near Teruel

Protected by ancient walls, medieval townships are suspended in Teruel's countryside amid acres of feral land. Getting to these mystical hamlets is an ordeal. Only one bus per day ventures here from Teruel and returns the next morning (see Teruel: Buses above). Therefore, you will have to spend the night, unless you juggle carefully the few train connections to Mora and Rubielos (see Teruel: Practical Information: Trains above). Some hitch, though *Let's Go* does not recommend it as a means of travel. Amid the reddish desert hills, traffic is heaviest between Teruel and Albarracín; hitchers have posted themselves with placards at the end of Camino de la Estación, beginning of the road for Zaragoza. For Mora de Rubielos and Rubielos de Mora, hitchers favor the end of the aqueduct bridge on the road to València.

Albarracín

Thirty-five km west of Teruel, castellized Albarracín was once a powerful Islamic city; it now lives mainly on memories of grandeur amid its stone houses, small churches, and dispersed towers. The **tourist office** is on C. Catedral, 5 (tel. 71 02 51), near Pl. Mayor. (Open 10:30am-2pm and 5-8pm. Summer free guided tours 11am, 2:30pm, and 5:30pm.) The **post office** can be reached at 71 07 77. The **Red Cross** is at Ctra. Teruel, s/n (tel. 71 00 62). The **Guardia Civil** is stationed on C. San Juan, s/n (tel. 71 00 03).

Mora de Rubielos

Forty km on the other side of Teruel, **Mora de Rubielos,** also battlemented, has the largest and best-preserved 15th-century castle in the neighborhood. There's **camping** at **El Morrón-Barrachinas** (tel. 80 03 62). (100ptas per person, 500ptas per tent, and 200ptas per car. Open June 15-Aug. 31.) Mora de Rubielos has no tourist office; check in Teruel or make inquiries at the **Ayuntamiento** in Pl. Villa, s/n (tel. 80 00 00). The **post office** is at C. Las Parras, 20 (tel. 80 01 71).

Rubielos de Mora

Local connoisseurs insist the most *preciosa* of the medieval towns around Teruel is **Rubielos de Mora,** 15km east of Mora de Rubielos. All of its 600 souls live in an unrestored and unscathed architectural setpiece from medieval days, complete with two city gates and a handsome 16th-century town hall (courtyard, dungeon, and all).

The Rubielos de Mora **tourist office** is at C. Nevatería, 1 (tel. 80 40 96; open July-Aug. 10am-2pm and 5-7pm; Sept.-June Mon.-Fri. 10am-2pm). The **Guardia Civil** is at C. Huerta Nueva, s/n (tel. 80 40 02). For all three towns, the **telephone code** is 974.

Huesca

Known far and wide as a convenient stopover on the way to the mountains, Huesca is as spectacular as cornflower-blue embroidery on bathroom curtains. The town, suspended between Jaca to the north and Zaragoza to the south, does not pretend to be a powerful tourist magnet, but there's plenty to keep visitors alive as they wait for connections.

The **Museo Provincial,** reputed to be the best of its kind in Spain, exhibits archeological artifacts from every few seconds of Iberian civilization up to the last century. (Open Tues.-Sat. 9am-2pm. Admission 200ptas.) Huesca also serves as a springboard for visitors to the **Castillo de Loarre** (see Near Jaca) or the nearby ruins of **Castillo de Montearagón.** The castle is 3km east of town down Ctra. 245. You'll have to walk or hitch. (Always free and open.)

Calle Zaragoza and **Coso Alto/Bajo** will soon become your favorite streets. The train station is a 10-minute walk down C. Zaragoza from the center, and the bus station is roughly at the midway point, set back from the street across Pl. Navarra. At the top of Calle Zaragoza, Coso Alto diddles off to the left, and its counterpart Coso Bajo to the right. Most of the shops and cafés stretch along this boundary between the old city and the new. To get to the *museo* turn right on Coso Bajo and follow it to the first major intersection; the Pl. Toros will be to the left. Continue and turn left at the first traffic light, right on C. Desengaño past the basketball courts, then left under the water tank.

Many *hostales* and *casas particulares* live, day in and day out, off C. Lizana, three blocks down Coso Alto and a right. In the summer long-term residents fill many *hostales,* so you might want to call ahead. The newly renovated **Hostal El Centro,** C. Sancho Ramirez, 3 (tel. 22 68 23), a right from Coso Bajo, has large singles complete with sturdy desks. (Singles 1500ptas, with showers 1700-1900ptas. Doubles with bath 3250-3750ptas. Triples with bath 4400ptas. Breakfast 300ptas.) Reasonable rooms with nice sinks are yours at **Pensión Augusto,** C. Aínsa, 16 (tel. 22 00 79), off C. Lizana. (Singles 1900ptas. Doubles 2700ptas.)

Huesca wears its green badge with pride, even in its choice of restaurants. Many restaurants amass just beyond the far end of Av. Parque, which runs off Pl. Navarra. **Posada Magoria,** C. Valle de Ansó (tel. 37 00 49), whips up a vegetarian *menú* (900ptas); there's delectable *crema de champiñón* (cream of mushroom soup), *ensalada de maiz y aspárragos* (corn and asparagus salad), and *requesón de pastores* (farmer's cheese). **Ceres,** C. Padre Huesca, 7 (tel. 24 26 21), serves *canelones de ralladura de verdura* (grated vegetable canelloni), *aspárragos gratinados* (asparagus au gratin), and *buñuelos de plátano* (banana doughnuts) among other fleshless options (full à la carte meals around 1300ptas).

Carrie Nation would have a field day in the *barrio* around C. Zaragoza. At **Zombis,** on C. Argensola, the bartender is rightly proud of his record collection (saved from death by fire a few years ago), and also pours a mean vodka on the rocks.

Back on the Coso Alto, at #23, the English-speaking staff of the **tourist office** (tel. 22 57 78) will ply you with pamphlets on the mountains. (Open Mon.-Fri. 8:15am-2:30pm.) The **post office** (tel. 22 59 87) is at Coso Alto, 14-16, at the corner of C. Moya (open Mon.-Fri. 9am-9pm, Sat. 9am-7pm). The **postal code** is 22002; the **telephone code** 974. There are **lockers** here (open 5-9pm, 200ptas). For the **municipal police** dial 22 30 00. The **Red Cross** can be reached at 22 40 25, 22 11 86, or, in an **emergency,** 22 22 22.

RENFE **trains** (tel. 24 60 23) have to back in and out of Huesca's siding on their way to Jaca (3 per day, 2 1/4 hr., 565ptas); Sabiñánigo (3 per day, 2hr., 565ptas); and Zaragoza (5 per day., 1 1/4 hr., 410ptas). **La Ocense** (tel. 22 70 11) runs **buses** to Sabiñánigo (2 per day, Sat.-Sun. 3 per day; 11/4hr.; 460ptas) to connect with the 11:30am mail bus to Torla, the closest point to the Ordesa park (catch the 9:45am Ocense bus to be sure to make the mail). **La Alta Aragonesa** (tel. 22 70 11) runs to and from Benasque (2 per day, 3 1/2 hr., 1060ptas).

Aragonese Pyrenees

Despite scanty train and bus transport, the Aragonese Pyrenees draw both mountaineering aficionados and daystrollers to their famous peaks. Although the area is slightly more touristy than many parts of the Catalan Pyrenees and the Navarrese Pyrenees, there are many isolated stretches; cliff faces, grand canyons, and icy snow-melt rivers fill the lower valleys between Jaca and Huesca. These build to a crescendo at the magical name of "Ordesa," the grand old national park.

Hikers should, as always, beg, borrow, or steal an *Editorial Albino* map. Tourist offices in Huesca and Jaca also hoard information on local mountain-climbing clubs. Skiers have five major resorts at their poletips: Astún, Cerler, Panticosa, Candanchú, and Formigal. The pamphlets *Ski Aragón* and *El Turismo de Nieve en España,* free at tourist offices, give the low-down on all of these. Other forms of transit through the mountains are more time-consuming. A car or lots of time are crucial to do justice to the valleys; Huesca and Jaca provide very limited, infrequent access by bus. If you don't have a car, Ordesa is still worth the even slower connection by the mail buses.

Jaca

Pilgrims to Santiago once recuperated from the trek through the Pyrenees at this first major stop on their route, the ancient capital Kingdom of Aragón. Today the pilgrimage has reversed directions; most people now head through Jaca *toward* the Pyrenees for spectacular hiking and skiing. Local people are welcoming, and there's a sense of camaraderie among the many travelers who use Jaca as a base for exploring the mountains. The Tour de France gets confused every twenty years or so and dips into Spain, and in 1991 it ended a stage here in Jaca, only 29km from the French border. Jaca's fuels the fledgling warriors from its large military academy in its many bars and cafés.

Orientation and Practical Information

If you arrive by bus, you'll be dropped conveniently at the edge of the city's heart on **Avenida de la Jacetania,** which loops around downhill to become **Avenida de Oroel.** When Av. Oroel reaches the bottom of the hill it connects with **Avenida Regimiento Galicia** and **Avenida Primo de Rivera,** one broad street that completes the circle by running back uphill to Av. Jacetania. Within this circle, the central artery for shops and restaurants is **Calle Mayor.**

Tourist Office: Av. Regimiento 2 (tel. 36 00 98), past C. Mayor. Friendly English-speaking staff. Useful map, lots of hiking information. Open Mon.-Fri. 9am-2pm and 4:30-8pm, Sat. 10am-2pm and 5-8pm, Sun. 10am-2pm; Sept.-June Mon.-Fri. 9am-1pm and 5-7pm, Sat. 10am-1pm and 5-7pm. Closed afternoons on festival days. The Ayuntamiento at C. Mayor, 24, also proffers a city plan when the tourist office is closed.

Travel Agent: Viajes Abad, Av. Regimiento Galicia, 19 (tel. 36 10 81). **Viajes Aran,** C. Mayor, 46 (tel. 35 54 80, 35 55 10). Both schedule bus tours to San Juan de la Peña (July-Aug. only).

Currency Exchange: The banks cluster on Av. Jacetania.

Post Office: C. Correos, 13 (tel. 36 00 85), Av. Regimiento Galicia heading downhill from C. Mayor. Open Mon.-Fri. 8am-3pm, Sat. 9am-1pm. Lista de Correos in same building. Open Mon.-Fri. 8am-3pm, Sat. 9am-1pm. **Postal Code:** 22700.

Telephones: Summer phone center on Av. Oroel, left from the bus garage an Av. Jacetania and down the hill (open July 1-Sept. 15 10am-2pm and 4-10pm). **Telephone Code:** 974.

Trains: City buses run 6 times per day between the station and downtown (6:30am-8:25pm, 50ptas); catch the shuttle by the bus station or on Av. Primo de Rivera. If you're walking, take Avenida de Juan XXIII from the station past three ornate traffic islands before joining Av. Primo de Rivera at the fork (just past Restaurante La Abuela 2); stay right until the Ciudadela comes into view then take the left fork (Av. Primo de Rivera), which eventually crosses C. Mayor. **RENFE** (tel. 36 13 32) is at the northeast end of Av. de Juan XXIII. To: Ayerbe to connect to Loarre (3 per day, 1 1/2 hr., 340ptas); Huesca (3 per day, 2hr., 565ptas); Zaragoza (3 per day, 3hr., 955ptas); Madrid (1 per day, 6 1/2 hr., 3500ptas). Ticket booth open 10-11am and 5-7pm.

Aragón

Buses: La Oscense (tel. 22 70 11). To: Sabiñánigo (2-3 per day, 15 min., 130ptas); Huesca (2-3 per day, 1 hr., 590ptas); Zaragoza (2-3 per day, 2 1/2 hr., 1130ptas). You can connect through Puente La Reina to Pamplona (2 per day, 2hr., 625ptas), and through the same juncture to Ansó, Hecho, and Siresa.

Taxis: Pedro Juanín, Av. Rapitán, 17 (tel. 36 32 95 or 36 18 48). 2000-3000ptas per hr.

Car Rental: Aldecar, Av. Jacetania, 60 (tel. 36 07 81), left from the bus station and downhill. Wheels are invaluable for Pyrenees expeditions. Seat, Ford, or Volkswagen 2500ptas per day. 25ptas per km. Mandatory insurance 1000ptas per day, 13% tax. Valid international license required. Must fill the tank and return the car to Jaca. **Don Auto,** C. Correos, 4 (tel. 35 50 27, 36 26 04), near the post office. 4 x 4 rental 12,500ptas per day. 200km free per day, 30ptas per additional km, 30% more if under 25. Rates are lower for rentals of at least 3-4 days.

Bike/Moped Rental: Nuero Jaca, Av. Regimento Galicia, 15 (tel. 36 27 69). Rents mountain bikes and organizes excursions. 500ptas per hr., 1500ptas per half day, 2500ptas per day. 2 hr min. **Deportes Goyo,** Av. Juan XXIII, 17 (tel. 36 04 13). Rents regular and mountain bikes, as well as motorbikes. Organizes mountain bike excursions on weekends and festival days.

Horse Rental: Caballos de Yjuez (tel. 36 24 55), 7km from Jaca in Castiello de Jaca, 50m from the train stop on the Camino de la Garcipollera. Rents horses, organizes excursions. Ask for information at the tourist office.

Supermarket: Compre Bien, C. Rey del Carmen, 16, 1 block from Av. Regimento Galicia off C. Correos. Open Mon.-Fri. 9:30am-1:30pm and 5-8pm, Sat.-Sun. 9am-2pm and 5-8pm.

Laundromat: Lavomatique, Av. Escuela Militar de Montaña, 1 (tel. 36 01 12), part of Bar Santi to the left of the bus station. Wash and dry 500-600ptas. Open 9am-10pm. **Lavandería,** C. de Ramiro I, 3. Wash and dry 1300ptas. Open Mon.-Sat. 9:30am-2pm and 4:30-8pm.

Hiking Club: Guías de Montaña (tel. 48 53 58), in Biescas. Organizes excursions throughout the Pyrenees and sells detailed maps.

Sports Center: Centro Deportivo, Av. Perimetral (tel. 35 53 06). Skating rink (tel. 36 10 32). Call to check if open in summer.

Study: Year-round, the University of Zaragoza runs 1-month courses in Jaca on Spanish life and culture. From 75,060-101,364ptas, including accommodation in student residence. Contact: La Universidad de Zaragoza, Jaca, Huesca, 22700, Spain (tel. 36 01 96, fax 35 57 85).

Ski Conditions: Teléfono blanco (tel. (976) 20 11 12).

24-Hour Pharmacy: Check listings in local paper. Failing that, take your medical prescription to the local police in the Ayuntamiento off C. Mayor; they will escort you to one.

Medical Services: Ambulatorio (tel. 36 04 90 or 36 07 95), downhill from C. Mayor and to the left of Av. Primo de Rivera.

Red Cross: (tel. 36 11 01), outside town on Llano de la Victoria.

Police: Policía Municipal, C. Mayor, 24 (tel. 35 81 00), in the Ayuntamiento. **Policía Nacional:** tel. 091. **Guardia Civil:** (tel. 36 13 50), on the highway to France, following Av. Primo Rivera from town towards the train station.

Emergencies: tel. 092.

Accommodations and Camping

Jaca's *hostales* and *pensiones* are mainly grouped around C. Mayor and the cathedral. Lodgings are scarce mainly during the town's *fiesta* June 24-29 and the biennial Festival Folclórico in late July and early August. Book rooms weeks ahead.

Albergue Juvenil de Vacaciones (HI), Av. Perimetral, 6 (tel. 36 05 36), by the skating rink. From the bus station, follow Av. Jacetania to the sculpture at the top of a flight of stairs; from the bottom the cluster of white buildings with red shutters comes into view. From C. Mayor in the center take C. Zocotín and follow it through various plazas to the edge of town. 900ptas per person. Symbolic locks. Swarms with youth groups; summer camp to the max. Tightly-packed doubles, triples, and quints encourage camaraderie. Winter heating. Members 550ptas, over 25 750ptas. Nonmembers 2000ptas. Breakfast and one additional meal 1500ptas. Reception in the smoke-filled bar open 1-4pm and 7pm-midnight.

Hostal Villanúa (HI) (tel. 37 80 16), on Camino de la Selva in Villanúa, about 15km north of Jaca. Buses and trains to Canfranc stop here. Open 7 months a year, including summer. Call ahead as it fills with groups July-Aug. 3-day max. stay. Members only. 450ptas per person, over 25 650ptas. Breakfast 600ptas, over 25 800ptas.

Habitaciones Martínez, C. Mayor, 53 (tel. 36 33 74). Management gushes over *Let's Go* travelers. Bar downstairs is occasionally noisy but always friendly; a good way to meet locals. New rooms down the street with elegant bedspreads. 2000ptas per person. Older rooms above bar are smaller. 1200ptas per person.

Hostal París, Pl. San Pedro, 5 (tel. 36 10 20). From C. Mayor, turn left on C. Obispo. Mattresses a bit lumpy but comfortable. Wood floors. Winter heating. Singles with shower 1600ptas. Doubles 2650ptas. Triples 3500ptas. Breakfast 275ptas.

Hostal Residencia Galindo, C. Mayor, 45 (tel. 36 37 43). Large, bright rooms. Excellent 950ptas *menú* in the restaurant below. Winter heating. Singles 2000ptas. Doubles 4000ptas, with bath 4500ptas.

Hostal Residencia El Abeto, C. Bellido, 15 (tel. 36 16 42), 1 block toward Av. Jacetania from C. Mayor. Modern, smallish rooms in shades of scarlet, some with views. Rooms elusive in Aug. Winter heating. Singles 2000ptas. Doubles 3200ptas, with bath 4200ptas.

Camping: Peña Oroel (tel. 36 02 15), 31/2km down the road to Sabiñánigo. Wooded grounds. First-rate facilities. 445ptas per person, per tent, and per car. Open Holy Week and mid-June through mid-Sept. **Camping Victoria** (tel. 36 03 23), 11/2km from Jaca on Highway C-134 (direction of Pamplona). Just beyond a garage. Groovy view of the foothills. 400ptas per person and per car, 375ptas per tent.

Food

Most of Jaca's restaurants center on **Calle Mayor,** with a few along Av. Primo de Rivera and Av. Juan XXIII. Regional specialties include *costillas de cordero* (lamb chops) and *longanizas* (short spicy sausages). There is a produce **market** on C. Fernando el Católico, Fri. 9am-2pm. From C. Mayor head down Av. Primo Rivera and turn right.

Crepería El Bretón, C. Ramiro I, 10. The French owner makes authentic dinner crepes (*galettes,* 300-800ptas) and dessert crêpes (250-500ptas). Salads 600ptas. Open 6pm-1am.

Croissanterie Cafetería Demi-Lune, Av. Regimiento Galicia (tel. 36 36 19), in the same clump of shops as the tourist office. Ideal for a quick snack or a full meal. Delightful café popular with locals of all ages. Substantial croissant sandwiches 190-260ptas, sweet dessert ones 45-185ptas. Warning: croissant *vegetal* comes with ham. Open 7:45am-2pm and 3:30-11:30pm.

Casa Martínez, C. Mayor, 53 (tel. 36 33 74). Small family-run dining room above the bar and beneath the *pensión* has checkered tablecloths. The *señora* cooks a terrific 700ptas *menú*. Open only in high season 1-4pm and 8pm-12:30am.

Restaurante Vivas, C. Gil Berges, 3 (tel. 36 05 31), left off C. Mayor from Av. Primo Rivera. Elegant decor (purple tablecloths). Arrive early to snag a courtyard table. Serenaded by a band of cardboard silhouettes. *Platos combinados* 725-800ptas. Open 1-3:30pm and 8-11:30pm.

Sights

The pentagonal fortress referred to as **La Ciudadela** or Castillo de San Pedro puts Jaca on the touristy map. Built in 1590 and ensconced in a grassy knoll, the citadel originally served as a fort protecting Jaca (then part of France) from Spanish attackers. It overlooks the battlefield known as *Las Tiendas* (The Tents) where Moors were repelled around 760. The victory is celebrated every first Friday in May with an all-female reenactment. These days, nobody's attacking the citadel, still used by the military, but you can't be too sure; a hundred Spanish soldiers and officers stand guard. (Tours in Spanish 11am-noon and 5-6pm. Free.)

The Romanesque **catedral** is modest but noteworthy. Begun in 1063, it influenced most designs for churches built along the Jacobean route. The Baroque period brought a new altarpiece and the clashing ribbed vaulting. Four masses are held roughly every hour each morning, an evening mass at 7pm. In the sealed cloister, the **Museo Diocesano** has intricate 13th-century ironwork and Romanesque wall paintings. (Open Tues.-Sun. 11am-1:30pm and 4-6:30pm. Admission 200ptas.)

The **Festival de San Juan y San Pedro** (June 24-29) is Jaca's most important, and it draws dozens of youth groups, bands, and costumed street performers to the city. The day after, C. Mayor is a nearly impassable, sticky mess of confetti and strewn bottles.

Every odd-numbered year at the end of July and beginning of August, people from all over the world spend a week dancing around town during the **Festival Folclórico de los Pirineos.** Traditional dance groups and bands come from the five continents to give national folkloric performances, in grass skirts, kilts, kimonos, balalaikas, and patchwork dresses.

Near Jaca

Iglesia de San Juan de la Peña

The **Iglesia de San Juan de la Peña** is difficult to reach, but find a way. The church, about 23km from Jaca, has been wedged into its mountainside for nearly 1000 years. Inside is the end of the line for all of Aragón's kings. Be careful not to confuse the *monasterio viejo* with the new one 1km uphill. You can check at the tourist office for information about travel agencies that organize excursions in July and August. The rest of the year, you can get partway there by taking the Jaca-Huesca bus as far as Desvío de Santa Cruz, which leaves you 11km to cover. (Church open June-Sept. 10am-2pm and 4-7pm; Oct.-May Wed.-Sun. 11am-1:30pm and 4-6pm. Free.)

El Castillo de Loarre

In the 11th century, King Sancho Ramírez built a castle to protect himself from Moorish attacks. **El Castillo de Loarre** (5km from the town of Loarre), perched atop a solid rock mount, is made nearly impenetrable by sharp cliffs at its rear and 400m of thick walls to the east. The building's outer walls follow the turns and angles of the rock so closely that at night an attacker might have only seen the silhouette of an awesome stone monolith.

A crypt opens to the right of the steep entrance staircase. The remains of Demetrius were stashed here after the French saint died in Loarre. A narrow staircase leads from the crypt into the magnificent **capilla.** A strip of checkered masonry curves directly above the several dozen capitals that line the apse, and a maze of passages and chambers honeycombs the rest of the castle. You can climb up to the battlements of both towers; the only access designed for the larger of the two is a narrow, arched footbridge from the smaller tower. Attackers needed to gain control of the first tower in order to cross to this final retreat, but given enough time, the castle's defenders could dismantle the footbridge. Be careful when climbing the wobbly steel rungs to the roof. Use equal caution descending into the **sótano** (dungeon). This dark, doorless chamber was probably used to hoard supplies, but feel free to imagine prisoners being thrown through the hole in the ceiling (20 ft. above) and left to rot. (Castle open June-Aug. 10am-1:30pm and 4-8pm; March 15-May and Sept.-Oct. 15 10am-1:30pm and 4-7pm; Jan.-March 15 11am-2:30pm. Free.)

Reaching **Loarre** isn't easy. By **train,** the closest town is **Ayerbe,** 7km away. Trains run from Jaca and Huesca. From Ayerbe, you can trek all the way to Loarre (about 2 hr.) or walk to Bar Pirineos on the main plaza and ask for a taxi. A **bus** from Huesca to Ayerbe passes through Loarre. You can **camp** near the castle in the lovely pine forests. The castle is 5km from the town by a very circuitous road; the more direct walk from Loarre takes 45 minutes.

Valle de Hecho

This unspoiled, craggy valley cuts the Aragonese Pyrenees with the **Río Aragón Subordán** roughly 20km west of Jaca, the closest hiking area to the city. From early July to early August, the villages in the valley host the annual **Simposio de Escultura y Pintura Moderna,** a festival that turns the surrounding hills into a huge open-air museum. An enormous party kicks off the festival in the first week of July, when villagers come to Hecho to feast on roast lamb and fried bread. By the end of August, when it ends, the symposium splatters nearly all of the valley's towns with modern painting and sculpture. The rest of the year the fruits of this labor lie scattered about the village, particularly next to the brightly painted studio on the *carretera*.

The town of **Hecho,** the valley's geographical and administrative center, cultivates its eclogic charm. Although diehard service-oriented restaurants translate their menus for foreign guests, the majority of residents brush tourists off like flies. Few people on the tourist caravan stop at the **Museo Etnológico,** which displays old photographs of valley residents and the meanest-looking collection of farming implements you've ever seen. To get there, go up the hill from Pl. Fuente on C. Aire. (Open 11am-2pm. Admission 100ptas.)

The best of Hecho's *hostales,* **Casa Blasquico,** Pl. Fuente/Pl. Palacio, 1 (tel. (974) 37 50 07), is right next to the bus stop, unmarked. The Spanish proprietor, possessing the obligatory German shepherd, also speaks English and French and offers comfortable, brightly colored rooms; her cooking rivals her linguistic abilitites. She has, however, only six rooms, which are nearly always full. (1600ptas per person. Doubles 2700ptas.) Up C. Aire all the way to the top of town at **Hostal de la Val,** they'll hit you for 4500ptas for a single with shower and 4000ptas for a double with shower. **Camping Valle de Hecho** (tel. 37 53 61), at the entrance to Hecho, has new facilities in a convenient location (400ptas per person, per car, and per tent).

Only 2km up the road from Hecho is **Siresa,** less pretentious and more tranquil than its neighbor. Octagenarians chatter on every available bench.

Townspeople built **Iglesia de San Pedro de Siresa** way back in Charlemagne's day. The church's caretaker, who lives in the white house around the corner, holds the key. The **Hostal Pirineo** (tel. 31 51 13), above the bar of the same name, right up the street at the very entrance to town, offers large rooms for up to four people for 3000ptas with access to hot showers. Inquire for rooms at the restaurant on past the bar, which has a 900ptas *menú*.

The **bus** from Jaca to Hecho continues here, arriving at 6:45pm and departing at 6:45am for Jaca.

Between Hecho and Siresa, carved wood signs mark the beginning of trails to Picoya, La Reclusa, Lenito, Fuente de la Cruz, and Ansó. These do not show up in the cartographic guide to the area, which is just as well. Although not particularly difficult, they are overgrown with brambles, eroded in places, covered with rocks, infested by flies, and scorched by the sun.

From Siresa, the road weaves up the valley, passing through a number of tunnels, and the rock formation known as the **La Boca del Infierno** (The Mouth of Hell). After about 9km, you'll reach the **Valle de Oza,** a crescent of meadows with the grounds of **Camping Selva de Oza** (tel. 37 51 68; open June to mid-Sept. 400ptas per person and per tent, 450 per car). The site gives you hot showers, a store, and even a restaurant. You can swim with, play with, or kill and eat the fish in the river that flows nearby.

Trails into the mountain leave from near the campground; go prepared with the red *Guía Cartográfica de las Valles de Ansó y Hecho,* published by *Editorial Alpino*. Nearly every bookstore, grocery store, and general store carries it. The campsite arranges excursions, but you'll have more fun on your own. North of the site, you can hike along the peaks of the French border, from **Pic Rouge** (2177m) to **Pic Lariste** (2168m) to **Pic Laraille** (2147m), which has a stupefying view of the **Ibon de Acherito,** a glimmering lake framed by alpine bush. If you follow the guidebook and take a car part of the way, the actual hiking time for these should be around three hours to the summit. To climb **Castillo de Acher** (2390m), a square-topped mountain that resembles a waitress in the sky, follow the forest road toward the **Torrente de Espata,** amble along the path by this stream, cut up the mountainside on the zigzag path to the ridge, follow the ridge past the **Refugio Forestal,** and go left at the fork. Several steep, narrow paths ascend to the summit (2 hr. to the top). Plan to spend most of the day making the journey from the campsite and back. For a real romp, consider scaling **Bisaurin,** the highest peak in the neighborhood. From the rocky, snow-capped peak you can practice casting parental looks over Old Aragón, the sumptuous Peña Forca (2391m), the isolated Pico Orhy (2015m), and the cosmic Castillo de Acher (2390m).

Valle de Ansó

Filled with mountain supply stores, **Ansó,** a collection of white plaster and stone houses with wrought-iron balconies and colorful garden boxes, presides over its very own valley 12km east of Hecho. Finally elected into the Kingdom of Aragón at the end of the 10th century, this placid town has never seen many visitors. Ansó once led a wilder life, however. Until recently, residents wore traditional costumes and spoke their own dialect. In 1900, the town boomed with 1700 residents; it's now down to 500 (but who's counting?). Sheep-herding dogs spread themselves on most street corners, ocular proof of the village's rural economy.

At Ansó's **Museo de Etnología,** inside the town church, mannequins model traditional garb next to candlesticks, spinning wheels, weaving looms, costume jewelry, wood carvings, and religious books. (Open July-Aug. 10:30am-1:30pm and 3:30-8pm. At other times of the year, knock three times on the brown door opposite the church entrance, and ask the curator to show you around. Admission 100ptas.)

Although few travelers decide to spend the night here, Ansó still maintains many *hostales.* The **Posada Magoría,** C. Chapitel, 8 (tel. (974) 37 00 49), is by far the best value. Its owner, Enrique Ipas, is not only fluent in both English and French, he is also the vice-president of the Pyrenean Conservation Society, and will regale you with stories of local flora and fauna. (3000ptas with *media pensión.*) Next door, the **Hostal Estanés,** Po. Chapitel, 9 (tel. (974) 37 01 46), keeps comfortable rooms. (Singles 1100ptas. Doubles 1900ptas. Meals 850ptas.)

The **post office** is next door (open Mon.-Fri. 9am-1pm and Sat. 9am-noon). The **bus** making the rounds of these valleys from Jaca stops here after Hecho and Siresa at 6:45pm and leaves for Jaca at 6:15am.

In Zuriza, 15km north of Ansó, the exquisite campground **Centro Multisport** rubs elbows with a mountain stream 2km away from the Río Veral, a broad river suitable for fishing and boating. The site also provides dormitory accommodations and an *hostal*. From the campground, it's a dayhike to the **Mesa de los Tres Reyes,** a series of peaks close to the borders of France, Navarre, and Aragón. From Zuriza, the Fountain of Linza lies north, and east of this the Collado de Linza, a break between two smaller peaks. Hereabouts the terrain alternates between the shallow **Agujero de Solana** (Hole of Solana), the steep summit of **Escoueste,** and other quirky peaks. From Zuriza, you can also make the arduous trek to **Sima de San Martín** on the French border. To enjoy the area without a strenuous hike, walk 2km south of Ansó to the fork in the road. Just above the tunnel toward Hecho, you can see the weird, weather-sculpted rock formation called **El Monje y la Monja** (The Monk and the Nun). Sweep all lurid thoughts from your mind. In the other direction, the road from Ansó leads into Navarra and to Isaba and Roncal.

Parque Nacional de Ordesa y Monte Perdido

There is something very primeval about Ordesa. If any park is worth riding along with the mail and then facing another 8km on foot, this is it. With miles of trails crossing poplar-covered mountain faces, cascades, and rivers, the park is deservedly popular, but find the right path and you can be completely alone. Located just south of the French border roughly midway between Jaca and Ainsa, Ordesa cuts deeply into the highest mountains of the Pyrenees, rising from a valley etched by the Río Arazus toward some of the most magnificent peaks in the country.

The park is a perfect base for hikers of all levels, from summer picnickers to daredevil alpinists who pack a pickaxe before a toothbrush. Hiking boots are a must for most of the well-marked trails. The best time of year to visit the park is from mid-July through August, when the storms have passed and the weather is almost perfect (although warm clothes are still needed). Arrive early (7-8am) to avoid the crowds on the principal paths.

Buses go only as far as **Torla,** a small stone village 8km short of the park; a local mail-delivery bus leaves Sabiñanigo at 11:55am Monday through Saturday and returns around 3:30pm. Sabiñánigo connects easily by bus and train to Jaca and Huesca (1 bus per day from Jaca, 20min., 120ptas; all trains from Zaragoza to Huesca and Jaca stop in

Sabiñánigo, which is 10min. away from Jaca). From Torla, walking is the only way to get to the park. The lovely riverside path is accessible by crossing the main bridge in Torla itself, at the bottom of a very rocky path leading down past the Hostal Bella Vista. Once you've crossed the bridge, follow the track off to the left for about 1km: this turns into the steep path, which becomes gentler and shadier later.

Although camping in the open is prohibited, the many *refugios* (mountain huts, usually without facilities) allow overnight stays. The 120-bed **Refugio Góriz,** about four hours from the parking lot, also has a hotel on its site (rooms 3000ptas). Unattended *refugios* are little more than a roof over your head.

Torla's range of accommodations is greater. With the *refugio* name and feel while still in town, **Refugio L'Atalaya,** C. Francis, 45 (tel. 48 60 22), offers 21 beds clumped together in several large wooden bunks (800ptas per person, hot showers, and a few bugs included). The French owners also serve a good *menú* (1050ptas) and breakfast (400ptas). Cobblestoned C. Francia is the only road in Torla off the highway to the park—go left up it and you will find the entrance to the *refugio* on your right after a block, under some wooden beams. If you fancy a room of your own, consider **Fonda Ballarín,** C. Capuvita, 11 (tel. 48 61 55), with comfortable beds; thick wool blankets; clean, checkered wooden floors; and an English-speaking owner. (Singles 1380ptas. Doubles 2350ptas. Mid-Sept. to June 31 1300ptas; 2200ptas. Breakfast 250ptas.) To get there continue on past Refugio L'Atalaya to the small plaza and go up the hill to the left of the building with the stone arches—you'll see the bright flowers and sign. **Hostal Residencia Bella Vista** is indeed that—from its spot at #6 on the Av. Ordesa to the park (tel. 48 61 53) you will have a commanding view of the river valley. (Singles with large bath 2500ptas. Doubles 4500ptas. Prices lower off-season. Breakfast 350ptas.) Two **campgrounds** lie just outside of "town." There's angling in the river at **Camping Río Ara** (tel. 48 62 48), about 1km down the paved path from its sign off Av. Ordesa. (Open April-Nov; 325ptas per person, per tent and per car, Aug. 350ptas.) After you cross the bridge, stay on the paved road to get to the reception. More upscale with a hotel, a pool, and tennis courts is **Camping Ordesa** (tel. 48 61 46), a bit farther along Av. Ordesa. (Open April 1-Oct. 15. 425ptas per person, per tent, and per car; children 300ptas.)

The Instituto Nacional para la Conservación de la Naturaleza (**ICONA**) is the control center for the park. They have an office in Torla during the summer on C. Francia in the bank building (tel. 48 62 12; open 8am-3pm), besides the station at the trailhead (on the edge of the parking lot). The information booth at the entrance to the park should be open in summer. All of these places should be able to give you a trail map (300ptas) and information. The indispensable *Editorial Alpino* guide is on sale (475ptas) at the souvenir shop by the parking lot. Ask the tourist office for their collection of pamphlets on the local fauna *Animales del Parque Nacional de Ordesa y Monte Perdido* (free). You could come across wild boar, vipers, unicorns, eagles, and vultures.

The **post office** is open 10am-1pm. The **postal code** is 22376. A **telephone center** in Torla is in the second plaza along C. Francia. The **telephone code** for the area is 974.

Circo de Soaso and Other Hikes

If you only have a day to spend in Ordesa, the **Soaso Circle** is the most practical hike, especially for first-time mountaineers. Frequent signposts along the wide trail clearly mark the six-hour journey. The trail slips through more topographical zones than Biosphere II: forests, waterfalls, cliffs, and plateaus. Although delightfully simple and satisfying in sunny weather, the trail becomes slippery and rather dangerous after rainfall. Check weather forecasts before starting out, and remember that in the winter, heavy snow can make the trail impassable. Less intrepid types who want to cut the hike by two-thirds (to about 2 hr.) may return to the parking lot instead of continuing past. Whichever route you choose, try to arrive at the park early, since the entire Soaso Circus resembles Picadilly Circus by noon.

If you prefer a private mountain hike to a communal, multilingual trek, try the **Circo Cotatuero** or the **Circo Carriata.** Both of these four-hour hikes take you through brilliant mountain scenery and towering waterfalls. More experienced hikers might attempt the **Torla-Gavarnie** trail, a six-hour haul all the way to Gavarnie, France. The

Ordesa-Gavarnie trail is even longer; plan to spend at least 10 hours. An even more rugged climb begins at the Refugio Góriz and climbs Monte Perdido (3355m). Count on eight hours there and back. For any of these hikes, the *Editorial Alpino* topographical map is an absolute must. Those who would rather enjoy the mountain splendor without strenuous involvement can hitch a **mule ride** around Ordesa Valley during July and August; inquire at the information office if it's open.

Aínsa

The same mail-delivery bus that stops off at Torla later continues, rain or snow or wind or shine, to the delightful village of Aínsa. It's difficult to imagine that Aínsa was once a major city; but a thousand years ago it was the undeniable capital of the Kingdom of Sobrarbe (incorporated into Aragon in the 11th century). The subtly restored **casco antiguo,** or old city, sits high above the Rio Ava on a dry plateau.

The city's strategic strength is evident in the ruins of the 11th-century **castillo.** Unofficial steps allow a sensational view from the top of its ancient walls, at the far end of the *casco antiguo* across the **Plaza Mayor.** The grand plaza used to be in the center of town, but the houses between it and the castle were destroyed in the 1860s. Today the plaza is stranded by a grassy park next to the castle, while the rest of the *casco antiguo* stretches back on the opposite side. In summer it often plays host to large tourist groups bused in from Jaca.

In 1811, priests consecrated the **Iglesia de Santa María** just across the Pl. Mayor from the castle. Its expansion in the 16th century pilfered the masonry of the nearby Iglesia de San Salvador. Several column bases transformed into capitals for the new church portal; the inscriptions are consequently upside-down. Inside you'll find the crypt's six original 16th-century capitals. There's a **torre,** but only short non-claustrophobes may want to brave its innards. From the plaza in front of the church, there is a stairway to the left of the church archway providing basic training for those planning Pyrenean mountain-climbing expeditions.

Every odd-numbered year the town holds a fiesta celebrating the victory against the Moors in 724. The **Morisma** takes place from September 14-16 and includes theatrical representations of the vanquishment, including multicolored costumes.

The mail-delivery bus drops you at the crossroads of the highways that run through Aínsa. Follow signs from there for the *casco antiguo* and Plaza Mayor to get to the old section of town. The stairs right next to the post office go up the hill; when you pass under an archway, C. Mayor is the left-hand fork, and that will take you uphill to Pl. Mayor.

Hostal Residencia Ordesa, Av. Ordesa, 22 (tel. 50 00 09), past the post office, has big hallway bathtubs and an 800ptas *menú.* (1750ptas per person. Doubles 3500ptas with bath. Oct.-June 1500ptas; 3500ptas with bath. Breakfast 300ptas.) At the crossroads is **Hostal Dos Ríos,** Av. Central, 2 (tel. 50 00 43), with compact, well-kept modern rooms painted bright white and interesting little chairs. (Singles 1800ptas, with bath 2750ptas. Doubles 3100ptas, with bath 3700ptas.)

Restaurante Bodegas del Sobrarbe on C. Mayor is typical of the *casco antiguo* establishments. It serves *platos combinados* (a whopping 1300-1900ptas) and a 1450ptas *menú* (open 12:30-4pm and 8:30-11pm).

The **tourist office,** Av. Pirenáica, 1 (tel. 50 07 67), is at the crossroads of the town's two highways. The helpful staff can advise you on transportation and excursions, and has a large supply of brochures on the region. (Open Tues.-Sat. 10am-1:30pm and 4:30-8pm, Sun. 10am-1:30pm, Mon. 4:30-8pm. Hours are irregular mid-Sept. to May.) The **post office,** Av. Ordesa (tel. 50 00 71), is virtually opposite the bus stop on the way to the old town. The **postal code** is 22340. A **telephone center** is located on Av. Central before the bridge, past Hostal Dos Ríos. The **telephone code** is 974. The **Red Cross** (tel. 50 00 26) is located on Av. Ordesa on the outskirts of town. The **Guardia Civil** is posted in Barrio Banasto (tel. 50 00 55).

The **mail bus** (300-400ptas) leaves at 6:45am for Barbastro to points south, and at 2:30pm for Sabiñánigo, which connects by train with Jaca and Huesca.

Valle de Benasque

The Valle de Benasque is a hiker's dream come true. Countless numbers of trails of all levels wind through the surrounding mountains, and the area teems with *refugios*. Tourists fearing its serious mountaineering reputation often are scared away from the valley. But the Río Esera gorge and the astounding variety of mountain landscapes titillate the beginning hiker. Snow-covered peaks 2km high tiptoe down the edges of the valley; cascades shoot over the sides of pine-covered hills. As always, be sure to get *Editorial Alpino's* excellent topographical map of the valley (475ptas) in any of Benasque's stores before starting your hike.

Benasque, at the valley's center, makes a practical base: most trailheads originate from the paved roads between Benasque and **Cerler,** the ski resort 8km north of Benasque.

Tres Hermanas, three sisterly peaks with only one eye between them, guard the valley. If you start early from Benasque, you can hike 8 1/2km down the valley road, cross the river on the camping area bridge, and climb up, up, and away following the falls of the Río Cregueña. Four sweaty hours later you will reach **Lago de Cregueña** (2657m), the largest and, you'll be convinced, highest lake in the Maladeta massif.

The pilgrimage to Mount Aneto (3404m), the highest peak in the Pyrenees, begins each morning at about 5am, when the experts set out from the **Refugio de la Renclusa** (tel. 55 14 90) to conquer the mountain. The *refugio* itself is a 30-minute trek from the end of the paved street that runs from the main road past the bus stop. If lugging heavy supplies and equipment up a mountain face isn't your idea of fun, head downhill to the road and follow signs to **Forau de Aigualluts.** This tranquil pond, 50 minutes from the *refugio* trailhead at the end of a tumbling waterfall, stoically withstands the onslaught of hundreds of gallons per minute. Two gaping black holes (*foraus* in Aragonese) keep the pond calm by pulling the water underground and releasing it in Val d'Arán. A more strenuous hike from the *refugio* leads to the peak of **Sacroux** (2675m). Even if snow prevents you from reaching the top and peering into France, the rush of the **Torrents de Gorgutes** and the sight of Lago Gorgutes make the four-hour climb worthwhile. *(Refugio open June 22-Sept. 24. 900ptas per person, discount for club members. Breakfast 450ptas. No showers, but a nice hose.)* Call 55 12 15 for information about any of the valley's *refugios*.

Although Benasque is the practical base for the BMWs and expensive off-road vehicles that frequent the trails of the town's peak-priced lodgings and restaurants, inexpensive lodgings are still available. At the literal rock bottom are the cement floors of the *literas*. **Fonda Barrabes,** C. Mayor, 5 (tel. 55 16 54), left from the bus stop, where an investment of 600ptas gets you a place in one of their *literas:* a well-used mattress; a blanket; possibly three bedfellows on the same wooden bunk; and a sink with water melted from the surrounding peaks. For just a little less than three times the price, you can get a real room, floor, and access to a hot shower. (Singles 1275ptas. Doubles 2545ptas.) The owner, a Basque California transplant, chatters in English, French, Spanish, or Basque. Downstairs, the restaurant offers relief from surrounding prices with *bocadillos* (275-325ptas) and *platos combinados* (650-850ptas). But wait, there's more. During the town's **Fiesta Mayor** in honor of San Marcial on June 30, in a Fonda Barrabés *litera* you'll be in an excellent position to hear the marching brass band if a torrential rainstorm in the midst of the revelry should detain them downstairs at 4am.

Campers undoubtedly get the best view in town, with 200m rock faces instead of bedroom walls. **Camping Aneto** (tel. 55 11 41) is about 3 1/2km out of town on up the hill past the Cerler turnoff, with facilities for both summer and winter camping. (350ptas per person, per tent, and per car.) **Camping Ixeia** is a little farther past Aneto. (Open June-Sept. 325ptas per person, per tent, and per car. Call (961) 54 68 09 in València if you need information during the off-season.) You can also pitch your tent in the wild open spaces for a maximum of two days, except in the Plan del Hospital, Plan d'Estany, Estós, and Vallibierna.

Benasque's **tourist office** (tel. 55 12 89) has volumes of information on local hiking. To get there, face the Galerías Barrabés mountain supply store in the main highway intersection and go past it on the right. After a block the office is on your left (open Mon.-

Fri. 10am-2pm and 5-8pm). There's a mapboard of the town near the fountains by the bus stop if the office is closed. The **post office** (tel. 55 12 37) is in the Ayuntamiento building (open Mon.-Fri. 10am-noon, Sat. 11am-noon for urgent telegrams only). The **postal code** is 22440. A **telephone center** is on C. Mayor near the bus stop (open July-Sept. 10am-1:30pm and 5-8pm). The **telephone code** is 974. The **Red Cross** is at 55 12 85, the **ambulance** at 55 10 01. Signs point to the offices of the **Guardia Civil** (tel. 55 10 08) from the main highway intersection.

La Alta Aragonesa (tel. 22 70 11) runs **buses** to and from Huesca (2 per day, 31/2hr., 1050ptas).

Catalunya (Catalonia)

Hemmed in by the Pyrenees to the north and the Riu Ebro delta to the south, Catalunya is a privileged land. This prosperous region has always proudly held itself apart from the remainder of the country, retaining its own uniquely Catalan culture and tongue.

Colonized by Greeks and Carthaginians, Catalunya (or Tarraconensis) was one of Rome's favored provinces. Only briefly subdued by the Moors, Catalunya's counts achieved independence in 874 and were recognized as sovereign princes in 987. Having nabbed the throne of Aragón in 1137, Catalunya was thenceforth linked to the rest of Spain; yet Catalan *usatges* or *fueros* (legal codes) remained in effect. It took a Bourbon, Felipe V, to suppress Catalunya's privileges as punishment for siding against him in the War of the Spanish Succession (1700-1713).

A revival of fortunes accompanied the opening of the American empire for trade with all Spanish cities (late 18th century), when Catalunya rapidly developed into one of Europe's premier manufacturing centers (chiefly textiles). Industrial expansion through the 19th century underpinned a flowering of the arts and sciences that came to be regarded as a Catalan *Renaixença* (Renaissance). Since then, however, Madrid has displaced Barcelona as the country's leading financial and manufacturing center, and more recently challenged Barcelona's preeminence in publishing and high fashion.

Having fought on the losing side in the Civil War, Catalunya lost its autonomy in 1939; Catalan instruction was suppressed in all but the universities and publication in the language was limited to specialized areas. Since autonomy was recovered in 1977, media and arts in Catalan have flourished. The language is once again official in Spain (it's not a dialect; rather, dialects of it are spoken in València) and is spoken everywhere in Catalunya. The region is almost entirely bilingual in Catalan and Castilian.

Some worry that the use of Catalan in institutions such as universities will discourage talented Spaniards elsewhere from teaching, studying, or doing research there, effectively sealing off the principality from the wider world. Vargas Llosa has spoken of the growing fascism of Catalunya. Others, however, argue for more autonomy for the region, and some people even rally for total political independence. Discussions in bars and cafés vociferously revolve around this issue. The most visible display of Catalan nationalism was the 1992 Olympics: Catalan president Jordi Pujol took out full-page ads in newspapers around the world that refered to the "country" of Catalunya, "Freedom for Catalunya" banners were not an uncommon sight, and Catalan was accepted as one of the four official languages at the Games.

Lovers exchange books and roses to honor the region's patron, St. George, on the Festa de Sant Jordi (April 23). On September 11, Catalans really whoop it up for Diada, La Festa Nacional de Catalunya, set aside to affirm the region's political autonomy.

Whether by air, rail, bus, ferry or road, transportation in Catalunya is superb; only in the Pyrenees and on the Costa Brava do you need a car.

Barcelona

Grand and sprawling, Barcelona embodies Catalunya's artistic genius and commercial resourcefulness. Its long reputation as Spain's most cosmopolitan, sophisticated, and progressive city has weakened of late, but it still wins the prize for the most self-confident.

Barcelona was a Carthaginian enclave until the Romans elbowed in sometime during the 4th century BC. By the Middle Ages the city was the capital of a fat commercial empire, but the discovery of the Americas turned the Atlantic into the hip trade route and left the poor Mediterranean to starve. Not until the 19th century did the Industrial Revolution's textile mills restore Barcelona's glory, feeding a budding bourgeoisie that then spat the money back at a geniusy generation of architects, artists, and musician.

The city tore down its medieval walls in 1859. While authoritarian planner Ildefons Cerdà laid out his stiff grid of streets, the brilliant architects of *Modernismo*, led by native son Antoni Gaudí, responded with exuberant, fantastical creations. The 20th century brought political unrest and the rise of anarchism when, during the Spanish Civil War, the anti-Fascist coalition operated out of Barcelona. In the latter part of the 20th century the city has been receptive to the political activism of feminists, gays, and other groups.

Barcelona used the 1992 Olympics to reposition itself as a European capital. Substandard hotels were given to the wrecking ball, new parks and sculpture gardens were planted, pedestrian zones expanded, and over 50 monuments restored. The Passeig Marítim—once a little-used dock—is now a seaside promenade with palm trees, benches, and cafés. Even street lamps and store signs were redesigned for citywide aesthetic coherence. After thorough renovations, Barcelona 1993 will finally be open to the sea and have a slick transport system, while two generations of Catalan and foreign architects are busy making the city a showcase of contemporary urban design. Much as Paris has been described as the capital of the 19th century, self-possessed Barcelona may well be remembered as the capital of the 1990s.

Orientation

The hub of the city, **Plaça de Catalunya,** is easily accessible from either train station. Most trains come into **Estació Sants,** a 30-minute walk from Pl. Catalunya. Sants is handily on the green L3 **Metro** line, which will whisk you to Pl. Catalunya (Direction: Montbau; 5am-11pm, weekends and holidays 5am-1am; 90ptas, weekends and holidays 100ptas). For late arrivals the N2 bus of the **Nitbus** service shuttles to Pl. Catalunya as well (every 1/2 hr. 11:30pm-4am, 120ptas). To get to the N2, exit Sants to Plaça Joan Peiró, then walk down Carrer de Sant Antoni to Plaça de Sants. Cross Carrer de Sants (which cuts through the plaza) to catch the bus going in the right direction.

Estació de França is the terminus for trains arriving from Paris, Zurich, and Brussels. The quickest route to Pl. Catalunya is the **Metro** from Barceloneta (turn left as you exit the station, take the third left, and the station is about 200m down the street) on the yellow line (L4). Take L4 in the Roquetes direction and switch to the red line (L1) at Urquinaona; Pl. Catalunya will be the next stop in the Av. del Carrilet direction. (For more details, see Getting Around: Metro and Bus.)

Flying travelers arrive at **Aeroport El Prat de Llobregat,** 12km southwest of Barcelona and well connected to the city by train, bus, and taxi. (See Getting There: By Plane.)

Accommodations are most easily reached on foot from França. The narrow and winding streets of **Barri Gòtic** are a 10- to 15-minute walk away, while the more centrally located *hostales* of the Rambles are 15 minutes away. From the exit of França, both neighborhoods lie to the left down Avinguda Marqués de l'Argentina, which becomes Passeig d'Isabel II. At Plaça d'Antoni López (marked by the enormous central post office labeled *Correos*) the wide street to the right, Via Laietana, runs along the edge of Barri Gòtic, which is most easily entered at Plaça de l'Angel by Carrer Jaume I (next to Hotel Suizo, which flies a red neon sign and a bevy of Helvetian flags). To the Rambles, from Pl. Antoni López continue down the palm-tree-lined Passeig de Colom

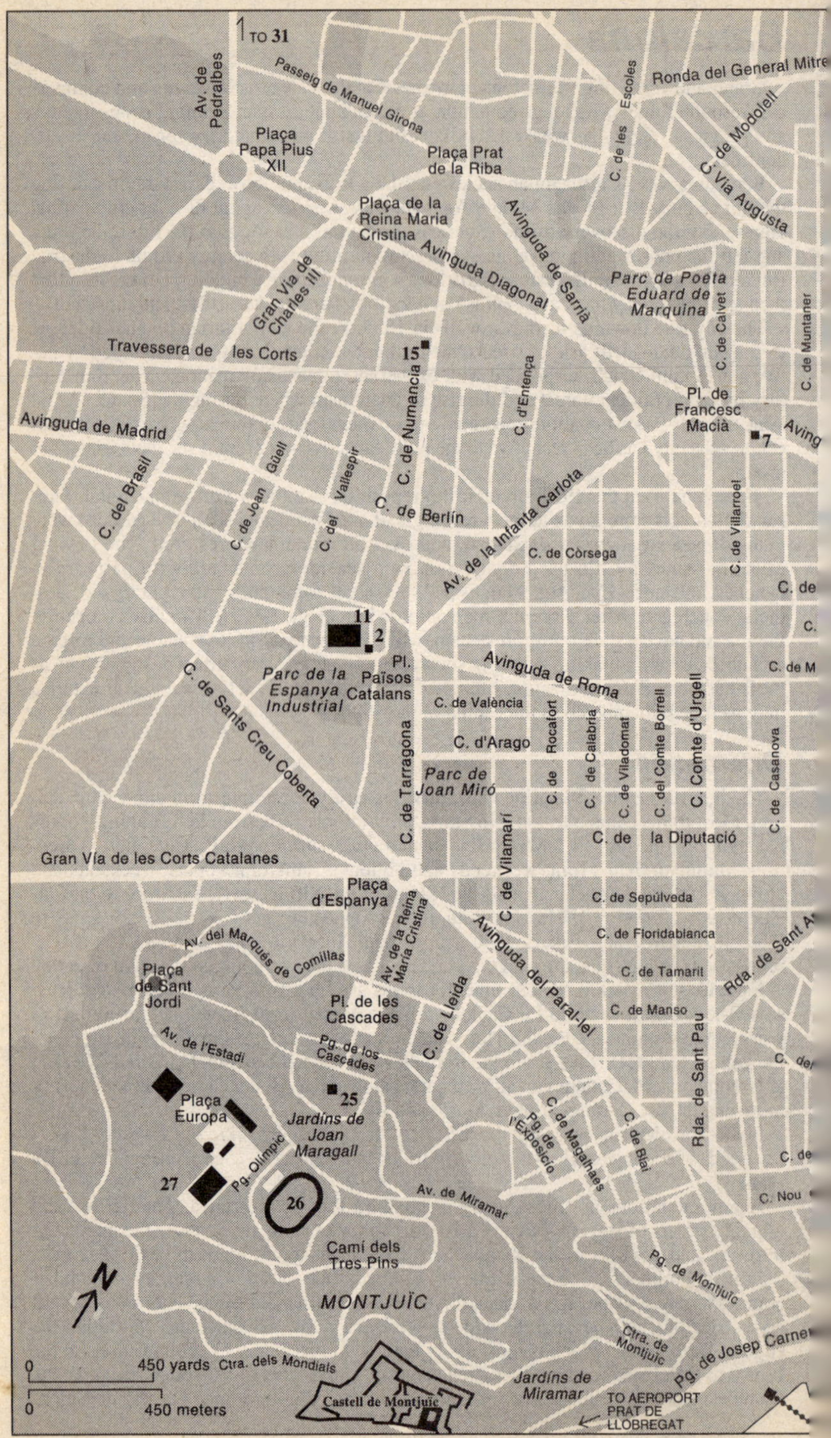
TO 31
Av. de Pedralbes
Passeig de Manuel Girona
Escoles
C. de les
Ronda del General Mitre
C. de Modolell
Vía Augusta
Plaça Papa Pius XII
Plaça Prat de la Riba
Plaça de la Reina Maria Cristina
Avinguda Diagonal
Avinguda de Sarrià
Parc de Poeta Eduard de Marquina
Gran Via de Charles III
C. de Calvet
C. de Muntaner
Travessera de les Corts
15
C. de Numancia
C. d'Entença
Pl. de Francesc Macià
7
Aving
Avinguda de Madrid
C. del Brasil
C. de Joan Güell
C. del Vallespir
C. de Berlín
Av. de la Infanta Carlota
C. de Villarroel
C. de Còrsega
C. de
C.
11
2
Pl. Països Catalans
Parc de la Espanya Industrial
C. de Sants Creu Coberta
Avinguda de Roma
C. de M
C. de València
C. d'Arago
C. de Rocafort
C. de Calabria
C. de Viladomat
C. del Comte Borrell
C. Comte d'Urgell
C. de Casanova
Parc de Joan Miró
C. de Tarragona
C. de la Diputació
Gran Vía de les Corts Catalanes
Plaça d'Espanya
C. de Vilamarí
C. de Sepúlveda
C. de Floridablanca
Av. de la Reina Maria Cristina
Avinguda del Paral·lel
Rda. de Sant A
Av. del Marquès de Comillas
Plaça de Sant Jordi
Pl. de les Cascades
C. de Lleida
C. de Tamarit
C. de Manso
Av. de l'Estadi
Pg. de los Cascades
Rda. de Sant Pau
C. de
25
Plaça Europa
Jardins de Joan Maragall
Pg. de l'Exposició
C. de Magalhaes
C. de Blai
Pg. Olímpic
27
26
Av. de Miramar
C. Nou
Camí dels Tres Pins
Pg. de Montjuïc
N
MONTJUÏC
Ctra. de Montjuïc
Pg. de Josep Carner
0
450 yards
Ctra. dels Mondials
0
450 meters
Castell de Montjuïc
Jardins de Miramar
TO AEROPORT PRAT DE LLOBREGAT

Bus 24 pl Cataluña → Trav de Dalt
to park

Barcelona

1. Regional Tourist Office
2. City Tourist Office
3. City Tourist Office
4. Budget Travel: TIVE
5. American Consulate
6. Canadian Consulate
7. U.K. Consulate
8. American Express Office
9. Main Post Office
10. Estació de França
11. Estació de Sants
12. Estació de la Plaça de Catalunya
13. Estació del Passeig de Gràcia
14. Police Station
15. Youth Hostel
16. La Seu
17. Palau de la Generalitat
18. Ajuntament
19. Santa María del Mar
20. Museu Picasso
21. Gran Teatre del Liceu
22. Museu Marítim
23. Temple Expiatori de la Sagrada Família
24. Palau de la Música Catalana
25. Palau Nacional
26. Estadi Olímpic
27. Palau Sant Jordi
28. Vila Olímpica
29. Auditori Municipal
30. Teatre Nacional de Catalunya
31. Museu-Monestir de Pedralbes
32. Museu d'Art Modern
33. Museu d'Art Contemporani
34. Hospital de Sant Pau

towards the Monument de Colom (Columbus: the guy in the raincoat standing on top of a tall pole pointing south over the water). The tree-lined **Rambles** with their wide central boulevard lie on the right.

Barcelona's layout is quite simple and is best described by imagining yourself perched atop Columbus's head, viewing the city hemmed in by the Serra de Collserola before you with the Mediterranean at your back. The city slopes gently upward from the harbor to the mountains; on most *avingudas,* this fact should help you get your bearings. From the harbor, Rambles de Santa Monica, Caputxins, Sant Josep, Estudis, and Canaletas make up one continuous boulevard extending to Pl. Catalunya known as **Las Rambles,** lined with newsstands, cafés, and flower shops. To the right of the Rambles is **Barri Gótic,** whose narrow and meandering streets reach past Via Laietana all the way to Parc de la Ciutadella and Estació de França. Beyond the Parc is the **Vila Olímpica** with its two new towers (the tallest buildings in Barcelona), numerous housing complexes, office buildings, and waterfront condominiums. On the left side of the Rambles towards the port is **Barri Xinès,** the city's red-light district. Beyond it rises a picturesque hill called **Montjuïc,** site of the Museu d'Art de Catalunya, the Fundacío Miro, Poble Espanyol, public gardens, and an amusement park.

From Pl. Catalunya, fanning up towards the mountains away from Las Rambles, the **Eixample** is bordered along its lower edge by the Gran Via de les Corts Catalanes and is bisected by Passeig de Grácia, with its numerous shops and cafés. The upper limit of the grid-planned neighborhood is Avinguda Diagonal, which separates the Eixample from the older neighborhood of **Gràcia,** in the foothills of the mountains that encircle Barcelona. In this mountain range, the peak of **Tibidabo,** the highest point in Barcelona, provides the most privileged aerie from which to view the city.

Barcelona is a relatively safe city and concerns about safety should not prevent you from enjoying it at all hours. Pickpocketing is the most common crime, mainly on and near the Rambles and in the train stations. The city has largely succeeded in its vigorous efforts to rid itself of petty thieves, but precautions are advised. Distraction is the pickpocket's primary tool. Standard ploys include dropping coins on the ground, smearing mustard on the victim's shirt and offering to clean it off, volunteering to serve as a "guide," prostitutes grabbing at men's crotches, and strangers giving women flowers. Keep valuables in your lap while sitting at an outdoor café and a firm grip on them while watching the street shows on the Rambles. Plaça Reial and Carrer Escudellers should be altogether avoided after dark, and Barri Xinès is not safe for lone walkers at night. There is no need to go looking for entertainment in these seedy neighborhoods; the areas where the city lives it up (see **Entertainment**) are always safe. Barcelona is well-patrolled and well-lit at night.

Practical Information

Getting There

By Plane

All domestic and international flights land at **El Prat de Llobregat** (tel. 370 10 11), 12km southwest of Barcelona. The quickest way between the city and the airport is via **RENFE** trains (every 1/2 hr., 20min., 220ptas). The first train to Barcelona leaves at 6:12am and the last one at 10:42pm, with stops at **Estació Central-Sants** (Metro: L1, L5; on the southwestern edge of the city), then **Plaça de Catalunya** (Metro: L1, L3; smack in the middle of Barcelona). The Red Automatic Purchase Machines, which have instructions only in Catalan or Castilian and take only ptas, are otherwise the most convenient way to buy tickets. The elevated enclosed walkway to the trains is accessible from inside the national terminal, which is less than 100m from the entrance of the new international terminal to your right.

Trains to the airport from Pl. de Catalunya run between 6:35am and 10:05pm, while those from Sants run between 5:42am and 10:12pm. Tickets to the airport are dispensed at the "Aeroport" window in Sants (8am-10pm); otherwise wait at Recorridos Cercanías window or purchase your ticket from one of the automatic ticket machines.

The bus is less expensive and is the only late-night service available besides a taxi. However, it's less frequent and is subject to traffic delays weekday mornings and weekend afternoons (every 40min.; 40min.; 90ptas, Sun. and holidays 100ptas). From the airport to **Plaça de Espanya** (Metro: L1, L5), take bus EA between 6:20am and 9pm or bus EN between 10:15pm and 2:40am. The bus departs from the airport in front of the domestic flight terminal. Bus EA leaves Pl. Espanya from 7am to 9:40pm, bus EN from 10:50pm to 3:15am. The stop at Pl. Espanya is on the corner between Gran Via de Les Corts Catalanes and Av. Reina María Cristina. A taxi ride between Barcelona and El Prat costs around 2000ptas. (See Taxis below.)

Iberia, Pg. Gràcia, 30, (tel. 301 39 93; national reservations 302 76 56). Metro: Pg. Gràcia (L3, L4), at intersection of Pg. Gràcia and Gran Via de les Corts Catalanes. To: Madrid (frequently all day, 13,150ptas); València (3 per day, 10,100ptas); Sevilla (4 per day, 18,025ptas); Lisboa (4 per day); New York (1 per day); London (5 per day); Paris (4 per day); Rome (2 per day); Geneva (2 per day). Open Mon.-Fri. 8am-9pm; Sat. 8am-3pm.

By Train

The RENFE 24-hr. information line stores general train information (tel. 490 02 02; some English spoken). **Estació Sants** (Metro: Sants-Estació, L3, L4; open 6am-11pm) is the hub of domestic and international traffic, while **Estació França** (Av. Marqués de L'Argentera, s/n; Metro: Barceloneta, L3; open 6am-11pm) is the endpoint for travel to and from Paris, Zurich, and Brussels.

At Sants, domestic and international train tickets are sold. To: Madrid (1 *rápido* per day, 8hr., 4355ptas; 3 *talgos,* 6 3/4 -7 1/2 hr., 6295-6545ptas; 3 *estrellas,* 10hr., 4355-6055ptas); Sevilla (4 per day, 12-14 1/2 hr., 6300-9000ptas); València (11 per day, 4-5 1/2 hr., 1900-3500ptas); Paris (2 per day, 13-15 1/2 hr., 9000ptas); Milan (at 7:40pm, 18hr., 9000ptas); Zürich (at 7:40pm, 13 1/2 hr., 12,000ptas).

The commuter **Ferrocarrils de la Generalitat de Catalunya (FFCC)** (tel. 205 15 15), or Catalan State Railways, with main stations at Pl. Catalunya and Pl. Espanya, are indispensable if you're going to Montserrat, Sant Cugat or Tarrassa. Connections with the metro are marked by a double-arrow symbol. The commuter line for Tibidabo charges the same as the metro and you can use your 10-ride metro pass; beyond Tibidabo, however, fares go up.

By Bus

Buses are generally less expensive than trains but are a bit slower.

Enatcar, Estació del Nord, Vilanova, s/n (tel. 245 25 28). Metro: Arc de Triomf (L1). Open Mon.-Fri. 9am-1pm and 4-7pm, Sat. 9am-1pm. To: Madrid (2 per day, 12hr., 6600ptas); València (10 per day, 8hr., 2375ptas).

Iberbus, Av. Paral-lel, 116 (tel. 441 54 94). Metro: Paral-lel (L3.) Open Mon.-Fri. 9am-1pm and 4-7pm, Sat. 9am-1pm. To: London (1 per day, 25 hr., 13,500ptas); Paris (1 per day, 15hr., 9300ptas); Rome (1 per day, 24hr., 13,300ptas).

Auto Transport Julià, Pl. Universitat, 12 (tel. 317 64 54). Open Mon.-Sat. 8am-8pm. Metro: Universitat (L1). To Lisboa (on Fri., 20hr., 10,475ptas).

Sarfa, Pl. Duc de Medinaceli, 4 (tel. 318 94 34). Metro: Drassanes (L3). On the corner with Pg. Colom. Open 7:30am-8:30pm. The most convenient way to get to one of several beach towns along the Costa Brava (2hr., 1000ptas).

By Ferry

Transmediterránea, Av. Drassanes, 6 (tel. 317 63 11). Metro: Drassanes (L3). Open Mon.-Fri. 9am-1pm and 5-7pm, Sat. 9am-noon. From the metro, Columbus points the way from his perch to Estació Marítima (tel. 412 25 24 for tickets and departures) behind the *Aduana* building on the wharf. During the summer daily voyages between Barcelona and Mallorca (8hr.), Menorca (9hr.), and Eivissa (9 1/2 hr.). *Butaca* (essentially an airline seat) is the cheapest at 5350ptas, but cabins are reasonably priced as well. The boats fill up quickly in the summer.

By Rideshare and Thumb

Barnastop, C. Pintor Fortuny, 21 (tel. 318 27 31), off the Rambles by the Hotel Ramada. Metro: Liceu (L3). Matches drivers with riders and can hook you up with other *Mitzfahrzentrales* (rideshare associations). 3ptas per km to driver on standard roads, 4ptas per km on highways. 1pta per km to Barnastop (min. 500ptas; max. 1800ptas). To: Paris (5500ptas); Geneva (4000ptas); Rome (5250ptas); Berlin (9000ptas). Open Mon.-Fri. 10am-2pm and 5-7pm, Sat. 11am-2pm.

Let's Go does not recommend hitchhiking as a safe mode of travel. Those who choose to hitch to France take the metro to Fabra i Puig, then Av. Meridiana to reach A-7. Those en route to Tarragona and València take bus #7 from Rambla Catalunya at Gran Via or ride the green line to Zona Universitaria, at the southern end of Diagonal, and head for A-7 south. The *autopista* access lies near here. With the proper sign, this approach also puts hitchers on the A-2 to Zaragoza, the beginning of the trek to Madrid. Hitchhiking on *autopistas* (toll roads) is illegal; they are marked with the letter A. Hitchhiking is permitted, however, on national (N) highways.

Getting Around

Maps

Don't bother to shell out 800ptas for *Un Plano de Barcelona* at a newsstand. Everything geographic you need to know about Barcelona is on one of the free *Ajuntament de Barcelona* (city government) maps, available in Catalan, Castilian, English, French, German, and Italian at all tourist offices.

Metro and Bus

Barcelona's extensive public transport system (tel. 412 00 00) will get you within walking distance of any point in the city quickly and cheaply. *Guía del Transport Públic,* available free at tourist offices and at the transport information booth in Pl. Catalunya, maps out all four of the city's metro lines and bus routes (day and night). Both metro and bus rides cost 90ptas (100ptas on weekends and holidays), and a 10-ride pass is 510ptas. Automatic ticket machines and all ticket windows sell passes. Make sure you hold on to your ticket or pass until you leave the metro, since riding the metro without any receipt carries a 1000ptas fine. Metro open Mon.-Fri. 5am-11pm; Sat.-Sun. and holidays 5am-1am. Individual bus routes vary, but day buses usually run 6am-10pm and night buses from 10:30pm-4:30am.

Taxi

Taxis are omnipresent and have a *Libre* sign in the windshield or a lit green light on the roof if they're not occupied. The yellow and black taxis can also be summoned by phone (tel. 358 11 11, 330 08 04, 491 00 00, or 300 38 11). The first 6 minutes or 1.9km cost 250ptas; then it's 100ptas per km.

Car Rental

Docar, C. Montnegre, 18 (tel. 322 90 08, 24-hr. reservations). Free delivery and pickup. 1900ptas per day, 19ptas each additional km. Mon.-Fri. 9am-7pm, Sat. 9am-1pm.

Tot Car, C. Josep Terradellas, 93 (tel. 405 34 33). Free delivery and pickup. 2100ptas per day, 21ptas each additional km. Mon.-Fri. 9am-1pm and 4-7pm, Sat. 9am-1pm.

Bicycle

Bike Rental: Bicitram, Av. Margués Argentera, 15 (tel. 792 28 41) near Parc Ciutadella. Bikes 350ptas 1st hr., 150ptas per additional1/2hr. Open Sat.-Sun. Oct.-May 10am-7pm; June-Sept. 10am-8:30pm.

Moped Rental: Vanguard, C. Londres, 31 (tel. 439 38 80), off. Av. Diagonal. Metro: Hospital Clinic (L3). Mopeds 2850ptas per day. Vespas 4000ptas per day. Open Mon.-Fri. 8am-8pm, Sat. 9am-1pm.

Tourist Offices

For general city information dial **010.** For general destination information dial **412 00 00.** Information on **cultural events** is dispensed at Palau de la Virreina, Rambla, 99 (tel. 301 77 75, ext. 243). (Metro: Liceu (L3), between La Boquería and C. Carme. Open June 24-Sept. 30 Mon.-Sat. 9:30am-9pm, Sun. 10am-2pm.) Year-round tourist information offices are:

Estació França, Av. Marqués de l'Argentera, s/n (tel. 402 70 00). Open 8am-8pm.

Estació Central de Barcelona-Sants, Pl. Països Catalans, s/n (tel. 490 91 71). Metro: Sants-Estació (L1, L5). Run by the Ajuntament de Barcelona with information on Barcelona only. Open 8am-8pm.

Aeroport El Prat de Llobregat, International Terminal (tel. 478 47 07); 25m to the left of the customs exit. Run by the Generalitat de Catalunya with information about Barcelona, Catalunya and the rest of Spain. Open Mon.-Sat. 9:30am-8pm, Sun. 9:30am-3pm.

La Gran Via de les Corts Catalanes, 658 (tel. 301 74 43). Metro: Urquinaona (L1, L4) or Pl. Catalunya (L1, L3, L5). Two blocks from the intersection with Pg. Gràcia, in the Eixample. Also run by the Generalitat office. Open Mon.-Fri. 9am-7pm, Sat. 9am-2pm.

Ajuntament, Pl. Sant Jaume (tel. 302 42 00, ext. 433). Metro: Jaume I (L4). Open Mon.-Fri. 9am-8pm, Sat. 8:30am-2:30pm.

Tourist Bus

Marked *Transports Turistics Barcelona,* four air-conditioned buses (bus #100) bop around the city with 15 stops at points of interest listed in a guidebook that comes with the ticket. The whole circuit (28km) takes two hours with buses passing each stop every 30 minutes. The ticket includes unlimited use of the Tram Via Blau, Funicular de Tibidabo, and the aerial tram to Montjüic; it'll also get discounted admission to Poble Espanyol, a guided tour through Barri Gòtic, the Golondrines boat tour of the harbor, and the city zoo. The easiest place to get on the bus is at Pl. Catalunya in front of El Corte Inglés department store. Tickets can be purchased on the bus. In service June 13-Sept. 27, 9am-9:30pm (the last bus leaves from Pl. Catalunya at 7:30pm). Full day 1000ptas, half day (after 2pm) 700ptas.

Budget Travel Offices

TIVE, C. Gravina, 1 (tel. 302 06 82). Metro: Universitat (L1). One block from Pl. Universitat off C. Pelai. Come here first and come early because in summer there's often a wait. Eurotrain tickets, cheap buses (Paris 7950ptas, Rome 11,350ptas, London 11,450ptas), flights, and ISICs (500ptas). Open June-Sept. 15 9am-2pm; Sept. 16-May 9am-1pm and 4-5pm.

Centre d'Informació: Assesorament per a Joves, C. Avinyó, 7 (tel. 402 78 03). More of a student tourist office than a travel agency. No tickets for sale, but plenty of free advice. Excellent library of travel guides, including *Let's Go*. English spoken. Open Mon.-Fri. 10am-2pm and 4-8pm.

Consulates

U.S.: Via Laietana, 33, 4th fl. (tel. 319 95 50; fax 319 56 21). Metro: Jaume I (L4). At the intersection of Av. Catedral and Laietana. Open Mon.-Fri. 9am-noon and 3-5pm.

Canada: Via Augusta, 125 (tel. 209 06 34). Metro: FFCC, Sant Gervase or Muntaner; any line from Pl. Catalunya except Tibidabo. At the intersection of C. Aribaud Augusta. Open Mon.-Fri. 9am-1pm.

U.K.: Av. Diagonal, 477 (tel. 419 90 44; fax 405 24 11). Metro: Diagonal (L3, L5). At the intersection of Pg. Gràcia and Diagonal. Open June-Sept. Mon.-Fri. 9am-2pm; Oct.-May 9:30am-1:30pm and 4-5pm.

Australia: Gran Via Carles III, 98 (tel. 330 94 96; fax 411 09 04). Metro: María Cristina (L3). At the intersection of C. Europa and Carles III by El Corte Inglés department store. Open Mon.-Fri. 10am-noon.

Money

American Express: Pg. Gràcia, 101 (tel. 217 00 70, client fax mail 415 37 00). Metro: Diagonal (L3, L5). The entrance is actually on C. Rosselló, around the corner from this address. Mail held 1 month free of charge for card and check holders. No charge for client fax mail. Multilingual ATM machine outside for 24-hr. service. Open Mon.-Fri. 9:30am-6pm, Sat. 10am-noon.

Currency Exchange: Currency exchange booths at the airport charge 500ptas. commission. In the international terminal, the money exchange is on the left just before customs (tel. 370 10 12). Open 7am-11pm. Exchange rates at travel agencies usually work on a percentage basis. **Viatges Marsans** on Rambles, 134 (tel. 318 72 16), 1/2-bl. from Pl. Catalunya, has a 3% commission on traveler's checks and 2% on bills. Open Mon.-Fri. 9am-1pm and 4-7pm. On Sun. you can change money at **Estació de Sants** (tel. 490 77 70, ext. 93) for a 1% commission on checks and bills (500ptas min. on checks, 400ptas on bills). Open Mon.-Sun. 8am-10pm, except Dec. 25, 26, and Jan. 1. The currency exchanges on the Rambles may be temptingly convenient on Sun., but they normally charge the maximum commission allowed by law (9.8%).

Communications

Post Office: Pl. Antoni López (tel. 318 38 31). Metro: Jaume I or Barceloneta (L4), at the end of Via Laietana near the port. Open for stamps (to the left and downstairs) Mon.-Sat. 8:30am-10pm, Sun. 10am-noon; for Lista de Correos (window #17) Mon.-Fri. 9am-9pm, Sat. 9am-2pm; for **telegrams** Mon.-Sat. 8am-10pm. To send **emergency telegrams** when post office is closed, go to Via Laietana, 1 (tel. 322 20 00). Metro: Urquinaona (L1, L4). Open Mon.-Fri. 10pm-midnight, Sat.-Sun. 8am-10pm. Most neighborhoods also have post offices; a useful one near the city center is at Pl. Urquinaona, 6. Metro: Urquinaona (L1, L4). Open Mon.-Fri. 9am-2pm and 4-6pm. **Postal Code:** 08002.

Telephones: Central Telephone Exchange, C. Fontanella, 4. Metro: Catalunya (L1, L3), just off Pl. Catalunya. Perennial lines open Mon.-Sat. 8:30am-9pm. Another telephone service is at Estació Sants. Metro: Sants-Estació (L3, L5). Also, **faxes** sent and received (tel. 490 82 73). Open 8am-10:45pm. Open 7:45am-10:45pm. **Telephone Code:** 93.

Emergency, Health, and Help

Police: New police station at Rambles, 43 (tel. 301 90 60), right across from the entrance to Pl. Real and next to C. Nou de la Rambla. Metro: Liceu (L3). Installed to deal with tourist concerns (English, French, German, and Italian spoken) and clean up the port end of the Rambles. **Municipal Police:** tel. 092. **National Police:** tel. 091.

Fire: tel. 080.

Ambulance: tel. 061.

Hospitals: Hospital Clínic, C. Casanova, 143 (tel. 454 25 80). Metro: Hospital Clínic (L5). Main entrance at intersection of C. Roselló and Casanova. **Hospital de la Santa Creu i Sant Pau,** at intersection of C. Cartagena and C. Sant Antoni Moria Claret (tel. 347 99 50). Metro: Hospital de Sant Pau (L5). **Médicos de Urgencia,** C. Pelai, 40 (tel. 412 12 12). Metro: Pl. Catalunya (L1, L3), close to the end of the street that meets the Rambles and Pl. Catalunya.

24-Hour Pharmacy: Drugstore, Pg. Gràcia (tel. 215 70 74). Metro: Pg. Gràcia (L3, L4). On the block between C. Mallorca and C. València. Night buses N4, N6, and N7 all pass by it.

Crisis Services: Informacions i Urgencies de Les Dones, C. Avinyó, 7 (tel. 402 78 27). Metro: Drassanes (L3). Turn left at the end of the Rambles down C. Clavé; C. Avinyó is the 3rd left after the church. Helps female victims of violent crimes. Open Mon.-Fri. 9am-1pm and 4-7pm.

STD treatment, Av Drassanes, 17-21 (tel. 441 29 97). Hotline number.

Gay and Lesbian Associations: Front d'Allibrement Gai de Catalunya, C. Villaroel, 63 (tel. 254 63 98). Metro: Urgell (L1). At the corner of C. Consell de Cant and Villaroel. **Grup de Lesbianes Feministes de Barcelona,** Gran Via de les Corts Catalanes, 549, 4th fl. (tel. 323 33 07). Metro: Pl. Catalunya (L1, L3). Less than 1 bl. from Pg. Gràcia heading away from Pl. Catalunya. Ask for information about Barcelona's brand new **ACT-UP** chapter at these places.

Other

El Corte Inglés: Pl. Catalunya (tel. 302 12 12). They have a good **map. Currency exchange:** 1% commission (250ptas min. charge). They also offer novels and guidebooks in English; haircutting; rooftop cafeteria; and **telephones.** Open Mon.-Sat. 10am-9pm.

Luggage Storage: At **Estació Sants** (Metro: Sants-Estacio (L1, L3)) and **Estació França** (Metro: Barceloneta (L1)). Small lockers 300ptas, large lockers 500ptas. Open 6:30am-11pm. **Sarfa,** Pl. Duc de Medinaceli, 4 (tel. 318 94 34). Metro: Drassanes (L3). Lockers 150ptas. Open 8am-8:30pm. **Alsina Graells Bus Terminal,** Ronda Universitat, 4 (tel. 302 65 45). Metro: Universitat (L1). Lockers 100ptas. Open 9am-1:30pm and 4-8pm. You can also leave your things at many of the hostels for about 150ptas per bag per day.

Lost Property: Objets Perduts (tel. 301 39 23), on the ground floor of the Ajuntament, Pl. Sant Jaume. Metro: Jaume I (L4). Open Mon.-Fri. 9:30am-1:30pm.

English Bookstore: Librería Francesa, Pg. Gràcia, 91 (tel. 215 14 17). Metro: Diagonal (L3, L5). Between C. Provença and C. Roselló. Good selection, including *Let's Go*. Open Mon.-Fri. 9:30am-2pm and 4:30-7:30pm, Sat. 9:30am-1:30pm. **Simons and K.O.,** C. La Granja, 13 (tel. 238 30 86). Metro: Lesseps (L3). Off Trav. de Dalt, near Pl. Lesseps at the end of C. Gran de Gràcia. Buys, sells, and trades English-language books and has the lowest-priced new Penguin paperbacks in the city! Open Sept.-July Mon.-Sat. 10am-7pm. **LAIE,** Av. Pau Claris, 85 (tel. 318 17 39). Metro: Urquinaona (L1, L4) or Pl. Catalunya (L1, L3, L5), 1 block from the Gran Via. It has the most extensive collection, but you pay for selection. Open Mon.-Sat. 10am-8pm. **Come In,** C. Provenza, 203 (tel. 453 12 04; fax 451 40 56). Guidebooks, paperbacks, magazines and newspapers, language reference books, and greeting cards.

Library: Institut d'Estudis Norteamericans, Via Augusta, 123 (tel. 227 31 45). Take the FFCC commuter train to Pl. Molina. Lots of American newspapers and periodicals, as well as a strong reference section. Open Sept.-July Mon.-Fri. 11am-1:30pm and 4-8pm. **Biblioteca Central,** C. Carme, 47 (tel. 317 07 78), next to Hospital de Santa Creu off the Rambles. Open Mon.-Fri. 9am-8pm, Sat. 9am-2pm.

Foreign Periodicals: Try the newsstands along the Rambles and Pg. Gràcia.

Women's Services: Ca La Dona Women's Center, Gran Vía de les Corts Catalanes, 549, 4th fl. left (tel. 323 33 07). **Llibrería de Dones Prolèg,** C. Dagueria, 13. Metro: Jaume I. Open Mon.-Fri. 10am-8pm, Sat. 10am-2pm. Women's bookstore that stocks a large feminist collection; English, French, and German books. Current and second-hand books. Workshops, seminars, signups, and notice board.

Religious Services: Catholic Mass in English, C. Anglí, 15 (tel. 204 49 62). Take bus #74 or #22 from Pl. Catalunya. Sun. 10:30am. Anglican Mass in English, St. George Church, C. Sant Joan de la Salle, 41 (tel. 400 61 48). Metro: Arc de Triomf (L1). Jewish services, Sinagoga de la Comunidad Judía, C. Avenir, 24 (tel. 200 85 13). Muslim services, Comunidad musulmana, Mezquita Al-Widadiyah, C. Balmes, 13 (tel. 318 67 09). Metro: Universitat (L1).

Laundromats: Lava Super, C. Carme, 63, off the Rambles by the Palau Virreina. Wash and dry 925ptas per 5kg. Open Mon.-Fri. 8am-8pm, Sat. 8am-2pm. Other places with similar prices and hours are **Lavanderiá Autoservicio,** at Rambles, 114B, **Lavanderiá Ramblas,** C. Ramelleres, 13, on Pl. Vicenç Martorell.

Showers: Public showers are nonexistent, but municipal swimming pools have shower facilities. (See Entertainment: Recreational Sports.)

Accommodations and Camping

1993 travelers will reap the benefits of 1992's Olympic frenzy. *Hostal* and *pension* owners madly spruced up their places, expecting a flood of tourists. Moreover, because the city of Barcelona issued its periodic statement of standards, many *hostal* owners rushed to upgrade to "one-star hotel" status. What you'll see is a lot of new paint, new furniture, and new bathrooms.

Hostels

Barcelona's hostels run the gamut; luxury and convenience come at a price.

Alberg Mare de Déu de Montserrat (HI), Pg. Mare de Deu del Coll, 41-51 (tel. 213 86 33), beyond Park Güell off Av. República Argentina. Take bus #28 from Pl. Catalunya, bus #100, or Metro L3 to Pl. Lesseps, then bus #25. The green line of the metro drops you at Vallcaraca; then walk up (and up and up and up...) Av. República Argentina and across C. Viaducte de Vallcaraca. At the end of a 20-min. commute, this gorgeous neo-Moorish villa doesn't disappoint. Stained-glass filtered light fills the brightly tiled atrium. 3-day max. stay. Reception open 7:30-9:30am, 1:30-3pm, 5-8pm, and 9-11pm. Curfew midnight, but door opens at 1 and 2am for the late-night crowd to slip in. 850ptas per person, over 26 1275ptas. Breakfast included. Sheets 300ptas. No reservations.

Alberg Juvenil Palau, C. Palau, 6 (tel. 412 50 80). Metro: Jaume I (L4). One block from Pl. Sant Jaume: take C. Ciutat to C. Templaris, then take the 2nd left. Still in its infancy (opened April 1992), this early blooming *hostal* has already developed refined service. Colorful interior with a big lounge. Curfew midnight. 4-6 people per room, 1200ptas per person. Breakfast included. Reservations with 1 night's deposit.

Albergue Internacional Pensión Colón, C. Colom, 3 (tel. 318 06 31). Metro: Liceu (L3). The area is very unsafe at night. Just off the Rambles at Pl. Reial. A combination youth hostel/1-star hotel in the thick of the Rambles. You can stay either in the *hostal* part (7-8 people per room,

1000ptas) or the pricier hotel part (doubles 4500ptas). Lockers available. Sheets 250ptas. Laundry 500ptas. Must be under 30 to stay in the *hostal*.

Hotel Kabul, Pl. Reial, 17 (tel. 318 51 90), off the Rambles. The area is very dangerous at night. Graffiti art and paintings on the walls, pool table and color TV in lounge, and new bathrooms. 4-8 bunk beds per room. Check-out noon. 1000ptas per person. 1000ptas deposit for keys to a locker. Laundry 500ptas.

Barri Gòtic and the Rambles

Ciutat vella (the old quarter) is the best hunting ground for cheap places to stay in the heart of the city, as well as for inexpensive food.

Hostal Marítima, Rambles, 4 (tel. 302 31 52). Metro: Drassanes (L3). Across from the metro station exit on the port end of the Rambles; follow the signs to the Wax Museum next door. Quiet, clean, spacious, and bright rooms in an easily accessible location. The speaker in each room can be turned off if the Doors and Dire Straits aren't your scene. Singles 1700ptas. Doubles 2800ptas, with showers 3500ptas. Triples 4200ptas, with showers 4800ptas. Laundry 700ptas. Reservations with 1 night's deposit.

Casa de Huéspedes Mari-Luz, C. Palau, 4 (tel. 317 34 63). Metro: Jaume I (L4) or Liceu (L3). One block from Pl. Sant Jaume. Take C. Ciutat to C. Templaris, then take the 2nd left. After dark approach only by Ferran or Jaume, not Escudellers. On the 4th floor, Mari-Luz and Fernando, the kind owners, offer basic rooms, sparkling new showers, use of their refrigerator, and a li'l extra TLC. 1200ptas per person (less in winter). Reservations for repeat visitors.

Pensión Fernando, C. Volta de Remedio, 4 (tel. 301 79 93). Metro: Liceu (L3). The 4th left off C. Ferran coming from the Rambles. Also run by Mari-Luz and Fernando, this *pensión* is as user-friendly as its spouse. It's currently being expanded to include an elevator, a more accessible street entrance, and new rooms. Catch some cancerous sun in the rooftop chairs. 1200ptas per person (less in winter). Reservations for repeat visitors.

Hostal-Residencia Pintor, C. Gignás, 25 (tel. 315 47 08). Metro: Jaume I (L4). Gignás is the street that narrows from C. Angel Baixeras behind the post office. Each spacious room features new paint and furniture, a balcony, and inexplicably thick red and black checked blankets. Singles and doubles 1500ptas per person.

Hostal-Residencia Romay, C. Avinyó, 58 (tel. 317 94 14). Metro: Drassanes (L3). Walk to the end of the Rambles and turn left onto C. Josep Anselm Clave, which becomes C. Ample. C. Avinyó is the 3rd left after the church on the right-hand side. This clean, big-windowed *hostal* has a tropical touch due to a couple of birds, colorful green and black wallpaper in the halls, and balconies in many of the rooms. Singles with showers 1500ptas. Doubles 2000ptas, with showers 2500ptas. Reservations with 1 night's deposit.

Hostal Drassanes, C. Ample, 7 (tel. 318 15 14). Right around the corner from Hostal-Residencia Romay and run by the same people. No birds here, but same great price. Good deals flock together.

Hostal Levante, Baixada de San Miguel, 2 (tel. 317 95 65). Metro: Jaume I (L4). From Via Laietana down C. Jaume I, turn left at the Ajuntament onto Pl. San Miguel. Baby-lovers will go wild over the owners' son Fabio; others will drool over the new bathrooms, handsome wood interior, and lounge with color TV. Quiet and airy. Singles 1800ptas. Doubles 3200ptas, with shower 4000ptas. Sept.-April: 1500ptas; 2800ptas, 3500ptas.

Hostal Layetana, Pl. El Gran Ramon Berenguer, 2 (tel. 319 20 12). Metro: Jaume I (L4). Up Via Laietana from the metro on the left-hand side and on Berenguer's left once you're in the plaza; right behind the Cathedral. Elevator, lounge with TV, and balconied doubles. Singles 1800ptas. Doubles 3000ptas, with showers 5000ptas. Showers 200ptas.

Pensión Segura, Junta de Comerç, 11 (tel. 302 51 74). Metro: Liceu (L3). From the metro walk down the Rambles, turn right at C. de Hospital; then take the 1st left after Pl. Sant Augustì. Choose your siesta—the huge central patio or the firm beds. Newly renovated and well-lit rooms, along with a breakfast of coffee, fresh-squeezed orange juice, and a croissant (345ptas), are wise preparation for a hard day's touring. Singles 1900ptas. Doubles 3000ptas, with bath 3500ptas. Reservations for more than 1 person with deposit (postal code: 08001).

Hostal Marmo, C. Gignás, 25 (tel. 315 42 08), 2 floors below Hostal-Residencia Pintor. Bubble-gum pink hallways raise expectations of something more sprightly than the dim rooms deliver. Singles 1500ptas. Doubles 2500ptas.

Hostal Dalí, C. Boquería, 12 (tel. 318 55 80). Metro: Liceu (L3). From the metro walk down the Rambles to Pl. Boquería and turn left. No drooping watches, only sagging beds and slouching couches in the TV room downstairs. Singles 1700ptas, with bath 2100ptas. Doubles 2800ptas, with bath 3000ptas. Reservations only by phone and held until 6pm same day.

Hotel Juventut, Junta de Commerç (tel. 301 84 99), across the street from Pensión Segura. A 1-star hotel that's a good deal for a group larger than 3. Frolic in huge rooms with new showers; lounge downstairs. Laundry 50ptas. Singles 4000ptas (better find some friends to room with). Doubles 5000ptas. Triples 6000ptas. Quads 7000ptas. Breakfast of coffee, juice, and toast included.

Hostal Benidorm, Rambles, 37 (tel. 302 20 54). Metro: Drassanes (L3). Just below Pl. del Teatre. A tad small and a tad old, but a low price and newly-renovated bathrooms. Singles 1400ptas. Doubles 2600ptas, with bath 3500ptas. Showers 200ptas.

Hostal Barcelona, C. Roser, 40 (tel. 442 50 75). Metro: Paral-lel (L3). Exit the metro on the C. Vila i Vila side and walk past the newspaper stand to C. Roser. In a serene residential neighborhood. Mattresses can't pass the princess test and you'll need a candelabra for the dark hallways at night, but there are strong showers and a new paint job. Singles and doubles 1500ptas per person. No reservations.

Hostal Meridiana, Av. Meridiana, 2 (tel. 309 51 25). Metro: Marina (L1). On the corner of Pg. Pujades and C. Meridiana, the entrance is located inside the gas station and up the stairs along the wall. In a quiet, secluded area (5min. from the Marina station, 20min. from Pl. Catalunya on foot, or a mere stone's throw from Parc de la Ciutadella). Large rooms, thin mattresses. Singles 1700ptas. Doubles 2200ptas. Reservations with 1 night's deposit (postal code: 08018).

Hostal Cisne, C. Marqués del Campo Sagrado, 9 (tel. 442 27 78). Metro: Paral-lel (L3). From the metro head up Rda. Sant Pau and take the 2nd left. A little remote, though on a pleasant, broad, well-lit street. Like Alice's Wonderland—labyrinthine layout and cavernous rooms with incongruously tiny beds. Immaculately clean. Singles to quads 2000ptas per person. Showers 100ptas. Reservations with 1 night's deposit (postal code: 08015).

Hostal Orleans, Av. Marqués de L'Argentera, 13 (tel. 319 73 82). Metro: Barceloneta (L4). Next to the Banc Sabanell. Two hefty advantages: it's a brief stagger across the street from Estació de França (train station), and there's a TV in every room. Singles 3000ptas. Doubles 4500ptas, with bath 6000ptas.

Hotel Peninsular, C. Sant Pau, 34 (tel. 302 31 38). Metro: Liceu (L3). From the metro walk down the Rambles past the market and C. Hospital, then turn right onto C. Sant Pau. A former monastery converted into a *Modernista* masterpiece—listed in the Generalitat's guide to *Modernista* architecture in Barcelona. The glass-covered inner courtyard is draped with hanging plants for 4 floors. The only drawback: the street is dark and generally unsafe at night. Singles 3585ptas. Doubles 7100ptas. Breakfast of coffee, juice, and toast included. Reservations with 1 night's deposit (postal code: 08001).

Hostal Rey Don Jaime I, C. Jaume I, 11 (tel. 315 41 61). Metro: Jaume I (L4). Take C. Jaume off Pl. Angel; next to Pl. Sant Jaume. Well-lit area with lots of police. This handily located *hostal* will soon be reclassified as a 1-star hotel. The price has already been upgraded. Singles 3300ptas. Doubles 4700ptas.

Hostal New York, C. Gignás, 2 (tel. 315 03 04). Metro: Jaume I (L4). C. Gignás is the street that narrows from C. Angel Baixeras behind the post office. Creaky elevator, flaking plaster, corroded bathroom fixtures, and dark hallways could be the setting for *Barton Fink*. Fine if you're running out of money and are too misanthropic to share a room elsewhere with others. 1000ptas per person.

Near Plaça de Catalunya

A bit more expensive than in the Barri Gòtic, accommodations here are more safe and modern, while still close to the action (and noise) of the Rambles. The metro stop is Pl. Catalunya (L1, L3) unless otherwise specified.

Hotel Toledano/Hostal Capitol, Rambles, 138 (tel. 301 08 72; fax 412 31 42). Right at the top of the Rambles behind the newsstand on the left as you look down the street. The owner's parrot says one word, *guapo* (handsome); this sums up the whole operation. TV, phone, and balcony in rooms. The *hostal* part is a great deal for groups of more than 1 person. Singles 2100ptas, in hotel 3100ptas. Doubles 3200ptas, in hotel 5200ptas. Triples 4100ptas, in hotel 6500ptas. Quads 4800ptas, in hotel 7500ptas. Reservations with 1 night's deposit.

264   Catalunya (Catalonia)

Residencia Australia, Ronda Universitat, 11 (tel. 317 41 77). A gregarious English-speaking owner shows that she cares with embroidered sheets and curtains, wooden boards under the mattresses, a spotless bathroom, ceiling fans in rooms, and winter heating. Singles 2150ptas. Doubles 3100ptas, with bath 3750ptas. Very difficult to find rooms here; reserve well in advance (postal code: 08007).

Pensión L'Isard, C. Tallers, 82 (tel. 302 51 83). Metro: Universitat (L1). Beaming with youth at the end of the street off Pl. Universitat. New mattresses, tiling, sinks, the works. The neighborhood quiets down at night. English and German spoken. Singles 1700ptas. Doubles 3000ptas. Reservations with 1 night's deposit (postal code: 08001).

Hostal Lausanne, Av. Porta de L'Angel, 24 (tel. 302 11 39). Head towards the *Telefónica* but turn right; look for the blue square sign next to Cellini jewelry. Bright and airy rooms and a tranquil terrace out back for catching the evening breeze. Couches and chairs in many rooms, but some doubles are cramped. Singles 1800ptas. Doubles 3000ptas, with bath 3500ptas.

Pensión Aris, C. Fontanella, 14 (tel. 318 10 17). Walk past the *Telefónica;* Aris is on the right. Ideal location, soundproofed by the 1 1/2 bl. between here and the Rambles. Spartan rooms need, and are getting, renovation. Aesthetics aside, it's a good price for the location. Singles 1400ptas. Doubles 2700ptas. Reservations with 1 night's deposit (postal code: 08010).

Pensión Guernia, Ronda Universitat, 29 (tel. 318 45 14). Metro: Universitat (L1). On the corner with C. Balmes. Paper fans on the walls plus paper balloons over the lights equals Far Eastern kitsch. Not quite on the level of *chinoiserie.* Only 7 bedrooms. 1500ptas per person. Showers 150ptas. Breakfast of coffee and bread 120ptas.

Pensión Santa Anna, C. Santa Anna, 23 (tel. 301 22 46), off the Rambles before Pl. Catalunya. High ceilings and spacious green rooms. Quiet-by-midnight rule. Singles 1700ptas. Doubles 3000ptas. Showers 200ptas. Reservations with 1 night's deposit.

Pensión Comtal, C. Comtal, 7 (tel. 302 42 44). Metro: Catalunya (L1, L3) or Uriquanaona (L1). One block from Fontanella on your right if you go down Laietana, or on your left if you go down Porta de L'Angel. Steep prices (for singles), but fans and heaters in the rooms assure a temperate stay. TV room with magazines. Singles 2500ptas. Doubles 3800ptas. Reservations with 1 night's deposit.

The Eixample

The most beautiful *hostales* are found here along wide, safe *avingudas*. Most have huge entryways with colorful tiles and steel and wood *Modernista* elevators.

Hostal Líder, Rambla Catalunya, 84 (tel. 215 19 23). Metro: Pg. Gràcia (L3, L4). Intersection with C. Mallorca is one of Barcelona's swankiest shopping areas. Sacrifice aesthetic delight to be the first one at the shops. Singles without showers 1700ptas. Doubles with showers 3200ptas.

Hostal-Residencia Oliva, Pg. Gràcia, 32, 4th floor (tel. 488 01 62), 1 handy block up the street from Metro: Pg. Gràcia (L4, L3). Above the Galas clothing store. Recently touched-up rooms in a courtly building. Sedate lounge with a long, polished wooden table encourages guests to write home or the great 20th-century novel; the statue of the *Fénix Español* across the street plays the muse. Some doubles are cramped. Singles 2000ptas. Doubles 4400ptas, with showers 5500ptas. Breakfast included. Reservations with 1 night's deposit (postal code: 08007).

Hostal-Residencia Palacios, Gran Via de les Corts Catalanes, 629bis (tel. 301 37 92). Metro: Pl. Catalunya (L1, L3, L5) or Urquinaona (L1, L4). Across from the main tourist office, its rooms are well-furnished, if a little dark. Singles 2100ptas, with showers 2440ptas, with bath 3710ptas. Doubles 3180ptas, with showers 4100ptas, with bath 4240ptas. Breakfast 250ptas.

Hostal-Residencia Windsor, Rambla Catalunya, 84 (tel. 215 11 98), above the Hostal Líder. This aristocratic place lives up to its name: crimson carpets, palatial quarters, and individually decorated rooms. Indeed. For the price, though, you might as well fly to England. Singles 2500ptas, with showers 3200ptas. Doubles 4500ptas, with showers 4900ptas, with bath 5500ptas. Reservations with 1 night's deposit (postal code: 08012).

Hostal-Residencia Montserrat, Pg. Gràcia, 114 (tel. 217 27 00). Metro: Diagonal (L3, L5, FFCC). Near Pl. Joan Carles I on the right side of Diagonal as you face Tibidabo. Stately reception area with large couches and color TV. Freshly painted bedrooms and older bathrooms. Singles with showers 2725ptas. Doubles with bath 4500ptas. Triples with bath 5850ptas. Breakfast 350ptas.

Gràcia

In Gràcia, an area five to 10 minutes by foot from Diagonal, families and travelers mingle in a relaxed, neighborhood setting. The *hostales* listed here are all small and elegant, and the quaint neighborhood bars and *pastelerías* remain "undiscovered." Stick around and you might even get a feeling for life in Barcelona.

Pensión San Medín, C. Gran de Gràcia, 125 (tel. 217 30 68), down the street from the Fontana (L3) Metro stops. The classiest rooms in the classiest area, well-carpeted and with huge windows, furniture, and a phone in each room. Singles 2000ptas, with bath 3000ptas. Doubles 3500ptas, with bath 4500ptas. Showers 200ptas.

Hostal Bonavista, C. Bonavista, 21 (tel. 237 37 57). Metro: Diagonal (L3, L5). Off the northern end of Pg. Gràcia—quiet, lush neighborhood. Well-kept rooms dotted with pictures of horses and old-fashioned cars. Singles 1600ptas. Doubles 2500ptas, with bath 3200ptas. Showers 300ptas.

Pensión Norma, Gran de Gràcia, 87 (tel. 237 44 78). Metro: Fontana (L3). So newly-renovated as to be austere. Rooms with life-size dressers and tables, but you can tell it's not your own room because a life-size house could never be this clean. Singles 2500ptas. Doubles 3500ptas.

Camping

While there is no camping in Barcelona, inter-city buses (150ptas) run to all the following locations in 20 to 45 minutes.

El Toro Bravo (tel. 637 34 62), just south of El Prat in Vildecans, accessible by bus L93 from Pl. Universitat or L90 from Pl. Goya. 450ptas per person and 500ptas per tent. **Filipinas** (tel. 658 28 95) at 450ptas per person and 500ptas per tent, and **La Ballena Alegre** (tel. 658 05 04) at 385ptas per person and 1750ptas per tent (open May 15-Sept. 30) are also 1st-class sites another km down the road.

Gavá, the town before Castelldefels south of Barcelona, has several campgrounds, all accessible by bus L90 from Pl. Universitat. **Albatros** (tel. 662 20 31) is a 1st-class campground on the beach. 405ptas per person, 490ptas per tent. Open May-Sept. **Tortuga Ligera** (tel. 662 12 29) is another 1st-class site on the beach. 475ptas per person, 550ptas per tent. Both sites are near the "Tortuga Ligera" bus stop. **Tres Estrellas** (tel. 662 11 16) is 2km closer to town, one stop past "Ballena Alegre". 570ptas per person, 600ptas per tent. Open April-Sept.

Camping Don Quixote (tel. 389 10 16), north of Barcelona. Take a RENFE local train from the Cercanías station. Get off at Monsolis, one stop past Mongat, about 15min. from the city. Third-class site near the beach. 420ptas per person and per tent. Open June 15-Sept. 15.

Food

Barcelona is a city where visitors and locals alike eat out; just about every block has four or five places to eat. They range from local bars with *tapas variadas* to luxurious restaurants that serve sorbet between courses. In the Eixample, *patisseries* and cafés offer expensively luscious treats under the shady trees. Closer to the port, bars and cafés are more crowded and more harried. The Barri Gòtic is plastered with 850-950ptas *menús*. Catalan specialities include *faves a la catalana* (lima beans with herbs), *butifarra con judias blancas* (sausage with white beans), and *escudella i carn d'olla* (a pork and chicken broth).

"La Boquería," officially the **Mercat de Sant Josep,** off Rambla Sant Josep, 89, is Barcelona's best market, with fresh fish and produce in an all-steel *Modernista* structure. The packed food stalls sell everything from dried fruit to pig's feet. (Open Mon.-Sat. 8am-2:30pm and 5-8pm.)

Be aware that food options shrink drastically in August, when restaurateurs and bar owners close up shop and take their vacations.

Barri Gòtic

You'll find oodles of *menús* for around 850ptas in the narrow and dark streets between the cathedral and the port. Carrer de Avinyò runs through the middle of the *barri*, between C. Ample and C. Ferran; it's called Carrer de les Gegants at its intersection with the latter. Metro: Liceu (L3) or Jaume I (L4).

Restaurante Bidasoa, C. Serra, 21. (tel. 318 10 63). Metro: Drassanes (L3). Take C. Josep Anselm Clavé off Pl. Portal de la Pau near the port and then your third left. This hidden treasure is buried in the maze-like streets of the Barri Gòtic. Glossy wooden tables and Catalan memorabilia on the walls complement some of the best local fare in town. Tremendously good fish. Full meals around 1000ptas. Wine 375ptas per liter. Open Sept.-July Tues.-Sun. 1-4pm and 8-11pm.

Restaurant Pitarra, C. Avinyò, 56 (tel. 301 16 47). Metro: Drassanes (L3). Turn left at the end of the Rambles down C. Clavé, which becomes C. Ample. C. Avinyó is the 3rd left after the church. Located in the former home of the great Catalan poet and founder of Catalan theatre Pitarra. The art lives on in epic dishes concocted by Señor Marc, former chef to Princess Sofia of Spain. Don't let the hauteur scare you off; the food is affordable, the presentation artful. The *escalopines ternera* (veal) is the most delicious 975ptas you can spend in Spain. *Paella* 1175ptas. *Vino de la casa* 750ptas. Meal for 2 about 3000ptas. Open Sept.-July Mon.-Sat. 1-4pm and 8-11:30pm.

Pakistani El Gallo Kirko, C. Avinyó, 19 (follow directions for Restaurant Pitarra). Built around part of the stone wall that the Romans erected around Barcelona in the 4th century, the PEGK specializes in *couscous,* curry, and spicy Pakistani food. Full meal will cost 500-1500ptas, but individual dishes are quite inexpensive, such as *arroz con pollo* (chicken and rice, 350ptas).

Els Quatre Gats, C. Montsió, 3-5 (tel. 302 41 40). Metro: Urquinaona (L1). From the metro walk down Via Laietana and take the 2nd right after the Palau de la Musica. The hangout of Picasso and other Lost Generation artists and intellectuals still maintains the same decor, with their works adorning the walls. *Menú* 1500ptas. Open Mon.-Sat. 1-4pm and 8-11:30pm.

Restaurante Self-Naturista, C. Santa Anna, 11-13 (tel. 302 21 30). Metro: Catalunya (L1, L3). Handsome variety of complete proteins at a self-service vegetarian cafeteria. Wholesome meatless *paella* (285ptas) and *albergina al forn* (baked eggplant, 210ptas). Natural *tartas* (cakes) 210ptas. Open Mon.-Sat. noon-10pm; count on a line from 2-3pm.

Can Conesa, C. Llibreteria, 1 (tel. 315 33 09), on the corner of Pl. Sant Jaume. This little nook distinguishes itself from myriad other sandwich shops with ultra-low prices and trademark crispy grilled *bocadillos* and *sobrassada* (ground sausage). Beer 95ptas per 1/3liter. Open Mon.-Sat. 8am-9:30pm.

Al Primer Crit, Banys Vells, 2 (tel. 319 99 33). Metro: Jaume I (L4). From Museo Picasso, follow C. Barra de Ferro off C. Montcada and take the 1st left. A zippy duplex that pipes cool jazz and dishes fresh market food. Exquisite homemade cakes 375ptas. Open Sept.-July Tues.-Sun. 8:30pm-midnight.

Restaurante Cafeteria Nervión, C. Princesa, 2 (tel. 315 21 03). Metro: Jaume I (L4). Right on the corner of Princesa and Via Laietana at Pl. L'Angel. Casual and inexpensive. Filling 2-course *menú* with bread, wine, and dessert for 675ptas, along with a slew of affordable *platos combinados* and breakfast. Open Sept.-July Mon.-Sat. 6-10am and 11am-10pm.

Restaurant Agut, C. Gignás, 16 (tel. 315 17 09), off C. Avinyò in the heart of the old town. A traditional Catalan meal under oil paintings that starving artists bartered for food. The menu changes weekly; dishes start at 650ptas. House wine 385ptas per liter. Open Aug.-June Mon.-Sat. 1:30-4:15pm and 9pm-midnight.

Restaurante Porto Mar, C. Josep Anselm Clavé, 19 (tel. 301 82 27). Metro: Drassanes (L3). At the port end of the Rambles turn left onto Clavé. Porto Mar is 2 blocks down on the left. Near the sea, named for the sea, decorated with boats, but not strictly seafood. Chicken and fish dishes. Ever-changing 2-course *menú* with bread, wine, and dessert 800ptas. Mon.-Sat. 1-5pm and 8-11pm.

Los Pergaminos, C. Ample, 19 (tel. 302 20 29). Metro: Drassanes (L3). Walk to the port end of the Rambles and turn left on C. Josep Anselm Clavé (which becomes C. Ample). A varying 850ptas 2-course *ménu* with bread, wine, and dessert packs the locals in for lunch. Open 1-5pm and 8pm midnight.

Between the Rambles and Ronda de Sant Antoni

Students and workers cluster here at lunch. The area around C. Talleres and Sitges, just one block off Rambla de les Canaletes, overflows with inexpensive places to eat, some of which advertise specials on chalkboards outside. Good Galician food is served off C. Luna and C. Joaquím Costa. Barri Xinès, the red-light district, begins roughly below C. Hospital.

Restaurante Riera, C. Joaquím Costa, 30 (tel. 242 50 58). Metro: Universitat (L1). Off Ronda de Sant Antoni near Pl. Universitat. The Riera family supplies a top-notch rudimentary feast. Showerstall blue tiles, shiny paint, and flocks of gregarious regulars. Meals change daily but a heaping plate of *paella* is always lurking around. 3-course meal with drink and homemade flan 550ptas. Open Sept.-July Sun.-Fri. 1-4pm and 8:30-11pm.

Restaurante Biocenter, C. Pintor Fortuny, 24 (tel. 302 35 67). Metro: Liceu (L3). Behind the store of the same name off the Rambles. It sounds threateningly holistic, but this terrific vegetarian restaurant is small and friendly. Even devout carnivores cherish their well-stocked salad bar (450ptas). The *plato combinado* (600ptas) entitles you to a small portion of any dish plus a trip to the buffet. Open Mon.-Sat. 1-4:30pm; extremely crowded after 2pm.

Restaurante Club Taurino, C. Xuclà, 5 (tel. 302 40 32). Metro: Catalunya (L1, L3), on a dark, narrow street between C. Fortuny and C. Carme, both off the Rambles. The Biocenter's alter ego, dedicated to bullfighters, whose pictures plaster the walls. Cheap *menú* 650ptas. Open Sun.-Fri. 1-4pm and 8:30-11pm.

Raim D'or Can Maxim, C. Bonsuccés, 8 (tel. 302 02 34). Metro: Catalunya (L1, L3). Take the 2nd right off Rambla Canaletas from metro station. Seats scarce among diners eating the 800ptas lunch *menú,* which includes tangy *gazpacho* or *pescadillos* (little fish fried in olive oil). Pizza is also popular. Open Oct.-Aug. Mon.-Sat. 1-4pm and 8-11pm.

Restaurante Xaloc, C. Sitjas, 6 (tel. 302 74 69). Metro: Catalunya (L1, L3). From the metro walk down the Rambles and take the 1st right onto C. Tallers, then the 1st left onto C. Sitjas. An upscale office worker's retreat with a vast array of entrees (400-1500ptas), a 900ptas *menú,* and mouth-watering desserts. Open Sept.-July, Mon.-Sat. 1-4pm and 8:30-11pm.

Restaurante Nuria, Rambles, 133 (tel. 317 43 77). Metro: Catalunya (L1, L3). Two doors down from Burger King at the upper end of the Rambles. Have it your way: *platos combinados* (600-1500ptas) in the sedate upstairs restaurant, or deli-style sandwiches (300-600ptas) and a bar in the rowdier downstairs. Restaurant open Mon.-Sat. 1-4pm and 8-11pm. Deli and bar open Mon.-Sat. 8am-1pm and 8pm-1am.

El Pollo Campero, C. Nov de la Rambla, 46. Metro: Liceu (L3), off the Rambles. A small, unassuming, touristless place almost sacrilegous to include in a guidebook. Your taste buds, stomach, and wallet won't care that it's not much to look at. 2-course *menú* with wine, bread, and dessert merely 550ptas. Luscious *paella* and *carne.* Open Mon.-Sat. 1-4pm and 8-10:30pm.

Restaurante Egipte, C. Jerusalem, 3 (tel. 317 74 80). Metro: Liceu (L3). From the metro walk up the Rambles past the Palau de la Virreina and turn left onto C. Carme; C. Jerusalem will be the 2nd left. Nothing Egyptian at all about the classic Spanish *menú* (2 courses with bread, wine and dessert, 895ptas). Open Sept.-July Mon.-Sat. 1-4pm and 8-10:30pm.

Restaurant Super Pollo a l'Ast, C. Santa Pau, 100 (tel. 242 44 79). Metro: Paral-lel (L3). In front of Església Sant Pau del Camp. It's hard to find; follow the barbeque scent. Not for the squeamish; spicy roasted chicken broils on spits outside. 1/2-chicken 500ptas. *Pollo al ajillo* (1/4-chicken roasted in garlic) 350ptas. Mixed salad 175ptas. 1/3liter of beer or soda 100ptas. Open Oct.-Aug. Wed.-Mon. 9am-11pm.

Bar Muy Buenas, C. Carme, 63 (tel. 242 50 53). Metro: Liceu (L3). Off Rambla Sant Josep near the market. *Faux* Gaudí undulating wood and stained glass welcome you into this otherwise old-fashioned and very good bar. *Platos* 500-1100ptas. Two-course *menú* 800ptas. Open Sept.-July Mon.-Sat. 8am-9pm.

The Eixample

The chi-chi aura is ever so soothing, although the restaurants tend to be pricier than those in the old quarter. Metro: Pg. Gràcia (L3, L4) or Diagonal (L3, L5).

Restaurant Les Corts Catalanes, Gran Via de les Corts Catalanes, 603 (tel. 301 03 76). Metro: Catalunya (L1, L3), just off Rambla Catalunya. Earthy-crunchy vegetarian staples such as *tarta de espinicas con guarnición* (savory spinach cake) and *zumo de zanahorias* (carrot juice). Salads 500-875ptas. Most pastas around 1000ptas. Desserts such as sweet spinach cake around 425ptas. Healthy eating don't come cheap. Mon.-Fri. 9am-11:30pm.

Bar-Restaurante Can Segarra, Ronda Sant Antoni, 102 (tel. 302 44 22). Metro: Universitat (L1). Next to Pl. Universitat. Sensational food in a small, informal dining hall up the stairs. Filling 750ptas lunch. *Gazpacho* 475ptas. Open Dec.-Oct. Fri.-Wed. 1-4pm and 8-11pm.

Buffet Comida, Gran Via de les Cortes Catalanes, 609 (tel. 301 33 99). Metro: Catalunya (L1, L3). Between Rambla Catalunya and Pg. Gràcia. Gorge at this all-you-can-eat buffet for 1800ptas (Sat.-Sun. 2000ptas). Open Mon.-Thurs. 1-3:30pm, Fri.-Sun. 1-3:30pm and 8:30-10:30pm.

Pizzería Argentina El Ceibo, C. Mallorca, 279. Metro: Diagonal (L3, L5) or Pg. Gràcia (L3, L4). 1 block from Pg. Gràcia. Outdoor tables in summer. South American specialties such as *empanadas* (meat turnovers) 135ptas. Assorted pizzas 600ptas. Open Sept.-July Mon.-Sat. 1-4pm and 8-11pm.

Charcuterìa L. Simò, Pg. Gràcia, 46 (tel. 216 03 39). Metro: Pg. Gràcia (L3, L4). On the right side as you walk up the street from the Metro. This air-conditioned gourmet eatery fuels Armani-clad clientele at the horseshoe-shaped bar. Culinary options are displayed in the window. Meat dishes about 700ptas. Salads and casseroles 400ptas per *ración* (portion). Open 8am-8pm.

Gràcia and Nearby Neighborhoods

You know you're in Gràcia when you hear fellow diners speaking Catalan, instead of Spanish, English, French, or German. The food is likewise authentic.

Can Suñé, C. Mozart, 20 (tel. 218 54 86). Metro: Diagonal (L3, L5). Take C. Goya off C. Gran de Gràcia, and then take the 2nd right. A petite family-run place with marble tables and ceiling fans. Neighbors gather to spin yarns and eat a different meal each day (including wine and dessert, 750ptas). *Paella* served Thurs. and Sun. Open 1-4pm and 8:30-11pm.

El Glop, C. Sant Lluís, 24 (tel. 213 70 58). Near the Joanic metro stop (L4) off C. Escorial. The 2-story rustic tavern specializes in *Asado de Tira* (lamb ribs, 725ptas) and other Catalan favorites such as *carne de cerdo* (sliced pork) cooked over an open flame. Try the *torrades* (big slices of toasted Catalan bread with tomatoes and cheese or sausage, 125-450ptas). Widely celebrated and always crowded. After 10pm, the wait may top 30 min. Open Sept.-July Tues.-Sun. 1-4pm and 8pm-midnight.

La Ceba/La Perla, C. La Perla, 10. Metro: Fontana (L3). Down the street from El Glop (C. La Perla becomes C. Sant Lluís as you head towards Joanic), in the direction of Fontana. An elegant little restaurant which specializes in *truiterias* (Catalan for tortillas)—36 kinds at last count—and ice cream desserts. Open Mon.-Sat. 1-4pm and 8:30-11:30pm.

Restaurante Pas de la Virreina, C. Torrijos, 53 (tel. 237 51 09). Metro: Fontana (L3), then take C. Asturias off C. Gran de Gràcia, follow it to its end and turn right. Good Catalan cuisine in a crepuscular basement restaurant. Unwind with the 3-course lunch special (850ptas). Open Oct.-Aug. 1-4pm and 9pm-midnight.

La Crêperie Bretonne, C. Balmes, 274 (tel. 217 30 48). FFCC: Pl. Molina, outside of Gràcia by about 5 blocks, next to Pl. Molina. Over 50 types of crêpes served in a French-style café (chocolate 350ptas, cheese 200ptas). Beer 200ptas. Open Sept.-July Tues.-Sun. 6pm-2am.

Sights

During the summer (June 13-Sept. 27) the easiest way to take in the major sights of Barcelona is to hop on the **Transports Turistics Barcelona,** sponsored by the city's Patronat de Turisme. (For fare and schedule information see **Tourist Bus** under Getting Around. Ajuntament tourist offices have a free pamphlet that maps out the bus route.) The bus stops 15 times, looping among all of the city's major attractions. The tourist offices have a wealth of information and pamphlets. *Barcelona: One and Only* is a *barrio* by *barrio* description of the city; *El Barcelonés* is the Reader's Digest version. For a thematic look, peruse *Discovering Romanesque Art in Catalonia, Routes of Gothic Art in Catalonia,* or *Discovering Modernist Art in Catalonia. Barcelona: Urban Spaces* is downright strategic in its layout of various walking itineraries. And don't leave the office without the Ajuntament's large map of the city, which lists all the museums and Gaudís in Barcelona.

Las Rambles

Dubbed "the most beautiful street in the world" by W. Somerset Maugham, this tree-lined boulevard runs from Pl. Catalunya to the Monument de Colom at the port. Actually made up of five distinct segments, its broad pedestrian lane is a bundle of urban nerves: street performers swallow knives, fortune-tellers survey palms, beggers hold out their hands, tourists fiddle with their fanny packs, old men lean on their canes, and policemen pretend they know what's going on. The superstitious and the sentimental gather around **Font de Canaletes** at the top of the Rambles near Pl. Catalunya. A drink from this elegant fountain insures you'll return to Barcelona at least once in your life.

About halfway down the Rambles towards the port, you'll see the **Gran Teatre del Liceu**, the Rambles, 61 (tel. 318 91 22), on your right. On opening night here in 1892, an anarchist launched two bombs from the upper balcony into the crowd of aristocrats, killing 22 and wounding many more. After executing five others for the crime, authorities finally found the real culprit, who cried *"Viva la anarquía"* before being hanged. Tours of the colossal neo-Baroque opera hall, which is undergoing considerable expansion, Monday or Friday from September through June. (Tours at 11:30am and 12:15pm. Admission 250ptas.) The *teatre* is one of Europe's leading stages, having nurtured the likes of José Carreras. Inexpensive seats or standing room for performances sometimes cost as little as 750ptas.

At the far end of C. Sant Pau stands Barcelona's oldest Romanesque church, the 10th-century **Església de Sant Pau,** once attached to a Benedictine monastery. The church is noted for the capitals of the entrance, the carved tympanum, and particularly the ornate **cloister** with lobed arches, dating from the 11th and 12th centuries. (No regular hours, but there's usually someone next door at C. Sant Pau, 101, Mon.-Fri. 6-8pm.)

The area to the right of Rambla Santa Mónica and Rambla de Caputxins (facing the port) is known as the **Barri Xinés,** or Barrio Chino, Barcelona's red-light district. **Plaça Reial,** to the left off Rambla de Caputxins, continues to draw naive tourists. Watch the architecture and palm trees as well as your bags, cameras, and valuables. Avoid the plaza at night. The ideal time to visit is Sunday from 10am to 2pm, when the stands of stamp collectors stud the porticoes.

At the port end of the Rambles the **Monument de Colom,** erected in 1886, towers over the city. Spotlights turn it into a firebrand at night. (Elevator to the top open 9am-9pm; Oct.-June 23 Tues.-Sat. 10am-2pm and 3:30-6:30pm, Sun. 10am-7pm. Admission 175ptas. Ticket office open until 1/2hr. before closing.) The **Museu Marítim** is nearby on Pl. Porta de la Pau, 1 (see Museums).

Barcelona's drive to recover and refurbish its seafront has not only resulted in Vila Olímpica, but also in **Moll de la Fusta,** which lies between Pg. Colom and the water. By shoving the coastal road underground, the city was able to open a wide new pedestrian zone that leads down to the docks past five new, scenic, and pricey restaurant-cafés. The cobblestone docks are ideal for a slow evening *passeig.*

You can ride westward on the small ferry **Las Golondrinas** through Barcelona's busy harbor, past a beautiful view of Montjüic to the isolated peninsula at the breakwater. (July-Sept. 11am-9pm; Oct. and April-June Mon.-Fri. 11am-6pm, Sat.-Sun. 11am-7pm; Nov.-March Mon.-Fri. 11am-5pm, Sat.-Sun. 11am-6pm. Every 1/2hr. Round-trip 300ptas.)

Barri Gòtic

Strictly speaking, the **Barri Gòtic** (Gothic Quarter) is the area surrounding the cathedral, the Ajuntament, and the Generalitat, but the name also extends to the area between the Rambles and Via Laietana. While streets such as **Carrer de la Pietat** and **Carrer del Paradís** have managed to preserve their medieval charm, cheap *pensiones,* souvenir stands, and bars swamp much of the area. The intrusion of modernity, however, gives the area a liveliness—and a livelihood—it would otherwise lack.

Since Roman times, the handsome **Plaça de Sant Jaume** has been the city's main square. It took its present form in 1823 and is dominated by two of Catalunya's most important buildings: the **Palau de la Generalitat** (seat of Catalan's autonomous government) and the **Ajuntament** (tourist information and lost and found also here).

The Gothic **Església Catedral de la Santa Creu** is on C. Bisbe next to the Generalitat (look for its high-flying jagged spires) and the smallish **Plaça de la Seu.** Charles Galtés designed the façade in the 15th century, almost 200 years after the first stone was set; Josep Mestres didn't finish the *església* until 400 years later (haste makes waste). The coats of arms painted on Pere Ca Anglada's elegant upper pews mark the gathering of the Knights of the Golden Fleece at Carlos V's summons in 1519. The marble choir screen in the chancel illustrates the death of Barcelona's patron saint and martyr, St. Eulália. Nowadays, St. Eulália spends her time in a 14th-century alabaster sarcophagus in the church crypt. The cathedral's **claustre** is one of the most beautiful sights in Barcelona. Magnolias grow in the middle, and fat white geese waddle around inside the iron fences. The petite **museu** (tel. 315 35 55) off the cloister houses religious treasures and the 15th-century *La Pietat,* painted by Bartolomé Bermejo. (Cathedral open 7:45am-1:30pm and 4-7:45pm. Cloister open 8:45am-1:30pm and 4-7pm. Museum open 11am-1pm. Admission 25ptas. Ask a guard to let you see the *coro* for 25ptas.)

On the opposite side of the Cathedral, on C. Comtes, is the **Palau Reial** (Royal Palace) of the counts of Barcelona, then of the kings of Aragón. Inside, the **Museu Frederic Marés** and **Museu d'Historia de la Ciutat** (see Museums) hold court. (Chambers of the royal palace open Tues.-Sat. 9am-8:30pm, Sun. 9am-1:30pm, Mon. 3:30-8pm. Admission 250ptas.)

Also on C. Comtes, the distinguished late Gothic **Palau del Lloctinent** (Lieutenant's Palace) has a Renaissance-influenced courtyard and fountain. The **Arxiu de la Corona d'Aragó** (Archives of the Kingdom of Aragón), one of the major repositories of medieval documents in the world, molders inside the palace. Behind it looms an imposing ensemble of buildings that form **Plaça del Rei.** The square's landmark is the Renaissance tower, wherein a rebellious peasant tried to assassinate King Ferran el Catòlic.

Barri de la Ribera

Turn-of-the-century urban planners separated this vivacious and venerated part of the old city from the Barri Gòtic proper when they built the Via Laietana in 1907. The area grew with Barcelona's development as a major sea power during the Middle Ages. With its horizontal lines, octagonal towers, and large, unadorned surfaces, the **Església Santa María del Mar** on Pl. Santa María is perhaps the zenith of 14th-century Catalan Gothic design. Entrance around back on Pg. Born. (Open 10am-12:30pm and 5-7:30pm, occasionally closed Sun. for concert preparations.)

Secular architecture is also well-represented by the monumental palaces on **Carrer de Montcada,** which begins around the back of the *església.* This style is noted for its plain facades, small courtyards, stairways supported by arches, and, here and there, delicately arcaded galleries. Especially interesting is **Palau Berenguer d'Agüilar** at #15. Its elegant courtyard is so akin to that of the Palau de la Generalitat that both have been attributed to the same architect. This same palace is also one of Barcelona's greatest tourist attractions for its **Museu Picasso** (see Museums). The **Museu Tèxtil i d'Indumentària** is across the street (see Museums). About a 15-minute walk from the museum up Via Laietana is the famed *Els Quatre Gats,* a café where Picasso and other fin-de-siècle artists and intellectuals hung out. (See Food.)

Nearby soars the **Palau de la Música Catalana** (tel. 268 10 00), designed by *Modernisto* Lluís Domènich i Montaner. Completed in 1908, the music hall is festooned with stained-glass cupolas, flowing marble reliefs, intricate woodwork, and dazzlingly colorful ceramic mosaics on the ceilings, walls, and floors. The palace is located at Sant Francesc de Paula, 2, just off of the intersection of Via Laietana and C. Jonqueres. (Open to the public by appointment only; call ahead. English spoken.)

Parc de la Ciutadella and Vila Olímpica

Fierce fighting and damage to the city convinced Felipe V to construct a large citadel in 1716 on what is now Pg. Picasso. Citizens left homeless by the fires that ravaged Barcelona relocated here, and the fortress became a symbol of the Bourbon king's strict treatment of Catalan insurgents. The peaceful promenades of **Parc de la Ciutadella** replaced the fortress after it was razed in 1868. The park hosted the 1888 Universal Exposition; it now harbors several museums and a zoo. EXPO '88 also bore the **Arc de Triomf,** just across Pg. Pujades from the park. The surrounding tree-lined plaza is used today by elderly locals who sip *café* and play *bocce.* Little Snowflake (*Copito de Nieve*), the only captive albino gorilla in the world, is the main attraction at the **Parc Zoològic** (tel. 309 25 00), south of the Plaça d'Armes. Dolphin and whale shows too. (Open 9:30am-7:30pm. Admission 700ptas.) On Pl. Armes is Barcelona's **Museu d'Art Modern** (see Museums).

On the northwest side of the zoo is the site of the Vila Olimpica, which housed 15,000 athletes for the 25th edition of the Summer Games. The village also contained several public parks, a shopping center, offices, strategically placed monumental buildings, a ring road connecting the East and West ends of the city, and a new dock from which the Olympic yachting races were won. Since the games packed up and moved off to Atlanta, Barcelona yuppies have begun to invade the neighborhood, which is known as **La Nova Icaria**. Perhaps the most radical transformation of Barcelona occasioned by the Olympics, the village—designed by over 20 leading Catalan architectural studios—has opened the city to 5km of the seafront (once covered by railroad tracks and warehouses) and correct its tendency to grow west (with its back to the sea).

The Eixample

The 1859 demolition of Barcelona's medieval walls symbolically ushered in a *Renaixença* (Renaissance) of Catalan culture. Hausmann-wannabe Ildefon Cerdà's design for a new Barcelona, *Pla de Reforma i Eixample* (plan for renovation and broadening), evinces a typically 19th-century notion of modernity. An aerial view of the Eixample area shows a regular grid of squares softened by the cropped corners of streets, which form octagonal intersections. Meanwhile, the flourishing bourgeoisie commissioned a new wave of architects to build their houses, reshaping the face of the Eixample with *Modernismo*. The best way to approach this macro-museum of Catalan architecture is with two handy-dandy guides available free at the tourist office. *Discovering Modernist Art in Catalonia* offers a cogent 24-page look at the main buildings. *Gaudí* is more a pamphlet than a guide, describing nine of the master's masterpieces.

Antoni Gaudí (1852-1926) led the Modernists with his curving, organic surfaces and blurring of artist and artisan. Nature served as the model for his floral motifs and undulating surfaces, but it was new technology that made sheet iron and concrete usable on a large scale. This combination spawned the outlandish-yet-structurally-sound contours of his buildings. Predating Frank Lloyd Wright's unified design approach, Gaudí designed every last detail of his works, including the furniture, lighting fixtures, decorative mosaics, and iron grillwork. His methods were unconventional: he fashioned some buildings by first making a small-scale model, turning it upside down, and then hanging sand bags from key stress points for balance. Gaudí's distinctive use of elaborate ornamentation and rich color make his work recognizable at a glance; his incomparable genius transcends the *Modernismo* tag. Fellow luminaries include Luis Domènech i Montaner, noted for his profusely decorated surfaces; and José Puig y Cadafalch, who developed an antiquarian style mingling local and foreign traditions.

Many modernist buffs argue that the **Casa Milà** apartment building (popularly known as **La Pedrera**—Stone Quarry), Pg. Gràcia, 92 (tel. 215 33 68), is Gaudí's masterpiece. The entrance to this buckling mass of rock is around the corner on C. Provença. Note the intricate ironwork around the balconies and the diversity of the front gate's egg-shaped window panes. The roof sprouts chimneys that resemble odd geological formations. Rooftop tours give a closer look at the *cascs prusians* (Prussian helmets), spiral chimneys inspired by the helmets worn in Wagner's operas. The arches are not structural; they point to other Gaudí buildings. (Rooftop tours Mon.-Fri. at 10am, 11am, noon, 4pm, and 5pm, Sat. at 10am, 11am, and noon; 1st and 3rd Sun. of the month at 11am and noon. Free.)

Gaudí's magnum opus, his life's work, is the **Temple Expiatori de la Sagrada Família**, on C. Marina between C. Mallorca and C. Provença (Metro: Sagrada Familia, L5). Gaudí seized another architect's neo-Gothic plans for the church and made it look like no other building on the face of the earth. For 43 years Gaudí obsessed over the Sagrada Familia, living in a small room here for his last 11 (he was killed by a trolley in 1925). He estimated the project would take at least 200 years to finish. The church's three proposed facades symbolize Jesus's nativity, passion, and glory; only the first is finished. Take the elevator or walk up the stairs to wander among the towers, bridges, and crannies of the facade. Since 1926, construction has progressed erratically, with the latest bout (since 1979) of activity along the side toward C. Mallorca. A furor has arisen over recent additions, such as the streamlined pyramid arch on C. Sardenya, that some say don't flow with the rest of the structure. In the museum is a model of the completed structure and various artifacts relating to the constructions. (Open 8am-9pm; off-season 8am-7pm. Admission to church, museum included, 400ptas.)

For a quick glimpse of buildings from the peak of *Modernismo,* check out the odd-numbered side of Pg. de Gràcia (called *la manzana de la discordia*—city block of discord), between C. de Aragò and Consell de Cent. The bottom two floors of the facade of **Casa Lleó i Morera** (1905; tel. 215 44 77), by Domènech i Montaner, were destroyed to house a store, but the upper floors sprout flowers, and winged monsters snarl on the balconies. Puig i Cadafalch opted for a cubical pattern on the facade of **Casa Amatller** (1900) at #41. Gaudí's balconies undulate and the tiles sparkle on #43, **Casa Batlló**. To see the interior, you need a letter of permission from Cátedra Gaudí, Av. Pedralbes, 7 (tel. 204 52 50; open Mon.-Fri. 8am-2pm). Then you may enter the *casa principal* (main apartment), where bent and swollen wood doors and the mushroom-shaped arch in front of the main fireplace make you think you're in a German Expressionist film. The conference room ceiling is a magnificent twirl of plaster that resembles an immense snail shell. Visits are permitted from 8 to 10am; no permission is required to peek into the building's entrance. **Fundació Antoni Tàpies** is just around the corner from *la manzana de la discordia* and the **Museu de la Música** is nearby on Av. Diagonal, 373 (see Museums).

Although the Eixample has become the city's financial hub, its tree-lined boulevards are still ideal for a slow evening stroll. **Gran Via de les Corts Catalanes** and the **Rambla de Catalunya** are filled with outdoor cafés and restaurants.

Montjuïc

Throughout Barcelona's history, whoever controlled this strategically located mountain ("hill of the Jews") ruled the city. Over the centuries, dozens of despotic rulers have modified the **fortress** built on top of the ancient Jewish cemetery at Montjuïc. Felipe IV's troops overcame rebelling citizens here in the 1640s, Felipe V snatched it away from the Catalans in 1714, and in this century Franco made it one of his local interrogation headquarters. Somewhere deep in the recesses of the structure, his *ben-eméritos* ("honorable ones," a.k.a. the Guardia Civil) shot Catalunya's former president, Lluís Companys, in 1941. Only in 1960 did Franco return the fortress to the city for recreational purposes. This act was commemorated with a huge stone monument expressing Barcelona's thanks; the reminder of forced gratitude is still visible from the castle battlements. To get to Parc de Montjuïc, go first to Pl. Espanya (Metro: L1, L3), then take bus #61, which comes every 10 minutes and stops at various points on the mountain. The walk up, along Av. Reina María Cristina, is direct but lengthy.

The **Fonts Luminoses** (Illuminated Fountains), dominated by the huge central *font mágica* (magic fountain), are visible from Pl. Espanya up Av. Reina María Cristina. The fountains are especially enchanting when light, water, and music blend in an hour-long sensory extravaganza. (Illuminated Thurs., Sat., and Sun. 9pm-midnight, music show at 10pm; mid-Sept. to May Sat.-Sun. 8-11pm, music show at 9pm.) The **Museu d'Art de Catalunya** is housed in the stately **Palau Nacional** (see Museums).

Following Av. Marqués de Comillas from the base of the fountains, you'll discover the recently reconstructed **Pavelló Mies van der Rohe,** designed by the German architect for his country's 1929 EXPO pavilion. Its simple lines and building materials (marble, onyx, chrome, glass, and water) were the talk of the show. (Open 8am-8pm; Sept. 25-June 23 8am-midnight.) Just across the hillside is **Poble Espanyol,** Barcelona's attempt to dissuade you from visiting the rest of Spain. Also built for the '29 EXPO, the "town" features replicas of famous buildings and sites from every Spanish region: a Plaza Mayor (with a self-service cafeteria), a Calle de la Conquista, a Plazuela de la Iglesia, and so on. Prices here are high, but think of all the travel money it saves, and you won't get another chance in Barcelona to see glassblowers and potters plying their trades. Studded with happening bars and clubs, it's also a favorite nighttime spot. (Open Mon. 9am-8pm, Tues.-Wed., and Sun. 9am-2am, Fri.-Sat. 9am-6am. Craftspeople close shop an hour early. Admission 600ptas; year-round pass 1200ptas.)

The stately **Palau Nacional** and **Museu d'Art de Catalunya** (see Museums) are closed for renovations. Meanwhile, the **Jardì Botánic,** behind the Palau Nacional, nurtures a variety of exotic plants. (Open Mon.-Sat. 9am-2pm and 3-7pm.) Up the road are the **Jardins Joan Maragall,** weedy with sculpture. (Open Sun. 10am-2pm.)

In 1929 Barcelona inaugurated the **Estadi Olímpic de Montjuïc** in its bid for the 1932 Olympic games. Over 50 years later, Catalan architects Federic Correa and Alfons Milá—who were also responsible for the overall design of the **Anella Olímpica** (Olympic Ring) esplanade—and Italian Vittorio Gregotti renovated the shell and lowered the playing field in order to maximize seating. Designed by Japanese architect Arata Isozaki, the **Palau d'Esports Sant Jordi** is the most technologically sophisticated of the Olympic structures. The dome resembles a slightly asymmetrical tortoise shell over a square base. The 17,000-seat arena blends in with the sloping hillsides of Montjüic, while the undulating outer fringes allude to *Modernista* architecture. About 100m down the road from the Olympic stadium is the **Fundació Miró** (see Museums).

Parc del Migdia, on the opposite side of the Olympic Ring from the Palau Nacional, is remote and peaceful, with a long view of the sea nibbling at the plains south of Barcelona. A team of architects, landscapists, botanists, and horticulturalists were hired in 1989 to design a new **Jardí Botànic** respectful of the mountain's topography on the southern slopes of Montjüic. The **Museu Arqueològic** is on the far side of the mountain (see Museums).

Further along Pg. Miramar, where the park comes nearest to getting wet, there's a popular amusement park. From the Fundació Miró, walk down Av. Miramar and take the *teleferic* (cable car) halfway up. (Open 11:30am-9pm; off-season Fri.-Sun. 11:30am-2:45pm and 4-7:30pm. Fare 250ptas, either halfway or all the way up.) If you come from Barcelona, ride the funicular (tel. 412 00 00; fare 150ptas) from Pl. Raquel Meller (Metro: Paral-lel (L3)) to Av. Miramar, where you can hop on the *teleferic*. The **Parc d'Atraccions** (tel. 241 70 24), C. Montjüic at the cable car's mid-station, amuses with every sort of ride, including bumper cars, a roller coaster, and a ferris wheel. (Open June 21-Sept. 14 Mon.-Thurs. 6pm-midnight, Fri.-Sat. 6pm-2am, Sun. noon-midnight; Sept. 15-March Sat.-Sun. noon-8pm; April-June 20 Sat.-Sun. noon-10pm.) Uphill the historically rich **castell** guards the **Museu Militar** (see Museums).

Gràcia

Barcelona swallowed Gràcia during the construction of the Eixample. Somehow the strong-minded area northwest of the Eixample was blissfully unaffected by Cerdà's street-widening and creation of open courtyards. Its narrow alleys and numerous plazas charm even as they confuse. The **Torre del Reloj** (Clocktower) on popular **Plaça Rius i Taulet** is a symbol of the Revolution of 1868. **Plaça del Diamant,** on nearby C. Astúries, is a poetic landmark made famous by Mercé Rodoreda's eponymous novel. At night local youths swarm to **Plaça del Sol** and the cafés and bars that skirt the edge of it.

Modernismo brushed across Gràcia, as you'll see at #13 and #15 Carrer Astúries. One of Gaudí's youthful experiments, **Casa Vicens,** stands at C. Carolines, 24-26. The house incorporates audacious variations on Islamic motifs. To get to Gràcia, take the metro to Fontana (L3).

Park Güell

This park (spelled in the English fashion because it was partly modeled on the English garden) was conceived as a garden city for 60 houses with a splendid view of the city and sea. Gaudí designed the roads and walls of the park, along with service buildings. His five-point plan includes an avenue, a promenade, a great square, two roads for vehicles, and various pedestrian walks. Although Gaudí started it in 1900, the park was not completed till after his death. Inside, an elegant white staircase, lined with patterned tiles and a frightening multicolored salamander, leads to a pavilion supported by 86 pillars. In the back of the park, sweeping elevated paths, supported by columns shaped like palm trees, swerve through large hedges and prehistoric plants. The **Casa-Museu Gaudí** is here (see Museums). The park is near Pl. Lesseps on C. Olot; take bus #24 from Pg. Gràcia or the metro to Lesseps (L3) and walk down Travessera de Dalt for about 1/2km and turn left up C. Llamard. (Park open May-Aug. 10am-9pm; April and Sept. 10am-8pm; March and Oct. 10am-7pm; Nov.-Feb. 10am-6pm. Free.)

Sarrià

Sarrià is the home of Barcelona's old money. In the 19th century wealthy families came here to summer in their graceful villas. Nowadays, Sarrià's well-to-do residents still talk about "going down to Barcelona." Sarrià was the last *barrio* to lose its independence and merge into Barcelona in 1921. A walk through the shady, peaceful streets reveals elegant mansions with manicured gardens, and a host of exclusive Modernist *colegios* (private schools).

Gaudí designed one of these schools, the **Colegio-Convento de Santa Teresa,** C. Ganduxer, 85, in the 1880s. The brick facade is composed of high windows elongated by rows of distinctive parabolic arches. Inside, arched corridors flank the courtyard.

The villa of **Bellesguard,** at C. Bellesguard, 46, is a good example of Gaudí's creative interpretation of Gothic Revival. The walls surrounding the villa used to belong to the royal summer residence of Margarita de Prades, wife of Martin I, King of Aragón. The **Finca Güell,** on Av. Pedralbes, 7, near Pg. Tilos and Pg. Manuel Girona, has an iron gate encrusted with a Gaudí dragon.

Off Pg. Bonanova, the **Planetarium Barcelona,** C. Escoles Pies, 103 (tel. 418 45 12), focuses on the stars. To reach the planetarium, take bus #22 from Pg. Gràcia or bus #64 from C. Aribau near the university. (Temporarily closed for renovations.)

Early this century, the city of Barcelona built a summer residence for King Alfonso XIII. **Palau Reial de Pedralbes,** Av. Diagonal, 686 (tel. 280 16 21), was modeled on Italian Renaissance *palazzi* and set in an ample garden. (Open Tues.-Sun. 10am-2pm. Admission 250ptas. Metro: Palau Reial, L3.)

The **Monestir de Pedralbes,** Baixada del Monestir, 9 (tel. 204 25 45), at the end of Pg. Reina Elisenda, has a Catalan Gothic single-aisle church and 14th-century three-story cloister. The artistic highwater is in the Capella Sant Miquel, where murals by Ferrer Bassa depict Mary's seven joys as well as some of her low moments. The monastery recently received a part of the private collection of paintings belonging to the escalator-man Thyssen-Bornemisza. (Open Tues.-Sun. 10am-2pm. Free.)

Tibidabo

The odd name comes from the smashing view it commands over Barcelona, the Pyrenees, the Mediterranean, and, on a clear day, Mallorca. In St. Matthew's Gospel, the devil tempts Jesus, "Haec omni tibi dabo si cadens adoraberis me." ("All this I will give to you if you fall down and worship me.") Tibidabo's huge **Temple del Sagrat Cor** is of little artistic merit; indeed, the souvenir shop and telescopes tucked away in the building's spires make its religious function an afterthought. The view of Montserrat and the Pyrenees from the bust of Jesus is an eyebrow raiser (round-trip elevator ride, 75ptas). There's another **Parc d'Atraccions** (tel. 211 79 42), but it doesn't compare to Montjuïc's. (Open July-Aug. Mon.-Thurs. 6pm-2:30am, Fri.-Sat. 6pm-3:30am, Sun. noon-11pm; Oct.-April Sat.-Sun. 11am-8pm. Admission with 9 rides 800ptas, unlimited rides 1900ptas.)

Designed to appeal to all ages and interests, the **Museu de Ciéncia** rests on its laurels in Tibidabo (see Museums). An FFCC train or buses #17, 22, and 58 from Pl. de Catalunya run to Av. del Tibidabo. To reach the mountain top, either wait 15 minutes for the *tramvia blau* (blue streetcar; 125ptas) or walk up Av. Tibidabo in the same time. At the top of the street, you have to take a funicular. (Operates 7:15am-9:45pm. Round-trip 400ptas.)

Museums

Casa-Museu Gaudí, Park Güell, C. Olot (tel. 317 52 21). Metro: Pg. Gràcia (L3,L4), then bus #24 (see Park Güell, Sights). Designed by Gaudí's associate Francesc Berenguer, the house where he lived from 1900-26 has an eclectic *Modernista* collection of designs, sensual furniture, a few portraits, and personal effects. Open April-Oct. 10am-2pm and 4-7pm; Nov.-March 10am-2pm and 4-6:30pm. Admission 150ptas.

Fundació Miró, Parc de Montjuïc, Pl. Neptú on Av. Miramar, s/n (tel. 329 19 08). Metro: Parallel (L3), then funicular from Pl. Raquel Meller to Av. Miramar (see Montjuïc, Sights). Designed by renowned Catalan Josep Lluís Sert and winner of an international competition, the unobtrusive white concrete building commands a panoptic view of Barcelona. The permanent collection includes work from all periods of Miró's career. Two new wings provide more space for his sculptures. The library and well-stocked art boookstore also help attract young artist-types and intellectuals. Open Tues.-Sat. 11am-7pm, Thurs. until 9:30pm, Sun. 10:30am-2:30pm. Admission 500ptas, students 250ptas.

Fundació Tàpies, C. Aragó, 255 (tel. 487 03 15). Metro: Pg. de Gràcia (L3,L4), between Pg. Gràcia and Rambla de Catalunya (see Eixample, Sights). Well-marked with an enormous array of tangled wire hanging over the entrance. Features Tàpies and prestigious exhibitions of 20th-century artists. Home of the automated wigwam; beware of Poliscar. Open Tues.-Sun. 11am-8pm. Admission 400ptas, students 200ptas.

Museu Arqueològic, Parc de Montjuïc, Pg. Santa Madruna, s/n (tel. 423 21 49). Metro: Espanya (L1, L3), then bus #61. East of the Palau Nacional (see Montjuïc, Sights). There's a fine collection of Carthaginian art from Eivissa. Several rooms are dedicated to relics found in the excavation of the Greco-Roman city of Empúries (near Girona). Open Tues.-Sat. 9:30am-1pm and 4-7pm, Sun. 9:30am-1pm. Admission 250ptas, Sun. free.

Museu Clarà, C. Calatrava, 27 (tel. 203 40 58). Metro: Pg. Gràcia (L3,L4), then bus #22. Home in Sarrià of sculptor Josep Clarà until his death. It contains dozens of the artist's coldly perfect busts and nude studies. Open Tues.-Sun. 9am-2pm. Admission 250ptas.

Museu d'Art de Catalunya, Palau Nacional, Parc de Montjuïc (tel. 423 18 24). Metro: Espanya (L1,L3), then bus #61 (see Montjuïc, Sights). The world's finest Romanesque art collection in a palace originally built for the 1929 EXPO. It was converted to a museum in order to preserve the Romanesque frescoes, Gothic altarpieces, and paintings of Catalunya's medieval churches scavenged from the world's museums. Barcelona waits for the unveiling of architect Gae Aulenti's remodeled product. The museum is currently closed for renovation.

Museu d'Art Modern, Plaça d'Armes in the Parc de la Ciutadella (tel. 319 57 28). Metro: Ciutadella (L4) (see Parc de la Ciutadella, Sights). Holds a potpourri of paintings and sculptures, mostly by Catalan artists of the last 100 years. Noteworthy works include *Plein Air* by Casas, Josep Llimona's *Desconsol, Els Primers Freds* by Blay Fabregas, and Isidre Nonell's paintings of Gypsy women. Open Tues.-Sat. 9am-7:30pm, Mon. 3-7:30pm. Admission 500ptas, under 18 free.

Museu de Cera de Barcelona (tel. 317 26 49), Rambla 4-6. Where Cleopatra mingles with C3P0. Open Mon.-Sat. 10am-2pm and 4-6pm, Sun. 10am-2pm. Admission 450 ptas.

Muse u de Ciéncia, C. Teodor Roviralta, 55, Tibidabo (tel. 212 60 50). FFCC train or buses #17, 22, and 58 from Pl. de Catalunya to Av. del Tibidabo, walk 2 blocks and turn left onto C. Teodor Roviralta, then go to the end of the street and up the stairs (see Tibidabo, Sights). One of Barcelona's most popular museums. Knob twisting, button pushing, and gadget fussing opens the mysterious world of science. If you can't understand the Catalan and Castilian instructions, stand back and let the first-graders show you the ropes. Open Tues.-Sun. 10am-8pm. Admission 450ptas, students 300ptas. Admission to museum and 1/2hr. planetarium show 750ptas.

Museu de Geologia, near the corner of Pg. Picasso and Pg. Pujades in the Parc de la Ciutadella, (tel. 319 68 95). Metro: Ciutadella (L4). The rock displays are geared toward those who already understand a good bit of geology. Open Tues.-Sun. 9am-2pm. Admission 250ptas; under 18 free.

Museu de la Música, Casa Vidal-Quadras, Av. Diagonal, 373, in the Eixample (tel. 416 11 57). Metro: Diagonal (L3,L5). The building by Caldafach conceals a collection of odd and antique instruments in a neo-Arabic setting. Open Tues.-Sun. 9am-2pm. Admission 250ptas.

Museu de l'Art de l'Espectacle, C. Nou de la Rambla, 3-5 (tel. 317 39 74). Metro: Liceu or Drassanes (L3) (see Las Rambles, Sights). The Palau Güell, bought by the city to house this museum of 19th- and 20th-century theater memorabilia, is one of the few Gaudí buildings you can actually enter. Completed in 1890, the design stirred great controversy with its both functional and ornamental parabolic arches; fungiform capitals; cast-iron window twirlies; and his trademark pinwheel-shaped roof extrusions. This is one of Gaudí's more conservative projects. Open Mon.-Fri. 11am-3pm and 5-8pm, Sat.-Sun. 4-8pm. Admission 200ptas.

Museu de Zoologia (tel. 319 69 50), at the corner of Pg. Picasso and Pg. Pujades in the Parc de la Ciutadella. Metro: Ciutadella (L4). An amusing reminder of the antiquated stuff-and-tag approach to museum displays. Almost everything that once swam, crawled, flew, or knew how to have a good time stares at visitors from behind glass cases. Open Tues.-Sun. 9am-2pm. Admission 250ptas; under 18 free.

Museu d'Historia de la Ciutat, entrance at C. Verguer (tel. 315 11 11). Metro: Jaume I (L4), next to Pl. del Rei, (see Barri Gótic, Sights). Sixth-century Visigoths buried the Roman ruins to make room for their cemetery; their buildings, in turn, became the foundations for medieval structures. Ruins of the Roman colony are in the basement; some well-preserved floor mosaics and villa walls are all that remain. On the upper floors of the museum is the **Capella de Santa Agueda,**

built to store the king's holy relics. Open Tues.-Sat. 9am-8:30pm, Sun. 9am-1:30pm, Mon. 3:30-8pm. Admission 250ptas.

Museu Etnològic, Parc de Montjuïc, Pg. Santa Madruna, s/n (tel. 424 64 02). Metro: Espanya (L1,L3), then bus #61 (see Montjuïc, Sights). Organizes temporary exhibitions on Asian and Hispanic cultures. Open Tues.-Sat. 9am-8:30pm, Sun. 9am-2pm, Mon. 2-8:30pm. Admission 250ptas.

Museu Frederic Marés, entrance at Pl. Sant Lu, 5-6 (tel. 310 58 00). Metro: Jaume I (L4). Housed in the Palau Reial, on the opposite side of the Cathedral (see Barri Gòtic, Sights). An idiosyncratic personal collection of the sculptor Marés. Roman busts and Iberian stone figurines eyeball the 12th- and 13th-century wooden religious sculptures next door. The crypt has a more Old Testament air, where a series of reliefs illustrate Adam and Eve. The 2nd and 3rd floors contain exhibits about daily life from the 15th to the 20th centuries. Open Tues.-Sat. 9am-2pm and 4-7pm, Sun. 9am-2am. Admission 200ptas.

Museu Marítim, Pl. Porta de la Pau, 1 (tel. 318 32 45). Metro: Drassanes (L3) (see Las Rambles, Sights). At the port end of the Rambles, the museum recounts Barcelona's maritime history with displays of old maps, compasses, and even a reproduction of the galley that Don Juan de Austria commanded in the Battle of Lepanto, 1571. The museum fills the old *drassanes,* the only extant example of a medieval shipyard in Europe. Open Tues.-Sat. 9am-1pm and 4-7pm, Sun. 10am-2pm. Admission 150ptas, students free.

Museu Militar, Castell de Montjuïc, Parc de Montjuïc (tel. 329 86 13). Metro: Paral-lel (L3), then funicular from Pl. Raquel Meller to Av. Miramar, then cable car all the way up to the *castell* (see Montjuïc, Sights). Replete with an extensive collection of antique and modern Spanish army weapons. Models of castles and lead soldiers for the more imaginative or bellicose. Open April-Sept. Tues-Sat. 10am-2pm and 3:30-8pm, Sun. 10am-8pm; Oct.-March Tues.-Sat. 10am-2pm and 3:30-8pm, Sun. 10am-7pm. Admission 50ptas.

Museu Picasso, in Palau Berenguer d'Aguilar, C. Montcada, 15-19 (tel. 315 47 61). Metro: Jaume I (L4) (see Barri de la Ribera, Sights). Here you can follow the artist's development, from his early textbook doodlings to his last exhibition posters. Thirty rooms of paintings and drawings include masterpieces such as the *Maids of Honor* series, Picasso's reinterpretation of Velázquez's *Las Meninas.* Lithographs and early works (especially Blue Period, which he initiated while living in Barcelona) make up a large part of the collection. Many aren't familiar with Picasso's ceramic work, which includes such curious inventions as his brightly painted bull-shaped plates and jugs. Open Tues.-Sat. 10am-8pm, Sun. 10am-3pm. Admission 500ptas, students and under 18 free.

Museu Tèxtil i d'Indumentària, C. Montcada, 12-14 (tel. 310 45 16). Metro: Jaume I (L4), almost across the street from the Picasso, in what used to be the Palau dels Marquessos de Llió (see Barri de la Ribera, Sights). For clothing enthusiasts, a rich assemblage of 16th-century Spanish costume, including shoes, purses, and other accessories. For others the building itself, a 14th-century palace, may be more interesting. Open Tues.-Sat. 9am-2pm and 4:30-7pm, Sun. 9am-2pm. Admission 250ptas.

Palau de la Virreina, the Rambles, 99 (tel. 301 77 75). Metro: Liceu (L3), on the corner of Carrer del Carme. This 18th-century palace, once a Peruvian viceroy's residence, displays the excellent Colecció Cambó with works by Raphael, Tintoretto, Titian, Van Dyck, Goya, and Zurbarán on the second floor. Changing exhibitions stop by as well. Open Mon.-Sat. 10am-2pm and 4:30-9pm, Sun. 9:30am-2pm. Admission 300ptas, students free. A tourist office here distributes information on cultural events (see Practical Information: Tourist Offices).

Entertainment

Every evening around 5pm, a man sets up a box in the middle of C. Porta de l'Angel before the Galerías Preciados and, as a crowd gathers, intersperses opera with voluble commentary. Nightlife in Barcelona starts then and there, and winds down about 14 hours later. Having caught word that the city is a perfect combination of exuberance and variety, international youth has poured in over the last few years. As the hip continue to flood the city, the nightlife only gets better.

The best source of information on movies, concerts, cultural events, bars, and clubs is the weekly *Guía del Ocio* (75ptas), available at all newsstands. Although in Spanish, the listings are comprehensible even to the Spanishless. The *Cine* section lists all the films currently playing in alphabetical order and, after each blurb, the movie house. For subtitled films, look for *V.O. subtitulada (versión original-subti* in Castilian); otherwise it's been dubbed. The *Arte* section lists all the currently open exhibitions and museums with phone numbers, hours, location, and fees. In the *Restaurantes* section, eateries are simply listed with phone numbers, hours, and address; the most useful sections are *Cenar de Madrugada* (late-night eateries) and *Restaurantes Abiertos en Domingo* (restaurants open on Sunday). The *Tarde/Noche* section has reams of bars and discos. These listings include the name, location, phone, and hours, but do not provide reviews.

Discos, Clubs, and Bars

The *passeig* is divided into two shifts: the post-siesta burst of energy (around 5-7pm), then a second wave after dinner (perhaps 9-11pm). The later *passeig* blends into the beginnings of a drink around 10 or 11pm, but only in a pub, café, or bar. After the bars wind down around 2am, the crowds flood the discos for another four- or five- hour stint. The swisher bars and discos tend to discriminate on the basis of hair and dress styles. Doorpeople may also invent a cover charge for men to prevent their numbers from overwhelming those of the women.

Where to take your *passeig* is yet another decision. Moll de la Fusta and the Rambles with their cafés and bars are a good starting point for a leisurely stroll in the direction of the Eixample, the densest concentration of nightlife. Other options include a more serene setting on Montjüic or the trendy Rambla de Catalunya with its chic cafés and clientele. The 700ptas cab ride up to *Mirablau* (see listings) is well worth every peseta to watch Barcelona light up in the evening.

The most fashionable, modern, and safe discos and clubs are located in the **Eixample.** Fish out your hippest garb and head out along **Carrer de Balmes, Avinguda Diagonal,** and any of their crossstreets. (Metro: Diagonal, L3, L5.)

Discos and Clubs

Otto Zutz, C. Lincoln, 15 (tel. 238 07 22). Metro: FFCC Muntaner. Uptown near Pl. Molina where C. Balmes intersects with Via Augusta. Large and flashy. Cover 2000ptas. Drink included. Open until 4:30am.

Fibra Optica, C. Beethoven, 9 (tel. 209 52 81). Metro: Hospital Clinic (L5). From metro walk up C. Comte Urgell, turn left at Diagonal; it's in Pl. Wagner 1 block up on the right. An early 20s crowd in a place that rivals Otto Zutz, but without the beautiful people. Cover 1700ptas. Drink included. Open Mon.-Fri. midnight-5am, Sat. midnight-7am.

Studio 54, Av. Paral-lel, 64 (tel. 329 54 54), on the opposite side of Barri Xinés from the Rambles. Metro: Paral-lel (L3). Unlike its New York counterpart, this disco has lost neither its popularity nor its cachet. Famous rock groups sometimes play here. Open Fri.-Sun. midnight-dawn; cover 1000ptas. Early sessions Sat.-Sun. 6:30am-10pm; cover 750ptas. Drink included.

Zeleste, C. Almogavers, 122 (tel. 485 05 12), a 15-minute walk from Pg. Lluis Companys, or take the NL bus (11pm-4:30am). Metro: Llancuna (L4). Located in an old warehouse, this dance club has rooftop terraces and live performances on occasion. The shindig takes off at 2:30am. Cover 1000ptas. Separate charge for live shows.

KGB, C. Alegre de Dalt, 55 (tel. 210 59 06). Metro: Joanic (L4). C. Alegre de Dalt is the first left off C. Pi i Margall from the metro. Caters to those who like their rock and roll loud and hard. Just don't make any jokes about "how many spies does it take to screw in a strobe light" and you'll be fine. Open Tues.-Sat. 10pm-4:30am.

La Paloma, C. Tigre, 27 (tel. 301 68 97). Metro: Universitat (L1). Less stuffy than most discos, this dance hall is just plain fun. It attracts a friendly group, usually from nearby towns. Spanish and Latin music only. Open Wed.-Sun. 11:15pm-2:30am, Fri.-Sat. 11:15pm-4am.

Bars

La Fira, C. Provença, 171 (tel. 323 72 71). Metro: Diagonal (L3, L5). On the block between C. Aribau and C. Muntaner. Bumper cars, swings, ferris wheel benches, and fun house mirrors salvaged from amusement parks. No carnival dress: avoid shorts or sandals. Open Mon.-Fri. 7pm-3am, Sat.-Sun. 7pm-4am.

Nick Havana, C. Rosselló, 208 (tel. 215 65 91). Metro: Diagonal (L3, L5). On the block between C. Balmes and Rambla Catalunya. Slick bar with blaring video screens and a dance space. See and be seen. Cocktails about 850ptas. Open 8pm-3am.

Monroe's Gallery-Bar, C. Lincoln, 3 (tel. 237 56 78). Metro: FFCC Muntaner. This popular gay bar is also a shrine to Marilyn Monroe, whose beauty mark spots every nook and cranny. Open 7pm-3am.

La Nostra Illa, C. Reig i Bonet, 3 (tel. 210 00 62). Metro: Joanic (L4). From the metro walk up C. Escorial; Reig i Bonet is the 3rd left. A women's bar that attracts all ages and plays all sorts of music. Open Mon.-Tues. and Thurs.-Fri. 7:30pm-1am, Sat.-Sun. 7:30pm-3am.

Mirablau, Pl. Funicular, s/n (Av. Tibidabo) (tel. 418 58 79). Take the FFCC to Av. Tibidabo and then hop on the *tramvia blau* or just hail a taxi from Pl. Catalunya (700ptas). An admirable view of Barcelona in a covered but open-air bar.

Sisisi, Av. Diagonal, 442 (tel. 237 56 73). Metro: Diagonal. A jazz bar with an appropriately cool and casual ambience. Drinks around 500ptas. Open 7pm-dawn.

Miramelindo, Pg. Born, 15. Right behind Església Santa María del Mar. Metro: Jaume I (L4). Two-floor tavern in a Spanish colonial style with soothing jazz in the background. Open 8pm-3am.

L'Ovella Negra, Sitges, 5 (tel. 317 10 87). Metro: Catalunya (L1, L3). From Catalunya, go down the Ramblas and take your first right at C. Tallers and Sitges is the first left. Rural tavern motif with foosball and pool tables. Open 8pm-3am.

La Cova del Drac, C. Tusset, 30. Metro: Diagonal (L3, L5). A jazz club with a small bar upstairs. Show starts at 10:30pm. Open Wed.-Sun. Cover 400-900ptas.

Xampanyeríes

Often translated "champagne bars," they're upscale bars that serve *cava*, the Catalan sparkling wine.

Xampau Xampany, Gran Via de les Corts Catalanes, 702 (tel. 265 04 83). Metro: Pg. Gràcia (L3). 40s swing music and an urbane atmosphere. Cava *brut nature* lets you rub elbows with the upwardly mobile of Barcelona. 500ptas per glass for the cheap stuff. Open 6pm-3am.

Xampanyet, C. Montcado, 15, off Pg. des Borne behind La Església de Santa María del Mar. A cozy ceramic-tiled establishment with only a few constantly occupied tables. The bubbly proprietor knows enough to teach a mini-course on *cavas* in Castilian. Open Tues.-Sun. 7pm-1am.

Bar Bodegueta, Rambla Catalunya, 100 (tel. 215 41 48). Metro: Pg. Gràcia (L3). This low-key wine and champagne cellar is a favorite with business people who come in for *tapas* and a drink after work. Cramped quarters and small tables, with overhead fans. Champagne bottles from 750ptas. Open Mon.-Sat. 7pm-1am.

Music, Theater, and Film

The **Gran Teatre del Liceu,** Rambla de Caputxins, 61 (tel. 318 92 77), founded in 1847, is one of the world's leading opera stages. Its season lasts from September through July. (Box office open Mon.-Fri. 8am-8pm, Sat. 8am-1pm. Metro: Liceu (L3). Advance schedules and ticket information are available by writing the theater at Sant Pau, Ibis, 08001 Barcelona.) Classical music is performed at the **Palau de la Música Catalana,** an extraordinary brick *Modernista* building, cleverly tucked away on C. Francesc de Paula, 2 (tel. 268 10 00), off Via Laietana near Pl. Urquinaona. Concerts cover all varieties of symphonic and choral music, and tickets run 500-5000ptas. Ask about free Tuesday night winter concerts and about the October music festival. (Box office open Mon.-Fri. 5-8pm.; Sept.-May Mon.-Fri. 11am-1pm and 5-8pm.) The **Conservatorio,** C. Bruc, 112, in the Eixample, is the one indoor classical music venue that operates during the dog days of summer.

Theatrical offerings in Barcelona are no less satisfying, for those who understand Catalan. The **Teatre Lliure** (Free Theater) claims notoriety and respect with years of innovative productions. It's at C. Montseny, 47 (tel. 218 92 51), in Gràcia. (Metro: Fontana L3.) Despite its name, shows are not free. Tickets range from 600-1100ptas, depending on the day. The season runs from Oct. to June. The **Teatre Poliorama,** or Teatre Català de la Comèda, offers light theater. Look for it at Rambla Estudis, 115 (tel. 317 75 99).

A new domed **Auditori** (concert hall) is going up on Plaça de les Glòries. Next door on Plaça dels Arts will be Ricard Bofill's **Teatre Nacional de Catalunya** (Catalan National Theater), a cyclopean, glass-enclosed Classical temple. It's an estimated three years before the two are functional. City watchers have long been on the edge of their seats for this extension of the Diagonal past the Pl. Glòries. The new square devoted to the arts is meant to supply Glòries with the shape and cultural weight to become a focal point for renewed investment in the neighborhood.

Barcelona doesn't close its stage doors when summer arrives, the theater simply moves outdoors. The **Teatre Grec,** on Montjuïc, the **Mercat de les Flors,** and the **Velòdrom d'Horta** (for the fabulous *Grec* season) are the three biggies. Grec, named for the classical Greek theater, produces theater, music, dance, films, folklore and a special program for young adults (Grec Jove). Prices start at 300ptas for the Banda Municipal concerts on Pl. Rei (behind the cathedral) and ascend to 3000ptas for concerts at the Velòdrom, which feature consecrated jazz and rock musicians. Buy tickets at the door or at the Palau de la Virreina, Rambla, 99 (tel. 301 77 75; open Mon.-Sat. 9:30am-9pm, Sun. 10am-2pm). The Palau distributes comprehensive schedules of events. For rock concerts held in the main soccer stadium or the sports palace, tickets are available in the booth on Gran Via at C. Aribau, next to the university. (Open 10:30am-1:30pm and 4-7:30pm.)

Films are popular in Barcelona. Besides Spanish and Catalan features, you should be able to find a Hollywood classic or the hottest new flick in English. It's customary to tip the usher (25ptas or so) who shows you to your seat. Also check the schedule of the **Filmoteca,** Av. Sarrià, 33 (tel. 430 50 07), run by the Generalitat, which screens classic, cult, exotic, and otherwise exceptional films. (Always subtitled if not a Castilian- or Catalan-language film. Metro: Hospital Clínic, L5. Admission 300ptas.)

Recreational Sports

Guia de l'esport, available free at the tourist offices, lists (in Catalan) sporty activities such as swimming, cycling, tennis, squash, sailing, hiking, scuba diving, and even white-water rafting and kayaking. Information is also available over the phone (Catalan or Castilian, tel. 415 73 73).

> **Swimming Pools: Covered: Piscina Municipal Marítím,** (tel. 309 34 12), Pg. Marítím, s/n. Metro: Ciutadella (L4), next to the hospital across the street from the beach. Open Mon.-Fri. 7am-9pm. Admission 270ptas. **Outdoor: Piscina Municipal Montjüic,** Av. Miramar, 31. Metro: Paral-lel (L3), and then take the funicular up Montjüic. The pool is down the road on the left side. Open June-Sept. 9am-7pm.

Shopping

Barcelona's reputation as a fashion capital second to Paris and Milan is only a fond memory, but mod attire can still be bought. Everything you want but can't afford is in the elegant shops along **Pg. Gràcia** and the **Rambla de Catalunya.** Things you can probably afford but may not want jam the tacky tourist traps along the Rambles.

> **Markets: An antique market** is held Thurs. 9am-8pm in Pl. Nova. The famous **Els Encants** flea market (metro: Glòries (L1)) bites Mon., Wed., Fri., and Sat. 9am-8pm on C. Consell de Cent at C. Dos de Maig, near Pl. Les Glòries. A **stamp and coin market** is held Sun. 10am-2pm in Pl. Reial. A **coin and book market** is held at the same time in the Mercat de Sant Antoni.
>
> **Centre Permanent d'Artesania,** Pg. Gràcia, 55 (tel. 215 54 08). A great—though not especially cheap—place for souvenirs. Here Catalan artisans display and sell their crafts. Open Mon.-Fri. 9am-2pm and 4-7pm, Sat. 11am-2pm and 5-7pm, Sun. 11am-2pm.
>
> **Carrer Banys Nous,** in the Barri Gòtic. On this street of tiny antique shops, prices and quality vary widely. Painters gather in Pl. Pi to sell their masterpieces. Sat. 11am-8pm, Sun. 11am-2pm.
>
> **El Corte Inglés,** Pl. Catalunya (tel. 302 12 12). The top department store in Barcelona. Huge, crowded, well-stocked, and staffed by multilingual salespeople. The view from the rooftop cafeteria is better than Olympus but the food is expensive. Open Mon.-Sat. 10am-9pm.
>
> **Galerías Preciados,** C. Portal de l'Angel. Inglés' department store rival. The bird-ridden pet shop wins points, but the rooftop cafeteria (serves a good buffet lunch), is a Corte Inglés wannabe. Open Mon.-Sat. 10am-9pm.
>
> **VIPS,** Rambla Catalunya, above Pl. Catalunya. Only a fraction of the floor space that the department stores have, but it crams books, records, a food store, and a café into its late-night locale. Open Sun.-Thurs. 8am-1:30am, Fri.-Sat. 8am-3am.

English Bookstores: see Practical Information.

La Lidia, Sardanas, and Fiestas

While few Catalans are bullfighting fans, Barcelona does maintain **Plaça de Toros Monumental,** a *Modernista* bullring on Gran Via at Pg. Carles I. Metro: Marina (L1). Spain's best matadors don't risk their entrails in a Barcelona show; go to Madrid, Sevilla, or Málaga for better action. If you don't mind a novice bullfighter, buy tickets at C. Muntaner, 24 (tel. 253 38 21), near Pl. Universitat, or at the box office (tel. 245 58 04) before the start of the *corrida*. (Open Thurs.-Sun. 10am-1pm and 4-8pm. Admission from 1300ptas.) Don't waste your money on expensive seats. The ring is small enough so that everyone can see. Bullfights normally take place on Sunday at 5:30pm; the season runs June to October. There is also a **museu** of bullfighting history here. (Open 10am-1pm and 3:30-6pm.)

One of Barcelona's most touristed sights is the *sardana*, Catalunya's regional dance. Teen-agers and grandparents join hands to dance in a circle in celebration of Catalan unity. You can see the **sardanas** in front of the cathedral, Pl. Sagrada Familia, or at Parc de la Ciutadella near the fountains Sundays at noon. Dances are also held in Pl. Sant Jaume on Sundays at 7pm, at Parc de l'Espanya Industrial on Fridays at 8pm, in Pl. Catedral on Saturdays at noon and 6:30pm, and in other locations throughout the city on Tuesday, Thursday, and Friday. Consult papers for current information.

Fiestas are as abundant as everything else in Barcelona. Before Christmas, **Fèria de Santa Lucía** fills Pl. Catedral and the area around Sagrada Familia with stalls and booths. **Carnaval** is celebrated wildly from February 7th to the 13th, but many Barcelonins head to the even more raucous celebrations in Sitges and Vilanova i la Geltrú. Soon thereafter comes the **Fiesta de Sant Jordi** (Saint George) on April 23, the feast of Catalunya's patron saint and Barcelona's answer to St. Valentine's Day. Men give women roses, and women reciprocate with a book. On May 11 is the **Festa de Saint Ponç**, when a traditional market of aromatic and medicinal herbs and honey is set up in C. Hospital, close to the Rambles. Barcelona's summertime eruption occurs on June 23, the night before **Día de Sant Joan.** Bonfires roar throughout the city, and the fountains of Pl. Espanya and Palau Reial light up in various colors in anticipation of fireworks on Montjüic. Next, city folk kick up their heels at Gràcia's **Festa Major** (Aug. 15-21). Lights blaze in the plazas and streets, while rock bands and Latin groups play all night.

In September, the **Feria de Cuina i Vins de Catalunya** brings wine and *butifarra* (sausage) producers to the Rambla de Catalunya. For one week you can sample fine food and drink for a pittance. The **Festa de la Verge de la Mercé** is celebrated on September 24, when fireworks again light up the city while the traditional *correfocs*, manic parades of people dressed as devils, whirl pitchfork-shaped sparklers. Buckets of water are hurled at the demons from balconies overlooking the fiery streets. In November, a **festival de jazz** swings the city's streets and clubs.

Near Barcelona

Montserrat

About an hour northwest of Barcelona, the unmistakable profile of the Montserrat mountain range juts out from the flat Riu Llobregat valley. Legendary site of the Holy Grail, local fable and landscape inspired Wagner's *Parsifal*. Beyond its geological and operatic importance, Montserrat's hallowed ground is revered as the home of *La Verge de Montserrat,* Catalunya's spiritual *patrona*. In the 10th century, a wandering mountaineer had a blinding vision of the Virgin Mary. The story began attracting pilgrims, and in 1025 a bishop and Benedictine abbot founded a **monastery** here. The present buildings date from the 19th century, although two wings of the old Gothic cloister survive. Today some 80 Benedictine monks tend a shrine to the Virgin, work in ceramics and goldsmithing workshops, and distill the herbal liqueur *Aromes de Montserrat*. For centuries the monastery has been a well-spring of Catalan culture.

The trains to the village stop near the mountainside. Then a cable car (whose price is included in the ticket to Montserrat) ascends majestically up the slope, although some maniacal hikers will brave the walk. The car lets you off at **Plaça Creu,** Montserrat's tourist-oriented commercial area; the steps beside the information booth lead up to **Plaça Santa María,** where the most important buildings stand. The *basílica's* spacious courtyard contrasts with the dark, cavernous interior, reverently aglow with dozens of suspended votive lamps (each one a gift of a city or institution). To the right of the main chapel glimmers the sacred 12th-century polychrome figure of Mary and child, *La Moreneta* ("the little dark lady"). Legend has it that an image of Mary carved by St. Luke was hidden in the caves of Montserrat by St. Peter. (*Basílica* open 8am-8pm. Free.) The *plaça* also boasts the **Museu de Montserrat,** which encompasses a eclectic range of art in its two sections—from Mesopotamian artifacts to paintings by El Greco, Caravaggio, and Picasso. Various artifacts from biblical lands are also on display, including a mummified crocodile more than 2000 years old. (Antiquities section open 10am-2pm. Modern section open 3-6pm. Ticket valid for both museums 300ptas.)

Another ride on the funicular (every 20min., 660ptas) to **Sant Joan** makes the apotheosis to the monastery and shrine. From there, it's a 15-minute walk to the hermitage along a path that overlooks the valley. The other funicular, also off the *plaça,* descends to **Santa Cova** (Holy Grotto), where the mountaineer allegedly discovered the image of Mary. The **Via Crucis** to the shrine is crowded with religious works illustrating the Stations by famous Catalan artists such as Gaudí. (Chapel open 9am-6:30pm; Nov.-March 10am-5:30pm. Funicular every 20min. 10am-1:20pm and 2:20-6:40pm; Nov.-March 10am-1:20pm, 2:20-4:40pm; 145ptas, round-trip 230ptas.) A path that starts near Pl. Creu leads down to Santa Cova; the walk takes about an hour.

A pilgrimage to some of the most beautiful areas of the mountain is possible only on foot. A lookout over Barcelona sits twenty minutes down the path between the two funicular stations; but the heavenly view from **Sant Jerónim** (the area's highest peak at 1235m) requires a little more legwork. The trail (well-marked with yellow-painted rocks) can be picked up from the top of the Sant Joan funicular or down in the village at the steps by the fountain in Pl. Santa María. The hike takes about two hours. There are mystical views of Montserrat's celebrated rock formations—enormous domes and serrated outcroppings that resemble human faces. On a clear day the spectacular view of the Baleares, the eastern Pyrenees, and central Catalunya will make you sing hosannas. The enlightened avoid hiking under the hot sun from noon to 2pm.

To spend the night, stop at the building marked **Despatx de Celles** on the walk from Pl. Santa María down to Pl. Creu (tel. 835 02 51, ext. 630; open 9am-1pm and 3-6pm). More a series of apartments than a hostel or hotel, up to 10 people may room together for extended periods of time. The rooms are ascetic, the view stupefying. (Singles 1090ptas. Doubles 1985ptas. Reservations recommended for Aug.) It is a five-minute walk up the hillside beyond the Sant Joan funicular to the adequate **campground** (tel. 835 02 51, ext. 582) with showers (300ptas per person and per tent).

The tempting fresh fruit and baked goods at the **food stands** next to the Despatx de Celles are a holy feast, but their exorbitant prices make budgeting travelers prefer a holy fast. Instead try the **Bar de la Plaça** behind the market (sandwich about 475ptas) and the all-you-can-eat **buffet** 100m down the road from Pl. Creu (Mon.-Fri. 1550ptas, Sat.-Sun. 1775ptas).

For more details on navigating your way through the mountains, go to the **information booth** on Pl. Creu (tel. 835 02 51, ext. 586), a providential and multilingual source of advice and the *Official Guide to Montserrat* (330ptas). (Open 9:30am-1:45pm and 3-6pm.) Other conveniences include a **post office** (open Mon.-Fri. 9am-1pm and 3-5pm, Sat. 9am-1pm) and a place to **change money** ("La Caixa" automatic exchange machine accepts Visa, AmEx, MC, and Eurocard). For an **ambulance** or mountain rescue team call 835 02 51 (ext. 162). The **Guardia Civil** is headquartered in the main square (tel. 835 00 85).

Trains to Montserrat leave Barcelona from Pl. Espanya (L1) stop (every 2 hrs., 9:10am-5:10pm, 1280ptas; with funicular to Sant Joan 1800ptas, children 1200ptas). These Ferrocarrils de Catalunya commuter trains are on the Manresa line; be sure to get off at the Aeri de Montserrat stop, *not* the Olesa de Montserrat just before it.

Sant Cugat del Vallès

Devotees of Romanesque art and architecture can happily worship the church at **Sant Cugat del Vallès,** just over the Serra de Collserola on Barcelona's coattails. This church boasts one of the largest Romanesque cloisters in Catalunya, with a double-decker forest of 13th-century columns supporting the breathtaking upper gallery, which wasn't completed until the 16th century. The most striking feature of the church is also its oldest: the soaring 11th-century Lombard bell tower, visible from any corner of the town. Visigothic, Biblical, and mythological motifs mingle in its intricate carvings, while the rose window breathes life into its facade. Arnau Gatell is the sculptor of all the figures in the cloister. (Cloister open Tues.-Sat. 9:30am-1:30pm and 3:30-5:30pm, Sun. 9:30am-1:30pm. Admission 100ptas.) FFCC **trains** depart Barcelona's Pl. Catalunya (Metro: L1, L3) for Sant Cugat (every 15min., Sat.-Sun. every 20min.; 5am-midnight).

Costa Brava

The jagged cliffs of the Costa Brava cut into the Mediterranean Sea from Barcelona north to the French border. Coined by journalist Ferran Agulló, the name for this "savage" coast rings of danger and natural isolation. Craggy precipices and hairpin turns render certain parts of the coast unnavigable even by the most modern land transportation; many buses zigzag between the coastal towns and safer inland routes. In winter the *tramontana,* a bitterly cold wind from the Pyrenees, can screech at 45 mph for four days straight across the Empordà, the flatlands that encompass Costa Brava. But the coast flaunts its better half in summer. In July and August, warm sun, cool sea breezes, and idyllic days attract vacationing European families. The rocky shores also traditionally attract artists; the Surrealist painter Salvador Dalí was a native of the region. Dalí's house in Cadaqués and a museum in Figueres house the largest collections of his work in Europe. In late September the water is still warm, the beaches are half-empty, and hostel owners face the prospect of room vacancies. Although accommodations and bus sevice are drastically reduced, this is the perfect time to visit the area.

RENFE stops at the southern tip of the coast at Blanes and again at Llançà and Portbou (up near the French border). Bus is the preferred mode of transportation here, though coverage is less than complete. Tossa de Mar makes a good starting point for southern Costa Brava. For the northern swath, Figueres is linked with Cadaqués by bus and Portbou by rail. Palafrugell is an inland connection to central Costa Brava. Local tourist offices distribute maps of off-road sights, camping areas and long-distance walking trails along the coast.

Tossa de Mar

In Tossa, a blissful beach resort on the lower part of the Costa Brava, year-round inhabitants entertain their guests with small-town sincerity. Beaches aside, the chief lure is the Vila Vella (old town), a collection of 14th- and 15th-century buildings and fortifications on the rocky peninsula by the beach.

Orientation and Practical Information

Tossa is near the southern corner of the Costa Brava, about 40km north of Barcelona. The bus is the quickest and easiest way there; service is relatively frequent (6-7 per day) from Barcelona. Service from Girona is so limited that travelers may wish to head for Lloret de Mar (10km south) first, and then catch the 15-minute ride from there to Tossa.

Buses arrive at **Plaça de les Nacions Sense Etat** at the corner of **Av. Pelegrí** and **Av. Ferran Agulló**; the town slopes gently down from there to the waterfront (a 10-minute walk). From the terminal there are two routes to the beach. Av. Pelegrí wends its way through the **old quarter,** a tangle of alleys near the walls of the Vila Vella. More directly, Av. Ferran Agulló runs parallel to the coastal *passeig* (promenade); walk away from the station and turn right at the circle onto **Av. Costa Brava,** which leads to the middle of the beach strip. **Passeig del Mar** curves, starting near the end of Av. Costa Brava, along the **Platja Gran** (Tossa's main beach).

> **Tourist Office:** Av. Pelegrí, 25 (tel. 34 01 08; fax 34 07 12), in bus terminal building at the corner of Av. Ferron Agulló and Av. Pelegrí. Godsend map of the city with indexed streets, accommodations, campsites, and services. English spoken. Open July-Aug. Mon.-Sat. 9am-9pm, Sun. 10am-1pm; Sept.-June Mon.-Sat. 10am-1pm and 4-7pm.
>
> **Post Office:** C. Bernats at corner with C. Maria Auxiliador off Av. Pelegrí, (tel. 34 04 57). Open Mon.-Fri. 8:30am-2pm, telegrams Mon.-Fri. 8:30am-2pm; for urgent telegrams, money orders, and Lista de Correos also open Sat. 9am-1pm. **Postal Code:** 17320.
>
> **Telephones:** Av. Costa Brava, 2, to the left just before you're speared on the statue of Neptune. Open 10am-1pm and 4-8pm. **Telephone Code:** 972.
>
> **Buses:** Av. Pelegrí at Pl. Nacions Sense Etat. **Pujol i Pujol** (tel. 36 57 90). To: Lloret del Mar (every 1/2 hr. 8:15am-8:15pm, 15 min., Mon.-Fri. 115ptas, Sat.-Sun. 130ptas). **Sarfa** (tel. 34 09 03). To Girona (8am, 1 hr., Mon. 430ptas, Sat. 495ptas) and Barcelona (7 per day 7:30am-6:30pm, 80 min., Mon.-Sat. 725ptas, Sun. 825ptas). Information for both companies at tel. 34 09 03.
>
> **Ferries:** The only direct way to St. Feliu and other points immediately north of Tossa, as buses first travel inland by way of Girona. **Cruceros** (tel. 34 03 19) has its booth on the main beach. To St. Feliu (45 min., 950ptas, round-trip 1350ptas) and points as far north as Palamos and as far south as Calella. The cliff views along the way are better than a 3-D movie. Schedules vary frequently, Sun. service is sporadic, and poor weather may cause all service to be cancelled. Check with the ticket booth near the Vila Vella end of the Platja Gran.
>
> **Laundromat: Lavandería Valentí,** Av. Catalunya, 25, off Av. Ferran Agulló at Av. Costa Brava. Look for the blue sign after the soccer field on the left. Open 10am-noon and 4-8:30pm.
>
> **Medical Services: Centre Medic Tossa,** C. S. Sabastià, 2 (tel. 34 14 48 or 34 23 04), off C. Maria Auxiliadora. English spoken. Open 10am-1pm and 5-8pm.
>
> **Emergency/Police:** In emergency, medical or otherwise, call the **municipal police,** C. Esglesia, 4 (tel. 34 01 35), in the Ajuntament building, first floor to the rear. English spoken. They will escort you to the current **24-hr. pharmacy.** The rules say you must have a doctor's prescription or they cannot help you get medicine. **Guardia Civil,** Ctra. Sant Feliu (tel. 34 03 29).

Accommodations and Camping

Small-town sincerity or no, Tossa is still a big-time resort and fills up completely in the summer. Travel agencies rent many *hostales* for the entire summer. Reservations by phone, letter, or through the multitude of travel agencies are a must, as some establishments are booked solid from late July to late August. The tourist office can provide a list of travel agencies and help you find available rooms during this period. Winter travelers should keep in mind that few rooms have heating. The alleys and cobblestone streets of the *ciudad vella*, near the Vila Vella, are the only areas worth contemplating for lodging.

> **Fonda Lluna,** C. Roqueta, 20 (tel. 34 03 65). From the castle walls take the stairs of C. Pont Vell and go left where it forks. Small rooms, big beds, grandparent-like attention, and a heartstopping rooftop view of the Vila Vella and the sea. Some guests have been coming for almost three decades. The gorgeous upstairs terrace provides special secret sea breeze laundry drying service. 1600ptas per person with bath. Breakfast included. Rates lower May-June. Open May-Aug.
>
> **Pensión Moré,** C. Sant Telmo, 9 (tel. 34 03 39). Large rooms with wash basins and views of the old quarter below. July-Aug. 1200ptas per person; Sept.-June 1000ptas per person.
>
> **Camping:** Five sites within a 7km radius of town. **Cala Llevador** (tel. 34 03 14), 3km from Tossa off the road to Lloret. The Pujol i Pujol bus to Lloret stops here. Palisaded with pines and openings to the sea. June 21-Aug. 27 585ptas per person and per tent; Aug. 28-June 20 420ptas per person and per tent. **Caravaning Camping Pola** (tel. 34 10 50), 4km from Tossa on the road to St. Feliu. June 27-Aug. 28 600ptas per person, 850ptas per tent; Aug. 29-June 26 450ptas per person, 650ptas per tent.

Food

Restaurants on Av. Ferran Agulló and the other main drags are mainly for tourists.

Restaurant La Salsa, C. Sa Sassola, s/n (tel. 34 08 85), on the corner of C. Estolt in the old quarter. The entrance is off the wide alley to the right. Lists 4 vegetarian *raciónes* (try the *berenjenas*—eggplant—625ptas) but serves fish, fowl, and quadrupeds as well.

Restaurant Marina, C. Tarull, 6 (tel. 34 07 57). Faces the right side of L'Església de Sant Vicenç—look for the green and white awning and tables out front. Fairly priced considering its choice location. It's crowded in the summer and doesn't take reservations. Arrive early or settle in for a wait. *Raciónes* 375-950ptas.

Sights and Entertainment

The **Vila Vella** is a *Monumento artístico-histórico nacional* dating from the 12th to 14th centuries. Inside its golden stone walls, a spiral of medieval alleys leads to the remains of an old Gothic church poised atop the cliff, the **Església de Sant Vincenç.** Also in the Vila Vella, on tiny Pl. Pintor J. Roig y Soler, the **Museu Municipal** (tel. 34 07 09) occupies a nifty old house with low, arched doorways, split-level floors, and confused stairs. Its collection of Roaring 20s art includes works by Olga Sakharov, Georges Kars, Togores, and Solá, plus the only painting by Chagall currently in Spain. Tossa's 4th-century BC Roman mosaics and other artifacts from the nearby **vila romana** keep cool in the museum basement. If you're in a high density mood, other mosaics and the foundations of the buildings themselves are at the excavation site off Av. Pelegrí. (Museum open Mon.-Sat. 10am-1pm and 4-8pm, Sun. 11am-1pm; Oct.-May Mon.-Sat. 10am-1pm and 3-6pm. Admission 150ptas, students, seniors, and groups 75ptas.)

Tossa has four resplendently clean **beaches**: Platja Grande, Platja del Reig, Mar Menuda, and Es Codolar. The tourist office supplies maps of nearby **hiking** paths. Several companies offer **boat** outings to nearby beaches and caves (7-8 per day, 1 hr., 800ptas). Tickets are available at booths on the Platja Gran. The currently fashionable discos are **Ely,** C. Bernats, 2 and Av. Costa Brava, 5 (tel. 34 07 11), and **Paradis,** C. Pou de la Vila, 12-14 (tel. 34 06 52), at the end of Pg. Mar in Hotel Rovira, but you'll find merrymaking everywhere after dark. For information about outdoor concerts and cultural festivals, contact the **Casa de Cultura,** Av. Pelegrí, 8 (tel. 34 09 05), in an historic red-tile roof building. (Open 4-6pm.) Local festivals take place on January 20 and 21, when the townsfolk make a 42km pilgrimage from Tossa to Santa Coloma in honor of St. Sebastian. This is followed on January 22 by a **Festa del Hivern** (Winter Fair) celebrating the feast day of St. Vincent, Tossa's patron saint. A **Festa del Estiu** (Summer Fair) is held June 30 and July 1 in honor of St. Peter. The **Aplec Sant Grau,** a traditional picnic in the hills, takes place on October 13. Make reservations for accommodations if you plan to come on these dates.

Lloret de Mar

Travelers make the 12km jaunt from Tossa to party down the coast at Lloret de Mar. Less pretentiously chic than its northern neighbor, this beach town of 16,000 bloats to 180,000 in July. By day, tourists cram into the winding back streets off the beach. Shops push everything from sunblock to three-foot sombreros. By night Lloret hooks 'em with 25 discos, 27 dance clubs, and five gay bars. For those more intimate moments, a winding path leads up the rocks on the right side of Platja de Lloret (the main beach).

Orientation and Practical Information

Buses arrive at the intersection of **C. de Blanes** and **Av. Just Marlés Vilarrodona.** The latter is a neon-lit string of clubs and hotels leading to the waterfront (turn left off C. de Blanes, about a 5-min. walk). The main beach, **Platja de Lloret,** is surprisingly pristine for such a promiscuous town. It runs the length of the shopping district, whose center is **Plaça de L'Església,** right behind the main tourist office.

Tourist Offices: Main office, Pl. Vila, 1 (tel. 36 47 72). In a yellow stucco building, **Casa de la Vila,** midway down the beach. They can help you find rooms in peak season, and their *Camins* brochure suggests trails that put the carousing behind you. Open July-Aug. 9am-9pm, June and Sept. Mon.-Sat. 9:30am-1pm and 4-7pm. If you arrive by bus you may find the **terminal branch** (tel. 36 57 88) more convenient; the entrance is to the right as you exit the station. Open Mon.-Sat. 9am-1pm and 4-7pm, Sun. 10am-2pm.

Post Office: Vincens Bou, 10 (tel. 36 46 78), in the grey building on the corner of C. de L'Oliva. Telegrams in the same building. Open Mon.-Fri. 8:30am-2pm, Sat. 8:30am-1pm. **Postal Code:** 17310.

Telephones: Office in bus terminal open 9am-1pm and 4pm-9pm. **Telephone Code:** 972.

Buses: Carretera de Blanes (tel. 36 44 76), at Av. Just Marlés Vilarrodona. **Rafael Mas** (tel. 36 41 42). To Girona (June 15-Sept. 15 Mon.-Fri. 5 per day, Sat.-Sun. 14 per day; Sept. 16-June 14 7 per day; 50min.; Mon.-Fri. 370ptas, Sat.-Sun. 420ptas); tickets on sale 15 in. before departure. **Sarfa** (tel. 36 42 95). To Barcelona (7-10 per day; 70min.; Mon.-Fri. 630ptas, Sat.-Sun. 720ptas). **Pujol i Pujol** (tel. 36 40 74). To Blanes (20 per day 7am-9:30pm; 15min.; 80ptas, Sat.-Sun. 90ptas) and Tossa (every 1/2 hr. 8:45am-8:15pm; 15min.; 115ptas, Sat.-Sun. 130ptas).

Ferries: Stands are on the beach in front of the tourist office. **Cruceros** (tel. 36 44 99). To Tossa (7 per day, 40min., round-trip Mon.-Fri. 850ptas, Sat.-Sun. variable) and Sant Feliu (11:50am, 1 1/2 hr., round-trip Mon.-Fri. 350ptas, Sat.-Sun. variable). In case of bad weather, call first. **Viajes Maritimòs** (tel. 36 90 95). To Tossa (July-Aug. 7 per day, round-trip 850ptas; Sept.-June Mon.-Sat. 7 per day, round-trip 850ptas) and Sant Feliu (variable, call first).

Moped Rental: Motos Catalunya, Ctra. de Tossa, 5 (tel. 36 36 58).

Laundromat: Lavanderia, C. dels Horts, 7, a little street between C. de L'Esperança and C. del Torrento, across from a Chinese restaurant. Pawn your jewelry to wash and dry. 1700ptas (yes, 1700) per load. Open Mon.-Sat. 9:30am-12:30pm and 4-7:30pm.

Red Cross: Ctra. Blanes (tel. 33 03 36).

Hospital: Vall de Venècia between C. Castell and C. Vidal i Barraquer (tel. 36 47 36). English spoken.

Emergency/Police: In an emergency, medical or otherwise, dial 092 for **municipal police,** C. Verge de Loreto, 3 (tel. 37 91 00), next to the market. English-speaking personnel will accompany you to the emergency room or the current **24-hr. pharmacy.**

Accommodations and Food

The over 30,000 rooms of Lloret have no room for you, particularly in July and August when reservations should be made one to two months in advance. Many people reserve summer rooms here as early as March. Most of the cheaper hotels and *pensions* are stacked atop each other near **Calle de la Fabrica.** Ask at the tourist office for a complete list (on the backside of their map) and call before walking 5-15 min. from the bus terminal. The waterfront area is a Babel of restaurants, from fast food to German.

>**Casa d'Hostes Alegría,** C. Migdia, 42 (tel. 36 74 72), a right turn off C. Conill i Sala from the waterfront. Located on a quiet side street, this tiny *pensión* doesn't even have a sign; look for the blue "CH" square on the wall. The rooms have comfortable beds and hot and cold running water. Student travelers are especially welcome. 1000ptas per person. Weekly 800ptas per person per night.
>
>**Hostal La Rosa,** La Fàbrica, 41 (tel. 36 44 92), on the next street over from the Alegría. Delightfully pink building with a restaurant downstairs. July.-Aug. singles 1600ptas, doubles 3000ptas; Sept.-June singles 1100ptas, doubles 1900ptas. Restaurant has *menú* for 700ptas.
>
>**Raimon's II,** Ctra. Tossa, 5, 3 blocks from the bus station on the right where Tossa meets C. Girona. A break from the glossy illustrated menus, where locals enjoy the simple, generous servings. Two-course *menú* with salad and beverage 880ptas.
>
>**La Parra Vinos,** C. Cervantes, 50 yds. behind the main tourist office. Typical of the near-beach restaurants; doubles as a bar. Specials 590ptas. *Menú* 850ptas. *Paella* for 2 1600ptas.

Sights and Entertainment

The beach is busy even on cloudy days, and Lloret doesn't allow mere nightfall to cramp its boogie: highrollers in the town's **casinos** tie their fate to a roll of the die, while patrons of the town's threescore discos dance for their preferred vice. **Clubs** are abundant in the maze of streets leading up from the beach.

Ask the tourist office about events at the **Casa de Cultura,** C. Enric Granados and C. Hipòlit Làzaro (tel. 36 79 09). The local holiday is **Festa Major** on July 24, when everything closes for the festivities.

Sant Feliu de Guíxols

A perilous but panoramic road twists 23km north between golden cliffs and frothy blue sea from Tossa to this little town. In Sant Feliu, which has the largest year-round population on the Costa Brava, tourists only slightly outnumber residents. Some ancestral boat building goes on in the side streets, but fishing boats are now more decorative than functional.

You can't see much of Sant Feliu's history in its buildings; successive invaders doggedly removed traces of the past. The **Monestir** church and monastery at Pl. Monestir (take Av. de Juli Garreta from the beach) is an architectural palimpsest patched together from the remains of various buildings. Most notable is the **Torre de Fum**, which stands behind the Visigothic and Roman walls. Follow the monastery walls to the right for the entrance to the **Museu d'Història** (free, open Sat. 5-8pm and Sun. 11am-2pm).

If you've come for Sant Feliu's beachy *platja*, arrive before 11am or you won't be able to find a vacant grain. It's a 20-minute walk to the new strip of sand called **Platja de Sant Pol.** A green Viñolas will convey you there from P. Marítim (every 1/2hr., 60ptas). The cove has unmediated access to the sea because it lacks marina and commercial docking. Next to Sant Pol, a 2km path scampers across the rocky hills, tumbling headlong into the blue water and tiny fingerlike coves. The walk leads to **La Conca,** another popular beach.

The Sunday before or the Saturday after July 16 (whichever falls closer), fishermen primp their ships as part of the **Processió de la Verge del Carme.** In summer, Sant Feliuians dance *Sardanes,* the local folkdance, one block from the beach in Pl. Espanya (mid-June to mid-Sept. Wed. 10:15pm). Throughout July and August classical music fills Sant Feliu's municipal theater in Pl. Monestir for the **Festival Internacional de Música de la Porta Ferrada.**

If by land your entry will be the Sarfa **bus station** on Ctra. Girona. If by sea you'll disembark mid-beach in front of the tree-lined waterfront promenade and pedestrian path, **Passeig del Mar.** Connecting the two points of entry is the **Rambla D'Antoni Vidal,** which leads from the middle of the pedestrian street to the Placeta de Sant Joan. From the beach take a left onto Passeig del Mar, then a right onto Rambla D'Antoni Vidal, following it to the semicircular *placeta.* A right again at the sign for Girona puts you on the Ctra. Girona; the bus station is three blocks away on the left.

Many hotel owners will discount prices if you remain five days or more, and reservations are suggested for July and August. **Fonda Alga,** C. Algavira, 16 (tel. 32 57 43), one block inland off C. Rutlla, which runs from Placeta de Sant Joan, has smallish doubles with bath and bright curtains and bedding (July-Aug. 1500ptas per person; Sept.-June 1200ptas per person). Less economical is **Hostal Zürich,** Av. Juli Garreta, 43-45 (tel. 32 10 54), just off Pl. Monestir. It has airy, well-lit rooms. (Singles 2500ptas, breakfast included. Doubles 4100ptas, with bath 5100ptas.) The café downstairs serves portly *bocadillos* (200-325ptas). Reasonably priced but slightly cramped is **Fonda Forta Ferrada,** C. Juli Garreta, 19 (tel. 82 18 32). The rooms are a little dark; windows and flowered bedspreads help brighten things (July-Aug. 1600ptas per person; Sept.-June 1200ptas per person).

Around the beach many restaurants serve *bocadillos* at middling to outlandish prices. **Nou Casino La Costancia,** Rambla Portalet, 2 (tel. 32 10 92) is a curious *Modernista* gambling emporium famous enough to earn its own postcards. A Moorish arch divides the outer world from a crowd of old men playing checkers and sipping beers in a bingo-hall atmosphere. (Beers 120-150ptas. Open 9am-1am; Oct.-May 9am-midnight. Closed one month in winter.) The main **market** is next to Pl. Espanya, the town's main square. (Open Mon.-Sat. 8am-2pm.)

The **tourist office** is on Pl. Monestir, 54 (tel. 82 00 51). From the beach take a left on Passeig del Mar to Av. Juli Garreta. Follow this to the *plaça*. (Open Mon.-Fri. 8am-8pm and 5-9pm, Sat. 8am-noon.) The *Guía del Sardanista* lists *coblas (sardana* groups) currently performing. The tourist office also compiles a monthly list of events. The **post office** is at Ctra. Girona, 15 (tel. 32 11 60; open Mon.-Fri. 8am-3pm, Sat. 9am-1pm). **Telegrams** may be sent from the post office during the same hours (tel. 32 06 78). **Telephone calls** can be made at Rambla Antoni Vidal, 44. (Open Mon.-Sat. 10am-1pm and 4:30-8:30pm, Sun. 10am-1pm.) The **telephone code** is 972. The **municipal police,** C. Callao, s/n (tel. 32 42 11) are on the outskirts of town; from Pl. Monestir head past the theater and across the parking lot on Ronda Martirs.

Sarfa, Ctra. Girona, 35 (tel. 32 11 87), runs **buses** to: Palafrugell (Mon.-Fri. 12 per day, 24min., 180ptas; Sat.-Sun. 6 per day, 205ptas); Girona (Mon.-Fri. 6-7 per day, 1 1/2 hr., 535ptas; Sat.-Sun. 8:45am-4:45pm, 615ptas); and Barcelona (Mon.-Fri. 8 per day, 1hr. 50min., 902ptas; Sat.-Sun. 8:30am-8pm, 1050ptas). **Teisa,** Pl. Monestir, runs buses to Girona (13 per day, 50min., Mon.-Fri. 315ptas, Sat.-Sun. 285ptas). **Cruceros ferries** (tel. 32 00 26) have a stand on the beach and sail south to Tossa (1 per day, 45 min., round-trip 1350ptas); Lloret (1 1/4 hr., round-trip 1725ptas); and Blanes (1 3/4 hr., round-trip 1775ptas). One-way fares are over half the round-trip price.

Palafrugell

40km east of Girona and 3km from the coast, Palafrugell prides itself on having been both maternity ward and nursery to Catalan literary patriarch Josep Pla. This is well and good, but tourists come to recline on the nearby beaches: **Calella**, **Llafranc**, and **Tamariu.** Tamariu and the rocky inlet of Aigua Xelida are the least crowded and most scenic of the three busy beaches. A string of cash-hungry sand strips stretch from the fishing port of Calella: Portbou, Port Pelegrì, El Golfet, Mala Espina, and Canadell. Llafranc, about 2km away, is more sedate. Palafrugell's inexpensive accommodations make it the best starting point for forays into the area.

Orientation and Practical Information

The pilgrim's progress in Palafrugell lies down **Carrer Torres Jonama** and **Plaça Nova.** From the traffic circle outside of town, C. Torres Jonama runs past the **Sarfa bus station,** from whose doors you should turn right and walk until you reach C. de Pi i Margall. Turn right and walk past the **Guardia Civil** and the **market** until you hit the **plaça,** the hangout of the town's pensioners.

From Palafrugell, buses frequently dash the paltry 4-5km to Llafranc, and the 1km from there to both Calella and Tamariu, leaving from the Sarfa station. The Calella and Llafranc bus leapfrogs Llafranc to stop in Calella first and then turns around to catch Llafranc on the way back to Palafrugell. There are multiple stops in Calella—watch for the inflatable beach balls to know when to get off.

Tourist Office: C. Carrilet, 2 (tel. 30 02 28). From the bus station take a left on C. Torres Jonama and follow it to the traffic circle. Turn left on the road out of town and look for the giant "I" for *informaciò*. **Summer branch office,** on Pl. Nova in the old Cinema Victoria. A superflux of information—good map of Palafrugell and beaches, and the *Guía Municipal* chock full of helpful facts. Both offices open June-Sept. Mon.-Sat. 10am-1pm and 5-9pm, Sun. 10am-1pm; C. Carrilet office also open Oct.-May Mon.-Sat. 10am-1pm and 5-7pm. Branches with the same summer hours are located in Llafranc, C. Roger de Llúria (tel. 30 50 08); Calella, Les Voltes, 4 (tel. 30 36 75); and Tamariu, C. Riera (30 50 07).

Post Office: C. Torres Jonama, 14 (tel. 30 06 07). Open for stamps, telegrams, and Lista de Correos Mon.-Fri. 8am-3pm, Sat. 9am-1pm. **Postal Code:** 17200.

Telephones: Pl. Camp. d'en Prats, at the end of C. Sant Sebastià, next to the bar in the middle of the *plaça*. Open Sept.-June 10am-1pm and 5-9pm, July-Aug. 9:30am-1pm and 5-10pm. **Telephone Code:** 972.

Catalunya (Catalonia)

Buses: Sarfa, C. Torres Jonama, 67-79 (tel. 30 12 93). To: Girona (8-11 per day 8am-7pm, 1hr., Mon.-Fri. 445ptas, Sat.-Sun. 505ptas); Tamariu (July-Aug. 6 per day; June-Sept. 4 per day; 8:05am-8:35pm, 15min., Mon.-Fri. 75ptas, Sat.-Sun. 90ptas); Calella and Llafranc (July-Aug. every 1/2 hr. 8am-8pm; June and Sept. 10 per day 8am-7pm; Oct.-May 6 per day 8am-7pm; 20min. to Calella, 25min. to Llafranc, Mon.-Fri. 75ptas, Sat.-Sun 90ptas); Sant Feliu (8-13 per day 7:45am-8pm, 1hr., Mon.-Fri. 190ptas, Sat.-Sun. 210ptas); Barcelona (4-8 per day 8am-5:30pm, 2hr. 20min., Mon.-Fri. 1090ptas, Sat.-Sun. 1245ptas); Figueres (3-5 per day, 1 1/2 hr., Mon.-Fri. 530ptas, Sat.-Sun. 605ptas); and L'Escala (take the Figueres bus, 45min., Mon.-Fri. 240ptas, Sat.-Sun. 280ptas).

Market: on C. Pi i Maragall, off Pl. Nova (Tues.-Sun. 7am-1pm).

Laundromat: C. Constancia, 16 (tel. 30 28 63), off C. La Caritat. Open Mon.-Fri. 9am-1pm and 4-8pm, Sat. 9am-1pm.

Medical services: Red Cross, C. Ample, 1. Call 30 19 09 for **ambulance.** The **ambulatorio,** Av. Josep Pla (tel. 30 48 16), provides more general medical care. Little English spoken.

Municipal police: Av. Josep Pla and C. Cervantes (tel. 61 31 01). One of 2 places on the Costa Brava with an *oficina de atención extranjera* (office for assistance to foreigners), the answer to the penniless, documentless, or clueless tourist's prayers. In an emergency dial 092.

Accommodations and Food

Palafrugell remains the cheapest and most welcoming center from which to visit Catalunya's mid-coast beaches. While even one-star *hostales* on the beach will cheerfully relieve you of 5000-6000ptas for a double in high season, Palafrugell's largely family-run operations are more reasonable.

Fonda L'Estrella, C. Quatres Cases, 13 (tel. 30 00 05), under the pink sign at the corner of C. La Caritat, off C. Torres Jonama. Not your average everyday *hostal*. The exterior rooms have rounded ceilings over wood-framed beds, and the brighter interior rooms border a courtyard of Moorish arches. July-Aug. 1300ptas per person; June and Sept. 1200ptas per person; April-May 1100ptas per person. Breakfast 350ptas.

Pensió Ramírez, C. Sant Sebastià, 29 (tel. 30 00 43), 2 blocks from and within earshot of Plaça Nova. Halls are papered in blue with printed white "paint spatters." Sparkling tiled bathrooms. 1200ptas per person, July-Aug. 1450ptas. Showers included. Reservations recommended in summer.

Hostal Platja, C. Sant Sebastià, 34 (tel. 30 05 26). Ornate arched entryway and quiet rooms with terraces. June singles with bath 2400ptas; July-Sept. 15 2500ptas. June doubles with bath 3300ptas; July-Sept. 15 3500ptas. Breakfast 450ptas.

Camping: Camping Kim on Font d'En Xecu (tel. 30 11 56 or 30 07 05), in Llafranc. Halfway down the hill toward the beach on C. Lluís Marquès Carbó are signs for this campsite. The left side of this street merges with C. Pere Pascuet, which empties into the sea. 510ptas per person, 350ptas per tent, 510ptas per car. Open April-Sept. **Camping Moby Dick,** C. Costa Verde, 16 (tel. 30 48 07), on the bus route off Av. Costa del Sol in Calella. Cheaper than surrounding grounds, it's a tree-filled park a 5-min. walk from the beach with roomy sites and good showers. 450ptas per person, 390ptas per tent, 460ptas per car. Open April-Sept.

Restaurant La Clau, C. Pi i Margall, 31, 2 blocks toward C. Torres Jonama, close to Pl. Nova. Simple. *Raciones* 500-1200ptas.

Piscolabis, C. Pi i Maragall, 18 (tel. 30 00 01), a half block from Pl. Nova. Locals come a-running for their *bocadillos* (sandwiches, 160-325ptas). Savory *sobrassada y queso* (Mallorcan sausage and cheese, 240ptas). Open Tues.-Fri. 7:30am-2pm and 4-11pm, Sat.-Sun. 5pm-midnight.

Sights and Entertainment

From the bus stop in front of Calella's Hotel Garbí, it's a 45-minute walk to the botanic gardens at **Castell i Jardins de Cap Roig.** After fleeing his homeland during the revolution, Russian Colonel Nicolas Voevodsky came to Spain and built this castle on the sea. He and his wife planted and pruned a splendid maze of paths and flower beds with their own hands. (Open 8am-8pm. Admission 150ptas.) The first of the signs leading you to the castle points to the right at the fork of Av. Costa Daurada and C. Consolat del Mar.

On Calella's waterfront, anglers spend the first Saturday in July crooning the old seafaring songs of the **Cantata de las Habaneras,** effectively scaring away most of the fish.

Palafrugell's Friday evening *passeig* ends up at the *plaça,* where young and old do the *sardana* (folk-dancing) at 10pm. The town's biggest party occurs from July 20 to 22, when the **Festa Major** bursts into the streets, including *sardana* and open-air dancing in the Plaça Nova. Calella's festivities take place on June 29 in honor of Sant Pere; Tamariu's on August 15, and Llafranc's on August 27-30 in honor of Santa Rosa.

Empúries and L'Escala

In the 7th century BC Greek traders landed on a small island on the northeast Iberian coast. As the settlement grew it moved to the mainland and became the prosperous colony of Emporion ("marketplace"), falling into Roman hands four centuries later. Remnants of both Greek and Roman cities, as well as a Visigothic early Christian basilica, today form the ruins of **Empúries,** a 40-hectare site. Excavation of the ruins continues, most recently fueled by the 1992 Olympic Games, whose torch formally entered Spain through the ancient Greek port. Amateur anthropologists can relive the past in the **Museu Monogràfic d'Empúries** (tel. 77 02 08), on the excavation grounds. The museum showcases a large collection of ceramics, artifacts, and weirdly complex doorlocks. Comely plaques throughout the ruins indicate the ancient urban plan without marring the overall effect of fountains, mosaics, and columns set against a backdrop of cypress trees and the Mediterranean Sea. (Grounds and museum open Tues.-Sun. 10am-2pm and 3-7pm; Oct.-May Tues.-Sun. 10am-1pm and 3-5pm. Admission 150ptas.)

Only half a km to the north is the start of the 18.5-sq. mi. **Parc Natural dels Aiguarnolls de l'Empordà,** a protected habitat with miles of marshland, lakes, and animal and plant species found only in this area (the unhappily named *fartet* fish, for example). Bird-watchers should strap on their binoculars: mornings and early evenings from March to May and August to October are choice watching hours. (Brochure on the park at the tourist office in L'Escala; Park Information Center tel. 45 12 31.)

L'Escala, a 2km walk south of Empúries, fully exploits the tourist potential of its beaches and nearby sights. This town of 4800 hosts classical concerts one night a week and live flamenco dancing (Tues.-Sun. 10pm) at **La Palmera,** C. La Tone, 62 (tel. 77 03 03). To see a more local Spanish dance, ask at the tourist office about the *sardanas,* which regularly occurs on summer nights at the *plaçà* next to the main beach.

Finding a room in L'Escala is taxing; many *pensiones* require that their summer guests pay full board. People who make reservations months in advance may find room at the **HI youth hostel,** Les Coves, 41 (tel. 77 12 00), set 100m from the ruins in a grove of trees. (Open Jan. 16-Dec. 15. Members only. 850ptas per person, over 25 1275ptas. Breakfast included. Filled with groups July-Aug. Call Girona youth office at 20 15 54 for reservations.) **Hostal Poch,** C. Gràcia, 10 (tel. 77 00 92), decorates its spacious rooms with antique furniture and fine ceramic tiles. (July-Aug. singles 1800ptas. Doubles 2700ptas.) **Hostal Mediterráneo,** C. Riera, 22-24 (tel. 77 00 28), is one of those barren but clean slumberamas with baths in every room and a dining area downstairs. (July-Aug. 1600ptas per person; April-June and Sept. 1300ptas per person. *Pensión completa* 3475ptas per person.) The nostalgic **Restaurant El Garìa,** C. Enric Serra, 16 (tel. 77 03 55), 2 blocks up from the *platja,* combines homey service, historical pictures of L'Escala on the wall and tuneful 40's Spanish swing (*paella* 700ptas, and seafood specialties).

The **tourist office** on Pl. Les Escoles, 1 (tel. 77 06 03) provides a useful map and an accommodations list. (Open July-Sept. Mon.-Sat. 8:30am-8:30pm, Sun. 9:30am-1:30pm; Oct.-June Mon.-Wed. and Fri.-Sat. 10am-1pm and 4-7pm, Thurs. 10am-1pm.) The **post office** is on Pl. Rei Marti, s/n (tel. 77 16 51; open Mon.-Fri. 8am-2pm, Sat. 9am-1pm). The **postal code** is 17130. Near the waterfront on Av. Ave María is a **telephone center.** (Open 9am-1:30pm and 5-10pm.) The **telephone code** is 972. For an **ambulance** call 75 92 02. The **municipal police,** C. Massanet, 24, take calls at 77 00 86.

Sarfa **buses** (tel. 77 01 29) depart from Av. Ave María, s/n, near the tourist office for: Figueres (3-5 per day, 45min., Mon.-Fri. 290ptas, Sat.-Sun. 335ptas); Palafrugell (3 per day, 45min., Mon.-Fri. 240ptas, Sat.-Sun. 280ptas); Girona (2 per day, 1 1/2 hr., Mon.-Fri. 340ptas, Sat.-Sun. 390ptas); Barcelona (2 per day, 2 1/2 -3hr., Mon.-Fri. 1195ptas, Sat.-Sun. 1360ptas).

Figueres (Figueras)

Tourists once ignored the rather nondescript and beachless Figueres, 40km north of Girona. But since the egomaniacal Salvador Dalí decided to build a museum for his works here, art buffs and wannabes swarm to see the largest single collection of Spain's most notorious Surrealist. Scandal-monger and snob, fascist and fop, Dalí was inspired by dreams and the new theories of Sigmund Freud. Transformed from old municipal theater into Surrealist playhouse, the **Museu Dalí** (tel. 51 18 00; fax 50 16 66) in Pl. Gala i S. Dalí parades the artist's capricious projects: erotically nightmarish drawings, extra-terrestrial landscapes, and even a personal rock collection. Probably nowhere else in the world can you walk up a set of stairs to stand underneath a camel, look through a peephole and see a room with a giant nose on the floor. The coin-operated black Cadillac with a five-foot hood ornament is an outsize toy; there's even a surprise for those who look on the side *opposite* the coin box. Dalí is not the only featured act—Evarist Vallés's thing for nails has mettle too. Follow C. Sant Llàtzer (to the train station) for six blocks, turn right on C. Nou and follow it to its end at the Rambla. Go diagonally to the right and take C. Girona, which goes past Pl. Ajuntament and becomes C. Jonquería. A flight of steps with a Dalí statue on the left leads to the museum. (Open July-Sept. 9am-8:15pm; Oct.-June 10:30am-5:15pm. Admission 500ptas, students and seniors 300ptas, groups 400ptas per person.) The same ticket is good for the **Museu de l'Empordà** (tel. 50 23 05), a few blocks back at Rambla, 1, which keeps some Roman bits and a collection of paintings from the 19th-century Catalan *Renaixença*. (Open July-Sept. 9am-8:15pm; Oct.-June 10:30am-5:15pm.)

If you find the Dalí museum too rich, try playing in the **Museu de Joguetes,** Rambla, 10 (tel. 50 45 85), a historical toy collection. (Open Mon.-Sat. 10am-12:30pm and 4-7:30pm, Sun. 11am-1:30pm and 5-7:30pm. Closed Tues. Oct.-June. Admission 300ptas, students and groups 200ptas, children under 12 150ptas.)

The nearest body of water in town is one of the municipal **swimming pools,** C. Cusi i Fortunet (tel. 50 90 01, 50 93 39), just behind the city park in the northeastern quarter of Figueres, across town from the train and bus station. (Outdoor Olympic-sized pool open June 20-Sept. 20 Mon.-Sat. 10am-8pm. Admission 350ptas, under 14 250ptas. Indoor pool 1 block away open year-round Mon.-Fri. 7am-11pm, Sun. 9am-2pm. Admission 300ptas.)

In September, the town hosts classical and jazz music at the **Festival Internacional de Música de l'Empordà.** (Call Joventuts Musicals at 50 01 17 for information and tickets or ask at the tourist office for their brochure.) In the first week of May, the **Fires i Festes de la Santa Creu** offers cultural events and art and technology exhibitions. The merrymaking at the **Festa de Sant Pere,** held June 28-29, is in honor of the town's patron saint.

Figueres is convenient to the many isolated sights of the Empordà countryside but Girona (only 45min. away by train) is preferable to Figueres for extended stays. The **HI youth hostel,** C. Anicet de Pagés, 2 (tel. 50 12 13), is a bit of a hike from the train and bus stations. Follow C. Sant Llàtzer past the park on your left, turn right on Ronda de Barcelona, turn left into the tourist office parking lot (called C. Mestre Falla beyond the post office), and finally take a left on C. Poeta Marquinà. The red brick building on your right hides rooms with kitchen facilities and awe-inspiring crimson trim. The hot showers and French television insure popularity with foreign visitors. (Lock-in 11pm-8am. Lockout 1-5pm. 775ptas, over 25 950ptas; nonmembers 300ptas extra. Sheets 300ptas, over 25 360ptas. Reserve 1 month in advance in July and Aug. through the Barcelona office at (93) 302 28 58 or call the hostel 2-3 days prior to arrival if you can get there by 8pm. Lights out at midnight, the final deadline for exceptions to curfew. 1 room available for a family of 4.)

Tourist-oriented restaurants near Plaçà del Sol serve expensive yet bland meals. One exception is **Restaurant-Cafeteria Dolç Glop,** C. Vilafant, 26 (tel. 51 08 03). Follow C. Lausaca (across from the tourist office), take the 100° right, and proceed for three blocks. No glop here; the *menú* (800ptas) includes simple but well-prepared omelettes, gazpacho, and chicken. (Open 6am-1am.) Only a few blocks from the Dalí museum bops the cheaper food of popular **Menestral,** C. Peralada, the casino-turned-diner with Spanish rock, a younger crowd, and hamburgers (500ptas).

The **tourist office** (tel. 50 31 55) on Pl. Sol. offers the standard good city map, list of accommodations, ranking of restaurants, and still more facts about Catalunya. (Open mid-June-Sept. Mon.-Sat. 9am-8pm; Oct.-June 20 Mon.-Fri. 8:30am-3pm, Sat. 9am-1pm.) During the summer use the **branch office,** in the bus station across the park from the train station. (Open Mon.-Sat. 9:30am-1pm and 4:15-7pm.) From the stations, the swiftest route to Pl. Sol is straight up C. Llàtzer (which becomes C. Collegi halfway up) to the Rambla de Barcelona. Turn right and discover the *plaçà* two blocks away.

Behind the main tourist office is the **post office** (tel. 50 54 31; open Mon.-Sat. 9am-2pm) and **telephones** (open Mon.-Sat. 9am-2pm and 5-10pm). The **postal code** is 17600; the **telephone code** 972. The **Red Cross** is at Santa Llogia, 67 (tel. 50 17 99 or 50 56 01). The **local police** (tel. 51 01 11, 50 98 58 or 50 99 62) share their building with the tourist office; the **emergency** number for the **municipal police** is 092.

Sarfa **buses** (tel. 50 01 59) spin to Cadaqués (2 per day, July-Aug. 4 per day; 1 1/4 hr.; 325ptas, Sat.-Sun. 370ptas). Teisa buses connect with Olot (1-3 per day, 70min.), where there's service to Ripoll, an entrance to the Catalan Pyrenees. RENFE **trains** (tel. 50 46 61) make for Girona (26 per day including 2 *talgos,* 25min.-1hr., 220ptas), Portbou (23 per day, including 2 *talgos;* 24-34min.; 105ptas), and Barcelona (15 per day, 1 1/2 -2hr., 710ptas).

Cadaqués

This charming cluster of whitewashed houses around a small bay has been filled with artists since Dalí built his house here. The teeny town remains picturesque—no condos or huge hotels, few noisy buses and no trains. However, high lodging prices make it better for a daytrip.

The bus to Cadaqués halts at a shack outside of town, where there's an excellent guidebook for sale (300ptas) with detailed maps of the city and much information (including a Catalan glossary). From the bus station, walk downhill to your left along Av. Caritat Serinyana until you reach the waterfront **Plaça Frederic Rahola.** There, a signboard map with indexed services and accommodations will orient you.

The **Museu Municipal d'Art** on C. Monturiol is currently closed for repairs. Ask for information at the tourist office about this collection of local and "Dalíesque" art. The **Museu Perrot-Moore,** C. Vigilant, 1, near the center of town, hoards a load of odd Dalí memorabilia, including the doodles in his chemistry book, pictures of him as a young tyke, and lithographs and posters of his work. (Open Easter week and June 15-Sept. 10 Mon.-Sat. 5-9pm only. Admission 300ptas, students 250ptas.) For either museum follow the signs from the mapboard on Pl. Frederic Rahola; otherwise, head toward the bay, hang a right on the waterfront road and another on C. Vigilant. For Dalí's house, stay on the waterfront road until you pass the bars and restaurants and C. Miranda appears on the left. Follow this road out of town to Av. Salvador Dalí; a right on this road arrives at the museum.

The **Festival Internacional de Música** sponsors nine concerts in the first two weeks of August, two given by students. (Tickets 800-1100ptas, the sole contemporary music concert free; for more information, call 25 83 15.) Throughout the summer, locals dance *sardanas* outdoors (Sat. 10pm) and hip-hop to live rock every other Thursday. Those determined to catch some rays can try the **Platja Gran,** near the town center, or, even better, **Sa Concha,** to the south of town.

Sleep is dear in Cadaqués. Most choose to make it a daytrip from Figueres. Rooms are nearly always available except on major Catalan weekend holidays. **Hostal Ubaldo,** C. Unión, 13 (tel. 25 81 25), has brightly colored doubles with bath (summer 4500ptas; Sept.-June rates lower; breakfast 400ptas). Take C. Vigilant up the hill and take the right fork. Near the water there is **Hostal Marina,** C. Riera de Sant Vicenç, 3 (tel. 25 81 99), directly ahead as you face the mapboard on Pl. Frederic Rohola. Its rooms are clean, some even balconied. (Singles 2000ptas, with shower 2300ptas. Doubles 3000ptas, with bath and/or shower 4000-5000ptas. Breakfast 350ptas.) **Camping Cadaqués,** Ctra. Portlligat, 17 (tel. 25 81 26), is on the left as one heads for Dalí's house from town; or ask the bus driver to let you off near it before you arrive in town. The grounds, only 1/2km from the beach, have a view, supermarket, and warm showers (100ptas). (Open March 20-Sept. 30, 450ptas per person, 1080ptas per tent.)

Piu Snack Bar, partly downhill on C. Caritat Serinyana, serves snacks. The staff deftly prepares such sandwiches as *Llam "Nareta"* (grilled chicken with tomato, 400ptas) before your wondering eyes.

The **tourist office,** C. Cotxe, 2 (tel. 25 83 15), off Pl. Frederic Rahola opposite the *passeig,* informs on local events. (Open during summer Mon.-Sat. 10am-1pm and 2-9pm, Sun. 10am-1pm; winter Tues.-Sat. 10am-noon and 5-7pm.) The **post office** is in the upper part of town on an alley off Av. Caritat Serinyana; they have no phone. (Open Mon.-Fri. 9am-2pm, Sat. 9am-1pm.) The town's **postal code** is 17488. **Telephone** cabins are on the beachwalk in Pl. Frederic Rahola; the **telephone code** is 972. **Bikes and mopeds** are rentable at Motos Cadaqués, Av. Salvador Dalí, s/n; go left on C. Miranda as you come up from town. Call the tourist office for information and prices (tel. 25 87 35; open April-Sept. daily, Oct.-March Sat.-Sun. 10am-1pm and 3-8pm). The **laundromat** number is 25 84 89. In an **emergency,** contact the solicitous **local police** (tel. 25 81 94) on Pl. Frederic Rahola beside the promenade. For **medical assistance,** call 25 80 97.

Sarfa **buses** (tel. 25 87 13 or 50 01 59) run to Figueres (2 per day, July-Aug. 4 per day; 1 1/4 hr.; 285ptas, Sat.-Sun. 325ptas) and to Barcelona (2 per day, July-Sept. 15 4 per day; 1365ptas, Sat.-Sun. 1555ptas). Buses disgorge passengers at the junction of Ctra. Port Lligat and Pg. Caritat Serinyana; the latter leads to the town center.

Llançà, Sant Pere de Roda, and Portbou

These towns are the extremities of the Costa Brava. 9km south of the French border, **Llançà** is the northernmost resort of magnitude of the Costa Brava, with many beaches and coves and a smattering of historical sights. The main beach, Platja del Port, opens onto a protected harbor. The town center lies in the opposite direction; look for the **Església** and the 14th-century **Torre de Llançà** to find the central **plaça.** The town's annual festival takes place on the outskirts, in the chapel of the 11th-century Romanesque hermitage **Sant Silvestre de Valleta i del Terrer.** To get there from town, take a right from the train station onto Ctra. Bisbal, cross the river on a bridge opposite the soccer field, and continue on the path up the hill. Near the top take the left fork for the hermitage (1 hr.).

From the bus and train stations, cross the highway and bridge and continue on Av. Europa until it forks: right goes into town, left to the port. For the harbor and beaches, follow the curve to the left and walk about 1km; there are signs for the port. The first street you'll meet in the town center is C. Rafael Estela. Follow it to the **telephones** (open 9am-1pm and 4:30-9pm) and to the Plaça Major.

Habitaciones Cau Pau, C. Puig d'Esquer, 4 (tel. 38 02 70), were built laboriously on weekends by the owner and his son for 10 years; comfortable and clean, they've a rooftop view (1200ptas per person). To get there take the first left as you enter town, C. Cabrafiqa, for three blocks, then turn left on C. Deciana; almost immediately, turn right on C. Puig d'Esquer. Overflow is channeled to more cramped rooms across town at the original location. For magnificent and clean rooms there's **Hostal Beri,** C. Creus, s/n (tel. 38 01 98), with bathrooms to get lost in. (Singles with bath 2500ptas, doubles with bath 4000ptas. Winter heating.) From Pl. Major, bear right on C. Nicolás Salmerón and follow it to the edge of town. At the crossroads take a sharp left till the sign comes into view.

Restaurante El Puerto, C. Castellar, 7, on the road to the port, caters mainly to tourists. There is good seafood such as *merluza* (hake) and *calamares* (squid). *(Menús* 895-975ptas; open 12:15-11pm.)

The mobbed staff in the **tourist office,** Av. Europa, 17 (tel. 38 08 55), on the road to the port, distribute a ludicrous map whose utter uselessness around the Pl. Major is surpassed only by the piece of abstract art on the signboard in front of the telephones. You'll reach the port all right, but there you'll stay. A new map is currently in the works. (Office open Mon.-Sat. 10am-1pm and 4:30-8pm.) The **post office** is in the municipal building on C. la Selva (open Mon.-Fri. 8am-3pm, Sat. 8am-2pm). The town's **postal code** is 17490. The **Red Cross** is at Platja Crifeu, s/n (tel. 38 08 31). The **local police** take calls at 38 13 13. The **Guardia Civíl** is installed at C. Nicolas Salmerón, 18 (tel. 38 01 22).

RENFE **trains** (tel. 38 02 55) run to and from: Portbou (17 per day, 10min., 90ptas); Figueres (17 per day, 20-30 in., 105ptas); Girona (17 per day, 1hr., 240ptas), and Barcelona (15 per day, 1 1/2 hr., 760ptas). **Autocares Estarriol** (tel. 50 04 03) run six buses per day from the train station to Port de la Selva (100ptas).

The glorious ruins of the monastery **Sant Pere de Roda** are 9km south of Llançà on the coast. The Benedictine monastery was built in the 10th and 11th centuries with unassailable walls girding it about. Visitors go batty over the monastery's view; on a clear day you can easily see Portbou to the north and Cadaqués to the south. If you don't have a car, getting there is an adventure. Catch the Autocares Estarriol **bus** (tel. 38 74 55) from the train station in Llançà (6 per day, 45ptas) and ask to be dropped off on the road to the *monestir.* From there make the hour-long hike; monastery maniacs, and anyone else, will be supremely rewarded. (Open Mon.-Sat. 10am-2pm and 4-7pm. Admission 80ptas.)

Seven km to the north, peaceful **Portbou** suffered a sea-change about a hundred years ago when the Barcelona-Cerbère railroad opened. Once a fishing community, Portbou now caters to fly-by-day tourists on their way somewhere else. The village spills around a small cove with a pleasant stone beach. The view from paths leading up from the grassy cliffs by the beach show a town dwarfed by the train station behind it. To get to the water, head out the lower level of the train station down the tree-lined C. Mercat and take the first left past the **post office,** Pg. Enric Granades, 10 (tel. 39 01 75). The **postal code** is 17497. Plaça Lluis Companys is right near the water. The **tourist office** there is phoneless, but well-stocked.

Hostal Juventus, Av. Barcelona, 3 (tel. 39 02 41) lies near the water. Walk two blocks from the train station and turn left on Av. Barcelona. The outer rooms just manage views of the nearby bay and bluffs. The same owners run a *croissanterie* downstairs with a panoply of baked goods in the morning. (1100ptas per person, triples 3000ptas. Arrive in the morning.) **Hostal Plaza,** C. Mercat, 15 (tel. 39 00 24), is on the left half a block from the train station. The rooms and facilities are clean; moreover, you can practice sweeping entrances on the wide tile staircase. (Doubles 2120ptas, with shower 2978ptas. July-Aug. call to reserve.) Those in need of a restorative drink will want to know of the many **cafés** lining Pg. Marítim—ask for directions at the tourist office.

The **Oficina de Turisme Juvenil** at the train station is scheduled to reopen soon. The **police** (tel. 39 00 91) and the **health center** share the same building at the end of Pg. Sardanes on the right side end of the beach. RENFE **trains** (tel. 39 00 99) pay calls to Llançà (10min., 90ptas) and various nearby beaches. At the two stops prior to Portbou are better beaches than in town.

Girona (Gerona)

Few travelers know what they're missing when, on their way from Barcelona to France, they bypass the stone alleyways of Girona. The medieval masterpiece reigns without vainglorious ceremony from the banks of the Riu Onyar, while its new city across the river is one of Spain's wealthiest mainland centers. The city was home to the renowned *cabalistas de Girona,* who for centuries spread the teachings of mystical Judaism in the West. Still a center of culture and education, artists and students from the University fill the city's cafes and strut throught the streets lined by Girona's trademark orange, yellow, and blue facades. Despite its allure, however, Girona fills only on cloudy days, when crowds wash in from the resorts on the Costa Brava.

Orientation and Practical Information

The coffee-colored **Riu Onyar** divides the new city from the old. The **Pont de Pedra** connects the two banks and leads directly into the old quarter by way of C. Ciutadans, C. Carreras Peralta, and C. Força, off which are located the **Cathedral** and the historic Jewish neighborhood known as the **Call.**

Girona is the transportation hub of the Costa Brava: all trains on the Barcelona-Portbou-Cerbère line stop here, seven different lines send scores of buses daily to the Costa Brava and nearby cities, and the major national and international car companies have offices here. The RENFE and bus terminals are off **Carrer de Barcelona** on the modern side of town. To get from there to the old city, pass through the **commercial district** by heading straight out of the station through the parking lot, turning left on C. Bailen and left again on C. Barcelona. Follow C. Barcelona for two blocks until it forks at the traffic island. The right fork runs via C. de Santa Eugenia to the **Gran Via de Jaume I.** Cross this at the Banco Central and you should be on **C. Nou,** which runs directly to the bridge **Pont de Pedra.**

Tourist Office: Rambla Llibertat, 1 (tel. 20 26 79), directly on the left as you cross Pont de Pedra from the new town. Vies for best in Catalunya; the staff has made Girona tourism its guiding passion. Transit schedules, restaurant and accommodations listings with locations marked on maps, and piles of brochures. English and all major European languages spoken. Least busy early afternoon. (Open Mon.-Fri. 8am-8pm, Sat. 8am-2pm and 4-8pm.) **Train station branch:** tel. 21 62 96. Downstairs, on the left as you face away from the RENFE ticket counter. Open summer Mon.-Fri. 9am-2pm. The office posts indexed street map when closed, with directions to the main office.

Budget Travel: Direcciò General de Juventut, C. Juli Garreta, 14 (tel. 20 15 54), 1 block from the train station, off C. Bisbe Tomás de Lorenzana. In an unmarked building, one flight up on the *entresol* (mezzanine). Railpasses, buses to Europe, HI cards (1800ptas), ISICs (500ptas), *Guide to Budget Accommodations* (500ptas). They also run Girona's youth hostel. Open Mon.-Fri. 8am-3pm; Oct.-May 9am-2pm.

Post Office: Av. Ramón Folch, 2 (tel. 20 32 36), at Gran Via de Jaume I. Turn right on the Gran Via if coming from the old city. Open Mon.-Sat. 8am-9pm for stamps and Lista de Correos. **Telegrams** upstairs. Open Mon.-Sat. 9am-9pm. **Postal Code:** 17001 for post office.

Telephones: Gran Via de Jaume I, 58. Turn left on the Gran Via if coming from the old city and walk half a block. Open Mon.-Sat. 9am-9pm. **Telephone Code:** 972.

Trains: RENFE, Pl. Espanya (tel. 20 70 93). To: Figueres (25 per day 6am-11pm, 26-52min., 220ptas); Portbou (24 per day 6am-11pm, 50-70min., 340ptas); Barcelona (27 per day 6:10am-10pm, including 2 *talgos;* 1-2hr.; 515ptas, *talgo* 1035ptas); Zaragoza (2 per day, including 1 *talgo;* talgo 6-7hr.; 3000ptas, *talgo* 4230ptas); València (1 *talgo* per day at 10:30am, 8hr., 4300ptas); Madrid (2 per day, including 1 *talgo;* 12 hr., *talgo* 9-10hr.; 5000ptas, *talgo* 7300ptas). To Jaca or Huesca: change in Zaragoza.

Buses: (tel. 21 23 19), around the corner from the train station. **Sarfa** (tel. 20 17 96). To: Tossa de Mar (1 per day, July 1 to mid-Sept. 3 per day; 430ptas, Sat.-Sun. 495ptas); Palafrugell (8 per day, July 1 to mid-Sept. 13 per day; 1hr.; 445ptas, Sat.-Sun. 505ptas); St. Feliu (6 per day, July 1 to mid-Sept. 11 per day; 535ptas, Sat.-Sun. 615ptas). From Palafrugell, you can make connections to Begur, Llafranc, Calella, and Tamariu. **Fills de Rafael Mas** (tel. 21 32 27). To: Lloret (3-5 per day; 55min.; 370ptas, Sat.-Sun. 420ptas). **Teisa** (tel. 20 02 75). To: Olot (8-14 per day; 1 1/4 hr.; 465ptas, Sat.-Sun. 490ptas); continues to Ripoll (3-4 per day, 23/4hr. from Girona, 720ptas); St. Feliu (15 per day every hr.; 315ptas, Sat.-Sun. 295ptas). **Barcelona Bus** (tel. 20 24 32). Express service to: Barcelona and Figueres (4-13 per day).

Car Rental: Most companies clustered around C. Barcelona near the train station. You must be over 21 (some companies 24) and have had your license for at least 1-2 years. **Hertz:** (tel 21 01 08), at the train station next to the branch tourist office. Rents Ford Fiestas and Fiat Unos (5500ptas per day, unlimited mileage). **Avis:** C. Barcelona, 35 (tel. 20 69 33). Rents Fiats and Opels (3990ptas for unlimited mileage). **Melció:** Sant Joan Bta. La Salle, 33-38 (tel. 20 04 43). Rents Marbellas (1800ptas per day, 18ptas per km). Fancy models available. Rates improve the longer you keep the car. All agencies charge approx. 1500ptas per day for mandatory insurance. Credit cards generally required.

Automobile Club: Real Auto Club de Catalunya, C. Barcelona, 30 (tel. 20 08 68), to the right from the train station. Their travel agent will help you rent a car.

Luggage storage: Lockers in train station (200ptas). Obtain token from *equipaje* booth right of RENFE counter. Check items that don't fit in locker at counter (200ptas). Open 8am-8pm.

Library: Casa de Cultura, Pl. Hospital, 6. From the Banco Central turn right onto Gran Via de Jaume I, then left; it's on the left side. Open July-Aug. 9am-2pm and 4-9pm, Sept.-June 10am-1pm and 4-9pm.

Laundromat: LASO, C. Balmes, 6 (tel. 20 51 25). From the train station turn right on C. Barcelona, then left 2 blocks down on C. Creu; C. Balmes is the 3rd right. There is a sign on the left near the end of the street. Wash and dry 734ptas a load. Open Sept.-June Mon.-Fri. 9am-1pm and 4-8pm, Sat. 9am-1pm.

Early Closing Day: On Mon. most museums are closed and shops are open only in the afternoon.

Red Cross: (tel. 22 22 22).

Medical Services: Hospital Municipal de Santa Caterina, Pl. Hospital 5 (tel. 20 14 50), across from library. **Hospital Doctor Josep Trueta** (tel. 20 27 00), on the highway to France. Interpreter in summer.

Police: Policía Municipal, C. Bacià, 4 (tel. 41 90 92). From Banco Central turn right on the Gran Via, then right on Bacià. In **emergency** dial 092.

Accommodations

Rooms are hardest to find in Girona from October to June when many small *pensiones* fill with local university students and workers. The majority of the budget rooms are in or around the historic quarter.

Alberg-Residència de Girona (HI), C. Ciutadans, 9 (tel. 21 80 03). In the heart of the old quarter, on the street which runs from Pont de Pedra. Unveiled with great fanfare in Oct. 1990. Snappily new and ultramodern inside, repainted stucco outside. High-caliber staff, high-fashion sheets. No lights-out curfew in VCR/TV room downstairs. 11pm curfew; but door is opened again at midnight and 1am. 850ptas, over 25 1275ptas. Self-service breakfast in cafeteria downstairs included. Dinner 625ptas, over 25 700ptas. Laundry on the top floor: wash and dry 500ptas per load. Reservations should be made 2-3 days in advance, especially from late May to early June when university students from the region come to Girona for exams.

Pensio Viladomat, C. Ciutadans, 5 (tel. 20 31 76), in the old town on the same street as the youth hostel. Yellow tilework, high ceilings, and big bare rooms. This jumbo edifice is primarily a student residence during the academic year and usually fills with groups in July and early Aug. Singles, 1650ptas. Doubles 2900ptas.

Hostal Coll, C. Hortes, 24 (tel. 20 30 86). Turn left on C. Santa Ciara just before Pont de Pedra; C. Hortes is 2 blocks away on the left. In the modern sector across the river from the Call. More accessible to nightlife, but almost uniquely devoid of character. Blah but functional rooms. Winter heating in halls. Avoid the annex down the street; rooms there are small, stuffy, and off a dark hallway. Doubles with bath 3000ptas.

Hostal Residencia Bellmirall, C. Bellmirall, 3 (tel. 20 40 09), next to the cathedral. The delightful and creative project of two Gironese artists tied in holy matrimony. The stone rooms are a florid mix of the husband's oil paintings and the wife's colorful needlework. Juice, croissants, and coffee served in an intimate breakfast room. July-Aug. singles with shower 2734ptas, doubles 4718ptas; Sept.-June 2576ptas, 4267ptas. Breakfast included.

Food

Partly because of Girona's blessed obscurity, the city's restaurants serve authentic, inexpensive Spanish cuisine. There are plenty of restaurants—including several al fresco—on **Plaça Independència,** the modern section of the city at the end of C. Santa Clara. A score of cafés lies along **Rambla de la Llibertat.** Many of the city's best restaurants huddle about the cathedral, especially along **Calle Força.** Several cafés and bars in the old quarter cater to university students. There's a **market** at the very end of Gran Via de Jaume I; turn right at Banco Central. (Open 8am-1pm.)

Café la Torrada, C. Ciutadans, 18, 1 block from the youth hostel. An artsy university crowd. Catalan menu only. Entrees 300-700ptas. *Pà amb escalivada:* anxoves de *l'Escala* (anchovy, red and green pepper, and onion sandwich, 400ptas). Open Mon.-Fri. 9am-4pm and 7pm-midnight, Sat.-Sun. 7pm-midnight.

El Pou del Call, C. Força, 14 (tel. 22 37 74). From the hostel take a left onto C. Ciutadans to Pl. l'Alí; continue on C. Carreras Peralta, which runs uphill before it intersects with C. Força. Owner, chef, and 25-year-old extraordinaire, Chico already holds claim to Girona's most original and affordable gourmet restaurant. In his elegant air-conditioned clubhouse, he drums up handsome specialties such as *ternera con hongos* (veal with mushrooms). House wine 300ptas per liter. Open Dec.-Oct. Tues-Sat. 1-4pm and 8:30-11pm, Sun. 1-4pm.

El Racò, C. Santa Clara, 47. Take C. Santa Clara left just before crossing Pont de Pedra into the old town and continue 21/2 blocks. Pasta, pizza (400-600ptas), salads (550ptas), and dessert crêpes (400-600ptas) prepared at counters while you watch. Open 1-4pm and 8pm-midnight.

L'Anfora, C. Força, 15 (tel. 20 50 10). The upstairs dining hall of wicker chairs, exposed stone walls, and Van Gogh prints was once the secret site of Jewish religious ceremonies. Bar hung with smoked hams. *Butifarra* 450ptas. Entrees 600-1500ptas. Open Jan.-Nov. Tues.-Sun. 12:45-4pm and 7:45-11pm.

Sights and Entertainment

Most of Girona's sights hobnob in the old city across the Riu Onyar from the train station. To take an historical tour, begin at the Pont de Pedra and turn left at the tourist office down tree-lined **Rambla de la Llibertat.** At the end of the *rambla,* turn right on C. Argenteria, cross C. Cort-Reial and continue straight on C. Bonaventura Carreras i Peralta. Up a flight of stairs, C. Força begins on your left. The **Call,** the Jewish medieval neighborhood, begins at C. Sant Llorenç, a right turn off C. Forçà onto a narrow alleyway. The entrance to **Casa de Isaac el Cec** (the Blind) is off C. Sant Llorenç about halfway up the hill. The probable site of the last synagogue in Girona, it now serves as a museum linking the baths, the butcher shop, and the synagogue, all of which surround a modern central patio. (Open Tues.-Sat. 10am-2pm and 4-7pm, Sun. 10am-2pm. Free.)

Girona's Jewish community became a leading center for the practice of Kabbalah, a mystical reading of the Scriptures which flourished in the 13th century. Its most influential teacher was Moses Ben Nahman, or Nahmanides, born in Girona in 1194. The Jewish community grew during the Middle Ages despite increasing harrassment from the city's Christian sector. In 1391 during an economic crisis when Jews were accused of deliberately spreading the plague and sapping the community's wealth, a mob of Girona's Christians killed 40 residents of the Jewish quarter. The violence culminated with the 1492 expulsion of all Jews from Spain by Queen Isabel and King Fernando. By the 16th century mass emigration, conversion to Christianity, and the Inquisition's *autos-da-fé* had virtually wiped out the once prosperous Jewish community. The city blocked off the streets of the *aljama,* or neighborhood, and converted the buildings for its own use. The process of reopening the streets and alleys that once were the Call started after Franco's death in 1975. The area off C. Forçà is the best place to see what's left of Jewish Girona's architecture.

Farther uphill on C. Força (which used to be the main road to Rome), signs lead to the **Museu d'Historia de la Ciutat,** which contains a small collection of antique printing presses, electric generators, and other piecemeal vestiges of the early days of the Industrial Revolution. Wrap up your visit with the pictorial history of a mummification workshop downstairs in the ex-Capuchin convent. The *treball de momificació* was one of only three such sites in the world. Medieval morticians dried out naked dead bodies in the small stalls that line the room. (Open Tues.-Sat. 10am-2pm and 5-7pm, Sun. 10am-2pm. Free.)

Just around the corner to the right, Girona's cyclopean Gothic **catedral** rises up a record-breaking 90 Roccoco steps from its *plaça*—the largest Rococo stairway in Europe. The northern **Torre de Charlemany** is the only structure which remains from the 11th century. The leftover was designed in the 15th century. The cavernous interior has but one rather than the customary three naves, making it the world's widest Gothic vault at 22m.

A door on the left leads to the trapezoidal cloister and the **Museu del Claustre**, which hoards some of Girona's most precious possessions: seven sculptures by the 15th-century Mercadante de Bretaña and Beato de Liébana's 10th-century *Libre de l'Apocalipsis,* an illuminated commentary on the end of the world. The museum's (and possibly Girona's) most famous piece is the intricate and animated **Tapis de la Creació,** which takes up the entire wall of Room IV. Woven in the 11th or 12th century, its illustrations depict the cycle of creation and biblical scenes. (Cathedral and museum open June-Sept. 10am-1:30pm and 4-7pm; museum closed Tues. afternoon. Admission to museum 200ptas, students 150ptas.)

From Pl. Catedral, head out through the Roman arch and take a right to the Romanesque **banys àrabs** (Arab Baths) on C. Ferran el Catòlic. Dating from the 13th century, each of the four rooms was kept at a different temperature for truly salubrious bathing. (Open Tues.-Sat. 10am-1pm and 4:30-7pm, Sun. 10am-1pm. Admission 100ptas.)

To reach the **Museu Arqueològic** (tel. 20 26 32), turn left from the *banys àrabs* and climb down the stairs. From the foot of the stairs walk through the gates of the Pl. Jurats and over the bridge. Housed in the Església de Sant Pere de Galligants on Pl. Santa Llucía, the museum is final resting place for the medieval tombstones that once marked graves of Jews on a nearby burial hill. The small section dedicated to artifacts from Empúries, the Greek trading colony, grovels for visitors to see its *anforas,* ceramic urns from the 2nd century BC. (Open Tues.-Sat. 10am-1pm and 4:30-7pm, Sun. 10am-1pm. Admission 150ptas, students free.)

The trees and meadows of the **Val de Sant Daniel** stretch north along the banks of the Galligant. Partly stepped and lined with cypresses, pines, and flower beds, the **Passeig Arquelògic** (archeological promenade) skirts the medieval wall on the eastern side of the river and overlooks the city. To reach the promenade, exit the *banys àrabs* and take the stairs to the base of the turret.

On the way back to the cathedral, turning right, the view of the river valley from the Portal de Sant Cristòfol is sure to slow your pace. The building on its eastern side is the **Museu d'Art,** which houses a large collection of 12th-century Romanesque wood sculpture and the **tabla de vidrerio.** This 14th century wooden tablet is the only known vestige of the laborious medieval stained-glass making process. Each page of the 15th-century book *Martirologi* is adorned with five delightfully humane paintings of abused martyrs. On the fourth floor, moody 19th-century landscapes and portraits of farmers hang side by side with modern Catalan works. (Open Tues.-Sat. 10am-7pm; Oct.-Feb. Tues.-Sat. 10am-6pm. Admission 100ptas, free Sun. 10am-2pm; students free.)

Girona takes its evening *passeig* seriously. The Rambla is the place to see and be seen, to chat amicably, to gossip, to complain about the greenhouse effect, to flirt, to desert one's dog, and to dance: there's a live band here every Wednesday in July at 10pm, and *sardanes* most Fridays all summer long.

After the *passeig,* there's dinner, and after dinner, there's bar-hopping, when the throngs move to the newer part of the city, near Pl. Ferran el Catòlic. Bars such as **Class, Croquis, Fractal,** and **Azimut** draw the biggest crowds. Then the wimpy go to bed and the rest shake their thing. Of Girona's four discotheques, the mightiest is **La Sala de Cel,** C. Pedret, 118 (tel. 21 26 64), off Pl. Sant Pere in the northern quarter of the city. It is in a venerable building with a small pool and garden. (Open Sept.-July Thurs.-Sun. nights.) The artsy I'm-in-the-mood-to-read-poetry crowd sticks around the bars and cafés of the old quarter.

For nine days in May, **jocs florals** (flower and poetry competitions) are held in the city, and the courtyards of Girona's fine old buildings open to the public. (Contact tourist office for this year's dates.) Also in May, the city hosts the **Curs Internacional de Música,** a series of six concerts, in La Mercé, the concert hall at Pujada de la Mercé, 12 (tel. 41 94 22). In June and July concerts take place in front of the cathedral, in the Jardins de la Devesa, and various other points in the city. (Admission free to 1200ptas.) Check with the tourist office for a schedule of events (for specific information, call 41 94 01). The **Parc de la Devesa,** on the western side of the river is, at 40 hectares, the largest urban park in Catalunya. Against a backdrop of towering 140-

year-old trees and broad paths, throughout the summer local bars set up outdoor terraces and sell refreshments to customers relaxing after an evening's stroll. Summer entertainment is also to be had in **Les Caseines,** the former military quarters now converted into public gardens. Take C. Joan Maragall from Pl. Ferran el Catòlic. On Rambla Llibertat near the tourist office a small jewelry and flower market vies for attention (Sat. mornings). The complete *sardana* guide, the *Guia d'Aplecs Sardanistes de les Comarques Gironines,* can be found at the tourist office, along with a complete listing of observed holidays and festivals. Girona's two biggest are July 25 for Sant Jaume and Oct. 29 for its Festa Major.

Catalan Pyrenees

Once upon a time, around the turn of the last millennium, a number of virtually independent counts ruled the mountains of upland Catalunya. By and large, the old counties of Pallars, Urgell, and Cerdanya remain in idyllic isolation. Sheep outnumber people here, wandering unattended through the rocky outcrops and snow-covered crags that cut through the steep green slopes. Badly paved roads and limited bus service prevent easy access to this section of the Pyrenees, but the splendor of Parc d'Aigüestortes, filled with clear glacial lakes and waterfalls, merits the journey.

Besides Catalan and Spanish, inhabitants of the ancient Catalunyan villages often speak French, while people in the Val d'Aran speak Aranese, a variant of the Gascon spoken in the Comminge region of France. Some of the region's gastronomic specialties also reveal French influence—pâtés, civets, and crêpes *(pasteres* or *pescajüs.)* These give way to equally hearty dishes such as *trinxat amb rosa* (creamed spinach and salt pork) in areas farther from the French border.

Romanesque castles, churches, and monasteries outnumber even sheep in the old medieval counties. This style emerged after the breakup of the Carolingian Empire in the latter part of the 10th century and dominated Europe until the end of the 13th century. Romanesque architecture mixed Roman building traditions with newer techniques necessary for the larger constructions of an expanding, optimistic society. Benedictine monks and the Knights Templar hired builders to spread Romanesque influence far and wide; it is the first truly European architectural style.

For each Catalan *comarca,* the Department of Commerce and Tourism distributes pamphlets with information on local winter sports or areas of scenic grandeur. Skiers will find the English-language guide *Snow in Catalonia* (free at tourist offices) especially useful. Cyclists should ask for *Valles Superiores del Segre/Ariège,* which covers the Alt Urgell, Cerdanya, and the Val de Ribes. Editorial Alpina publishes a series of indispensable topographical maps bound in red booklets.

Ripoll is the point of entry for the area. From Girona or the Costa Brava you can connect by bus; RENFE runs from Barcelona through Ripoll to Puigcerdà, where you are linked by bus to La Seu d'Urgell. The RENFE line connects to ski-resort Núria, and more complicated transport from Barcelona will get you to the lakes and hikes of the Parc Nacional d'Aigüestortes i Estany de Sant Maurici.

Ripoll

On the ear-popping road up to Ripoll, you'll pass by tiny hamlets and pastoral villages and over mountain streams running undisturbed through the valleys. It is surprising, then, when you round the bend and see the relative sprawl of Ripoll with its multi-story modern buildings. Both trains and buses drop you smack dab on the border between modern Ripoll and its rustic tubers.

Almost everyone comes to Ripoll to see the mouthwatering 11th-century portal of the **Monestir de Santa Maria.** This incredibly detailed archway depicts monstrous gargoyles and local animals in a 12-month calendar. These days, you may need to squint and exercise some imagination because time has taken its toll on the stone; but you should still be able to make out the figures of Christ and the apostles shepherding away. Inside, the fruits of 19th-century restoration meet with mixed reactions, but the

12th-century **claustre** is surprisingly well-preserved. (Church is always open and free. Cloister open Tues.-Sun. 9am-1pm and 3-7pm. Admission to cloister 50ptas.)

In the building to the left of the church, there is a second wonder at the top of a very long spiral staircase. The **Museu-Arxiu Folklòric** is worth a trip in itself. Simply by wandering around, you will unwittingly set off working scale models of old Ripollese mills, and by pressing the odd button you will be unexpectedly deafened by children singing local folk songs. Birds' eggs, toy soldiers, funny hats—it's all here. The curator is an extremely knowledgeable and quizzable man. (Open Tues.-Sun. 9:30am-1:30pm and 3:30-7pm. Admission 100ptas.) The monastery and the museum are both in Pl. Abat Oliba, the center of town. From the train or bus station, turn left on C. Progrés and follow the "*tots direccions*" signs until crossing a bridge. Follow Bisbe Morgades up the hill to the large Pl. Abat Oliva.

Fans of Antoni Gaudí will enjoy the tiny **Capilla de Sant Miquel de la Roqueta,** built by the mystic architect's disciple, Joan Rubió. The chapel is usually closed, but to see the outside, walk left down C. Progrés from the train station, turn right on C. Lleida, and left on C. Industria.

Ripoll's **Festa Major** falls on May 11; the following Sunday, the slightly cruel **Festa de la Llana** (Festival of Wool) amuses the town with shearing of indignant sheep in Pl. Ajuntament. On July weekends, the **Festival de Música** brings seven evenings of classical music to the cloisters. Montserrat Caballé, perhaps Spain's foremost diva, frequently makes an appearance. For more information, call the tourist office.

Most tourists stay only long enough to gape at the church portal. For longer stays, the best deal is **Habitaciones Ca La Paula,** C. Berenguer, 4 (tel. 70 00 11; Berenguer runs off Pl. Abat Oliba), at the corner of C. Pirineus, where some of the big rooms face the monastery. (900ptas per person, showers included.) There is camping 2km south of town at **Solana del Ter,** Ctra. Barcelona (tel. 70 10 62), in Colonia Santa María; follow the road from Pl. Gran, since there is no bus. (Open Dec.-Oct. 370ptas per person and per tent.) Many around the monastery's *plaça* serve scrumpy *bocadillos* and *tapas.* Try **Bar Stop** on Pl. Claré down C. Raguer Font for *platos combinados* (650ptas) and a snappy art deco interior done all in primaries. Ripoll's food and clothing **market** sets up on C. Berenguer (Sat. 9am-1pm).

The **tourist office** (tel. 70 23 51) is next to the monastery on Pl. Abat Oliva. (Open July-Sept. Mon.-Fri. 10am-1pm and 5-7pm, Sat. 10am-1pm; Oct.-June Mon.-Fri. 11am-1pm and 4-6pm, Sat. 11am-1pm.) The **post office** (tel. 70 07 60) is at the corner of C. Sant Bartomeu and C. Progrés. (Open Mon.-Fri. 8am-3pm, Sat. 9am-1pm.) The **postal code** is 17500; the **telephone code** 972. **Medical services** are administered at the Ambulatori de la Seguretat Social, C. Macià Bonaplata (tel. 70 01 59). An **ambulance** can be summoned at the **Red Cross** (tel. 70 04 71). The **municipal police** are at Pl. Ajuntament, 3 (tel. 70 15 15 or 70 06 00).

RENFE, Pl. Nova, 1 (tel. 70 06 44), serves Puigcerdà (9 per day, 1hr. 50min., 265ptas) and Barcelona (15 per day, 2hr., 505ptas). To reach Ribes de Freser and the Cremallera to Núna take the Puigcerdà train (105ptas). **Teisa** (tel. 20 02 75), 1 block down from RENFE, runs buses to Girona via Olot (3-4 per day, 2 3/4 hr., 720ptas, Sat.-Sun. 790ptas). Buses to Sant Joan de les Abadesses (8 per day starting at 7:55am; 20min.; 110ptas, Sat.-Sun. 120ptas).

Near Ripoll: Sant Joan de les Abadesses

In the 9th century Comte Guifré el Pelós ("the Hairy"), an equal-opportunity patron, endowed a convent 10km away to complement Ripoll's first monastery. His daughter Emma became the first abbess for Benedictine nuns. In the 12th century the Augustinians set up here, expanding and rebuilding most of the pre-existing structures. The **Santíssim Misteri,** a seven-piece polychromatic modern sculpture, is kept in the monastery's Romanesque church. Admission to the church and cloister (100ptas) allows you to visit the **museu** (tel. 72 00 13), a showcase for some richly embroidered cassocks, a gigantic mortuary cloth crafted for a bishop, and some humorous 16th-century choir stalls. (Open mid-June to Sept. 31 10am-1pm and 4-7pm, Oct. 1 to mid-June Sat.-Sun. 10am-2pm and 4-7pm.) The monastery may be reached by following the *rambla* to the circle at the end. At the other end of the *rambla,* turning right on the highway out of town, the untended ruins of *Sant Pol* are an unofficial picnic ground. The **tourist office**, at Rambla Comte Guifré, 1 (tel. 72 00 92), will give you a guide and a map, although you really won't need either. (Open 9am-1:30pm and 5-7pm.) Buses connect Sant Joan de les Abadesses to Ripoll (see above).

Núria

Near the French border and a tad north of Ripoll, Núria attracted only the religious hard-core fringe to its **Santuario** to the Virgen de Maria until 1931. These faithful pilgrims had to make the trip on foot or horseback during the summer. The installation of a second-hand *funicular,* the Cremallera (literally "the zipper"), left over from the 1929 World's Fair in Barcelona, brought major changes. By 1934, a luxurious lodge had been erected at the top of the new cable ride. After the Civil War, Núria enjoyed about 20 years of fame for its international ski competitions, but with the new popularity of bigger mountains and longer slopes, the town temporarily declined. Now accessible all year round, Núria offers hiking or skiing right from your doorstep. The **Cremallera** zips from the Ribes de Freser stop on the Barcelona-Puigcerdà line; the 45-minute scenic ride covers 1000m up.

From Núria, a modern cable line whisks straight to **Alberg de Joventut Pic de l'Aliga** (tel. (972) 73 00 48). The modern three-story youth hostel that has helped revive Núria's popularity since international ski competition moved elsewhere in search of bigger and longer slopes. Ping-Pong too. (850ptas per person, over 25 1275ptas. Hot showers. Breakfast included.) **Hotel Vall de Núria** (tel. (972) 73 03 26) provides the only other lodgings in the valley. (Doubles with bath 5000ptas.) Free **camping** is permitted near the hotel; shower and bathroom access is available for a nominal fee.

The lake near the shrine greets picnickers. Climbers prefer the four-hour hike to **Puigmal** (2913m). In 1988, 11 ambitious mountaineers climbed the peak on 6-ft. stilts, setting a new world record. **Pic d'Eina** is a shorter but equally strenuous hike through a stone gorge littered with yellow wild flowers.

Ten ski trails offer slopes ranging from *molt facil* (very easy) to *molt difficil* (very difficult or expert) at **Estació de la Vall de Nùria.** The "white phone" for ski conditions is in Barcelona at (933) 02 73 45. (Weekend lift tickets 1200ptas, weekdays 1000ptas.)

Information for the whole valley is available at (972) 73 07 13. Núria is equipped with full 24-hr. medical services, including a first aid dispensary, a pharmacy and a rescue group. The **Guardia Civil** in Ribes de Fresser is posted at C. Eres, 2 (tel. (972) 72 70 38).

Puigcerdà

There are few towns in Catalunya whose names are more difficult to pronounce and whose RENFE stations are more inconveniently placed. One and a half hours northwest of Ripoll by train, on the French border, Puigcerdà (something like Pushchair-DAH) commands the best vantage point from which to explore the teeny *comarca* of Cerdanya. A virtual nonentity until the turn of the century, the town then became a resort for well-to-do families from Barcelona and more recently for outdoor types from much farther afield. Come here if you hike, fish, hunt, kayak, ski, or enjoy gaping at a delicious view of the valley within a stone's throw of half a dozen bars.

Orientation and Practical Information

Puigcerdà's center squats squarely on top of a hill. It is roughly boxed in by the **Passeig 10 d'Abril** to the east, three *plaças* (Sta. María, dels Herois, and de Barcelona) to the north, and the **Plaça de l'Ajuntament** to the west. This *plaça* is nicknamed *El Balcón* (balcony) *de Cerdanya* because of its view of the valley and is a wickedly delovely place to watch bedraggled newcomers struggle up the hill from the RENFE station at the foot of the west slope. Most buses will also drop you off at the bottom of the hill (if you're lucky, they might continue to the top).

To reach Pl. Ajuntament from the train station, walk past the stairs in the station's *plaça* to the first flight of *real* stairs (between two buildings). Turn right at the top of these, and then look for the next set on your left, just before a sign for C. Hostal del Sol. Climb these to the top and turn left on C. Rabadans, where the final set of stairs winds up to the right.

With your back to the wall, **Carrer Alfons I** runs straight out of the left-hand corner of the *plaça*. It will lead you after one block to **Carrer Major,** the principal commercial street. Left on C. Major will convey you to **Plaça Santa Maria,** where road signs for Barcelona point to Plaça dels Herois, then Plaça de Barcelona. Continuing straight across C. Major on C. Alfons I leads to Passeig 10 d'Abril, the other main square in town.

Tourist Office: C. Querol, 1 (tel. 88 05 42), a right turn off Pl. Ajuntament with your back to the view. Good map packed with accommodations and entertainment listings. Open Mon.-Thurs. 10am-1pm and 4-7pm, Fri.-Sat. 10am-1:30pm and 4-8:30pm, Sun. 10am-2pm; Oct.-June Tues.-Thurs. 10am-1pm and 4-7pm, Fri.-Sat. 10am-1:30pm and 4-8:30pm.

Post Office: Av. Coronel Molera, 11 (tel. 88 08 14), off of Pl. de Barcelona on your left after 1 1/2 blocks. Open Mon.-Fri. 9am-2pm, Sat. 9am-1pm for telegrams only. **Postal Code:** 15720.

Telephone Code: 972.

Trains: RENFE (tel. 88 01 65) runs to Ribes de Freser to connect to Núria (7 per day, 1 1/4hr., 220ptas), Ripoll (7 per day, 1 1/2hr., 265ptas), Barcelona (6 per day, 4 1/2hr., 800ptas). To get to Jaca or Huesca you must first go to Zaragoza from Barcelona, a good full day of travel.

Buses: Alsina Graells (tel. (973) 35 00 20) runs 3 buses per day to La Seu d'Urgell and back (1 hr., 380ptas). First departs Puigcerdà at 7:30am; last returns from La Seu at 7pm. **Cerdanya** (tel. 302 65 45, 203 40 86) runs to Llívia 2 times per day (Mon.-Fri. 11:50am and 8:20pm, Sat.-Sun. 9:20am and 8:20pm; return Mon.-Fri. 5:30am and 2pm, Sat.-Sun. 6:30am and 5pm). Buses depart from in front of the train station; tickets are purchased once on board.

Car Rental: Suzuki off-road vehicle from **Touring 44,** C. Escoles Pies 19 (tel. 88 06 02 or 88 14 50), off Pl. Cabrinetly. 9500ptas per day with unlimited mileage. Insurance 1200ptas per day. Must be returned to Puigcerdà. Must be at least 23 and have possessed a license for at least 1 year. Open Mon.-Sat. 9am-1pm and 8:30-8pm.

Bike Rental: Casas, C. Espanya, 32 (tel. 88 03 96), off Pl. Herois.

Supermarket: Bon Preu, across from the post office on Av. Colonel Molera. Open Tues.-Sat. 9am-1pm and 4-8pm, Sun. 10am-2pm.

Early Closing Day: Shops are closed Mon. Sept.-June.

Ambulance: Pol. Indus. la Closa (tel. 88 21 35).

Red Cross at Av. Segre 8 on the outskirts of town to the right of Pl. Ajuntament with your back to the view (tel. 88 05 47, 89 41 53).

Medical Services: Centre Hospitalari, on Pl. Santa Maria (tel. 88 01 50 or 88 01 54). English spoken. A **pharmacy** is located on C. Alfons I (tel. 88 01 60); check the door there or ask the **municipal police,** Pl. Ajuntament (tel. 88 06 50), for the current **24-hr. Pharmacy.**

Accommodations

Since many visitors daytrip to Puigcerdà, you should be able to find a room easily, although high supply plus low demand equals high prices. The closest **HI youth hostel** is the Mare de Déu de les Neus in La Molina-Alp on Ctra. Font Canaleta (tel. 89 20 12), 500m from the RENFE station at La Molina, 30 minutes by train from Puigcerdà. (Members only. 775ptas. 170 beds. Slopes only 1km away.)

Pensión Domínguez, C. Major, 39 (tel. 88 14 27), up a flight of stairs. Only 4 rooms. On the main commercial strip so liable to be noisy. Doubles 2200ptas. Showers extra.

Hostal Residencia La Muntanya, C. Coronel Molera 1 (tel. 88 02 02) off Pl. de Barcelona. Paintings of pearly teared waifs weep at your bedside, but the rooms are clean. 1700ptas per person.

Hostal Residencia Estación (tel. 88 03 50), to the left from the train station. Location ideal if passing through; otherwise it's a strenuous hike along a rollercoaster road to town and back. Renovated in June 1991. Singles 1900ptas, with shower 2000ptas. Doubles 2800ptas, with shower 3600ptas. Triples 4300ptas with shower.

Food

The neighborhood of C. Alfons I is a cornucopia of bakeries, markets, and delis. The **market** is at Pg. 10 d'Abril, Sun. 9am-2pm.

Gourmet Cerdà, C. Alfons I, 9 (tel. 88 14 85). A deli. Fresh bread next door at **Palau** to make a giant *bocadillo.*

Bar-Restaurant Sant Remo, C. Ramón Cosp, 9 (tel. 88 00 05), right across from Fonda Cerdanya. Serves a wide variety of *tapas* and *bocadillos.* Ducks-and-bunnies decor in dining room upstairs. *Menú* 1200ptas.

Bar-Restaurant El Capritxo, C. Major, 55 (tel. 88 06 62). Follow C. Major beyond Pl. Santa María; the 2nd intersection. Atmosphere relaxed, food fine. Entrees 500ptas and up. Open Fri.-Wed. 9am-midnight.

Sights and Entertainment

Puigcerdà calls itself the capital of snow, and you can indeed ski in the country of your choice (Spain, France, or Andorra) at one of 19 ski areas within a 50km radius. Other winter sports include hockey and ice skating at the rink in **Club Polisportin Puigcerdà,** on the edge of town from Pl. Barcelona (tel. 88 02 43). In summer, the club offers soccer, tennis, and a heated indoor pool.

Between runs or at half time dash over to the **campanar,** the octagonal bell tower in Plaça de Santa Maria. This 42m-high 12th-century tower is all that remains of the Església de Santa Maria, destroyed in 1936 by fighting during the Civil War. Along Passeig 10 d'Abril, off Pl. Heroes, is the 13th-century **Convent de Sant Domènec,** whose large-scale renovation brought a regional museum, library, and archives to the town. **Església de Sant Domènec,** the largest church in Cerdanya, hulks next door. Its most interesting holdings are several Gothic paintings, probably by Guillem Manresa, and considered to be some of the best of their genre. On the outskirts of town, spanning the Riu Querol, is the **Pont de Sant Martí d'Aravó** with a Romanesque base and a Gothic superstructure. The two arches were constructed between 1326 and 1328.

Even travelers lucky enough to rent a 4 x 4 may want to park it and go for pony-rides or paddle boats around the **Estany,** the tree-lined lake up Av. Pons i Guasch from Pl. Barcelona. **Festa de l'Estany,** usually held the last Sunday of August, begins with a parade of floats, a concert, and some folkloric activity, and culminates with a swish fireworks display over the lake. On September 8 the town hoofs it up at the **Festivitat de la Verge de la Sagristia,** when everybody who knows how dances *sardanes* in the square. In July and August, devotees gather for *sardanes* every Wednesday at 10pm.

Near Puigcerdà

Six km from Puigcerdà is the little town of **Llívia,** a Spanish enclave in French territory. It owes its status to a legal technicality. The Treaty of Llívia of 1660 ceded half the villages in Cerdanya (33 in all) to France, but because Llívia was chartered as a *Vila* (town), it remained officially Spanish. The town has picturesque old streets, a fortified church with a 13th-century defense tower, and the small **Museu Municipal de Llívia.** The **Farmàcia Antiga** inside preserves early apothecarian equipment and a complete 19th-century drugstore. (Open 10am-1pm and 4-8pm. Admission 200ptas, students free.) The **tourist office** (tel. 89 60 11) is opposite the museum, upstairs in the Torre Bernat de So. The **telephone code** is 972. Every August orchestras, quartets, and choirs from all over Europe perform in the Romanesque church for the **Festival de Música Vila de Llívia.**

Other diversions pop up along the valley in the direction of La Seu d'Urgell. Hikers wander across the landscape above the small town of **Meranges** and ascend to **Estany de Malniu,** just below the glaciers along the Andorran border. There is a well-equipped **refugio** at Meranges.

Parc Nacional d'Aigüestortes i Estany de Sant Maurici

Ice-cold mountain lakes, gushing waterfalls, and stream-crossed trails make up the splendor of Parc Nacional Aigüestortes. 100km east of Ordesa and adjacent to the French border, the park is punctuated with some challenging peaks, but most hikes are easy enough for tyros to enjoy. A 2500m range divides the park in half. Informally, the eastern half is considered the Estany de Sant Maurici (the central lake), and the western half the Aigüestortes. You can cross the entire park in an eight- to 10-hour hike. Don't rely on the streamlined freebie maps from the information offices; the red *Editorial Alpino* guides, one for Montardo and Valle de Boí, the other for Sant Maurici, are essential for trails and *refugios* (300ptas at any bookstore in the Pyrenees). The brochure on the Parc published by the Generalitat de Catalunya, available at tourist offices throughout Catalunya, is useful. For general information on the park, contact the tourist offices of the Patronat de la Vall de Boí (tel. (973) 67 60 00).

The park deserves at least two days, and if you rely on public transport it's hard to see much in less than three. The mountains are often deceptive from afar, particularly in spring and fall. A couple hikers die each year when they lose the trail in a freak spring blizzard. Listen to local advice: bring warm clothing even for July and August and check with the Espot or Boi park office before heading out.

Estany de Sant Maurici

The official gateway to the eastern half of the park is the little town of **Espot**. Espot is actually a good 6 or 7km from the entrance proper, an arrangement that respects the tranquility of the park but is a thorn in the side of the traveler. The other bad news is that the Alsina Graells bus (the only public transport to the area) will not come any nearer than 7km from the *other* side of Espot, on Highway C-147. The good news is that a **jeep service** (tel. (973) 63 50 09) taxis into the park from Espot, and may well collect you from the bus stop to Espot as well. From Espot, they run to Estany Sant Murici (5000ptas per jeep) and to Amitges, another lake up in the north (12,000ptas per 8-person jeep). The launch pad of most hiking routes is Estany Sant Maurici. The **park information office** is on the main road on the right as you enter town. They will provide a good brochure and explanation of the park. (Open 9am-1pm and 3-6:30pm.) **Alsina Graells** buses (tel. (933) 01 65 45) leave Barcelona's Ronda de la Universitat, 4, for Espot (Mon.-Sat. at 7:30am, return at 5am and 3:45pm; 2100ptas) and from Lleida to Espot (tel. (973) 26 85 00). Buses stop in La Pobla de Segur, which RENFE serves from Lleida.

A night's rest in Espot prepares hikers for an early start on the park trails. **Residencia Casa Pagés Felip** (tel. (973) 63 50 93) packages rooms with breakfast (2000ptas per person during high season, negotiable the rest of the year). Cross the main Espot bridge, follow the road for two blocks, then turn left. **Camping La Mola** (tel. (973) 63 50 24) lies about 5km before the bus stop at Espot (425ptas per person, per car, and per tent), and **Camping Sol i Neu** (tel. (973) 63 50 01) is just beyond La Mola en route to the village. (Both open July-Sept.) Many farmhouses in the area take in travelers. Contact the tourist office in Vall de Boí for information.

Aigüestortes and Val de Boí

Gentle inclines in the western half of the park attract more cows and casual strollers than the Sant Maurici side. To compare the two halves of the park, take the main trail up Val de Sant Nicolau from Aigüestortes to the **Portarró de Espot,** the 2400m gateway between the two sides. The descent to Estany de Sant Maurici is steep and covered in patches of snow at the higher altitudes. This six- to eight-hour hike crosses the whole park, passing the **Estany Llong,** a llong llake indeed. Near its western tip is the park's first *refugio,* also called **Estany Llong.** (Open June 17-Oct. 10. Call the park administration at (973) 69 02 84 for information.) Near the end of the paved road at the entrance of Aigüestortes, are pine groves circled by winding streams; this tranquil sanctuary of twisted waters is the park's namesake.

Entering the park from its western side isn't much easier than the eastern approach. When it's running, the bus from Lleida drops off in **Boí,** a community of 150 people

11km from the park's entrance. **Viatges Aigüestortes,** Ctra. a Taüll (tel. (973) 69 61 06, 69 02 50, 69 63 50), to the left as you enter town, will drop you off and retrieve you at the park (600-725ptas per person, 6 person minimum). They also organize longer excursions into the park. The valley is high on the Romanesque church route, having an inordinate number in the villages surrounding Boí. **Sant Climent of Taüll,** uphill from Boí, is most noted. Boí maintains its pastoral feel, despite the nearby ski resort in Taüll. Amid low arches and cobblestoned streets stand accommodating accommodations with local families. Recommended is **Casa Guasch** (tel. (973) 69 60 42), whose *señora* lets you use her kitchen if the house isn't too full. The family knows the mountains well and can give you pointers in Spanish or Catalan (1500ptas per person). Next to the bus stop is **Hostal Residencia Pey** (tel. (973) 69 60 36; July-Aug. singles 2700ptas, doubles 4000ptas; lower off-season).

Pont de Suert, 17km south of Boí, offers most emergency services. The **Red Cross** can be reached at (973) 69 00 06.

Costa Daurada (Costa Dorada)

Sitges

A chic resort, Sitges earns its good name with long ocean-side walks, cobbled streets, and whitewashed houses, cheerfully decorated with flowers and ceramic tiles. This delightful town buzzes with activity year-round, and is also home to a lusty international gay community.

The water is a direct 10-minute walk from the train station via any street. In summer, the main **beaches** get crowded, but you can walk to less busy areas on your right as you face the water (west); nude sunbathing sprawls about 45 minutes away. Walk along the shore to the Solarium Club on your right, then over the hill or through the train tunnel and left. The beach is mixed stone and sand with some surf. The gay beach is over the next hill.

Vying with golden sands, the several museums are remnants of the village's past life as an artists' colony. Behind the Església del Evangelista on C. del Fonollar is the **Museu Cau Ferrat** (tel. 894 03 64), which contains works by Utrillo, Russinyol, and El Greco. In an annex next door, the **Museu Maricel del Mar** (tel. 894 47 57) has a fine collection of medieval paintings and sculpture. The **Museu Romàntic** (Can Llopis), on C. Sant Gaudenci, 1 (tel. 894 29 69), a bourgeois 19th-century house filled with period pieces, includes music boxes and 17th- to 19th-century dolls. Take C. Bonaire from the waterfront. (All three open Tues.-Sat. 10am-1pm and 4-6pm, Sun. 10am-2pm. Free.)

Sitges is most attractive during the spring **Festa de Corpus Christi,** when hundreds of thousands of flowers pave the streets. Sadly, this dazzling display of color and design lasts only one day. For raucous fun, visit during the **Festa Major,** held each year August 23 to 27 in honor of the town's patron saint (Bartolomé). On August 23 and 24, papier-mâché dragons, devils, and giants dance in the streets and fireworks light up the sky. Yet nothing compares to **Carnaval,** when Spaniards of every ilk and any province crash the town for a frenzy of dancing, street parties, outrageous costumes, vats of alcohol, and general frolicking.

Hostal Terminus, Av. Flores, 7 (tel. 894 02 93), across the train tracks left of the train station, has clean rooms and bathrooms for 1500ptas per person. The owner speaks English. Only 30m from the beach, an aristocratic villa called **Hostal-Residencia Lido,** C. Bonaire, 26 (tel. 894 48 48), off C. Parellades, purveys clean and well-lit rooms with telephones. (Singles 2500ptas. Doubles 3000ptas. Prices increase in Aug.) **Bar-Restaurant Can Gregori,** Pg. Villavueva, 41 (tel. 894 79 33), has a lion of a *menú* (700ptas) with bread, wine, coffee, and dessert. From the train station, turn right and the street becomes Pg. Vallanueva. (Open 1-4:30pm and 8-11pm.)

The modern **tourist office** at Bus Terminal "Oasis" waits in the Oasis shopping mall, Pg. Vilafranca (tel. 894 12 30). From the train station, turn right and go downhill until Oasis signs appear on the right. (Open July-Sept. 15 Mon.-Sat. 9am-9pm, Sun. 9am-2pm; Sept. 16-June 30 Mon.-Fri. 9:30am-2pm and 4-6:30pm, Sat. 10am-1pm.) The

LET'S GO® Travel
1992 CATALOG

When it comes to budget travel we know every trick in the book Discount Air Fares, Eurailpasses, Travel Gear, IDs, and more...

LET'S PACK IT UP

Let's Go Supreme

Innovative hideaway suspension with parallel stay internal frame turns backpack into carry-on suitcase. Includes lumbar support pad, torso and waist adjustment, leather trim, and detachable daypack. Waterproof Cordura nylon, lifetime guarantee, 4400 cu. in Navy, Green or Black.

A $165

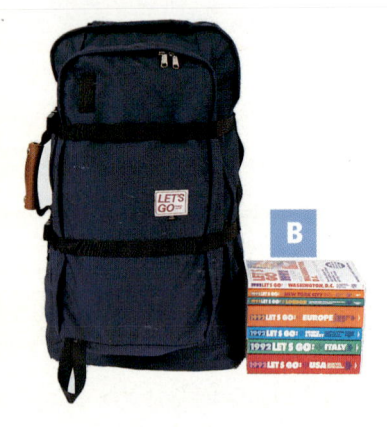

Let's Go Backpack/Suitcase

Hideaway suspension with internal frame turns backpack into carry-on suitcase. Detachable daypack makes it 3 bags in 1. Waterproof Cordura nylon, lifetime guarantee, 3750 cu. in. Navy, Green or Black.

B $119

Undercover NeckPouch

Ripstop nylon with soft Cambrelle back. 3 pockets. 6 1/2 x 5". Lifetime guarantee. Black or Tan.

C $9.95

Undercover WaistPouch

Ripstop nylon with soft Cambrelle back. 2 pockets. 12 x 5" with 30 x 13cm waistband. Lifetime guarantee. Black or Tan.

D $9.95

Let's Go Backcountry

Full size, slim profile expedition pack designed for the serious trekker. Parallel stay suspension system, deluxe shoulder harness, Velcro height adjustment, side compression straps. Detachable hood converts into a fanny pack. Waterproof Cordura nylon, lifetime guarantee, main compartment and hood 6350 cu. in. extends to 7130 cu.

E $195

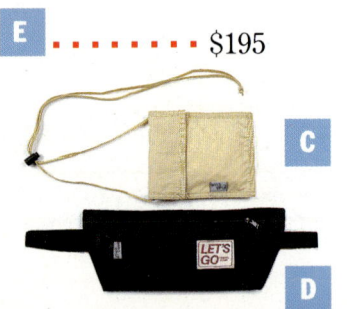

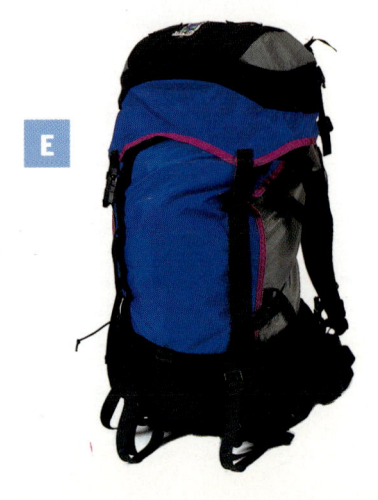

LET'S SEE SOME I.D.

1993 International ID Cards

Provides discounts on accomodations, cultural events, airfares and accident/medical insurance. Valid 9-1-92 to 12-31-93

F1	Teacher (ITIC)	$16.00
F2	Student (ISIC)	$15.00
F3	Youth (IYC)	$15.00

FREE "International Student Travel Guide."

LET'S GO HOSTELING

1993-94 Youth Hostel Card

Required by most international hostels. Must be a U.S. resident.

G1	Adult (ages 18-55)	$25
G2	Youth (under 18)	$10

Sleepsack

Required at all hostels. Washable durable poly/cotton. 18" pillow pocket. Folds into pouch size.

H	$13.95

1992-93 Youth Hostel Guide (IYHG)

Essential information about 3900 hostels in Europe and the Mediterranean.

I	$10.95

Let's Go Travel Guides

Europe; USA; Britain/Ireland; France; Italy; Israel/Egypt; Mexico; California/Hawaii; Spain/Portugal; Pacific Northwest/Alaska; Greece/Turkey; Germany/Austria/Swizerland; NYC; London; Washington D.C.; Rome; Paris.

J1	USA or Europe	$16.95
J2	Country Guide (specify)	$15.95
J3	City Guide (specify)	$10.95

LET'S GO BY TRAIN

Eurail Passes

Convenient way to travel Europe. Save up to 70% over cost of individual tickets. Call for national passes.

First Class

K1	15 days	$460
K2	21 days	$598
K3	1 month	$728
K4	2 months	$998
K5	3 months	$1260

First Class Flexipass

L1	5 days in 15	$298
L2	9 days in 21	$496
L3	14 days in 30	$676

Youth Pass (under 20)

M1	1 month	$508
M2	2 months	$698
M3	5 days in 2 months	$220
M4	10 days in 2 months	$348
M5	15 days in 2 months	$474

LET'S GET STARTED

Please print or type. Incomplete applications will be returned

International Student/Teacher Identity Card (ISIC/ITIC) (ages 12 & up) enclose:
1. Letter from registrar or administration, transcript, or proof of tuition payment. FULL-TIME only.
2. One picture (1 1/2" x 2") signed on the reverse side.

International Youth Card (IYC) (ages 12-25) enclose:
1. Proof of birthdate (copy of passport or birth certificate).
2. One picture (1 1/2" x 2") signed on the reverse side.
3. Passport number
4. Sex: M☐ F☐

Last Name _____ First Name _____ Date of Birth _____

Street _____ *We do not ship to P.O. Boxes. U.S. addresses only.*

City _____ State _____ Zip Code _____

Phone _____ Citizenship _____

School/College _____ Date Trip Begins _____

Item Code	Description, Size & Color	Quantity	Unit Price	Total Price

Shipping & Handling

If order totals: Add
Up to $30.00 . . . . . . $4.00
30.01-100.00 . . . . . . $6.00
Over 100.00 . . . . . . $7.00

Total Merchandise Price	
Shipping & Handling (See box at left)	
For Rush Handling Add $8 for continental U.S., $10 for AK & HI	
MA Residents (Add 5% sales tax on gear & books)	
Total	

Enclose check or money order payable to: Harvard Student Agencies, Inc.

Allow 2-3 weeks for delivery. Rush orders delivered within one week our receipt.

LET'S GO® Travel

Harvard Student Agencies, Inc., Harvard University, Thayer B, Cambridge, MA 02138
(617) 495-9649   1-800-5LET'S GO (Credit Card Orders Only)

Prices subject to change

post office (tel. 894 12 47) HQs on Pl. Espanya. (Open Mon.-Fri. 9am-2pm.) The **postal code** is 08870. There are **telephones** for international and domestic calls at C. San Pau, 19 (open 9am-midnight). The **telephone code** is 93. The **hospital** is on C. Hospital (tel. 894 00 03). The **municipal police**, on Pl. Ajuntament, can be reached at tel. 894 05 00. There is **train** service to Sitges from Barcelona (2 per hr., 50min., round-trip 440ptas).

Castelldefels and Vilanova i la Geltrù

Castelldefels, on the same train line as Sitges, has more grit and less glitter, but the enormous beach is only 20 minutes from Barcelona. The beach is perfect for young children and hydrophobes: the water extends forever without getting deep. When commuting, depart in the morning and return in early afternoon or late evening; train cars are often packed. The L93 bus leaves Barcelona's Pl. Espanya for Castelldefels (stop at Platja de Castelldefels, one-way 180ptas).

Catalunya's most important port after Barcelona and Tarragona, **Vilanova i la Geltrù** (90km southwest of Barcelona) is actually two cities smushed into one. La Geltrù is the elder, dates back to 1070, while the large and bustling Vilanova was born in 1274. The industrial side of the city cooperates graciously with its well-groomed beaches and vibrant cultural life.

The **beach,** ten minutes' walk from the train station, is emptiest on weekdays. The **Passeig Marítim** is the nightly setting for leisurely seaside promenades.

In the **Museu Balaguer,** Av. Victor Balaguer, s/n (tel. 815 42 02), opposite the train station, an Egyptian mummy shares space with paintings from the 17th century to the present, including El Greco's *Anunciació*. (Open Mon.-Sat. 10am-2pm and 4-7pm. Free.) Deep in the old city, the 13th-century **Castell de la Geltrù,** C. Torre, s/n (tel. 893 00 13), now safeguards a bronze mortar that maybe, just maybe, 12th-century alchemists used to grind drugs. There's also a 13th-century carved wooden altarpiece from Toledo, and some 20th-century paintings. (Open same hours as Museu Balaguer. Free.) **Casa Papiol,** Carrer Major, 32 (tel. 893 03 82), the house that landowner Francesc Papiol built at the beginning of the 19th century, takes us back to the tastes of turn-of-the-century bourgeoisie. (Open Tues.-Sat. 10am-1pm and 4-6pm, Sun. 10am-2pm. Free.)

The **tourist office** (tel. 815 45 17), right on the beach, can help find lodgings. (Open Mon.-Fri. 9:30am-1:30pm and 4-7pm, Sat. 10am-1pm.) **Taxis** can be summoned by phone (tel. 893 32 41). You can obtain an **ambulance** by calling tel. 893 12 16. The **municipal police** can be reached at tel. 893 00 00.

Tarragona

The Romans anointed Tarragona a provincial capital; this rocky mountain on the sea was both strategic for trade and invulnerable in war. Tarragona was one of the empire's finest cities; its architecture sumptuous, its population burgeoning, its wine world-famous. Unfortunately, the city peaked several centuries ago. Unless you're a Roman-ruin fanatic or rich enough to enjoy the highlife, the city is hardly exciting enough to justify the dingy budget restaurant scene, inadequate budget accommodations, and second-rate nightlife. Instead, centrifugal forces pull tourists northwest to Barcelona and southwest to València.

Orientation and Practical Information

The older part of the city sits on a hill surrounding the cathedral in view of the sea. The main thoroughways, **Rambles Nova** and **Vella,** run parallel to each other and perpendicular to the shore. Most of the city's sights are north of Rambla Vella (on the other side of Rambla Nova). Rambla Nova runs from the edge of the city to **Plaça Imperial Tarraco** (home of the bus station). As you face the sea, everything sloping downhill to the right of Rambla Nova constitutes the grid-patterned streets of the newer district.

To reach the center of the old quarter from the train station, take a right and walk 200m to the vertiginous (killer) stairs parallel to the shore. At the top of the stairs, walk past Rambla Nova, one block down Passeig de las Palmeres to Rambla Vella. Turn left on Rambla Vella. The third right ends at **Plaça de la Font,** a center of activity.

Tourist Office: Rambla Nova, 46 (tel. 23 21 43). Maps, brochures in English, and a razor sharp staff. Open July-Sept. Mon.-Sat. 10am-9pm, Sun. 11am-1:30pm and 5:30-9pm; Oct.-May Mon.-Fri. 10am-2pm and 4-8pm, Sat. 10am-2pm. The other office at C. Major, 39 (tel. 29 62 24), below the cathedral steps, is likewise useful. Open July-Sept. Mon.-Sat. 10am-1:30pm and 4-7:30pm, Sun. 11am-2pm. **Generalitat,** C. Fortuny, 4 (tel. 23 34 15), off Rambla Nova, 5 bl. from the sea end. Some Tarragona information, but best with regional information. Open Mon.-Fri. 8am-3pm and 4-8pm, Sat. 9am-2pm.

American Express: Viajes Eurojet, Rambla Nova, 30 (tel. 23 36 23, fax 23 38 08). 2% commission on traveler's checks. No charge to cardholders for receipt of a fax. Mail held for 1 month. Wires money. Open Mon.-Fri. 9am-1:30pm and 4:30-8:30pm, Sat. 9am-1pm.

Consulates: U.K., C. Reial, 33 (tel. 22 08 12). From in front of the train station turn left down C. Comerç; when it ends, go right onto C. Josep Anselm Clavé, which becomes C. Reial. Open Mon.-Fri. 10am-1pm.

Post Office: Pl. Corsini (tel. 21 01 49), 1 bl. below Rambla Nova off C. Canyelles. Lista de Correos and **telegrams** open Mon.-Fri. 8am-9pm, Sat. 9am-7pm. **Postal Code:** 43000.

Telephones: Rambla Nova, 74, at C. Fortuny. Open Mon.-Sat. 9am-9pm, Sun. 11am-2pm and 5-9pm. **Telephone Code:** 977.

Trains: Pl. Pedrera (tel. 23 36 43), on the waterfront at the base of the hill. Information office open 6am-10pm. To: Sitges (18 per day, 1hr., 275ptas); Barcelona (32 per day, 1 1/2 hr., 410ptas); Lleida (10 per day, 2hr., 540ptas); Zaragoza (10 per day, 3 1/2 hr., 1270ptas); València (10 per day, 4hr., 1370ptas); Madrid (5 per day, 8hr., 3875ptas; 2 *talgos* per day, 6 1/2 hr., 5800ptas); Córdoba-Málaga-Sevilla (3 per day, 5450ptas to Sevilla; 2 *talgos* per day, 8600ptas). **RENFE,** Rambla Nova, 40 (tel. 34 86 00). Tickets and inquiries. Open Mon.-Fri. 9am-1pm and 4-7pm.

Buses: Pl. Imperial Tarraco (tel. 22 91 26). **Transportes Bacoma** (tel. 22 20 72) serves most of these destinations. To: Barcelona (4 per day, 1 1/2 hr., 700ptas); Lleida (3 per day, 2 1/2 hr., 850ptas); València (10 per day, 3 1/2 hr., 1875ptas); Alacant (10 per day, 6 1/2 hr., 3545ptas); Madrid (1 per day, 10hr., 3540ptas); Málaga (3 per day, 14hr., 6855ptas).

Public Transportation: EMT Buses (tel. 54 94 80) runs 8 buses all over Tarragona. The tourist offices have a map with the routes. Runs 7am-10pm, 11pm on some routes. Mon.-Sat. 60ptas, Sun. 65ptas.

Car Rental: Gaui, C. Ramón y Cajal, 61 (tel. 21 42 58), off Rambla Nova. Seat Marbella special 2300ptas per day, plus 14ptas per km. Open Mon.-Fri. 8am-1pm and 4-7:30pm.

Luggage Storage: At the **train station,** 200ptas per bag. Open 6am-10pm.

English Bookstore: London House, C. Gasometre, 24 (tel. 22 73 71), on the corner of C. Canyelles by the Fòrum. Mostly English texts and dictionaries; small bunch of contemporary paperbacks. Open Mon.-Fri. 10am-1:30pm and 5-8pm, Sat. 10am-1:30pm.

Medical Assistance: Casa Socorro, a hospital at Rambla Vella, 14 (tel. 23 50 12). **Protecció Civil,** Pl. Imperial Tarraco (tel. 006), handles any emergency.

Police: Comisaría de Policía, Pl. Orleans (tel. 23 33 11). From Pl. Imperial Tarraco on the non-sea end of Rambla Nova, walk down Av. Pres. Lluis Companys, which runs between the bus station and the Govern Civil building. Take the 3rd left to the station.

Emergency: tel. 091 or 092.

Accommodations and Camping

Accommodations are quite cheap. Frankly, however, apart from the youth hostel, they aren't bargains—quality is sadly poor. The tourist offices have a list of accommodations.

Residencia Juvenil Sant Jordi (HI), C. Marqués Guad-El-Jelu (tel. 24 01 95). At the end of Rambla Nova, cross the traffic circle to Av. Pres. Lluis Companys and turn right after 2 bl. It's the 1st large building on the right. A youth recreation complex on the outskirts of Tarragona. Well-kept and well-lit facilities. Rows of spacious modern rooms for 4 or 6 people, with large closets and desks. Large TV screen attracts a boisterous local crowd. 3-day max. stay. Reception open 7am-8pm. Check-out 9:30am. Lockout 10am-2pm. Curfew strictly 11pm. 850ptas per person.

Breakfast included. Sheets 250ptas. 26 and over: 1000ptas; 300ptas. Make reservations for July-Aug.

Pensión Marsal, Pl. Font, 26 (tel. 22 40 69). Close to restaurants and monuments. Five floors of newly renovated rooms, all with full bath. Mind the stairs. Singles to triples 1500ptas per person; prices lower for 5th fl. rooms.

Pensión Mariflor, C. General Contreras, 29 (tel. 23 82 31). From the train station exit, turn left down Pl. Pedrera and right onto C. Barcelona (not the sharp right), then another right onto C. Contreras. Shabby neighborhood, but the rooms are adequate. Singles to quads 1000ptas per person.

Pensión la Unión, C. Unió, 50 (tel. 23 21 41). Coming from the seafront end of Rambla Nova, C. Unió is the 4th left. Grungy entrance, peeling walls, and sagging mattresses. It's cheap. Singles 1100ptas. Doubles 2000ptas.

Camping: Several sites conveniently line the road toward Barcelona (Via Augusta or CN-340) along the beaches north of town. To reach any of them, take bus #3A or 3B from Pl. Corsini, opposite the market (every 20min.; 60ptas, Sun. 65ptas). The closest is **Tarraco** (tel. 23 99 89), 2km away at Platja Rabassada. Facilities are well-maintained, and the beach is out the tent door. 440ptas per person, per tent, and per car. Open April-Sept.

Food

Rambles Nova and Vella are the most promising streets, but true seafood freaks with fishy priorities take bus #1 from Rambla Nova to **El Serrallo** (see Sights for walking directions), where the fresh daily catch is served up in the pricier restaurants of this fisher's neighborhood. Tarragona's **indoor market,** at Pl. Corsini by the post office, moves food and many other wares (plants, goldfish, baby ducks, candy, spiders; open Mon.-Thurs. 7am-1pm, Fri.-Sat. 7am-1pm and 7-9pm).

Groceries: Simago, C. Augusta, 13 (tel. 23 88 06), parallel to and running between Ramblas Nova and Vella. A supermarket with a vast selection. Open Mon.-Sat. 9am-8pm.

Bar Turia, Pl. Font, 26 (tel. 22 40 69), under Pensión Marsal. At lunchtime there's invariably a wait for the 3-course 650ptas *menú;* come early. Locals easily drown out the TV. Specials vary, but there's always a fish or meat option for the main course. Afternoon tables on the plaza. Prodigious *bocadillos* 200-300ptas. Open 1-3pm and 8:30-10:30pm.

Mesón El Caserón, Trinquet Nou, 4 (tel. 23 93 28), parallel to Rambla Vella (off Pl. Font). Decorous ceiling fans cool plain stomach-stuffing family-style eats. Roast Chicken 450ptas. Appealing *paella* 900ptas. *Menú* 850ptas. Wine 300ptas per bottle. Open Jan. 21-Dec.19 1-3:30pm and 8-10:30pm.

C'an Peret, Pl. Font, 6 (tel. 23 76 25). Not unlike Al's Diner: lively music, sandwiches (135ptas), and good desserts, viz., *churros con chocolate* (195ptas). Open Mon.-Fri. 11am-11pm.

Sights

Countless Roman and medieval remains lie on the city's Mediterranean edge. **Balcó del Mediterràni,** fringing Rambla Nova, commands a view of the lazy sea. From here as you face the water, the **Amfiteatre Romà** (Roman amphitheater) and the **Circ Romà** (Roman circus where chariots raced) are off to the left down Pg. Palmeres. The amphitheater used the sea as a backdrop. (Both open Tues.-Sat. 10am-8pm, Sun. 10am-2pm. Free.)

Continuing past the ruins, Pg. Sant Antoni winds its way up into the medieval quarter of the city. The first stop is the **Museu Arqueològic,** with a collection of ancient utensils, statues, friezes, and mosaics, including a ravishing *Cap de Medusa* (Head of Medusa). (Open July-Sept. Tues.-Sat. 10am-8pm, Sun. 10am-2pm; Oct.-June Tues.-Sat. 10am-1:30pm and 4-7pm, Sun. 10am-2pm. Admission 100ptas, Tues. free.) The museum adjoins the **Pretori Romà,** the governor's palace in the first century BC. Rumor has it that Pontius Pilate was born here during his father's term of office. Tunnels link the palace with the Roman circus. God only knows what evil went on here; the vaults were used as dungeons, both by the Romans and centuries later by Franco's Fascists. (Same hours as museum. Admission 100ptas.)

Nearby, cornered by narrow streets and lit by a huge rose window, it's yet another Romanesque-Gothic **catedral.** Dominating the ornate apse is the extravagantly detailed altarpiece, carved about 1430. The 19 chapels depict frozen moments in history by means of 12th- to 15th-century sculpture and a 10th-century Moslem *mihrab*. Just to the left of the church door is the whimsical, niftily gruesome *Processió dels rats*. The **Museu Diocesà,** in the east gallery, contains Roman and Iberian pottery, medieval and Renaissance religious icons, and medieval tapestries. (Cathedral and museum open July-Sept. Mon.-Sat. 10am-7pm; Oct.-June Mon.-Sat. 10am-12:30pm and 4-6pm. Admission 150ptas.)

Following the walls that encircle the old city, the **Passeig Arqueològic** weeds through all of Tarragona's history, from prehistoric foundations to a 20th-century statue. The ruins of the Roman city walls date from the 3rd century. Moorish and Christian towers guard the ancient gates; rusty cannon contrast with Roman statues. (Open July-Sept. Tues.-Sun. 10am-midnight; Oct.-June Tues.-Sat. 10am 1:30pm and 3-5pm. Admission 100ptas.)

For those more ontological visitors, farther out on Pg. Independència are the **Necròpolis** and **Museu Paleocristià.** The enormous early Christian burial site has yielded a rich variety of urns, tombs, and sarcophagi, the best of which go to the museum in its center. (Both open July-Sept. Tues.-Sat. 10am-8pm, Sun. 10am-2pm; Oct.-June Tues.-Sat. 10am-1:30pm and 4-7pm, Sun. 10am-2pm. Admission (Wed.-Mon.) 100ptas, or use ticket from the Museu Arqueològic.) Water signs might prefer the **Pont del Diable** (Devil's Bridge), a perfectly preserved Roman aqueduct. Take a bus from the corner of C. Christòfor Colom and Rambla Nova to San Salvador (every 15min.; 45ptas, Sun. 50ptas) and then walk 1km back towards Tarragona. The breathtaking structure's two tiers of weathered arches stretch for 217m through a pine forest.

The city hides a shocking amount of *Modernisme* behind its antiquity. As in Barcelona, head for the **Eixample** (expansion) district south of the old quarter; Rambles Nova and Sant Joan there have the densest concentration of the sinuous style. The neo-Gothic **Convent dels Carmelites,** the **Escorxador** (Slaughterhouse), and **Mercat Central** (Central Market—an iron structure with a magnificent arched entrance and fanciful wrought-iron gates) give the Romans a run for their money.

El Serrallo, Tarragona's fishing district, fans out next to the port. Narrow streets wind through the *barrio,* colorful fishing boats are moored in tidy rows at dock, and innumerable restaurants serve fresh fish. The best time to go is late afternoon, when fishers return to auction off the daily catch. Take bus #1 ("Náutico") or walk. From the train station, take C. Comerç and turn a long right on C. Reial (which starts as C. A. Clavé) until it hits C. Pere Martell; turn left, go one block, then duck under the bridge.

The rather hidden access to **Platja del Miracle,** directly below town, is along Baixada del Miracle, starting off Pl. Arce Ochotorena, beyond the Roman theater. **Platjas Rabassada, Sabinosa,** and **Llarga,** north of town, are larger beaches. To reach them, take bus #3A or 3B from Pl. Corsini. Everyone boos the new dirt-like sand laid down at Rabassada because it clumps. Sabinosa appeals to families, Llanga to windsurfers and other youngsters.

Entertainment

On Sunday afternoons Passeig de les Palmeres is packed with seagazers. Throughout the week at *passeig* time (about 7pm), Rambla Nova and the surrounding streets also teem with families and packs of roving teenagers. The cafés along Rambla Nova entertain many of the city's visitors into the small hours. Otherwise, the town is dead by midnight.

Moto Club Tarragona, Rambla Nova, 53 (tel. 23 22 30), near C. Comte de Rius, is a popular sidewalk café from which to admire the sunset at the end of Rambla Nova. (Open 7am-midnight.) Tarragona's innest disco is **La Canela,** in a warehouse on C. Sant Magí, 6 (tel. 21 76 00), off C. La Unió. (Open 7pm-2:30am.) Serious dance clubs are in **Salou** and **Torredembara,** two beach towns 10km south and north of Tarragona, respectively. Salou in particular is a blast, with fabulous beaches (easily reached by Plana bus from the main bus station). As the last bus returns at 10pm, you'll need to find a ride back.

July and August usher in **Festivales de Tarragona**—rock, jazz, dance, theater, and film—at the Auditori Camp de Mart near the cathedral. A booth on Rambla Nova sells tickets for the 10:30pm performances. One hour before the performance go to the location itself (contact the municipal tourist office for details).

Every odd-numbered year, on the Sunday closest to August 19 (Festa de Sant Magí), local cooks compete for the title of **Maestre del romesco,** the classic Tarragonese almond and pine nut sauce. The cook-off begins at 10am in El Serrallo. After the mid-afternoon verdict, the *romescaires* auction off their entries. The contest helps "define the gastronomic vitality of the sauce." Only the dancing in the streets and traditional music that follow can release the tension excited by this high-staked event. On even-numbered years, the first Sunday in October brings the **Concurs de Castells.** In this competition at the Plaza de Toros, groups of acrobatic buddies, all dressed in white pants and the same color shirt, try to build the highest human castle. These human towers also appear amidst dragons, beasts, and fireworks during the annual **Festa de Sant Tecla** on September 23, or **Diá de Sant Joan** on June 24.

Near Tarragona

Monestir Poblet

Monestir Poblet (tel. (977) 87 00 89), one of the largest Cistercian abbeys in Europe, is celebrated for its magnificent architecture. Ramón Berenguer IV founded the monastery in 1151, and the community grew rapidly. A favorite stopover between Zaragoza and Barcelona for the kings of Aragón, it was eventually selected as the royal burial place. In the middle ages Poblet became a model for depravity, and was plundered in the early 19th century. The lovingly restored buildings today form a splendid monastic complex.

Poblet also rose to fame for its library and scriptorium, almost without parallel in medieval Europe. The Cistercians' trademark habits, made from undyed cloth, earned them the nickname "White Monks," as opposed to the black-clad Benedictines. The Cistercians shunned dye along with all manner of materialistic and worldly things. Austerity was the guiding passion, in their lifestyle as in their architecture.

The monastery's buildings, of a handsome caramel color, are protected by a mile-long perimeter; a second wall surrounds the conventual annexes, and the innermost wall protects the monastery itself. Guided **tours** showcase the 12th-century kitchens and refectory, the cloister, the chapter house, the 13th-century library, and the royal tomb. The church's severe grandeur complements its most remarkable ornaments, a 16th-century carved alabaster altarpiece and the immense low arches in the cross vault. The four-tiered *retablo* was painstakingly created in 1527; the adjacent cloisters swathed in lovely scrollwork complete the serenity. (Open 10am-12:30pm and 3-6pm. Admission 200ptas. Students free. Closed Christmas Day.)

Hostal Fonoll, C. Ramon Berenguer IV, 2 (tel. 87 03 33), lies a little to the right of the monastery's entrance in Poblet (singles 2435ptas, doubles 3815ptas; open July-Sept.). The town, 48km from Tarragona, is a stop on the **bus** route from Tarragona to Lleida (1hr., 350ptas).

Monestir Santes Creus

Monestir Santes Creus (tel. (977) 63 83 29) was founded under the reign of Alfonso II thanks to the generosity of Guerau Alemany and other Catalan nobles who donated the land for the Cistercian monastery. Like Poblet, the three perimeter walls testify to Catalunya's embattled history. The monastery survived invasions from both Felipe and Napoleon, but in 1835 the monks abandoned it and the buildings were sacked and otherwise maltreated. A 20th-century restoration has preserved this architectural treasure that spans from Romanesque to Gothic. (Open 10am-noon and 3:30-6pm.)

To get here, after catching the 11am **bus** (tel. 22 20 72, 185ptas) from Tarragona to Valls, take the noon bus (150ptas) from Valls to Santes Creus (about 40km from Tarragona).

Illes Baleares (Balearic Islands)

Were EuroDisney to open in the Baleares, none of its residents would bat an eye. The islands have, at one time or another, been visited, settled, and invaded by every Mediterranean culture with a boat. Even a few northern European peoples have tried to slip the islands into their imperialistic pockets. Yet in spite of all the pressure from greedy nations, the Baleares remain Spanish. Whereas past cultures left numerous palaces, windmills, fortresses, and *talayots*, today's visitors contribute little more to the culture than broken bottles and fish 'n' chips.

The province's most important islands are Mallorca, Menorca, Eivissa (Ibiza), and Formentera. Although the numbers have dwindled somewhat, hundreds of thousands still descend upon the sun-drenched islands each summer, making for a prosperous economy. Those islanders neither running a restaurant or *pensión*, nor designing shoes and world-famous trinkets, work in the olive, fig, and almond groves that blanket the countryside. The Moors introduced the practice of growing cereals along with fruits; the islands now export both products to all of Europe.

Mallorca is home to the province's capital, Palma, and absorbs the bulk of invaders. Jagged Serra de Tramontana limestone cliffs line the north coast, while lazy bays scoop into the rest of the coastline. Condominiums obscure the beaches with clear turquoise water on the coast, while orchard upon orchard springs from fertile soil inland. Eivissa, once a haven of the counter-culture, successfully plays the decadent entertainment capital of the islands and has an active gay community. Meanwhile, Menorca leads a more private life. Wrapped in green fields and stone walls, it chuckles in complacent glee over its empty white beaches, hidden coves, and mysterious Bronze Age megaliths.

It's a cinch finding rooms on any of the islands until late July. The best weather shines in autumn and spring anyway, as summer days are hot and dry, save for the occasional northeasterly wind.

While island cuisine is simple, mayonnaise, a Menorcan innovation, puts the Baleares in the culinary hall of fame. *Pa-amb-oli* ("bread with oil," plus ham, tomato, or egg) makes a filling snack. More substantial foods include *sopes mallorquines,* a stocky vegetable soup ladled over thinly sliced brown bread, and *escaldums,* an appetizing chicken dish. Soft, spicy sausages, such as *camaiot, sobrassada* (Mallorcan *chorizo* spread), and *botifarrons* are picnicable. *Ensaimadas* are doughy, candied breakfast rolls or pastries smothered in powdered sugar. Most renowned are Menorca's gin and sweet liqueur distilleries.

Getting There

By Plane

Charters are the cheapest and quickest means of round-trip travel. Most deals entail a week's stay in a hotel, but some charter companies (called *mayoristas*) sell fares for unoccupied seats on flights booked primarily with full-package (airfare and hotel) passengers. These leftover spots are called "seat only" deals, and are most easily found in newspaper ads and by asking around at various travel agencies in any Spanish city (flights from Barcelona are cheapest and most frequent). Off-season (Oct.-May) round-trip fares can sink as low as 8000ptas; summer prices more than double that. The 1993 *Liberalización del Transporte* Act may mean the relaxation of stringent you-pay, you-stay policies if new companies get involved in the charter business.

Scheduled flights are far easier to book. Frequent departures cruise from Barcelona, Madrid and València, as well as Düsseldorf, London, Frankfurt, Hamburg, and Paris. **Iberia** and **Aviaco** handle all flights from Spain to the isles. From Barcelona a one-way ticket to Palma costs 7975ptas, to Menorca 8275ptas and to Eivissa 9125ptas. From València a one-way ticket to Eivissa runs 7550ptas, to Palma 9050ptas, and to Menorca

11,200ptas. From Madrid the one-way fares are a bit steeper: to Eivissa 12,900ptas, to Palma 14,300ptas, and to Menorca 16,825ptas. Another option, the *tarifa-mini* fare, discounts round-trip tickets by 40%, but only five or six seats open up per flight. They can sell out almost six months beforehand. If you do get one of these tickets, you must stay on the island at least one weekend (no changes allowed).

By Boat

Boat fares are about as cheap as charter flights. A disco and small swimming pool help while away the longer passage. **Transmediterránea** has the monopoly on movement between the mainland and all the islands except Eivissa and Formentera. Their ships depart from Barcelona (office at Estació Marítima, tel. (93) 317 42 62) and València (office at Av. Manuel Soto Ingeniero, 15, tel. (96) 367 39 72); any travel agent in Spain can book you a seat. Ships sail from both ports to Palma, Maò (Mahon), and Eivissa (Ibiza) City. All connections are direct except València-Maò, a painful 18-hour trip via Palma. Ships follow this schedule: Barcelona-Palma 10 per week; Barcelona-Eivissa 8 per week (4 in winter); Barcelona-Menorca 7 per week (2 in winter); València-Palma 7 per week; València-Eivissa 2 per week. The journey to the islands takes about 8-9 hours. The one-way fare for *butaca* (airplane-style seat) is 5350ptas. Reservations made a few days in advance help, although seats are often available until an hour before departure.

Flebasa in the city of Denia, on the coast just north of Alacant (tel. (96) 578 40 11), challenges Transmediterránea in Eivissa. The trip from Denia to Eivissa (3hr.) is the shortest, and their boats dock in Port Sant Antoni rather than Eivissa City. Denia lies on the FEVE rail line between València and Alacant. The high-speed ferry ticket comes with a bus connection from either of those cities or from Madrid, Albacete, and Benidorm (in summer). A one-way ticket from Madrid costs 7610ptas, from Alicante or València 6210ptas. Offices are at the ports of Denia (tel. (96) 578 40 11 or 78 41 00), València (tel. (96) 367 80 01), Alacant (tel. (965) 22 21 88), and Sant Antoni (tel. (971) 34 29 71 and 34 28 71). Travel agents also book for Flebasa.

Getting Around

Flying is the best way to island-hop. Planes are quicker, more comfortable, and cheaper than ferries. **Iberia** flies from Palma to Eivissa (3-4 per day, 20min., 4100ptas) and Maò (2-3 per day, 20min., 4100ptas). Note that the stopover in Palma between Menorca and Eivissa can last up to four hours (2-3 per day, 8200ptas). Planes fill a couple of days in advance in summer, so make reservations. If flying round-trip, ask if the *tarifa-mini* fare is applicable.

Seafarers sail **Transmediterránea,** whose ships connect Palma with Eivissa City (2 per week, 4 1/2 hr., 3900ptas) and Maò (1 per week, 6 1/2 hr., 3900ptas). Mallorca, Menorca, and Eivissa all operate extensive intra-island **bus** systems. Mallorca also has two narrow-gauge **train** systems that don't accept Eurailpass. Travel costs on Mallorca, Menorca, or Eivissa add up, as bus fares between cities range from 100 to 700ptas each way. **Cars, mopeds, and bikes** provide self-operated transport to the islands' remote beaches. A full day in a car such as a SEAT Panda should cost around 5000ptas, including insurance; on a Vespa or moped, 2000ptas; on a bicycle, 700ptas.

Mallorca

Out of all the Iberian vacation possibilities fit for a monarch, King Juan Carlos I of Spain chooses to take his holiday on Mallorca. The island's very name rings of wealth, royalty, and romance. Polish pianist Frédéric Chopin and French novelist George Sand spent months of their steamy love affair in the island's smaller towns. Kings and artists aren't the only vacationers on this island however; package tours and European vacationers stuff the 500km coastline, particularly in July and August.

The jagged edge of **Serra de Tramontana** stretches along the island's northwestern coast, hiding its white sand beaches and frothy water. Lemon groves and ancient olive trees cling to the hillsides in terraced plots. To the east, expansive beaches, some as long as 6km, open onto smooth bays; while the southeastern coast hides its beauty underground in giant caves. The calmer inland plains, dotted with windmills drawing water up for the almond and fig trees, form the agricultural heartland of a thriving economy.

Palma is a concrete jungle, the island's transportation hub with cheap and frequent buses fanning out to every quiet corner and several slow and scenic ferries to points on the southwest coast. For a group of three or four, a rented car can actually be cheaper for day trips; it's essential for beach hopping. More daring souls ride mopeds on Mallorca's crowded highways with brazen speed.

Palma

Mallorca's capital is a showy Balearic upstart, a city that delights in quashing every image of serene island living ever to grace a travel agency's wall. Its streets hustle with shoppers consuming conspicuously. Shops hawk leather coats and bags, designer clothes, jewelry, silverware, and car stereos. Even the city's namesake palm trees have gone commercial, picked up plastic roots, and moved to cheap hotel lobbies. Palma remains one of Spain's wealthiest cities, a true metropolis with a large year-round population, a well-preserved old quarter, fancy restaurants, and a swinging nightlife.

Orientation and Practical Information

To get to the town center from the airport, take bus #17 to Plaça d'Espanya (every1/2 hr. 7:05am-12:05am; 15min.; 165ptas, after 9pm and Sun. 190ptas). From the ferry dock, walk outside the parking lot and turn right on Pg. Maritim, then left onto Av. Antoni Maura, which leads to **Plaça de la Reina** and **Passeig des Born.** Pg. des Born leads away from the sea to **Plaça del Rei Joan Carles I. Avenida Rei Jaume III,** the business center, runs to the left. To the right, Carrer de la Unió leads after some stairs to the **Plaça Major,** the center of the pedestrian shopping district. Carrer de Sant Miquel connects Plaça Mayor to **Plaça d'Espanya,** where you will sooner or later catch a bus.

Tourist Office: Govern Balear, Av. Rei Jaume III, 10 (tel. 71 22 16), off Pl. Rei Joan Carles I. Superb information about all the islands. Emergency help looking for rooms from mid-July to Aug. Essential tourist provisions: map, bus and train schedules, a multilingual pamphlet describing the beaches, a monthly list of all sporting and cultural events on the island, and a pamphlet with 20 hiking excursions. English spoken. Open Mon.-Fri. 9am-8pm, Sat. 10am-1:30pm. Branch office at the **airport** (tel. 26 08 03). Open Mon.-Sat. 9am-9pm, Sun. 9am-2pm; off-season Mon.-Sat. 9am-8pm, Sun. 9am-2pm. The English-speaking staff at **Municipal,** C. Sant Dominic, 11 (tel. 72 40 90), are likewise helpful. *A Palma,* their monthly cultural calendar, is brimful with facts. Open Mon.-Fri. 9am-8:30pm, Sat. 9am-1:30pm. The **information booth** (tel. 71 15 27) in Pl. Espanya is a branch of this operation. Open Mon.-Fri. 9am-8:30pm, Sat. 9am-1:30pm. **Free telephone service** (English spoken): (900) 32 13 21.

Budget Travel: TIVE, C. Jerónim Antich, 5 (tel. 71 17 85), near Pl. Bisbe Berenguer de Palou toward Pl. Espanya. Student IDs (ISIC 500ptas), HI cards (1800ptas), and mainland flights. Go elsewhere for inter-island travel and charters. Open Mon.-Fri. 9:30am-1:30pm.

Consulates: U.S., Av. Rei Jaume III, 26 (tel. 72 26 60). Not a full consulate. Passports and visas in Barcelona. Open Mon.-Fri. 4-7pm. **U.K.,** Pl. Major, 30 (tel. 71 24 45), through the arcades off one corner near the Teatre Principal. A full consulate. Open Mon.-Fri. 9am-2pm; Nov.-May Mon.-Fri. 9am-1pm and 4-6pm.

American Express: Viajes Iberia, Pg. Born, 14 (tel. 72 67 43). Can't accept wired money. Holds mail for 1 year. Cashes all traveler's checks with 2% commission. Open Mon.-Fri. 9am-1:30pm and 4-7pm, Sat. 9:30am-1pm.

Post Office: C. Constitució, 6 (tel. 72 10 95). Parcels upstairs, open Mon.-Fri. 9am-9pm, Sat. 9am-2pm. Lista de Correos downstairs at window #7; open Mon.-Fri. 9am-9pm, Sat. 9am-2pm. **Postal Code:** 07000.

Telephones: Av. Rei Jaume III, 20. Open Mon.-Sat. 9:30am-1:30pm and 5-9pm. Also at C. Constitució, 2. Open Mon.-Sat. 9:30am-8:30pm, Sun. and holidays 10am-2pm. **Telephone Code:** 971 for all the Baleares.

Mallorca 313

Flights: Aeroport Son San Juan (tel. 26 46 24); 8km away from downtown Palma. Take bus #17 from inside the bus station at Pl. Espanya (every 1/2 hr. 6:30am-10:30pm, 30min., 175ptas). **Iberia**, Pg. Born, 10 (tel. 28 69 66 or 71 80 00 for reservations). Open Mon.-Fri. 9am-1:45pm and 5-6:45pm, Sat. 9am-12:45pm. **Spantax**, tel. 26 77 00 or 28 50 08. **Aviaco**, tel. 26 50 50.

Trains: Ferrocarril de Sóller, C. Eusebio Estada, 1/6 (tel. 75 20 51), off Pl. Espanya. To Sóller (5 per day, 650ptas). Avoid the 10:40am "tourist-train"—prices inflate to 10,400ptas for the privilege of a 10-min. stop in Mirador del Pujol d'en Banya. **FEVE** (tel. 75 22 45), on Pl. Espanya, goes inland to Inca about once every 40min., on weekends once per hr. (195ptas). **RENFE** maintains an information and bookings office at Pl. Espanya (tel. 75 88 17).

Buses: Transportes de Palma (tel. 29 57 00) runs municipal buses with terminals at Pl. Espanya and Pl. Reina. Standard city fare 90ptas, 10-trip tickets 570ptas. Prices to outlying areas are slightly higher. Buy tickets aboard or in Pl. Espanya kiosks. Service 6am-9pm. **Inter-city buses** are coordinated from **Servicios de Carreteras** (tel. 75 22 24) at Pl. Espanya. Buy tickets here or aboard. (Office open Mon.-Sat. 9am-1:30pm and 3:30-7:30pm.) **Playa-Sol**, Pl. Espanya (tel. 29 64 17), serves Andraitx and Maglluf. **Autocares Llompart**, C. Arxiduc Lluís Salvador, 1 (tel. 20 21 25), near Pl. Espanya, links Valldemosa, Port de Sóller, and Deià. **Autocares Grimalt**, Av. Alejandro Rosselló, 32 (tel. 58 02 46), off Pl. Progrés, serves towns in southeastern Mallorca. **Autocares Carbonell**, C. Arxiduc Lluís Salvador, 24 (tel. 75 50 49), covers southwestern Mallorca, including Bangalbufar. **Armint**, Pl. Espanya (tel. 54 56 96), serves Alcúdia and other towns in northern Mallorca. Fares from 150ptas (Valldemossa) to 760ptas (Costa del Pins).

Ferries: Transmediterránea, Moll Vell, 5 (tel. 72 67 40). Bus #1 runs along Pg. Marítim to the Moll Pelaires. Tickets sold Mon.-Fri. 8:15am-1pm and 5:15-7pm, Sat. 9am-noon. Ferries dock at Moll Pelaires (part-way around the bay south of the city), where you can buy tickets until shortly before sailing. To: Eivissa (2 per week, 4 1/2 hr., 3900ptas); Maò (Sun. at 9am, 6 1/2 hr., 3900ptas); Barcelona (1-2 per day, 8hr., 5350ptas).

Taxis: tel. 75 54 40, 71 04 03, 40 14 14. Airport fare is about 1400ptas.

Car Rental: Atesa, Pg. Marítimo, 25. Take bus #1 from Pl. Espanya and ask the driver to let you off at the auditorium. Cheapest car, Equis, 4900ptas per day. Open 9am-1pm and 5-8pm. Tourist offices have a list of others.

Moped Rental: Medped, Av. Joan Miró, 388 (tel. 40 25 85). From Pl. Espanya take bus #3 to Pl. Gomila. Mopeds 2800ptas per day. Open Mon.-Sat. 9am-7pm.

Luggage Storage: RENFE office, Pl. Espanya (tel. 76 85 10). Small locker 200ptas, big locker 300ptas. Automatic system, open 24 hrs.

English Bookstore: Book Inn, C. Horts, 20 (tel. 71 38 98), right off La Rambla. An impressive selection of literature, but most Jackie Collins and other beach reading has long been snatched up. Children's books too. Open Mon.-Fri. 10am-1:30pm and 5-8pm, Sat. 10am-1pm.

Library: Bibliotéca de la Caixa, Av. Alejandro Rosselló, 4 (tel. 46 28 29). Open Sun.-Fri. 11am-1pm and 4:30-8:30pm.

Laundromat: London Laundry, C. Montsenyor Palmer, 3 (tel. 73 87 95), off the waterfront in Es Jonquet. 7kg 1100ptas. Open Mon.-Fri. 9am-1:30pm and 4:30-8pm, Sat. 9am-2pm.

Women's Center: Central Informació Drets de la Dona, C. Portella, 11, 2nd fl. (tel. 72 25 51), near Parc de la Mar. At the end of Av. Antoni Maura by the waterfront, turn left up the stairs to D'alt Murada and take the 2nd left; 3 doors down from the Museu de Mallorca. Rape crisis assistance available in English. Open Mon.-Fri. 9am-1:30pm and 5-7pm.

Medical Assistance: Hospital Provincial Sa Misericordia C. Misericordia, s/n (tel. 17 35 01). From Pl. Espanya walk to C. Olmos (OMS on most maps), turn right onto Pg. La Rambla, left onto C. Bisbe Campins and another left onto C. Misericordia. English spoken.

24-hr. Pharmacy: See listings in *Diario de Mallorca* (local paper, 90ptas).

Emergency: tel. 091 or 092.

Police: Municipal, on Av. Sant Ferran, s/n (tel. 28 16 00).

Accommodations

Finding a room in Palma is a snap; likely possibilities abound on **Passeig des Born** and **Plaça de la Reina**. For 300-400 ptas more and a bus commute (#3 from Pl. Espanya, every 10min.) to the center of town, some *hostales* by **Parc Gomila** on Av. Joan

Miró offer fairly luxurious lodging five minutes from the city's nightlife. Make reservations for late July and August when you're competing with the rest of Europe.

Alberg Juvenil Platja de Palma (HI), C. Costa Brava, 13 (tel. 26 08 92), in El Arenal. Take bus #15 from Pl. Espanya (80ptas) and ask the driver to let you off at Hotel Acapulco. Poorly-lit rooms and showers only a water conservationist could love. Dunk at the beach instead—only 2 blocks away. Curfew 11pm. 850ptas, nonmembers 1100ptas. Breakfast included. Open Dec.-Oct.

Hostal Bonany, C. Almirante Cervera, 5 (tel. 73 79 24), in El Terreno 3km from the center of town and 5 min. from the nightlife. Take bus #3, 20, 21, or 22 from Pl. Espanya to the beginning of Av. Joan Miró, walk up C. Camilo José Cela, take the 1st right, then the 1st left. Sleepy residential street with a receiving line of shrubs, palm trees, and cacti. Sizeable rooms, all with baths and balconies. Courtyard and swimming pool. Doubles 3250ptas. Hearty breakfast (bread, coffee, eggs, cheese, and juice) 400ptas.

Hostal Ritzi, C. Apuntadores, 6 (tel. 71 46 10), off Pl. Reina. Central location. Meticulous British owner keeps a classy place that attracts guests that teeny boppers might call old. Wallpapered rooms contain eclectic period furniture. English books, games, and videos entertain. Well-heated in winter. Singles 1500ptas. Doubles 2600ptas, with shower 2800ptas, with bath 3000ptas.

Hostal Residencia Pons, C. IV, 8 (tel. 72 26 58), at the end of C. Apuntadores, which starts at Pl. Reina. No 2 rooms alike, and there's a piano in the salon (no *Chopsticks* allowed). 1200ptas per person. 100ptas extra for 1-night stay. Showers 275ptas.

Hostal Apuntadores, C. Apuntadores, 8 (tel. 71 59 10). Next door to the Ritzi. Pink walls and tiled floors help obscure that the place is aging. Large rooms are enticing. 1500ptas per person. Oct.-May: 1200ptas. Lower rates if you stay more than a few days.

Hostal Goya, C. Estanco, 7 (tel. 72 69 86), off Pg. Born. Cheapest thing you can buy with Goya's name on it. Bare-walled, aging *hostal.* Singles 900ptas. Doubles 1600ptas.

Camping

Unless you can drive stakes into concrete, you'll have to go outside Palma to camp. The two campgrounds stake out more hospitable terrain in the absolutely gorgeous **Badia d'Alcúdia,** over 50km northeast of Palma on the opposite corner of the island. First-class site **Platja Blava** (tel. 53 78 63) is located at kilometer 8 of the highway between Alcúdia and C'an Picafort. (740ptas per person and per tent.) Four buses leave daily for C'an Picafort from Palma (450ptas). **Club San Pedro** (tel. 58 90 23) is a third-class site just outside of Colònia de Sant Pere. (Open June 15-Sept. 30; 675ptas per person and per tent.) To get here from Palma hop on one of the C'an Picafort buses and take the the connecting bus to Colònia de Sant Pere.

Food

Menus come in German, French, and English, as well as Catalan and Spanish, but the food in such touristy places is unadulterated Mallorcan. Mom-and-pop operations serve tourists and locals alike along the side streets, especially around **Pg. Born.** Two **markets** vie for customers, one in Pl. Olivar, off C. Padre Atanasio near C. Pl. Espanya; the other across town by Pl. Navegació in Es Jonquet. (Both open Mon.-Sat. 7am-2pm.)

Groceries: Pryca, Av. General Riera, 156-172. Take bus #16 from Pl. Espanya. Open Mon.-Sat. 10am-10pm.

Casa Regional Murciana, Av. Antoni Maura, 24 (tel. 71 48 54), on the street that empties into the port from Pl. Reina. Local families and workers favor this sociable dining room. Carefully hidden on the 2nd floor so tourists miss it. *Menú del día* 600ptas. Murcian *paella* 700ptas. Open Dec.-Oct. Tues.-Sun. 1pm-midnight.

Celler Payés, C. Felipe Bauzá, 2 (tel. 72 60 36). Take C. Pintor Guillem Mesquida off Pl. Reina and turn right. Another townsfolk favorite. Bowl of spiced olives with every 900ptas meal. Open Mon.-Fri. 1-4pm and 8:30-11pm, Sat. noon-4pm.

Celler Sa Premsa, Pl. Bisbe Berenguer de Palou, 8 (tel. 72 35 29), between Via Roma and Pl. Espanya off C. Falangista Laportilla. *Mallorquin* eatery. Screaming customers surround strategically placed giant wine-filled vats. Three-course *menú del día* 850ptas. Famous *sopas mallorquinas,* a heartier than hearty vegetable soup (435ptas). Open Mon.-Fri. noon-4pm and 7-11:30pm.

Bodega Casa Payesa, C. Moliners, 3, in an alleyway off C. San Miguel at C. Verge de la Salut. An island of domesticity; 5 small tables and TV. Full meal just 550ptas. *Menú* with *paella* option 550ptas. *Bocadillos* 100-120ptas. Open 8am-8pm.

Bon Lloc, C. Sant Feliu, 7 (tel. 71 86 17). Excellent vegetarian *pastel de calabacín* (zucchini in a pastry crust), *arroz Iziki con algas* (Iziki rice with seaweed), and *mousaka*. Full a la carte meals about 1400ptas. Open Tues.-Sat. 1-4pm and 9-11pm.

Merendero Miñonas, C. Miñonas, 4. An infinitesimal booth on a small street 1 block from and parallel to C. Constitució. *Pa-amb-oli i tomate* (tomato and olive oil on bread) 75ptas. *Sobrassada* (soft Mallorcan chorizo spread), 145ptas. They'll wrap up sandwiches for the beach. Large selection 110-140ptas. Open Mon.-Fri. 7:30am-8:30pm, Sat. 7:30am-2pm.

C'an Joan de S'aigo, C. Sans, 10 (tel. 71 07 59), near Pl. Coll. Old-fashioned ice cream and pastry parlor with an indoor fountain and caged songbirds. *Gelat de Metla* (Mallorcan almond ice cream) 140ptas. Open Wed.-Mon. 8am-9pm.

Sights

While there are no beaches in Palma proper, some respectable ones are a mere bus ride away. The beach at **El Arenal** (Platja de Palma, bus #15), 11km to the southeast, is popular, but prepare to fend off underpaid PR people who roam there with handouts on bars and nightclubs. The clear-watered **Palma Nova** and **Illetes** beaches (buses #21 and 3 respectively) are 15 and 9km southwest.

The **Barri Gòtic** (medieval quarter) around the cathedral and Palau Almudaina is a tangle of tight streets, stairways, and plazas, half-covered by the overhanging carved wooden eaves of elegant townhouses still occupied by aristocracy. The Gothic **catedral** at C. Palau Reial dramatically looms atop the hill overlooking Palma and its bay. At night its traceries are illuminated. Begun in 1230, the cathedral—one of the largest Gothic ones in the world—wasn't finished until 1601. Gaudí, creator of Barcelona's Sagrada Familia, modified the interior and the ceiling ornamentation in *Modernista* fashion to blend smoothly with the stately exterior. The relics of St. Sebastian, Palma's patron saint, and pieces of the True Cross lie in the **tresor.** The tombs of the last two monarchial Jaumes (Jaume II and Jaume III) and of the last Avignon Pope also rest here. (Cathedral and treasury open Mon.-Fri. 10am-12:30pm and 4-6:30pm, Sat. 10am-1:30pm. Admission for both 250ptas.) The **Museu Diocesà** (tel. 71 40 63), behind the cathedral on C. Palau, is pure eclecticism. Among its 15th-century statues and tableaux are an alligator killed and stuffed in 1776; the autographs of Napoleon Bonaparte, Emperor Mçximilian of Mexico, Queen Victoria, and Louis Philippe D'Orleans; and a collection of American quarters. (Open Mon.-Fri. 10am-1pm and 3-7pm, Sat. 10am-1pm. Admission 200ptas.)

The **Banys Arabs** (Arab sauna baths), in the same area at C. Serra, are the island's only well-preserved Moorish legacy. (Open 10am-7pm. Admission 100ptas.) Also in the Barri Gòtic is the graceful **Llotja,** on Pg. Sagrera near the waterfront, a 15th-century commodities exchange. **Palau Sollerich,** a few blocks away at C. Sant Caietá, 10, displays contemporary art and sponsors frequent exhibits. (Open Tues.-Fri. 11am-1:30pm and 5-8:30pm, Sat. 11am-1:30pm and 5-8:30pm. Free.) In the heart of the old quarter, **Església de Sant Francesc,** in the *plaça* of the same name, is a cavernous 13th-century Gothic structure altered in the 16th and 17th centuries with the incorporation of a Plateresque and Baroque facade. (Open Mon.-Sat. 9:30am-1pm and 3:30-6:45pm.)

Although Palma has more to offer in medieval and Renaissance sights than in modern ones, the **Col leccion March, Art Espanyol Contemporani,** C. Sant Miguel, 11 (tel. 71 26 01) has an enviable collection. The thirty-six works are each by a different 20th-century Spaniard, including Picasso, Dalí, Miró, Juan Gris, *and* Antoni Tapies—posthumous patron of the Poliscar. (Open Mon.-Fri. 10am-1:30pm and 4:30-7:30pm, Sat. 10am-1:30pm. Admission 200ptas.)

Overlooking the city and bay and set in a park, **Castell Bellver** (tel. 23 06 57) served as summer residence to Mallorcan kings in the 12th century; for centuries thereafter it housed distinguished but involuntary guests. Floodlit at night, the castle contains a **Museu Municipal** of archeological displays. Buses (#3, 21, 22, or 23) leave from C. Joan Miró and walk up C. Camilo José Cela. (Castle and grounds open 8am-sunset.

Museum open Mon.-Sat. 8am-8pm. Admission 120ptas.) Built by the Moors and later occupied by Mallorcan kings, **Palau Almudaina** cannot be visited, save for the museum and chapel. In the palace gardens fountains form an arcade of water and a shaded arbor leads to a pond. A little way outside of town is Palma's **Poble Espanyol,** C. Capitán Mesquida, 39 (tel. 73 70 75), a smaller reproduction of its parent in Barcelona, with scaled-down samples of Spanish architecture. Buses #4 and 5 pass nearby along C. Andrea Doria. (Open 9am-8pm. Admission 325ptas, under 12 250ptas.)

Entertainment

Monthly publication *Is la Guia* (199ptas) is the first place to check for entertainment listing or specific events. The municipal tourist office dutifully keeps a less comprehensive list of sporting activities, concerts, and exhibits.

Although Palma went tourist-happy years ago, the traditional Spanish *passeig* is still the early evening pastime of choice. **Parc de la Mar,** between the illuminated cathedral and the waterfront, affords a spectacular view and an essential breath of fresh air before a night in smoke-filled bars.

Let down every last hair at **ABACO,** C. Sant Joan, 1 (tel. 71 59 11), in the Barri Gòtic near the waterfront. This Edenesque, indulgent bar-palace is like a Dalí canvas gone Baroque, fulfilling the most exuberant of fantasies. Drinks appear amid elegant furniture, cooing doves and ducks, piles of fresh fruit and flowers, and hundreds of dripping candles, all to the accompaniment of Handel, Bach, et al. Fruit nectars cost 700ptas, cocktails 1300-1400ptas; but wandering the chambers is free.

Salsa is the latest rage in Palma, and those who have the gusto head to **El Rincón Latino** on C. Industria near Pg. Mallorca and C. Argentina. *Caipirinha,* a zingy Brazilian lemon cocktail (700ptas), oils the hips until the 6am coda (Fri.-Sat.; Wed. and Thurs. 4am; opens at 11pm; no cover). The rest of Palma nightlife is in the **El Terreno** area, centered on Pl. Gomilia and along C. Joan Miró with a motherlode of nightclubs. **Minim's,** Pl. Gomila, 3A (tel. 73 16 97) is a magnet for the rich and extravagant, the favorite watering hole of King Carlos's children. **Plato** (across the street at Pl. Gomilia, 2) keeps a lower, more local profile as a pub-disco fashionable with Spaniards hoping to avoid tourists. At Pl. Gomiia, 1, **Tito's Palace** (tel. 73 76 42) is an indoor colosseum of mirrors and lights with windows overlooking the water. Hats off to the gay bar **Sombrero,** C. Joan Miró, 26 (open 9pm-3am, no cover). The divine **Baccus,** around the corner on C. Lluis Fábregas, 2, attracts lively lesbian and gay hedonists (open until 3am). Finally, the thirtysomething crowd heads to the waterfront for **Victoria Boite,** Pg. Maritim (tel. 45 12 13), directly below Tito's. Fluorescent blue lights and 70s tunes are staying alive in this couch-filled pad (cover 1500ptas).

Residents will use any occasion as an excuse to throw a party. One of the more colorful bashes, **Día de Sant Joan** (June 24), involves a no-expense-spared fireworks display the night before, followed by singing, dancing, and drinking in Parc del Mar below the cathedral.

Western Coast

The westernmost end of Mallorca, punctuated by **Illa Dragonera,** plunges abruptly into the water from the Serra de Tramontana. Stone walls stitched across the slopes support terraced olive groves, and villages crouch in protected pouches on the hillside. This area is perilously close to the aggressively developing Palma; the metropolis is starting to swallow some areas between the Badia de Palma and western Cap Tramontana.

Cap de Cala Figuera and the surrounding area is best explored on foot. *A Rambler's Paradise*, available from the Ajuntament tourist office in Calvia (across the *plaça* from the bus stop; open Mon.-Fri. 9am-2pm and 4-7pm, Sat. 10am-1pm), describes several hikes of varying difficulty past natural and historic sights. The Playa-Sol company (tel. 29 64 17) runs **buses** from stops around Pl. Espanya in Palma as far south as Magaluf (lines #1, 2, and 3 every 15-30min., 175ptas), about 8km from the cape's end. Palma's only official nude beach, **Platja del Mag,** is near the tip of the cape, about 5km south of Magaluf near Portals Vells.

Playa-Sol buses stop on C. Eusebio Estada, next to the Sóller train in Palma, and continue to **Andraitx** and **Port de Andraitx,** 5km apart and about 30km from Palma (bus #4, every 1/2 hr., 270ptas). These towns are handy transport bases for exploring the many capes between Cap d'es Llamp and the tip of the island. Sharp cliffs that plunge into the water jut from **Sant Telm,** a small village up the coast. (4 buses per day from Andraitx, 70ptas.) Bus #4 leaves from Palma at 9:05am; the last back to Palma returns at 5:15pm (one-way 290ptas).

The rugged northwest coast of the island lacks tourists and is the shortest day trip from Palma. The road to **Banyalbufar** twists through the southwestern end of the Serra de Tramontana. Banyalbufar produces its own *malvasía,* a wicked answer to sherry. A Moorish watchtower just off the main road gazes out to sea south of Banyalbufar. An uncrowded beach lies below the town's quiet hills. **Hotel Barronia,** C. Barronia, 16 (tel. 61 81 46), on the main road, has cool, relaxing rooms and a sea view. (Singles 2500ptas. Doubles with bath 3820ptas. Open April-Oct.)

On the bus route to Banyalbufar lies the country estate of **Sa Granja** (tel. 61 00 32), outside the town of Esporlas, now a crafts, arts, and farming exhibit of ancient Mallorcan ways of life. The 600ptas admission includes all the *buñuelos* (doughnuts) you can eat, and all the homemade wine (seven kinds) you can quaff. Every Wednesday and Friday (3-6pm), the oasis comes alive with folk dancing, eating, drinking, and general carousing, all for 900ptas. (Open 10am-6pm.) Autocares P. Carbonell **buses** leave twice per day (8:30am and 4pm, once Sun. at 10am; 235ptas) for Banyalbufar from Bar Río, C. Arxiduc Lluís Salvador, 24 (tel. 75 50 49), near Pl. Espanya in Palma. They stop at Sa Granja on the way. September 10 is feast day for Banyalbufar's patron saint.

Valldemosa

Eighteen tortuous km from Banyalbufar, Valldemosa's weathered houses huddle in the harsh yet beauteous Serra de Tramontana. Little in this ancient village hints at the passion that shocked the townsfolk in the winter of 1838-39, when tubercular Frédéric Chopin and his lover George Sand (with her two children in tow) stayed in the **Cartoixa Reial** (tel. 61 21 06), loudly flouting the monastic tradition of celibacy. The monastery's museum assembles innumerable Chopin memorabilia, including a picture of the famous hands and piano upon which they played. There are short piano recitals here in the summer (4 per day; Mallorcan dance instead on Mon. and Thurs. mornings). Chopin's love shack was also a monastery, don't forget, and you can inspect the former monks' quarters, a 16th-century printing press, and an 18th-century pharmacy with island-blown glass bottles.

The **Museu Municipal** inside the monastery collects dust and documents on the royalty who once lived in town. Next door is **Palau del Rei Sancho,** a Moorish residence converted into a palace by Mallorcan kings. (Cartoixa Reial open Mon.-Sat. 9:30am-1pm and 3-6:30pm; Oct.-May 9:30am-1pm and 3-5:30pm. Museum open 1/2 hr. longer. Admission to everything 775ptas. Admission to piano recitals 175ptas.)

On the night of July 28, the *carro triumfal* (triumphal carriage) rolls through the town's streets, carrying a local girl dressed as little Santa Catalina. The festivities of the raucous **Festival de Santa Catalina** end on the last Sunday in July with a piano concerto by a world-famous pianist in the Chopin reclusory. Past ivory-ticklers were Aaron Copland and Arthur Rubinstein.

Valldemosa lacks many basic services (i.e., no tourist office), but the **post office** is at Pl. Ruben Carío, 21, down the street from the museum. (Open for Mon.-Fri. 8:30am-11:30pm.) Autocares Llompart **buses** (tel. 20 21 25) to Valldemosa leave from Palma at the bar at C. Arxiduc Salvador, 1 (5 per day, 150ptas).

Near Valldemosa, 10km north on the bus route to Sóller, vogues the artists' hangout, **Deià** (5 buses per day, 80ptas). Tourists frequent its overpriced restaurants, all on the main road, for lunch. Some walks through this unspoilt town and surrounding area afford a sensational view of miles and miles of twisted olive trees. Mallorcan folklore holds that only the thousand-year-old trees have witnessed the true history of the island.

Sóller, Port de Sóller, and Sa Calobra

Another 30km up the coast, **Sóller** hums with tourists all day long. There's not much to see but the **catedral** in Pl. Constitució, which resembles a sandcastle. (Open Mon.-Fri. 10am-12:30pm and 2:30-5pm, Sat. 10am-12:30pm.) If you stay in town, make sure it's for the **Ferias y Fiestas de Mayo.** Starting on the Friday nearest the second Sunday in May, the Christians beat the Moors in a reenactment of the 1561 battle; seacraft land, houses are sacked, and there's much fighting in the streets. Everyone dresses up, dances wildly, and then atones for it the next day at high Mass. The celebration winds up at the end of the week, but concerts and unchoreographed pillaging continue throughout the month. Sóller celebrates its patron **Sant Pere** with marching bands and festivities on June 29. For the first two weeks in August, the Ajuntament of Sóller hosts an international **Festival de Dança Folclorica** with dancers from all of Spain, Europe, and Asia.

The **tourist office** in the town hall on Pl. Constitució, 1 (tel. 63 02 00), supplies a map and keeps a list of the few **accommodations** in Sóller. They can suggest some scenic hikes through the valley's handsome citrus and olive orchards; one manageable route steps to **Fornalutx,** about an hour up the valley. (Tourist office open Mon.-Sat. 9:30am-1:30pm.) The **post office** is on C. Cristobal Piza at C. Rectoria, about two blocks from Pl. Constitució. (Open Mon.-Fri. 9am-2pm, Sat. 9am-1pm.) The **police** (Guardia Civil) can be reached at 63 41 41 and 63 41 42; the **Red Cross** at 63 08 45. Six **trains** per day take you to Sóller from Palma (350ptas; tel. 63 01 30 for information).

The half-hour walk to **Port de Sóller** from the beach is therapeutic, but many people prefer to rumble along on the **trolley.** The port lies at the bottom of the valley absorbing most of the tourists. A beach lines the small, semicircular bay, where windsurfers zip back and forth. The **tourist office** (tel. 63 42 82) is at C. Canonge Oliver, one block in from the trolley's last stop (open Mon.-Fri. 10am-1pm). One of the only accommodations not flooded by foreign package-tourists is the spotless **Hotel Generoso,** Marina, 4 (tel. 63 14 50), where every room has a full bath and terrace. (Open March-Oct. Singles 2240ptas. Doubles 3560ptas. Breakfast 450ptas.) You can continue exploring the coast by **boat** (tel. 63 20 61 for information) in summer. Round-trip excursions leave Port de Sóller for Sa Calobra (3 per day, 1320ptas) and Cala Deia (Tues. at 10am and 3pm, 875ptas). Llompart **buses** link Port de Sóller to Palma via Valldemosa (5 per day, 315ptas) and to Port Pollença via Lluc (3 per day).

If your parents saw the road to **Sa Calobra,** they'd reach for the Valium. This asphalt serpent drops 1000m to the sea over 10 hairpin kms, writhing back underneath itself in the process. The **boat** from Port de Sóller is easier on the nerves (see above). Sa Calobra's tiny inlet shelters several worthless restaurants, but a five-minute hike through tunnels cut in the stone cliffs leads to the **Torrent de Pareis,** a pebble-strewn canyon ending in a bit of coast. In winter it becomes a river, but in summer it makes a super beach with water so clear you can see the shadows of boats on the bottom.

Lluc

The **Monestir de Lluc** (tel. 51 70 25), 20km inland in Escorca, tucks into the mountains, remote from the frenetic coastal bustle. This is Mallorca's Montserrat, home of the 700-year-old image of *La Verge de Lluc,* whose carved wood has turned a dark brown over the years (hence its nickname, *La Moroneta,* The Dark Lady). She darkens in a room behind the main altar in the basilica. The in-house **museu** aggregates somewhat interesting prehistoric remains, 15th-century ceramics, and 14th-century religious treasures. (Open 10am-6:30pm. Admission 200ptas.) Behind the monastery, **Via Crucis** winds around a hill with a view of the valley of olive trees and jingling goats. Gaudí designed the path's stations of the cross.

Only the monks and a few pilgrims sleep with you in the progressive **monastery** (tel. 51 70 25), a privileged place to bed down; unmarried couples are allowed. (True pilgrims stay for a donation. Others: Doubles 1175ptas, with bath 1750ptas. Quads 1875ptas, with bath 2300ptas.) The monks can point you to **campgrounds** nearby. Although prices at the monastery's **restaurant** are a bit steep, the small food store sells

groceries. To get to the monastery from Palma, take the 10am or 4pm **train** to Inca, which arrives in time for the two daily connecting **buses** to Lluc.

Northern Gulfs

Two peninsulas of land point audaciously at Menorca, forming large, beautiful bays on Mallorca's northern edge. The package tours and condo developments that overrun these beaches have missed a secluded cove or two in their haste. A highway connecting Palma to the eastern shore stretches directly across the flat southern plain and passes through inland Inca.

Pollença

From the top of **El Calvari**, there's a visual *festa* down into the northern gulfs, straight beyond Porto de Pollença into the bay, and even into Alcúdia and the bay beyond. At the bottom of the stairs is the **Ajuntament** (tel. 53 01 08; open Mon.-Fri. 8am-3pm), where you'll learn everything you ever wondered about the area. **Museu Miguel Costa Llobera,** C. Llobera 9, is the famous poet's birthplace. You must write beforehand for permission to enter. The **post office** is at C. Sant Josep, 3. (Open Mon.-Fri. 9am-9pm, Sat. 9am-2pm.)

Porto de Pollença's long beaches and short strip of residential development make for a relatively uncrowded beach of fine white sand and rambunctious surf. The area hosts a **festival de música** from July to September. In the port, tickets are available at **Casa Penya** (tel. 53 19 91).

Hostal Corro, C. Joan XXIII, 68 (tel. 53 10 05), off C. Elano (tributary of the waterfront), at the bus stop, has expansive rooms with sinks (1200ptas per person, with bath 1600ptas; breakfast 300ptas). **Hostal Juma,** Pl. Major, 9 (tel. 53 00 07), doubles with bath (2300ptas). Down the hill, **Autocares Villalonga,** C. Sant Isidoro, 4 (tel. 53 00 57), pays calls to Porto de Pollença (5 per day, 470ptas). Meals tend to be expensive, but off C. Joan XXIII toward the waterfront, **Bar-Restaurante Mibar,** Ctra. de Formentor, 18 (tel. 53 39 71), whips up cheap à la carte specialties and a 750ptas *menú*. They also make Falstaffian English breakfasts for 550ptas. (Open Jan.-Nov. 9am-midnight.)

The **tourist office,** at Pl. Miquel Capllonch, 2 (tel. 53 46 66), off C. Atilio Bover from the waterfront, weeds through bus schedules and plans excursions in a single bound. (Open May-Oct. Mon.-Fri. 9am-1pm and 4-7pm, Sat. 9am-1pm.) The **post office** is on C. Llevant, 15. (Open for stamps Mon.-Fri. 9am-9pm, Sat. 9am-2pm; for **telegrams** Mon.-Fri. 8am-9pm, Sat. 9am-2pm.) **Maria's,** C. Joan XXIII, 52 (tel. 53 24 68), near Hostal Corro, rents two-wheeled vehicles. (Bikes 600ptas per day, 2200ptas per week. Mopeds 2000ptas per day, 10,500ptas per week. Open March-Oct. Mon.-Sat. 9am-1pm and 3-7pm, Sun. 9am-1pm and 6-7pm.) Right on the beach, a summertime **telephone kiosk** handles international calls (open April-Oct. 9:30am-10pm).

At the end of **Cap Formentor** 15km northeast of Porto de Pollença, *miradores* (lookouts) overlook spectacular fjords. Before the final twisting kilometers, the road drops down to **Platja Formentor,** where a canopy of evergreens runs nearly to the edge of the water. Here the sand is softer, the water calmer, and the crowds smaller than at Port de Pollença. Some people say you can taste it in the *sangría*. Call Armenteras **buses** (tel. 54 56 96) for information to Formentor from Palma and Porto de Pollença. Hydrophiles can also take the boat to Formentor from Porto de Pollença (tel. 86 40 14, 5 per day, 650ptas). One boat per day heads to Formentor at 10am (1075ptas).

Alcúdia

The site of the ancient Roman city of Pollentia, and a base for beaching and boating nearby, **Alcúdia** might be one of the most sensible places on the island to settle down for a few days. Fourteenth-century ramparts encircle the town itself and the remains of Pollentia and the Roman amphitheater line the road to the port. Loops of isolated coves and beaches string their way around the point of Alcúdia. In the Bon Aire section of town resides Mallorca's only HI youth hostel outside of Palma. Signs to the **Alberg Victoria,** Ctra. Cap Pinar, 4 (tel. 54 53 95), lead east from the town center; it's on the right of a hillside road 4km from Alcúdia (1hr. walk or 800ptas taxi ride). The hostel lolls only 100m from an empty beach on the Badia de Pollença; you have to reserve at least six months in advance to get a bed in July or August. (Open mid-June to Sept. Members only 800ptas. Breakfast included.) A long hike from the youth hostel leads to the spiritual center of Alcúdia, **Ermita de la Victoria,** tucked away in a pine grove near the notable **Museu Arqueológic** next to the church. (Open Tues.-Sat. 10:30am-1:30pm and 3:30-6:30pm, Sun. 10:30am-1:30pm. Admission 100ptas, under 12 free.)

Port d'Alcúdia, the beach and boating area 1km south, has less crowded and only slightly more expensive accommodations; the trusty tourist office has the master list. At C. Teodoro Canet, 41, on the road that leads up to Alcúdia, **Hostal Calma** (tel. 54 53 43) includes breakfast with its spacious rooms. Reserve well in advance for the summer. (Singles with bath 1700ptas. Doubles with bath 2400ptas. Breakfast 350ptas. Open mid-March to mid-Dec.) **C. Hostelería,** off the waterfront at the bus stop for the tourist park, is true to its name. **Café Paris** (tel. 54 78 79) has bright wainscoting and elegant tablecloths. The French owner whips up a 750ptas *menú*. (Open April-Oct. 11am-4pm and 6pm-midnight.)

The **tourist office** is near the waterfront at Av. Pere Mas Reus, on the corner with Ctra. Ata, at the third stop on the bus after the tourist port. They speak English. (Open April-Sept. Mon.-Sat. 9am-7pm.) An equally helpful and much more mobile **tourist van** parks outside the tourist port. (Open Tues.-Sun. 10am-1pm and 5-8pm. Tues. and Sun. mornings parked at the town market instead.) The summertime **telephone kiosk** also tinkles at the tourist port (open 9:30am-1:30pm and 4-11pm). Rent bikes at 600ptas per day (better than chickens) from **Reina Bike Rental,** C. Teodoro Canet, 27 (tel. 54 55 72, open in summer 9am-1pm and 5-8pm). **Medical attention** in Port d'Alcúdia can be had at **Casa del Mar,** C. Ciudadela (tel. 54 59 68).

Armenteras **buses** (tel. 54 56 96) for Alcúdia and Port d' Alcúdia leave Pl. Espanya in Palma (Mon.-Sat. 10 per day, Sun. 4 per day; 440ptas and 470ptas). The bus between Alcúdia and Porto de Pollença runs reliably (every 15min., 80ptas), and some buses continue on to Cap Formentor. Bus service to the south goes only as far as C'an Picafort. All buses in Port d'Alcúdia pass along waterfront Pg. Marítim and through the center of Alcúdia proper.

Eastern Coast

As the tourist swarm sweeps east, it swamps dozens of small coastal towns in its wake then seeps underground, down to the eerie Plutonian landscapes of the region's many caves. Buses connect most of the major towns and beaches.

Artá

In the northern end lies the dreary town of **Artá,** which features a dull **Museu Regional** (open Mon.-Fri. 10am-noon), bland Gothic church, and uninspiring Castell Fortalesa Almudaina. Fortunately for spelunkers and laypeople alike, the magnificent **Covas de Artá,** Mallorca's best caves, burrow just 10km away. The labyrinth of vaulted chambers with imposing stalactites and stalagmites (mites go up, tites go down) draws far fewer explorers than the Covas del Drach and exudes a macabre and mysterious beauty (tours 9:30am-7pm, winter 9:30-5pm; 450ptas). Aumasa **buses** (tel. 55 07 30) leave Pl. Espanya in Palma for Artá (Mon.-Sat. 4 per day, 625ptas) and continue to Cala Ratjada (110ptas more), with the same number of return trips.

Platja and **Costa de Canyamel,** just south of the Covas del Artá, form part of a classy German beach development; the hotels charge a fortune, but the magnificent sites on the seaside hilltops tempt unofficial campers. The **tourist office** on Pl. Pins (tel. 56 30 33) hands out a list of lodgings. (Open Mon.-Fri. 9:30am-1:30pm and 4-7pm, Sat. 9:30am-1:30pm.)

Porto Cristo

Porto Cristo and its famous **Covas del Drach** lie 25km south. The port contains nothing but excursion buses, bothered tourists, a crowded beach, and much too much SPF 30. Hop a boat to Cala Millor (1 per day at 12:30pm, returns at 3pm; round-trip includes food and drink, 1500ptas).

Porto Cristo's **aquari** (tel. 57 02 10) is just off the road to the caves (1km outside town). Inside is one of the most extensive marine-life collections in Spain; outside are some of the gaudiest murals. (Open 9am-7pm. Off-season 11am-3pm. Admission 500ptas, under 9 250ptas.) The **Covas del Drach** (Caves of the Dragon) (tel. 82 07 53 or 82 16 41) are fairyland stalactite caverns where towering white cities, forests, angel wings, and childhood memories emerge from stone. Tours last one hour and include a Chopin boat concert on the Stygian lake. (Tours daily on the hr. 10am-5pm, except 1pm. Admission 700ptas.) The **Covas dels Hams** (Caves of the Baits) outside Porto Cristo on the road to Manacor have more sap and less soul. Three buses connect directly to the caves from Pl. Espanya in Palma (Sun. 1 per day, round-trip 1140ptas).

The **tourist office**, C. Gual, 31 (tel. 82 09 31), has a map, list of its superb restaurants, and list of accommodations. (Open in summer Mon.-Fri. 8:30am-3pm, Sat. 9am-1pm.) The **post office** is at C. Zanglada, 10 (tel. 57 07 64), off C. Navegantes. (Open Mon.-Fri. 9am-9pm, Sat. 9am-2pm.) For **medical attention,** call the Red Cross at 82 07 84. **Buses** connect Port Cristo with **Ca'n Picafort** (1 per day at 4pm), **Palma via Manacor** (Mon.-Sat. 5 per day, Sun. 2 per day; 1hr.; 455ptas), and various beaches nearby, including **Cala Ratjada** (2 per day Mon.-Sat.).

Southeastern Mallorca

The eastern coast of Mallorca's southeastern peninsula is a scalloped fringe of bays and caves. Many harbor the island's most recent resort developments, where the new hotel towns aspire to some architectural integrity. A walk of 1-2km, however, puts plenty of sand between you and the thickest crowds. **Autocares Grimalt** buses (tel. 58 02 46) leave Cafetería Alcalá, Av. Alejandro Rosselló, 32 (tel. 46 35 27), in Palma, for **Santanyí,** an inland town whose Porta Murada defensive wall testifies to the piracy that once plagued the region (5 per day, 515ptas); **Cala d'Or,** an inlet of pinewoods and massive boulders (4 per day, 630ptas); and **Porto Petro,** on the beach (3 per day via Cala d'Or, 610ptas). Santanyí erupts for the yearly patron saint feast day (July 25).

Rounding **Cap de Salinas,** Mallorca's southernmost point, the long leg of coastline back to Palma begins. Miles of inaccessible and isolated sand lie between here and **Cap Blanc,** beyond which ill-humored, rocky cliffs fend off Palma's southern suburbs. The grandsons of Joan March, an infamous Spanish banker, own most of the southeastern interior.

One Grimalt bus runs (at 7:30am) from Cafetería Alcalá in Palma to Colonia Sant Jordi (520ptas). From Colonia Sant Jordi, a boat ventures to **Cabrera,** a 30 sq. km island that is the largest in a small archipelago of 17. Uninhabited except for a small military installation, it has a gruesome history. Besides the many shipwrecks that poke up from the ocean floor, 8000 French prisoners of war died here during the Peninsular War in 1809; the Spanish abandoned them on the island with no food. A monument to the dead stands by the port. Nearby looms a 14th-century fortress used as a pirates' den. The boat excursion leaves the port at Sant Jordi (June-Sept. Wed.-Mon. 9:30am, Tues. 9am, return at 6pm; 1 1/2 hr.; round-trip a whopping 2600ptas). Restaurante Miramar (tel. 64 90 34) in Sant Jordi dispatches tickets.

Inland

The interior landscapes of orchards, vineyards, and wheat fields make up Mallorca's heartland. Ancient stone walls, crumbling and rudimentary, divide the inland valleys into individual farms, where windmills and sloppy haystacks dot chunks of hillside fig, olive, and almond groves. The pastel almond blossoms flourish in February, their petals covering the island like fragrant confetti.

Inca

Inca lies just south of the Serra de Tramontana, panting for the moisture barred by the mountains. Halfway between Palma and Alcúdia and at the end of a railway, it attracts many visitors with its inexpensive leather goods and the busy Thursday-morning market. Snack food connoisseurs flock to Inca to snatch up *galletes d'oli*, locally produced cookies that resemble overfed American goldfish crackers. The main streets parallel to the railroad tracks—**Carrer de Colom** and **Carrer de Vicent Ensenyat**—lined with factory outlet leather shops, where you can buy everything from books and combs to whips and chains. Inca lies 35 minutes by train from Palma (Mon.-Sat. 20 per day, Sun. 16 per day; 220ptas). Five buses per day make the trek from Inca to Alcúdia.

Manacor

Manacor rises out of this scenic landscape as the industrial backbone of inland Mallorca. As part of its grand scheme to lure the masses away from the beaches, Manacor has developed a booming artificial pearl industry. The factories are open for visits and purchases. The largest, **Perlas Majorca**, Via Roma, 48 (tel. 55 02 00), is on the road to Palma on the edge of town. (Open Mon.-Fri. 9am-2:30pm and 3-7pm, Sat.-Sun. 10am-1pm. Free.) Closer to town, you can visit **Perlas Orquídea**, on Pl. Ramón Llull, 15 (tel. 55 04 00). (Open Mon.-Fri. 9am-7pm, Sat. 9am-1pm, Sun. 9:30am-1pm. Free.) There's not much else to see except for the turreted Gothic **catedral** and adjoining **Museu Arqueológic** (open Mon.-Sat. 10am-1pm).

Aumasa **buses** depart from Pl. des Cos, 4 (tel. 55 07 30), for Palma (7 per day, 2 on weekends and holidays; 455ptas), and Porto Cristo (10 per day, 115ptas).

Near Manacor: Petra and Felanitx

Rocking nearby is **Petra**, the hometown of Fray Junípero Serra, the man responsible for the Spanish presence in California. The house of this ecclesiastical Johnny Appleseed, who founded a chain of West Coast Franciscan missions—the seedlings of San Francisco, Monterey, and San Diego, among others—is now a museum. The unadorned **Ermita de Bonany**, or "cathedral of the mountains," is a one-hour walk into the splendiferous hills, alive with the sound of music. July 21 brings the patron saint's feast to Petra when the town gathers together and celebrates Santa Práxedes. The town also commemorates the birth of Sena on the Sunday closest to November 24. (Four Aumasa **buses** per day leave Pl. Espanya in Palma for Petra; Sun. 2 per day, 360ptas.)

About 15km to the south of Manacor, on route C714, lies the city of **Felanitx** and its 16th-century convent of Sant Antoni. The town lounges at the foot of Puig de Sant Salvador, capped by the **Santuari de Nostra Senyora de San Salvador** and the **Castell de Santueri**. The monastery (tel. 58 06 56) overlooks the southern coast, the island of Cabrera, and the Bay of Alcúdia. Some accommodations are available and the hostelry serves a simple but hearty lunch.

Should you take a liking to the sequestered life, another monastery, the **Santuari de Nostra Señora de Cura** (tel. 66 09 94), goes about its humble routine 30km east of Palma. The sanctuary is open most daylight hours, but if it's closed (usually around lunchtime), ask to be let in at the convent. If you don't have a car or motorbike, you'll have to take a **bus** to Lluchmajor and then hike, take a taxi, or pray for divine intervention.

Menorca

The northernmost of the major Baleares, Menorca has managed to retain its sloping green pastures and rugged stone fences, unobstructed by the condominiums, luxury hotels, and flashy discos that lure masses to Mallorca and Eivissa. The lengthy coastline (224km) cradles the province's least frequented beaches, some of which can be reached only by foot or boat. Over 200 stone monuments lie scattered about the island, souvenirs from Menorca's Bronze Age visitors.

Maò

Maò's whitesplashed houses and mellow inhabitants mingle a gentility long forsaken by most tourist-plagued cities. From atop a steep bluff, the city overlooks a harbor that now serves partly as a submarine base for the Spanish navy. The British occupied this capital city for almost a century in the 1800s and left Georgian doors, brass knockers, and wooden shutters in their wake. They introduced the gin distilleries that industrialized the production of indigenous liqueurs such as *calent,* a sweet potion made from anise, cinnamon, and saffron. British-style pubs and the city's early bedtime testify to a continuing influence.

The British never relinquished the area as a vacation spot and almost outnumber locals in summer. However, their numbers are dropping as they abandon Menorca for American resorts. Although no beaches are within walking distance from the city, extensive bus service fans out from Maò, making the city a convenient base for a seaside vacation.

Orientation and Practical Information

Many streets retain their Castilian names; we give both in case of confusion. No buses traverse the 7km between the airport and town (850ptas a taxi). One main highway spans the 45km across the island between Maò and **Ciutadella,** on the west end of Menorca, and passes through the towns of **Alaior, Es Mercadal,** and **Ferreires** en route.

For the center of Maò from its port, climb the path across from the ferry station. To reach **Plaça de l'Esplanada,** the hub of the city, continue on Carrer Rector Panedes (C. Rector Mort) to **Plaça Bastió.** Walk into the *plaça* and turn right at the far right-hand corner of the square onto Carrer de Sa Comedia (C. San Bartolomé). The first left is Carrer de la Lluna, which leads to Carrer de ses Moreres (C. Dr. Orfila). Two blocks to the right is Pl. de l'Esplanada; the tourist office is on the far side.

Tourist Office: Pl. Esplanada, 40 (tel. 36 37 90), near the corner across from the bus station. Marked only by a small brass sign. Valuable maps of Maò's street maze, pamphlets on archeological sites and island entertainment, and bus schedules. Open Mon.-Fri. 9am-2pm and 5-7pm, Sat. 9:30am-1pm. Summer office at the **airport** (tel. 36 01 50) purveys similar materials. Open June-Oct. 8am-11pm. **Municipal information:** tel. 900 30 05 84. English operator available upon request.

American Express: Viajes Iberia, C. Nou, 35 (tel. 36 28 48, 36 28 45, fax 35 25 31), 2 doors from Pl. Reial. 2% commisssion on AmEx and other traveler's checks. Cardholder mail held for 2 months. Open Mon.-Fri. 9am-1pm and 4-7pm, Sat. 9:30am-1pm.

Post Office: C. Bonaire, 11-13 (tel. 36 38 95), on the corner with C. Esglésias. From Pl. Esplanada, take C. Moreres (C. Dr. Orfila) until it becomes C. Hanover, then take the 1st left. Stamps on the 1st fl., Lista de Correos on the 2nd. Open Mon.-Fri. 9am-9pm, Sat. 9am-2pm. **Postal Code:** 07700.

Telephones: Several booths in Pl. Esplanada, 64. Open Mon.-Sat. 10am-1pm and 5-10:30pm, Sun. 6-10:30am. **Telephone Code:** 971.

Airport: (tel. 36 01 50), 7km out of town. Main office open 7:15am-9:30pm. To Palma (6 per day; 20min.; 4100ptas, round-trip 8200ptas) on Aviaco or Iberia. Also summer flights to Barcelona and Madrid. Any travel agent issues tickets. In summer advance booking is essential. For information and reservations, call Aviaco at the airport (tel. 36 01 50, ext. 1225). Many travel agencies offer charter flights.

Buses: Transportes Menorca (TMSA), C. Josep M. Quadrado, 7 (tel. 36 03 61), off Pl. Esplanada. To: Alaior and Son Bou (5 per day, 120ptas); Es Mercadal (5 per day, 185ptas); Ferreires (5 per day, 240ptas); Ciutadella (5 per day, 375ptas). Other lines to Platja Punta Prima (9 per day, 150ptas) and Villacarlos (every 1/2 hr., 80ptas) depart from Pl. Esplanada. **Autocares Fornells** (tel. 37 66 21), on Pl. Esplanada. To: Fornells (Mon.-Sat. 3 per day, Sun. 2 per day; 175ptas); Platja Es Grau (3 per day, 6 on Sun.; 80ptas); and other points. **Torres,** Camí de Maò, 42 (tel. 38 47 20). All buses leave from Pl. Esplanada. To: Caleta Sontandria (7 per day, 340ptas); Cala Blanca (7 per day, 340 ptas); Cala Blanes and Forcat (9 per day, 340ptas); Cala Bosch and Son Xoriquer (10 per day, 375ptas). The tourist office hands out a complete bus schedule with exact times. Buy all tickets aboard the buses.

Illes Baleares (Balearic Islands)

Ferries: Transmediterránea (tel. 36 29 50), at Estació Marítima along Moll (Andén) de Ponent. To: Barcelona (June-Sept. 6 per week, off-season 2 per week; 9hr.; deck-class 5350ptas) and Palma (Sun. at 4:30pm, 6 1/2 hr., 3900ptas), continuing to València (9 more hr.). Easier to fly. Open Mon.-Fri. 8:30am-1pm and 5-7pm; Sat. 8am-noon; Sun. 8:30am-noon and 3-5pm, off-season 3-5pm.

Taxis: Taxi stand, (tel. 36 12 83, 36 71 01 in Maò or tel. 36 28 91 in Ciutadella). Flat rates for any given route. Hail one on or near Pl. Esplanada.

Bike and Moped Rental: Essential to get to the isolated parts of the island. Scores of places in town, all with similar prices. Try **Gelabert,** Av. J.A. Clavé, 12 (tel. 36 06 14), off Pl. Esplanada. Bicycles 700ptas per day, 4200ptas per week. Mopeds and motorcycles 1500ptas per day, 9000ptas per week. Prices lower Oct.-May. Open Mon.-Fri. 9am-1pm and 4-8pm, Sat. 9am-2pm. Complete list of all vehicle rental places at the tourist office. There are only 9 gas stations on Menorca; the tourist office has a pamphlet of their locations. Open 6am-10pm; Oct.-May 7am-9pm. 24-hr. service rotates among the stations (one of them is always in Maò) and is listed in the *Menorca Diario Insular* (local paper, 80ptas, newsstands in Pl. Esplanada).

English Bookstore: English-Language Library, C. Deya (Costa d'en Ga), 2 (tel. 36 27 01), off Pl. Reial. Sells a few paperbacks but lends anything you'd like to read. Open Mon.-Sat. 9am-1pm.

Laundromat: 215, Antic Estació Marítima, at the port in a large yellow building behind the **food market** of the same name. 7kg wash 800ptas, dry and fold 700ptas. Open 9am-1pm and 6-9pm.

Red Cross: tel. 36 11 80.

24-hr. Pharmacy: See listings in *Menorca Diario Insular* (local paper, 80ptas, newsstands in Pl. Esplanada).

Medical Assistance: Residencia Sanitaria, (tel. 37 35 00), C. Barcelona, s/n. Near the waterfront, 1 block in from Pg. Marítim. English spoken.

Emergency: tel. 091 or 092. **Fire:** tel. 36 39 61.

Police: Municipal (tel. 36 39 61), Pl. Constitució. **Guardia Civil** (tel. 36 11 00), Ctra. Sant Lluís.

Accommodations

There are few *pensiones,* but space is a problem in August only. Call a few days in advance. The tourist office also keeps a list of accommodations.

Casa-Huéspedes Company, C. Rosari, 27 (tel. 36 22 67), off C. Sant Roc, which runs from Pl. Bastió. Each of the 7 rooms has a different homey touch: a chair-to-curl-up-in here, a lovely wooden table there. Singles 1200ptas. Doubles 2200ptas. Prices slightly lower off-season.

Hostal-Residencia Jume, C. Concepció 6 (tel. 36 32 66), near Pl. Miranda. Take C. Anuncivay off C. Infanta. The TV room, lounges on each floor, ice-cream freezer, bar, and pool table nudge sluggish social lives. Modern rooms, all with full bath. Singles 1700ptas. Doubles 3300ptas. Oct.1-June 14: 1500ptas; 3000ptas. Breakfast 325ptas.

Hostal Orsi, C. Infanta, 19 (tel. 36 47 51). From Pl. Esplanada, take C. Moreres (C. Dr. Orfila) straight as it becomes C. Hanover. Turn right at Pl. Constitució, and follow C. Nou through Pl. Reial. Hard-working English couple keep it clean and inviting. Handy rooftop sunning patio, plus new sinks and mirrors. Mattresses are so firm. Really. Singles 1850ptas. Doubles 2900ptas, with shower 3400ptas. Triples 3900ptas. Oct.-May: 1500ptas; 2500ptas, with shower 2900ptas; 3300ptas. Breakfast 350ptas.

Hotel la Isla, C. Santa Catalina, 4 (tel. 36 64 92). Take C. Concepció from Pl. Miranda. Flower frenzy rooms and bathrooms match the island's pastel scheme. There's a restaurant below (full meal 800ptas!). Singles 1500ptas, new room with bath 1650ptas. Doubles 2900ptas, new room with bath 3300ptas. Oct.-May: 1300ptas, 1500ptas; 2200ptas, 2900ptas.

Bar-Hostal Roca, C. Carmen, 37 (tel. 35 15 39). Around the corner from Hostal la Isla, its rooms are on the spartan side; many are directly over the bar downstairs. 1000ptas per person.

Hostal Reynés, C. Comerç, 26 (tel. 36 40 59). No sign out front. Tranquil, with a large dining area. The jungle of plants downstairs gets more light than the rooms. Singles 1900ptas. Doubles 2600ptas. Triples 3700ptas. Oct.-May: 1200ptas; 2000ptas; 3400ptas. 3 meals per day 2600ptas.

Food

Bars around **Plaças de la Constitució and Esplanada** serve filling *platos combinados* for 400-650ptas. The **market** off Pl. Carme hawks fruits, vegetables, and sandwich meats. Try *formatge maonès* (a local cheese), *sobrassada* (soft Mallorcan chorizo spread), *caldereta de langosta* (lobster stew), *crespells* (biscuits), and *rubiols* (pastry turnovers filled with fish or vegetables).

La Huerta, C. Joan Ramis (Sa Rovellada de Baix), 64 (tel. 36 28 85). Take C. Rovellada de Dalt (Comte de Cifuentes) off Pl. Esplanada and make a sharp right at the 1st intersection. Toothsome dining in front of a wide-screen TV. Enticing 2-course meal with bread, drink, and dessert 720ptas. Open Mon.-Fri. 1-3:30pm and 8:30-10:30pm.

Ristorante Pizzeria Roma, Andén de Levante, 295 (tel. 35 37 77). Down by the port, next to the stairs from Costa de Llevant. Among many waterside joints, this popular one stands out for its authentic Italian pizza (although some complain it's short on the tomato). Basic pizza 300ptas. Fishy special<italicxd1 fruta del mar pizza with mussels, prawns, crawfish, and capers 825ptas. Open 12:30pm-12:30am. *Menús* served 3:30-7pm.

Mas i Glop, C. Alaior, 10 (tel. 36 64 57), right off the Pl. Bastió. *Al fresco* dining. Choice among the *platos combinados* (550-700ptas), *menú* (850ptas), and *paella* (2100ptas for two) a stumper. Open Mon.-Sat. 8am-midnight.

El Turronero, C. Nou, 22-26 (tel. 36 28 98), off Pl. Reial. They've been making *turrón* (nougat) candy and ice cream since 1894. Double scoop of *turrón*-flavored ice cream 175ptas. Catch the *turrón* fever. Open Mon.-Fri. 9am-2pm and 4-10pm, Sat.-Sun. 9am-2pm and 7-10pm.

Sights and Entertainment

The **Museu Arqueològic Provincial de Belles Artes,** in the cloister of Església de Sant Francesc, contains chiefly Spanish ceramics from Alcora and Talavera, plus Aztec, Mayan, and Roman artifacts. (Currently closed for repairs.)

Església de Santa María la Major in Pl. Constitución, founded in 1287 and rebuilt in 1772, trembles to the 51 stops and 3006 pipes of its disproportionately large **organ**, built by Maese Juan Kilburz in 1810. A **festival de música** in July and August showcases this immense instrument. Festival concerts are given Fridays at 10pm; seats cost a minimal fee, but as the sound carries into the surrounding streets, you can listen from a nearby café.

Up C. Sant Roc, **Arc de Sant Roc** straddles the streets and reminds those who pass under it of the fortifications necessary to defend the city from marauding Catalan pirates. Closer to Pl. Esplanada, the **Ateneu Científic, Literari y Artístic,** C. Comte de Cifuentes, 25 (tel. 36 05 53), a private cultural society, hoards old pirate maps. The bad news is that the choice booty is probably long looted, and the sign outside says "members only." The good news is that all are welcome to admire their collection of books, stuffed birds, and preserved fish. (Open Mon.-Sat. 10am-2pm and 3-10pm. Free.) For the live version (fish, that is), head down to the **aquari** at the port, Moll de Ponent, 73 (tel. 35 05 37). (Open May-Oct. Mon.-Fri. 10am-3pm, Sat. 10am-2pm. Admission 200ptas, under 12 100ptas.) The aquarium is lined with small tables because every evening at 8pm it does a little quick-change into the **aquarium bar** where you can tipple under the stare of unblinking fish. (Open nightly 8pm-3am.)

Other recreations include an hour-long **boat tour** of the harbor. (2 tours per day, 800ptas, under 12 350ptas.) Buy tickets at the Xoriguer Gin Distillery, Moll de Ponent, 93 (tel. 36 75 78, see hrs. below), or the Mad Hatter Bar, Moll de Ponent, 62 (tel. 36 58 65, open Mon.-Sat. 9am-7pm, Sun. 9am-3pm). A more satisfying trip goes out of the harbor to the island beach **Illa d'en Colom.** The steep price covers lunch on the boat with wine and a splash of Menorcan gin (2500ptas, under 12 1250ptas). Ships leave at 10am and return by 5pm. Buy tickets at the aquarium.

The **Xoriguer** distillery brews its magic Menorcan gin on the waterfront at Moll de Ponent, 93 (tel. 36 21 92) in huge copper vats bubbling over wood fires. There are 15 subtly different local brews (free samples). (Distillery and store open Mon.-Fri. 8am-7pm, Sat. 8am-1pm; off-season 9am-2pm.)

From May to September, artisans with pottery, glass vases, and paintings display their work alongside neon T-shirts, jewelry, tablecloths, shoes, and assorted knickknacks in **mercadillos** held every day in the main square of at least one locale on the island. (Maó Tues. and Sat.; Ciutadella Fri.; Alaior Thurs.; Mercadal Sun.; Ferrieres Tues. and Fri.; Es Castell Mon. and Wed.; Es Migjurn Wed.; and Fornells Thurs.) The art is cheaper than the T-shirts.

Menorca turns into a pumpkin by midnight. The bars cluster along the port across from the ferry. One favorite is **Baixamar,** Moll de Ponent, 17 (tel. 36 58 96; open 7am-3am; Oct.-May 10am-1am). The only proper disco in Maò is **Si,** C. Virgen de Gracia, 16 (tel. 36 13 62) just off C. Infanta. It has low vaulted ceilings, a small dance floor, and strange, undulating benches along the sides. People squeeze in only on Saturdays after 2am; not for the claustrophobic or weak of heart. (Open midnight-5am. Cover with drink 1000ptas.)

Most nightlife isn't in Maò, but rather in neighboring Villacarlos. **Factory,** C. Sa Sinia de Muret (tel. 36 63 68), a 15-minute walk from Maò (follow C. Es Cós de Grácia and turn left at its end), sports a series of water-encircled islets for dancing to Euro-sounds. (Open Oct.-May weekends 11pm-6:30am. Cover with drink 1500ptas.) The biggest crowds converge on **Pacha** in Sant Lluís, 5km from Maò. (Open nightly midnight-5am. Cover with drink 1200ptas.) Jazz is at the **Jazz Club El Casino** (tel. 36 00 53) in Sant Clement (in summer Tues. and Thurs.). Sant Clement is about 4km out of town on the bus line to Cala'n Porter. Unfortunately, as the last bus leaves shortly after 8pm, many end up looking for a ride back to town.

Maò's **Verge del Carme** celebration, July 16, floats a colorful armada of trimmed boats into the harbor. The **Festa de Nostra Senyora de Gràcia** swings out September 7-9.

Ciutadella (Ciudadela)

One-time capital of the island, Ciutadella still thinks it's important and retains a corresponding air of dignity. Forty-five km west of Maò on the opposite side of the island, this city is both larger and more commercial with its sprawling plazas and long throughways. Still, the picturesque port—a finger of water poking into the belly of the old town—arcaded streets, stately residences, and 14th-century Gothic cathedral make it a pleasing base for excursions to nearby sights and fantastic beaches.

Orientation and Practical Information

The bus from Maò drops visitors off at C. Barcelona. To reach **Plaça des Born,** which connects to the city center of **Plaça de Colom/Plaça deis Pins,** turn left off C. Barcelona onto C. de Mao and walk straight until you hit the plaza.

Tourist Office: A caravan in Pl. Born (tel. 38 10 50). They disburse maps and transportation advice. Open Mon.-Fri. 9am-2pm.

Post Office: Pl. Born (tel. 38 00 81). Open Mon.-Fri. 9am-2pm, Sat. 9am-1pm.

Telephones: Plexiglass telephone office in Pl. Colom/Pins. Open June-Oct. 15 10am-1pm and 5:30-10pm.

Buses: Transportes Menorca, C. Barcelona, 8 (tel. 38 03 03). Between Maò and Ciutadella (6 per day, 375ptas). Buses to coastal points such as Cala Blanca (75ptas), Cala Bosch (95ptas), and Cala Santandria (75ptas) depart from Pl. Colom/Pins (every hr. 9am-7pm).

Taxis: tel. 38 44 35, 38 11 97. Try Pl. Colom/Pins.

Bike/Moped Rental: Bicicletas Tolo, C. Sant Isidor (de ses Cadufes), 28-34 (tel. 38 15 76). Bikes 500ptas per day, 2750ptas per week. Mopeds 3200ptas for 2 days, 9900ptas per week. Open Mon.-Fri. 8am-1pm and 3:30-8pm, Sat. 8am-1pm.

Red Cross: tel. 38 19 93.

24-Hour Pharmacy: Farmàcia Martí, Pl. Pins, 20 (tel. 38 03 94).

Medical Assistance: Ambulance (tel. 38 44 49).

Police: Pl. Born, Ajuntament building (tel. 38 10 95). **Guardia Civil** (tel. 38 02 99).

Accommodations and Food

Pensiones here tend to be small, intimate affairs; call in advance. Choice eateries spread their umbrellas and chairs along **C. Marina,** on the town's narrow, sailboat-filled harbor. Nondescript sandwich bars sulk in **Pl. Born** and its environs.

Hotel Geminis, C. Rossinyol, 4 (tel. 38 58 96). Take C. del Sud off Av. del Capital Negrete, then a quick right onto C. Rossinyol. Phone, heater/fan, light wood furniture, and full bath in every room. Singles 2600ptas. Doubles 3800ptas. Off-season: 1900ptas; 3400ptas. Breakfast of croissant and *café* included.

Bar ses Persianes, Pl. Antrux, 2 (tel. 38 14 45), off Av. Jaume I El Conqueridor. Bright white walls don't make the smallish scrubbed rooms feel any bigger. Bar with A/C below serves breakfast. Doubles 2500ptas, off-season 2000ptas.

Nou Port, C. Marina, 103. Cheaper *menús* than many of its neighbors offer (675-900ptas), yet the food doesn't suffer. Open May-Oct. 10am-11:30pm.

Bar La Guitarra, C. Dolores, 1 (tel. 38 13 55). The sign reads, "Try our meals the way *we* do them." Whether you take it as a threat or promise depends on how adventuresome you are: Menorcan cheese and sausage, ox tongue with peas, rabbit in onion sauce, stuffed cabbage rolls, etc. Open March-Jan. Mon.-Sat. 9am-3pm and 6:30-11pm.

Restaurante El Horno, C. Forn, 10 (tel. 38 07 67), off C. Mirador. On the site of the city's first bakery, this low, stone-ceilinged basement now battens a selective clientele. *Tortilla con queso* (380ptas), *pollo al Kiev* (1100ptas). Open Mon.-Sat. noon-3pm and 7-11pm, Sun. 7-11pm.

Café Balear, C. Marina, on the harbor's mouth. The only place to satisfy that craving for yeast water (*caña,* 125ptas) or Menorcan gin and tonic (350ptas). Open 6am-11pm.

Sights and Entertainment

The archeological sites of **Torre Trencada** and **Torre Llafuda** preserve Bronze Age remnants just 6km inland from Ciutadella. Both were formerly *talayot* (rounded towers for overlooking the countryside) settlements that housed the Stonehenge-ish *taulas.* The **taulas** are two enormous rectangles of rock carefully balanced on each other (for 3000 years) in the shape of the letter "T". Meanwhile, the most important prehistoric site on Menorca crumbles 4km from the city: the **Naveta dels Tudons,** the oldest building in Europe (despite some cosmetic restoration). Originally a dwelling, later a burial tomb, these community-tomb ruins are today the most complete among numerous similar community tombs on the island. Buses don't come near these sights; consider hiking along the tranquil C. Cami Vell de Maò.

From the first week in July to the first week in September, Ciutadella hosts the **Festival de Música d'Estiu,** featuring some of the world's top classical musicians and ensembles, in the Claustre del Seminari. Tickets (900-1500ptas) are sold at Foto Born, C. Bisbe Vila, 14 (tel. 38 17 54).

Beaches

Buses from Maò will easily take you to some of the more popular beaches. (For more information see Practical Information: Buses.)

Es Grau is a small sandy bay about 8km north of the town, frequented mainly by Menorcans. Autocares Fornells buses leave from Pl. Esplanada in Maò for Es Grau (3 per day, 6 on Sun.; 80ptas). Once there, catch a boat (500ptas) out to the **Illa d'en Colom,** a tiny island with more beaches. (Boats leave June-Sept. every 20min. 10am-7:20pm. Buy tickets at Bar C'an Bernat at the beach.)

Punta Prima, to the south, is a wide, often crowded beach served by Transportes Menorca buses (6 per day, 150ptas).

Platges de Son Bou, a gorgeous string of beaches with crystal waters on the southern shore. There is a 5th-century Christian **basílica** in the nearby settlement of Son Bou.

Cala Santa Galdana is the narrow beach 9km south of Ferreires, from which you can walk to the untouched **Cala Macarella,** about 1/2hr. west. Galdana is accessible by public transportation from Ferreires.

Cala'en Porter's huge bluffs are closer to Maò and connected by bus. Open beaches curve underneath. Here the **Covas d'en Xoroi,** a Swiss cheese of spooky prehistoric dwellings, gaze down on the sea.

Cales Cores is a 30min. walk to the east (left facing the sea) from Porter's, with the best sand to tan ratio on the shore.

Cala Bosc's jagged cliffs plummet into the clear pale-blue water, a perfect backdrop for a refreshing Mediterranean swimming hole.

Arenal d'en Castell, a sandy ring around calm water perfect for unofficial camping (although near hotels), sits on Menorca's northern shore behind a thin barrier of pine trees. The coastal ravines and cliffs are honeycombed with caves where prehistoric Menorcans ate, drank, slept, and died. Autocares Fornells buses to Castell leave from Pl. Esplanada (5 per day Mon.-Sat., 2 on Sun.;180ptas).

Excursions

Islanders say Menorca's gloomy interior more closely resembles Hamlet's Denmark than the Spanish mainland. Since Menorca is rainier than the other Baleares, here the old stone walls cross green hillsides splotched with whitewashed houses. Much of the land remains unpopulated and ideal for hiking. Excellent **topographical maps** (250ptas per quadrant) are sold at **Cós 4,** Cós de Gràcia, 4 (tel. 36 66 69), in Maò (open Mon.-Fri. 10am-1pm and 6-8pm, Sat. 10am-1pm). The maps mark island houses as well as archeological sites.

A small chapel dedicated to Menorca's saint caps **Mont Toro,** the island's highest peak. At the foot of the road leading to the shrine is **Es Mercadal,** a brilliant white town and departure point for the road to **Fornells,** a port situated on a rocky cove on the northern part of the island. Es Mercadal is on the TMSA bus route to Ciutadella (185ptas), while Autocares Fornells runs buses (which also stop in Es Mercadal) to Fornells from Pl. Esplanada in Maò (3 per day, 2 on Sun.; 185ptas). TMSA runs frequent buses to Ferreires (240ptas) and Sant Cristòfol (200ptas).

Prehistoric settlements stand like monumental rock gardens on the grassy slopes. They are built around *talayots,* great mounds of stone that may have covered burial sites, and *taulas,* massive stone slabs that form capital T's of undetermined significance. Visit near dusk when these cities are most eerie. Particularly creepy is the **Torre d'en Gaumes,** 14km from Maò off the route to Son Bou. To get there, hike or take the Son Bou bus. Walk 20min. from Mào's town center to **Trepuco,** the most accessible site off the road to Villacarlos. The tourist office provides a brochure in English that describes the major monuments on the island and how to locate them.

Eivissa (Ibiza)

Once upon a time, Eivissa slept in obscurity as a haven for hippies who scorned Mallorca. Although still ever-so-slightly bohemian, Eivissa is now essentially a summer camp for tourists. Overpriced and overrated, this is the one island in the Baleares to skip. Tourism has plummeted dramatically here, yet local entrepreneurs continue to charge exorbitant prices. As with most of Mallorca, tourism is divided between package tours and rich Europeans who own apartments on the island; this makes for slim budget pickings.

The island has three major towns: Eivissa City, the capital and home of the fashion-conscious; Santa Eulària, the origin of many a beach-bound bus; and Sant Antoni Abat, crawling in the evening with British youth high on testosterone. The adjacent island of Formentera is a tiny, sparsely populated annex of Eivissa that makes a convenient day trip by ferry. All that's left of Eivissa's natural charm are the hilly, pine-covered landscapes, not the beaches. Seaweed plagues the east coast, coral the west, and cancerating flesh the south.

Eivissa City

Nobody in their right mind hangs out in this hot, bare city when there are so many beaches about. When the sun sets, the boutique-lined streets near the port turn into an outrageously scanty display: bangles, braids, and bronzers; ear, nose, and nipple rings.

Orientation and Practical Information

Three sections comprise Eivissa City. Standing on the Transmediterranea dock at Estació Marítima with your back to the port, directly in front of you is **Sa Penya.** This former fishing village (stretching from Estació Marítima along the waterfront to the old walls) is now the soul of the old city and the center of much of the nighttime activity.

La Marina, the commercial district, is down Pg. Marina to the right towards the center of town. Passeig Vara de Rei and Avinguda d'Espanya are the main promenades. The **D'alt Vila** (high city) climbs up and behind the old walls.

The bus from the airport drops you off on C. Vicente D. Serra. From here, cross the street and walk two blocks away from C. Serra to Avinguda Isidoro Macabich. To get to the waterfront, turn left down Av. Isidoro Macabich, which becomes Av. Bartolomé Roselló and runs straight down to La Marina.

The local paper *La Prensa de Ibiza* (90ptas) has an *Agenda* page that lists the precise bus schedule for the whole island; the complete ferry schedule; the schedule of all domestic flights to and from Eivissa for the day; water and weather forecasts; 24-hr. pharmacies in Eivissa, Sant Antoni, Santa Eulària and Formentera; 24-hr. gas stations on the island; and a listing of phone numbers for the police, the Red Cross, the ferry companies, and taxis. The most convenient newsstand is across the street from the tourist office on Pg. Vara de Rei.

Tourist Office: Pg. Vara de Rei, 13 (tel. 30 19 00), on the long promenade that runs southeast from the harbor. Good maps and advice to get you to the nearest beach. Open Mon.-Fri. 9:30am-1:30pm and 5-7pm, Sat. 10:30am-1pm. Also a small booth at the **airport** (tel. 30 22 00, ext. 118), across from international arrivals. Open May-Oct. 8am-midnight.

Consulate: U.K., Av. Isidoro Macabich, 45 (tel. 30 18 18). Not a full consulate, but provides and sends passport and visa application forms to Palma. Open Mon.-Fri. 9am-3pm.

Post Office: C. Madrid, 23 (tel. 30 02 43), off Av. Isidoro Macabich. Open for stamps and Lista de Correos Mon.-Fri. 9am-8pm, Sat. 9am-3pm. Open for **telegrams** (tel. 72 20 00) Mon.-Fri. 9am-9pm, Sat. 9am-7pm. **Postal Code:** 07800.

Telephones: Kiosk for international and domestic calls on C. Carlos II near the waterfront, opposite the Formentera ferries. Open 10am-midnight, Oct.-May 10am-10pm. Another kiosk at Playa Figueretas south of the city. Open 10am-midnight; Oct.-May 10am-10pm.

Flights: tel. 30 22 00. Buses to the airport (7km south of the city) run from Av. Isidoro Macabich, 20 (every hr. 7am-10pm). Buses to town (every hr. on the 1/2 hr. 7:30am-10:30pm, 1/2 hr., 80ptas). To: Palma (7 per day, 20min., 4100ptas); Barcelona (5 per day, 1/2 hr., 9125ptas); València (2 per day, 1/2 hr., 7550ptas); Madrid (3 per day, 1hr., 12,900ptas); Alacant (4 per week, 7475ptas). **Iberia,** Av. España, 34 (tel. 31 13 54). Open for tickets and reservations Mon.-Fri. 9:30am-3:15pm and 4:30-7:45pm, Sat. 8am-1pm. Iberia's airport booth open 24 hrs.

Buses: The 2 main bus stations are on Av. Isidoro Macabich, one at #42, the other in front of #20. For an exact schedule see the *Agenda* page of *La Prensa*. Intercity buses run from #42 (tel. 31 20 75) to: Sant Antoni (Mon.-Sat. every 15min., Sun. every 1/2 hr.; 135ptas.); Santa Eulària (Mon.-Fri. every 1/2 hr., Sat.-Sun. every 11/2 hr.; 135ptas); Sant Miquel (Mon.-Fri. 4 per day, 2 on Sat.; 150ptas); Sant Mateu (Mon.-Sat. 1 per day; 170ptas). Buses to nearby beaches (80ptas) leave from #20 (tel. 34 03 82) to: Salinas (every hr.); Platja d'en Bossa (every 1/2 hr.); Cap Martinet (Mon.-Sat. 7 per day, Sun. 8 per day); Can Misses (Mon.-Sat. 7 per day, Sun. 2 per day).

Ferries: Estació Marítima, at the end of Av. Bartolomé Roselló (tel. 30 40 96). All boats except Flebasa's leave from here. **Transmediterránea,** Av. B. V. Ramón, 2 (tel. 31 16 50), at C. Lamine y Cayne. To: Barcelona (summer 6 per week, 5350ptas); València (summer 2 per week, 5350ptas); Palma (summer 4 per week, 3900ptas). **Ferries Pitiusos** (tel. 32 26 72) runs between Eivissa/Formentera and Gandía. Private boats leave for Sant Antoni, Santa Eulària, and some east coast beaches, but their schedules are erratic—bus is quicker and cheaper. To get to **Flebasa** (tel. 34 28 71), take the bus from Eivissa City to Sant Antoni. The office is at the docks in Edificio Faro I. (Open 9am-1:30pm and 4:30-8pm.) June 15-July 31 and Sept. 1-15 they sail to Denia (1 per day at 8pm, 3hr., 5860ptas), with bus connections to València (350ptas), Alacant (350ptas), Benidorm (250ptas), Madrid (1750ptas), and Albacete (1750ptas). Also offers 20min. ferries to Formentera (mid-June to mid-July, every 1/2 hr., 1400ptas).

Car and Motorbike Rental: Crucial for getting off the beaten path. Most places in town have similar prices. **Casa Valentín,** C. B.V. Ramón (tel. 31 08 22), the street running parallel to and 1 block off Pg. Vara de Rei. Mopeds 2240ptas per day, 2000ptas per day for more than 5 days. Panda or Marbella car 5264ptas per day. Open Mon.-Sat. 8:30am-1pm and 4-8pm, Sun. 9am-noon and 6-8pm.

Taxis: tel. 30 70 00, 30 66 02.

Laundromat: Master Clean Lavandería Autoservicio, C. Felipe II, 12 (tel. 31 07 36). Wash and dry 1000ptas per kg. Laundry must be dropped off by 2pm for next-day service. Open Mon.-Fri. 9am-2pm and 4:30-8pm, Sat. 9am-3pm.

Red Cross: tel. 30 12 14

Hospital: Hospital Can Misses, Av. Espanya, 49 (tel. 39 70 00 or 39 70 53). Heading out of town on Av. Espanya, the hospital is on the left at the corner with C. Extremadura. **Emergency Medical Clinic,** Pg. Vara de Rei, 18 (tel. 30 31 31).

Police: In emergency tel. 091. **Policiá Municipal,** C. Madrid (tel. 092), by the Post Office. **Guardia Civil** (tel. 30 11 00), on C. Aeropuerto.

Accommodations

As tourists take a hint and steer clear of the island, beds have emptied and prices sunk. The best deals are outside the city at the one-star resort hotels near the beaches. The cheapest rooms are near the port on the streets around **Pg. Vara de Rei.** The only crunch time is in August.

Hostal Marina, Moll del Port, 4 (tel. 31 01 72), across from Estació Marítima. Convenient location. Art-sprinkled rooms above the restaurant overlook the water. Newly-furnished annex rooms located 1 street in. Doubles 2500ptas, with bath 4000ptas. Meals in their aromatic restaurant 1000ptas.

Hostal Residencia Sol y Brisa, C. B.V. Ramón, 15 (tel. 31 08 18), off Av. Ignacio Wallis, 1 block from Pg. Vara de Rei. Two plant-filled entrance alcoves front sparkling facilities within. Singles 1200ptas. Doubles 2200ptas. Off-season: 1200ptas; 1600ptas. Hot showers 200ptas.

Hostal España, C. B.V. Ramón, 1 (tel. 31 13 17), down street from Sol y Brisa. Dim stairs and dim but big baths. Singles 1200. Doubles 2350ptas.

Hostal Las Nieves, C. Joan d'Austria, 18 (tel. 31 58 22), and **Hostal Juanito,** C. Joan d'Austria, 17. C. Joan d'Austria runs parallel to the right of C. B.V. Ramón from the waterfront. They're like twins. Escape from the mutagenic sun into the clutches of deepest darkness, no matter what the time of day. The owners are renovating; hopefully they'll toss in some new lightbulbs. Large rooms. Singles 1000ptas. Doubles 2000ptas.

Camping: Keen in Eivissa, a habit acquired in the hippie 60s. Five sites across the island. **Es Cana** (tel. 33 98 72), **Florida** (tel. 33 11 54), and **Cala Nova** (tel. 33 17 74) are close to Santa Eulària (see Santa Eulària). Cala Bassa (tel. 34 45 99) is 6km west of Sant Antoni on the bay and Payes (tel. 30 18 70) is on the remote northernmost point of the island, Cala Portinatx.

Food

Whereas a bed is fairly cheap here, a bite is horribly expensive. Full meals rarely cost less than 1200ptas in the port and downtown areas. Seemingly quaint restaurants up in Sa Penya and D'alt Vila proffer exquisite fare in elegant settings for no less than 1500ptas per person. A **fruit and vegetable market** usurps Pl. Constitució, near the old gate to the D'alt Vila in Sa Penya. (Open April-Sept. Mon.-Sat. 9am-2pm; some stands stay open until 8pm.)

Some Eivissan dishes worth hunting down are *sofrit pagès,* a deep-fried lamb and chicken dish; *flao,* a lush lemon- and mint-tinged cheesecake; and *graxonera,* the celebrated cinnamon-dusted pudding made from eggs and bits of *ensaimada* (candied bread). Vegetarians soak up lipids, amino acids, and co-enzymes from substantial *sopas mallorquines,* an almost waterless vegetable "soup" ladled over thin slices of brown bread. An icy *horchata de chufa* (a drink made from almonds) will cool your jets.

Restaurante Victoria, C. Riambau, 1 (tel. 31 06 22), off Av. Ramón i Tur, 1 block in from the waterfront. Señora Josefa makes Julia Child look comatose. She's been cooking all the meals herself for over 40 years. *Sopas mallorquines* 375ptas. Absolutely rapturous local desserts: *flao* or *graxonera* 300ptas. Open Mon.-Sat. 1-4pm and 8pm-midnight.

Restaurante Fonda Cán Costa, C. Cruz, 19 (tel. 31 08 65), *gloria!* it's down the street from Victoria. Underground, the family owners hover about a crackling fire and grill fresh specialties. Chicken or pork chops a mere 400ptas. Mixed salad 275ptas. Open Mon.-Sat. 12:30-3pm and 8-11pm.

Restaurante Cock's, C. Vicente Soler, 5 (tel. 31 01 73), off La Marina. The outdoor café has *sol y sombra* (sun or shade) seating, a front-row view of the harbor, and a most ample 950ptas *menú*. Open Mon.-Sat. noon-4pm and 7pm-12:30am, Sun. 7pm-12:30am.

Fonda Sport, C. B.V. Ramón, 3 (tel. 31 16 25), off the end of Pg. Vara de Rei, near the water. Unimaginative decor, but zesty homemade soups start off a generous 750ptas *menú*. Entrees about 450ptas. Open Mon.-Sat. 12:50-3pm and 9-11pm.

Pasteleria la Canela, C. Aragon, 54 (tel. 30 50 40). C. V.B. Ramón becomes C. Aragon as it heads away from the port. Delectable bakery and snack stop. Ham and cheese or bacon croissant 95ptas. Hypercaloric desserts. Open Mon.-Sat. 9am-1pm and 4:30-8:30pm.

Sights and Entertainment

High above **D'alt Vila's** (the old quarter's) narrow, twisting streets and 16th-century walls, a huge 13th-century belfry chimes above the **catedral**. The vista takes in the whitewashed neighborhood, puffing boats, Platja Figueretas, hazy Formentera, the business district, and the fields beyond. (Open Mon.-Sat. 7-11am and 6-8pm, Sun. 7am-1pm and 6-8pm.)

Puig des Molins is in the western part of the city on Via Romana, which runs off the Porta Nova at the foot of the *D'alt Vila*. The museum displays Punic, Roman, and Iberian art, pottery, and metals. Tours every half-hour to the 4th-century BC Punic-Roman **necropolis** behind the building. (Both open Mon.-Sat. 10am-1pm and 5-8pm; Oct.-May 10am-1pm and 4-7pm. Admission to each 200ptas.)

The rising sun in the east marks the exodus of sun-worshipers to the nearby tanning grounds. One of the closest and cleanest beaches is in **Salinas** (9 buses per day, 85ptas). Buses also split for former hippie hangout **Cala Llonga** (9 per day, 150ptas) and other beaches such as **Cala Olivera** and **Platja Talamaca**. Aigües Blanques, 10km north of Santa Eulària, is the island's only official nude beach, but people get naked everywhere on Eivissa.

The crowds return to Eivissa City by nightfall. **Clothing stores** pulse like late-night discos, luring tourists inside and scaring them off with price tags. The elbows push into most **bars** along C. Major and the next street parallel, Carrer de la Verge. Live jazz wails through the smoky air of **La Cantina** under Teatro Pereyra on C. Comte Roselló every night after 10pm. Gay nightlife hovers around Sa Penya; the bars **Exis** and **Gallery** are especially throbbing.

Eivissa's **discos** are notorious and cost a fortune. Hip-looking people sometimes get free passes to one of the smaller discos or a discount to one of the bigger ones, which start to fill around 1am. The nationally acclaimed **KU** (they even have their own bumper stickers) hulks massively just outside town on the road to Sant Antoni, with its own swimming pool (high season cover 3500ptas). Tourists coagulate at **Pacha**, Pg. Perimetral in New Eivissa (tel. 31 36 12), the newest of the high-society discos (cover 3000ptas).

Sant Antoni Abad

British package tours storm Sant Antoni's huge crescent beach, busy harbor, and stirring night scene. During the day it's too hot to be anywhere but the beach. Since sand space dwindles exponentially towards noon, many people relocate to beaches further out. All buses and boats leave from the central part of the waterfront, C. Balanzat at C. Progrés. They go to **Cala Bassa,** a sandy beach on a thin strip (8 buses per day on the 1/2 hr., 100ptas; 4 boats per day, 225ptas) and **Cala Conta,** a slightly rocky beach (bus 100ptas; boat 250ptas). Boats sail for Portinatx (2 per week, 900ptas) and Formentera (1 per day, 1100ptas). Several times per day buses serve Cala Tarida, a protected inlet at the base of forested hills (100ptas) as well as Cala Gració (80ptas), Port des Turrent (80ptas), and Santa Eulària (210ptas).

A national monument on the outskirts of town north of the waterfront, the underground **Capella de Santa Inés** haunts visitors with eerie devotion. Ask about tours at the tourist office. If you have your own wheels, explore **Cueva de Ses Fontanelles,** just north of Platja Cala Salada, where faintly colored prehistoric paintings cover the walls. (Open. Free.)

Rollicking nightlife is a welcome alternative to hellishly sunny days. Low energy types head for the **cafés** that line Carrer Balanzat, one street in from the waterfront, and sip cool drinks. The **bar** scene and streetside drinking prevail on Calles Vara de Rey and de la Mar, where people jockey for free passes (just ask around—in any language—for a free *entrada*). Dancers skip off to discos around midnight. Those in the know head to **Es Paradis** (tel. 34 28 93), off Av. Dr. Fleming, a large semi-enclosed garden of bushy plants and white pillars where exhausted patrons crash on the pillows around the dance floor. The "free" passes don't guarantee you'll make it past the doorperson. (Open June-Sept. 11:30pm-6am. Cover with drink 1500ptas, Aug. 2000ptas.) The less selective disco **Playboy 2**, C. Sant Antoni (tel. 34 08 35), off C. Progrés, draws a younger, more talkative crowd. (Open May-Sept. 11pm-5am. Cover 1000ptas.)

Sant Antoni blows its patron-saint fuse on August 24, **Diá de Sant Bartolomé**, with four days of dancing, music, fireworks, and sports such as soccer and sailing.

Rooms in Sant Antoni are better values than those in the capital. One high-quality hotel is **Hostal Nicolao**, C. Valencia, 11 (tel. 34 08 45). Follow C. Progrés uphill from the bus stop and take the fourth right. Large, modern rooms with comfortable beds, terrace, and full bath (1000ptas per person; breakfast 250ptas). Closer to the waterfront, three generations of a warm family look after freshly painted rooms, flowery bedspreads, and darling terraces at **Hostal Roig**, C. Progrés, 44 (tel. 34 04 83). (Singles 1200ptas. Doubles with shower 2300ptas, with bath 2600ptas. Open July-Sept.) The closest **campsite** is at Cala Bassa (tel. 34 45 99), 6km outside the city. (350ptas per person and per tent. Open May-Oct.)

Pizzerias and hamburger stands line the shore and work their way inland. **Grill Sant'Antoni**, C. Bisbe Cordona, 8 (34 04 51), off C. Miramar near the waterfront, is a bit expensive, but the *pollo a la parilla* (grilled chicken, 700ptas) and fresh seafood have quite a reputation. (Open May-Oct. 1-4pm and 7pm-midnight.) For a quick snack, **Bar 1900**, down the street from Grill Sant'Antoni on the corner with C. Miramar, flips up ten kinds of crepes (200-300ptas; Grand Marnier liqueur 250ptas; ham, egg, and cheese 275ptas). (Open May-Oct. 5pm-midnight; bar open 9am-midnight.) The indoor **Mercat des Clot Mares** stalls at the corner of C. Progrés and C. Santa Rosalia. (Open Mon.-Fri. 8am-2pm and 6-9pm, Sat. 8am-3pm; Oct.-May Mon.-Thurs. 8am-2pm, Fri. 8am-2pm and 5-8pm, Sat. 8am-3pm.)

The equipped **tourist office** (tel. 34 33 63) on the waterfront, next to the bus station, is open Mon.-Fri. 9:30am-8:20pm, Sat.-Sun. 9:30am-1pm; off-season 9:30am-1:30pm. The **post office** is on C. Mar at C. Sant Rafael (open Mon.-Fri. 9am-2pm, Sat. 9am-1pm). For **international phone service,** the kiosk is on the beach across from the tourist office (open 10am-midnight). **Motos Reco,** C. Ramón y Cajal, 14 (tel. 34 03 88), off C. Miramar, rents mopeds and motorcycles. (Mobilettes 2000ptas per day, insurance and tax included. Open May-Sept. 8am-2pm and 4-9pm.) **Centro Médico Salus**, C. Faro (tel. 34 00 00) handles round-the-clock medical emergencies. The **police** are on Av. Portus Magnus (tel. 34 08 30).

Santa Eulària des Riu

Some of Eivissa's most popular beaches are here in its northeasterly corner. Eivissa's only river flows into the sea south of this town. Occasionally the waters get murky, and seaweed lines the shore and numerous coral formations.

Boats and buses connect Santa Eulària to the northern beaches. Buses leave from C. Mariano Riquer Wallis, right up the street from the beach; boats leave from the waterfront near the edge of the boat basin. **Cala Llonga**, a long sandy cove, lies five km south (10 buses per day, 80ptas; 9 boats per day, 20min., 250ptas). Five km north of town, the overpopulated **Es Caná** sucks in backpackers and families alike with white sand and an overpriced Wednesday craft market (buses every 1/2 hr., 80ptas; boats every hr., 250ptas). **Cala Nova** is a 10-minute walk from Es Caná. Four buses per day serve **Cala Llenya** (160ptas). Most awestruck visitors to **Aigües Blanques** are moved to strip by its beauty. To get here, ask to be let off nearby on the bus route to Figueretas (4 buses per day, 160ptas).

Cala Nova's **campsite** (tel. 33 17 74) is just 50m from the beach (1km from large hippie-market; 390ptas per person and per tent). The beautiful pine-canopied **Florida** (33 11 54) at Es Cana hugs the beach. (300ptas per person and per tent. Open April-Oct.) Or try **Es Cana** (tel. 33 98 72), on the bus route to Es Cana. (475ptas per person, 450 per tent. Open May-Oct.) The town's two-star **Hostal Rey**, C. Sant Josep, 17 (tel. 33 02 10), is immaculate with enormous singles. (July-Aug. 1700ptas per person; June and Sept. 1500ptas; April-May and Oct. 1300ptas. Continental breakfast 350ptas.) **Hostal Central**, C. Sant Vincent, 24 (tel. 33 00 43), serves breakfast with eggs, bread with three marmalades, salami, and pots of coffee (300ptas). The flower-tiled bathroom in each room glimmers. (Doubles 3000ptas; winter 2500ptas. Full meals about 850ptas. Winter heating.) Local sources say there's only one place to eat—**Restaurante Ca'n Miquel**, C. Sant Vincent, 49 (tel. 33 03 29), off Pl. Espanya. The 540ptas *menú* includes two juicy courses, bread, wine, and dessert (open 1-4pm and 8:30-11pm). Not much goes on after 11pm.

The award-winning **tourist office** is on the same street as the bus stop, C. Mariano Riquer Wallis, 4 (tel. 33 07 28). (Open July-Sept. Mon.-Fri. 9:30am-1:30pm and 4:30-7:30pm, Sat. 9:30am-1:30pm; Oct.-June Mon.-Fri. 9:30am-1:30pm and 4:30-7pm, Sat. 9:30am-1:30pm.) The **post office** is at Av. General Franco, 1 (tel. 33 00 95; open Mon.-Fri. 8:30am-2pm). The international and domestic **telephone kiosk** rings on C. Juan Tur. (Take C. Dr. R. Curtays from the bus stop. Open 10am-2pm and 3-11pm.) The **medical emergency** center neighbors the tourist office at C. Mariano Riquer Wallis, 6 (tel. 33 24 53). The **municipal police** protect and serve at Sant Jaume, 2 (tel. 33 08 41).

Boats and buses dash between Santa Eulària and Eivissa City. The bus stops on C. Mariano Riquer Wallis. (Buses every 1/2 hr., 135ptas; boats 14 per day, every 1/2 hr., 45min., one-way 450ptas.) Boats drift from Santa Eulària to Formentera (3 per day, round-trip 1900ptas.)

València

València prizes water above all else. Lovely fountains and pools grace carefully landscaped public gardens in many of the region's cities. Spring and autumn floods of rivers bring soil down the alluvial plain, nurturing València's famous orange groves and geometrically patterned vegetable orchards, known as *huertas*. Since Roman times, irrigation canals have formed a broad network for water distribution. Dunes, sand bars, rock promontories, and lagoons (including the celebrated rice-growing Albufeira) mark the great bay of its coast. The traditional *Tribunal de les aigües* governs the distribution of the water, using an intricate set of rules to decide each grove's allotment. Each Thursday at noon, the *Tribunal* congregates in the capital by the Apostle's Door of the cathedral in Plaça de la Mare de Deu.

This proverbial land of water, light, and love has attracted Phoenicians, Carthaginians, Romans, Visigoths, and Moors; El Cid ruled it for five years in the 11th century. Although conquered by Aragón in the 13th century, the region retained a large, agricultural *morisco* population. València suffered for siding with losing sides in both the War of the Spanish Succession and the Civil War, not recovering its autonomy until 1977.

Since then, regional pride has caused an increasing usage of *valenciá*, a dialect of Catalan that differs mainly in certain spelling conventions; only diehard regionalists call it a distinct language. The language is spoken more in the north than the south, more inland than on the coast. The trend in official publications and signposts is toward bilingual or strictly *valencià* usage.

València's rice dish, *paella*, is known throughout the world and Alacant's varied nougat *turrones* are the traditional Christmas candy throughout Spain.

València

Surrounded by the famed orange groves of the *huerta*, this lively, modern city is graced by numerous ancient buildings, museums, and monuments. Decorous palaces and broad avenues alternate with narrow medieval alleys. Greenthumbs are the majority in València; lushly exuberant parks and gardens are a local obsession.

Spain's third-largest city has served many masters. Founded by the Greeks, it slipped in and out of the hands of Carthaginians, Romans, Visigoths, and Moors at one time or another. El Cid took the city in 1094 but lost it eight years later. Jaume I of Aragón eventually seized it back from the Moors in 1253. València has since become its own master. In the Middle Ages, the silk industry flooded the city with stupendous wealth, transforming it into an agricultural and industrial capital.

Orientation and Practical Information

Those with foresight arrive in València by train, since Estació del Nord is close to the town's center. Avinguda M. de Sotelo runs from the station to **Plaça del Ajuntament,** where the city tourist office is located. From the bus station, ride EMT municipal bus #8 (65ptas) to the same plaza.

From Pl. Ajuntament, the most tourist-relevant sections of the city fan out towards Río Túria in three directions. If you stand in the center of the plaza with the Ajuntament to your left and the water fountain in front of you, **Carrer Barcas (Barques),** which becomes **Carrer Joan d'Austria,** is the glitzy commercial area to your right. **Carrer de Sant Vicent,** straight ahead of you, veers off to the right to the cathedral at Plaça de Zaragoza. Finally, **Avinguda M. Cristina,** also in front of you, stretches off to the left towards the humongous central market **(Plaça del Mercat)** and the older parts of the city.

Choose your map: the tourist office's vague, sparsely labeled map, El Corte Inglés' free high-quality map, or the indexed Bayarri map (450ptas at newsstands). The municipal bus network connects the main parts of town, but most service stops around 10:30pm. Seven late-night bus lines run every 40 minutes until 1:40am.

Regional Tourist Office, C. Pau (Paz), 48 (tel. 352 40 00), just off Pl. Porta del Mar. A slick office with provincial and national information. Free accommodations service 9am-9pm. Open Mon.-Fri. 10am-2pm and 4-8pm, Sat. 10am-2pm. **City Tourist Office:** Pl. Ajuntament, 1 (tel. 351 04 17). Dedicated crew. Open Mon.-Fri. 8:30am-2:30pm and 4:15-6:15pm, Sat. 9am-1pm.

El Corte Inglés: on C. Poeta Quintana. Walk to the end of C. Joan d'Austria, where it meets Pl. Los Pinazo, and turn left onto C. Poeta Quintana. Free **map. Currency exchange:** 1% commission (250ptas min. charge). They also offer novels and guidebooks in English; haircutting; both cafeteria and restaurant; and **telephones.** Open Mon.-Sat. 10am-9pm.

Budget Travel: IVAJ, C. Hospital, 11 (tel. 386 97 00). From the train station, head left on C. Xàtiva, which becomes C. Guillem de Castro, and turn right on C. Hospital. The last word in student travel discounts. Several travel handbooks in English. ISIC 500ptas. HI card 500ptas, over 25 1000ptas. Open Mon.-Fri. 9am-11:30am and 4:30-6:30pm.

Consulate: U.S., C. Pau (Paz), 6 (tel. 351 69 73). Not a full consulate. Passport and visa applications forwarded to Madrid. Open Mon.-Fri. 10am-1pm.

American Express: Duna Viajes, C. Cirilo Amorós, 88 (tel. 374 15 62, 374 15 63; fax 334 57 00). Next to Pl. America on the edge of Río Turia. 2% commission on AmEx traveler's checks. Accepts wired money. Cardholder mail held for 1 yr. Fax service for cardholders. Open Mon.-Fri. 9:30am-1:30pm and 5-8pm, Sat. 10am-1:30pm.

Post Office: Pl. Ajuntament, 24 (tel. 351 67 50). Open for stamps Mon.-Fri. 8am-9pm, Sat. 9am-2pm; for Lista de Correos Mon.-Fri. 9am-8pm; for **telegrams** (tel. 352 20 00 off-hrs.) Mon.-Fri. 8am-midnight, Sat.-Sun. 8am-10pm. **Postal Code:** 14600.

Telephones: Pl. Ajuntament, 27. Open Mon.-Sat. 9am-11pm, Sun. 10am-2pm and 6-9pm. Also, **faxes** (fax 394 27 44) sent and received. **Telephone Code:** 96.

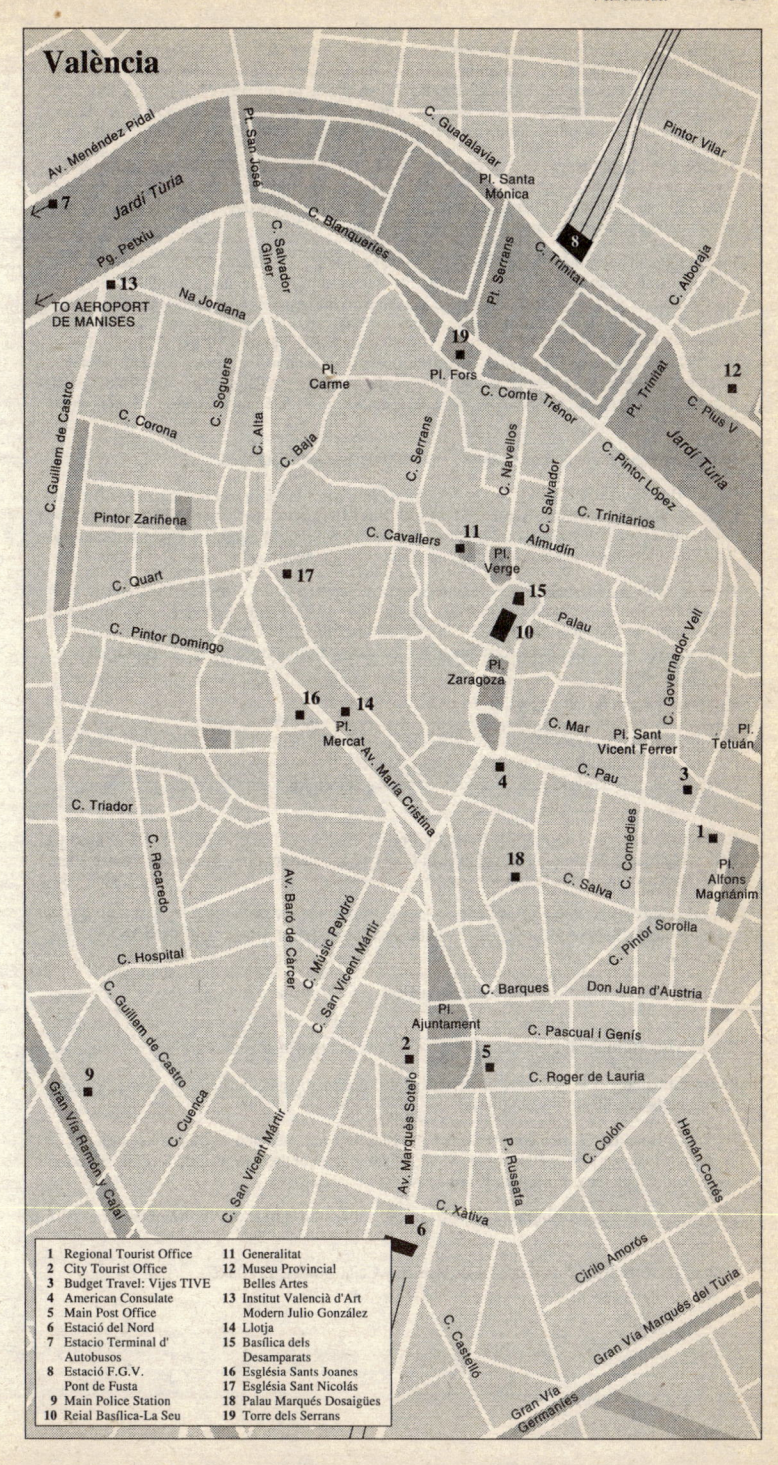

València

#		#	
1	Regional Tourist Office	11	Generalitat
2	City Tourist Office	12	Museu Provincial Belles Artes
3	Budget Travel: Vijes TIVE	13	Institut Valencià d'Art Modern Julio González
4	American Consulate		
5	Main Post Office	14	Llotja
6	Estació del Nord	15	Basílica dels Desamparats
7	Estacio Terminal d' Autobusos	16	Església Sants Joanes
8	Estació F.G.V. Pont de Fusta	17	Església Sant Nicolás
9	Main Police Station	18	Palau Marqués Dosaigües
10	Reial Basílica-La Seu	19	Torre dels Serrans

Flights: The airport is 15km southwest of the city (tel. 350 95 00). CVT buses (tel. 340 47 15) link the airport with the bus station in València (almost every hr. 6:35am-9:05pm from airport, 6am-8pm from bus station; 200ptas). **Iberia,** C. Pau (Paz), 14 (tel. 352 97 37). Open Mon.-Fri. 9am-1:30pm and 4-7pm, Sat. 9am-1:30pm. To: Palma de Mallorca (5 per day, 9500ptas); Barcelona (2 per day, 10,100ptas); Madrid (4 per day, 10,375ptas); Sevilla (2 per day, 13,800ptas).

Trains: Estació del Nord, C. Xàtiva, 15 (tel. 351 36 12). Information open 7am-10:30pm. To: Barcelona (11 per day; 4-6hr.; *talgo* 3500ptas, *rápido* 2500ptas); Madrid (12 per day, 5-71/2 hr., 3000-3500ptas); Málaga (2 per day, 10hr., 5000ptas); Sevilla (2 per day; 8 1/2-9 1/2 hr.; morning *rápido* 6200ptas, evening *exprés* 4850ptas.

Buses: Estació Terminal d'Autobuses, Av. Menéndez Pidal, 13 (tel. 349 72 22), across the river, a 25-min. walk northwest of the town center. From town center, get on municipal bus #8 (65ptas) at Pl. Ajuntament, 22. **Autores** (tel. 349 22 30) sends 15 buses per day to Madrid (5hr., 2400ptas). **Bacoma** (tel. 348 79 79) runs 4 buses per day to Málaga (11hr., 5550ptas) and Sevilla (12hr., 5140ptas). **Enatcar** (tel. 340 08 55) offers 10 trips daily to Barcelona (4 1/2 hr., 2375ptas). **Ubesa** (tel. 359 26 11) makes several stops along the Costa Blanca on its way to Alacant (12 per day, 2 1/4-3 hr., 1600ptas). International service from **Julia Tours** to: Paris (1 per day, 15,030ptas); Rome (1 per day, 16,550ptas); Geneva (3 per week, 11,925ptas); London (3 per week, 15,550ptas).

Luggage Storage: At the **bus station.** Lockers 100ptas. Open 7am-9pm.

Public Transportation: EMT Buses (tel. 352 83 99). Most leave from Pl. Ajuntament, 22. Bus #8 runs to the bus station at Av. Menéndez Pidal. Bus #19 runs to Las Arenas and Malvarosa. Buy tickets aboard or at any newsstand (65ptas, 10-ride ticket 450ptas). Regular service stops around 10:30pm. 7 late-night buses run 10:30pm-1:40am (every 40min.).

Ferries: Transmediterránea, Av. Manuel Soto Ingeniero, 15 (tel. 367 07 04). To Palma de Mallorca (Mon.-Sat. at 11pm, 9hr., 5350ptas). Or buy tickets (on day of departure only) at the port office, Estación Marítima (tel. 367 39 72). Take bus #4 from Pl. Ajuntament. Ask travel agent for **Flebasa** (tel. 367 86 01) ferry schedule to the Baleares, leaving from Denia (6210ptas includes 3hr. bus to Denia).

Taxis: tel. 370 36 00, 370 33 33, 357 13 13.

Car and Moped Rental: Motoauto, C. Actor Mora, 20 (tel. 348 10 71). Take bus #6 or 16 from Pl. Ajuntament. Seat Pandas 4000ptas per day. Mopeds 1500ptas per day. *Ciclomotores* 1800ptas per day plus 12% tax and 500ptas insurance per day. Open Mon.-Fri. 9am-1pm and 5-8pm, Sat. 9am-2pm.

English Bookstore: The English Book Centre, C. Pascual y Genis, 16 (tel. 351 92 88), off C. Barcas (Barques). Volumes upon volumes of literature and fiction. Open Mon.-Fri. 10am-1:30pm and 4:30-8pm, Sat. 10am-1:30pm.

Laundromat: Lava Super, Gran Via Germaníes, 35 (tel. 341 86 48), behind the bull ring next to the train station. Self-service 5kg load 750-800ptas. Open Mon.-Fri. 9am-2pm and 4:30-8pm, Sat. 9am-noon.

Women's Center (Instituto València de la Dona): C. Naquera, 9 (tel. 391 48 87). Open 8am-9pm.

Rape Crisis Hotline: Tel. 900 58 08 88 for a hotline and free legal counsel.

24-hr. Pharmacy: Check listing in *Levante* (local paper, 100ptas) or the *farmacias de guardia* schedule posted outside any pharmacy.

Hospital: Hospital Clínico Universitario, Av. Blasco Ibañez (tel. 386 26 00), at the corner of C. Dr. Ferrer. Take bus #30 or 40 from Av. M. de Sotelo in front of the train station. English-speaking doctor is often on duty. **First Aid,** Pl. América, 6 (tel. 322 22 39).

Emergency: tel. 091. **Ambulance** (tel. 352 67 50, 350 01 00). **First Aid,** Pl. América, 6 (tel. 322 22 39).

Police: Jefatura Superior, Gran Via de Ramón y Cajal, 40 (tel. 351 08 62).

Accommodations

The business of València is business, so rooms are not hard to find during high tourist months. If coming for the papier mâché orgy in March, reserve well in advance. Avoid the areas by the *barrio chino* (red-light district) around Pl. Pilar. The best options cluster around **Pl. Ajuntament** and **Pl. Mercat**.

> **Alberg Colegio "La Paz" (HI),** Av. Port, 69 (tel. 369 01 52), nearly halfway between town and the port. Take bus #19 from Pl. Ajuntament and ask the driver to signal the stop. Forbidding fortress disguises a peaceful ambience inside. 2-4 people per room. Lockout 10am-5pm; lock-in before 8:30am. Curfew midnight. Supposedly members only, but student IDs accepted. 850ptas per person. Breakfast included. Sheets 250ptas. Open July-Aug.

Near Plaça del Ajuntament

> **Hostal-Residencia Universal,** C. Barcas (Barques), 5 (tel. 351 53 84), so conveniently off the plaza. Three floors of the most pleasing budget rooms in town. High, ornate ceilings, multicolored floors, and freshly painted walls; new sinks and mattresses. Irresistible! Singles 1600ptas. Doubles 2600ptas, with shower 3200ptas. Triples 3600ptas. For students, 1 shower per day free. For others, 1 shower free, then showers 200ptas.

> **Pensión Paris,** C. Salvá, 12 (tel. 352 67 66), at the end of C. Pintor Sorolla near C. Barcas (Barques). *Nouveau* hotel with aggressively scrubbed rooms. Light ceramic floors, bright wooden furniture, and neatly folded towels on the beds. Singles 1600ptas. Doubles 2600ptas, with bath 3200ptas.

> **Hostal España,** C. Embajador Vich, 5 (tel. 352 93 42). Take C. Barcelonina off Pl. Ajuntament and go left when it ends. Neighborhood is dark at night. Rooms are an endearing mix of textured wallpaper, plaid blankets, shiny new mirrors, and antique desks. Only 7 rooms. Singles 1200ptas. Doubles 2200ptas.

> **Hostal Alicante,** C. Ribera, 8 (tel. 351 22 96). Parallel with Av. M. de Sotelo and off C. Xátiva going right from the train station. A step up in price and quality. Marble entry staircase, gleaming mosaic floors, and hanging lamps in the rooms. Currency exchange. Singles with shower 1800ptas. Doubles with shower 2800ptas, with bath 3300ptas. July-Aug. prices 30% higher, during winter trade fairs 15% higher.

Near Plaça del Mercat

> **Hostal del Rincón,** C. Carda, 11 (tel. 391 60 83), just past Pl. Mercat on the left coming from Pl. Ajuntament. A real live hotel with well-furnished, no-frills rooms that are cleaned daily. Singles 800ptas. Doubles 1550ptas. Triples 2100ptas.

> **Hospedería del Pilar,** Pl. Mercat, 19 (tel. 331 66 00), at the far end coming from Pl. Ajuntament. Hosting guests since 1886. Well-lit rooms, good security, toasty winter heating, and large saloon attest to its graceful maturity. 800ptas per person. Showers 150ptas. Singles with shower 1500ptas. Doubles with shower 2800ptas.

> **Hostal-Residencia El Cid,** C. Cerrajeros, 13 (tel. 392 23 23), 1 bl. from Pl. Redonda. The outgoing owner, tailed by his dog Snoopy, speaks some English. Flowery rooms are clean, though some are dim. Singles 950ptas. Doubles 1800ptas, with shower 2100ptas, with bath 2900ptas.

Food

València, of course, gave birth to *paella*. Since chefs jealously guard their secret recipes (some have been in the family for centuries), the hometown of the classic saffron rice dish is the only place where you can savor the real thing. Valencian custom dictates that this dish be eaten only at midday—just try to get some after sunset. Unbeknownst to most tourists, *paella* is just one of 200 Valencian rice specialties. Other local specialties include *arroz a banda,* a rice and fish dish with garlic, onion, tomatoes, and saffron, and *all i pebre,* eels fried in an oil, paprika, and garlic sauce.

Another regional favorite is *horchata,* a sweet, milky-white drink pressed from locally grown *chufas* (earth almonds). Chufamaniacs pop over to **Alboraya,** a neighborhood 4km from the center where all the *chufas* grow (take bus #70 from Pl. Ajuntament), to suckle a frosty glass in one of the many *horchaterías*. The most frequented is **Horchatería Daniel,** C. La Horchata, 41 (tel. 185 88 66; *horchata* 125ptas; open March-Nov. 10am-2:30am, Dec. and Feb. Sat.-Sun. 4pm-1am).

As in any other town, the eateries around Pl. Ajuntament are mediocre and overpriced, and the best restaurants inhabit the old city. Buckets of fresh fish, meat, fruit, and cereals sell at the **Mercat Central** on Pl. Mercat. Prices are low. (Open Mon.-Thurs. 7am-2pm, Fri. 7am-2pm and 5-8:30pm, Sat. 7am-3pm.)

Groceries: Mercadona, C. General Tovar, off La Puerta del Mar. Open 9:15am-9pm.

Comidas Eliseo, C. Conde de Montornes, 9 (tel. 392 33 58), off Pl. San Vicente Ferrer, at the end of C. Mar from Pl. Zaragoza. Narrow, white-tiled hall that serves a full meal with *paella*, beverage, bread, and fruit for the price of a commonplace sandwich and *agua* elsewhere (500ptas). Open Mon.-Sat. 1-11pm.

La Utielana, Pl. Picador de Dosaigües, 3 (tel. 352 94 14). Take C. Barcelonina off Pl. Ajuntament, turn left at its end, then turn right into an unmarked, fenced entry. Devilish to find. Cheap and classy meals in a SoHo-ish setting—modern art on the walls and blue lighting. Come early before the midday *paella* (700ptas) is licked dry. Three-course *menú* 725ptas. Open Sept.-July Mon.-Fri. 1-4pm and 9-11pm, Sat. 1-4pm.

Café Valiente, C. Xátiva, 8 (tel. 351 21 17). Every afternoon you'll wait 10 to 15min. for one reason only: rich *paella* scooped up fresh from giant round pans (with chicken 450ptas, with assorted garnishes 495ptas). Equal to any 4-star restaurant in the city. Stainless-steel bar. *Paella* served 1-4pm.

Cafeteria Xátiva, C. Xátiva, 14 (tel. 394 19 64). From the train station, 1 block to the left, downstairs. Bulging plates of food dished out in a dining room bulging with locals. *Menú* 825ptas. *Paella* 500ptas. Open 8am-11pm.

La Lluna, C. Sant Ramón (tel. 392 21 46). Behind the hanging-bead curtain is a veggie restaurant to moon over. The 675ptas *menú*, comprised of 4 courses and whole-grain bread, is served only on weekday afternoons. Most entrees 300-375ptas. Open Oct.-July 1-3:30pm and 8-11:30pm.

Comidas Esma, C. Zurradore, 5 (tel. 331 63 52), near Pl. Dr. Callado just off Pl. Mercat. Humble, wholesome dining. Full meal with hefty bowls of homemade soup and freshly grilled *emperador* (swordfish; 650ptas). Open mid-Sept. to mid-Aug. Mon.-Sat. 1-4pm and 8:30-10:30pm.

Centro Aragones, C. Don Joan d'Austria, 18 (tel. 351 35 50), off C. Barcas (Barques). A 1-room clubhouse 2 floors up. Join other folks at the wide communal table. High-quality *menú* (including—surprise!-*paella*) 650ptas. Open Mon.-Sat. 1:30-4pm.

Sights

Touring València on foot is a breeze, as most of the city's monuments are near each other. North (across the river) to south tours finish near the hotels and restaurants in the core of the city.

Taxonomists frequently lose it when they see the **Jardì Botànic** (tel. 391 16 57), a University-maintained open-air botanical garden that cultivates 43,000 plants (300 precisely labeled species) from around the world. (Open June-Sept. 10am-9pm and Oct.-May 10am-6pm. Admission 50ptas, students free.) Off C. Monforte over the Pont del Real bridge, the neoclassical **Jardì Monteforte** (tel. 360 48 33) blends geometric hedges, ivied arbors, orange trees, flower beds, fountains, a lily pond, and sculpture. (Open Mon.-Sat. 10:30am-6pm, Sun. 10:30am-2:30pm and 4:30-7pm. Free.) One block farther, the banks of the now diverted **River Túria** are nearly transformed into one of the world's largest urban parks, soon to be completed.

At the **Jardins del Real** (tel. 362 35 12), off C. Sant Pius V on the north bank, yaks, emus, baboons, swans, and flamingos go about their bodily functions in a small zoo. (Open 10am-9:30pm. 330ptas.) Next to the park, on C. Sant Pius V, the compelling **Museu Provincial de Belles Artes** (tel. 360 57 93) displays superb 14th- to 16th-century Valencian "primitives" (influenced by Flemish painters' marked attention to clothing) and works by later Spanish and foreign masters—a Hieronymus Bosch triptych, El Greco's *San Juan Bautista,* Velázquez's self-portrait, Ribera's *Santa Teresa,* and a slew of Goyas. (Open Oct.-July Tues.-Sat. 10am-2pm and 4-6pm, Sun. 10am-2pm; Aug. Tues.-Sun. 10am-2pm. Free.)

Across the old river and west, the **Institut Valencià d'Art Modern Julio González (IVAM),** C. Guillem de Castro, 118 (tel. 386 30 00), is a dynamic modern art museum with a permanent collection of works by 20th-century sculptor Julio González and frequent temporary exhibits of 20th-century art and photography. The institute also administers another smaller modern art museum in a rehabilitated convent, the **Centre del Carme** at C. Museo, 2, to the east off Pl. del Carmen. (Open Tues.-Sun. 11am-8pm. Admission 250ptas, students 150ptas; Sun. free.)

In Pl. Fors, a few blocks west of the Centre del Carme, the **Torre dels Serrans** (Watchman's Tower) stands watch; the arch-like structure built in the 16th century was a fortified entryway to the city. The Aragonese began the Gothic and Neoclassical **seu** in Pl. Zaragoza shortly after the *Reconquista*. Seized by a fit of Romantic hyperbole or simply of vertigo, French novelist Victor Hugo counted 300 bell towers in the city from the **Micalet** (the cathedral tower) in Pl. Reina—actually there are only about 100. (Tower open 10am-1pm and 4:30-7pm. Admission 100ptas.) The **Museu de la Seu** (Cathedral Museum, tel. 391 81 27) squeezes a great many treasures into not very much room. Zillions of statues, religious figurines, and paintings of the Nativity invade each other's space in the first gallery. In the second gallery gleams an overwrought tabernacle made from 1200kg of gold, silver, platinum, emeralds, and sapphires, all donated by most generous city residents. The tabernacle is paraded through the streets on Corpus Christi; the bells attached to its base announce its presence. One of Spain's several Holy Grails and two Goyas round out the wonders. (Open Mon.-Sat. 10am-1pm and 4-6pm; Oct.-Feb. 10am-1pm. Admission 100ptas.)

Behind the cathedral on Pl. Mare de Déu, **Basílica de la Mare de Deú dels Desamparats** (Basilica of Our Lady of the Forsaken) is an elliptical edifice with a dark interior. Immediately on the right, you'll find the **Palau de la Generalitat** (Provincial Palace) at C. Cavallers, 2. The courtyard is open to the public, but you must make an appointment to see the gilded, Asian-Renaissance blend of its acclaimed ceilings. (Courtyard open Mon.-Fri. 9am-8pm. Views of the ceiling possible for groups only by appointment Mon.-Fri. 9am-2pm; call 386 34 61.)

The **Ajuntament** dominates its eponymous plaza. Built in 1925, the façade features the little bat that residents consider a good luck symbol. Within, to the left of the lavish marble staircase is the **Saló de Festes,** where dignitaries gather. The yawnable **Museu Històric** (tel. 352 54 78), in the older part of the building, showcases the 30kg shield of James I and the city's first map, charted by an insomniac monk. (Museum open Mon.-Fri. 9am-2pm. Free.)

Not far from the cathedral, at the **Església Parroquía de Sant Esteban,** in Pl. Sant Esteban, El Cid married off his daughters. Next to the train station and linked to the bullring is the **Museu Taurino** (Bullfighting Museum), at C. Dr. Serra, 16, which was the first of its kind when it opened in 1929. Among displays of bulls' heads and matador equipment hang several gory photos of the death of Manuel Granero, last of the great Valencian fighters, killed in 1922. (Open Mon.-Fri. 10:30am-1:30pm. Free.)

Nearby, the old **Llotja de la Seda** (Silk Exchange, tel. 391 36 08) testifies to València's medieval prominence in the silk trade. Handsome, twisted pillars mask the upper chambers, with a masterfully sculpted ceiling, accessible by staircase from the Patio los Naranjos. (Open Tues.-Fri. 10am-2pm and 4-6pm; Sun. and holidays 10am-1:30pm. Free.)

A riot of Rococo, the **Palau del Marqués de Dosaigües,** a few blocks east on C. Rinconada de García Sanchis, houses the national **Museu de Ceràmica** (tel. 351 63 92). Like the Adams House swimming pool, this extravagantly Rococo-interiored museum is often closed for renovations, but will allegedly reopen by 1993. Two blocks down stands the old **Universitat.** València recently inaugurated the **Palau de la Mùsica** (concert hall), a dead ringer for England's Crystal Palace, in the middle of the Jardi del Túria.

Entertainment

València's most illustrious traditional event is undoubtedly **Las Fallas,** March 12-19. The city's neighborhoods compete to build the most elaborate and satirical papier-mâché effigy; over 300 such *ninots* spring up in the streets. Parades, bullfights, fireworks, and street dancing enliven the annual excess, and on the final day—*la nit del foc* (fine night)—all the *ninots* simultaneously burn in one last, clamorous release. The inferno exorcises social ills and brings luck for the agricultural season.

In the area around the **Plaza de los Fueros,** at the foot of the Puente de Serrano, clusters of bars, with their tables spilling into the narrow streets, look like fireflies on a summer's night. The bars and cafés of **C. Roteros** buzz the loudest. It's wiser to tackle the labyrinth of the old city in groups; while fireflies are harmless, dark streets aren't.

The newer sections of the city around Pl. Cánovas del Castillo and over the Túria near the university on Av. Blasco Ibañez are fertile ground for discos. One favorite disco is **Woody,** C. Menéndez y Pelayo, 137 (tel. 361 85 51), with a blinking 70s-type dance floor. (Open Fri.-Sat. 6:30-9:30pm and 11:30pm-7am. Early session 800ptas, late session 1000ptas.) **Distrito 10,** C. General Elfo, 10 (tel. 369 48 62), is another hot spot of mirrors, three floors of balconies, and a gigantic video screen. (Open Sept.-July Thurs.-Sat. 6-9:30pm and midnight-7am, Sun. 6-9:30pm. Early session 400ptas, late session 1500ptas.) Meanwhile, **Club Perdido,** C. Sueca, 17, past the train station, jazzes it up. Lesbians favor **Carnaby Club,** Poeta Liern, 17. Gay men congregate at **Balkiss,** C. Dr. Monserrat, 23 (tel. 391 70 80). **Movies** are popular. Countless cinemas show foreign and art films and host festivals. Ask at the tourist office for information on the Mostra de València de Cine Mediterrani and the Independent Film Festival.

During **Semana Santa** (Holy Week), the streets are clogged by lavishly attired monks riding platforms enacting Biblical scenes, and by children performing the miracle plays of St. Vincent Ferrer. The festival of **Corpus Christi** features *Rocas,* intricate coaches that double as stages for religious plays. The **Fira de Juliol** (July Fair) brings fireworks, cultural events, bullfights, and a **batalla de flurs,** a sort of violent girly skirmish in which girls on passing floats throw flowers at the crowd, which flings them back. For information on activities in the city, consult the *Qué y Dónde* weekly magazine, available at newsstands (100ptas), or *La Cartelera,* a weekly entertainment supplement to the daily paper *Levante* (125ptas for both).

Near València

Sagunt

Sagunt provoked the Second Punic War. Spaniards still puff with pride over the city's inhabitants, whose courage is rivaled only by Masadans (and they had a big mountain to help them). In the third century BC residents of Sagunt held out for months on end against Hannibal's besieging Carthaginians. There are conflicting stories about the outcome of this violent story of local pride and valor. Some sources say that on the brink of total destruction, Sagunt's women, children, and elderly threw themselves into a burning furnace; others insist that the residents chose starvation over defeat. Roman ruins still mark the hill just above the town (25km north of València).

To get to the center of town from the train station, turn right at the exit. Then turn left at the traffic lights onto the diagonal street (C. Vicent Fontelles), heading the wrong way down a one-way street to La Glorieta next to the **Ajuntament.** On the opposite side of the Ajuntament from La Glorieta, the town slopes upward to the old town and peaks at the refurbished medieval **castell.** Along the way, the limestone **Teatre Roman** presents classical theater productions every summer (ask at tourist office for details). The **Museu Arquelògic,** a national monument, boasts a collection of epigraphs; the Roman, Iberian, and Hebrew inscriptions go back to the Bronze Age. (Museum open June-Sept. Tues.-Sat. 10am-8pm, Sun. 10am-2pm; Oct.-May Tues.-Sat. 10am-2pm and 4-6pm, Sun. 10am-2pm. All free.)

Platjas, including the Puerto de Sagunto (which won an EEC award for "best beach"), beckon by the port (4km away). Buses leave from outside the Ajuntament (every 1/2 hr., 70ptas). In summer, a number of nameless restaurants set up shop on the beach along Av. Mediterrani and Pg. Marítim.

The **tourist office** (tel. 266 22 13), Pl. Cronista Chabret, proudly answers questions. (Open Mon.-Sat. 9:30am-2pm and 4-8pm, Sun. 10:30am-1pm; off-season Mon.-Fri. 9:30am-2pm and 4-6:30pm.) Frequent RENFE **trains** from València headed for Castelló and Barcelona stop in Sagunt (tel. 351 36 12, 1/2 hr., 220ptas), as do Vallduxense **buses** (tel. 349 37 38; 1/2 hr., 250ptas).

The province of València is famous for its colorful, hand-decorated ceramics largely thanks to the small town of **Manises,** which fairly bursts with family-owned ceramics ateliers and stores. The town's main square is a sop to those who detest souvenir hunting. CVT **buses** (tel. 340 47 15) leave almost hourly from València (1/2 hr., 150ptas), but **trains** from València along the line to Riba-Roja de Túria (20min., 105ptas) are more frequent and arrive at Manises's decorative ceramic-filled train station. You can also find fine ceramics closer to València at the famous **Fábrica Lladró** workshop in Tavernes Blanques (take bus #16 from Pl. Ajuntament in València).

The Levant

The polluted, overcrowded **platjas** close to València lie along the coastal strip known as the **Levant.** Most popular are **Les Arenes** and **Malvarosa,** both on the bus #19 route from Pl. Ajuntament. Equally crowded, but more attractive, is **Salér,** a long, pine-bordered strand 14km from the city center. Cafeterias and snack bars line the shore, with shower and bathroom facilities nearby. Mediterráneo Urbano buses (tel. 349 72 22) make for Salér from València's Pl. Puerto de la Mar, 1 (every 1/2 hr., 25min., 105ptas) on the way to El Perello.

Albufeira

See the **Albufeira,** Spain's largest lagoon (13km south of València). Rice fields rim the edges, fish and wild fowl populate the waters, and the scenery is splendid. Mediterráneo Urbano **buses** (tel. 349 72 22) from Pl. Puerto de la Mar, 1, València, stop here on the way to El Perello (every 1/2 hr., 40min., 140ptas). *All i pebre* (garlic eels fried in pepper sauce) are particularly delectable in the nearby village of **El Palmar,** another stop on the bus route from València (50min., 140ptas).

Cullera

The rapidly growing town of **Cullera,** south of València, has the most panoramic castle in the entire region. The 13th-century **castell** perches high above the new city on a rocky hilltop, commanding a spectacular vista of sea, rolling hills, orchards, and the river that slices through to the sea. (Closed, to reopen 1993.) Attached to the castle is the 19th-century **Santuari de la Verge,** displaying sundry religious treasures that the castle's residents collected over the years. (Both open Tues.-Sat. 10am-1pm and 4:30-7:30pm, Sun. 10am-2pm. Free.) You can get to Cullera on the Cercaníes **train** from València to Gandía (every hr., 35min., one-way 220ptas).

Morella

Amid miles of rolling green hills, a lone massive rock holds court. An ancient village is sprinkled about the outcropping, at whose top cliffs mingle with grand stone walls in truly superlative Spanish castle. The **castle** is unlike any other in the world, and the sight of it dazzles even the most jaded castlemasters. This stunning natural fortress has attracted settlers from Celts to Romans to Moors. Indeed, the history of Morella is the history of its fortress, the tenacious crown of the city and a trophy highly valued by the greatest of conquerors. El Cid stormed it in 1084 in one of his most powerful attacks on the Moors, and Don Blasco de Alagón took the town in the name of Jaume I in 1232. Weather-worn walls twirl in an almost vertical spiral to the pinnacle. The walk is rigorous but rewarding. (Entrance is up the hill from the church. Open 10am-sunset. Free.)

Getting around town is complicated; the streets curve and slope and twist. The elegant main street, **Carrer Don Blasco Alagón,** is halfway up the slope. **Calle Cuesta de San Juan** intersects C. Alagón and descends toward Puerta San Mateo.

Up C. Colomer from C. Alagón at Plaza Benedicto XV stand the two magnificent Gothic portals of **Basílica de Santa María la Mayor,** built by a sculptor and his son on a bet. Twin *mudéjar* doors with studded iron fittings open into the most beautiful Gothic church in València. The **museu** gathers ancient relics of Morella's past. (Open 11am-1:30pm and 4-7pm. Admission including guided tour 200ptas.)

Oldest among the town's noteworthy remains are the Paleolithic **pinturas rupestres** (cave paintings) in Morella la Vella (Old Morella, 4km away). Halfway there, leftovers of the 13th-century Gothic **acueducto**, with 16 towers and six gates, arch above the road.

The two inexpensive hotels usually have vacancies except during Easter and August. **Fonda Moreno,** C. San Nicolás, 12 (tel. 16 01 05) has ancient rooms, polished, uneven floors, and wooden ceilings (doubles 1400ptas). The less expensive **Hostal El Cid,** Puerta San Mateo, 3 (tel. 16 00 08), offers guests cheerless but passable rooms. (Downhill from the bus stop. Singles with bath 2300ptas. Doubles with bath 4200ptas.) **Campers** can pitch a tent and whack a mole in the small pine-filled lot opposite the municipal swimming pool, outside the city walls and downhill from Pl. Generalísimo (pay the facilities entrance fee at the pool). Bring blankets, for even in summer the nighttime temperature plummets to 10°C.

Hungry? Fonda Moreno's **Restaurante Casa Escori** doles out a portly three-course meal of local specialties as its *menú* (700ptas). (Open 1-3pm and 9-10:30pm.) Or else wait until Sunday for the town **market** on C. Alagón (8am-1:30pm).

The **tourist office** (tel. 17 30 32), at Puerta de San Miguel, works it Tues.-Sat. 10am-2pm and 4-8pm. The **telephone code** is 964. Call a **Red Cross ambulance** at 16 03 80, Ganio Hostal Nou. The **Guardia Civil** goosestep at C. San Agustin, 31 (tel. 16 00 11). Morella's 3500 inhabitants don't get around much, so trains don't even bother with the town. The closest train station is in **Vinarós,** 70km away on the coast between València and Barcelona. A **bus** runs from Vinarós to Morella at 4pm (2 1/2 hr., about 1000ptas). Otherwise, a bus travels from Castelló (2 per day at 7:30am and 3:30pm, 3hr., about 1000ptas). If going by **car,** know that Highway 232 from Vinarós skirts Morella's walls.

Xàtiva (Játiva)

The last foreigner of note to come through Xàtiva was Felipe V, and he burned it to the ground. With an imposing mountainous backdrop and land that lends itself equally to *huertas* (orchards) and to vineyards, its no wonder that Felipe was just one in a long line of conquerors. Although it's quite accessible as a day trip from València, few tourists visit the city, and its quiet charm remains intact.

Once the second-most populous city in València, this city of palaces and churches sits amidst verdant hills. Hills mean trees and trees mean paper; Xàtiva was one of the first places in Europe where paper was made. Baroque painter José Ribera (1591-1652) and Borgia Popes Calixtus III and the infamous Alexander VI hailed from Xàtiva.

Orientation and Practical Information

Xàtiva is an inland town 64km south of València and 102km north of Alacant, easily approachable by rail. The town divides into two parts: the old village, at the foot of the hill with the castles and ancient walls; and the modern village, separated from the old section by the main street, **Avinguda de Jaume I.** To get here from the train station in the modern section, go straight up Baixada de L'Estació and turn left at its end.

When traveling to Xàtiva, bring a copy of your passport or a student ID: museum caretakers and various other bureaucrats record document numbers to prove to the government that foreigners actually visit this town.

Tourist Office: C. Noguera, 10 (tel. 227 33 46). From Av. Jaume I, take Portal de Lleó and continue straight up the hill as it becomes C. Padre Urios. Great maps, lousy hours. Open June 15-Sept. 15 Tues.-Sun. 9am-2:30pm; Sept. 16-June 14 Tues.-Fri. 9am-2pm and 4-6pm, Sat.-Sun. 9am-2pm. City maps available any time of day at the **Policía Nacional.**

Post Office: Av. Jaume I, 33 (tel. 227 51 68). Open for stamps and Lista de Correos Mon.-Sat. 9am-2pm; for **telegrams** Mon.-Fri. 9am-3pm, Sat. 9am-1pm. **Postal Code:** 46800.

Telephone Code: 096.

Trains: RENFE, Av. Cavaller Ximén de Tovia (tel. 227 33 33). To València (35 per day; 1hr.; 265ptas, round-trip 375ptas) and Madrid (3 per day, 7 1/2 hr., 2800-3200ptas).

Buses: At corner of Av. Cavaller Ximén de Trovia and C. Don Carles Santhou; down the street to the left of the train station. Many companies serve the small nearby towns. **Iberbus** (tel. 287 41 10) goes direct to Gandía (at 9:30am and 6pm, 1 1/4 hr., 325ptas). Call the bus station in València (tel. 349 72 22) for schedule from there to Xàtiva.

Red Cross: tel. 227 02 39.

Hospital: Lluis Alcanyis, Ctra. Alzira (tel. 227 25 11), about 5km from the town center.

Medical Assistance: Ambulance (tel. 227 10 95).

Police: Baixada del Carme behind the Ajuntament at Av. Jaume I, 33 (tel. 092).

Accommodations and Food

Call before coming if you plan to stay the night. There's only one *pensión*: **Margallonero**, Pl. Mercat, 42 (tel. 227 66 77), which looks out on the city's active market plaza. Despite its monopoly, the large, well-furnished, utterly flowery rooms are reasonably priced. (1400ptas per person.) The restaurant below is one of the most economical in town (full meal 1000ptas).

Xàtiva's traditional desserts are unmistakably Arabic in origin. *Harnadi* is a pudding of squash, sweet potato, nuts, and raisins. *Al Monchamena* tastes like a sweetened omelette. The city's version of *paella* is *arroz al horno,* baked, slightly drier, and loaded with chickpeas. Get it from **Casa Floro,** Pl. Mercat, 46 (tel. 227 30 20), next door to the Margallonero (400ptas). Their *menú* is 1000ptas. (Open Mon.-Sat. 1-4pm.) Every Tuesday and Friday a **market** sells on Pl. Mercat. (Open 8am-1pm.)

Sights and Entertainment

The 18th-century mansions of **Carrer Moncada,** one block in and parallel with Av. Jaume I, reflect Xàtiva's formerly-capital glory. In its heyday, it housed the city's affluent and showcased all of Xàtiva's public events. At the end of the street, where C. Moncada meets Pl. Trinitat, the small 15th-century **Font Gotica** dribbles out water, looking more like an upside-down ice cream cone than the city's sole medieval remnant. Behind it, the 18th-century Baroque **Palau d'Alarco** once housed the city's richest family. The angled courtyard lets lounging visitors spy on the rambunctious *carrer.*

A walk up C. Sanchis is **Colegiata de Santa María,** a giant church known in town as *La Seu.* In front, the city's two popes scheme in bronze. Constructed from 1596 to 1920 (haste makes waste), the ornate *colegiata* is more a religious museum—paintings and figurines lurk in numerous nooks and crannies, as well as on the ceiling. (Open 7:30-10:45am and 7-9pm.)

The **Museu Municipal l'Almodi**, in a 16th-century palace on C. Corretgeria, 46 (tel. 227 65 97), off Pl. Calixto III, holds four floors of chronologically diverse Spanish paintings, including three Riberas. Here the townspeople avenged Felipe V's 1707 destruction of the town by hanging his portrait upside down. (Open June-Sept. Tues.-Sun. 9am-2:30pm; Oct.-May Tues.-Fri. 11am-2pm and 4-6pm, Sat.-Sun. 11am-2pm. Free.)

The striking ramparts atop the hill in back of town lead to the city's **castell,** made up of two sections, the **castell machor** (larger), on the right as you come in, and the pre-Roman *castell chicotet* (smaller). The former, used from the 13th through 16th centuries, bears the scars of many a siege and earthquake. Its arched stone **prison** has held some famous wrongdoers, including King Fernando el Católico and the Comte d'Urgell, would-be usurper of the Aragonese throne. Referred to in Verdi's *Il Trovatore,* this man spent his final decades here before being buried in the castle's chapel. (Open Tues.-Sun. 10:30am-2pm and 4:30-7pm; off-season Tues.-Sun. 10:30am-2pm and 3:30-6pm. Free.)

Although Xàtiva is a small town, partying people refuse to be tied down. **El Verde Limón,** Pl. Cayetano, a tavern inside an ancient house, blends a mean *agua de Valèn-*

cia: O.J., champagne, gin, and whatever else the owner feels like splashing in. (Open 7:30pm-2:30am, Fri.-Sat. 7:30pm-4am). The discos thrash all weekend long. Walking distance from the town center on Ctra. Xàtiva Novetlé, **Almassara** is a huge ex-factory that's the first choice of twentysomething insomniacs. (Opens at 1am. Cover 300ptas.) Traditionalists go to **Elite** (cover 300ptas) and dance to Spanish favorites. The annual **Fira**, in honor of the Virgin Mary, is August 15-20, complete with requisite bullfights, street theater, and fireworks.

Gandía

Gandía is the capital of **La Sofor**, a verdant region of València. The town is best known as the hangout of the Borgias, especially of Francisco de Borgia (who renounced his title and wealth to become a Jesuit). For five centuries an agricultural and commercial dilettante, Gandía now yields cash crops galore: sugar cane, oranges, silk, burlap, beach condos, and mulberries.

Orientation and Practical Information

Everything you need is a stone's throw from the train station on **Marqués de Campo**. Everything you want is at the **beach**, 4km away.

Tourist Office: Marqués de Campo (tel. 287 77 88), across from the train station in a small brick building. Detailed map. Open Mon.-Fri. 10am-2pm and 4-7pm, Sat. 10am-2pm. A beach branch (tel. 284 24 07) does business at Pg. Neptuno, on the water. Open May-June and Sept. 10am-1pm and 5-7:30pm; July-Aug. Mon.-Sat. 9am-9pm, Sun. 10am-1pm and 5-8pm.

American Express: Viajes Gandía, Pl. Escoles Píes, 5 (tel. 287 47 88; fax 287 03 98). From the train station, turn right onto Marqués de Campo and follow it as it bends left into the plaza. 2% commission on AmEx traveler's checks. Money wired. Cardholder mail held 1 yr. Open Mon.-Fri. 9am-12:30pm and 4:30-8pm, Sat. 9am-12:30pm.

Post Office: Pl. Jaume I, 7 (tel. 287 10 91), a few blocks behind the Ajuntament. Open for stamps and Lista de Correos Mon.-Fri. 9am-2pm; for **telegrams** 8:30am-8:30pm.

Trains: the **RENFE** variety (tel. 286 54 71) depart from Marqués de Campo to València (31 per day; every 1/2hr.; 1hr.; 340ptas, round-trip 500ptas).

Buses: UBESA (tel. 287 16 54) leaves from Marqués de Campo, just down the street from the train station, to: València (14 per day, 1 1/4 hr., 575ptas); Alacant (5 per day, 3hr., 960ptas); Barcelona (1 per day, 7-8hr., 3300ptas); Costa Brava towns (several per day). **Auto Res**, Marqués de Campo, 12 (tel. 287 10 64). Buses stop at the beach at Pg. Marítim en route to Madrid (6 per day; 6hr.; 2820ptas, round-trip 5095ptas).

Ferries: Ferries Pitiusos, Port de Gandía (tel. 284 45 00). Chugs to Sant Antoni Abad on Eivissa (Ibiza) Mon.-Fri. at 10pm, Sat. at 9pm (5220ptas).

Bike/Windsurfer Rental: At the HI hostel in Platja de Piles (see Accommodations). Bike 500ptas per hr. Windsurfer 600ptas per hr.

Emergency: tel. 091.

Police: tel. 287 19 35.

Accommodations

HI cardholders rejoice even at the thought of Gandía's hostel. A few green-eyed *hostales* look on jealously from the port on the side farthest from the beach. Make reservations in the summer, especially August, or go bedless.

Alberg Mar i Vent (HI), C. Doctor Fleming, s/n (tel. 289 37 48), in Platja de Piles, a town just south of Gandía. Take the La Amistal bus (tel. 287 44 10), which departs from the right of the train station (for exact times check with the tourist office; 75ptas). Simple flattery does not do justice to this hostel/beachfront resort. Water laps at the door, there's an outdoor patio and basketball court, and they rent bikes and windsurfers (see Practical Information listings). Alcohol is strictly prohibited. 3-day max. stay. Curfew 3am (midnight in winter). 730ptas per person. With 3 meals per day 1615ptas. Over 26: 870ptas; 2100ptas. 125ptas to camp. Sheets 140ptas. Open Jan. 11-Nov. 30.

Habitaciones Constantia, C. Levante, 21 (tel. 284 02 65). From the tourist office, hop the La Marina bus and ask the driver to let you off at the C. Levante stop (75ptas). Some rooms are electric-blue, some blindingly white—all 3 singles and 2 doubles are *enorme*. 1600ptas per person.

Hotel Europa, C. Levante, 12 (tel. 284 07 50), down the street from Constantia. A real hotel with its own real dining area. Doubles with real bath 4000ptas. Open April-Sept.

Camping: The tourist office has directions to and details about the 3 campsites near the beach. The cheapest is **L'Alqueria** (tel. 284 04 70) at 370ptas per person and per tent. Open April-Sept.

Food

When you've sick of *paella,* make the move to Gandía. Restaurants here offer *fideuà,* a pasta and shellfish specialty covered with hot broth, and the invariably expensive but tempting *zarzuela,* a platter of assorted shellfish and squid with salsa sauce.

Adasor Josman, C. Ermita, 16 (tel. 284 05 30). From the tourist office, take the La Marina bus and ask for the C. Levante stop; Levante becomes C. Ermita as it nears the highway. On weekends this *pollería* (chicken store) practically gives it away. Whole chicken with french fries for 4 people 850ptas! (French fries only on weekends.) Whole chickens perpetually 650ptas. Open Mon.-Sat. 9am-2:30pm and 6:30-10pm, Sun. 9:30am-1:30pm.

Bar-Restaurante Nati, C. del Mar, 25 (tel. 289 34 09), in Platja de Piles near the HI hostel; right at the bus stop. *Paella* 600ptas. *Bocadillos* 175-300ptas.

Sights and Entertainment

What is there other than the **beach?** Wedged between blue sea and tiled Pg. Marítim, fine sands stretch for several km from the port to the condos. Auto Res buses (tel. 287 10 64 for details) to Madrid, which leave from Marqués de Campo, 12, pause at Pg. Marítim, which runs the length of the beach.

To evoke some of Gandía's former glory, visit the **Palau de Sant Duc** (tel. 289 12 03), on C. Sant Duc in town (5min. from the train station; head south on C. Magistrat). Its mix of Gothic, Renaissance, and Baroque styles reflects renovations from the 14th to the 17th centuries. Now a Jesuit college, the palace was once inhabited by the Borja (Borgia) family, as well as Doña Constanza, the ne'er-do-well old aunt of King Jaume II. (Guided visits July-Sept. Mon.-Sat. 11am, noon, and 6pm; Oct. and May-June 11am, noon, and 6pm; Nov.-April 11am, noon, and 6:30pm. Admission 150ptas.) A **Museu Arquelògic** should open by 1993. Check with the tourist office.

No discos strobe in Gandía proper, although numerous **bars** line C. Gutiérrez más. (Follow Marqués de Campo to the end, turn right onto C. Magistrat Catala, and take the fifth right onto C. Gutiérrez Más.)

Alacant (Alicante)

Beyond the polished pedestrian thoroughfares, inlaid with meticulously cleaned red tiles, lies the old city—paradoxically a modern urban snarl of lively streets at the foot of the *castillo*. Grittier than their counterparts in the new quarter, these streets are full of historic buildings and mouthwatering food. The beaches are nearby, the lodging is plentiful and cheap, and the nightlife moves at a good clip.

Orientation and Practical Information

Esplanada de Espanya stretches along the waterfront between two large jetties. Behind it, the old quarter is a web of streets and *plaças* off the main avenue, **Rambla Méndez Nuñez,** where nearly all services and points of interest cluster. Be wary—Alacant is a port city where prostitutes and hash-pushers make a living—but don't panic: the situation is by no means threatening if you're not looking to get involved.

València

Tourist Office: Oficina de Información Turística, C. Portugal, 17 (tel. 522 38 02), by the bus station. The staff is clueless, but that's OK—ask for *Alicante at your Fingertips*, their invaluable guide to anything and everything. Open Mon.-Fri. 9am-9pm, Sat. 9am-3pm; Oct.-June Mon.-Fri. 9am-1pm and 4:30-7:30pm. **Tourist Office,** Esplanada d'Espanya, 2 (tel. 521 22 85). Information about the coast. Maps and accommodations listings for Alacant. They'll make room reservations for anywhere in Alacant or València. Open Mon.-Sat. 10am-2pm and 4-8pm, Sun. 10am-2pm; Sept. 16-June 14 Mon.-Fri. 9am-2pm and 5-7pm, Sat. 9am-1pm.

El Corte Inglés: Maisonnave, 53. The usual beautiful **map. Currency exchange:** 1% commission (250ptas min. charge). They also offer novels and guidebooks in English, haircutting, both cafeteria and restaurant, and **telephones.** Open Mon.-Sat. 10am-9pm.

Budget Travel: TIVE, Av. Aguilera, 1 (tel. 522 74 42), near the train station off Av. Oscar Esplá. No tickets sold. ISIC 500ptas. HI card 1800ptas. Open Mon.-Fri. 9am-1:30pm and 5-8pm.

Consulate: U.K., Pl. Calvo Sotelo, 1 (tel. 521 60 22), in the center of town at the end of C. Dr. Gadea, which runs from the waterfront. Open Mon.-Fri. 8:30am-2:30pm.

Post Office: Pl. Gabriel Miró (tel. 520 21 93), off C. Sant Ferran from the Rambla. Open Mon.-Fri. 9am-2pm and 4-6pm, Sat. 9am-2pm. **Telegrams** (tel. 522 20 00). Open Mon.-Fri. 8am-9pm, Sat. 9am-7pm, Sun. 9am-2pm. **Postal Code:** 03000.

Telephones: Av. Constitució, 10 (tel. 004). Open 9am-10pm. Another office at the **bus station.** Open Mon.-Sat. 8am-9pm, Sun. 10am-2pm and 5-9pm. **Telephone Code:** 96.

Flights: Aeroport Internacional El Altet (tel. 528 50 11), 17km from town. **Alcoyana** (tel. 513 01 04) sends 13 buses per day between the airport and Av. Constitución (departs town 7am-10pm, departs airport 6:30am-9:20pm; 110ptas). **Iberia,** C. F. Soto, 9 (tel. 521 85 10). To: Palma de Mallorca (5 per day, 9975ptas); Barcelona (3 per day, 11,600ptas); Madrid (4 per day, 13,200ptas); Sevilla (2 per day, 12,600ptas).

Trains: RENFE, Estació Término, Av. Salamanca (tel. 592 02 02), west of the city center. To get to Rambla Méndez Nuñez from here, walk down wide Av. General Mola past Plaça dels Lucers and onto Av. Alfons X El Sabio. Near the end, turn right on C. Torregrosse, which becomes the Rambla as you approach the water. Information open 7am-10pm. Most destinations require a transfer. Direct to: Murcia (14 per day, Sat.-Sun. 9 per day; 1 1/2 hr.; 340ptas); València (6 per day, 3hr., 955ptas); Madrid (6 per day, 9hr., *talgo* 4300ptas); Barcelona (4 per day, 11hr., 3800ptas). **Ferrocarrils de la Generalitat Valenciana, Estació de la Marina,** Av. Villajoyosa, 2 (tel. 526 27 31), far from town. Take bus C-1 from Pl. Espanya. Local service along the Costa Blanca to: San Juan (70ptas), La Vila Joiosa (255ptas), Benidorm (335ptas), Calp (510ptas), and Denia (745ptas). Railpasses not accepted. Departures every hr. 6:15am-8:15pm. Only 7 of these trains go as far as Calp and Denia. Round-trip tickets discounted 15%. Also **night trains** to discos on the beaches near Alacant.

Buses: C. Portugal, 17 (tel. 513 07 00), west of the city center. To reach Rambla Méndez Nuñez from here, turn left onto Carrer d'Italia, cross Avinguda Dr. Gadea, and follow Carrer Sant Ferran to its end. Confusion galore because each company serves different destinations; international destinations too. For the Costa Blanca, go to **UBESA** (tel. 522 01 43). 16 buses per day to: La Vila Joiosa (270ptas), Benidorm (355ptas), and Calp (520ptas). Also to: Xábia (9 per day, 725ptas); Denia (5 per day, 830ptas); València (12 per day, 1545ptas). **Molla** (tel. 522 08 51). To Elx (every 1/2 hr., 170ptas). **Albaterense** (tel. 522 69 72). To: Villena (395ptas); Orihuela (380ptas); Murcia (550ptas). **Enatcar** (tel. 522 00 77). To: Madrid (7 per day, 5-6hr., 2500ptas); Granada (7 1/2 hr., 2790ptas); Córdoba (9hr., 3810ptas); Sevilla (2 per day, 11hr., 4865ptas); Barcelona (6 per day, 8hr., 3790ptas).

Ferries: Transmediterránea, Esplanada d'Espanya, 2 (tel. 520 60 11). To Eivissa (4 per day, 2 3/4 hr., 5350ptas). **Flebasa** (tel. 514 48 35). Service from Denia (includes bus from Alacant to Denia, otherwise 350ptas) to Eivissa (1-2 per day, 3hr., 5570ptas). Open Mon.-Fri. 9am-1pm and 5-7pm, Sat. 9am-noon.

Taxis: tel. 525 37 98. 900-1000ptas to Platja Sant Joan.

Luggage Storage: At the **bus station** (150ptas per bag). Open 6:45-10pm.

Lost Property: Municipal Police, C. Julien Besteiro, 2 (tel. 528 44 11).

Medical Services: Hospital Clínico, C. Alicant Sant Joan (tel. 524 42 00). **Ambulance** (tel. 521 17 05, 523 06 01).

Emergency: tel. 091.

Police: Commisaría, C. Médico Pascual Pérez, 33 (tel. 514 22 22).

Accommodations and Camping

While there seems to be a *pensión* or *casa de huéspedes* on every corner in town, the number of clean rooms that are prostitute-free is considerably smaller. The tourist office keeps accommodations listings. Stay away from most places along C. Sant Ferran (where theft and prostitution are common) and around the Església de Santa María; opt instead for the newer section of town. Arrive early for a good room, especially in the summer.

Residencia Juvenil, Av. Orihuela, 97 (tel. 528 12 11). Take bus B from Pl. Espanya, or from the corner of C. Portugal and C. Lorenzo (70ptas). HI card required. Max. stay 5 days. Curfew 10pm (card for 810ptas allows you to ignore curfew—the power of money). 730ptas per person, with breakfast 810ptas, with 3 meals 1615ptas. Over 25: 870ptas; 1180ptas; 2100ptas.

Habitaciones México, C. Primo de Rivera, 10 (tel. 520 93 07), off the end of Av. Alfons X El Sabio. Finely decorated hallways and pristine rooms with fresh towels and complimentary soap. Gregarious owner speaks some English and invites all to use her kitchen. Communal washing space for the hygiene-conscious and a book swap for the literary. Singles 1400ptas. Doubles 2500ptas, with bath 3000ptas. Sept. 16-May 14: 1100ptas; 2200ptas, 2500ptas.

Residencia la Milagrosa, C. Villavieja, 8 (tel. 521 69 18), across from Església de Santa María. A miracle in this area. Every time you think you've wandered into the owner's living room, it turns out to be another lovely, flowery lounge in the *residencia*. Kitchen facilities. Singles only in winter 800-1000ptas. Doubles 2000ptas. Hot showers 250ptas (cold free).

Hostal Ivorra, C. Sant Vicent, 49 (tel. 20 38 22), off the intersection of the Rambla and Av. Alfons X El Sabio. Low price and good location. Lime green tiled floors and balconies add zing to otherwise bland rooms. Sinks, mirrors, and showers (weak) could be better. 800ptas per person.

Hostal Ventura, C. Sant Ferran, 10, 5th floor (tel. 520 83 37), off the end of the Rambla near the water. Bullfight-crazy interior decorator did good with the large, well-furnished rooms. New washbasins and comfortable beds. Doubles 2600ptas, with bath 3000ptas. Triples (all with bath) 4500ptas. Reservations accepted with deposit. Postal code: 03002.

Hostal Portugal, C. Portugal, 26 (tel. 592 92 44), across from the bus station. Angular rooms, some with electric fans. Sun-kissed dining area/lounge with color TV and a large collection of clocks. Singles 1500ptas. Doubles 2500ptas, with bath 3000ptas. Breakfast 250ptas.

Camping: Camping Bahía (tel. 526 23 32), 4km away on the road to València. Take bus C-1. 400ptas per person and per tent. Open March 15-Oct. 15.

Food

More tourists' stomachs are filled on the main pedestrian thoroughfare than anywhere else. Smaller family-run establishments in the **old city** (between the cathedral and the steps to the castle) and on side streets around town are a less traveled route. Locals devour *tapas* in the **C. Mayor**—the ambrosial cucumber and almond soup garnished with a single purple grape flutters many a heart.

The **market** near Av. Alfonso X El Sabio sells fresh fish, meats, and produce, plus sandwich meats and bread.

Groceries: Simago, Av. Alfonso X El Sabio, 27 (tel. 520 86 55). The trusty chain supermarket. Open Mon.-Sat. 9am-8:30pm.

La Venta del Lobo, C. Sant Ferran, 48 (tel. 514 09 85). A 2-room neighborhood grill ambitious enough to prepare specialties from all over Spain. Try *gazpacho Andaluz* for a taste of the south (370ptas) or Valencian *paella*. Wolf down the house specialty dessert *lobo loco,* an incredible flan boat doused in fruit, chocolate ice cream, nuts, and whipped cream (385ptas). Open Tues.-Sat. 1-5pm and 8:30pm-12:30am, Sun. 1-5pm.

Restaurante Misto Vegeteriano, Pl. Santa María, 2. Creative vegetarian fare. Your big chance to eat in the shadow of the Església de Santa María. *Menú* 850ptas, 40ptas more for a trip to the impressive salad bar. Open Tues.-Sun. 1-4:30pm and 8pm-midnight.

Restaurante Rincón Castellano, C. Sant Francesc, 12 (tel. 521 90 02). The best of 6 great restaurants all in a row. 2-course *menú* 825ptas. Wolves happily devour a full kilo of roast lamb (serves 2, 980ptas). Open 12:30-4pm and 7:30pm-midnight.

Casa Miguel, C. Poeta Quintana, 4 (tel. 520 05 13). Mostly vegetarian. Yummy and low-in-fat *ensalada de arroz* (rice salad) and *hervido de verduras* (steamed vegetables). Full à la carte meals around 1000ptas. *Menú* with bread, fruit, and juice 775ptas. Open Mon.-Fri. 1-4pm and 8-10pm, Sat. 1-4pm.

Pizzeria-Restaurante le Palme, C. Sant Vicente, 14 (tel. 520 02 09). A realish Italian place with maps of the ol' boot on the walls. 28 kinds of pie, including the "surprise" pizza, which nobody can quite figure out. 575-1100ptas. Generous single servings for take-out 150ptas.

Sights

Complete with drawbridges, clandestine tunnels, fishy passageways, and urine-splashed dungeons, the **Castell de Santa Bárbara** isn't just another castle. The Carthaginians were the first lucky holders of this 200-meter-high fortress. After they left, the military used the castle as a prison. Now most of the fortress has been reconstructed; there's a dry moat, a dungeon, and a spooky ammunition storeroom to review. Even if the citadel doesn't overwhelm, the view makes Alacant look like the Rió of Spain.

Less bellicose attractions are the expositions held here, often showcasing *Artistos Alicantinos*. Also in the castle, the miniscule, dull **Museu de les Fogueres de Sant Joan** (St. John) displays statuettes of the famed martyr. A paved road from the old section of Alacant leads to the top; most people take the elevator by the beachfront (200ptas). (Castle open Mon.-Fri. 10am-8:30pm, Sat. 10am-2pm; Oct.-May Mon.-Fri. 9am-7pm, Sat. 10am-2pm. Museum open Tues.-Fri. 10am-1pm and 5-7pm. Admission 25ptas—includes both.)

The **Concatedral de San Nicolás de Bari,** 1 block north of Méndez Núñez on C. San Isidro, reflects the sober Renaissance style of Agustín Bernadino, while the Baroque communion chapel lavishly compensates. Intricate wood carvings embellish the door to the cloister. (Open Mon.-Fri. 10am-12:30pm and 6-8:30pm, Sun. 9am-11:45pm.) For keen contrast, visit the **Església de Santa María,** built on the ruins of an Arab mosque. A melange of architectural styles, it harmonizes a Gothic nave, a Baroque façade, and a Renaissance marble baptismal font. (Open for Mass 9-10:30am and 6-7:30pm:)

Inside the Neoclassical **Palau del Consell Provincial,** a museu arqueològic (tel. 512 13 00) houses coins and paintings from excavations throughout the province. (Open Tues.-Sat. 9am-2pm. Free.) A delightful bunch of Calders, Mirós, and drawings by Picasso and Braque fraternize in the **Museu Colecció "Art del Segle XX"** (art of the 20th century; tel. 521 45 78), at the east end of C. Mayor. (Open Tues.-Sat. 10am-1pm and 5-8pm, Sun. 10:30am-1:30pm. Free.)

If Alacant's beach doesn't suit you, hop bus C-1 in Pl. Espanya (70ptas) or board the Alacant-Denia train (80ptas) for the 6km long **Platja de Sant Joan.** If crowds have soiled every square inch, try the **Platja del Saladar** in Urbanova. Buses from the Alacant bus station make the trip to Urbanova (3 per day, 35min., 80ptas).

Entertainment

In summer, nightlife centers on the **Platja de Sant Joan. Ferrocarriles de la Generalitat Valenciana** runs special night trains from Estacío de la Marina to several points along the beach (every hr. 11:15pm-5:15am, 70ptas). A taxi from Alacant to Platja de Sant Joan costs 900-1000ptas each way and can be shared by up to four people.

Voy Voy and **Caligula,** neighbors on Av. Niza at the "Discoteca" stop on the night train, swing with outdoor bars, decibels of music, and dancing. (Open until 6am. Beer 350ptas.) **Copity** and **Va Bene** are other jazzy discos, both along Av. Condomina, a long walk or short taxi ride away from the "Condomina" stop on the night train.

In Alacant itself most discos charge 1000ptas cover on weekends, but disco employees sometimes hand out free passes on Pl. Esplanada. The hottest one is **Buggatti,** C. Sant Ferran, 27 (tel. 521 06 46), featuring neon-lined bars and candle-lit tables. (Cover including 1 drink 1000ptas. Open nightly until 5:30am.) Gay men convene at **Jardine-**

to on C. Baron de Finestrat; for dancing, ask for directions to the sometimes-gay disco **Memphis,** or try **Rosé,** on C. Sant Joan Bosco.

From June 21 to 29, the town bursts with bacchanalian celebration for the **Festival de Sant Joan,** comprised of romping *fogueres* (symbolic or satiric effigies). The figures burn in a *crema* on the 24th; but the charivari continues with breathtaking and hazardous nightly fireworks, and lights and decorations that festoon the streets. On the last day a marching band and parade of candy hurlers whet people's appetites for next year's festival. The **Verge del Remei** takes place on August 5; pilgrims trek to the monastery of Santa Faz the following Thursday.

Near Alacant

Monestir de Santa Faz (tel. 526 49 12) allegedly has a shred of the controversial handkerchief of Saint Verónica, which supposedly preserves an imprint of the face of Jesus. Call before you arrive. To cover the 5km from Alacant, pick up the **bus** for "Muchamiel" at the beginning of the beach.

Tabarca, an island, makes a fine beachy daytrip. Crucero Kon-Tiki boats (tel. 521 63 96) leave from in front of the Esplanada de Espanya (6 per day, winter 1 per day; round-trip 1000ptas).

Xixona, 13km away from Alacant, is the home of the wondrous **Torrones El Lobo** (tel. 561 02 25), a nougat factory. Drool over free samples of the traditional Spanish Christmas candy (called *turron*) that has turned Xixona into a household word. The nougat makes Three Musketeers look like synthetic, granulated glop. Guided tour every 1/2 hr. Open 10am-1:30pm and 4-7pm.

Agost, fifteen km northwest of Alacant, has a **pottery museum** (tel. 569 11 99) and a *bojitos* (white clay jars) **factory.** (Factory open Tues.-Sat. 11am-2pm and 5-8pm; off-season Tues.-Sat. noon-2pm.)

Covas de Canalobre (tel. 569 92 50) are spectacular stalagmited caves 24km north of Alacant. One of Europe's great speleology centers, the caves lie 700m above the tiny village of **Busot,** hanging off a splendid view of the coastline. Open 10am-8pm. Admission 400ptas. Alcoyana **buses** (tel. 522 01 04) run from Alacant's Pl. Mar to the caves.

La Vila Joiosa (Villajoyosa), a happy and unspoilt town, sits north of Alacant, on the bus and train routes to Calp. The town is full of low buildings and friendly villagers who either like or pretend to like foreigners. Lots of ice cream and *churros con chocolate* joints. Ferrocarrils de la Generalitat Valenciana **trains** (hourly, 255ptas) and UBESA **buses** (16 per day, 270ptas) run from Alacant.

Costa Blanca

South of València, smooth beaches and juicy vineyards spread. The "White Coast," which extends from Denia through Calp and Elx down to Torrevieja, is named for the color of its sand, although some think it refers to its pasty summer colonists (mainly English, Germans, Belgians, and Scandinavians). Areas of great natural beauty border the tourist spots, but grabby developers are beginning to construct heinous high-rises on the vacant land. A rail line out of Alacant (not RENFE) connects most towns, as does the extensive UBESA bus line.

Elx (Elche)

Although most residents spend their days making shoes, Elx is best known for its 500,000 palm trees, which put Beverly Hills's to shame. The male palms produce enough fronds to supply the entire country on Palm Sunday, and the females bear enough dates to fill gift boxes around the world. The *Dama d'Elx,* Spain's finest example of pre-Roman sculpture, also hails from here (23km from Alacant).

Witness the **Misteri de Elx,** a medieval mystery play performed in **Basilica de Santa María** every August 11-15. (The *fiesta* **Nit de l'Alba** falls on August 13.) During even-numbered years, you can also watch it October 31 and November 1. Of the several parks and public gardens that fill odd corners of the city, the most beautiful is the **Hort del Cura** (Orchard of the Priest), where magnificent trees shade colorful flower beds.

The **tourist office** is at Pg. de la Estació, Parque Municipal (tel. 545 27 47; open Mon.-Fri. 9am-2:30pm and 4-7pm, Sat. 10am-1:30pm). The **post office** is in Parque Project (tel. 544 69 11), near the Pont de Canalejas. **First aid** comes from C. Reina Victoria, 6 (tel. 444 45). The **police station** is in Parque Project (tel. 44 70 70). The **central train station, Estació Parque,** is at Pl. Alfons XII, but there's also the **Estació Carrus** on Av. Llibertat. The **bus station** on Av. Llibertat serves Alacant (every hr. on the hr., 170ptas).

Calp (Calpe)

Steping into Calp is like stepping into a Dalí landscape. Ten km south of Moraira and 62km northeast of Alacant, the town cowers beneath the **Peñó d'Ifach** (327m), a gargantuan flat-topped protrusion of rock whose sheer faces drop straight to the sea. Luckily the throngs stampeding neighboring resorts spare Calp. **Platja Levant,** a white beach with lovely surroundings, has plenty of room and windsurfing.

If you decide to climb the big rock, wear sneakers and bring water (don't bring excess baggage). The hike takes over an hour. Hike during the day, since ghosts in goats' clothing haunt the rock and butt unwary travelers over the cliff at full moon.

Farther north are the hard rock and caves of the easterly **Cabo de la Nao.** From here you can see Eivissa. Around the bend from the *cabo,* a castle and watchtower have protected the old fishing village of **Moraira** from freeloading pirates for centuries (several buses from Calp per day, 150ptas). The fortress village of **Guadalest,** 25km inland from Calp, offers jaw-dropping views of the surrounding countryside (1 bus per day from C. Circumvalació).

The most reasonable inns and restaurants march up the steep incline toward the older *pueblo.* Avoid the bland food and high prices by the seaside. **Fonda Pati,** Av. Gabriel Miró, 34 (tel. 583 17 84), on the road that leads up to town, looks like a miniature semi-enclosed row of cabanas. (Singles 1500ptas. Doubles 2000ptas.) Tent-toters can try **Camping La Merced** (tel. 83 00 97), a second-class site 400m from the beach (330ptas per person, tent included).

Bar Larios, C. José Antonio, 44 (tel. 583 51 45), up the steep slope to the left, is a large local hangout that jingles with silverware and an electric gambling machine. *Menú del día* 575ptas. Larios also serves a truly luxurious *menú especial* for 900ptas, featuring a mean *zarzuela de pescados.* (Open 8am-10pm.)

The **tourist office** on Av. Ejércitos Españoles, 66 (tel. 583 12 50), between the old town and the beach, speaks inspiringly of other beaches near Calp. (Open July-Sept. Mon.-Sat. 9:30am-9pm; Oct.-May Mon.-Fri. 9am-12:30pm and 3:30-7:30pm, Sat. 10am-1pm.) The **American Express** office is at **Viajes Gandía,** Av. Gabriel Miró, 25 (tel. 583 04 12; fax 583 51 51). They hold mail for six months and cash AmEx checks for a 2% fee. (Open Mon.-Fri. 9:30am-1pm and 4:30-8pm, Sat. 9:30am-1:30pm.)

Five UBESA **buses** per day zip from Alacant to Calp (520ptas), stopping 2km from the beach at C. Capitán Pérez Jorda. **Trains** also connect the two cities (1 3/4 hr., 510ptas). From the train station, municipal buses (75ptas) coast downhill through old Calp to the beach.

Denia

Halfway between València and Alacant on the promontory that forms the Golfo de València, Denia is primarily a family resort where only a few bright rowboats interrupt the sweep of *platja.* The town is named by the Greeks for Diana, the goddess of the hunt, the moon, and purity. The first stretch north of Alacant is disappointing, but apartments soon become villas, and sandy coves swarm with fish.

A **museu arquelogico** resides within the dungeon of the 18th-century **castell.** (Enter off C. Sant Francesc. Open 10am-1:30pm and 5-8:30pm; Oct.-May 10:30am-1pm and 3:30-6pm. Admission 100ptas.) If you feel the beginnings of a claustrophobic attack, one bus per day (at noon) travels 9km down the coast to the hidden cove of **Xàbia** (Jávea). The return trip is at 5:45pm. Denia holds a mini **Fallas** festival March 12-19, burning effigies at midnight on the final day. During the second week of July, the **Festas de la Santísima Sangre** (Holy Blood) include street dances, concerts, mock battles, and wild fireworks over the harbor. From August 14 to 16 are the colorful parades and religious plays of the **Festas de Sant Roque**.

Denia is no haven for the budget traveler; the few affordable hotels usually fill in summer. The tourist office has a list of accommodations; else try **Pensión el Comercio,** C. Lavia, 43 (tel. 578 00 71), about halfway between the tourist office and bus station. All its roomy rooms have baths tiled in a brilliant shade of blue. (Singles 1650-2035ptas. Doubles 2700-3600ptas.) There are also several campgrounds in the area. **Camping Las Marinas** (tel. 578 14 46) is the closest to town, a 3km bus ride (55ptas) from Platja Jorge Joan. (July-Sept. 375ptas per person and per tent; April-June 400ptas; Oct.-March 320ptas.) Eating, too, costs a bundle; **C. Marqués de Campo** cooks the least expensive fare. The morning **market** operates on C. Magallanes, one block north of C. Marqués de Campo.

The **tourist office,** on C. Patricio Ferrandiz (tel. 578 09 57), near Pl. Jorge Joan, will set you up with a beach and a bed. (Open Mon.-Sat. 10am-2pm and 5-8pm, Sun. 10am-1pm; Oct.-June Mon.-Fri. 10am-2am and 4:30-7:30pm, Sat. 10am-1pm.) The **post office** also does **telegrams** at C. Patricio Ferrandiz, 59, west of the tourist office. (Open Mon.-Sat. 10am-2pm.) A **telephone** service operates next to the train station in summer. (Open 9am-2pm and 5-9pm.)

The **train station,** down the road at C. Calderón, has service to Alacant (6 per day, 2hr., 745ptas). The UBESA **bus station** at Pl. del Arxiduc Carles serves València (5 per day, 1600ptas) and Alacant (4 per day, 830ptas). Denia is the embarkation point for Flebasa **ferries** (tel. 578 40 11) to Eivissa. (July 16-Sept. 15 2 per day, June 16-July 15 and Sept. 16-Oct. 15 1 per day, April 9-June 15 and Oct. 16-Nov. 8 3 per wk.; 3 hr.; 5220ptas.)

Murcia

Murcia is a region of demented fortunes. Four centuries ago, mysterious forces unleashed a bizarre wave of plagues, floods, and earthquakes. The earthquakes uncovered a rich supply of minerals and natural springs. Unknown persons came up with the clever plan to convert floods into a system of irrigation canals that water every acre from the capital city to the wine towns of Yecla and Jumilla. Suddenly Murcia's nickname is "La Huerta de Europa" (Europe's Orchard). Thermal spas, pottery factories, and paprika mills pepper the lively coastal towns and orange- and apricot-filled countryside. Although it's flanked by the Mediterranean and the Mar Menor (a tiny sea separated from the larger one by a landstrip dubbed La Manga (The Sleeve), the province still suffers from dryness. The Costa Cálida (Hot Coast), although not geographically isolated, keeps to itself. The entire region, where the gap between rich and poor is one of the greatest in Spain, could be a tourist hotspot, but isn't. *Murciano,* a dialect akin to Andaluz, further isolates the population from their *Valencià*-speaking neighbors to the north.

Murcia

Springing up from a carpet of citrus orchards, the town of Murcia was no big deal until the 13th century, when the Moors and then the Christians spontaneously declared it the region's capital. Murcia has no castle and few monuments; it opened its university almost as an afterthought following World War I.

Instead, the city's virtue lies in the intangible: the absence of postcard or souvenir stands; congenial, much-swept plazas; and extra-long *siesta* hours. Get it while you can; tourist officials have targeted Murcia and are plotting to aggressively promote its unspoiled coast. A small caveat—Murcia is part of the aptly named Costa Cálida (hot coast), and while some Murcian apologists maintain the appellation refers to the water, it's the town that roasts in summer.

Orientation and Practical Information

To the dismay of weary travelers, most places of interest scatter around the town periphery. The Río Segura cuts the town into north and south halves, with most sights and services in the northern half. **Gran Vía de Alfonso X El Sabio** is a broad avenue running from Plaza S. Domingo north to the giant Plaza Circular. The cathedral is in **Plaza Cardenal Belluga**.

The **train station,** across the river at the southern edge of the city, and the bus station, at the western edge, are both 15 minutes from the center. A municipal **bus system** of 33 routes connects just about everything, including other towns within 15km.

> **Tourist Office:** C. Alejandro Séiquer, 4 (tel. 21 37 16), off Pl. Cetina near the cathedral. Enthusiastic and not yet bored by foreigners. Truck-loads of slick pamphlets on the city, province, and Costa Cálida. Free posters. Open Mon.-Fri. 9am-2pm and 4:30-6:30pm, Sat. 9am-1pm.
>
> **El Corte Inglés:** Av. Libertad, s/n. The old standby gives away **maps. Currency exchange:** 1% commission (250ptas min. charge). They also offer novels and guidebooks in English; haircutting; both cafeteria and restaurant; and **telephones.** Open Mon.-Sat. 10am-9pm.
>
> **Budget Travel: TIVE,** C. Manresa, 4 (tel. 21 32 61). Open Mon.-Fri. 9am-2pm; Sept.-July Mon.-Fri. 8am-3pm.
>
> **Post Office:** Pl. Circular, 8a (tel. 24 12 43), at the end of Gran Vía Alfonso X El Sabio, in modern building on the far left side of the giant traffic plaza. Open for stamps Mon.-Fri. 9am-2pm and 5-8pm, Sat. 9am-2pm; for Lista de Correos (in back) Mon.-Fri. 10am-2pm, Sat. 10am-1pm; for **telegrams** Mon.-Fri. 8am-9pm, Sat. 9am-7pm. **Postal Code:** 30001.
>
> **Telephones:** C. San Lorenzo, 16, 1 bl. up C. Alejandro Séiquer and right from Turismo. Open Mon.-Fri. 10am-2pm and 6-9pm, Sat. 10am-2pm. **Telephone Code:** 968.
>
> **Flights:** Airport in San Javier, 40km southeast of Murcia on the Mar Menor. Buses from Murcia's bus station (21 per day, 300ptas) only go to San Javier, 2km short of the airport. Taxi it from there. **Iberia** (tel. 24 00 50), Av. Alfonso X El Sabio, 11, Edificio Velázquez. Open Mon.-Fri. 9:30am-1:30pm and 4:30-7:30pm, Sat. 9:30am-1:30pm.
>
> **Trains: Estació del Carmen,** C. Industria (tel. 25 21 54). For the tourist office, take bus #9 or 11 to the town center; or walk straight on C. Diego Hernández, right on C. Floridablanca, left on Alameda de Colón, and cross the Puente Viejo (15min.). To: Lorca (13 per day, 1hr., 340ptas); Alacant (18 per day, 1 1/2 hr., 340ptas); València (2 *talgos* per day, 3hr., 2375ptas; 2 express per day, 4 1/2 hr., 1320ptas); Barcelona (2 *talgos* per day, 6 3/4 hr., 5600ptas; 2 express, 10hr., 3120ptas); Madrid (2 *talgos,* 5hr., 4045ptas; 1 express, 8 1/4 hr., 2250ptas).
>
> **Buses:** Sierra de la Pila (tel. 29 22 11), behind the Museo Salzillo. For the tourist office, take bus #3 from the station to the center (15min.). Ask the information window which booth sells tickets to your destination. To: La Manga (6 per day, 3 on Sun.; 1 1/2 hr.; 455ptas); Mazarrón (8 per day, 6 on Sun.; 1 1/4 hr.; 370ptas); Yecla (8 per day, 1hr., 640ptas) via Jumilla (490ptas); Lorca (10 per day, 1 1/2 hr., 490ptas); València (6 per day, 3 1/2 hr., 1570ptas); Almería (4 per day, 4 1/2 hr., 1900ptas); Granada (4 per day, 5hr., 2040ptas); Málaga (4 per day, 8hr., 3200ptas); Sevilla (3 per day, 9-10hr., 4090ptas).
>
> **Public Transportation:** Municipal bus system has 33 routes to get folks anywhere, including other towns within 15km. Fare 70ptas, 20-trip ticket (not valid Sun.) 100ptas. #3 from bus station to city center. #9 or 11 from train station to city center.
>
> **Taxis:** tel. 24 88 00.
>
> **Luggage Storage:** At the **bus station** (100ptas per bag). Open 7am-10:30pm.
>
> **Late-Night Pharmacy:** Check listings in *La Opinión de Murcia* (local paper, 85ptas).
>
> **Hospital:** Av. Intendente, Jorge Palacios, 1 (tel. 25 69 00).
>
> **Emergency:** tel. 23 75 50.
>
> **Police: Municipal,** C. Isaac Albéniz, 10 (tel. 26 66 00). **Nacional** (tel. 091).

Accommodations

As Murcia steams up and empties out in summer, finding a room is a breeze. When winter blows in, competition is a bit stiffer. The prices are high year-round.

Hostal-Residencia Hispano, C. Radio Murcia, 3 y 7 (tel. 21 61 52), near the casino in the heart of town. Not to be confused with the 3-star Hispano around the corner. Commodious rooms all have fresh towels, phones, and TV. Winter heating. Singles 2500ptas, with shower 3500ptas, with bath 4000ptas. Doubles with shower 4500ptas, with bath 5000ptas.

Hostal-Residencia Murcia, C. Vinadel (tel. 21 99 63), off Pl. Santa Isabel. Same phone-TV-luxury deal as above. Better furnished but not as classy overall. Singles 2500ptas. Doubles 5000ptas, with bath 6300ptas.

Hostal Consuelo, C. Alfaro, 14 (tel. 21 18 23), off Pl. Julián Romea in the center of town. Distinctly out of place in a refined neighborhood. Scuffed floor, sagging beds, and chipped plaster. It's called budget travel for a reason. Singles 1200ptas. Doubles 1500ptas. Hot showers 200ptas.

Food

Most Murcians don't have potassium, iron, or vitamin deficiencies because they load up on veggies and produce from the surrounding countryside. In fact, *paella murciana* means vegetarian *paella*. Along with the greenery, locals nibble on *hueva de mujo* (millet roe), a local delicacy. Sample the harvest at the **market,** on C. Verónicas near the river. (Open Mon.-Sat. 9am-1pm.)

El Tío Sentao, C. La Manga, 12 (tel. 29 10 13), near the bus station, hidden on a teensy street off Pl. Agustinas. Dusty metal beams crisscross the strange, graffiti-splashed dining room. Fresh vegetables from baskets around the room make a filling meal (700ptas). Beware the powerful chaser of local *vino de Jumilla*. Open 1-5pm and 8-11:30pm.

Casino de Murcia, in the casino at C. Trapería, 22 (tel. 21 22 55). Stop in between hands at the tables. No need to cash in all your chips; great *menú* 800ptas. Open 1-4pm.

Mesón el Corral de José Luís, Pl. Santo Domingo, 23 (tel. 21 45 97). Chefs in the open kitchen toss together Murcian cuisine. Local handicrafts complement the regional specialties. Daily *menú* 1000ptas. Open July-Aug. Sun.-Fri. 1:30-4pm and 8-11:30pm; Sept.-June 1:30-4pm and 8-11:30pm.

Restaurante La Parranda (tel. 22 06 75), Pl. San Juan near Pl. Cruz Roja on the banks of the river. Lots of outside tables on an elegant and quiet plaza. Squiggly-shaped bar inside. Full meal on weekdays 800ptas at bar, 1100ptas at table. Open June-July Sun.-Fri. 1-4pm and 8pm-midnight; Sept.-May Tues.-Sun. 1-4pm and 8pm-midnight.

Sights and Entertainment

The quirky and palatial **Casino de Murcia,** C. Traperiá, 22 (tel. 21 22 55), began life as a social club for the town's 19th- and 20th-century bourgeoisie. The fabulous rooms inside were each designed according to a particular theme. Mammoth, impossibly ornate chandeliers fill the would-be Versailles ballroom. A handsome English billiard room offers a whiff of Pall Mall, while the Arabic patio and its multicolored glass doors simulate the Alhambra. Red leather chairs and dark wood make for a most Oxfordian library. Women are lucky enough to recess in the luxurious gilt powder room. (Open 9am-11pm. Free.)

Next door to the casino, four hundred years of procrastination made Murcia's **catedral** (tel. 21 63 44) in Pl. Cardenal Belluga an odd confusion of architectural styles: an oft-photographed Baroque façade, a Gothic entrance, and Renaissance tower (open 10am-1pm and 5-7pm).

Museo Salzillo at C. Andrés, 1 (tel. 29 18 93), on Pl. San Agustín near the bus station, is devoted to the 18th-century polychrome wood sculptures by Murcian Francisco Salzillo. (Open Mon.-Sat. 9:30am-1pm and 4-7pm, Sun. 11am-1pm; Admission 100ptas.) The **Museo de Arqueología de Murcia,** Gran Vía Alfonso X El Sabio, 7 (tel. 23 46 02), one of the finest in Spain, chronicles the province from prehistoric times. (Open Tues.-Sat. 9am-2pm and 5-7pm, Sun. 9am-2pm. Admission 75ptas, EEC citizens free.) The **Museo de Bellas Artes,** C. Obispo Frates, 12 (tel. 23 93 46), contains works by Spanish artists of the 19th and 20th centuries. (Open Tues.-Sat. 9am-2pm and 5-7pm, Sun. 9am-2pm. Admission 75ptas.)

Beaches on the Costa Cálida are a snap to reach. **La Manga** (the sleeve) is the beach-peninsula 40km long and only 500m wide that closes off the shallow Mar Menor. Another large and popular beach is **Puerto de Mazarrón,** farther south. Buses for both beaches leave from the bus station in Murcia (6 per day to La Manga, Sun. 3 per day; 550ptas. 8 per day to Mazarrón, Sun. 5 per day; 390ptas).

On Wednesday and Saturday nights students blow off work and head to the bars near **Calle Saavedra Fajardo,** south of the university. When they get drunk enough, they move to the discos on **Gran Vía Alfonso X el Sabio.** During Holy Week, processions of vivid costumes and floats march through Murcia's streets. On the day before Easter starts the **Exaltación Huertana,** a week-long harvest celebration that brings jazz and theater to the already crowded streets.

Near Murcia: Parque Natural Sierra España

Just outside of Murcia, the Río España courses through rocky mountains dotted with the pines and sagebrush of the Parque Natural Sierra España (highest elevation 1585m). The flowers explode into dazzling color in springtime, the best season to visit the park. Snow occasionally falls between December and February, blanketing the park at its least crowded time of year. Accommodations range from camping and a hostel to mountainside refuges. Near Alhama de Murcia is a 5km trail from Carmona to Fuente Bermeja, where the youth hostel is located (**Albergue Juvenil el Valle;** tel. (908) 16 44 92; 500ptas per person). Ask about **camping** at the tourist office. From Murcia's bus station you can travel as far as Alhama (225ptas) or Totana (335ptas).

Lorca

The usual battles between Romans and Visigoths, Christians and Muslims, left Lorca without an orange grove, much less a full-fledged *huerta* (orchard), to its name. Today lots of quaint dwellings and almost sinister hills provide plenty of quirky pleasures. Each conquering force left its own peculiar imprint on the large, piecemeal **castillo** on Lorca's central hill. The Moors built the **Torre Espolón** shortly before the city fell to Alfonso el Sabio of Castilla, who conceitedly ordered the **Torre Alfonsina** be built. The ruins of Lorca's first church, the **Ermita de San Clemente,** deteriorate at the castle's eastern edge. (Open 9am-sunset. Free.)

Once Granada fell, inhabitants left the fortresses. Nearly the entire population picked up and moved to the bottom of the slope, leaving in their wake three idyllic churches, **Santa María, San Juan,** and **San Pedro.** Starting anew, Lorcans erected six monasteries and the **Colegiata de San Patricio.** Of the many well-preserved private residences, **Casa de Guevarra's** curving pillars and intricate carvings have a special flair. The interior has just been renovated. (Open Mon.-Fri. 10am-2pm and 5-8pm. Free.)

In town, there's a landmark on every corner. The **Columna Miliaria** on Pl. San Vicente marked the Roman road to Cartagena. Unfortunately, most of Lorca's historic buildings are now only walls crumbling into the dry landscape. Like the capital, Lorca has wild and colorful **Holy Week** processions. On Good Friday, religious groups stage extravagant productions of Bible stories.

Shining ceramic tiles and rooms with new wicker furniture are the siren calls of **Hostal del Carmen,** C. Rincón de los Valientes, 3 (tel. 46 64 59), off C. Nogalte (1200ptas per person). **Hostal Felix,** Av. Fuerzas Armadas, 146 (tel. 46 76 50), on the far side of the river, has air-conditioned halls and winter heating, phones, desks, and tightly made beds. (Singles 1100ptas. Doubles with bath 3000ptas. Breakfast 200ptas.)

The **Restaurante Casa Cándido,** C. Santo Domingo, 13 (tel. 46 70 02), 150m down the road from the tourist office, gives birth to fresh food. The shining crystal and cast-iron chandeliers embellish a full three-course meal (900ptas; open July-Aug. Mon.-Sat. 1-3:30pm and 8:30-11pm; Sept.-June 1-3:30pm and 8:30-11pm).

The **tourist office,** in Casa de Guevarra on C. Lópes Gisbert (tel. 46 61 57), gives out a detailed map. (Open Mon.-Fri. 10am-2pm and 5-8pm.) The **post office** is across the street on C. Musso Valiente. (Open Mon.-Sat. 9am-2pm.) **First aid** pampers the wounded at C. Abad Los Arcos (tel. 46 60 79). In **emergency,** call 091. The **police** come running from C. Villascusa, s/n (tel. 44 33 92).

The **train station,** Estación Sutullana (tel. 46 69 98), is one block from town at the end of C. Poeta Carlos Mellado, off Av. Juan Carlos I. Trains leave for Aguilas (3 per day, 1hr., 105ptas) and Murcia (8 per day, 1hr., 340ptas). Trapemusa **buses** (tel. 46 92 70) leave for Murcia (every hr., 1 1/2 hr., 455ptas) from outside the train station.

Andalucía

Between the jagged Sierra Morena and the deep blue sea, Andalucía has always radiated an intoxicating charm. The ancient lost kingdom of Tartessos—the Tarshish mentioned in the Bible for its fabulous troves of silver—grew wealthy on the Sierra Nevada's rich ore deposits. Greeks and Phoenicians colonized and traded up and down the coast, and Romans later cultivated wheat, olive oil, and wine on the fertile soil watered by the Guadalquivir (Betis to the Romans). Home of serveral emperors and writers of the caliber of Seneca and Quintilian, Baetica was one of the Roman Empire's richest, most sophisticated provinces.

Andalucía owes its name and not much more to the Vandals, who flitted through on their way to North Africa, where they were promptly exterminated. Arabs thereafter called the region Vandalusia (House of the Vandals). Although it is true the Moors remained in control of eastern Andalucía longer than elsewhere (711-1492), the region is as much Roman as Moorish in heritage. The system of irrigation, the cool patios, and the characteristic alternation of white and red stone (as at the Córdoba Mosque) are all in fact Roman (the horseshoe arch is Visigothic). The Moors maintained and perfected these techniques; more importantly they assimilated and elaborated the wisdom and science of Classical Greece and the East, which made the European Renaissance possible.

Owing to the long summers, regional cooking is light, depending on such delicacies as *pescaíto frito* (lightly fried fish) and cold soups as *gazpacho* served *con guarnición* (with garnish), often spooned by the waiter at your table. There are many varieties beside the tomato-based one, but perhaps the most sublime is attributed to Málaga. Called *ajo blanco* (white garlic), it is a bread and garlic soup lent a creamy white color by pureed blanched almonds and garnished with peeled grapes.

Sevilla

Sevilla may convince you that otherworldly cities do exist: brilliant light, whitewashed grace, jasmined balconies, orange trees laden with fat glowing globes, subtropical parks. Site of a small Roman acropolis founded by Julius Caesar, thriving seat of Moorish culture, focal point of the Spanish Renaissance, and guardian angel of traditional Andalusian culture, Sevilla has never failed to spark the imagination of newcomers. Jean Cocteau included it with Venice and Peking in his trio of magical cities. St. Teresa denounced it as the work of the devil. Moorish historian al-Saqundi proclaimed that even the milk of birds could be found here. *Carmen, Don Giovanni, The Barber of Seville,* and Zorilla's tragically racy play *Don Juan Tenorio* are only a few of the artistic works inspired by the metropolis. The 16th-century maxim *"Qui non ha vista Sevilla non ha vista maravilla"*—who has not seen Sevilla has not seen a marvel—remains true five centuries later.

Orientation

In the past few centuries the city has expanded to incorporate a number of neighboring villages. But these communities, now *barrios* of the city, have not lost their distinctive character. **Río Guadalquivir** flows roughly north-south through Sevilla. Most of the city, including the alleyways of the old **Barrio de Santa Cruz,** are on the east bank; some of the most active nightlife and least expensive food are on the west bank in **Barrio de Triana** and **Barrio de los Remedios.** The **catedral,** next to Barrio de Santa

Andalucía

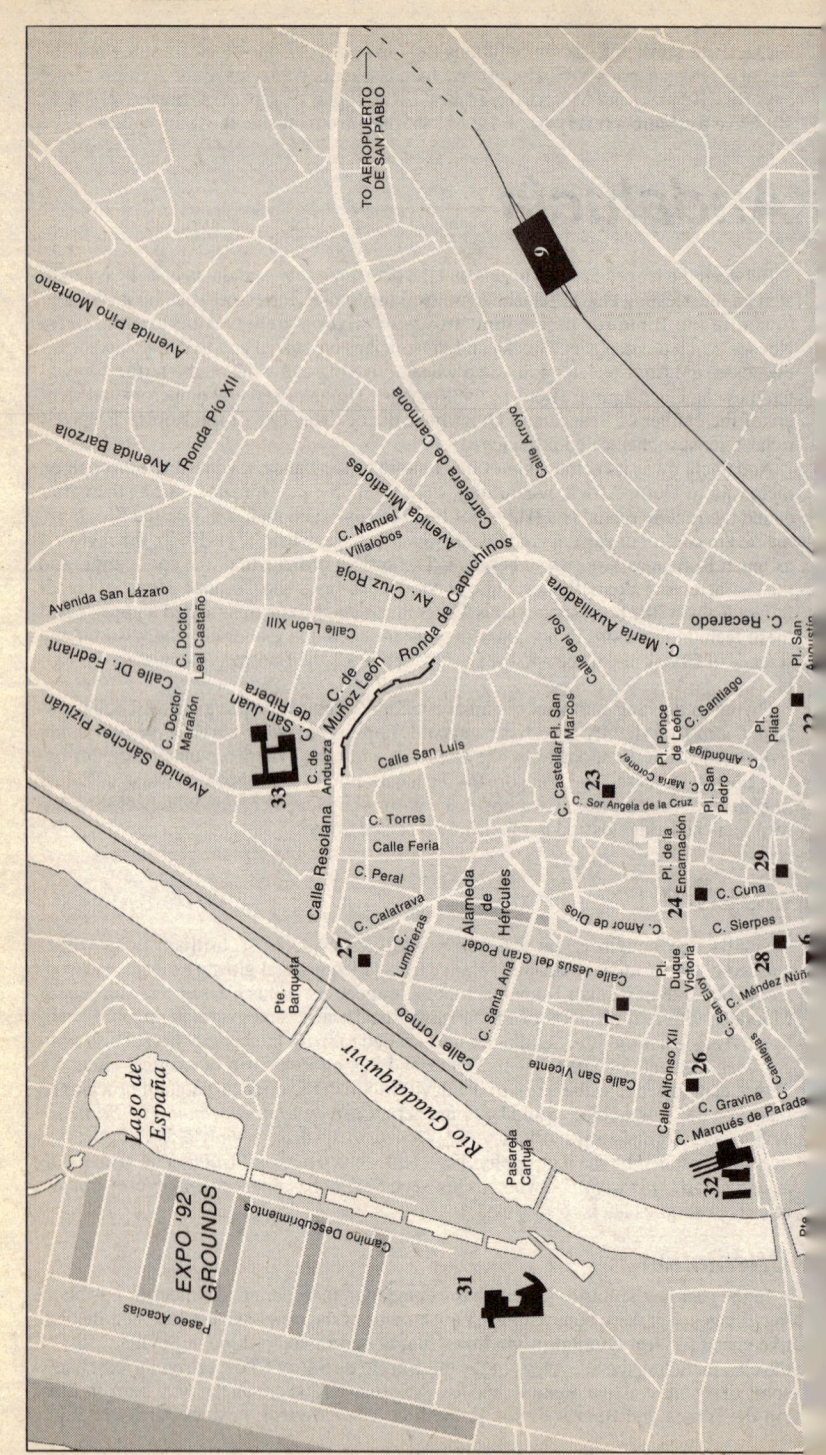

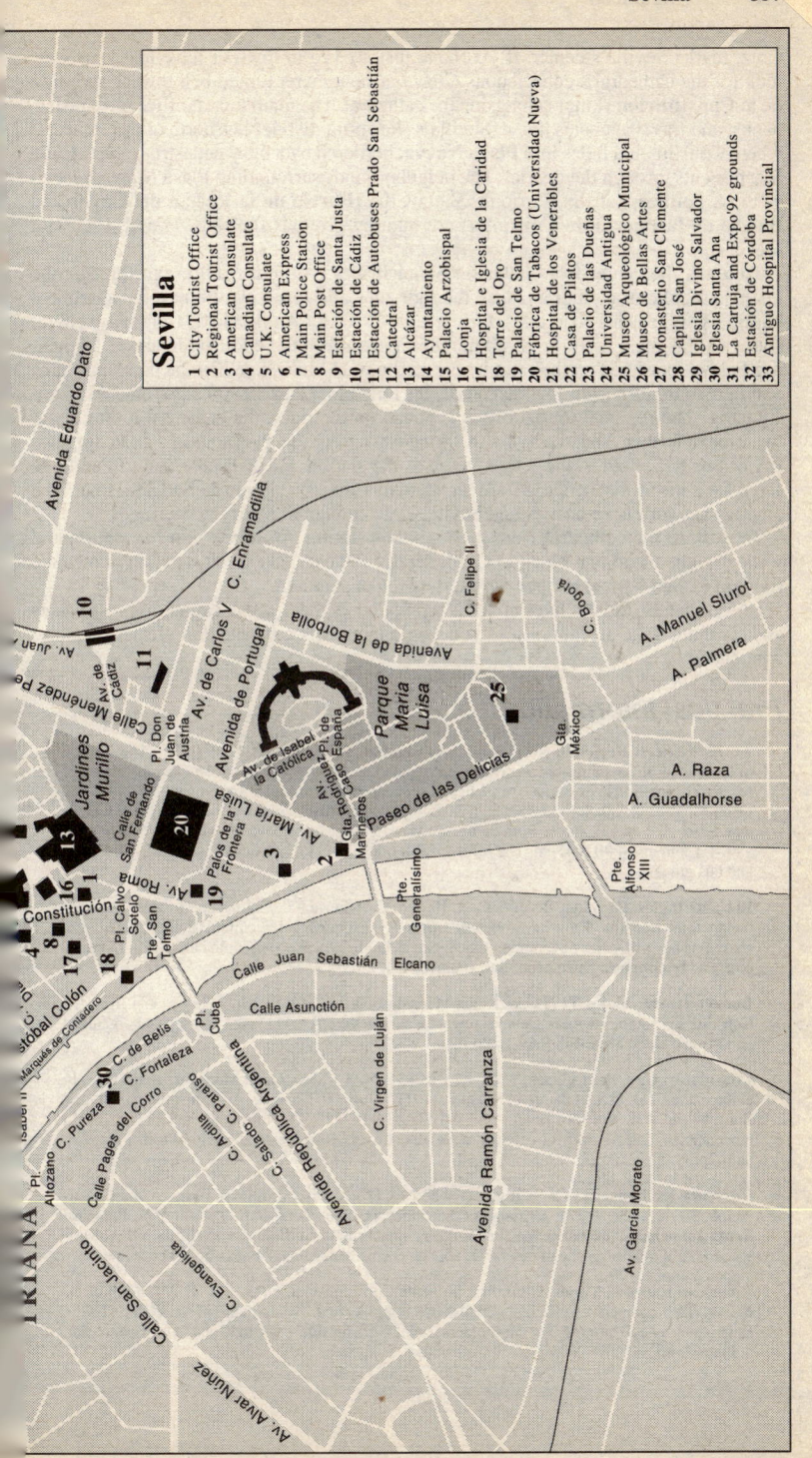

Sevilla

1 City Tourist Office
2 Regional Tourist Office
3 American Consulate
4 Canadian Consulate
5 U.K. Consulate
6 American Express
7 Main Police Station
8 Main Post Office
9 Estación de Santa Justa
10 Estación de Cádiz
11 Estación de Autobuses Prado San Sebastián
12 Catedral
13 Alcázar
14 Ayuntamiento
15 Palacio Arzobispal
16 Lonja
17 Hospital e Iglesia de la Caridad
18 Torre del Oro
19 Palacio de San Telmo
20 Fábrica de Tabacos (Universidad Nueva)
21 Hospital de los Venerables
22 Casa de Pilatos
23 Palacio de las Dueñas
24 Universidad Antigua
25 Museo Arqueológico Municipal
26 Museo de Bellas Artes
27 Monasterio San Clemente
28 Capilla San José
29 Iglesia Divino Salvador
30 Iglesia Santa Ana
31 La Cartuja and Expo'92 grounds
32 Estación de Córdoba
33 Antiguo Hospital Provincial

Cruz, marks Sevilla's center. If you have just arrived in town or have lost your way, look for the cathedral's conspicuous *Giralda* (the minaret turned bell tower). **Avenida de la Constitución** skitters alongside the cathedral. The main tourist office, post office, banks, and travel agencies line it. Sevilla's **shopping district** lies north of the cathedral where Constitución fades into **Plaza Nueva**, bordered by a busy pedestrian zone; **Calle Sierpes** cuts through the district. The neighborhoods surrounding Plaza Nueva, as well as those northeast of the Barrio de Santa Cruz (**Barrio de la Puerta del Carne** and **Barrio de la Puerta de Carmona**) are hunting grounds for *pensión* and restaurant seekers.

To reach the center from Estación Santa Justa (a 40-min. walk), exit through the main, parabolic front door and take the right on Calle José Laguillo past the apartment buildings. When this road ends, turn left on C. María Auxiliadora. Continue straight ahead on this main road for 25-30 minutes as it turns into C. Recaredo and C. Menéndez Pelayo, bordered on the right by the Jardines de Murillo. When the park ends at C. San Fernando, turn right. At the end of this long block, take a soft right onto Av. Constitución. The regional tourist office is ahead on the right; the cathedral looms about two blocks farther. You can avoid this long walk from the train station by catching bus EA or bus #70, both to the left as you exit the station. EA will take you to Puerta de Jerez, near the tourist office; #70 to the main bus station at Prado de San Sebastián. The city bus network is extensive, and Sevilla large enough to justify mastering it.

To walk to the cathedral from the main bus station (10 min.), exit the station and walk straight ahead one block to C. Menéndez Pelayo. Take a left here, an immediate right on C. San Fernando, then a right on Av. Constitución.

Unfortunately, Sevilla lives up to its reputation as the Spanish capital of pickpockets and car theft. Take precautions, as you would in any big city, and don't leave valuables unattended.

Practical Information

Tourist Offices: Regional, Av. Constitución, 21B (tel. 422 14 04, fax 422 97 53), 1 block south of the cathedral. Gushing staff with excellent regional and city information. Stocks separate maps for Sevilla and Barrio de Santa Cruz. English spoken. Most crowded at opening and in afternoon. Open Mon.-Fri. 9:30am-7:30pm, Sat. 9:30am-8pm, Sun. 10am-2pm and 5-8pm. **City,** Po. Delicias, 9 (tel. 423 44 65), across from Parque de María Luisa by Puente del Generalísimo. Mon.-Fri. 9am-1:15pm and 4:30-6:45pm. The **information booth** in Estación Santa Justa stocks city maps and bus guides.

El Corte Inglés: Pl. Duque de la Victoria, 10, near C. Alfonso XII; C. Luis de Morales, 122, near the football stadium. They have a **map. Currency exchange:** 1% commission (250ptas min. charge). They also offer novels and guidebooks in English; haircutting; both cafeteria and restaurant; and **telephones.** Open Mon.-Sat. 10am-9pm.

Budget Travel: Viajes TIVE, Av. Reina Mercedes, 53 (tel. 461 59 16). Take bus #34 from Av. Constitución south down Po. Delicias toward Cádiz. Also offers language courses and organized excursions. Open Mon.-Fri. 9am-1:30pm.

Consulates: U.S., Po. Delicias, 7 (tel. 423 18 83 or 423 18 85). Open Mon.-Fri. 10am-1pm. In emergencies, call U.S. embassy in Madrid at (91) 577 40 00. **Canada,** Av. Constitución, 30, 2nd floor, #4 (tel. 422 94 13; in emergency (91) 431 43 00). **U.K.,** Pl. Nueva, 8B (tel. 422 88 75). In emergencies, call Madrid for referral in Sevilla. Covers New Zealand affairs. Open Mon.-Fri. 9am-2pm.

Currency Exchange: El Corte Inglés (see above). **Oficina de Cambio de Banesto,** Av. Constitución, 30 (tel. 422 26 23), across from the cathedral. Open Tues.-Sun. 9:30am-8pm. **Estación Santa Justa** has an exchange machine for large-denomination bills and an ATM for VISA, Mastercard, AmEx cash card, and others. Of course, during office hours, banks offer better rates.

American Express: Viajes Alhambra, Teniente Coronel Seguí, 6 (tel. 421 29 23), north of Pl. Nueva. Two counters of efficient, English-speaking service. Holds mail (postal code: 41001). Emergency check-cashing for cardholders and 24-hr. outside cash machine. Open Mon.-Sat. 9:30am-8pm.

Post Office: Av. Constitución, 32 (tel. 421 95 85), across from the cathedral. Open for stamps and most mail services Mon.-Fri. 8am-9pm, Sat. 9am-7pm. Open for Lista de Correos Mon.-Fri. 8am-9pm, Sat. 8am-2pm. Open for **telegrams** (national tel. 422 00 00, international tel. 422 68 60) and **faxes** Mon.-Fri. 8am-9pm, Sat. 9am-8pm. **Postal Code:** 41070.

Telephones: Pl. Gavidia, 7, near Pl. Concordia. Open Mon.-Fri. 10am-2pm and 5:30-10pm, Sat. 10am-2pm. **Telephone Code:** 95.

Flights: Aeropuerto San Pablo, (tel. 451 61 11), 12km from town on Ctra. Madrid. Take bus EA (Especial Aeropuerto) to the airport from Puerta de Jerez, near the regional tourist office. Or from Av. Kansas City, near Estación Santa Justa (approximately every hr. 6:30am-10:30pm, 300ptas). **Iberia,** C. Almirante Loco, 2 (tel. 422 89 01, reservations 421 88 00), in front of Torre del Oro. To Madrid (10 per day, 11,475ptas); Barcelona (at 5 per day, 18,025ptas).

Trains: Estaciónes Plaza de Armas (Córdoba) and San Bernardo (Cádiz) have been converted to other purposes; all train service is now centralized in **Estación Santa Justa,** Av. Kansas City, s/n (information tel. 441 41 11, reservations 442 15 62). Spacious, elegant, efficient with vaulted ceilings. Services: **Information booth, luggage storage, telephone office, cafeteria, exchange machine** for large-denomination bills, **ATM** for Visa, Mastercard, AmEx cash card, and others. Bus #70 links Estación Santa Justa and the Prado de San Sebastián bus station. Bus EA makes for the airport and for Puerta de Jerez, near the regional tourist office. Both buses stop on Av. Kansas City, to the left as you exit the station. There's now special high-speed AVE (*Alta Velocidad Española*) train service between Sevilla and Madrid that reduces travel time to 2 3/4 hr. (6 per day, 6000-8400ptas). To: Osuna (4 per day, 1 1/2 hr., 505ptas); Córdoba (16 per day; *AVE* 50 min., *talgo* 1 1/2hr., *tranvía* 2hr.; 1415ptas, 660ptas); Cádiz (13 per day; *talgo* 13/4hr., *tranvía* 2hr.; 1600ptas, 890ptas); Algeciras (2 per day, 1810ptas); Málaga (6 per day, 3-4 hr., 1305ptas); Granada (3 per day, 4-5hr., 1530ptas); Madrid (5 per day; *talgo* 6 hr., *expreso* 6-8hr.; 5240ptas, 3745-5660ptas); Barcelona (4 per day, 10-13hr.; *talgo* 8600ptas, *rápido* 8570ptas, *expreso* 6175ptas). **RENFE,** C. Zaragoza, 29 (tel. 421 79 98), near Pl. Nueva. Open Mon.-Fri. 9am-1:15pm and 4-7pm.

Buses: Prado de San Sebastián, C. José María Osborne, 11 (tel. 441 71 11). Bus #70 links Estación Santa Justa and Prado de San Sebastián. Has helpful information service. **Empresa Alsina Graells** (tel. 441 88 11). To: Córdoba (Mon.-Fri. 16 per day, Sat. 8 per day, Sun. 12 per day; 1 3/4 hr.; 800ptas, round-trip 1300ptas); Granada (6 per day, 3 1/4-4 1/2 hr., 1950-2310ptas); Málaga (16 per day, 4hr., 1615-1910ptas); Almería (4 per day, 7 1/2-9 hr., 3805ptas). **Transportes Comes** (tel. 441 68 58). To: Jerez de la Frontera (9 per day, 1 3/4-2 1/2 hr., 1000ptas); Algeciras (5 per day, 3 1/2 hr.,1875ptas). **Enatcar Becoma** (tel. 441 46 60). To: València (3 per day, 10-11hr., 5135ptas) and Barcelona (2 per day, 18hr., 7755ptas). **Servibus** (in kiosk outside of station by buses). To: Madrid (13 per day, 6 1/2 hr., 2090ptas). **Empresa Los Amarillos** (tel. 41 52 01). To: Arcos de la Frontera (2 per day, 2hr., 760ptas); Ronda (3 per day, 3hr., 1035ptas); Marbella (2 per day, 4hr., 1485ptas). **Estación de Empresa Damas,** in new bus station by Puente del Cachorro bridge, next to the old Córdoba train station (tel. 490 80 40 or 490 77 37). To: Huelva (12-13 per day, 1 1/2 hr., 715ptas).

City Buses: Extensive network. Most lines converge on Pl. Nueva, Pl. de la Encarnación, or in front of the cathedral on Av. Constitución. Most buses run every 10 min. 6am-11:15pm. Limited night service every hr. midnight-3am. City bus guides stocked at the regional tourist office, city tourist office, the information booth at Estación Santa Justa, and at most tobacco shops and kiosks. Fare 100ptas, 10-trip *bonobús* 450ptas.

Taxis: Tele Taxi (tel. 462 22 22). **Radio Taxi** (tel. 458 00 00). All Sevillan cabs metered. Starting fare 240ptas, 45ptas per km, service after 10pm and on Sun. 25% surcharge.

Car Rentals: Avis, Av. Constitución, 15B (tel. 421 65 49), next to the regional tourist office. Open Mon.-Fri. 9am-1pm and 4-7:30pm, Sat. 9am-1pm. **Ital,** Av. República Argentina, 9 (tel. 427 75 51). Open Mon.-Fri. 9am-1pm and 4-8pm, Sat. 9am-1pm. **Hertz,** Av. República Argentina, 3 (tel. 427 88 87), and at the airport (tel. 451 47 20). Most companies require a credit card, a minimum age of 23 yrs., and 1 yr. of driving experience.

Bike Rental: El Ciclismo, Paseo Catalina de Ribera, 2 (tel. 441 19 59), at north end of Jardines de Murillo. Also sells and repairs bikes. 1500ptas per day (some mountain bikes available). Open Sept.-July Mon.-Fri. 10am-2pm and 5-8pm, Sat. 10am-2pm.

Moped Rental: Alkimoto, C. Recaredo, 28 (tel. 441 11 15). Rentals 2750ptas and up per day, depending on the model. Insurance 825-2700ptas extra per day. Required 25,000ptas deposit plus credit card. Minimum age 18 years with a driver's license.

Hitchhiking: As always, *Let's Go* cannot recommend hitchhiking due to the risks involved. Those who choose to hitch toward Madrid and Córdoba take bus #70 out Av. Kansas City by the train station. This road becomes the highway. Those heading to Granada and Málaga take bus #23 to Parque Amate and walk away from the park to the highway (about 20 min.). Those hitching to

Cádiz take bus #34 to Heliopolis and walk west to the bridge. Those heading for Huelva take bus C1 to Pachina; cross the bridge and walk straight ahead until you reach the highway.

Ride-sharing: Compartecoche, C. Amparo, 22 (tel. 421 48 95 or 421 54 94), near Pl. Encarnación. Open Mon.-Fri. 11am-1:30pm and 5-8pm.

Luggage Storage: At the main bus station, 140ptas per day, open 6:30am-10pm. At the train station, small locker 200ptas, medium locker 300ptas, large locker 500ptas per day; open 24 hr.

Lost Property: C. Almansa, 21 (tel. 421 15 64). Or contact municipal police (tel. 461 54 50).

English Bookstore: Librería Beta, Av. Constitución, 27 (tel. 456 07 03), 1 block from the tourist office. Decent selection of novels and Penguin Classics. Open Mon.-Fri. 9:30am-2pm and 4:30-8:30pm, Sat. 10am-2pm and 5:30-8:30pm; winter Mon.-Fri. 10am-2pm and 5-8pm. **Librería Vértice,** C. Mateos Gago, 24A, behind the cathedral. Choice literature and Penguin Classics selection. Open Sept.-June Mon.-Fri. 10am-1pm and 5-8pm, Sat. 11am-2pm; July Mon.-Fri. 10am-1pm and 5-7pm, Sat. 11am-2pm; Aug. Mon.-Fri. 10am-1pm, Sat. 11am-2pm.

Public Library: C. Alfonso XII, 19 (tel. 421 16 54). No materials in English. Open Mon.-Thurs. 10am-1:30pm and 5-8pm, Fri-Sat. 10am-1:30pm.

Women's Center: C. Alfonso XII, 52 (tel. 421 33 75). Information on feminist and lesbian organizations and gay matters, as well as legal and psychological services for rape victims. Also employment listings for women.

Religious Center: Iglesia del Señor San José, C. San José, 17 (tel. 422 03 19). Catholic mass in English Sat.-Sun. 7pm; confession in English daily.

Market: Supermercado Antonio de Pablo, Av. República Argentina, 12-13, 1 block past Puente de San Telmo in Barrio Triana.

Laundromat: Lavandería Robledo, C. F. Sánchez Bedoya, 18 (tel. 421 81 32), 1 block west of the cathedral, across Av. Constitución. Wash and dry 5kg 950ptas. Open Mon.-Fri. 10am-2pm and 5-8pm, Sat. 10am-2pm. **Lavandería Sevilla,** C. Castelar, 2 (tel. 421 05 35), 2 blocks off Av. Constitución. Self-service and full service same price: 5-6 kg 1000ptas. Open Mon.-Fri. 9:30am-1:30pm and 4:30-8:30pm, Sat. 9:30am-1:30pm.

Public Toilets: Off Av. Constitución, underground, between the cathedral and the Palacio de la Lonja. Semi-clean and completely free.

Swimming Pool: Piscina Municipal "Sevilla," Av. Ciudad Jardín, 81 (tel. 463 58 92), near the Gran Plaza (bus #23 or 25). Admission 425ptas, children under 10 250ptas. Open June-Sept. 11am-7pm.

24-Hour Pharmacy: 5-6 pharmacies are open each night all night on a rotating basis. Check list posted at any pharmacy in the city.

Hospital: Hospital Universitario, Av. Dr. Fedriani, s/n (tel. 437 84 00). English spoken.

Medical Assistance: Casa de Socorro, C. Menéndez Palayo, s/n (tel. 441 17 12).

Emergency: tel. 091.

Police: (tel. 428 93 00), Av. Blas Infante, an extension of Av. República Argentina in Barrio Triana. English theoretically spoken.

Accommodations and Camping

EXPO '92 sent accommodations prices skyrocketing. Where they'll settle down is anyone's guess. Rooms in Sevilla have always been dearer than those elsewhere in Andalucía, and it's likely that prices will stay very high in '93. There are reasons to be optimistic, however, as many hotel and *hostal* owners did not do as well as they'd hoped during EXPO.

As usual, during Semana Santa and the Feria de Abril, rooms vanish and prices soar. Make reservations if you value your footleather. Usually, a simple call a day or two ahead will suffice, but for Semana Santa and the Feria de Abril, you should call several months ahead. If you're really stuck, ask tourist officials about *casas particulares* that open their doors for special occasions.

Sevilla Youth Hostel (HI), C. Isaac Peral, 2 (tel. 461 31 54), a few km out of town. English spoken. Members 644ptas, over 26 825ptas; nonmembers 2035ptas; camping 477ptas.

Barrio de Santa Cruz

Look to these pedestrian streets for charm as well as convenience. Only those with a crowd fetish should prowl this area during the first few days of the *feria*.

Huéspedes Buen Dormir, C. Farnesio, 8 (tel. 421 74 92). From the cathedral follow Mateos Gago, bear left on the main thoroughfare, then turn right on Fabiola; look for the alley opposite #10. Room size varies radically. Terrace upstairs. Over 50 birds fill the lobby; but they sleep at night. Singles 2000ptas (some cheaper but hotter ones on the terrace). Doubles 4000ptas, with bath 5000ptas.

Hostal-Residencia Córdoba, C. Farnesio, 12 (tel. 422 74 98). Family-run with modern bathrooms, stained-wood doors, and spacious rooms. Courtyard. Singles 2500ptas. Doubles 4000ptas, with bath 5500ptas. Triples 9000ptas.

Hostal Toledo, C. Santa Teresa, 15 (tel. 421 53 35), off Pl. Santa Cruz. Lovely location on a quiet street, darling courtyard, and well-furnished. Most rooms with bathrooms. Singles with bath about 3500ptas. Doubles with bath about 5000ptas.

Hostal Residencia Monreal, C,. Rodrigo Caro, 8 (tel. 421 41 66). From the cathedral, walk northeast on C. Mateos Gago to the 1st block on your right. Centrally located. Somewhat dark rooms conceal particularly sleepable beds. Bar and restaurant open all day. Singles about 2700ptas. Doubles about 4400ptas, with bath about 5200ptas. Breakfast 500ptas.

Hostal Goya, C. Mateos Gago, 31 (tel. 421 11 70). A lounge to sprawl in, with new red leather furniture and daytime mood lighting. Singles with shower 3710ptas. Doubles with shower 6680ptas. Triples with shower 10,020ptas.

Pensión Fabiola, C. Fabiola, 16 (tel. 421 83 46). Basic, clean rooms, many recently refurbished. A plant-filled patio with lurking cat. Some interior rooms swelter in summer. Singles 4500ptas. Doubles 7500ptas. Triples 12,000ptas. Ask for the biggest room for groups of more than 3. Showers 450ptas.

Barrios Puerta de la Carne and Puerta de Carmona

These *barrios* are more spacious and frequently have more rooms available than the Barrio de Santa Cruz, though they are only a 5-minute walk north. The main thoroughfares are C. San Esteban, C. Santa María la Blanca, and Av. Menéndez Pelayo, and the plazas Alfalfa, Pilatos, and Curtidores. From the bus station to *hostal*-laden C. Archeros, exit the bus station and turn right on C. Menéndez Pelayo. Take the second left after the park breathes its last onto C. Santa María la Blanca, then the third right onto C. Archeros.

Hostal Bienvenido, C. Archeros, 14 (tel. 441 36 55), near Pl. Curtidores. Welcoming managers willing to negotiate prices. Rather small, dark rooms but free and abundant zeitbangers available on the thatched-roof terrace upstairs. Singles 2000ptas. Doubles 3000ptas.

Pensión Archero, C. Archeros, 23 (tel. 441 84 65). Spacious rooms face an open courtyard. Singles 1800ptas. Doubles 3000ptas.

Casa Saez, Pl. Curtidores, 6 (tel. 441 67 53). Bright, clean rooms with only a slightly musty odor. *Dueña* takes pride in her reasonable prices; for extended stays, get all the details in writing. Singles 2500ptas. Doubles 4000ptas. Triples 7000ptas.

Hostal Bonanza, Sales y Ferre, 12 (tel. 422 86 14), in the depths of a maze but perhaps worth the hike. From Pl. Pilatos, head down C. Caballerizas and through Pl. San Ildefonso, where the street becomes C. Descalzos. From Pl. Cristo de Burgos, Sales y Ferre is on your left. Perky owner. Odd *Dating Game*-vintage furniture. Nice TV-less lounge recently upgraded to more hotel-like quality. Singles 5000ptas. Doubles 6000-7000ptas.

Hostal Javier, C. Archeros, 16 (tel. 441 23 25). Well-decorated with oil-paintings and prints. Rooms are well-furnished and comfortable. Doubles 6500ptas, with bath 8000ptas.

Near Plaza Nueva

The streets radiating from Pl. Nueva seem to be monopolized by the hotelier guild. The quarter is airy, elegant, and discretely lively.

Pensión Hostal Nevada, C. Gamazo, 28 (tel. 422 53 40). From Pl. Nueva, take C. Barcelona, and turn right on C. Gamazo. Naturally cool courtyard with leather sofas and large fan collection. Dark tapestry-laden rooms. Singles 3500ptas. Doubles 6000ptas, with shower 6000ptas, with bath 7000ptas. Triples 9800ptas.

El Centro

Shoppers flock to here by day; by nightfall it heaves a sigh of relief. Tourists rarely venture this far from the cathedral, although the shops and street musicians make it worthwhile. The shopping area reaches critical mass at the Plaza Duque de la Victoria, the intersection of C. San Eloy, C. Alfonso XII, C. Laraña, and C. Velázquez, an extension of Av. Constitución.

Pensión Lis, C. Escarpín, 10 (tel. 456 02 28), off Pl. Encarnación. Brightly tiled eye-bugging entry. Singles with basic shower 3000ptas. Doubles with shower 6000ptas. Triples with shower 7000ptas.

Hostal La Gloria, C. San Eloy, 58 (tel. 422 26 73). Striking exterior with ornate wood trim in brick orange. Flawlessly tiled floors and firm beds. Slight bathroom stench mars an otherwise pleasant atmosphere. Night attendant. Singles 4000ptas, with bath 5000ptas. Doubles 6000ptas, with bath 9000ptas. Hot showers 500ptas, but they usually don't collect.

Near Estación de Córdoba

The backstreets around the erstwhile Estación de Córdoba (now converted into exhibition space) are near EXPO grounds. C. Gravina is parallel to C. Marqués de las Paradas and one block farther away from the old station.

Hostal Romero, C. Gravina, 21 (tel. 421 13 53). Potted plants, antique furniture, and hanging brass pots embellish the typically Sevillian inner courtyard. Rooms are basic. 2000ptas. Doubles 3500ptas. Triples 5000ptas.

Hostal Residencia Gala, C. Gravina, 52 (tel. 421 45 03). Shiny wood front door beckons with a sultry come-hither look. Clean bathrooms. Some rooms lack windows, but the place somehow keeps cool. Singles 2500ptas, with bath 3500ptas. Doubles 4000ptas, with bath 4500ptas.

Hostal Gravina, C. Gravina, 46 (tel. 421 64 14). Common bathrooms are a little shabby, but the rooms are dandy. Flowered chairs and cheery Arabian tiles brighten the entranceway. Singles 1500ptas. Doubles 2800ptas.

Hostal Residencia Los Gabrieles, Pl. Legión, 2 (tel. 422 33 07), directly facing the station. Expansive digs. Price includes up to 3 religious icons per room. Singles 4000ptas. Doubles 7000ptas.

Elsewhere

Hotel Simón, C. García de Vinuesa, 19 (tel. 422 66 60), across Av. Constitución from the cathedral. An 18th-century mansion with beautiful inner courtyard and corked fountain that spews out ferns. Laundry service available. Singles 3600ptas, with bath 5800ptas. Doubles 5800ptas, with bath 9000ptas.

Camping Sevilla, Ctra. Madrid-Cádiz, km 534 (tel. 451 43 79), 12km out of town near the airport. From Estación Prado de San Sebastián, take the Empresa Casal bus toward Carmona (approximately every hr. 7am-9:30pm, 225ptas) or bus #70, which stops 800m away at Parque Alcosa. A happy medium between metropolis and outback. Grassy sites, hot showers, supermarket and swimming pool. 490ptas per person, 460 per car and per tent. Children 390ptas.

Club de Campo, Av. Libertad, 13, Ctra. Sevilla-Dos Hermanas (tel. 472 02 50), 12km out of town. Take the Los Amarillos bus direct (not the indirect one) to Dos Hermanas (about every 45 min. 6:30am-midnight, 100ptas). Grassy site, swimming pool. 340ptas per person, per car, and per tent. Children 260ptas.

Camping: Camping Villsom, Ctra. Sevilla-Cádiz, km 554, 8 (tel. 472 08 28), closer to Itálica than to Sevilla about 14km out of the city. Take the Los Amarillos bus that goes to Dos Hermanas via Barriada (every 20-25 min. 6:30am-midnight, 115ptas). Adults 355ptas. 370ptas per car and per tent. Children 310ptas. Hot showers included. Free pool.

Food

In Sevilla you can feast on the best of Andalusian cuisine. The city is perhaps particularly renowned for its jams, pastry, and candy (some made in the many convents) sol in **Plaza del Cabildo** near the cathedral. It's a cinch to find more salubrious foo groups anywhere in Sevilla—good *bar-restaurantes* gravitate around venerable Est ación de Córdoba on **Calle Arjona** and **Avenida Marqués de Paradas,** throughou **Barrio Santa Cruz,** and on many streets of **El Arenal** and **Puerta de Carmona.** Afte hours try the Centro—particularly the area around C. Sierpes. Your tourist tocsi should sound the nearer the bullfight and flamenco paraphernalia get to becoming wallpaper.

Barrio Triana is Sevilla's favored venue for the *tapeo* (tapas-bar hopping), a gloriously active alternative to sit-down dining. On or near the waterfront promenade C. Betis, there are **Río Grande,** with outdoor tables overlooking the river and the city's monumental profile; **El Morapio,** a friendly haunt with *corrida* decor; **La Primera de Puente; La Tertulia;** and finally **Akela.** *Sangría* in Sevilla is especially delicious (thirst is the best garnish) and omnipresent, as is another refreshing summer drink, *tinto de verano,* a blend of red wine and Casera (sweetened tonic water, sometimes fruit-flavored).

Mercade del Arenal is near the bullring on C. Pastor y Leandro, between C. Almansa and C. Arenal. Look there for *toro de lídia* (fresh bull meat from next door) and screaming vendors. Merchants also hawk excellent fresh produce, fish, meat, and baked goods at **Mercadillo de la Encarnación.** (Both open Mon.-Sat. 9am-2pm.)

Near the Cathedral

Restaurants close to the cathedral cater exclusively to tourists. Better prices than in Barrio Santa Cruz are in the back street establishments between the cathedral and the river.

Cervecería Giralda, C. Mateos Gago, 1 (tel. 422 74 35), behind the cathedral. Andalusian tiled walls and Moorish arches. Locals can't seem to hide this place from the tourists. Entrees 800-1200ptas, delicious *tapas* 175-200ptas. Divine *champiñones a la plancha* (grilled mushrooms in garlic and olive oil, 250ptas). Open 9am-midnight; kitchen open 1-4:30pm and 8pm-midnight.

Restaurante El Baratillo, C. Pavia, 12 (tel. 422 96 51), on a tiny street off C. Dos de Mayo. You'd never know it existed if it weren't for the local raves. Small, informal bar with bad art and good inexpensive food. Surprisingly generous *menú* 450ptas, including bread and beverage. *Platos combinados* 300-550ptas. Meals served Mon.-Fri. 8-10pm, Sat. noon-5pm.

Pizzería Renato, C. Pavia, 17 (tel. 421 00 77), on the corner of C. Dos de Mayo. Facing the post office, take the first right, and continue straight through the golden archway onto C. Dos de Mayo or follow your nose. Elegant stained-wood paneling, a marble fireplace, and a bottle-stacked mantle. Several-topping pizzas will stuff (480-700ptas). *Lasagna al horno* (750ptas) comes sizzling straight out of the oven, smothered with superb cheese sauce. Open Thurs.-Tues. 1:15-3:45pm and 8:30-11:45pm, Sat. 8:45pm-midnight.

Bar-Mesón El Serranito, C. Antonia Díaz, 11 (tel. 421 12 43), beside the bullring. Take C. García Vinuesa across from the cathedral and split left on C. Antonia Díaz. The stuffed bull's head was a gift from the *matador*—a friend of the owner. Behind the bar framed images of the Virgin Mary compete with hanging hams and other bullfighting paraphernalia. *Platos combinados* 750ptas. Meat and fish dishes about 900ptas. Open Mon.-Sat. noon-4:30pm and 8pm-midnight.

Mesón La Barca, C. Santander, 6, across C. Temprado, up from Torre del Oro. Ample portions, small restaurant. *Platos combinados* 600ptas. Rare Andalusian specialty, *estofado de venado* (venison, red wine, garlic, and vegetable stew; 750ptas). Open Sun.-Fri. 10am-midnight.

El Mesón, Dos de Mayo, 26 (tel. 421 30 75). Photos of bullfighting elite on the walls, samples of their rivals on the table. Formally dressed waiters serve bull steak fresh from the Pl. Toros. Otherwise have the excellent *gazpacho andaluz* (650ptas). *Cola de toro* (bull's tail) 1450ptas, *estofado de toro* (bull stew) 1100ptas. No *menú.* Food 15% cheaper at the bar. Open Mon.-Sat. 12:30-4:30pm and 8pm-midnight; winter Tues.-Sun. 12:30-4:30pm and 7:30-11:30pm.

Cafetería Postal, C. Almirantazgo, 10 (tel. 422 03 92), across Av. Constitución from the cathedral. Thick, rich *chocolate* and chortle-prompting *churros,* crispy and greaseless. *Churros* with *chocolate* or *café* 210ptas per *ración.* Open for *churros* 8am-1pm.

Barrios Puerta de la Carne and Puerta de Carmona

Although this area is just minutes from the Barrio Santa Cruz, the food is much less expensive.

Casa Diego, Pl. Curtidores, 7 (tel. 441 58 83). Gobs of tourists. The *sopa de picadillo,* an Andalusian broth with eggs and bread (325ptas), is a delicious prelude to the house specialty, *brochetas* (breaded meat or fish strips, 700ptas). *Menú* 950ptas. Open April-Oct. Mon.-Fri. 1-4pm and 8:30-11:30pm, Sat. 1-4pm; Nov.-March Mon.-Fri. 1-4pm and 8-11pm, Sat. 1-4pm.

El 3 de Oro, C. Santa María la Blanca, 34 (tel. 442 68 20), down from C. Menéndez y Pelayo. Loud self-service cafeteria with ceramic art. Superb *paella* 550ptas and Andalusian dishes 525-725ptas. *Menú* 1050ptas. Open 8am-1am.

Bar Las Filipinas, C. Santa María la Blanca, 19, across from El 3 de Oro. The radio sings, the TV shouts, the slot machines bing, the waiters yell, and the customers chow. Informal and rambunctious. *Platos combinados* 450-550ptas. *Menú* with fried fish or *paella* 650-700ptas. Open Wed.-Mon. 6am-1am, Tues. 6am-4pm.

El Centro

Just beyond the usual tourist coops, this area belongs to business people and shoppers by day and young people on their *paseo* by night.

Jalea Real, Sor Angela de la Cruz, 37 (tel. 421 61 03), near Pl. Encarnación. From Pl. Encarnación, head 150m east on C. Laraña, and turn left immediately before Iglesia de San Pedro. Excellent vegetarian—fruits and veggies coming out of the walls. Garlicky, creamy *gazpacho* 350ptas, *panqueques de champiñones* (fluffy, sweet mushroom pancakes, 600ptas). Excellent, 2-course lunch *menú* with whole-wheat bread, wine, and dessert 1150ptas. Gargantuan *platos combinados* 650ptas. Open Tues.-Sat. 1:30-5pm and 8:30-11:30pm, Sun. 1:30-4:30pm.

La Bodeguita de Pollos, C. Azofaifo, 9 (tel. 421 30 44), off C. Sierpes in a quiet alley. Tame but TVed atmosphere. A penniless chicken lover's bliss. Cloth tablecloths and cramped leg room. Zesty foods. Half-chicken, fries, salad and beverage 650ptas. *Gazpacho* in a glass 150ptas. Meals served 1-4:30pm and 7-11pm.

Rincón San Eloy,C. San Eloy, 24 (tel. 421 80 79). Singing is explicitly prohibited, but barking waiters can still just barely be heard above the din of the crowds. Airy courtyard, old wine barrels, massive beer taps, and bullfight posters. Pork chop and fries 350ptas. Other *platos combinados* 700ptas, medium-sized *menús* without dessert 700ptas. Open noon-4:30pm and 7-11:30pm.

Barrio de Triana

This charming old *barrio,* on the far side of the Río Guadalquivir, was once a separate village. Despite increasing crowds, local pride and ambience are managing to hold out. *Tapas* bars, *freidurías* (fried-fish vendors), and terrific sunsets reflected in the river.

Freiduría Santana, C. Pureza, 61 (tel. 433 20 40), parallel to C. Betis, 1 block away from the river. This wee green and red fried-fish stand is jammed with locals. The line is worth it: 11 kinds of fried fish, all fresh and delicious. Free-sample-slipping *señora* eases the wait. Open Sept.-July Tues.-Sun. 7pm-midnight.

Casa Manolo, C. San Jorge, 16 (tel. 433 47 92), north of Puente Isabel II. Local favorite; a madhouse during *fiestas.* Screaming math whizzes tally bills with chalk on the 25m-long metal bar. Meat locker displays the merchandise for inspection. *Menú de la casa* 1430ptas, *pescado frito* (fried fish) 750ptas. Meals served Tues.-Sun. 9am-midnight.

Café-Bar Jerusalem, C. Salado 6, at Virgen de las Huertas. Kick-back bar with an international crowd and inventive *tapas. Shoarmas,* a.k.a. *"el bocadillo hebreo"* (250-400ptas). A savory change from standard Sevillian fare, though hardly kosher. Open Wed.-Mon. 8pm-3am.

El Puerto, C. Betis, s/n (tel. 427 17 25). Outdoor terrace overlooking the river, resplendent with palm trees and sculpted shrubs á la Disneyland. Young people crowd the bar inside. Delicious seafood entrees. *Boquerones fritos* (fried smelts, 1000ptas). 1/4- *pollo asado* (roast chicken, 450ptas), *pollo al chilindrón* (chicken with sweet red peppers, 500ptas). *Menú de la casa* 2500ptas. *Bocadillos* (sandwiches) 375-500ptas. Open Tues.-Sun. 1-4pm and 8:30pm-midnight.

Barrio Los Remedios

This neighborhood, across the river from the center and south of Barrio Triana (Av. República Argentina is the divide), is lively, modern, and middle-class.

El Amanecer, C. Asunción, 76 (tel. 445 93 79). Cross Puente de San Telmo, head left down C. Asuncíon several blocks. Tourists dissolve in the local, middle-class clientele like a sodium chloride matrix in water. Outdoor dining also available. Enchiladas 350-450ptas, tacos 250-350ptas, large selection of hamburgers 300-550ptas. Open Sun.-Thurs. 1pm-midnight, Fri.-Sat. 1pm-3am.

El Panchito, Pasaje Monte Carmelo, 5 (tel. 428 10 09), parallel to C. Asunción and about 2 blocks from Pl. de Cuba. Owned, managed, and frequented by North Americans. Casual and fun. Aztec-design tapestries within. Outdoor tables on large plaza. Most *platos* about 250ptas. *Taco Texano* loaded with beans, cheese, onions, tomatoes, and lettuce 225ptas. Open Sun.-Thurs. 8:30pm-2am, Fri.-Sat. 8:30pm-4am.

Elsewhere

Bar El Camborio, C. Baños, 3 (tel. 421 75 34), directly off Pl. Gavidia. The standard Sevillian tourist tri-themed decor scheme: the bullfighting wall, the flamenco wall, and the religious imagery wall. Comfortable A/C. *Platos combinados* from 300ptas. Lunch *menú* 650ptas, supper *menú* 750ptas. Open Mon.-Sat. 1-4pm and 7:30-11pm.

Bodegón Alfonso XII, C. Alfonso XII, 33, near the Museo de Bellas Artes. Dark-stone walls with columns and arches. Fleet waiters sprint the dizzying circuit from kitchen to counter to you. *Serranita*, a ham and pork burger with green pepper and tomato (with french fries, 250ptas). Ponderous *tortillas* (Spanish egg and potato omelette) with bread and tomato 275ptas. *Menú* 600ptas. Breakfasts with ham and eggs about 350ptas. Meals served Mon.-Sat. 8am-noon, 1-4pm, and 8-10pm.

Restaurante Chino Palacio Imperial, C. Marqués de las Paradas, 55 (tel. 421 88 16). Chinese lamps glow through a black dragon maw. Attentive servers slink about amidst the red and magenta decor. Numerous dishes for under 500ptas. *Menú* 700ptas. Filling *arroz frito de tres delicias* (fried rice with ham, eggs, peas, and carrots—I count 4 *delicias<noitalicxd1* 405ptas). Open 11:30am-4:30pm and 7:30pm-midnight.

Sights

The Acropolis

Renaissance-era and later urban planning is manifest in the broad avenues and wide open squares of Menéndez Pelayo, Constitución, Alfonso XII, and Reyes Católicos, where monuments have room to breathe. This airiness stands in contrast to the shady, twisting, crowded alleyways of those parts of town that have retained their Moorish layout. This Moorish area is sometimes called the Acropolis owing to the dense concentration of monuments.

Christians razed an Almohad mosque to clear space for Sevilla's **cathedral** in 1401, although the famed minaret known as **La Giralda** survived. The tower and its twins in Marrakech and Rabat are the oldest and largest surviving Almohad minarets (the lower walls are 2.5m thick). In 1565, it was crowned by a Renaissance belfry with classical arches and a bronze orchestra of 25 bells. A well-preserved stone ramp—built to permit ascent on horseback—leads to the equally well-preserved tower and belfry. (Open same hours as the cathedral; on same ticket. Entrance to the left after entering the cathedral's main door.) The conquerors demonstrated their religious fervor by constructing a church so great that, in their own words, "those who come after us will take us for madmen." It took more than a century to build Sevilla's cathedral, the fourth-largest (after St. Peter's in Rome, St. Paul's in London, and the pastiche of St. Peter's in the Ivory Coast), and the largest Gothic, edifice ever built. Black and gold coffin-bearers block the entrance, guarding one of Sevilla's most cherished possessions, the **Tumba de Cristóbal Colón** (Columbus's Tomb).

Green and gold floor tiles creep geometrically across the gilt oval chamber of the **cabildo** (chapter house) to the east, a magnificent Renaissance space. The cathedral is a treasury of Spanish, Flemish, and German architecture, painting, and sculpture. The collection of oversized hymn books intimidates everybody next door. Paintings by Murillo and Ribera cover the walls of the **Sacristía Mayor.** Behind the wooden partitions on either side, a disembodied head of John the Baptist watches visitors enter the **tesoro** and guards two keys that Jewish leaders presented to the city of Sevilla after King Fernando III ousted the Muslims in 1248. The neighboring **Sacristía de los Pintores** maintains a collection of minor canvases by old masters, including Zurbarán and Goya. The Baroque organ in the center of the cathedral is a colossal piece of hand-me-down mahogany left over from a 19th-century Austrian railway.

The barred **Portal Principal** at the back of the cathedral faces Av. Constitución. North of the portal, the **Capilla de San Antonio de Padua** celebrates the Portuguese-born saint notorious for demonstrating his exuberance by preaching to fish. The cathedral's only other Arab legacy is the adjoining **Patio de los Naranjos** (Courtyard of the

Orange Trees) north of the church. It has intricately carved Almohad walls and a Moorish gate facing C. Alemanes. Just before the exit is the domed **Capilla Real** (Royal Chapel). (Cathedral open 9:30am-8pm. Admission, including detailed guide to the cathedral, 1000ptas.)

Facing the Pl. Virgen de los Reyes, the **Palacio Arzobispal** was built in the 16th century; the sumptuous Baroque staircase and facade were added a century later. The main hall is hung with 17th-century paintings by Zurbarán, Murillo, Herrera el Viejo, Bassano, and Willaert. Opposite the palace and screened by orange trees is the **Convento de la Encarnación,** whose 14th-century church integrates the lobed windows of a mosque, visible from outside. The church is outfitted with a Neoclassical retable and 17th- and 18th-century sculptures and paintings.

The 9th-century crenellated walls of the **Alcázar** face the south side of the cathedral. Founded as early as 712 by the Almohads to control the Guadalquivir, the Mudejar palace-fortress is the oldest palace still used by European royalty. The walls and several interior spaces, including the **Patio de las Muñecas** (Courtyard of the Dolls) and the **Patio del Yeso** (Courtyard of Plaster), remain from the primitive Moorish fortress. Of later Christian additions, one of the most exceptional is the **Patio de las Doncellas** (Maid's Court). Court life in the Alcázar traditionally revolved around this spacious, colonnaded quadrangle ringed by foliated archways, adorned with stucco and glistening tilework, roofed with coffered ceilings, and soothed by a central fountain. Kaleidoscopic chambers open off the central patio. More impressive is the golden-domed **Salón de los Embajadores** where Fernando and Isabel welcomed Columbus upon his homecoming from America. Private quarters and the building's most exquisite carvings fill the nearby **Patio de las Muñecas.** The rooms open to the public display portraits, a unique collection of hand fans, and a bed purportedly slept in by Queen Isabel. **Jardines** stretch away from the residential quarters on all sides; muddle through the elaborate myrtle maze. (Open Tues.-Sat. 10:30am-5pm., Sun. 10am-1pm. Admission 600ptas. Students free.)

Between the cathedral and the Alcázar, the 16th-century **Lonja** was built by Felipe II as a *Casa de Contratación* (commercial exchange) for the American trade. In 1784 it was turned into the *Archivo General de Indias* (Archive of the Indies), a collection of over 30,000 documents relating to the discovery and conquest of the "New World." Highlights include letters from Columbus to Fernando and Isabel. (Open Mon.-Fri. 10am-1pm. Researchers Mon.-Fri. 8am-3pm. Free.) Modern art fans should go next door, to the **Museo de Arte Contemporáneo,** C. Santo Tomaso, 5; there are some fab Mirós on the top floor. (Open July-Sept. Tues.-Fri. 10am-2pm; Oct.-June Tues.-Fri. 10am-7pm, Sat.-Sun. 10am-2pm. Admission 250ptas. Students free.)

On C. Temprado, off C. Santander, two blocks west of the Lonja, is the **Hospital de la Caridad,** a compact 17th-century complex of arcaded courtyards. Its founder, Don Miguel de Mañara, is popularly belived to be the model for the classic Sevillian legend of Don Juan. He was allegedly converted to a life of piety and charity after stumbling out of an orgy into a funeral cortège that he was told was his own. Above the entrance of the **Iglesia de San Jorge** inside hangs Valdés Leal's *Finis Gloria Mundi*: the corpses of a peasant, a bishop, and a king putrefying beneath a stylized depiction of Justice and the Seven Deadly Sins. The dome is painted in fresco by Leal and there are paintings by Murillo, including the remarkable *Moses Striking Water from the Rock* and on the south side *The Miracle of the Loaves and Fish*. The ornate **altar mayor** (main altar) includes a grisly sculpture of Jesus. Don Miguel is buried in the crypt. (Open Mon.-Sat. 10am-1pm and 3:30-6pm, Sun. 10:30am-12:30pm. Admission to church 200ptas.)

Barrio de Santa Cruz

The tourist office has a special map for this neighborhood of winding alleys, flower pots, wrought-iron *cancelas* (gates), befountained courtyards, and excellent art galleries. King Fernando III forced Jews fleeing Toledo to live in this ghetto. Haloed with geraniums, jasmine, and ivy, every street corner in the *barrio* bears a reminder of history and legend. On **Calle Susona,** a glazed skull above a door recalls the beautiful Jewess Susona who fell in love with a Christian knight. Susona warned her lover when she learned her father and friends planned to kill several inquisitors, including her knight.

Bloody reprisal was unleashed on the ghetto, as a result of which Susona's whole family was slaughtered. The distraught woman requested her skull be placed above her doorway in atonement for her betrayal. According to legend the actual skull remained there until the 18th century. This street leads to **Plaza Doña Elvira,** site of a theater where Sevillian Lope de Rueda's works, precursors of Spain's Golden Age, were staged. A turn down C. Gloria leads to Pl. Venerables, location of the 17th-century **Hospital de los Venerables.** Founded as a rest home for priests, the hospital church is adorned with a choice ensemble of Seville School art. Juan Valdés Leal painted the ceiling frescoes (including those in the sacristy), his son Lucas the wall frescoes and the staircase dome. The great polychrome wood carver Martínez Montañés is represented by his sculpture of *St. Stephen.*

Calle Lope de Rueda is graced with two noble mansions; beyond them lies **Plaza de Santa Cruz,** one of the quarter's largest. St. Teresa of Avila forgot her cloak here, so now the **Convento de San José** on C. Santa Teresa (off Pl. Santa Cruz) religiously cherishes the wrap, along with her portrait by Father Miseria. Fans of saccharine Baroque painter Murillo will admire the **Casa Murillo's** collection of his work. Murillo died here after falling from a scaffold while painting ceiling frescoes in Cádiz's Iglesia de los Capuchinos; he was buried in the Pl. Santa Cruz church. (Closed in '92, to be reopened in '93.) **Iglesia de Santa María la Blanca** on the square of the same name was built in 1391 on the foundations of a synagogue. It features red marble columns, Baroque plasterwork by Pedro and Miguel Broja, and a Murillo *Last Supper.*

Sierpes and the Aristocratic Quarter

The **Ayuntamiento** on Pl. San Francisco has 16th-century Gothic and Renaissance interior halls, a richly decorated domed ceiling in the chapter room, and a Plateresque facade. Off Pl. San Francisco, pedestrian **Calle Sierpes** has always been and probably will always be shoppers' turf. At the beginning of the street a plaque marks the spot where the royal prison was located; some scholars believe Cervantes began *Don Quijote* there.

Fronted by a Montañés sculpture, **Iglesia de El Salvador** stands on the square of the same name one block east of Sierpes. The 17th-century church was built on the foundations of the city's main mosque, of which the courtyard and the belfry's base remain. As grandiose as a cathedral, it's adorned by outstanding Baroque retables, sculpture, and painting, including Montañés' *Jesús de la Pasión.*

Iglesia de la Anunciación and the **Antigua Universidad** line the somewhat degraded Plaza de la Encarnación. Blanco White, early 19th-century writer of the acerbic *Letters from Spain,* is one of the university's most renowned alumni. Designed in 1565 for the Jesuits, the brick church served for two centuries as the church of the old university next door. There is a pantheon here for illustrious Sevillians, including painter Gustavo Adolfo Bécquer.

North of Barrio Santa Cruz off Pl. Pilatos, the **Casa de Pilatos** is the most sumptuous Sevillian palace (after the Alcázar of course). Tradition has it the palace was modeled on the praetorium of Pontius Pilate in Jerusalem; in fact the name derives from a plaque the Marqués de Tarifa placed on the building to commemorate his trip to the Holy Land in 1521. The palace is a majestic melange of Gothic, Mudejar, and Renaissance, with a considerable collection of Roman antiquities, Renaissance and Baroque paintings, period furniture, several courtyards, and a pond. (Open 9am-9pm; Oct.-April 9am-7pm. Admission 400ptas.) If you arrive during visiting hours and the gate is closed, use the metal bellpull. Sundry palaces at #2 and #5 on C. Esteban lead to **Iglesia de San Esteban.** The lobed arches and 16th-century Mudejar altar tiles make it one of Seville's finest Gothic Mudejar churches.

La Macarena

This neighborhood, named for the Roman Macarios who owned an estate here, is a richly endowed quarter often overlooked by tourists. C. María Coronel leads to **Convento de Santa Inés,** whose simple courtyard leads to the revolving window from which cloistered nuns sell patented puff pastry and coffee cakes. Legend has it the founder was pursued so insistently by King Pedro el Cruel, she poured boiling oil on her face to disfigure it.

The so-called *ruta de los conventos* (route of the convents) traverses this quarter. **Convento de Santa Paula** includes a church with Gothic, Mudejar, and Renaissance elements, a magnificent coffered ceiling, and sculptures by Montañés. The **museo** has a *St. Jerome* by Ribera. Here the nuns push marmalades and angel's hair pastry. Opposite the belfry of the Iglesia de San Marcos rises **Convento de Santa Isabel**. The Baroque church has a retable done by Montañés. Nearby on C. San Luis stands the exuberantly Baroque **Iglesia de San Luis** with octagonal glazed-tile domes, a strong contrast to the restrained Iglesia de Santa Marina opposite.

Nearby C. Dueñas leads to yet another great Sevillian mansion, **Palacio de las Dueñas**. Decorated with Mudejar plasterwork and fine tapestries and paintings, the house was the birthplace of 20th-century poets Manuel and Antonio Machado.

Between the Puertas de Macarena and Córdoba on the Ronda de Capuchinos ring road is a stretch of restored **murallas,** built by the Almohads in the 12th century and successively enlarged by the Almoravids and the Christians. Seven square towers reinforce the walls; the polygonal **Torre Blanca** has brick decoration and vaulted ceilings. A large garden beyond the walls leads to the **Hospital de las Cinco Llagas,** one of the most spectacular Renaissance buildings in the city now being primped to house the Andalusian parliament.

Back within the walls toward the river is **Alameda de Hércules,** in a quarter punctuated by many Mudejar churches. The city's traditional red-light district abuts it.

El Arenal, San Lorenzo, and Triana

The **Torre del Oro** (Gold Tower), on P. Cristóbal Colón, beside the river, is a 12-sided crenellated tower built by the Almohads in 1220 to reinforce a wall leading from the Alcázar. A glaze of golden tile once sheathed its squat frame; today a tiny yellow dome is the only reminder of its original splendor. For an attack of claustrophobia, climb to the top and visit the **Museo Náutico,** with engravings and drawings of Sevilla's port in its heyday. (Tower and museum open Tues.-Fri. 10am-2pm, Sat.-Sun. 10am-1pm. Admission 100ptas.)

The inviting riverside esplanade **Marqués de Contadero** stretches along the banks of the Guadalquivir from the base of the tower. Bridge-heavy one-hour boat tours of Sevilla leave from here (500ptas). Immortalized by Golden Age writers Lope de Vega, Quevedo, and Cervantes, **Arenal** and (across the river) **Triana** were Sevilla's bustling and chaotic seafaring quarters in the 17th century The tiled boardwalk leads to **Plaza de Toros de la Real Maestranza,** a veritable temple of bullfighting. Home to one of the two great schools of *tauromaquia* (the other is in Ronda), the plaza fills to capacity for the 13 *corridas* of the Feria de Abril and for weekly fights in the summer (on Thursdays and Sundays). (Open to visitors April 24-Oct. 12 Mon.-Sat. on non-bullfight days from 10am-1:30pm. Tours every 30 min. Admission 200ptas.)

The **Museo Provincial de Bellas Artes,** Pl. Museo, 9, contains Spain's finest collection of works by Seville School painters, notably Murillo, Leal, and Zurbarán and aliens El Greco and Dutch master Jan Breughel. To reach the museum, walk toward the river along C. Alfonso XII, lined with a number of palaces along this stretch. (Open Tues.-Fri. 10am-2pm and 4-7pm, Sat.-Sun. 10am-2pm. Free.) The Museo de Bellas Artes has been undergoing major renovations for the last couple of years. The actual distribution of works may well change by 1993.

Several blocks away in Pl. San Lorenzo is **Iglesia de San Lorenzo,** remarkable for Montañés's lifelike sculpture *El Cristo del Gran Poder.* Worshipers kiss Jesus's ankle through an opening in the bulletproof glass. Semana Santa culminates in a procession with this statue. (Open 8am-1:30pm and 6-9pm. Free.)

Across the river is the former potters', tilemakers', and gypsy quarter called Triana, now much gentrified. The riverside promenade **Calle Betis** with its many outdoor terraces is an ideal spot from which to view Sevilla's monumental profile. Originally comissioned by King Alfonso X el Sabio (the wise), the **Iglesia de Santa Ana** (two blocks from the river), was thrice renovated between the 13th and 16th centuries.

Elsewhere

In 1929, Sevilla made elaborate plans for an Iberian-American world's fair. When Wall Street crashed, so did the fair, but the event left the city the lovely landscapes of the **Parque de María Luisa**. Innumerable courtyards, turquoise-tiled benches, and tailored tropical gardens fill this expanse of manicured greenery.

On the park's northeastern edge, the twin spires of **Plaza de España** poke above the Sevillian skyline. The plaza's colonnade, checkered with terracotta tiles, curves toward the neighboring park, and a narrow moat, spanned by four bridges, encircles the pavilion. The enclosed area is overlaid with brickwork and punctuated in the center by a large fountain. Boaters putt around the miniature canal (275-300ptas per hr.).

Sevilla's **Museo Arqueológico,** inside the park at Pl. de América, shows off a small collection of pre-Roman and Roman artifacts excavated in the surrounding provinces. (Open Tues.-Sun. 10am-2pm. Admission 250ptas, students and under 21 free.) Off the far north end of the park, across C. San Fernando, some of the **Universidad de Sevilla's** humanities faculties are housed in the vast 18th-century tobacco factory, the largest civic building in Spain. It set the stage for Bizet's *Carmen*. A block or so toward the river down Palos de la Frontera is 17th-century **Palacio de San Telmo,** built as a training school for sailors. St. Telmo, patron saint of sailors, hovers over the door amid a maelstrom of marine monsters and allegorical figures. Within, there's an imposing courtyard, pillared hall, and chapel with large Zurbarán. The 1992 Sevilla Universal Exposition (EXPO) occupied a 538-acre site on Isla de la Cartuja, named for the 15th-century Gothic-Mudejar **Monasterio de la Cartuja de Santa María de las Cuevas,** with Renaissance and Baroque additions. First burial place of Christopher Columbus, moated by two branches of the Guadalquivir, it lies within walking distance northwest of the city center. The theme of the EXPO was "The Age of Discoveries," following a linear view of human progress in technology. Beginning in 1993, the site will become a scientific and technological park.

Entertainment

Movies, Theater, and Music

The tourist office distributes *El Giraldillo,* a free monthly magazine on entertainment in Sevilla with complete listings on music, art exhibits, theater, dance, fairs, and film.

Avenida 5 Cines, C. Marqués de las Paradas, 15 (tel. 422 15 48), and **Cine Cristina,** C. Almirante Lobo, 1 (tel. 422 66 80), both show predominantly foreign (i.e. American) films dubbed into Spanish. **Cine Corona,** in the mall between C. Salado and C. Paraiso in Barrio de Triana, screens subtitled films, often in English. Shows at most theaters run from early afternoon to late at night and cost around 500ptas. For information on all three cinemas, call 427 80 64.

For theater, the venerable **Teatro Lope de Vega,** near Parque María Luisa, has long been the city's leading stage. (Ask about scheduled events at the tourist office or check the bulletin board in the university lobby on C. San Fernando.) The grand new **Teatro de la Maestranza,** on the river next door to the Plaza de Toros, is a splendid concert hall designed to accommodate both orchestral performances and full-fledged stagings of opera. On spring and summer evenings neighborhood fairs are often accompanied by free **open-air concerts** in Barrios de Santa Cruz and Triana.

Bars

On warm nights after sundown Sevillians gather in *bars, terrazas,* and *chiringuitos.* **Plaza del Salvador,** C. Alvarez Quintero, three blocks north of the cathedral, fills with revelers toting drinks from the two tiny bars on the plaza. Others flock a few blocks to the east on C. Alcaicería to **Plaza Alfalfa,** a district brimming with *tapas* bars and cafés, including several in a row on C. Perez Galdos. In Barrio Santa Cruz, the areas on and around **C. Mateos Gago** and **C. Argote de Molina** are always worth a late-night visit, as is the smaller area across Av. Constitución from the tourist office. A bevy of *terraza* bars takes over Barrio de Triana near Puente Isabel II and line **Calle Reina**

Mercedes and the **Jardines de las Delicias,** both down Po. Delicias away from the cathedral. *Chiringuitos* are outdoor bars that pipe in their own dance music. They are a typically *Costa* phenomenon that has invaded the big cities. There's a cluster on the east bank of the river between Puente del Generalísimo and Puente de San Telmo that has loud dance music and a lively pick-up scene. (Beer 125-175ptas. Open Mon.-Thurs. until about 5am, Fri.-Sat. until about 6:30am.)

> **La Carbonería,** C. Levies, 18, a few blocks west of C. Menéndez y Pelayo, off C. Santa María la Blanca. Established 30 years ago to encourage artists and musicians censored during Franco's dictatorship, the locale now functions as a popular nightspot, with jazz, folk, and other shows nightly (flamenco Sun.-Tues.). On hot nights the large garden courtyard is packed with a crowd of mixed ages.
>
> **Antigüedades,** C. Argote de Molina, just north of the cathedral. A new decorative theme every other week (such as hanging bones and flying golden trumpets) and modern-art oddities displayed through upstairs balconies. Beer 150ptas, mixed drinks 400ptas. Open weeknights until 3am. Open Fri.-Sat. until about 4am.
>
> **Las Columnas,** corner of C. Mateos Gago and C. Rodrigo Caro. Hordes of people most nights block access inside; try joining the overflow outside.
>
> **Abades,** C. Abades, 15 (tel. 421 50 96). Not just another bar in Barrio de Santa Cruz; it's your excuse to visit an 18th-century mansion. For background music you can choose between the fountain in the elegant courtyard or the strains of classical music in one of the comfortable dens.
>
> **Casa Morales,** C. García de Vinuesa, 11, one block from the cathedral. Small tables dwarfed by 5m-high barrels is the setting for regional wine sampling (100-130ptas per glass). More of a quiet *bodega* than a loud bar. *Tapas* are not served; however, some customers bring *pescada frita* (fried hake) from the stand next door.

Nightclubs

You don't have to look far to find dancing here. As in other Spanish cities, most clubs don't get busy until well after midnight. Peak hours are between 2 and 4:30am, and many thrive until daybreak. Foreigners, especially Americans and women, are often admitted to discotheques without having to pay cover; English-speakers in particular are thought to raise the "cool" quotient. **El Coto,** C. Luis de Morales, 118, across from El Corte Inglés near the football stadium (cover 800ptas, Sun. 1200ptas), and **El Río,** C. Betis, 69 (2nd of 2 sessions starts after midnight; cover 500ptas) are hotspots. In summer, people avoid the indoor pressure-cookers only to pack such places as **E.M.** and **Out,** both small, outdoor discos on the far side of the *Feria* grounds in Barrio de los Remedios (cover about 500ptas). Currently, the most popular last stops for the liminal hours of the morning are the two outdoor discos by Parque de María Luisa on Po. Delicias, **Alfonso XII** and **Líbano.**

The gay scene is coming out strong in Sevilla; several gay and lesbian bars have opened in the last couple years. Most can give you information on the others and some carry a local guide to gay life in Sevilla. Several are popular with foreigners. Rumor has it that **Itaca,** C. Amor de Dios, near C. Lope de la Vega in el Centro is the best gay disco in town (show Wed. at 1am). **Conos,** C. Santa Ana in el Centro is a disco bar with a video room (opens at 8pm). **Lamentable,** Pl. Alfalfa., **Poseidon,** C. Marqués de las Paradas, and **Califas,** C. Menendez Palayo by C. Santa Maria la Blanca are mixed bars that open around 8-9pm.

If, after a night of partying, you get the urge to read a non-Spanish newspaper, use a clean restroom, buy a cassette tape, or purchase some non-perishable groceries, bear in mind that a branch of the Spanish chain of modern convenience stores called **VIPS** is at C. República Argentina, 25, three blocks from Pl. Cuba in Barrio Remedios. (Open 9am-3am. The adjoining café serves expensive hamburgers and sandwiches for 500-600ptas; *platos combinados* for 900ptas.)

Flamenco

The lightning-fast footwork of Sevilla's flamenco *bailaores* dazzles the eyes; rhythmic guitar, pulsating handclaps, and wailing *cantaores* fill the ears. There are two ways to see flamenco: go to a professional show or visit a local club. Unfortunately for the budget traveler, good flamenco doesn't come cheap. The best show in town and the only one with professional dancers is on the western edge of Barrio Santa Cruz at **Los Gallos,** Pl. Santa Cruz, 11 (tel. 421 69 81). The cover (3000ptas) includes one drink (1st show 9:30pm, 2nd at midnight; if you pay for the first, the second is free). Arrive early to get a good seat. You'll find similar prices at **El Arenal,** C. Rodó, 7 (tel. 421 64 92), with daily performances (10pm-1:30am), and **Patio Sevillano,** P. Cristóbal Colón, 11 (tel. 421 41 20; shows at 7:30, 10, and 11:30pm). Some sort of folk music or flamenco is performed at **La Gitanilla,** C. Ximénez de Encisco, 11, in Barrio de los Remedios, across the river; take bus #42 from Pl. Encarnación, Pl. Nueva, or Av. Constitución.

La Lidia

Several booths on C. Sierpes, C. Velázquez, and Pl. Toros sell **bullfight** tickets. Prices depend on the coolness of both your seat and the matador. To avoid the scalper's 20% markup, buy tickets at the bullring. However, the booths might be the only source of tickets for a good *cartel* (line-up). Prices run from 10,000ptas for a *barrera de sombra* (front row seat in the shade) to 1500ptas for a *grada de sol* (nosebleed seat in the sun). *Corridas de toros* (bullfights) or *novilladas* (cut-rate fights with young bulls and novice bullfighters) are held on the 13 days around the Feria de Abril and into May, often during Corpus Christi in June, nearly every Sunday in June, and again near the end of September during the Feria de San Miguel. For information on dates and prices, go to **Plaza de Toros de Sevilla** or call 422 31 52.

Festivals

Sevilla swells with tourists during the *fiestas*. The world-famous **Semana Santa** (Holy Week) festival can inspire even the most parade-pooped tourist. Celebrations last from Palm Sunday to Good Friday with penitents in hooded cassocks guiding bejeweled floats, lit by hundred of candles, through the streets. A central float carries a likeness of the city's patron, the *Virgen de la Macarena*. Masked marchers are members of ecclesiastical guilds, each of which venerates a different image of Jesus from an episode of the Passion. Penitents march through the streets a total of eight times conducting 99 floats from their neighborhoods to the cathedral and back. Book your room well in advance of the festivities, and expect to pay about triple the ordinary price.

Two or three weeks after Semana Santa, the city rewards itself for its lenten-like piety with the six-day carnivalesque **Feria de Abril** (April Fair). Circuses, bullfights, and flamenco shows roar into the night in a showcase of local customs that began in the 19th century as part of a popular revolt against foreign influence. The fairgrounds are on the southern side of Barrio Los Remedios, near the river. A spectacular array of flowers and lanterns festoons over 1000 kiosks, tents, and pavilions. Although most of the *casetas* (booths) are for private neighborhoods or organizations, if you wander around enough you're bound to find a party overflowing into the street. Horsemen costumed in traditional garb ride about the grounds, carrying *señoritas* in ruffled Gypsy dresses. The lights and the party begin Monday at midnight. The activity on the fairgrounds runs Tuesday to Saturday from around 9:30am to 2pm, and at night the festivities spill into town.

Spain's biggest festival, the **Romería del Rocío,** takes place 50 days after Easter on Pentecost. Caravans of pilgrims trundle over the Spanish countryside to converge on the tiny village of **El Rocío,** 60km west of Sevilla. They come to venerate the *Blanca Paloma* (white dove), a sacred image of the Virgin in the town's shrine. Pilgrims from the Barrio de Triana in Sevilla are some of the loyal participants that make the annual procession. Activities at the sacred shrine extend from Saturday afternoon to Monday morning and include candle-light parades, mass, traditional dance, and general chaos. Buses run five times per day to the new bus station on C. Torneo next to the old Córdoba train station.

Near Sevilla

Itálica

The ruins of the first important Roman settlement in Iberia, Itálica lies only 9km northwest of Sevilla. Founded in 206BC, the city was the birthplace of emperors Trajan and Hadrian. The Romans promptly became the town's aristocracy, the Iberians its underclass. The city walls, Nova Urbs, and other edifices were constructed between 300 and 400 AD, otherwise known as the *apogeo* (apogee). In the centuries that followed Itálica's power declined, and by the 5th century Sevilla had become the region's seat of power.

Archeological excavations begun in the 18th century continue today. The well-preserved **anfiteatro**, one of Spain's largest, seats 25,000. Classical theater is still performed here; check Sevilla's *El Giraldillo* for schedules. A handful of colorful **suelos mosáicos** (mosaic floors) remain in some buildings. Other mosaics and relics have been moved to Sevilla's Palacio Lebrija and Museo Arqeológico. (Site open April-Sept. Tues.-Sat. 9am-6:30pm, Sun. 9am-3pm; Oct.-March Tues.-Sat. 9am-5:30pm, Sun. 10am-4pm. Admission 250ptas. Students and EEC citizens free.)

Take Empresa Casal's **bus** toward the village of Santiponce, and tell the driver you want to go to Itálica. Catch the bus in front of #53 C. Marqués de las Paradas, near Sevilla's old Plaza de Armas or Córdoba train station. (Buses run Mon.-Fri. 6am-11pm every 1/2 hr., Sat.-Sun. 7:30am-midnight, every hour; 30 min.; 100ptas.)

Carmona

The ancient city of Carmona, an hour east of Sevilla, presides on a high hill above the gold and green countryside that surrounds it. Once a thriving Arab stronghold, it was later the favorite 14th-century retreat of Pedro el Cruel. Predictably, Moorish Mudejar palaces mingle with Christian Renaissance mansions amidst a skein of streets still partially enclosed by fortified walls. **Puerta de Sevilla,** a horseshoe-shaped passageway, burrows through the ramparts, to the right and up C. San Pedro as you leave the bus stop. The adjoining **Alcázar de la Puerta de Sevilla** dates back to the reign of Augustus in the first century BC (open Fri.-Sat. 11am-1pm, Sun. 11am-2pm). Opulent Baroque mansions lie farther uphill past the Alcázar, while the **Alcázar del Rey Don Pedro,** a fortress of Almohad origin, is at the eastern edge of town. Just west of the town limits, by the ruins of the most important **Necrópolis Romana**, is the **Museo Arqueológico.** The museum contains urns and such from over a thousand tombs (including some pre-Roman burial mounds) that were unearthed at the necropolis. (Roman necropolis and museum open Tues.-Sat. 10am-2pm and 4-6pm, Sun. 10am-2pm.)

Accommodations are generally cheaper and easier to find than in Sevilla. Bedrooms and common bathrooms at **Pénsion Comercio,** C. Torre del Oro, 56 (tel. 414 00 18), just inside the Puerta de Sevilla and to the left, are spic, span, and spacious. It comes with a rapturous view of the Alcázar from the terrace and a restaurant downstairs. Breakfast 350ptas, *platos* 400-600ptas, *menú del día* 1100ptas. (Singles 1500ptas, with bath 2000ptas. Doubles 3000ptas, with bath 4000ptas.) **Pensión Hoyos,** C. San Pedro, 3 (tel. 414 12 54), has basic rooms, slightly dirty floors, and odd metal bed frames. It's just to the right from the bus stop. (Singles 1200ptas, with bath 1500ptas. Doubles 2000ptas, with bath 3000ptas. Showers 200ptas.)

Tourist information is available from the **Casa de la Cultura,** Pl. Descalzas, s/n (tel. 414 22 00). From the bus stop, head right up C. San Pedro, pass through the Puerta de Sevilla, and take C. Prim to the left. Keep going until Pl. San Fernando, then take C. Martil L. (on the far size of the plaza) down to Pl. Descalzas. (Open Mon.-Fri. 8am-3pm, Sat. 8am-1pm.) The **post office** is at C. Prim, 29 (tel. 414 15 62; open for stamps, Lista de Correos and telegrams Mon.-Fri. 8am-3pm, Sat. 9am-2pm). **Postal code** is 41410; **telephone code** 95. For **medical assistance,** at C. Paseo de La Feria, s/n, call 414 09 97. The **police,** Pl. San Fernando, s/n, take calls at 414 00 08.

Carmona is a convenient, one-hour **bus** ride from Sevilla. (Mon.-Fri. 23 per day, Sat. 10 per day, Sun. 7 per day; 250ptas.) In Sevilla, buses leave across the street from the south side of the station. In Carmona, buses leave from in front of Bar La Parada at C. San Pedro, 31. For information call Empresa Casal at 441 06 58.

Ecija

Hemmed in by hills and the Río Genil, Ecija lies in a depression of the fertile *campiña* midway between Sevilla and Córdoba. Long an unusual temptation for sloganeers, Ecija has been tagged the *"sartén de Andalucía"* (frying pan of Andalucía) and *"la ciudad del sol"* (city of sun) for its torrid summers, as well as *"la ciudad de las torres"* (the city of towers) for its whopping number of *azulejo* and Baroque brick belfries (11). The city prospered during the Renaissance and even more so during the 18th century, periods when most of the city's many churches and palaces were built. Nearly every block in Ecija has its very own local belfry or distinguished palace or church. Los Siete Niños de Ecija, Spain's baddest gang of outlaws, was allegedly once based here. Ecija's prosperity and proximity to major cultural centers has induced its moneyed classes to remain, which explains the general air of prosperity evident in shops and dress.

The center of town is Plaza de España, lined by old houses, shops, a casino, and the Iglesia de Santa María; it is appropriately known as "El Salón" (The Drawing Room), where locals gather for the evening *paseo.* The Neoclassical **Ayuntamiento** lords it over the south side of the square. There's a Roman mosaic and a Renaissance coffered ceiling within. A **tourist information booth** (tel. 483 30 62) inside to the left dispenses brochures, including three self-guided tours of the city's representative monuments starting from Plaza de España. (Open Mon.-Fri. 9am-2pm, Sat.-Sun. 10am-2pm.)

Next to the Ayuntamiento, the Baroque **Iglesia de Santa María** is known for its facade and ostentatious altar and choir. **Iglesia de la Concepción,** directly south of Pl. España, sports a Renaissance façade and Mudejar coffered ceiling. In the southeastern quarter of town, **Palacio de Benamejí** is distinguished by its size, its marble portal, and its flanking towers. The guard on duty will usually let you see the impressive collection of old carriages inside. Regarded as an exceptional example of Andalusian Gothic Mudejar, the nearby **Iglesia de Santiago** has a Baroque courtyard and belfry. To the north, the **Palacio de Peñaflor** is resplendent with a curving balconied facade painted in fresco, a pink marble Baroque portal, and a striking courtyard and staircase. (Open Mon.-Fri. 10am-1pm and 5-8pm.) Battles rage over the relative merits of the city's many belfries. The consensus seems to be that the **Iglesia de San Gil's** is the most graceful and **Iglesia de San Juan's** the most beautiful.

Between Pl. España and Palacio Peñaflor, **Fonda Santa Cruz,** C. Practicante Romero Gordillo, 8 (tel. 483 02 22), is installed in a typical Ecijan two-story house with a courtyard, potted plants, a fountain, and a florid wrought-iron gate; to enter, ring the bell. (Singles 1200ptas. Doubles 2400. No winter heating.) On a sidestreet about one block west of Pl. España, **Bar Chico,** C. San Francisco, 9 (tel. 483 00 03), is excellent both for morning breakfast and evening *tapas* (100ptas). Service is amiable and brisk, the clientele varied and lively, the food always *en su punto* (on the money). Typical Ecijan breakfast fare is a *mollete* or *torta de manteca* (local English muffins) with butter and jam (150ptas). Another 150ptas buys a tall glass of fresh-squeezed orange juice. The owner reputedly sings *zarzuelas* (arias) as he works.

Osuna

It's easy to imagine the Dukes of Osuna sallying forth from their mountaintop retreat to scour the countryside for the *osos* (bears) that once lumbered about the land. Only Osuna's handsome stone mansions remain to reveal its former status as a cushy ducal seat.

Crowning the hilltop, the **Iglesia Catedral** has dominated the horizon since its erection in 1535. The third Duke of Osuna was protector for a time of the renowned Valencian painter Ribera, hence the church's possession of four excellent Riberas. The dukes had their very own private chapel built beneath the main one, complete with pulpit and choir. The neighboring 16th-century mausoleum holds the Duke of Osuna's treasures. By far the most intriguing of the chambers is the **Panteón Ducal,** a morbid sepulchre with low ceilings. Only three empty spaces await the remaining nobility. Goya's portrait of this family—his most assiduous private patrons—now hangs in the Prado. The only duke not buried here lies in a marble sarcophagus upstairs because his coffin couldn't fit through the sepulchre's entrance. (Open Tues.-Sun. 10am-1:30pm and 4-7pm; winter Tues.-Sun. 10am-1:30pm and 3:30-6:30pm. July-Aug. closed Sun. afternoons. Admission by guided tour only, 150ptas.)

Downhill from the church's entrance is the **Monasterio de la Encarnación.** A resident nun will show you room upon room of polychromed wooden sculptures and silver crucifixes, but the must-sees are the 18th-century statue of *Cristo de la Misericordia* in the adjoining Baroque church and the Sevillian *azulejo* tiles in the shadow of the sun-filled patio. (Open Tues.-Sun. 10am-1:30pm and 4-7pm; winter Tues.-Sun. 10am-1:30pm and 3:30-6:30pm. July-Aug. closed Sun. afternoons. Admission 125ptas. Divine sweets really made by monks 250-350ptas.)

The **Museo Arqueológico,** on the road to the hilltop from Plaza Mayor, houses a collection of Roman artifacts found in the vicinity and replicas of pieces sent on to Madrid and Paris. (Same hours as the Iglesia and the Monasterio. Admission 125ptas.)

Best suited to daytrippers, Osuna has few beds. Hike past the Pl. Mayor to reach **Hostal Cinco Puertas,** C. Carrera, 79 (tel. 481 12 43). Although it has comfortable rooms; the bar below sends up a bit of noise. (Singles 1770ptas. Doubles 2975ptas, with shower 3435ptas.) The convenient restaurant charges faintly stiff prices. The *gazpacho flamenco* (400ptas) and the *cocido* (stew) are particularly good. **Restaurante Mesón del Duque,** Pl. Duquesa, 2 (tel. 481 13 01), on the road to the Museo Arqueológico and Iglesia Colegial supplies a *menú* (1200ptas), several fish dishes (500-900ptas), and a panoply of tortillas (400ptas). Flower-filled view of the plains from an outdoor terrace. (Open Tues.-Sun. 1-4:30pm and 9-11:30pm.) The **market** adjoins Plaza Mayor (open Mon.-Sat. 8am-2pm).

A new **tourist office** near the bus station will have opened by '93, but you'll have to obtain the telephone number and schedule from the temporary tourist office at C. Sevilla, 22 (tel. 481 22 11). Mail away at the **post office,** C. San Agustín, 4 (tel. 481 09 61), between Pl. Santa Rita and Pl. Mayor (open Mon.-Sat. 9am-2pm). The **postal code** is 41640; the **telephone code** 95. For **medical assistance,** call Hospital Ntra. Sra. de la Merced, C. Carrera, 84 (tel. 481 09 00). In an **emergency** dial 091. The **municipal police** are at 481 00 50, on Pl. Mayor.

Halfway between Sevilla and Antequera, Osuna is an easy daytrip from either. **Trains** stop at the small, desolate station on Av. Estación (tel. 481 03 08), a 15-minute walk from the center. To reach Pl. Mayor from the train station, walk up Av. Estación, which curves right onto C. Mancilla. When you hit a small plaza with Hostal Granadino, turn left onto C. Carmen and then right onto C. Sevilla. There are trains from here to Sevilla (4 per day, 1 1/4 hr., 540ptas), Málaga (2 per day, 1 3/4 hr., 635ptas), Granada (2 per day, 3 1/4 hr., 905ptas), and Bobadilla (4 per day, 45min., 340ptas). The new **bus station** is at Av. de la Constitución, s/n (tel. 481 01 46), a 10-minute walk from the center. To reach Pl. Mayor from the bus station, exit the back of the station where the buses pull in, walk up the ramp and go downhill. When you reach little Pl. Santa Rita, head right on the main road, Carerra Caballos. **Empresa diaz Paz** or **Dipasa** (tel. 481 01 46) runs buses to Sevilla (12 per day, Sat. 7 per day, Sun. 5 per day; 1 1/2 hr.; 700ptas). Other **empresas** stop here for connections to Málaga (3 per day, 2 1/2 hr., 1000ptas), Granada (3 per day, 3 1/2 hr., 1350ptas), and Antequera (6 per day, 1hr., 550ptas).

Córdoba

Córdoba, one of the oldest cities on the Iberian Peninsula, has seen Christianity, Islam, and Judaism meet in harmony and strife for centuries. The city's first inhabitants lived in the caves of the nearby Sierra Morena. In 152 BC Roman Praetor Claudius Marcellus, considered by many the founder of Córdoba, proclaimed the city capital of Roman Ulterior Spain. With Romanization Córdoba became a major cultural center, producing such luminaries as the playwright Seneca. It was under the Muslims (711-1263) that Córdoba once again emerged as a seat of intellectual and political power, capital of the western Caliphate (929-1031) when the Ummayads broke with Baghdad. During and following its medieval "Golden Age," Córdoba was birthplace to many of

Córdoba 375

Córdoba

1. Provincial Tourist Office
2. Municipal Tourist Office
3. Main Post Office
4. Telephones
5. Train Station
6. Bus Station (Transportes Ureña and Empresa Bacoma)
7. Bus Station (Alsina-Graells Sur)
8. Medical Assistance (Casa de Socorro)
9. Youth Hostel
10. Mezquita
11. Alcázar
12. Sinagoga
13. Museo de Bellas Artes
14. Museo Julio Romero de Torres
15. Posada del Potro
16. Museo Taurino y de Arte Cordobés
17. Cristo de los Faroles
18. Museo Arqueológico
19. Palacio del Marqués de Viana
20. Puente Romano

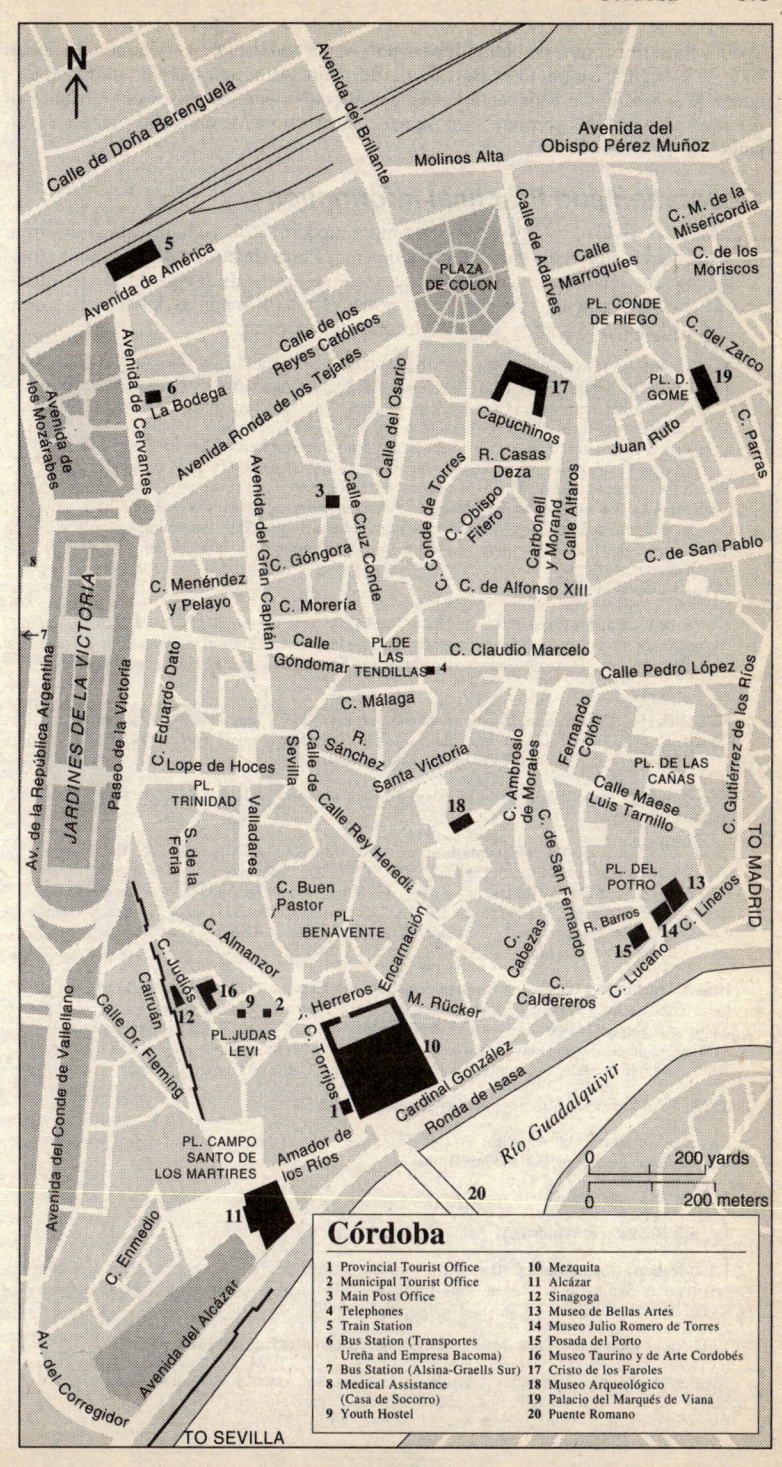

Spain's most illustrious, including Jewish philospher and theologian Maimonides, poet Luís de Góngora, and painter Bartolomé Bermejo. Although the Christians reconquered Córdoba in the 13th century, vestiges of *convivencia* (coexistence) remain. On the anniversary of the *mezquita*'s (mosque's) construction, Muslims and Catholics still gather for joint services.

Orientation and Practical Information

Córdoba is divided into two parts: the more modern northern half, extending from the train station on **Avenida de América** down to **Plaza de las Tendillas** in the center of the city; and the older, mazelike southern half called the **Judería** (old Jewish quarter). This famous tangle of narrow streets extends from Pl. Tendillas down to the banks of the Guadalquivir, winding past the Mezquita and Alcázar.

Tourist Offices: Provincial, C. Torrijos, 10 (tel. 47 12 35), on the western side of the Mezquita. To get to the tourist office from the train station (15-20min.), turn left onto Av. de América, then take the first right onto Av. del Gran Capitán, which widens into a pedestrian street. At the end of this wide walkway, turn left onto C. Góndomar, which ends at Pl. Tendillas. There, turn right onto C. Jesús y María, a street whose name becomes C. Saavedra and then Blanco Belmonte, and then bear left onto C. Céspedes, which ends at the Mezquita. Follow its large wall to the right and then around the corner to the left. The tourist office will be halfway down this road (Calle Torrijos) on the right, near the entrance to the Mezquita. Abundant information on Córdoba and all of Andalucía. English spoken. Open Mon.-Fri. 9:30am-2pm and 5-7pm, Sat. 10am-1pm; winter Mon.-Fri. 9:30am-2pm and 3:30-5:30pm, Sat. 10am-1pm. **Municipal,** Pl. Judas Levi (tel. 47 20 00; ask the switchboard operator for ext. 209 or *oficina municipal de turismo*), 2 blocks west of the Mezquita. Open Mon.-Fri. 8am-3pm.

Currency Exchange: Cajasur, C. Medina y Corella, s/n, near the tourist office. 1% commission if you change more than 50,000ptas (min. charge 500ptas). Open Mon.-Fri. 8:30am-2pm. Dozens of banks along Av. del Gran Capitán, Ronda de los Tejares, and near Pl. Tendillas also change money.

Post Office: C. Cruz Conde, 15 (tel. 47 82 67), just north of Pl. Tendillas. Open for stamps and Lista de Correos Mon.-Fri. 8am-9pm, Sat. 9am-7pm. **Telegrams:** tel. 47 20 09 or 47 03 45. Open Mon.-Fri. 8am-9pm, Sat. 9am-7pm. **Postal Code:** 14070.

Telephones: Pl. Tendillas, 7. Open Mon.-Fri. 9:30am-2pm and 5-11pm, Sat. 9:30am-2pm. **Telephone Code:** 957.

Trains: Av. América, 130. (**Information:** tel. 49 02 02.) To: Sevilla (16 per day, *AVE* 50min., 1700-2300ptas; *talgo* 1 3/4 hr., 1415ptas; *rápido* 1 /2 hr., 1025ptas; *tranvía* 2hr., 660ptas); Málaga (8 per day, *talgo* 2-3hr., 1915ptas; *rápido* 3hr., 1395ptas; *tranvía* 3hr., 955ptas); Algeciras (2 per day, 5 1/2 hr., 2095ptas); Madrid (5 per day, 4 1/2-8 hr., *talgo* 4100ptas; *expreso* 2950ptas); València (3 per day, 4110ptas; *rápido* T. de Oro, 10:12am, 5615ptas). **RENFE,** Ronda de los Tejares, 10 (tel. 47 58 54). Open Mon.-Fri. 9am-1:30pm and 5-7:30pm.

Buses: Transportes Ureña and **Empresa Bacoma,** Av. Cervantes, 22 (tel. 47 23 52). To: Sevilla (3 per day, 2-3hr., 1055ptas); Jaén (5 per day, 3hr., 790ptas); Madrid (3 per day, 5 1/2 hr., 2840ptas); València (3 per day, 4075ptas); Barcelona (6pm, 6700ptas). **Alsina-Graells Sur,** Av. Medina Azahara, 29 (tel. 23 64 74). To: Sevilla (16 per day, 2-3hr., 800ptas); Granada (8 per day, 3-4hr., 1485ptas); Málaga (2 per day, 3 1/2 hr., 1295ptas); Cádiz (7:30am, 1870ptas).

Taxis: Tendillas (tel. 47 02 91) or **Gran Capitán** (tel. 41 51 53).

Car Rental: Hertz, Av. América, s/n (tel. 47 72 43), next to the train station. Open Mon.-Fri. 8:30am-1pm and 5-8pm, Sat. 9:30am-1pm.

Luggage Storage: Paquete-Exprés, next to the train station, 200ptas per locker.

English Bookstore: Windsor, C. Santa Victoria, 4 (tel. 48 53 11).

Laundromat: Cordobesas, C. Barroso, 2, midway between Pl. Tendillas and the Mezquita. Not self-service; 5kg 1250ptas. Open Mon.-Fri. 9am-1:30pm and 5-8:30pm, Sat. 9:30am-1:30pm; winter Mon.-Fri. 9:30am-1:30pm and 4:30-8pm, Sat. 9:30am-1pm.

Late-Night Pharmacy: On a rotating basis. Refer to list posted outside every pharmacy.

Medical Assistance: Urgencias Avenida de América, Av. América, s/n (tel. 47 23 82), 1/2 km east of the train station. **Urgencias Santa Victoria,** C. Jerez, s/n (tel. 20 38 05), in *sector sur* on the other bank of the Guadalquivir. **Ambulance:** tel. 29 55 70.

Fire: tel. 080.

Emergency: National Police, tel. 091. **Municipal Police,** tel. 092.

Accommodations and Camping

Córdoba is especially crowded in summer. Call ahead for reservations. The following prices include hot showers.

Residencia Juvenil Córdoba (HI), Pl. Judas Levi (tel. 29 01 66; fax 29 05 00), next to the municipal tourist office. Hostel heaven: impeccably clean, brand-new glass building with white marble floors in the heart of the Judería. Each room has 2 firm beds and a sink. Nice dining room. 3-day max stay. No curfew. Must evacuate room for cleaning 10am-noon. Membership required, but may be purchased on the spot (500ptas, over 25 1000ptas). Call to reserve in the summer. 715ptas per person, over 25 885ptas. With breakfast 850ptas, over 25 1150ptas. *Media pensión* 1300ptas, over 25 1550ptas. *Pensión completa* 1675ptas, over 25 2100ptas.

Near the Train Station

Most places are cheap and feel safe, but bring the earplugs.

Casa de Huéspedes Córdoba, Av. Cervantes, 22 (tel. 47 72 04), diagonally across from the train station. Trapezoidal rooms on perhaps the noisiest street in existence. Singles 1200ptas. Doubles 1700ptas. Triples 2500ptas.

Hostal Perales, Av. Mozárabes, 15 (tel. 23 03 25). Turn right down Av. América as you exit the train station, and go past the park until you reach Av. Mozárabes and the big yellow sign on the left. Clean, verging on institutional. Washbasins in each room. Singles 1200ptas. Doubles 2200ptas.

In the Judería

The Judería's white-washed walls, narrow twisty streets, and proximity to the major sights make it the most pleasing and convenient area to stay in Córdoba. Accommodations cluster around **Calle Cardenal González.**

Huéspedes Martínez Rücker, Martínez Rücker, 14 (tel. 47 25 62), just east of the Mezquita. Airy, arboreal courtyard. Charming furnishings and rooms. Singles 1500ptas. Doubles 3000ptas.

Hostal-Residencia Séneca, C. Conde y Luque, 7 (tel. 47 32 34), 2 bl. north of the Mezquita. Impeccably maintained, but some rooms tiny. Breakfast with the patio-based crawling turtle. Owner speaks English. Singles 1875ptas. Doubles 3500ptas, with bath 4500ptas. Triples 4950ptas. Breakfast included.

Hostal Mari 2, C. Horno de Porros, 6 (tel. 48 61 85 or 48 60 04), between C. Cardenal González and C. Calderos. Simple, adequate rooms. Patrons may use the washing machine. Some parking—a rarity in the Judería. No check-in 2-4pm. Singles start at 1000ptas. Doubles 2000ptas. Triples 3000ptas.

Fonda Rey Heredía, C. Rey Heredía, 26 (tel. 47 41 82), on a narrow street parallel to the northeastern corner of the Mezquita. High ceilings, full-length mirrors, spacious courtyard, and jigsaw puzzle decor. Some windowless rooms get a little stuffy in the summer, but most have fans. Modern bathrooms. Singles 1500ptas. Doubles 3000ptas. Triples 4000ptas. Open Feb.-Nov.

Hostal El Portillo, C. Cabezas, 2 (tel. 47 20 91), off C. Caldereros, the continuation of C. Rey Heredía near the river. Lush patio and stained-glass window. Rooms have lace curtains and small beds. Bathrooms could be cleaner. Singles 1500ptas. Doubles 3000ptas. Triples 4000ptas.

Hostal Mari, C. Pimentera 6 and 8 (tel. 47 95 75), off C. Calderos, the continuation of C. Rey Heredia near the river. Simple, clean rooms and verdant garden. Singles 1250ptas. Doubles 2500ptas.

Off Plaza de las Tendillas

Hotels in this busy plaza enjoy the atmosphere of modern Córdoba, yet are only five minutes north of the Judería. The *terrazas* bounded by Renaissance-style buildings make popular local hangouts.

Hotel Residencia Boston, C. Málaga, 2 (tel. 47 41 76; fax 47 85 23), on Pl. Tendillas. This 2-star hotel's prices are more suited for a *hostal*. Stuffed with amenities: A/C, winter heating, TV, telephones and baths in modern rooms. Laundry service available. Full-time concierge. Singles with small bath (no TV) 1900ptas, with TV 2300ptas. Doubles with bath 3900ptas.

Hostal Residencia La Paz, C. Morería, 7 (tel. 47 61 79), off the plaza on a pedestrian side street beside C. Cruz Conde. Old paintings, antique lamps, and religious memorabilia from *pueblos* around Córdoba create an eerie atmosphere. Owner, a dead ringer for Alfred Hitchcock, will narrate stories about his bric-a-brac. Large tapestry-laden rooms with winter heating, away from the noisy street. Doubles 2650ptas, with shower 3180ptas, with bath 3445ptas. Triples with shower 4770ptas.

Hostal Las Tendillas, C. Jesús y María, 1 (tel. 47 30 29), on Pl. Tendillas. Not distinctive, but rooms and bathrooms are respectable. Deafening plaza revelry below. Refrigerator in hall; overnight laundry service. Singles 1300ptas. Doubles 2400ptas. Triples 3300ptas.

Elsewhere in Córdoba

Hostal Maestre, C. Romero Barros, 16 (tel. 47 24 10; fax 47 53 95), near the Plaza del Porto, between C. San Fernando and the plaza. Clean rooms with windows, washbasins, and fans. Patio with gas stove and refrigerator. Sink and clothesline on terrace for washing clothes. Parking. Singles 1600ptas, with bath 2000ptas. Doubles 2800ptas, with bath 3800ptas. Triples 3800ptas, with bath 4800ptas.

Campamento Municipal, Av. Brillante (tel. 47 20 00); ask for *Camping Municipal*). About 2km north of the train station: turn left on Av. América, left again at Av. Brillante, then walk uphill. Buses #10 and 11, which leave from Av. Cervantes near the station, run to the campsite. Pool next door. 365ptas per person, per tent and per car, under 11 265ptas.

La Campiña, Ctra. Aldea de Quintana a Santaella at km 11 (tel. 31 51 58), somewhat smaller and farther away from the city, also has a swimming pool. Bus to the campsite leaves from Av. República Argentina, 34 (tel. 23 14 01 for bus info). 325ptas per person and per car, children 275ptas.

Food

The famous Mezquita attracts more high-priced eateries than Mohammed did followers. These restaurants offer some of the best specialties, but if you're counting pesetas, branch out into the Judería. Many establishments here still offer *platos combinados* at a moderate 600ptas. For an afternoon beer, try the outdoor **cafés** along Pl. Tendillas and Pl. de la Corredera.

The regional specialties of Córdoba beckon to the visitor more insistently than a muezzin. High on any must-eat list are *gazpacho, salmorejo* (a *gazpacho*-like sauce topped with hard-boiled eggs), and *rabo de toro* (oxtail meat simmered in tomato sauce). The nearby towns of Montilla and Moriles produce superb sherries (about 150ptas per glass): a light, dry *fino;* a darker *amontillado;* a sweet *oloroso;* and a creamy *pedro ximénez*. Córdoba is swimming in nonalcoholic drinks as well: *horchata de chufa* (a sweet sedge-based orgeat), *horchata de almendra* (an almond orgeat), and *granizados* (iced drinks, known in the U.S. as slushies). For about 125ptas, you can indulge your sweet tooth in a light *pastel córdobés* (Córdoba pie) at any *confitería*.

Groceries: Supermercado Gama, C. Medina Azahara, 3 (tel. 23 36 36). Open Mon.-Fri. 9am-1:30pm and 5:30-8:30pm, Sat. 8am-2pm.

Sociedad de Plateros, C. San Francisco, 6 (tel. 47 00 42), between C. San Francisco and the top end of Pl. Potro. Big and bustling. Casual atmosphere attracts families by day and British students by night. Wide selection of *tapas*. Fresh fish, including *japuta*, almost every day (450ptas). Half-glass of wine 75ptas. Bar open 8am-4:30pm and 6:30pm-1am; meals served 1-4pm and 8:30-10pm.

Taberna Salinas, C. Tundidores, 3 (tel. 48 01 35), just south of the Ayuntamiento. A shining example of traditional Cordovan cooking: *salmorejo, carne con tomate,* and a surprisingly excellent spinach and garbanzo mash. Service a bit rushed, but the patio setting is calm. *Raciones* 500-600ptas. Open Mon.-Sat. noon-4pm and 8pm-midnight; winter Mon.-Sat. noon-4pm and 7:30-11:30pm.

Mesón-Restaurante El Tablón, C. González, 75 (tel. 47 60 61). An exception to the never-eat-near-the-Mezquita rule, on the southern corner of the Mezquita. Slightly slow service, but air conditioning makes the wait enjoyable. *Platos combinados* (600ptas) are carefully-prepared and big enough to fill a budgeting belly. Open noon-4pm and 7:30-11pm; winter noon-4pm and 7:30-10:30pm.

La Hostería de Laurel, C. Sevilla, 2 (tel. 47 30 40), 1 block west of Pl. Tendillas. Large, friendly bar with *tapas* (150-200ptas), including *salmorejo,* tortilla with potato and green peppers, and tuna meatballs. Owner makes wine from local grapes and wall decorations from local deer. The back hosts pool tournaments between English and Irish locals weeknights after 10pm. Wine 80-150ptas. Open Mon.-Sat. 8am-4pm and 8pm-midnight.

Taberna Juramento, C. Juramento, 6 (tel. 48 54 77), through eastern exit of Pl. Corredera and to the left. Vintage neighborhood bar with *tapas,* fish and meat *raciones* (375ptas), tortillas (250ptas), and salads (250-350ptas). Crowded on Sun. afternoons, when local families spill into the street waiting for a table. Open Thurs.-Tues. noon-5:30pm and 8:30pm-12:30am.

Cafetín Halal, C. Rey Heredía, 28 (tel. 47 76 30). A lone lingering outpost of Islamic influence. Locals drink herbal teas in low-key Arabic decor. Arabic sofa-tables and over 30 kinds of aromatic tea. Daily *menú* with *couscous* (800ptas) gets mixed reviews. Open noon-11pm.

Meson de las Cabezas, C. Cabezas, 17 (tel. 47 83 56), in the bottom of the Judería. Dark, dirty, musty, and wonderful. 10 kinds of wine and not much else. Cheerful host, deep chairs, and a quiet patio fountain. Half-glass of wine 50ptas. Open Tues.-Sun. 10:30am-3pm and 7-11pm.

Sights

Begun in 784 under the reign of Abderramán on the site of a Visigothic basilica, the **Mezquita** was intended to surpass all other mosques in grandeur. Over the next two centuries the spectacular golden-brown building was gradually enlarged to cover an area equivalent to several city blocks—the largest mosque in the Islamic world of that time. The airy space is enclosed by a massive wall reinforced with thick, square towers. The 14th-century Mudejar door, **La Puerta del Perdón,** opens to the north. A high crenellated wall on the north side of the Mezquita encloses the fabulous **Patio de los Naranjos** (open to the public all day). Arcaded on three sides, the courtyard features carefully spaced orange trees, palm trees, and fountains. Inside, 850 pink and blue marble, alabaster, and stone columns—no two the same height—support hundreds of red-and-white-striped two-tiered arches. Caliphal vaulting, greatly influential in later Spanish architecture, appears for the first time in the **Capilla Villaviciosa,** in the center of which is the **Mihrab** (chamber where the Koran was guarded). A prayer arch roughly facing Mecca resembles a keyhole. The intricate gold, pink, and blue marble Byzantine mosaics shimmering across its arches were given by the Emperor Constantine VII to the Córdoba caliphs. Three domes supported by woven lobed arches with typically Caliphal dense openwork enclose the *mihrab,* the lighted central dome.

When Córdoba was conquered by the Christians in 1236, the Mezquita was converted into a church. The **Capilla Mayor** (High Chapel) was enlarged in 1384, substituting ogival elements for arches and columns. In 1523 more drastic alterations stuck a full-blown Renaissance cathedral in the middle of the mosque. The uneasy hybrid disappointed even Carlos V, who originally authorized it. "You have destroyed something unique to create something commonplace," he reportedly griped. You can survey the whole cathedral/mosque mélange (along with the city's white houses and Indian-corn-colored roofs) from the **torre.** (Open April-Sept. 10am-7pm; Oct.-March 10am-1:30pm and 3:30-5:30pm. Admission 500ptas, ages 8-11 250ptas, free Sun. 10am-1pm.)

Just west of the Mezquita and closer to the river lies the **Alcázar.** This palace for Catholic monarchs was constructed in 1328 during the campaign for the conquest of Granada; between 1490 and 1821 it served as headquarters for the Inquisition. Its walls surround a manicured hedge garden with flower beds, terraced goldfish ponds, multiple fountains, and palm trees. Inside, the museum displays 1st-century Roman mosaics and a 3rd-century Roman marble sarcophagus. (Open May-Sept. Tues.-Sat. 9:30am-1:30pm and 5-8pm, Sun. 9:30am-1:30pm; Oct.-April 9:30am-1:30pm and 4-7pm. Gardens illuminated May-Sept. 10pm-1am. Admission 200ptas. Free Sun.)

The **Torre de la Calahorra,** south of the Alcázar and across the river, is a museum offering a kitschy multi-media review of Córdoba's history. One room houses a large-scale, detailed model of the Mezquita in its pre-cathedral heyday. Headphones are available in four languages. (Open May-Sept. 10am-2pm and 5:30-8:30pm; Oct.-Apr. 10:30am-8:30pm. Tower tour 250ptas; with multivision film 500ptas.)

The **Museo Taurino y de Arte Cordobés,** at Pl. Maimonides, is dedicated to *la lidia*, with galleries full of the heads of bulls who killed matadors and other unfortunates. Some rooms devote themselves to the *tauromaquia* of legendary Córdovan matadors, including Manolete. A copy of his tomb is exhibited beneath the hide of Islero, the bull that killed him. (Open May-Sept. Tues.-Sat. 9:30am-1:30pm and 5-8pm, Sun. 9:30am-1:30pm; Oct.-April Tues.-Sat. 9:30am-1:30pm and 4-7pm, Sun. 9:30am-1:30pm. Admission 200ptas, free Tues.)

Tucked away on C. Judíos, the **Sinagoga** is a solemn reminder of the expulsion of Spanish Jewry in 1492. The temple is decorated with Mozarabic patterns and Hebrew inscriptions from the psalms. The statue of Maimonides which marks the site was used as the model for the New Israeli Shekel. (Open Tues.-Sat. 10am-2pm and 3:30-5:30pm, Sun. 10am-1:30pm. Admission 50ptas.) Across from the Sinagoga sits **El Zoco,** a series of leather, ceramics, and silversmithing workshops within a beautiful courtyard. (Open Mon.-Fri. 10am-2:30pm and 4:30-8pm, Sat.-Sun. 10am-2pm.)

The **Museo Arqueológico** is on Pl. Paez, several blocks northeast of the Mezquita. Housed in a Renaissance mansion, the museum contains a chronological exhibit of tools, ceramics, statues, coins, jewelry, and sarcophagi, including intriguing stone carvings of lions that date from 500 BC. (Open Tues.-Sat. 10am-2pm and 5-7pm, Sun. 10am-1:30pm. Admission 250ptas. EEC citizens free.)

The **Museo de Bellas Artes** in Pl. Potro now occupies the building that was once King Fernando and Queen Isabel's Charity Hospital. Its small collection displays a couple of original Goya prints, an early 17th-century sculpture of a christ-child by Juan de Mesa y Velasco, and canvasses by Cordoban "primitives." (Open May-Sept. Tues.-Sat. 10am-2pm and 6-8pm, Sun. 10am-1:30pm; Oct.-April Tues.-Sat. 10am-2pm and 5-7pm, Sun. 10am-1:30pm. Admission 250ptas. EEC citizens and children under 12 free.) Also in the plaza, the **Museo Julio Romero de Torres** exhibits the major works (all portraits of Cordoban women) of this native artist. The **Posada del Potro,** a 14th-century inn mentioned in *Don Quixote,* is next door. It now contains the excellent collection of *guadameciles* formerly in the Museo Taurino.

North of the Palacio del Marqués de Viana, in Pl. Capuchinos, is the **Cristo de los Faroles.** Four large lanterns flank the crucifix, known for the anomalous two nails in the feet. This plaza, one of the most famous religious shrines in Spain, is frequently the site of all-night vigils.

The townspeople take great pride in their traditional *patios,* many dating from Roman times. These open-air courtyards offer hidden, tranquil pockets of orange and lemon trees, flowers, and fountains in the old quarter of the city. You'll find the most beautiful patios at the **Palacio del Marqués de Viana,** Pl. de Don Gome, 2. (Open June-Sept. Thurs.-Tues. 9am-2pm; Oct.-May Thurs.-Tues. 10am-1pm and 4-6pm, Sun. 9am-2pm. Closed 1st week of June. Admission 250ptas.)

Entertainment

To see some of the best **flamenco** in Spain, head for the **Tablao Cardenal,** Cardenal Herrero, 14 (tel. 48 03 46), facing the Mezquita. Professional dancers shimmy through the small and intimate room. (Shows Tues.-Sat. at 10:30pm. 2000ptas, including one drink.) The tourist office keeps a schedule of **bullfights** at Las Califas bullring; tickets range from 800 to 120,000ptas. The Feria in late May is an especially busy time for bullfighting.

For classical or traditional music, Córdoba's Municipal Orchestra gives Sunday morning **concerts** in the Alcázar (winter 11am). In the summer, the **Palacio de Viana** has frequent and free chamber music concerts on Fridays at 8:30pm. The city's open-air theater hosts concerts and festivals, including the irregularly scheduled **Festival Internacional de Guitarra** in June or July. For information and tickets stop by the office at F.P.M. Gran Teatro, Av. Gran Capitán, 3 (tel. 48 02 37 or 48 06 44; admission 400-1200ptas). You may also call the **ayuntamiento** at 47 20 00 and ask the switchboard operator for the Area de la Cultura.

The newest addition to Córdoba's cultural life is the **Filmoteca** on C. Medina y Corella, 5, just west of the Mezquita. On most nights one movie is screened in its original language, often subtitled in Spanish. Two films are shown Wednesday night. A beautiful old palace houses the Filmoteca, along with a phoneteca and a film library. (Information and tickets 80 03 00. Screenings at 8:30pm, or 8pm in winter. Admission 150ptas, 10-show pass 1000ptas.)

Although nightlife tends to be scattered throughout Córdoba, the Brillante area (uphill from and north of Av. América) has become popular due to the opening of many new bars. In addition, Pl. Tendillas and the area immediately north and west of C. Cruz Conde are filled with outdoor cafés and *terrazas*. Of Córdoba's festivals, **Semana Santa**, with its floats and parades, is the biggest. But Cordovans are proudest of their **Festival de los Patios,** in the first two weeks of May, when the city erupts with classical music concerts, flamenco dances, and a city-wide decorated-patio contest. Late May brings the week-long **Feria de Nuestra Señora de la Salud** (Fair of Our Lady of Good Health), for which thousands of Cordovan women don colorful, traditional apparel. Dozens of stands and a carnival attract large crowds every night. Córdoba celebrates its patroness in early September with the **Feria de Nuestra Señora de la Fuensanta.** The **Concurso Nacional de Arte Flamenco** (National Flamenco Contest) is held every third year during May.

Near Córdoba

Medina Azahara

Constructed in the 10th century by Abderramán III for the favorite wife in his harem, Azahara, the *medina* was considered one of the greatest palaces of its time. The pleasure palace, built into the Sierra Morena 8km northwest of the city, was divided into three terraces: one containing the palace, another the living quarters for the thousands of servants and attendants, and the third enclosing the *medina's* gardens. The site was planted with almond groves because Azahara was born in Granada and loved the snow in the Sierra Nevada. When spring came, the almond groves turned white, reminding Azahara of her beloved snow. The site was first excavated in 1944; before then, its existence had been mere rumor.

The **Salón de Abd al-Rahman III,** the grand hall on the lower terraces, is almost completely reconstructed to its original intricate and geometrical beauty. On first excavation these lofty ceilings were compacted into rubble only five feet high. Even with the rest of the palace in ruins, the structure retains its ancient grandeur. (Open Tues.-Sat. 10am-2pm. Admission 250ptas. EEC citizens free.)

Reaching Medina Azahara takes some effort; call ahead to make sure it's open (tel. 23 40 25). The O-1 bus (schedule information tel. 25 57 00) leaves from Av. Cervantes for Cruce Medina Azahara, stopping 3km from the site itself (about every hr. 6:30am-10:30pm, 90ptas). Don't jump any brick walls in the area; Ramón Sánchez keeps his fighting bulls here.

Almodóvar del Río

Thirteen km from Córdoba on the rail line to Sevilla, the impenetrable **castillo** at Almodóvar del Río crowns a solitary, rocky mount, commanding views of the countryside and the whitewashed houses of the village spiral below. The castle is a remarkably well-preserved example of Gothic-Mudejar architecture. On the second Sunday in May the town celebrates the **Romería de la Virgen de Fátima** with a parade from Cuatro Caminos to Fuen Real Bajo roads. Frequent trains run to Almodóvar del Río from Córdoba (7 per day, last train back at 10:12pm; 20min.; 125ptas).

Jaén

Capital of one of the few landlocked provinces in Andalucía, Jaén excels in the grainy fecundity of its countryside. Moreover, the city is Spain's olive capital; olive trees are absolutely everywhere. The mountains are just beyond the checkerboard of barley, hops, and wheat fields: Sierra Morena and Valdepeñas to the north, Sierras de Segura and Cazorla to the east, and Sierras de Huelma and Noalejo to the south. The

Moors called it *Geen* (caravan route), since this rugged terrain was the crossroads between Andalucía and Castilla. Even now Jaén identifies itself in relation to its illustrious neighbors; everywhere posters and signs declare it "the gateway to Andalucía." Sadly, there's no reason to linger in a gateway. Jaén is soporific.

Orientation and Practical Information

Best not to judge this provincial capital, 99km north of Granada, by its drab new city. Jaén is dominated by Castillo Santa Catalina, a 3km vertical crawl from the town center. **Paseo de la Estación** and **Avenida de Madrid** are the two main arteries in the new quarter. **Plaza de las Batallas** is a few blocks south (uphill) from the train station on Po. Estación; even farther south is the **Plaza de la Constitución,** the center of the new city. From the bus station on Av. Madrid, turn right (uphill) on Av. Madrid which also runs into Plaza de la Constitución. While many hostels and restaurants favor Pl. Constitución, the **barrio antiguo** and some other points of interest lie west of the plaza, at the bottom of the slope.

Tourist Office: C. Arquitecto Berges, 1 (tel. 22 27 37), off. Po. Estación. From the train station, walk south (uphill) on Po. Estación. Turn right on C. Arquitecto Berges after Pl. Batallas but before Pl. Constitución. From the bus station, walk uphill and take the first right on C. Pio XII; 2 bl. later it becomes C. Arquitecto Berges. English- and French-fluent staff has boundless info. Free maps and brochures. Open Mon.-Fri. 8:30am-2:30pm.

Post Office: Pl. Jardinillos (tel. 22 01 12), west of Pl. Constitución. Open Mon.-Sat. 9am-2pm. **Postal Code:** 23071.

Telephone Code: 953.

Trains: Po. Estación (tel. 25 56 07), at the bottom of the slope. RENFE has cut all southbound trains. To Madrid (2 per day, 4-5hr., 1500-1900ptas) and Sevilla (1 per day, 1300ptas). For other points outside Andalucía, go through the town of Esperluy, on the Madrid-Sevilla line. To Esperluy (3 per day, 1/2 hr., 200ptas). For other points in Andalucía, go via the town of Linares, north and east of Jaén.

Buses: Pl. Coca de la Piñera (tel. 25 01 06), just off Av. Madrid. To: Ubeda (9 per day, 11/2hr., 450ptas) via Baeza (1hr., 380ptas); Granada (9 per day, 1 3/4 hr., 745ptas); Málaga (4 per day, 4hr., 1710ptas); Córdoba (4 per day, 4hr., 750ptas); Sevilla (3 per day, 5hr., 1845ptas); Madrid (8 per day, 5hr., 1845ptas); Barcelona and València (2 per day, call **Bacoma** at 22 52 53 for times and prices).

Public Transportation: Although almost everything is within walking distance, a private company called **Urbanos** (tel. 25 43 03) runs a local bus service from stops such as Pl. Batallas and Pl. Constitución 7am-11pm.

Taxis: Service from Pl. Constitución (tel. 26 50 17).

Late-Night Pharmacy: 1/2 bl. downhill from Pl. Constitución on Po. Estación. Open 9:30am-2pm and 4:30-8pm.

Hospital: Hospital Provincial Princesa de España, Ctra. Madrid (tel. 22 26 50, 22 27 08).

Emergency: tel. 091.

Police: C. Arquitecto Berges, 13 (tel. 25 16 01).

Accommodations

A number of budget accommodations here seem ready for the wrecking ball; luckily competition for rooms isn't fierce.

Hostal Carlos V, Av. Madrid, 4 (tel. 22 20 91). The Emperor himself would have deigned to stay in these clean, classy rooms with embroidered bedspreads. No Titians on the walls, but all rooms have bath. Singles 1500ptas. Doubles 2500ptas.

Hostal Martín, C. Cuatro Torres, 5 (tel. 22 06 33), off Pl. Constitución. Big beds in slightly dingy rooms. Singles 1600-1700ptas. Doubles 2500-2600ptas.

Fonda La Española, C. Bernardo López, 9 (tel. 25 84 34), west of the cathedral off C. La Parra. A plastic flower frenzy close to the town's pedestrian area. Small rooms could use some renovation. Singles 1300ptas. Doubles 2600ptas, with bath 3000ptas.

Food

Not a vegetarian establishment in sight, but herbivores needn't fret. Most restaurants serve several types of salad, including a succulent local specialty called *ensalada de pimientos asados* (roasted sweet red pepper salad). **Calle Nueva,** a pedestrian side street a half-block downhill from Pl. Constitución, is lined with bars and restaurants to suit every taste and budget.

La Gamba del Oro, C. Nueva, 3 (tel. 26 16 13). A no-nonsense eatery with fried *raciones* of every conceivable fish under the sea for 600ptas. Savor a cold beer and 1/4 kg *calamares* for 400ptas. Open noon-4pm and 8:30pm-midnight.

Freiduría Pitufos, inside Café-Bar Los Mariscos, C. Nueva, 2. *Pitufo* means a dwarf or short person. *Churros y café* 150ptas. Irresistible desserts. Open 7am-midnight.

Sights

Dating from the 11th century, Spain's largest **hamman** (baths) have only recently been excavated and restored in Jaén. Originally for the public rather than private, they lack the decorative detail of the better-known *hamman* in Granada and Córdoba, although they have the same nifty star-shaped holes in the ceiling. Much of the original structure remains. Enter through the Renaissance **Palacio de Villadompardo**. Better yet, skip the lame baths and check out the **Museo de Artes y Costumbres Populares,** also in the palace. There's a permanent exhibition of costumes from the world over. (Open Tues.-Fri. 10am-2pm and 5-8pm, Sat.-Sun. 10am-2pm. Free with EEC passport or student ID.)

Between the train station and Pl. Batallas, at Po. Estación, 29, the **Museo Provincial** displays a dubious range of works, from prehistoric artifacts to Expressionist paintings. The famous *Toro Ibérico de Poruna* and *Sarcófago Paleocristiano de Martos* are exhibited here; they were discovered in a nearby Tartessian necropolis. (Open Tues.-Sat. 10am-2pm and 4-7pm, Sun. 10am-2pm. Free with EEC passport or student ID.)

Catedral de Santa María, a few blocks southwest of Pl. Constitución, features a remarkably intricate façade by Pedro Roldán, flanked by twin bell towers. The chapels within are upstaged by massive fluted Roman columns. The **Museo de la Catedral** is blessed with sculptures by Martínez Montañés and canvases by Alonso Cano. (Cathedral open 8:30am-1pm and 4:30-7pm. Museum open Sat.-Sun. 11am-1pm. Both free.)

The **Castillo de Santa Catalina** is being renovated yet again, but may be open by 1993. The castle was once an Arab palace from which a *taifa* was ruled. **Iglesia de la Magdalena** and **Iglesia de San Juan** were both built on the foundations of mosques and anchor neighborhoods worth a stroll. Both churches are in the northwest of the city, just east of the Carretera de Circunvalación. The **Monestir de Santa Clara,** just west of the tourist office, near the Plaza de los Jardinillos, has a lovely coffered ceiling and an image called *Cristo del bambú* which has been attributed to the School of Quito. (Ring the convent bell and a concierge will open the monastery.)

Ubeda

On a ridge above the olivey Guadalquivir valley, Ubeda encloses narrow cobbled streets, ivied remnants of medieval walls, and a passel of old palaces and churches. A stop on the crucial trade route linking Castilla with Andalucía in the 16th century, the town battened on the American gold shipped up from Sevilla. The resulting showpiece owes its existence to Spanish Renaissance architecture and town planning. Shortly thereafter, economic anorexia hit the town as traders bagged the worn Ubeda route. Hence the origin of the Spanish idiom for remoteness—"go via the hills of Ubeda." Few tourists do.

Orientation and Practical Information

You'll find plenty of beds along **Calle Ramón y Cajal** or on **Plaza de Andalucía**, both of which are northeast of the bus station. The old district is downhill, to the southeast.

To reach C. Ramón y Cajal from the bus station, walk two blocks left (uphill) to a large street, then two blocks right to a big, six-way intersection. Calle Ramón y Cajal is the second road from the left. To reach Pl. Andalucía from the bus station, start from the same six-way intersection and take the second road from the right. At the big stone building on your left (Hospital de Santiago), turn left onto Calle Obispo Cobos. This leads to Pl. Andalucía.

Tourist Office: Pl. Ayuntamiento (tel. 75 08 97), next to the Ayuntamiento. Head for Pl. Andalucía, look for the sign, and follow C. Real to the bottom. Open Mon.-Sat. 8am-2:30pm.

Post Office: C. Trinidad, 1 (tel. 75 00 31). Left on C. Trinidad as you face Iglesia de la Trinidat in the Pl. Andalucía. Open for mail and **telegrams** Mon.-Fri. 9am-2pm, Sat. 9am-1pm. **Postal Code:** 23400.

Trains: No train service to Ubeda. The nearest station is in Linares, 40min. northwest by bus (see below).

Buses: C. San José, s/n (tel. 75 21 57). To: Baeza (7 per day, 15min., 80ptas); Linares train station (6 per day, 40min., 175ptas); Jaén (7 per day, 1hr., 450ptas); Córdoba (3 per day, 2 1/2 hr., 1105ptas); Sevilla (3 per day, 5hr., 2175ptas); Madrid (2 per day, 51/2 hr., 2225ptas); Barcelona (4 per day, 12hr., 5615ptas).

Taxis: Service available from Pl. Andalucía (tel. 75 12 13), but major points of interest are within walking distance.

Late-Night Pharmacy: C. Rastro, 5 (tel. 75 01 51), 1 bl. uphill from bus station on right. Open 9am-2pm and 5:30-8pm.

Medical Services: Residencia Sanitária (tel. 75 11 03).

Police: (tel. 75 00 23), in the Ayuntamiento next to Turismo.

Accommodations and Food

Despite Ubeda's isolation, lodgings are generally expensive and inconveniently located.

Hostal Victoria, C. Alaminos, 5 (tel. 75 29 52). From Pl. Andalucía, C. Gradas leads to C. Alaminos if you veer right on C. Muro. This totally new *hostal* goes batty with color TV, A/C and winter heating, and baths for every room. Singles 1400ptas. Doubles 2400ptas.

Hostal Sevilla, C. Ramón y Casal, 9 (tel. 75 06 12). Carpeted halls lead to decent-sized rooms, some with phones. Large TV lounge. Singles with bath 1900ptas. Doubles with bath 3000ptas.

A roster of regional specialties: *andrajos* (a soup made with ground chickpeas), *pipirrana* (a sauté of tomato, green pepper, onion, egg, and tuna salad). The **market** is down Corredera de San Fernando from Pl. Andalucía. (Open Mon.-Sat. 8am-2:30pm.)

Marisquería La Isla, C. Ramón y Casal, next to Hostal Sevilla. An air-conditioned, landlocked island of superb *raciones* and *platos combinados* (500-900ptas). Mainly fish. Open noon-3pm and 7-11pm.

Cafetería Atalaya, C. Rastro, 2 (tel. 75 36 96), on Pl. Andalucía. Locals salivate when they think about Atalaya's outdoor dining, congenial service, and varied menu. Open late August-early July 8am-12:30am. Dining room open 2-5pm and 9-11pm.

Sights

Stateliness and balance mark Pl. Vázquez de Molina, the town's historic center (follow signs from Pl. Andalucía). **Palacio de las Cadenas** now serves as the town hall. Vázquez's palace has an attractive, open-air courtyard below. To the south, at the wide end of Pl. Vázquez de Molina, is **Iglesia de Santa María de los Reales Alcázares**, with chapels enclosed by grilles wrought by maestro Bartolomé.

Just as impressive is Gothic **Iglesia de San Pablo,** on Pl. 1 de Mayo, with its Plateresque, concave southern portal. The magnificent chapels within are embellished with intricate wrought-iron grilles. (Open 9am-1pm and 7-9pm. Free.)

Carlos V commissioned an enormous palace here, but when the architect died (shortly after finishing the plans) construction fell to his lackey, Vandelvira, a developer of the Spanish Renaissance style. The result is a characteristically severe, monumental profile. Only the **Sacra Capilla del Salvador,** at the narrow end of the square, and the main façade remain. (Chapel open 5-7pm. If the front door is closed, go around the side and ring the sacristy bell.)

Ubeda is well-placed for jaunts into the Andalusian wilds. Numerous whitewashed villages and ruins dot the mountainous countryside to the east and south, outside *Let's Go's* turf. **Quesada,** 15km south of Cazorla, is a balm to the urbanite seeking blissful oblivion among whitewashed houses and Roman, Islamic, and Christian ruins. **Orcera,** less than 100km east of Ubeda, is a traditional highland village devoted to the wood trade. These scraps of Eden lie amid the national parks in the Sierras de Cazorla y Segura.

Baeza

Baeza is charmingly unaware of its allure. Despite the noteworthy monuments on every street corner and the winding, walled streets, accommodations are scarce, backpackers are rare, and the tourist director isn't really sure when the bus leaves for the train station. There are few places in Spain as picture-perfect, and as utterly uncorrupted by tourists, as this town.

Orientation and Practical Information

Plaza del Pópulo, at the entrance to the city coming from Jaén, is surrounded by the well-preserved **slaughterhouse** and the former city hall, which is now the tourist office. Eroded stone lions guard the central fountain, and Princess Imilce, wife of Hannibal, strikes a pose atop the fountain's pillar. Next to this is the main **Paseo de la Constitución,** where the entire town turns out in the evenings to take refreshment and shoot the bull.

Tourist Office: Pl. de Pópulo (tel. 74 04 44). Free maps and brochures. English and French spoken. Open Mon.-Sat. 8am-2:30pm.

Post Office: C. Julio Burell, 19 (tel. 74 08 39). **Telegrams. Postal Code:** 23440.

Telephone Code: 953.

Trains: Estación Linares-Baeza (tel. 65 01 31), 8km from town. Buses run to the train station, but schedules are uncertain, as are RENFE schedules, due to the madness of 1992. Consult *Guía RENFE* or call the train station for schedule information.

Buses: Av. Puche y Pardo, 1 (tel. 74 04 68), at the uphill end of C. San Pablo, in the north of the city. To get to the station, walk north on Po. Constitución to Pl. España. C. San Pablo leads north out of the plaza. To: Ubeda (9 per day, 15min., 75ptas); Jaén (9 per day, 45min., 360ptas); Granada (6 per day, 1 3/4 hr., 1050ptas). To reach Córdoba and most other major cities, you must switch in either Jaén or Ubeda.

Late-Night Pharmacy: Farmacia Lorite, C. Julio Burell, 41 (tel. 74 03 93), 1 bl. downhill from the bus station on C. Julio Burell. Not that late.

Hospital: Sor Felisa Cien, 1 (tel. 74 01 58).

Police: C. Cardenal Benavides, 7 (tel. 74 06 59).

Accommodations and Food

Accommodations and restaurants are scarce—but then, so are tourists.

Hostal Residencia Comercio, C. San Pablo, 21 (tel. 74 01 00), on the street leading from Po. Constitución to the bus station. In a 4-story building. Halls decked out with pots of brass. Large, attractive rooms, some furnished with turn-of-the-century antiques. Poet Antonio Machado snored here in 1912. Singles with shower 1200ptas. Doubles 2300ptas, with bath 2700ptas.

Restaurante la Gondola, Pl. España, 7. *Churros* and croissants (160ptas), *platos combinados*, pizzas, *menús* (850ptas), and ice cream. Open 8:30am-2am.

Bar La Paz, Po. Constitución, 6. Outdoor tables. *Platos combinados* (500ptas) for misers. Backgammon champs come from far and wide.

Sights

Fortunately for the lazy, most of Baeza's monuments practically smother each other. If a monument is closed, ask in the tourist office; the Ayuntamiento may open it.

In the heart of the city, just north of Pl. Constitución, is the **Palacio de Jabalquinto,** now the Seminario. Somewhere on the ornate Plateresque façade and sober patio are written the names of its graduates, along with a caricature of an unpopular professor, in bull's blood. At night, this area is suffused with mystery and calm; bats flutter about and eye succulent necks. Across from the Palacio, poet Antonio Machado taught French at the Renaissance **Universidad** (founded in 1595 and disbanded in the 19th century). The amphitheater bears a fine Mudejar ceiling. (Open 9am-2pm.)

The **Ayuntamiento,** formerly the town jail and court, is pierced with magnificent Plateresque windows; the cornice is lined with portrait medallions. Other Renaissance structures line Cuesta de San Felipe on its way to the **catedral,** a soaring, brightly colored thing whose interior was remodelled by Vandelvira and his groupies.

Iglesia de San Andrés is faced with a Plateresque south portal. But perhaps most remarkable are the Gothic paintings in the **sacristía** and the choir stalls from the now-vanished Santa María del Alcázar. The church's square—**Plaza de la Fuente de Santa María**--is named for its 16th-century fountain. The glint of gold in the cathedral's *retablo* is blinding. (Church open 10am-2pm and 5-7pm. Free, but 100ptas donation requested.) For a death-defying view of rolling hills of olive groves and the surrounding mountain ranges on the horizon, face the cathedral, take the street that winds behind it to the right, and follow the arrows to the end of C. Plaza Santa Catalina.

Cazorla

High in the hills 52km east of Ubeda, Cazorla clings to the edge of **Parque Natural de las Sierras de Segura y Cazorla.** Indeed, this puny town of pastel houses doesn't have much of an identity other than its relation to the park.

Cazorla's squares are three, each within five minutes of the others. Buses screech into the main square, **Plaza de la Constitución.** Facing the peaks from here, **Plaza de Corredera** lies down the street to the right (south) and **Plaza del Mercado** is behind and downhill (southwest).

For most, Cazorla's enticement is the **Parque Natural,** a protected woodland and game reserve well-watered by springs and scented with thyme, lavender, rosemary, and other Mediterranean flora. The mighty Río Guadalquivir—Andalucía's lifeline—wells up here. Hunting, fishing, and camping are permitted in designated areas, and hiking along marked paths. For more info on the park, storm the park office at **La Agencia de Medio Ambiente,** C. Martino Falero, 11, the white building with green trim a few blocks uphill from Pl. Constitución. (Open Tues.-Sun. 11am-2pm and 5-8pm.) **Buses** run to Cotorios, in the middle of the park. (Mon.-Sat. 2 per day at 6:30am and 2:20pm, 1 1/2 hr., 350ptas. Return Mon.-Sat. 2 per day at 8am and 5pm.)

Two ancient castles stand like forlorn sentinels within hiking distance of town. Sometimes called Castillo de las Cinco Esquinas, the **Castillo Moro** overlooks Cazorla. The ruins of Renaissance **Iglesia de Santa María,** by Vandelvira, are in the south of the city.

The comforts for which you'll pay at **Hostal Guadalquivir,** C. Nueva, 6 (tel. 72 02 68), include beautifully stained wood trim everywhere and colorful tiles in bathrooms. (Singles 1800-2000ptas, with bath 2400-2700ptas. Doubles with bath 3200-3600ptas. Breakfast 325ptas.) Walk downhill from Pl. Constitución to Pl. Mercado and follow the signs. **Hostal Betis,** Pl. Corredera, 19 (tel. 72 05 40), has vast rooms with good views of the mountains. (1000ptas per person.) The owner runs a *comedor* for guests only. *(Menú* 700-800ptas. Breakfast 175ptas.)

Tapas bars and cafeterias rule on Pl. Corredera and Pl. Constitución. A fresh fruit and veggie **market** resides tautologically in Pl. Mercado. (Open Mon.-Sat. 8am-2pm.)

Although Cazorla has no tourist office, a private tour guide company named **Quercus,** C. Juan Domingo, 2 (tel. 72 01 15), associated with the Forestry Department, provides tourist information free from its second-floor office in Pl. Constitución. (Open 10am-2pm and 5-8pm.) They also sell detailed maps of Cazorla and the Parque Natural (350ptas) and topographic maps (1000ptas). The company arranges excursions by Land Rover to the park (for groups of at least five, 2 per day in morning and afternoon, 5hr., 2100ptas per person). The **post office** is at C. Mariano Extremera, 2 (tel. 72 02 61), behind the Ayuntamiento in Pl. Corredera. The **postal code** is 23470; the **telephone code** 953. There's a **pharmacy** at Pl. Corredera, 17 (tel. 72 00 09), to the right after entering the square. (Open 9am-2pm and 5-8pm.) The nearest **hospital** is Centro de Salud José Salcedo (tel. 72 10 61 or 72 20 00), a few km away. The **police** are in Pl. Corredera (tel. 72 01 81).

The easiest way to Cazorla is by **bus** from Ubeda (3 per day, 1 1/4 hr.), Jaén (3 per day, 2 1/4 hr.), and Granada (2 per day, 4hr.). Before boarding buses departing Cazorla, buy your ticket at the small window on ground level, to the left of the tour guide office as you face it.

Granada

The 40,000 students of its University help make Granada a lively provincial capital. The city center is noisy with the construction of new highways, while the bustling pedestrian area around the cathedral is easier on the ears. But above all, the city houses the extraordinary Alhambra complex, built by the Moors at the brilliant pinnacle of their culture and civilization.

Conquered by the Moors in 711, the town then blossomed into one of Europe's wealthiest and most refined cities. Granada's rulers took increasing precautions as the Christians fought back, adding layer upon layer of fortifications. By the 15th century Granada was the last Muslim outpost in Iberia, surrounded and besieged by the troops of a unified Christian kingdom. But trouble was brewing in the harem. Unluckily for the Moors, the ruling Sultan Moulay Abdul Hassan was so in love with a concubine named Zoraya that he couldn't concentrate on his work. He ignored civic duty and began publicly repudiating his wife. Aïcha (the queen) soon caught on, drummed up local support, deposed him, and thrust her young son Boabdil on the throne. Fernando of Aragón took advantage of the disarray and captured Boabdil, winning the city.

Those charitable Christians burned every mosque and most of the lower city, but the hills overlooking the city escaped unscathed. Spain's most famous attraction, the spectacular palatial city known as the Alhambra, was abandoned for hundreds of years until its rediscovery in the 19th century.

Traces of Granada's rich heritage remain on two other neighboring hills across the Río Darro. The Albayzín, a maze of Moorish houses and twisting alleys, is Spain's best-preserved Arab settlement and the only part of the Muslim city that survived the Reconquista. More recently it was the center of Granada's Republican resistance during the Civil War. Nearby, footpaths in the Gypsy Quarter wind up to cactusy caves atop the hill of Sacromonte. The top of the hill has scattered ruins of the Muslim city walls.

388　　Andalucía

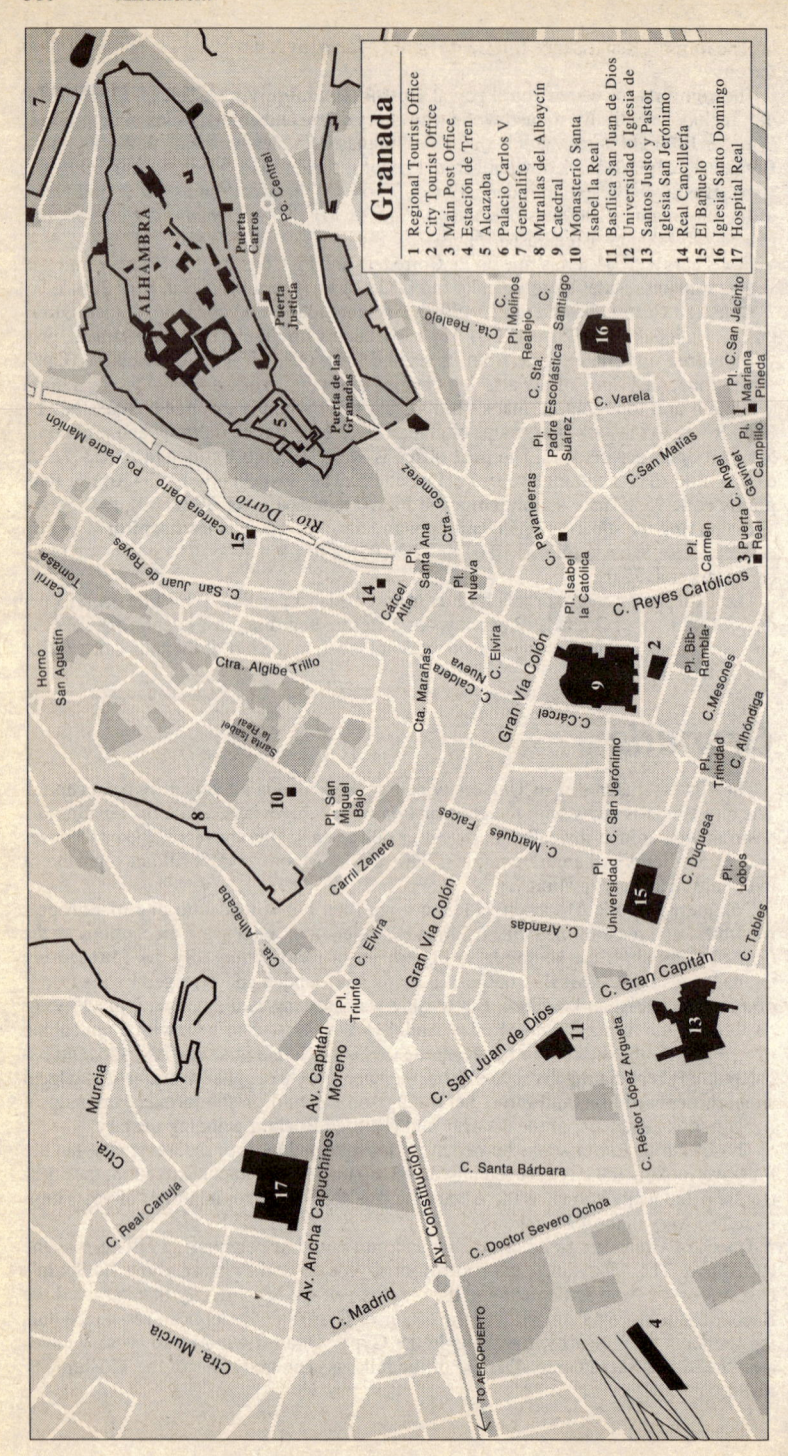

Granada

1. Regional Tourist Office
2. City Tourist Office
3. Main Post Office
4. Estación de Tren
5. Alcazaba
6. Palacio Carlos V
7. Generalife
8. Murallas del Albaycín
9. Catedral
10. Monasterio Santa Isabel la Real
11. Basílica San Juan de Dios
12. Universidad e Iglesia de Santos Justo y Pastor
13. Iglesia San Jerónimo
14. Real Cancillería
15. El Bañuelo
16. Iglesia Santo Domingo
17. Hospital Real

Orientation and Practical Information

The center of Granada is **Plaza Nueva**, framed by handsome Renaissance buildings and outfitted with a wide variety of hotels and restaurants. Plaza Nueva sits just north of **Plaza de Isabel la Católica**, which is at the intersection of the two main arteries, **C. Reyes Católicos** and **Gran Vía de Colón**. A few blocks south of that, **Puerta Real** is the 5-way intersection of C. Reyes Católicos, Calle de Recogidas, Calle los Mesones, Calle Acera de Darro, and Calle Angel Ganivet.

From RENFE and all bus stations except Alsina Graells, follow Av. Constitución to Gran Vía de Colón, turn right and walk the 15-20 minutes into town. From the Alsina Graells bus station, turn right on Camino de Ronda and left three full blocks later at the gas station onto C. Recogidas, which becomes C. Reyes Católicos at Puerta Real.

Municipal **buses** cover nearly all areas of town. Bus #11 connects a number of major streets, including Carretera de Madrid, the train and bus stations, and the town center. Since the Alhambra, Albayzín, and Sacromonte hills are all near each other and the town center, the best way to explore is on foot. If solo, avoid the small streets at the foot of the Albayzín northeast of Pl. Nueva after dark.

Tourist Office: C. Libreros, 2 (tel. 22 59 90), in a passage between the southwest corner of the cathedral and Pl. Bib-Rambla. Bulletin boards in the window. Patient staff speaks English, French, German, Arabic, and Russian. Open Mon.-Sat. 9am-2pm; winter Mon.-Fri. 10am-1pm and 4-7pm, Sat. 10am-1pm. High-tech **branch office** at the Patronato, Pl. Mariana Pineda, 10 (tel. 22 66 88). Open Mon.-Fri. 10am-1:30pm and 5-7pm, Sat. 10am-1pm.

Budget Travel: Viajes TIVE, C. Martínez Campo, 21 (tel. 25 02 11). BIJ tickets and assorted information. Open Mon.-Fri. 9am-1pm and 4:30-8:30pm.

Currency Exchange: Hipercor supermarket, C. Arabial at the corner with Sta. Clotilde, near the bus station. Good rates and long hours. Open Mon.-Sat. 9am-9:30pm.

American Express: Viajes Bonal, Av. Constitución, 19 (tel. 27 63 12), at the north end of Gran Vía de Colón. Entrance on side street. If you're a cardholder, you can buy traveler's checks with personal checks. No commission on changing AmEx traveler's checks; worse rates than many banks. Cardholder mail held. Open Mon.-Fri. 9:30am-1:30pm and 5-8pm. Currency exchange Mon.-Fri. 10am-1pm.

Post Office: Puerta Real (tel. 22 48 35; fax (58) 22 36 41). Open for stamps and Lista de Correos Mon.-Fri. 8am-9pm, Sat. 9am-2pm; for **telegrams** Mon.-Fri. 8am-9pm, Sat. 9am-7pm, Sun. 9am-2pm. **Faxes** also sent and received. **Postal Code:** 18070.

Telephones: C. Reyes Católicos, 55, 1 bl. towards Pl. Nueva from Pl. Isabel la Católica. Open Mon.-Sat. 9am-2pm and 5-10pm. **Telephone Code:** 958.

Flights: (tel. 44 70 81), 17km west of the city. Salidas bus (tel. 13 13 09) shuttles there from Pl. Isabel la Católica (2 per day, Sun. 1 per day; 200ptas). Call them or ask tourist office for departure times. Taxi to the airport about 1800ptas. **Iberia,** Pl. Isabel la Católica, 2 (tel. 22 75 92). Open Mon.-Fri. 9am-1:45pm and 4-7pm. To Madrid (2 per day, 45min., 11,375ptas) and Barcelona (2 per day, 1 1/4 hr., 16,275ptas).

Trains: Av. Andaluces (tel. 23 34 08), off fat Av. Constitución northwest of the city center. To: Málaga (3 per day via Bobadilla, 4hr., 455ptas); Córdoba (3 per day, 4hr., 1225ptas); Sevilla (3 per day, 4hr., 1420ptas); Algeciras (2 per day, 5hr., 1480ptas); València (3 per day, 8-12hr., 4450ptas); Madrid (2 per day, 6-8hr., 3255-4595ptas); Barcelona (2 per day, 13hr., 5880ptas).

Buses: The usual mess of companies.

Alsina Graells, Camino de Ronda, 97 (tel. 25 13 58), near C. Emperatriz Eugenia. In Andalucía: Málaga (15 per day, 2 1/2 hr., 1120ptas); Salobreña (7 per day, 1 1/4 hr., 645ptas); Almuñecar (6 per day, 1 1/2 hr., 545ptas); Nerja (2 per day, 2hr., 780ptas); Almería (7 per day, 4hr., 1000ptas); Córdoba (7 per day, 3 1/2 hr., 1485ptas); Sevilla (8 per day, 4-5hr., 1950ptas).

Bacoma, Av. Andaluces, 12 (tel. 28 42 14), near the train station. To: Alicante (4 per day, 7hr., 2790ptas); València (4 per day, 9hr., 4100ptas); Madrid (5 per day, 6hr., 2550ptas); Barcelona (3 per day, 14hr., 6550ptas).

Autedía, C. Rector Martín Ocete, 10 (tel. 28 05 92), off Av. Constitución. To: Guadix (12 per day, 1 1/4 hr., 450ptas), Almería (2 per day, 3 1/2 hr., 1235ptas); Baeza (8 per day, 2 1/4 hr., 810ptas).

Autocares Bonal, Av. Constitución, 34 (tel. 27 31 00). Tickets sold at Ventarrillo bar. To Veleta in the Sierra Nevada (at 9am, 1hr., 580ptas). Departs from Po. Salón near the Monumento de la Constitución.

Public Transportation: Municipal buses (80ptas, book of 10 tickets 450ptas). Lifesaving bus #11 connects Ctra. Madrid, the train station, all bus stations, and the city center. Stops are clearly marked.

Taxis: Tele-Taxi (tel. 28 06 54).

Car Rental: Atesa, Pl. Cuchilleros, 1 (tel. 22 40 04). Cheapest car 3900ptas per day plus 25ptas per km. Must be 21 or over.

Ridesharing: Mitzfahrzentrale, C. Elvira, 85 (tel. 29 29 20), 1 bl. east of Gran Vía de Colón. An unofficial agency that helps arrange rides. Give them at least 2 days' notice.

Hitchhiking: The tourist office has information on buses to places where some people sometimes supposedly allegedly conceivably maybe possibly hitch. *Let's Go* does not recommend hitchhiking as a safe means of travel.

Luggage Storage: At the **train station** (200ptas).

English Bookstore: Librería Urbano, C. Tablas, 6 (tel. 25 29 09), off Pl. de la Trinidad. Decent selection of literature and fiction, with some guidebooks. Open Mon.-Fri. 9:30am-2:30pm and 4:30-9pm, Sat. 9:30am-2:30pm.

Women's Services: Servicio Sociales, C. Lepanto (tel. 24 81 65), in the Auntamiento off Pl. Carmen. Open Mon.-Fri. 8am-2pm.

Laundromat: Lavandería Autoservicio Emperatriz Eugenia, C. Emperatriz Eugenia, 26 (tel. 27 88 20). Exit Alcina Graells bus station to the left and turn at the 1st right. Wash and dry 500ptas per load. Open Mon.-Sat. 9am-2pm and 4-8pm. **Lavomatique,** C. La Paz, 19. From Puerta Real, walk 2 bl. away from Pl. Nueva and turn right on C. Puentezueles. It's the 7th left. Wash and dry 500ptas per load. Detergent 75ptas per load. Open Mon.-Fri. 9am-2pm and 4-8:30pm, Sat. 9am-2pm.

Swimming Pool: Piscina Neptuno (tel. 25 11 12), next to flamenco club Jardines Neptuno, near the intersection of C. Recogidas and Camino de Ronda. Adults 500ptas, children 400ptas. Open June-Sept. 11am-7:30pm.

Red Cross: C. Escoriaza, 8 (tel. 22 22 22).

Late-Night Pharmacy: Farmacia Nuña González, Camino de Ronda, 83 (tel. 25 48 43), down 1 full bl. from Alsina Graells bus station. Exit bus station to the right. Open 9:30am-1:30pm and 5-8pm. For later pharmacies, check listings in any local paper.

Medical Services: Clínica de San Cecilio, Ctra. Jaén (tel. 28 02 00).

Police: Municipal, C. Duquesa, 21 (tel. 092). **Guardia Civil** (tel. 25 11 00). **Policía Nacional,** Pl. Campos (tel. 091). Theoretically, English and French spoken.

Accommodations and Camping

Except during Semana Santa, there's an ample supply of accommodations. A number of *Pensión* and *fonda* owners skulk at the train and bus stations, but don't feel compelled to deal with them.

Residencia Juvenil Granada (HI), Camino de Ronda, 171 (tel. 27 26 38). Inconveniently located. From the Alsina Graells station, exit left and walk 15min. down Camino de Ronda. From the other bus stations and RENFE, head away from town on Av. Constitución, continuing on C. Málaga. Camino de Ronda starts on the left and crosses the tracks. Sign over arch reads "Junta de Andalucía Instalaciones Deportivas." In a white building across the field on the left. If gate is locked, go around to the back. All rooms are doubles with winter heating and showers. Occasional music blares over hallway speakers. Room keys left unguarded on foyer table. Reception always open. Must evacuate rooms 10am-12:30pm for cleaning. No curfew. 644ptas per person, over 26 825ptas.

In the Alhambra

Pensión Doña Lupe, Av. del Generalife, s/n (tel. 22 14 73). Such a good deal that we wanted to put it on the back of the book. All the clean, expansive rooms have baths, TV, and winter heating. Pool. English-speaking owner. Students and/or *Let's Go* users: singles 1000ptas, doubles 1950ptas. Breakfast included.

Along Cuesta de Gomérez

The most convenient budget hotels are directly off **Pl. Nueva,** on the street that leads to the Alhambra. The area fills quickly in summer, and the racket of tour buses en route to the Alhambra starts early in the morning. To reach this area, walk to Pl. Nueva, or take bus #11 from the train/bus stations and disembark at the cathedral. The cathedral isn't visible from a bus window; either count stops or look at each stop for the purple signs pointing to the entrance.

Hostal Residencia Britz, Cuesta de Gomérez, 1 (tel. 22 36 52). Big rooms, power showers, lusciously ornate furniture, and modern appliances. Communally, enjoy a vending machine, TV room, and attentive management. Great but noisy views of Pl. Nueva. Singles 1855ptas. Doubles 2965ptas, with bath 3975ptas.

Hostal Residencia Gomérez, Cuesta de Gomérez, 10 (tel. 22 44 37). Kept sparkly clean by young, multilingual, singing proprietor. Front door keys available for night owls. Singles 1000ptas. Doubles 1800ptas. Hot showers 100ptas.

Hostal Navarro-Ramos, Cuesta de Gomérez, 21 (tel. 25 05 55). A schemey rope mechanism unlocks the door to a hidden world of spacious, simply decorated rooms. Privacy, quiet courtyard, and several showers. Singles 1100ptas. Doubles 1800ptas, with bath 2800ptas. Hot showers 150ptas.

Pensión Gomérez, Cuesta de Gomérez, 2, 3rd fl. (tel. 22 63 98). Cool, small, and lush with plants. Curfew 2am. Singles 1200ptas. Doubles 2000ptas, with bath 2900ptas. Hot showers 100ptas. Winter heating.

Near the Cathedral

Just west of the cathedral and the Capilla Real, streets bubble with activity by day, but settle down at night; even so, they still feel safe after dark. Budget *hostales* multiply like horny rabbits. A whole farm of them (about 1000ptas per person) line **Calle Lucena,** northwest of Pl. Trinidad—they're usually occupied during the academic year. Take bus #11 from the train or bus station to reach the cathedral.

Huéspedes Romero, C. Sillería, 1 (tel. 26 60 79), overlooking Pl. Trinidad (not to be confused with the C. Sillería off Pl. Nueva), at the end of C. Mesones. Each room is unique. Large double beds and tiled floors. Appetizing aromas from the kitchen fly around the rooms. Beg for one of the roof rooms. 1100ptas per person.

Pensión Muñoz, C. Mesones, 53 (tel. 26 38 19), east of Pl. Trinidad. The managers recently painted the place and bought new mattresses. Lovely sitting room with TV. 1100ptas per person.

Hostal-Residencia Lisboa, Pl. Carmen, 27 (tel. 22 14 13), across C. Reyes Católicos. Hefty, clean, and homey. New bathrooms tiled in glossy green. Phones and winter heating in all rooms. The outside rooms are sound barriers to the plaza. Singles 1855ptas. Doubles 2978ptas, with bath 3975ptas.

Hostal Plaza Isabel, C. Colcha, 13 (tel. 22 30 22), at the corner with Pl. Isabel la Católica. Everyone's raving about this spacious *hostal.* The location couldn't be any more central and the shrewd new owners just installed new beds, paint, and the works. Singles 1200ptas. Doubles 2200ptas.

Hostal Residencia Zacatín, C. Ermita, 11 (tel. 22 11 55), right off Pl. Bib-Rambla. Follow C. Zacatín; enter from the Alcaicería alleyway. Quiet; some rooms face private courtyard. Bathrooms a bit raggedy but clean. Singles 1200ptas, with bath 1800ptas. Doubles 2200ptas, with shower 2800ptas, with bath 3200ptas.

Hostal Roma, C. Navas, 1 (tel. 22 62 77), near Pl. Carmen. Colorful tile livens up the bottom floor. Bathrooms could be in better shape. Singles 2500ptas. Doubles with bath 3000ptas. Breakfast 1500ptas.

Off Calle San Juan de Dios

This area is the closest to the train station. From the station, head straight along Av. Andaluces, turn right onto Av. Constitución, then right onto **Calle San Juan de Dios** (10min.). Although it does feel quite safe, this is the seediest area that we list.

> **Hostal Residencia San Joaquín,** Mano de Hierro, 14 (tel. 28 28 79), 5th street on the left off C. San Juan de Dios. Erstwhile 15th-century count's estate, with 3 gorgeous indoor patios and much foliage. Only slightly decaying. Many college students during the academic year. Sprawling premises make supervision difficult; leave your valuables at the front desk. All rooms have bath. 1400ptas per person. Lunch or dinner with a tub of wine 700ptas.
>
> **Hostal las Cumbres,** C. Cardenal Mendoza, 4 (tel. 29 12 22), the 3rd left off C. San Juan de Dios. Everything new, including the lickable stained wood and linoleum stairway. Pleasantly piney smell of ammonia. Winter heating. Singles 1800ptas. Doubles 3200ptas.

Camping

Buses serve five campgrounds within 5km of Granada; check the departure schedules at the tourist office.

> **Sierra Nevada,** Av. Madrid, 107 (tel. 15 09 54). Lots of shady trees, modern facilities, and free hot showers. If the town fair is here stay elsewhere, or forget about REM sleep. 415ptas per person, per tent and per car. Youngsters 315ptas. Open March 15-Oct. 15.
>
> **El Último,** Camino Huétor-Vega, 50 (tel. 12 30 69). Free swimming pool. 350ptas per person, per tent, and per car.
>
> **María Eugenia,** Ctra. Nacional 342 (tel. 20 06 06), at km 292. 350ptas per person, per tent, and per car. Brats 250ptas.
>
> **Los Alamos** (tel. 20 84 79), next door to María Eugenia at km 290. 350ptas per person, per tent, and per car. Offspring 250ptas. Open April-Oct.
>
> **Reina Isabel,** Ctra. Granada at km 4 (tel. 59 00 41), in nearby Zubia. 375ptas per person, per tent, and per car. Kids 275ptas. Open March 1-Oct. 31.

Food

As in the rest of Andalucía, the accent is on fresh (usually fried) fish. *Tapas* rule. Most of Granada hits the bars on **Campo del Príncipe** (several blocks south of Pl. Nueva) late in the evening. Ice cream fans head to the mirrored walls of **Heladería Walther,** two blocks east of Puerta Real off Pl. Batallas, or the popular **La Veneciana** (commonly called "Los Italianos"), Gran Vía, 4 (50-300ptas). The **market** overflows from Pl. Romanilla beside the cathedral, until the architectural dig at the usual spot on C. San Agustín is done. (Open Mon.-Sat. 8am-3pm.)

Tortilla Sacromonte is an omelette composed of calf brains, ham, shrimp, and numerous green vegetables. Other *platos típicos: sesos a la romana* (batter-fried calves' brains) and *rabo de toro* (bulls' tail).

> **Groceries:** C. Ribera del Genil, s/n, next to Galerías Preciados. Open Mon.-Sat. 9:30am-1:30pm and 5-8:30pm.

Near Plaza Nueva

These casual family-type joints have both bars and *comedors* (dining areas). The prime location ups your ante, but portions are generally generous.

> **Restaurante Alcaicería,** C. Oficios, 6 (tel. 22 43 41). One of the most highly regarded fooderies in town and a wise place to pick up the check. Enter through the vine-covered archway and follow the sounds of the guitar. Menú 1400ptas. Chickpea and lemon specialty 750ptas. Open 1-4pm and 8-11:30pm.
>
> **Rincón de Pepe,** Escudo de Carmen, 17 (tel. 22 07 63), off Pl. Carmen. *Conejo al ajillo* (rabbit in garlic sauce, 625ptas). *Raciones* 400-600ptas. Open noon-4pm and 7:30-10:30pm.
>
> **La Nueva Bodega,** C. Cetti Merién, 3 (tel. 22 59 34), on a small side street parallel to C. Reyes Católicos and 2 bl. toward town from Pl. Nueva. Numerous locals at the large bar. Tangy *menús* 675-1000ptas, eminently munchable *bocadillos* around 200ptas. Prices much lower at the bar. Open noon-midnight.

Restaurante-Café Boabdil, C. Hospital de Peregrinos, 2 (tel. 22 81 36), 2 bl. west of Pl. Nueva. Street tables flood with tourists and car exhaust. A/C and a TV at the bar. *Menús* 850-1000ptas. Meals served Fri.-Wed. noon-11pm.

Restaurante-Bar León, C. Pan, 3 (tel. 22 51 43), on a small side street parallel to C. Reyes Católicos and 1 bl. toward town from Pl. Nueva. The kind of place where you want to settle in for a while. Meals from 650ptas. Open late July to mid-June Thurs.-Tues. 1-4pm and 7:30-11pm. *Tapas* at bar Thurs.-Tues. 12:30-4pm and 7-11pm.

Elsewhere

El Ladrillo, Placeta de Fatima off C. Pagés in the Albayzín. Follow the main street from the foot of the Albayzín to the top of the hill (15min.). Thunderous evening hangout. Whopping rations of delicious fresh seafood. Mountainous *media barco* (a platter for 2 of diverse fried fish) 750ptas. *Ensalada* 350ptas. Open 1-4pm and 8-midnight.

Restaurante Vegetariano Raíces, C. Pablo Picasso, 30 (tel. 12 01 03), 15min. from Puerta Real. Face post office, turn right, and follow Acera del Casino. When it ends flow into the intersection with C. Pablo Picasso and turn left. (Bus #11 indirectly wends its way to C. Pablo Picasso.) Marvellous vegetarian food. By day it's a cross between Wall Street and a wrinkled tea party. By night crunchy types talk civil disobedience and sip fruit drinks. Filling 4-course *menú del día* includes mystery tea concoction (700ptas, Sat.-Sun. 900ptas). Veggie burger and fries 330ptas. Open Mon.-Tues. and Thurs.-Sat. 1:30-4pm and 9-11:30pm, Wed. 1:30-4pm; winter Mon.-Tues. and Thurs.-Sat. 1:30-4pm and 8:30-11pm, Sun. 1:30-4pm.

Pulcinella Trattoria, Dr. Martín Lagos, 3 (tel. 25 52 60), at the corner of C. Frailes, off C. Recogidas. Blaring classical music and dapper waiters. Copious Italian menu and food *para llevar* (to go). *Mejillones alla marinara* (mussels in tomato sauce) 560ptas. Pizzas 475-630ptas. Open 1:30-4pm and 8pm-midnight.

Las Girasoles, C. San Juan de Dios, 24 (tel. 29 34 10). Dull interior, unbeatable prices and hours. *Menú* 600ptas. *Bocadillos* 125-175ptas. Open 7am-midnight.

Sights

The Alhambra Complex

The **Alhambra** (tel. 22 75 27) is both the name for the hill that dominates Granada and the sprawling palace-fortress atop it. From the Arabic for "red," it refers to the clay extracted from the hill used for building. Enter the Alhambra through Puerta de Granada, off Cuesta de Gomérez, and climb to the well-marked main entrance. Some monuments are closed to the public and viewing time is limited. (Alhambra open Mon.-Sat. 9am-7:45pm, Sun. 9am-5:45pm; Oct. 1-May 31 9am-5:45pm. Admission 500ptas, but unused portions of the ticket are valid for return visits; Sun. after 3pm free. Separate 525ptas ticket required for illuminated nighttime admission: Tues., Thurs., and Sat. 10pm-midnight; winter Sat. 8-10pm. Daytime admission to Generalife only, 125ptas. Box office shuts down about 45min. before closing time.)

The Alcazaba

Against the silvery backdrop of the Sierra Nevada, the Christians drove the first Nazarite King Alhamar from the Albayzín to this more strategic hill. Here he built a fortress called the Alcazaba, the oldest section of today's Alhambra.

In the Alcazaba, the **Torre de la Vela** (watchtower) has the finest view of Granada and the Sierra Nevada. The bells of the tower were rung to warn of impending danger and to control irrigation phases. The Alcazaba was once a separate palace with its own entrance; its massive battlements were later transformed into a guard house and palace garrison. Napoleon stationed his troops here, but before leaving he blew up enough of the place to ensure the end of the palace's reign as an effective military outpost. Exit through **Puerta del Vino** (wine gate), where inhabitants of the Alhambra once bought tax-free wine.

The Alcázar

The next addition to the Alhambra, the Alcázar (Royal Palace) was built for the great Moorish rulers Yusuf I (1333-1354) and Mohammed V (1354-1391). Legend has it that an unexplained force murdered Yusuf I in an isolated basement chamber of the Alcázar, so his son Mohammed V was left to complete the palace.

The entrance is east of the Patio de Machuca, leading into the **Mexuar,** a great pillared council chamber. This area was demolished after an explosion in a nearby gunpowder mill. The Mexuar opens onto the Patio del Cuarto Dorado (Patio of the Gilded Hall). Off the north side of the patio, foliated horseshoe archways of successively diminishing width open onto the **Cuarto Dorado** (Gilded Hall) itself, decorated by Carlos V in Mudejar style. Its opulent starry wooden ceiling is inlaid with ivory and mother-of-pearl.

To the east lies the **Patio de los Arrayanes** (Courtyard of Myrtles), a wide open space with a bubbling fountain at either end. Also at either end, the palace shows an elaborately carved wood façade, the 14th-century **Fachada de Serallo**. The long and slender **Sala de la Barca** (Boat Gallery), with a boat-hull ceiling, flanks the north side of the courtyard.

Adjoining the Sala de la Barca to the north, the **Sala de los Embajadores** (Hall of Ambassadors) is where King Fernando and Christopher Columbus discussed the route to India. This perfectly square hall is one of the most magnificent rooms in the palace, every surface intricately wrought with inscriptions and ornamental patterns and topped by an incredible carved wooden dome. On the ground floor of the **Torre de Comares,** it's interrupted by enormous, rounded windows that offer views in all directions.

East of the Patio de los Arrayanes, the Galería de los Mozardos leads to the **Patio de los Leones** (Courtyard of the Lions), the most photographed swatch of the palace and once the center of the sultan's domestic life. The grandeur continues: a symmetrical arcade of horseshoe arches and white marble columns border this courtyard, while a fountain supported by 12 marble lions tinkles in the middle.

At the far end of the courtyard, the **Sala de los Reyes** (Hall of the Kings) shelters the sultan's bed. South of the courtyard, in the **Galería de Abencerrajes,** Sultan Moulay Abdul Hassan piled the heads of the sons of his first wife (16 of them) so that Boabdil, son of his second, could inherit the throne. The (metaphorically) bloodstained room has another doozy of a ceiling. On the north side of the courtyard, the resplendent **Sala de las Dos Hermanas** was named for twin marble slabs embedded in its floor. It also has a staggering honeycomb dome made of thousands of tiny cells. From here a secluded portico overlooks the Jardines de Daraxa.

Passing the room where Washington Irving resided, a balustraded courtyard leads to the 14th-century **Baños Reales** (Royal Baths), the center of court social life. Light shining through star-shaped holes in the ceiling once refracted through steam to create indoor rainbows.

Just outside the east wall of the Alcázar, in the **Jardines del Partal,** lily-studded pools drip beside terraces of roses shadowed by the soaring **Torre de las Damas** (Ladies' Tower).

The Palacio de Carlos V

After the Christian Reconquista drove the Moors from Spain, Fernando and Isabella respectfully restored the Alcázar. Little did they know, two generations later omnipotent Emperor Carlos V would demolish parts of it to make way for his Palacio de Carlos V, a Renaissance masterpiece by Pedro Machuca (a disciple of Michelangelo).

Although glaringly incongruous amidst all the Moorish splendor, experts seem to agree that the Palacio is one of the most beautiful Renaissance buildings in Spain. Ringed with two stories of Doric colonnades, it's Machuca's only surviving effort. Inside, a **museum** of Hispano-Arabic art contains the only original furnishing from the Alhambra, a spectacular vase (admission 250ptas).

El Generalife

Up the hill past the Alhambra's main entrance and through **Callejón de los Cipreses** and the shady **Callejón de las Adelfas** is the lush palace greenery of the Generalife, the spacious summer retreat of the Sultans that crowns the Alhambra's twin hill, *el cerro del sol* (the sun hill). Aben Walid Ismail designed El Generalife in 1318. The two buildings converse across the **Patio de la Acequia** (Courtyard of the Irrigation Channel), embellished with a narrow pool fed by fountains forming an aqueous archway. Canals, fountains, and water jets criss-cross the lovely gardens.

The Cathedral Quarter

Back in the town proper, rich in Gothic carving and gilded floral ornaments, the **Capilla Real** (Royal Chapel) was Fernando and Isabel's private chapel. During their prosperous reign, they funneled almost one-quarter of the royal income to the chapel's construction.

Inside, the cool gray marble figures of the 16th-century **royal mausoleums** repose behind an elaborate screen. The figures of Fernando and Isabel recline to the right; beside them sleep their daughter Juana la Loca (the Mad) and her husband Felipe el Hermoso (the Fair). The tombs lie in the crypt directly below, accessible by a small stairway on either side. To the horror of the rest of the royal family, Juana insisted on keeping the body of her handsome husband with her for an unpleasantly long time after he died. Friends had a hard time convincing the insanely jealous wife that Felipe was actually dead. After they pried him from her arms, the remains of his body were laid to rest here.

The highlight of the chapel, Queen Isabel's private **collección de arte,** is exhibited next door in the sacristy. The collection favors Flemish and German masterpieces of the 15th century, especially the exquisite Memling, Bouts, and Roger van der Weyden. Drool over the glittering **alhajas reales** (royal jewels) in the middle of the sacristy: the queen's golden crown, scepter, and jewelry box, and the king's sword. (Open 10:30am-1pm and 4-7pm; Oct.-Feb. 10:30am-1pm and 3:30-6pm. Admission 150ptas, Sun. morning free.).

The adjacent **catedral** dwarfs the Capilla Real. The first purely Renaissance cathedral in Spain boasts massive Corinthian pillars supporting an astonishingly high vaulted nave. Its frosty whiteness gives it the look of an overexposed snapshot. You can adjust the lighting with coin-operated electric switches beside each chapel (25ptas per viewing). Admission is good for the cathedral's **tesoro** and **museo** to boot. (Open 10:30am-1pm and 4-7pm; Oct.-Feb. 10:30am-1pm and 3:30-6pm. Admission 150ptas.)

The 16th-century **Hospital Real** is divided into four tiled courtyards. Above the landing of the main staircase, the Mudejar coffered ceiling echoes those of the Alhambra. Nearby rise the twin spires of **Basílica de San Juan de Dios,** a very Baroque temple with a crazy Churrigueresque *reredos.* The 14th-century **Monasterio de San Jerónimo** is just around the corner; badly damaged by Napoleon's troops, it's recovered admirably. (All three are at the end of C. San Juan de Dios. *Monasterio* open 10:30am-1pm and 4-7pm; Oct.-Feb. 10:30am-1pm and 3:30-6pm. *Iglesia* open 8:30-10am and 6:30-8:30pm. Hospital open Mon.-Fri. 8am-3pm.)

The Albayzín

The Moors built their first fortress on a hill called the Albayzín, the old Arab quarter. After the Reconquista, a small Moorish population clung to the neighborhood until their expulsion in the 17th century. The tourist office provides a detailed guide to the Albayzín on request. Be cautious here at night.

The best way to explore the maze is to proceed along C. Darro off Pl. Nueva, climb up Cuesta del Chapiz on the left, then wander aimlessly through Muslim ramparts, cisterns, and gates. On Pl. Nueva, the 16th-century **Real Cancillería** (or Audiencia) was the Christians' Ayuntamiento. The arcaded patio and stalactite ceiling are notable. Behind the Plateresque façade of Casa Castril is the **Museo Arqueológico,** C. Darro, 41, with funerary urns, coins, Classical sculpture, Carthaginian alabaster vases, Muslim lamps, and ceramics. (Open 10am-2pm.)

Cármenes—traditional whitewashed Arab villas with luxuriant walled gardens—characterize the neighborhood. Bus #12 travels from beside the cathedral to C. Pagés, at the top of the Albayzin. From here, walk down C. Agua through the **Puerta Arabe,** an old gate to the city at Pl. Larga. The terrace adjacent to **Iglesia de San Nicolás** affords the city's best view of the Alhambra, especially in winter when glistening snow covers the Sierra Nevada. To the west of San Nicolás, **Monasterio de Santa Isabel la**

Real, founded by Queen Isabel in 1501, is a domed church with an exceptional coffered ceiling and Plateresque Gothic facade.

Entertainment

Entertainment listings are near the back of the daily paper, the *Ideal* (85ptas), under the heading *Cine y Espectáculos.* The Friday supplement lists even more bars, concerts, and special events. The tourist office distributes a monthly culture guide. Discos tend to be overpriced and unpopular.

Avoid the **Cuevas Gitanas de Sacromonte** (gypsy caves). Once home to a thriving Gypsy community, the hill is now just a snare for gullible tourists.

You can get drunk in the Albayzín. Exclusive **Casa de Yanguas,** on C. San Buenaventura off Cuesta del Chapiz, with terraces, balconies, and even a rotating art exhibit surrounding its 15th-century Moorish patio, competes with **Carmen de Aben Humeya,** off Pl. San Nicolás, for the title of Most Romantic Bar in Spain. (Drinks at both start at 600ptas.) **Casa Arabe,** also in the Albayzín off C. Pages, is also in the running. The university crowd tarries at pubs and bars in the area bounded by **Calle Pedro Antonio de Alarcón, Callejón de Nevot,** and **Calle de Melchor Almagro.**

Granada's **Corpus Christi** celebrations, processions, bullfights and other fun, are well-known. The **Internacional Festival de Música y Danza** (mid-June to early July) sponsors open-air performances of classical music and ballet amid towering shrubbery in the gardens of the Alhambra's Generalife. This refined culture bit has also taken over the new **Auditorio Manuel de Falla** (tel. 22 00 22), one of Spain's premier concert halls. Cheaper seats for most performances are available from Edificio Hermanitas de los Pobres, Gran Capitan, 24, Granada 18002 (tel. 20 68 47). Their office is at C. Gracia, 21 (tel. 26 74 42). Travel agencies can also hook you up for a small fee.

Near Granada

On the outskirts of Granada stands **La Cartuja,** a 16th-century Gothic Carthusian monastery. A marble with rich brown tones and swirling forms (a stone unique to nearby Lanjarón) marks the sacristy of Saint Bruno. To reach the monastery, take **bus** #8 from in front of the cathedral. (Open 10:30am-1pm and 4-7pm; Oct.-Feb. 10:30am-1pm and 3:30-6pm.)

Federico García Lorca's birthplace is outside of town in tiny **Fuentevaqueros,** near the airport. The ancestral house has recently been converted into a disappointing **museo** of photographs, manuscripts, and possessions of the poet, who was shot by right-wing forces near Granada at the outbreak of the Civil War. (Open to 15 people every 1/2 hr. July 1-Sept. 30 Tues.-Sun. 10am-1pm and 6-8pm; Oct. 1-March 31 Tues.-Sun. 10am-1pm and 4-6pm; April-June 30 Tues.-Sat. 10am-1pm and 5-7pm. Admission 100ptas.) **Buses** (125ptas) run to the house from the train station almost hourly.

Guadix and Purullena

There are 7000 **caves** in the Guadix region and 2000 in **Guadix** itself. Forty percent of the population lives in privately-owned caves. People began moving into caves because they couldn't afford houses; the fad spread like the plague. Dug into soft clay hills 55km east of Granada, the caves have the whitewashed exteriors of typical Andalusian houses and feature three or four rooms. Due to the clay's natural insulating quality, the caves are toasty in winter and cool in summer. Some of the structures date back more than 1000 years.

From the bus station, walk along Carretera de Almería (which becomes Avenida de Medina Olmos) to the white arch of **Puerta de San Torcuato.** Uphill perches **Plaza de las Palomas** (Dove's Square, a.k.a. Plaza de la Constitución). Farther up, you'll come to the decorative cannon and Plateresque facade of the 16th-century **Iglesia de Santiago.** Atop the hill, a 9th-century Moorish **Alcazaba** pokes its crenellated towers above the roofs of the old town. Climb to the top for a superb view of the cave dwellings in Barrio de Santiago to the south. Inexplicably, a fishy sculpture of the Virgin Mary occupies the uppermost turret of the fortress.

Crowning the hill is the recently opened **Cueva Museu** in Pl. Ermita Nueva. Here visitors simulate cave life and examine costumes and tapestries from the region.

Guadix makes a fine daytrip from Granada, but if you're tired visit **Hostal Río Verde**, Ctra. Murcia, 1 (tel. 66 07 29), on La Cruce (the traffic circle where all the highways meet). Large white rooms are shockingly quiet given the location (1500ptas per person). If you're hungry visit **Restaurante Accitano**, C. Jardín, 3 (tel. 66 00 07), on the corner across from Puerta de San Torcuato (*menú* 800ptas; served 1:30-4pm and 9-11pm). **Serrano** on the opposite corner fries up delish *churros* before your eyes (with coffee or hot chocolate, 150ptas).

The new **tourist office** (tel. 66 26 65) on Ctra. Granada helps in English, French, Italian, or Castilian. (Open Mon.-Sat. 9am-2pm; winter Mon.-Fri. 10am-1pm and 4-6pm.) The **post office** is on Pl. Palomas, officially Pl. Consitución (tel. 66 03 56; open Mon.-Sat. 9am-2pm). The **postal code** is 18500.

Come here by **bus** from Granada (12 per day, 1 1/2 hr., 450ptas), Almeriá, Sevilla, and Jaén. The bus station in Guadix is at Urbanización Santa Rosa (tel. 66 11 02), near Ctra. Almería. The **train station** (tel. 66 06 25) is a 20-minute walk down Ctra. Murcia. Trains run to Granada (3 per day, 1hr., 410ptas), Almería (6 per day, 1 1/2-2 1/2 hr., 480-860ptas), Sevilla, Madrid, and Barcelona.

Purullena, 7km down the road from Guadix to Granada, is the site of more cave living and a bizarre tufa landscape of lunar-looking pocked stones. Shops lining the road peddle Andalusian ceramics, brass, and animal hide souvenirs. A **campsite** is being prepared and should be open by summer 1993. Granada-Guadix **buses** stop here.

Sierra Nevada

The peaks of Mulhacén (3481m) and Veleta (3470m), the highest mountains of the Sierra Nevada (Snowy Range) and of all Spain, sparkle with snow and groan with tourists most of the year. The most popular approach to the Sierra Nevada is the highway from Granada to Veleta. The alternative is the southern approach through the Alpujarras. The first option is quick and easy; the second time-consuming and circuitous, but more rewarding. Sierra Nevada is currently expanding its ski facilities to accommodate the 1995 Alpine Ski Championships.

The most detailed, inexpensive **hiking map** of the Sierra Nevada was printed by the Federación Española de Montañismo (350ptas) but is now out of print. If you can't find it in bookstores in Granada, you'll have to settle for something less. **Librería Estudios**, C. Mesones, 53 (tel. 26 74 08), Granada, sells a detailed but pricey 4-part map of the Sierra Nevada printed by the Dirección General del Instituto Geográfico Nacional (1200ptas). (Open Mon.-Fri. 10am-1:30pm and 5-8:30pm.)

Before you go, call to check on **road and snow conditions** (tel. 48 01 53 in Spanish and English) as well as hotel vacancies. Bring warm clothes.

Veleta

Near the foot of Granada's Alhambra, the highest road in Europe begins its ascent to one of the highest peaks. The road starts as a normal everyday *camino* through the arid countryside, then climbs the face of the Sierra wall. Due to snow, the very top of Veleta is driveable only in August and September.

The Autocares Bonal **bus** (tel. 27 31 00) from Granada to the top of Veleta is a fantastic bargain (at 9am, round-trip 580ptas). Buy tickets in the bar El Ventorrillo, next to Palacio de Congresos. (See Granada: Practical Information: Buses for details.) The bus runs only up to the resort community of **Prado Llano** (19km from the peak), stopping at a **cabina-restaurante**. From mid-June on, the road is clear up to an altitude of at least 2700m, leaving a snowy, treacherous, three-hour hike to the top. The bus driver sometimes will drive to the top if a few people request it (extra 200ptas charge). The bus stops for four hours before the return (at 5pm, 1hr.) Those bored by hiking after the first five minutes shouldn't attempt this excursion, as there's no escape other than the return bus.

During ski season (Nov. to mid-May), a network of **ski lifts** operates from the cabin-restaurant to the peak of Veleta and several intermediate points (all-day lift ticket 2500-5000ptas). **Ski rentals** are in the Gondola Building and in Pl. Prado Llano. This is the brightest and southernmost ski resort in Europe—wear sunscreen or suffer DNA mutations. The entire resort of Prado Llano closes in summer. Check **weather conditions** through Federación Andaluza de Esquí, Po. Ronda, 78 (tel. 25 07 06) or through the station on the mountain (tel. 44 91 00). The cheapest of the area's accommodations is the lodge **Albergue Universitario,** Peñones de San Francisco (tel. 48 01 22; mandatory *pensión completa* 3500ptas; reserve early in winter).

When the snow has melted, peak shading **Capileira** in the southern valley of the Alpujarras is hikeable. The walk is a good 25km among rock-strewn meadows with wild goats and birds behind every boulder. Even in summer, the wind is severe and temperatures drop considerably at night.

Las Alpujarras

The small white houses of the poor, secluded Alpujarra villages huddle together on the southern slopes of the Sierra Nevada. Settled by mountain Berbers in the Middle Ages, they are of an architectural style found only here and in the Algerian and Moroccan Atlas. The beauty of these settlements is due to their isolation; until the 50s, travel there was possible only by foot or mule. Made famous by British writer Gerald Brenan's account in *South from Granada,* the villages are opening to tourism. Local gastronomic *especialidades* include *sopa alpujarreña* (broth with eggs, croutons, and ham) and *plato alpujarreño* (ham, fries, eggs, sausages, and salad).

Silkworms love the climate of the Alpujarra. As soon as a worm nibbles on a bit of mulberry tree, gobs of silk come out its anus. Although villagers used to spin the silk in their own homes, they later sent most of the cocoons directly to Almería or Granada to be processed.

Villages in this area are also notorious for their strict adherence to local custom and superstition. According to Brenan, the ninth male child is widely known to have a special grace. In addition, anybody named María is particularly adept at curing the evil eye. When a child comes down with this affliction (beautiful children are most prone), only the cooperation of four Marías can remove the curse (only one need be a virgin). If the Marías don't come fast enough, the crown of the child's head may fall in and start to decompose. To start the cure, the virgin María puts the child in a basket of *torvisco* (a plant that is thought to belong to the devil), and lifts the poor young thing into the air. The other three Marías then slip in, lay the child upon a fresh bed of *torvisco,* and usher the priest into the room. If the fresh herb dries out after the priest's blessing, everybody can rest assured; the Marías have triumphed.

Gerald Brenan regularly walked between the villages, but even by **bus** you should plan on at least a two-day trip. The Estación Alsina Graells in Granada, Av. Constitución, 19, runs buses to all the major villages; to reach the most elevated—such as Pampaneira, Bubión, Capileira, Portugos, and Trevélez—take the Murtas bus (2 per day at noon and 5pm). Plan for a night in the mountains; the single return bus to Granada leaves early the next morning. From July to September, **Viajes Ecomar** (tel. 22 30 91) organizes a Sunday excursion from 9am to 8pm (3000ptas, midday meal included). Reservations are required. Unfortunately, this is the only form of public transportation between the villages. The locals, aware of the transportation problem, often sympathize with hitchers. *Let's Go* does not recommend hitchhiking as a safe means of travel.

Lanjarón

Lanjarón is famed throughout Spain for its mineral water, gulped by the gallon throughout Andalucía. Spaniards used to flock to the village by the gross to cure themselves of kidney ailments and rheumatism. A town of 4200 people and 23 hotels, not-so-secluded Lanjarón is close to the highway connecting Granada to the coast. If you're stuck here overnight, try **Hotel El Sol,** Av. Generalísimo, 32 (tel. 77 01 30), which has firm beds, marble floors, winter heating, and phones in all rooms. (Singles with bath 2040ptas. Doubles with bath 3710ptas.) If driving, take the left-hand turn just before Orjiva. If taking the **bus** to Ugijar via the main highway, you'll have to disembark here to take advantage of the tourist route.

Pampaneira
As the road winds in serpentine curves up to Pampaneira, the lowest of the Alpujarras villages (1059m), the scenery suddenly becomes dramatic. **Casa Alfonso,** José António, 1 (tel. 76 30 02), is the best place to stay. The large, clean rooms, all doubles, are kept warm in winter with knit quilts and central heating. (Doubles 3000ptas. *Pensión completa* 3000ptas per person.)

Bubión
Bubión looks out over the snow-covered peaks of the high Sierra. Ask around for *casas particulares* (about 900ptas per person). **Casa Teide,** C. Francisco Pérez Garrión (tel. 76 30 37), the local favorite, hosts diners in high style at tables around a lush rose garden *(menú* 800ptas, potent *gazpacho* 140ptas, homemade whiskey ice cream cake 300ptas).

Capileira
Three kilometers up the road lies the wonderful village of Capileira, a good base for exploring the region and the closest thing to a tourist center in the Alpujarras. Jagged, cobbled alleys wind up the slope amid ivy and chirping birds; on either side, the peaks loom above while the valley plummets below. You can enjoy the latter vista from your bedroom window at **Mesón-Hostal Poqueira,** C. Dr. Castillo, 6 (tel. 76 30 48), with fresh, wainscoted rooms, all with bath and winter heating. (Singles 1500ptas. Doubles 2500ptas.)

The road through Capileira continues up the mountainside. By June, the road may be clear enough to make the two-hour climb to **Mulhacén,** Spain's highest peak. Proceed with extreme caution when approaching the summit; the wind is gusty, the snow slippery, and the drop to the other side unpleasantly murderous. To reach the trail, follow the signs marked "Sierra Nevada;" the well-marked fork for the road to Mulhacén branches to the right after 20km. The hike from Capileira down to the **gorge** is also scary. There's no clearly marked trail and at times the going is rough. For the most comfortable (and indirect) route, take the road to Bubión and the path from there to Pampaneira (3 times faster than the road).

Pitres and Portugos
In Capileira, buses back up and continue along the highway through Pitres, a cozy cliffside hamlet. Spain's highest official campground (1295m), **Balcón de Pitres** (tel. 76 61 11) sits at the cliff's edge. (375ptas per person, 350ptas per tent and per car.) The lookouts are spectacular, but keep the barfbag handy or avoid this stretch altogether if you're prone to motion sickness. You can rehydrate in the the town of **Portugos** at **Hostal Mirador de Portugos,** Pl. Nueva, 5 (tel. 76 60 14; *pensión completa* 3600ptas per person). Portugos' *fuente agria* (bitter fountain) spouts water that looks and tastes metallic owing to the mineral wealth of the soil.

Trevélez
The highway stops at the township of Trevélez (1476m), continental Spain's highest community, renowned for its cured ham. Covens of witches used to cast spells in this village; supposedly there is a direct correlation between the number of witches in an Alpujarran village and its altitude above sea level. For a wonderful view of the village, cross the stone bridge over the Río Chico de Trevélez and continue along the opposite side of the gorge. On the road into town, clean and modern **Hostal Mulhacén** has spacious rooms and a terrace with a view of the valley. (Singles 800ptas. Doubles 1800ptas, with bath 2500ptas. Showers included. Good meals reasonably priced.) **Camping Trevélez** (tel. 76 50 75), Ctra. Trevélez-Orgiva, km 1, is open year-round with a bar, restaurant, and lots of shade. (350ptas per person, 275ptas per tent and per car.)

On June 13, Trevélez celebrates the **Fiesta de San António** with a costumed dramatization of the Moorish-Christian conflict. Skilled actors on horseback make their horses rear up and neigh.

Yegen, Laroles, and Ugijar

On a mountaintop outside Berchules, **Yegen,** the world's most scenic playground, offers bizarre vistas and a nameless cheap *pensión*. Thereafter, the road forks to the larger agricultural villages of **Laroles** to the north and **Ugijar** to the south. Ulysses supposedly stopped in Ugijar one day to patch up his ships. Although it's far from the sea, he picked this village because the river bed supposedly has a high gold content. If you're driving, this eastern portion of the Alpujarras is most directly accessible via the somewhat dilapidated highway originating in the village of Lacalahorra near Guadix.

Málaga

More style than substance, the city is known gastronomically for wine (not cuisine), known economically for tourism (not industry). Poor Málaga, once celebrated by Hans Christian Andersen, Rubén Darío, and native poet Vicente Aleixandre, has lost its looks. Its concrete arms extend down the coast, its beaches are unpleasant, its streets crowded and dirty. Nonetheless, the town deserves a visit. As the second largest city in Andalucía and the transportation hub of the Costa del Sol, Málaga makes an ideal base for Costa-del-Sol-searching.

Orientation and Practical Information

To see the city at its best, stroll the length of the palmy **Paseo del Parque;** it'll take you below the **Alcazaba,** the local Moorish palace. Po. Parque turns into **Alameda Principal** just east of the **Plaza de la Marina.** The city center, containing most sights and the cathedral, is north of Alameda Principal. The Río Guadalmedina flows north-south through the town.

Tourist Office: Pasaje de Chinitas, 4 (tel. 221 34 45), off Pl. Constitución. Enter through Pasaje Chinitas and take the first alleyway to the right. Long list of *fondas* and a guide to the city's *centro histórico*. Efficient English-, French-, German-, and Italian-speaking staff. Open Mon.-Fri. 9am-2pm, Sat. 9am-1pm. A small office at the **bus station** hands out brochures and transportation information. Open 8am-10pm.

El Corte Inglés: Av. Andalucia, 4-6. **Map,** map, map. **Currency exchange:** 1% commission (250ptas min. charge). **Supermarket.** They also offer novels and guidebooks in English; haircutting; both cafeteria and restaurant; and **telephones.** Open Mon.-Sat. 10am-9pm.

Budget Travel: Viajes TIVE, C. Huéscar, 2 (tel. 227 84 13), next to El Corte Inglés. Books international plane, train, and bus tickets. ISIC 500ptas. HI card 1800ptas. Open Mon.-Fri. 9am-1pm; for information only Sat. 9am-noon.

Consulates: U.S., C. Ramón y Cajal, Edificio El Ancla, Apto. 502 (tel. 247 98 91), in nearby Fuengirola. **Canada,** Pl. Malagueta, 3 (tel. 222 33 46). **U.K.,** Duquesa de Parcent, 8 (tel. 221 75 71), Edificio Duquesa.

American Express: Viajes Alhambra, C. Especería, 10 (tel. 222 22 99), near C. Nueva. 2% commission on cash. Mail held 1 yr. Accepts wired money. Open Mon.-Fri. 9am-1:30pm and 5-8pm, Sat. 9am-2pm.

Post Office: Av. Andalucía (tel 235 91 07), a tall building just over the bridge from the city center. Open for stamps and Lista de Correos Mon.-Fri. 8am-9pm, Sat. 9am-2pm; for **telegrams** Mon.-Fri. 9am-9pm, Sat. 9am-3pm. **Postal Code:** 29070.

Telephones: C. Molina Larios, 11, next to the cathedral. Open Mon.-Sat. 9am-9pm, Sun. 10am-1pm. See also El Corte Ingles. **Telephone Code:** 95, recently changed from 952. The lost digit 2 has been added to the front of the local numbers, so if you see numbers in old publications without a two as the first number, tack one on.

Málaga **401**

Flights: south of the city (tel. 213 61 66, 213 61 67). Buses flit between the cathedral and the airport (every 1/2 hr. roughly 6:30am-11:30pm, 110ptas). Train service to the airport and back is just as frequent (6:30am-10:30pm, 90ptas). To Madrid (10 per day, 45min., 12,300ptas) and Barcelona (4 per day, 1 1/4 hr., 17,550ptas). **Iberia,** C. Molina Larios, 13 (tel. 221 37 31), beside the cathedral. Open Mon.-Fri. 9am-1:15pm and 4:30-7:15pm, Sat. 9am-1:15pm.

Trains: C. Cuárteles (tel. 231 25 00), southwest of the city. To get to the town center, take bus #3 or 4 from the park opposite the station to Po. Parque; debark at Pl. Marina. Or else walk down C. Cuárteles, turn left on Po. Matadero (fronting the river), cross Puente Tetuán, and you'll be on Alameda Principal (15min.). **RENFE,** C. Strachan, 2 (tel. 221 31 22), is less crowded, more convenient for getting tickets and information. Open Mon.-Fri. 9am-1:30pm and 4:30-7:30pm. To: Antequera (2 per day, 1 1/2 hr., 410ptas); Granada via Bobadilla (2 per day, 3 1/2 hr., 955ptas); Sevilla (5 per day, 2 1/2-3 1/2 hr., 1400-1900ptas); Córdoba (8 per day, 2 1/2 hr., 955-1915ptas); Madrid (5 per day, 5-9hr., 4110-7200ptas); Barcelona (3 per day, 11-14hr.; *talgo* 8600ptas, express 6435ptas).

Buses: Enormous central bus station, Po. Tilos (tel. 235 00 61), behind RENFE. To get to the town center, walk 2 bl. straight ahead from the exit and turn right onto Alameda Principal. To: Granada (14 per day, 1 1/4 hr., 1120ptas); Córdoba (2 per day, 2 1/2 hr., 1295ptas); Antequera (7 per day, 1 1/2 hr., 395ptas); Sevilla (9 per day, 3 1/2 hr., 1620ptas); Almería with stops along the Costa del Sol (5 per day, 4 1/2 hr., 1620ptas); Madrid (5 per day, 7-9hr., 2686ptas); Valéncia (4 per day, 11hr., 5066ptas); Barcelona (3 per day, 18hr., 7505ptas). Buses leave every 1/2 hr. for Torremolinos (29 per day, 1/2 hr., 100ptas) and Fuengirola (29 per day, 1 1/4 hr., 230ptas).

Public Transportation: Municipal buses run until midnight. Fare 85ptas, book of 10 tickets 475ptas.

Taxis: Tele-Taxi (tel. 233 64 00). From Pedregalejos to town center 800-1000ptas. From town center to airport 900-1000ptas.

Luggage Storage: At the **train station,** 200ptas per day.

Women's Services: Centro Asesor de la Mujer, C. Carretería, s/n (tel. 221 93 39), the street off Po. Sta. Isabel near the bridge. Open Mon.-Fri. 9am-2pm.

Medical Assistance: tel. 222 44 00. **First Aid:** tel. 229 03 40, 222 64 98.

Emergency: tel. 091 or 092.

Police: tel. 091.

Accommodations and Camping

Málaga's affordable rooms tend to look somewhat run-down. *Pensión* owners often frequent the train station in hopes of enticing travelers to rent a room. If the price seems high (over 1500ptas for a single), straighten your spine and bargain like crazy. Many budget establishments cluster north of **Paseo del Parque** and **Alameda Principal.**

Hostal Residencia Chinitas, Pasaje Chinitas, 2 (tel. 221 46 83), on an alley off Pl. Constitución. Look for the big yellow sign. A *hostal* with humor: the bathroom is dubbed "sala de pensar" (thinking room). Mellow reception area with a VCR and movie collection. Clean rooms. Singles 1300-1500ptas. Doubles 2400-2800ptas.

Hostal Residencia Lampérez, C. Santa María, 6 (tel. 221 94 84), off Pl. Constitución, on a small alley beside Pasaje Chinitas. Rather in need of renovation and some 200 watt bulbs, but preferable to most places in town. Fairly quiet location. Singles 1100ptas. Doubles 1800ptas. Pitiful showers 150ptas.

Hostal Residencia Larios, C. Marqués de Larios, 9 (tel. 222 54 90). Centrally located between Alameda Principal and Pl. Constitución. Bright, clean rooms with squeaky hard beds. Splashes of crimson everywhere—bedspreads, tablecloths, et al. TV room with sofas. Rooms without windows may be cheaper, but get frightfully stuffy in summer. Prices not including IVA. Singles 1850ptas. Doubles 3000ptas, with bath 3800ptas. Showers officially 250ptas, but they often don't charge.

Camping: Balneario del Carmen, Av. Juan Sebastián El Cano (tel. 229 00 21), 3km from the center. Take bus #11 and ask the driver to signal the stop. 400ptas per person, children 200ptas; 400ptas per tent and per car.

Food

For inexpensive food, try the *pasajes* of the older section of town around **Plaza de la Constitución** and **Calle Granada,** and also on the streets behind **Paseo Marítimo.** Those in the know dine on the beachfront in **Pedregalejos,** near the eastern edge of town, where a row of crowded and inexpensive restaurants snatches up the day's catch. (Take bus #11 from Po. Parque.)

Local cuisine features the pasture and the sea. Sample *arroz a la marinera* or *choto* (goat meat with oil, vinegar, garlic, and almonds) and *malagueño* and *moscatel,* Málaga's sweet wines. Some places rustle up the Málagan mountain specialty: pork loin preserved in its own fat. The main **market,** near the town center between the river and Alameda Principal, gets really crowded after noon, but the selection is still pretty good. (Open Mon.-Sat. 8am-2pm.)

> **Groceries: El Corte Inglés,** Av. Andalucía, 4-6. Open Mon.-Sat. 10am-9pm.
>
> **El Tormes,** C. San José, 6 (tel. 222 20 63), off C. Granada. Lively local favorite with good food, ceiling fans, and some elbow room. Andalusian *menú:* appetizer, 2 entrees, salad, dessert, bread, and drink 800ptas. Open Tues.-Sun. 1-5pm.
>
> **La Cancela,** C. Denis Belgrano, 3 (tel. 222 01 50), off C. Granada. Outdoor tables in a pleasant alley. Extensive soup and tortilla list and *menú.* Fried squid 545ptas. Small portion of *pollo al jeréz* (chicken in sherry sauce) 400ptas. Open Thurs.-Tues. 1-4pm and 8-11pm.
>
> **La Tarantella,** C. Granada, 61 (tel. 222 22 01). Deeply decorated with pictures of the olden days. A/C. Appetizing pizzas (515-685ptas) and crispy greens. Gargantuan *insalata mista* (400ptas) a meal in itself. Open noon-4pm and 8:30pm-midnight.

Sights and Entertainment

Anchoring the end of Paseo del Parque, the hefty **Alcazaba,** a fortified palace built for Moorish kings, contains a museum of Roman and Moorish art surrounded by flowering purple blossoms, palms, and cacti. (Open Mon.-Sat. 10am-1pm and 5-8pm, Sun. 10am-2pm. Admission 25ptas.) For a better view and a sweatier climb, amble up the crumbling walkway at the side of the Alcazaba to the lofty Moorish **Castillo Gibralfaro.** From its walls you can see the concrete coastline of the Costa del Sol and most of Málaga's urban sprawl, including the bullfight ring and cruise-ship docks. Thieves and other shifty types prowl the castle walls at night; think twice about strolling here come evening. Microbus H also heads for the castle every hour from the cathedral. (Open 10am-2pm. Free.)

On Pl. Obispo, the **catedral,** a pastiche of Gothic, Renaissance, and Baroque styles, has fondly been dubbed "the little lady with one arm" because no one ever bothered to finish the second tower. Pedro de Mena's 17th-century choir stalls positively glitter. The arches behind the altar swing open, exposing the chapels behind. To find the one-armed holy spot, from Alameda Principal near Pl. Marina, turn onto C. Molina, which ends at Pl. Obispo. (Open Mon.-Sat. 10am-12:40pm and 4-5:30pm. Admission 100ptas.)

The **Museo de Bellas Artes,** C. San Agustín, 6, in the old palace of the Counts of Buenavista, hoards a wealth of mosaics, sculptures, and paintings, including works by Murillo, Ribera, and native son Picasso. (Open 10am-1:30pm and 5-8pm. Admission 250ptas, EEC students under 21 free.) Picasso was born here in the Plaza del Merced. According to the tourist officials, even though Picasso beat it out of Málaga when he was quite young, he always "felt himself to be a true *Malagueño*". The Ayuntamiento bought **Picasso's birthplace** and plans to convert it to a museum. Meanwhile, diehard fans can visit the unadorned house (tel. 228 39 00; open 11am-2pm and 5-8pm).

The most popular beach stretches to the east at **Pedregalejos.** (Take bus #11.) After dinner in the restaurants along the beach, students swamp the bars a few blocks down. Others forage inland to **Calle Juan Sebastián Elcamo** in the **Echevarría** district, where crowds coagulate at around 1am when the discos open. The unconventional prefer **Calle Beatas,** off C. Granada, where eclectic bars cater to diverse tastes in music and fashion. The *Guía de Ocio* (150ptas), sold at newwstands, lists the week's events around town.

Near Málaga: Garganta del Chorro

In the hierarchy of remarkable geological formations, the **Garganta del Chorro** (a.k.a. El Chorro, 70km northwest of Málaga) stands high. One of Spain's premier natural wonders, the gorge is overwhelming and the walk exhilarating; best of all, virtually no tourists spoil the experience. The gorge is remote, the entrance to the walkway hard to find, and the route somewhat dangerous, yet the toil is worth it. Those susceptible to vertigo or afraid to stroll through functioning train tunnels are guaranteed to be scared stiff. If none of this dampens your appetite for adventure, bring some rope and update your will before leaving.

Nobody seems to know exactly why there is a walkway precariously attached to the sheer sides of a 300 foot gorge. Finding the safer part of the **Camino del Rey** (Road of the King) is a bit tricky. Half of the walkway is unsturdy, full of holes, and liable to collapse at any moment. You can get to the other half only via bridges and narrow, forbidding train tunnels (put your lips to the track before passing through). Fortunately, a prudent search undertaken with the *Guía RENFE* in hand leads to an unforgettable thrill.

The **bartender** at El Chorro's train station knows a number of ways to hike the 2km to the gorge, but the easiest route starts along the gravel road behind the station. Follow it down, past the eight-odd houses in town, and past the hairpin turn that leads to the power station. The road begins to head uphill and becomes a winding construction road; follow as it degenerates into a rocky trail. This trail continues to the train tracks and iron bridge at the outermost side of the gorge (10-15 min. walk). At this point you have a choice:

> 1) You can throw caution to the wind and enter the dilapidated end of the Camino del Rey, the most dangerous rotting wooden walkway in existence.
>
> 2) You can safely enter the widest and most impressive end of the gorge.**

To pursue option #2, follow the tracks through a short series of tunnels until you can see, at the base of the gorge, a wide and deep section of luminescent green water, surrounded by rocks and a meadow. Several downward paths squiggle on the other side of the next tunnel, whose opening rock-wall face draws intermediate to advanced rock climbers. On the left end of the next and last tunnel wobbles a footbridge to the safe half of the walkway. Be extremely careful when crossing: the bridge, though sturdy, has no railings and spans only about 4 ft. The wind can gust pretty violently through this 100-ft. dropoff.

Mostly dilapidated and at times downright scary, the *camino* remains reasonably safe if treated with respect. Large groups should spread out to avoid overburdening the platforms. If you have rope, tie it around each person's waist as a security measure. This surviving portion of the walkway proceeds through the most breathtaking part of the gorge. Masses of rock, sculpted by water and wind, poise 300 ft. over the trickling stream at bottom. Near the end, a staircase with green railings swirls down for a better view of the fish swimming at the bottom. The path ends at a small power station at the mouth of the gorge, a one and a half hour hike from the train station (2hr. via the more dangerous route).

If you choose to camp unofficially by the gorge, try to find a place to stash your pack before hitting the camino. The nearest town with cheap lodgings is tiny **Alora,** 13km away. There, **Bar Valle del Sol,** C. Carambuco, 35 (tel. 249 73 47), off C. Camino Nuevo, rents decent, small rooms (800ptas per person). **Bar La Reja,** C. Soto Mayor, 11, near the fountain in the main square, serves a tasty meal for about 750ptas.

Two **trains** per day travel from Málaga to El Chorro (1:45pm and 7:45pm) and two return (3:20pm and 7:20pm). El Chorro can't be daytripped from Antequera via public transportation. A bus from Antequera to Alora leaves at 6:45am, and the train from Alora to El Chorro leaves at 2:27pm and 8:19pm, but no bus returns to Antequera from

---

**Choose this option.

Alora. No trains return to Antequera from El Chorro. Some people hitchhike to the gorge from Antequera or nearby towns. *Let's Go* does not recommend hitchhiking as a means of travel.

By car, follow signs to El Chorro until the dam by the train station. To reach the *camino* at the other end of the gorge, follow signs for 8km to the **Pantano de Galtanejo**. You'll bump up against a pair of artificial reservoirs near **Lago Conda de Guadalhorce**. Just before the highway reaches the reservoirs, it wiggles through a rock-hewn tunnel. The dirt road wandering off to the right immediately before the tunnel leads to that same small power station by the mouth of the gorge. A footpath leads from the left of the locked entrance to the station, then to the right away from the small dam, and finally to one extreme of the Camino del Rey.

Costa del Sol

The coast has sold its soul to the Devil, and now he's starting to collect. Artifice covers its once-natural charms as chic promenades and hotels seal off small towns from the shoreline. The former Phoenician, Greek, Roman, and Arab port caters to an international clientele with wads of money and tons of attitude. Although the Costa del Sol officially extends from Tarifa in the southwest to Cabo de Gata east of Almería, the name most often refers to the resorts from Marbella, in the province of Málaga, to Motril, in the province of Granada.

North of Málaga, the hills dip straight into the ocean. The environment is less spoiled in the northeastern half, but beaches are usually rockier as well. To the more convenient south, water washes almost entirely against concrete. Nothing can take away the coast's major attraction, however: abundant sun that makes for eight months of spring and four of summer per year.

Sun-freaks swarm everywhere in July and August; make reservations or be ready for a search. Prices double across the board in high season. Some sleep on the beaches (solo travelers and women should be cautious), a practice that is winked at on the outskirts of less elegant areas. Alternatively, ask around for *casas particulares*. June is the best time to visit, when summer weather has come to town but most vacationers haven't.

Trains go far as Málaga, Torremolinos, or Fuengirola; private bus lines supply connections along the coast itself. Railpasses are not valid, but prices are reasonable.

Salobreña

Salobreña seems mysteriously unaffected by tourism. In fact, the town is too listless to be affected by much of anything.

From the bus stop head left (away from the mountains) on the main drag that connects the bus stop with the beach. Take the first right about five minutes later, connecting with **Calle Fábrica Nueva**. A left curve on C. Fábrica Nueva leads to: the market, beach (coarse gravelly sand), Ayuntamiento, Pensión, and castle. A right curve on C. Fábrica Nueva leads to Pensión Palomares or Mesón Chacho.

Presiding over the town, a restored **castillo** rarely slips from view. Fragrant flowers brighten its shady walkways, where concerts and theater take place in July. (Open summer 10am-10pm; winter 10am-1pm and 4-9pm. Admission 100ptas.)

Since most visitors rent nearby apartments in summer, rooms aren't too difficult to find. Most cluster around C. Fábrica Nueva, which winds through town. **Pensión Arnedo**, C. Nueva, 19 (tel. 61 02 27), uphill of C. Fábrica Nueva, has mammoth beds with floral bedspreads and views of the town, the mountain, and the coastline. (800ptas per person. If it looks pretty empty, feign indifference and owner may offer a better price.) At friendly **Pensión Palomares**, C. Fábrica Nueva, 48 (tel. 61 01 81), a trail of urns leads to essentially clean but crepuscular rooms. (Singles 1100ptas. Doubles 2100ptas. Bargaining may work.) In July and August, **Camping Peñón** (tel. 61 02 07), across from the beach, may be packed. To be a part of its community—hot showers, small store, café, and peacocks—you'll have to give them 330ptas per person, 300ptas per child, and 330ptas per car and per tent. (Open late April-Oct.)

Blanco y Negro, Av. García Lorca, 18, up the street from the tourist office, offers a sating *menú* for an unbeatable 600ptas. Morning types win the best pick of fish, meats, and fruit at the **market** (open Mon.-Sat. 9am-1pm).

The **tourist office** is in a miniscule stucco building at Pl. Goya, s/n (tel. 61 03 14, 82 83 45), around the corner to the right from the bus stop. (Open 10am-2pm and 5-8:30pm; winter Tues.-Sun. 11am-1:30pm and 5-9pm.) The **Red Cross** is in a reassuring shack on the beach. The **hospital** number is 82 83 32; call for an **ambulance** at 82 83 02. The **police** answer at 61 10 59.

Buses stop on an exit road from the highway into town. Destinations include Almuñécar (10 per day, 15min., 110ptas), Granada (8 per day, 1 1/4 hr., 555ptas), and Málaga (6 per day, 2hr., 720ptas).

Almuñécar

A steadily growing town with character (unlike its boring sister Salobreña), Almuñécar is a rarity on the Costa del Sol. The well-preserved old quarter makes up for the high-rises in the background, and brightly colored boats moor alongside the beach.

Still in use, the 1900-year-old 8km-long **acueducto** (1km to the west off the highway) watered the ancient Roman town and its salt-manufacturing industry. **Castillo de San Miguel** was enlarged by Renaissance monarchs and now gathers Almuñécar's tombstones. Closed to the public, but kind of nice to think about. The ruins of a Roman salt factory—just a heap of rocks—and reproductions of characteristic Andalusian houses occupy **Parque El Majuelo.** The **museo arqueológico** sleeps in the Cueva de Siete Palacios.

Almuñécar is justly proud of its **Parque Ornitológico,** just inland from the Peñón del Santo, where birds munch tropical fruit and squawk up a racket. (Open July 1-Sept. 15 11am-2pm and 6-9pm; Sept. 16-June 30 11am-1:30pm and 4-7pm. Admission 300ptas, children 150ptas.)

The extensive beaches blend fine gray sand and fist-sized stones, but they're still more *Let's Go*-ish than the glitzy resorts west of Málaga. The two main beaches are **Puerta del Mar** and **San Cristóbal,** split by the **Peñón del Santo.** Puerta del Mar is on the east side of the *peñón,* while San Cristóbal lies on the west side. Most streets across from the bus station eventually end at the beach; but the easiest way to get there is via Av. Europa straight from the bus station (signs points to "Playa San Cristóbal").

Ready for more beach? Farther down Po. Puerta del Mar to the east lies **Playa de Velilla.** Five buses per day run to the town of **La Herradura,** 4km west along the main road to Málaga. The sand here doesn't feel dramatically different, but you'll melt at the thrilling landscape. Two of the three largest official **nude beaches** on the Costa del Sol are near Almuñécar—Playa "Trópico de Europa" and Playa de Cantarriján, each just a few km away. If you're into that kind of thing, telephone the Asociación Naturista de Andalucía at (951) 25 08 08, or write to Apartado 301, Almería, 04070.

The closest-to-budget accommodations cluster around Pl. Rosa, directly behind the *paseo* that overlooks Playa Puerta del Mar. Among the rather dilapidated choices, **Fonda Casa Ruiz,** C. San José, 9 (tel. 63 11 52), stands out as the good egg. From Pl. Rosa, follow Baja del Mar to its end and turn left; then take the first little side street to the right. Despite the broken sign and shabby exterior, it has passable bathrooms, a rooftop terrace, and live music from across the street every summer evening. The owner prides herself on being a skillful cook. (1300ptas per person, with breakfast 1500ptas, with 3 meals 2900ptas.) More new and posh is **Hotel R. Carmen,** Av. Europa, 19 (tel. 63 14 13, 63 25 11), halfway to the beach on the left from the bus station. Faux marble tiles and bright halls lead from a plant-filled entryway through a homey TV room. All rooms have phones and clean, modern baths tiled in soothing blue floral prints. (Singles 1500-2500ptas. Doubles 2500-4000ptas, depending on season.)

Plenty of restaurants stud Po. Puerta del Mar (a.k.a. Po. Altillo), where you can enjoy the day's catch from a terrace peering over the coast. **Bar Meson Entre Amigos** (tel. 63 10 29), Pl. Teatro off Po. Altillo (see sign), serves portly portions, a *menú* (775ptas) and *pollo con manzana* (1/2-chicken with apples; 600ptas). (Open 1-3pm and 8-11:30pm.) Locals favor the restaurants along Playa Velilla, 2km east around the point past the water slicks. **Restaurante Casa Paco,** in the seventh block of the *paseo* across from the beach, has astounding *paella* for two (1650ptas). *Menú* 800ptas. (Open 2-4pm and 7:30-11pm.) Most of these places serve *hirimoyas* (custard apples) and *nísperas* (Japanese pears), the exotic fruit unique to Almuñécar's subtropical climate. Teenagers stir up mischief around **Pl. Rosa** and **Bajo del Paseo,** a row of bars, cafés, and cheesy restaurants on the beach.

The **tourist office** (tel. 63 11 25) reigns from a mauve mansion called La Najanra on Av. Europa, s/n, one block inland from Playa San Cristóbal. (Open Mon.-Fri. 10am-2pm and 4-7pm.) The **post office** (tel. 63 04 59) is on Pl. Liury Gargan, 2, next to Edificio Puerta del Mar on the east end of the *paseo* overlooking Playa Puerta del Mar. (Open Mon.-Fri. 9am-2pm, Sat. 9am-1pm.) The **postal code** is 18690, and the **telephone code** is 58. In a medical emergency, rush to the **municipal hospital,** Ctra. de Málaga (tel. 63 20 63). The **police** can be reached at 63 03 33.

Buses call at Granada (7 per day, 2 1/2 hr., 665ptas), Almería (4 per day, 3 1/2 hr., 990ptas), Málaga (7 per day, 2hr., 620ptas), and Nerja (7 per day, 45min., 240ptas). The station (tel. 63 01 40) is at the corner of Av. Costa del Sol and Av. Europa.

Nerja

Nerja, 50km east of Málaga, is a resort, no doubt about it, but the town's elegance has yet to bow to the raw commercialism infesting resorts to its west. Nerja embalms a peaceful old quarter, proffers some sandy beaches, and kicks its heels to a lively nightlife, all with a little less hype.

The focal point is the **Balcón de Europa,** a clifftop promenade that looks out over 14km of coastline. Follow the signs from the street across from the bus station. At night the terrace becomes a lively *paseo* where you can see and be seen. Below the cliff is a really gorgeous series of small caves, best explored from the marvelous promenade **Paseo de los Carabineros** (off the stairs left of the tourist office).

Long **beaches,** mostly of gravel or coarse sand, have clear, brilliant turquoise water. To reach them from the Balcón, cut through town westward to the Playa Torrecilla apartments; from there follow the shoreline for 15 minutes. Much closer but even more packed is **Playa del Salón,** through an alley off the Balcón to the right of Restaurante Marissal. **Playa Burriana** is a large, sandy beach a short hike to the east. Sacrifice glamour for elbow room. From the tourist office, follow C. Hernando de Corabeo to a dirt road behind a few newly constructed apartments.

Nerja's **accommodations** are pricey. **Pensión Maria Jose,** C. Animas, 5 (tel. 252 23 66) is a bargain at 1500ptas per person (off-season 1000ptas). Spacious rooms, a TV lounge, and plants to green the halls. **Hostal Nerjasol,** C. Arropiero, 4 (tel. 252 21 21), off C. Pintada, boasts a rooftop terrace, clean baths in each room, jaunty halls, and winter heating. (Singles 1500-2000ptas. Doubles 2500-4000ptas.) For *casas particulares,* arrive in the morning and ask at bars, or ask the inhabitants as they wash their doorsteps in the morning. Some rent rooms or have a buddy who does (about 900ptas per person).

Overpriced restaurants along the Balcón de Europa tempt passersby with terraces and views. Locals slip out after 9pm to avoid the foreigners and eat at **Marisquería La Familia,** Diputación Provincial, 17 (tel. 252 00 46), west of the Balcón. Abundant seafood *menú* 750ptas. Their fresh fish dishes start from 700ptas. (Open 1-3:30pm and 6:30-11:30pm.) You can also spot locals at the **market,** 2 blocks up C. San Miguel from the bus stop.

The **tourist office** (tel. 252 15 31) is at Puerta del Mar, 2, beside the Balcón de Europa. English, French, and German are spoken fluently. (Open Mon.-Fri. 10am-2pm and 6-8pm, Sat. 10am-1pm; winter Mon.-Fri. 10am-3pm, Sat. 10am-1pm.) The **post office** (tel. 252 17 49) is at C. Almirante Ferrandiz, 6. (Open Mon.-Fri. 9am-2pm, Sat. 9am-1pm.) The **postal code** is 29780. The **telephone kiosk** is next to the Ayuntamiento by the Balcón de Europa. (Open summer 10am-2pm and 5:30-10pm; winter 11am-2pm and 5:30-9pm.) The **telephone code** is 95. The **Book Center,** C. Granada, 30, is a hip place to buy, sell, and swap used English books. There's a **message board** that might just possibly have a message for you. (Open Mon.-Sat. 10am-1:30pm and 5-9pm.) For **first aid,** call 252 09 35. **Police** headquarters are in C. Pescia (tel. 252 15 45); English and French spoken, at least by receptionist.

Fairly frequent **buses** travel here from Málaga (10 per day, 1 1/2 hr., 380ptas), less frequently from Almería (4 per day, 3hr., 1230ptas) and Granada (2 per day, 905ptas). The small bus station is at C. San Miguel, 3 (open erratically, but bus schedules posted in the window).

Near Nerja

Just 5km east of Nerja pose the tremendous, cathedralline **Cuevas de Nerja**. The cave is a huckster's paradise, with piped-in music and photographers snapping and selling your picture (400ptas each, in cave-shaped frames). The caves are a primitivist's wet dream; the caverns consist of large chambers winding around a huge column of limestone. They're filled with weird rock formations created over millions of years by deposit and erosion, and one reputedly has the world's largest stalactite (65m). (It's technically the widest column, a merged stalagmite and stalactite. Refer to the 1989 edition of the *Guinness Book of World Records* for more details.) One cave is used as an amphitheater for music and ballet performances in July and August. Intrepid explorers have just discovered a new section of caves, reportedly four times as large as the already known one. Look for the archeological exhibit of primitive art and tools in the cave. (Caves and exhibit open June 1-Sept. 30 10am-6pm; Oct. 1-May 31 10:30am-1:30pm and 3-6pm. Admission 400ptas, ages 6-12 200ptas.) **Buses** run to and from Nerja (every hr., 80ptas).

Maro is an unspoiled speck of a village near the cave that has not one single solitary attraction. Paths from the town lead to nearly empty rocky beaches and coves. North of Nerja, the tiny village of **Frigiliana** crowns a hill 5km away. Only two small gift shops have put down tourist-hungry roots among the glistening white buildings and patterned, cobblestoned streets. Take a **bus** from Nerja (Mon.-Sat. 6 per day, 70ptas).

Ther's some great swimming west on the coastal road toward Málaga. Near the city itself, the beaches deteriorate into narrow, rocky strips, exposed to the roar of traffic.

Torremolinos

Is it Fort Lauderdale or is it Andalucía? Infamous Torremolinos, a nightmare landscape of overpriced kiosks, concrete high-rises, and pretentious boutiques, is the nearest alternative to Málaga's dull beaches. By late morning (in season), the sand on the stretch of unappetizing beach disappears beneath a carpet of bodies. At sundown the plastic nightlife takes over, and Torremolinos turns torrid with pulsating disco and flamenco until 4am.

Fortunately there are a couple of welcoming, reasonably priced *hostales* free of airbrushed seascapes. **Hotel-Residencia Castilla,** C. Manila, 3 (tel. 238 10 50), is modest and fairly quiet. To get there from Plaza Costa del Sol, take C. María Barrabino (a pedestrian side street which becomes Av. Europa) uphill, then turn left on C. Buenos Aires, and right on C. Manila. (Singles 1500ptas. Doubles 2500ptas. Hot showers included.) A little cleaner and in better condition is **Hostal-Residencia Guillot,** Pasaje Rio Mundo, 4 (tel. 238 01 44), on Pasaje Pizarro off the main plaza, Pl. Costa del Sol. A friendly owner maintains its large rooms and, when he's feeling racy, adds a postcard to the postcard-plastered ceiling. (Singles 1800-2200ptas. Doubles 2400-3700ptas.)

The tourist-oriented restaurants in town cost limbs, so head to the older, residential part of town for meals. Most of the restaurants and bars are uphill of Pl. Costa del Sol, especially around Av. Europa. **Bar-Restaurant Lanjarón** at Av. Europa, 12 (tel. 238 21 31), serves dirt-cheap, refreshing *gazpacho* (125ptas) and medium-sized *raciones* (400-600ptas) amidst a crowd of local men and women. (Open 1-4:30pm and 7:30-11pm.)

The **tourist office** is in the big commercial complex La Nogalera at Bajos la Nogalera, 517 (tel. 238 15 78). From the Empresa Portillo bus terminal, walk right, and take the first major left after Pl. Costa del Sol. The office is around the corner, waiting to inform you in English, Castilian, French, German, Italian, or Portuguese. (Open Mon. and Thurs.-Fri. 9am-3pm, Tues.-Wed. 9am-3pm and 5-7:30pm, Sat. 9:30am-1pm.) The **post office** is on Av. Palma de Mallorca, 23 (tel. 238 45 18), the continuation of the main road on the other side of Pl. Costa del Sol. (Open for stamps, *certificados*, and Lista de Correos Mon.-Fri. 8am-3pm, Sat. 9am-1pm; for **telegrams** Mon.-Fri. 8am-9pm, Sat. 9am-2pm.) The **postal code** is 29602, the **telephone code** 95. For **medical assistance,** call an ambulance at 238 38 38. You can reach the **local police** at 237 60 00.

Frequent **buses** run to Málaga, Fuengirola, and Marbella depart from the Empresa Porillo bus terminal just northeast of Pl. Costa del Sol (tel. 238 09 64).

Fuengirola

Thirty km southwest of Málaga, Fuengirola is closer to Torremolinos than anywhere else on the coast but isn't as lame. The beach crowds almost as much, however, and budget accommodations just don't exist. **Camping Fuengirola,** on Ctra. Nacional 340, km 207 (tel. 247 41 08), is large and wooded (390ptas per person, car, and tent; 320ptas per child).

The **tourist office** (tel. 246 74 57) occupies a corner of Parque de España. From the bus station, head toward Av. San Isidro, which becomes Av. Condes at Parque de España. (Open Mon.-Fri. 9:30am-1:30pm and 4-8pm.) The **post office,** C. Velande, s/n (tel. 247 43 84), is across Av. Ramon y Cajal from the bus station. (Open for stamps and Lista de Correos Mon.-Fri. 9am-2pm, Sat. 9am-1pm; for **telegrams** Mon.-Sat. 9am-9pm.) The **postal code** is 29640, the **telephone code** 95. The **hospital** responds to 247 29 29. The **police** answer 247 31 57. **Buses** hop over from Málaga or Marbella all the time (see Torremolinos).

Marbella

Glamorous Marbella, popularly considered the jewel of the Costa del Sol, has one function: the fleecing of the British, Germans, French, Swedes, and Americans who descend upon it each season in a vain attempt to rub elbows with the rich and famous. The city extorts *pesetas* quickly, efficiently, painlessly, and in five different languages, but it's also possible to steal away from this snooty city with a budgety good time. Of late, its controversial mayor has "cleaned up" the "marginal" elements (drug dealers, prostitutes, undesirables, etc.), but cleanliness comes at a price—the police presence here is overwhelming.

Orientation and Practical Information

Marbella glitzes 56km south of Málaga. To get to the town center from the bus station, take a left on Avenida Ricardo Soriano until it becomes **Avenida Ramón y Cajal.** The old town is on the left; the waves crash to the right.

Tourist Office: Av. Miguel Cano, 1 (tel. 277 14 42), opposite C. Huerta. From the bus station, walk left down C. Ricardo Soriano, the main road. Av. Miguel Cano is the 6th right. English, French, German, and Italian spoken. The office distributes an indexed map and guide to Marbella as well as some information on Andalucía. Open Mon.-Fri. 9:30am-9:30pm, Sat.-Sun. 10am-8pm.

American Express: Av. Arias Maldonado, 2 (tel. 282 14 94, 282 28 20), off Av. Ricardo Soriano. Holds mail for cardholders. Open Mon.-Fri. 9:30am-1:30pm and 4:30-7:30pm, Sat. 10am-1pm.

Post Office: C. Alonso de Bazán, 1 (tel. 277 28 98). Open Mon.-Fri. 9am-2pm, Sat. 9am-1pm; for **telegrams** Mon.-Fri. 8:30am-8:30pm, Sat. 9am-1pm. **Postal Code:** 29600.

Telephones: Kiosks every couple of blocks along the beach. Open June-Sept. 10am-2pm and 5-10pm. **Telephone Code:** 95.

Buses: Av. Ricardo Soriano (tel. 277 21 92). To: Málaga (every 1/2 hr., 1 1/2 hr., 435ptas); Torremolinos (every 1/2 hr., 1hr., 325ptas); Fuengirola (every 1/2 hr., 1/2 hr., 240ptas); Puerto Banús (every 1/2 hr., 15min., 70ptas); San Pedro de Alcántara (every 1/2 hr., 70ptas); Estepona (every 1/2hr., 190ptas); Ronda (4 per day, 1 1/2 hr., 445ptas); Gibraltar (1 per day in morning to La Línea, 1450ptas); Granada (4 per day, 2 1/2 hr., 1395ptas); Sevilla (2 per day, 2 1 /2 hr., 1485ptas); Cádiz

(3 per day, 3hr., 1620ptas); Madrid (5 per day, 8-11hr., 2965-4845ptas); Barcelona (2 per day, 20hr., 7935ptas) via València (13hr., 5480ptas).

Taxis: tel. 277 44 88.

Red Cross: tel. 277 45 34.

Hospital: Clínica Marbella, Av. Severo Ochoa, 22 (tel. 277 42 00).

Emergency: tel. 092.

Police: C. Serenata, s/n (tel. 277 31 94).

Accommodations and Camping

If you don't have reservations, especially from mid-July through August, arrive early and pray. The area in the old part of town behind Av. Ramón y Cajal, is loaded with little *hostales* and *fondas,* all of which fill up quickly. Several cheap guest houses line **Calle Ancha, Calle San Francisco, Calle Aduar,** and **Calle de los Caballeros,** all of which are uphill on C. Huerta Chica, across C. Ramón y Cajal from the tourist office road. People at bars often know of *casas particulares:* the lively **English Pub** and **The Tavern,** face to face on C. Peral can advise you in English.

Hostal del Pilar, C. Mesoncillo, 4 (tel. 282 99 36), in an alley behind the English Pub. C. Mesoncillo is the 2nd left off C. Huerta Chica. Friendly English management and a relaxing bar/lounge make for a sociable, youth-hostelish ambience. Mattresses on the roof (in warm months) 800ptas per person. Singles 1500-1900ptas. Doubles 2400-2900ptas. Triples about 3600ptas. Well-prepared English breakfasts served all day 150-500ptas.

Casa-Huéspedes Aduar, C. Aduar, 7 (tel. 277 35 78). Positively overflowing with roses in summer. Unexceptional rooms open onto a brand-new, tiled, and plant-filled courtyard on the first floor; balconied rooms upstairs. Singles 2000ptas. Doubles 2800ptas. Oct.-March: 1400ptas; 2100ptas.

El Castillo, a couple bl. uphill from the Aduar. Same owners. Horny tomcats wail and the confused roosters crow from sunset until dawn. The windowless rooms get a little stuffy in summer, but the other rooms are fine, and all have nice bathrooms inside. Singles with bath 1500-2000ptas. Doubles with bath 2700-3500ptas.

Camping Marbella (tel. 283 39 98), 2km east on N-340. Coming by bus from the Fuengirola direction, it's on the left just before Mirabella; push the button to signal the driver to stop. A 2nd-class site. 410ptas per person, 675ptas per tent.

Food

The municipal **market** is down the first left off C. Huerta Chica.

Bar El Gallo, C. Lobatas, 46 (tel. 282 79 98). Heaven in Marbella. Loud TV and louder locals, but lipsmacking good food. *Ensalada mixta* 300ptas. *San Jacobo* (pork stuffed with ham and swiss) and fries 400ptas. Open 9am-midnight, but meals not served at all times.

Bar Taurino, C. Leganitos, 1, toward the top of C. Aduar. Boisterous local crowd inspired by bullfighting posters. Whopping tortillas 325ptas. Mountain of *paella* 450ptas. Tasty *tapas.* Open 9am-11pm.

Restaurante Sol y Sombra, C. Tetuán, 7 (tel. 277 00 50). Not particularly inexpensive, but good fresh fish dishes (400-1100ptas) and a 1000ptas *menú del día.* Open 1-4pm and 8-11:30pm.

Sights and Entertainment

Marbella caters to fat-walletted tourists who like a little melanoma. Aside from some 3rd-century **baños** at the western city limits, don't look for much in the way of historical titillation. The eastern section of the old town, just up from the church, is worth exploring. A massive Arab **wall** once protected the town, and numerous houses with beautiful courtyards huddle against its crumbling remains.

Marbella has a chic promenade over the beach, leaving its most valuable asset starved for space. If the press of flesh stifles, hop on the Fuengirola bus, stop at **Playa de las Chapas,** 10km east, and walk in either direction to find an open stretch. Even here, the sand's rough and the beaches are rocky. If you choose to stay in Marbella for the evening, visit **Old Vic,** Av. Ansol, 2, for some Spanish neon disco. The **Feria y Fiesta de San Bernabé** (mid-June) is the big event of the year, with fireworks and concerts.

Near Marbella

If you're a pickpocket or seeking the life of the rich and famous, take the bus to **Puerto Banús,** 7km west. This international yacht harbor crawls with bars, discos, and the jet set. Try not to be hungry here; restaurants are shamefully bad and shamelessly expensive. **Joe's Bar** pickles a slice of American atmosphere. Popular discos include **Willy Salsa,** at km 186 on highway N-340, and **¡Oh! Marbella,** in Hotel Don Carlos (open summer only). Most discos don't charge at the door, but a small drink costs at least 700ptas. Public transportation ends at 10:30pm, and a cab back to town from Puerto Banús costs about 1100ptas. From nearby discos, it varies between 700 and 1000ptas.

Antequera

The whitewashed houses and occasional church towers of Antequera broil in a valley below a Moorish fortress. Although Romans named the city, civilization here began much earlier—*dólmenes* (funerary chambers built from rock slabs) constructed 5000 years ago stud the outskirts of town. Antequera makes a fine bivouac for forays into the surrounding mountains, and there are few sunsets more beautiful than those captured through the hills from the top of the Moorish fort.

Orientation and Practical Information

Antequera straddles the crossroads of Córdoba, Granada, Sevilla, and Málaga (rail travelers, however, will notice that RENFE has made Bobadilla the major switching point). It's a 10-minute hike up a slow, shadeless hill (Av. Estación which becomes C. Cruz Blanca) from the station to town. At the top, forge dead ahead to Plaza las Descalzas, the plaza just east of the tourist office. Turn right at C. Encarnación to reach **Plaza San Sebastián,** the town center.

The bus station sits atop a neighboring hill. To reach Plaza San Sebastián from the bus station, walk down the hill to the bullring, then turn left onto the **Alameda de Andalucía.** At the fork, follow **Calle Infante Don Fernando** (the right branch) until it runs into the plaza. If you dislike climbing with luggage in the heat, arrive by bus and leave by train—or take a cab (about 350ptas).

Tourist Office: on Pl. Coso Viejo, s/n (tel. 284 21 80), just inside Museo Municipal off C. Nájera near Pl. Descalzas. They distribute maps and some information about the surrounding countryside. Open Tues.-Fri. 10am-1:30pm, Sat. 10am-1pm, Sun. 11am-1pm.

Post Office: C. Nájera (tel. 284 20 83), down the street from the tourist office. Open for stamps, *certificados,* Lista de Correos, and **telegrams** Mon.-Fri. 8am-3pm, Sat. 9am-1pm. **Postal Code:** 29200.

Trains: Av. Estación, in the north of the city. To: Granada (3 per day, 1 1/2-2 hr., 540ptas); Málaga (3 per day, 410ptas); Sevilla (2 per day, 2 1/2 hr., 905ptas); Algeciras (2 per day, 4hr., 955ptas). At Bobadilla (3 per day, 105ptas) are a number of other connections. For information call the nearby Bobadilla station (tel. 272 00 22).

Buses: Po. García del Olmo (tel. 284 31 82), near the Parador Nacional. To: Bobadilla train station (5 per day Mon.-Sat., 15min., 150ptas); Granada (5 per day, 2hr., 745ptas); Málaga (15 per day, 1hr., 400ptas); Sevilla (9 per day, 2 1/2 hr., 1150ptas); Córdoba (2 per day, 2hr., 950ptas).

Taxis: tel. 284 10 76 or 284 10 08.

Hospital: Hospital Municipal San Juan de Dios, C. Infante Don Fernando (tel. 284 44 11).

Emergency: tel. 091.

Police: Municipal (tel. 284 11 91 or 284 12 89).

Accommodations.

Most establishments lie between the museum and the market. All charge moderate if not rock-bottom prices, and many serve meals.

Pensión Toril, C. Toril, 5 (tel. 284 31 84), off Pl. Abastos. Clean, bright-bulbed rooms and free parking in new garage. English-speaking proprietor goes off about the area's attractions. The best place to stay in Antequera. Singles 1000ptas. Doubles 2000ptas, with bath 2500ptas.

Hostal Manzanito, C. Calvo Sotelo, 5 (tel. 284 10 23), on Pl. San Sebastián. Utterly central, with high-tech showers, jaunty flowered bedspreads, and a TV lounge. Singles with shower 2200ptas, with bath 3000ptas. Doubles 3400ptas, with bath 4800ptas.

Hostal Reyes, C. Tercia, 4 (tel. 284 10 28). Portly, clean rooms with sleek, shiny metal tables and chairs like a spaceship. Singles 1200ptas. Doubles 2200ptas, with bath 3500ptas.

Food

Most places to eat are economical. Stop by the **market** on Pl. Abastos (open 8am-2pm) for a savory nibble of *queso de cabra* (goat cheese).

Pensión Toril, C. Toril, 5 (tel. 284 31 84). Well-prepared and inexpensive fare. Larger-than-life *menú* (650ptas), whopping *platos combinados* (500ptas), and generous drinks (75ptas). Open 1-4pm and 7:30-9:30pm.

Manolo Bar, C. Calzada, 24 (tel. 284 10 15). Quirky and popular local bar serving evening *tapas* and drinks. Great rock-n-roll. Eclectic decor includes photo of owner dressed as a cowboy and pinball machine parts on wall. *Tapas* 175ptas. Drinks 125-300ptas. Open Tues.-Sun. 4:30pm-12:30am.

Café-Restaurante Don Sancho, in Pl. Cristobal Toril off C. Infante Don Fernando. *Raciones* 500-600ptas. Sedate and sophisticated. Local specialties galore: gazpacho-like *porra antequerana* (450ptas) and *bienmesabe*, a sweet almond and egg cake traditionally made by local nuns (375ptas). House specialty is the *sopa Don Sancho* with seafood (450ptas.). Open Tues.-Sun. 1-4pm, 8pm-midnight.

Sights

Antequera's three ancient **cuevas de dólmenes** dodder along as the oldest and best-preserved tombs in Europe. Crudely cut rock slabs form both the antechamber (the storeroom for the dead's possessions) and the burial chamber. Actual remains and artifacts decompose in museums in Málaga and Sevilla, although it was probably bad luck to move them there. **Cueva de Menga** dates from 2500 BC. Pious and muscular ancients lugged the mammoth 200-ton roof over 5 mi. to the burial site. The four figures engraved on the chamber walls typify Mediterranean Stone Age art. The elongated **Cueva de Viera,** discovered in 1905, bears equally monstrous proportions. Bring a flashlight to explore the dark recesses. Small, flat stones cement the circular interior walls and domed ceiling of **Cueva de Romeral,** which dates from 1800 BC.

To reach the Cuevas de Menga and Viera, follow the signs toward Granada to the edge of town (a 10-min. walk from the market), or catch the bus for Barrio de los Dolmenes (50ptas) and watch for a small sign on C. Granada next to the gas station. To reach Cueva de Romeral from the other *cuevas,* continue on the *carretera* to Granada for another 2km or so. Just past Almacenes Gómez, one of the last warehouses after the flowered intersection, a gravel road cuts left and bumps into a narrow path bordered by 50-ft. high fir trees. Take this path across the train tracks to reach the cave. (Cuevas de Menga and Viera open Mon.-Sat. 9:30am-2pm and 3-6pm, Sun. 10am-2:30pm. Cueva de Romeral open Tues. 4-6:30pm, Wed.-Sat. 9:30am-2:30pm and 4:15-6:30pm, Sun. 10am-2pm. All caves free. Tips appreciated.)

Back in town, all that remains of the Arab **Castillo Santa María** are two towers and the wall between them. At the top of the wall you can feast on the beautiful view of farmland capped by a neighboring mountain peak. Along a shady, cypress-lined stairway downhill looms the Renaissance **Iglesia de Santa María.** (Open only during Mass on Sun. and holidays.)

Down the street from Pl. San Sebastián in Pl. Coso Viejo, the deserted **Museo Arqueológico** is home to the tourist office. The building still houses some local pieces, such as the *Efebo de Antequera,* a 1st-century Roman bronze figure. (Open Tues.-Fri. 10am-1:30pm, Sat. 10am-1pm, Sun. 11am-1pm. Admission 100ptas.)

Near Antequera: Sierra de Torcal

A gargantuan garden of windsculpted boulders, the Sierra de Torcal glows like the suface of a very weird distant planet. The central peak of **El Torcal** (1369m) hogs most of the horizon, but the smaller clumps of rounded rocks are even more spectacularly unusual. Clouds often smother the summit, but the mist only adds to the magnificent spookiness. Like an uninhabited planet, the Torcals are usually tourist-free. Don't wear sandals on these hot but rocky trails in summer, and bundle them feet up well in winter.

Close to the summit, two circular trails await wisely shod feet. The path marked with yellow arrows takes about an hour and is 2 1/2 km long; the path marked with red arrows takes over two hours and is 4 1/2 km long. Both paths begin and end 13km from Antequera at the *refugio* at the base of the mountain. Two-thirds of the 13km can be covered by **bus;** take the bus (from Antequera) for Villanueva de la Concepción, and ask the driver to let you off at the turnoff for El Torcal (150ptas). Buses leave Antequera only at 1pm and 6:30pm; the return bus leaves Villanueva de la Concepción at 7:45am and 3:30pm. (Call Empresa for details at tel. 233 92 47.)

Hitchhikers have helped their way back to Antequera by making friends with other tourists in the bar of the *refugio,* though of course this entails risks and we don't recommend that you try it. (Bar open in summer at the owner's whim.) There are no towns or turnoffs before Antequera, so anyone heading east on the road is going all the way. Taxi to the *refugio*—with time to watch the sun set—costs about 1800ptas.

Ronda

Ronda tops a rocky massif split by a spectacular 1000-ft. gorge, while far below the Río Guadalevín twinkles. An earthquake split the rock and made the city a natural fortress.

Ronda's history runs as deep as the gorge. Pliny and Ptolemy mention it as *Arunda* (surrounded by moutains). During the Muslim occupation, the sneaky Al Mutadid ibn Abbad annexed the city for Sevilla by asphyxiating the previous lord in his bath. German poet Rainer Maria Rilke wrote his *Spanish Elegies* here, and Orson Welles had his ashes buried on a bull farm outside of town.

Only an hour from the resorts of the Costa del Sol, Ronda is both a welcome diversion from crowded beaches and a good base for exploring some of the *pueblos blancos* to the south.

Orientation and Practical Information

Ronda is in the donut-hole of Andalucía, 125km southeast of Sevilla, 60km northwest of Marbella, 75km west of Antequera, and 98km north of Algeciras. The old and new parts of the city connect by three bridges: one Roman, one Moorish, and one new (the **Puente Nuevo**—1735). On the new side of the city, **Carrera Espinel** (the main east-west drag) runs perpendicular to **Calle Virgen de la Paz.**

Both the train and bus stations rumble on the western side of the new city. To reach the tourist office and the center of town from the train station, turn right on Av. Andalucía and follow it past the bus station (where the name changes to C. San José) until the street ends. Here, take a left on C. Jerez, follow it past the Alameda del Tajo (city park) and Pl. Toros (C. Jerez will change names to Virgen de la Paz) until it hits **Plaza de España.** Carrera Espinel intersects C. Virgen de la Paz directly across from the *corrida de toros,* immediately before Pl. España.

Tourist Office: Pl. España, 1 (tel. 287 12 72). English- and French-speaking staff know a lot about Ronda and a little about surrounding towns. Open Mon.-Fri. 10am-2:30pm.

Post Office: C. Virgen de la Paz, 20 (tel. 287 25 57), across from Pl. Toros. Open for stamps, Lista de Correos, and **telegrams** Mon.-Fri. 8am-3pm, Sat. 9am-1pm. **Postal Code:** 29400.

Telephones: Orbase, S.L., C. Mariano Soubirón, 5 (tel. 287 46 70), off C. Virgen de la Paz. A few booths in a tobacco shop. Expensive, but they accept plastic. Open 9am-2:30pm and 5-9:30pm. **Telephone Code:** 52.

Trains: Station, Av. Andalucía (tel. 287 16 73). **Ticket office,** C. Infantes, 20 (tel. 287 16 62). Open Mon.-Fri. 10am-2pm and 5-7pm, Sat. 10am-1:30pm. To: Málaga (3 per day, 2hr., 720ptas); Algeciras (6 per day, 3hr., 545ptas); Granada (3 per day, 4hr., 950ptas); Sevilla (at noon, 4 1/2 hr., 1200ptas). Change at Bobadilla for destinations other than Algeciras.

Buses: Av. Concepción García Redondo, 2. **Empresa los Amarillos** (tel. 287 22 64). To Málaga (2 per day, 825ptas) and Sevilla (4 per day, 3hr., 1025ptas). **Empresa Portillo S.L.** (tel. 287 22 62). To Marbella (6 per day, 430ptas). **Ferron Coin** handles most local connections and the cheapest route to Málaga (3 per day, 750ptas).

Taxis: tel. 287 23 16.

Car Rental: Francisco Sánchez, C. Los Remedios, 26 (tel. 287 13 43).

Hitchhiking: Let's Go does not recommend hitchhiking as a safe means of travel. Those heading to Sevilla, Jerez, and Cádiz follow C. Sevilla out of the Mercadillo. Those panting for Granada walk up Carrera Espinel and take the 3rd right after the tree-lined Av. Martínez Stein. Those destined for Málaga and the Costa del Sol zip across the highway leading downhill from Barrio de San Francisco.

Luggage Storage: At the **bus station** (100-150ptas). Open 8am-7:45pm.

Laundromat: Lavandería Andaluza, C. Almendra, 23, 1 bl. past Hostal Ronda Sol on the same street. Dry clean only. About 200ptas per item. Open Mon.-Fri. 9:30am-2pm and 5-8:30pm, Sat. 9:30-2pm.

Swimming Pool: Piscina Municipal, Av. Málaga, s/n. Av. Málaga is the continuation of Carrera Espinel. On the left as you enter the city from Málaga or Marbella. Admission 225ptas, children 175ptas. Open June 5-Sept. 5 10am-8pm.

Medical Services: First Aid (tel. 287 17 73). **Clínica Comarcal,** Ctra. Burgo (tel. 287 15 40).

Emergency: tel. 091.

Police: Av. Málaga, 9 (tel. 287 13 70).

Accommodations

Almost all accommodations are bunched in the new city along the streets perpendicular to **Carrera Espinel.** Expect difficulties only during the Feria de Ronda in September.

Fonda La Española, C. José Aparicio, 3 (tel. 287 10 52), on a side street around the corner from Turismo. What a deal! Sparkling clean with spacious rooms and a sundeck view of El Tajo. Curfew 1am. 1000ptas per person. Hot showers included.

Pensión La Purísima, C. Sevilla, 10 (tel. 287 10 50), next to La Española. Airy hallways and solid beds. A bargain if you get a room away from street. Singles 800-1000ptas. Doubles 1600-2000ptas. Showers 150ptas.

Hostal Morales, C. Sevilla, 51 (tel. 287 15 38), near the corner with C. Lauria. Friendly management. Spotless. Modern bathrooms and a tiled courtyard. Singles 1200ptas. Doubles 2400ptas.

Hostal Ronda Sol, C. Cristo, 11 (tel. 287 44 97), near the corner with C. Sevilla. Sunken courtyard, plants, and rooms with matching furniture. Annoying showers alternate between blistering hot and icy cold, but they're included in the price. Singles 1200ptas. Doubles 2200ptas.

Hotel El Tajo, C. Cruz Verde (the official name is C. Ramón y Cajal, but locals refuse to call it that), 7 (tel. 287 62 36), off Carrera Espinel. Fancy, fancy. Modern rooms in a huge hotel with elevator and garage. All rooms have phones. Singles with bath 2500ptas. Doubles with bath 4000ptas.

Food

Affordable *menús* and *platos combinados* are tough to find because so many rich people come here. Owners think they can charge tons of money and people will simply pay the prices. Well, we're here to say no. Please support the budget eateries that clatter conveniently near the center of town around **Plaza de España.**

Snack bars and bakeries line **Carrera Espinel** near Pl. España. **Gestoria Harillo,** #36, serves pastry to flaky perfection. The ice cream at **Heladería La Ibense,** next door, is creamy and delicious. **Café Alba** at #44 has *churros* in the morning that are taller than some 8-year-olds.

> **Groceries: Super Márquez,** Carrera Espinel, 13. Open Mon.-Fri. 9am-2pm and 4-7pm, Sat. 9am-noon. More of this supermarket chain throughout town.
>
> **Cervecería Marisquería "El Patio,"** Carrera Espinel, 100 (tel. 287 10 15). A/C inside, patio outside. Grilled swordfish 625ptas. Potent garlic chicken 425ptas. Open Thurs.-Tues. noon-4pm and 8pm-1am.
>
> **Pizzeria Piccola-Capri,** C. Villanueva, 18 (tel. 287 39 43). Pizza, fresh pasta, and Spanish specialties. Come here for the view of the Puente Nuevo. Caviar pizza 575ptas. *Menú* 800ptas. Open noon-4pm and 8pm-midnight.
>
> **Mesón Santiago,** C. Marina, 3 (tel. 287 15 59), off Pl. Socorro. Pl. Socorro is the 1st left off Carrera Espinel from C. Virgen de la Paz (C. Jerez). Delectable. Vine-covered terrace in the summer, cozy fireplace in winter. *Filete de ternera* (veal cutlet) 850ptas. Open noon-5pm.

Sights

Ronda's most dramatic sight, the precipitous gorge carved out by the Río Guadalevín, dips under three stone bridges. The most impressive of these, the 18th-century **Puente Nuevo,** hangs nearly 100m high and binds the city's old and new quarters.

In the old city (to the left across the bridge), a colonnaded walkway leads to the **Casa del Rey Moro** (House of the Moorish King), which, notwithstanding its name and Moorish façade, dates from the 18th century. From the gardens in back, 365 steps descend to *la mina* (the mine), a spring that once served as the town's water supply. Four hundred Christian prisoners were employed at one time to perform the arduous task of drawing water. Across the street, behind a forged iron balcony and a stone façade portraying four Peruvian Incas, stands the 18th-century **Palacio del Marqués de Salvatierra.** The palace floor sparkles with ceramic tiles. (Open Mon.-Wed. and Fri.-Sat. 11am-2pm and 4-6:30pm, Sun. 11am-1pm. Tour every 1/2 hr., min. 6 people. Admission 200ptas.)

Cobbled steps descend from the turnoff to the Puente San Miguel to Ronda's sci-fi **baños árabes.** The roofs are punctured with star-shaped holes and capped with skylights. The 14th-century saunas still function but are currently undergoing restoration (may reopen in 1993). Enter through the unmarked brown door under the dilapidated plaster wall at the bottom of the street; a yellow sign reads "Ministerio de Cultura Monumento en Restauración." (Open Tues.-Sun. 10am-2pm and 4-7pm. Free.)

On the way back up the cobbled steps, Ronda's second and third bridges appear on the right: the 17th-century **Puente Viejo** (rebuilt over an earlier Arab bridge) and the Roman **Puente San Miguel.** The former was as much an architectural achievement for its time as the Brooklyn Brige—one head architect died in the collapse of a scaffold, while another committed suicide so he would never have to build another such bridge in his life.

Calle Marqués de Salvatierra leads to the **Iglesia de Santa María,** a large 16th-century hall-church crowned by a Renaissance belfry, in the heart of Ronda's old city. Just inside the entrance bends a small arch, the only vestiges of a mosque once on the site. Inside the cathedral is *Virgen de los Dolores* by Martínez Montañés. (Open 10am-7pm. Knock for the caretaker, who'll admit you for 100ptas.) The balcony on the tower side of the church overlooks Pl. Cuidad, former parade grounds of the castle.

Back toward the new city, **Giralda de San Sebastián** pokes out as part of a former mosque converted into a church after 1485, when Ronda was captured by the Christians. Nearby, toward the Puente Nuevo, is **Palacio Mondragón,** once owned by Don

Fernando Valenzuela, one of Carlos III's ministers. The Baroque façade, bracketed by two Mudejar towers, hides 15th-century Arab mosaics. (Open 8am-2pm; in off-season 8am-3pm.)

Ronda's beautiful **Plaza de Toros,** is the site where local hero Pedro Romero invented modern bullfighting *a pie* (on foot) and used the *muleta* (red cape) for the first time. Inside the 1784 structure the **Museo Taurino** tells his glorious story and highlights Cayetano Ordóñez, apotheosized by Hemingway as the matador in *The Sun Also Rises*. (Open 10am-7pm; Oct.-May 10am-2pm. Admission 200ptas; free for children and seniors after Fri. 3pm.)

Perhaps the calmest, certainly the coolest, spot in town is the shady green **Alameda del Tajo** on C. Virgen de la Paz. Complete with drinking fountains, flower gardens, subtropical plants, and a view of the gorge, the park is overrun by ducks, swans, canaries, doves, roosters, pheasants, and the occasional vulture. **Paseo de Blas Infante,** at the bottom of Carrera Espinel by the bullring, has the better view.

Entertainment

Excitement lurks in the discos and pubs near Pl. España. **Café Tenorio,** C. Tenorio, 1, to the right of the bridge in the old quarter, blasts rock music in a rustic bar with an exquisite pool table. In early September crowds flock to the **Plaza de Toros,** where *corridas goyescas* (bullfights in Goyesque costumes) and flamenco contests explode as part of the **Feria de Ronda** celebrations. The **Corpus Christi** festivities revolve around Alameda del Tajo and C. Virgen de la Paz.

Near Ronda

Cuevas de la Pileta

A subterranean prehistoric museum of bones, stalagtites, stalagmites, and paleolithic paintings, the Cuevas de la of Pileta hollow out 25km west of Ronda along the road to Ubrique. Discovered in 1905 by the grandfather of the present owner, the caves were populated by the late Ronda-ites 25,000 years ago. Inside, rocks and water drip together in vaguely recognizable shapes, resembling a Venus de Milo here, a gorilla there. The highlight of the expedition is surely the "Cámara del Pez" (Chamber of the Fish), named for its enormous prehistoric painting. Bring a flashlight or torch, bundle up, and don't wear sandals, high heels, or ill-fitting footwear. Upon arrival at the caves, climb to the mouth to see if the guide is inside. If no one is about, walk to the farm below and rouse the owner, who'll make appropriate arrangements. (Open 9am-2pm and 4-7pm. Admission and 1hr. tour 500ptas.)

To reach the caves from Ronda, take the **train** to **Benjaón** (4 per day—the 7am will spare you the midday heat on the hike, 340ptas) and steel yourself for the grueling 7km uphill climb to the cave entrance. From the station, take the wide dirt road leading uphill and bear right at the rotary in the middle of town. The uphill road to the cave is just outside of town—it's only 4 1/2 km from here. You'll have to ask directions in town. By **car,** take highway C-339 north (Ctra. de Sevilla heading out of the new city). About 13km out of town is the turnoff to Benjaón and the caves, in front of an abandoned bar-restaurant. Don't leave valuables in your car during the tour.

You can also take the **bus** to Benjaón on Amarillo at 8:30am and 1:30pm (190ptas). The approach through the barren stone massifs of the Serranía de Ronda is stupendous. The road winds through the town of Montajaque; the turnoff to the caves is just outside of town.

Serranía de Ronda

South of Ronda, the rocky Serranía de Ronda extends east to west. With the exception of the area between Ronda and Ubrique, where wind and rain have created a polymorphic landscape, the terrain is composed of mountainous brown rock and sparse vegetation. Only at the heights do the *pinsapos,* famous native pines, spruce up the mountains with greenery.

The southern stretch from Ronda south to San Pedro de Alcántara climbs up along a fantastic coast overlooking the valley of the Pío Guadalmedina. Explore other routes as well.

Highway toward Málaga: The **Mirador de Guardia Forestal** lookout point is spectacular.

Road to Jerez and Sevilla: Winding among the Serranía foothills, the road passes through the village of **Zahara de la Sierra,** dominated by the lovely **Iglesia de Santa María de la Mesa.**

Highway C-341: Dazzling local scenery and three choice *pueblos blancos* (Knights Templar country) to boot. **Benadolid** has a handsome, cliffside Moorish castle to its credit; **Algatocín** chimes with a 18th-century stone bell tower; and **Gaucín** wraps around a humongous rock scattered with Moorish ruins.

Olvera

Olvera's wave of white houses washes up a hill and breaks over the green and gold of surrounding farmlands, in bright contrast to the rows of orange houses lining the hillside. Procure the key to the **Castillo Arabe** from the caretaker who lives on Pl. Iglesia, 2, to the left of the castle gate. She's also pocketed the keys to the 17th-century church across from the plaza (donations expected). The top of the castle has a fabulous view of the town set against acres of olive groves.

The best place to stay—and you may want to stay for a long time—is **Pensión Maqueda,** C. Calvario, 35 (tel. 213 07 33; 900ptas per person). **Pensión Olid,** Llana, 13 (tel. 213 01 02), proffers immaculate rooms, friendly management, and an architecturally remarkable shower curtain. (Singles 1000ptas. Doubles 2000ptas. Showers 150ptas.) **Bar-Restaurante Manola,** in Pl. Andalucía between the hotels and the castle, stirs up a *menú* (650ptas) and entrees (500-700ptas). Los Amarillos **buses** take on Olvera from Ronda (at 1:15pm, 385ptas).

Setenil de las Bodegas

Nearby, the village of **Setenil de las Bodegas** perches on a mountain encrusted with caves. Troglodytes first inhabited Setenil's caves; façades and later free-standing houses branched off the grottoes. There are still long rows of chalk-white houses built into the hillsides. The village stretches along a dramatic gorge cut by the waters of the sparkling Río Guadalporcún. The riverside streets or *cuevas* burrow under the gorge's cliff walls, creating long, covered passageways: **Cuevas Sombra, Cuevas del Sol,** and **Cuevas de Cabrerizos.** The 15th-century **Iglesia de la Encarnación,** atop the biggest rock, has darling views of the village below.

Back in town, broiled lamb and fries are 325ptas at **Bar Las Flores** (on the top of the other side of the village from the church). In August, folk dancers storm the streets. From Ronda, Ferron-Coin **buses** serve Setenil (Mon.-Fri. at 8:45am and 9:30am). By **car,** take Ronda's C. Sevilla to C-339 North. For Olvera and Setenil, take either the turn for El Gastor or the longer route by the dramatic outcropping of the village of Zahara.

Algeciras

Most people come to Algeciras to leave. If Morocco is next on your agenda, consider spending your last Spanish evening in Tarifa or Véjer de la Frontera. Algeciras does make a sensible jumping-off point for exploring Gibraltar, however. Buses run between the two every half hour, and the city appears not quite so uninhabitable when the alternative is spending your last pesetas in an overpriced Gibraltar *pensión*. If you do stay in this grimy port town, venture into the city, where health and company improve dramatically as you move away from the dope fiends at the port.

Orientation and Practical Information

Avenida Virgen del Carmen, where the banks, hotels, and restaurants are, stretches all along the coast. Near the port, its name changes to **Avenida La Marina.** The train tracks and Calle Juan de la Cierva run perpendicular to this street and the coast, and the train and Comes bus stations are located on its extension.

Algeciras 417

All services necessary for transit to Morocco are clustered around the port, accessible by a single driveway. Purchase tickets immediately prior to departure; advance purchase is unnecessary. Be wary of impostors who peddle ferry tickets. You'll need about 30 minutes to clear customs and board, 90 minutes if you have a car.

Tourist Office: C. Juan de la Cierva, s/n (tel. 60 09 11), the gigantic tube-shaped pink and red building. To reach the tourist office from the train or Comes bus stations, follow the tracks toward the port for a few hundred meters. From the port itself, cross the tracks as you exit and the tourist office is just up on the right. French and English spoken. Big map with all essentials clearly marked. Lots of Andalucía brochures. Open Mon.-Fri. 9am-2pm, Sat. 10am-1pm.

Budget Travel: No office, but many of the travel agencies sell BIJ tickets. Try **Tourafrica** (tel. 65 22 00), on Av. Marina. Open Mon.-Sat. 7am-9pm, Sun. 9am-1pm, 4-8pm.

Currency Exchange: For *pesetas* or *dirhams,* go to a bank along Av. Virgen del Carmen around the market or Pl. Alta. Travel agencies get away with atrocious exchange rates.

Post Office: C. Ruiz Zorilla, s/n (tel. 66 31 76). From the train station, hang a left on the street leading to Málaga. It becomes C. Ruiz Zorilla. Open for Lista de Correos and **telegrams** Mon.-Fri. 9am-8pm, Sat. 9am-6pm. **Postal Code:** 11080.

Telephones: Just inside the exit to the port terminal building. Open 8am-10pm. **Telephone Code:** 956.

Trains: RENFE (tel. 63 02 02), all the way down C. Juan de la Cierva and its connecting street. To: Málaga (2 per day with connections in Bobadilla, 5hr., 1225ptas); Sevilla (3 per day with connections in Bobadilla, 1710ptas); Granada (2 per day, 2 1/2 hr.,1470ptas); Madrid (2 direct night trains per day, 4065-4820ptas).

Buses: Empresa Portillo, Av. Virgen del Carmen, 15 (tel. 65 10 55), 1 1/2 bl. to the right as you leave the port complex. To: Marbella (at 11:45am, 580ptas); Málaga (11 per day, 5 1/2 hr., 1015ptas); Granada (2 per day, 1980ptas); Almería (at 11:45am, 2600ptas). **Empresa La Valenciana,** Viajes Koudubia (tel. 60 34 00) in port complex. To: Jerez de la Frontera (6 per day, 21/ 4hr., 905ptas); Sevilla (6 per day, 3 1/4 hr., 1650ptas); Madrid (at 8:30pm, 10hr., 3300ptas). **Empresa Comes** (tel. 65 34 56), under Hotel Octavio on C. San Bernardo, the continuation of C. Juan de la Cierva. To: Tarifa (11 per day, 45min., 185ptas); La Línea (for Gibraltar every 1/2 hr., Sun. every hr.; 50min.; 185ptas); Cádiz (9 per day, 2 1/2 hr., 1040ptas). **Empresa Bacoma,** at the Tourafrica office on the port (tel. 65 27 55). To Barcelona (3 per day, 8520ptas). Shortened schedule weekends and holidays.

Ferries: To Ceuta (Mon.-Sat. 9 per day, Sun. 5 per day; mid-Sept to late June 6 per day; 80min.; 1500ptas, children 750ptas, 6300-7900ptas per car, 1600-2400ptas per motorcycle) and Tangier (April-Oct. 8 per day, Nov.-March Mon.-Sat. 4 per day; 2 1/2 hr.; Class A 3440ptas per person, Class B 2700ptas per person, 8500ptas per car, 2400ptas per motorcycle). 50% discount for children 4-12, 20% with Eurail pass. No cars and no service on board in stormy weather. Limited service on Sun.

Luggage Storage: In the port complex, by the stairs of the embarkation platforms. Bags must be locked or well-secured. 50ptas per small, 75ptas per medium, and 100ptas per large bag. Open Mon.-Tues. and Thurs.-Sat. 7:30am-1pm and 3:30-8:30pm; Wed. 7:30am-8:30pm; Sun. 8am-1pm.

English-Language Periodicals: Kiosk on C. Juan de la Cierva across from Turismo, next door to the Casa Alfonso Restaurant. Limited selection.

24-Hour Pharmacy: None. Regular pharmacy on C. Cayetano del Toro at C. Tarifa. Open Mon.-Fri. 9am-1:30pm and 5pm-8:30pm.

Hospital: Residencia Sanitaria (tel. 69 57 22).

Emergency: tel. 091.

Police: Municipal, C. Ruiz Zorilla (tel. 66 01 55), next to Pl. Andalucía. **National,** Av. Fuerzas Armadas, 6 (tel. 091).

Accommodations

Lots of convenient *casas de huéspedes* and *hostales* bunch around **Calle José Santacana,** parallel to Av. Marina and one block inland, and **Calle Duque de Almodóvar,** 2 blocks farther from the water. Consider asking for a back room, as would-be mods cruise the narrow streets on Vespas at ungodly hours. The beach in Algeciras isn't the best place to camp. Police patrol the waterfront and when they don't, unsavories do.

Hostal Vizcaíno, C. José Santacana, 9 (tel. 65 57 56). From the port, follow the train tracks and take the 2nd street to the right. Attractive foyer and front TV room. Rooms on top floor glow with outside light, but the lower rooms are rather gloomy. Whimsical light fixtures make disco ball patterns at night. Owners may allow you to store your things for a few weeks if you're coming back to town. Singles 850ptas, with shower 900-1000ptas. Doubles with shower 1800ptas.

Hostal Residencia González, C. José Santacana, 7 (tel. 65 28 43). Another decent bargain close to the port. Roomy, tasteful quarters and new wood furnishings. Singles 1500ptas, with shower 1800ptas. Doubles 2400ptas, with shower 3000ptas.

Hostal Levante, C. Duque de Almodóvar, 21 (tel. 65 15 05), 2 streets inland from C. José Santacana. Modern, multi-fauceted bathrooms, with demonic miniature soaps. Brightly lit rooms. Enormous color electric babysitter gets all six Spanish channels. Beds sag a tad. Singles 1500ptas, with bath 2000ptas. Doubles 2100ptas, with bath 3000ptas. Showers free.

Hostal La Plata, C. Cayetano del Toro, 29 (tel. 66 21 52), 1 bl. inland from C. Duque de Almodóvar. New wood furnishings, firm beds, and clean, modern bathrooms. Spiffy tiled entryway and TV room. Singles 1500ptas, with shower 2000ptas. Doubles with shower 3000-3500ptas.

Food

Relish your final taste of *paella,* or welcome yourself back from Morocco with a *medio pollo asado* (baked 1/2-chicken) sold in many places along **Avenida Virgen del Carmen,** near the port.

Casa Alfonso, C. Juan de la Cierva (tel. 60 31 21), the big green building near the tourist office. For no-nonsense eating with the people who run the port. Tortillas (250-400ptas) make a substantial meal. Complex system where you can assemble a personalized *menú* (700ptas). Open Sun.-Fri. noon-midnight; winter Sun.-Fri. noon-11pm.

Restaurante Casa Sánchez, Av. Segismundo Moret, 6 (tel. 65 69 57), on the corner of C. Río, 1 bl. inland from C. José Santancana. Lively local joint with low-key service. *Menú del día* with salad, 2 courses, fruit, bread, and wine 700ptas. *Gazpacho andaluz* 225ptas. Open Fri.-Wed. noon-11:30pm.

Restaurante Montes, C. San Juan, 16 (tel. 65 42 07), off Ctra. Málaga. One of three Montes joints on the block. Lots of scrumptious dead fish laid out in an ice coffin. Handsome table settings. Family atmosphere. *Menú* with two main plates 900ptas. Various tortillas 450ptas. Fish dishes 650-800ptas. Open noon-5pm and 7:30pm-midnight.

Sights

Some of the Spaniards forced to leave Gibraltar in 1704 settled in Algeciras around the beautiful **Plaza Alta,** crowned in the middle by a handsome blue- and gold-tiled fountain. Many outdoor cafés and *heladerías* line nearby **C. Regino Martínez,** the main *paseo.*

Accessible only by car, the nicest **beach** around borders the tiny village of **Getares,** 5km south of Algeciras off the main road. The mile-long sand strip is relatively uncrowded. A city bus (tel. 66 22 57) swings out that way in summer.

Advertised with great pomp and circumstance throughout Andalucía, the **Fiesta de Algeciras** during the last week of June shimmies with fairs, carnival rides, and dancing.

Gibraltar

The gateway to the Atlantic commands a breathtaking view of the Straits of Gibraltar all the way to the Moroccan coast. Nicknamed "Gib" by the locals, this British colony is a microcosm of modern Britain, complete with bobbies, fish 'n' chips, a changing of the guard, and Marks and Spencer. Gibraltar takes its Britishness very seriously, but unlike their counterparts in London, citizens can switch in and out of the Queen's English and Andalusian Spanish. The history of the Rock leaves tension unresolved today: residents look up to Britain and down on mainland Spaniards, there's a massive

Gibraltar

British military presence, and Moroccans work in horrific conditions at sweatshop wages.

The Ancients considered the Rock of Gibraltar one of the Pillars of Hercules, marking the very end of the world. The Moors fortified Gibraltar into an important strategic base following the 711 invasion. After they recaptured the Rock from the Moors in 1462, the Spanish Christians pocked the peninsula with military wares to ward off Barbary pirates and Moorish retaliation. English troops stormed Gibraltar's shores during the War of the Spanish Sucession, and the Treaty of Utrecht (1713) solidified Britain's hold on the enclave. When control of Hong Kong passes to China, Gibraltar will become the last outpost of Britain's empire.

A 1967 vote showed that the populace overwhemingly favored its British ties over becoming part of Spain (12,138 to 44). In 1969, General Franco sealed off the border and forbade any contact between Spain and Gibraltar. After a decade of negotiations and 16 years of isolation, however, the border reopened at midnight on February 4, 1985. Now tourists and residents both can cross *la línea* freely. However, the Spanish government is far from relinquishing its claim to *El Peñón*.

Orientation and Practical Information

Buses run to **La Línea,** the nearest Spanish town on the border, from the Empresa Comes station in Algeciras behind Hotel Octavio (every 1/2 hr., 40min., 185ptas). From the bus stop on the Spanish side, walk directly toward "the Rock;" the border is 10 minutes away. After passing through Spanish customs and Gibraltarian passport control, walk across the airport runway and cross the overhead pedestrian bridge.

To get downtown, continue along Winston Churchill Avenue to Corral Lane. Turn right on Corral, and head left through **Landport Tunnel.** Gibraltar's **Main Street**, a commercial strip containing most services and hotels, begins at the far end of the large parking lot past the shops on the left.

The currency used here is the Gibraltar pound, equivalent to the British pound sterling. Pesetas are accepted everywhere.

Tourist Office: 18-20 Bomb House Lane (tel. 742 89), in the Gibraltar Museum. Bomb House Lane is across the street from the cathedral and Marks and Spencer on Main Street. Open Mon.-Fri. 10am-6pm. Sat. 10am-2pm. This office is a bit better equipped than the information office, though neither has much in the way of maps. The best free maps are at the **Queen's Hotel,** farther down the peninsula (see Accommodations below). **Information Center**, to the right of Landport Tunnel through the auto and pedestrian arches. Open Mon.-Fri. 9am-6pm, Sat. 10am-2pm.

Currency Exchange: (See Orientation, last paragraph.) Banks on Main St.; most close at 3:30pm, reopening Fri. only 4:30-6pm. **Gib Exchange Ctr., Ltd.,** John Mackintosh Sq., 6A (tel. 735 17), has comparable rates. Open Mon.-Fri. 10am-7pm, Sat. 10am-5pm. Candy shop **Ransom's** also changes currency. Open 8am-10pm.

American Express: Bland Travel, 83 Irish Town (tel. 726 17; after-hours emergency calls are forwarded to England if necessary). Holds mail and sells traveler's checks, but doesn't cash them. Open Mon.-Fri. 9am-6pm; off-season 9am-5pm.

Post Office: 104 Main St. Sells Gibraltar stamps in sets for collectors. Possibly the easiest Poste Restante address on earth (not one number): Name, Poste Restante, Gibraltar (Main Post Office). Open for most services Mon.-Fri. 9am-3:15pm, Sat. 10am-1pm; winter Mon.-Fri. 9am-5pm, Sat. 10am-1pm.

Telephones: Conspicuous red booths on many corners and pay phones in most pubs. More expensive but without the hassle of coins is **Gibraltar Telecommunications International Ltd.,** 60 Main St. (tel. 756 87), across the street from Benetton. **Faxes** also sent. Open Mon.-Fri. 9am-5pm. **Telephone Code:** From Britain (010) 350. From Spain first dial 07 (or from Algeciras *only* 7), as the Rock is considered a foreign destination. The USA Direct code is 88 00.

English Bookstore: The Gibraltar Bookshop, 300 Main St. (tel. 718 94). Superior choice of classics such as *Let's Go.* Open Mon.-Fri. 9:30am-7pm, Sat. 9:30am-4pm.

English-Language Periodicals: Sacarelo News Agency, 96 Main St. (tel. 787 23). The most globe-trotting selection of papers and magazines in town. Open Mon.-Fri. 9am-7pm, Sat. 9am-3:30pm, Sun. 1:30-5pm.

Laundry: Wun-Tun Laundrette, 6 Crutchetts Ramp (tel. 425 14), near the beginning of Main St. Capacious washers and dryers. Wash and dry £4.10 self-service, £5.10 full-service. Open Mon.-Sat. 9am-6pm; winter Mon.-Sat. 9am-9pm.

Hospital: St. Bernard's Hospital (tel. 797 00), on Hospital Hill.

Police: 120 Irish Town St. (tel. 725 00), by MacKintosh Sq.

Accommodations

Camping is illegal, and the two affordable places in the area are usually full. Realistically, you have two alternatives: 1) Stay in Algeciras, only a bus ride away. 2) Ask around the restaurants near the bus station in La Línea for information about *casas particulares*.

Toc H Hostel, Line Wall Rd. (tel. 734 31). South on Main St., right just before the arch at Referendum Gate, then left in front of the Hambros Bank. Grandfatherly proprietor knows everyone in Gibraltar and runs the hostel for pleasure. A bohemian place with shackey lodgings, but prices are unbelievably low. The only trouble is getting in; some boarders have unpacked for good. Show up by 9:30am with your lucky rabbit's foot. Cold showers only. £3 per person. £15 per week.

Miss Serruya Guest House, 92/1a Irish Town (tel. 732 20). From Main St., turn right onto Tuckey's Lane, then left before the stairs. Only 4 cramped rooms. Even tiny snorelets filter through the paper-thin walls. Often the only cheap rooms available on the Rock. Singles £10. Doubles £14.

Queen's Hotel, 1 Boyd St. (tel. 740 00), facing the cable car station. Game room, sun deck, and free parking. Luxurious, spacious rooms with swish lights, plush furnishings, and winter heating. Common bathrooms aren't quite as nice. Singles £24, with bath £33. Doubles £33, with bath £38-44. Hot showers included. Breakfast £3-4.

Bristol Hotel, 10 Cathedral Sq. (tel. 768 00). The place is immense, so beds are usually available until late in the day. Modern rooms with showers, carpets, and color TV. Posh sitting room with pool table. Swimming pool across the street, sauna in the hotel. Singles with shower £42, with bath £46. Doubles £53, with bath £60. Continental breakfast £2.50.

Food

Visitors can scarf Chinese, English, French, Indian, Spanish, and Italian cuisine for a (high) price. Even fast food is expensive.

Smith's Fish and Chips, 295 Main St. (tel. 742 54). Run by a cheerful lad who dishes out rotund servings of solid English slop. Nibbling good fish or crispy chicken. A photo shows Prince Charles and Princess Di's motorcade passing in front of the shop on their honeymoon. Fish and chips (£2.95) plus some vegetarian dishes. Open Mon.-Fri. 11am-10pm, Sat. noon-3pm.

Uptown Chicago, 10 Cannon Lane (tel. 789 51), off Main St. Cheery primary-colored ice cream parlor decor with outdoor seating. Fine English grub and fab service. King-size burger with fries and salad £3.35. Spare ribs with chips and garnish £3.75. Expansive English breakfast £2.95. All food cheaper if take-away. Open Mon.-Fri. 9am-10pm, Sat. 9am-5pm.

Ye Olde Rock, Mackintosh Sq. (tel. 718 04), near the tourist office. Horrendous name. "Atmospheric" British pub with beer mugs hanging from the rafters. Hot pie with chips and salad £2.50. Sandwiches merely 90-110p. Open Mon.-Sat. 10am-11pm, meals served 10am-4pm.

Sights

From the northern tip of the monstrous massif known as **Top of the Rock,** there's a truly remarkable view of Iberia and the Straits of Gibraltar. **Cable cars** carry visitors from the southern end of Main St. to the Top of the Rock, making a stop at Apes' Den (every 10min. Mon.-Sat. 9:30am-5:15pm; £3, round-trip £4). Get the one-way ticket and walk down. The price of the cable car is better than it seems because it includes admission to St. Michael's Cave and the Apes' Den, and because newly installed toll booths charge £3 per car and £3 per walking person.

The ruins of a Moorish wall crumble on down the road from the cable car station to the south, where the spooky chambers of **St. Michael's Cave** cut into the rock. Creepy giant stalactites drip to such depths that the Romans thought the cavern bottomless. The cave metamorphosed into a hospital during the 1942 bombardments; now it's an auditorium complete with colored lights and corny music. If lucky, you'll hear a flute arrangement of "Maneater." The first Neanderthal skull ever discovered was unearthed here. To reach St. Michael's from the Top of the Rock, take gravelly St. Michael's Road and stick to the right. (Open 10am-7pm; off-season 10am-5:30pm. No entrance 15min. before closing. Admission £1.50.) Next door, a café with a view sells pricey refreshments.

Take a U-turn down to Queen's Rd. to the **Apes' Den,** where a colony of wild primates (technically monkeys) clamber lithely about the sides of rocks, the tops of taxis, and tourists' heads. The tailless Barbary apes have inhabited Gibraltar since before the invasion of the Moors. The British believe they'll control the peninsula only as long as the animals survive. When the ape population came dangerously close to extinction in 1944, Churchill ordered reinforcements from North Africa. (Admission 50p.)

Farther north on Queen's Road, the **Moorish castle** refuses to relinquish its majestic presence over the city. The Moors built the castle in 1160. The fortress has always been the symbol of mastery in Gibraltar and has flown the British flag since 1704. (Closed to the public.) A labyrinth of steep stone alleyways through Gibraltar's **old town** leads back to the commercial rush on the north end of Main St.

The **Gibraltar Museum** at the tourist office on Bomb House Lane has hedonistic 14th-century **Moorish baths** and other items of interest about Gib's history. (Open Mon.-Fri. 10am-6pm, Sat. 10am-2pm. Admission £1, students and children 50p.)

At the southern tip of Gibraltar, **Europa Point** commands a nearly endless view of the straits, guarded by three machine guns and a lighthouse. On a clear day you can see Africa. Take buses #3 or #1-13 from Line Wall Rd., just off Main St., all the way to the end (every 15min., 30p).

Tucked at the foot of the great white cliff on the northern end of the peninsula, **Catalan Bay** is a beach swarming with British tourists. Several seaside cafés and grocery stores sell snacks and beverages. Smaller but slightly less crowded, **Sandy Bay Beach** is just a short hike up the road. You can get to the most spacious crescent of sand, **Eastern Beach,** by foot from Catalan Bay. To reach the beach, take buses #1B, 4A, or 4B from Line Wall Rd. toward Catalan Bay (every 15min. 8:45am-8:45pm, 30p).

Entertainment

Pubs linger along Main St. (1/2-pint of beer 60-70p). The early evening crowd people-watches from **Angry Friar,** 287 Main St. across from the Governor's Residence (tel. 715 70), which occasionally has live music, and a jazz band most summer Sunday nights. The name alone warrants patronage by ecclesiastophiles. Don't miss having your photograph taken with the picture of the fist-shaking MONK. (Open 10am-midnight, food served 10am-3pm.) As evening wears into night, pub-hoppers slide on down to the **Horseshoe Bar** with its video jukebox at 193 Main St. (tel. 774 44; open Sun.-Thurs. 9:30am-midnight, Fri.-Sat. 9:30am-1am).

Films screen at the **Queen's Cinema** (Wed.-Fri. at 10pm; £3 stalls), Boyd St. (tel. 757 61), near the Queen's Hotel across from the cable car station. The **Casino** lies up the hill from the cinema.

Tarifa

The southernmost city in continental Europe ranks with the streets of downtown Chicago or the moors of England as one of the world's great windsurfing centers, and in fact, many windsurfers prefer Tarifa since it has a beach. Only a 45-minute bus ride west of Algeciras, Tarifa is a wannabe clone of a California surf town, complete with locals clad in thongs and tongas so brief you can tell their religion. T-shirts announce that Tarifa has "365 windy days a year." But the same winds taunt sunners and swimmers who would otherwise clog the uncongested beaches.

To reach **Plaza de Mateo,** the main square, from the bus station, take a right before the ivy-covered main gateway to the Moorish old town. A sign on the left side of the street will direct you to the long plaza of palm trees, playgrounds, and good cafés. At the bottom of the square swaggers a statue of Guzmán el Bueno, the town's hero. The stone pile to your left is his **castillo.** In the 13th century, the Moors kidnapped Guzmán's son and threatened to kill him if Guzmán didn't surrender the castle. Guzmán chose his country over his son. The castle is not open to visitors, but you can look out from its ramparts to Morocco (entrance Mon.-Fri. noon and 1pm). To get here, follow the street on your left from the castle's main gate and climb the stairs through the lovely gardens of **Plaza de Santa María.** The wetter action treks 200m north at **Playa Lances,** 5km of cool orange sand and turquoise water. Beware of high winds and undertow.

La Casa Concha, C. San Rosendo, 4 (tel. 68 49 31), one block off Pl. El Bravo, offers inexpensive lodging. From the bus stop, take an immediate left through the aforementioned ivied arch; C. San Rosendo is a few blocks down on the right. (Singles 1250ptas. Doubles with bath 3000ptas.) You can also find affordable rooms on the main strip, Batalla del Salado. If you visit in August, call ahead or arrive early. A number of official **campgrounds** lurk a few km to the north on the beach (375-400ptas per person). The police seem remarkably tolerant of short-term, unofficial camping closer to town.

For simple yet sating victuals head to **Méson el Carnicero,** Edificio Av., 3, for the filling 600ptas *menú*. Exit the bus station to the left and take the 6th right off Batalla del Salado. *Tubo de cerveza* 100ptas, with *tapa* 125ptas. (Open Sat.-Thurs. 11am-4:30pm and 7:30pm-midnight.)

The small **information kiosk** near the intersection of Batalla del Salado and Av. Andalucía (by the ivied arch) can be reached through the Ayuntamiento (tel. 68 41 86, ext. 51). The tourist office is usually open Mon.-Fri. 11am-1pm and 7-9pm, but if closed, head to the **Ayuntamiento** on Pl. Santa María for a map and advice. The **police** uphold law and order from the Ayuntamiento building (tel. 68 41 86). In case of **medical emergency,** dial **Casa del Mar** at 64 37 79. The **post office,** C. Colonel Moscardó, 9 (tel. 68 42 37), is near the town center. (Open Mon.-Fri. 8am-3pm, Sat. 9am-2pm.) The **postal code** is 11380.

Transportes Generales Comes buses make for Algeciras (9 per day, 1/2 hr., 185ptas) and Cádiz (8 per day, 2hr., 850ptas) from the **bus station** at Batalla del Salado, 19 (tel. 68 40 38).

Véjer de la Frontera

Véjer de la Frontera is the archetypal charming and tourist-free Andalusian village. Whitewashed houses scatter at the base of a handsome Moorish castle, and an elegant church pokes above an imposing rock spike. The view from the outskirts of town is, predictably, smashing. (Perhaps the best countryside vista is along the Corredera near the bus stop.) Favorite evening pastimes in Véjer: 1) gaping at the sunset from the esplanade, 2) the colorful bars around **Plaza de España**, the **Mercado de Abastos,** and especially the **Plazuela** just uphill from the bus stop.

The **Castillo Moro** offers the usual assortment of battlements and crenellated walls, along with a blinding view of the town's glowing white houses. (Open July-Aug. 10am-2pm and 4-9pm, or ask at Ayuntamiento.) **Iglesia del Divino Salvador** is a peculiar mix of Romanesque, Mudejar, and Gothic styles, unlike the peculiar mixes of these styles in other towns. The castle and the church are brilliantly illuminated at night. (Open for mass Mon.-Fri. 8:30pm, Sat. 9pm, Sun. 11am.)

The village throws some slightly bizarre fiestas. As soon as the **Corpus Christi** revelry ends in June, Véjer shoots off the **Candelas de San Juan,** in which a firecracker-filled mannequin is burnt over a huge bonfire. Amid much pomp and ceremony in Pl. España, a committee reviews the mannequins prepared by the village children and selects the most beauteous for the esteemed honor. A marching band escorts the inanimate winner through the village before its demise. Véjer loves its children and teaches them well. In spring come the delirious **Semana Santa** and **Feria de Abril** celebrations, with dancing in the streets and the running of a bull.

Sra. Luisa Doncel keeps clean and secure (3-key system) **rooms** in the nameless *pensión* on C. San Filmo, 12 (tel. 45 02 46). C. San Filmo begins at the stone stairs to the right of the Auto-Servico across from the bus stop. If Doña Luisa is not around, ask at #10 or #14. (Singles 1200ptas. Doubles 2600ptas.) More expensive, but also more luxurious, with its TV room and winter heating, is the modern **Hostal La Janda** (tel. 45 01 42), at C. Hermanos Machado, 16. From the Plazuela above the bus stop, follow C. Juan Relinque to the right. Continue uphill to a plaza, then take C. Rivas de Neira uphill to the right. This turns left and becomes C. San Ambrosio. The *hostal* is at the top of the hill next to Restaurante Quijote. (All rooms are doubles, but a lone person may be able to get a double room with bath for 1500ptas. Doubles with bath 3000-3500ptas.)

Locals recommend **La Posada** (tel. 45 01 11), on the Corredera a few buildings downhill of the Plazuela. Cute-as-a-bunny wood carvings hop around the bar and ornate dining room, where *menús* cost 900ptas, and 350ptas buys a monster tuna-topped *ensalada mixta*. (Open 1:30-4pm and 8-11pm.)

The occasional flamenco music seems strangely out of place in the **Janis Joplin Bar** at C. Marqués Tamarón, 16—after 10pm they get rockin' with one of their 400-plus classic rock tapes and albums. Frequented by well-dressed locals, the club looks much like a cave inside, tastefully decorated with hippie art (Hendrix prints, Janis & Bobby photos, etc.). To get to this groovy little pad from the Plazuela, climb C. Ntra. Sra. de la Oliva and bear left. (Open 7pm-2am 3am 4am 5am ...)

Véjer's tourist office is in the **Ayuntamiento** on Pl. España (tel. 44 72 75). (Open Mon.-Fri. 8:30am-2:30pm.) The **post office** (tel. 45 02 38) is located at C. Juan Bueno, 22A. (Open for telegrams and Lista de Correos Mon.-Fri. 8am-3pm, Sat. 9am-2pm.) The **postal code** is 11150. In case of medical emergency, call the **Centro de Salud** at 45 01 07, Av. Andalucía, 8. The **police** eat donuts in the Plazuela at the entrance to the pueblo; their number is 45 04 00.

Buses run inland almost every hour from Cádiz (80 min., 470ptas) and Algeciras (1 1/4 hr., 580ptas). Sadly, some buses let you out by the highway at **La Barca de Véjer.** Taxis charge 500ptas to take you up the hill, a fee that can be split among several passengers. It's money well spent, as the walk up can be murderous with a backpack. If you do decide to make the 30-minute trek, climb up the stone steps to the left of the restaurant. Leaving Véjer, you won't have to walk downhill, since all buses come up to a stop on the **Corredera,** the main road running on and along the mountain. For bus departures, buy your ticket in the tiny office beside the big hotel in the **Plazuela,** then wait at the stop nearby on the Corredera. (To Cádiz: 8 per day; Sevilla: 1 at 6:45am, 1500ptas.)

Cádiz

Blessed with a spectacular seaside location and beautiful bay, Cádiz seems somehow fatigued and grey. New, modern, upscale shopping districts contrast with some worn and less-inspiring streets. Yet, Cádiz has an energetically progressive streak: Cádiz' inhabitants fought fiercely against the Fascists during the civil war, and today they consistently vote for leftist parties. Socially, the city has a reputation for a roaring nightlife, open gay life, and the most extravagant carnival in all of Spain.

Over 3000 years ago, few Phoenician merchants would have guessed that their newly-founded commercial port would become so darn liberal. The town was frequented by Hannibal and the Romans; but when Rome fell, so did Cádiz. It continued to decline under assorted invasions. At last, with the discovery of America, the "City of Explorers" won a monopoly over trade to make it the wealthiest port in Europe. Unfortunately, England targeted Cádiz in its struggle with Spain. In 1587, Sir Francis Drake torched the Spanish Armada here, and the port was invaded several times by the British navy during the 17th century.

Cádiz was instrumental in liberating the very colonies which it had exploited for centuries. When Napoleon occupied Spain, Cádiz resisted (as did other regions) by proclaiming a provisional *junta* to rule the country. The radical *Constitución de 1812*

424   Andalucía

(providing for universal suffrage, including the colonies) was drawn up here even while French cannon bombarded the peninsula. Latin American creoles in attendance were influenced by this document and moved first to resist Napoleon and then Fernando VII.

Orientation and Practical Information

Cádiz is accessible by bus and train from Sevilla, Jerez de la Frontera, and Algeciras. To reach **Plaza San Juan de Dios** (the center of town) from the bus station, exit to the left, walk along Avenue del Puerto until you pass a park (Paseo Canalejas), and then head almost two blocks to the plaza.

Tourist Office: C. Calderón de la Barca, 1 (tel. 21 13 13). From the bus station on Pl. Independencia, cross over to Pl. España and walk uphill on C. Antonio López. The office is across Pl. Mina on the corner of C. Calderón de la Barca. From the train station, follow Av. del Puerto north toward the town center all the way to Pl. España, then follow directions given above. Some English spoken. Open Mon.-Fri. 9am-2pm and 5-7pm, Sat. 10am-1pm.

Post Office: Pl. Flores, in the same plaza as the market. The two lion-mouthed mail slots outside gulp down letters without even chewing. Open for Lista de Correos Mon.-Fri. 9am-3pm, Sat. 9am-2pm; for stamps and **telegrams** Mon.-Fri. 8am-9pm, Sat., 9am-7pm. **Postal Code:** 11080.

Telephones: C. Sacramento, 41. Open Mon.-Fri. 9am-2pm and 5:30-9:30pm, Sat. 9am-2pm. **Telephone Code:** 956.

Trains: Pl. Sevilla, s/n, off Av. Puerto. RENFE (tel. 25 43 01). To: Jerez de la Frontera (18 per day, 45min., 265ptas); Sevilla (8 per day, 2hr., 760ptas); Málaga (3 per day, 5hr., 1650ptas); Granada (3 per day, 6hr., 1860ptas); Madrid (*expreso* at 10:15pm, 9 1/2-10 hr., 4660ptas; *talgo* at 1:50pm, 8hr., 6610ptas); Barcelona (*rápido* at 7:00am, 14 1/2 hr., 9510ptas; *expreso* at 6:25pm, 17 1/2 hr., 6760ptas).

Buses: Transportes Generales Comes, Pl. Hispanidad, 1 (tel. 21 17 63, 22 46 00, or 22 46 01). To: Puerto de Santa María (Mon.-Sat. 19 per day, Sun. 7 per day; 40min.; 160 ptas); Rota (Mon.-Sat. 8 per day, Sun. 3 per day; 1 1/4 hr.; 385ptas); Arcos de la Frontera (Mon.-Sat. 6 per day, Sun. 3 per day; 2hr.; 565ptas); Jerez de la Frontera (Mon.-Sat. 15 per day, Sun. 8 per day; 1hr.; 300ptas); Algeciras (8 per day, 2 3/4 hr., 1040ptas); Sevilla (11 per day, 1 1/4 hr., 1000ptas); Córdoba (1 at 4:30pm, 4 1/2 hr., 1870ptas); Málaga (3 per day, 5hr., 1650ptas); Granada (1 at noon, 8hr., 3080ptas). **Transportes Los Amarillos,** Av. Ramón de Carranza, 31 (tel. 28 58 52), across from Jardines de Canalejas. To: Sanlúcar de Barrameda (8 per day, 1 1/4 hr., 315 ptas); Chipiona (8 per day, 1 1/2 hr., 385ptas); Puerto de Santa María (6 per day, 1 1/4 hr., 145ptas); Arcos de la Frontera (2 per day, 3hr., 735ptas).

Taxis: tel. 21 21 21, 22 10 06, or 27 20 21.

Luggage Storage: The train station has medium size lockers.

Pharmacy: Farmacia S. Matute, Pl. San Juan de Dios, 2. Open Mon.-Fri. 9:30am-1:30pm and 5-9pm; winter Mon.-Fri. 9:30am-1:15pm and 4:30-8pm, Sat. 9:30am-1:15pm.

Medical Assistance: Casa de Socorro, C. Benjumea, 11 (tel. 21 10 53) or Av. López Pinto (tel. 23 10 80).

Emergency: tel. 091 or 092.

Police: National, Av. Andaluciá, 28 (tel. 28 61 11), in new city. **Municipal,** tel. 22 81 06, by Campo del Sur in new city.

Accommodations

Singles and triples are scarce here, but many *hostales* huddle around the harbor and **Plaza San Juan de Dios.** Call months in advance for February's carnival.

Pensión Marqués, C. Marqués de Cádiz, 1 (tel. 28 58 54), off Pl. San Juan de Dios. Plants in the patio; no plants in the oldish high-ceilinged rooms. Glaring green and white interiors with floor tiles that could use help. Singles 1100ptas. Doubles 2200ptas. Cold showers 100ptas, hot showers 150ptas.

Hostal Barcelona, C. Montañés, 10 (tel. 21 39 49), off Pl. Candelaria. A Barbie dream house: teeny plastic cups, miniature soaps, big pink beds, pink towels, and a large balcony. The central patio is dark. Singles 1595ptas. Doubles 2925ptas. Showers 250ptas.

Camas Cuatro Naciones, C. Plocia, 3 (no tel.), right next to Pl. San Juan de Dios. Same two-tone decor as the cathedral. Aquatic blue rooms, with lots of light in those facing the street. Fading yet functional at rock-bottom prices. Singles 1200ptas. Doubles 2500ptas.

Food

The area around Pl. San Juan de Dios is fertile foraging territory. The dozens of stands or bars (called *peñas*) near Playa de la Caleta, in Barrio de la Viña to the southwest, and on C. La Palma sell the city's notorious **pescado frito** (fried fish).

Restaurante Pasaje Andaluz, Pl. San Juan de Dios, 9 (tel. 28 52 54). The bare decor, metal tables on the plaza, and white tiled walls disguise one of Cádiz's best restaurants as a shower stall. *Menú* of plenty (paella, veal chop, fries, bread, wine, dessert; 600-800ptas). Amazing *almejas* (clams, 450ptas) and snapping good *judías* (green beans). Open 1-4:30pm and 8-11pm; Oct.-June Sat.-Thurs. 1-4:30pm and 8-11pm.

Novelty Café, Pl. San Juan de Dios, s/n (tel. 28 54 54), at the corner of C. Nueva. Self-service inside, metal chairs and tables for service outside. Prices and *menús* scribbled on walls and windows. Plenty of farinaceous dishes assist cellulite accumulation. *Menú* 600-850ptas. Spaghetti and macaroni 200-2500ptas. Open Thurs.-Tues. 11am-4pm and 8-11pm. Closed every other Tues.

Restaurante Fanny, C. Barrocal, 2 (tel. 29 59 51), near Pl. Candelaria. The first corner on the left off C. Obispo Urquinaona. Flash white tablecloths, paneling, and friendly service. *Paella* or fried fish, a veal chop, fries, bread, and dessert, 800ptas. Open Mon.-Sat. 1-4pm and 8:30-10:30pm.

Sights and Entertainment

The winding, cobbled streets of the **Ciudad Vieja** form a labyrinth of seaside dives and tiny shops. Across from the tourist office on C. Antonio López, in Pl. Mina, the **Museo de Bellas Artes y Museo Arqueológico** hang a fulsome collection of Murillo, Rubens, and Zurbarán. (Open Tues.-Sun. 9:30am-2pm. Admission 250ptas. EEC citizens free.) To the south on C. Santa Inés, 9, the **Museo Municipal Histórico** flaunts an enormous, painstakingly-wrought 18th-century ivory-and-mahogany model of the city. (Open Tues.-Fri. 9am-1pm and 5-8pm, Sat.-Sun. 9am-1pm; winter Tues.-Fri. 9am-1pm and 4-7pm, Sat.-Sun. 9am-1pm. Free.) Around the corner and two blocks downhill on C. Rosario, works of Goya, Cavallini, and Camarone hang at **El Oratorio de Santa Cueva.** (Open Mon.-Sat. 10am-1pm. Admission 50ptas.)

Continue down C. Rosario and turn right on C. Padre Elejarde to reach the 18th-century **catedral,** with an imperious gold dome and Baroque facade. The treasury bulges with stupefying valuables. One piece, the *Custodia del Millón,* is said to be set with a million precious stones. Believe it or not, composer Manuel de Falla is buried in the crypt. (**Museo de la Catedral** open Mon.-Sat. 10am-1pm. Guided tours every 1/2-hr. Cathedral mass Mon.-Sat. 6:30pm, Sun. noon and 6:30pm. Admission 200ptas, children 100ptas. No shorts or bare shoulders allowed during mass.)

Cádiz's balustraded **seaside paseo** runs along the north and east sides of the city, fronting the panoramic Atlantic and the far shore of the bay of Puerto de Santa María. Exotic trees, fancifully sculpted hedges, and even a couple of chattering monkeys fill the neighboring **jardines públicos.** To reach the finest part of the beach, catch local bus #1 (toward Cartadura) at Pl. España or points east, get off at "Balneario," and turn right on C. Glorieta Ingeniero La Cierra. If you prefer to hike to the beach (about 30 min. from Pl. España), walk east to Pl. Constitución and continue along Av. Cayetano del Toro. Although it doesn't show up on Turismo's map, the sprawling **Paseo Marítimo,** along the beach east of Plaza Constitución, is home to the city's best bars, discos, cafés and *terrazas*.

The gray of winter gives way to dazzling color in February when Cádiz hosts one of the most Rabelaisian **carnavales** in the world. Costumed dancers, singers, and residents take to the streets in a week-long frenzy of festivity that makes New Orleans' Mardi Gras look like Thursday night bingo.

Costa de la Luz

As the Costa del Sol continues its pell-mell degeneration, discriminating eyes stray to the Costa de la Luz. Although this coastline can't compete with the sun coast's warm waters, its long, sandy beaches are relatively tourist-free.

Heavy winds and industrialization mar the shoreline, leaving only a few beaches such as Rota, Chipiona, and Sanlúcar de Barrameda top-notch. While hotels and restaurants jack up their prices 15-20% for the summer season, they're still substantially cheaper than on the Costa del Sol. Don't camp unofficially by the ocean because police are suspicious of backpackers. Courtesy of the shore's large fishing industry, sea creatures are everywhere. Especially scrumptious are *chocos*, a variety of squid, and fresh *sardinas a la plancha*.

El Puerto de Santa María

El Puerto de Santa María snuggles comfortably behind Cádiz in the *Bahía de Cádiz;* even the wind is calmer than in the bustling city southwest. El Puerto's modern attraction is its casino, the only major one on the Costa de la Luz. The city has also some historical claims to fame. One of Columbus's pilots in 1492 was Juan de la Cosa, *de facto* owner of El Puerto de Santa María. Columbus's second voyage to the New World departed from El Puerto. After the discovery of the New World, El Puerto became Spain's largest mercantile center.

The tourist office will direct you to the locations of the dozen or more palaces built by traders after the discovery of the New World and by prominent families after the discovery of the British market. **Iglesia Mayor Principal** has a Baroque front topped with a one-armed nude and two sidekicks. (Church open 10am-noon and 8-9:30pm. Free.) Alfonso X El Sabio (The Wise) built the **Castillo de San Marcos** in the 13th century. Visitors can survey the city from the castle's tower. (Castle open July 1-Sept. 30 Mon., Wed., and Sat. 11am-1:30pm, Oct. 1-June 30 Sat. 11am-1:30pm. Free.) The **Museo Municipal Arqueológico** displays local artifacts. (Open Mon.-Sat. 9:30am-1:30pm. Admission free.) To visit one of El Puerto's two *bodegas* that offer tours (Mon.-Fri. 10am-1pm), make a reservation with **Bodega Terry** (tel. 48 30 00) or the **Bodega Osborne** (tel. 85 52 11).

Several *hostales* lie off C. Virgen Milagros and C. Palacios in the town center. To get to the town center from the train station (about 10 min.), follow the signs straight ahead and then to the left on C. Virgen de los Milagros. From the bus stop, simply walk away from the water. The plant-filled patio at **Hostal Loreto,** on C. Ganado (tel. 54 24 10), just north of C. Virgen de los Milagro, is roasty good; the rooms are modern, clean, and comfortable. (Singles 2500ptas. Doubles 5000ptas.)

When quelling the rumbling in your tummy, avoid the numerous overpriced restaurants near the water. **Casa Adriano,** C. Pozas Dulces, 20 (tel. 54 34 17), on the way from the train station to the tourist office, specializes in rabbit (525ptas) and fish and gets rave reviews from locals. The *menú* (750ptas) is served on turquoise tablecloths in a full-fledged dining room. Sit in the back to avoid the noise from the street. (Open Tues.-Sun. 1-4:30pm and 8pm-midnight.) Baked whole chickens are sold from the stand at C. Ganado, 29 (575-600ptas; irregular hours, but generally open 7-10:30pm, sometimes early afternoon). Don't even try to sneak out of town without visiting **La Tortillería** at C. Palacios, 4. This bar serves mouthwatering specialty tortilla sandwiches (150-225ptas; open Mon.-Fri. 9am-3pm and 8pm-closing, Sat. noon-3pm and 8pm-closing, Sun. 8pm-closing).

El Puerto's **tourist office** is at C. Guadalete, 1 (tel. 54 24 13, 54 24 75), off Av. Bajamar, near the bus stop. From the train station, go directly left on the Ctra. Madrid and, at the fork, to the right onto C. Pozas Dulces. Stay to the left and follow the water for about 5-10 minutes. The tourist office is on the right, salivating over its map and list of *hostales* with addresses, telephone numbers, and sample prices. (Open 10am-2pm and 6-8pm; winter 10am-2pm and 5:30-7:30pm.) The **post office** deals on Pl. Polvorista, 3 (tel. 85 53 22). The **telephone kiosk** (tel. 54 30 14) is in the middle of the palm-lined *paseo del parque* on the way from the train station to the tourist office. (Open July-

Aug. 10am-3pm and 6pm-midnight; off-season 10am-2pm and 6-10pm.) The **telephone code** is 956. In case of a medical emergency, rush to the **Clínica Santa María del Puerto** at C. Valdés, s/n (tel. 85 13 11). The **national police** are on Av. Constitución (tel. 091), while the **municipal police** can be alerted at C. Manuel Alvarez, 58 (tel. 092).

El Puerto's bus station is more of a **bus stop,** directly between the water and the tourist office on Av. Bajamar. The bar on the corner lists current bus schedules. Buses connect El Puerto to Cádiz (every 1/2 hr. 7:15am-9:30pm, 40min., 180ptas), Jerez de la Frontera (6 per day), Rota (8 per day), Sanlúcar (8 per day, 35min.), and Chipiona (8 per day, 50min.). If arriving by bus from Jerez, you may be dropped off in front of El Puerto's **train station** on Pl. Estación, at the intersection of Av. Estación and Carretera de Madrid. Trains depart for Jerez (23 per day, 11min., 105ptas), Cádiz (23 per day, 1/2hr., 220ptas), Sevilla (12 per day, 1 1/2 hr., 590-1060ptas), Madrid *(expreso* at 10:49pm, 9 1/2 hr., 4495ptas; *talgo* at 2:18pm, 7 1/2 hr., 6295ptas), and Barcelona *(rápido* at 7:25am, 14hr., 9230ptas; *expreso* at 6:58pm, 17 1/2 hr., 6500ptas). A ferry ("El Vapor") links El Puerto with Cádiz, departing near the bus stop and tourist office. (Mon.-Sat. at 9am, 11am, 1pm, and 3:30pm, Sun. at 9am, 11am, 1pm, 3:30pm, and 5:30pm; 45min.; 160ptas. Departures from Cádiz Mon.-Sat. at 10am, noon, 2pm, 6:30pm; Sun. 10am, noon, 2pm, 4:30pm, and 6:30pm.)

Rota

A series of very fine white beaches rims the calm, clear water of Rota, a small town midway between Jerez and Cádiz (about 30 minutes from each). The local American naval base perverts the character of this prosperous town; a large number of bars and discos clearly cater to the sailors. Americans should not advertise their citizenship here—the local Spanish population isn't particular in distinguishing between military and civilian. English is widely, if begrudgingly, spoken. Rota's 13th-century **Castillo de Luna** (Castle of the Moon) and medieval walls are diverting when the sun, sand, and soldiers wear you out.

To get downtown from the bus station, exit to the left, immediately take a soft right onto C. Calvario, and follow it for about 15 minutes. Pass the beach on the left, and continue for five minutes to the town's hub, **Pl. España** (past the stone arch from Pl. Andalucía). Nightlife centers on **Av. Sevilla,** which runs parallel to another beach on the west side of town. To get to Av. Sevilla from Pl. Andalucía, walk down C. Blas Infante to the end, turn right and walk about 10 minutes.

Not much room in tiny Rota for travelers. It might be best to return to Jerez or Cádiz for the night, but first check **Hostal de Española,** C. García Sánchez, 9 (tel. 81 00 98), the continuation of C. Charco, near Pl. España. The clean rooms are on a quiet pedestrian street away from the bars. (Singles 1250ptas. Doubles 2500ptas.)

Diners in Rota join naval people at the moderately priced restaurants and fast-food establishments along Av. Sevilla, or they munch with the locals. One excellent local spot, **Cafe-Bar Rota,** C. Calvario, 18 (tel. 81 17 55), serves nine different *platos combinados* (under 500ptas) in a no-nonsense, no-frills setting. (Open Sun.-Fri. 9am-midnight.)

The **city tourist office** in Viajes TourAfrica, on Pl. Triunfo, can give you the scoop on Cádiz, Jerez, elsewhere in Andalucía, and on Rota's May fair and festival. (Open Mon.-Fri. 9am-1pm and 5-8pm, Sat. 10am-1pm.) There is a full-fledged tourist office at C. Blas Infante, 1, on Pl. Andalucía. (Open Mon.-Fri. 9am-1pm and 5-7:30pm, Sat. 10am-1pm.) In case of **emergency,** call tel. 091. Find the **municipal police** at 82 91 26.

Buses connect Rota with Jerez (3 per day, 255ptas), Cádiz (Mon.-Sat. 7 per day, Sun. 3 per day; 385ptas), Sevilla (2 per day; 980ptas), El Puerto de Santa María (Mon.-Sat. 7 per day, Sun. 3 per day; 1/2 hr.; 220ptas), and Chipiona (3 per day, 145ptas). The pristine white stucco and tiled bus station is just off Pl. Triunfo, near the beginning of C. Calvario.

Chipiona

For nine months of the year, Chipiona is a quiet, pleasing, unpretentious seaside village. Around the end of June, like maggots to meat, tens of thousands of tourists creep across the beaches and invade the *pensiones* until September. Maybe they all heard that the water here has curative powers; Chipiona was a popular 19th-century spot for taking the waters.

Iglesia de Nuestra Señora de la O, constructed in 1640, stands in Pl. Juan Carlos I. Gothic architecture buffs may prefer the **Santuario de Nuestra Señora de Regla,** still the site of daily Mass. (Open 8am-noon and 5-9pm.) In July the town celebrates the **Festival de la Virgen del Carmen** and August brings the **Festival del Moscatel.** During July and August, accommodations are scarce. Try one of the *hostales* by the beach or defer to one of the local scouts at the bus station. Impeccably kept and filled with plants and stained wood, **Hostal Gran Capitán,** C. Fray Baldomero González, 3 (tel. 37 09 29), off Pl. Juan Carlos I, occupies a lovely old Andalusian house. Rooms are individually decorated with religious icons and decorative candles. Prices are more than reasonable for the quality and location. (Singles with bath 2500ptas. Doubles with bath 4000ptas. Open mid-April to Oct. 31.) A municipal **campground,** Carretera a Rota at 3km (tel. 37 23 21), sits in a nearby pine grove about 800m from the beach. It has a pool and a supermarket. (425ptas per person and per tent, children under 11 365ptas; electricity 350ptas.)

Restaurants line Playa Cruz del Mar (at the end of C. Isaac Peral) and the area around Pl. Palomas and Pl. Pío XII. Ordering a glass of *vino moscatel* says "I'm a tourist" but is quite all right. **Restaurante El Gato,** C. Pez Espada, 9-11 (tel. 37 07 87), is Chipiona's best. Lap up its specialties, *viz.,* local seafood and *bellota* ham (from acorn-fed piggies). Most dishes 700-900ptas. (Open 1-5pm and 8pm-midnight.)

Chipiona's **tourist office** (tel. 37 08 80) is in the municipal library at Plaza Pío XII, on pedestrian shopping street C. Isaac Peral. (Open Mon.-Fri. 9am-1pm and some afternoons and Sat. mornings.) To get here from La Valenciana bus station, exit to your left, take a left around the corner and continue for two blocks; Pl. Pío XII is down and to the right. From the Los Amarillos station exit to the left, take C. Victor Pradera up two blocks, and then turn left. Finally, if the bus haps to leave you at the stop outside town, walk down Av. del Ejercito for two blocks and take a right on C. Miguel de Cervantes, which becomes C. Isaac Peral. Meanwhile, the **Ayuntamiento** (on Plaza Juan Carlos I, close to C. Isaac Peral, 2 blocks from the beach) gives away maps.

The **post office** is on C. Padre Lerchundi, 15A (tel. 37 14 19), near Pl. Pío XII. (Open Mon.-Fri. 8am-2pm, Sat. 9am-1pm.) The **postal code** is 11550. The friendly staff at the **telephone** center (tel. 37 19 87) on Pl. Juan Carlos I sell postcards and birdseed for the plaza's doves. (Open 9am-2pm and 6-11:30pm.) **Taxis** are summoned at 37 00 18 or 37 11 20. In a **medical emergency,** call an **ambulance** at 37 17 04, or find the **Red Cross** (tel. 37 04 81). at Av. Cruz Roja, 35, 1 block inland from Pl. Regla. For **local police** (tel. 37 10 88), go to C. Virgen de Consolación. Los Amarillos **buses** (tel. 37 02 92) operate from Av. Regla, while La Valenciana buses (tel. 37 12 83) depart from Pl. San Sebastian to Sanlúcar (12 per day, 20 min., 75ptas) and Jerez (12 per day, 1 hr., 240ptas).

Sanlúcar de Barrameda

The best way to approach Sanlúcar de Barrameda is by sea. Unfortunately, you'll be approaching from the opposite side, so be prepared for a disappointment. Rugged old-town charm *is* tucked behind those industrial outskirts. Magellan embarked from here for his globe-circling journey, and Columbus used this port on his third trip to the New World. In additon to launching famous voyagers, Sanlúcar is celebrated primarily for its huge *langostinos* (king prawns) and *manzanilla*—this savory sherry, served at any *bodega* (wine cellar) in the old city, has a unique tangy aftertaste ascribed to the sea-salt in Sanlúcar's soil.

Orientation and Practical Information

Unlike most Spanish towns, the streets of Sanlúcar run in a shocking direction—straight—and all are parallel or perpendicular to the Guadalquivir. The primary parallel drag is **C. San Juan,** which runs about 12 blocks inland from the river between Plaza La Salle and **Plazas del Cabildo** and **de San Rogue** (the town gathering spots). **Calzada del Ejército** is the main perpendicular thoroughfare, starting one block north of Pl. Cabildo and blasting a wide promenade through town down to the water.

Tourist Office: Calzada del Ejército, s/n (tel. 36 61 10). From the small Los Amarillos bus station, walk straight ahead on C. San Juan until Pl. Cabildo on the left. Cross the plaza and follow Calzada del Ejército. La Valenciana buses will leave you on Calzada del Ejército, just 150m from the office. The office, in its own building along the middle of the dirt promenade, provides an upside-down yet functional map, information on Parque Nacional de Doñana, and a brochure on Sanlúcar. Open Mon.-Fri. 10am-2pm and 6-8pm, Sat.-Sun. 10am-1pm. Closed weekends in winter.

Post Office: Av. Cerro Falon, 61 (tel. 36 09 37), 3 blocks east of the tourist office. Open for Lista de Correos, stamps, **telegrams,** and packages Mon.-Fri. 8am-3pm, Sat. 9am-2pm.

Telephones: Calzada del Ejército, next door to tourist office. Open May-Sept. 10am-3pm and 6pm-midnight. **Telephone Code:** 956.

Buses: Los Amarillos, Pl. Salle (tel. 36 04 66), at the end of C. San Juan. To: Chipiona (Mon.-Fri. 7 per day, Sat.-Sun. 4 per day; 15min.; 75ptas); Cádiz (Mon.-Fri. 8 per day, Sat.-Sun. 4 per day; 1 1/4 hr.; 315ptas); Sevilla (9 per day; 2hr.; 745ptas). **La Valenciana** ticket office (tel. 36 01 96), C. San Juan, 12. Buses operate from Calzada del Ejército, by the tourist office. To: Chipiona (Mon.-Sat. 9-11 per day, Sun. 6 per day; 15min.; 70ptas); Jerez de la Frontera (Mon.-Sat. 11 per day, Sun. 7 per day; 40min.; 180ptas); Sevilla (3 per day; 845ptas).

Taxis: C. San Juan (tel. 36 11 02); C. San Jorge (tel. 36 00 04).

Pharmacy: C. San Juan, 26 (tel. 36 04 25). Open Mon.-Fri. 9:30am-1:30pm and 5-9pm; winter 9:30am-1:15pm and 5-8pm.

Hospital: Hospital de San Diego, Centro de Salud (tel. 36 44 44).

Police: Juan de Argüeso, 11 (tel. 36 25 26). **Municipal,** Cuesta de Belén (tel. 36 01 02).

Accommodations

No true budget accommodations exist, and most places extort double room fees from a lonesome traveler if only double rooms remain.

Hostal La Blanca Paloma, Pl. San Roque, 9 (tel. 36 36 44). Spacious, clean rooms with white marbley floors, some with jumbo balconies. Singles 2500ptas. Doubles 4000ptas.

Hotel Los Helechos, Pl. San Roque, 9 (tel. 36 13 49). This recently renovated Spanish home mixes old charm with modern conveniences: lounge with international cable TV, patio, bar/restaurant, and parking garage. All rooms with phones. Singles with shower 4800ptas. Doubles with shower 7800ptas, with bath 8000ptas.

Hostal Río, C. Santo Domingo, 35 (tel. 36 15 81), on the same road as C. San Juan but 2 name changes later. Bare, big rooms, most with balconies; all bear flowery bedspreads. Concerned management supplies nifty no-slip pads in some shower stalls. Singles 2500ptas, with bath 3000ptas. Doubles with showers 4000ptas, with bath 5500ptas.

Food

Bar-restaurants and *tascas* serving *tapas* and *raciones* fill **El Barrio,** the area uphill and away from the river, circumscribed by Calles San Nicolás, Bolsa, Rubiños, Barrameda, and San Antonio o Pirrado. For a sit-down meal head for the side streets off **Calle San Juan.**

Bar-Restaurante El Cura, C. Amargura, 2 (tel. 36 29 94), by Pl. de San Rogue. Old-fashioned fans and family atmosphere. Signs above the bar spell out 9 combination plates (375ptas). *Paella* 450ptas, fried seafood dishes 350-900ptas. Open 7am-midnight.

Bar-Restaurante La Parada, Pl. Paz, 4-5 (tel. 36 11 60). Always crowded with locals and hundreds of ham shanks doing the Virginia reel on the ceiling. Long menu of tremendously big *raciones* posted on the wall (350-500ptas). Open Oct. 1-Aug. 31 Tues.-Sun. noon-5pm and 8pm-12:30am.

Sights and Entertainment

Sanlúcar is a strange bird on the Costa de la Luz, possessing the secret of joy in its beach and historic sights. Two impressive palaces, **Palacio Infantes Orleans,** built by the 19th-century Bourbons, and the 15th-century Renaissance **Palacio de los Duques de Medina Sidonia**, grudge match with the enormous 14th-century **Iglesia de Nuestra Señora de la O** for the attention of sun-struck tourists. Until recently the Palacio de los Medina Sídonia was inhabited by the duchess and the family's rich archives; the entire complex has since been ceded to a foundation associated with the University of Madrid.

Sanlúcar is ususually perky for a small town; it bops with people sitting on terraces, outdoor bars, etc. until after midnight, even on schooldays. The city's numerous festivals testify to the residents' fondness for merry-making. The **Feria de la Manzanilla** in May liberates the most alcohol, but Corpus Christi, in June, explodes the biggest fanfare. In August, horseracing thunders along the beach, and the **Festival de la Exaltación del Río Guadalquivir** enlivens the streets with a flamenco competition, popular dances, and bullfights in tribute to Andalucía's great river.

Parque Nacional de Doñana, one of the most important natural reserves in Europe, extends north of Sanlúcar. A boat connects the Doñana beach to the north end of the Sanlúcar beach (200ptas), but enrollment in an organized tour is required to enter the park. For a four-hour, 3300ptas guided tour, contact **Tourafrica,** C. San Juan, 8 (tel. 36 25 40) or **Agencia de Viajes Ocio y Vacaciones,** Calzada del Ejército, s/n (tel. 36 02 25). Significantly cheaper, but also many kilometers away, are the administrative offices of Parque Doñana in El Acebuche (tel. (955) 43 04 32), which also organize tours. Yet another way to visit Doñana is to approach the park from Sevilla, taking a bus that passes through the picturesque towns of **Almonte** and **El Rocío.** From El Rocío you can see the endless expanse of marshes that becomes Western Europe's largest lake in winter. (Park open except during the week-long festival of the Romería del Rocío in May.)

A **ferry** crosses the Río Guadiana into Portugal from **Ayamonte,** an attractive seaside artists' colony (fare 90ptas per person, last at 11pm), but most border-crossers now use the spanking new bridge (completed in 1992) 5km further north.

Jerez de la Frontera

During the reign of Henry VII the English developed the taste for sherry. British families have since elbowed in on production of these Andalusian wines, and even mangled the name, originally derived from this Spanish town. You can still visit fermenting sherry in the *bodegas* (wine cellars) throughout Jerez. One of Andalucía's most commercial cities, Jerez is also handy for exploring four popular tourist circuits: the *ruta de los pueblos blancos* (route of the white villages); *ruta del toro* (route of the bulls); *ruta de la Sierra* (route of the Sierra); and, of course, *ruta del vino* (wine route).

Orientation and Practical Information

From the bus station, exit north onto Calle de la Cartuja, and turn left. C. Cartuja becomes C. de la Medina, which beelines for **Plaza Romero Martínez** (the commercial city center). **Plaza del Arenal** is two blocks left on Calle de la Lencería. From the train station exit to the left and take the first right on C. Herrera. The bus station is one block up, then follow the directions above.

Tourist Office: C. Alameda Cristina, 7 (tel. 33 11 50), on a palm-lined *paseo*. From Pl. Romero Martinez take C. Honda to the right and continue as it swerves to the right. Friendly and well-staffed, with highly technical data on brandy and sherry production, the royal equestrian school, etc. English spoken. Open Mon.-Fri. 8am-3pm and 5-8pm, Sat. 10am-2pm; winter Mon.-Fri. 8am-3pm and 5-7pm, Sat. 10am-2pm.

Post Office: Main office is on C. Ceron (tel. 34 22 95, 32 14 10), off the Pl. Romero Martínez. Open for stamps and Lista de Correos Mon.-Fri. 8am-7pm, Sat. 9am-2pm. Open for **telegrams** Mon.-Fri. 9am-9pm, Sat. 9am-7pm. **Postal Code (main office):** 11480. Another office beside the train station sells stamps and accepts packages.

Flights: Ctra. Jerez-Sevilla (tel. 15 00 00, 15 00 20). Connections to Madrid, València, Tenerife, Las Palmas, Palma de Mallorca, Zaragoza, and Barcelona. Flights to London (the "sherry express") Wed. and Fri. **Iberia,** Pl. Arenal, 2 (tel. 33 99 12). **Aviaco** (tel. 15 00 08), at the airport.

Trains: Pl. Estación (tel. 34 23 19), at the eastern end of C. Medina after its name changes to C. Cartuja. **RENFE,** C. Tornería, 4 (tel. 33 48 13). To: Cádiz (19 per day, 45min., 240ptas.; *talgo* at 10:10pm, 810ptas); Sevilla (15 *rápidos* and *expresos* per day, 1 1/4 hr., 515-645ptas; *rápido T. Oro* at 7:38am, 1hr., 825ptas; *talgo* at 2:31pm, 1hr., 910ptas); Madrid (2 per day, 9-11hr., 4365ptas; *talgo* at 2:31pm, 7 1/2 hr., 6175ptas); Barcelona (*expreso* at 7:12pm, 16 3/4 hr., 6575ptas; *rápido T. Oro* at 7:38am, 12 3/4 hr., 9195ptas).

Buses: C. Cartuja, the continuation of C. Medina, at the corner of C. Madre de Dios (tel. 34 10 63). To: Sanlúcar (11 per day, 1/2 hr., 180ptas); Arcos de la Frontera (17 per day, 6 on Sun., 1/2 hr., 240ptas); Cádiz (18 per day, 8 on Sun., 1hr., 300ptas); Sevilla (8 per day, 1 1/2 hr., 750ptas); Ronda (4 per day, 3hr., 1065ptas).

Taxis: tel. 34 48 60.

Car Rental: Hertz, C. Sevilla, 29 (tel. 34 74 67). **Avis,** C. Sevilla, 25 (tel. 34 43 11). **Europcar,** C. Honda, 18 (tel. 30 34 66).

Red Cross: Av. Cruz Roja (tel. 34 54 74).

Medical Assistance: Ambulatorio de la Seguridad Social, C. José Luis Díez (tel. 34 84 68).

Fire: tel. 33 66 00.

Emergency: tel. 091 or 092.

Police: National Police (tel. 091), **Municipal Police** (tel. 092).

Accommodations

Finding a bed in Jerez is as easy as pie and much less expensive than in Sevilla to the north. Look along C. Medina, near the bus station, and C. Arcos, which intersects C. Medina at Pl. Romero Martínez.

Albergue Juvenil (HI), Av. Carrero Blanco, 30 (tel. 34 28 90). In something of an urban wasteland, 25 min. from downtown or 10 min. via bus L-8 (leaves near the bus station every 15 min., 65ptas). Prices are outrageous if you don't have an HI card, and no cards are available here. Two people per room (in low season you may get a single), pool and sports facilities, TV and video room, and a rooftop terrace. Full of local students. Under 26: 714ptas per person, full *pensión* 1625ptas. Over 26: 885ptas, full *pensión* 2100ptas. Nonmembers: 2035ptas, full *pensión* 3180ptas.

Hostal Las Palomas, C. Higueras (tel. 34 37 73), 5 blocks from the bus station down C. Medina. Glittery clean, with modern bathrooms. Bed jumping won't bust head, but beware of low doorways designed by some vengeful Andalusian elf. Patio with plants, TV, and singing canaries and a lounge on every floor to entertain guests. Singles 1600ptas, with bath 2000ptas. Doubles 2800ptas, with shower 3200ptas.

Pensión Los Amarillos, C. Medina, 39 (tel. 34 22 96), down the street from the bus station. Green halls, yellow windows, red-check bedspreads, and blue beds make for Crayola heaven. Color TV in converted dining room. Cheap, clean, and convenient with hosts who can't wait to exhibit all the in-house sherry paraphernalia. Singles 1000ptas. Doubles 2000ptas.

Food

Tapas-hoppers bounce in, out, and all around **Plaza del Arenal,** or northeast on Av. Alcalde Alvaro Domeqo around **Plaza del Caballo.** *Vino de Jerez* means an inexpensive local sherry.

Restaurante Económico, C. Fontana, 4 (tel. 30 33 11), between C. Medina and C. Arcos, near Pl. Romero Martínez. Tablecloths, TV, bullfighting prints in 1 room; seafood oil-paintings in the other. Four-course *menú* 575ptas. Open Mon.-Sat. 1-4pm and 8-11pm.

Bar Serrano 2, C. José Luis Díez, 7 (tel. 33 10 99), off Pl. Arroyo, between Pl. Romero Martínez and the cathedral. The locals come to enjoy outdoor tables on the shady plaza. Leather aficionados drool over the chairs inside. Pork chop *plato* 550ptas. Fish *platos* 450-750ptas. *Menú* 800ptas. Meals served 6:30pm-midnight.

Sights and Entertainment

Like Napa Valley, California, the reason to come here is to see the *bodegas*. Multilingual tour guides distill the complete sherry-making process, and you tipple free sherry. The best time to visit is early September, during the harvest; avoid August when many of the *bodegas* close down. Maps showing *bodega* locations are available in many of the town's travel agencies. Group reservations for the hour-long tours must be made at least one week in advance. All wine-cellars are open to the public Mon.-Fri. during certain hours only.

Harveys of Bristol: C. Arcos, 53 (tel. 15 10 30). No reservations required. Particularly charming tour guides. Admission 250ptas. Tour at noon. Closed the first 3 weeks of Aug.

González Byass: Manuel María González, 12 (tel. 34 00 00). Reservations required. No charge. Tours at 9:30am and 11am.

B. Domecq: San Ildefonso, 3 (tel. 33 19 00). Reservations required. No charge. Tours at 9am and 11:30am.

Williams and Humbert, Ltd.: Nuño de Cañas, 1 (tel. 33 13 00). No reservations required. Admission 300ptas. Tours 10am-1:30pm; call for exact times.

Wisdom and Warter, Ltd.: C. Pizarro, 7 (tel. 18 43 06, fax 18 11 79). No reservations required. Guided tours in English and French. Admission 200ptas. Tours 10am-2pm.

For more sober pleasures, join the monks in their 16th-century **Iglesia de Santo Domingo** on C. Marqúes de Casa Arizon near the tourist office. (Open Mon.-Fri. 7:30-10:15am and 7:30-8:40pm.) To the south, one block past Pl. del Arenal, lies the 11th-century **Alcázar,** the Moorish **Torre Octagonal** (Octagonal Tower), and the Almohad **Baños árabes** (Arabic baths). (Open Mon.-Sat. 10:30am-1:30pm and 5-8pm, Sun. 10:30am-1:30pm.) Near the elaborate Alcázar is the imposing Baroque **catedral,** built on the site of a major Arab mosque with a Mudejar belfry. (Open for mass at 6pm and all morning on Sun.) The **Zoológico Alberto Durán,** C. Taxdirt, s/n (tel. 18 23 97), is both a huge park and the King of Andalucía's zoos, plus botanical gardens. (Open June-Aug. Tues.-Sun. 10:30am-8pm; Sept.-May Tues.-Sun. 10:30am-6:30pm. Admission 400ptas, children and seniors 200ptas.)

During the last week of April or the first week of May, the **Real Escuela Andaluza de Arte Equestre** (Royal Andalusian School of Equestrian Art) sponsors a **Feria del Caballo** (Horse Fair), with shows, carriage competitions, and races of Jerez-bred Carthusian horses. (Shows at noon every Thurs. Admission 1400-1700ptas.) Dress rehearsals are almost as impressive (Mon.-Wed., Fri. at 11am; admission 375ptas). The **Festival de Teatro, Música y Baile** in September celebrates flamenco dancing, which supposedly originated in Jerez. Beautiful sculptures are borne through the streets during **Holy Week** in March or April. Also, during the second week in September, the town erupts in the **Fiestas de la Vendimia,** a celebration of the season's harvest.

Arcos de la Frontera

The road to Arcos snakes through fields of sunflowers and sherry-grape vines. Abruptly the town appears on a giant spike undercut on three sides by the Río Guadalete. The premier *pueblo blanco* on the *ruta de los pueblos blancos* (route of the white villages), Arcos de la Frontera is a historic monument, a maze of alleyways, medieval ruins, and stone arches.

Orientation and Practical Information

Arcos twiddles its thumbs on the highway between Jerez (30km away) and Antequera, accessible by bus from either city and from Cádiz. To reach the center of town from the bus station, turn left on Calle de los Corregidores and walk uphill to Calle Muñoz Vásquez. This becomes Debajo del Corral, the first part of the Corredera, and leads into the old quarter. Most of the town's restaurants are in the rotunda area, and the pensiones are off the **Corredera,** halfway to the old quarter.

Tourist Office: C. Cuesta de Belén, 1a (tel. 70 22 64), on the continuation of the Corredera. As you exit the bus station, turn left, left again at the end of the street, and walk uphill on the Corredera 10-15 min. Good map of the old city and all essential information on food and lodgings. Some English spoken. Open Mon.-Sat. 9am-2pm; winter Mon.-Fri. 9am-3pm, Sat. 9am-2pm.

Post Office: C. Boliches, s/n (tel. 70 15 60), parallel to the Corredera, near the tourist office. Open Mon.-Fri. 9am-2pm, Sat. 9am-1pm. Open for **telegrams** Mon.-Fri. 9am-3pm, Sat. 9am-2pm. **Postal Code:** 11630.

Telephone Code: 956.

Buses: On C. Corregidores, about a 15min. walk downhill from the old quarter. To: Jerez (Mon.-Sat. about every 1/2 hr. 6:45am-7:30pm, Sun. 9 per day; 35min.; 240ptas); Cádiz (Mon.-Sat. 9 per day, Sun. 5 per day; 600ptas); Sevilla (2 per day, Sun. 5pm only; 1hr.; 760ptas); Costa del Sol (Mon.-Sat. at 4pm).

Taxis: tel. 70 13 55 or 70 00 66.

Luggage Storage: Consigna, at bus station (10ptas per bag). Open Mon.-Sat. 8:30am-7:30pm.

Medical Assistance: Red Cross, Av. Cruz Roja. (tel. 70 03 55). **Ambulatorio de Seguridad Social:** C. Calvario (tel. 70 05 55).

Police: C. Nueva, s/n (tel. 70 16 52).

Accommodations

Arcos has surprisingly few beds for a city that thrives on tourism. Except for the Fonda del Comercio, budgeters live on the hill opposite the old town. It's a long uphill walk from the bus station.

Fonda del Comercio, C. Debajo del Corral, 15 (tel. 70 00 57). High-beamed ceilings, antique furniture, and thick white-washed walls. Singles 1100ptas. Doubles 2200ptas. Call ahead or arrive early.

Hostal Málaga, Av. Ponce de León, 5 (tel. 70 20 10). From the bus station, exit to the right from the bus station, take an immediate right uphill, then a left uphill onto Av. Manuel Mancheño. At the intersection, take a sharp right onto the highway, which becomes Av. Ponce de León (20 min.). Modern new rooms with mod wood furniture, A/C, shiny bathrooms, and a terraza with a view. Singles 2500ptas. Doubles 5000ptas.

Hostal Voy-Voy, Av. Ponce de León, 9 (tel. 70 14 12), also uphill next to the Málaga. Recently remodeled rooms strut their A/C and sharp bathrooms. Good restaurant below. Management is sick of "I go" jokes. Singles 2500ptas. Doubles 5000ptas.

Food

A clique of bars in the old quarter shun the company of other good eateries at the bottom end of the Corredera by the rotunda.

Bar Alcarvan, C. Nueva, 1 (tel. 70 33 97). In a cave carved into the side of the mountain a googleplex years ago. Solid rock ceiling and walls witnessed the transition between *Homo Habilis* to *Neanderthal*. Delectable *tapas* 175-200ptas, including local cheeses and roasty good *chicharrones* (spiced pork). Open Tues.-Sun. 11am-3pm and 7:30pm-1am.

Mesón Camino del Rocío, C. Debajo del Corral, 8 (tel. 70 19 16). An Egyptian-Spanish couple serve Egyptian and Spanish dishes amid Middle Eastern decor. A/C. Felafel and lamb shish kebab 725ptas. Andalusian or Arabic dishes 825-1200ptas. Open 11:30am-5pm and 8pm-12:30am.

Café-Bar El Faro, C. Debajo del Corral, 14 (tel. 70 00 14). Filling meals in this hermitage with A/C and color TV. Hams are on the walls. Good, garlicky *pez espada con patatas* (swordfish with fries, 600ptas). *Platos combinados* 400-600ptas. Gigantic *menú* with *gazpacho, pollo en salsa* (chicken in sauce), *pescado frito* (fried fish), a drink, and bread, 850ptas. Open for meals 11:30am-4:30pm and 8pm-midnight.

Sights

The old town begins, or abruptly ends, at **Plaza del Cabildo,** a rectangular esplanade hanging over a cliff. **Iglesia de Santa María** and a privately-owned **Castello Moro** face the dandy view of olive groves and low hills. Built in 1553, the church's unique interior melange of Gothic, Renaissance, and Baroque styles is sheathed by a late-Gothic facade. (Open for mass Mon.-Sat. 8:30pm, Sun. noon and 8:30pm; winter Mon.-Sat. 8pm, Sun. noon and 8pm. Spanish-speaking guide available. Open Mon.-Fri. 11am-2pm and 4:30-7pm. 150ptas.)

Christians built the late Gothic **Iglesia de San Pedro,** on the site of an old Arab fortress on the northern edge of the old quarter. Baroque Murillos, Zurbaráns, Riberas and Pachecos decorate the interior. (Same hours as Iglesia de Santa Maria. 150ptas.) In the attached **tower,** the town bell-ringer usually lets visitors climb the tight spiral staircase that leads to the belfry. Even the spindly-legged find the view worth the effort. (Open 9am-3pm and 4:30-9pm.) In the twisting alleys of the old quarter, heraldic emblems mark medieval *palacios* or nobles' dwellings. Also, the tourist office can make arrangements for tours of 16th- and 17th-century **convents.**

When the monuments start to blur, the patio at the **Parador de Arcos Nacional,** Pl. Cabildo (tel. 70 05 00), in the heart of the old quarter shelters the weary. The **Galeria de Arte Arx-Arcis** (tel. 70 06 81), on C. Magdalena Amaya exhibits local *artesanía*. (Open Mon.-Fri. 10am-2pm and 4-7pm.) A 13th-century *alfombra* (rug) factory, C. Maldonado, 7, weaves and sells rugs, tapestries, and other local crafts. (Open Mon.-Fri. 10am-2pm, Sat. 11:30am-2pm.)

Bornos, a hillside hamlet 11km to the northeast, is the next town along the *ruta de los pueblos blancos*. To dip in the freshwater lake, climb down the hill and turn left on the dirt road. A bar at the end of the road is cleverly disguised as a straw hut. Swim only in the area directly in front of the bar; dangerous whirlpools swirl other parts of the lake. **Buses** for Bornos are run by both Comes and Los Amarillos from the bus station (11 per day, Sun. 5 per day; 20min.; 150-200ptas).

Extremadura

Extreme, harsh. Its very name, referring to the "far end" of the Río Duero, which flows from western Spain into Portugal, rings with the qualities that define the region. Unspoiled natural beauty is the area's most attractive quality: mighty rivers, forests, and rolling plains here have yet to suffer from industrialization; towns are few and far between. The climate is as tough as the landscape, and temperatures above 100°F are common in summer.

A strategic frontier zone for centuries, it fell to Tartessians, Celts, Romans, Muslims, and Christians, all of whom left behind monuments, bridges, and castles. From Extremadura came most of the *conquistadores* who forged into the New World, such as Hernán Cortés and Francisco Pizarro (exploiters of Mexico and Peru). Also from Extremadura, María Escobar was the first person to plant wheat in Peru and Inés de Suárez helped capture Santiago del Nuevo Extremo (today Santiago de Chile) by beheading imprisoned Araucanians as a threat to other defending indigenous tribes.

Just as Extremadura prospered during the Age of Empire, its fortunes sagged with Spain's decline. Many stately structures from that period now house storks, nuns, cultural centers, and schools. The storks themselves are coming to be perceived as regional treasures. With only 5000 pairs left in the whole country (one-third of the total in the 1940s), local governments sweat over who will deliver the babies; in their panic they have cooperated with ecological groups and energy boards to create a new system of electric lines that kills fewer birds.

Extremadura is administratively and culturally divided into the provinces of Cáceres (also known as Alta Extremadura) and Badajoz (Baja Extremadura). During the Spanish Civil War, Cáceres fell with virtually no fighting while the province of Badajoz fiercely resisted Franco. Since the region became one after Franco's death, only soccer rivalries have divided its people.

The most traditional dishes of Extremaduran cuisine come from the wild: rabbit, partridge, lizard with green sauce, wild pigeon with herbs, and *faisán a la Alcántara* (pheasant with a truffle and port wine sauce). *Extremeño* soups are scrumptious: *cocido* (chickpea stew) warms in winter as the many varieties of *gazpacho* (including an unusual white one) cool in summer. Consommés and tomato-fig soup are enjoyed year-round. Cáceres favors *migas,* a spicy bread and *chorizo* (paprika sausage) concoction. Montánchez sausages are renowned in Spain; hence, the nickname for an Extremaduran is *choricero* (sausage-maker). Fruit, especially melon, is remarkable throughout the region.

Tourists have ignored the haunting landscape of the region, but the Junta de Extremadura is doing its best to provide potential visitors with up-to-date information. Brochures and street maps for all the region's towns are available from any one town's tourist office. Museum hours can still be erratic and budget lodgings scarce, but Extremadura's ancient cities make it an unusual and provacative destination.

Cáceres

In the wilds of Extremadura, the thriving provincial capital and university town of Cáceres (pop. 70,000) is the closest thing to the big city. Since the mid-80s, the old city (*ciudad monumental*) has been carefully protected as part of the UN-designated Patrimonio de la Humanidad; the hand of modernity is almost invisible within the walls of the medieval city. Beyond, the elegant new city wears its expansion well, although it's less interesting to the sightseer.

Because of its central location, Cáceres makes a good base for exploring the rest of Extremadura. From here you can enter Portugal via Badajoz, with several daily road and rail connections to Elvas, or by train via Valencia de Alcántara, due west of here. Valencia de Alcántara's station is the last Spanish stop on the Madrid-Lisboa line.

Orientation and Practical Information

The **ciudad monumental** (old city) lies east of **Plaza Mayor** (Plaza del General Mola on old maps). The plaza is 3km north of the bus and train stations, which face each other across the Carretera de Sevilla, in the south of the city. Bus #1, from the stop between the two stations (every 15min., 45ptas), runs to a small plaza just up stone steps from Pl. Mayor. Alternatively, a shuttle bus from the bus station runs to **Plaza de América** (south and west of Plaza Mayor), hub of the new downtown area.

Walkers head towards the city (north) on the Carretera de Sevilla until it runs into the Plaza de América. From here, purple *Ciudad Monumental* signs point north up the grassy and tree-lined Avenida de España toward Pl. Mayor. When the avenue ends, bear right on Calle de San Antón, then right again on Calle de San Pedro.

> **Tourist Office:** Pl. Mayor, 33 (tel. 24 63 47), east side of the plaza, to the right of the steps up to the old city gate. Staff more helpful than their maps, which cover only the old city and its vicinity. Open Mon.-Fri. 9am-2pm and 5-7pm, Sat.-Sun. 10am-2pm.
>
> **Post Office:** C. Miguel Primo Rivera, 2 (tel. 22 50 71). Open for stamps and Lista de Correos Mon.-Fri. 9am-2pm and 4-6pm, Sat. 9am-2pm; for **telegrams** Mon.-Sat. 9am-2pm. 24-hr. telegrams (tel. 22 20 00). **Postal Code:** 10004.
>
> **Telephone Code:** 927.

Trains: Av. Alemania (tel. 22 50 61), across the highway from the bus station 3km south of the old city. Fares listed are *talgo* 2nd class, *estrella* (seated, not sleeper). To: Mérida (3 *regional* per day, 1hr., 340ptas; 1 *talgo* per day at 7:28pm, 50min., 860ptas); Plasencia (3 *regional* per day, 1 1/2 hr., 860ptas); Badajoz (1 *regional* per day at 1:45pm, 2hr., 660ptas); 1 *talgo* per day at 7:28pm, 2hr., 1215ptas); Sevilla (2 per day, 5hr., 1565ptas); Madrid (3 *regional* per day, 4hr., 1865ptas; 2 *talgos* per day, 3 1/2 hr.; 1 *estrella* per day, 5hr.); Lisboa (1 *talgo* per day, 5 1/2 hr., 3190ptas; 1 *estrella* per night; 5hr., 2335ptas).

Buses: Ctra. Sevilla (tel. 24 59 54), across the highway from the train station 3km south of the old city. To: Mérida (5 per day, 1hr., 650ptas); Trujillo (4 per day, 1hr., 390ptas); Plasencia (2 per day, 1½hr., 630ptas); Badajoz (4 per day, 2hr., 700ptas); Valencia de Alcántara (2 per day, 2 1/2 hr., 680ptas); Guadalupe (2 per day, 3hr., 1000ptas); Salamanca (6 per day, 4hr., 1350ptas); Sevilla (6 per day, 4 1/2 hr., 1915ptas); Madrid (7 per day, 5hr., 2040ptas); Valladolid (4 per day, 5 1/2 hr., 2295ptas).

Public Transportation: Buses (45ptas). #1 runs from a stop between the train and bus stations on Ctra. Sevilla to the plaza just above Pl. Mayor (every 15min.).

Taxis: Pl. Mayor (tel. 24 30 63). 24-hr. service.

Car Rental: Avis, in the train station.

Red Cross: tel. 24 78 58.

24-Hour Pharmacy: One of the four in Pl. Mayor is open 24 hrs. Most post the *farmacia de guardia* listing in their windows.

Medical Services: Casa de Socorro, C. Badajoz, 1 (tel. 24 30 38). **Hospital Provincial** (tel. 24 50 25).

Emergency: tel. 091.

Police: Comisaría de Policía, Av. Virgen de la Montaña, 3 (tel. 22 60 00).

Accommodations

Here are few tourists and equally few *hostales* from which to choose. **Plaza Mayor** is the epicenter. Many residents from nearby towns fill the town's lodgings on weekend visits; call a day or two in advance. The only bed in the *ciudad monumental*—the Parador Nacional—costs 12,000ptas per double.

Albergue Colegio Donoso Cortés (HI), Rda. San Francisco (tel. 22 16 07). Follow C. Pacheco south from Pl. Colón to Pl. San Francisco. Clean mattresses rival undercooked pasta for firmness. Crowded with local university students, so call ahead. 3-day max. stay. 550ptas. Non-members 650ptas.

Pensión Márquez, Gabriel y Galán, 2 (tel. 24 49 60), sign visible at low end of Pl. Mayor. Several balconied rooms right on the plaza. Faded floor tiles, candle holders and miniatures clutter the walls. Noise from the streets and the cozy *comedor* make for a laid-back atmosphere. Bathrooms are small, and the plaza blares at night. Singles 1000ptas. Doubles 2000ptas. Showers 200ptas. Breakfast 150ptas. Lunch or dinner 600ptas.

Pensión Carretero, Pl. Mayor, 22 (tel. 24 74 82). A well-worn and well-kept Spanish house. Rooms are somewhat larger and more numerous than those in the Márquez, but they are also more sterile and stuffy. Curfew 1am. Singles 1150ptas. Doubles 1800ptas. Showers 150ptas.

Hostal Residencia Almonte, C. Gil Cordero, 6 (tel. 24 09 25), 15min. south of Pl. Mayor, off noisy Pl. América. A gigantic, hotel-like, 90-room monster with unrestrained luxuries in every room: full bath, phone, electric oscillating fan, fluffy towel, firm bed. Rooms *per se* lack decoration. Garage, laundry service, elevator, cafeteria/TV lounge with A/C and Canal+ to boot. Singles 2200ptas. Doubles 3300ptas. Triples 4300ptas. Quads 5300ptas. Jan. 1 until (not including) Semana Santa: 2000ptas; 3000ptas; 4000ptas; 5000ptas.

Hostal Residencia La Princesa, C. Camino Llano, 32 (tel. 22 70 00). From Pl. America head down Rda. Carmen to Pl. Conquistadores, bear left on C. Colón, and turn left on C. Camino Llano, the last unmarked street. From Pl. Mayor, take C. Pintores past Iglesia de San Juan, follow the left-hand branch down and to the left onto C. Camino Llano. Don't forget the candelabra—the hallways are looooong and dark. Antiseptic-smelling rooms, some with phones. Singles 1575ptas, with bath 1800. Doubles with bath 2800-3000ptas. Triples with bath 4200ptas. Breakfast 175ptas.

Hostal Goya, Pl. Mayor, 33 (or12) (tel. 24 99 50). Some doubles are quite posh, with a balcony on the plaza, a salon with sofa, TV, phone, bath, and large double bed. The runtier rooms, particularly the overpriced singles and back rooms, don't have it so good—but they do have bath, phone, and TV. Singles 3600ptas. Doubles 3900ptas. Triples 5200ptas.

Food

Like accommodations, restaurants are scarce. Aside from smoky bars and cafés, few establishments serve meals. Within the old city walls there's only a pair of expensive restaurants and a couple of taverns, catering largely to the *parador* clientele (see the notable exception below). On Wednesdays the weekly **market** unfurls on Pl. Marrón, two and a half blocks north of Pl. Mayor. The permanent local market, **Mercado de Abastos,** is on C. San José at C. Piedad. (Open Mon.-Sat. 8am-2pm and 4-7pm.)

Groceries: Mostazo, several locations. Most central at Pl. Duque, just behind the low end of Pl. Mayor. Mostazo's specials are tough to beat. Open Mon.-Sat. 9am-2pm and 5:30-8:30pm, Sun 10am-2pm. **Super Spar,** C. Parras, 4, at junction of C. San Antón and C. San Pedro. Larger and less expensive, but farther from Pl. Mayor. Open 9am-2pm and 5-9pm.

La Callejina del Beso Extremeño, C. Anoha, in the *ciudad monumental,* up the street from the *parador.* Shares an entrance with the Restaurante Palacio del Vino. Music and decently-priced *raciones* like *champiñones al ajillo* (375ptas). Heap of *frite extremeño* 700ptas. The iron cages lining the wall are surely the remnants of a 16th century pet store. Open noon-1am.

El Gran Mesón Restaurante, C. General Ezponda 7, just off Pl. Mayor. A dilemma of a *ménu* choice (800 or 1100ptas) in a "typical" *mesón* with swinging hammocks and the requisite wooden tables and bar. Bar open noon-midnight. Meals served 1:30-4pm and 9-11pm.

El Puchero, Pl. Mayor, 9 (tel. 24 54 07), diagonally across from Turismo. A relaxed *cafetería* with tables on the plaza and a downstairs restaurant with a warm ambience. House specialty *carne San Jacobo* (pork cutlet stuffed with ham and cheese) 550ptas. *Platos combinados* 550-800ptas. Restaurant open 1-4:30pm and 9pm-midnight. *Cafetería* open 11am-2am.

El Adarve, C. Sánchez Garrido, 4 (tel. 24 82 45), off C. Pintores near Pl. Mayor. A standard bar that serves filling, no-frills *bocadillos* (200ptas and up), *tapas* (150ptas and up), and *raciones* (550ptas and up). Restaurant with limited menu open 1-3pm and 7-9pm. Bar open 7:30am-11pm.

Sights

The stork-filled, golden **barrio antiguo** (a.k.a. *ciudad monumental* or old city) is one of the most harmonious architectural ensembles in Europe. Surrounded by Almohad walls built on Roman foundations, the *barrio* is Arabic in its narrow, winding streets opening onto small squares and feudal in the churches, towers, ancestral mansions, and fortified palaces introduced by rival clans. Roman, Arabic, Gothic, Renaissance, and even Native American influences have left their stamp.

Enter the old town from the eastern side of Pl. Mayor. The Almohad **Torre del Horno** and **Torre de Bujaco,** are two of five rectangular towers preserved in the western wall. The steps between these towers lead to one of the citadel's main entrances, **Arco de la Estrella,** an unusual twisted Baroque stairway. The star-shaped lantern near the entrance marks the spot where Queen Isabel la Católica swore she would respect the *fueros* (city charters) in exchange for recognition of her sovereignty. Before Isabel and Fernando came to town, the city was autonomous, governed by 12 men elected on the first day of every year.

Between the 14th and 16th centuries Cáceres was flooded with *hidalgos* (nobles) who built dozens of fortified palaces and towers including Palacio de la Generala, Casa de los Ovando-Perero, Casa Espadero-Pizarro, and Casa del Mono. The testosterone-ridden aristocracy resolved their disputes more often than not through violence, prompting the monarchs to remove all battlements and spires from local lords' houses as punishment. Due to Don Golfín's loyalty to Isabel, his **Casa y Torre de las Cigueñas** (the House and Tower of Storks) was the only one allowed to keep its battlements. The fowl build impressive nests on its spires every spring. The Golfín clan's showy **Palacio de los Golfines de Abajo** gratefully bears the coat of arms of Isabel and Ferdinand. The **Palacio de los Golfines de Arriba,** another Golfín-owned palace, is farther uphill, near C. Olmos and C. Adarros de Santa Ana. Here, on October 26, 1936,

Francisco Franco was proclaimed head of the Spanish state and Generalísimo of its armies.

In the 15th and 16th centuries the taste for fortified palaces gradually yielded to one for smaller, comfier mansions. Examples include Casa de Aldana, Casa del Sol, Casa de Ulloa, and Casa de Carvajal. The **Casa de los Toledo-Moctezuma** is outside the old town through Arco de la Estrella, down the street to the right. Inside the **Casa de las Veletas** (House of Weathervanes), the absorbing **Museo de Cáceres** exhibits fascinating memorial stones *(estelas)* that were hoisted up after the death of a great prehistoric warrior. Other rooms hold a few Celtiberian stone animals (relatives of the bull in Salamanca), Roman and Visigothic tombstones, one El Greco, and a variety of randomish crafts. The museum's *pièce de résistance* is the 11th-century Arab *aljibe* (cistern) downstairs, which supplied Cáceres with water until 1935. It catches rainwater by means of an intricately designed drainage system. If you could filch all the coins at the bottom and send them back to us, we'd be happy. (Open Tues.-Sat. 9:30am-2:30pm, Sun. 10:15am-2:30pm. Admission 200ptas.)

In front of Arco de la Estrella, **Plaza de Santa María** suns itself between stone buildings. A statue of San Pedro de Alcántara, one of Extremadura's two saints, eyes the plaza from an outside corner pedestal of **Catedral de Santa María**. His big toes are shiny because locals have rubbed or kissed off all the dirt, bird turd, and oxidation— touching them is said to bring good luck. The cathedral itself, built between 1229 and 1547, has Romanesque columns, a Renaissance ceiling, and a exquisite pine and cedarwood altarpiece. Cáceres's nobility decays beneath the floor. (Open for several masses per day Mon.-Sat. 7:30am-9pm, Sun. 10am-1pm and 7:30-8:30pm.)

Legend has it that the Orden de Santiago—first known as Los Frailes de Cáceres (The Friars of Cáceres)—was established in the **Iglesia de Santiago Matamoros**, outside the city walls on Pl. Santiago. A Gothic retable by Berruguete can be viewed during services only.

Uphill is **Plaza de San Jorge,** named for the dragonslayer and patron saint of the city whose likeness is bolted to its niche, lest it be pinched by rival Plasencians eager to rob the city of its saint's protection.

Entertainment

On warm evenings at around 10 or 11 residents and tourists pack the *terrazas* on the fringes of **Plaza Mayor,** especially those at the lower end (such as **Mesón Los Portales, Mesón Los Arcos** and **Berlin**) until the wee hours. As the night heats up and temperatures drop down, the town drifts toward the discos along **Calle General Ezponda** and the crowded pubs that line the two little alleys connecting Pl. Mayor with Pl. Duque.

El Corral de las Cigüenas, Cuesta de Aldana, 6, is perhaps the only place for drinks and socializing after dark in the *ciudad monumental*. Melrose Place types frequent its sizable *terraza*, surrounded by high ivied walls. Dining here is expensive (*platos combinados* 800ptas and up, *raciones* 600ptas and up). Beers are 300ptas, mixed drinks 500ptas. (Open from 8pm on.)

Plasencia

Alfonso VIII of Castilla founded this city in the 12th century "for the pleasure of God and men." His wish, in Latin, gave this lively town its name and established Castilian influence in newly reconquered Extremadura. Not only men, but all people, will find the town pleasing: it may not have the obvious appeal of Cáceres, but its well-preserved sandstone and whitewashed buildings with wrought-iron balconies and thriving bar scene make it an amiable introduction—or farewell—to Extremadura.

Orientation and Practical Information

Plasencia perches over the Río Jerte. From **Plaza Mayor,** streets radiate toward what used to be the city gates. To reach the town center from the bus station, turn left (coming out of the main lobby, upstairs), take the right-hand fork (Av. Vera), cross the main road, then follow C. Sol all the way to Pl. Mayor (15min.). The train station is about 11/2 km from the town center, just off the road to Cáceres; to reach the town center, turn left at the bottom of the lane from the station, cross the bridge, pass under the **Ermita de la Salud** (arch just across the street to the left), and follow C. Trujillo up past Turismo to the plaza. Alternatively, catch the bus (every 20min, 60ptas) just opposite the gas station at the bottom of the lane. It stops at **Puerta Talavera;** pass through and take C. Talavera to Pl. Mayor.

Tourist Office: C. Trujillo, 17 (tel. 41 27 66), downhill from Pl. Mayor. Open Mon.-Fri. 9am-2pm and 4-6pm, Sat. 9am-2pm; winter Mon.-Sat. 9am-2pm.

Post Office: Av. Alfonso VIII, 18 (tel. 41 23 77). Open for stamps and Lista de Correos Mon.-Fri. 9am-2pm, Sat. 9am-1pm; for **telegrams** Mon.-Fri. 8am-8pm, Sat. 9am-1pm. **Postal Code:** 10600.

Telephone Code: 927.

Trains: Estación de Palencia (tel. 41 00 49), off Ctra. Cáceres (tel. 41 00 49). To: Cáceres (6 per day, 1 1/2 hr., 455ptas) and Madrid (5 per day, 3 1/2 hr., 1530ptas).

Buses: Av. Vera (tel. 41 45 50). To: Cáceres (7 per day, 1 1/2 hr., 630ptas); Madrid (1 per day, 4 1/2 hr., 1700ptas); **Auto Res** (42 05 97) runs 5 buses per day Valladolid-Sevilla and back, stopping in Salamanca (3hr., 1030ptas); Mérida (3hr., 840ptas); Zafra (4hr., 1500ptas); Valladolid (5hr., 1660ptas). For connections to the rest of Extremadura, go to Cáceres.

Taxis: At Pl. España (tel. 41 21 73), Puerta del Sol (tel. 41 13 77), and Puerta de Talavera (tel. 41 13 78).

Luggage Storage: At the **train station** (lockers 300ptas).

Medical Services: Residencia Virgen de la Puerta (tel. 41 36 50). **Hospital Provincial** (tel. 41 31 00). **Ambulance** (tel. 41 23 07, 41 30 74, 41 28 76).

Police: Policía Municipal (tel. 41 00 33). **Nacional** (tel. 41 29 18). **Guardia Civil** (tel. 41 33 58).

Accommodations

You will have no problem finding a bed, but standards aren't so high.

Hostal La Muralla, Berrozanas, 6 (tel. 41 38 74), the 2nd street to the left off C. Quesos, near the lower end of Pl. Mayor. Large place maintained by diligent manager. Well-lit, clean rooms with new furniture and modern baths. TV lounge. Top floor toasty in summer and sometimes ant-infested. Singles 1000ptas. Doubles 2000ptas, with bath 2550ptas. Breakfast 150ptas. Dinner 725ptas.

Fonda Santa María, C. Trujillo, 15 (tel. 41 24 40), next to the tourist office. Rooms are rather small and dark, but the hammock-like beds are clean. Only 1 bathroom for the 8 rooms and family. Singles 800ptas. Doubles 1200-1400ptas. Prices flexible. Hot showers 150ptas.

Pensión Blanco, C. Resbaladeros, near Puerta Berrozanas and around the corner from Hostal la Muralla. Cramped, dim singles, large, airy doubles, and a huge dog that howls at the moon and everything else. Long tables and mini chairs in dining room that's a cross between a kindergarten and a monastery. Singles 900ptas, with shower 1000ptas. Doubles 1800ptas, with shower 2000ptas. Breakfast 150ptas. Dinner 650ptas.

Food

Plasencia is famous (locally) for its remarkable number of bars per capita. Many can be sleuthed out on **Calle Patalón,** the 2nd left down C. Talavera. **Pl. Mayor** is swamped by *mesones* that serve typical *tapas* and *bocadillos (raciones* 500ptas). It's too hot to eat much in the summer. The **market** is in Pl. Abastos Copa, just up the street from the tourist office (open Mon.-Sat. 8am-2pm and 5:30-8pm).

Rincón Extremeño, C. Vidrieras, 6 (tel. 41 11 50), off Pl. Mayor. Small dining room with tightly packed tables. Simple *menú* 600-750ptas. Open 1:30-4pm and 9pm-midnight.

Bar La Ría, C. Sol, 32, off Pl. Mayor. Coca-Cola decor with a large TV. Unbelievably inexpensive, refreshing *tapas* (25-200ptas). Open 11am-11pm or midnight.

Restaurante-Bar Mi Casa, C. Patalón, 15 (tel. 41 14 50). Unfinished wood furniture, crispy white tablecloths, and fresh flowers. *Menú* 850ptas. *Cabrito al horno* (roast baby goat) 750ptas. *Cochinillo asado* (roast suckling pig) 700ptas. Open 1-4pm and 9pm-midnight.

Sights and Entertainment

Sightseeing in Plasencia means sitting in the plaza watching the rest of the town sit in the plaza. Real sights-hounds motor to one of the more unusual architectural clusters in Spain: the 13th-century Romanesque **catedral vieja** and the Gothic **catedral nueva** (1498), down C. Trujillo and left at C. Blanca. A door in their shared wall connects the two churches. The new church was blocked up before it was finished, hence its squat appearance east of the old church. Master carver Rodrigo Alemán fashioned the **choir stalls** in the new cathedral. The front pews were covered with biblical scenes on one side, more mundane ones on the other. Legend has it that his impatient employer confined the Jewish convert to the church until he finished his work. Rodrigo took the opportunity to mock the Church with these grotesque and vaguely obscene carvings. Then, it's said, he built a flying machine and jumped from the belfry to his death. (Open 9am-noon and 5-8pm; winter 9:30am-12:30pm and 4-5:30pm. Free.)

Through the door in the left aisle, the old cathedral, now the **Museo Diocesano**, holds a collection of vestal garments, gold chalices, and old Bibles, plus a larger-than-life statue of Santa Ana slaying Satan. (Informative optional tour in Spanish. Open same hours as *catedral nueva*. Admission 100ptas.)

In Pl. San Nicolás, the **Palacio del Marqués de Mirabel** is still used as a private residence by the *marqueses* when they visit town. The 2-room *museo* and lovely courtyard garden are open to the public. On display are deer heads chopped by a former *marqués* and some European sculptures and paintings. The bust of Carlos V is allegedly by Pompeye Leoni. Across the terrace, there's a medieval kitchen and pantry. (No regular hours. Ring the bell and the caretaker may give a personal tour; a tip is appreciated. Best to visit 10am-2pm and 5-7pm.) The new **Museo Etnográfico** displays crafts from northern Extremadura. (Open Mon.-Sat. 11am-2pm and 5-8pm; winter Mon.-Sat. 11am-2pm and 5-6:30pm.)

El Parque de la Isla, an island/park in the river, is pleasant for picnics; however, most of its accoutrements (soccer field, basketball and tennis courts, café, and benches) are half-finished or half-hearted. Vendors journey from all over Extremadura to display their arts and crafts at the open-air **mercado** every Tuesday in the Pl. Mayor.

The **Fiesta del Martes Mayor,** on the first Tuesday in August, celebrates the town's founding. The parties and fairs actually last from Saturday to Saturday. Less well-known, but just as much fun, are the **ferias y fiestas** in early June, with rides, bullfights, and music.

Trujillo

Native son Francisco Pizarro, conqueror of Peru, is from this "cradle of the Conquistadors"—along with over 600 other plunderers of the New World. A recent influx of wealthy Spaniards has helped Trujillo restore the many churches, fortresses, and *conquistador* palaces that reflect its bygone glory as a wellspring of empire.

Orientation and Practical Information

Trujillo is accessible only by bus or car. The bus station is on the road to Badajoz at the foot of the hill. To get to the **Plaza Mayor,** turn left as you exit the station and go uphill on Calle de Pardos, past the Iglesia y Convento de la Encarnación and the small Plaza de Aragón, onto Calle de Romanos. Turn right at the end of C. Romanos onto Calle de la Parra, then left on Calle de Hernando Pizarro (15min.).

Tourist Office: Pl. Mayor (tel. 32 06 53), in the arcade on Pizarro's right. Extremely helpful. No English, some French spoken. Open Wed.-Mon. 11am-1:30pm and 5-8pm.

Post Office: C. Ruiz de Mendoza, Po. 7 (tel. 32 05 33), across C. Encarnación from the bus station. Open for stamps, Lista de Correos, and **telegrams** Mon.-Fri. 9am-2pm, Sat. 9am-1pm. **Postal Code:** 10200.

Telephone Code: 927.

Buses: C. Marques Albayda, s/n (tel. 32 12 02), off C. Encarnación. To: Mérida (5 per day, 1hr., 580ptas); Plasencia (Mon.-Fri. 1 per day, 1 1/2 hr., 570ptas); Cáceres (12 per day, 40min., 360ptas); Badajoz (5 per day, 2hr., 1035ptas); Guadalupe (2 per day, 2hr., 600ptas); Madrid (14 per day, 4 1/2 hr., 1800ptas).

Taxis: tel. 32 02 74.

Luggage Storage: Although it seems odd, the **municipal police** store backpacks during the day in their jail. Contact any agent on Pl. Mayor.

Swimming Pool: Piscina Pública, C. Montanchez, off C. Encarnación (3 bl. west of the bus station). Olympic-size, lots of grass for sunning, and a snack bar. Mon.-Fri. 280ptas, Sat.-Sun. 325ptas. Open 11am-9pm.

Red Cross: tel. 32 11 77.

Medical Services: Centro de Salud de la Seguridad Social, C. Ramón y Cajal (tel. 32 00 89). C. Ramón y Cajal is the road to Cáceres. **Hospital,** by the road to Montánchez.

Police: Ayuntamiento, C. Hernández Pizarro, 2 (tel. 091 or tel. 32 01 08).

Accommodations

There are few lodgings in Trujillo and even fewer tourists.

Hostal Trujillo, C. Francisco Pizarro, 4 (tel. 32 22 74), off C. Encarnacíon (5min. from the bus station). A suit of armor at the top of the stairs guards impeccable, newly renovated rooms and baths. Singles with shower 2100ptas. Doubles with bath 3180ptas. Triples 3180ptas.

Pensión Boni, C. Domingo de Ramos, 7 (tel. 32 16 04), off Pl. Mayor. Convenient location, commodious rooms. One single 1500ptas. Doubles 2500ptas, with bath 3000-4000ptas. Breakfast 200ptas. Lunch or dinner 950ptas.

 Hostal Residencia-Restaurante Emilia, C. General Mola, 26 (tel. 32 00 83), a few bl. farther down C. Encarnacíon past Hostal Trujillo. Shiningly clean—even the stone staircase is scrubbed daily. Stark, spacious brown and white rooms. Old bathroom fixtures still flush and spray. Singles 1850ptas, with bath 2200ptas. Doubles 2850ptas, with bath 3300ptas. The restaurant in the back is intimate, with booths, a fireplace, and a small patio. *Menú* 850ptas. Entrees about 650ptas. Open 1-4pm and 9-11:30pm.

Food

Fooderies cling to the **Plaza Mayor.**

Groceries: Supermercado Natividad Garcia Arias, C. Merced 1 (tel. 32 05 81). Open Mon.-Sat. 9:30am-2pm and 5-8pm. **Eurospar,** next door to the bus station. Open Mon.-Sat. 9am-2pm and 5-9pm, Sun. 9:30am-2pm.

Mesón-Restaurante La Troya, Pl. Mayor, 10 (tel. 32 14 65). Famed throughout Extremadura for mammoth amounts of blue-ribbon food. Bar designed as the façade of a Spanish house, a theme continued throughout the restaurant with red tiles, potted plants, and plates on the walls. *Menú* includes 3 courses, wine, mineral water, and a waffer-thin mint (1500ptas). No à la carte. Open 1-4:30pm and 9-11:30pm.

Cafeteria Nuria, Pl. Mayor, 36 (tel. 32 09 07). 'Tis a gift to be simple.... *Bocadillos* 250-325ptas. *Platos combinados* 600ptas. Scrumptious *granizado de limón* (lemon granité) 150ptas. Open 8am-1am; off-season 8am-11pm.

Sights

Trujillo's **Plaza Mayor** inspired the one built in Cuzco, Perú, after Francisco Pizarro defeated the Incas: palaces, arched passageways, and one wide flight of steps surround an ample, stone-paved space and center fountain. The **Estatua de Pizarro,** the gift of an American couple, was sculpted in 1927. At night the eerie church clock tower keeps vigil over the lit fountain and statue.

When Pizarro died in Peru, he urged his younger brother and companion in arms, Hernando, to erect a memorial church on the southwestern corner of the plaza. Hernando built the **Palacio de la Conquista** instead. Co-owned by eight descendants of Pizarro, this is the foremost of the clan's several *Casas de Pizarro* in Trujillo. Architectural highlights include the masonry by the second-floor corner balcony, which includes depictions of the Pizarro gang, and the priests, Incas, condors, and pumas carved into the woodwoork in the **Salón de Perú.** Downstairs, the guide may show you the stables, which predate the existing house and feature some exciting old latrines. (Open 10:30am-2pm and 4:30-8pm; winter 10:30am-2pm and 4-7pm. Small donation requested.)

Festooned with storks' nests, **Iglesia de San Martín** dominates the northeastern corner of the plaza. The church contains several historic tombs, but not—contrary to the dearly held Extremaduran belief—the tomb of Francisco de Orellana, the first European to explore the Amazon. *Conquistador* graves in Spain are few; Orellana, like most of his fellow explorers, died abroad. (No regular hours. Open in the morning and for services).

Across the street, the **Palacio de los Duques de San Carlos** was given by its owners to the few remaining Hieronymite cloistered nuns, who became homeless when their convent rotted. If you ring the bell hard, one of the two nuns will show you around the patio (whose 18th-century stonework includes a couple of Visigothic chunks) and up a winding staircase. One ancestor of the Duke is said to have climbed it on horseback. Emperor Carlos V stayed here a couple of times and had his coat of arms painted on the ceiling. The seven smokestacks atop the house signify the different religions defeated by conquering Spaniards in the New World. (Open 9am-1pm and 4-7pm. Donation of at least 100ptas requested.)

Just behind Iglesia de San Martín, the spectacular **castillo** (built by the Arabs) is just an uphill climb away. On the way up is a cultural center in the house of Francisco Pizarro's father, one Captain Gonzalo de Pizarro. Here on the summit of Trujillo's 517m granite hill, the air is thick with swallows, storks, and buzzards. Vultures pick at rotting animal corpses just over the ridge. Some of the castle walls are extremely well-restored. The battlements and ramparts offer a view of the unspoilt landscape that overwhelms even the most jaded of travelers. Stone-wall sheep tracks lead across the plains. Inside the walls lie remnants of the castle's *aljibe* (cistern) and the entrance to the lower-level dungeons. In 1232, the Virgin Mary infused Fernando III's troops with the strength to drive the Moors from the city; in return the town erected a shrine to her inside one of the castle turrets. The **Madonna** twirls round (for 25ptas).

West on C. Ballesteros is Gothic **Iglesia de Santa María**. Sra. Tomasa, the caretaker, points out the places assigned to Fernando and Isabel for mass during their brief residence in the city. Pizarro is said to have been christened on a stone font here. Legend has it that the giant soldier Diego de Paredes picked up the fountain and carried it to his mother at age 11 (yeah right); the giant was buried here after he twisted his ankle and fell to his death. The church's 27-panel Gothic retable at the high altar was painted by master Fernando Gallego. (Open Mon.-Sat. 10am-2pm and 4-7pm, Sun. Mass at 11am. Admission 75ptas. If the church is closed, inquire at the house directly to the right of the church steps.)

The fascinating free **Museo de la Coria** (with your back to Santa María's facade, walk two blocks up and turn right) explores the historical relationship between Extremadura and Latin America. Fifteenth-century maps, drawings, and modern photo exhibits arranged around the sunny, plant-filled cloister describe (in rather triumphant Spanish) the region's decisive impact on New World history. (Open Sat.-Sun. 11:30am-2pm.)

Guadalupe

One day in 1300, cowherd Gil Cordero found his lost cow, apparently dead, on the banks of the Río Guadalupe. Just as he began to skin the animal, the Virgin Mary appeared and told him to find the local priests, for in the ground under the cow's body lay an image of the Holy Mother. This image had, according to the story, been a gift of Pope Gregory the Great to St. Isidore of Sevilla, and had been buried before the Islamic conquest. The cow revived, the cowherd fled, the image was found, and the pilgrims haven't stopped coming.

In 1340 at the Battle of Salado, Alfonso XI invoked the Virgin's aid and defeated a superior Muslim army. In gratitude he commissioned the sumptuous **Real Monasterio de Santa María de Guadalupe,** a church/castle/fortress to house the shrine on the site. The monastery and town came to unite all of *hispanidad* in the 15th century; it became customary to grant all licenses for foreign expeditions here. It was also here that Fernando and Isabel signed their contract with Christopher Columbus. Columbus, in turn, named the island of Turugueira "Guadalupe" in 1493 and also brought the first Native American converts to be baptized here in 1496. The rest of the *Conquistadors* took with them the Virgin's new nickname, Guadalupe. In 1836, the monastery was temporarily dissolved, and part of the complex was used for stables. The Franciscans moved into the lavish monastery early in this century.

Today, this small mountain town depends on agriculture and the thousands of tourists who visit its monastery. Guadalupe is a *very* small town, and one you've gone through the monastery (twice), strolled the back streets (idly), and had drinks at a *terraza* (a few), you may find yourself twiddling your thumbs until tomorrow's bus.

Orientation and Practical Information

Two hours east of Trujillo and a three-hour bus ride southwest of Madrid, Guadalupe rests on a mountainside in the Sierra de Guadalupe. From Madrid, most travelers rush through the monastery as a daytrip, although the transportation can be tricky. Others go with organized bus tours or simply drive. From Trujillo, bus schedules force an overnight stay.

Everything you need in Guadalupe is within 100m of the bus stop. The multi-purpose Ayuntamiento lies on the outside of the curve of **Avenida Don Blas Pérez,** the town's main thoroughfare (better known as **Carretera de Cáceres**). Around the corner and down the hill is the restaurant-lined **Plaza Mayor,** shaded by the monastery's basilica on one side and open to the mountains on the other.

Tourist Office: Pl. Mayor, 1 (tel. 36 73 25). Plenty of brochures on the rest of Extremadura. Open Tues.-Fri. 9:15am-2pm and 5-7pm, Sat.-Sun. 9:15am-2pm.

Post Office: Ayuntamiento, Av. Don Blas Pérez, 2 (tel. 36 71 42). Open for stamps, Lista de Correos, and **telegrams** Mon.-Fri. 9am-2pm, Sat. 9am-1pm. **Postal Code:** 10140.

Telephone Code: 927.

Buses: On either side of the street just uphill from the Ayuntamiento. **Empresa Doalde** (tel. Madrid 468 76 80). To Madrid's Estación Sur (at 9am and 3:30pm, 3hr., 1700ptas). **S.A. Mirat.** To Cáceres (Mon.-Fri. at 6:30am and 4:30pm, 3hr., 850ptas) via Trujillo (2hr., 600ptas).

Swimming Pool: Ctra. Villanueva (tel. 36 71 39), 3km downhill from town. 250ptas, children 125ptas. Open June-Sept. 11am-8pm.

Medical Services: Contact 1 of 2 town doctors (tel. 36 71 97, 36 74 68) or the **Guardia Civil** (tel. 36 70 10). **Ambulance** (tel. 36 71 95).

Police: Ayuntamiento (tel. 36 70 06).

Accommodations and Food

Plaza Mayor is the place to be. Finding a room is difficult only during Semana Santa. *Migas* (bread spiced with pepper, garlic, and *chorizo,* fried and eaten with a spoon), *caldereta extremeña* (simmered stew of goat and lamb), and Guadalupan *gazpacho* (prepared with raw eggs, *migas,* vinegar, and oil) are regional specialties.

> **Mesón Típico Isabel,** Pl. Mayor, 18 (tel. 36 71 28). Modern rooms, all with newly renovated private baths. Singles 2000ptas. Doubles with shower 2500ptas, with bath 3000ptas. Bar serves amazingly huge *raciones* (400ptas) and toothsome *caldereta* (350ptas). Open 8am-1am.
>
> **Hostal Cerezo,** Gregorio López, 12 (tel. 36 73 79), between the Ayuntamiento and the plaza. Dreamy. Nuzzle up to the immaculate rooms, all with baths and many with views. Bare it all for the strong, hot showers. Singles 2000ptas. Doubles 3000ptas. Triples 3600ptas. Restaurant-bar *menú* 750ptas. A la carte available.
>
> **Mesón Extremeño,** Pl. Mayor, 3 (tel. 36 73 60). Small rooms with chipping paint above a sometimes raucous bar. Singles 800ptas. Doubles 1500ptas. Classy bar-restaurant with tables inside and out. *Caldereta* 700ptas. Open 10am-1am.
>
> **Restaurante Lujuán,** C. Gregorio López, 21 (tel. 36 71 70), across from Hostal Cerezo. Rather bland, modern decor—yet locals rate the food among the best in town. *Menú* 800ptas. *Cordero asado* (roast lamb) 850ptas. Open 7:30am-10pm.
>
> **Bar-Restaurante Guadalupe,** Pl. Mayor, 32 (tel. 36 70 80). From Pl. Mayor, walk down the street farthest to the left. Elysian patio dining area with fountain and crawling ivy. *Gazpacho* 200ptas. *Caldereta* 750ptas. Restaurant open 1-4pm and 7-10pm. Bar open 9am-midnight.

Sights

The **Real Monasterio de Santa María de Guadalupe's** anything-but-ascetic display of riches reflects the bygone wealth and power of the Church. Construction began in the 14th century, but haphazard renovations and additions continued through the 18th century.

The **basílica** of the monastery hulks over Pl. Mayor, connected by a wide set of stairs. Inside is a severe, 18th-century retable, designed by El Greco's son. You'll see the *coro* on the official tour, wherein lie ornate Churrigueresque wood chairs and the magnificent ceiling painting of Juan de Flandes. (Basilica open 8:30am-8:30pm; Oct.-May 9am-6pm. Four masses per day. Free.)

The rest of the monastery complex is only accessible by guided tour (in Spanish), leaving from the main entrance to the left of the basilica. The first stop, is the **Museo de Libros Miniados,** home to the monastery's old hymn-books and an enormous four-sided revolving *facistol* (bookstand). Each of the 86 four-ft.-high tomes (20 on display) weighs about 40kg and contains 15th-century Gregorian chants. The shortened shepherd's crook in the corner was used as a bookmark.

The **Claustro Mudéjar** is the focal point of the complex and the only place photos are permitted. Encircled by towers, the cloister combines an arcade of Almohad arches with an inspiring Gothic garden temple, raised in 1905 by a Hieronymite monk. Twenty Franciscan monks, who ousted the Hieronymites in 1908, live behind the green windows on the uppermost floor. Just off the cloister in the old refectory, the **Museo de Bordados** (Embroidery museum) boasts a marvelous collection of opulent ecclesiastical garments. The gems and gold thread were laced into the *frontal rico* by the famous 15th-century fingers of Friar Diego of Toledo.

The 17th-century **sacristía** is a breathtaking monument to the painter Zurbarán, who loved painting Hieronymite monks. *Apoteósis de San Jerónimo* and *Los Azotes en el Juicio de Dios* hang in the **Capilla de San Jerónimo,** at the far end of the sacristy. In the **relicuario** are some of the odder gifts presented at the Virgin's shrine through the centuries and the icon's wardrobe (her clothes are changed several times a year for religious festivals). Overhead, the 19th-century Italian chandelier, made of *cristal de Murano,* is from one of the most famous glass-works of Venice.

At this point, one of the Franciscan friars actually assumes control of the tour and leads it up two flights to the incredibly luxe Baroque mansion, **Camarín de Nuestra Señora** (Alcove of Our Lady). The dense decoration took 40 long years to finish; the walls are decorated with carved marble and jade motifs. Eight polychrome statues of biblical characters stand in the corners; nine paintings depicting scenes from the Virgin's life line the walls.

The **Imagen de Nuestra Señora Santa María de Guadalupe** is raised upon a golden throne in a small chapel off the Camarín. Legends date the tiny, plain sculpture back to the first century AD and trace its path through the groping hands of Cardinal Gregorio in Constantinople in 590 to the Sevillan monks who buried it near the river to prevent its capture by Muslims. Modern technology dates it to the end of the 12th century. Mary is painted black so that the light of God's glory can better reflect off her face onto the populace (little do they know that black actually absorbs light, not reflects it). The handpainted tiles on the back of the throne depict various visitors to the shrine, including Cervantes and St. Teresa. The latest plaque shows Pope John Paul II, who visited Guadalupe in 1982. (Monastery open 9:30am-1pm and 3:30-7pm; Oct.-March 9:30am-1pm and 3:30-6pm. Admission 200ptas.) The Virgin of Guadalupe's special day is September 8; be prepared for huge crowds, rockets, and Madonna-mania.

Badajoz

> *Badajoz, I will never forget you, no matter how long I am away from you. What beautiful trees there are that surround you! The valley of your delightful river opens out like a split in an embroidered tunic.*
> —Anonymous 11th-century poet

Invasions, surrenders, acts of bravery, betrayals, and massacres all once were the talk of Badajoz, the capital of Baja Extremadura. More than 3000 people are said to have been killed here by Franco's troops in the aftermath of one of the bloodiest battles of the Civil War. Many of the victims were executed in the old bullring.

Apparently quite a beauty in the 11th century, Badajoz hasn't managed to cope with urbanization, modernization, and emigration with much grace. Whereas many Extremaduran towns could be described as "poor but proud," Badajoz is simply poor. While there's less to see here than in other Extremaduran cities, the nightlife is the region's best. Badajoz is often a necessary stopover en route to or from Portugal—the border is only 7km to the west, and the town of Elvas, Portugal only 11km beyond.

Orientation and Practical Information

Plaza España is the heart of the old town, across the Guadiana river from the train station. From the Pl. España, Calle Juan de Rivera leads to **Plaza Libertad** (5min.). To get from the train station to the center of town, follow Avenida de Carolina Coronado straight to the Puente de Palmas, cross the bridge, and continue straight along Calle Prim and its continuation. Turn left on Calle Juan de Rivera for the Plaza España, right for the Plaza Libertad (35min.).

Tourist Office: Pl. Libertad, 3 (tel. 22 27 63). Better city maps than the one in the "Badajoz" pamphlet; mountains of glossy brochures. Staff helps with lodgings if you want them to. Open Mon.-Fri. 9am-2pm, Sat.-Sun. 9am-2pm.

Post Office: Po. General Frans, 4 (tel. 22 23 09), across from the tourist office. Open for stamps and **telegrams** (tel. 22 26 56) Mon.-Fri. 8am-9pm, Sat.-Sun. 9am-2pm. **Postal Code:** 0605.

Telephone Code: 924.

Trains: tel. 23 71 70. Take the hourly bus (70ptas) or a taxi (about 360ptas) from the station across the river. If you want to walk, see the directions in Orientation. To: Mérida (8 per day, 1 1/2 hr., 265-860ptas); Cáceres (3 per day, 2 1/2 hr., 660ptas); Lisboa (2 per day, 5 1/2 hr., 1900ptas); Madrid (5 per day, 5hr., *expreso* 3135ptas, *talgo* 4100ptas).

Buses: tel. 25 86 61, south of the city center. To reach Pl. España from the station, turn left after exiting, then right, then left onto the main C. Damion Tellez Lafuente. It becomes C. Fernando Cazadilla and then C. Pedro de Valdivia, which bears right and runs uphill to Pl. España (15min.). Buses #3, 6a, and 6b (every 15min., 60ptas) run between the station and Pl. Libertad, the stop just past broad Av. Huelva. To: Zafra (6 per day, 45min. 620ptas); Mérida (8 per day, 45min., 515ptas); Cáceres (3 per day, 1 3/4 hr., 700ptas); Madrid (10 per day, 4hr., 2725ptas); Sevilla (8 per day, 4 1/2 hr., 1700ptas).

Hospital: Pl. Minayo, 2 (tel. 21 81 16), between Pl. Libertad and Pl. España

Police: tel. 091.

Accommodations

Most *hostales* lie near **Plaza España**. Three acceptable *pensiones* (some with curfew) and a lone *hostal* huddle on **Calle Arco Agüeros,** in the heart of the open-air party (described in Sights and Entertainment below). You won't sleep here until 3, 4, or 5am unless you get an interior room and put your pilla over your head.

Hotel Cervantes, Pl. Cervantes (tel. 22 37 10). From Pl. España, take C. San Blas to the plaza. This 2-star hotel has pleasant overstuffed furniture and cool tile floors. All rooms with bath, phone, and winter heating. Singles 2700ptas. Doubles 4000ptas.

Pension Orrego, C. Arco Agüeros, 41 (tel. 22 08 32), follow directions for Hostal Niza below. Has the nicest rooms on the street, graced by faded wedding pictures. Singles 900ptas. Doubles 1600ptas.

Hostal Niza, C. Arco Agüeros, 34 (tel. 22 38 81), the street off C. San Blas to the right, coming from Pl. España. Solid beds, large rooms, and lofty ceilings. Singles 1070ptas. Doubles 1800ptas.

Food

Restaurants mingle with accommodations in and around the Plaza España.

La Bellota de Oro, C. Zurbarán, 5 (tel. 22 10 25). A lively, smoky atmosphere. *Menú* 625ptas. Open 1-4pm and 8pm-midnight.

Café Bar La Ría, Pl. España, 7 (tel. 22 20 05). Another popular hangout, with large picture-coded *platos combinados* (600-750ptas). Open 8am-1am.

Sights and Entertainment

Badajoz complies almost dispiritedly with the requisite cathedral/castle/museum points of interest. In one of Spain's least attractive Plazas de España, the bleak 13th-century **catedral** looms, fortress-like. Each of the 85 chairs is carved to represent a saint. There's also some hand-carved wooden choir stalls and an impressive pipe organ. (Open 8am-1pm and 7-8pm with three masses per day.)

To the west of Pl. Espana on C. Meléndez Valdés is the **Museo de Bellas Artes,** ashamed at the silly copies of Zurbarán and Caravaggio that fill its ground floor. Charming works by local 19th-century artists hang above. (Open Mon.-Fri. 8:30am-2:30pm, Sat. 9am-1pm. Free.)

The ruins of the **Alcazaba** now house the newly reopened **Museo Arqueológico,** which displays fragments of Roman and Visigothic architecture from local digs. Although not as impressive as Mérida's museum, the collection is well-presented with detailed Spanish descriptions of the exhibits. (Open Tues.-Sun. 10am-3pm. Admission 200ptas. EEC citizens with ID and all under 21 free.) Nearby hovers the **Torre del Apéndiz,** nicknamed **Torre de Espantaperros** ("to shoo away Christian dogs"). Its octagonal shape is similar to the Torre de Oro in Sevilla.

Heading uphill from the center of town, the neighborhood becomes increasingly poor and deserted—Plazas Alta and San José, just outside the castle walls, are particularly ruinous, and the walls of the Alcazaba aren't in great shape. Visit when the museum is open; avoid the area altogether after dark. To get to the Alcazaba, follow the road leading uphill (parallel to the highway) from the Puerta de Palma. The road everntually runs into C. San Antón, which leads up to the right past the walls to the main entrance.

Nightlife rages. It spillls out from the bars and literally fills the streets of the *centro* for several blocks; no one bar or club is exceptionally popular. **Calle San Blas,** off Pl. Mayor, is stuffed with teens passing around *minis* (300ptas) of *cerveza* or *sidra*. **Calle Zurbarán,** off Pl. Mayor and perpendicular to C. San Blas, is wall-to-wall with twentysomethings milling about while dodging the cars and *motos* that insist on parting the Red Sea at 30mph. Barhoppers also clog the zone between these two streets, especially along **Calle Martín Cansado.**

Mérida

As a reward for services rendered, Caesar Augustus granted a group of veteran legionnaires the privilege of founding a city in Lusitania, comprised of Portugal and part of Spain. They chose a lovely little place surrounded by several hills on the banks of the Río Guadiana and called their new home "Augusta Emerita." Strategically located, Mérida became the capital of Lusitania. The nostalgic soldiers set out to adorn their "little Rome" with bridges, baths, aqueducts, temples, a hippodrome, an arena, and the famous amphitheater where plays are still performed.

Although the modern town lacks the splendor of its renowned classical ancestor, Mérida's ruins and world-class *Museo Romano* both merit a pause. In July and August, the *Festival de Teatro Clásico* attracts some of Europe's finest classical and modern troupes, which perform tragedies by the Greek triumvirate (Aeschylus, Euripides, and Sophocles).

Orientation and Practical Information

Deep in the heart of Extremadura, Mérida is 73km south of Cáceres and 59km east of its provincial capital, Badajoz. **Plaza de España,** the town center, is near the Río Guadiana, two blocks up from the **Puente Romano.**

Anybody in the whole wide world can figure out how to get to Turismo from Pl. España. Head up Calle Santa Eulalia, which becomes a pedestrian shopping street, and bear right at the little circle onto Calle J. Ramon Melida. Turismo is on the right, across the street from the *Museo Romano* next to the *teatro romano* entrance.

Tourist Office: C. P.M. Plano (tel. 31 53 53). Multilingual. Small maps and theater schedules (but no tickets). Lists of accommodations. Open Mon.-Fri. 9am-2pm and 5-7pm, Sat.-Sun. 9am-2pm.

Post Office: Pl. Constitución (tel. 31 24 58). Open for stamps and Lista de Correos Mon-Sat. 9am-2pm; for **telegrams** Mon.-Fri. 9am-8pm. **Postal Code:** 06800.

Telephone Code: 924.

Trains: C. Cardero. To reach Pl. España from the station, follow C. Valverde Lillo down from the end of C. Camilo José Cela. **RENFE** office (tel. 31 81 09), 2 bl. downhill from Hotel Cervantes and across C. Marquesa de Pinares/Av. Extremadura. To: Cáceres (2 *regional* per day, 1hr., 340ptas; 1 *talgo* per day at 8:53am, 1hr. 860ptas); Badajoz (6 per day; 1hr.; *regional* 265ptas, *talgo* 860ptas); Sevilla (1 per day, 4hr., 1225ptas); Madrid (5 per day; 6hr.; *expreso* 2890ptas, *talgo* 3810ptas).

Buses: Av. Libertad (tel. 37 14 04, 30 04 04), 1km from the center. To reach Pl. España, it's a hike across either the suspension bridge in front or the Roman bridge to the right. To: Badajoz (8 per day, 1hr., 450ptas); Zafra (5 per day, 1hr. 500ptas); Cáceres (5 per day, 2hr., 580ptas); Sevilla (7 per day, 3hr., 1505ptas); Madrid (7 per day, 5 1/2 hr., 2310ptas).

Taxis: tel. 37 11 11. 24-hr. service.

Medical Services: Residencia Sanitaria de la Seguridad Social Centralita (tel. 38 10 00). **Ambulance,** El Madrileño (tel. 31 57 58, 31 11 08).

Emergency: tel. 092 or 091.

Police: Ayuntamiento, Pl. España, 1 (tel. 38 01 00).

Accommodations

Hostales go incognito in Mérida. The best place to look is around **Plaza de España,** but you could spend days wandering the side streets without seeing any blue-and-white square signs. Budget triples do not exist.

> **Pension El Arco,** C. Santa Beatriz de Silva, 4 (tel. 31 01 07). Follow the signs to the *parador;* just before passing under the arch, look right. Wacky Mérida-baroque decor runs from posters of Extremadura to pictures of dignitaries who've stayed the night to tactful reminders concerning your behavior. Rooms are small, simple, neat, painfully decorated, and the least expensive in town. Electric fans, too. Singles 1200ptas. Doubles 2400ptas. Showers 125ptas.
>
> **Hostal-Residencia Senero,** C. Holguín, 12 (tel. 31 72 07), take street to left of Hotel Emperatiz (on Pl. España) through its twists to C. Holguín. Spanish tile interior. Clean and comfortable, with wood furniture. Cool patio. All rooms with bath. Singles 1800ptas. Doubles 3500ptas. Winter: 1800ptas; 3000ptas.
>
> **Hostal Bueno,** C. Calvario, 9 (tel. 31 10 13), a bit out of the way. From Pl. España pass under the arch and continue past the *parador* and around the corner of the post office to C. Almendralejo. Turn left, then immediately right on C. Calvario. A modest establishment whose rooms, all with bath, are a bit dim and cramped, but clean. Singles 2000ptas. Doubles 3500ptas. Winter: 2000ptas; 3000ptas.

Food

Restaurant options are plentiful—for those not on a budget. Sleuth out meals and pop *tapas* around **Plaza España** and **Calle Juan Ramón Melida,** near the *teatro romano*. The **market** is on C. San Francisco, off C. Lillo (open 8am-2pm and 4-7pm).

> **Casa Benito,** C. San Francisco next to the market. Gawk at the photos, prints, and posters of all things taurine that cover every inch of wall space—some images date back to the beginning of the century—while sipping *caña* (75ptas) and munching a spicy *pincho* (200ptas). Ivy-shaded terrace and small dining room for meaty meals. Open for eating 1-4pm and 9-12pm. Bar open all day and into the night.
>
> **Bar Restaurante Briz,** C. Féliz Valverde Lillo, 5 (tel. 31 93 07). Typical Extremaduran fare and more ubiquitous bar-restaurant atmosphere. *Caldereta* (lamb stew) 750ptas. Hefty *menú* (800ptas) specializing in *callos* (tripe). Open Mon.-Sat. 1-5:30pm and 9:15pm-midnight.
>
> **Cafeteriá Lusi,** on a little plaza just behind Pl. España on the Hotel Emperatriz side. The *menú* (900ptas) is uninspired, but it's a popular spot in the evening for *tapas* (150-200ptas) and cool drinks *(caña* 70ptas). Open 10am-2am.

Sights

¿Is it Rome or is it Extremadura? The best view of the **Acueducto de los Milagros** is from the road from Cárceres. Farther up the river are the three remaining pillars of the **Acueducto de San Lázaro.** Over the wide, shallow Río Guadiana, the **Puente Romano,** one of the Romans' largest bridges, is still the main access to town from the south.

Rafael Moneo's award-winning **Museo Nacional de Arte Romano,** whose brickwork and rounded arches deftly evoke Roman taste, almost steals the show—truly delightful. The relics from the Roman theater, amphitheater, and circus, as well as detailed explanations and diagrams of each structure (in Spanish), sit in the nearby brick atrium. The **tombstones** are fascinating. On one of them is a prayer to the goddess Proserpina to avenge the thefts endured by the supplicant in his lifetime, complete with an itemized list of the losses ("Tunics 6, linen capes 2," etc.). A Roman road passes under and through the museum. To get here, follow C. Santa Eulalia from Pl. España and bear right up C. Juan Ramón Melida. (Open Tues.-Sat. 10am-2pm and 5-7pm, Sun. and holidays 10am-2pm. Admission 200ptas, EEC citizens and students with ID free.)

The **teatro romano** lies across the street, a gift from Agrippa to the city. The semicircle of tiers (seating for 6000) faces a *scaenaefrons,* an impressive marble colonnade built backstage. The Romans actually plagiarized some of the architectural ideas of the Greek theater. A Roman's idea of a fun night out did not include dry recitations of *Antigone*; instead, they revelled in the consumptive antics of Christian-eating lions. The

Spanish were slightly more conventional in their taste, and preferred a well-acted tragedy over the spontaneous sort of Roman hijinks. Seats are divided into three sections, originally used to separate social classes. The *teatro clásico* performances, somewhat less graphic than those of ancient Rome, take place here June through August at 11pm. (Tickets 800-2000ptas. Box office open 10am-1pm and 6-11pm.) Next to the theater and in worse shape is the 14,000-seat **Anfiteatro Romano**. Inaugurated in 8 B.C., the amphitheater was used for man-to-man gladiator combat and *venationes,* contests between men and wild animals. The corridors at both ends of the ellipse hold gloomy pre-combat waiting rooms. (Both open 8am-9:30pm; Oct.-March 8am-6pm. Admission 200ptas. The same ticket is valid for the Alcazaba; see below.)

Northeast of the theater complex is the **circo romano,** or hippodrome. Once filled with 30,000 crazed spectators cheering their favorite charioteers, the arena now resembles a large parking lot. Diocles, the all-time best Lusitanian racer, got his start here and wound up in Rome with 1462 victories. (Open. Free.)

Down the banks of the Guadiana, near the elegant *terrazas* of Pl. España, is the **Alcazaba,** a Moorish fortress built to guard the Roman bridge. The Moors showed their usual canny good sense by using building materials left behind by the Romans and Visigoths. The *aljibe* (cistern) held water filtered from the river. (Open Mon.-Sat. 8am-1pm and 4-7pm, Sun. 9am-2pm; Oct.-March Mon.-Sat. 9am-1pm and 3-6pm, Sun. 9am-2pm. Admission 200ptas.)

Los Pueblos Blancos

So named for their blindingly whitewashed walls, the *pueblos blancos* are a series of small, tranquil towns in southern Extremadura. Any of these towns make good daytrips from Mérida or Badajoz, or even from Sevilla or Cáceres. A car helps, since public transportation schedules don't always permit early arrivals and/or late departures. You may also want to come armed with a town map (available at any of the larger Extremaduran or Andalucían tourist offices), as the few tourist offices in these villages have limited, irregular hours. The slim *Guía de Hoteles, Campings, Agencia de Viajes y Restaurantes* lists all you need to know about budget lodgings (free at tourist offices in Badajoz, Mérida, and Cáceres).

Zafra

Unpretentious Zafra has few spectacular sights, but has a certain suffuse beauty. A major market town since the Middle Ages, Zafra has not one, but two central squares. Misnamed **Plaza Grande** has palms to relieve the austerity of the balconied stone 17th- and 18th-century mansions that line it. Small cafés sit in the shade at the fringes of the arcades. **Plaza Chica** is made up of smaller 15th to 17th century mercantile buildings with Mudejar windows and arcades; a *vara* (medieval yardstick) once used in Zafra's markets is embedded in one of them.

The Gothic **Colegiata de la Candelaria,** a small church near the two plazas, has an uninspired 16th-century interior, apart from the retable (1644) by Zurbarán. The crafty nuns who run the *colegiata* sneakily keep the interior shrouded in obscurity. For a better look at the retable, pop 25ptas into the timed light fixtures. From Plaza Grande, follow C. Tetuán then turn right on C. Conde de la Corte. (Open 10:30am-1pm and 8-10pm. Free.)

C. Sevilla links Pl. Grande to verdant **Plaza España,** lined with restaurants and hotels. The **Alcázar,** a 15th- and 16th- century structure, once home to the noble Suárez de Figueroa family (Duques of Feria; their fig leaf appears as a motif throughout town), is two blocks to the left on C. Campo Marín. Although the building is now a luxury *parador,* the staff at the reception desk will happily point out the lavish, echoing *capilla* with its coffered cupola, the *Sala Dorada* (Gilded Hall; open when not occupied by guests), and Juan de Herrera's luscious Renaissance courtyard.

If stranded in Zafra try **Hostal Rafael,** C. Virgen de Guadalupe, 7a (tel. 55 20 52). Rooms are small but clean and the *hostal* is equipped with a bar that serves various refreshments. The bus station and tourist office sandwich the site, off C. Campo Marín on the left as you walk from the former and the right from the latter. (Singles 2400ptas. Doubles 3800ptas, with bath 5300ptas.)

The **tourist office** (tel. 55 10 36) is in a small adobe building in Pl. España. Good with accommodations, weak on sights, and neither English nor French spoken. (Open Mon.-Fri. 11:15am-2pm and 6:15-8pm, Sat. 11:15am-1:30pm.) Across the street at #12, the **post office** (tel. 55 02 78) does **telegrams**. (Open Mon.-Fri. 8am-3pm and Sat. 9am-2pm.) **Telephone booths** scatter themselves all over; some cluster at the edge of Pl. España and C. Campo Marín. In a **medical emergency** dial 55 49 04. For **police** call 55 45 13.

The **bus station** (tel. 55 39 07) is a 15-minute walk from Turismo. From the station walk left, then right on C. Antonio Chacón; Parque de la Paz is on the left and the Alcázar on the right before Pl. España. To Mérida (5 per day, 1hr., 630ptas), Badajoz (8 per day, 1hr., 620ptas), Sevilla (7 per day, 2 1/2 hr., 1040ptas), and Madrid (2 per day, 7hr., 2500ptas). The **train station** (tel. 55 02 15) is also 15 minutes from Turismo. Turn right out of Turismo, walk through the park, then turn left. To: Mérida (2 per day, 1hr., 340ptas), Badajoz via Mérida (2 per day, 3hr., 825ptas), Sevilla (2 per day, 2hr., 1110ptas), and Madrid (1 per day, 7 1/2 hr., 2345ptas).

Llerena

Known under the Caliphate of Córdoba as Ellerina, Llerena flourished under Maestre Pelay Pérez Correa, who made it the center of the military Orden de Santiago; remains of 14th-century walls are proof of Llerena's strategic importance as a frontier town. The Baroque style here gets a peculiar vernacular twist, incorporating Mudejar elements in its balconies, wrought-iron grilles, and courtyards. From Zafra, **buses** run here (4 per day, 1 1/4 hr., 480ptas).

Plaza Mayor is a textbook of Mudejar architecture with brick, octagonal pillars, and *alfiz* (rectangular moulding) prominent. Facing the square, 14th- to 15th-century Gothic **Iglesia de Nuestra Señora de Granada** has brilliant *aljimez* (windows divided by slender columns) and balustrades. (Open for mass only.) Admirers of 16th-century polychrome wood sculpture seek out the 16th-century Gothic **Convento de Santa Clara** for its one Martínez Montañés. Portocarrero started the **Palacio del Maestre** in the 15th century, but 16th-century alterations furnished the palace with a galleried courtyard.

Jerez de los Caballeros

The discovery of several *dólmenes* in the area suggest that Jerez de los Caballeros was the site of some kind of mysterious prehistoric settlement. The Phoenicians called it Ceret, corrupted eventually to Xerisa. Numerous mosaics, funerary steles, and inscriptions remain from the Romans. Like so many towns in this part of Extremadura, Jerez owes its profile, its noble character, and the martial resonance of its full name to a military order, the Orden Militar del Temple. The entire town was given as a bonus to the order by Alfonso IX of León when he captured it from the Moors in 1230. Famous Jerezites include Hernando de Soto, explorer of Florida, and Núñez de Balboa, regarded as the first European to discover the Pacific.

Tourists come to see the 13th-century **Castillo Fortaleza** and intricately decorated brick, painted stucco, mosaic, and *azulejo* Baroque church **torres** (notably those of San Miguel, San Bartolomé, and Santa Catalina). The castle was built by heavenly Knights Templar in the 13th century. When the pope abolished the order in the 14th century, the Knights were put to death in the church towers. (*Castillo* open mid-morning to 8pm. Churches open for mass only.) The town is also dense with palaces, fountains, convents, and hermitages that blend Gothic, Renaissance, and Baroque features with a strong Andalusian influence.

The **tourist office** is open Mon.-Fri. 9am-3pm and 6-8pm. Four **buses** per day go to and from Zafra and one from Mérida.

Olivenza

Founded by the strong and brave and beautiful Portuguese Knights Templar, swiped by Castilian Knights Templar, and ceded to Portugal in 1297 by the Treaty of Alcañices, the fortified town of Olivenza passed into Spanish hands definitively in 1801 as spoils from the War of Oranges. But five centuries of Portuguese rule have left their stamp on this town, rich in Manueline style (see Portugal: Art and Architecture).

Two gates remain of the **fortaleza** built by King Dinis in the early 14th century. The town's trapezoidal **castillo** dates from the 15th century; its corners are anchored by square towers and there's a courtyard. It houses an unusual **Museo Etnográfico.**

Namesake of the Manueline style, King Manuel I commissioned **Santa María de la Magdalena** in the early 16th century, notable for its tall, slender, fluted pillars and the heraldic motifs in the vaulting. The lateral aisles are decorated with Portuguese *azulejos*. **Santa María del Castillo** was erected in the 13th century for King Dinis and altered to a late-Renaissance aspect in the 16th; the Virgin's family tree is represented in the Capilla del Evangelio as 12 polychrome wood sculptures that stand for the 12 tribes of Israel. The town's civic architecture is well represented by the **Palacio de los Duques de Cadaval,** now the Ayuntamiento, a pure Manueline mansion with the arms of Portugal on the façade.

The **tourist office** is open Tues.-Fri. 10am-2pm and 5-7pm, Sat. 10am-2pm.

PORTUGAL

US $1 = 112.76 escudos ($)
CDN $1 = 101.59$
UK £1 = 230.12$
AUS $1 = 88.79$
NZ $1 = 66.33$

100$ = US $0.89
100$ = CDN $0.98
100$ = UK £0.43
100$ = AUS $1.13
100$ = NZ $1.51

Once There

Tourist Offices

The national tourist board is the **Direção General do Turismo (DGT)**. Their offices are in virtually every city; look for the **"Turismo"** sign. They'll give you free maps that usually include brief descriptions of sights and useful phone numbers. Many Turismos keep lists of approved accommodations and can point you to a *quarto*. They may stock maps and brochures for the whole area, even for the whole country. Finding an English speaker at these offices should be no problem.

The principal student travel agencies are **TURICOOP**, R. Pascoal de Melo, 15-1° DT, 1000 Lisboa (tel. (1) 53 92 47 or 53 18 04; fax (1) 57 47 16; telex 13566); and **TAGUS Juvenil** (for addresses, see Planning Your Trip: Useful Addresses: Travel Services). Again, English is spoken at these offices.

Embassies and Consulates in Portugal

If you're seriously ill or in trouble, contact your consulate, not your embassy (whose function is solely diplomatic). They can provide legal advice and medical referrals and can contact relatives back home. In extreme cases, they may offer emergency financial assistance. Embassies are in Lisboa; consulates (if any) are in other major cities. Embassies and consulates keep regular business hours: open from Monday to Friday, out to lunch from 1:30 to 3pm, and closed by 5:30 or 6pm.

U.S. Embassy: Av. Forças Armadas, 1200 Lisboa (tel. (1) 72 66 00).

Canadian Embassy: Av. Liberdade, 144/56, #4, 1200 Lisboa (tel. (1) 347 48 92).

British Embassy: R. São Domingos a Lapa, 35-37, 1296 Lisboa (tel. (1) 39 60 89). **Consulates,** Av. Varco, 2, CP 417 9000 Funchal, Madeira (tel. (9) 12 12 21); Av. Boavista, 3072, Porto 4000 (tel. (2) 68 47 89).

Australian Embassy: Av. Liberdade, 244, 4th fl., 1200 Lisboa (tel. (1) 52 33 50).

New Zealand Embassy: Refer to the embassy in Rome, via Zara, 28, Rome 00198 (tel. (39-6) 440 29 28).

Getting Around

Train

Caminhos de Ferro Portugueses, Portugal's national railway, operates throughout the country, but aside from the Braga-Porto-Coimbra-Lisboa line, it's wisest to take the bus. Trains are less comfortable, less frequent, often slower, and reach fewer destina-

Getting Around 453

tions than buses; on the other hand, a second-class train ticket is generally less expensive than the bus fare.

Unless you own a Eurailpass, the return on round-trip tickets must be used before 3am the following day. The fine for riding without a ticket is at least 4500$. Tykes under 4 travel free; ages 4-11 pay half price for their own seat. **Youth discounts** are only available to Portuguese citizens; this stipulation is strictly enforced and checked.

With a first-class **Eurailpass**, a supplementary fee, and an advance reservation, you can take convenient express trains. But unless you're planning to travel much outside of Portugal and Spain, Eurail won't save you money. (For more information, see Getting There: From Europe: Train.)

Bus

Who's on that bus? It's us! Buses are the way to go. Overall more comfy than trains, they run frequently and are super cheap. Get this: you'll pay 1520$ to sit on a train for six hours from Lisboa to Porto, *or* you can get there one hour faster for just 1480$ (slick, deluxe *expresso* 1650$).

Rodoviária, the national bus company, links just about every town, while a superflux of private regional companies—**Cabanelas, AVIC, Mafrense,** among them— cover the more obscure routes. Express coach service *(expressos)* between major cities is especially good. City buses are really inexpensive and may run to small nearby villages. Rodoviária's headquarters in Lisboa are at Av. Casal Ribeiro, 18-B (tel. (1) 54 54 39).

Car

Traveling by car in Portugal is not for the faint of heart; Portugal has the highest accident rate per capita in Western Europe. Off the main arteries, the narrow, twisting roads may prove difficult to negotiate. Moreover, parking space in cities is nonexistent, and Portuguese drivers fulfill their reputation for rash and risky maneuvers. The Portuguese AAA is called the **Automóvil Clube de Portugal.**

Gas comes in super (97 octane), normal (92 octane), and unleaded. Prices are high by North American standards (about 200$ per liter). Officially you need an **international driver's license** to drive in Portugal (see Planning Your Trip: Documents).

Renting a car involves the extra costs of insurance and tax. A major rental company in Portugal and Europe is **Europcar,** whose U.S. affiliate is National Car Rental. **Avis, Hertz,** and other major companies are in the larger cities and in airports. Rates start at about US$200 per week (not including insurance and tax), but local companies may be less expensive. It costs less (for some reason) to reserve your rental in the U.S. before coming to Portugal. The driving age is 18, but you must be 21 to rent a car and have had a driver's license for at least one year. The following companies offer information on reservations.

Auto-Europe, P.O. Box 1097, Camden, ME 04843 (in the U.S. and Canada tel. (800) 223-5555; elsewhere (207) 236-8235; fax (207) 236-4724).

Avis (tel. (800) 331-1212). You must reserve while still in the U.S.

Europe By Car, 1 Rockefeller Pl., New York, NY 10020 (tel. (800) 223-1516 or (212) 581-3040). Student and faculty discounts.

Hertz Rent-A-Car (tel. (800) 654-3131).

Kemwel Group, 106 Calvert St., Harrison, NY 10528-3199 (tel. (800) 678-0678 or (914) 835-5454). Rents, leases, and sells most makes of cars. The good rental rates are even lower if reservations are made.

National Car Rental (tel. (800) 227-7368).

Moped and Bicycle

Touring by **moped** is less popular here than in the rest of Europe, so don't expect to find rentals easily.

Although in coastal areas and on the flatlands **bicycles** are an obvious choice, roads are often in deplorable condition (some still cobblestoned); often only a mountain bike will do. Also, watch out for motorists who aren't used to driving alongside of cyclists. Even experienced pedal-pushers should beware of the hot Mediterranean climate of southern Portugal.

There are few bike stores outside of Portugal's major cities. You'd best be packing a suitable bike helmet and a tough bike lock (the best are made by Kryptonite, US$35-US$50), a strong pump, and various spare parts and tools. Wise cyclists bring along a basic bike repair book and the relevant gadgetry.

Airlines count a bicycle as your second free piece of checked luggage. As a third piece, it'll cost US$85 each way. The bike can't weigh over 70 lbs. and must be boxed (normally boxes are available at the airport). Policies vary, so call individual airlines.

A number of books about bicycle travel in Europe recommend particularly senic and cyclable roads. *Europe by Bike: 18 Tours Geared for Discovery,* by Karen and Terry Whitehill (The Mountaineers Press, Seattle $10.95), is a fairly accurate aid for planning your trip and outfitting your bike.

Hitchhiking

> *Let's Go* does not recommend hitching as a means of travel. The information presented below and throughout the book is not intended to do so.

Opportunities to hitch in Portugal are few and far between. Although some tourists try to hitchhike, most locals stick to buses, which are already surprisingly inexpensive. Rides are reportedly easiest to come by between smaller towns. Thumbers often get results by approaching people for rides at gas stations near highways and rest stops.

The dangers of hitchhiking should not be underestimated. Drivers have raped, sexually assaulted, and killed passengers. If you choose to solicit a ride, avoid doing it alone. Experienced hitchers sit in the front, and never get in the back seat of a two-door car. If the driver begins to harrass them, they ask firmly to be let out. They report that, in an emergency, opening the door on the road may surprise a driver enough to slow down. Pretending you're about to vomit may also help, they say.

Accommodations

Tourist offices keep lists of all recognized youth hostels, hotels, *pensões, pousadas,* and campgrounds. Sometimes they can inform on *quartos* (rooms in private homes).

Youth Hostels

The **Associação Portuguesa de Pousadas de Juventude (APPJ),** the Portuguese Hostelling International affiliate, runs the country's HI hostels. A bargainous bed in a *pousada de juventude* costs 850-1350$ per night, 750-1000$ in off-season (breakfast included). Lunch or dinner cost 750$. Rates are slightly higher for guests 26 or older (i.e., over 25). Hostels are typically some distance away from the town center. Check-in hours are from 9am to 12:30pm and 6pm to 9pm. Most hostels enforce a lockout 10:30am to 6pm, and early curfews (11pm or midnight) may cramp your style if you club-hop. Don't expect much privacy.

To reserve beds in swamped high season (July and August), obtain an **International Booking Voucher** from APPJ (or your home country's HI affiliate) and send it to the desired hostel four to eight weeks in advance of your stay. If traveling between October 1 and April 30, call or write ahead to make sure the hostel's open. Groups should contact APPJ's national reservation service (address below) at least 30 days in advance, giving the exact number of males and females in the group and the dates desired.

To stay in a hostel, an **HI card** (3000$) is mandatory. In Portugal they're sold only by APPJ's Lisboa office (see address below), so you may want to get one before leaving home (see Planning Your Trip: Documents: HI Membership). Also required is a **sleepsack,** so either bring your own or rent one from the hostel—in listings we'll write "Sheets 200$." (To make a cheap sleepsack, see Planning Your Trip: Packing.) Don't confuse *pousadas de juventude* with their sneakily—named opposites, *pousadas* (the Portuguese equivalent of the Spanish *parador,* historic buildings that were converted into pricey hotels).

For **information** such as hostel addresses, contact APPJ, R. Andrade Corvo, 46, 1000 Lisboa (tel. (1) 53 97 25). (See also Planning Your Trip: Documents: HI Membership.)

Pensões and Residencias

Pensões, also called *residencias,* will likely be your mainstay. They're far cheaper and offer fewer amenities than hotels; only slightly more expensive than youth hostels and offer a private room. All are rated by the government on a three-star scale and required to prominently post their category and legal price limits. During high season, many *pensõe* owners won't reserve rooms by phone. Travellers with foresight book at least one month in advance and get written confirmation.

Hotels

Hotels in Portugal are expensive. A quality establishment typically includes showers and breakfast in the price. Most rooms without bath or shower have a sink and bidet. Generally you must vacate your room by noon the following day. When business is slack, try bargaining down in advance; the "official price" is merely the maximum allowed.

Camping

The Portuguese love to camp. They see it as a social activity rather than a solitary survival exercise, and their 168 official campgrounds *(parques de campismo)* come brimful of amenities and comforts. Virtually all have a supermarket and café and most enjoy access to a beach. Many inland sites possess river bathing or pools. With such facilities, it's wise to arrive early; urban and coastal parks may require reservations. Recently police have been cracking down on illegal camping, so don't try it close by one of the official campgrounds. Larger Turismo branches stock the **Roteiro Campista**, an indispensable multilingual guide to all official campgrounds; or write to the Federação Portuguesa de Campismo, Apartado 3168-1304, Lisboa Codex (tel. (1) 86 23 50 or 364 23 74; fax (1) 888 10 76).

Orbitur-Intercâmbio de Turismo, S.A., a private company, administers 15 of Portugal's poshest, best-run, and most expensive campgrounds (bungalows available). For reservations write to Orbitur at Av. Almirante Reis, 246 r/c, Dío. Lisboa 1000 (tel. (1) 89 05 75 or 84 29 38; fax (1) 848 18 81).

Alternative Accommodations

Quartos: Rooms in private residences, just like *casas particulares* in Spain. Sometimes the only choice in small or less touristed towns, particularly in southern Portugal. Turismo can usually help find them, although at times officials prefer to direct tourists to hotels. Restaurant proprietors and bartenders often supply names and directions.

Pousada (literally, resting place): A castle, palace, or monastery converted into a luxurious government-run guest house. Portugal's version of the Spanish *parador nacional.* Pricey *pousadas* play up local craft, custom, and cuisine. You pay for the exceptional surroundings: they generally cost as much as the most expensive hotels. Most require reservations. For information contact ENATUR, Av. Santa Joana Princesa, 10-A, 1700 Lisboa (tel. (1) 848 90 78).

Turismo de Habitação Regional helps tourists find rooms, apartments, or entire houses, many of them mansions. This practice is most common in the Algarve and the provinces north of the Ribatejo.

Food and Drink

Olive oil, garlic, herbs, and sea salt routinely season local specialties. As a whole, the aromatic Portuguese cuisine is heavy on herbs and light on spices.

Typical Fare

Sopas (soups) are hearty and filling. Thick *caldo verde,* a potato and cabbage or kale mixture with a slice of sausage and olive oil is a northern specialty. Sweating sightseers cool off with southern *gaspacho.* **Sandes** or **sandwiches** (sandwiches) here are smaller than their Spanish counterparts, but a *bifana* or *prego no pão* (a meat sandwich) is a fiesta on a roll.

Main dishes run a delectable gamut. Seafood lovers get their fix from grilled *peixe espada grelhado* (Madeiran scabbard-fish), *lagosta suada* (steamed lobster), *pescada frita* (fried hake, a particularly delish Atlantic fish), *linguado grelhado* (grilled sole), *polvo* (boiled or grilled octopus), and *mexilhões* (mussels). Cod lovers snarf *bacalhau* (roasted, boiled, or fried cod served with potatoes). Bold gourmands shouldn't miss *chocos grelhadas* (grilled squid) or *lulas grelhadas* (also grilled squid), a Portuguese specialty.

Pork fiends indulge in *bife de porco à alentejana,* made with clams in a coriander sauce. Those who prefer chicken fork into *frango assado* (roasted on a spit) and *frango no churrasco* (barbecued). The entire country feeds on *cozida à portuguesa* (boiled beef, pork, sausage, and vegetables) in winter. Ballsy connoisseurs plop a dollop of *piri-piri* (mega-hot) sauce on the side. In the country, an expensive delicacy is freshly roasted *cabrito* (baby goat). There are scores of variations on *feijoadas,* bean stew with pork and sausage. No matter what you order, *batatas* (potatoes), prepared in a billion different ways, will accompany it.

Queijos (cheeses) are fresh and delectable. The soft, chewy *serra* comes from ewe's milk and costs many a ducat, while tangy *cabreiro* takes its name from goat's milk. *Alvorca* is a blanket term for hard cheeses made from cow's, goat's, or ewe's milk. The only cheese reminiscent of cheddar is *queijo São Jorge* from Açores.

Portugal's favorite **dessert** is *pudim,* a rich caramel custard. The Costa Verde's own *toucinho de céu* (bacon of heaven) combines egg, almond, and sugar in a prodigiously sweet tart. The almond groves of the Algarve produce their own version of marzipan. For something different, try *peras* (pears) bathed in sweet Port wine and served with a sprinkling of raisins and filberts on top.

Dining Hours and Restaurants

The Portuguese eat earlier than the Spanish. The midday meal (dinner, "lunch" to Americans) is served between noon and 2pm, supper between 7:30 and 10pm.

A good meal costs 900-1100$ just about anywhere. Oddly, prices don't vary much between ritzy and economy restaurants in Portugal. Half portions **(meia dose)** cost more than half-price but are often more than adequate—a full dose is enough for two. Other cheapo options? The ubiquitous **prato do dia** (special of the day) and **menú** (appetizer, bread, entree, and dessert) satisfy hungry people. The **ementa turistica** (tourist *menú)* is usually a way to rip off foreigners, although it's a lot of food (inevitably the most expensive option at 1500$). The standard pre-meal bread, butter, cheese, and paté usually served at restaurants will up your bill.

Although restaurant prices certainly won't drive you to this, concocting a meal from the outdoor food stalls is the most inexpensive option. Attention vegetarians—every town you visit is likely to have a **mercado municipal** (open-air market); get there before noon for the choicest produce. For groceries, shop at the **mercado** (supermarket).

Drinks

Portuguese **vinho** (wine) costs a pittance by North American standards. Sparkling *vinho verde,* (literally "green wine"—the name refers to its youth, not its color) comes in red and white versions; the red may be obnoxious to the unaccustomed palate but the white is delicious by anybody's standards. The Adega Cooperatives of Ponte de Lima, Monção, and Amarante make the best. Excellent local table wines are Colares, Dão, Borba, Bairrada, Bucelas, and Periquita. Ordering the overpriced Mateus Rosé marks you instantly as a foreigner ignorant of Portuguese vintages. If you can't decide, experiment with the **vinho de casa** (house wine), a reliable standby.

Port, pressed (by feet) from the red grapes of the Douro Valley and fermented with a touch of brandy, is a dessert in itself. Chilled white port makes a snappy aperitif. A unique heating process gives **Madeira** wines their odd "cooked" flavor. Try the dry Sercial and Verdelho as aperitifs, and the sweeter Bual and Malmsey as dessert wines.

Bar lingo is rather specialized. If it's beer you want, order bottled Sagres or Super Bock. Ask for it **fresco** (cool), or it may come *natural* (room temperature). A small glass of beer is a **fino** or an *imperial,* while a tall glass is a **caneca.** When it's time to sober up, order a **bica** (cup of black espresso) or a **galão/cafe com leite** (coffee with milk, served in a glass).

Communications

Mail

The most reliable way to send a message is actually via telegram (see below); the least is by surface mail, which may take over two months. Mail sent from small towns takes longer than from major cities such as Lisboa; overall, mail service tends to be faster than Spain's. Stamps are sold only at post offices *(correios).* A "CTT" sign at the post office indicates that it does telegrams and has telephones—nearly all do.

Air mail: *Via aerea.* Takes 6-8 business days to reach the U.S. or Canada. Postage 120$.

Surface mail: *Superficie.* Takes up to 2 months.

Postcards: *Cartão postal.* Takes a bit longer than a letter. Postage 120$.

Registered or express mail: *Registrado* or *certificado.* The most reliable way to send a letter or parcel home. Takes about 5 business days.

Overnight mail: Only available in large cities.

General Delivery mail: *Posta Restante.* Letters or packages held for pick-up at the post office that handles general delivery for a town. Letters should be addressed as follows: LAST NAME, First Name; Posta Restante; City Name; Postal Code; COUNTRY; AIR MAIL. When you pick it up, always ask for mail under both your first and last names to make sure it hasn't been misfiled. You can have mail forwarded to another Posta Restante address if you must leave town whilst expecting mail. Takes 2 wks. Charge of 20$ per piece picked up.

American Express: Mail (no packages) for cardholders may be sent to some AmEx offices, where it'll be held. This service may be less reliable than Posta Restante. A directory of which offices hold mail can be had from any AmEx office, or contact their main office at 65 Broadway, New York, NY 10006 (tel. (800) 528-4800). They'll keep mail for one to three months after receipt.

Telegraph

A telegram, the most reliable means of communication, costs the same as a three-minute international call. Telegrams may be sent from most any **post office**, whose signs will read "CTT." A message of 10-15 words costs a flat fee of about 1300$ plus a 68$ per word charge.

Fax

Fax is virtually nonexistent in Portugal; only big city post offices are likely to have machines.

Telephone

Country Code: 351.

Directory Assistance: 118.

Local Operator: 142.

International Operator: 099 for inside Europe; 098 for elsewhere.

Emergency (Police, Fire, Medical): 115.

Phone booths are located at phone offices, on the street, and in some post offices, marked by signs saying Credifone. The **Credifone** system uses magnetic cards rather than coins (few pay phones accept coins any more) that are sold at locations posted on the phone booth. Local calls cost 17.5$ by Credifone, or 20$ by coin. Phone calls from bars and cafés cost whatever the proprietor decides to charge, typically 30-35$; there's usually a posted sign that indicates the rates.

Direct-dialing from a phone booth is the least expensive way to make an international call. You may have difficulty reaching the U.S. from anywhere other than Lisboa. Call the operator beforehand to get an idea of how much your call will cost. Then dial 098 for Europe, 097 for everywhere else; + country code + city code + phone number. Handy calling cards let you make calls even when you don't have a pocket full of coins, but their rates are higher.

AT&T calling card: To call the U.S., dial toll-free 05 017 1288; then give the operator the number you want to reach and your calling card number. For Canada, the U.K., Australia, and New Zealand, consult the international operator.

MCI calling card: To call the U.S., dial toll-free 05 018 120 33; then give the operator the number you want to reach and your calling card number.

Collect calls *(pago no destino)* are charged are billed according to person-to-person *(chamada pessoa à pessoa)* rates but are still cheaper than calls from hotels.

Telecom Portugal is an overpriced telephone office, similar to *Telefónica* in Spain.

Overseas Access is a telephone service offered by EurAide, P.O. Box 2375, Naperville, IL 60567 (tel. (708) 420-2343). European travelers pay a registration fee (US$15) and a weekly (US$15) or monthly (US$40) fee. Anyone who wants to get in touch with you calls a "home base" in Munich and leaves a short message (US$1 per minute); you get the message by calling the home base as often as you like. Calls to Munich from Iberia are clearly cheaper than overseas calls. If you buy a Eurail pass from them, the initial fee is waived and the monthly rate is US$25.

More Money

Bills come in denominations of 500, 1000, 2000, 5000, and 10,000$. Coins come in 1, 2 1/2, 5, 10, 20, 50, 100, and 200$.

Banking hours are officially Monday through Friday 8:30am-3pm, but play it safe and visit between 8:30-11:45am and 1-2:45pm. All banks are closed on Saturdays.

Value-Added Tax (VAT)

The Value-Added Tax (VAT) is a sales tax levied on goods and services in the European Economic Community, at a rate that depends on the item. Stores, restaurants, and lodgings include VAT in posted prices, unless otherwise noted. In Portugal the rate is 2-16%. The *factura* is an official bill which lists the price of your purchase separately from the amount of VAT. Ask at stores and tourist offices about VAT refunds—a rare possibility with many restrictions (e.g., hefty minimum amount spent). The tax on accommodations and other "services" is not refundable. Prices quoted in *Let's Go* include VAT except where noted.

Tipping

Most restaurants will add a service charge to your bill. It's customary to round off the sum to the next highest unit of currency and leave the change as a tip. Everyone else deserves a tip too: train or airport porters 100-150$ per bag, taxi drivers 15% of the meter fare, movie theater ushers 15-20$, and hotel chambermaids 200$ per day (optional).

Life and Times

History

Way Back

Portugal was colonized by a succession of civilizations—Phoenicians, Celts, Greeks, and Carthaginians—long before the **Romans** won the peninsula in the Second Punic War (218-202 BC). The Romans brought the Latin language to the land they called "Lusitania."

The Moors and the Reconquista

When the Roman Empire crumbled in the early 5th century, Visigoth invaders assumed a shaky dominance, then fell to the Moors in 711 AD. Four centuries of Moorish rule left heavy stone castles throughout the country and hundreds of Arabic words in the Portuguese language. With the help of the Crusaders, **Dom Afonso Henriques** eventually overpowered the Moors and declared himself ruler of the Kingdom of Portugal at Guimarães, site of the first Christian victory (1143). The speedy Christian **Reconquista** ("reconquering") united Portugal by the 13th century, as **Dom Dinis** (1279-1325) ensured the unity of the nation, established a university, and exterminated that powerful, mystery-shrouded bunch of troublemakers, the **Knights Templar**.

The Age of Discovery

In 1415, Portuguese forces captured the North African city of Ceuta. Ambitious Prince Henry, his imagination fired by this new conquest, launched a famous school of navigation and exploration at Sagres, earning himself the nickname **Henry the Navigator** and inaugurating the Age of Discovery.

Portuguese adventurers drove into Africa in search of wealth, glory, and a mysterious messianic figure named Prester John, the mythic ruler of a Christian paradise thought to be hidden in the African interior. Portugal established (and exploited) colonies in Madeira, the Azores, and Guinea-Bissau before Bartolomeu Dias found an ocean route around Africa's Cape of Good Hope in 1487. **Vasco da Gama** led the first European naval expedition to India in 1498, and Portugal beefed up its empire with numerous colonies along the East African and Indian coasts. Two years later **Pedro Alvares Cabral** stumbled into Brazil then, on a roll, Portugal became the first European nation to establish trading contacts with Japan. With riches pouring in from far and near, Lisboa blossomed into one of Europe's most ornate cities. King Manuel the Fortunate commissioned buildings and monuments, artists slapped on symbols of maritime conquest, and *voilà*, Portugal had perfected its **Manueline** style.

The House of Bragança

Meanwhile, Spanish, English, and Dutch merchant fleets competed ferociously with Portugal for control of the **spice** trade. By the late 16th century, the debt-ridden country had lost it and the Golden Age of Portugal went out with a whimper. In 1580, paper-pushing Habsburg Felipe II inherited the Portuguese crown, uniting the entire Iberian peninsula under Spanish rule. For 60 years the Habsburgs dragged Portugal into their ill-fated wars; when the dust cleared, Portugal had lost a good part of its empire.

In 1640 the **House of Bragança** engineered a nationalist rebellion, assumed the throne, and erected a pole topped by a stone pig in their hometown (see Trás Os Montes: Bragança). The clever dynasty handed over Tangier and Bombay to the English, sealing an alliance with Spain's worst enemy. In the next two decades the nation gave up Ceylon and Malabar to the Dutch. Still, Portugal's empire was not entirely defunct. Brazil's gold, not to mention the booming slave trade (the first slave market was in Lagos), financed the "enlightened" despotism of **João V** (1706-1750), who lavished the dough on massive, flamboyant architectural projects.

The great **Earthquake of 1755** devastated Lisboa and killed as many as 50,000. The catastrophe, unparalleled in Portuguese history, shook European faith in both God and humanity; some even suggest that it brought an end to the more naïvely cheery aspects of Enlightenment thought. Dictatorial minister **Marquês de Pombal** led Lisboa's reconstruction, rebuilding the capital (or at least the Baixa district) in typically griddy Neoclassical style.

Napoleon, then More Trouble

When Napoleon's army invaded in 1807, the Portuguese royal family fled to Brazil, where they hid until the French were driven out. The timid monarchs returned to Lisboa in 1821, only to face even more problems. One year later, in the New World's only bloodless revolution, Brazil declared its independence.

As the empire disintegrated, behind-the-scene machinations at court left Portugal itself in disarray. When Prince Pedro flubbed the marriage arrangement between his seven-year-old daughter Maria da Gloria and his brother Miguel, a squabble over succession to the crown mushroomed into the **War of the Two Brothers** (1826-1834). Eight gory years later, with Pedro pushing up the daisies and Miguel in exile, Maria ascended to the throne at the age of 15. But even **Queen Maria's** staunch opposition could not stop the formation of a shaky party government.

Recent History

The monarchy wasn't ended, nor the **First Republic** established, until 1910. The new government granted universal male (of course) suffrage and managed to wrangle some power from the Catholic Church. The world disapproved when the Republic booted out the Jesuits and other religious orders, while governmental conflicts with workers' movements heightened tensions at home. The Republic wobbled along until it was overthrown in a 1926 military coup led by Antonio Carmona.

When Carmona died in 1951, conservative economist and star University of Coimbra student **António Salazar** succeeded to the dictator's chair. His *Estado Novo* (New State) gave women the vote for the first time, but did little else to end the country's authoritarian tradition (his secret police had a ball). The regime improved life for the wealthy while the working class, peasantry, and colonized peoples of Africa suffered. Salazar spent what money didn't go into his own pocket on costly wars that snuffed out colonial rebellions.

A slightly more liberal **Marcelo Caetano** continued the increasingly unpopular African wars after Salazar's death in 1970. On April 25, 1974, a left-wing military coalition overthrew Caetano in a quick coup. The **Captain's Revolution** sent Portuguese splashing euphoric graffitti on government buildings; today, every town in Portugal has its own Rua 25 de Abril. The Marxist-socialist armed forces established a variety of civil and political liberties and withdrew from Africa by 1975. But civil wars in Angola and Mozambique continued, and hundreds of thousands of *crioulos* (overseas Portuguese) and African refugees streamed into the country.

Portugal's first elections (1978) plopped the more conservative Social Democrats into power under charismatic **Mario Soares.** Foreign debt, inflation, and unemployment skyrocketed. Doares instituted "100 measures in 100 days" to resuscitate the country by stimulating industrial growth. The year 1986 brought Portugal into the European Economic Community, ending its long isolation from more affluent Northern Europe. Soares won new elections to become the first civilian president in 60 years.

Art

The **Age of Discovery** (15th-16th centuries) promoted cultural exchange with the rest of Renaissance Europe. Flemish masters such as **Jan van Eyck** brought their talent to and left their influence in Portugal, and Portuguese artists polished their skills over in Antwerp. King Manuel's favorite, **Jorge Afonso,** the most famous High Renaissance artist, whipped up typically ordered, realistic portrayals of human anatomy. Afonso's best work hangs at the Convento de Cristo in Tomar and the Convento da Madre de Deus in Lisboa. In the late 15th century, **Nuno Gonçalves** revived a primitivist school that went against the humanist grain of the Renaissance.

The Baroque era spawned intricate woodwork. Many a tree died for **Joachim Machado's** elaborately carved crêches in the early 1700s. On canvas, the portrait flourished. Nineteenth-century artist **Domingos António de Sequeira** painted historical, religious, and allegorical subjects too; his technique would later inspire French Impressionists. Porto's **António Soares dos Reis** brought Romantic sensibility to sculpture in the 1800s.

Cubism, Expressionism, and Futurism trickled into Portugal despite vicious censorship by Salazar's henchmen. In recent years, **Maria Helena Vieira da Silva** has won international recognition for her abstract paintings; **Carlos Botelho** is well-known for his street scenes of Lisboa.

Architecture

Few Moorish structures survived the Christian Reconquista, but Moorish elements persist in the tilework, church ceilings, and castle windows of later periods. Colorful **azulejos** grace many walls, ceilings, and thresholds. Carved in fabulous relief by the pre-Reconquista Moors, these ornate tiles later took on flat, glazed Italian and Northern European design.

Portugal's "national style," the **Manueline,** celebrates the exploration and imperial expansion that took place under King Manuel the Fortunate. This hybrid style frappés an Islamic and Gothic heritage with the influences of Italy, Flanders, and the Spanish Plateresque—and a sprinkle of marine motifs (anchors, knotted ropes, seaweed). The amalgamation found its most elaborate expression in the church and tower at **Belém,** built to honor Vasco da Gama. Close seconds are the Mosteiro dos Jerónimos in Lisboa and the Abadia de Santa Maria de Vitória in Batalha. Groups of architects collaborated to design these, among them **Diego Boytac, João de Castilho,** and the brothers **Diego and Francisco Arruda.**

Today Portuguese architect **Alvaro Siza** blends diverse Portuguese traditions, relying heavily on Modernism's functionality. His adorned houses line the streets of Porto and the Malagueira District at Évora.

Literature

Poetry holds a proud place in Portugal's literary tradition. Bards and balladeers entertained royalty with troubadour art for centuries and it was the poet-king **Dinis I** who made Portuguese the region's official language in the 12th century. Portuguese poetry bloomed with the Age of Discovery, most notably in the verse letters of **Francisco de Sá de Miranda** (1481-1558) and the musical lyrics of **Antonio Ferreira** (1528-1569). **Luís de Camões** celebrated the Indian voyages of Vasco da Gama in the greatest epic poem of Portuguese literature, *As Lusíadas* (The Lusiads, 1572).

Prose historians used great flourish and varying degrees of accuracy to chronicle the exploits of the Portuguese discoverers. An explorer himself, **João de Barros** detailed his wild adventures in *ásia*. **Gil Vicente,** the country's first known playwright, wrote light if idealized dramas about peasants, the pastoral life, and nature. The witty realism of Vicente's *Barcas* trilogy (1617-1619) influenced his contemporaries Shakespeare and Cervantes, and his works in Castilian earned him a distinguished place in the Spanish literary pantheon.

Spanish hegemony, intermittent warfare, and imperial decline conspired to make the literature of the 17th and 18th centuries somewhat less triumphant in tone. But **Almeida Garrett,** the dandy leader of the Romantic school, breathed life into patriotic literature with his accounts of Portuguese heroism. A lyric poet, dramatist, politician, revolutionary, frequent exile, and legendary lover, Garrett is credited with reviving drama in Portugal; his most famous play is *Frei Luiz de Sousa* (Brother Luiz de Sousa, 1843).

Political thinkers dominated the rise of the literary **Generation of 1870.** The Generation's most prominent novelist, **José Maria Eça de Queiroz,** inaugurated Portuguese social realism in works such as *O Primo Basilio* (Cousin Basilio, 1878) and *A Cidade e as Serras* (The City and the Mountains, 1901).

Portuguese modernism has not forsaken the tradition of lyric poetry. **Fernando Pessoa** wrote in English as well as Portuguese and developed four distinct styles under four different names: Pessoa, Alberto Caeiro, Ricardo Reis, and Alvaro de Campos. This multiple personality of the literary world introduced free verse to Portuguese poetry and lent a distinctly anti-bourgeois tone to the vanguard. **José Regio** waxed messsianic in the collection *Poemas de Deus e do Diabo* (Poems of God and the Devil), in which poets are frequently compared to Jesus. Contemporary writers **Aquilino Ribeiro** and **Miguel Torga** have risen to international fame with their entertainingly satirical novels.

Music

The best known expression of Portuguese music is **fado,** solo ballads accompanied by acoustic guitar. Symbolically named for fate, *fado* is identified with the peculiarly Portuguese state of mind that goes by the name of *saudade* (yearning or longing), and is characterized by tragic, romantic lyrics and mournful melodies—the Portuguese version of the blues. The Alfama district of Lisboa and Coimbra are the two modern centers of *fado*.

Apart from its folk tradition, the music of Portugal never managed to emerge from its general international obscurity. Opera, under the sponsorship of the Jesuits, soon assumed its position as the most popular and sophisticated Portuguese musical form. **António José da Silva,** who eventually fell victim to the Inquisition in 1739, was one of the most celebrated operatic composers. Music for keyboard instruments flourished as well, thanks in large part to the influence of Italian composer **Domenico Scarlatti,** who was brought to Lisboa by King João V. Scarlatti's preeminent Portuguese contemporary, Coimbra's **Carlos Seixas,** thrilled 18th-century Lisboa with his talent and contributed to the development of the sonata form. Sousa Carvalho's student **Domingo Bontempo** introduced new symphonic innovation from abroad and helped establish the first Sociedade Filarmónica, modeled after the London Philharmonic, in Lisboa in 1822.

The French invasion and civil war in the 19th century meant bankruptcy for the Church and the court, the two main sources of patronage. Since then, musical activity has been limited to local and popular spheres. New composers such as **Luís de Freitas Branco,** leader of the Neoclassical movement, have helped revitalize the Portuguese music scene.

Final Note

Note: *Let's Go* provides a glossary in the back of the book for all terms used recurrently in the text.

Lisboa (Lisbon)

Although modern problems assail Lisboa—the traffic, smog, and urban decay that most visitors notice—there is still something imperial about the city. It's appeal certainly doesn't come from any wealth of historic buildings, since most were destroyed during the great earthquake of 1755, but rather from the city's relaxed urbanity and from the care with which Lisboans have retained many of their traditions. The city meticulously maintains the black and white mosaic sidewalks, pastel building façades, and cobbled medieval alleys (some barely an arm's length wide), and streetcars still run down the broad avenues and narrow lanes.

While legend has it that Ulysses founded the city, historians and archeologists say that the Phoenicians were the first to stick their flag in Lisboa's soil, sometime in the 12th century BC. Successively conquered by Greeks, Carthaginians, Romans, and Arabs, Lisboa later flourished as a trade center during 300 years of Moorish rule. Dom Afonso III completed the Moorish expulsion in the Algarve, however, and in 1255 made Lisboa the capital of the Kingdom of Portugal.

The city's golden age began toward the end of the 15th century when Portuguese navigators pioneered the exploration of Asia and the New World. Then, on November 1, 1755, a huge earthquake struck. Many were at Mass; hundreds perished immediately as churches collapsed on their congregations. A tidal wave gulped the lower part of the city and drowned those that fled to the Tejo. Close to 50,000 ultimately died in the catastrophe that reduced Lisboa to a pile of smoldering rubble. Under the authoritarian leadership of the Prime Minister, the Marquês de Pombal, the city quickly recovered, and magnificent new squares, palaces, and churches were speedily rebuilt.

Over the past two centuries Portugal lost large portions of its overseas empire, most significantly Brazil in 1822. When Mozambique and Angola won their independence in 1974, hundreds of thousands of refugees, both African and Eurocolonist, streamed to the Portuguese capital. This, combined with the demise of the long-standing dictatorship in 1974, lends Lisboa a cosmopolitan air.

Orientation and Practical Information

Getting around Lisboa requires patience and well-developed leg muscles. The **Baixa,** or Lower Town, is Lisboa's downtown and the old business district. Its grid of small streets begins at the **Rossio** (the main square, comprised of the connecting **Praça Dom Pedro IV** and **Praça da Figueira**) and ends at Praça do Comércio, near the Rio Tejo (Tagus River). **Praça dos Restauradores,** a major square, is just north of the Rossio. Elegant Art Nouveau buildings color the newer business district, which centers on the broad avenues that radiate from the northern **Praça Marquês de Pombal.** The old and new business districts are connected by **Avenida da Liberdade,** a broad, tree-lined boulevard that begins its uphill climb at Pr. Restauradores.

Lisboa's swish shopping district, the **Chiado,** is linked to the Baixa by the Ascensor de Santa Justa. Rua do Carmo and Rua Garrett are the two most famous streets. (Buildings in this area were destroyed in the Great Fire of 1988 and much construction is currently taking place.)

West of Rua da Misericórdia spreads the **Bairro Alto,** or Upper District, a populous working-class area of narrow streets, tropical parks, and Baroque churches. To the east, the **Alfama,** Lisboa's famous medieval quarter, stacks tiny whitewashed houses along a labyrinth of narrow alleys and stairways beneath the city's *castelo.* **Belém** (Bethlehem), formerly an autonomous town (about 6km west of Praça do Comércio), is home to the Mosteiro dos Jerónimos, as well as several museums and palaces.

Orientation and Practical Information   465

A detailed map is an absolute necessity in this town. The twisty streets change names about every three steps. The **Falk city map** (sold in Estação Rossio, 500$) is street-indexed. If you plan to stay for any length of time, consider investing in a *bilhete de assinatura turístico* (tourist pass), good for unlimited travel on CARRIS buses, trolleys, funiculars, and the subway (1700$ for 7 days, 1200$ for 4 days). The passes are sold in CARRIS booths (open 8am-8pm), located in most network train stations and the busier metro stations (e.g., Restauradores).

Tourist Office: Palácio da Foz, Pr. Restauradores (tel. 346 33 14, 342 52 31). Metro: Restauradores. English and French spoken. Bus schedules and *pensão* lists. Open Mon.-Sat. 9am-8pm, Sun. 10am-6pm. Busy branch offices at Estação Santa Apolónia (open Mon.-Sat. 9am-7pm) and the airport (open 24 hrs). **National Tourist Office Headquarters,** Av. António Augusto de Aguiar, 86 (tel. 57 50 86). Same services as Restauradores office. Open Mon.-Fri. 9:30am-12:30pm, 2:30-5pm.

Budget Travel: Tagus (Youth Branch), Pr. Londres, 9B (tel. 89 15 31). Metro: Alameda. Books flights on TAP and British Airways. English spoken. **Tagus (Main Office),** R. Camilo Castelo Branco, 20 (tel. 352 55 09). Both offices open Mon.-Fri. 9am-6pm, Sat. 9am-1pm.

Embassies: U.S., Av. Forças Armadas (tel. 726 66 00). **Canada,** R. Rosa Araújo, 2, 6th floor (tel. 56 38 21). **U.K.,** R. São Domingos à Lapa, 37 (tel. 66 11 22). Also handles New Zealand affairs. **Australia,** Av. Liberdade, 244, 4th floor (tel. 52 33 50).

Currency Exchange: Estação Santa Apolónia, on the platform. Enormous lines here and at the airport branch. Both open 24 hrs. The main post office, most banks, and travel agencies also change money (often for a 750$ fee and 68$ tax). Banks open Mon.-Fri. 8:30-11:45am and 1-2:45pm.

American Express: Star Travel Service, Pr. Restauradores, 14 (tel. 346 03 36, 446 03 37). Metro: Restauradores. This branch office of Star Travel handles all AmEx services. Travellers checks sold and cashed; mail held. English spoken. Main office on Av. Duque de Loulé, 47 (tel. 356 30 23). Metro: Rotunda. Both offices open Mon.-Fri. 9am-12:30pm and 2-6pm.

Post Office: Correio, Pr. Comércio (tel. 346 32 31). Open for Posta Restante Mon.-Fri. 9am-7pm. Branch office at Pr. Restauradores open for **telegrams,** international express service, stamps, and telephones 8am-10pm. **Postal Code:** 1100 for central Lisboa.

Telephones: Central exchange at Pr. Dom Pedro IV, 68. Metro: Rossio. On the corner to the right of the National Theater as you face away from the theater. Staff explains the arcane telephone system in Portuguese only. For **telegrams,** dial 183. Open 8am-11:30pm. Credifone cards come in 50 units (750$) or 120 units (1725$). Local calls consume at least 1 unit. Do not confuse this card with the TLP card, which is valid in Lisboa and Porto only. One phone (marked with stickers) also accepts MC, Visa, and Eurocard. **Telephone Code:** 01.

Airport: Aeroporto de Lisboa (tel. 80 20 60), on the northern outskirts of the city. Local buses #44 or 45 stop to the right and then upstairs as you exit the airport (20min. from downtown). The express bus *(linha verde)* is expensive at 275$ but faster; it stops directly in front of the exit. All 3 lines head for the Baixa. Taxis are cheaper for more than 2 people (about 750$ to the Baixa). Major airlines have offices at Pr. Marquês de Pombal and along Av. Liberdade. **TAP Air Portugal** (airport tel. 88 91 81; information 80 41 21). To: Faro (8500$); Funchal (16,000$); Porto (7500$); London (APEX round-trip £264); New York (APEX round-trip US$713). **Iberia** (tel. 56 20 16; reservations 53 95 71).

Trains: Information (tel. 87 60 25). Sort of confusing; a bunch of stations. **Santa Apolónia** (on banks of the Tejo near Alfama) for all international, northern, and eastern lines. **Cais do Sodré** for Estoril and Cascais (every 15min., 40min., 145$). **Barreiro** for the Algarve and southern lines. To reach Barreiro, take a ferry across the Tejo (135$, free if coming into Lisboa from the south); ferries leave from Pr. Comércio every 5-10min. **Rossio** (between Pr. Restauradores and Pr. Dom Pedro IV) for Sintra (every 10min., 45min., 145$) and western lines. Detailed schedules and some assistance available at Rossio. French and English spoken. Open 8am-11pm. To: Évora (6 per day, 3hr., 695$); Portalegre (4 per day, 4 1/2 hr., 1200$); Porto (6 per day, 6hr., 1520$); Lagos (5 per day, 6 1/2 hr., 1500$); Faro (6 per day, 7hr., 1450$); Badajoz, Spain (4 per day, 5hr., 2600$); Paris (1 per day, 27hr., 21,000$).

Buses: Rodoviária, Av. Casal Ribeiro, 18 (tel. 57 77 15). To find it, from Pr. Marquês de Pombal take Av. Fontes Pereira de Melo to Pr. Duque de Saldanha and bear right around the roundabout. Metro: Picoas. A 1/2 hr. walk from Pr. Restauradores. To: Évora (6 per day, 2 1/2 hr., 1000$); Coimbra (8 per day, 3hr., 1100$); Portalegre (3 per day, 4hr., 1250$); Lagos (5 per day, 5hr., 1800$); Porto (5 per day, 5hr., 1480$); Faro (5 per day, 5 1/2 hr., 1700-2000); Braga (2 per day, 6hr., 1720$). Private company **Caima,** R. Bacalhoeiros, 19, runs express buses to the Algarve and

Lisbon

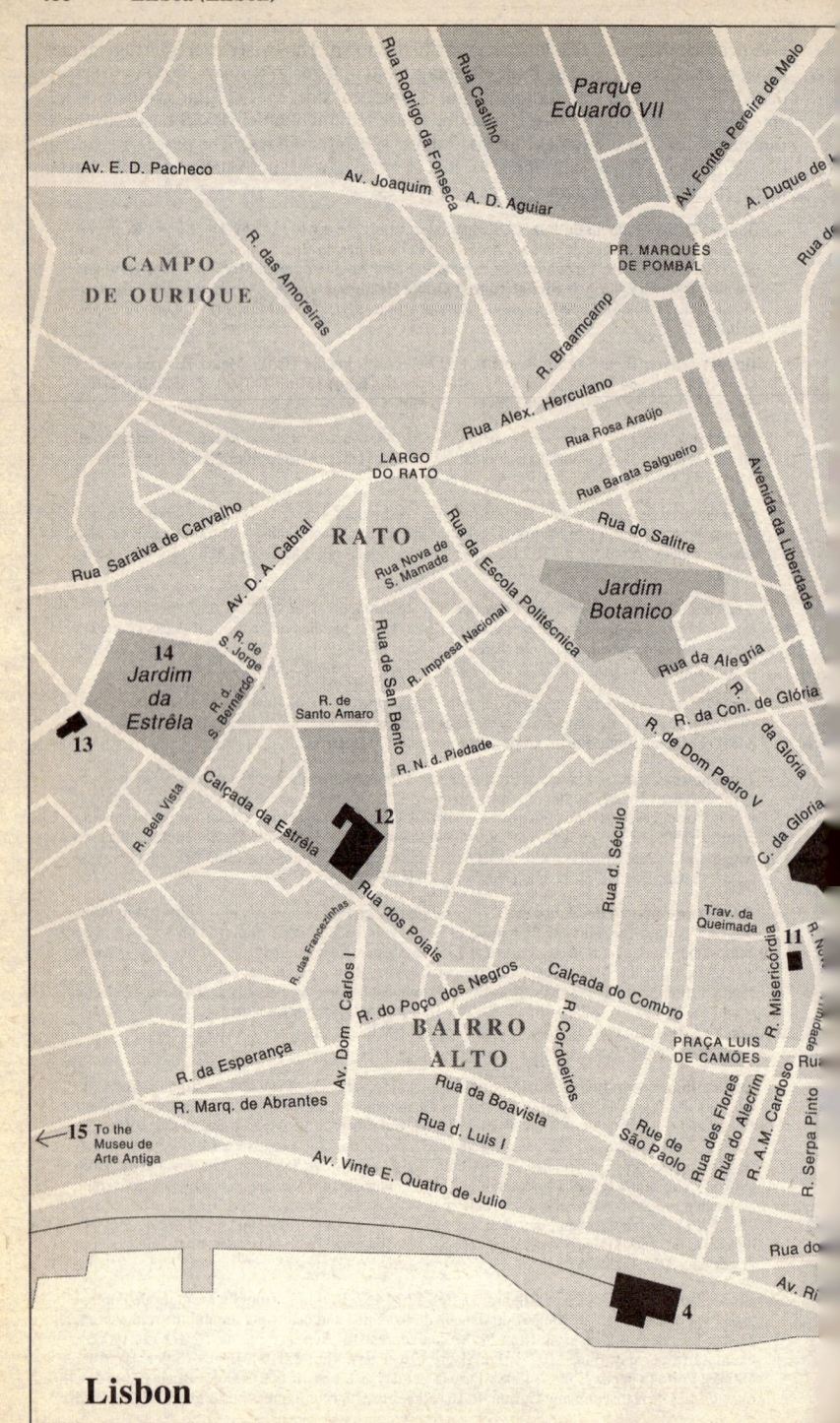

Lisbon

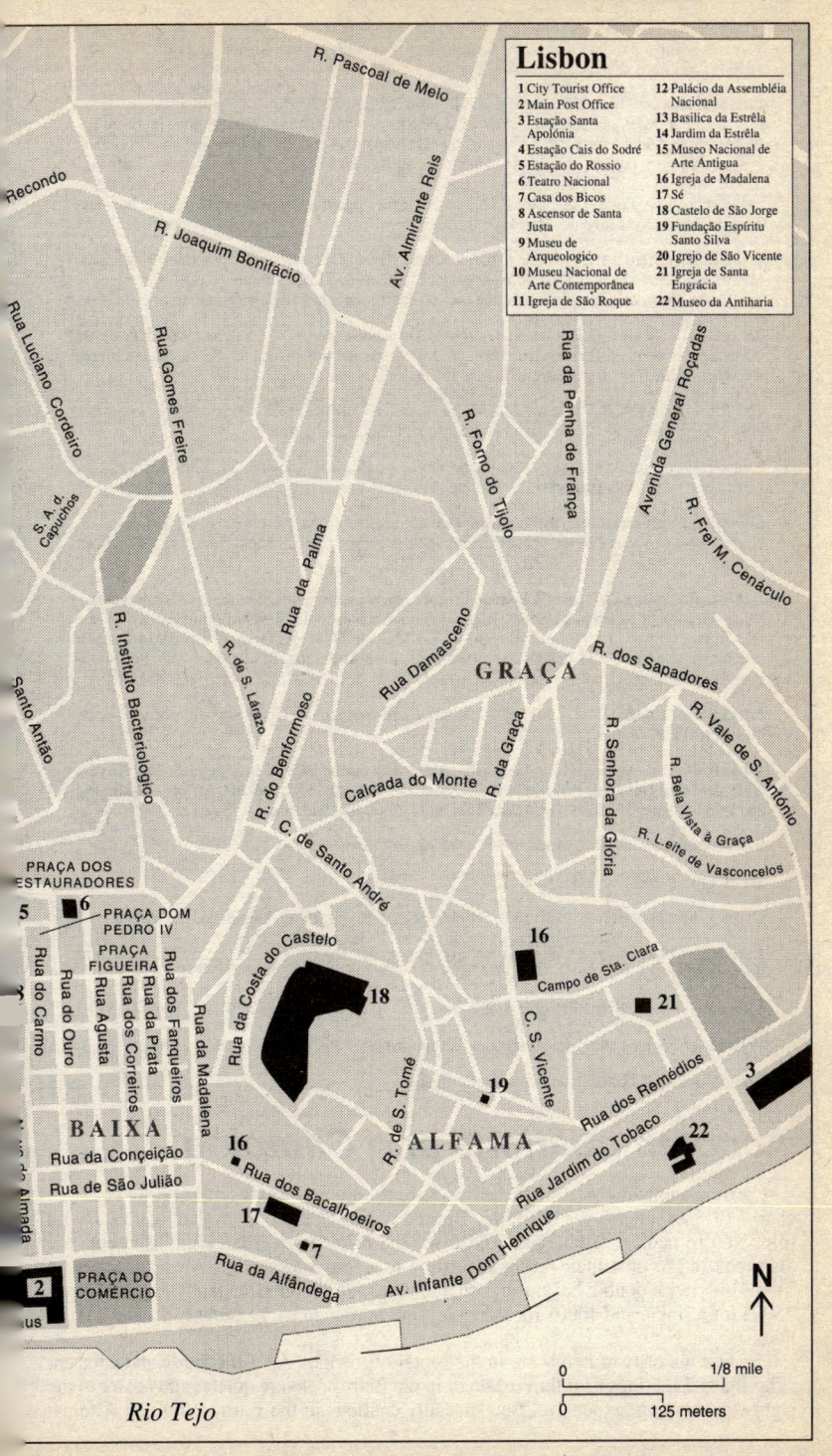

1. City Tourist Office
2. Main Post Office
3. Estação Santa Apolónia
4. Estação Cais do Sodré
5. Estação do Rossio
6. Teatro Nacional
7. Casa dos Bicos
8. Ascensor de Santa Justa
9. Museu de Arqueologico
10. Museu Nacional de Arte Contemporânea
11. Igreja de São Roque
12. Palácio da Assembléia Nacional
13. Basílica da Estrêla
14. Jardim da Estrêla
15. Museo Nacional de Arte Antigua
16. Igreja de Madalena
17. Sé
18. Castelo de São Jorge
19. Fundação Espíritu Santo Silva
20. Igrejo de São Vicente
21. Igreja de Santa Engrácia
22. Museo da Antiharia

Porto (they show movies). This is the fastest way to the Algarve from Lisboa. To Porto (6 per day, 1650$) and Lagos (6 per day, 2000$).

Public Transportation: Buses, Av. Casal Ribeiro, 18 (tel. 57 77 15). 130$ within the city. From Estação Santa Apolónia, take #9, 39, or 46 to Pr. Restauradores; #59 to Estação Rossio. From Estação Cais do Sodré, take #1, 2, 32, 44, or 45 to Pr. Restauradores; #17 to Estação Santa Apolónia. From the airport, take #8, 22, 44, 45, or express bus (green line, 275$) to town center. **Subway:** 55$ at window, 45$ from vending machines. Book of 10 425$ at window, 410$ from machines. "M"=Metro stop. Follows Av. Liberdade, then branches into lines that cover the modern business district. Pickpockets love the Metro.

Trolleys *(eléctricos):* Everywhere. Offer beautiful views of the harbor and older neighborhoods. Many cars seem to be of pre-World War I vintage. #28 is good for sightseeing (stops in Pr. Comércio, 110$). **Funiculars** *(elevadores)* link the lower city with the hilly residential areas (30-78$).

Taxis: Rádio Táxis de Lisboa (tel. 82 50 61), **Autocoope** (tel. 793 27 56), and **Teletáxi** (tel. 82 80 16). 24-hr. service. Taxis swarm along Av. Liberdade and throughout the Baixa, but are scarce elsewhere. Fare 550$ from Estação Rossio to central bus station.

Car Rental: AABA, R. Padre António Vieira, 44 (tel. 65 38 40). 3900$ per day, 39$ per kilometer plus 17% tax. Must be 23 and have had license 1 yr. Hair-raising traffic.

Luggage Storage: At **Estaçãos Rossio** and **Santa Apolónia**. Lockers 390$, 500$, and 850$ for up to 48hr. At the **bus station**, 130$ per bag per day.

Shopping Center: Amoreiras Shopping Center de Lisboa, Av. Duarte Pacheco. 330 shops including a humongous Pão de Açucar supermarket, a couple English bookstores, and a 10-screen cinema.

English Bookstore: Livraria Clássica Editora, Pr. Restauradores, 17. Metro: Restauradores. Wide selection of paperback classics, best-sellers, and travel books, mostly Portuguese with some French and English. **Livraria Británica,** R. São Marçal, 83, across from the British Institute in the Bairro Alto (tel. 32 84 72). Open 9:30am-7pm; June-Aug. Mon.-Fri. 9:30am-7pm. See Shopping Center above.

Library: Av. Duque Loulé, 22-B (tel. 57 01 02). English-language. Open Aug.-June Mon. 2-8pm, Tues.-Fri. 12:30-6pm.

Laundromat: R. Augusto Rosa, 11. Wash in shiny new machines 500$ per 5kg load. Large dryers 300$ per load. **Lavatax,** R. Francisco Sanches, 65A (tel. 82 33 92). Metro: Arroios. Wash, dry, and fold 800$ per 5kg load. Open 9am-1pm and 3-7pm, Sat. 9am-noon.

Public Toilets: In the Rossio and other major squares. Some subway stations.

Weather and Sea Conditions: tel. 150.

Crisis Lines: Poison (tel. 79 50 143). **Suicide** (tel. 54 45 45). **Drug Abuse** (tel. 726 77 66).

Late-Night Pharmacy: Throughout the city. Emergency service only. Police will direct you to the nearest one.

Medical Services: British Hospital, R. Saraiva de Carvalho, 49 (tel. 60 20 20; at night 60 37 85).

Police: R. Capelo, 3 (tel. 346 61 41). English spoken.

Emergency: call 115 from anywhere in Portugal.

Accommodations and Camping

A government-imposed price ceiling supposedly restricts what hotel owners can charge for particular types of rooms. But the ceiling is more myth than reality. If you think you're being overcharged, ask to see the printed price list. Establishments are also required to post their rating according to a four-star system. Most places have rooms only with double beds; some charge more for double occupancy. Expect to pay 2500$ for a single and 4000$ for a double, and more in fancier *residenciais* and smaller hotels.

The vast majority of hotels are in the center of town on **Av. Liberdade** and adjacent side streets. Lodgings near the *castelo* or in the Bairro Alto are quieter and nearer to the sights, hence more expensive. Be especially cautious in the Bairro Alto, the Alfama, and the Baixa after dark. Many streets are isolated and most are poorly lit. If the central accommodations are full, head east to the *pensões* along **Av. Almirante Reis.**

Beach aficionados with tents or lots of cash may want to use **Estoril** or **Cascais** as a base. These affluent suburbs are about 20km away from Lisboa and mercifully free of the capital's noise and smog. Food and lodging prices here are up to 50% higher than those in the city.

> **Pousada da Juventude de Catalazete (HI),** Estrada Marginal (tel. 443 06 38), in the coastal town of **Oeiras.** Take a train from Estação Cais do Sodré to Oeiras (20min., 95$), exit the station through the underpass, and turn right under the sign "Praia" (beach). Head left to the first of several signs pointing the way. Follow the street as it curves downhill to the highway along the beach, turn left at the underpass, and walk through the INATEL tourist compound; the hostel is at the far end of the enclosed area. Rooms are a bit cramped. Moonlight views of the ocean from the patio rival those from The Love Boat's Aloha deck. Reception open 9:30-10:30am and 6-10:30pm. Curfew midnight. June-Sept., Holy Week, and Christmas 1250$; Oct.-May 1000$. Breakfast included. Lunch or dinner 700$. Reservations advisable; make them through Lisboa's HI office, R. Andrade Corvo, 46 (tel. 57 10 54).

Baixa

Dozens of *pensões* surround the three connected plazas—**Pr. Restauradores, Pr. Dom Pedro IV,** and **Pr. Figueira**—that form the nexus of Lisboa's downtown. Many pre-war buildings with decrepit exteriors have been renovated within. Most have fewer than 20 rooms. Quality varies greatly. For a good night's sleep, bring soundproofing.

> **Residência Mucaba,** Av. Liberdade, 53, 2nd fl. (tel. 346 56 47), convenient to Pr. Restauradores. Warehouse-like surroundings, but modern interior. Gleaming baths. Singles with shower 4000$, with bath 5500$. Doubles with shower 4200$, with bath 6000$. Oct.-May 25% discount.
>
> **Pensão Arco Banderia,** R. Arco Bandeira, 226, 4th fl. (tel. 342 34 78), south of Pr. Dom Pedro IV, under the arch (Archo Bandeira) on the left. Strangely quiet for the central location. Singles 2300$. Doubles 3500-3900$.
>
> **Pensão Prata,** R. Prata, 71, 3rd fl. (tel. 346 89 08), 2 bl. from Pr. Comércio. A yellow awning hides the sign. Sun-kissed rooms in a peaceful apartment setting. Some use of kitchens permitted. Singles 2800$, with shower 3300$, with bath 3800$. Doubles 3000$, with shower 3500$, with bath 3800$. Triples with bath 4500$. Winter 25% discount.
>
> **Pensão Campos,** R. Jardim do Regedor, 24, 3rd fl. (tel. 346 28 64), on the busy pedestrian street between Pr. Restauradores and R. Portas de Santa Antão. Cozy, well-furnished rooms and spic and span bath. Singles 2500$. Doubles 3000$, with bath 4000$.
>
> **Pensão Beira Minho,** Pr. Figueira, 6, 2nd fl. (tel. 346 90 29), beside the Rossio at the northern end of the *praça* through a flower shop. Nicely renovated rooms. Small, windowless singles are well-lit and magically cheerful. Singles 2000$, with bath 3950$. Doubles 2600$, with bath 4600$. Breakfast included.
>
> **Residencial Florescente,** R. Portas de Santo Antão, 99 (tel. 342 66 09), 1 bl. from Pr. Restauradores. 120 rooms. Rooms with windows are cleaner and better furnished. Lively social scene. Singles and doubles 4000$, with shower 5000$, with bath 6000$, with bath and A/C 7500$.
>
> **Pensão Residencial Estrela do Mondego,** Calçada do Carmo, 25, 2nd fl. (tel. 346 71 09), 1 bl. from Estação Rossio. Be wary of stairs. Neat, carpeted rooms with big windows. Five-person room a bargain if you can recruit enough bedmates. Singles 2000$. Doubles 3500$, with bath 4000$.
>
> **Pensão Pemba,** Av. Liberdade, 11 (tel. 342 50 10). Dank staircase, decent rooms. Singles 2000$. Doubles 3000$. Triples 4000$.

In and around the Bairro Alto

The Bairro Alto is quieter than the Baixa and has a sense of community lacking in the town center, but it's inconvenient to transportation. Fools with heavy luggage may want to forgo the hike uphill or the inconvenience of waiting for *elevadores*. Don't wander off alone here at night—this area has a reputation for muggings.

Pensão Estrela de Chiado, R. Garrett, 29, 4th fl. (tel. 342 61 10). The climb upstairs is hell but worth it. Clean rooms with hot water. Rooms with veranda have views of *castelo*. Singles 1500$. Doubles 3000$, with bath 4000$.

Pensão Globo, R. Teixeira, 37 (tel. 346 22 79), on a small street parallel to R. S.P. Alcântara at the top of the funicular. Immaculate, beguiling singles 3500$, with shower 4000$.

Pensão Londres, R. Dom Pedro V, 53 (tel. 346 55 23). Take the funicular by Palácio da Foz in Pr. Restauradores. Facing away from the funicular, walk right (west) up to R. Dom Pedro V. Ideal for sedentary types and gluttons; right near the parks and the city's best inexpensive restaurants. Rooms of varying size on 4 floors. Singles 3000$, with bath 4000$. Doubles 4500$, with bath 5500$. Breakfast included.

Hotel Suisso Atlântico, R. Gloria, 3 (tel. 346 17 13), 1 bl. from Pr. Restauradores. A worthwhile extravagance. Modern rooms and currency exchange for guests. All rooms with bath. Singles 6700$. Doubles 8700$. Breakfast included.

Near the Castelo (Mouraria)

This neighborhood has narrow streets, flowered balconies, and amazing views. The hilly streets will torture those who don't travel light. The *pensões* aren't as bad as they look from the grimy streets they're on. Beware of this area at night.

Pensão Ninho das Águias, R. Costa do Castelo, 74 (tel. 886 70 00), near Escada do Marquês da Ponte de Lima. A long, winding stairway mounts to the patio with aviary, flowering garden, and stupendous views of Lisboa. Rooms are in high demand—make reservations weeks in advance. All rooms are doubles and have phones. Doubles 4500$, with shower 5500$, with bath 5700$.

Pensão Residencial Brasil Africano, Trav. Pedras Negras, 8, 2nd fl. (tel. 886 92 66), off R. Madalena. Conveniently located near the cathedral and the Baixa. Don't judge the hotel by the outside; it's been renovated. Spacious, comfortable rooms with balconies. Singles 1500$. Doubles 2700$, with bath 3780$.

Camping

Staple all your valuables to your person.

Parque da Câmara Municipal de Lisboa-Monsanto (tel. 70 20 61, fax 70 20 62), on the road to Benfica. Lisboa's municipal campground has a swimming pool and a reasonably priced supermarket. Take bus #43 from the Rossio to the Parque Florestal Monsanto. 300$ per person, 250$ per tent, 200$ per car.

Clube de Campismo de Lisboa Costa da Caparica (tel. 290 01 00), 5km out of Lisboa (take the bus from Pr. Espanha; Metro: Palhavã, 15min.). Beaches. Shade. Pool. Fun. 600$ per person, per tent, and per car.

Food

Lisboa has some of the least expensive restaurants of any European capital. Two can often feed for the price of one, and Portugal's burgeoning wine industry broadens the selection each year. A full dinner costs about 1500$ per person. The *prato do dia* (special of the day) and *ementa turística* (tourist menu) are usually reasonable deals.

Restaurants in the **Baixa** are more elegant and more expensive than those in other districts, catering largely to tourists. The **Bairro Alto** feeds many locals. Restaurants there, as in the **Alfama,** are correspondingly small, dark, and (relatively) cheap. Batten on seafood specialties such as *bacalhau cozido com grão* (cod with chickpeas and boiled potatoes), a local classic. Other culinary delights are *amêijoas à bulhão pato,* a steamed clam dish, or *creme de mariscos,* seafood chowder with tomatoes.

If you want to buy food, take bus #40 to **Mercado Ribeira,** a market complex on Av. 24 de Julho outside the Cais do Sodré (open Mon.-Sat. until 2pm). There's a larger market in Cascais on Wednesday morning (5min. from the train station). Go early for the freshest crisps. For groceries, try the jumbo **supermarket Pão de Açucar,** in Amoreiras Shopping Center de Lisboa, Av. Duarte Pacheco.

Baixa

The nearer the water, the cheaper the restaurants. The southern end of town near the port and the area bordering the **Alfama** are particularly inexpensive. Some bargain places line **Rua dos Correiros,** parallel to R. Prata, and neighboring streets. One block from Pr. Restauradores, on **Rua das Portas de Santo Antão,** many superb (and expensive) seafood restaurants stack the day's catch in their windows. Many of the Baixa's restaurants are not open on Sunday and close around 9pm or 10pm on weekdays.

> **Groceries: Supermercado Expresso,** R. Jardim do Regidor, a block around the corner from R. das Portas de Santo Antão. The quality of the groceries doesn't quite match the glitter of the storefront coffee-counter and outdoor café, but it's central and offers more than the ordinary pastry shops in the city. Open 9am-11pm.
>
> **Adega Popular 33,** R. Conceiçao, 33 (tel. 32 84 72), 2 bl. from Pr. Comércio. Green awning. Small and popular. The least expensive food on the block. Delicious *lulas grelhadas* (grilled squid) 700$. Entrees 550-850$. 1/2-portions available. Open Mon.-Fri. 8am-9:30pm.
>
> **Restaurante Bonjardim,** Trav. de Santo Antão, 12 (tel. 342 74 24), a side street off Pr. Restauradores. Supremely delicious roast chickens (980$). No 1/2-fowls. Nibbly good appetizer is *chouriço asado na brasa* (roast sausage, 290$). Open 11am-3pm and 6:30-10:30pm.
>
> **Adega do Atum,** R. Bacalhoeiros, 8D, off R. Madalena, 1 bl. north and parallel with R. Alfandega. A local hangout in a sun-splashed square not far from the port. Fish barely dead. Try their *chocos assados con tinta* (roast squid in their own ink). Entrees 500-850$. Open Mon.-Sat. 7am-midnight.
>
> **Porto de Abrigo,** R. Remolares, 16-18 (tel. 346 08 73), near Estação Cais do Sodré. One of the most popular riverside eateries. *Pato com arroz* (duck with rice and olives) 1480$. Other entrees 980-1580$. Open Mon.-Sat. noon-3pm and 7-10pm.
>
> **Restaurante Chekiang,** Estação Rossio, Store #108 (tel. 32 69 57). Turn left just before the escalator and go down the next down stairway. Hidden. Radical Chinese cuisine in a sleepy atmosphere. Chicken with mushrooms 850$. Sweet-and-sour fish 800$. Opulent glazed fruit desserts 280-440$. Open 11:30am-3pm and 7-10:30pm.
>
> **O Baleal,** R. Madalena, 277 (tel. 87 21 87), 1 bl. toward the Mouraria from Pr. Figueira. Enter through a passage flanked with tanks of lobsters. Exceptionally clean, bright, and cheery. Fresh fish. Entrees 680-1650$. Open Tues.-Sun. 8am-10pm, Sat. 8am-4pm.
>
> **Lua de Mel,** R. Prata, 242-248 (tel. 87 91 51), on the corner with R. Santa Justa. A snack bar and A/C! Quite possibly the freshest, most scrumptious pastries in the city (85$). Sweet as honey. Sandwiches 170-340$. Fruit salads and ice cream sundaes 450$. Open Tues.-Sun. 7am-midnight.

Bairro Alto

Although the Bairro has its share of places to throw a glamourous *soirée,* it also has far more small and medium-sized restaurants than the Baixa. The district's hilly, narrow streets are quieter and less congested. Many inexpensive local haunts line **Calçada do Combro,** the neighborhood's main westward artery. Climb up **R. Misericórdia** to the adjacent side-streets for places that are dimmer, mustier, and cheaper.

> **Casa da India,** R. do Loreto, 49-51, off Pr. Camões. Local crowd files in for the no-frills food. Chew on a chunk of *orelha polvo* (octopus ear) and pop in a few *caracois* (snails). The old stalwart *bitoque* (steak and egg, 600$). Entrees 620-1500$. Open Mon.-Sat. 9am-10:30pm.
>
> **Lua Nova,** Trav. Queimada, 4 (tel. 346 57 92), off R. Misericórdia, a couple blocks down from Calçada da Gloria. Bring a mini flashlight so you can read the menu. Great for a cheap dinner before hitting the nearby *fado* houses. Entrees 750-950$. Open July 16-June 30 Mon.-Sat. 10am-10pm.
>
> **Bota Alta,** Trav. Queimada, 37 (tel. 342 79 59), on the far side of R. Misericórdia. Hold out as you walk past the wafting aromas of its rivals. Worthwhile if expensive. *Sopa Alentejana* (garlic soup) 240$. Entrees 1080-2150$. Open Mon.-Fri. noon-2:30pm and 7-10:30pm.
>
> **Xêlê Bananas,** Pr. Flores, 29. Walk down R. S. Marçal from R. Escola Politécnica to one of Lisboa's quaintest squares. Popular with the truly choosy. Entrees 1000-1500$. Open Mon.-Fri. 12:30-3:30pm and 7:30-11pm, Sat.-Sun. 7:30-11pm.

A Pérola do Bonjardim, R. Cruz dos Poiais, 95A (tel. 60 84 80), off R. Poiais, a continuation of Calçada do Combro. Stucco and tile family-ish restaurant in a darling neighborhood. Delectable entrees (600-1000$) and *pratos do dia* (650-700$). Open Mon.-Sat. 7am-midnight.

Casa de Pasto de Francisco Cardoso, R. Século, 244 (tel. 32 75 78), off R. Dom Pedro V. Genuine neighborhood hangout. Walls inscribed with proverbs. Omelettes 650$. Sangria 500$. Mouthwatering pastries 180$. Open 8am-midnight.

Alfama

The winding streets of the Alfama conceal a number of extremely small, unpretentious restaurants. Lively discussions and chatter echo through the damp, narrow alleys. Theft plagues the Alfama, so come here by day without handbags, cameras, or snatchable diamond earrings.

Mestre André, Calçadinha de Sto. Estevão, 6 (tel. 87 14 87), off R. Remédios. Eclectic yet tasteful adornment of old movie posters and stills. Their *murcela frita*, an ugly but savory little blood sausage (395$), and *truta grelhada* (grilled trout, 775$) are favorites among regulars. Brazilian background music. Outdoor seating and grill on a stone terrace above the street. Open Mon.-Sat. noon-3pm and 7-10:30pm.

Dragão da Alfama, R. Guilherme Braga, 8 (tel. 86 77 37), near Igreja São Estevão. Monstrous platters of classic fish entrees (700-1400$). *Peixe espada grelhada* (grilled swordfish) 950$. Around 10pm, a woman with a voice like a woolly mammoth belts out some tear-welling *fado*. Open Mon.-Fri. noon-4pm and 7pm-midnight, Sat. noon-4pm.

Os Minhotos, R. Remédios, 31 (tel. 87 55 80), next to Mestre André. Less sophisticated than its neighbor. Simple good dullard food cooked on an outdoor grill. Fresh *lulas* (squid) or *bacalhau cozido* (boiled cod, 650$). Other entrees (550-900$) are a steal. Open Mon.-Sat. 11am-4pm and 7pm-midnight.

Sights

Old Center

Lisboa's 18th-century heart shows the city's modern and sophisticated, side. The center of bustle is the **Rossio,** or **Praça Dom Pedro IV,** the city's main square. Cattle market turned public execution stage turned bullfight arena turned carnival ground, the plaza is now the domain of drink-sipping tourists looking for some action. Three sides of the *praça* are lined with limestone and tile buildings built by the Marquês do Pombal's edict after the 1755 earthquake. On the fourth side, the **Teatro Nacional** marks the former site of the Palace of the Inquisition. A statue of Gil Vicente, Portugal's first dramatist, straddles the building. **Dom Pedro IV** maintains a surprisingly stoic countenance considering his position atop a tall Corinthian column in the center of the *praça*. According to popular belief, the statue is actually a likeness of the Emperor Maximilian of Mexico, purchased for a rock-bottom price after the Mexican soldiers executed the Austrian-born archduke.

After the earthquake Pombal created the **Baixa,** the grid of streets south of the Rossio, to facilitate communication between the town center and the river. The grid of perpendicular streets, each one designated for a specific trade, was the very height of Enlightenment urban design. Two centuries later, pedestrians toss litter on the wide mosaic sidewalks and cars drag race down the Marquês' stately streets. **Rua Augusta,** now restricted to pedestrians, is lined with shops selling furs, shoes, and perfume and leads past a triumphal arch to **Praça do Comércio.** According to a Lisboa saying, "God gave the Portuguese the Tagus, and in gratitude they made the Terreiro do Paço." Now known by its popular name, Pr. Comércio, this street lies prostrate before the towering statue of Dom José I, cast in 1755 from 9400 pounds of bronze. The center of the *praça* has since been converted to a sports pavillion, so the mighty equestrian figure currently oversees bleachers and a parking lot.

From the northwest corner of Pr. Comércio, R. Alfândega leads to the late Gothic **Igreja da Conceição Velha.** Its effusively Manueline portal represents Mary protecting miscellaneous clerics and royals with her mantle. The church's interior has a handsome vaulted chancel and a statue (in the second chapel on the right) of Nossa Senhora de Rastelo. The figure came from a small church in Belém where great Portuguese navigators all spent their last terrified night in prayer before shipping out.

The **Casa dos Bicos** (House of Beaks), the area's prominent 16th-century landmark, is devoted to temporary exhibits of the most durable bird part. (Open Mon.-Sat. 10am-noon and 2:30-6:30pm. Admission varies with the exhibit.)

North of the Rossio, **Praça dos Restauradores** commemorates the 1640 "restoration" of Portugal's independence from Spain with an obelisk and a bronze sculpture of the Spirit of Independence. Here begins **Avenida da Liberdade,** the city's most imposing boulevard. Its malls of flowering shrubs, palm trees, swan ponds, and fountains were at one time the city's favorite promenade. Although this mile-long avenue has seen better days, it's still delightful. The avenue ends at **Praça do Marquês do Pombal** in the center of a bustling commercial district.

Chiado and Bairro Alto

Boxed in a fanciful Gothic tower by Eiffel, the beloved **Acensor de Santa Justa** connects the Baixa to the Chiado. (Every 5min., 1/2 min., 35$.) From the upper terrace, a narrow walkway leads under a huge flying buttress to the 14th-century **Igreja do Carmo,** largely destroyed in the 1755 earthquake. Although roofless, it retains its dramatic Gothic arches. A ramshackle **Museu Arqueológico** here includes Dom Fernando I's tomb, black from a treatment inflicted for photographic purposes. (Open Tues.-Sun. 10am-6pm. Admission 300$.)

One block south, wealthy R. Garrett has an embarrassment of riches. The Art Nouveau coffee houses give it a vaguely Prague-ish flavor. Portuguese writer Eça de Queiroz used to get wired at **A Brasileira** at #120-122, perhaps the most famous of the city's 19th-century coffeehouses. Two blocks south (left) on R. Serpa Pinto, the **Museu Nacional de Arte Contemporânea** invites visitors to moon at the 19th-century Portuguese paintings and sculpture. (Open Tues.-Fri. 10am-12:30pm and 2-5pm. Admission 300$, students free.)

Back to R. Garrett, past a square (Pr. Camões) guarded by two churches, and right on R. da Misericórdia is **Igreja de São Roque.** Roque's intervention saved the Bairro Alto from the devastation of the great quake. Inside the church, the bewildering *trompe l'oeil* ceiling isn't really a series of domes—it's just a flat wooden roof!! Rumored to be the costliest ever, the notorious **Capela de São João Baptista** (fourth from the left), ablaze with precious gems and metals, caused a stir upon its installation in 1747. Three different ships delivered the chapel to Lisboa after it was built in Rome from agate, lapis lazuli, alabaster, *verde antica,* and mosaics. Adjoining the church, the small **Museu de São Roque** has its own share of gold and silver. (Open Tues.-Sun. 10am-noon and 2-5pm. Admission 50$, students and seniors free.)

At the end of the Travessa do Convento de Jesus (off Calçada do Combro), flowered balconies and hanging laundry frame **Igreja das Mercês,** a handsome 18th-century travertine building. Its small *praça* overlooks the neoclassical **Palácio da Assembléia Nacional** (House of Parliament).

Past the Parliament on Calçada da Estrela, **Basilica da Estrela** (1796) steals the sky with an exquisitely shaped dome poised behind a pair of tall belfries. Half-mad Maria I lived in mortal fear that she would die without giving birth to a male heir. "If only I could squeeze out just one baby boy," Mary said to anyone who would listen. She made fervent religious vows promising God anything and everything. When her son was born she actually came through, with this church. The narrow proportions of its richly decorated nave make the light all the more spectacular. Ask the sacristan to show you the gigantic 10th-century *presépio* (manger scene). (Open 7:30am-1pm and 3-8pm. Free.)

Across from the church, **Jardim da Estrêla's** wide asphalt walkways wind through lush flora and flocks of pigeons. The park is popular for Sunday strolls and nastyish P.D.A. on the benches. Behind the park tropical plants, cypress trees, and odd gravestones mark the **Cemitério dos Ingleses** (English Cemetery; ring bell for entry). Its musty Victorian chapel dates from 1885. The cemetery's most famous decaying flesh belongs to the novelist Henry Fielding, who came to Lisboa in 1714 on a rather unsuccessful convalescence trip.

It's a half-hour walk down Av. Infante Santo and a 10-minute jaunt to the left of Calçada da Pampulha to find Portugal's national museum, the **Museu Nacional de Arte Antiga** on R. Janelas Verdes. A representative collection of European paintings ranges from Gothic primitives to 18th-century French masterpieces. The most prized possession is the six-panel *Adoration of St. Vincent* by Nuno Gonçalves, one of Portugal's greatest painters. Other notable works are the ghoulish 16th-century *O Inferno* and the few choice Breughels in Room VIII. (Open Tues.-Sat. 10am-1pm and 2-5pm. Admission 300$, free for students.) Buses #40 and 60 stop to the right as you leave the museum and head back to the Baixa.

Alfama and Mouraria

The **Alfama,** Lisboa's oldest quarter, covers the hill in tiers beneath Castelo de São Jorge on the southern slope facing the Rio Tejo. Between the Alfama and the Baixa is the quarter known as the **Mouraria** (Moorish ghetto), established after Dom Afonso Henriques and the Crusaders expelled the Moors in 1147. A few words of warning: don't even think about walking through the Alfama without getting lost; wandering aimlessly among the winding medieval streets is a delightful way to spend the rest of your life. Also remember that this area is dangerous at night; stash your money somewhere deep in your underclothes.

The best way to enter this part of the city is from the street alongside the 16th-century **Igreja de Madalena** at the eastern end of the Baixa's R. Conceição. Behind the Madalena rises the delicately proportioned **Igreja de Santo António da Sé** (1812), built over the saint's supposed birthplace. The construction was funded with money collected by the city's children, who fashioned freaky miniature altars bearing images of the saint to place on their doorsteps—a custom still re-enacted annually on June 13, the saint's feast day. Near the entrance is a **museum** devoted to the saint's life and miracles. (Open Mon.-Sat. 8am-6pm. Mass in Latin with Gregorian chants Fri. noon.)

Directly beyond the little church looms the stolid 12th-century **sé,** one of the few buildings that made it out of the earthquake alive. Gothic chapels, pierced by lancet windows, surround the Baroque choir and shelter medieval royal tombs.

The restored **Castelo de São Jorge** looks down at Lisboa from its hill a few blocks up from the cathedral. Built in the 5th century by the Visigoths and enlarged by the 9th-century Moors, this castle was the principal lap of luxury for the royal family from the 14th to the 16th centuries. High up on its windswept esplanade shaded by olive trees, the castle gardens are home to odd-looking albino peafowl. (Open April-Sept. 9am-9pm; Oct.-March 9am-7pm. Free.)

From here it's a short walk to Lisboa's famous medieval quarter, the **Alfama,** former home to the Moorish aristocracy. Unfortunately the earthquake crushed most of the area's noble architecture. Just the outline of its pre-urban planning tangle is visible in the labyrinth of balconies, archways, terraces, and courtyards. Since the *Reconquista*, when this neighborhood became the noisy residence of fishers and sailors, only the fervent voice of the *fado* recalls this district's past.

To reach Largo do Salvador from Largo das Portas do Sol, take the ramp or stairway down to Beco de Santa Helena and turn left on R. Castelo Picão. From here, R. Regueira descends to a small *praça*. The square adjoins **Beco do Carneiro** (Sheep Alley), which is so narrow that the eaves of the buildings on either side touch one another, and **Beco do Mexias,** where a doorway leads to a fountain in which the local women do their washing. Rua da Regueira ends at R. Remédios. Turn right past an open square to **Rua de São Pedro,** the Alfama's main fish market street. A small opening (to the right, midway down the street) leads to **Igreja de São Miguel,** with a Rococo gilt altar screen and a ceiling crafted of Brazilian jacaranda wood. (Ask the sacristan to turn on the lights.) Rua de São Pedro ends at Largo de São Rafael, enclosed on one side by the remains of an old Moorish tower. To return to Largo das Portas do Sol, climb R. da Adiça.

The **Fundação Espírito Santo Silva,** a decorative arts museum, borders the Largo Portas do Sol. The collection is kept in a palace that survived the earthquake to become a veterinary hospital and later home to 17 successive families. It's a kooky place—each irregularly shaped room is littered with furniture and decorations from the heyday of the aristocracy. Portuguese artisans carved most of the 18th-century tables and chairs from Brazilian jacaranda wood. The tapestries are especially beautiful; a 16th-century Flemish work represents Vasco da Gama romping about India. (Open Tues.-Sat. 10am-1pm and 2:30-5pm, Sun. 1-5pm. Admission and multilingual tours free, but tip the guide.)

Left from the museum down the Travessa de São Tomé (along the trolley tracks) is the **Igreja de São Vicente de Fora** (1582-1627), dedicated to Lisboa's patron saint. The church's two-towered Renaissance façade (the dome collapsed during the earthquake) conceals a gracefully proportioned nave that sets off a Baroque high altar and organ. Beyond the cloister broods the **Panteão de Bragança,** filled with the remains of the later kings and queens of Portugal. Ask to see the deathly still *sacristia,* with fabulous 18th-century walls inlaid with Sintra marble—perhaps the only part of the complex worth the admission. (Open 9am-1pm and 3-7pm. Admission 200$.)

Igreja de Santa Engrácia, a tad to the east, took so long to build (1682-1966) that it gave rise to the famous expression, "endless like the building of Santa Engrácia." Designated the Portuguese National Pantheon, the church commemorates the "low-born" heroes of the country alongside the royal Panteão de Bragança. (Open Tues.-Sun. 10am-5pm. Admission 200$.)

Take a #13 bus from Estação Santa Apolónia for the 10-minute ride to **Convento da Madre de Deus.** Founded at the beginning of the 16th century and heavily restored after the earthquake, the convent complex houses an excellent tile museum, the **Museu Nacional do Azulejo.** The Baroque interior of the church, reached through a fine Manueline doorway, is a riot of oil paintings, *azulejos,* and gilded wood. The rapturous excess continues in the *coro alto* (chapter house) and the **Capela de Santo António,** where bright *azulejos* and paintings make the place eye-buggingly busy. (Complex open 10am-5pm. Admission 300$, Sun. 10am-2pm and students free.)

Belém

Rising from the banks of the Tejo behind a sculpted garden worthy of a king, **Mosteiro dos Jerónimos** stands as Portugal's most refined celebration of the Age of Discovery. Begun by Manuel I in 1502 to give thanks for the success of Vasco da Gama's voyage to India, this exhibit remembers the exuberant age when Portuguese navigators mapped the word. The monastery showcases Portugal's own Manueline style, combining Gothic forms with early Renaissance details. Sailor symbolism is everywhere: ropes, anchors, coral, and algae.

The south door of the church is a sculptural anachronism—Henry the Navigator mingles with the Twelve Apostles under carved canopies on both sides of the central column. In the vast interior, six octagonal columns spring open like palm trees to support an elaborately creased roof 25m above. The pagoda-style tombs in the chancel and transepts and the various fruit and vegetable encrustations throughout the church typify Manueline exoticism.

The symbolic tombs of Luís de Camões and navigator Vasco da Gama lie in two opposing transepts. Camões, who is considered the Portuguese Shakespeare, chronicled Portugal's discoveries in lyric poetry. The studly poet had so many affairs with ladies of the court that he was forced to flee to North Africa to escape their vengeful husbands. He died a pauper somewhere in Asia. The fact that his body was never recovered is considered something of a national tragedy.

Even flashier than the church's interior are the octagonal cloisters, some of the most overdone in Europe. Vaulted throughout, the two stories are lavishly decorated with fantastic sculpture. The complex is 40 minutes from Pr. Comércio by trolley #16, 15 minutes by train (every 15min., 95$) from Estação Cais do Sodré. (Open Tues.-Sun. 10am-6:30pm; Oct.-May 10am-1pm and 2:30-5pm. Admission 400$, Oct.-May 250$; students and seniors free.) The monastery faces the sword-shaped **Monumento dos**

Descobrimentos, built in 1960 to honor Prince Henry the Navigator. An elevator (225$) ascends to the top.

The petite **Museu da Marinha** exhibits a humdrum collection of nautical maps and replicas. (Open Tues.-Sun. 10am-5pm. Admission 300$, students and seniors 200$.) Across the square, **Planetário C. Gulbenkian** instills visitors with hope that there is life on other planets. (Sat.-Sun. shows at 4 and 5pm in English and French; Wed. at 11am, 3pm, and 4:15pm in Portuguese; admission 300$, under 19 150$, under 11 and seniors free; headphones 200$.)

One door over, the lucky **Museu Nacional de Arqueología e Etnología** has a whole bunch of cave-man skulls and some other less interesting stuff. (Open Tues.-Sun. 10am-5pm. Admission 400$, students free.)

The **Torre de Belém,** built to protect the seaward entrance of the Portuguese capital, rises from the Tejo's north bank. It's a half-hour walk along the railroad tracks from the monastery. The six-cornered turrets, copied from originals in India, and the Venetian balconies and windows demonstrate the crafty eclecticism of Manueline architects. Climb the narrow, winding steps to the top of the tower for a panoramic view. (Open Tues.-Sun. 10am-1pm and 2:30-5pm. Admission 400$, Oct.-May 250$; students and seniors free.)

Before leaving Belém, consider visiting the **Museu Nacional dos Coches,** retirement home of 74 carriages ranging from the gilded Baroque coach that bore the Portuguese ambassador from Rome in 1716 to the simpler carriages of the late 18th century. (Open Tues.-Sun. 10am-1pm and 2:30-5:30pm. Admission 400$; Oct.-May 250$.) The **Palácio Nacional da Ajuda,** a royal palace constructed in 1802, is a short bus ride away in the hills overlooking Belém. Its 54 rooms make a rather disgusting display of decadence considering the neighborhood's impoverishment. (Open Tues.-Sun. 10am-5pm. Admission 85$.) Trolley #18 ("Ajuda") stops behind the palace and will return you to town.

Entertainment

The paper *Sete,* available from kiosks in the Rossio, publishes listings of concerts, movies, plays, exhibits, and bullfights. The **Teatro Nacional de Dona Maria II** (tel. 32 37 46) at Pr. Dom Pedro IV stages performances of classical Portuguese and foreign plays. (Tickets 500-4000$, 50% student discount.) Every night in June and less frequently during the rest of the summer, **folk concerts** and **dance performances** move and shake the Palácio de Congressos de Estoril. The Fondação Gulbenkian also sponsors classical and jazz concerts year-round. Opera reigns at the **Teatro São Carlos,** R. Serpa Pinto (tel. 346 59 14, 1-7pm)—the largest theater in Lisboa—from late September through mid-June.

Fado

Fado is a melancholy wailing expressive of *caudade,* an enigmatic Portuguese emotion that can't be translated. The sensational tales of lost loves and faded glory performed by *fadistas* are Lisboa's trademark, Portugal's blues. Occasionally some inspired or misguided or drunken audience members join in with spontaneous outbursts of their own *fado.* In some establishments nobody feels melodramatic enough until after midnight. On weekends, book in advance by calling the venues or the municipal tourist offices. The Bairro Alto also has many *fado* joints off **R. Misericordia,** particularly on side streets radiating from the Museu de São Roque.

Arcadas do Faia, R. Baroca, 54 (tel. 32 19 23). Cover charge 2500$. Open Mon.-Sat. 8pm-2am.

Sr. Vinho, R. Meio a Lapa, 18 (tel. 67 26 81), in nearby Madregoa. Minimum food and drink charge 2500$. With appetizers at 1100-2800$, this isn't hard to reach. Open 8:30pm-2am.

Parreirinha da Alfama, Beco do Espírito Santo (tel. 86 82 09) and **Pátio das Cantigas,** R. São Caetano, 27. Less exclusive but more commercialized than places in the Alfama.

Nightlife

Lisboa certainly ain't Madrid, but you won't be bored late at night. June is the month of *feiras populares,* outdoor night fairs with plenty of eating, drinking, and dancing to live music (the **Festas de Santo António).** There's a lively one called "Oreal" at **Campo das Cebolas,** near the waterfront in the Alfama. (Open June Mon.-Fri. 10pm-1am, Sat.-Sun. 10pm-3am). The Elevador da Glória stops at a *feira* in the **Bairro Alto** with a view of the illuminated Av. Liberdade. This one goes until 3am all month, except on June 13 (St. Anthony's feast day), when it continues all night (as do the rampaging crowds around the *castelo).*

Cafés

Most cafés close before your grandmother goes to bed. Dawdlers linger at the **Pastelaria Suiça,** on the eastern side of Pr. Dom Pedro IV (the Rossio), a boisterous gathering place mobbed until midnight. Bring your well-thumbed Camões volumes across the square to **Café Nicola,** a famous meeting spot for 19th-century Portuguese writers. **A Brasileira,** on R. Garrett, attracts a more bohemian crowd. On weekends a roving guitar player serenades late-night coffee drinkers.

Bars

Those in search of rowdier nightlife shouldn't be deceived by the after-dinner lull. Nothing starts up until after midnight—primarily on weekends, of course. Nightlife clusters around **Rua Diario das Notícias** in the Bairro Alto.

> **Boris, Travessa Água da Flor,** 20. A small but trendy place where the drunken singing carries into the street. Open 9pm-2am.
>
> **Mascote do Bairro,** R. Diario das Noticias, 136. Diagonally across the street from Boris. Calmer, roomier, and more down-to-earth than Boris.
>
> **A Tasca-Bairro Alto Tequila Bar,** Trav. Queimada, 13-15. More than just tequila slammers. Brownies and beer are 100$, cookies and coffee half that. Best for pre-disco drinking. Open 6pm-2am.

Discos

> **La Folie Discoteca,** R. Diario das Noticias, 122-4. Runneth over with a bar, A/C, and the latest international music. The 800$ cover charge includes two beers or one mixed drink. Open Tues.-Sun. 10pm-4am.
>
> **Loucuras,** Av. Alvares Cabral, 35 (tel. 68 11 17), southwest of Largo do Rato. A multi-roomed mirrored extravaganza decorated entirely in black. Cover 600$ for pub, 1000$ for disco. Open Fri.-Sat. 11pm-4am as a disco, plus Sat.-Sun. 4-8pm as a pub.
>
> **Memorial,** R. Gustavo de Matos Sequeira, 42A (tel. 396 88 91), one block south of R. Escola Politécnica in the Bairro Alto. A hip gay and lesbian disco-bar. The lights and Europop blast from 10pm, but the place doesn't get moving until after midnight. The 1000$ cover charge includes two beers or one drink. Open 10pm-4am.

Shopping

Bookworms burrow for three glorious weeks in the **Feira do Livro** (Parque Eduardo VII, late May-early June). In June, the Alcântara holds the **Feira Internacional de Lisboa,** while in July and August the **Feira de Mar de Cascais** and the **Feira de Artesania de Estoril** take place near the casino. Bargaining is the name of the game. The *fritadas* (Portuguese doughnuts) and freshly baked bread are fair staples. Burrowers, prowlers, and packrats should catch the **Feira da Ladra** (flea market), held at Campo de Santa Clara (Tues. and Sat. 7am-3pm; take bus #12 or trolley #28).

Mercado Ribeira, an open-air market just outside Estação Cais do Sodre, is festive with fresh fruit and abundant food. (Open Mon.-Sat. until 2pm. Freshest pickings in the morning.) The **Amoreiras Shopping Center de Lisboa,** Av. Duarte Pacheco, boasts 330 shops (see Practical Information).

Estremadura

An angry Atlantic foams below the sharp cliffs and whitewashed fishing villages along the Costa de Prata (Silver Coast) of Estremadura. Mornings dawn misty and grey here, but the gloominess dissipates by midday. The people of Costa de Prata cling tightly to their traditions, despite or perhaps because of the tourists.

Along the coast this culture thrives in such towns as Nazaré and Peniche. Inland, medieval strongholds and monumental monasteries remain at Óbidos and Alcobaça. The beach towns of Estoril and Cascais are part wealthy Lisboan suburb and part wealthy resort. These, along with the castles of Queluz, Mafra, and Sintra, make pleasant daytrips from Lisboa. Below the Tejo and south of Lisboa lies the Setúbal Peninsula, an industrial and fishing center often bypassed by tourists. Setúbal itself is the best base for daytrips to the picturesque fishing village of Sesimbra; the Serra da Arrábida, a mountainous area with sparkling beaches; and the resort and beaches of Troia. Accommodations are quite expensive in these smaller towns.

Sintra

After Lord Byron sang its praises in the epic poem *Childe Harold,* dubbing it "glorious Eden," Sintra became a must for 19th-century English aristocrats on the Grand Tour. While the town's popularity has made it a bit self-conscious, Sintra retains the air of a fairy-tale city and makes a delightful daytrip from Lisboa.

Orientation and Practical Information

Sintra (30km northwest of Lisboa and 15km north of Estoril) is connected by train to Lisboa's Estação Rossio (every 5min., 45min., 145$). From the train station take a left and follow signs down a winding road to the town center (10min.). Be aware that theft is common in this heavily travelled area; many backpackers stow their gear in the tourist office for safety during the day.

Tourist Office: Pr. República (tel. 923 39 19, fax 923 51 76), in the same building as the **regional museum.** Paintings on the ground floor and archeological exhibits on the upper floor. English and French spoken. The staff will help you find a room in a private home. Open June 1-Sept. 30 9am-8pm; Oct. 1-May 31 9am-7pm.

Post Office: Pr. República (tel. (01) 923 52 52) across from the tourist office. **Telephones** inside and in a trailer outside. Open Mon.-Fri. 9am-12:30pm and 2:30-6pm. **Postal Code:** 2710.

Currency Exchange: Banco Totta e Açores, R. Padarias, 4, on a side street off the main *praça*. Open Mon.-Fri. 8:45-11:45am and 1-2:45pm.

Trains: Estação de Caminhos de Ferro, Av. Dr. Miguel Bombarda (tel. 923 26 05), at the northern end of the city. To: Lisboa (every 5min., 45min., 145$), Óbidos, Figueira da Foz (8 per day), and the northern beaches (change at Cacém). No direct service to Estoril or Cascais (see below).

Buses: Rodoviária, Av. Dr. Miguel Bombarda, across the street from the train station. To Cascais (10 per day, 1hr., 265$) and Estoril (13 per day, 40min., 260$). Green-and-white **Mafrense** buses depart from stops to the right of the train station as you exit. To Mafra (11 per day, 45min., 320$), with connections to points north.

Hospital: Largo Dr. Gregório de Almeida (tel. 923 34 00).

Emergency: tel. 115.

Police: Largo Dr. Virgilio Horta on corner of R. Costa (tel. 923 07 61).

Accommodations and Camping

The youth hostel is inexpensive but far away from the city center. *Pensões* are pricier here than almost anywhere else in the country. Turismo has a list of *quartos* (singles 3000$, doubles 3500$).

> **Pousada da Juventude,** Sta. Eufémia (tel. 924 12 10), 2 long km out of town. Up winding streets beyond São Pedro. Get Turismo to show you on the map. Meals served. TV in lounge. Reception open 9am-noon and 6pm-midnight. Lockout midnight. Singles 1100$. Doubles 3000$. Low season: 900$; 2500$.
>
> **Pensão Nova Sintra,** Largo Afonso d'Albuquerque, 25 (tel. 923 02 20), facing the square east of the train station. Charming terrace, clean rooms—some with stupendous views of the *castelo*. Singles 3200$. Doubles 5200$. Breakfast included.
>
> **Casa de Hóspedes Adelaide,** R. Guilherme Gomes Fernandes, 11 (tel. 923 08 73). Turn left as you leave the train station and walk to the yellow *câmara*. The *pensão* is around the corner to the left opposite the police station. All rooms with A/C. Doubles 2500$, with bath 3000$.
>
> **Residencial Sintra,** Trav. dos Avelares (tel. 923 07 38), in the São Pedro de Sintra neighborhood above the town center, beneath the Palácio da Pena. Well-furnished rooms and beautiful garden. Singles with bath 5600$. Doubles with bath 6600$. Breakfast included.
>
> **Camping: Camping Capuchos** (tel. 86 23 50), near Convento da Capuchos 10km from Sintra. Very few of the usual amenities and quite a ways from Sintra. 550$ per person, under 18 320$ per person.

Food

Cheap places haunt the street behind the train station on the other side of the tracks. In the town center, a wider range of eateries live on side streets such as **Rua Padarias.** There's a local **market** in the small square behind the buildings facing the Paço Real. The **Mercado Municipal** is open 8am-8pm on the 2nd and 4th Sunday each month in São Pedro, 1.5km from Sintra.

> **Casa da Avó,** R. Monserrate, 44 (tel. 923 12 80), near the fire station. Fewer tourists than most local restaurants. Best *frango assado* (roast chicken, 750$) around; other *pratos do dia* up to 1100$. *Sopa de legumes* (vegetarian soup) 100$. Open Fri.-Wed. 9am-10pm.
>
> **Restaurante Alcobaça,** R. Padarias, 9 (tel. 923 16 51), on the street running uphill from Pr. República. *Ensopada de borrego* (lamb stew, 1200$). Most entrees 850-1800$. Open Thurs.-Tues. noon-4pm, 7pm-midnight.
>
> **Casa da Piriquita,** R. Padarias, 5 (tel. 923 06 26). Toothsome bakery and old auntie-ish tea-room. *Queijadas* (cheese and cinammon filling) and *travesseiros* (egg filling), Sintra's traditional pastries, about 100$. Open Thurs.-Tues. 9am-10:30pm.

Sights

Although tourists swarm across this playground of Portugal's bygone aristocracy; Sintra's attractions are so numerous that it remains a memorable place to visit. Between the train station and the town center stands a storybook village hall with the conical chimneys of the **Paço Real (Palácio Nacional)** looming behind. Once the summer residence of Moorish sultans and harems, the palace and its complex gardens were torn down during the Reconquista and replaced with a vaguely Moorish, mostly Gothic and Manueline building. Not much to look at on the outside (the chimneys look like giant bullhorns), the palace's interior is pure whimsy.

According to legend, the impressive **Sala das Pêgas (Hall of Magpies)** came to be when Dom João I was caught by his wife as he kissed one of the ladies of the court. Although he claimed that it was merely a gesture of friendship, the court ladies made it a subject of scandalous gossip. To spite them, the king caricatured them as magpies. A more serene bird motif is echoed in the **Sala dos Cisnes (Hall of Swans),** a banquet hall where 27 swans in different positions (you didn't think it possible) decorate the ceiling. The patio is a work of Moorish genius. (Open Thurs.-Tues. 10am-1pm and 2-4:30pm. Tickets sold 10am-4:30pm. Admission 400$, Oct.-May 200$; Sun. free.)

From the Paço Real, the 3km ascent to the **Castelo dos Mouros** and the **Palácio da Pena** (crowning one of the highest peaks in the Sintra range) begins. The lush flora is best seen on foot, but outside the Paço Real taxis (round-trip 2000$, will wait 1hr.) and buses (May-Sept. at 10:45am, 3pm, and 4pm; one-way 135$) will whisk there and back.

To reach the **Castelo dos Mouros,** walk up R. Monserrate and take the first right (signs point to Monserrate and Seteais); hang a left shortly thereafter on Calçada dos Clérigos. Continue climbing a short distance past the small 12th-century Igreja de Santa Maria until the sign for the *castelo.* From here, follow the trail through the dense forest. The 7th- to 8th-century castle of the Moors commands a glorious view of the countryside. Returning to the fork in the forest path, take a right turn and walk (10min.) until the path exits onto a road where you can either continue the climb to the Palácio da Pena (10min.) or make a slight detour to a small park. Take care: this path, though scenic, is steep and strenuous. It shouldn't be attempted if you're tired, a heavy smoker, lazy, very pregnant, or in poor health. Also avoid taking this path after dusk, since the tortuous maze of paths becomes a tortuous maze of invisible paths.

The **Palácio da Pena** was built in the 1840s by Prince Ferdinand, the queen's German consort, on the site of a 17th-century convent. Nostalgic for his country, the prince commissioned an obscure German architect to design this folly; it combines the aesthetic heritages of both Germany and Portugal. The utterly fantastic result would do loony King Ludwig proud: a Bavarian castle embellished with Arab minarets, Gothic turrets, Manueline windows, and a Renaissance dome. The rooms inside contain the usual assortment of royal Portuguese, Indo-Portuguese, and Sino-Portuguese furnishings, plus overstuffed Victorian junk; they're definitely worth seeing if only for the cloister and chapel, which remain from the original convent. (Open Tues.-Sun. 10am-5pm, none admitted after 4:30pm. Admission 400$, Oct.-May 200$; students with ID and seniors free.)

To get back to town take the narrow road straight down. A 15-minute detour up a trail to the right along this road (look for the "Sta. Eúfemia" sign) leads past a ruined convent to a **capela,** built on a ridge to mark the miraculous appearance of Santa Eúfemia in the 18th century. The view from here is incredible—Lisboa, the Rio Tejo, Cascais, and the coastline—but an even more impressive scene can be spied along the path to the **Cruz Alta** (a stone cross built on a rocky peak 520m above sea level). On the way down you'll pass the **Igreja de São Pedro,** which preserves 17th-century *azulejos* of Bible scenes. From there, R. Trindade leads past a small convent and then rejoins the road you came up on.

Near Sintra

Queluz, 13km west of Lisboa, is famous for its **Paço Real** (a.k.a. Palácio Nacional de Queluz), built in the late 18th century by Portuguese architect Mateus Vicente Oliveira. Queen Maria I, fondly known as "the pious" (a.k.a. "the crazy"), commissioned this pink and white Rococo wedding cake. It is now, alas, somewhat shabby and overrun by Portuguese children on field trips. The building, furnishings, and grounds are clearly French in inspiration. Of historical interest is the room where Pedro I, first emperor of Brazil, was born and died. The **tourist office** (tel. 436 34 15) is in here too (the Palácio, not Pedro's room). (Both open Wed.-Mon. 10am-1pm and 2-5pm. Admission June-Sept. 400$; Oct.-May 200$. Students free.) To **train** here from Lisboa take the Sintra line from Estação Rossio (every 15min., 1/2 hr., 145$). Turn left and follow the signs to the palace.

Cabo da Roca, 11km from Sintra, is the westernmost point on the European continent. Spectacular views of the ocean hurling itself against the cliffs you'll see here. The cape—mobbed on Sunday—is accessible by **bus** from Sintra (10 per day, 1hr., 260$) and a 3km hike or bus from Cascais (see Estoril and Cascais).

Estoril and Cascais

The reputations of these two towns as playgrounds for the rich and famous shouldn't deter you from spending a day at the beach. Although they bristle with luxury hotels, at least they're relaxed and informal. Turn-of-the-century villas and tropical gardens prevail in these pleasure havens a half-hour west of Lisboa.

Estoril

There's little to do in Estoril but soak up the sun, shield yourself from the sun, and spend money at overpriced restaurants and hotels. High-energy people sometimes walk the flowery paths of **Parque do Estoril,** the public garden.

Smash the piggy at Estoril's famed **casino,** reputedly the largest and most luxurious in Europe. The glass and marble gaming-palace tempts from just above the park; it contains a restaurant, bars, a cinema, and a room of slots. Foreigners must cough up a passport; all must be 18 years old for the slot machines and 21 for the game room. (Entrance fees are 20$ to the bingo room, 400$ to the game room, and 150$ to the slot machine room. Open 3pm-3am.)

You can find a reasonably priced room at **Pensão Costa,** R. Olivença, 2, on the corner of Estrada Marginal uphill from the train station (tel. 468 16 99; singles and doubles 4000$, with shower 5000$; Oct.-June 25% discount). **Pensão Marilus,** R. Maestro Lacerda, 13 (tel. 468 27 40), is on the side street off Av. Bombeiros Volunários. A large dog guards the harmless neighborhood. (Singles 2500$. Doubles 6000$. Oct.-May 25% discount; breakfast included.) **Pensão Residencial Continental,** R. Joaquim Santos, 2 (tel. 468 00 50), is two blocks away from the water from Marilus, at the end of the street on the left. In a grand old building surrounded by a well-kept garden, the clean rooms have phones and high ceilings. Common bathrooms are gigantic. (Singles 3500$. Doubles 6000$. Breakfast included.)

Up Estrada Marginal from the station, east of the park on the corner of Av. Bombeiros Voluntários, is **Restaurante Esplanada** (tel. 468 18 54), where you can gobble a hefty dinner of baked fish (tourist menu 1400$; open 7am-midnight).

The **tourist office** on Arcadas do Parque (tel. 468 01 13), across from the train station, has an English-speaking staff and maps of Estoril and Cascais. (Open Mon.-Sat. 9am-8pm, Sun. 10am-6pm; Oct. 15-June 14 9am-7pm, Sun. 10am-6pm.) **Trains** from Estoril to Lisboa's Estação Caís do Sodre (1/2 hr., 145$). **Buses** for Sintra depart from in front of Estoril's train station (every 45min., 40min., 260$).

Cascais

Cascais is more historic than its twin (fraternal). The **Museo do Palácio de Castro Guimarães,** in the city's lush municipal garden, has an exotic setting for its fine collection of 17th-century Portuguese and Indo-Portuguese silver and furniture. (Admission Tues.-Sat. 120$, Sun. free. Open Tues.-Sun.) Nearby, the small Manueline **Igreja da Assunção** is decorated with vibrant 18th-century *azulejos*.

About 1km west of town on the shore lies the **Boca do Inferno** (Maw of Hell), a huge mouth carved in the rock by the incessant Atlantic surf. Sadly, the supposedly dangerous sight is swamped with tourists. Less crowded is **Praia do Guincho,** an immense stretch of sandy beach 8km to the west. Its dangerous undertow and cold water make it less than ideal for a swim, but it's perfect for windsurfing and it offers a good view of **Cabo da Roca** (see Near Sintra). Here the Serra de Sintra ends abruptly in a sheer cliff 150m above the sea. A little farther from Praia do Guincho, at a bend in the way flanked by small restaurants, a road leads to **Praia do Abano,** well worth the 2km walk. **Buses** to Praia do Guincho leave from the train station in Cascais (every hr.; 20min.; book of 5 tickets 650$, book of 10 1300$).

Pensão le Biarritz, Av. Ultramar, 555 (tel. 483 22 16) is on the outskirts of town. From the train station, walk up Estrada Marginal to Av. 25 de Abril; follow that road up to Av. do Ultramar, then turn right. (Singles 3500$, doubles 5000$.) On the same street but closer to town is the pricier, hotel-like **Pensão Residêncial Casa Lena** at #329 (tel.

486 87 43; doubles 6500$, with bath 7500$; triples 8000$; breakfast included). **Restaurante Pereira,** R. Bela Vista, 30 (tel. 483 12 15), an uphill walk from the Alameda, serves plain but hearty meals. (Open Fri.-Wed. noon-4pm and 7pm-midnight.)

The **tourist office** (tel. 486 82 04), at Av. Combatentes da Grande Guerra, is located on the site of an archeological dig in Paços do Concelho. Rodoviária **buses** leave from Sintra's Av. Dr. Miguel Bombarda, across the street from its train station, for Cascais (10 per day, 1hr., 265$).

Mafra

In a country famous for its modest charms, Mafra comes as a shock. The unremarkable town is the site of a huge **complex,** like Spain's El Escorial, that houses a palace, a royal library, a marvelous cathedral-sized church, and a hospital. With 2000 rooms, the building is so monstrous that it took 50,000 workers 13 years (1713-1726) to complete under the whip of architect Johann Friedrich Ludwig. This Herculean task gave rise to a school of sculpture known as the Mafra School.

The exterior of the magnificent Baroque **igreja** has fallen into grime-covered disrepair, but the belfries remain eloquent. The design for the extravagant dome was actually snagged from Bernini's unexecuted plan for St. Peter's in Rome. The interior is one of Portugal's finest, richly decorated with bas-reliefs and statues of Carrara marble. (Open Wed.-Mon. 10am-1pm, 2-5pm, closed on national holidays. Admission June-Sept. 300$, Oct.-May 200$; students with ID free.)

Access to the rest of the building is through a door to the right as you exit the church. The **hospital's** beds are bizarrely arranged like side-chapels, so patients can hear mass. (Note the slots placed between the bedboards to make a night's sleep easier on the spinal cord.)

The **sala dos troféus,** furnished with the antlers and skins of stags from chandeliers to chairs, is a must-see, but is outdone by the small **cells** where monks of yore used to scourge their mortal vileness with chains, switches, and other paraphernalia.

As the Portuguese-speaking guides (who accompany all visitors) tour the complex, they dwell lovingly on Mafra's pride and joy, the 40,000-volume **biblioteca** (library). It contains numerous 15th-century Bibles in assorted languages, as well as the monks' fine collection of murder mysteries.

To reach **Turismo** walk right after exiting the museum, then take the first left on Av. 25 de Abril. The staff hoards many shiny brochures and information on accommodations. (Open 9:30am-7pm.) Green and white Mafrense **buses** stop in front of the church. They serve Lisboa's Largo Martim Moniz and Estação Rossio (1 per hr., 1 1/2 hr., 470$).

Setúbal

Lucky Setúbal is the home of spanking new Ford and Renault factories. Along with the exhaust-sputtering salt and cement plants and the port, these factories make the city an key commercial center. Industry doesn't net tourists, most of whom head straight for the Algarve. Yet the city is a matchless base for daytrips to the mountainous Serra da Arrábida and the beaches of Troía.

Setúbal was born in the first century AD as a Roman port connecting the iron mines of the Alentejo and the merchant ships of the Mediteranean. Abandoned in later centuries then occupied by the Moors, the town became part of the Portuguese kingdom in the 13th century.

Orientation and Practical Information

Avenida Luísa Todi, a broad boulevard with a strip of park and cafés down its middle, runs parallel with the Rio Sado through the city. North of Av. Todi runs **Avenida 5 de Outubro**, containing the **Praça do Quebedo** (home to the train station and tourist office) and the bus station. Between Av. Todi and Av. 5 de Outubro sits the **Praça de**

Bocage in the heart of the city. Av. Todi, Av. 5 de Outubro, Pr. Quebedo, and Pr. Bocage bound a bunch of narrow streets that are the old city.

Tourist Office: Largo do Corpo Santo (tel. 52 42 84), off Pr. Quebedo and across from the train station. English spoken. Pamphlets of Setúbal and the Costa Azul. Open Mon.-Sat. 9am-7pm, Sun. 9am-12:30pm.

Currency Exchange: Banco Borges e Irmão, Av. Todi, 290. Coming from Pr. Bocage onto Av. Todi, it's on the left. Open Mon.-Fri. 8:30am-3:30pm.

Post Office: Av. Mariano de Carvalho (tel. 52 27 78), on the corner with Av. 22 de Dezembro. Open for Posta Restante and telephones Mon.-Fri. 8:30am-6:30pm, Sat. 9am-12:30pm. **Postal Code:** 2900.

Telephones: In the post office. **Telephone Code:** 065.

Trains: Pr. Quebedo, across from the tourist office, for local trains. **Estação de Setúbal,** Pr. Brasil (tel. 52 68 45). To: Lisboa (28 per day, 1 1/2 hr., 235$); Faro (4 per day, 4hr., 1225$); Évora (13 per day, 2hr., 680$).

Buses: Rodoviária Subalentejo, Av. 5 de Outubro, 5 (tel. 52 50 51). For the tourist office, walk down the street towards Pr. Quebedo, passing R. Cap. Araújo, and turn right. To: Lisboa (every 1/2 hr., 1hr., 470$); Évora (5 per day, 2 1/2 hr., 720$); Faro (7 *expressos* per day, 4hr., 1500$); Porto (6 *expressos* per day, 6hr., 1720$).

Ferries: Transsado, Doca do Comércio (tel. 52 33 84), off Av. Todi at the east end of the waterfront. 36 trips back and forth between Setúbal and Troía per day (15min.; 85$ per person, 45$ per child, 400$ per car).

Taxis: tel. 333 34, 314 13, or 523 55. Often found near train and bus stations.

Luggage Storage: At the **bus station,** 80$ per bag.

English Bookstore: Livraria Telis, R. Serpa Pinto, 8 (tel. 52 85 55), on a street off Pr. Bocage to the east. Petite stock of maps and paperbacks in English. Open Mon.-Fri. 9am-7pm, Sat. 9am-1pm.

Laundromat: Tinturária Domini, R. Tenente Valadni, 9 (tel. 52 42 77), off Pr. Bocage to the north. Dry cleaning only. 500$ per shirt, 600$ per pants. Open Mon.-Fri. 9am-7pm, Sat. 9am-1pm.

Hospital: R. Camilo Castelo Branco (tel. 52 21 33).

Emergency: tel. 115.

Police: Av. Todi (tel. 52 20 22), at the corner with Av. 22 de Dezembro, on the roundabout across the street from the Mercado Municipal.

Accommodations and Camping

Summer prices are higher, but there are plenty of rooms for all. Many *pensões* and *casas de hóspedes* (boarding houses) are unused to foreign travellers seeking rooms for a night.

Residencial Todi, Av. Todi, 244 (tel. 52 05 92). Centrally located with plain but clean rooms. The noisy ones overlook the street. Doubles 3500$, with bath 4000$. **Pensão Residencial Avenida,** Av. Todi, 87 (tel. 52 25 40). Wood floors, airy ceilings, and huge windows (if you're lucky). Distinctly spartan with a common bathroom, but it's all clean and there's gallons of hot water. Singles 2000$. Doubles 3000$.

Residencial Bocage, R. São Cristão, 14 (tel. 52 15 98, fax 52 18 09). Tidy rooms overlooking a quiet square 1 bl. north of Av. Todi and 1 bl. east of Pr. Bocage. All rooms have bath. Singles 4900$. Doubles 5900$. Oct.-May: 3900$; 4900$. Breakfast included.

Camping: Toca do Pai Lopes (tel. 52 24 75), run by the Câmara Municipal de Setúbal. At the western end of Av. Todi on the road to Outão. The standard amenities and crowds. Right on the beach. Reception open June-Aug. 8am-10pm; Sept.-May 9am-9pm. 200$ per person, 160$ per tent, 200$ per car. Sept.-May: 150$; 110$; 150$. Free showers.

Food

Cheap meals wait in the narrow streets of the old town, especially off **R. A. Castelões** (off Pr. Bocage). Fresh grilled seafood costs more on Av. Todi. The **Mercado Municipal** vends fresh produce at open stands on the corner of R. Ocidental do Mercado and Av. Todi, next door to Pingo Doce supermarket.

> **Groceries: Pingo Doce,** Av. Todi, 149. Very big and well-stocked. Open Mon.-Sat. 8am-9pm, Sun. 8am-8pm.
>
> **A Torre,** Av. Todi, 275 (tel. 308 01). The left half is fancier and more pricey, the right is an inexpensive *cervejaria*. *Pratos económicos* (budget meals) 450-650$. *Caracóis* (snails) too. Open 9am-10:30pm.
>
> **Jardim de Inverno,** R. Álvaro Luz, 48-50 (tel. 393 73), off R. A. Castelões. The green garden motif doesn't keep this bustling *cafetaria-restaurante-bar* quiet. Reasonably priced fare attracts everyone. Tourist menu 1300$. Entrees 600-900$. Open 9am-7:30pm.
>
> **Laçarote,** R. Álvaro Luz, 34 (tel. 380 84), down the street from the above. Vast miscellany of foods make up for the jaundiced decor. Pizza from 350$. Crepes from 160$. *Pratos do dia* 670$. Open 10am-7:30pm.

Sights and Entertainment

The red stone **Igreja de Jesús** occupies Praça Miguel Bombarda at the western end of Av. 5 de Outubro like a defrocked priest. Begun in the 15th century as part of a larger monastic complex, its maritime-motif decorations and faux-rope pillars and vaulting mark the beginnings of the Manueline style.

Next door, the **Museu de Setúbal** (a.k.a. Convento de Jesús) occupies the rest of the old monastic complex. (Closed in 1992 for renovations.) Here the **cloister,** built from the 15th to the 17th centuries, is closed whilst being restored. The **library** boasts 12,000 volumes of valuable first editions, municipal archives as far back as the 14th century, and a celebrated collection of autographs. (Closed in 1992.) (Open Tues.-Sun. 9am-noon and 2-5pm. Free.)

The most impressive sight in town is the **Castelo de São Filipe.** Take Av. Todi to its western end, turn right, and continue to the crossroads. Then take Estrada do Castelo Road uphill about 600m (30min.). Built by serious Spanish king Felipe II in 1590, this national monument is a luxury *pousada* where you can part with 22,500$ each night for a double (some rooms are in the old dungeon). The views from the walls of Setúbal, the Troía across the river, and the Serra da Arrábida mountains are worth the exertion. (Always open. Free.)

Setúbal is known for its cement factory, not its nightlife. The two cinemas sometimes show the same feature (280$). **Cinema Jupiter,** Av. 22 de Dezembro, 96 (tel. 52 34 19), is more convenient than **Cinema Charlot,** R. Dr. António Gamito, 9-11 (tel. 367 59). The **Feira de Santiago** in the last week of July and first week of August is an industrial and agricultural party. More entertaining are the amusement park, bullfighting, and folk dancing that accompany it.

Óbidos

In 1228, Queen Isabella so admired Óbidos's beauty that her husband, King Dinis, gave it to her, beginning a tradition (lasting until 1833) in which Óbidos was part of the queen's dowry. Long a favorite retreat of the royal couples, Óbidos died and rose again as a luxury resort turned national monument. Caravans of tour buses now come to pay their respects to the embalmed city. No tourist pamphlet can honestly claim that this town of fantastically clean streets, expensive restaurants, and multilingual inhabitants is "typically Portuguese." Óbidos is just an exhibition piece: mosey around the walls, appreciate its beauty, snap some pictures and, after a few hours, leave. You'll eat and sleep more cheaply in nearby towns such as Caldas da Rainha (6km) and have more fun at the beaches around Peniche (20km).

Óbidos

When you see the formidable **walls,** you'll understand why Portugal's first king, Dom Afonso Henriques, was humbled in several attempts to capture the town from the Moors. He only succeeded when forces at the main gate diverted the guards' attention, while others, disguised as cherry trees, tiptoed up to the castle. Taking notice of the advancing trees, the astute Moorish princess, gazing out her window at the time, asked her father if trees walked. The distracted king just didn't listen. By the time he realized what was happening, Afonso's men had broken through the castle door, later named *Porta da Traição* (Door of Betrayal). You can walk around the entire town on the walls.

The main entrance to the town has always been **Porta Da Vila.** Rua Direita, the main street, runs from here through the entire walled town to the Sant'Iago Igreja and the inner fortress. The 17th-century **Igreja de Santa Maria** was built on the foundations of a Visigothic temple and later used as a mosque. Nun Josefa de Óbidos's graceful, vividly colored canvases fill the retable to the right of the main altar. (Open 9:30am-12:30pm and 2:30-7pm; Oct.-May 9:30am-12:30pm and 2:30-5:30pm. Free.) The nearby fountain bears the arms of Queen Leonor.

Igreja de São Pedro was built on the site of a Gothic temple that toppled in the earthquake of 1755. Only the broken arch at the *praça* portal remains. Slightly below the church, the **Museu Municipal** houses Portuguese paintings and Gothic religious sculptures from the 16th to 18th centuries. (Open 10am-12:30pm and 2-5pm. Admission 50$. Students, seniors, under 12, and Wed. free.) At the eastern end of R. Direita is **Igreja de Sant'Iago,** open only once a year for the **Festival de Música Ântiga** in October. Nearby is the remains of the **castelo,** built in the 12th century as a fortress on the Atlantic coast. The stronghold gradually lost its strategic importance as the ocean receded 7km through silting.

Places to stay are few and dear. Private rooms are the best option. **Agostino Pereira,** R. Direita, 40 (tel. 95 91 88), rents inexpensive rooms. He has a pleasant lounge and well-stocked bar. Use of washing machine and kitchen plus winter heating. (Singles 3000$. Doubles 3500-4000$. Reserve at least 3 days in advance.)

Óbidos is a hungry traveler's nightmare. The fact that locals aren't in the restaurants should tell you something. There's a tiny **mini-market** near the town's main gate and two larger ones wedged between handicraft shops on R. Direita. Otherwise, **Café Restaurante 1 de Dezembro,** on Largo São Pedro (tel. 95 92 98), serves food simply and well. *Prato do dia* 1100$ (1/2-portion 600$). Óbidos patents a wild cherry liqueur called *ginga,* even sweeter and more syrupy than the national norm. It may make you thirstier than you already are.

The **tourist office** (tel. 95 92 31) is in an adobe house on the main street, R. Direita, right before Pr. de Santa Maria. The competent staff speaks English. (Open 9:30am-1pm and 2-6pm.) The **post office** (tel. 95 91 99) is nearby in Pr. de Santa Maria. (Open Mon.-Fri. 9am-12:30pm and 2:30-6pm.) The **postal code** is 2510 and the **telephone code** 062. Some regard **hitchhiking** from here east to Caldas or west to Peniche an option, though we don't recommend it. The nearest **hospital** is in Caldas da Rainha (tel. 83 21 33). In an **emergency,** call 115. For **police,** dial 951 49.

Óbidos is an easy two-hr. **train** ride from Lisboa's Estação Rossio. Take a commuter train to Torres Verdes, then change trains for Óbidos (8 per day, 2 3/4 hr., 590$). The train station is 10 minutes outside town to the north. To get there from the town center, at the far end of R. Direita from the Porta da Vila walk out the gap in the walls. Turn right, then left, then walk down a steep flight of stairs on the hillside. Only Lou Ferrigno could manage the walk with luggage. The station is unattended; buy tickets aboard the train. Frequent **buses** connect via Caldas da Rainha (6 per day, 20min., 115$) to Lisboa, Santarém, and Nazaré. The incoming bus lets you off down some stairs from the main gate, but the bus stop for departures is a little farther down on the main road.

Peniche

Portugal's second-largest fishing fleet is based in Peniche, a dreary seaport 24km west of Óbidos. The town crests a high and rugged peninsula of the same name, and wide beaches skirt the cliffs. Many travelers overlook Peniche as they hurry through to the Ilhas Berlengas, but the town's monuments and beaches are mysteriously beginning to attract tourists in greater numbers. Maybe it's Peniche's bleak industrial nature that comes as a relief after all the marvels to the south.

Salazar, Portugal's longtime Fascist dictator, chose Peniche's formidable 16th-century **Fortaleza** as the site for one of his four high-security political prisons. Its high walls and bastions later became a camp for Angolan refugees and now house the **Museo de Peniche.** The highlight of the museum is undoubtably the fascinating anti-Fascist Resistance exhibition. A series of photo panels accompanied by Portuguese text trace the dictatorship and underground resistance movements from the seizure of power in 1926 to the coup that toppled the regime on April 25, 1974.

The round lookout tower perched above the ocean contains the notorious **Segredo de Peniche** (Secret of Peniche) punishment cell, the scene of a more dramatic liberation story. In 1954 Communist political prisoner Dias Lourenço made a daring breakout from the isolation cell, plunged into the icy waves far below, and waded through a sewage tunnel to the town. He was eventually recaptured and imprisoned once again. An international campaign for his release drew attention to the tribulations of the Portuguese. The fortress is at the far end of Rua José Estevão, near the dock where boats leave for the Berlengas. (Museum open Tues.-Sun. 10am-noon and 2-7pm; Oct.-June Tues.-Sun. 10am-noon and 2-5pm. Admission 90$, under 15 free.)

The largest church in town is **Igreja de São Pedro** (two blocks from the docks where R. Marquês de Pombal hits R. Nossa Senhora de Conceição), a 16th-century Manueline building with paintings of the life of St. Peter. The **Parque do Murraçal** winds over to the Baroque **Igreja de Ajuda,** gilded with *azulejos* depicting biblical, classical, medieval and pastoral scenes. The church is opposite the primary school just off R. 25 de Abril.

For sun and surf, head to either of the town's three beaches. **Praia de Peniche de Cima,** along the northern crescent, is more beautiful and has warmer water, but a deadlier undertow. The beach merges with another at **Baleal,** a small fishing village popular with tourists. The southern **Praia do Molho Leste** is much colder but safer. Beyond it is the crowded **Praia da Consulação**. The strange humidity at this beach is supposed to cure all sorts of bone diseases. In the past decade an improved economy has revived the art of tatting hand-made lace, once an important craft. The town's patron saint is Our Lady of the Safe Journey, protector of fishermen; the **Festa de Nossa Senhora da Boa Viagem,** held Saturday through Tuesday on the first weekend in August, brings arts and crafts, music *(fado),* fireworks, and a temporary amusement park.

Pensões fill up quickly in July and August; try to arrive early in the day. Women and children roam the streets offering beds in their homes. The closest **HI youth hostel** (tel. 42 21 27; 1150$ per person, Oct.-May 800$) is at Praia da Areia Branca, 13km south. The hostel is accessible by the local bus to Lisboa (9 per day, 1/2 hr., 385$). **Residencial Cristal,** R. Gomes Freitas de Andrade, 14-16 (tel. 78 27 24), sparkles three blocks inland of Pr. Jacob Rodrigues Pereira, the square on the other side of the park from Turismo. Its plain rooms are mighty clean, although the private baths are considerably more so than the common ones. (Singles 2500$, with bath 3000$. Doubles with bath 4500$. Oct.-May: 2000$; 2800$; 4000$.) **Pensão Felita,** Largo Professor Francisco Freire, 12 (tel. 78 21 90), is one block from the bus station. Turn right from the bus station on R. Estado Português da India and right again. The large bright rooms are all loosely beige. Some rooms with bath. (Singles 2800$, with bath 3500$. Doubles 3500$, with bath 5000$. Breakfast included.) An overcrowded **municipal campground** (tel. 78 95 29), 1 1/2km outside of town, fronts a beach and has a small market. Eight buses per day speed to the campground from a stop one block to the right of Turismo. Otherwise it's a 40-minute walk through the *jardim público* and across the Ponte Velha; once across turn right, then left at the T in the road. Go straight ahead a long,

long time until the Mobil station, behind which you can collapse in the comfort of the *campismo.*

For bargain meals, **Casa Canhoto** (open 10am-10pm), on R. 13 de Infantaria, serves savory treats from an outdoor grill. The *espetadas de lulas grelhadas* (squid kebab, 650$) and the *sopa de peixe* (fish soup, 120$) are especially good. Terrific cheap restaurants also line **Av. Mar.** The **market** has fresh produce; from the tourist office walk up R. Paulino Montez, then turn right on R. António da Conceição Bento. (Open Tues.-Sun. 7am-1:30pm.)

Turismo, R. Alexandre Herculano (tel. 78 95 71), is hidden in a garden behind the gas pumps. (Open 9am-8pm.) The **post office** (tel. 78 70 11), on R. Arquitecto Paulino Montez, is around the corner from the bus station. Posta Restante and **telephones** lie within. (Open Mon.-Fri. 9:30am-12:30pm and 2:30-6pm.) The **postal code** is 2520 and the **telephone code** 062. The **hospital** (tel. 78 17 00, 78 17 08) is on R. Gen. Humberto Delgado, off R. Arquitecto Paulino Montez. For **medical assistance,** dial 78 18 27. In an **emergency,** dial 115. The **police** (tel. 78 95 55) are on R. Marquês de Pombal off Pr. Jocab.

The **bus station** (tel. 78 21 33) is on R. Estado Português da India. To reach Turismo, turn left on Largo Bispo Mariana and left again at the public garden. Buses travel to Lisboa (15 per day, 2 1/2 hr., 750$), Caldas (4 per day, 1hr., 450$), and Santarém (2 per day, 1 1/2 hr., 670$).

Near Peniche: The Peninsula and Ilhas Berlengas

The best way to savor the rough ocean air is to walk all the way around the peninsula (8km). Start hiking at **Papôa,** a small, rocky peninsula that juts out to the north of Peniche. Stroll out to the tip, where orange cliffs protrude from a swirling blue sea. Nearby lie the ruins of an old fortress, **Forte da Luz.**

The **Santuário de Nossa Senhora dos Remédios** stands at the edge of a Portuguese ghost town. In this unusually tiny chapel, *azulejo* panels cover the walls and cylindrical ceiling, glowing in the crepuscular gloom. Only six pews fit inside the chapel proper; another six are in the sunlit anteroom, where prominently placed signs invite pilgrims to seek reconciliation with God and to be quiet.

Cabo Carvoeiro, the most popular and dramatic of Peniche's natural sights, and its **farol** (lighthouse) punctuate the extreme western end of the peninsula. Next door is a conveniently situated snack bar where you can watch the waves crash on the rocks below as you relish *ginga* (the syrupy cherry liquor of Óbidos). There are stunning views both from the **Nau dos Corvos** (Crow's Ship), an odd rock formation and a popular bird roost, and from the top of the lighthouse.

Ilhas Berlengas

Out of the Atlantic Ocean 12km northwest of Peniche rises the rugged, terrifying beauty of the Ilhas Berlengas (Berlenga Islands). One minuscule main island, numerous reefs, and isolated rocks form an archipelagic home for thousands of screeching seagulls, wild black rabbits, and a small fishing community.

The main island, encircled by sparkling surf, is traced with deep gorges, natural tunnels, and rocky caves. For 600$ to 800$ per person (groups of 8-10), a motorboat will chug from the castle pier to explore some of the island's scenic wonders. Unfortunately you can't swim here. The island is fringed with two protected **beaches,** the better one by the landing dock, the other by the castle. You can rent underwater fishing and skin-diving equipment in Peniche. The tiring trek to the top of the island yields a gorgeous view of the 17th-century **Fortaleza de São João Batista,** now a hostel on an islet.

The private **hostel** that occupies the old fortress is a spectacular place to sleep. The government tried running it as a luxury *pousada,* but the effort failed due to the utter lack of facilities and the strenuous 20-minute hike from the ferry landing. Bring a sleeping bag. The hostel has a kitchen, but no cooking utensils; the small canteen and snack bar stock basic food. (Spartan singles 700$, with bath 800$. Bunks in 6-bed dorms 600$. Open June 1 to mid-Sept. Advance reservations must be made from Peniche's Turismo.) The island has a small, barren **campground** on a series of rocky terraces above the ferry landing and beach. If you stay here, be prepared to be shat on by scores of seagulls. They may attack those who stray off by themselves. Always look mean and carry a stick to ward them off. Inquire and make reservations from Turismo in Peniche. (Open June-Sept. 20.) **Pavilhão Mar e Sol** (tel. 720 31) is the lone restaurant here. It also offers unaffordable rooms with private showers. (Doubles with breakfast 12,500$, with *diário completo* 15,000$.)

Near the boat landing there's a tiny **supermarket** as well as **public bathroom** facilities. From Peniche's public dock, the Berlenga **ferry** makes three trips per day to the island in July and August (9am, 11am, and 5pm, returning 10am, 4pm, and 6pm), and one per day in June (10am, returning 6pm) and September 1-20 (10am, returning 5pm). In July and August, the ferry gets so crowded that you may have to queue up at 7am. A same-day round-trip ticket (1500$; 1700$ for chair) for the 9am ferry means you'll return on the 4pm ferry; if you go at 11am, you return at 6pm. To stay overnight, buy a 900$ one-way ticket for the 5am boat and pay your return fare on board a 10am return boat. The crossing can be rough. If you intend to stay the night, bring a flashlight. The 30-minute walk from the bar near the boat landing to the hostel is lit only by periodic flashes from the lighthouse.

Caldas da Rainha

Most famous for its sulfur springs, the town takes its name, "Baths of the Queen," from Queen Leonor, who luxuriated in the thermal springs here in 1484. The first lady then ordered (and sold her jewels to finance) the construction of the world's first **thermal hospital** where victims of rheumatism, respiratory ailments, and skin afflictions came to be cured. The ailing and the curious can still sample the treatments at the Hospital Thermal Rainha Dona Leonor. (Bath 490$; pay at the cashier upstairs.) Downstairs, an attendant shows you to a small private room where you can soak in the steaming, sulfurous, and disgustingly smelly water. The tubs are equipped with an optional water massage. An hourglass marks time in 20-minute segments, but you can stay as long as you like, provided there's no wait. After your bath, the attendant will advise you to lie down in one of the reclining chairs in the lobby and to drink liquids at room temperature for the rest of the day. These moments of rest are most important; your body needs to regain its equilibrium. To reach the hospital, walk downhill on R. Liberdade from Pr. República, the town's main square. The hospital (tel. 340 40) is at the bottom of the ramp on the left. (Open for baths Mon.-Fri. 8am-6pm, Sat. 8am-noon.)

Through the tunnel on the left side of the hospital façade is its old chapel, **Igreja de Nossa Senhora do Pópulo.** The church was another Leonor commission, probably as a spiritual counterpart to the baths' physical therapy. An enthusiastic English-speaking guide spurts an architectural history of the little chapel. Arabic tiles and arches shine out from the early Manueline design. (Inquire at the hospital for permission to visit; usually open only for mass. Free.)

Caldas is best known to the Portuguese for its traditional ceramics. The town's prestige in ceramics has long been unrivaled, and most art museums throughout the country house at least a few characteristic pieces from Caldas. Its kilns produce chiefly for handicraft shops nationwide. You can shop here for high quality pieces at low, low prices, or view the finished products at the **Casa da Cultura** on Largo Rainha Dona Leonor, across from the hospital. (Open during exhibits 10am-12:30pm, 2-6:30pm, and 8pm-midnight. Free.) More pieces are displayed at the **Associação de Artesãos das Caldas da Rainha** gallery in the building just inside the park gate from the Casa da Cultura. A leaflet here lists the local artists and their *ateliers*. (Open June-Sept. 10:30am-1pm and 3:30-8pm.) Caldas hosts the **Feira Nacional de Cerâmica** for four days in the middle of July.

Believe it or not, well-rounded Caldas is also a center of modern sculpture. The work of native son António Duarte occupies the beautiful, modern, and undiscovered **Atelier-Museu Municipal António Duarte.** Most of Duarte's sculpture explores the range of facial and anatomical expression. (The museum has no fixed hours. Ring the doorbell at any reasonable hour and the guard will cheerfully let you in; you'll probably have the whole place to yourself. Free.) Less compelling, the **Museu de Cerâmica** across the street traces the history and manufacturing process of Caldas clay. (Open Tues.-Sun. 10am-noon and 2-5pm. Free.) The two museums put the park between themselves and the center of town; from R. Camões or Largo Rainha Dona Leonor, walk clockwise around its periphery.

Parque Dom Carlos I is a popular sanctuary. Nearby, the **Museu de José Malhôa** houses a collection of modern Portuguese paintings, sculpture, and ceramics. (Open Tues.-Sun. 10am-12:30pm and 2-5pm. Admission 200$; students with ID, seniors, and Sun. morning free.)

Residencial Europeia, R. das Mantras, 64 (tel. 347 81), is on the main pedestrian shopping street off Pr. República. New if uninspired rooms. (Singles 4000$. Doubles 5000$. Triples 6500$. Breakfast included.) **Orbitur** (tel. 88 23 67) runs a campground in Parque Dom Carlos I. From the Hospital Thermal continue on R. Camões until the small roundabout. Turn left on Av. Visconde de Sacavem, walk past the tennis courts and *voilà*. (Reception open 8am-10pm. 420$ per person, 355$ per tent and per car. Hot showers 60$. Open Jan. 16-Nov. 15.)

Yet another quirky property makes Caldas distinctive—it's the fruit capital of Portugal. Even if you don't want to buy any produce, visit the large **Mercado da Fruta** in Pr. República. Local vendors and shoppers amass each morning for frenzied haggling fits. No-frills meals are wolfed at **Churrasqueira Zé do Barrete,** Trav. da Cova da Onça, 16 (tel. 83 23 37), off the busy pedestrian shopping thoroughfare R. Almirante Cândido dos Reis. Half-*frango no churrasco* (barbecued chicken) is just 750$ (500$ for a 1/2-dose). (Open Mon.-Sat. 9am-10:30pm.) The town's sweets (*cavacas*, like Burgos' sugared egg yolks) are famed and loathed throughout the country. For **dessert** head for one of the dozens of pastry stores around Pr. República.

The **tourist office** (tel. 83 10 03) is at Pr. 25 de Abril, in the municipal campground two blocks down on the left away from the bus station. (Open Mon.-Fri. 9am-7pm, Sat.-Sun. 10am-1pm and 3-7pm.) The **post office,** R. Heróis da Grande Guerra (tel. 83 21 56), is across the street from the bus station. (Open Mon.-Fri. 8:30am-6:30pm.) The **postal code** is 2500 and the **telephone code** 062. **Taxis** (tel. 83 10 98) run 24 hrs. a day. You may want one from the train station to the campground (250$). Dirty laundry is deloused at **Lavanderia Luso-Americana,** R. Henrique Sales, 13 (tel. 83 21 74; 400$ per kg.). The **hospital** (tel. 83 21 33) is on the first street to the right after the police station. In an **emergency,** call 115. The **police** (tel. 316 22) are headquartered at R. Diário de Notícias, just off Pr. República.

The **train station** (tel. 236 93) is on the northwestern edge of town. To reach the tourist office from here, take Av. Independência Nacional, which veers right and changes into R. Dr. Miguel Bombarda. Continue straight ahead onto R. Almirante Cândido dos Reis. Eight trains per day connect Caldas to Lisboa (2 1/4 hr., 635$). The train station has **luggage storage** facilities (115$ per 4hr., 180$ per day). The **bus station** (tel. 310 67) is on R. Heróis da Grande Guerra. For the tourist office, turn left as you exit the station and left again two blocks later onto R. Almirante Cândido dos Reis. Frequent bus service to Óbidos (14 per day, 20min., 90$) and Sintra (8 per day, 1 1/2 hr., 590$).

Nazaré

Nazaré has always lived for the sea; now it fishes for tourists. In summer its beach quarter explodes with foreigners. Meanwhile, the *Nazarenses* continue to paint their long, narrow wooden boats in bright colors and preserve their unique form of dress. The typical male fisher, barefoot and clad in plaid pants rolled up to the knees, wears a black stocking cap in which he keeps tobacco, matches, hook and line, and, in the bulging hem, money. Women typically don seven petticoats, a thick shawl, and large gold earrings. Visitors debate whether these people cling to their traditions in spite of tourism or because of it.

Orientation and Practical Information

Nazaré is situated on a long, populated, and windy beach. On a cliff north of town lies the **Sítio,** the old town, which preserves a sense of calm and tradition less prevalent in the resort further south. To get from the bus station to the tourist office (10min.), walk to **Avenida República** along the beach, then turn right. Turismo awaits between the two major *praças.* The nearest train station (Valado), 5km away on the Lisboa-Figueira da Foz line, serves both Nazaré and Alcobaça. Regular buses shuttle between the three points (115$).

> **Tourist Office:** Av. República (tel. 56 11 94). English- and French-speaking staff provide maps and little else. Open 9:30am-12:30pm and 2-6pm; July-Aug. 10am-10pm.
>
> **Currency Exchange: Viagens Maré,** Centro Comercial Maré, Store #10 (tel. 56 19 28), next to Hotel Maré on R. Mouzinho de Albuquerque, off Pr. Souza Oliveira (the next square after Pr. Arriaga from the bus station). Open Mon.-Fri. 9am-7pm.
>
> **Post Office:** Av. Independência Nacional (tel. 56 16 34). From Pr. Sousa Oliveira walk up R. Mousinho de Albuquerque, which veers to the right. The post office is just past Hotel Central. Open for Posta Restante and telephones Mon.-Fri. 9:30am-12:30pm and 2:30-6pm. **Postal Code:** 2450.
>
> **Telephones:** In the post office. **Telephone Code:** 062.
>
> **Trains:** tel. 473 31, in the town of Valado dos Frades on the Nazaré-Alcobaça bus line. To Lisboa (4 per day, 3hr., 720$) and Figueira da Foz (5 per day, 2hr., 500$). Change in Figueira da Foz for other destinations.
>
> **Buses:** Av. Vieira Guimarães (tel. 511 72), perpendicular to Av. República. Express service to: Lisboa (5 per day, 2hr., 950$); Coimbra (1 per day, 2hr., 880$); Porto (2 per day, 3 1/2 hr., 1160$). Regular service to: Valdos dos Frades (11 per day, 115$); Alcobaça (15 per day, 1/2 hr., 170$); Caldas da Rainha (5 per day, 1 1/4 hr., 350$); Leiria (13 per day, 1 1/4 hr., 470$) with connections to Óbidos and Peniche.
>
> **Luggage Storage:** In the **bus station** 80$ per bag.
>
> **Laundromat: Lavandaria Nazaré,** R. Branco Martins (tel. 527 61), off R. Trineiras, which is in turn off Av. República. Wash and dry 400$ per 3kg load. Dry clean: 600$ per shirt, 500$ pants. Open Mon.-Sat. 9am-7pm.
>
> **Hospital:** (tel. 56 11 16) in the Sítio above the back on the cliff.
>
> **Emergency:** tel. 115.
>
> **Police:** (tel. 56 12 68), near the market.

Accommodations and Camping

By stepping off the bus, you unwittingly signal a phalanx of room-renters to stampede. Although prices (singles 2000$, doubles 3500$) are lower than at *pensões,* a "room" may be anything from a comfortable bedroom with bathroom and shared kitchen to a prison-like cell. In theory, you should insist on seeing your quarters before settling the deal. Once they take you home, though, they consider the deal sealed. As always, bargain and never pay more than the lowest prices for a room in a *pensão.*

> **Pensão Central,** R. Mouzinho de Albuquerque, 85 (tel. 55 15 10). Gigantic, primly furnished rooms with cramped but decent bathrooms. Winter heating. Singles 2850$, with bath 4250$. Doubles 4350$, with bath 7000$. Breakfast included.
>
> **Residencial Marina,** R. Mouzinho de Albuquerque, 6A (tel. 55 15 41), down the street from the above. Cheery, spacious rooms decked out with carpets and modern furniture. Pristine baths. Singles 3500$. Doubles 5000$. Open May-Oct.
>
> **Pensão Mar Alto,** Pr. Dr. Manuel de Arriaga, 25-28 (tel. 55 12 59), on a main square parallel with the beach. Austere rooms are carpeted and smell reassuringly of detergent. Singles 2500-3750$. Doubles 3900-6300$.
>
> **Pensão Europa,** Pr. Dr. Manuel de Arriaga, 23 (tel. 55 15 36), next to Pensão Mar Alto. Cramped, bright rooms with lofty ceilings. Bedrooms noticeably cleaner than baths. Some rooms overlook the beach. Singles 2500-4000$. Doubles 3000-5000$.

Camping: Orbitur's Valado site (tel. 56 11 11), a 2km uphill climb from town. 420$ per person, 355$ per tent, 360$ per car. Hot showers 60$. Pines shade the bungalows. Bus service is sketchy, so take a taxi at night. A newer and closer site, **Vale Paraíso,** Estrada Nacional, 242 (tel. 56 15 46), includes swimming pools, a restaurant-bar, and a supermarket. 470$ per person, 430$ per tent, 390$ per car. Mid-Sept. to Dec. 20% discount. Open June-Dec.

Food

As long as you stick to fresh fish, you'll eat well anywhere. The tourist restaurants along the beach and in the main square are more expensive than the small places along the side streets and near the bus station. For fresh fruit and vegetables, shop at the large **market** across from the bus station. (Open 8am-1pm; in winter Tues.-Sun. 8am-1pm.)

A Casinha da Graça, Av. Vieira Guimarães, 30L (tel. 55 22 11), across the street from the bus station. Fresh flowers atop every checkerboard picnic table; a toy family is always about to step out of the little house. Delicious *caldeirada* (fish stew) 850$. Other entrees 700-1000$. Open 8:30am-9:30pm.

Casa Santos, R. Occidental, 19A, a narrow street 1 bl. toward the water from the bus station. Sardines and Salad served with a Smile (520$). *Sopa de peixe* (fish soup) 125$. Open noon-midnight.

Forno d'Orca, Largo Caldeiras, 11 (tel. 55 18 14). From Pr. Souza Oliveira, follow Trav. do Elevador toward the funicular. The outdoor patio is in the small square immediately on your right. One of the best of the beach-quarter restaurants. Generous helpings of *lulas à Sevilhana* (squid) or *ameijos ao natural* (clams) 750-1300$. Open 8am-midnight.

O Frango Assado (a.k.a Casa dos Frangos), Pr. Dr. Manuel de Arriaga, 20 (tel. 55 18 42). Heavenly barbecued chicken *piri-piri* (1050$ per kg—to go only). Even though they cut the chicken, you'll still have to rip, peel, and gnaw like a beast. Open noon-9pm.

Sights and Entertainment

The demented, stairway-shaped funicular (every 15min. until 1am, $70) climbs from R. Elevador off Av. República to the **Sítio,** all there was of Nazaré before the tourist boom. Here are the uneven cobbled streets and weathered buildings of a less refined quarter. The striking façade of **Igreja de Nossa Senhora da Nazaré** fronts a large square, site of the annual festival dedicated to Nazaré's patron saint (2nd week in Sept.). The church itself, above a semi-circular staircase, rises from a handsome portico that wraps around three sides of the building. An elegant coffered dome shelters the interior, which is carved with grapevines. The motif is repeated on the twisted columns of the high altar.

On a side street leading off the *praça* to your right facing the church, the **Museu Dr. Joaquim Manso** displays miniature fishing boats and other fishing paraphernalia. (Open 10am-12:30pm and 2-7pm; Oct.-May Tues.-Sun. 9:30am-12:30pm and 2-6pm. Admission 300$; students, seniors, and Sun. free.)

The tiny, whitewashed **Ermida da Memória** stands in a corner of the square diagonally across from the church. The hunter Dom Fuas Roupinho built the chapel out of gratitude to Our Lady of Navaré, who took time out of her busy schedule to save him from falling off a cliff when he was chasing a deer. *Azulejos* cover the closet-like room from floor to ceiling. One hundred and twenty meters above the sea is a breathtaking aerie from which to view the lower town's orange-tiled roofs, the town profile, and the coastline.

Around 7:30pm, visit the **port** at the southern end of the Praia quarter to witness the return of fishing boats through the surf. The shorefront market holds lively actions where local restaurateurs bid for the best catches of the day.

Back in the tourist quarter, Av. República, the **beach-side promenade** is cluttered with fun-seekers at all hours. By day cars, tour buses, local vendors, and tanned fools infest the thoroughfare, trying to burrow their way to the sanctity of the beach. Stay in the populated area if you're swimming, as sewage collects on the water surface elsewhere.

Cafés in Pr. Souza Oliveira bustle with *bica*-sippers until 1am. Of course, you might want to graduate to **Discoteca Jeans Rouge** (opens at 11:30pm), up the street from the *praça* and dance away the early morning. Every Thursday and Friday at 10pm, a local group performs **traditional dances** called *viras* at the Casino, a festival hall, on R. Rui Rosa. (Admission 500$). The **Salão Mar-Alto** next to Hotel Nazaré also hosts *viras* every Tuesday, Thursday, and Saturday at 10am; Friday is *fado* night. Bulls fight at the **Praça de Touros** (bullring) in the Sítio every other Saturday or Sunday in early summer and every Saturday from mid-July to mid-September. Tickets (from 1500$) go on sale at the kiosk in Pr. Sousa Oliveiro.

Near Nazaré: Alcobaça

Unlike Nazaré, Alcobaça is a peaceful little town built on rolling hills away from the sea and its sunseekers. Dom Afonso Henriques donated the land for the great Cistercian **Mosteiro de Santa Maria,** one of the finest sights in Portugal, as an offering of thanks for the recapture of Santarém from the Moors.

Behind the abbey's handsome Baroque façade, only the main doorway and rose window remain from the original Gothic structure. Inside, the 350-ft. long and 70-ft. high nave, the largest in Portugal, dozes in elegantly diffuse light. The simple lines of the interior may at first seem barren, but the sleek, chalk-white Mosteiro has a powerful appeal (there is, however, a Manueline door in the rear of the nave for those who experience Manueline withdrawal). A forest of slender columns uphold the vaulted ceiling. In the transept are the two jewels of the church: the 14th-century **sarcophagi** of Inês de Castro and Dom Pedro I. While Pedro was prince, he had an adulterous affair with his wife's handmaiden, Inês. Pedro's father didn't punish the assassins who slit Inês's throat, but upon attaining the crown Pedro personally ripped out their hearts and ate them (hence his nickname, "the Cruel"). He then revealed that he and Inês had been secretly wed, and in a ghoulish ceremony had her body exhumed and brought to court where coutiers were made to kiss her rotting hand. Pedro then meticulously dressed his beloved in royal robes, plopped her on a throne, and made her his queen. She was reinterred in an exquisitely carved tomb in the king's favorite monastery. The king had his own tomb placed opposite hers so that they could reunite at the moment of resurrection.

A doorway on the north side of the church leads to the **claustro,** worth every *escudo* of the entrance fee. The central courtyard is the Claustro do Silêncio. The impressive *cozinha* (kitchen) has two massive chimneys that can cook five or six roasting steers at a time. A six-ton marble table hulks at the center of the room, and at its feet flows a branch of the Rio Alcoa, amazingly routed into the kitchen floor.

Enormous terracotta statues painted by monks in the 17th and 18th centuries fill the **sala do capítulo** next door. The **refeitório** has ribbed vaulting and an ingenious staircase built directly into the wall leading to a pulpit. (The monks ate in silence whilst listening to readings from the Scriptures.) The last of the chambers is the **Sala dos Reis** (Room of the Kings), whose 17th-century *azulejos* depict the founding of the convent. Larger than life statues of the kings of Portugal, sculpted by more of these artistic monks, look down from an upper ledge. Since many were damaged by Napoleonic vandalism, those of uncertain identity bear question marks next to their names. To get to the monastery from the bus station turn right, then right again, cross the river and pass through tree-lined streets with many restaurants. (Monastery open 9am-6:30pm; Oct.-March 9am-5pm. Admission 300$, Oct.-March 200$; students, teachers, and seniors free.)

The **Museu Nacional do Vinho,** Portugal's only museum devoted to the history and production of wine, lies about 1km outside of town on the road to Batalha. Tours wind through the musty, warehouse-like museum, stopping at ancient wine presses and giant 1000-liter storage jars. The resin-coated rooms once served as enormous (55,000 liter) wine vats, each devoted to a specific wine-producing region. Unfortunately, the museum skips the all-important imbibing stage of the wine cycle—there's no tasting. At the end you can, however, purchase a bottle or two (from 350$). (Tours often in Portuguese only; the multilingual guide is elusive. Try calling ahead at tel. 422 22 to schedule a tour with him. Open Mon.-Fri. 9am-12:30pm and 2-5:30pm. Free.)

At **Pensão Alcoa,** R. Araújo Guimarães, 30 (tel. 427 27), by Pr. República, an elderly couple offers passable accommodations between dark wood floors and ceilings.

(Singles 700$. Doubles 1400$.) Cheerful rooms with winter heating welcome the traveler at **Pensão Corações Unidos,** R. Frei Antonio Brandão, 39 (tel. 421 42), on a street radiating away from the monastery's entrance. Bathrooms and windows could be cleaner. (Singles 2500$, with bath 3500$. Doubles 4000$, with bath 5500$. Breakfast included.) **Pensão Mosteiro,** nearby on Av. João de Deus, 1 (tel. 421 83), just up from Turismo, has similarly bright and heated rooms. (Singles 2000$, with bath 3000$. Doubles 5000$. Breakfast included.) A municipal **campground** (tel. 422 65) spreads itself near a stand of trees a block behind the market. The site is woefully sandy and barren. (210$ per person, 700$ per tent, 150$ per car. Showers 55$.)

O Ovo Batido, R. Dr. Brilhante, 35 (tel. 436 62), is a quick self-serve place with filling meaty dishes. *Carne de vaca assado* (roast beef) is 650$. Turn left out of the bus station and left again; it's two blocks down on the corner. (Open Tues.-Sun. 8am-8pm.) Similar restaurants lie across from the bus station; more stylish ones cluster in and around Pr. Dom Afonso Henriques, in the shadow of the monastery. For reputedly the freshest fruit in Portugal (measured in time from tree to market), forage at the **market** just across the small park north of the bus station. (Open Tues.-Fri. 9am-1pm.) Monday and Saturday are the town's big market days (8am-4pm).

Turismo (tel. 423 77) kneels in Pr. 25 Abril opposite the monastery steps. The staff are multilingual and keep a list of accommodations. (Open 9am-7pm; Oct.-May 10am-1pm and 3-6pm.) The **post office** (tel. 597 435) is on an adjacent corner. It provides Posta Restante and **telephones.** (Open Mon.-Fri. 8:30am-6pm.) The **postal code** is 2460 and the **telephone code** 062.

The **bus station** (tel. 422 21) is on Av. Manuel da Silva Carolino, a five-minute walk from the center of the old town. To reach Turismo from here, turn left from the station exit, walk down the slope, then turn left again. Follow R. Dr. Brilhante across the bridge to Pr. Republica. Through the portal, the sight of the monastery towers will guide you to Pr. 25 Abril, the square in front of the monastery. You can **store luggage** at the station (80$). Buses to: Nazaré (14 per day, 1/2 hr., 170$); Batalha (6 per day, 45min., 300$); Leiria (6 per day, 1hr., 385$); Lisboa (3 *expressos* per day, 2 1/2 hr., 880$). Frequent buses (14 per day, 115$) run to the **train station,** 5km north in Valado dos Frades, halfway between Nazaré and Alcobaça.

Beira Alta and Beira Baixa

The **Beira Alta** ("high edge") and **Beira Baixa** ("low edge") are just about the only regions in Portugal that shiver under snowfall. Desolate and poor, these mountainous provinces have always been more traditional than most of the country. Yet a recent agricultural boom has transformed the region into a quirky center of upward mobility.

Boom or no boom, the transportation system remains downright archaic. Train connections are few and far between, while the trains themselves are ancient and wheezing (some pull passenger cars that date from the 30s). This mode of travel is picturesque but insufferably slow and crowded. Except for the route between Figueira da Foz and Coimbra, buses are quicker, more reliable, and more expensive. Beware the sharp curves and steep hills.

If the transportation system doesn't scare you off, you'll be rewarded by small hamlets, beautiful scenery, and a refreshing absence of tourists. Farmers terrace the mountainsides for grape cultivation and fill the horizon with the silvery sheen of olive trees. The success of the Portuguese wine trade blooms everywhere; new cars and new concrete houses crowd the streets of mountain towns.

Coimbra

Coimbra's old town sits on a hill, a combination of medieval churches and monumental Fascist architecture. Below the old town sprawls the rest of the city. Despite its modest size, Coimbra has the grime, filth, and noise of a town three times its size—at least it's a university town, with English-language bookstores and foreign flicks in the cinemas.

The University (founded in 1290) earned great fame throughout medieval Europe. Founded in Lisboa and tossed back and forth between the two cities, the university settled here for good and became Portugal's most exclusive center of learning. Its alumni include Luis de Camões, Portugal's great epic poet, and Salazar, Portugal's great Fascist dictator (who as an impoverished student had one of the highest GPAs in the university's history).

Orientation and Practical Information

The steep streets of Coimbra rise in tiers above the Rio Mondego. Coimbra's center, a tangle of narrow streets, is roughly split into two areas. The lower town lies between the triangle formed by the river, **Largo da Portagem**, and **Praça 8 de Maio**. The upper town spreads on the adjoining hill, accessible through the **Arco de Almedina**. Coimbra has two train stations: Coimbra-A, near the town center by the bridge, and Coimbra-B, 3km nothwest of the center. Resign yourself to getting lost at least twice.

Tourist Office: Largo Portagem (tel. 238 86), an olive-green building 2 bl. east of Coimbra-A off Av. Emídio Navarro. Patient staff has a stash of good maps. Information on accommodations and daytrips. English and French spoken. Turismo headquarters for central Portugal. Open Mon.-Fri. 9am-6pm, Sat.-Sun. 9am-12:30pm and 2-5:30pm.

Currency Exchange: Hotel Astória, across the *largo* from Turismo. 800$ charge per transaction. Open 24 hrs. Bank rates are better; try **Montepio Geral**, C. Estrela, around and up from the Turismo. 500$ charge per transaction. Open Mon.-Fri. 8:30am-3pm.

Post Office: R. Olímpio Nicolau Rui Fernandes (tel. 297 80), just past the Manga rotunda. Central office is in the pink powder puff on Av. Fernão de Magalhães. Both open Mon.-Fri. 8:30am-6:30pm, Sat. 9am-12:30pm. One of several branch offices at Pr. República for Posta Restante. Open Mon.-Fri. 9am-12:30pm and 2:30-6:30pm. **Postal Code:** 3000.

Telephones: In post offices. **Telephone Code:** 039.

Trains: Estação Coimbra-A Largo das Âmeias (tel. 272 63). From the front entrance follow Av. Emidio Navarro along the river all the way to Turismo. **Estação Coimbra-B** (tel. 349 98). Trains from cities outside the region stop only in Coimbra-B, while regional trains stop at both stations. Frequent shuttles connect the two (5min., 85$). To: Aveiro (14 per day, 40min., 380$); Figueira da Foz (1 per hour, 1hr., 240$); Viseu (5 per day, 2 1/2 hr., 635$); Porto (14 per day, 3hr., 725$); Lisboa (14 per day, 3hr., 1080$); Paris (1 per day, 22hr., 15,835$).

Buses: Av. Fernão de Magalhães (tel. 270 83). To reach the tourist office, turn right from the station and follow the avenue to Coimbra-A and then Largo da Portagem (15min.). To: Lisboa (16 per day, 3hr., 1100$); Porto (5 per day, 6hr., 900$); Évora (5 per day, 6hr., 1350$); Faro (4 per day, 12hr., 2220$).

Public Transportation: Buses and street cars. Fares: 150$ (single ticket bought on board); 435$ (book of 10). Special tourist passes also available. Ticket books and passes sold in kiosks at Largo da Portagem and Pr. República, among other places. Main lines are #1 (Portagem-Universidade-Estádio); #2 (Pr. República-Fornos); #3 (Portagem-Pr. República-Santo António dos Olivais); #5 (Portagem-Pr. República-São José); and #7T (Palácio da Justiça-Estádio-Tovim).

Taxis: Táxis de Coimbra (tel. 266 22). 24-hr. service. Many loiter outside Coimbra-A.

Car Rental: Avis (tel. 347 86). What could be more convenient than this office in Coimbra-A, right outside the platform door? Cars start at 4800$ per day, plus 48$ per km, 1600$ for insurance, and the usual 17% tax. Open Mon.-Fri. 8:30am-12:30pm and 2:30-7pm.

Hitchhiking: Hitchers trying to get to Lisboa have been sighted on Av. Inês de Castro, just across the bridge. Those going to Porto waste hours on Estrada Nacional 1, near R. Padrão. *Let's Go* does not recommend hitchhiking as a means of travel.

Luggage Storage: At the **bus station** 100$ per day. At **Coimbra-A** 135$ per 4hr., 210$ per day.

Bookstore: Many good ones line R. Ferreira Borges. **Livraria Bertrand,** Largo da Portagem, 9 (tel. 230 14), 1 bl. from Turismo. Good selection of English and French classics such as *Let's Go*. Classical music in the background. Open Mon.-Fri. 9am-7pm.

Swimming Pool: Piscina Municipal (tel. 71 29 95). Take bus #5 São José, #1 Estádio, or #7T Solum from Largo Portagem outside the tourist office. The pool is near the stadium. Terrific but often packed 3-pool complex. Open July-Aug. 10am-1pm and 2-7pm; June and Sept. Mon.-Sat. 10am-1pm and 2-7pm, Sun. 2-7pm; Oct.-May Mon.-Sat. 12:30-3pm. Admission 150$, under 6 or over 60 free.

Crisis Lines: Poison (tel. (01) 795 01 43). **Suicide Prevention** (tel. (02) 82 35 35). Both are in Lisboa.

Hospital: Hospital da Universidade de Coimbra (tel. 72 32 11, 72 32 12). Near the Cruz de Celas stop on lines #3, 7, 7T, and 29.

Emergency: tel. 115.

Police: R. Olímpio Nicolau Rui Fernandes (tel. 220 22), facing the market and post office.

Accommodations and Camping

Notoriously cheap and seedy *pensões* line **Rua da Sota** and the surrounding streets across from Coimbra-A. Anything decent starts at 2000$ for doubles; pay less and pay the consequences. Fortunately for the downmarket set, an excellent HI youth hostel recently flung open its doors.

Pousada de Juventude (HI), R. António Henriques Seco, 14 (tel. 229 55). From either Coimbra-A or Largo Portagem, take bus #7, 8, 29, or 46, then walk from Pr. República up R. Lourenço A. Azevedo, left of the Santa Cruz park, and take the 2nd right. Great neighborhood. Enormous sunlit rooms (84 beds), large patio, TV room with VCR, bar, and gray parrot (Jacó). The young warden is an avid photographer—the black & whites in the halls are his. Reception open 9am-noon and 6pm-midnight. Bag dropoff all day. Curfew midnight. Lockout noon-6pm. 1250$ per person; Oct.-May 1000$. Breakfast included. Kitchen and laundry facilities.

Pensão Rivoli, Pr. Comércio, 27 (tel. 255 59), in a mercifully quiet pedestrian plaza off busy R. Ferreira Borges, which originates in Largo da Portagem. Neat, well-furnished rooms with white walls. Lockout 1am, but you can borrow a key. Singles 1800$. Doubles 3600$.

Residencial Internacional de Coimbra, Av. Emídio Navarro, 4 (tel. 255 03), in front of Coimbra-A. Bring ear plugs or insulation materials. Renovated *pensão* with plain, comfy rooms and fresh-smelling baths. Fluorescent lighting. Some rooms have a river view. Singles and doubles up to 3200$, with bath 4500$.

Residência Lusa Atenas, Av. Fernão de Magalhães, 68 (tel. 293 57), on the main avenue between Coimbra-A and the bus station, 3 bl. north of the former and 10min. south of the latter. More like Sparta than the name suggests. Bare, wan bulbs, but comfy rooms with high ceilings. Uncanny cleanliness. Small private baths in each room. Winter heating. Singles 1500$, with bath 2500$. Doubles 3500$, with bath 4500$. Triples 5500$. Breakfast included. **Pensão Flor de Coimbra,** R. Poço, 5, 2nd fl. (tel. 238 65), diagonally across Largo das Âmeias down R. Poço. Quality of furniture varies from sculpted wood to red plastic. All rooms have bath. Doubles 3500$; Oct.-May 2500. No reservations by phone.

Camping: Municipal Campground (tel. 71 29 97), corralled in a recreation complex ringed by noisy avenues with the stadium and swimming pool. The entrance is at the arch off Pr. 25 de Abril; take the same buses as for the pool. The small market is open only during the summer. Reception 9am-10pm; Oct.-Mar. 9am-6pm. 190$ per person, 120$ per tent, 230$ per car. Showers free.

Food

Scout out **Rua Direita,** running west off Pr. 8 de Maio; the side streets to the west of Pr. Comércio and Largo da Portagem; and the university district around **Praça da República.** There are university *cantinas* (cafeterias) at several locations, including one in the old college courtyard. Those passing for students—no problem in late June through July, when the university hosts foreign programs—will receive a better-than-average cafeteria meal for a mere 130$. Unfortunately, lines are usually long (with *Let's Go*-reading imposters), especially during the summer session. As with accommodations, be aware that many budget establishments in Coimbra are located in dark neighborhoods where no one should walk alone at night.

Churrasqueria do Mondego, R. Sargento Mór, 25 (tel. 233 55), off R. Sota, 1 bl. west of the Largo Portagem. The paper placemats map out a monumental tour of the city. Frequented by truck drivers, students, and tourists. Unceremonious service. Their *frango no churrasco* (barbecued 1/2-chicken) leaves Colonel Sanders squawking in the dust (330$). The plucky ask for a brushing of *piri-piri* sauce (it's *hot*). Grilled fish served at the counter. *Menú* 600$. Open noon-3pm and 6-10pm.

Restaurante Adega Funchal, R. Azeiteiras, 18 (tel. 241 37), on a side street off Pr. Comércio. A notch up from the others; unimpressive exterior conceals an elegantly rustic atmosphere. Generous helpings of A-1 Portuguese cuisine include *chanfana carne de cabra regional* (goat broiled in red wine, 900$) or *escalopes de vitela com champignons* (tenderloin of veal with mushrooms, 1200$). 1/2-portions available. Open 7am-2am.

Restaurante Democrática, Trav. Rua Nova, 5-7 (tel. 237 84), on a tiny lane off R. Sofia (1st full left after city hall). Quite popular. Most entrees 690-950$. For something different try *espetadas de porco á Africana* (pork kebabs African-style) 800$. Specialties change daily. Open Mon.-Sat. noon-3pm and 7-10pm.

Restaurante Flor de Coimbra, R. Poço, 5 (tel. 238 65), in Pensão Flor de Coimbra on the 2nd fl. down the hall on the left. Caught in a time warp. Low prices and ancient decor. *Frango assado* (roast chicken) 450$, 1/2-dose 300$. Soup 70$. Open noon-2pm and 7-9pm.

Café Santa Cruz, Pr. 8 de Maio (tel. 336 17), in what used to be part of the cathedral (still has vaulted ceiling and stained-glass windows). The most famous café in Coimbra. Espresso-worshipping has replaced more conventional prayer. Filled with professors and students. Coffee 55$. Open 7am-2am.

Sights

To reach the old center of town, pass through the **Arco de Almedina,** the remnant of a Muslim town wall, next to the Banco Pinto e Sotto Mayor on R. Ferreira Borges. The gate leads to a stepped street named Rua Quebra-Costas (Back-Breaker Street). Up a narrow stone stairway looms the hulking 12th-century Romanesque **Sé Velha** (Old Cathedral). Around noon a guide leads visitors interminably around the principal tombs and friezes as gloomy Gregorian chants drone in the background. (Open 9:30am-12:30pm and 2-7pm. Admission 150$.)

From Pr. Sé Velha, R. Borges Carneiro (behind the cathedral) leads to the **Museu Machado de Castro,** famous for its Gothic and Renaissance sculptures. Close your eyes near the one of St. Bartholomew's bloody demise if you're contemplating a meal. There's some 17th- and 18th-century porcelain on the second floor. Creepy lighting illuminates the ancient sculptures in the underground passageways of the old Roman forum. (Open Tues.-Sun. 10am-12:30pm and 2-5:30pm. Admission 200$, seniors and students free.)

The **Sé Nova** (New Cathedral), across from the museum in Largo da Feira, was built for the Jesuits in the late 16th century. The façade gets progressively more elaborate as it goes up; each builder tried to outdo his predecessor. The interior is austere and self-consciously antique. (Open 9am-12:30pm and 2-5pm. Free.)

Rua São Pedro, flanked by the grim façades of the new university buildings, leads to the **Porta Férrea** (Iron Gate), a door to the old courtyard of the **universidade.** Now the law school, these buildings housed Portugal's royal palace when Coimbra was the capital (1324-1537). The staircase at the right leads up to the **Sala dos Capelos,** where portraits of Portugal's kings hang below a beautifully painted 17th-century ceiling. (Open 9am-noon and 2-6pm.) Past the Baroque clock tower are the **capela da universidade** (university chapel) and the 18th-century **biblioteca da universidade** (university library). The library shelters 143,000 books in three lofty halls painted with Chinese motifs. Press the buzzer to the left of the door to enter. (Open 9am-12:30pm and 2-5pm.) From the university it's a short walk downhill alongside the **Aqueduto de São Sebastião** to the **Jardim Botânico's** sculpture and fountains.

The **Mosteiro de Santa Cruz** (Monastery of the Holy Cross) on Pr. 8 de Maio, at the far end of R. Ferreira Borges in the lower city, is a 12th-century monastery with all the usual fixin's: a splendid barrel-vaulted **sacristia** (sacristy), an ornate **tumulos reals** (where the first two kings of Portugal lie buried), and a 16th-century **claustro.** Up the staircase in the cloister's corner is the *coro alto,* where the choir stalls are decorated with gilded reliefs of episodes from the voyages of Vasco da Gama. (Open 9am-noon and 2-6pm. Admission to sacristy, tombs, and cloister 50$.)

In the 14th century, Holy Queen Isabel ordered the construction of the great **Convento de Santa Clara-a-Velha.** The queen's architects, just out of grad school and a little nervous about such a large responsibility, managed a marvel of medieval architecture—smack on top of a swamp. The convent sinks a little deeper each year; today it's more than half underground. (Open 10am-7pm.) As soon as the citizens of Coimbra realized what was going down, they rushed to build the **Convento de Santa Clara-a-Nova** (1649-1677) to replace the vanishing convent. The new convent's gloomy Manueline church contains both the old 14th-century Gothic tomb of the queen—barely discernible through a wrought-iron grill in the back—and a new silver one topping the high altar. (Open 8am-1pm and 3-7pm.)

Just past Santa Clara-a-Velha, a toy castle gateway leads to **Portugal dos Pequenitos,** a nationalistic little park filled with miniatures. Models reproduce Portugal's most famous historical monuments; a miniature house characterizes each region of the country; and a mini-museum is devoted to each former Portuguese colony. (Open 9am-7pm. Admission 300$.)

Entertainment

The most popular late-night coffeehouse, **Café Santa Cruz,** Pr. 8 de Maio, occupies what once was a chapel. Underneath its handsome vaulted ceiling, students occasionally sing *fado* (see Food listings). To hear the most unrestrained and heartfelt singers, go after dinner to **Diligência Bar,** R. Nova, 30 (tel. 276 67), off R. Sofia. (Open until midnight.)

The happening discos are **Via Latina**, R. Almeida Garret, 1 (tel. 321 98) near the Santa Cruz garden, for the younger crowd; and **Scotch** (tel. 81 31 36), across the river near Convento Santa-Clara-a-Nova. Both places are at their peak between midnight and 2am. Sometimes there's a cover charge. Beers are about 350$ and mixed drinks about 500$.

Students run wild through the streets during Coimbra's famous weeklong festival, the **Queima das Fitas** (Burning of the Ribbons) in the first or second week of May. The festivities begin when graduating students burn the narrow ribbons they received as first-years and receive wide, ornamental ones in return. The continuing carousing features midnight *serenatas* (groups of black-clad serenading youth), wandering musical ensembles, and parades. There are scheduled concerts and folkdancing as well. Another good time to come to Coimbra is during the **Festas da Rainha Santa,** held in even-numbered years in the first week of July. Throughout this religious festival, live choral music echoes through the festooned streets.

Near Coimbra

Conímbriga

The largest Roman settlement yet to be excavated in Portugal, Conímbriga lies only 10km south of Coimbra. Archaeology freaks squeal as ongoing excavations uncover more of the site each year. Outside the 4th-century town wall, a luxurious villa on the right, several smaller shops and houses, and the baths (complete with sauna and furnace room) on the far left are easily discernible. Some of the mosaics are remarkably elaborate and well preserved. The floor plan of the ruins, unfortunately, is incomprehensible. Maps (sold at the entrance, 150$) are some help, but not much. (Ruins open 9am-1pm and 2-8pm. Admission Tues.-Sun. includes museum 300$; Mon. ruins only 150$. Sun. morning, students, and seniors free.)

The nearby **Museu Monográfico de Conímbriga** displays artifacts unearthed in the area. It has a rather expensive restaurant-cafeteria. (Museum open Tues.-Sun. 10am-

1pm and 2-6pm. Admission Tues.-Sun. includes ruins 300$; Sun. morning, students and seniors free.)

AVIC **buses** (tel. 201 41, 201 42) run direct to Conímbriga from Coimbra. They depart opposite Hotel Astória (Mon.-Fri. at 9:05am, Sat.-Sun. at 9:35am; 210$). The return bus leaves the ruins Monday through Friday at 12:55pm, weekends at 5:50pm. Rodoviára has more frequent service (Mon.-Fri. every hr., Sat.-Sun. 3 per day; 1/2 hr.; 190$) from Coimbra to **Condeixa,** a town 2km from the ruins. Condeixa is a stop en route to Leiria or Figueira da Foz. The last bus returns to Coimbra at 7:55pm. Since the bus stop in Condeixa is near the highway, some people hitch back to Coimbra. *Let's Go* does not recommend hitchhiking as a means of travel.

Floresta de Buçaco

Foliage-shaded, rocky paths have drawn solitary wanderers to the Floresta de Buçaco for centuries. Nearly 400 years ago the Carmelite monks selected the forest, filled with exotic flora from around the world, as the perfect site for *desertos* (isolated dwellings for penitence and absolute silence). The decrees are still visible, carved indelibly into the Portas de Coimbra, and silence still reigns over the woodland. The forest became national property after the abolition and expulsion of all religious orders in 1834.

The bishop of Coimbra gave the Carmelites the **convent** in 1628. Inside are stained glass by Machado de Castro in the chapel and many paintings by the monks themselves. Note the cork on the walls and doors of the cubicles, applied to mute distracting noises and keep out the humidity. In 1810 Wellington spent a cool and quiet night here after defeating Massena. (Open 9am-noon and 2-7pm. Admission 80$.)

After Dom Carlos shooed away the monks, he used the convent for a hunting lodge. His son Dom Manuel II built the exuberant **Palaçio de Buçaco** that adjoins the old convent in a flamboyant display of neo-Manueline architecture. The overwrought excess of the palace, now a luxury hotel, is the perfect stone counterpart to the forest's natural abundance. The *azulejos* that adorn the outer walls depict scenes from *Os Lusíadas,* the great Portuguese epic about the Age of Discovery.

If you want an unforgettable **lunch** for an unaffordable price (fixed *menu* 5000$), dine at the Palácio (make reservations in morning). Otherwise, bring food and picnic by the Fonte Fria.

The hotel/palace has maps of the forest. Landmarks are the **Fonte Fria** (Cold Fountain), whose waters ripple down entrance steps, the **Vale dos Fetos** (Fern Valley) below, and the **Porta de Reina** (Queen's Gate). The most robust walkers trek one hour along the Via Sacra to a sweeping panorama of the countryside. The little 17th-century chapels represent stations of the cross.

Bus service from Coimbra to Buçaco continues to Viseu (5 per day, Sat.-Sun. 3 per day; 1hr.; 395$) beginning at 7:45am (Sat.-Sun. at 9am). Buses leave from Buçaco's station on Av. Fernão de Magalhães, a 15-minute walk from downtown (last bus back to Coimbra leaves Buçaco at 6pm, Sat.-Sun. at 5pm).

Luso

A 4km walk downhill from Buçaco brings you to Luso**,** a pleasant old-fashioned spa town with a couple of inexpensive restaurants and *pensões*. Luso's **tourist office** (tel. (03) 93 01 33) is on R. Emídio Navarro, in the center of town. (Open Mon.-Fri. 9:30am-1pm and 2-6:30pm, Sat.-Sun. 10am-12:30pm and 2-6:30pm.) **Buses** back to Coimbra stop a couple blocks above the tourist office on the same street.

Leiria

Capital of the surrounding district and an important transportation center, Leiria is an agreeable, if unspectacular, suburban town spread out in a fertile valley 22km from the coast. Leiria's proximity to the seashore and the museum towns of Batalha and Alcobaça make it a good base for both culture vultures and beach leeches.

Although both Romans and Moors hung out in Leiria, neither group left much behind. The city's oldest and most magnificent historic pile is the **castelo,** a granite fortification built by Dom Afonso Henriques after he greedily snatched the city from its Muslim owners. The castle rests dramatically atop the crest of a volcanic hill overlooking the northern edge of town. Later proprietors introduced a touch of high Gothic to the original severe Castilian style in an attempt to make the castle more livable. After its final occupants left for greener pastures, the castle was left to ruin for hundreds of years; now only the **torre de menagem** (homage tower) and the **sala dos namorados** (lovers' hall) remain. (Castle open 9am-6:30pm. Admission 100$.)

Down a winding road from the castle, the medieval **sé** is simple but eloquent. The bare interior is restful for eyes tired by Manueline histrionics. The cathedral sits off Largo Cónego Maia, two blocks away and visible from the bus station.

The **Santuário de Nossa Senhora de Encarnação** sits upon a wooded hill on the southern edge of town. Outside, the sanctuary looks fairly ordinary, but wow, take a gander at the marvelously colorful inside. The murals painted above the choir illustrate three local miracles attributed to Mary. To get in, try the unbolted door on the southern wall; the church seems to have no official hours. The clean and *confortável* **Pousada de Juventude (HI)** on Largo Cândido dos Reis, 7D (tel. 318 68) offers members the cheapest beds in town and the occasional cat. Kitchen and laundry facilities are available. (Reception open 9-10:30am and 6-10pm. Lockout noon-6pm. 800$ per person.) From the bus station walk to the cathedral. Then exit Largo da Sé (next to Largo Cónego Maia) on R. Barão de Viamonte, a narrow street lined with many shops. Largo Cândido dos Reis is about six blocks away on the right. **Pensão Alcoa,** R. Rodrigues Cordeiro, 24 (tel. 326 90) is four blocks to the right of the youth hostel on the corner of R. Barão Viamonte. All 14 rooms have telephone, radio, and central heating. (Singles 3000$. Doubles 6000$. Breakfast included.)

Café-Restaurante Casa Nova, R. Barão de Viamonte, 53 (tel. 252 63) serves up hearty food. From the bus station, follow the directions for the youth hostel to reach this street. Delicious Portuguese standards such as *bife á cortador* (grilled steak, 950$) and *bacalhau* (cod, 850$) come with heaps of rice, salad, and fries. (Open Sun.-Fri. noon-3pm and 7-10pm.) For fruit and vegetables, shop at the **market** (Tues. and Sat. 9am-1pm) in Largo da Feira opposite the gymnasium, located on the far side of the castle from the bus station. The **tourist office** (tel. 81 47 48) is across the Jardim Camões in the modern building that looks out on the fountain. The staff has cool-looking maps and schedules for buses going to the beaches of Vieira and Pedrógão. (Open Mon.-Fri. 9am-7pm, Sat.-Sun. 10am-1pm and 3-7pm; Oct.-April Mon.-Fri. 9am-6pm, Sat.-Sun. 10am-1pm and 3-6pm.) The **post office** (tel. 323 55) is on Av. Combatentes da Grande Guerra, three blocks from the youth hostel. (Open Mon.-Fri. 8:30am-6:30pm, Sat. 9am-12:30pm.) The **postal code** is 2400 and the **telephone code** 044. For medical assistance, call the **hospital** (tel. 81 22 63), on R. Tomás Coelho. **Police** (tel. 81 24 47) have a little nook on Largo São Pedro, just below the entrance to the castle.

Buses leave (tel. 323 76) from just off Pr. Paulo VI in the new part of town. To: Batalha (6 per day, 15min., 150$); Fátima (5 per day, 1/2 hr., 280$); Nazaré (4 per day, 45min., 385$); Coimbra (6 per day, 1hr., 725$); Lisboa (3 *expressos* per day, 2hr., 950$); Porto (6 per day, 3 1/2 hr., 1100$).

Leiria is on the Lisboa-Figueira da Foz **train** line. To Lisboa (7 per day, 3 1/2 hr., 840$) and Figueira (9 per day, 1 1/4 hr., 335$). The train station is 3km outside town in a dismal suburb. Buses for the station leave across the street from Turismo (approximately every hr. between 7:15am and 11:45pm, 10 min., 65$). **Taxis** (tel. 328 57) are on call 24 hrs. to zip to the train station from the bus station for 350-450$.

Batalha

The **Mosteiro de Santa Maria da Vitória,** Batalha's architectural delight, rises from the fertile Vale de Lena. Massive and elaborate in gold-hued stone, the *mosteiro* was built by Dom João I in 1385 to commemorate his victory against the Spanish. The complex of cloisters and chapels remains one of Portugal's greatest national monuments.

The church **façade** soars upward in a high but heavy Gothic and Manueline style, opulently decorated right up to the dozens of bell-like spires. Napoleon's uncouth troops used the stained glass windows for target practice and turned the nave into a latrine and a brothel. The **Capela do Fundador,** immediately to the right of the church's entrance, shelters the sarcophagi of Dom João I and his English-born queen, Philippa of Lancaster, daughter of John of Gaunt and relation of many British sovereigns. Life-size marble effigies lie on top, their heads resting under intricately carved Gothic *baldechins* (canopies). In the recesses of the chapel's south side are the tombs of their children, notably that of the Infante Dom Henrique—Henry the Navigator. The rest of the monastery complex is accessible via a door in the north wall of the church. Dense Manueline tracery covers the broad Gothic arches of the **Claustro de Dom João I.** Sculpted by Afonso Domingues, the delicate columns mark the very beginning of the Manueline style. The **sala do capítulo,** just off the cloister, is a large square room daringly designed to avoid all central supports. Its construction was so dangerous—the roof fell in twice— that only prisoners condemned to death were employed to build it. Here two Portuguese soldiers stand stonily at the tomb of two unknown Portuguese soldiers. A small Aladdin's lamp with the "Flame of the Nation" flickers, patriotically fed by Portuguese olive oil. On the wall hangs a mutilated crucifix from a World War I battlefield in Flanders where Portuguese soldiers fought and died.

To the north of the royal cloister, past the barrel-vaulted granary (now used as an exhibition hall), is the sober **Claustro de Dom Afonso V.** From here you can go outside to visit the chapels behind the chancel of the church. The **Capelas Imperfeitas** (Unfinished Chapels) surround a central octagon of massive buttresses designed to support a large dome. The project was dropped like hotcakes when Manuel I ordered his workers to build a monastery in Belém. The chapel in the 2 o'clock position flaunts the most flamboyant stonework in the entire complex and gives some idea of how the finished structure would have looked. (Monastery complex open 9am-5:30pm; Oct.-May Mon.-Fri. 9am-5pm. Admission 400$, Oct.-May 250$; students and seniors free.)

Batalha is devoid of cheap beds or even a campground. If marooned here, sleep at **Pensão Vitória** (tel. 966 78), on Largo de Misericórdia in front of the bus stop. The clean rooms are suitably bare and monastic. The **restaurant** below does wonders with *pudim* and is a handy place to wait for the bus. (Singles 3000$. Doubles 6000$. Winter: 2500$; 5000$.)

The **tourist office** (tel. 961 80), in the shopping mall complex at the freeway entrance, has some serious bus information. From the exit of the monastery walk right until the freeway. (Open Mon.-Fri. 10am-1pm and 3-7pm, Sat.-Sun. 10am-1pm and 3-6pm; Oct.-April Mon.-Fri. 10am-1pm and 3-6pm, Sat.-Sun. 10am-1pm and 3-5pm.) The **post office** (tel. 961 11) is just around the corner. (Open Mon.-Fri. 9am-12:30pm and 2:30-6pm.) The **postal code** is 2440 and the **telephone code** 044. The **hospital** is at tel. 962 46. In an **emergency,** dial 115. For **police,** call 961 34. The **bus stop** is at Café Frazão (tel. 965 05), across from Pensão Vitória on Largo da Misericórdia. Batalha's central location makes for convenient connections to: Leiria (8 per day, 15min., 150$); Fátima (4 per day, 40min., 210$); Alcobaça (6 per day, 45min., 300$); Nazaré (9 per day, 1hr., 410$); Tomar (4 per day, 1 1/2 hr., 450$); Lisboa (3 *expressos* per day, 2hr., 800$).

Fátima

Only Lourdes rivals this holy site in attracting millions of faithful Christian pilgrims each year. Unlike Santiago de Compostela, its Spanish competitor, Fátima has become a huge religious amusement park. The miracles believed to have taken place here are modern-day phenomena, well-documented and witnessed by thousands of people. In this once-humble setting three children—Lucia, Francisco, and Jacinta—sat tending their sheep while most of Europe concerned itself with war. On May 13, 1917, Mary appeared before them to issue a call for peace and to warn the world of the tragic events that would stem from Russia's godless communism. Not surprisingly, the incident aroused its share of heated controversy. The three children remained steadfast in their belief despite skepticism from the clergy and attacks from the press. Word of the vision spread throughout Portugal. Bigger and bigger crowds flocked to the site as Our Lady of Fátima returned to speak to the children on the 13th of each month, promising that a miracle would occur on her final appearance in October. On that morning 70,000 people gathered under a torrential rain storm; at noon, the sun spun around in a furious light spectacle and appeared to sink toward the earth. When the light returned to normal, everything was dry and no evidence remained of the morning's rain. The townspeople were convinced by the "fiery signature of God" and built a chapel at the site to honor Mary.

Fátima's exalted status was recognized by the Vatican in 1930, and the town has since received two papal visits, in 1967 and 1982, on the anniversary of the first apparition. To this day, the eves of the 12th and 13th of each month witness torch-lit processions of believers. The Pope has credited the Lady of Fátima with saving him after the attempt on his life in 1981; he made a silver-and-glass votive offering of the bullet now on display here. She apparently also had a hand in the demise of communism.

An astounding religious complex dominates the town. The sanctuary is set in vibrant parks enclosed by tall leafy trees, blocking out the surrounding commercial areas. At the end of its sunken asphalt football-field-sized plaza rises the **Basílica do Rosário** (1928) whose very construction is intended to awe. The *azulejo*-covered walls of the colonnade focus all attention on the tower. A crystal cruciform nightlight perches atop the tower's seven-ton bronze crown. Inside, the off-white stone hall with its tall cylindrical ceiling leads to the blinding high altar. The centerpiece of this striking edifice is a painting of Mary appearing before the three shepherds. Visitors must be conservatively dressed. Clothes that are tight-fitting, short, or in any way flashy are forbidden, as are "extravagant hats." (Open 7am-8pm.)

Sheltered beneath a metal and glass canopy, the original **Capelinha das Aparições** (Little Chapel of the Apparitions) was built in 1919. Masses are given here all morning in six languages. The information booth on the left as you face the chapel has the schedule of foreign-language confessions. (Open 9am-7pm.)

The **Museu de Cera de Fátima** (wax museum) tells Fátima's incredible story quite realistically in a series of vivid scenes like a Fantasyland ride in Disney World. Something you wouldn't find at the Magic Kingdom is the disturbing "Vision of Hell"—a fiery, fluorescent pile of contorted bodies rasping in agony from behind an iron screen. The many scenes of the children at prayer and depicting the deaths of Francisco and Jacinta in the flu epidemic that swept Europe are carpeted with coins. (There's now a movement to have them canonized.) To get here from the bus station, turn right at the exit and then take the first left uphill; make a right on R. Jacinta Marto. An adjacent gift shop sells plaster saints and postcards bearing the caption *"Rezei por ti em Fátima"* ("I prayed for you in Fátima"). (Open 9:30am-6:30pm; Nov.-March Mon.-Fri. 9:30am-5pm., Sat.-Sun. 9:30am-6pm. Admission 500$.)

Last, but absolutely not least, the **Museu-Vivo Aparições** uses light, sound, and special effects to recreate that famous apparition. As you face the Basilica the museum lies on your left. Walk through the belt of trees to Hotel Fátima. The museum is in the basement of the shopping complex on the left. (Open 9am-8pm, Nov.-April 9am-6pm. Soundtracks in English, French, German, Italian, or Spanish. Admission 350$.)

Aljustrel, the small village where the famous young trio lived, is 1km away. The entire town has been turned into a museum exhibit. To reach Aljustrel, walk past Turismo along Av. D. José Alves Correia da Silva.

The only time rooms are scarce is during the grand celebrations on the 13th of May and October, the first and last appearances of Mary. On these nights, some people discreetly **camp** in the parks around the sanctuary as a last resort. Fátima has a whopping number of *pensões-restaurantes* and *hoteles;* all are in the town around the sanctuary, a simple right turn out of the bus station. **Pensão Santo Amaro,** R. Francisco Marto, 59 (tel. 53 25 27), near the rotunda de Santa Teresa on the edge of town, is hotel-like in comfort but not in price. All the carpeted rooms have phones, immaculate full baths, and winter heating. (Mon.-Fri. singles 3500$, doubles 4000$. Sat.-Sun.: 4500$; 5000$. Nov.-April 20% discount. Breakfast included.) The cheapest rooms in town are right above the bus station itself, at **Pensão a Paragem** (tel. 515 58). The rooms, ornamented only by a crucifix, are clean. You'll be serenaded by diesel engines and suffocated by their exhaust. (Singles 2000$. Doubles 3500$. Triples 5000$.) For a bite to eat, drop by **O Portal,** R. Santa Isabela, off R. Francisco Marto. American dramas unfold on the TV overhead as viewers eat inexpensive *feijoadas* (pork and beans) for 850$. (Open Mon.-Sat. 9am-midnight, Sun. 9am-7pm.)

The **tourist office,** Av. Dr. José Álves Correia da Silva (tel. 53 11 39), is a 10-minute walk down the avenue from the bus station. It looks like a roadside diner. (Open 9am-7pm; Oct.-April 10am-6pm.) The modern **post office,** R. Cónego Formigão (tel. 53 18 10), is on the left before Turismo. The office has Posta Restante and **telephones.** (Open Mon.-Fri. 8:30am-6pm, Sat. 3-8pm, Sun. 9am-noon; winter Mon.-Fri. 8:30am-6pm.) The town's **postal code** is 2495 and the **telephone code** 049. The nearest **hospital** (tel. 421 30) is in Ourém. In **emergency** dial 115. The **police station** is on R. Francisco Marto (tel. 53 11 05).

Fátima's **bus station** (tel. 53 16 11) is listed as "Cova da Iria" on all schedules, while the "Fátima (est.)" listing refers to the **train station** (tel. 461 22), some 20km out of town. Buses run to: Fátima (est.) (6 per day, 45min., 275$); Leiria (5 per day, 45min., 280$); Batalha (3 per day, 40min., 210$); Tomar (3 per day, 1hr., 385$.); Lisboa (5 per day, 2 1/2 hr., 980$); Porto (3 per day, 3 1/2 hr., 1200$).

Figueira da Foz

Figueira is a resort. For the young there's a 1km by 3km beach; for the rich there are condos and a casino. The city is perhaps the only Portuguese "party" town—in the most neon, late-night sense of the word (11 discos, 10 bars, and 3 movie theaters at last count).

Orientation and Practical Information

Packed with hotels and "aparthotels," **Avenida 25 de Abril** is the busy lifeline that separates town from beach. Four blocks inland and parallel to the avenue, **R. Bernardo Lopes** harbors semi-affordable *pensões* and restaurants. Much of the action in Figueira happens in a casino-cinema-disco complex on this street.

Tourist Office: Av. 25 de Abril (tel. 226 10), next to Aparthotel Atlântico at the very end of the airport terminal-like complex. Useful map of the slanty street variety. Open 9am-midnight; Oct.-May Mon.-Fri. 9am-12:30pm and 2-5:30pm.

Currency Exchange: Aparthotel Atlântico or **Grande Hotel da Figueira,** Av. 25 de Abril, near Turismo, change money after hours.

Post Office: Main office at Passeio do Infante Dom Henrique, 41 (tel. 220 00), off R. 5 de Outobro. Open for Posta Restante and telephones Mon.-Fri. 8:30am-6:30pm, Sat. 9am-12:30pm. **Postal Code:** 3080.

Telephones: In the main post office and in a Telecom trailer on the esplanade 1 bl. from Turismo. Trailer open 2-7pm. English spoken. **Telephone Code:** 033.

Trains: Largo Estação (tel. 233 13), near the bridge. An easy 20-min. walk to Turismo and the beach. Keeping the river to the left, Av. Saraiva de Carvalho becomes R. 5 de Outubro at the fountain then curves into Av. 25 de Abril. Frequent connections to Coimbra (19 per day, 40min., 240$) and Lisboa (8 per day, 3hr., 1120$).

Buses: Terminal Rodoviário (tel. 230 95). Three rights. Facing the church, turn right on R. Dr. Santos Rocha, then right on Largo Luis de Camões, then right on R. 5 de Outubro, which curves into Av. 25 de Abril. To: Leiria (9 per day, 1 1/4 hr., 560$); Coimbra (2 per day, 2hr., 600$); Faro (1 per day, 12hr., 2400$); Lisboa (3 per day, 3 1/2 hr., 1000$). **AVIC** (tel. 251 13) serves Aveiro (5 per day, 2hr., 585$). **AFGA,** R. Miguel Bombarda, 79 (tel. 277 77), near the post office. To: Porto (1 per day Mon.-Fri., 2 hr., 980$); Lisboa (2 per day, 3 1/2 hr., 1080$); Évora (1 per day, 7hr., 1540$); Faro (1 per day, 10hr., 2220$).

Taxis: tel. 235 00. 24-hr. service. From the bus or train station to the campground 500$.

Bike Rental: AFGA, R, Miguel Bombarda, 79 (tel. 277 77). Rents pink bikes. 1000$ per 1/2-day, 1500$ per day. Special rates for weeklong rentals or groups. Open Mon.-Fri. 9:30am-1pm and 3-7pm.

Hospital: Nearest is in Gala, across the Rio Mondego (tel. 221 33, in emergencies 242 81).

Emergency: tel. 115.

Police: R. Joaquim Carvalho (tel. 220 22), near the bus station and park.

Accommodations and Camping

Prices depend on the time of year; July and August are the most expensive. Arrive early to check on vacancies; many managers won't reserve a room by phone in high season.

Pensão Residencial Bela Figueira, R. Miguel Bombarda, 13 (tel. 227 28), 2 bl. from the beach. Gorgeous, comfortable rooms and spotless bathrooms. Cool outdoor terrace. English-speaking manager. Central heating. Singles 1400-4000$, with bath 1750-5000$. Doubles 2500-5750$, with bath 3000-6750$. Breakfast included. *Diário completo* 1100$ per meal.

Pensão Paris, R. Lopes Guimarães, 23 (tel. 226 11), off R. Miguel Bombarda, 2 bl. from Bela Figueira. Bargainish rooms are simple but spacious, modern, and utterly white. Baths are impeccably maintained. Charming back patio for meals. Singles 2500$, with bath 4200$. Doubles 4800$, with bath 6500$. Open June 15-Sept. 15.

Pensão Residencial Rio-Mar, R. Dr. António Dinis, 90 (tel. 230 53), perpendicular to R. Bernardo Lopes. Spacious and comfortable (albeit old and dark) rooms. Lounge, TV, and a grand breakfast room downstairs. Doubles with bidet 3300$, with shower 4200$, with bath 5800$. Discount 40-50% in winter. Breakfast included.

Camping: Parque Municipal de Campismo (tel. 327 42). Keeping the beach at your left, walk up Av. 25 de Abril and turn right at the roundabout on R. Alexándre Herculano. Turn left at Parque Santa Catarina going up R. Joaquim Sotto-Mayor past Palácio Sotto-Mayor. About 2 1/2km inland. An excellent site complete with an Olympic-size pool, tennis courts, kennel, market, pharmacy, and currency exchange. Reception open 8am-8pm, Oct.-May 8am-7pm. Silence reigns 11pm-7am. June-Sept. each party must have a minimum of 2 people. 250$ per person, 200$ per tent, 250$ per car. Showers 100$.

Food

The restaurants in town are more expensive than the Portuguese norm. Hope lies in the direction of **R. Bernardo Lopes.** The local **market** sells food beside the municipal garden on R. 5 de Outubro. (Open Mon.-Sat. 7am-7pm; in winter Sun.-Fri. 8am-5pm, Sat. 8am-1pm.)

Groceries: Supermercado Ovo, on the corner of R. A. Dinis and R. B. Lopes. Beach town necessities: eggs, sunscreen, alcohol. Open Mon.-Fri. 9:30am-1:30pm and 3:30-7:30pm.

Restaurante Rancho, R. Miguel Bombardo, 40-44 (tel. 220 19), 2 bl. up from Turismo. Packed with locals at lunchtime. Hefty, delicious entrees (450-720$) such as *chocos grechados* (grilled squid, 500$). Open Mon.-Sat. 6am-midnight. **Restaurante O Escondidinho,** R. Dr. António Dinis, 62 (tel. 224 94), hidden inside the gate. Close encounters with tourists from all over Europe. Portuguese and Goanese Indian cuisine. Curry and *piri-piri* (hot sauce) dishes 750-1575$. Open Tues.-Sun. 12:30-2:30pm and 7-10pm.

Restaurante Astória, R. Bernardo Lopes, 57. Limited menu, but filling meals. The manager uses an intercom or yells orders to the cook through the wall. *Frango assado* (grilled chicken, 450$) or mixed salad (400$) cheaper at the bar. Open 9am-1am.

Restaurante Bela Figueira, in the *pensão*. Another Indian-Portuguese place. Try their *chamucas* (meat-filled appetizer, 105$) and their splendid *caril de gambas com coco e arroz* (shrimp, coconut, and rice curry, 1100$). Prices slightly higher on the terrace.

Sights and Entertainment

There are few cultural attractions to keep visitors out of the cancerous sun. The under-rated **Museu Municipal do Doctor Santos Rocha** houses everything from ancient coins to decadent fashions of Portuguese nobility to Ensley Eikenbergs. The museum coddles its archeological exhibits, primarily the ceramic vases excavated in Figueira da Foz and Caldas da Rainha, like a mother would her newborn child. The building lies in Parque Abadias, smack in the middle of the residential district; the museum entrance faces R. Calouste Gulbenkian. (Open Tues.-Sun. 9am-12:30pm and 2-5:30pm. Free.) **Casa do Paço,** Largo Prof. Vitar Guerra, 4 (tel. 221 59), is decorated with 6888 Delft tiles that serendipitously washed ashore after a shipwreck. (Open 9:30am-12:30pm and 2-5pm. Free.) The modest exterior of the **Palácio Sotto-Mayor** belies the shameless extravagance inside. Lavish green marble columns line the main hallway, and the opulent ceiling is slathered with paintings and decorative panels trimmed in gold-leaf. (Open Tues.-Sun. 2-6pm. Admission 100$.)

The **casino** on R. Bernardo Lopes (tel. 220 41) gobbles up money in a modern complex that also contains a nightclub (1750-2500$ cover charge) and a cinema (admission 300$). It costs 162$ for the slot machine and 20$ for bingo. To gamble you must be over 18 and show proper ID. There's also a show, usually music, at night. (Open 3pm-3am.)

Figueira's party mode shifts from high gear to warp speed during the **Festa de São João** (June 19-24). People frolic in the streets at all hours; more organized activities occur at the fair. Finally, at 5am, a huge rowdy procession heads for Buarcos, where all involved take a so-called *banho santo* (holy bath) in the ocean. For 10 days in September, the **Festival de Cinema de Figueira da Foz** screens international flicks.

Near Figueira da Foz

From the nearby village of **Buarcos,** which also has a large beach, you can watch fishers haul in the day's catch. The thick walls were built to protect the town from pirates who took great joy in pillaging Bucaros throughout the 17th century. The **tourist office** (tel. 250 10) guards the entrance to town on R. Tomás Aquino. (Open June-Sept. 9am-8pm.) Frequent **buses** for Buarcos leave from Figueira's train station and stop along Av. 25 de Abril.

The forested region north of Figueira in **Serra da Boa Viagem** (4km) has several vantage points with spectacular panoramas of the shoreline below. Farther north, the **Lagos Quiaios** region delights throngs of naturalists and weekend picnickers with a pool-spotted countryside. These jaunts are best made by bicycle. (See Figueira: Practical Information: Bike Rental.)

Aveiro

If you like salt, you'll love Aveiro. An important seaport in the 16th century, the town gradually declined as silt sealed off its estuary. Although initially disastrous to the community, the phenomena created the vast *ria* (estuary) that extends 45km up the coast, protected by a long sand bar. Islands, salt marshes, sand dunes, and an occasional pine forest now speck the water. Aveiro proper is graced with a few charming canals, which will tempt the delirious and the untraveled to draw comparisons with Amsterdam.

Along these aged waterways, streamlined *barcos moliceiros* drift laden with salty seaweed (residents make their living collecting it for fertilizer), their brightly painted bows rising high and curling into fearsome horns. Smaller *barcos saleiros* whisk through the canals past the glistening white salt beds. *Marnotos* (people who work the salt pans) gather salt into baskets and transport it to warehouses along the Canal de São Roque.

Orientation and Practical Information

Salt country is 200km north of Lisbon and 60km south of Porto. Trains are most convenient for travel in and out of Aveiro and the Rota da Luz region. Aveiro is split by the *canal central* and Avenida Dr. Lourenço Peixinho, which runs from the train station to **Praça Humberto Delgado** (actually a bridge). North of the *canal central* lies the fishermen's quarter, **Beira Mar.** The town's southern port is the "new" residential district, which actually contains all the historical monuments.

> **Tourist Office:** R. João Mendonça, 8 (tel. 236 80, 207 60). Both a regional and city tourist office. Sells tickets for boat trips on the *ria* (1750$). Maps and lodgings information. English- and French-speaking staff. Open 9am-9pm; Sept. 15-June 15 Mon.-Fri. 9am-9pm, Sat. 9am-1pm and 2:30-5:30pm.

Aveiro

Currency Exchange: Hotel Paloma Blanca, R. Luís Gomes de Carvalho, 23, (tel. 38 19 92), not far from the train station. 24-hr. service at bank rates.

Post Office: Pr. Marquês de Pombal (tel. 231 51). Cross the main bridge and walk up R. Coimbra past the town hall. Open for Posta Restante and **telephones** Mon.-Fri. 8:30am-6:30pm, Sat. 8:30am-12:45pm. **Postal Code:** 3800.

Telephones: In the **post office. Telephone Code:** 034.

Trains: Largo Estação (tel. 38 11 56), at the end of Av. Dr. Lourenço Peixinho. To find Turismo (1km), walk up Av. Dr. Lourenço Peixinho (the leftmost street) until Pr. da República. R. João Mendonça runs parallel to and beside the canal. Also, buses run from the train station to the bridge into the rest of town. To: Águeda (8 per day, 160$); Coimbra (22 per day, 1hr., 380$); Porto (30 per day, 1/2 hr., 430$); Viseu (5 per day, 4hr., 680$); Lisboa (20per day, 5hr., 1300$).

Buses: Nearest Rodoviária station is in Águeda, 19km away. Eight buses and trains per day go from the train station to Águeda (160$). **AVIC-Mondego,** R. Comandante Rocha Cunha, 55 (tel. 237 47), runs from the train station to the Águeda station to Figueira da Foz (5 per day, 2 1/4 hr., 585$) and Praia da Mira (5 per day, 45min., 450$).

Ferries: From Forte da Barra to São Jacinto (about 1 per hr., last one back at 7:30pm; 125$). Despite their tantalizing proximity, there is no service between São Jacinto and Barra—only from Forte da Barra.

Taxis: Res-Assillo (tel. 52 18 84).

Laundromat: Lavandaria União, Av. Dr. Lourenço Peixinho, 292 (tel. 235 56), near the train station. Wash and dry 350$ per kg. Open Mon.-Fri. 8am-1pm and 1:30-7:30pm, Sat. 8am-1pm.

Hospital: Av. Dr. Artur Ravara (tel. 271 67), near the park across the canal.

Emergency: tel. 115.

Police: Pr. Marquês de Pombal (tel. 211 37).

Accommodations and Camping

Pensões are generally uncrowded, but reservations can't hurt during festivals and in the dead of summer.

Pensão Palmeira, R. Palmeira, 7-11 (tel. 225 21). From R. Morais (perpendicular to R. José Estêvão, parallel to R. João Mendonça), turn left 1 bl. before the church. Cheerful rooms in a recently renovated establishment. Many rooms have TV. Singles 4500$, with bath 6500$. Doubles 5000$, with bath 7000$. Triples 8000$.

Residencial Estrêla, R. José Estêvão, 4 (tel. 238 18), on the *praça*. Grand stairway with oval skylight. Rooms are pleasing despite bare walls and floors. All rooms on top floor have low slopey ceilings; some are cramped. Bathrooms could use some Ajax and elbow grease. Singles 4000$. Doubles 5000$, with bath 6000$. **Residencial Santa Joana,** Av. Lourenço Peixinho, 227 (tel. 286 04), 1 bl. from the train station. Modern, appealing rooms have carpeting and furnishings in subdued colors. All have bath and winter heating; many have phone and TV. Singles 3500$. Doubles 5000$.

Camping: São Jacinto (tel. 482 84; fax 481 22), on the beach in the direction of Ovar. Sometimes crowded. 420$ per person, 355$ per tent, 360$ per car.

Food

Seafood restaurants are common but can be expensive. Scrounge for cheaper gruel around **Av. Dr. Lourenço Peixinho** and **R. José Estêvão.** Aviero is known for its *ovos moles* (sweetened egg yolks).

Restaurante Snack-Bar Amazonas, R. Capitão Sousa Pizarro, 15, Store #2 (tel. 276 60), on a street leading to the park. Serving prodigious portions day in and day out. One entree easily satisfies two diners. Half-portions available. Hamburgers 250-330$. Meatless *salada Niçoise* 450$. Open Mon.-Sat. 8am-midnight.

Restaurante Salimar, R. Combatentes da Grande Guerra, 6 (tel. 251 08), 1 bl. from Turismo. Nautical decor. Fragrant *bacalhau no churrasco* (barbecued cod) 880$. Bubbling orange-red broth swimming with seafood called *arroz de marisco* 1200$ (for 2 people 2000$). Open 9am-midnight.

Restaurante Zico, R. José Estêvão, 52 (tel. 296 49). The "in" place (by Aveiro standards). Especially favored by families and young folk. Pork on *prego de porco* (pork steak with fries, 600$) or try Portuguese shish kebab, *espetada mista no churrasco* (1/2-portion 630$). Save room for the caloric desserts. Open Mon.-Sat. 6am-midnight.

Sights and Entertainment

Across from Turismo in Pr. República, the regal **Paço do Concelho** (town hall) radiates a somber elegance with its 18th-century French windows and bell tower. **Igreja da Misericórdia** vies for attention with its simple yet striking blue façade. Seventeenth-century Lisboeta tiles cover the walls and complement the white window frames.

The real thriller is the **Museu de Aveiro,** in the old Convento de Jesus. While its assorted religious pieces aren't especially rousing, the exuberant, flamboyant gilt Baroque woodwork that covers the church interior is perhaps the most beautiful in Portugal. In 1472 King Afonso and the Infanta Joana, who wished to become a nun against his will, fought it out here. Beneath *azulejo* panels depicting the story, the beatified St. Joana's Renaissance tomb is one of the most famous works of art in the country. Sculpted in white marble in a checkered pattern reminiscent of the Indo-Portuguese style, the tomb is supported by the heads of four angels. (Open Tues.-Sun. 9am-12:30pm and 2-5pm. Admission 200$, seniors and students free.)

The nearby **Igreja das Carmelitas** displays 18th-century *azulejos* in a remarkably symmetrical interior. The ceiling of the nave and the chancel is decorated with paintings depicting the life of St. Teresa.

For four weeks beginning in mid-July, the salty city shakes with the **Festa da Ria** (river festival). Dancers groove on a floating stage in the middle of the *canal central*. The *festa* changes its tune in the third week, with the **Feira de Artesanato da Região de Aveiro (FARAV),** a mammoth region-wide handicrafts fair. It climaxes the final weekend in mid-August with a fabulous *moliceiro*, rowing, and sailing regattas.

The neighboring **beach** towns and the national park, **Dunas de São Jacinto** (sand dunes), merit daytrips. **Buses** leave for the beaches from a stop by the canal near the tourist office. The bus stops at Forte da Barra (free), where a **ferries** run to the town of **São Jacinto** (no cars in summer). There, a pathetic prehistoric *trolley carro* (tram pulled by a tractor, free) drives to the beach and the dunes. (See Practical Information: Buses and Ferries.) By foot, head directly away from the port (20min. to reach the beach). The dunes are 15 minutes to the right of the beach.

Viseu

Huddled in the wooded hills of Portugal's famous Dão wine country, the provincial city of Viseu preserves its old district of flowery balconies and narrow streets. In summer, locals congregate in chatty outdoor cafés on the shady *rossio*. Reasons to come here are few and far between, except as a convenient stopover en route to Spain.

Orientation and Practical Information

Viseu is 60km east of Aveiro. To get to the town center from the bus station, go right (uphill) along wide **Avenida Dr. António José de Almeida** until you reach the **rossio,** the main boulevard, bordered by a wall that shimmers with 19th-century *azulejos*. If arriving from the south, think about taking the express bus from Coimbra—the train is painfully slow.

Tourist Office: Av. Calouste Gulbenkian (tel. 42 20 14), uphill along the avenue from the *rossio*. Distributes decent maps and a colorful English booklet about the city (150$). English and French spoken. Open Mon.-Fri. 9am-12:30pm and 2:30-6pm.

Currency Exchange: Agência de Viagens Novo Mundo, Largo General Humberto Delgado, 2 (tel. 251 93), next to the post office. Open Mon.-Fri. 9am-12:30pm and 2-6pm.

Post Office: R. Combatentes da Grande Guerra (tel. 248 20), downhill from Turismo. Open for Posta Restante and **telephones** Mon.-Fri. 8:30am-6:30pm. **Postal Code:** 3500.

Telephones: At the **post office**. **Telephone Code:** 032.

Trains: The nearest stations are at Nelas (tel. 94 44 40) and Mangualde (tel. 62 32 22). Buses run to them.

Buses: Central de Camionagem, Av. Dr. António José de Almeida (tel. 270 85). Rodoviária to: Coimbra (5 per day, 2hr., 700$); Porto (2 per day, 2 hr., 780$); Vila Real (2 per day, 2 1/2 hr., 880$); Lisboa (5 per day, 5 hr., 1300$); Portalegre (1 per day, 5hr., 1380$).

Laundromat: Tinturaria a Nova Económica, Av. C. Gulbenkian, 32 (tel. 42 28 20), downhill from the tourist office. Dry cleaning only. 300$ per shirt. 500$ per pants. Open Mon.-Fri. 9am-12:30pm and 2:30-7pm, Sat. 9am-noon.

Hospital: Largo Dr. Eduardo Correia (tel. 42 41 24).

Emergency: tel. 115.

Police: S. Martinho (tel. 42 20 41).

Accommodations

This may be a town where you should grit your teeth and shell out a few extra *escudos* for someplace decent.

Residencial Bela Vista, R. Alexandre Herculano, 510 (tel. 42 20 67), 10min. uphill from Turismo. Hotel runs like a well-oiled machine. Ugly building. All rooms are quiet and have bath, carpeting, TV, phone, and a peculiar antiseptic smell. Winter heating. Singles 4000$. Doubles 7000$. Breakfast included.

Residencial Visiense, Av. Alberto Sampaio, 31 (tel. 42 19 00). From the bus station, turn right at the end of the *rossio*, then up some cement stairs on the left. Looks abandoned, but no! In fact bright and commodious, with carpeting and windows. Winter heating. Singles 3000$. Doubles 4500$, with bath 5000$. Breakfast included.

Camping: Fontelo-Orbitur (tel. 261 46), on the northeast edge of town. From the *rossio* follow R. Formosa to the Santa Catarina rotary. Continue straight on what is now N16-E80 or R. 5 de Outubro, and after roughly 200m take a sharp left (30min.). Fab facilities in an attractive woods. Small market and laundromat. 420$ per person, 355$ per tent, 360$ per car. Showers 60$.

Food

Affordable restaurants and bars litter the avenues up the hill west of the *rossio*. Misers shop for food at a super-duper **market** on Av. Capitan Silva Pereira. Bread and cheese shops are nearby.

Restaurante O Cortiço, R. Augusto Hilário, 36 (tel. 42 38 53), in the old town. The cuisine and rustic interior are *tipico*. Entrees 850-1300$. Open noon-3pm and 7-11pm.

Restaurante O Hilário, R. Augusto Hilário, 35 (tel. 265 87), next door. Menu longer than this book. Try *vitela con ervilhas à beirão* (veal with peas) 800$. Scrumpy appetizer *morcela caseira frita* (fried homemade blood pudding) 180$. Open 9am-10pm.

Sights

Most sights rest on the **Ardo da Sé** (cathedral square), built at the town's rocky pinnacle and surrounded by its oldest homes and buildings.

In the 16th century, Viseu nurtured one of the great Portuguese schools of painting. Fine canvases, including works by Vasco Fernandes, hang in the **Museu de Grão Vasco,** next to the cathedral. Observe divine 14th- and 15th-century wood and terracotta sculptures and 19th- and 20th-century paintings, including works by Alberto Sousa. (Open Tues.-Sun. 10am-12:30pm and 2-5pm. Admission 250$; students, seniors, and Sun. free.)

Next door, the solid **sé** dominates the old town. Extensively fiddled with since the 12th century, the interior bears Baroque altars and a Manueline ceiling of *trompe l'oeil* knotty cables. A staircase in the north transept ascends to the **coro alto** (upper choir), where there is a four-sided, 16th-century lectern of Brazilian jacaranda wood. Adjacent to the church, *azulejos* plaster the columned Renaissance **cloister.** Up the stairs to the left of the altar, the **tesouro** (treasury) rolls in wealth. Portugal's only combination museum guide-magician pulls escudos out of orifices as he whisks groups through the cathedral's collection of religious art. The priceless exhibits include a 12th-century Bible, astounding medieval statuettes, and a gruesome silver case displaying the 11th-century forearm bones of São Teotónio, the first Portuguese saint. (Treasury open 9am-noon and 2-5pm. Tour 100$. Cathedral open until 7:30pm.)

The glorious white façade and twin towers across from the cathedral belong to **Igreja da Misericórdia** (1775), the center of community social gatherings. In the evenings, young people pour out of the door between Corinthian columns to mingle in the parking lot.

Douro and Minho

Although their landscapes and shared Celtic past invite comparison with neighboring Galiza, Douro and Minho are more populated and faster developing, defying popular conception. Extending north from the Rio Douro and south from the frontier Rio Minho, these regions are relatively wealthy and correspondingly rich in monuments and historic towns. The Kingdom of Portugal came into being here when Afonso Henriques defeated the Moors in 1143 in Guimarães and declared himself ruler.

Hundreds of trellised vineyards in these fertile rolling hills grow grapes for the famous *porto* and *vinho verde* wines. Houses covered in brilliant tiles (called *azulejos*) dot the town streets. The traditional female costume—including layer upon layer of gold necklaces encrusted with charms—attests to the region's mineral wealth. The mild climate of this region is too cool to attract the beach crowd until July, and only a few ambitious travelers ever make it past Porto to the beautiful towns of the interior: Vila Nova de Cerveira, Braga, and Guimarães.

Porto (Oporto)

Portugal's second city is an attractive harbor town, despite being the industrial and commercial hub of the north. Porto is magnificently situated on a dramatic gorge cut by the Rio Douro, 6km from the sea. Granite church towers pierce the skyline, closely packed orange-tiled houses tumble down to the river, and three of Europe's most graceful bridges span the gorge above. Gérard Eiffel supplied the soaring lines of the oldest one, the Ponte de Dona Maria Pia, completed in 1877.

Like its name, Porto epitomizes the European port city—at once grimy and alluring, shabby and stately. The city's industrious reputation is illustrated by the proverb: "Coimbra sings, Braga prays, Lisboa shows off, and Porto works." For the 1415 invasion of Ceuta, residents slaughtered all their cattle, gave all the meat to the Portuguese fleet, and kept only the entrails (tripe) for themselves. The tasty and ever-popular dish *tripas à moda do Porto* commemorates the culinary self-sacrifice; to this day the people of Porto are known as "*tripeiros*" (tripe-eaters).

Porto's greatest fame, however, springs from the taste of its *vinho*. Developed by English merchants in the early 18th century, the Port wine industry across the River Douro in Vila Nova de Gaia drives the city's economy.

Orientation and Practical Information

Constant traffic and a chaotic maze of one-way streets fluster even the most easily oriented of travelers. At the heart of Porto, **Avenida dos Aliados** forms a long rectangle bordered on the north by **Praça General Humberto Delgado** and on the south by **Praça da Liberdade.** The **Estação São Bento** lies smack in the middle of town, just off Pr. Liberdade. The **Ribeira**, or Esplanade, district is a few blocks to the south, directly across the bridge from **Vila Nova de Gaia,** the *adega* area of wine houses.

Porto (Oporto) 509

Tourist Office: R. Clube dos Fenianos, 25 (tel. 31 27 40), on the west side of city hall. Doting staff doles out maps, accommodations advice, and info on wine production tours. Open Mon.-Fri. 9am-7pm, Sat. 9am-4pm, Sun. 10am-1pm; Oct.-June Mon.-Fri. 9am-12:30pm and 2-5:30pm, Sat. 9am-4pm.

American Express: Star Travel Service, Av. Aliados, 210 (tel. 200 36 37, 200 36 89), near the post office. Open Mon.-Fri. 9am-12:30pm and 2-6pm.

Currency Exchange: An office at the **airport** provides service Mon. 9am-8pm, Sat. 9am-4pm. Also, there's an **automatic exchange machine** (open 24 hrs.) on Pr. Liberdade, right outside Banco Espírito Santo e Commercial de Lisboa.

Consulates: U.K., Av. Boavista, 3072 (tel. 68 47 89). Handles Canadian and Commonwealth affairs. Open Mon.-Fri. 9:30am-12:30pm and 3-5pm.

Post Office: Pr. General H. Delgado (tel. 208 02 51), across from Turismo. Posta Restante 50$ per item. A fascinating collection of postal uniforms on display. Open for stamps Mon.-Fri. 8am-10pm. **Postal Code:** 4000.

Telephones: Pr. Liberdade, 62. Open 8am-11:30pm. Also at the post office. **Telephone Code:** 02.

Flights: Aeroporto Francisco de Sá Carneiro (tel. 948 21 41), accessible by bus #44 and 56 from Pr. Lisboa. **TAP Air Portugal,** Pr. Mouzinho de Albuquerque, 105 (tel. 608 02 00). To Lisboa (7500$) and Madrid (33,100$).

Trains: Estação de São Bento (tel. 200 27 22), centrally located 1 block off Pr. Liberdade. Receives some trains, mostly locals and nearby regional routes. ALFA runs buses to Viseu (3 per day, 3 1/2 hr., 850$). All trains pass through **Estação de Campanhã** (tel. 56 41 41), Porto's main station west of the center. Frequent connections to Estação São Bento (5min., 80$). To: Aveiro (19 per day, 1 1/2 hr., 290$); Viana do Castelo (13 per day, 2hr., 505$); Braga via Nine (9 per day, 2hr., 290$); Coimbra (12 per day, 2 1/2 hr., 725$); Lisboa (5 per day, 4 1/2 hr., 1520$); 8 ALFA per day, 3 1/4 hr., 2760$); Madrid via Entroncamento (2 per day, 12hr., 7100$); Paris (1 per day, 27hr., 18,500$). ALFA trains are both faster and more luxurious; some have bar service.

Buses: Garagem Atlântico, R. Alexandre Herculano, 366 (tel. 200 69 54). To: Coimbra (11 per day, 1 1/2 hr., 900$); Viseu (2 per day, 2hr., 780$); Lisboa (4 per day, 5hr., 1480$). **Estação de Camionagem** (tel. 200 61 21), 1 bl. from Av. Aliados. To Braga (every 1/2 hr., 1 1/2 hr., 520$) and Viana do Castelo (13 per day, 2hr., 600$). **Cabanelas,** R. Atenou Comercial do Porto (a.k.a. Travessa P. Manuel; tel. 200 43 98), 1 bl. from R. Sá da Bandeira. To Vila Real (7 per day, 4hr., 800$).

Public Transportation: *Passe Turistico* discount pass is available for the Porto transportation system (trolleys, buses, etc.). Good for 4 days 1210$; for 7 days 1680$.

Taxis: tel. 48 80 61. 24-hr. service. Taxi stand on Av. Aliados. Fare to youth hostel 500-600$.

English Bookstore: Livraria Diário de Notícias, R. Sá de Bandeira, 5, across from Estação São Bento. Good selection of travel books (including *Let's Go* guides), maps, and paperbacks. Open Mon.-Fri. 9am-12:30pm and 2:30-7pm; winter Mon.-Fri. 9am-12:30pm, Sat. 9am-1pm. **Livraria Britânico (The English Bookshop),** R. José Falcão, 184. Vast choice of paperbacks, plus hardcovers and mags. Textbooks for the studious. Open Mon.-Fri. 9am-7pm, Sat. 9am-1pm.

Laundromat: Penguin, Av. Boavista (tel. 69 50 32), in shopping center Brasília. Follow the same route to the youth hostel, but walk uphill 1 bl. further to the roundabout. The *only* self-service place in town. 1000$ per 5.5kg load. Open Mon.-Sat. 10am-11pm.

Public Showers and Toilets: Pr. Liberdade (in the middle of the garden in the traffic island), Pr. Batalha, and Largo do Viriato. Open 24 hrs.

Swimming Pool: Piscina Municipal, R. Almirante Leute do Rêgo (tel. 49 33 27). Admission 190$, Sat.-Sun. 230$. Open 10am-12:30pm and 2-6:30pm.

Drug Abuse Hotline: tel. 49 12 12.

24-hr. Pharmacy: tel. 166.

Medical Services: Hospital de Santo António, R. Prof. Vicente José de Carvalho (tel. 200 52 41). **Hospital de São João,** A1 Prof. Hernâni Monteiro (tel. 48 71 51). **Ambulance** (tel. 115).

Emergency: tel. 115.

Police: R. Alexandre Herculano (tel. 200 68 21).

Accommodations and Camping

Summer is a challenge. Most of the city's *pensões* lie west of Av. Aliados. Rates for singles are absolutely criminal, and the city's single HI youth hostel is on the small side.

Pousada de Juventude do Porto (HI), R. Rodrigues Lobo, 98 (tel. 606 55 35), about 2km from the center of town. Take bus #3, 19, 20, or 52 (10min., 125$) from the stop on the lower west end of Pr. Liberdade and hop off at R. Júlio Dinis (driver knows the hostel stop). Fine kitchen facilities and small cozy rooms. Game room and library for a plush touch. A constant flow of people keeps the place lively. If you arrive in town after 10am, don't bother—it'll be full. Three-day max. stay. Reception open 9-10am and 6pm-midnight. Curfew midnight. 1200$ per person; Oct.-June 950$. Breakfast included. Your reservation may be unexpectedly cancelled if a large group arrives.

Pensão São Marino, Pr. Carlos Alberto, 59 (tel. 32 54 99). From Turismo turn left on Travessa Cedofeita, and again onto R. Oliveiras; a few doors away from Banco Borges. Some of the bright, carpeted rooms look onto the *praça*. All have bath, phone, and winter heating. Singles 3000-4000$. Doubles 3500-5500$. Breakfast included.

Pensão Estoril, R. Cedofeita, 193 (tel. 200 51 52, 200 27 51), on a street radiating from Pr. Carlos Alberto. Colossal, bright rooms in an elegant building with sea-green carpeting. All rooms have radios and winter heating. Lounge with satellite TV. Singles with shower 2400$, with bath 2600$. Doubles with shower 3000$, with bath 3600$. Breakfast 280$.

Pensão dos Aliados, R. Elísio de Melo, 27 (tel. 200 48 53, fax 200 27 10), on the left as you walk up Av. Aliados. Living room with TV. Noise, noise, noise! Sumptuous rooms with telephones and wall-to-wall carpeting. All rooms with bath. Singles 4000$. Doubles 4500$. Breakfast included. In summer reserve several days in advance.

Residencial Vera Cruz, R. Ramalho Ortigão, 14 (tel. 32 33 96), on the side street before Turismo. The rooms exemplify Portuguese grandeur: dim, dank opulence. All rooms have phone, TV, and winter heating. Singles 5000$. Doubles with shower 5900$, with bath 6200$. Breakfast included.

Pensão Brasil, R. Formosa, 178 (tel. 31 05 16). From Av. Aliados take R. Passos Manuel (which begins just above the Pr. Liberdade) until Pr. Dom João I. Turn left on R. Sá de Bandeira, the street at the far end of the *praça*, and R. Formosa is the second right. Some of the cheapest rooms in Porto, but not the worst. All doubles have baths and are cleaner and brighter than singles. Winter heating. Singles 2500$, with bath 3500$. Doubles with bath 4500$.

Residencial Porto Rico, R. Almada, 237 (tel. 31 87 85). From Av. Aliados, go up R. Elísio de Melo after 2 left-hand blocks and turn right on R. Almada. Small, homey rooms, all with full bath, phone, and TV. Don't cross the landlady. Singles 4500$. Doubles 4800$. If your Portuguese is good, try to get the native-Portuguese price. Singles 4000$. Doubles 4500$.

Pensão Residencial Monte Sinai, R. Alexandre Herculano, 144-146 (tel. 200 82 18, 201 88 61), near the Batalha. These old high-ceilinged rooms come with full baths and phones. Front rooms look out onto a busy (read noisy) street. Singles 2500$. Doubles 3000$.

Residencial Grande Oceano, R. da Fábrica, 45 (tel. 28 24 47), 100m from Pl. Liberdade. No great ocean view. If you're lucky enough to get a room with a veranda you'll see the grimy side street below. Tackily colored rooms all have full baths. Singles 1500-2000$. Doubles 2000-2500$.

Camping: Prelada, Parque de Prelada (tel. 81 26 16), 5km from the beach. Take bus #6 from Pr. Liberdade. 390$ per person, 310$ per tent, 320$ per car. **Salgueiros** (tel. 781 0500), near Praia de Salgueiros in Vila Nova de Gaia, is less accessible, less equipped, but closer to the surf. 130$ per person and per tent, 100$ per car. Open May-Sept.

Food

The most colorful restaurants border the river in the Ribeira district, particularly on **Cais de Ribeira, Rua Reboleira,** and **Rua de Cima do Muro.** You'll find budget fare in much rowdier and seedier surroundings near Praça da Batalha on **Rua do Cimo de Vila** and **Rua do Cativo.** Cheaper eateries surround the **Hospital de Santo António** and **Praça de Gomes Teixeira,** a few blocks west of Pr. Liberdade. Adventurous gourmands savor the city's specialty, *tripas à moda do Porto* (tripe and beans).

An outdoor food and handicrafts **market** lines Cais de Ribeira daily (8am-8pm). Replete with flowers, fruit, and fish, the **Mercado de Bolhão** bustles on the corner of R. Formosa and R. Sá de Bandeira (See Accommodations: Pensão Brasil for directions; open Mon.-Fri. 7am-5pm, Sat. 7am-1pm).

Churrasqueira Moura, R. Almada, 219-223 (tel. 200 56 36). Toothsome, dirt-cheap meals (most under 1000$) include *frango no churrasco* (barbecued chicken with fries, 670$). Mongo jar of *Piri-piri* (hot sauce) to slather on the chicken. Open Mon.-Sat. 11:30am-10pm.

Restaurante Abadia, Trav. Passos Manuel, 22 (tel. 200 87 57). From the Turismo walk down Av. Aliados, take a left on R. Passos Manuel after Pl. D. Yoão I; at the end of the 1st street on the left. Waiters, white tablecloths, and the *menú* win. No niblets here—exuberant portions are all authentically Portuguese. *Bacalhau à gomes de sá* (1700$) or *marmota frita* (900$). Open noon-2pm and 7:30-10:30pm.

Máximo Restaurante-Café, R. José Falcão, 115 (tel. 38 04 24). From the bus station continue up the hill and turn right on R. José Falcão. White walls, black designer lamps and chairs, and green-gray marble tables could easily be in SoHo. The food is equally ambiguous: hamburgers (380-740$), salads (250-620$), daily specials (600-900$). No innards here. Open 8am-10:30pm.

Taberna Típica, R. Reboleira, 12 (tel. 32 03 73). Stone walls and nautical decor fit the riverside location. *Arroz de polvo* (octopus rice) is a specialty, and won't cost you an arm and a leg as it did the octopus (unless your leg is 850$). Satisfying *pratos do dia* 425-525$. Open Thurs.-Tues. 11am-3pm and 7pm-midnight, Wed. 11am-3pm.

Restaurante Boa Nova, Muro dos Bacalhoeiros, 115 (tel. 200 60 86), across the square from Típica. Serves wine from huge, wooden barrels. The dining room downstairs serves *carapaus fritos* (fried whitefish, 600$). Open Mon.-Sat. 9am-midnight.

Taberna do Bebobos, Cais da Ribeira, 21-25 (tel. 31 35 65). Stone walls and candlelight. *Lulas ribeirinho* (braised squid) 1200$. *Sardinhas* (grilled sardines) 750$. Open Mon.-Sat. noon-2:30pm and 7-9:30pm.

Brasa Churrasqueira, Pr. Batalha, 117, east of Estação São Bento at the end of R. 31 de Janeiro. Barbecue smoke marks the spot. Whole roasted chicken 600$, 1/2-chicken 450$. Open Wed.-Mon. 9am-10pm.

A Brasileira, R. Bonjardim, 18 (tel. 200 71 46), 1 bl. from Estação São Bento. The café interior is an enticing opera-set mixture of Art Deco and turn-of-the-century Edwardian. A great place for morning coffee and pastries. Open Mon.-Sat. 8am-9:30pm.

Sights

In the town center, monumental commercial buildings dwarf the bustle below. Domes, towers, and mansard roofs proclaim a late 19th-century verve, although the avenue was actually developed in the 1920s. The neo-Renaissance **prefeitura** tops off this *belle-époque* time capsule.

South past the alluring blue and yellow *azulejo* façade of **Igreja dos Congregados** is one of Porto's oldest residential districts. Ponderous and fortified, the heavy Romanesque husk of Porto's 13th-century **sé** glowers on a hill above the Ribeira. The Capela do Santíssimo Sacramento to the left of the high altar shines with solid silver and plated gold. During the Napoleonic invasion, crafty townspeople whitewashed the altar to protect it from vandalism. Drippingly ornate choir stalls fill the chancel. The late 14th-century cloister is wrapped in *azulejo* panels. (Open 9am-noon and 2-5:30pm. Admission to cloister 100$.)

Narrow R. Dom Hugo runs just behind the cathedral through the old city and past the **Casa-Museu de Guerra Junqueiro.** This house holds an unexceptional collection of 17th- to 19th-century furniture, pottery, and tapestries. (Open Tues.-Thurs. 10am-12:30pm and 2-5:30pm, Fri.-Sat. 10am-12:30pm and 2-6pm, Sun. 2-6pm. Admission 50$; students, seniors, and Sat.-Sun. free.) Out-of-town exhibits visit the museum space at the **Casa Dom Hugo** across the street. (Open Tues.-Sun. 9am-12:30pm and 2:30-5pm. Free.)

The narrow street in front of Igreja dos Grilos leads to R. Mouzinho da Silveira. From here follow signs to the **Palácio da Bolsa** (Stock Exchange), the epitome of 19th-century elegance. The exchange was built in 1834 over the ruins of the old convent of Igreja de São Francisco. Magnificent parquet floors of inlaid Brazilian wood smell of cedar and jacaranda. Almost elliptical in shape, the sparkling Sala Arabe took 18 years to decorate. Modeled after the Alhambra in Granada, its ornate gold and silver walls are covered with plaques bearing two Arabic inscriptions. The red squares read "Glory to Allah;" the blue ovals read "Glory to Queen Maria II." The tour visits the Pátio das

Nações, the former trading floor, but the action is closed to visitors. (Open Mon.-Fri. 9am-6pm, Sat.-Sun. 10am-noon and 2-5pm; Oct.-May Mon.-Fri. 9am-5pm, Sat.-Sun. 10am-noon and 2-4pm. Admission 300$, students free.)

Next door to the Bolsa stands **Igreja de São Francisco.** Originally Gothic but remodeled in the 17th and 18th centuries, the church glitters with one of the most elaborate gilded wood interiors in Portugal. (Open Tues.-Sat. 9am-5pm. Admission 100$.)

Home of the municipal archives and a tiny museum, the much-restored **Casa do Infante** (birthplace of Prince Henry the Navigator) stands south of Igreja de São Francisco past Pr. Infante Dom Henrique on R. Alfandega. (Open Mon.-Fri. 9am-noon and 2-5pm.) A few feet away, a marvelous quay filled with shops and restaurants skirts the **Ribeira** (Esplanade). To see more of the Ribeira, take trolley #1 from the nearby Igreja de São Francisco. The cars run along the river to the Foz do Douro, Porto's beach community.

Just up R. Taipas from the museum and church rises the 82m **Torre dos Clérigos** (Tower of Clerics). Built in the middle of the 18th century and long the city's most prominent landmark, its granite tower glimmers like a splendid processional candle. Mount the 200 steps for a vista of the city and the Rio Douro valley. (Open Mon.-Fri. 7:30-9:30am, 10:30am-noon and 3:30-8pm, Sun. 10am-1:15pm and 8:30-10:30pm. Free.)

On R. D. Manuel II, past the churches and a forested park, the **Museu Nacional de Soares dos Reis,** built in the 18th century as a royal residence, houses an exhaustive collection of painting and sculpture. In addition to its array of 19th-century Portuguese canvases, the museum exhibits works by the 19th-century sculptor Soares dos Reis, sometimes called Portugal's Michelangelo. Soares dos Reis cast identical twin statues of Dom Afonso Henriques; one lives here, the other in the 10th-century castle in Guimarães. His best-loved piece is of a boy frozen in marble; his most innovative is *O Desterrado* (The Exiled). The museum also contains an excellent group of Portuguese paintings that correspond to most of the 19th-century movements. Check out the early-late period of the geniusy young Henrique Pousão. (Closed for reconstruction.)

Most of Porto's *caves* or *adegas* (wine lodges) lead free tours of the wineries, where both red and white Port are aged and blended in huge oak barrels. After touring the processing and bottling factories, you'll sample various vintages in the tasting rooms, of course. Now as always, only human feet crush the grapes (á la Lucy and Ethel). A dash of brandy supplies the extra kick. Most of the 80-odd Port lodges ferment across the river, in **Vila Nova de Gaia.** (Walk across the lower level of the Dom Luís I bridge and take a sharp right.) The listings below are only a fraction of the countless *caves* open to the public. For more information, ask the tourist office or let your fingers do the walking.

> **Sandeman** (tel. 30 40 81), Largo Miguel Bombarda off Diogo Leite. Stocks the best Port and runs almost too-organized tours. All true MTV buffs make the pilgrimage for the grape-crushing music video. Reservations necessary for large groups. Open 9:30am-1pm and 2-5:30pm. Free.
>
> **Cálem** (tel. 39 40 41), Av. Diogo Leite, the first warehouse on the street. Multilingual guides. Tours 9:30am-5:30pm. Free.
>
> **Ferreira,** Av. Diogo Leite, 70 (tel. 370 00 10, ext. 315 Turismo). The crowds are smaller here than at Sandeman's and the Port is nearly as good. Open Mon.-Fri. 9:30am-12:30pm and 2-5pm and Sat. 9:30am-noon. Free.

Braga

In Braga, religion and commerce come wrapped in green hills with elegant vest-pocket parks. This is also the Portuguese city with the highest concentration of hair stylists. In recent years the city has undergone a face-lift with the works; modern bars and discos are moving in on Baroque turf. Yet, Braga still sniffs that it is "aristocratic to the backbone," and flaunts its pedigree to prove it.

In Roman times the city was an administrative center. After the Moors sacked the town in 716, it remained a backwater for four centuries until designated the seat of a newly created archdiocese. Since then it has become known amongst residents as "*a cidadé dos arcebispos.*" Archbishop Dom Diogo de Sousa built many of the city's Baroque churches, most of the buildings around the southeast, and turned 16th-century Braga into Portugal's Rome. Braga's people are considered by some the most pious, by others the most fanatic, and by all the most politically conservative in the country.

Orientation and Practical Information

Praça da República lies in the heart of the city. Wide **Avenida da Liberdade** runs north to south from the *praça* to the hills of Pinheiro da Gregória. Perpendicular to Av. Liberdade, Avenida Central runs along a tapering park leading into **Largo da Senhora-a-Branca.** If you follow R. do Souto, a pedestrian thoroughfare lined with luxe stores, it becomes **Rue Dom Diogo de Sousa** and then **Rua Andrade de Corvo**, leading straight to the train station.

Tourist Office: Av. Central, 1 (tel. 225 50), at the corner of Av. Liberdade. Large maps. English spoken. Open 9am-7pm; winter Mon.-Fri. 9am-7pm, Sat. 9am-5pm.

Currency Exchange: Hotel Carandá, Av. Liberdade, 96 (tel. 61 45 00), a 10-min. walk from the *praça*. No commission. Open 8am-10pm. **Banco Borges and Irmao,** Pr. República, across the street from Turismo. Open Mon.-Fri. 8:30am-2:30pm.

Post Office: Av. Liberdade (tel. 27 56 54), 2 bl. south of Turismo. Open Mon.-Fri. 8:30am-6:30pm, Sat. 9am-12:30pm. Open for Posta Restante (at the building's last door on the left around the corner on R. Dr. Gonçalo Sampaio) Mon.-Fri. 9am-noon and 2-5pm. **Postal Code:** 4700.

Telephones: In the post office building, and in a kiosk under the Arcada on the *praça*. **Telephone Code:** 053.

Trains: on Largo Estaçao (tel. 785 52). To walk 15min. to Turismo, turn right up R. Andrade Corvo and continue under the arch. The Pr. República hangs at the end of R. Souto; Turismo is across the avenue. Virtually everything requires a change of train at Nine, 1/2 hr. to the west. To: Barcelos (16 per day, 1hr., 200$); Porto (13 per day, 1 1/2 hr., 560$); Viana do Castelo (11 per day, 2hr., 380$); Vila Nova de Cerveira (8 per day, 3hr., 560$); Valença (8 per day, 3hr., 635$, with 2 daily connections to Vigo, Spain); Coimbra (12 per day, 4hr., 905$). At 7:45am and 5:20pm there's an **Inter-Cidades** train that goes with few stops to Porto and then to Lisbon.

Buses: Central de Camionagem (tel. 61 44 62), a few bl. north of the center. To reach the tourist office, as you leave the station from the upper level, follow Av. General Norton de Matos (on your left) up to a small square. Continue straight and R. Chãos ends at Pr. República. **Rodoviária.** To: Porto (every 1/2 hr., 1 1/2 hr., 530$); Guimarães (11 per day, 1hr., 300$); Campo do Gerês a.k.a. São João do Campo (5 per day, 1 1/2 hr., 450$); Coimbra (4 per day, 3hr., 1080$); Lisboa (4 per day, 8hr., 1720$); Faro (2 per day, 13hr., 2620$). **Hoteleira do Gerês,** a private company, sends blue and white buses. To Gerês (10 per day, 1 1/2 hr., 470$). A host of other private companies, with offices on the upper level of the bus station, also provide service.

English Bookstore: in **Feira Nova** supermarket (see Food listings).

Hospital: Hospital São Marcos (tel. 61 33 33), Largo Carlos Amarante.

Emergency: tel. 115.

Police: Campo de Santiago (tel. 61 32 50).

Accommodations and Camping

Braga resounds with *pensões*. The cheapest are concentrated around the **Hospital de São Marcos,** the more expensive around Av. Central. This conservative town may look upon single people, platonic couples, and those living in sin with suspicion.

Pousada de Juventude (HI), R. Santa Margarida, 6 (tel. 61 61 63). From Turismo walk down Av. Central until the tapering park peters out, then turn left on Largo Senhora-a-Branca. Popular with people traveling to or from Peneda-Gerês National Park. Relaxing, modern hostel with spotless kitchen and bath facilities. The warden is a god; he'll store your stuff if you go to Gerês. Reception open 9-10:30am and 6pm-midnight. 1150$ per person; Oct.-May 850$ per person. Breakfast included. Reservations recommended July-Aug.

Residencial dos Terceiros, R. dos Capelistas, 85 (tel. 704 66, 704 78), across the street from the Terceiros church and diagonally across the *praça* from Turismo. Simple, new, and neat. All rooms have full bath, some with TV. Singles 6000$. Doubles 6700$. Oct.-June 20: 4000$; 5300$. Breakfast included.

Residência Grande Avenida, Av. Liberdade, 738 (tel. 229 55, 230 99), around the corner from Turismo. Reception on 3rd floor. A classy *pensão* run by amiable folk. Elegant mirrors and furniture. Singles 2350$, with bath 3500$. Doubles 4000$, with bath 5500$. Breakfast included. Reserve 2 weeks ahead in summer.

Casa das Velinhas, R. São Bento, 23 (tel. 239 19), Largo Carlos Amarante. Only for the hardcore, the dim but decent rooms are the cheapest in town. The owners also run the restaurant and tavern downstairs. Hot water is limited, so bathe at odd hours. Singles 1500$. Doubles 2000$.

Residencial Inácio Filho, R. Francisco Sanches, 42 (tel. 238 49). From the *praça* walk down R. do Souto 1 bl.; R. Francisco Sanches is the 1st perpendicular pedestrian street. Small, well-kept, and conservative establishment. Doubles 3200$, with bath 3500$.

Hotel Carandá, Av. Liberdade, 96 (tel. 61 45 00, fax 61 45 50). ¡Splurge! Oh baby—melt in the comfort of these rooms with A/C, radios, TVs, phones, sparkling baths, and terrific views of the city and Bom Jesús. Singles 5300$. Doubles 7800$. Oct.-March: 4600$; 6500$. Breakfast included.

Camping: Parque da Ponte (tel. 733 55), 2km down Av. Liberdade from the center, next to the stadium and the municipal pool. Buses to and from station stop 20m from the entrance every 1/2 hr. Market and laundry facilities. 250$ per person, 180$ per tent, 205$ per car. Showers 115$. Electricity 160$.

Food

Braga has many scintillating cafés, several superb restaurants, and little in between. As usual, scout the old city for authentic Portuguese fare. A municipal **market** invades Pr. Comércio, two blocks from the bus station (open Mon.-Sat. 7am-3pm). This *praça* has a number of restaurants which serve typically heavy Minhoto dishes.

Groceries: Feira Nova, av. Padre Júlio Fragata (tel. 61 68 13). From Praça Comércio walk 20min. down Av. Central and continue straight as it becomes R. S. Vitor and R. D. Pedro V. Take a left onto Av. Padre Júlio Fragata. Big supermarket with good prices. Open Mon.-Fri. 10am-10pm, Sat. 9am-11pm, Sun. 9am-9pm.

Café Vianna, Pr. República, under the arcade across the *praça* from Turismo. A snappy café with pink marble and mirrors. Horrifyingly offensive statue of a black waiter wearing a red bow-tie, gloves, striped pants, and a vest—the only hint of diversity in this town. The café serves a real breakfast (350-700$), lunch, and dinner (entrees 300-1000$). At night it turns into a popular bar/disco, sometimes with live music. Open Mon.-Sat. 8am-2am; winter Mon.-Sat. 8am-8pm and 10pm-2am.

Restaurante A Marisqueira, R. Castelo, 3-15 (tel. 221 52), 1st right off R. Souto. Come for the simplicity and the rotating, enormous *prato do almoço* (lunch entree, 650$). Other tasty entrees 800-1000$. Open noon-11pm.

A Brasileira, Largo Barão de São Martinho, in the square before R. Souto. Romantic café studded with intelligentsia; the subject of a famous essay. No real meals. Open Mon.-Sat. 7am-midnight.

Restaurante tia Rosalina, R. dos Chãos, 25-31 (tel. 225 41). One-half block up on the left as you go from Turismo up the steep hill to the train station. This new restaurant has old stone walls, but the rustic atmosphere doesn't slow the waiters down. No-frills food. Tourist menu 1800$. Entrees 600-1400$. Open noon-10:30pm.

Sights and Entertainment

When Braga isn't ablaze with religious fervor or rollicking students, the city lolls in an affluent lull. Amidst one of Portugal's wealthiest cities, ultra-modern buildings jostle historical monuments. Braga's **sé,** Portugal's oldest cathedral, is a heavy granite structure modified many times since its construction in the 11th and 12th centuries. Hollow, pyramid-like ribs top unusual Baroque towers. The city had a 900th birthday bash for the altar on August 28, 1989. There are guided tours in Portuguese to its **tesouro, coro alto,** and **capelas.** Under the stale fluorescent hum of the treasury, several remarkable pieces hide among the usual crammed assortment of vestments and reliquaries (i.e., scraps of the dead bodies of saints). The tour begins in the **sala forte** (strong room), which contains the archdiocese's most precious paintings and relics. Foremost among these is the *Cruzeiro do Brazil,* the plain iron cross of Pedro Alvares Cabral's ship when he discovered Brazil in 1500; it was used in the first Portuguese mass in the New World. For formaldehyde fans, the treasury's real treat are the two *cofres cranianos* (brain boxes), one of which contains the 6th-century brain of São Martinho Dume, the first bishop of Braga. Rumor has it that an inner-circle of internationally acclaimed scientists are trying to clone a new São Martinho Dume from a few cells of the cerebral tissue. The *coro alto* (upper choir) has a pipe organ with 2424 fully functional pipes still used at Mass.

Adjacent to the church, off a Renaissance cloister, moulder two historic *capelas tumulares* (tomb chapels). The **Capela dos Reis** (Kings' Chapel) guards the 12th-century stone sarcophagi of Conde Dom Henrique and Dona Teresa, the dear parents of Portugal's first king, Dom Afonso Henriques. Less precious to Portugal's national soul but certainly more arresting are the mummified remains (note the protruding teeth and long fingernails) of a 14th-century archbishop. The Moorish-patterned **Capela de Nossa Senhora da Glória** next door protects the carved tomb of an archbishop. (Treasury and chapels open 8:30am-6:30pm; Oct.-June 8:30am-12:30pm and 1:30-5:30pm. Admission 200$.)

The street behind the chapel leads to a square flanked by the somewhat less morbid 17th-century **Capela de Nossa Senhora da Conceição** and the picturesque **Casa dos Coimbras.** The chapel has an interior faced with *azulejos* depicting the story of Adam and Eve and a finely carved *Entombment of Christ.* (Open Mon.-Fri. 9:30am-1pm and 2:30-7pm.)

The Rococo facade of **Igreja de Santa Cruz** gleams across from the monumental **Hospital de São Marcos** on Largo Carlos Amarante. Statues of the Twelve Apostles crown the latter's Baroque facade. Of a completely different spirit is the **Casa dos Crivos** (House of Screens) on R. São Marcos, with its Moorish latticed screen window coverings.

Curvaceous and colorful, the **Jardim de Santa Bárbara** prefaces an archaic set of free-standing arches. Around the corner in the spacious **Praça do Município,** the **Câmara Municipal** (City Hall) and **Biblioteca Municipal** eye each other from either side of a graceful fountain.

A block and a half down R. de Souto on the right stands the **Largo do Paço,** an archbishop's palace turned University of Minho administration building. The **Salão Medieval,** a stone-walled auditorium, looks like something out of King Arthur's court, with heavy black iron chandeliers hanging from ornate ceilings. (Open Mon.-Fri. 9am-noon and 2-8pm.)

Braga's most famous landmark is actually 5km out of town. Here, on a hillside carpeted in greenery, the 18th-century **Igreja do Bom Jesús** overlooks the city. The main attraction here is not the chapel itself, but the long, slow walk up the granite-paved pathway that forks into two zigzagging stairways. For no money down, you get 1) a solemn climb, and 2) some blaring commercialism at the top. A funicular ferries cheaters up and down for 60$. From Braga, buses labeled "#02 Bom Jesús" depart from the stop in Largo Carlos Amarante, in front of Hospital de São Marcos (at 10 and 40min. past the hr.; 175$, book of 10 550$). The bus stops at the bottom of the stairway and the funicular.

The **Mosteiro de Tibães** is lost in an unspoiled forest. In contrast to the resplendent monasteries of Alcobaça and Batalha, this 11th-century Benedictine monastery reflects centuries of neglect. Stone tombs rattle eerily underfoot the weathered **claustro.** Adjoining the cloister is a magnificently preserved **igreja,** with high, narrow, cylindrical ceiling and ornate high altar. Through the kitchen and the back woods is another chapel. (Open Tues.-Sun. 9am-noon and 2-7pm. Guided tour free.) A city bus rides 6km from Braga to the monastery. Buses labeled "Sarrido" leave from Pr. Conde de Agrolongo, 1 block west up R. Capelistas from Pr. República. The stop itself is in front of the "Arca-Lar" store, with the schedule posted (roughly every 2hr., 165$).

Entertainment

Braga's nightlife belies the city's conservative reputation. Nothing gets started before 10pm. Discos, pubs, and cafés clutter **Avenida da Liberdade;** try **Trigonometria** for one. Farther down under the Hotel Turismo is the disco **Club '84.** College students crowd these popular spots after they finish their homework.

Braga's Holy Week, at once solemn and festive, features a great religious procession similar to the more famous one in Sevilla, Spain. There's a busy schedule of processions and concerts all week long. The streets are decorated entirely in purple and black. (Ask at Turismo for a detailed program.) During the **Festival de São João** (June 23-24), the entire main avenue becomes a makeshift disco carnival of dancing, drinking, popsicle-eating celebrants. Be sure to polish your air-cushioned, squeaky plastic mallet before this festival. Everyone joins in the squeak 'n peep rubber-duck melée on the last night of the festival.

Near Braga: Parque Nacional Peneda-Gerês

An unspoiled expanse of mountains, lakes, vegetation, and wildlife, **Parque Nacional de Peneda-Gerês** occupies the Vale do Alto Minho just south of the Spanish border at Portela do Homem, 43km north of Braga. You'll have to trust Turismo that deer, wild boars, and wild ponies make their home here—they're far too clever to come out for a snapshot. We didn't see any either—the whole thing could be a hoax. Hiking routes between the main village of Gerês and the *miradouro* (lookout point) of Pedra Bela (6 1/2km) twist past glistening waterfalls and natural pools. On summer weekends, a bus connects several of the villages that inhabit the huge park.

The Hoteleira do Gerês bus company runs excellent **minibus tours** that pass through key sights in the park (5 per day, 3 different circuits; 2-4 1/2 hr.; 650-800$). Hoteleira's office is in the village Gerês (tel. 391 35), across from the Hotel Parque and a few blocks down from Turismo. Inquire there or at their office/garage in Braga at Rua dos Chãos, 38 (tel. 220 61).

A line of *pensão-restaurantes* stapled together forms the village of **Gerês.** In addition to their straight-room prices, most offer *diário completo* (rooms plus three meals a day) at excellent rates. **Pensões Príncipe** and **Ponte** (tel. 39 11 21), two neighboring buildings under the same management, offer clean, undistinguished digs with wood floors. (Singles 2200$. Doubles 3500$, with bath 5000$. Breakfast included. *Diário completo* 5000$. Open May-Oct.) About a 15-minute walk downhill from the tourist office, **Pensão Casa da Ponte** (tel. 39 11 25; no relation to Pensão Ponte) has dark, heated rooms with carpet and bath. This is one of the few *pensões* in Gerês open all year. (Singles 3900-4200$, doubles 4700$-5200$. Breakfast included. *Diário completo* option.)

The **tourist office** (tel. 39 11 33) encamps in the horseshoe arcade. (Open Mon.-Sat. 9am-12:30pm and 2:30-6pm, Sun. 9am-12:30pm.) The multilingual staff has an accommodations list, but the National Park administration office up the street upstages them with their better trail map and more thorough information. (Open Mon.-Fri. 9am-noon and 2-5pm.) Gerês' **post office,** downhill from Turismo, has **telephone** booths. (Open Mon.-Fri. 9am-12:30pm and 2-7:30pm.) The **postal code** is 4845 and its **telephone code** 053. The nearest **hospital** (tel. 64 71 01) is in the town of Vieira do Minho. The **police** answer to 39 11 37. The private **bus** company Hoteleira do Gerês (tel. 220 36) runs buses to Braga's bus station (every hr., last departure for Braga at 9pm; 1 1/2 hr., 435$).

An **HI Youth Hostel** (tel. 353 39), called Vilarinho das Furnas, borders the park 16km east of the main village in **São João do Campo** (a.k.a. **Campo do Gerês** in maps and bus schedules). On a clear day, you can see Braga and Bom Jesús from the mountaintop—simply breathtaking. (1200$ per person. Breakfast included. Lunch or dinner 500$.) Portuguese youth groups sometimes book the place solid in summer, so call ahead. Rodoviária Nacional **buses** (5 per day, 1 1/2 hr., 465$) connect São João do Campo with Braga, but no direct link with Gerês exists. From there, you must take a blue-and-white Braga-bound bus, get off at the Rio Caldo stop, and catch Rodoviária's bus coming from Braga to São João do Campo.

The park's spartan **campground,** in Vidoeiro (tel. 39 14 93), teeters off a steep, poorly maintained mountain road often inaccessible to campers and trailers. (324$ per person, 216-540$ per tent, 324$ per car. Open mid-April to Oct.)

Guimarães

Guimarães (an hour southwest from Braga by car) is a mid-sized country town known throughout Portugal as the "cradle of the nation." In 1143 Dom Afonso Henriques proclaimed himself the first King of Portugal after defeating the Moors. Unfortunately, this nativity also signaled a return to a time when the Moorish enlightenment would no longer hold sway in Iberia.

Guimarães predates the kingdom of Portugal by a couple of centuries. The Galician countess Mumadona founded a Benedictine monastery here in the 10th century and supervised the construction of the **castelo** (castle), the keep of which remains intact. This impressive granite structure perches on a rocky hill near the center of town. It's viewed as Portugal's foremost historical monument because Dom Afonso Henriques emerged from the womb within its walls. (Open Tues.-Sun. 10am-12:30pm and 2-5pm. Free.)

While the castle protected its inhabitants from the Normans and the Moors, it provided few creature comforts. So the Dukes of Bragança, the local noble family of a less bellicose age, built a palatial manor house, the **Paço dos Duques de Bragança** next door. The elegant 15th-century *paço,* modeled after the late Gothic palaces of Northern Europe, was toasted as one of the finest noble houses in Portugal. The crown confiscated the property in 1483 after the second Duke of Bragança died, then left it to rot for 200 years. By the 17th century, the local Capuchin friars received permission to use its dilapidated stones for the construction of their monastery. Scavenging and vandalism continued until 1880 when the government declared the *paço* a historic monument and began restoration. Inside, there's a museum of 15th-century Portuguese aristocratic life and an astonishing collection of furniture, silverware, crockery, and weapons. Don't miss the 15th-century D'Aubisson tapestries. In the boat-roofed banquet hall, tables that once seated 15th-century nobles now serve the presidents of Portugal at their regular conventions. During dinnertime, at least a quarter of the 39 fireplaces burn in order to heat the chilly building. (Open 10am-5:30pm. Admission 300$, Oct.-May 200$; students, seniors, and Thurs. free. Mandatory tour is available in various languages.)

The **Museu de Alberto Sampaio,** located in the Renaissance cloister of the **Igreja Colegiada de Nossa Senhora da Oliveira,** is back in the center of town. The church entrance fronts an arched medieval square and outdoor temple. Like the castle, the church was commissioned by Mumadona, that scandalously ambitious 10th century Galician countess. (Open Tues.-Sun. 9am-noon and 3-6pm. Free.) Next door, the museum collects late Gothic and Renaissance art. Its star is a massive bas-relief triptych in gold-plated silver from the 14th century. The 15th-century Gothic chapel of São Braz holds the granite tomb of Dona Constança de Noronha, first duchess of Bragrança. The courtyard *oliveira* (olive tree) symbolizes the patron saint of Guimarães. (Open Tues.-Sun. 10am-12:30pm and 2-5pm. Admission 200$. Students, seniors, and Sun. morning free.)

Guimarães offers few budget accommodations or restaurants; try not to spend the night. If you get stuck or are suddenly hit by a fit of narcolepsy, a bunch of church *padres* run the boarding house-like **Casa de Retiros,** R. Fransisco Agra, 163 (tel. 51 15 15). From Turismo, head through Pr. Toural and straight up R. de Santo Antônio; R. Francisco Agra is narrow and curves left when you reach the traffic circle. The tidy bedrooms come with full bath, radio, phone, heating, and crucifix. The 11:30pm curfew isn't negotiable, and unmarried couples might not be permitted to share quarters. (2000$ per person. Breakfast included.) For a refreshment in summer try the outdoor **café** (open 9am-10pm) under a canopy of trees in the Jardim de Alameda, in front of the Turismo. **Restaurante Alameda** serves full meals in a spiffy dining room overlooking the Jardim (entrees 700-1200$, tourist menu 1500$).

The **tourist office** (tel. 41 24 50), hidden by signs pointing to various cities, is on Av. da Resistência á Fascismo, facing Pr. Toural. The maps and the guides are absolutely free. (Open 9am-12:30pm and 2-5:20pm.) Find the **post office** at Rua de Santo António, 89 (tel. 41 50 32; open Mon.-Fri. 8:30am-6:30pm, Sat. 9am-12:30pm). The **postal code** is 4800 and the **telephone code** is 053. Call the **hospital**, on Rua Dr. Joaquim de Meira, at tel. 51 26 12, **emergencies** at tel. 115, and the **police** at Rua Moleirinho (tel. 51 33 34).

To get to the tourist office from the **bus station** (tel. 51 62 29), follow the long street on the bank in front of you, Av. de Londres, then turn right at the intersection with a small garden in the traffic island. Rodoviária Nacional dispatches buses every half hour (last one at 8:25pm) for Braga (45min., 300$). Several private companies go everywhere else. The **train station,** a 10-minute walk south of Turismo down Av. Afonso Henriques (tel. 41 23 51), has hourly service to Porto (17 per day, 1 3/4 hr., 405$).

Barcelos

There are two and only two reasons to visit this little town, 22km west of Braga. 1) The **Milagre do Galo** (Miracle of the Cockerel), which occurred in the 14th century; and 2) the **Feira de Quinta Feira** (Thursday Fair).

In the 14th century, a pilgrim on his way to Compostela was unfairly accused of theft and condemned to death. He panicked, wept, then prayed to São Tiago (Saint James). "The judge is about to feast on roast capon," Saint James curiously replied. In a fit of inspiration and valor, the pilgrim rushed to the judge's house and exclaimed, "By my innocence, may this cockerel stand up and crow!" Of course it did. The judge went hungry, the pilgrim went free, and the cock of Barcelos became an unofficial national symbol. The *galo de Barcelos,* black or red with floral designs, comes in shrink-wrapped packages of all shapes and sizes with "tourist" stamped on the front. The **handicraft center** (tel. 31 18 82) sells pottery, baskets, and embroidery (most all in the likeness of the legendary fowl) from the 15th-century *Torre de Menagem* (Homage Tower) in the main *plaça*. (Handicraft center open Fri.-Sat. 9am-12:30pm and 2-7pm.) The grateful pilgrim erected the cross to São Tiago now in the **Museu Arqueológico**. (Open 10am-noon and 2-6pm.)

If you come to see the cock, come on a Thursday. The largest open-air market in the country is held in the central, sprawling Campo da República. Sadly, these **Thursday Fairs** have become over-commercialized and kitschy. Wheelers and dealers of clothes, shoes, ceramics, rugs, and fresh fruit do what they can to bring the town to life (6am-7pm).

Pensão Bagoeira, Av. Dr. Sidónio Pais, 57 (tel. 81 12 36) has cheery if noisy rooms (singles 3000$, breakfast included). The cheaper **Residencial Arantes,** Av. da Liberdade, 35 (tel. 81 13 26), near Largo Bom Jesús de Cruz, has spotless rooms with carpeting and comfortable beds. (Singles with shower 2800$, with bath 3600$. Doubles with shower 3600$, with bath 4750$. Breakfast included.) If local food gives you a *frisson,* munch at **Restaurante Bagoeira,** Av. Dr. Sidónio Pais, 57 (tel. 81 12 36), in the eponymous *pensão*. Entrees such as *rojoes* or *cabrito assado* run 900-1200$. (Open 8am-10:30pm.)

The **tourist office** is diagonally across from the church on the *praça*, in the very *Torre de Menagem* which contains the handicraft center. (Open Mon.-Wed., Fri. 9am-12:30pm and 2-7pm, Thurs. 9am-5:30pm, Sat.-Sun. 9am-1pm and 2-7pm; Oct.-May 9am-12:30pm and 2-5:30pm.) The **post office** is on Rua Cândido dos Reis, 28 (tel. 81 24 44), off Av. da Liberdade. (Open Mon.-Fri. 9am-12:30pm and 2-5:30pm.) The **postal code** is 4750 and the **telephone code** is 053. Call the **hospital** on Av. Combatentes da Grande Guerra at 81 071 through 81 073. Dial 115 in an **emergency**. The **police** swing their sticks next to the Rodoviária bus office (tel. 81 22 00).

Buses are the quickest and most convenient way to get to Barcelos. Find the bus stop by the Rodoviária office (tel. 814 310) on Av. Dr. Sidónio Pais, which faces the large fairground. To get to Turismo, turn right as you get off the bus and make a left at the square. Buses connect Barcelos to Braga (every hr., 1/2 hr., 300$). The only way to reach Viana do Castelo is by the bus to Esposende (7 on Thurs.); from there Auto-Viação do Minho runs up the coast to Viana (9 per day, 30min., 325$) and south to Porto

(4 per day, 1 1/4 hr., 530$). The **train station** is located at the end of Av. Alcaldes de Faria, which becomes Av. dos Combatentes da Grande Guerra as you approach downtown. It's a good half-hour walk: head left around the fairground onto Av. da Liberdade to the square. Trains run to Braga via Nine (13 per day, 1 1/4 hr., 200$) and Viana do Castelo (15 per day, 1hr., 300$).

Viana do Castelo

If you think there are no beach-seeking tourists on the Costa Verde, think again, bucko. Although July and August are a scene, you can usually catch the heat and just miss the crowds in June and September. The town is immaculate; hardly a street lacks some assiduous youth washing the ancient walls or sweeping the walk. Besides the city beach, there is easy access to the less crowded sandy stretches north and south of town. Yes, come to Viana—it has the lively social scene of a beach town without the rampant commercialism of a seaside resort.

Orientation and Practical Information

Avenida dos Combatentes da Grande Guerra, the main avenue, glitters from the **train station** south to the **port,** on the Rio Lima. The **old town** lies east of the avenue; to the west lie the fortress and sea. Most food and accommodations are dispensed from side streets off Av. Combatentes.

Tourist Office: Pr. Erva (tel. 82 26 20), 1 bl. east of Av. Combatentes. From the main station take the 3rd left, then a sudden right. Maps and lists of lodgings in English and French. (Handicraft center connected to the office by courtyard.) Open Mon.-Fri. 9am-6pm, Sat. 9:30am-6pm, Sun. 9:30am-12:30pm; Sept.-June Mon.-Fri. 9am-12:30pm and 2:30-6pm, Sat. 9am-12:30pm and 2:30-6pm, Sun. 9:30am-12:30pm.

Currency Exchange: Automatic exchange machine outside Caixa Geral de Depósitos on the main boulevard. **Banco Nacional Ultramarino,** Pr. da República, on the main square. Open Mon.-Fri. 8:30am-3:30pm.

Post Office: Av. Combatentes (tel. 82 27 11), across from the train station. Open Mon.-Fri. 8:30am-6:30pm, Sat. 9am-12:30pm. **Postal Code:** 4900.

Telephones: In the post office. **Telephone Code:** 058.

Trains: (tel. 82 22 96), at the northern end of Av. Combatentes, directly under Santa Luzia hill. To get to Turismo, walk down the street, turn left after 4 blocks onto R. Picota, and take the 1st right. To: Vila Nova de Cerveira (7 per day, 1hr., 240$); Barcelos (15 per day, 1hr., 220$); Porto (12 per day, 2 1/2 hr., 505$); Vigo, Spain, via Valença (2 per day, 2hr., 1070$).

Buses: Rodoviária (tel. 250 47). To Braga (8 per day, 1 1/2 hr., 530$). **AVIC** (tel. 82 97 05) and **Auto-Viação do Minho** (tel. 82 88 34) face off on Av. Combatentes. To: Lisboa (2 per day, 6hr., 2000$); Porto (every hr., 1 1/2 hr., 660$). Except for *expressos* (which leave from Av. Combatentes), all buses leave from **Central de Camionagem,** on the eastern edge of town, 15-min. walk to the train station. From the bus station walk left, passing through a pedestrian underpass, or take the bus (100$).

Hospital: Av. Abril, 25 (tel. 82 90 81).

Emergency: tel. 115.

Police: R. de Aveiro (tel. 82 88 41).

Accommodations and Camping

Aside from during the week of the Romaria de Nossa Senhora da Agonia in mid-August, accommodations in Viana are easy to find but not particularly cheap. Most young people stay in private homes that charge reasonable rates, especially for longer stays. Many of the small, informal *pensões* (usually a few rooms above the family restaurant) are slightly cheaper but far worse in quality.

Residência Viana Mar, Av. Combatentes, 215 (tel. 82 89 67). Large, clean, and efficient. Some noise from the avenue may filter into the rooms. Telephone, TV, and winter heating. Singles 3500$, with bath 6000-7000$. Doubles 3750$, with bath 5500$. Triples with bath 7000-8500$. Oct.-May: 3000$, with bath 4500$; 3500$, with bath 5000$; 6000-7500$.

Pensão Guerreiro, R. Grande, 14-1° Andar (tel. 220 99), on the corner of Av. dos Combatentes and R. Grande. Rooms are old with high ceilings and big windows. Hot and cold water. Singles 1800$. Doubles 3000$. Sept.-June: 1500$; 2500$.

Residência Laranjeira, R. General Luís do Rego, 45 (tel. 82 22 61), 1 block down from the train station on your left. Sparkling large rooms. Winter heating. Doubles 5300-6000$. Triples 7000-7950$. Winter:4500-5500$; 6000-7000$.

Pensão Vianense, Av. Conde da Carreira, 79 (tel. 82 31 18), the first right out of the train station. Small, plain rooms with cracked paint and pale wood furniture. Above a restaurant of the same name. Singles 2250$. Doubles 3500$. Oct.-May 1500$; 2500$. Breakfast included.

Pensão Residencial Magalhães, R. Manuel Espregueira, 62 (tel. 82 32 93), 3 blocks from the train station on the left. English-speaking management runs a great *pensão* with spacious, carpeted rooms and a clean but antiquated common bath. Singles 3000$, with bath 4000$. Doubles 3900$, with bath 4700$. Triples 5100$, with bath 6500$. Nov.-June: 2250$, with bath 3000$; 3000$, with bath 3500$; 4000$, with bath 5000$.

Camping: Two campsites wash up near the Praia do Cabedelo, Viana's ocean beach across the Rio Lima. Take the 60$ ferry and hike the 1km from the terminal, or hop a "Cabedelo" bus (80$) from the bus station or behind the train station near the funicular stop. **INATEL** (tel. 32 20 42), off Av. Trabalhadores. July-Aug.: 180$ per tent, 300$ per trailer. Oct.-May 105$; 215$. June and Sept.: 150$, 260$. Showers 70$. Tents available for rent. Open Jan. 16-Dec. 15. **Orbitur** (tel. 32 21 67). Closer to the beach, better equipped, and a lot more expensive. 420$ per person, 355$ per tent, 360$ per car. Showers 60$. Open Jan. 16-Dec. 15.

Food

Bloodthirsty diners should attempt one of the heftier local specialties, *arroz de sarabulho,* rice cooked in blood (it sounds just terrible but looks "seasoned") served with sausages and potatoes. A less gross specialty is *arroz de marisco,* rice cooked with different kinds of shellfish. The large municipal **market** is in Pr. Dona Maria II, several blocks east of Av. Combatentes. (Open Mon.-Sat. 8am-3pm; Friday is the big day.)

Groceries: Brito's-Auto-Serviço, R. Manjovos, 31 (tel. 231 51). From the train station walk down Av. Combatentes; take the 5th side street on the right. Everything from flatware and plastic flora to water and frozen dinners. Good array of wine. Open 8am-12:30pm and 2:30-8pm.

Baskin-Robbins, Pr. Erva, 1 bl. east of Av. Combatentes, across the *praça* from Turismo. Ice cream.

Restaurante "O Vasco," R. Grande, 21 (tel. 246 65), on the side street across from Pensão Guerreiro. Until the food arrives, the highly white interior (walls, tables, and chairs) and glass ornaments look like the local clinic. Specialties such as *polvo cozido* (boiled octopus) and *rojoes à moda do Minho* (Minhoized mixed roast meat) are a pennypincher's wet dream (entrees 550-1000$). Open 11:30am-12:30pm.

Restaurante Diplomático, Av. Rocha Páris, 202 (tel. 256 56), 3 bl. east of Av. Combatentes. Filled with indulging peoples. Entrees 900-1200$, but the complete *prato do dia* only 500-750$. Open 8am-midnight.

Dolce Vita, R. Poço, 44 (tel. 248 60), across the *praça* from Turismo, hence the tourists. Viana's answer to pizza or spaghetti (475-1100$). Portuguese dishes 900-1150$. Open noon-10pm; off-season noon-3pm and 7-10pm.

Sights

Even in a country famous for charming squares, Viana's **Praça da República** is exceptional. In the center of the recently repaved square spouts a 16th-century fountain encrusted with sculpture and crowned by a sphere bearing a Cross of the Order of Christ. The small **Paço do Concelho** (1502), formerly the town hall, seals the square to the east, while diagonally across stands **Igreja da Misericórdia** (1598, rebuilt in 1714). Granite caryatids support its playful, flowery façade.

The **Museu Municipal,** west of Av. Combatentes da G. Guerra on Largo São Domingos, occupies the former 18th-century palace of Dr. Barbosa Maciel. Dr. Barbosa contracted Policarpo de Oliveira Bernardes, the most sought-after *azulejo* painter of his day, to design the allegorical muraled interior. Amid the small museum's array of 18th-century furnishings and artwork, its prize possession is the collection of famous, coveted *cerâmica de Viana*. To judge from his collection of crucifixes and pietàs, the illustrious doctor seems to have had a fascination with blood and gore. (Open Tues.-Sun. 9:30am-noon and 2-5pm. Admission 110$. Tour included.)

The cliff-like **colina de Santa Luzia** rises north of the city, crowned by an early 20th-century neo-Byzantine church. The view of the town and Rio Lima is glorious. Those with a keen sense of direction can shorten the steep walk by taking the stairs that link some of the switchbacks in the road. To reach the hilltop, take either the long stairway or the funicular, next to each other 200m behind the train station. (Walk through the station, over the tracks, and up a set of stone steps.) Two cars inch their way up and down (9am-7pm every hr. in the morning, 2 per hr. in the afternoon; 60$). The basilica sheds the solemnity of most churches; its vibrant interior seems more regal than religious.

For a better view of the ocean visit **Castelo de S. Tiago da Barra.** From the train station take the second right off Av. Combatentes (R. Gen. Luis do Rego) and follow this street five blocks until it hits a field. Built in 1589 by Spanish Philip II, the walls of the *castelo* rise to the left, from which you can gaze at the harbor and ocean.

Hungry insects prowl the nearby gravelly **praia** on Rio Lima. For more enjoyable sunbathing and swimming, take the **ferry** behind the parking lot at the end of Av. Combatentes to the ocean beach Praia do Cabedelo. (Ferries every 1/2 hr. May-June and Oct.-Dec. 7:50am-7:55pm; July-Sept. until midnight; Jan.-April until 5pm; 60$ per ride.)

Although Cabedelo is OK, true beach connoisseurs abandon Viana altogether for the beaches to the north. Fortunately, Viana puts you within easy daytrip range of **Vila Praia de Âncora, Moledo,** and **Caminha,** some of the cleanest and least crowded beaches on the Costa Verde. The coastal rail line has frequent stops as far north as Vila Nova de Cerveira and Valença. Vila Praia de Âncora, the largest and most popular of the three adjacent beaches is also the closest to Viana (16km), with two rail stops, the main "Âncora" station and the "Âncora-Praia" *apeadeiro* (just a platform, not a full station) where the beach beckons just a few blocks away. Moledo and Caminha, just two and four local stops north of Âncora, respectively, are equally gorgeous but less popular (because the train lets you off 1-2km from the sand). Creepingly slow *suburbano* (local) **trains** serve all three beach towns; regional trains stop only at Âncora-Praia (7 per day, 25min., 135$).

Vila Nova de Cerveira

Tiny, tranquil Vila Nova de Cerveira gazes at Spain from the south bank of the Rio Minho. While the once-strategic town offers little more than lovely scenery, its youth hostel makes an excellent base for trips to the handsome beaches of Âncora, Moledo, and Caminha, and to the even smaller towns of the Alto Minho interior.

Two of Vila Nova's landmarks stand on the steep hills above the town: a whimsical sculpture that looks like Bambi and the ruins of the **Monte Picoto monastery** and chapel. Ballsy trekkers can reach both via hiking trails. Both deer and monastery are by the noted Portuguese architect and sculptor José Rodrigues, who was associated with the nearby art school. Back in town, the luxe Pousada Dom Dinis occupies a runt of a **castelo** that originally sprung up in the 16th century as a look-out over Spain.

The pristine, modern **HI youth hostel,** Largo 16 de Fevreiro (tel. 961 13), has large rooms, a riverview veranda, a grassy patio, TV with VCR, and kitchen rights for guests. Angela, the cheerful warden, could easily have trained the Turismo staff. (Reception open 9am-noon and 6pm-midnight. 1000$ per person. Breakfast included. Reservations recommended.) From the train station turn left, then left again at the Fonseca Porto minimarket opposite the TURILIS office (20min.). The nearest **campground** (tel. (058) 92 24 72) digs in 4km away in Vilar de Mouros, an out-of-the-way village called the "Woodstock" of Portugal, betwixt here and Caminha. (350$ per person, 300$ per tent, 250$ per car.) The most popular alimentary scene is the **Café-Restaurante A Forja** on R. 25 de Abril (entrees 650-1000$; open Tues.-Sun. 8am-11pm).

Vila Nova's **tourist office** is at R. Antônio Douro (tel. 79 57 87), kitty-corner from Igreja de São Roque. From the train station turn left and then left again at the first and only major intersection. Grab a map from the clueless staff and flee. (Open Mon.-Sat. 9:30-11:30am and 2:30-6pm.) The **post office** (tel. 79 51 11) is next door to the bank on Pr. Alto Minho (open 9am-12:30pm and 2:30-6pm). The **postal code** is 4920; the **telephone code** is 051. Looking for the **hospital** (tel. 79 53 51)? It's on the main highway past the edge of town. The **police** (tel. 79 51 13) preside over Largo 16 de Fevreiro. Take the last street on the left as you skip out of town.

The **train station** (tel. 952 65), off the highway 1/2km east of town is a conduit to: Valença (9 per day, 25min., 130$, with 2 daily connections to Vigo, Spain); Vila Praia de Âncora (9 per day, 40min., 150$); Viana do Castelo (9 per day, 1hr., 240$); Porto (9 per day, 2 1/2 hr., 680$). Three private **bus** companies serve the same route as the train—upriver to Valença and down the coast to Porto. **Turilis** buses leave from the Turilis travel agency (tel. 79 55 50) across the highway from the youth hostel. **AVIC** and **A. V. Minho** depart from Café A Forja, Av. 25 de Abril (tel. 79 53 11), between the hostel and the town center. All to: Valença (6 per day, 15min., 285$); Porto (4 per day, 2hr., 825$); Lisboa (3 per day, 7hr., 1950$). A **ferry** (1/2 hr.; 60$ per person, 280$ per car) shuttles between Vila Nova de Cerveira and the Galician town of Goyan, with bus connections to Vigo and A Garda.

Near Vila Nova de Cerveira: Alto Minho

Within easy reach of Vila Nova de Cerveira, **Valença do Minho** dutifully guards the entrance to northern Portugal. Stone arches and cannon portals intermittently cut through the three concentric ramparts of these infamous 17th-century fortifications. From Valença, a winding road rises to the breath-taking summit of **Monte do Faro,** which overlooks the coastline, the Vale do Minho, and the Galician mountains. The town has earned some notoriety as a smuggling center, chiefly for Spanish cigarettes and Portuguese wine. Inquire at **Turismo,** Av. Espanha (tel. 233 74; open 9am-7pm, off-season Mon.-Sat. 9:30am-12:30pm and 2:30-6pm) about cheap rooms in **casas particulares. Pensão Rio Minho** has fine rooms and is conveniently next to the train station. (Singles 2500$. Doubles 3000$.) **Restaurante Bom Jesus,** on Largo do Bom Jesus (Muralhas) is within the walls and serves lunch and dinner every day. Entrees 950-1690. Valença is a stop on the Porto-Vigo **train** line (11 trains per day from Viana to Valença, 2 of which continue to Vigo; 335$).

For an unforgettable daytrip, hop a bus to **Ponte de Lima**. This highly picturesque town straddles the Rio Lima in the middle of the *vinho verde* region. A 15-arch Roman bridge spans the river, which is nearly 1/2km wide here. **Igreja de São Francisco,** now a museum for temporary exhibits, has carved wood altarpieces and two unusual wooden pulpits. If you decide to stay overnight, inquire at **Restaurante Catrina** (tel. 94 12 67), near the bridge facing the river. The owner keeps lovely rooms in his hotel (doubles 3500$). The **tourist office** (tel. 94 23 35) in Pr. República stocks information on accommodations and will arrange for a private home rental if you decide to move in. (Open 9am-8pm; off-season Mon.-Sat. 9:30am-12:30pm and 2:30-6pm.) For a meal, there's **Restaurante Encanada** (tel. 94 11 89), near the park, next to the market and with a veranda overlooking the river and the Roman bridge. They serve enormous portions (about 750-1100$). The *sarrabulho* (rice and sausage) and the *bacalhau* (cod) are particularly good. Ponte de Lima hovers smack in the middle of *vinho verde* country.

Trás-Os-Montes

The country's most desolate, rough, and isolated region, Trás-Os-Montes ("behind the mountains") is lightyears off the beaten path. Bragança and Vila Real, the two largest towns, are cold in winter and hot in summer. Getting back here is half the fun; train service is slow and rickety (where it exists at all), and roads are twisty and treacherous. Few tourists pass by, although the region is mobbed with returning emigrants in August.

Bragança

The grand 12th-century castle dominating the town is evidence of its importance during the Middle Ages. Amid the rough terrain of the Serra da Nogueira, the town is named for the royal dynasty that ruled Portugal for three centuries, until the abolition of monarchy in 1910.

Orientation and Practical Information

The **Praça da Sé** is the heart of town. **Avenida Cidade de Zamora** lies a couple of blocks north of Pr. da Sé. To the west is the **new quarter**, up Rua Almirante Reis on Avenida João da Cruz. The **castle complex** sits on a hill west of Pr. da Sé. To get there, take **Rua Combatantes de Grande Guerra** and Rua T. Coelho.

Tourist Office: Av. Cidade de Zamora (tel 282 73), northeast of the center. From Pr. da Sé take R. Abilio Beça, turn left on R. Marqués de Pômbal (2nd street), then right on Av. Cidade de Zamora. In a little bungalow in the middle of the street. Maps and pamphlets on surrounding areas and help with accommodations. English and French spoken. Open Mon.-Fri. 9am-12:30pm and 2-7pm, Sat. 10am-12:30pm and 3-6pm; Oct.-May Mon.-Fri. 9am-12:30pm and 2-5pm, Sat. 10am-12:30pm.

Currency Exchange: Many banks line Av. João da Cruz. Open Mon.-Fri. 8:30am-3pm. **Hotel Bragança,** Av. Francisco Sá Carneiro, keeps later hours.

Post Office: R. 5 de Outubto, s/n (tel. 234 72), on the corner with Av. João da Cruz and R. Almirante Reis. Open for Posta Restante, express mail, and **telephones** Mon.-Fri. 8:30am-6pm, Sat 9am-12:30pm. **Postal Code:** 5300

Telephones: At the **post office. Telephone Code:** 073.

Trains: Largo da Estação, Av. João da Cruz (tel. 223 27), the opposite end of the street from the post office. No trains dare come here, however. The nearest station is in Mirandela. Buses run from here to Mirandela (5 per day, 2 1/2 hr., 490$). From Mirandela there are trains to Porto (4 per day, 8hr., 1300$).

Buses: Hotel Brangança, Av. Francisco Sá Carneiro. The reception desk sells tickets and has schedules. Buses leave from across the street. To: Vila Real (3 *expressos* per day, 2 1/2 hr., 980$); Porto (3 *expressos* per day, 4 1/2 hr., 1200$); Viseu (4 *expressos* per day, 4hr., 1200$); Coimbra (4 *expressos* per day, 5 3/4 hr., 1540$); Lisboa (4 *expressos* per day, 7 1/4 hr., 2120$). For bus to Mirandela, see Trains above.

Hospital: Hospital Distrital de Bragança, Av. Abade de Baçal (tel. 221 33), before the stadium on the road to Chaves.

Emergency: tel. 115.

Police: Joverno Civil building, R. José Beça (tel. 223 54).

Accomodations

Most *pensões* cluster about **Praça da Sé** and up **Rua Almirante Reis**.

Pensão Rucha, R. Almirante Reis, 42 (tel. 226 72), on the street connecting Pr. da Sé to Av. João da Cruz. Great old style lodgings at 19th-century prices. Clean. The museum-like *cozinha antiga* (old kitchen) warms guests in winter. Grand breakfast room. Singles 1800$. Doubles 3500$. Breakfast included.

Residencial Nordeste Shalom, Av. Abade de Baçal (tel. 246 67), on the road to Chaves across from the stadium and before the train bridge. Satellite TV, modern baths, parking, and a lounge are luxurious amenities for Bragança. Breakfast included.

Hospedaria Brigantina, R. Almirante Reis, 48 (tel. 243 21), up the street from the Rucha. Three floors of basic, antiseptically clean rooms. Singles 1500$. Doubles 2500$. During July and August call in advance.

Food

The region is celebrated by epicureans for *presunto* (raw bacon), *salpicão* (sausages), and *cozido* (a stew of boiled meats and vegetables). Traditional Portuguese fare prowls the **Praça da Sé**. More modern cafés and restaurants sit on their fashionable asses along **Avenida Jãoa da Cruz**.

Restaurante Poças, R. Combatentes da Grande Guerra, 200 (tel. 224 28), off the Pr. da Sé to the east. Classic grub in a no-frills setting. *Costeleta de vitela grelhada* (grilled steak) 900$—better than the Whistle Stop. Most entrees 750-1100$. Open noon-3pm and 7-10pm.

Restaurante La'em Casa, R. Marquês de Pombal (tel. 221 11). Rustic decor and user-friendly food. *Bacalhau dos amigos* (friendly codfish) 1350$. Entrees 900-1800$. Open noon-2pm and 6pm-midnight.

Café Chave d'Ouro, Pr. da Sé on the corner with R. Combatentes. No sign out front, but it's the café everyone knows. Gulp down breakfast with the rest of the town. *Café* (coffee) 60$. *Sumo de laranja 100%* (fresh-squeezed orange juice) 200$. *Batidos* (shakes) 250$. Open Mon.-Sat. 7am-midnight.

Sights and Entertainment

High above the rest of town, the handsome, brooding **castelo** is a 10-min. walk from the center of town down R. Combatentes and R. T. Coelho. The 15th-century **Torre de Menagem** (Homage Tower) stands at the center of the 12th-century inner walls. The castle currently houses the **museu militar** (military museum), a random bunch of paraphernalia ranging from medieval battle swords to a World War I machine gun nest. There's a bird's eye view of Bragança and the surrounding countryside from the top of the tower. (Open Fri.-Wed. 9am-noon and 2-5pm. Admission 100$, students with ID 50$.)

The medieval **pelourinho** (pillory) outside the *torre* looks like a honey dripper and bears the coat of arms of the House of Bragança. Impaled atop the whipping post is a prehistoric granite pig. In the Iron Age people were bound to the pig as a sort of punishment.

The **Domus Municipalis,** behind the church opposite the *torre*, contained water hoarding cisterns in the 13th century, but it later became the municipal meeting house. The pentagonal building is actually just one bench-filled room above the cisterns. (If it's closed, the *senhora* across the street at #40 has the key; be sure to tip her.)

Four blocks from the gates of the castle on R. Serpa Pinto, the **Museu Abade de Baçal** displays a small but eclectic collection. The beds are in rooms IV and X. A few more granite pigs (not on poles), some Portuguese paintings, and mannequins in regional costume round out the collection. Strollers take over the garden out back. (Open Tues.-Sun. 10am-12:30pm and 2-5pm. Admission 200$, students with ID free.)

What do folks do in Bragança to unwind? Many hunt hares, gallinules (aquatic birds), and partridges; the rest wait for the **Festas de Nossa Senhora das Graças,** a week of frolicking wrapped up the night of August 21.

Vila Real

The not-so-lively town of Vila Real swings its feet over the edge of the gorges of the Corgo and Cabril Rivers in the foothills of the Serra do Marão. This modest community, made affluent by a recent agricultural surge, serves as the principal commercial center for the southern farms of Trás-Os-Montes. The old town center is ringed by new boroughs reaching into the hills; the main street swoons with the heady scent of rosebeds, and its few cafés brim with youth. The town's black pottery with a leaden sheen is coveted throughout Portugal. Vila Real makes a good point of departure for excursions into the fertile fields and rocky slopes of the Serras do Alvão and Marão.

Orientation and Practical Information

Vila Real is poised north of Viseu and 100km east of Porto. The old town centers on **Avenida Carvalho Araújo,** a broad tree-lined avenue that streams from the post office (off the corner of a small rotunda with fountain) downhill to the Câmara Municipal.

Tourist Office: Av. Carvalho Araújo, 94 (tel. 32 28 19; fax 32 17 12). Good town map and information about Parque Natural do Alvão and the Sogrape winery. English and French spoken. Open 9:30am-7pm; Oct.-March 9:30am-12:30pm and 2-5pm; April-May 9:30am-12:30pm and 2-7pm.

Currency Exchange: Realvitur, Largo do Peoledo, 2 (tel. 37 44 14), 4 bl. uphill from Turismo and to the right. Same rates as the banks but longer hours. Open Mon.-Fri. 9am-7pm, Sat. 9am-1pm.

Post Office: Av. Carvalho Araújo (tel. 32 22 01), up the street and across from the tourist office. Open for Posta Restante and **telephones** Mon.-Fri. 8:30am-6:30pm. **Postal Code:** 5000.

Telephones: At the **post office. Telephone Code:** 059.

Trains: Av. 5 de Outubro (tel. 32 21 93). To get to the town center, walk straight up Av. 5 de Outubro over the iron bridge onto R. Miguel Bombarda, and turn left on R. Roque da Silveira. With the river on the left, continue to bear left until Av. Primeiro de Maio. Trains crawl and almost everything requires a change at Régua. To: Porto via Régua (5 per day, 3hr., 770$); Bragança with changes in Régua, Tua, and from Mirandela by bus (4 per day, 8hr., 940$).

Buses: Rodo Norte, R. D. Pedro de Castro (tel. 32 22 47), on a square directly uphill from Turismo. To: Guimarães (3 per day via Amarante, 630$); Porto (3 per day, 3 1/2 hr., 800$); Lisboa (2 per day, 7hr., 1750$ lunch included). **Rodoviária,** out of Ruicar Travel Agency, R. Gonçalo Cristovão, 16 (tel. 3712 34), near Rodo Norte uphill on the right. To: Viseu (4 per day, 2 1/2 hr., 880$); Coimbra (2 per day, 4 1/2 hr., 1100$); Lisboa (2 per day, 8hr., 1720$; Bragança (3 per day, 2 1/2 hr., 980$).

Taxis: (tel. 32 12 96). They queue along R. Araujo Carvalho. To Mateus (450$).

Hospital: Hospital Distrital de Vila Real (tel. 34 10 41) in Lordelo, north of the town center.

Emergency: tel. 115.

Police: Largo Comandante Amarante (tel. 32 20 22).

Accommodations and Camping

Several cafés along **Avenida Carvalho Araújo** advertise rooms upstairs, and three *pensões* line the **Travessa São Domingos,** the side street next to the cathedral.

Residencial Encontro, Av. Carvalho Araújo, 78 (tel. 32 23 25), a few doors down from Turismo. A hyperactive family keeps these renovated rooms and modern baths next to the most fashionable (read: noisiest) café in town. Singles 2500$. Doubles with bath 5000$. Breakfast included.

Residencial Real, R. Combatentes da Grande Guerra, 5 (tel. 37 38 78), 2 streets behind the tourist office, above an eponymous café. New and clean. All rooms with TV and shower. Singles 4500$. Doubles 6500$. Triples 9000$. Oct.-May: 3200$; 4500$; 6000$.

Pensão Mondego, Trav. São Domingos, 11 (tel. 32 30 97), off Av. Carvalho Araújo across from the cathedral. For those who like bells in the morning. Bright, carpeted rooms. Peculiar wallcoverings. Singles 2500$. Doubles 3000$.

Residencial São Domingos, Trav. São Domingos, 33 (tel. 32 20 39). Look under the yellow restaurant awning: it's actually an overpriced piano bar. Steeply raked floors make furniture tilt—at least you're not wearing gold high heels. Carpeted downstairs rooms with bath; intolerably hot upstairs rooms (in summer) with spartan, bare wood floors. The common bath gets a B- for cleanliness. Winter heating. Singles 2000$, with bath 3000$. Doubles with shower 3600$, with bath 4800$. Breakfast included.

Camping: Municipal campground (tel. 32 47 24), just northeast of town on a bluff above the Corgo River. Get on the Av. Marginal and follow the signs. Free swims in the river or the new pool complex. 300$ per person, 180$ per tent and per car.

Food

A superflux of cafés offer the town's only evening entertainment. The restaurants around **Avenida António de Azevedo** and **Primeiro de Maio** cook for little in exchange. Across the street from the bus station, the huge **market** is open Tues.-Fri. 9am-noon.

Restaurante Nova Pompeia, Rua Carvalho Araujo, 82 (tel. 37 28 76), next to the tourist office above popular café Nova Pompeia. Low prices, middling environs, high A/C. Most entrees 600-870$. *Prato do dia* 500-520$. *Lulas grelhados* (grilled squid) 690$. Open Mon.-Sat. 11:30am-2:30pm and 7-10:30pm.

Restaurante Churrasco, R. António de Azevedo, 24 (tel. 32 23 13), on a back street parallel to Av. Carvalho Araújo in the commercial sector. Charred chickens beckon from the display window. *Espetadas no churrasco* (shish kebab) 900$. Entrees 800-1400$. Open Mon.-Sat. noon-3pm and 6:45-11:30pm.

O Aldeão, R. D. Pedro de Castro, 70 (tel. 247 94). Follow Av. Carvalho de Araújo as it branches left past the post office and turns into R. D. Pedro de Castro. Haughty and formal exterior is an optical illusion; relaxed on the inside. *Bife grelhado* (grilled steak) 900$. Entrees 700-900$. 1/2-portions available. Open Sun.-Fri. 8am-11:30pm.

Sights

At the lower end of Av. Carvalho Araújo looms the 15th-century **sé,** with its simple interior divided by thick, arched columns. Two blocks east of the cathedral stands the **Capela Nova** (New Chapel), with a bizarre floral façade. At the end of R. Combatentes da Grande Guerra loiters **Igreja de São Pedro,** decorated with 17th-century *azulejos*. At the end of each June potters sell their distinctively dark regional ceramics at the **Feira São Pedro.**

Near Vila Real

The village of **Mateus,** 3km east of Vila Real, has garnered world renown for its rosé wine and cheesy TV commercials. The **Sogrape Winery,** on the main road from Vila Real 200m from the turnoff for the Palácio Mateus has a terrific free tour of the wine-processing center (with unlimited free tasting). (Open July.-Sept. 9am-noon and 2-4pm; winter 9am-noon and 2-5pm. Don't bother going during harvest time, late Sept.-early Oct., when you'll be ignored.)

Up the road from the Sogrape Winery and surrounded by its vineyards glitters the Baroque **Palácio Mateus.** Inside the mansion hangs an original 1817 edition of Luís de Camões's *As Lusiadas,* Portugal's most famous literary epic, with a display of Fragonard illustrations alongside their original engraving plates. Unfortunately, visitors must take a tedious hour-long tour of the palace. In the 18th-century chapel on the grounds, the 250-year-old **remains** of a certain São Marco, a Spanish soldier, recline fully dressed in a glass case. How unsavory. (Open 9am-12:30pm and 2-6pm. Admission to mansion and gardens 750$ per person, to gardens alone 550$. Per car: 1450$; 1250$.)

Cabanelas (tel. 32 22 57) operates seven **buses** per day from Vila Real to Mateus and back again (one-way 75$). They leave from the Câmara Municipal in the morning, from Cabanelas bus station in the afternoon. Many people walk between the two towns. The road loops, so follow the signs south from Vila Real's train station or north from the main highway out of town.

Vila Real makes an ideal base for those hardy souls who wish to explore the **Parque Natural do Alvão,** a protected area spreading to the heights of the Serra do Alvão and Serra do Marão. The hill town of **Lamas de Olo,** teetering 1000m above sea level, is a four-hour trudge straight up. Mysterious granite dwellings live in this area, nearby the spectacular **Rio Olo gorge.** No buses serve this region, nor are there any *pensões*.

Ribatejo and Alentejo

The meadowed Ribatejo (named *riba do Tejo*—bank of the Tagus—by its first settlers) is a fertile region that fills most of the basin of the Tejo and its main tributary, the Zêzere. Although farmed intensely—yielding grains, vegetables, olives, and citrus fruits—the area is best known in Portugal as a pastureland and breeding ground for Arabian horses and great black bulls.

Huge Alentejo *(além do Tejo* means beyond the Tagus) covers almost one-third of the Portuguese land mass, but with a population barely over half a million it remains the least populous region. The requisite olive and cork trees and whitewashed hamlets dot the rolling hills. Aside from the mountainous west, the region is a vast granary, though severe droughts, resistance to contour farming, and overplanting of soil-drying eucalyptus trees have severly affected its agricultural capacity. Ambitious plans to irrigate large tracts of land with water from the Tejo and the Guadiana have been stalled by Lisboa's refusal to cooperate with local governments. Several medieval towns grace the Alentejo Alto, while Beja is the only major town on the seemingly endless Alentejo Baixo plain.

Santarém

Capital of the Ribatejo province and its major town, Santarém sits on a rocky mound overlooking the Rio Tejo. The name Santarém stems from Santa Iria, a nun who was accused of lapsed virtue and cast into the river. (After she washed up in Santarém her water-logged body was autopsied and pronounced innocent). Santarém, Beja, and Braga were the three ruling cities of the ancient Roman province Lusitania. This flourishing medieval center boasted 15 convents, making it today the capital of Portugal's Gothic style. It's also the primary market for the produce of this fertile region.

Orientation and Practical Information

The core of this swiftly growing town is formed by the densely packed streets between **Praça Sá da Bandeira** and the park **Portas do Sol,** below which flows the Río Tejo. **Rua Capelo Ivêns,** which begins at the *praça,* contains the tourist office and many *pensões*.

Tourist Office: R. Capelo Ivêns, 63 (tel. 231 40). English-speaking staff disperses information on accommodations and festivals. Open 9:30am-12:30pm and 2-6pm, Sat.-Sun. 9:30am-12:30pm and 2-5:30pm.

Post Office: R. Dr. Teixeira Guedes (tel. 230 01). Turn right from the front door of Turismo; it's at the next intersection. Open for all services and **telegrams** Mon.-Fri. 8:30am-6:30pm, Sat. 9am-12:30 pm. **Postal Code:** 2000.

Telephone Code: 043.

Trains: (tel. 231 80), 2km outside town with connecting bus service from the bus station (every 45min., 10min., 130$). Otherwise take a taxi (300$); on foot it's a steep climb up dangerous roads. To: Lisboa (every hr., 1hr., 460$); Tomar (every 2hr., 1hr., 345$); Portalegre (5 per day via Entroncamento, 3hr., 815$); Faro (7 per day, 4hr., 1665$); Porto (7 per day, 4hr., 1225$).

Buses: Rodoviária Tejo, Av. do Brasil (tel. 220 01). Convenient location. To reach Turismo, walk through the park and cross busy Av. Marquês Sá da Bandeira. Turn right and then left, taking R. Pedro Canavarro uphill, and make a right on R. Capelo Ivêns. To: Lisboa (5 *expressos* per day, 1hr., 750$; others every hr., 1 1/2 hr., 650$); Tomar (2 per day, 1 1/2 hr., 680$); Caldas da Rainha (3 per day, 1 1/2 hr., 550$); Faro (3 per day, 7hr., 1920$).

Taxis: Omnitour (tel. 255 50, 235 50). 24-hr. service. From bus station to train station 300$.

Hitchhiking: *Let's Go* does not recommend hitchhiking as a means of travel. Those headed to Lisboa start on R. Prior de Crato in the western quarter of the city. Those headed to Porto take R. Alexandre Herculano in the north of the city. Don't hold your breath, and if you're a solo woman, don't hitchhike at all.

Luggage Storage: On the **bus station** platform (80$ per day). At the **train station**, on the right as you exit (230$ per day).

Laundromat: Tinturaria Americana, R. João Afonso, 15 (tel. 235 02). At the post office walk down R. Elias Garcia, then take the first left. Dry cleaning only. Shirt 250$, pants 400$. Open Mon.-Fri. 9am-1pm and 2:30-7pm, Sat. 9am-3pm.

Hospital: Av. Bernardo Santareno (tel. 270 61). From Pr. Sá de Bandeira walk up R. Cidade da Covilhã and follow as it becomes R. Alexandre Herculano.

Emergency: tel. 115.

Police: Campo Sá da Bandeira (tel. 220 22). Follow the signs from the bus station about 100m.

Accommodations and Camping

Staying the night here can be expensive. During the Ribatejo Fair (10 days starting the first Friday in June) prices for rooms increase 10-40%; Turismo can help find a double in a private house for about 3000$ (1500-2000$ during the rest of the year). True budget *pensões* leave plenty to be desired; those with amenities are often worth the extra money.

Pensão do José, (a.k.a. **Pensão da Dona Arminda),** Travessa do Frois, 14 and 18 (tel. 230 88), under sign that reads "rooms." On a mercifully quiet street off R. Capelo Ivêns, 1 bl. from Turismo. Bright and clean. Singles 2000$. Doubles 3500$.

Hotel Abidis, R. Guilherme de Azevedo, 4 (tel. 220 17), down the street from the Central. A 19th-century conception of luxury complete with phones in most rooms. Well-decorated living room with fireplace. Only 2 rooms without bath. Singles 2500$, with bath 4250$. Doubles 4200$, with bath 7000$. Breakfast included.

Residencial Beirante, R. Alexandre Herculano, 5 (tel. 225 47). From the bus station, turn left towards the Mercado Municipal, then another left. Each room has a TV, a phone, and a sparkling bathroom. Worth every *escudo*. Singles 3500$. Doubles 5000$. Breakfast included.

Residencial Victoria, R. do Segundo Visconde de Santarém, 21 (tel. 282 02), in a quiet residential neighborhood 5min. from the town center. From the bus station, turn right on R. 25 de Abril and left on R. Duarte Pereira; follow through 2 name changes, making the penultimate possible right onto R. Segundo Visconde. Recently renovated and decorated with the owner's needlework. Spotless rooms have bath, phone, TV, heating, *and* A/C. Singles 4000$. Doubles 4500-7000$, depending on the season. Cheaper rooms in the old half of the *residencial*.

Residencial Muralha, R. Pedro Canavarro, 12 (tel. 223 99), between Av. Marquês Sá da Bandeira and R. Capelo Ivêns. Modern furniture reminiscent of the glorious 1970s. All rooms are carpeted and have bath, phone, and patio. Singles 2500$, with shower 3200$, with bath 3250$. Doubles 3200$, with shower 3900$, with bath 4500$. Breakfast included.

Camping: Parque do Campismo Municipal, Largo do Município. From the bus station turn left on Av. Brasil, take the 1st right on an unmarked street that leads past the park to R. Cidade da Covilhã. Turn left, then right after the Jardim da República. The campground is small and primitive, but rarely full. 30$ per person, 50$ per tent, 30$ per car. Showers 25$.

Food

Eateries cluster in and around **Rua Capelo Ivêns**. The **municipal market**, in the colorful pagoda-thing on Largo Infante Santo near the Jardim da República, supplies fresh produce and vegetables from the surrounding countryside. (Open Mon.-Sat. 8am-2pm.)

> **Restaurante Caravana,** Travessa do Frois, 24 (tel. 225 68), a side street off R. Capelo Ivêns; another entrance in the square around the corner. Toothsome food in a refreshingly clean, modest restaurant. Entrees 650-800$. *Frango corado* with fries (ruddy chicken 750$). Open Sun.-Fri. 8am-10pm.
>
> **Restaurante Cascata,** R. António Maria Batista, 3 (tel. 241 43), left out of the bus station and left again. A neighborhood restaurant with an attached *quiosque*. Informal family-style dining. *Plato da Dia* 700-850$. Open Sun.-Fri. 8am-10:30pm.
>
> **Restaurante Pigalle,** R. Capelo Ivêns (tel. 242 05). Always bustling with people snacking or boozing it up. Entrees (750-1200$) are 100$ less at the *balção* (bar) than at the table. Open Mon.-Sat. 8am-midnight.
>
> **Restaurante Solar,** Largo Emílio Infante de Câmara, 9-10 (tel. 222 39), the 2nd left off R. Teixera Suedes from the post office. Fresh, high-quality food at a stand-up counter or in padded chairs. *Truta grelhada* (grilled trout, 800$), *bife de perú* (turkey, 800$). Open Sun.-Fri. 9am-10:30pm.

Sights and Entertainment

The austere facade of the **Igreja do Seminário dos Jesuitas** dominates Santarém's main square, Praça Sá da Bandeira. Stone friezes carved like ropes separate each of its three stories, and Latin mottoes from the Bible embellish every lintel and doorway. To the left of the church, the former **Colégio dos Jesuitas** conceals two enormous, overgrown palm trees crammed into a tiny cloister. (Church usually open 9am-5pm, cloister 2-5pm. If either is closed, enter the door to the right of the main entrance and ask Sr. Domingos to unlock it for you.)

A statue of the Marquês Sá da Bandeira embellishes the center of the *praça*. Standing back-to-back with him, the street before you on the left is R. Serpa Pinto. Follow it to the wonderful **Praça Visconde de Serra Pilar,** formerly Pr. Velha. Centuries ago, this commercial area was the only place where Christians, Moors, and Jews mixed for social and business affairs. The 12th-century **Igreja de Marvila** has a 16th-century Manueline portal and a 17th-century *azulejo* interior. (Closed for restoration, expected to reopen by summer 1993.) The early Gothic severity of nearby **Igreja da Graça,** contrasts with Marvila's exuberance. In the chapel to the right of the chancel is the tomb of Pedro Alvares Cabral, the explorer who discovered Brazil and one of the few *conquistadores* who managed to stay alive long enough to be buried in his homeland.

Off R. São Martinho stands the medieval **Torre das Cabaças** (Tower of the Gourds), so-called because of the eight earthen bowls installed in the 16th century to amplify the bell's ring. Across the street, the **Museu Arqueológico de São João do Alporão** squats in a former 13th-century church. The main exhibit is the elaborate Gothic "tomb" of Dom Duarte de Meneses, swirling tracery and stone flames rising from pointed arches. Meneses was hacked apart while fighting the Muslims. The museum houses only what little of his dismembered remains his comrades could salvage from the battlefield: one tooth. The molar is entombed in the glass case across the aisle. (Open Tues.-Sun. 9am-1pm and 2-5pm. Free.)

Santarém shimmies with festivals. Feed your sweet tooth at the **sweets fair** (from the last Wednesday to Sunday in April) featuring calories from all over Portugal. At the same time, **Lusoflora** displays flowers from all over the world, accompanied by regional music, folk dancing, and a sailing exhibition. The largest festival is the **Feira Nacional de Agricultura** (a.k.a. **Feira do Ribatejo),** a national agricultural exhibition. People come for the ten-day bullfighting and horseracing orgy (starting the first Friday in June.) Smack your lips and put some meat on those spindly bones at the **Festival e Seminário Nacional de Gastronomia** (Oct. 20-Nov. 2), in which each region of Portugal has a day to prepare a typical feast and entertainment.

Tomar

For centuries the mysterious Knights Templar schemed and plotted from their lair in this small town straddling the Rio Nabão. Most of Tomar's monuments reflect its former status as the den of that secretive religious order. The warrior-monks first settled here in the 12th century, after helping the first king of Portugal, Dom Afonso Henriques, oust the Moors. It was not until the 14th century, however, when the Templars were fervently persecuted throughout the rest of Europe, that they made Tomar their headquarters. Grand-Master Infante D. Henrique used the order's revenue to help finance the discoveries. Yet this powerful, enigmatic order fell into disfavor with the monarchy, and was forced to regroup as the seemingly more subservient Order of Christ. The celebrated convent-castle of the Knights Templar is one of the great masterpieces of Portuguese architecture.

The order's decline continued. The Napoleonic army ruthlessly trashed the Knights' priceless paintings and sculptures when it seized the castle. The Order of Christ, the last militant religious order of Christian Europe, was officially disbanded in 1834. Today the only vestiges of centuries of intrigue are the main streets tiled with the Cross of Christ (the Knights' symbol and Portugal's banner during the age of exploration).

Orientation and Practical Information

The **Rio Nabão** divides Tomar. The train and bus stations and most accommodations and sights lie on the west bank. **Rua Serpa Pinto** connects the Ponte Velha (old bridge) to the main square, **Praça da República.** Several blocks south of and parallel to Serpa Pinto, **Avenida Dr. Cândido Madureira** runs from the central roundabout to the entrance of the **Mata Nacional** (national forest), which is crowned by the convent-castle.

Tourist Office: Av. Dr. Cândido Madureira (tel. 31 32 37), facing Parque Mata Nacional. Perhaps the most comprehensive map on the Portuguese mainland. Open Mon.-Fri. 9:30am-12:30pm and 2-6pm, Sat.-Sun. 10am-1pm and 3-6pm; Oct.-May 9:30am-12:30pm and 2-6pm, Sat. 10am-1pm.

Currency Exchange: Hotel dos Templários (tel. 331 21), next to Parque Mouchão. **Banco Nacional Ultramarino,** R. Serpa Pinto, across from Café Paraíso. Open Mon.-Fri. 8:30am-3pm.

Post Office: Av. Marquês de Tomar (tel. 31 23 24), across from Parque Mouchão. Open Mon.-Fri. 9am-11:30 and 2-6pm. **Postal Code:** 2300.

Telephones: At the post office. **Telephone Code:** 049.

Trains: Av. Combatentes da Grande Guerra (tel. 31 28 15), the southern edge of town. To reach Turismo, turn right at the door, left on R. Torres Pinheiro, and continue until Av. Dr. Cândido Madureira; Turismo is 2 bl. on the right. Tomar is the northern terminus of a minor line, so most destinations require a transfer at Entroncamento; you can buy the ticket for both legs here. To: Lisboa (11 per day, 2hr., 725$); Coimbra (9 per day, 2hr., 680$); Porto (5 per day, 4 1/2 hr., 1165$); Faro (via Lisboa, 9hr., 1815$).

Buses: Av. Combatentes da Grande Guerra (tel. 31 27 38), next to the train station. To: Fátima (3 per day, 1/2 hr., 380$); Leiria (2 per day, 45min., 470$); Lisboa (6 per day, 2hr., 1000$); Coimbra (2 per day, 2hr., 680$); Porto (1 per day, 4hr., 1250$); Lagos (1 per day, 8hr., 2200$).

Taxis: Tel. 31 30 71; 31 51 48; 31 28 86. Taxi stand at R. dos Arcos.

Hitchhiking: Doncha ya dare hitch. Foro Lisboa, Av. D. Nonu Alves Perreira (which becomes E.N. 110) near the garage at the south end of town. For Porto, R. Coimbra, near Pr. Santo André. For Leiria, Av. Marquês de Tomar, near the public garden at the north end of town.

Hospital: Av. Cândido Madureira (tel. 31 30 74).

Emergency: tel. 115.

Police: R. Dr. Sousa (tel. 31 34 44), behind the *câmara municipal*.

Accommodations and Camping

Finding a place to stay is only a problem during the Festival dos Tabuleiros. Usually Tomar is a buyer's market, so try bargaining prices down.

Residencial União, R. Serpa Pinto, 94 (tel. 31 28 31, fax 31 12 99), near Pr. República. A wall of old glass looks out on the central courtyard from the large breakfast room. Simple wood furniture in the bright rooms and white-tiled, immaculate baths. Plush lounge, well-stocked bar, lovely period furniture: amazing luxury. All rooms with bath, telephone, satellite TV, and central heating. Singles 3500$, with bath 4000$. Doubles 4500$, with bath 5000$. Triples 6000$. Oct.-May 20% discount. Breakfast included. Reserve several days ahead July-Aug.

Pensão Nuno Alvares, Av. Nuno Alvares, 3 (tel. 31 28 73), 1 bl. to the right of the bus and train stations. Slightly run-down but quite clean. Large rooms; those facing the avenue are extremely noisy. Singles 1800$. Doubles 2400$, with bath 3200$. Breakfast included.

Pensão Tomarense, R. Torres Pinheiro, 15 (tel. 31 29 48), 1 bl. from Nuno Alvares. Large and noisy rooms facing the street. Large and quiet rooms in back with a splendid view of the castle on the hill and the old town. The kind owners speak some English and French. One common bath with hot water; primitive private baths. Singles 1700$, with bath 2200$. Doubles with bath 2700$. Breakfast included.

Residencial Luz, R. Serpa Pinto, 144 (tel. 31 23 17), down the street from União. Cheerful *pensão* with large rooms. Somewhat dim and overfurnished, but excellent location. All rooms with shower and phone. Singles 2500$, with bath 3000$. Doubles 4000$, with bath $4500. Gargantuan 4- and 6-person rooms with bath 1500$ per person. Oct.-May 20-25% discount.

Pensão Luanda, Av. Marquês de Tomar, 13-15 (tel. 31 29 29). Quiet, location across from the park and river. Cool, modern interior with marble steps. Windows are double-glazed to ensure quiet. All rooms have pristine bath, phone, TV, and central heating. Singles 3500-4500$. Doubles 5250-6000$. 3-person suites 10,000-10,500$. Oct.-May 10% discount.

Camping: Parque Municipal de Campismo (tel. 31 39 50), across Ponte Velha near the stadium and the swimming pool, on the river. Exit off E.N. 110 on the east end of the Nabão bridge. Thickly forested campground with a pool. Reception 8am-8pm. Hot water 7am-11pm. 200$ per person, 100$ per tent, 200$ per car. Showers free. 14km south of Tomar alongside a 1030m dam, **Castelo do Bode** (tel. (041) 942 44) enjoys a fine view of the Zêzere valley and river swimming. 450$ per person, 160$ per tent, 190$ per car.

Food

Tomar is the picnic capital of Portugal. The **market** (open Mon.-Sat. 8am-2pm,), on the corner of Av. Norton de Matos and R. Santa Iria on the other side of the river has all the fixins. Friday is the big market day (8am-5pm). A section of Parque Mouchão is set aside just for picnickers.

Restaurante Estrela do Céu, Pr. República, 21. Possibly the most original menu in the entire region. The ex-Sheraton cook invents delights that make Babette look gastronomically illiterate. Rustic decor. *Lonbinhos à corredora* (veal with orange, red pepper, and carrot) is one of the specialties. Hefty portions. Entrees 990-1600$. Open 11am-midnight.

Restaurante A Bela Vista, Fonte Choupo, 6 (tel. 31 28 70), across Ponte Velha on your left. Dine on the riverside patio under a grape arbor with a handsome view of the castle. Appealing chicken curry (900$). Diverse entrees 750-1600$. Open Thurs.-Mon. 10am-3:30pm and 7-9:30pm, Tues.-Wed. 10am-3:30pm.

Snack-Bar Tabuleiro, R. Serpa Pinto, 140 (tel. 31 27 71), near Pr. República. Dim, rather seedy-looking place that serves delicious meals. Mouth-watering *bitoque de porco* (595$) comes in an earthenware bowl topped with an egg and buried in a heap of fries. Other dishes 500-700. Open Mon.-Sat. 9:30am-10pm.

Restaurante Piri-Piri, R. Moinhos, 54 (tel. 31 34 94), off R. Serpa Pinto. Simple but pleasant decor with long, flowing drapes. Great *truta grelhada* (grilled trout) 750$. Sure to be fresh. Open Wed.-Mon. noon-3pm and 7-9:30pm.

Estroia de Tomar, R. Serpa Pinto, 14. A pleasant place to have a drink. Home-made pastries include *beija-me depressa* (kiss me quickly). Ice cream 100$ per scoop, 110$ per "American" scoop (?). Open 8am-midnight.

Sights and Entertainment

It's worth trekking in from the far corners of the earth to see the **Convento de Cristo** grounds, established in 1320 as a refuge for the disbanded Knights of Templar. An effusively ornamented doorway opens to the heart of the complex, the Byzantine-Romanesque **Templo dos Templares** or **Charola**. Modeled after the Holy Sepulchre in Jerusalem, the *templo* contains an ornate octagonal canopy that protects the high altar. The Knights supposedly attended Mass on horseback, each under one of the arches.

A 16th-century Manueline **coro** extends north from the rotunda. Here you'll find all the rich seafaring symbolism of the style: seaweed, coral, anchors, rope, and even artichokes (eaten by mariners to prevent scurvy). On the west wall, the design culminates in two great stained-glass windows. Below stands the **Janela do Capítulo** (chapter window), Portugal's best-known "window"—an unjustly plain word for this elaborate, exuberant tribute to the Golden Age of Discoveries.

To the south of the nave rises the main cloister, constructed between 1557 and 1566, called **Claustro dos Felipes** for King Felipe II of Castille, who was crowned here as Felipe I of Portugal during Iberia's unification (1580-1640). Considered one of Europe's masterpieces of Renaissance architecture, its graceful spiral staircases, Tuscan columns, and Ionic pillars frame a large fountain.

Tucked behind the Palladian main cloister and the nave is **Claustro Santa Barbara,** where insanely grotesque gargoyle rainspouts writhe in pain as they vomit up a fountain of water. On the northeast side of the church is the Gothic **Claustro de Cemetério,** the only part of the complex that dates from the time of Henry the Navigator.

Monks scrubbed their stockings in the adjoining **Claustro de Lavagem** (Laundry Cloister); water was supplied by the **Aqueducto dos Pegões** (1593-1614), part of which you can see by leaving the convent and walking to the right. Allow at least two hours to tour the grounds. (Open 9:30am-12:30pm and 2-6pm; Oct.-Feb. 9:30am-12:30pm and 2-5pm. Admission 300$, Oct.-Feb. 200$; Sun. mornings free.)

On the way back into town you'll pass the **Capela de Nossa Senhora da Conceição** (1540-50), an excellent example of early Renaissance architecture. The church is closed to the public, but the convent loans out the key.

Tomar's **Museu Luso-Hebraico,** in the 15th-century Sinagoga do Arco at R. Dr. Joaquim Jaquinto (a.k.a. R. da Judiaria), 73, is Portugal's only significant reminder of what was once a great European Jewish community. Jews worshiped only for a few decades before the ultimatum of 1496: convert or leave. The building then served as a prison, a Christian chapel, a hayloft, and a grocery warehouse until its classification as a national monument in 1921. Two years later, a man named Samuel Schwarz purchased the synagogue, devoted most of his life to its restoration, and donated it to the state in 1939. Timely gift: the government awarded Schwarz and his wife Portuguese citizenship, assuring them sanctuary during World War II. The museum's single square room, with its vaulted ceiling supported by four columns, owes its remarkable acoustic resonance to the pair of fist-sized holes at each corner—actually the mouths of clay amphoras embedded in the walls. The museum now keeps an unexceptional collection of old tombstones, inscriptions, and donated pieces from around the world. (Open 9:30am-12:30pm and 2-6pm. At other times, ring at #104 and the engaging, multilingual Sr. Vasco will gladly open the synagogue.)

Pyromaniacs light up over the **Museu dos Fósforos,** an exhibition of the world's largest matchbox collection. It's in the Convento de São Fransisco, just across from the train and bus stations. (Open Sun.-Fri. 2-5pm. Free.)

For a week in either June or July, handicrafts from the entire country, folklore, *fado,* and theater storm the city during the **Feira Nacional de Artesanato.** Yet Tomar's best-known festival is the **Festa dos Tabuleiros** (Feast of Trays), when girls dressed in white parade down the streets with willow baskets balanced on their heads. They pile each basket nearly 2m high (at least 30 loaves of bread). The festival recalls the "giving of bread to the poor," a custom begun by Queen (later Saint) Isabel in the 14th century. Thousands travel to Tomar for the festival, which is held every other odd year for the first two weeks of July. The festival was last held in 1991; the next one is in 1995.

Évora

From the rolling plain of cork and olive trees, Évora rises like a megalith on a hill. Considered Portugal's foremost showpiece of medieval architecture, the town also contains the Roman Temple to Diana, labyrinthine streets winding past Moorish arches, and a 16th-century university. Haunting the otherwise cheerful city is the macabre Capela de Ossos (Chapel of Bones), Iberia's largest ossicle studded paradise. Since the days when the outlaw Moor-ouster Gerald the Fearless shoved lances into the city walls in order to scale them, Évora has had few worries, apart from its worsening drug problem. The city remains unspoiled by the steady trickle of tourists daytripping from Lisboa, about 140km to the west.

Orientation and Practical Information

Évora is easily accessible from Lisboa; several trains per day ply the routes from Lisboa and Faro, and the town is also linked by rail with Estremoz, Portalegre, and Elvas to the north.

No direct bus connects the train station to the center of town. To avoid hiking 700m up R. do Dr. Baronha, hail a taxi (350$) or flag down bus #6, which fords the tracks two blocks over (75$; book of 10 tickets 315$). Near the edge of town, R. do Dr. Baronha turns into R. da República, which leads to the main square, **Praça do Giraldo**. From the bus station, simply proceed uphill to the *praça*. In the old town on the hill, dozens of winding, often narrow, and steep side streets lead in and out of the *praça*, home to most of the monuments and lodgings.

Tourist Office: Pr. Giraldo, 73 (tel. 226 71). Pathetically illegible map, with guided tour of monuments. List of rooms in private homes. Open Mon.-Fri. 9am-7pm, Sat.-Sun. 9am-12:30pm and 2-5:30pm; Oct.-May Mon.-Fri. 9am-6pm, Sat.-Sun. 9am-5:30pm.

Post Office: R. Olivença (tel. 233 11), 2 bl. north of Pr. Giraldo. Exit the *praça* and walk up R. João de Deus, keeping to the right. Pass under the aqueduct and make an immediate right uphill. Open for mail, Posta Restante, telephone, and **telegrams** Mon.-Fri. 8:30am-6:30pm. **Postal Code:** 7000.

Telephones: At the post office. **Telephone Code:** 066.

Currency Exchange: Automatic exchange machine outside Turismo. Open 24 hrs. **Banco Fonsecas e Burnay,** Pr. Giraldo, 52, across the *praça* from Turismo. Open Mon.-Fri. 8:30am-3pm.

Trains: (tel. 221 25), 1 1/2 km from town center. To: Lisboa (5 per day, 3hr., 695$); Faro (1 per day, 6hr., 1225$); Beja (4 per day, 1 1/2 hr., 535$); Estremoz (4 per day, 1 1/2 hr., 375$).

Buses: R. República (tel. 221 21), opposite Igreja de São Francisco. To: Lisboa (7 per day, 2 1/2 hr., 1000$); Faro (4 per day, 5hr., 1250$); Vila Real de Santo António (2 per day, 7hr., 1480$); Beja (5 per day and 1 *expresso*, 1 1/2 hr., 750$); Elvas (6 per day, 2 1/2 hr., 780$).

Taxis: tel. 73 47 34. From bus station to train station 350$. 24-hr. service.

Luggage Storage: In the **bus station** basement (80$ per day).

Laundromat: Lavévora, Largo D'Alvaro Velho, 6 (tel. 238 83), off R. Miguel Bombardo. 350$ per kg. Open Mon.-Fri. 9am-1pm and 3-7pm.

English Bookstore: Nazareth, Pr. Giraldo, 46 (tel. 222 21). Small English and French sections upstairs. A superflux of guidebooks and mysteries. Stationery too. Open Mon.-Fri. 9am-1pm and 3-5pm.

Swimming Pool: (tel. 323 26). A splendid complex of 5 pools on the outskirts of town. Admission 150$, under 13 100$. Open June-Sept. Wed.-Mon. 10:30am-7:30pm. Frequent summer bus service (75$; book of 10 315$).

Hospital: R. Velasco (tel. 250 01, 221 32, 221 33), close to city wall and intersection with R. D. Augusto Eduardo Nunes.

Emergency: tel. 115.

Police: R. Francisco Soares Lusitánia (tel. 74 11 20), near the Temple of Diana.

Accommodations and Camping

Most *pensões* reside on side streets around the **Praça do Giraldo.** They're crowded by June, so it's wise to reserve several days ahead. Prices drop about 20% in winter. *Quartos* (rooms in private houses) cost 2000-3500$.

> **Pensão Giraldo,** R. Mercadores (tel. 258 33), 2 bl. from Turismo. Small, tidy rooms just off the *praça.* Singles 2200$, with shower 3000$, with bath 3900$. Doubles 3500$, with shower 4900$, with bath 5500$.
>
> **Residencial Diana,** R. Diogo Cão, 2 (tel. 220 08, fax 74 31 01). From the Turismo cross the *praça* and follow R. de 5 D'Outubro up towards the cathedral; take the 3rd right. Recently renovated, this *residencial* combines *fin de siècle* charm with modern amenities. Lofty ceilings and pristine baths. The owner also runs the *salão de chá* (tea room) across the street. Singles 6500$. Doubles 7500$. Oct.-May: 5750$; 6750$.
>
> **Pensão Os Manueis,** R. Raimundo, 35 (tel. 228 61), around the corner from Turismo and upstairs from a restaurant. The main building with rooms and baths is startlingly clean and sunny. The annex across the back street is less so, but rooms are still spacious. Singles 3000$, with bath 5000$. Doubles 3500$, with bath 5500$.
>
> **Pensão Policarpo,** R. Freiria de Baixo, 16 (tel. 224 24), on a quiet side street in the shadow of the *sé.* Facing the *sé,* turn right on the street that curves to the left; Freiria is the last right before you find yourself back behind the cathedral. You may need to ask the way. A spruced-up 15th-century noble's house. Educated management speaks Portuguese, English, French, German, Italian, and Spanish. Central heating. Private parking lot. Singles 3500$, with shower 4500$, with bath 5500$. Doubles 4500$, with shower 5500$, with bath 6500$. Triples 8000$. Breakfast included.
>
> **Pensão Residencial O Eborense,** Largo da Misericórdia, 1 (tel. 220 31), first right as R. República hooks a left into the center of town. Ducal mansion turned renovated pension. Grandiose and plant-covered stone stairwell leads up to a exquisite outdoor balcony. Rooms small and cozy with high ceilings and rugs. All rooms with bath and heating. Singles 6450$. Doubles 7900$. Breakfast included.
>
> **Camping Orbitur** (tel. 251 90), a two-star park on Estrada das Alcáçovas, which branches off the bottom of R. Raimundo. 40-min. walk to town; only 1 bus daily. Washing machines. Small market. Reception open 8am-10pm. 420$ per person, 355$ per tent, 360$ per car. Shower 60$.

Food

Many budget restaurants cook in and around the **Praça do Giraldo.** ¡Warning! Food is strangely salty in Évora—bring your diuretics. A **public market** is usually in the small square in front of Igreja de São Francisco (cool bone place) and the public gardens. You will find produce, flowers, and a wild assortment of local cheeses (including *queijo de cabra,* goat cheese).

> **Café-Restaurante A Gruta,** Av. General Humberto Delgado, 2 (tel. 281 86), outside the city wall on the way to Pr. de Touros. Follow R. República toward the train station and turn right at the end of the park. It's in a cave! Inhale the thick aroma of roasting fowl as you pass by the monstrous grill. Lip-smacking *frango no churrasco* (barbecued chicken) buried under a heap of fries is a satisfying meal for two (900$). Half-chicken (500$). Open Sun.-Fri. 7am-3pm and 5pm-midnight.
>
> **Restaurante O Garfo,** R. de Santa Catarina, 13-15 (tel. 292 56). Leave the square via R. Serpa Pinto and take the 1st right. Giant tea drinking fork on the wall. Serene service of massive portions. *Gaspacho à Aleutejana com peixe frito* 875$. Entrees 850-1050$. Open 11am-10:30pm.
>
> **Restaurante A Choupana,** R. Mercadores, 16-20 (tel. 244 27), off Pr. Giraldo. Elegantly prepared Portuguese nouvelle cuisine. *Trutas do Minho* (Minhoesque trout) 680$. Mind the astronomical cover charge (it may reach 800$). To avoid it, reject the bread and small salad. Entrees 680-1300$. 1/2-portions 600$. Open 10am-2pm and 7-10pm.
>
> **Restaurante Aquário,** R. de Valdevinos, 7 (tel. 294 03). From Turismo cross the *praça,* take R. 5 D'Outubro, and turn right. What a relief to stumble into this petite, shady *restaurante* on a hot summer day. Great for a meal or just a sweat-dabbing drink break. Meat kebabs with salad and fries 840$. Other entrees 820-1400$. Swoony desserts. Open 9am-10pm.

Sights

Évora earns the title "museum city" for its streets brimming with monuments and architectural riches. Wooden tombstones cover the floor of **Igreja Santo Antão** at the northern end of **Praça do Giraldo**. Its fortress-like outer bulk conceals a serene, vaulted interior space.

Off the east side of the *praça*, Rua 5 de Outubro leads to the colossal 12th century **sé**. Two asymmetrical towers, one capped by a conical, tile-covered dome, the other encircled by a series of turrets, frame a deeply recessed porch. The Twelve Apostles that adorn the porch are masterpieces of medieval Portuguese sculpture. Between the nave and the chancel soars an octagonal tower supported by squinches (arches across the corners of the tower). The **claustro** of the cathedral (accessible by a small door to the right of the entrance) is in a ponderous 14th-century Romanesque style. Small circular openings with Moorish latticework pierce part of the area above the arcade. Dark staircases spiral to the cloister's roof. The **Museu de Arte Sacra,** in a gallery above the nave, houses the cathedral's treasury and astonishing 13th-century ivory *Virgem do paraíso*. (Cloister and museum open Tues.-Sun. 9am-noon and 2-5pm. Admission 200$.)

Adjacent to the north side of the cathedral lounges the 16th-century Episcopal palace, now the **Museu d'Évora**. Its varied collection includes Roman artifacts unearthed in the nearby countryside and 16th- and 17th-century European paintings. Upstairs, the prize of the painting collection is a series of 13 canvases illustrating the life of Mary. (Open Tues.-Sun. 10am-12:30pm and 2-5pm. Admission 300$, seniors and students free.)

Across from the museum, Évora's most famous monument, the 2nd-century **Templo de Diana**, stands outlined against the sky. It was used as a slaughterhouse for centuries.

Facing the temple is the town's best-kept secret, **Igreja de São João Evangelista** (1485). The church is the private property of the Cadaval family, who live in their ancestors' ducal palace next door. (Open 9am-noon and 2-6pm; 125$.) The interior is covered with dazzling *azulejos* that depict the life of St. Lawrence Giustiniani, patriarch of Venice. The *trompe l'oeil azulejo* window still confuses the Cadavals. Ask to see the church's assorted hidden chambers. A visit to the crypt, filled with the crumbling bones of bygone monks, is the perfect appetizer for the infamous Capela de Ossos. (Exhaustive guided tour includes small museum next door. Ring bell of house to get in.)

On the west side of the *largo,* down a flight of steps, is the **Convento de Nossa Senhora do Carmo** (1665), decorated with a Baroque version of Manueline motifs that look like ribbons on a Christmas package. On R. Misericórdia stands the 16th-century **Convento de Nossa Senhora da Graça.** Not much remains of the original interior except three rear windows. Miniature ceiling coffers recede sharply, creating an illusion of depth. (Open Tues.-Sun. 9am-noon and 2-5pm. Admission 300$).

The *piece de resistance* of a visit to Évora is, of course, the **Igreja Real de São Francisco**. Its austere bulk represents the finest example of Manueline Gothic architecture in southern Portugal—far more importantly, it encoffins the rapturously perverse **Capela de Ossos** (Chapel of Bones). Some osseophiles come all the way to Portugal just to see this grisly masterpiece. Above the door an inscription reads: "*Nós ossos que aqui estamos, pelos vossos esperamos"* ("We bones here awaiting lie, your own bones and you to die"). Three tireless Franciscan monks ransacked assorted local cemeteries for the remains of 4000 people in order to construct it. Enormous femurs neatly panel every inch of wall space, while rows of skulls and an occasional pelvis line the capitals and ceiling vaults. Baby tibias fill cracks of empty space. The decayed and shriveled corpses of an adult and an infant dangle ghoulishly on one wall. The three innovative founders grimace at skeptics from the stone sarcophagus to the right of the altar. Outside the chapel on a wall, a collection of shorn human braids are thank-yous to St. Francis for prayers answered. Some are over a hundred years old, others are fresh from the scalp. (Church and chapel open Mon.-Sat. 8:30am-1pm and 2:30-6pm, Sun. 10-11:30am and 2:30-6pm. Admission to chapel 25$; 50$ to take pictures.)

Just south of the church sprawls a dreary **Jardim Público.** At the northeast end of the park, an exit leads to R. Raimundo, past the 17th-century **Igreja Conventual de Nossa Senhora das Mercês.** The multicolored tile interior is now a museum of decorative arts. (Open Thurs. and Sat.-Sun. 10am-12:30pm and 2-5pm. Free.) From here either continue onto Pr. Giraldo or explore the neighboring side streets, where the stone pavements, whitewashed houses, and connecting arches have changed little since the 13th century, when this was the Jewish quarter of town.

Entertainment

Although most of Évora turns into a pumpkin when the clock strikes midnight, **Xeque-Mate,** R. Valdevinos, 21 (2nd right off R. 5 de Outubro from the *praça*), and **Discoteca Slide,** R. Serpa Pinto, 135, keep the music blaring until 2am. Only couples and single women need apply. Both clubs charge 800$ for admission and two beers. Évora's most popular café-bar hangout is **Portugal,** R. João de Deus, 55.

Évora's festival, the **Feira de São João** (last week of June), celebrates the arrival of summer with a full-fledged, Portuguese-style country grange fair. Labor organization tents and shiny tractors on display accompany the usual fair trappings: rides and pink cotton candy. Farmers and butchers sell pungent Portuguese meats and cheeses to regional dancers and onlookers alike. The Feast of São Pedro is the climax; after a bullfight and fireworks display, the dancing lasts 'til dawn.

Near Évora

On a prominent hill 35km northeast of Évora, the tiny village of **Evoramonte** clings to its massive **castelo.** Originally Roman, the castle was remodeled in the 14th and 16th centuries, and now has three lovely vaulted Gothic halls. Evoramonte is famous in Portuguese history as the place where liberal Dom Pedro IV secured the throne for his niece after forcing his reactionary brother to abdicate. The house where the 1834 agreement was signed bears a commemorative plaque. Although this hamlet is a lovely place to pass a few hours, only those with cars can get back to town. A morning **train** or **bus** (245$) doesn't return to Évora until the next day.

Évora's most cosmopolitan neighbor, **Monsaraz,** overlooks the Guadiana Valley from a hilltop on the border between Portugal and Spain. The road enters the town through a pointed gateway and leads to the main square. On the south side lies the **Municipio** with an arched veranda and a splendid coat of arms. The surprisingly large 16th-century **Igreja Paroquial** contains the late 13th-century marble tomb of Gomes Martin, decorated with carved figures in a funeral procession. On R. Direita, a virtually intact 16th-century street, the former **Tribunal** houses a recently discovered allegorical 13th-century fresco. The 18th-century **Hospital da Misericórdia,** opposite the parish church, has a beautiful meeting hall and a chapel of very fine gilded Baroque woodwork.

A *quarto* in Monsaraz costs 800-1200$ per person. **Estalagem d. Nuno,** R. José Fernandes Caeiro, 6 (tel. 551 46), is more expensive. (Singles 3000$. Doubles 4500$. Breakfast included.) Round-trip public transportation is a pain here as well. A **bus** runs at 11am and 1:15pm from the station in Évora with a return trip the following morning (round-trip 400$).

Elvas

Within the fortified walls of Elvas you can eat the local sugarplums and share outdoor cafés with the Spaniards who storm the border to buy sheets and towels at far lower Portuguese prices. The town blankets the crown of a steep hill, baking under the Alentejo sun. Arid heat forces people into the shade of canopied sidewalks and restricts business to the cooler morning and early evening hours. Despite the 17th- and 18th-century reinforced battlements, the town retains the character of its Moorish past and has a number of extraordinary churches.

Orientation and Practical Information

Conveniently situated 15km west of the border, Elvas is often a necessary stopover on the voyage to or from Badajoz, Spain (1hr. by bus). Infrequent buses (75$) connect Elvas' train station to the town center. The bus station is on **Praça da República** (the main square), no more than a five-minute walk from the *pensões* and restaurants. Many stores and restaurants line the busy **Rua da Cadeia** and the two streets perpendicular to it, **Rua da Carreira** and **Rua do Alcamim,** just south of the *praça*.

Tourist Office: Pr. República (tel. 62 22 36). Well-armed with detailed maps and pamphlets about the rest of Portugal. Open Mon.-Fri. 9am-7pm, Sat. 10am-12:30pm and 2-5:30pm, Sun. 10am-12:30pm and 2:30-5:30pm; winter Mon.-Sat. 9am-7pm, Sun. 10am-1pm.

Currency Exchange: Hotel Dom Luis, Av. Badajoz (tel. 62 27 56), near the aqueduct. Late-night service.

Post Office: R. Cadeia (tel. 62 21 11), at the end of the street across from the hospital. Open for mail and Posta Restante Mon.-Fri. 8:30am-6pm. **Postal Code:** 7350.

Telephones: At the post office. **Telephone Code:** 069.

Trains: Fontainhas (tel. 62 28 16), 3km north of city. Connected to Pr. República by bus (every 2hr. noon-10pm, 75$). To: Badajoz, Spain (2 per day, 1hr., 450$); Évora (2 per day, 3hr., 310$); Portalegre (4 per day, 1 1/2 hr., 345$); Lisboa (4 per day, 5 1/2 hr., 840$).

Buses: Pr. República (tel. 628 75), next to Turismo. To: the Spanish border at Caia (4 per day, 20min., 130$); Évora (3 per day, 2hr., 780$); Portalegre (2 per day, 1 1/2 hr., 550$); Lisboa (5 per day, 4hr., 1200$); constant connections to Badajoz (15min., 80ptas).

Hospital: R. Feira (tel. 62 21 77), through the arch, then right.

Emergency: tel. 115.

Police: R. Andrés Gonçalves (tel. 62 26 13).

Accommodations and Camping

Despite Elvas' modest fame, inexpensive accommodations are usually full. As always, try renting a room in a private home. Politely and firmly bargain the price of a single down to 2500$ maximum, and pay no more than 3500$ for a double. The few existing *pensões* are boarding houses for semi-permanent residents, with owners utterly unaccustomed to one-nighters.

Joaquina T. Dias (quartos), R. João d'Olivença, 5 (tel. 62 47 22), 1st left below the bus station next to "O Escondidinho" restaurant. Pink beds, haphazard religious iconography, cramped baths, and quiet. Singles 2000$. Doubles 3000$. Oct.-May: 1500$; 2500$.

Lucinda da Conceição Travancas (quartos), R. Aires Vareza, Páteo 2 (tel. 62 37 36). Right off R. João d'Olivença, 1st left below the bus station. Rooms are cool and clean, with oak furniture. Singles 2000$. Doubles 3500$, with bath 4500$.

Maria Garcia (quartos), R. Aires Varzea, 5 (tel. 62 21 26), across the street from Lucinda's. Frolic in the cheerful and immaculate bathrooms to escape the bare and dingy rooms. Singles 2000$. Doubles 3500$.

Camping: Parque da Piedade (tel. 62 37 72), a few km southwest of town. Less-than-clean facilities. As always, watch your belongings. 150$ per person, 200-300$ per tent, 200$ per car. Cold showers and water free. Open May-Sept. **Varche,** a small hamlet just off the main highway about 4km east of Elvas. Once the royal family's garden, the site overlooks the checkered Spanish plains. English owners in process of renovating cottages; for now, pitch a tent under an orange tree or park a trailer in the olive grove. Take the Rodoviária bus to Elvas, which stops in Varche, and ask at **Café/Restaurante Pepé** for directions to **Quinta de Torre das Arcas**; or take the road behind **Casa dos Frangos,** a chicken-coop/restaurant on the highway, and bear right where the smooth road ends. Inquiries can be made through RJ and ME Cornwell, Apt. 180, Elvas 7350, Portugal.

Food

Unless you go to the hotel, you'll eat cheaply. Every Monday fresh produce is sold at an outdoor **market** near the aqueduct.

Groceries: Supermarkets line R. da Cadeia.

Canal 7, R. Sapateiros, 16 (tel. 62 35 93), on a street just east of Pr. República. Good warm food served by a good warm family in a neighborhood joint. Whole chicken to go 550$, 1/2-chicken with fries (sitting down) 425$. Other entrees 450-700$. Open Mon.-Sat. noon-3pm and 7-9pm.

Bar Os Elvenses, R. Évora, 2. Follow R. Carreira (west of R. Alcamin) and bear left at the fork in the street. Filling meals (700-900$) in a sun-drenched interior patio. *Febras de porco* (grilled pork) 800$, -portion 450$. Open Thurs.-Tues. 10am-10pm.

O Vinho Verde, R. Tabolado, 4 (tel. 62 91 69), around the corner from Os Elvenses. Loud TV reverberates throughout this local bar. Entrees 500-800$. *Bitoque* 500$. Open Mon.-Sat. 8am-3pm and 5-9:30pm.

Estalagem Dom Sancho, Pr. República, 20 (tel. 62 26 86), across the narrow corner of the *praça* from Turismo. Plush old Portuguese inn with an interior courtyard. Often booked on summer evenings when Spaniards hop over to spray some *pesetas* around. Entrees 900-1200$. Tourist menu 1800$. Open noon-3pm and 7-10pm.

Sights

Elvas' primary spectacle is the **Aqueduto da Amoreira,** a colossal, four-tiered structure that emerges from a hill at the entrance to the city. Nearly 8km long and 31m high in places, its construction began in 1529 and took almost a century. Haughtily flaunting the city seal, the aqueduct is the largest in Europe and considered one of the most beautiful. Lisboa's largest shopping center, Amoreiras, is styled after it.

Igreja de Nossa Senhora da Assunção dominates the main square, which is itself covered with mosaics. Reconstructed in the 16th century in Manueline style, the church interior is decorated with abstract *azulejos* and covered by a beautifully ribbed and vaulted ceiling. Behind the cathedral and uphill to the right is **Igreja de Nossa Senhora da Consolação,** also known as **Freiras.** Ostensibly Renaissance, the octagonal interior actually explodes, mosque-like, in multicolored geometric tiles. In the three-sided *praça* in front of the church stands another of the city's unique monuments: built in the 16th century, the **pelourinho** is an octagonal pillory that culminates in a pyramid. From here, narrow streets cluttered with colorful houses lead uphill to the **castelo.** Enlarged in the 15th century, it was originally constructed by the Moors on the site of a Roman fortress. To the right of the entrance, hidden behind some plants, is a stairwell leading up to the castle walls where you can walk around the periphery and ogle.

Walking to the left as you leave the castle, follow the alleys skirting the city walls and pass under the Arco do Miradeiro. Downhill, just below the **Cemetério dos Ingleses** (Graveyard of the Englishmen, so-named for the Protestant Peninsular War soldiers buried there), is the **Ordem Terceira de São Francisco,** also known as **Igreja dos Terceiros.** Ask the sacristan to unlock the cemetery gate. From here there is an amazing view of **Forte da Graça,** high on a hill north of the city. The church itself, built in 1741, has a flashy interior including a richly gilded Baroque high altar. The sacristan likes to show-off the small garden in the back with its *azulejo*-ed altar. (All churches and the *castelo* open 9:30am-12:30pm and 2:30-7pm; Oct.-May 9:30am-12:30pm and 2:30-5:30pm.)

The **Museu Arqueológico e Etnológico** is around the corner from Pensão Central on Largo do Colégio (the entrance is between the library and a large church). Hagiophiles drool over the life-size paintings of saints now haunting the ex-convent's wide corridors. The museum rooms display, among other items, Roman mosaics and artifacts from Africa and the Portuguese Far East. (Open Mon.-Fri. 9am-1pm and 3-6pm, Sat. 10am-1pm. Admission 150$.)

Entertainment

Elvas dies at night.

Portalegre

Relative to its heyday as an important Moorish fortress and thriving center for the region's wool tapestry and silk industries, modern Portalegre is a snore. The city's only movie theater closed in spring 1989 for lack of attendance. Located in the foothills of the Serra de São Mamede just 24km from the Spanish border, most of its inhabitants depend on agricultural work or employment in the chemical plant and cork factory that protrude above the urban skyline.

Some of Portalegre's traditional skills have been preserved in modern commercial enterprise: a tapestry factory in what was once a Jesuit monastery churns out cloth masterpieces that take up to two years to produce; the cork factory carries on the age-old industry of converting cork-oak bark into bottle-stoppers. Cork from this factory is partially responsible for livable temperatures aboard United States NASA spacecraft.

Orientation and Practical Information

All traffic through Portalegre intersects at the *rossio* in the center of the new town. The old, walled section of the city spreads up a gently sloping hill several blocks south of here. Most sights are located in this charming part of town. **Avenida República** heads north in the other direction.

Tourist Office: Largo de Santana, 23 (tel. 21 815, fax 240 53), 1km from the bus station. Follow directions to the youth hostel, then continue downhill and turn right at the 1st intersection. After you pass the police station, turn left; the office is at the foot of the hill. Photocopied maps and glossy pamphlets about surrounding villages. Open Mon.-Fri. 9am-7pm, Sat.-Sun. 10:30am-7pm.

Currency Exchange: União de Bancos Portugueses, R. Nuno Alvares Perreira, 8. On the corner 1 bl. from the bus station towards town. Open Mon.-Fri. 8:30am-3pm.

Post Office: Av. Liberdade (tel. 211 11), above the *rossio* and little park with the WWI monuments. Open Mon.-Fri. 8:30am-6pm. **Postal Code:** 7300.

Telephones: In the post office. **Telephone Code:** 045.

Trains: (tel. 961 23), 13km south of the city. Mon.-Sat. 4 buses per day go to the bus station, Sun. 3 per day (20min., 170$.) To: Elvas (4 per day, 50min., 345$); Évora (4 per day, 4hr., 725$); Lisboa (4 per day, 6 1/2 hr., 1200$); Sautarém (4 per day with change in Entroncamento, 4 1/2 hr., 815$).

Buses: R. Nuno Alvarez Pereira, near the *rossio*. To: Estremoz (2 per day, 1 1/2 hr., 558$); Évora (2 per day, 2 1/2 hr., 720$); Beja (2 per day, 4 1/2 hr., 950$); Lisboa (3 per day, 5 1/2 hr., 1250$); Viseu (1 per day, 5hr, 1380$).

Luggage Stoage: Depósito de Volumes at the **bus station**. 80$ per bag per day.

Taxis: (tel. 223 75). In the *rossio*. Expensive, but you may have no choice. To the train station 20min., 1200$.

Hospital: Av. Santo António (tel. 212 19).

Emergency: tel. 115.

Police: Pr. República (tel. 215 47), in the building of the Governo Civil.

Accommodations and Camping

Budget accommodations are a scarcity.

Pousada de Juventude (HI) Pr. República (tel. 235 68), 1km from the bus station. Smack below the cork factory, an infallible landmark, in a former convent. From the *rossio* follow the signs for the police, then take your first left to a small park and playground. Walk uphill under the trees; when they end turn left up the flight of stairs. At the top, walk straight ahead toward the palms. The hostel is just past the graveyard of buses. Go through the gates to a sorry-looking building complex, and the hostel will be on the left. This place is great: very clean and often completely empty. Fickle hot showers. Enthusiastic warden loves company. Kitchen facilities. Open 8-10am and 6-11pm. 800$ per person. Breakfast included.

Mansão Alto Alentejo, R. 19 de Junho, 59 (tel. 222 90). Three left-hand bl. from the main tourist office. Pleasant, family-run *pensão* in heart of the old city. Heartwarming rooms beam with colorful, floral-painted furniture. Winter heating. Singles 2000$, with bath 3000$. Doubles 3300$, with bath 4300$. Breakfast included.

Pensão Nova (Residencial São Pedro), R. 31 de Janeiro, 28-30 (tel. 216 05). Follow the signs from the *rossio* to the reception at Pensão Nova. Two other nameless buildings on the *rossio* are under the same ownership. All rooms sunny and tastefully furnished; many overlook a well-manicured park. Singles 2700$, with bath 3400$. Doubles 4000$, with bath 6000$. Breakfast included.

Camping: Quinta de Saúde (Orbitur) (tel. 228 48), 4km northeast of town on E.N. 246-2. 370$ per person, 320$ per tent, 345$ per car. Electricity 250$. Showers 60$. Discounts up to 70% Oct.-March. Open Jan. 16-Nov. 15.

Food

Bars around the *rossio* serve beer, *bicas* (small espressos), and light meals. Restaurants in the old town offer more traditional settings and meals. Portalegre's children grow strong on the *açorda Aleutejana,* garlic soup with bread and an egg in it. The **municipal market,** near the São Bernardo convent, sells fresh produce, fish, and meat (Wed. and Sat. 6am-3pm).

Groceries: Plaça Nova, R. Nuno Alvares Pereira, 12. First building on the right from the bus station. Despite the name it's a small supermarket. Open Mon.-Fri. 9am-7pm, Sat. 9am-1pm. Groceries also at **R. Gerência de Antunes,** 10, in the old town.

Restaurante O Abrigo, R. Elvas, 74 (tel. 227 78), near Mansão Alto Alentejo. Modest exterior cloaks a surprisingly attractive dining room with A/C. Delicious *açorda Alentejana* 200$. Entrees 600-1050$. Tourist menu 1290$. Open Wed.-Mon. 10am-3pm and 5:30-10pm.

Cervejaria Cordas, Av. Liberdade, 47 (tel. 235 12). Clean new dining room with A/C next to a stand-up bar (the *cervejaria* part). Instantly packed at lunch. Entrees 700-1200$. *Plato do dia* 700$. *Açorda Aleutejana* 150$. Meals served noon-3pm and 7:30-10:30pm.

Restaurante "Stop", R. Don "Nuno" Alvares Pereira, 11-15 (tel. 213 64), across from the bus station. Like an elementary school classroom without the finger-paintings. Tasty *lulas* (squid) 650$. "Open" Mon.-Sat. noon-2pm and 7-10pm.

Restaurante Alpendre, R. Janeiro, 19 (tel. 216 11). Expensive appetizers, but every mouthful of scrumpy spreads and warm bread makes it worthwhile. Local specialties (850-1200$) are worth an extra escudo. Open noon-10pm.

Sights

The huge granite pillars of the **sé** block the western end of the old town. Its late-Renaissance façade is recessed between two towers with narrow slit windows. A terrace behind the *sé* (entered through an archway of the bishop's residence) looks toward the **Penha de São Tomé,** a rocky hill with 289 steps leading up to a small church, a rather dehydrating climb. (Open 8-11am and 3:30-6pm. Free.)

The **Museu Municipal,** flanking the cathedral, displays a fine collection of sacred art that once belonged to the city's convents. The museum is definitely worth the one-hour guided tour (in Portuguese only), if only to see the ivory reliefs illustrating the *Slaying of the Innocents* and the *Ascension of the Virgin.* (Open Tues.-Sun. 9:30am-12:30pm and 2-6pm. Admission 150$, children and seniors free.)

A little farther north you'll find the **Palácio Amarelo** (yellow palace), now decaying, famed for its beautiful 17th-century wrought-iron grilles. Across the old quarter, near the youth hostel, the **Casa do Poeta José Régio** is a house museum containing a collection of the poet's religious art. (Open Tues.-Sun. 9:30am-12:30pm and 2-6pm. Admission 150$, seniors and children free.)

A decrepit 17th-century Jesuit college near the *rossio* is now the headquarters of **Fábrica Real de Tapiçaria** (royal tapestry factory), where paintings are reproduced in woven cloth with 5000 shades of thread. Patrons pay about US$2000 per square meter for the finished product. To get there, head uphill and turn left off R. 31 de Janeiro. Enter at #26, climb the wide stairway and ring at the unmarked brown door on the left. (Open Mon.-Fri. 9am-noon and 2-5pm.) Not far from the factory, uphill past the manicured park and playground on the right, 1739 *azulejos* decorate the huge Manueline interior of the **Convento de São Bernardo.** The tomb of the founding bishop lies within the church, encrusted with religiosity despite scandalous rumors that he fathered a child with one of the convent's nuns

Near Portalegre

Buses run between most towns once or twice per day on weekdays. On weekends schedules change or service stops entirely. If you're an aspiring orienteer, you'll find that hiking between towns is one of the best ways to explore the area. Footpaths between the villages are numerous. The warden at the youth hostel is a fount of information on jaunts in the hillsides and may even take guests out for daytrips.

Marvão

If you have time to visit only one hilltown in Portugal, let it be Marvão. This border stronghold, 21km northwest of Portalegre and only 6km from Spain, preserves its full medieval character in a remarkable setting. Massive walls still encircle this great military outpost of the Middle Ages and trap hundreds of years of history within stone borders. The 13th-century **castelo** sits above the western edge of town. Below the town walls, terraced fields and patchwork pastures stretch to the horizon. Simply maahvelous.

Marvão's **tourist office** (tel. 932 26) shares the white chapel at the foot of the castle with the two-room **Museu Municipal.** The museum displays local paleolithic finds and folk costumes still worn during festivals, alongside the usual Roman and medieval bric-a-brac. (Both open 9am-12:30pm and 2-5:30pm. Museum admission 150$, students free.)

Turismo's cheerful multilingual staff stocks information on the only inexpensive accommodations in town—rooms in private houses. The town allows free **camping** inside the castle walls in summer as long as there is no more than a tent or two. **Pensão Dom Dinis** (just down R. Dr. Matos Magalhães from Turismo, tel. 932 36) is a grand hotel with stone floors and steps. (Comfy singles and doubles with bath 7200-8000$. Annex one block below contains more modest singles and doubles from 6000$, triples from 7800$. Breakfast included.) Among the town's good **restaurants** is the nameless one (tel. 931 60) at the end of Travessa da Praça. (Go through the door on the left from the large stone terrace at the end of the street. Open 8am-midnight.)

The largest of Marvão's many seasonal **festivals** is Nossa Senhora da Estrêla, held Friday to Monday on the first or second weekend in September. A Luso-Spanish folk dancing fair is held in July. The **Festival da Castanha** (Chestnut Festival) the second weekend in November treats visitors to unlimited free wine, roasted chestnuts, and ham sandwiches.

Portagem and Beirã

Leaving Marvão, you can hike down a Roman road starting from the local hospital, next to the old convent on the switchback road just below the town walls. The 40-minute walk leads to the main highway through the town of **Portagem,** where a right turn will bring you to the **Piscina Fluvial do Sever,** a free outdoor swimming pool filled with water from the passing river.

Beirã, 12km from Marvão, is Portugal's border stop on the Madrid-Lisboa train line. A bus leaves the train station for Beirã's town center at 7am and 1pm, continuing on to Castelo de Vide and Portalegre (170$). Although stops in every intervening village make the ride rather tedious, the rural scenery compensates. The jovial owner of the station's *cantina* runs the spacious, usually empty **pensão** (tel. 921 30) upstairs. (Singles 2000$. Doubles 2500$.)

Castelo de Vide

The old walled town of Castelo de Vide stretches along the top of a foothill of the Serra de São Mamede, 20km due north of Portalegre and 13km west of Marvão. The town has a history of being kicked around faster than a hot potato. Don Afonso traded it to his brother around 1300 for some prime southern real estate and Dom Fernando pawned it off on the Order of Christ a century later. A maze of streets and tiny white houses picks its way to the Gothic windows and doorways of the **Judiaria.** Once one of Portugal's most important Jewish quarters, this section of town still preserves its medieval aura, although now only a plaque identifies its vacant, two-room synagogue. Just below this area, the **Fonte da Vila** (1586) dominates an intimate square surrounded by old houses.

In the center of town at Praça Dom Pedro V, **Igreja de Santa Maria** sticks up its nose at two 17th-century buildings, the Baroque **Palácio Torre** and the **Hospital Santo Amaro.** Despite its monumental size, the church's whitewash interior is comparatively modest. The pink-and-gray marble columns are actually just molded plaster with a paint job. View the landscape below from the **castelo de vide** (castle of vine) for which the town is named. The inner ring of fortifications has the highest lookout point (open 9am-8pm; Oct.-May 10am-5:30pm). Follow the signs from the center of town; it's not far from the synagogue to the castle.

Casa de Hóspedes Cantinho Particular, R. Miguel Bombarda, 9 (tel. 911 51), on a street off the square opposite Turismo, is a family-run *pensão* with about a dozen rooms and a homey atmosphere. (Singles 2000$. Doubles 3000$. Breakfast included.) The ground-floor **restaurant** serves a homemade *plato do dia* for 700$; other entrees start at 600$. (Open 8-10am, noon-3pm, and 7-10pm; Oct.-May Thurs.-Tues. 8-10am, noon-3pm, and 7-10pm.) The **tourist office** (tel. 913 61) is in the center of town on R. Bartolomeu Alvares da Santa near the square. (Open 9am-12:30pm and 4-7pm; Oct.-May 9am-12:30pm and 2-5:30pm.) The friendly staff can arrange for *quartos* in private houses (about 1000$ per person). A **bus** runs from Beirã to Castelo de Vide en route to Portalegre (170$).

Flor da Rosa

Built by the Knights of Malta in 1356, the former monastery of Flor da Rosa rises 24km west of Portalegre. The extraordinary complex consists of an imposing barrel-vaulted church, a Gothic cloister, and a splendid Manueline chapter house and refectory. Abandoned when the church ceiling collapsed in 1897, the monastery was left to the elements until 1940, when a massive reconstruction began. The enthusiastic caretaker launches into a proud stone-by-stone account of the mighty effort. (Admission 100$.)

The nearest train station is 3km away in **Crato** (tourist office tel. 971 61). From there you'll have to walk to the monastery. **Buses** from Portalegre also run to Crato, leaving in the early evening and returning the next morning.

Beja

Beja has long been known for its strong communist bent. Bitter disputes erupted here between landlords and farmers after the 1974 revolution, when the exploited farmers occupied and confiscated many of the large estates. Fourteen years later, political graffiti still covers the buildings of this serene, charming town. Old homes and modern shops sit in amity on narrow, winding streets. Perhaps to ensure the town's recent pacification, a German Air Force base sits on the town's outskirts, courtesy of the NATO exchange program.

Orientation and Practical Information

Beja is connected by direct highways to Lisboa (193km to the northwest), Évora (78km to the north), and to the Spanish border at Ficalho (65km due east). Transportation to the Algarve is easier by bus than by train.

Rua de Mértola and **Rua de Capitão João Francisco de Sousa** mark the center of town. The streets are unmarked and confusing, especially in the town center. The **train station** is in the eastern corner of town; those with heavy bags might want to taxi it to the town center (250$) rather than walk a half-hour uphill. The **bus station** is at the southern edge of town. To reach the center from the bus station, walk past the statue and turn left onto Av. do Brasil. After one block, turn right at the new white building and go past the post office on the left; continue up the curving street. At the intersection, take a left on R. Capitão J.F. de Sousa (with a small pedestrian square); keep to your right and watch for the tourist office.

Tourist Office: R. Capitão João Francisco de Sousa, 25 (tel. 236 93). Featureless map. Open Mon.-Fri. 9am-8pm, Sat. 10am-12:30pm and 2:30-6pm; Oct.-May Mon.-Fri. 10am-6pm, Sat. 10am-12:30pm and 2:30-6pm.

Travel Agent: Agência de Viagens Páx-Júlia, R. Capitão João Francisco de Sousa (tel. 224 54), across from Turismo, is a jack of all trades: **currency exchange,** car rental, and bookings. Open Mon.-Fri. 9am-12:30pm and 2-6:30pm.

Post Office: Largo do Correio (tel. 38 92 56), down the street from Pensão Rocha. Open for Posta Restante and **telephones** Mon.-Fri. 8:30am-6:30pm. **Postal Code:** 7800.

Telephone Code: 084.

Trains: (tel. 32 50 56), on the eastern edge of town. To: Lisboa (5 per day, 4hr., 860-950$); Évora (6 per day, 1hr., 535$); Faro (2 per day, 5 1/2 hr., 945$).

Buses: R. Cidade de São Paulo (tel. 32 40 44, 32 26 01), at the roundabout on the corner of Av. Brasil. To: Lisboa (4 *expressos* per day, 3hr., 1100$); Évora (3 per day, 2hr., 630-750$); Faro (5 per day, 3 1/2 hr., 1080$); Real de la Frontera, Spain (1 per day, 1 1/2 hr., 680$). Connections to Spain and France.

Taxis: tel. 224 74; about 300$ from train station to town center.

Car Rental: see **Agência de Viagens Páx-Júlia** above.

Luggage Storage: At the **bus station** on the platform 100$ per day.

Swimming Pool: Av. Brasil (tel. 236 26), near bus station and camping. In a fine complex with park and restaurant. Admission to park 50$, for park and swimming 200$. Open Thurs.-Sat. 9am-8pm.

Hospital: R. Dr. António F.C. Lima (tel. 32 21 33, midnight-8am tel. 32 28 24). Signs point the way from the bus and train stations.

Emergency: tel. 115.

Police: R. D. Nuno Alvares Pereira (tel. 32 20 22), 1 bl. downhill from Turismo and a couple of meters to the left.

Accommodations and Camping

Almost all hotels (and restaurants) are within a few blocks of the tourist office and the central pedestrian street. Deviant *pensões* cluster around **Pr. República.** Places fill quickly, so reserve several days in advance. The tourist office keeps an up-to-date list of accommodations and prices.

Residência Bejense, R. Capitão João Francisco de Sousa, 57 (tel. 32 50 01), down the street from the tourist office. Worth every red *escudo*. Luxuriously spacious rooms with carpeting. Lavish interior with classical dining room and mirrored hallways. Access to kitchen and TV lounge. All rooms with phones; only 3 rooms without private bath. Singles 2500$, with bath 3500$. Doubles with bath 4500$.

Pensão Tomás, R. Alexandre Herculano, 7 (tel. 246 13), turn right 1 bl. up from the intersection. Naked floors, but bright rooms with comfortable furnishings. Recently renovated, immaculate bathrooms. Doubles 3400$, with bath 4800$.

Casa de Hóspedes Rocha, Largo D. Nuno Alvares Pereira, 12 (tel. 242 71), up the curving street from the post office. Clean although a little worse for wear. Singles 1500$. Doubles 3000$. Triples 3500$.

Residencial Coelho, Pr. República, 15 (tel. 240 31). Room quality varies; some view the *praça*. All rooms with bath. Singles 3600$. Doubles 4800-5500$. Triples 7200$. Quads 8400$. Breakfast included.

Camping: on the southwest side of town at the end of Av. Vasco da Gama (tel. 243 28), past the stadium. Small, shady, and clean. 324$ per person, 216$ per tent and per car.

Food

Most restaurants keep limited hours here (noon-2pm and 7-10pm). The local specialty is *migas de pão,* a sausage and bacon dish cooked with bread. There's the municipal **market** in a building a block up from the bus station and one block right. (Open 6am-1:30pm.)

Café Saiote, R. da Biscayinha, 45 (tel. 258 87), off the intersection of Sousa and Mértola. Small, family-run restaurant. Hefty pig steak and cholesterol-rich fries 500$. Entrees 300-500$. Open 9am-3pm and 7pm-midnight.

Restaurante Tomás, R. Alexandre Herculano, 7 (tel. 246 13), beneath the *pensão*. A stylish, award-winning restaurant offering fish and meat dishes (860-1600$). Excellent *carne de porca à alentejano* (1000$). Wide variety of desserts. Open noon-3pm and 7-10pm.

Restaurante Alentejano, Largo dos Duques do Beja (tel. 238 49), across from the Museum as you walk down the steps. Simple restaurant with reasonable prices (entrees 650-850$). Everything apart from *bife de porco à Americana* (750$) is authentic Portuguese fare. Open Sat.-Thurs. noon-3pm and 7-10pm.

Churrasqueria O Alemão, Largo dos Duques de Beja (tel. 234 76). Walk down the stairs by the museum; ahead to the right. Terribly busy. Heavy Teutonic cuisine 500-900$. 1/2-chicken 380$. Open 11am-midnight.

Sights

The outstanding **Museu Rainha D. Leonor,** in the former Convento da Nossa Senhora da Conceição, is the site of sex and intrigue, but no murder. In 1669, a nun allegedly had a steamy affair with a French officer and confessed her story in the racy *Letters of a Portuguese Nun*. The letters were said to be translated into French from the Portuguese, although this is unlikely. They became an immediate literary success in France; the poet's identity is unknown. The museum has built the cell window through which some fanciful designer imagined the lovers exchanged secret vows of passion.

Inside, the gilded church's 18th-century *azulejo* panels depict the lives of Mary and St. John the Baptist. Nearby are fine intaglio marble altars and panels of *talha dourada*. Moorish *azulejos* and a Persian-style ceiling make the chapter house look like a mini mosque. The rest of the varied collection includes three paintings attributed to Ribera and some fine Roman sculpture. The 19th-century costumes on the second floor are worn by mannequins that bear a striking resemblance to the young Bette Davis. (Open Tues.-Sun. 9:45am-1pm and 2-5:15pm. Free. Ticket also good for the **Museu Visigótico** behind the *castelo*.)

One block northeast of the convent is the adobe-like **Igreja de Santa María** (13th-century, rebuilt in 15th century). Its corner column is emblazoned with a miniature bull, the city's symbol. From here Rua D. Aresta Branco leads past handsome old houses to the city's massive **castelo,** built around 1300 on the remains of a Roman fortress. It still flaunts an enormous crenellated marble keep, vaulted chambers, and stones covered with mysterious cryptic symbols (probably some sort of code). The interior walls are covered with ivy. (Open 10am-1pm and 2-6pm; Oct.-March 9am-noon and 1-4pm. Admission 100$.)

Back in the center of town a Manueline column enhances the long **Praça da República.** On one side stands **Igreja de Misericórdia,** built in 1550 as a market hall. Exiting the *praça* to the southeast leads to **Rua do Touro** and **Rua D. Afonso Costa,** a.k.a. **"Rua das Lojas"** (Street of Shops).

Algarve

This southern coast is in the process of selling its soul to commercial capitalism. After the Moors were driven from Portugal, the Algarve remained a quiet backwater of fishers; but increasing tourism and overdevelopment are destroying its trademark fishing villages. Portuguese often come in September, while in July and August foreigners predominate, lured by the region's beaches and sunny, hot, and dry weather. Ocean winds cool the mornings, while clear skies bless the evenings.

Aside from the mobbed resorts, plenty of villages welcome budget travelers, particularly between Lagos and Sagres (for instance, Salema and Burgau). Other inexpensive spots are Sagres (ravishing isolated beaches and sheer cliffs) and the region between Olhão and the Spanish border (also the least developed).

Reaching more remote beaches is a snap, as EVA has extensive bus services with convenient schedules and low fares. The train costs less than the bus but only connects major coastal cities, and in some towns the station is a hike from the center.

Algarve's cuisine relies on the sea. Ubiquitous *sardinha assada* (grilled sardines) often accompanies *caldeirada,* a chowder of fish and shellfish, potatoes, and tomatoes perked up with onion and garlic. Chefs stir up *cataplana* (a wild combination of clams, ham, and sausage, flavored with onions and paprika) and *carne de porco à Alentejana* (pork and clams marinated in a wine and coriander sauce). Specialties include *lulas* or *chocos* (squid), sometimes soaked in its own ink, *robalo* (bass), *peixe espada* (swordfish), and *anchova* (anchovy). Full-bodied local wines, such as Cartaxo, go for little; watch out for English-run establishments, which may charge a pretty penny for similar booze. Also keep an eye on official prices to avoid paying an extra "tourist tax" tacked onto meal, accommodation, and transportation costs.

Hotels and *pensões* usually fill during the peak months of July and August; use the reasonably priced *quarto.* Ask at tourist offices or bars, keep your eyes peeled for signs, or take your chances with the room-pushers who accost incoming travelers at bus and train stations. If you're staying for a month or more with two or three friends, renting an apartment may be affordable (a four-room apartment rents for up to 200,000$).

Tourist offices sell *The Algarve News* (local paper, 105$). It runs articles on trendy clubs, local festivals, special events, and nude beaches. Topless bathing is the fashion here, but bottomless (especially for women) is illegal, offensive to locals, and punishable with a jail term.

Faro

Zillions of northern Europeans begin their holiday in Faro, the Algarve's capital and largest city. Relatively few bother to stay longer than it takes for a package tour to ship them to Albufeira or Lagos. Unlike the rest of the Algarve, Faro remains a Portuguese provincial city.

The city grew in importance from the 13th to the 16th centuries. After the English made off with a bunch of valuable books from the bishop's library (which would become some of the first holdings of Oxford's Bodleian library), they burnt Faro to the ground in 1596. Built afresh, the city crumbled again in an 18th-century earthquake.

Orientation and Practical Information

Faro's commercial center surrounds **Doca de Recreio,** the small dock of empty fishing boats. The main road into town, **Avenida da República,** runs past the train station and bus depot, spilling into a delta of smaller streets at the **Praça D. Francisco Gomes** (a pedestrian mall). **Rua D. Francisco Gomes** and **Rua de Santo António** are the major pedestrian thoroughfares. Turismo is on **Jardim Manuel Bivar,** the town's small park.

Tourist Office: R. Misericórdia, 8 (tel. 80 36 04), at the far end of Jardim Manuel Bivar. The staff speaks English and can help with accommodations. Open Mon.-Fri. 9:30am-8pm, Sat.-Sun. 9:30am-5pm; Oct.-May 9:30am-5:30pm.

American Express: Star Agency, R. Conselheiro Bivar, 36 (tel. 80 55 25), off Pr. D. Francisco Gomes. Holds mail. Authorizes personal checks for cashing at local banks. No cash advances. Open Mon.-Fri. 9am-12:30pm and 2:30-6pm.

Post Office: Largo Carmo (tel. 82 41 26), across from Igreja de Nossa Senhora do Carmo. Open for Posta Restanta and telephones Mon.-Fri. 8:30am-6:30pm. **Postal Code:** 8000.

Telephones: R. Misericórdia, 1 (tel. 82 06 38), opposite the tourist office. Air-conditioned, comfortable cabins. Stay out of the staff's way. Open Mon.-Fri. 9am-6pm. **Telephone Code:** 089.

Flights: Airport (tel. 80 02 10), 7km west of city. Buses #16, 17, and 18 drive from the street opposite the bus station to the airport (every 20min. 7:10am-7:56pm, 20min., 125$). From airport to the bus station, similar frequency and schedule. **TAP Air Portugal** (tel. 80 32 49), next to Pensão Algarve on R. D. Francisco Gomes. Open Mon.-Fri. 9am-12:15pm and 2-5:45pm. To: London (1 per day, round-trip 85,100$); Lisboa (one-way 13,500$); Madrid (1 per day via Lisboa, 35,800$). Student discounts up to 50%.

Trains: Largo da Estação (tel. 82 26 53). To get to Turismo, turn right and walk along the harbor. To: Lisboa (5 per day, 7hr., 1450$); Albufeira (8 per day, 45min.-1hr., 250$); Vila Real de Santo António (10 per day, 1 1/2 hr., 380$); Lagos (8 per day, 2 1/2 hr., 500$).

Buses: EVA, Av. República (tel. 80 33 25). To get to Turismo, turn right and walk along the harbor. To: Lisboa (3 per day, 7hr., 1700-2150$); Beja (4 *expressos* per day, 3hr., 1080$); Albufeira (14 per day, 1hr., 600$); Olhão (15 per day, 20min., 150$); Vila Real de Santo António (9 per day, 1hr., 600$). **Caima** (tel. 81 29 80), across the street and 1 door over, is their rival. To: Lisboa (every hr., 4 1/2 hr., 2000$); Porto (every hr., 8 1/2 hr., 2750$); Braga (every hr., 10hr., 2800$).

Taxis: Rotaxi (tel. 82 22 89). From bus station to airport about 800$.

Laundromat: Sólimpa, R. Letes, 43 (tel. 82 29 81). Up R. Primeiro de Maio, straight through the *praça*. Wash and dry 300$ per kg. 2kg minimum. Open Mon.-Fri. 9am-1pm and 3-7pm, Sat. 9am-1pm.

Hospital: R. Leão Pinedo (tel. 82 20 11), north of town.

Emergency: tel. 115.

Police: R. Bernardo de Passos (tel. 82 20 22), off R. 5 de Outubro.

Accommodations and Camping

Rooms vanish in high season. Tourist office's top-20 list of *pensões* helps. Lodgings are concentrated near the bus and train stations.

Residencia Pinto, R. 1 de Maio, 27 (tel. 82 28 20), off Pr. D. Francisco Gomes. Cramped but cozy rooms with clean common bath. Singles 2000$. Doubles 3000$. Triples 3500$. Oct.-May: 1500$; 2500$; 3000$.

Pensão Oceano, Travessa Ivens, 21 (tel. 82 33 49), off R. 1 de Maio. Tidy, cheerful rooms with Scandinavian furniture. All rooms have bath and telephone. Singles 4000-5000$. Doubles 6000-6500$. Oct.-June: 3000$; 4000$. Breakfast included.

Pensão Tivoli, Pr. Alexandre Herculano, 6 (tel. 82 85 41), 3 bl. from Turismo on the corner with R. Alexandre Herculano. Old decor but fresh paint. One common bath. The ingenious elderly owner has rigged a string with pulleys to open the street door from the top of the stairs. Doubles 3000$. Showers 500$.

Pensão Algarve, R. D. Francisco Gomes, 4 (tel. 82 33 46), 2 bl. from Turismo on the *praça*. Convenient location. Under renovation. Carnivorous insects from the harbor devour unsuspecting guests. Fire engines serenade at night. Singles 3000$. Doubles 3500$, with bath 5000$.

Pensão Residencial O Faráo, Largo da Madalena, 4 (tel 82 33 56). From D. Francisco Gomes, follow R. Cancelheiro Bivar to the eensy Largo. This *pensão* with a makeover has a luxurious reception area in marble and glass, and a terrace overlooking the city where lodgers breakfast. The rooms have distinctive tiles; all have sparkling new bathrooms. Some overlook the quiet square & fountain. Singles 7000$. Doubles 7500-8500$. Quads 12,800$. Oct.-May: 3000-3500$; 4000$.

Camping (tel. 81 78 76) sprawls on the beach, Praia de Faro. 75$ per person, 40$ per child; 75$ per tent; 50$ per car. Showers 25$. Reception open 9am-9pm.

Food

Almonds and figs grow on trees. Faro has some of the Algarve's chattiest cafés, flocks of them on **Pr. D. Francisco Gomes.** At the **market,** locals buy and sell everything from dried octopus to small semis. (Open Mon.-Fri. 9am-1pm.)

> **Restaurante Snack-Bar Centenário,** Largo Teneiro Bispo, 4-6 (tel. 82 33 43), on R. Lethes. Wood furniture in tiled rooms. Simple food. Wide assortment of fish and meat dishes 800-1200$. A full portion would fill even Mr. Creosote. Open noon-11pm.
>
> **Restaurante Fim do Mundo,** R. Vasco da Gama, 53 (tel. 262 99), off Pr. Ferreira de Almeida. The sign overhead wails "Frango" (chicken). Chicken with fries 1100$. Take-out too. *Péru* (roast turkey, 650$). Open Mon. noon-3pm, Wed.-Sun. noon-3pm and 5-10pm.
>
> **Restaurante Dois Irmãos,** Largo Terreiro do Bispo, 14, r/c (tel. 82 33 37), across from Restaurante O Centenário. More flair than its neighbors. Entrees 840-1480$. *Arroz de polvo* (octopus rice) 840$. Open noon-11pm.
>
> **Restaurante Chelsea,** R. D. Francisco Gomes, 28 (tel. 82 84 95). Elegant sidewalk café downstairs, blue and white Art Deco restaurant upstairs. Cheerful service. *Arroz de marisco* (seafood rice, 950$) and *platos do dia* (650-700$). Open noon-3pm and 6:30-11pm.
>
> **Restaurante Peking,** Av. República, 168 (tel. 82 70 51), between bus station and *praça*. Chow mein to die for. Entrees 800-1750$. Owners speak English. Open July-May noon-3pm and 7pm-midnight.

Sights and Entertainment

Near the small harbor and public garden, the 18th-century **Arco da Vila** pierces the old wall. A narrow road leads through an Arab portico to the Renaissance **sé,** which sits forlornly in a deserted square. One day, not long ago, archeologists unearthed traces of Neolithic civilization under the cathedral; lo and behold, the site was also sacred to Romans, Visigoths, and Moors. The simplicity of the Renaissance interior is relieved by the Capela do Rosário (right), decorated with 17th-century *azulejos,* a red Chinoiserie organ, and sculptures of two Nubians bearing lamps.

The **Museu Arqueológico e Lapidar** (behind the church) stockpiles a hodge-podge of Roman and earlier artifacts, religious paintings, *azulejos,* and military memorabilia in a two-story Gothic-Renaissance cloister. The prize piece, a 30- by 20-foot Roman mosaic, has a room all to itself. (Open Mon.-Fri. 9am-noon and 2-5pm. Admission 125$.)

Across from the old city and facing the huge and dusty Largo de São Francisco stands the mighty **Igreja de São Francisco,** whose hulking façade belies a delicate interior. The chancel extends into a long, tunnel-shaped room leading to the elaborate high altar. (Open Mon.-Sat. 10am-1pm.) The **Capela dos Ossos** in **Igreja de Nossa Senhora do Carmo** is a wall-to-wall macabre bonanza of crusty bones and fleshless monk skulls borrowed from the adjacent cemetery. (Open 10am-1pm and 3-5pm. Free.) Nearby, **Igreja de São Pedro** displays *azulejos* of St. Peter and twin pulpits atop curving stairs.

The city's **Museu de Etnografia Regional,** occupying an entire wing of the District Assembly Building, introduces guests to the folklife of the Algarve. (Open Mon.-Fri. 9:30am-12:30pm and 2-5:30pm. Admission 100$, students with ID and seniors free.) The **Museu da Marinha** crowns the Departamento Marítimo do Sul (next to Hotel Eva) with the history of Portuguese boats. Here the boat that bore imperialists up the Congo River in 1492 (the horror, the horror), the mightiest galleon of the 16th century, and the single vessel that outclassed the Turkish navy in 1717 highlight a time when the Algarve was on the cutting edge of technology. (Open Mon.-Fri. 9:30am-12:30pm and 2-5:30pm, Sat. 9am-1pm. Free.)

Numerous sidewalk **cafés** line the pedestrian walkways off the garden in the center of town. For dancing, try the boisterous (and somewhat expensive) **Scheherazade,** in Hotel Eva on Av. República (tel. 82 34 76; open Thurs. 10pm-midnight, Sun. 4-7pm).

Thursday night is folklore and *fado* night. The fine **beach** hides on an islet off the coast. Take bus #16 from the stop in front of the tourist office (every hr. until 8pm, 125$).

Near Faro: Albufeira

To this, the largest seaside resort in the Algarve, tourists come hell-bent on relaxation. The occasional Portuguese fisher seems oddly out of place amongst tourists rubbing elbows, barrelling through bars, and killing the night. White high-rises plaster the hills surrounding Albufeira far above **Rua 5 de Outubro,** the main concourse. All essential services serve near the tunnel blasted through the rocks to the beaches.

The last holdout of the Moors in southern Portugal, Albufeira tries desperately to preserve graceful Moorish architecture in the old quarters of town. Tiny minarets pierce the small Byzantine dome of **Santana;** an exquisite filigree doorway heralds the **São Sebastão;** an ancient Gothic one fronts the **Misericórdia;** and a barrel-vaulted interior receives worshippers into the **Matiz.**

Albufeira's fine beach, **Praia dos Barcos,** is edged with rocky coves. Despite new construction and commercialization, the center remains cheerful (if packed with tourists). Local artisans sell their wares in the **tropical park** at Largo Engenheiro Duarte-Pacheco.

The hottest clubs in town, **Disco Silvia's** and **Club Disco 7 1/2,** face off on R. São Gonçalo de Lagos. The steep 600$ cover includes one drink. A dandy mingling spot is the **Fastnet Bar** on R. Cândido dos Reis (tel. 58 99 16; open 10am-2am). They net tourists with tequila sunrises, blue Hawaiians, and a whopping good *karaoke*. Bands perform almost nightly on the outdoor stage in the *largo*. The tourist office sells **bullfight** tickets (May-Sept. Sat. 5:30pm, tickets 2500-5000$).

Many places are booked solid through travel agents from the last week in June through mid-September. The modern **Pensão Albufeirense,** R. Liberdade, 18 (tel. 512 079), one block from the *largo* through Travessa 5 de Outubro, has a garish interior, comfortable rooms, and a TV lounge. (Singles 4000$, with bath 4500$. Doubles 6000$, with bath 6500$. Money changed at 5% commission.) **Camping Albufeira** (tel. 58 76 27, fax 58 93 93) is a few km outside town on the road to Ferreiras. More like a crowded shopping mall than a peaceful retreat, the place boasts four swimming pools, three restaurants, three tennis courts, a supermarket, and an inflated price tag. (625$ per person, per car, and per tent.) The new campground effectively prohibits unofficial camping on nearby beaches. It's about halfway between Albufeira and the bus station; ask the driver to stop here.

Budget restaurants spill across the old fishing harbor east of the main beach. **Cantinho Algarvio,** Travessa Cais Herculano (tel. 547 97) serves up a nifty *salade Niçoise* and other entrees for 700-1000$, as well as *costeleta de Vitela* (T-bone steak, 1100$). (Open 9am-midnight.) Chicken-and-chips buffs patronize the small family-run **Caravela** (tel. 51 56 94), on the corner of R. 5 de Outubro and R. Padre Semedo Azevedo three blocks from Turismo. (Open Mon.-Sat. noon-midnight.) There's an open-air fruit and vegetable **market** near the park at Largo Engenheiro Duarte-Pacheco. (Open 1st and 3rd Tues. each month 9am-1pm.)

The **tourist office,** R. 5 de Octubro, 5 (tel. 51 21 44) has an English-speaking staff. They've maps and brochures and keep a list of *quartos* (about 3000-3500$). (Open 9:30am-8pm; Oct.-May 9:30am-7pm.) The **post office** (tel. 521 11) ships packages from next door. (Open Mon.-Fri. 8:30am-6pm.) The **postal code** is 8200; the **telephone code** is 089. The **hospital** patches people up on R. Henrique Calado, off R. Bernardino de Sousa (tel. 51 21 33; for **ambulance** tel. 58 63 43). In an **emergency** dial 115. The **police** (tel. 51 22 05) are on R. Henrique Calado opposite the hospital.

The **train station,** 6km inland, is accessible from the center by bus (every 30min., 115$). Albufeira is on the Lagos-Vila Real de Santo António line. Frequent departures to Faro (45min., 300$) and Lagos (1 1/2 hr., 450$). The **bus station** (tel. 51 43 01) is at the entrance to town, up Av. Liberdade; walk downhill to reach the center. EVA buses head to Faro (every hr., 1 1/2 hr., 600$), Portimão (7 per day, 1hr., 550$), and Lagos (7 per day, 1 1/2 hr., 650$).

Lagos

For many many moons, swarms of Europeans have sojourned here to worship the almighty Sun, god of Lagos. Although half-buried under pilgrims, Lagos is less touristed than Albufeira and closer to the beach than Faro. The port and old town pickle a measure of local color; along the narrow pedestrian streets, cosmopolitan bars burble to English pop or sway to jazz. To the west, rock tunnels through the sheer cliffs connect secluded sandy coves, while 4km of uninterrupted beach lounges to the east.

Founded by the Romans, Lagos thrived under the Moors as the largest port between Portugal and North Africa. During the Age of Discovery, the city's shipyards built caravels that came close to falling off the earth. Capital of the Algarve for two centuries, the city was a key port in the slave trade until it was destroyed by the 1755 earthquake.

Orientation and Practical Information

Running the length of the river, **Avenida dos Descobrimentos** carries traffic in and out. Rua das Portas de Portugal marks the gateway leading into **Praça Gil Eanes** and the town's glitzy tourist center. Most restaurants, accommodations, and services hover about the *praça* and **Rua 25 de Abril;** they are usually mobbed.

> **Tourist Office:** Largo Marquês de Pombal (tel. 76 30 31); take the side street R. Lina Lectão (off Pr. Gil Eanes) which leads to the Largo. A 20-min. walk from the train station, a 15-min. walk from the bus station. Brochures, maps, and transport information about Lagos and the Algarve. List of *quartos*. Changes money and traveller's checks. English spoken. Crowded. Open Mon.-Fri. 9:30am-7pm, Sat.-Sun. 9:30am-12:30pm and 2-5:30pm.
>
> **Budget Travel: Club Algarve,** R. Marreiros Neto, 25 (tel. 76 23 37), uphill from the tourist office. English spoken. Standard student discounts on TAP and British Airways. Open Mon.-Fri. 9am-12:30pm, 2:30-6:30pm.
>
> **Currency Exchange:** see **Tourist Office** above. **Caixa Geral de Depósitos,** Pr. Gil Eanes. Cash advances. 500$ commission on cash, 100$ commission on traveler's checks. Open Mon.-Fri. 8:30am-3pm.
>
> **Post Office:** R. Portas de Portugal (tel. 76 31 11), between Pr. Gil Eanes and Av. Descobrimentos. Open Mon.-Fri. 9am-6pm; for Posta Restanta 9am-noon. **Postal Code:** 8600.
>
> **Telephones:** In an air-conditioned building across from the post office. Open 9am-11pm. **Telephone Code:** 082.
>
> **Trains:** tel. 76 29 87. On the eastern edge of town across the river from the bus station. To: Lisboa (5 per day, 6 1/2 hr., 1500-2200$); Vila Real de Santo António via Faro (11 per day, 3hr., 850-900$); Évora (3 per day, 4 1/2 hr., 1400$); Beja (3 per day, 3 1/2 hr., 945$).
>
> **Buses: Rodoviária** (tel. 76 29 44), on the eastern edge of town. To Lisboa (4 per day, 5hr., 1800$) and Sagres (12 per day, 1hr., 385$). A private company also runs to Portimão (10 per day, 1/2 hr., 235$). Its blue and white buses leave from in front of the Messe Militar on Av. Descobrimentos, near Pr. República.
>
> **Taxis:** tel. 76 35 87, 76 32 19.
>
> **Car Rental: Hertz-Lagos,** Rossio de S. João Ed. Panorama, 3 (tel. 76 30 08), behind the bus station. Cars 5000-11,000$ per day. Cars are useful for the western tip of the Algarve (Sagres and Cabo São Vicente).
>
> **Bike/Moped Rental: Motolagos,** R. S. José d'Armas (tel. 76 03 65) and a booth on R. 25 de Abril. Must be 16 to rent. Mountain bikes 1700$ per day. Motorbikes 2000$ per day. **Moto Sonho,** R. Dr. Yoaquim Telo, 27 (tel. 76 75 71). Off R. Cândido dos Reis and next to Hotel Riomar. Mopeds 1500$ per day, 9500$ per week.
>
> **Laundromat: Lavandaria Luso-Britânica,** Pr. Gil Eanes, 11 (tel. 76 22 83). Wash and dry 1100$ per 4kg load. Dry cleaning: pants 1500$, shirt 320$. Open Mon.-Fri. 9am-1pm and 3-7pm, Sat. 9am-1pm.
>
> **Medical Services: Hospital,** R. Castelo dos Governadores (tel. 76 30 34), next to Igreja Santa María. **Ambulance** (tel. 76 01 15). English spoken.
>
> **Police:** General Alberto Silva (tel. 76 29 30), near Pr. da República. English spoken.

Accommodations and Camping

In the summertime, *pensões* fill up and cost a bundle. Rooms in *casa particulars* go for 1500-3500$. Some are surprisingly comfortable, with sparkly bathrooms and hot showers. The best deals come from haggling with owners who wait at train and bus stations and at the tourist office. Make sure that there's hot water and that the location is somewhere remotely near downtown.

Residencial Solar, R. Anónio Crisógono dos Santos, 60 (tel. 76 24 77, 76 39 17). From the bus station, exit through the back and take a left. After a block the street forks; follow the sign on the right. New-furnished rooms have full baths. Views of the town, river, and sea from the rooftop terrace. Singles 4000$. Doubles 6000$. Oct.-May: 2000$; 2500-3000$. Breakfast included.

Residência Marazul, R. 25 de Abril, 13 (tel. 76 97 49), near Turismo. Elaborate wainscoted interior. Immaculate rooms, some with small terraces overlooking the street. Spotless baths. Access to hedonistic, wicker-chaired lounge. Watch your step on the polished staircase. Singles 5000-7700$. Doubles $7200-8000$. Oct.-May: 2500-4700$; 2750-5000$.

Caravela Residencial, R. 25 de Abril, 8 (tel. 76 33 61). Small, carpeted rooms around a sunny central courtyard. Exceptionally clean. Singles 3020$. Doubles 4200$, with bath 4620$. Discount about 20% in winter. Breakfast included.

Residencial Rubi Mar, R. Barroca, 70 (tel. 631 65), down R. 25 de Abril and then left on Travessa da Senora da Graça. Run by an English couple who have decorated like Camelot. Some rooms have ocean view. Singles 5000$. Doubles 5500$. Oct.-May: 3500$; 4000$. Breakfast included.

Camping: Sites are crowded and expensive, resembling high-tech shantytowns. Jam-packed **Parque de Campismo do Imulagos** (tel. 76 00 31) is annoyingly far away but linked to Lagos by a free shuttle bus. (Reception 8am-10pm; 738$ per person, 410$ per car.) Nearer town on the beautiful Praia Dona Ana is **Camping da Trinidade** (tel. 76 38 92). 300$ per person, 350$ per tent, 270$ per car. Free showers. On a beach 1 1/2km west of Praia da Luz, peaceful **Camping Valverde** (tel. 78 92 11) costs 460$ per person, 400$ per tent and per car (guarded, free showers). **Quinta dos Capricos** (fax (082) 651 22), 18km west of Lagos, is less crowded and near a terrific beach (470$ per person, per tent, and per car). The no-frills, guarded plot of land has a small market. The bus from Lagos to Sagres stops on the road nearby in Salema.

Food

Overpriced places in and around Praça Gil Eanes and Rua 25 de Abril cater to foreign tourists and have menus in several languages. The search for an inexpensive Portuguese meal may take you far and wide.

Restaurante Escondidinho, hidden in a dead-end alley in front of the GNR (tel. 76 03 86). From the *praça* walk down A. Descobrimentos (upstream) and turn left up R. da Capelinha; on the left. Truly Portuguese, yet welcoming to foreigners. In the running for the Best of Algarve. Toothsome grilled fish. Catch of the day (entrees 800-1200$). All-you-can-eat sardines at lunch 500$.

Mullens, R. Cândido dos Reis, 86 (tel. 76 12 81). A Lagos hot spot. Servers dance to the tables with huge portions of spicy food. The crowd quivers with a carnal pulse. Chicken *piri-piri* (smothered in hot sauce) 995$. Open noon-2pm and 7-10:30pm.

Restaurante O João, R. Silva Lopes, 15 (tel. 76 1067). Oak tables and tile floors. Be daring—hamburgers *à casa* (850$). Variegated entrees 850-1200$. Open 10am-4pm and 6pm-midnight.

Pizzaria O Pic Nic, Pr. Gil Eanes, 24 (tel. 76 12 85). O Tou Rists eat O Piz Za He Re. Floor-length windows, oak trim, and hefty tables. Smoky. Frenzied staff. Individual pizzas from 750$. Open 9am-2pm.

Restaurante Ao Natural, R. Silva Lopes, 29 (tel. 76 26 64). Stylish tropical rooftop terrace has live music and bar. Veggie-lusters do the fruit salad breakfast 450$. Vegetarian plate 895$. Vegetarian chili with brown rice 750$. Open 9am-12:30am.

Restaurante A Capoeira, R. 25 de Abril, 76 (tel. 76 34 70). You'll think you never left the East End of London. Steak and kidney pie 1300$. 1/2-chicken 1200$. Good soup 300$. Open 11am-11pm.

Sights and Entertainment

The statue marking the entrance to Lagos at **Praça Gil Eanes** is King Dom Sebastião, who inherited the throne as a young tyke in 1557. His precarious reign ended when he set out to conquer Morocco and never returned. Sebastião's death marks the beginning of 60 years of Spanish rule.

Only the altar of **Igreja de Santo António** survived the 1755 earthquake; workers painstakingly rebuilt everything else exactly as before. Extraordinary gilded woodwork embellishes the interior. Adjoining the church, the **Museu Municipal** exhibits costumes, weapons, and mutant animal fetuses. The guides are friendly and knowledgeable. (Open Tues.-Sun. 9:30am-12:30pm and 2-5pm. Admission 200$, free Sun. and to students and seniors.) On either side of Pr. da República, near Igreja de Santa María da Misericórdia, molder the evil remains of the 16th-century **Antigo Mercado de Escravos,** modern Europe's first slave market.

Ancient weathered cliffs surround the **beaches.** Follow Av. dos Descobrimentos (the main waterside avenue) west until the sign for **Praia de Pinhão.** Follow this to the shore and continue on the paths until you find a suitable cove. The rocks afford tremendous views of the inlets. **Praia Dona Ana's** sculpted cliffs and grottoes appear on at least half of all Algarvian postcards. It drowns in kid piss during the summer.

More good beaches await at **Salema** and **Burgau,** small towns on the way to Sagres. Several convenient **buses** per day roll between Lagos and Sagres. The trip takes about an hour and costs 380$. Be warned, though, that bus schedules aren't posted at the Sagres stop; plan your return trip while still in Lagos.

The streets of Lagos pick up late into the evening; the area between Pr. Gil Eanes and Pr. Luís de Camões bursts with cafés. **Café Gil Eanes,** Pr. Gil Eanes, 20 baits especially large crowds. Stop by **Shots in the Dark,** R. 1 de Maio, 16, parallel to and behind R. Cândido dos Reis, to hang out with the international backpacking crowd. Every Saturday in summer, posters all over the Algarve announce a **bullfight** at Largo da Teira, a 15-minute walk or 600$ taxi ride from the town center (5:30pm, admission 2500$).

Sagres

Marooned on the barren southwest corner of Europe, Sagres has evolved into the international backpackers' capital. Its dramatic, desolate location atop a bleak scrub-desert promontory sends tour groups and upscale travelers running. In fact, there's little to do here besides loll on the gorgeous little beaches between the cliffs and socialize at night with wild young travelers in cafés and bars.

Prince Henry the Navigator's polygonal stone **fortaleza** dominates the town like a big vulture. From this cliff-top outpost Prince Hal stroked his beard and formulated his plan to map the world. Vasco da Gama, Magellan, Diaz, and Cabral apprenticed in the school of navigation he founded here. The 15th century fortress is always open.

Mercifully uncrowded beaches fringe the peninsula hereabouts, and the two main beaches are close to Sagres. The most popular spot, **Mareta,** is at the bottom of the road from Kiosk do Papa; rock formations jut far out into the ocean on both sides of this sandy crescent. **Tonel** is along the road to the cape.

By day, the young set invades **Café Conchinha** (tel. 641 31) in Pr. da República. When the café closes at 8pm, the crowd walks across the square to cavort at the lively restaurant-bar **Rosa dos Ventos** *(bitoque,* pork and fries, 750$). Another popular nightspot is **The Last Chance Saloon,** a hunting ground that blasts English dance tunes and overlooks the beach. The small bar hops by 11pm.

No more youth hostel—only *quartos* to shelter your bones. Windows everywhere display signs for them in three or four languages. Many are in boarding houses with guest kitchens, and prices range from 1500-3000$ for singles and doubles, from 3000-4000$ for triples. Experienced hagglers can talk prices down 2000$. If you aren't accosted at the bus stop, look for the signs or ask at the Turinfo office on Praça da Liberdade. **Fransisco Casimir** (a black-clad 86-yr.-old) offers singles and doubles for 1100$ and triples for 2000$ at his little boarding house. He'll trundle you and your bag over there in the back of his motor tricycle, when he's not stealing his friends' crutches. Also consider **Ofélia Viagos,** Bairro da Liberdade, 62 (tel. 643 85), off Rua Comandante Matoso a few blocks from the bus stop. She has three rooms with private baths (1500-2000). **Camping** unofficially is tricky, as police get off on hassling illegal campers who set up on the main beaches or in the fields. Sleep peacefully instead at the guarded ground near town, close to the beach, just off E.N. 268. (Tel. 76 43 51, fax 76 44 45. 350$ per person and per tent, 300$ per car. Showers 80$.)

Restaurante-Bar Atlántico (tel. 76 42 36) is one of the best of the bargain restaurants on the main street in town, serving heaping portions of *ameijoas ao natural* (plain clams, 900$). **O Dromedário** R. Comandante Matoso (tel. 76 42 19), whips out thick fruit shakes (300-480$), sandwiches, and original wholemeal pizzas (540-900$). The pizza has proved such a hit that on the patio in back the owners opened **Bossa Nova,** a pizza restaurant with a wider variety and similar prices. The **market** is off the same street; turn left at R. do Correio.

The very helpful **tourist office** (tel. 76 41 25) in the fortress **exchanges currency** from 9:30am to 7:30pm (Oct.-May 9:30am-6:30pm). The **post office** (open Mon.-Fri. 9am-12:30pm and 2:30-6pm) is a left turn at R. do Correio, which is down the street from O Dromedário. The **telephone code** is 082. The GALP station at the roundabout and the Kiosk do Papa across from O Dromedario rents both **bicycles** and **mopeds.** (Bicycles 1000$ per day; mopeds 1800$ per day.) **Rodoviária buses** (tel. 76 29 44) travel here from Lagos (12 per day, 1hr., 385$).

Near Sagres

Powerful Atlantic winds bring cooler temperatures and large rolling waves to the dazzling coastline west of Sagres. The limited presence of humans has preserved fields of cacti and desert flowers. Red rock cliffs tower 70m above the pounding waves.

Cabo de São Vicente

On the way down to the cape from Sagres, **Beliche,** a 17th-century fortress with a tiny chapel, affords an excellent view of the coastline. To the right of the entrance, stone stairs tumble down the rocky cliff to Beliche's beautiful beach, in a perfect horseshoe cove.

Crowning the southwestern tip of continental Europe, **Cabo de São Vicente** was once believed to be *o fim do mundo* (the end of the world). At the far end of the cape, the second most powerful lighthouse in Europe throws its beam 60 miles out to sea beckoning sailors home. (No fixed hours. Get permission to climb to the top from keeper at the gate, who disappears noon-2pm.) No buses connect the cape with Sagres. Nevertheless, hiking the scenic 6km along a paved road from Sagres takes only about an hour. Or you can explore on a rented bike or moped (see Sagres).

Carrapateira and Odeceixe

Don't tell anybody about undiscovered **Carrapateira,** 16km north of Sagres on the western coast, where you can camp in the summer. To get here, take the road (turn-off at Vila do Bispo) or the bus for Aljezur to the small village of Carrapateira, and proceed 1km down a small dirt road to the coast. At the top of the road, **Restaurante O Cabrita** marks the turn-off. O Cabrita doses up tired walkers with an iodine jolt from freshly caught fish grilled on an open-air barbecue. The *robalo* (bass), *anchova* (anchovy), and roast goat (for which this place is named) are other specialties. Entrees 650-900$. (Open Tues.-Sun. noon-midnight.)

A more distant yet equally well-kept secret is **Odeceixe,** 20km north of Carrapateira, the northernmost beach in the Algarve. You can **Camp** (tel. 941 45) on the beach where the river meets the sea. Take the road by the edge of town at the bridge marked "camping"—it's a 4km hike. (330$ per person, 270$ per tent and per car. Free showers.) Infrequent **buses** pass through town (1 per day each to Lagos and Sagres) and stop at the station across from the **post office** (R. Estrada Nacional, 19). Roomrenters plaster the town center, **Largo Primero do Maio,** with advertisements. (Doubles 800-925$.)

Olhão

Olhão prospered during the Napoleonic war with a lucrative smuggling trade. Today citizens have gone mainstream; it's the largest fishing port and fish canning center in the Algarve. Believe it or not, the dauntless fisherpeople of Olhão go from the shores of their heavenly beaches all the way to Newfoundland to catch cod.

Olhão's handsome **Igreja de Nossa Senhora do Rosário** (1681-1698), at the mouth of Olhão's main street, **Avenida da República,** is smack in the middle of the Muslim quarter. The drab, modern buildings that line the avenue exemplify the "new" city's efficiency. The area between the church and the Ria Formosa has more character.

At dusk mosquitoes approach from the water to feast on the unwary; they seem particularly attracted to tourists. The same could be said of the drug dealers and prostitutes who haunt the parks and bars in this area. Ferries at the pier leave for the gorgeous beaches spread across three nearby islands. **Ilha da Armona,** the easternmost island, hosts a lively summer community that crowds around the ferry dock but leaves miles of oceanfront almost deserted, illustrating the human need for companionship. You can easily rent bungalows and rooms in private homes here. (Ferries every hr., round-trip 160$.) **Ilha do Farol** (the one with the offshore lighthouse) also has plenty of beaches. (Ferries every 2hr., round-trip 240$.) **Ilha da Culatra,** an island fishing community, is legendary among a small group of backpackers and seafarers for its hospitality and fine bars. Its ocean beach, even more deserted than those of its neighbors, makes an ideal unofficial campsite. (Ferries every 2hr., round-trip 170$.)

Residencial Bicuar, R. Vasco da Gama, 5 (tel. 71 48 16) has small but luxurious rooms, most with small patios. (Singles and doubles with bath 4000$; reservations advisable July-Aug.) From the front door of Turismo, turn right onto R. Comércio and walk back toward the church, taking your first right on R. de São Pedro; it's the first block on your left. **Pensão Residencial Helena,** R. Dr. Miguel Bombarda, 42 (tel. 70 26 34) has rooms that could launch a thousand ships. Classically ornate hallways and an opulently furnished living room sparkle with chandeliers and glow with heat in winter. Its street begins on the same block as Turismo, then bears left at a confusing spidery intersection. (Singles 1700$. Doubles with bath 3200$. Breakfast included.) Campers bed at **Parque dos Bancarios,** outside of town off E.N. 125. These highly recommended, guarded sites have access to the ocean. (Tel. 70 54 02, fax 70 54 05. 450$ per person, 300$ per tent, 350$ per car. Oct.-May: 225$; 150$; 175$. Showers included.)

Casa de Pasto on Pr. Patrão Joaquim Lopes (tel. 71 24 70), near the river opposite the market buildings, serves decent entrees (700-900$; open Mon.-Sat. 8am-3pm and 7-11pm). Between the city gardens along the river, two robust red brick buildings house the fresh produce **market.** (Open Mon.-Sat. 7am-1pm.)

The **tourist office** (tel. 71 39 36) is on Largo Sebastão Martins Mestre, an offshoot of R. Comércio. The brusque, English-speaking staff has maps and ferry schedules. (Open Mon.-Fri. 9:30am-12:30pm and 2-5:30pm, Sat. 9:30am-noon.) The **post office** (tel. 71 20 13) is at Av. República, 17, on the corner with R. 18 de Julho (open Mon.-Fri. 8:30am-6pm). The **postal code** is 8700 and the **telephone code** 089.

The **bus station** is on R. General Humberto Delgado, one block west of Av. República. For the tourist office, turn right leaving the station and right again on Av. República, whose left fork is R. Comércio. (To Faro every 1/2 hr., 20min., 150$; and Tavira every hr., 1hr., 260$.) The **train station** is one block north of the bus station on Av. Combatentes da Grande Guerra; a left takes you to Av. República, and a right deposits you downtown.

Tavira

Farmers on motor scooters tease police by riding over the Roman pedestrian bridge: that's about as raucous as Tavira gets. Evenly split by the slow Gilão river, this community can't even work up a sweat over the recent influx of backpackers. White houses fringe this enchanting city's river banks and festively Baroque churches speckle the hills above. Tavira is an important fishing port; in mid-afternoon, fishers sit in small riverfront warehouses repairing nets alongside their beached craft. Sidestreets trace the skeleton of a Moorish fortress from which the town sprang.

The seven-arched **Ponte Romana** leads from the center of town around Pr. República across the river to fragrant Pr. 5 de Outubro. Up the stairs at the opposite end of the square is the imposing **Igreja do Carmo**. Its elaborately decorated chancel resembles a 19th-century opera set where false perspectives give the illusion of windows and niches supported by columns. (Open only for mass.) On the other side of the river, steps opposite the tourist office lead to **Igreja da Misericórdia**, whose superb Renaissance doorway glowers with a variety of heads sprouting from twisting vines and candelabra. (Open 9am-noon and 2-5:30pm.) Just beyond, the remains of the city's **Castelo Mouro** now enclose a lovely garden (open 9am-5pm). Dusk is such a lovely time to visit the river-hugging Rua José Pires Padinha, the peaceful park, and the cafés and shops.

To reach Tavira's excellent **beach** on an island 2km away, take the "Tavira-Quatro Aguas" bus from Pr. República. The ferry between Quatro Aguas and **Ilha da Tavira** runs until 8pm (10 per day, 5min., 125$ round-trip; keep ticket stub for the return).

Tavira has one of the finest *pensões* in the Algarve, **Pensão Residencial Lagôas Bica,** R. Almirante Cândido dos Reis, 24 (tel. 222 52), on the far side of the river. There's a spectacular view of the city from the rooftop terrace. Demand is high. When rooms fill up the owners direct supplicants to rooms in private homes (1500-2500$). To reach the *pensão* from Pr. República, cross the bridge and continue straight down R. A Cabreira; turn right and go down two blocks. (Immaculate singles 2000$. Doubles 3500$, with bath 4500$. Outdoor hand-laundering and drying facilities.) **Pensão-Residencial Castelo,** R. Liberdade, 4 (tel. 239 42), across the street from Turismo, is comparable. Some of the clean wainscoted rooms are fitted with patios and carpets. More views. (Doubles 4000$, with bath 4500$. Winter: 1800$; 2500$.) The city's **campground** (tel. 235 05), with its entourage of snack bars and restaurants, sprawls on the beach of the island 2km from the *praça*. (Open May-Sept.; 100$ per person, 300$ per tent.)

Restaurante Bica, underneath the Pensão Lagôas, serves excellent entrees from 950$ (open 9:30am-midnight). Seek and ye shall find equally reasonable cafés and restaurants on Pr. República and opposite the garden on R. José Pires Padinha.

Turismo (tel. 225 11) stands conveniently on Pr. República, just up and across the street from the bus station. Ask nicely for maps and bus schedules. (Open 9:30am-8pm; Oct.-May 9:30am-7pm.) **Buses** leave from the *praça* for Faro (12 per day, 1hr., 2350$). **Trains** leave every hour for Vila Real de Santo António (1hr., 205$) and Faro (25min., 250$). To get to Turismo from the station, walk down Av. Dr. Teixeira and then R. Liberdade.

Vila Real de Santo António

Vila Real is a bore. At the mouth of the Rio Guadiana opposite the Spanish border, the town makes a convenient transfer point to other destinations. The Marquês de Pombal founded the city in 1774 and planned its *praça* and streets after his design for the Baixa in Lisboa. The exciting plan backfired; most of the place has faded into a dreary grid of straight streets and nondescript buildings. Vila Real was further emasculated with the recent completion of a bridge 5km north; nobody uses Vila Real's ferry to Spain anymore. This town is indeed a fitting complement to the swampy, dreary countryside that surrounds it.

The **Pousada de Juventude (HI),** R. D. Sousa Martins, 40 (tel. 445 65) is on the fifth street into the grid and then five blocks to the left from the tourist office. (Reception 8am-10pm; lockout noon-6pm; decent quarters 1050$, breakfast included.) **Residência Félix,** R. Dom Manuel Arriaga, 2 (tel. 437 91), across from the tourist office, has clean rooms. (Singles and doubles 3500$.) Two streets down at R. Teófilo Braga, 3, **Residência Baixa Mar** (tel. 435 11) rents singles for 4300$ and doubles for 5000$. These are the only *residências* in Vila Real. If you are shut out, Don't Panic—

ask after *quartos* at the tourist office. Cheap restaurants dot the pedestrian R. D. Manuel de Arriaga. **Restaurante Monumental** on Praça do Marquês de Pombal stays open later than most places in town. (Entrees 700-900$.)

The **tourist office** (tel. 432 72), at the exit of the border control station, will **exchange money** and locate *quartos*. (Open 8am-7:30pm.) The **postal code** is 8900, the **telephone code** 081.

Trains service Lagos (4 per day, 4 1/2 hr., 815$) and Faro (11 per day, 2 1/2 hr., 380$). For trains to Spain (an hour ahead of Portugal in summer), first cross the river by **ferry** to Ayamonte, a delightful fishing town and art colony. (In summer, ferries run 7:10am-1am; 130$ per person, 650$ per car.) From Ayamonte, you can take a bus in the main square direct to Sevilla, or to Huelva (every hr., 390ptas) with connections to Sevilla (summer 8 per day, 710ptas). Pesetas are sold in banks along the port in Ayamonte. Although it still runs, the ferry is useless; a bridge was completed last year linking Spain and Portugal 5km north of Vila Real.

Buses from Vila Real to the rest of the Algarve are more expensive, more reliable, and faster than trains. They zip to Faro (9 *espressos* per day, 1hr., 620$; via Tavira, 2hr., 320$), Lagos (8 per day, 4hr., 860$), and Lisboa (4 per day, 7 1/2 hr., 1900$). The last bus leaves at 6:30pm for Faro. Buses leave from the esplanade to the right of the tourist office.

MOROCCO

US $1 = 8.75 dirhams (dh)　　　　1dh = US $0.11
CDN $1 = 7.88dh　　　　　　　　1dh = CDN $0.13
UK £1 = 17.86dh　　　　　　　　1dh = UK £0.06
AUS $1 = 6.89dh　　　　　　　　1dh = AUS $0.15
NZ $1 = 5.15dh　　　　　　　　　1dh = NZ $0.19

Once There

Tourist Offices

Most cities have a centrally located **Offices Nationales Marocaine de Tourisme (ONMT)**. They may give you a free map and offer info on sights and markets, accommodations, and official guides. They also change money when banks are closed. Many towns also have a **Syndicat d'Initiative,** a city tourist office, who'll do the same.

Embassies and Consulates in Morocco

If you're seriously ill or in trouble, contact your consulate if possible, not your embassy (whose function is mainly diplomatic). They can provide legal advice and medical referrals and can contact relatives back home. In extreme cases, they may offer emergency financial assistance. Embassies are in Rabat; consulates (subdivisions of a country's embassy) are in other major cities. Embassies and consulates keep regular business hours: open from Monday to Friday, out to lunch from 1:30 to 3pm, and closed by 5:30 or 6pm.

U.S. Embassy: 2 av. Marrakech, Rabat (tel. (7) 76 22 65). **Consulate,** 8 blvd. Moulay Youssef, Casablanca (tel. (7) 22 14 49).

Canadian Embassy: 13 rue Joafar Essadik, Agday, BP 709 Rabat (tel. (7) 77 13 76 or 77 13 77).

British Embassy: 17 blvd. de la Tour Hassan, BP 45, Rabat (tel. (7) 72 09 05). **Consulate,** 9 rue Amerique du Sud, Tangier (tel. (9) 93 58 95 or 93 58 97); 60 blvd. D'Anfa, BP 13 762, Casablanca (tel. (7) 26 14 40 or 26 14 41).

Australian Embassy: Refer to Canadian Embassy (above).

New Zealand Embassy: Refer to British Embassy (above).

Orientation

Large cities break up into a number of separate quarters. Years of French imperialism left behind a **ville nouvelle** (new city) in every town, a district that contains the snazzier hotels and tourist centers. The **medina** (old city) is likely to be labyrinthine, and contain sights such as *mederas,* medieval Qur'anic schools (the major tourist attraction for non-Muslims, who are sometimes forbidden to enter mosques). Adjoining the medina is the **mellah** (old Jewish quarter). The **kasbah** is the area surrounding the old fortress. In addition to handicraft **souks** (markets), nearly every city has a weekly *souk* where residents and those from outlying villages meet to transact business.

Many streets, especially those in European colonist tongues, are currently being renamed. *Rue* and *calle* may be called *zankat, derb,* or *sharia.* Also, many stores or restaurants may have no street number; these are only identifed by their street corner or square.

Stores in all cities and most towns sell **toiletries** such as toothpaste, shampoo, and shaving cream. **Toilet paper** is sold in all grocery stores (2-3dh per roll).

Getting Around

Train

Trains are far and away the swiftest and comfiest way to travel; service is fairly reliable and surprisingly prompt throughout Morocco. Second-class fares are only a bit more expensive than the corresponding CTM bus fare. In first- and second-class cars, there are non-smoking compartments. Couchettes cost 35dh extra. Only speed-freaks ride the fourth-class (Economie) trains, which take absolutely forever to go nowhere and have the creature comforts of a freight car. Tickets bought on the train, instead of at the ticket counter, carry a 10% surcharge. Alas, the national rail company, **Office National de Chemin de Fer (ONCF),** has a somewhat limited network.

A **Eurailpass,** good for discounted train travel in Europe, is not valid for train travel in Morocco. **InterRail** passes, previously used for train travel in Morocco, are dead as of fall 1992.

Bus

Buses have more frequent, more extensive service than trains, but you sacrifice comfort for convenience. Before you get on any bus, check on return service and connections from your destination to avoid being stranded like a shipwreck victim washed up on a desert island. Many routes run only once or twice per day. Try to take a bus that originates at your point of departure so it won't be full by the time it gets to you.

Most buses make at least one 20-minute stop. If you wish to explore or stretch your legs, tell the driver you're continuing on the bus—else you'll be left blubbering in a dust cloud as the vehicle speeds off. Remember that each bus company has its own information window, as in Spain, so you'll have to window-hop for destinations and schedules.

Compagnie de Transports du Maroc (CTM): Morocco's national bus company. The fastest, most luxurious, and most expensive. No reservations necessary.

SATAS: The second largest company. Operates primarily in southwest Morocco. Equal to CTM in speed and reliability, but slightly less comfortable.

Cars publiques: The term for countless other private bus companies. They run both from city to city and from big city to nearby towns and villages. Aside from CTM and SATAS, most companies offer five cramped seats per row and terrible ventilation. Buses often average under 50km per hour, since they stop wherever anyone wants to get on or off. Ludicrously cheap (about 10dh per 100km).

Collective taxis: Similar, and a good alternative to a bus. See Taxis below.

Car

When exploring remote areas (especially south of Marrakech and inland from the Atlas Mountains), groups of four or more should consider renting a car. Most rentals are manual transmission; automatics are rare or nonexistent. **Gas** costs about 6.15dh per liter.

The **police** often pull private vehicles over for security checks; this is routine throughout Morocco, especially in and around major northern cities. All police officers speak French. You may be interrogated about your travel plans and even searched. A good way to dissolve the tension is to ask directions to your destination immediately after you're stopped. *Always drive with your passport and car papers.* If you're stopped for a traffic violation, you may have to pay the fine on the spot; make sure you get a receipt. By law, **seatbelts** are required outside major towns.

Routes goudronées (principal roads), designated with a "P," are paved and connect most cities. **Bonne pistes** (secondary roads), designated with an "S," are less smooth. You may have to contend with tortuous mountain roads made yet more hazardous by loose gravel. In spring, in such regions as the Sahara, frequent flash floods can make roads impassable. Only swimmers or those with water wings should drive in this area.

Buy several detailed **maps,** and ask people if the routes you intend to take are passable. Sometimes roads marked on maps have a way of turning into riverbeds and mule tracks. On the other hand, many roads marked as impassable on old maps have been recently cleared and paved.

In the desert, bring along at least 10 liters of bottled water per person and per radiator, a spare tire, and extra fuel (remember to allow for the expansion of gasoline in the heat). Move rapidly over sand; if you start to bog down, put the car in low gear and put the pedal to the metal. If you come to a stop in soft sand, it's better to get out and push than to sink into tire trenches. Don't try to drive or park on beaches.

Renting a car is not too difficult. **Afric Car, Moroloc,** and **Locoto** are the large Moroccan companies; in Casablanca, explore the cut-rate rental agencies or the international companies (Avis or Hertz). **Europcar,** whose U.S. affiliate is National Car Rental, rents a Renault IV, the most common budget car, at about 1560dh for three days of unlimited mileage, and 2695dh per week. If not included in the price, mandatory insurance costs about 70dh per day. Reserve a few days in advance and bargain. It's cheaper to reserve rental cars from the Americas or the European continent, but many companies are reluctant to insure driving in Morocco. Most companies require renters to be at least 25, although at Kemwel you need only be 21.

North Americans should try **Europe By Car,** which allows you to purchase the car from the company for a prearranged period, after which the company buys the vehicle back. The rates are low and the insurance terms good, but you must pay at home and pick up the car before you get to Morocco. For phone numbers of rental companies, see Once There: Getting Around for Spain or Portugal.

Taxi

> **Petits taxis:** For travel within a city. Screamingly inexpensive. Drivers are required by law to turn on the meter. If drivers try to fix a price instead, they may overcharge. Fares usually 5-7dh, rarely over 10dh; about 50% surcharge on night fares.
>
> **Grands taxis:** For travel anywhere. Always agree on a price before hopping in. To avoid being overcharged sleuth out standard charges. Fares about twice as much as for *petits*.
>
> **Collective taxis:** Good for long-distance trips. A bus/mini-van hybrid. They have specific destinations and depart when full (about 6 people). If the driver wants to leave before the cab is full, make sure he or she won't jack up the fare. Seats are cramped, but collective taxis are far faster than buses and more convenient for many routes. A good way to meet other travelers and Moroccans. They depart from marked taxi stands. Pay upon arrival, and pay no more than other passengers. Fares are reasonable, about 15% more than CTM bus fares.

Hitchhiking

> *Let's Go* does not recommend hitching as a means of travel; the information presented below and throughout the book is not intended to do so.

No one hitches in Morocco. Other forms of transportation are inexpensive by European and North American standards. Don't pick up hitchers either.

The dangers of hitchhiking should not be underestimated. Drivers have raped, sexually assaulted, and killed passengers. If you choose to solicit a ride, avoid doing it alone. Experienced hitchers sit in the front, and never get in the back seat of a two-door car. If the driver begins to harrass them, they ask firmly to be let out. They also report that, in an emergency, opening the door on the road may surprise a driver enough to slow down. Pretending you're about to vomit may also help, they say.

Accommodations

Most lodgings that *Let's Go* lists in Morocco are passably clean—not spotless. Rooms may be grimy, roachy, or verminous; sinks and baths may have rusty water and toilets may be no more than a hole in the ground. A room's quality may inspire you to bargain despite already low rates; acting less than eager often helps.

Sometimes a proprietor will let you sleep on the roof for a fraction of the price of a room, an especially attractive option in the Sahara. Do some comparison shopping; hotels are rarely full to capacity.

Youth Hostels

The **Fédération Royale Marocaine des Auberges de Jeunesse (FRMAJ)** is the Moroccan Hostelling International (HI) affiliate. A bargainous bed costs 15-25dh per night, a few dh more for non-members. Moroccan hostels vary widely in quality and are sometimes far from the town center. Reception is only open for limited hours, so call ahead. Curfews and lockouts are rare. To reserve beds in swamped high season (July and August), obtain an **International Booking Voucher** from FRMAJ (or your home country's HI affiliate) and send it to the desired hostel four to eight weeks in advance of your stay. There are hostels in Casablanca, Fes, Marrakech, Rabat, Meknés, and some smaller cities and towns.

Whether officially or unofficially, non-members can stay in Morocco's youth hostels. Some hostels sell **HI membership cards** (75dh) on the spot; else buy one at FRMAJ's main offices (see addresses below). Mandatory is a **sleepsack;** but since linens are rented by hostels less commonly than in Europe, you'll have to bring your own. (To make a cheap sleepsack, see Planning Your Trip: Packing.)

For **information** such as hostel addresses, contact FRMAJ, blvd. Oqba Ben Nafii, Meknés (tel. (52) 46 46 98); or at the Casablanca hostel, 6 pl. Amiral Philibert (tel. (7) 22 05 51). (See also Planning Your Trip: Documents: HI Membership.)

Hotels

As a rule, the cheapest hotels are in the **medina.** Owners sometimes charge per room rather than per person, hence it's economical to find roommates. An acceptable rate for a budget room is 30dh. Often rooms are rented by the week at 50% of the per-night price. There are two categories of hotels.

> **Classé:** Government regulated and rated on a scale of 1-5 stars. Within each rating there's an additional A-B rating. Maximum prices are set by the government. A large, comfy room in a 1-star hotel costs 50-55dh; a slightly better room and private shower 76dh. A deluxe 4-star hotel with poolside café, bellhops, and red carpets costs 180-240dh. The price list and listings of all *classé* hotels *(Royaume du Maroc: Guide des Hotels)* are free at tourist offices.
>
> **Non-classé:** Not regulated, rated, nor price-fixed by the government, so they don't need to meet uniform standards. Much less expensive than *classé*. A high standard *non-classé* hotel should cost no more than 40dh per night.

Showers, when available, cost 3-4dh; in cheaper places hot water is available only during certain hours. **Hammam** (public Turkish baths) or **bains-douches** (individual public showers) run 3-4dh and are a handy source of hot water. There are laundromats in the large cities, but often a worker in your hotel will do **laundry** (20-30dh). Agree on the price beforehand.

Camping

Campgrounds are the cheapest lodging (3-5dh per person and per tent). Besides the usual site for tents, "camping" often refers to a place where you can rent a small hut or bungalow. The ritzier campgrounds boast a superflux of amenities (e.g., pools and nightclubs). Be ready to share your space with scads of Northern European teens. Avoid off-the-road camping; even where it's legal; too many tourists have returned from a quick skinny-dip to find their clothes, passport, or airplane ticket absent. Those camping unofficially try to pick a spot where there are others nearby.

Food and Drink

Moroccan chefs lavish aromatic and colorful spices (pepper, ginger, cumin, saffron), honey, and sugar on their concoctions. The climate and cuisine may upset sensitive digestive tracts. Drink plenty of purified water. *Sidi Ali*, heavily chlorinated mineral water sold for about 4dh per bottle, is widely available and refreshing. If the bottle isn't completely sealed, it doesn't take Harriet the Spy to realize that it's probably full of tap water. Although the water is said to be safe in the north, unpurified water anywhere is likely to wreak havoc on your stomach. A policy of peeling all fruit and cooking all vegetables will probably stand your stomach in good stead.

Typical Fare

Couscous is named for the covered ceramic bowl in which it's cooked and served. *Bonjour, ma petite couscous! Man, I love that couscous! ¡Te amo couscous! Mi piace couscousetta!* Diners around the world praise Morocco's national dish in every language. Made of semolina grain, onions, beans, fruit, and nuts, here it's served with a sprinkling of saffron-flavored chicken, beef, lamb, or fish. Another lovable specialty is any meat and poultry mixture blanketed in **tajine**, the scrumptious fruit and vegetable stew of olives, prunes, or artichokes. *Tajine* beats *couscous* hands down at a restaurant—the latter is better when made in a private home.

Rich **kefta** (balls of delicately seasoned ground meat, sometimes in a stew) draw mouthfuls of saliva for just 6-8dh. A steaming bowl of **harira,** a savory soup of chicken and chickpeas, costs 3-4dh. **Poulet** (chicken), whether *roti* (roasted on a spit with olives) or *limon* (lemoned), rules the roost. Gobble a little *mechoui,* a whole lamb spitted and roasted over an open fire, or *pastilla,* a pastiche of squab, almonds, eggs, butter, cinnamon, and sugar under a thin pastry shell.

For a lighter repast, slurp sweet natural yogurt with mounds of peaches, nectarines, or strawberries (2dh or more per glass), or try a finely minced, liberally spiced Moroccan salad. Snackers choose among gross briny olives (about 1dh per scoopful), roasted almonds, and cactus-buds (1dh per bud) when the munchies strike. For a righteous low-calorie dessert, munch on fresh fruit such as grapes, honeydew melon, watermelon, plums, apricots, figs, and dates (remember to peel).

Meals and Restaurants

A **"complete"** meal includes: your choice of entree *(tajine, couscous,* or perhaps a third option); salad or *harira;* a side of vegetables; and yogurt or *eine* orange for dessert. If a service charge isn't automatically included, a 10% tip will suffice.

Every medina has one-table cubbyholes where miserly gluttons can stuff themselves on **brochettes** (grilled lamb, beef, or brain shish kebab in a pita) for 15dh. Dingy-looking medina eateries often hide rapturous meals.

Although Moroccan cuisine emphasizes meat, **vegetarians** won't starve, shrivel up, and die. Markets sell fresh fruit and packaged yogurt. Restaurants and food stalls prepare salads and serve a variety of omelettes and lentil dishes.

If you're lucky enough to be invited to a traditional rural feast or into a **private home** (don't be led into an unfamiliar area; see Additional Concerns: Hustlers and Guides for necessary cautions), don't expect utensils. Scoop up mouthfuls of food with pieces of bread or simply shovel with the middle three fingers of your right hand (never ever use the left, which is used as toilet paper by Moroccans). The third cup of mint tea signals the end of a visit.

Drinks

Although Muslims are forbidden alcohol by their religion, French, Spanish, and local wines *may* be sold in more northern towns. Alcohol is quite scarce, except in swish restaurants.

Introduced by the English in the 18th century, the ritual of preparing **tea** with sprigs of fresh mint and great quantities of sugar figures prominently in daily Moroccan life (1.50-2dh per glass, 3dh per pot). In hot weather, gulp tureens of water (bottled, *bien sûr*). Freshly squeezed orange juice (2-4dh per glass) is also ubiquitous.

Communications

Mail

The most reliable way to send a message is via telegram (see below); the least is by surface mail, which may take over two months. Sending mail from Morocco to Israel is forbidden due to Arab League policy. Post offices *(le poste)* and shops that sell postcards sell **stamps.**

>**Air mail:** *Par avion.* Takes 10-14 business days to reach the U.S. and Canada. Postage for a letter 4.5dh.
>
>**Surface mail:** *Par terre.* Takes up to two months.
>
>**Postcards:** *Cartes postales.* Take longer than letters. Postage 4.5dh.

Registered or express mail: *Recommandé* or *exprès postaux*. The most reliable way to send a letter or parcel. Slightly faster than regular air mail.

General Delivery mail: *Poste Restante*. Letters or packages held for pick-up. Letters should be addressed as follows: LAST NAME, First Name; Poste Restante; City Name; Postal Code; COUNTRY; AIR MAIL. When you pick it up, always ask for mail under both your first and last name to make sure it hasn't been misfiled. You can have mail forwarded to another Poste Restante address if you must leave town whilst expecting mail. Takes 2 wks. Fee 1 1/2 dh per item picked up.

American Express: Mail (no packages) held for cardholders at some AmEx offices. For more details, see this section in Once There: Communications for Spain or Portugal.

Telegram

A telegram *(telegramme)* is the most reliable means of communication. Telegraph offices are inside **post offices.**

Telephone

Country Code: 212.

Directory Assistance: Contact the local operator. Generally, only Arabic spoken.

Emergency (Police): 19.

Phones in Morocco are less than predictable. **Pay phones** are strictly coin-operated—phonecards and calling cards are useless. International calls can't be made from pay phones.

Make international calls, **direct-dial** (an *appel* call) or **collect calls** from the local telephone office, which is always found in the **post office.** Either option costs about the same. There are usually long lines; allow plenty of time (up to 1 or 2 hours). A rare sight, spotted in Rabat and Casablanca, is the phone booth from which you can make international calls. (1) Lift the receiver and wait for the dial tone. (2) Dial 00 and wait for a musical tune, but start dialing before it ends or you'll be disconnected (like *Jeopardy*). (3) Dial: country code + area code + phone number.

The most convenient—and expensive—way to call long distance (especially in rural areas) is to go to a luxury **hotel** and ask them to place the call for you. They typically levy a hefty commission (as much as 50%).

More Money

Don't try the black market for currency exchange—you'll be ripped off or robbed. Exchange money at **banks,** where rates are uniform and they don't charge commission. Banking hours are Monday through Friday 8:30-11:30am and 3-5:30pm.

It's illegal to import or export *dirhams;* keep receipts and you can re-exchange *dirhams* at the border (but only up to half the amount for which you have receipts).

Value-Added Tax (VAT)

The Value-Added Tax (VAT) is a sales tax levied on goods and services in the European Economic Community, at a rate depending on the item. VAT is included in posted prices, unless otherwise noted. Ask at stores and tourist offices about refunds of VAT on goods—a rare possibility with many restrictions (e.g., hefty minimum amount spent). Prices quoted in *Let's Go* include VAT except where noted.

Tipping

You should tip in Morocco, but it's hard to know when. Here is an illustrative example: You *should* tip: when a bus station employee drags you through crowds to a bus that's about to leave (2-3dh). You don't have to tip: when someone demands 5dh for showing you to a cab 10 feet away. You don't owe guardians of monuments anything unless they give you a tour—unlike official guides, they're paid by the government. However, a 2-3dh tip is always appreciated, and many times a few *dirhams* open locked gates. Pens, cigarettes, nuts, and aspirin, especially in rural areas, also work wonders.

Bargaining and Shopping

Haggling takes time. Sometimes pretending to head to another shop quickens the process. Bartering is effective in both cities and rural areas. American cigarettes, crappy digital watches, jeans, and t-shirts with English printing are particularly coveted. Never go shopping with an official or unofficial guide, who will collect at least 30% in commission. If you decide to take your chances and later find you've been grossly overcharged while accompanied by an official guide, report this promptly to the tourist office and demand a refund. Don't purchase anything if you see loiterers whom a shopkeeper might think are your guides. Local boys follow tourists unobtrusively, stand outside the shop, and later claim a commission without ever exchanging a word with the buyer.

Additional Concerns

Hashish

The most famous hashish fields in the world lie in the Rif (which rhymes with *kif,* the Arabic word for marijuana). Although *kif* and hash (sometimes called "chocolate" or the Arabic word for hash, *shit*) are often openly smoked, drugs are *not* legal for foreigners or locals. Moroccan law forbids the transport of drugs, and foreigners are officially always in transport. Dealers surround all foreigners and try to peer pressure them into smoking. Although it may be tempting to indulge, getting caught with dope in Morocco is no fun. Say you don't smoke, and never admit to having drugs on you: many dealers are narcs.

Police and military personnel make frequent road checks throughout the country. Sometimes entire buses are stopped and searched. Police are far more stringent with tourists than they are with locals, and possession of just a few grams, even a pot seed, is a serious offense—punished by up to six years in jail. You can also get thrown in jail if you are in the company of someone who gets busted. If arrested, you'll find American diplomatic officials remarkably unsympathetic and legally unable to help. Moreover, the U.S. embassy refuses to contact a detainee's family unless s/he personally requests this, an opportunity you may not get. Never bring drugs from Morocco into Spain (duh).

Hustlers and Guides

Especially in Tangier, Fes, and Marrakech, tourists are continually approached by hustlers and guides. Many visitors find this one of the most trying aspects of Moroccan travel. Moroccan hustlers are famed the world over for their talents—the best speak flawless French, competent English, and a few words of every other European tongue. Don't fall for the old line "if you buy a *djellabah,* you'll look less like a tourist and be hassled less." Other hoaxes include invitations to authentic Moroccan suppers (departure fee charged) or introductions to bargain rug stores (overpriced). Never allow yourself to be led to faraway neighborhoods on any pretense; your companion may refuse to lead you back unless you pay through your nose. Never, ever, accept an offer of hashish or other drugs. Drug-dealers often moonlight as informants for the police.

Facing the extreme poverty in Morocco, you might have difficulty distinguishing the genuine beggar from the slick grifter. Beware of people who are too insistent, who claim they're students (or Club Med employees or art teachers) wanting to practice English, or whom you meet on a train (and offer to show you around town on arrival). "Moroccan hospitality" is sometimes a genuine interest in visitors and can result in friendships made; but it's also a well-known scam. Tips written here may already be passé, so be wary of newer and sneakier techniques.

When dealing with hustlers, firmly explain that you know where you're going and don't need help. Some hustlers answer dismissals with questions like "What's your damage?" or with threatening retorts. Never be rude or patronizing, and don't lose your temper. Don't be frightened or too adamant in your refusals unless it's called for. A visitor who's interested is far less likely to run into problems than one who reveals belligerence and suspicion in every action.

There are almost no situations for which a guide is required and few for which a guide is helpful. Unofficial guides are illegal, often ill-informed, and sometimes dangerous. Don't leave a car or valuables in any spot you can't find again by yourself. If someone proffers something you don't want, make your refusal absolutely clear from the start. An iffy answer will be taken as a yes. You're almost always better off with *Let's Go* and a map.

In a few instances you may want a guide: for the huge, labyrinthine medina of Fes, or when you have only a day in town and want to zip from sight to sight. Sometimes having a guide keeps the hustlers away. For off-road trips into the desert and climbs up Mt. Toubkal, guides are required. In these cases, go to the local tourist office for a competent and honest **official guide.** Always go to the tourist bureau; don't be taken in by bureaucratic-looking name tags and papers. As always, agree on the price before starting out—the tourist office fixes rates at 30dh per half-day, 50dh per day. Official guides may make a commission on anything you buy or eat, so additional purchases will cost you more.

Women Travelers

Women traveling alone or with other women may experience a more threatening form of hustling. Exercise extreme caution, and don't walk in deserted areas. Always wear a bra; both genders should take care to cover bare knees and shoulders. Take any offer seriously and refuse it firmly. If harassment persists, protest loudly, especially in the presence of onlookers. Memorize the **emergency phone number** for Morocco: 19. (For more tips, see Planning Your Trip: Specific Concerns: Women Travelers.)

Festivals and Holidays

Ramadan is the holy month of Islam. Muslims fast from sun-up to sundown (roughly 4:30am to 8:30pm) to cultivate spiritual well-being, compassion, and charity. Eating, drinking, smoking, and sex are forbidden until the sun sinks too low for a black thread and a white thread to be distinguished from each other. Ramadan after dark is another story: a siren prompts every Moroccan to swill a bowl of *harira,* and the feasting, along with religious services, begins. City streets explode with pedestrians, music, and wild festivities. **The Night of Power,** on the 27th day of Ramadan, honors the transmission of the Qu'ran from God to Muhammad. Muslims illuminate all mosques to initiate their children into the fasting ritual. When the new moon comes out the king proclaims the end of the holy month, and the public holiday **Aid el-Saghir** marks the end of the daylight fast. Families celebrate with enormous breakfasts and gifts to children.

Nearly all Muslims fast to observe Ramadan. City services continue to operate for the most part, but restaurants and cafés that cater to locals close down during the day. Ramadan falls at a slightly different time each year (it's calculated using the Islamic *(hijri)* lunar calendar) so that over the course of three decades it will make a full cycle. In 1993, Ramadan falls between February 22 and March 24; the night of power this year is March 19th.

Non-Muslim travelers should be extremely sensitive to their host country during Ramadan. Eat, drink, and smoke as unobtrusively as possible. Respect for Moroccans' religious practices guarantees your own well-being; in rural areas, where locals are not accustomed to tourists, a lack of sensitivity can provoke outright hostility. In large cities such as Tangier and Rabat, many restaurants stay open all day during Ramadan.

Elsewhere in the country, all but the fancier tourist establishments close from dawn to dusk.

Local Islamic holidays something like Catholic patron saint days are called **moussems.** *Moussems* last several days and feature group pilgrimages to local shrines, street bazaars, and agricultural fairs. The rowdier *moussems* treat observers to music-and-dance events that may include charging cavalcades of costumed, armed equestrians. Most *moussems* fall in summer; exact dates vary with the Islamic calendar and the decisions of local governments. The **Meknes festival** (actually held in an outskirt called Tissan around Sept. 14-20), is the grandest of Moroccan *moussems*. During summer's **Aid el-K'bir** (The Big Feast), each family slaughters a sheep to commemorate Abraham's biblical sacrifice. Also catch the **Marrakech Folklore Festival,** which starts the first Friday in June and continues for two or three weeks. Be wary of *moussems* and other small holidays that are more tourist traps than expressions of religious zeal. Moroccan political festivals include the **Fête du Trone** (November 18) commemorating the Muhammad V's return to Morocco after a long exile, and **Independence Day** (March 2), marking Morocco's liberation from French colonialism.

Friday is the Muslim day of rest, and at least within the medina most places will be closed. Since Morocco is adapting to Western calendars, Sunday is an appropriate day of rest for non-Muslims. Office hours are usually from 8am to 2pm in summer and from 8am to noon and 4 to 6pm in off-season and during Ramadan.

Conversion calendars from Muslim to Gregorian and back are available from the Islamic Center of New York, 1 Riverside Drive, New York, NY 10023 (tel. (212) 362-6800). The booklet *Leisure in Morocco,* free at most Moroccan tourist offices, contains helpful information on dates and places of annual *moussems,* as well as weekly *souks.* Also check local French-language newspapers.

Life and Times

History

Way Back

Gold, spices, aphrodisiac rhinoceros horn, salt, ebony, ivory, and, of course, camels made Morocco a wealthy pitstop in the trade route between Africa and Europe. **Berbers** native to the mountains and plateaus met up with Phoenician and Carthaginian colonists on the North African coast by 500 BC. The Romans who followed left behind economic prosperity and a ruin or two. After Titus sacked the Temple in Jerusalem in the 3rd century BC, Jews trickled into the Moroccan cities.

The Arabs

Vandals and Byzantines controlled the area until 683 AD, when the Arabs swept in under **Uqua Ibn Nabir**. Nabir and his cohorts converted the native Berbers to Islam, founded Qur'anic schools, and made Arabic the dominant language. Berber princess and prophetess **Kahina** killed herself at the news of the Arab conquest in 702. The many southern Africans in the country share a common history: Arab slave traders kidnapped their ancestors from Mali, Guinea, the Sudan, and Senegal.

Idris (I) Ibn Abdallah, a distant relation to Muhammad the Prophet, fled from the Abbasid rulers (one Islamic dynasty) of Baghdad to found his own Idrissian dynasty and the Kingdom of Fes (789). The Moors later displaced the dynasty from their control room in Spain.

The Golden Age Ends

By the 11th century **Almoravids** from the Western Sahara had quashed Spanish-Muslim control and founded their own kingdom in Marrakech. In 1163, High Atlas Berbers or **Almohads** established the greatest of the western Islamic empires, ruling from Tripoli to Castilla, well into the 13th century. A golden age of Berber **Merinid** and **Wattasid** rule (1244-1554) ignited a cultural and intellectual boom and strengthened the link between Morocco to Spain.

As the Christian Reconquista overtook Iberia, the Spanish turned against the "heretics" across the way. A second wave of Jewish immigrants, the **Sephardim,** arrived in Morocco after Catholic Monarchs Fernando and Isabel booted them out of Spain in 1492. The Wattasids recruited an army of refugees and converted (or mercenary) Christians to battle the imperialistic Spanish. By the early 1500s, however, the weak-chinned Habsburgs had established control over Morocco's ports and a number of inland territories.

Colonization

The **Saadis** drove out some foreign influence and reunited the country. Under **Ahmed el Mansour**—a.k.a. Ahmed the Gilded—Morocco expanded its trade in slaves and gold in Timbuktu and parts of the Sudan. When the **Alawite dynasty** overthrew the Saadis in 1659, they took over Marrakech and the area around Fes, controlled by religious mystics or **marabouts.** The Alawite dynasty rules to this day.

But constantly warring European rulers conspired to dissolve Moroccan unity. England nicked Tangier in 1662 as part of a settlement with crumbly Spain. **France** gradually imposed itself on northern Africa, winning a major battle at Isly in 1844. After the death of Sultan Hassan of Rabat in 1893, his 13-year-old son **Abd el-Aziz,** an expert at bicycle polo, ascended the throne. The French took advantage of the poor preteen, snarfed up Moroccan territories right and left, and eventually occupied Casablanca. By 1912 they had exiled the ruling vizier, Abd el-Hafid, and secured an official protectorate in the **Treaty of Fes.** The equivalent **Treaty of Algeciras** gave the Spanish the same rights.

Recent Years

In 1921, **Abd el Krim,** now considered the founder of modern Morocco, organized a rebel army in the Rif Country. Although Krim's rebels claimed nearly 30,000 Spanish lives, the troops of Major Francisco Franco (future Fascist dictator of Spain) aligned with Marshall Pétain's French army and forced the rebels into submission (1926).

Moroccan nationalism brewed under increasingly chaotic European rule. **Sultan Muhammad V** founded the Independence Party in 1944 and ignited the nationalist movement, but the French deported the nationalist leaders and exiled Muhammad in 1952. The ensuing popular unrest (combined with revolt in Algeria) forced the French to abandon their hard line. Muhammad returned to the throne on November 18, 1955 and signed a **treaty of independence** for French Morocco on March 2, 1956. The independence of most of Spanish Morocco followed one month later.

Muhammad V's successor, **King Hassan II,** tried to introduce a democratic constitution in the 60s, but two abortive military coups and divisions within the government delayed the first parliamentary elections until 1977. Meanwhile, Morocco's own expansionist claims in the phosphate-rich Western Sahara began to crumble. In response to attacks from the nationalist **Polisario Front,** the Moroccan army built a 1500-mile concrete and barbed wire wall to fence off the rebel army. In the escalating conflict Morocco broke off diplomatic relations with **Algeria,** whose support for the Polisario Front included military as well as diplomatic aid. A United Nations committee interceded on behalf of the rebels, and Algeria and Morocco reinstated uneasy relations in 1988. Negotiations for an independent Western Saharan state continue today.

Art and Architecture

Abstract design bloomed in Morocco centuries before its heyday in Europe and the Americas. Beautiful buildings glorify God, and an Islamic ban on representational images, inspired by Islam's opposition to idolatry of any kind, led to an incredible ingenuity in geometric and calligraphic decoration. As a result, colorful geometric patterns swirl across tiles, woodwork, stone, and ceramic. In less doctrinaire times, Almoravid artists slipped in designs that vaguely resemble leaves and flowers.

Calligraphy, particularly elegant renderings and illuminations of Qur'anic verse, became another outlet for creativity as well as for religious devotion. The more puritanical 12th-century Almohads introduced an interlocking almond-and-hexagon pattern to which all calligraphy was to conform. The Merinids who followed relaxed the formalism to include both floral and geometric strains, as manifest in the curved and straight-edged **zallij** (mosaic tiles).

The spirit of compromise also influenced architecture, which mixes the decorative simplicity of Islam with the airiness of Berber spaces. Led by the caliphs of Damascus, most rulers of the Moorish empire embarked upon the construction of full-blown **djemma** or **mosques** by the 8th century AD. Two hundred years later, Fes residents built the first Moroccan mosques, el-Andalus and the Kairouyyin.

Any place where Muslims pray is a mosque, or *masjid*. The word is best translated as "place of prostration." The direction facing Mecca, in which all prayer is spoken, is called the *qibla*. It is marked by a niche, the **mihrab.** The *imam* (leader of prayer) gives a sermon *(khutba)* on Friday from the *minbar* (pulpit). There are two basic designs for mosques: the Arab style, based on Muhammad's house, which has a pillared cloister around a courtyard (hypostyle); and the Persian style, which has a vaulted arch (an *iwan*) on each side. There are no absolute religious restrictions on non-Muslims entering mosques, but other restrictions are often adopted for practical reasons in areas with mobs of tourists. Prayer is not a spectator sport, and visitors should stay away during times of worship and always wear modest dress (women need to cover their heads and arms, and neither sex may wear shorts).

Attached to most mosques are the Qur'anic schools known as *mederas* (singular, **medrassa**). To promote Sunni Orthodoxy and religious scholarship, Merinid sultans built these tiny residential colleges in the 14th century. Classrooms, libraries, and the prayer hall surround a central courtyard and fountain. Most Merinid *mederas* display the same devotional artistry as the rest of the mosque complex; the Saadien *medrassa* in Marrakech displays a range of wood and marble carving.

Sultans reserved their most dazzling designs for **palaces,** typically a long, symmetrical series of reception and dwelling rooms studded with decorative gates, hidden gardens, and tiny pools and fountains. Royals built each palace as a testament to the owner's individuality, and the diversity of palatial styles is amazing. More functional than a palace but still highly ornmental, a **bab** is a gate in the walls of a Moroccan city.

Literature

Western translators have shamefully ignored Moroccan literature. Among the few works available in English, *Love With a Few Hairs, M'hashish,* and *The Lemon* are **Mohammed Mrabet's** snatches of contemporary Moroccan life. Historian **Youssef Necrouf's** *The Battle of Three Kings* is an entertaining account of medieval violence and intrigue.

Reading Matter

Guidebooks

Because our map of Morocco doesn't include the Western Sahara, *Let's Go* is banned from Moroccan bookstores. Buy before you go.

If worse comes to worst, you may want to check out some of the practical guidebooks of our competitors. Hachette's *Guide Bleu* is unbelievably thorough (an English edition was last printed in 1966) and available in all major Moroccan cities. Christopher Kininmonth's *Morocco: The Traveller's Guide* introduces Moroccan culture in laconic English.

Travel Narratives

Writing Moroccan guidebooks was popular among European and North American literati. Edith Wharton's *In Morocco* is a collection of episodic descriptions of Rabat, Salé, Fes, and Meknés. Walter Harris's *Morocco That Was,* a turn-of-the-century journalist's diary, features a wry account of a Brit's kidnapping by the international bandit Raissouli. *The Voices of Marrakech* by Bulgarian Nobel Prize recipient Elias Canetti eloquently records a European Jew's encounter with Moroccan Jews.

History

Plenty of Western histories of Morocco give one-sided perspectives on Islam and colonialism. *Saints of the Atlas* by Ernst Gallner describes in rather florid prose the conversion to Islam of the Atlas Mountain Berbers. David Montgomery Hart's *The Aith Waryagher of the Moroccan Rif* and Vincent Sheehan's *An American Among the Riffi* provide little-known trivia on the Riffian rebellion. Gavin Maxwell's *Lords of the Atlas* rivetingly recounts the rise and fall of the colonial puppet leader from 1893 to 1956. Banned in Morocco, it might be seized by local authorities if they find it in your possession.

Tangier

Tangier is certainly more familiar with drug-trafficking and prostitution than your average vacation spot. In the 1950s nearly 100 brothels thrived until they were forcibly shut down, and hashish flowed freely into town via the Rif mountains. Be prepared for minor culture shock when you step off the ferry: hustling wide-eyed tourists has become a formidable industry here. A city of shifty characters and fishy smells, Tangier is for those whose sensibilities delight in the sinister.

With the marriage of English King Charles II to Portugal's Princess of Braga, Tangier became a British possession. Although by 1912 the Brits, the French, and the Spanish had established themselves in Morocco, Tangier miraculously preserved a neutral status. A 1923 statute recognized the city as an international zone to be administered by a council of six Moroccan Jews, six Muslims, and representatives from seven European nations.

A smuggling nucleus in the 40s and 50s, the city's image of illicit activities gives thrill-seekers a delicious frisson. Tangier's foreign community began to dissolve after Morocco gained independence in 1956. Nevertheless, a lively expatriate community still enlivens the new city's boulevards and cafés.

Orientation and Practical Information

An hour by hydrofoil and two and a half hours by ferry from Spain, Tangier's main virtue is its train and bus service to points south. When leaving town, allow plenty of time (1-1 1/2 hr. in summer). Obtain a boarding pass from the ferry company representative at the port. Beware of hustlers trying to sell customs departure cards: they're free from customs agents and ferry company representatives. Try to get rid of your last *dirhams* before you come to the port, since travel agents never adhere to the official rates. Disembarking entails the same procedure in reverse, minus the boarding pass. The port area is filled with "guides," "students," and others who insist that you need someone to show you around. The easiest way to get to the center of town is to hop into one of the blue *petits taxis* in front of the port. Negotiate the fare in advance (about 3dh).

The **port** is directly below the **medina**. The **Grand Socco** is the medina's commercial center, a busy square. The sprawling **ville nouvelle** extends from the port area in all directions, particularly to the east along the beaches of the bay. The **train station** is the large, white building about 2 blocks to the left of the port as you exit; the **bus station** is on av. Louis Van Beethoven, about 2km from the port and medina. To get to the bus station from the port, walk along the beach on av. D'Espagne. Turn right on av. Beethoven.

Buses serve the entire city, but it's safer to use the abundant *petits taxis* as long as you have a general idea of where you're going. All roads to Tangier have an old European name and a new Moroccan name. Nearly all street signs give the old name, while most good maps record the new.

Tourist Office: 29 blvd. Pasteur (tel. 93 29 96), 20min. from the port. Walk straight ahead along the beach on av. d'Espagne from the port's exit. Take the 1st right after Hôtel Biarritz onto rue Magellan; at the end turn left. Blvd. Pasteur is ahead. Barely helpful; very sketchy map. Open July-Aug. Mon.-Fri. 9am-3pm; Sept.-June Mon.-Fri. 8:30am-noon and 2:30-6:30pm; Ramadan Mon.-Fri. 9am-3pm. **Librairie des Colonnes** (see English Bookstore below) across the street sells decent maps.

Consulates: U.K., 9 rue Amerique du Sud (tel. 93 58 95, 93 58 97), near Grand Socco. Money sent from Britain takes just 2 days. Varying hours. Open Mon.-Fri. 9am-noon. The **U.S.** Consulate is closed, but in emergency try the **Voice of America** radio station, 29 rue El Achouak (tel. 93 59 04).

Currency Exchange: Many hotels change money, some at a hefty commission. Travel agencies near the port are required to change money at official rates but sometimes give you less, especially if you're exchanging *pesetas* for *dirhams* or selling *dirhams* back to them. If you suspect overcharging, demand a receipt. Beware of hustlers that offer to change money.

American Express: Voyages Schwartz, 54 blvd. Pasteur (tel. 93 34 59). Open for mail pickup Mon.-Fri. 9am-12:30pm and 3-7pm, Sat. 9am-12:30pm; during Ramadan Mon.-Fri. 9am-12:30pm and 3-6pm, Sat. 9am-12:30pm. Like all Moroccan AmEx offices, this is a branch office and can't receive wired money. Cardholders may buy traveler's checks with personal checks.

Post Office: 33 blvd. Mohammed V (tel. 93 56 57), the downhill continuation of blvd. Pasteur. Open Mon.-Fri. 8:30am-12:15pm and 2:30-5:45pm.

Telephones: 33 blvd. Mohammed V, to the right and around the corner from the post office. Open 24 hrs. **Telephone Code:** 9.

Trains: av. d'Espagne (tel. 93 45 70), to the left exiting the port. 2nd-class fares to: Rabat (4 per day, 5-8hr., 79dh); Casablanca (4 per day, 6-9hr., 81.5dh); Marrakech (4 per day, 9-12hr., 134dh); Meknes (3 per day, 5hr., 56dh); Fes (3 per day, 6hr., 67dh).

Buses: rue Louis Van Beethoven by pl. de la Ligue Arabe, 2km from the port. For bus information, ask only policemen or the blue-coated personnel. Give baggage directly to the ticket taker and tip 1-3dh per bag. **CTM** buses to: Rabat (5 per day, 5hr., 66dh); Casablanca (5 per day, 6hr., 87dh); Fes (2 per day, 5 1/2 hr., 66dh). CTM and private company buses leave every hr. for Tetuan and Ceuta (1hr., 18dh). **CTM office,** av. d'Espagne (tel. 93 24 15, 93 11 72), near the train station next to the entrance of the port. Information and tickets sold. Open 5am-midnight.

Ferries: Voyages Hispamaroc, blvd. Pasteur (tel. 93 59 07, 93 27 18, 93 31 13; fax 94 40 31), below Hôtel Rembrandt. English spoken. Open Mon.-Thurs. 7am-7pm, Fri. 7am-noon, Sat. 7am-2pm. To: Algeciras (7 per day, 2 1/2 hr., Class B 2790ptas or 196dh); Tarifa (Mon.-Thurs. at 3:30pm, 1hr., 196dh); Gibraltar (Fri. at 9am, Sat.-Sun. at 4:30pm; 2 1/2 hr.; 220dh). Also, tickets are sold at any travel agency.

Taxis: Fast transport to points not served by rail (Tetuan, Ceuta, Asilah). About 100dh, which can be shared by 5-6 people. Be prepared to haggle. Pick-up points along blvd. Pasteur, Grand Socco, at the port, and by the bus station.

Car Rental: Avis, 54 blvd. Pasteur (tel. 93 30 31). **Hertz,** 36 av. Mohammed V (tel. 93 33 22). Both charge 210dh per day plus 2.30dh per km; 2695dh per week with unlimited mileage. Insurance 70dh per day.

Luggage Storage: At the **bus station** (3dh per bag). Open 4am-midnight.

English Bookstore: Librairie des Colonnes, 54 blvd. Pasteur (tel. 93 69 55). See directions under Tourist Office above. A superb collection of maps and guidebooks, mostly in French. Novels and books on Moroccan culture. Open Mon.-Fri. 10am-1pm and 4-7pm, Sat. 10am-1pm.

Red Cross: 6 rue El Monsoui Dahbi (tel. 93 11 99).

Late-Night Pharmacy: 22 rue de Fes (tel. 93 26 19), through tiny windows in the green wall on the left side of the entranceway. Open Mon.-Fri. 1-4pm and 8pm-9am, Sat.-Sun. 8pm-9am.

Medical Services: Hôpital Al-Kortobi, rue Garibaldi (tel. 93 10 73, 93 42 42). **Ambulance** (tel. 15).

Police: tel. 19.

Accommodations and Camping

In and Near the Medina

The medina's accommodations are cheaper, dirtier, and closer to the port than the more appealing options in the *ville nouvelle*. The most convenient hotels cluster near **rue Mokhtar Ahardan,** formerly **rue des Postes,** off the Petit Socco. Several hostels on this street cost under 30dh per person. At night the medina can be unsafe.

To enter the medina from the port area, make a U-turn around the CTM office and head west up the ramp along rue de Cadiz. Take the set of stairs on the left, just before the lower gate entrance to the Kasbah. At the top of the steps is rue des Postes. From the tourist office, head toward pl. de France and turn right on rue de la Liberté, which leads downhill into the Grand Socco, a noisy square. Cross the square and take the first right down rue Semmarine to the Petit Socco. Rue des Postes begins at the end of the Petit Socco closest to the port.

Hôtel Palace, 2 rue Mokhtar Ahardan, (tel. 93 61 28). We love it. Sizeable, spotless rooms. Deceptively clean bathroom—tiles, naturally the color of grime, are actually scrubbed fanatically. Inexplicably high beds. Attractive courtyard. Singles 40dh. Doubles 80dh. Hot showers 5dh.

Hôtel Continental, 36 rue Dar el Baroud (tel. 93 10 24). From the Petit Socco take rue de la Marine downhill toward the port to the Continental's blue gate. Veer to the left at the raised overlook. Perhaps the grandest hotel in town, dignified if past its prime. Large Art Deco rooms with views of the Mediterranean. Full of permanent expatriates. Often swamped by tour groups, so call ahead. Singles 87dh. Doubles 110dh.

Pension Miami, 126 rue Salah Eddine el-Ayoubi (tel. 93 29 00). The most palatable of the budget hotels on the block. Turquoise and magenta rooms, handsomely carved ceilings, and a balconied cloister on each floor. The only drawback is the hole in the floor (bathroom). Singles 30dh. Doubles 50dh. Hot showers 5dh.

In the Ville Nouvelle

Av. D'Espagne (straight ahead from the port and across from the train station) has decent rooms at decent prices. The best values lie farther up, in the heart of the new city.

Hôtel Valencia, 72 av. D'Espagne (tel. 93 07 70). Located near the port, train station, and medina. Richly decorated interior and first-rate modern rooms. Clean baths with natty miniature soaps. TV room. Singles 68dh, with toilet 103dh, with shower 84dh. Doubles 84dh, with toilet 125dh, with shower 103dh.

Hôtel Cecil, 112 av. d'Espagne (tel. 93 10 87), 10min. from the port along the waterfront. Remodeled interior features bright blue ocean wave motif on each and every wall. Bathrooms still desperately need remodeling. Spacious rooms in a palette of sky blue and dark yellow are carpeted and newly furnished. Singles 60dh. Doubles 120dh.

Hôtel de Paris, 42 blvd. Pasteur (tel. 93 81 26), across from the tourist office. The rooms—some with balconies overlooking the boulevard—are spacious, clean, and comfortable, but can be noisy. Large windows let in lots of light. Firm beds. Singles 60dh, with toilet 95dh, with shower 74dh. Doubles 74dh, with toilet 110dh, with shower 95dh.

Hôtel El Muniria, rue Magellan (tel. 93 53 37), take the first right after Hôtel Biarritz on av. d'Espagne, and follow as it winds uphill. Jack Kerouac, Allen Ginsberg, and William S. Burroughs—whom the owner calls "a terribly boring lot"—slept here. Prodigious rooms and beds with terraces overlooking the bay. Cushy lambswool mattresses. Singles 100dh. Doubles 120dh. Hot showers included.

Camping

Camping Tingis (tel. 94 01 91), 2km from the beach on the Malabata road near Mar-Bel, has showers, a pool, a grocery store, modern facilities, and tight security. Be careful walking to the beach—there have been muggings and rapes in the deserted woods. 10dh per person, 6dh per tent and per car.

Camping Miramonte (tel. 93 71 38) is less deluxe, but set in a lovely green site 1km from the town center (the route is well-marked with signs). Bar, grocery store, and restaurant. Reception open 8am-noon and 3-8pm. 10dh per person, 6dh per tent, 5dh per car.

Food

In and Near the Medina

For the greatest variety and lowest prices, hop like a bird from one stall to the next along the **Grand Socco.** Standard Moroccan fare is also served in passable budget restaurants along **rue Mokhtar Ahardan** and just outside the medina on **rue Salah Eddine el-Ayoubi,** which begins across from the train station and runs uphill to the Grand Socco.

Restaurant Hammadi, 2 rue de la Kasbah (tel. 93 45 14), the continuation of rue d'Italie just past the walls of the medina. Extravagant interior: luxe Moroccan carpeting, plush cushions, low tables, elegant candlelight. Arabic background music. Impeccable service, exalted food. Specialties are *tajine* (35dh) and *couscous* (30-35dh). Beer and wine. Service 19%. Open Mon.-Sat. (sometimes Sun.) noon-3pm and 8pm-1am.

Restaurante Africa, 83 rue Salah Eddine el-Ayoubi (tel. 93 54 36). A bamboo screen shields the entrance, and imitations of Prado paintings cover the walls. Abustle with travelers and Moroccans. Lipsmacking soup precedes delicious lamb *couscous.* Beer and wine. Whopping 4-course *menu du jour* 40dh. Open 9am-12:30am.

Restaurant Ahlen, 8 rue Mokhtar Ahardan (tel. 93 19 54), near the Petit Socco. Immense salads (3.50dh), lamb *couscous* (18dh), and chicken (16dh). Mainly Moroccan clientele. Open 9am-10pm.

Restaurant Andalus, rue du Commerce, an alley off rue Jaman Kebir at the Petit Socco and rue Mokhtar Ahardan. Small dining grotto buzzing with feverish brouhahas. If it's not the noise outside, it's the flies inside. Hefty sizzling brochettes 16dh. Full meal (entree, bread, olives, peas, and fries) 24dh. No set hours.

In the Ville Nouvelle

Tangier's former status as an international zone shows in *ville nouvelle* cuisine. For hot sandwiches, try the storefronts off **boulevard Pasteur.**

L'Marsa, 92 av. d'Espagne (tel. 93 23 39). Popular restaurant and café. Outdoor dining on the front patio and overhead terrace. Attentive service by bowtied waiters. Eclectic menu includes pizzas (20-35dh), spaghetti (22-24dh), Moroccan delicacies, and Italian ice cream treats in 10 flavors (8-20dh). Open 11am-11pm.

La Grenouille, 3 rue el-Jabba el-Quatania, just off blvd. Pasteur. Look for the green frog. A mélange of Moroccan, French, and English dishes popular with expatriates. Delicious *coq au vin* 40dh. Satisfactory *menu* 50dh. Service 19%. Open Tues.-Sun. noon-2:30pm and 7pm-midnight.

El Dorado, 21 rue Allal ben Abdellah (tel. 94 33 53), near the Chella hotel. Up the street across from the post office. Fancied by locals for *kebab* and *couscous.* Belt-loosening meals 40-50dh. Luscious fresh fruit for dessert. Open 11am-3pm and 6:30-11pm.

Sights

In and Near the Medina

Although you don't need a guide to show you around, it's dangerous to wander through the medina or on the beaches at night. Restrict any nighttime exploration to the *ville nouvelle.*

The medina's commercial center is the **Grand Socco,** a busy square and traffic circle cluttered with fruit vendors, parsley stands, and *kebab* and fish stalls. Bordering the square to the northeast is the **main market,** where the perfume of fresh spices wafts through narrow rows of orange, mint, fig, and melon stalls. The adjacent indoor **fish market** swims with live crab, squid, eel, shark, and ray.

In the colorful **Fes Market,** local merchants sell fresh fruits, vegetables, flowers, fish, and meat to Tangier's European community. To reach the market from the Grand Socco, head uphill on rue de la Liberté across pl. de France and onto rue de Fes—the market is 2 blocks down on the right. A more festive **country market** comes to town on Thursday and Sunday in the Dradeb district, when Rifian Berbers ride into town to sell their pottery, parsley, olives, mountain mint, and fresh fruit. To reach the Dradeb market, head west from the Grand Socco along rue Bou Arrakia and northwest on rue de la Montagne.

To the northwest, where rue Bou Arrakia joins the Grand Socco (through the door marked #50), a cache of 17th- and 18th-century bronze cannon hides in the shady **Jardins de la Mendoubia** (formerly the Jardin du Tribunal du Sada). **Rue Bou Arrakia,** the junk-dealer's alley, is lined with a motley collection of rare motercycle parts, used batteries, brass bedposts, and other random bits.

To reach the **Kasbah,** enter the next large gate to the right of the #50 gate. Veer to the left, then follow rue d'Italie north from the Grand Socco all the way through **Bab Fahs,** the Moorish gateway, and up the steep incline of rue de la Kasbah. This street ends at the horseshoe-shaped **porte de la Kasbah,** which is guarded by particularly industrious hustlers. Rue Riad Sultan runs from the main portal alongside the Jardins du Soltane, where artisans weave carpets (open Mon.-Sat. 8am-2pm; off-season 8:30am-noon and 2:30-6pm; admission 5dh), to **place de la Kasbah,** a sunny courtyard and adjacent promontory with a view of the Atlantic all the way to Spain. With your back to the water, walk straight ahead and right toward the far corner of the plaza. Just around the corner to the right, the perky **Mosque of the Kasbah's** octagonal minaret pokes up.

Near the mosque is the main entrance to the **Dar el-Makhzen,** an opulent palace with handwoven tapestries, inlaid ceilings, and foliated archways where the ruling pasha of Tangier once resided. The **Museum of Moroccan Art,** inside the palace, has a first-rate collection of Fes ceramics, Berber and Arabic carpets, copper and silver jewelry from Marrakech, and Andalusian musical instruments. Also inside, the **Museum of Antiquities** is a collection of ancient tools documenting the archeological history of Tangier. (Palace open Wed.-Mon. 9am-1pm and 3-6pm. Free.)

The **Old American Legation,** 8 rue America, lies south of pl. de la Kasbah in the far corner of the medina. Enter the medina from the archway off rue du Portugal, and look for the yellow archway emblazoned with the U.S. seal. The stone battlements were built in the 1600s by the Portuguese. A stately cross between the White House and a Moroccan palace, the United States' first ambassadorial residence (1777) displays a wonderful collection of antique maps and works by 20th-century American artists who lived in Morocco. Downstairs is the correspondence between Sultan Moulay ben Abdellah and George Washington that led to Morocco being the first country to recognize America's independence. The curator explains everything in English. (Open 9am-1pm and 4-6:30pm. 5dh tip is expected.)

The **Forbes Museum of Military Miniatures** (owned by late tycoon Malcolm Forbes) contains the world's largest collection of toy soldiers. Whoopee. Sundry historic battles are meticulously represented in miniature. Gardens behind the museum offer a spectacular view of the ocean and were the setting of a James Bond movie. To get here from the Kasbah, at the top of rue de la Kasbah, turn left onto rue de la Corse. Bear right at the fork onto H. Assad Ibn Farrat and continue straight ahead past a hospital on the right and then a sports stadium on the left (15min.). The museum is in the white mansion farther up on the right. (Open Fri.-Wed. 10am-5pm. Free.)

In the Ville Nouvelle

British expatriates frequent **St. Andrew's Church**, an Anglican house of worship designed by British imperialists to look like a mosque (1 bl. southwest of the Grand Socco on rue d'Angleterre). The Lord's Prayer is carved on the chancel arch in decorative Arabic. A garden shades the tombs of some of prominent British residents, including Walter Harris, the celebrated chronicler of Morocco. (Tours by caretaker 9:30am-12:30pm and 2:30-6pm. Tips appreciated.)

The city's most recent monumental construction is the towering **New Mosque,** an ochre and white structure on **place el-Koweit,** southwest of the Grand Socco along rue Sidi Bouabib. A gift from the king of Kuwait, the mosque occupies the largest site of any house of worship in North Africa.

Entertainment

Av. d'Espagne runs along Tangier's expansive **beach.** Stick to the main portions frequented by tourists—the deserted areas are prime locations for muggings. Watch all your belongings carefully.

The most popular evening activity is to settle into a **café** on **boulevard Pasteur,** sip mint tea, and watch the crowds. The passing throng is particularly thick during Ramadan. If you don't mind paying twice as much for a pot of tea (5-6dh), you can enjoy the atmosphere at one of the two teahouses where Tangier's intelligentsia come to sip and quip: **Café de Paris,** 1 pl. de France (open until 1am), and **Madame Porte,** on av. Prince Moulay Abdellah at rue el-Mou Hanabi (open until midnight).

Folk music and dance performances are at a more traditional setting at the **Morocco Palace,** av. du Prince Moulay Abdellah, just off blvd. Pasteur. Belly-dancers, beanie-twirlers, and Berber singers perform to the rhythms of lute, violin, tambourine, and bongo drums. (Open nightly from 10pm. Best on Sat. Cover including 1 drink 45dh.)

If thirsty for alcohol, but tired of the noise, try the **Negresco,** 20 rue Mexique (93 80 97), a relaxed place that plays quiet folk music and serves free hors d'oeuvres. (Beer 18dh, mixed drinks 30-35dh. Open 10am-1am.) For serious drinking there's no place finer than **Dean's Bar** (2nd right on rue de la Liberté coming from the Grand Socco). Come to where Tennessee Williams, Errol Flynn, and Ian Fleming all drowned their sorrows in tepid gin—it's not the place for those looking to get merely tipsy on a beer or two.

Asilah

Only 46km south of the tensions of Tangier, Asilah soothes the soul of the harried tourist with its quiet streets, white-washed buildings bright with frescoes, nearby beaches, and mellow local demeanor. Tourism has made some inroads here, but the presence of the Minister of Finance and Portuguese dignitaries in the summer have kept the town hassle-free; self-appointed guides are pretty easy-going and merchants eager to sell their leather and carpets are neither persistent nor hostile. Although the town isn't quite the unspoiled resort it was a few years ago, it remains a tranquil base for tea-sipping and exploring the beaches and ruins along Morocco's northwest Atlantic coast.

Orientation and Practical Information

There's no tourist office. The town is small enough that a map is unnecessary. The main street into town is **boulevard Mohammed V,** which ends at the town's center, **place Mohammed V,** a traffic circle. The road to the right leads to a fork in the road in the medina. To the right is **rue Zallakah,** which leads to the port. To the left is **Avenue Hassan II,** tracing the walls of the medina.

Post Office: Hard to find. From av. Hassan II, take the 1st immediate left; at Hotel Las Palmas turn right onto rue Ben Zagour, which ends at a small plaza on the right. Open Mon.-Thurs. 8am-3pm, Fri. 8am-12:30pm. **Telephone Code:** City Code 9.

Currency Exchange: BMCE, pl. Mohammed V. Traveler's checks cashed without commission. Open Mon.-Thurs. 8:15-11:30am and 2:15-4:30pm, Fri. 8:15-11:15am and 2:45-4:45pm.

Trains: The station is 3km from town on the Asilah-Tangier highway, near a strip of campgrounds. A taxi from town coasts about 10dh. A bus (3dh) connects the station to town, but it leaves from in front of the station immediately after the train arrives. To Tangier (5 per day; 1hr.; 1st class 15dh, 2nd class 10dh) and Casablanca, with connections to Rabat and Marrakech (5 per day).

Buses: CTM, off av. Liberté on the way out of town to the highway. CTM and private buses to Tangier (every 1/2 hr.) leave from in front of the office. To Casablanca (14 per day, 4 1/2- 5 1/2 hr., 77.50dh). Buses depart with surprising promptness and sometimes leave early at the driver's whim.

Taxis: pl. Mohammed V, across from the bus station. *Grand taxis* only. To Tangier or Larache about 100dh. To train station 10dh.

Pharmacy: Pharmacie Loukili, av. Liberté (tel. 91 72 78), 1 bl. from pl. Mohammed V across from the police station. Open Mon.-Fri. 9am-1pm and 4-8:30pm.

Police: Service de Police, av. Liberté at blvd. Mohammed V (tel. 19), 1 bl. from pl. Mohammed V. Helpful if you arrive at night.

Accommodations and Camping

To rent rooms in a small pension or private home (30-35dh per person), ask around the waterfront or along **rue Zallakah** by the walls of the medina; you can usually get homemade meals for a little extra. Still, be careful with your valuables. Otherwise, a variety of reasonably priced hotels lie within walking distance of the beach.

Hôtel Marhaba, 9 rue Zallakah (tel. 91 71 44), on the right as you approach the medina from pl. Mohammed V. The most popular place with travelers: prime location, low rates, more than adequate rooms, and perfectly clean bathroom. Owner may let you dry laundry on the terrace. Singles 40dh. Doubles 60dh.

Hôtel Asilah, 79 av. Hassan II (tel. 91 72 86). From rue Zallakah, turn left and follow the walls of the medina along av. Hassan II. Enter on a side street. Small, spartan rooms with cool blue and aqua green walls that make you want to go swimming. Pink Moroccan-style lounge with puffy cushions along the walls and a balcony. Large terrace has excellent view of medina walls. Singles 40dh. Doubles 60dh.

Hôtel Sahara, 9 rue Tarfaya (tel. 91 71 85). Take blvd. Mohammed V from pl. Mohammed V, turn right at av. Liberte and left at the next block. Handsome new wood beds. Smallish rooms, some lacking windows. Baths are modern, newly-tiled, and squeaky clean. Lounge in the TV room on plump pillows and read their copy of *Let's Go*. Singles 54dh. Double 75dh. Hot showers 5dh.

Asilah is bursting with campgrounds, some of which rent small, inexpensive "bungalows" to those without tents or sleeping bags. Most campgrounds line up near or on the shore towards the train station; others are along the road to Cape Spartel.

Camping Echrigui (tel. 91 71 82), 700m from the train station toward town, where the new port finally ends. On a glorious beach, and the walk to town isn't too bad. Young, English-speaking manager. Office has cushiony salon/lounge. 8dh per person, 9dh per tent, 9dh per car. Bungalows with bath and hot shower 70dh, with electricity 100dh.

Food

The cheapest and most authentic restaurants clutter **av. Hassan II**, along the walls of the medina. Famished souls eat their hearts out in one of the tiny stalls with green doors for 20dh. A fruit and vegetable **market** lurks further down on av. Hassan II.

Resaurant Café Rabie, 9 av. Hassan II, near beginning of medina walls. The chicken, beef, and fish dinners are hypercheap (16-25dh). Soup and chips 7.50dh. Sidewalk patio across the street.

Restaurant Najoum, directly below the Marhabe hotel. Savory swordfish 35dh. English spoken. Fast service. Open 7am-11pm.

La Alcazabah Restaurant (tel. 91 70 12), at beginning of rue Zallakah by the medina and port. Reputedly the best restaurant in town, but bus tours from Tangier have upped the price. Sit inside or upstairs on a terrace overlooking the street and the port. Wine served. Fixed menu 150dh. Service charge 10%. Open 8:30am-3:30pm and 6:30pm-2am.

Restaurant Lixus, pl. Mohammed V (tel. 91 73 79). Bland atmosphere, sizable portions (20-30dh). Equally sizable dining room. Open 8am-10pm.

Sights

Asilah has but two attractions: its nearby **beaches** and its shining medina. The beaches just north of town are smooth, sandy, sprawling delights. The beach company is generally congenial, but don't bring a passport or valuables along—there are sometimes muggers, and it's safer to have your hotel management lock things in their safe. Also, men tend to leer at and harrass any women who swim. Five km south of Asilah, an enclosed cove called **Paradise Beach** has fine sand and clear water. The walk down the coast takes one hour, or catch a horsecart in town (about 100dh).

The **medina**, bounded by heavily fortified stone walls, is easy to navigate. Just enter—unescorted—through **Bab Hamar** at the intersection of av. Hassan II and rue Zallakah. Intricately painted stalactite arches and bright tiled burial markers decorate the Portuguese **Palais de Raissouli** on the coastal side of the medina across from the *bab*. (Open only Sundays in off-season 9am-2pm.)

Apart from the regular town market, there's a Sunday morning Berber market at **souk el-Had el-Gharbia,** 9km inland from Asilah. Berbers from as far away as the Rif mountains converge on the enclosed area by the tiny village to peddle their wares. The scanty vestiges of the once-sizeable Roman metropolis **Admercuri** sprinkle a dusty road 2km farther inland. Ask local children to point the way. There's no public transport to the market.

In August, artists from all over the world flock here for the famous **cultural museum festival.** Painters cover the white walls with murals, and jazz and folk musicians sprinkle sound along the beach.

Fes

Fes is why you came to Morocco. Here is the medina of medinas, a mixed bag of delights and frustrations, chaos and exultation. Artisans bang out sheets of brass, donkeys strain under crates of Coca-Cola, *muezzins* wail, and children balance trays of dough on their heads. The air smells: the perfume of brochettes on open grills, acrid whiffs of hash, the stench of tanning lye, and the sweet scent of cedar shavings.

The city exploits its uniqueness. Tourism predominates, and it's nearly impossible for travelers to simply roam unattended about the medina. Fes is a "must see" and for that reason, you may feel more like an outsider and a reject than ever.

Orientation and Practical Information

Fes is an extreme case of the modern Moroccan paradox: the French-built **ville nouvelle** is broad and orderly, the **medina** is knotty and tangled. The CTM bus station is in the heart of the new city (near the budget hotels); the other bus station lies near **Bab Boujeloud,** the main entrance to the medina. The train station is on the outskirts of the *ville nouvelle.*

You can reach Bab Boujeloud from the *ville nouvelle* either by *petit taxi* (10dh) or by bus #2 or 9 (1.40dh) from the stop on **Avenue Hassan II,** near **plaza de la Résistance** (the hub for most city buses). Bus #18 runs from pl. de la Résistance to Bab Ftouh at the opposite end of the medina, near the Andalous Quarter. Bus #3 roars to pl. des Alaouites.

The old city is divided into two walled-off sections, Fes el-Bali and Fes el-Jdid. **Rue Tala Kebira,** which runs southwest-northeast from Bab Boujeloud to the Karaouyine Mosque, traverses the ninth-century **Fes el-Bali** (Old Fes). **Avenue des Français**, just outside Bab Boujeloud, leads to Bab Semmarin, the entrance to the **Fes el-Jdid** (New Fes).

Tourist Office: ONMT, pl. de la Résistance (tel. 62 34 60), at av. Hassan II. From the CTM bus station, turn left onto blvd. Mohammed V and right past the post office onto palm-lined av. Hassan II. From the train station, head straight ahead on rue Chenguit, bear left at pl. Kennedy along av. France, and turn left on av. Hassan II. From Bab Boujeloud Gare Routière, walk to nearby pl. de l'Istiqlal and catch bus #2 or 9; a *petit taxi* is 8dh. English-speaking staff tries to stick tourists with sketchy maps; newsstands in the *ville nouvelle* sell better ones. Open Mon.-Fri. 8am-3pm; mid-Sept. to June Mon.-Fri. 8:30am-noon and 2:30-6pm; Ramadan Mon.-Fri. 9am-3pm. **Syndicat d'Initiative,** blvd. Mohammed V, BMCE building (tel. 247 69). Not as well stocked. Official guides found here (40dh per 1/2-day). Open Mon.-Fri. 8am-3pm; mid-Sept. to June Mon.-Fri. 8:30am-noon and 2:30-6pm.

Currency Exchange: BMCE, pl. Mohammed V, across from the Syndicat d'Initiative. Handles VISA/Mastercard transactions and traveler's checks. Open 8:15am-1:45pm; winter 8:30am-noon and 3-5pm. **Les Merinides** (tel. 64 52 25), in the Borj Nord. Open 5-10pm.

Post Office: At the corner of av. Hassan II and blvd. Mohammed V in the *ville nouvelle.* Open for stamps and Poste Restante Mon.-Fri. 7am-2:30pm; Sept. 16-June Mon.-Fri. 8:30am-6:45pm. Open for **telegrams** Mon.-Fri. 8:30am-9pm. **Branch offices** at pl. d'Atlas and in the medina at pl. Batha. Open same hrs.

Telephones: In the **main post office**; enter from blvd. Mohammed V. There's a long line for telephone calls, and an even longer wait for a connection. Open 8:30am-9pm. **Telephone Code:** 06.

Flights: Aérodrome de Fes-Saiss (tel. 62 47 12, 62 47 99), 12km out of town along the road to Immouzzèr. Bus #16 leaves from pl. Mohammed V (3dh). Collective taxi (7dh per person). **Royal Air Maroc** (tel. 62 55 16, 62 55 17), av. Hassan II.

Trains: av. des Almohades (tel. 62 50 01), at rue Chenguit. 2nd-class trains are more expensive than buses, but more comfortable. To: Casablanca (11 per day, 4 1/2-5 1/2 hr., 87dh); Rabat (12 per day, 3 1/2 hr., 62.50dh); Meknes (12 per day, 1hr., 15dh); Oujda (7 per day, 6hr., 83.50dh); Tangier (5 per day, 5 1/2 hr., 84dh).

Buses: CTM (tel. 62 20 41, 62 20 42) and private bus companies, blvd. Mohammed V in the *ville nouvelle* and just outside Bab Boujeloud. To: Rabat (7 per day, 3hr., 47.50dh); Casablanca (7 per day, 5hr., 69dh); Marrakech (2 per day, 8hr., 95-110dh); Meknes (4 per day, 1hr., 15dh); Tangier (3 per day, 6hr., 66dh); Oujda (at 12:30pm, 6 1/2 hr., 62dh).

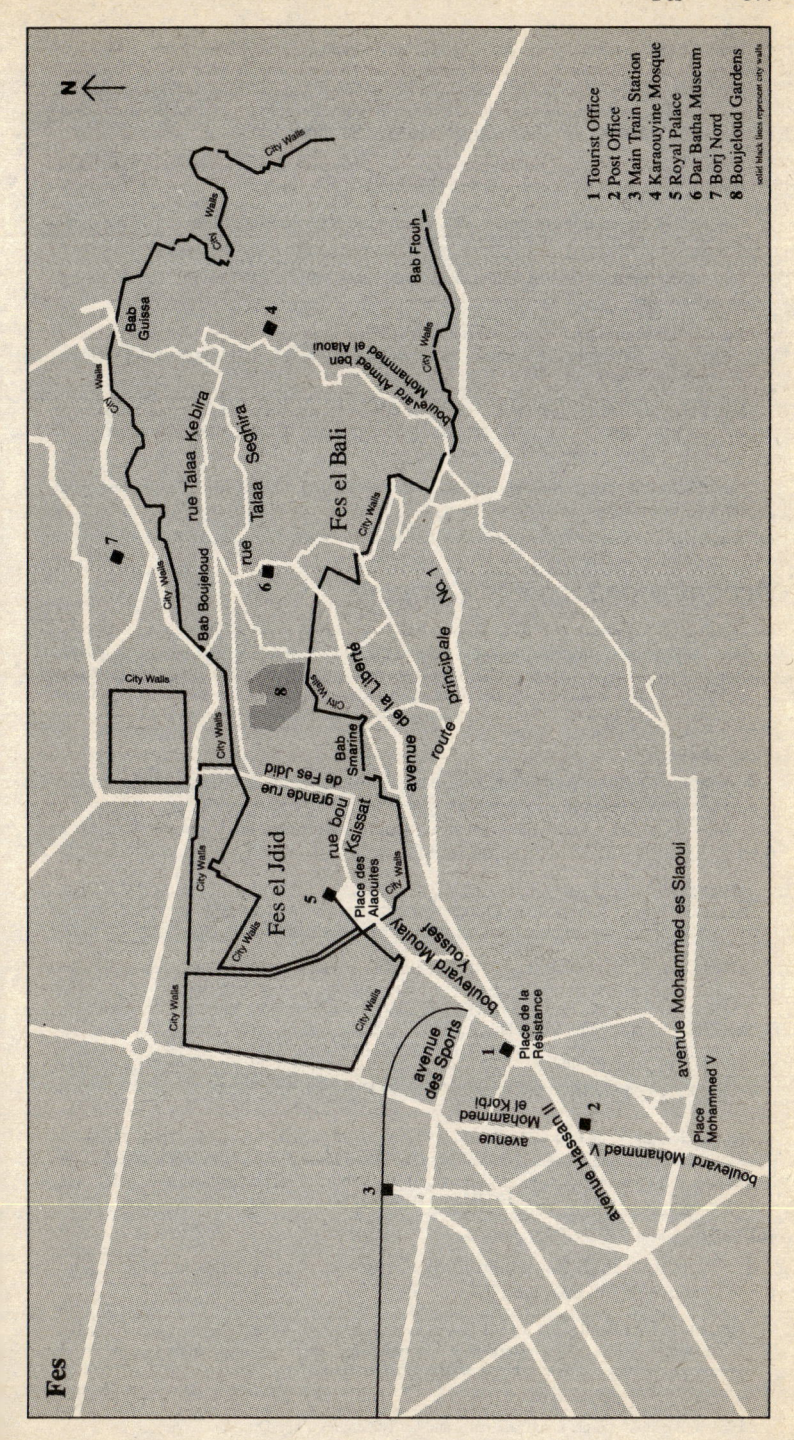

Fes

1 Tourist Office
2 Post Office
3 Main Train Station
4 Karaouyine Mosque
5 Royal Palace
6 Dar Batha Museum
7 Borj Nord
8 Boujeloud Gardens

solid black lines represent city walls

Public Transportation: Numerous buses (1.40dh; fares double after 8:30pm, Sept. 16-June after 8pm). Pl. de la Résistance is the hub. #2 or 9 from av. Hassan II near the plaza to Bab Boujeloud. #18 from the plaza to Bab Ftouh at the opposite end of the medina, near the Andalous Quarter. #3 from the plaza to pl. des Alaouites. #4 or 9 from *ville nouvelle* (in front of Grand Hôtel) to Fes el-Jdid (Bab Semmarin). #16 from pl. Mohammed V to the airport (3dh).

Taxis: Major stands at the post office, the Syndicat d'Initiative, Bab Boujeloud, and Bab Guissa. Fares double after 8:30pm; Sept. 16-June after 8pm.

Car Rental: Hertz, Hôtel de Fes, av. des Forces Armées Royales (tel. 62 28 12), off the southwestern end of av. Hassan II. Renault IV for 3 days with unlimited mileage 1560dh.

Luggage Storage: At the **bus station,** blvd. Mohammed V in the *ville nouvelle*. 1.50dh per bag. Open 6am-11pm.

English Bookstore: 68 av. Hassan II (tel. 208 42), near pl. de la Résistance. All genres: novels, poetry, plays, guidebooks, and phrase books. English-speaking staff. Open Mon.-Fri. 8:30am-12:30pm and 3-7pm.

Swimming Pool: Municipal Pool, av. Sports, next to the stadium and near the train station in the *ville nouvelle*. Crowded. Open July-Sept. 15. Admission 5dh. **Camping Moulay Slimane** (tel. 62 47 12). Call ahead to see if there's water today.

Late-Night Pharmacy: Municipalité de Fes, blvd. Moulay Youssef (tel. 233 80), just uphill from the Royal Palace. Open 8pm-8am.

Police: tel. 19.

Accommodations and Camping

Auberge de Jeunesse (HI), 18 rue Abdeslam Serghini (tel. 62 40 85), in the *ville nouvelle*. From the ONMT tourist office cross the street, turn left onto blvd. Abdallah Chefchaouni, walk 4 bl., turn left, and look for the sign. English-speaking proprietors. Reasonably clean rooms. Shower dribbles hot water in winter only. Reception open 8-10am, noon-3pm, 6-midnight (10pm in winter). HI card and 2 photos (75dh) sold on the spot. 15dh per person. Nonmembers 17.50dh.

Ville Nouvelle

The nondescript new city is a long haul from the medina, but appealing during the old city's tourist season. In August rooms here fill up entirely. Cheap lodgings clump conveniently on or just off the west side of **blvd. Mohammed V** between av. Mohammed es-Slaoui, near the bus station, and av. Hassan II, near the post office.

Hôtel Excelsior, 107 rue Larbi el Kaghat (tel. 62 56 02), 6 bl. up blvd. Mohammed V from the bus station toward the post office. Clean rooms with stucco walls. Acceptable toilets and showers. TV room. Singles with shower 65dh. Doubles with shower 78dh, with full bath 96dh.

Hôtel Central, 50 rue Nador (tel. 62 23 33), en route to the above. Plain rooms with ample beds; slinky satiny bedspreads and cool-ass oval windows. Strong, lukewarm showers. A bit noisy thanks to blvd. Mohammed V. Singles 50dh, with shower 65dh, with bath 75dh. Doubles 68dh, with shower 78dh, with bath 96dh.

Hôtel CTM, rue Ksarelkbir (tel. 62 28 11). On intimate terms with the bus station. Dark hallways belie the wide-open rooms. Expect street noise. Singles 50dh, with shower 65dh. Doubles 68dh, with shower 78dh.

Hôtel Olympic, blvd. Mohammed V (tel. 62 24 03, 62 45 29), 1 bl. toward av. Hassan II from pl. Mohammed V. Bright, modern rooms with excellent bathrooms, brass beds, phones, and winter heating. Restaurant below. Choose your fixture: Singles with toilet 72dh, with shower 105dh, with bath 133dh. Doubles with toilet 102dh, with shower 123dh, with bath 155dh. Breakfast 17dh.

Fes el-Bali

Step right up to **Bab Boujeloud** for budget rooms. Cheaper, noisier, and dirtier than the *ville nouvelle*, but near the medina.

Hôtel du Jardin Public, 153 Kasbah Boujeloud (tel. 63 30 86), a small alley across from the Bab Boujeloud bus station. A prehistoric hotel with relatively sanitary rooms, some with good views. Moroccan showers and toilets. Singles 30dh. Doubles 60dh.

Hôtel Erraha (tel. 63 32 26), 1 bl. farther from the *bab*, on the right as you approach. Staff babbles French. Passable rooms, but small, bare, and stuffy. Singles 40dh. Doubles 70dh.

Fes el-Jdid

Escape the Bab Boujeloud hustlers here. The lively main street, **grande rue de Fes Jdid,** runs from Bab Smarine to Bab de Kakene, near the Boujeloud gardens.

> **Hôtel du Commerce,** pl. des Alaouites (tel. 62 22 31), near the Royal Palace. The cleanest and most pleasant place in the medina. Paintings of weeping Pierrots in the hall. Mauve stucco. Clean tiled showers. Some rooms have sunset-watching terraces overlooking the Royal Palace. Singles 30dh, with terrace 50dh. Doubles 60dh. Showers 4dh.
>
> **Hôtel le Croissant,** 285 grande rue de Fes Jdid (tel. 62 56 37), just 30m from Bab Smarine. Hot and cheap. Some rooms have balconies on the street; better rooms are off a renovated court in back. Pastel green rooms are bare-bones basic. Singles 20dh. Doubles 40dh.

Food

Ville Nouvelle

Cheap food huts skulk on the little streets to either side of **blvd. Mohammed V.** See also **Rue Kaid Ahmed**, on the left a few blocks down blvd. Mohammed V from the main post office. For a marvelous breakfast, snarf some pastries at the **Boulangerie Patisserie Epi D'or** at 81 blvd. Mohammed V, then proceed 40 minutes downhill to **Café Zanzi Bar** on rue Abdelkrim el-Khattabi, where you can sip some of the best coffee and mint tea in town.

The busy, aromatic **municipal market** is where the city's households stock up on fresh fruit, veggies, fish, meat, and spices. It's opposite Café Zanzi Bar, just off blvd. Mohammed V.

> **Restaurant CTM,** rue Ksar El Kbir under Hôtel CTM. Substantial food at super prices. A great place to gastronomically delight a stomach after a long and harrowing bus ride. *Tajine marocaine,* salad, and bread 40dh. Open 9am-10pm.
>
> **Rotisserie La Rotonde,** rue Nador (tel. 62 05 89), up the street from Hôtel Central. Hole-in-the-wall with skewered chicken torsos pirouetting by the front door, instead of on a spinning hot plate. Fast food (almost as fast as our format) munchies. Succulent bubbling 1/4-chicken, sauce, bread, and rice 12dh. Prices lower for take-away. Open 9am-9pm.
>
> **Restaurant Es Saada,** 42 av. Slaoui, a couple bl. off blvd. Mohammed V on the right. Eat outside to escape the boring interior. Lipsmacking, plenteous *menu* 47dh. *Mechoui* only 50dh. Service charge 12-20%. Open 6:30am-11pm.
>
> **Restaurant Roi de la Bière,** 59 blvd. Mohammed V (tel. 62 53 24). Gobs better than the adjoining café on the corner. Wood-panelled walls, Art Deco *élan*. Entrees 20-45dh. *Menu* 50dh. Open noon-3pm and 6pm-midnight.
>
> **A la Tour d'Argent,** 30 av. Slaoui (tel. 62 26 89). One of the finest French restaurants in town. Less-than-grand ambience, *viz.,* pinball machines. Patio on the street. 3-course *menu* 50dh. Try their specialties: *tajine d'agneaux* or *poulet aux amandes* 35dh. Service charge 15%.

Fes el-Bali and Fes el-Jdid

Food stalls line the beginning of **Tala Kebira** and **Tala Seghira,** the two streets that split off rue Serrajine at the mouth of the *bab*. Choose from *couscous, harira,* brochettes, *kefta-burgers,* and a jumble of oily, diced tomatoes and cucumbers known as *salade.* Stalls on Tala Seghira sell chunks of *pastilla* (candy). Look for budget fare just inside **Bab Boujeloud.** If no prices are posted, ask for them before before you order. The quiet cafés around the **Place des Alaouites** specialize in almond juice and milk (3.50dh), a most nutritious beverage.

> **Restaurant des Jeunes,** 16 rue Serrajine (tel. 63 49 75), on the right as you enter the *bab*. Stellar reviews. *Tajine* 25dh. Other entrees 20-25dh. *Pastilla* (when available) 30dh. Open 6am-midnight.
>
> **Restaurant Bouayad,** 26 rue Serrajine (tel. 63 62 78), on the right and farther down from the above. Good *tajine* or *couscous* 25dh. Salad 2dh. Locals loiter around the clock. Open 24 hrs.

Sights

The medina is the most difficult to navigate in Morocco. Guides skulk everywhere. "Do you want to see the medina?" they ask. You can hire an **official guide** at the ONMT tourist office or the Syndicat d'Initiative. A morning tour costs 40dh and ends at noon. Especially in summer, visit the medina in the morning, when it's at its liveliest. A "full day" tour costs 80dh.

If pride or a sense of adventure compels you to strike out on your own and being lost doesn't faze you, prepare yourself for constant harassment by hustlers. Bring water, emergency provisions, a compass, and a good map. Begin in the morning so you'll have plenty of time to find a way out.

Take a *petit taxi* to Babouissa, and work your way to the Kairouyine Mosque. Or take bus #2 or #9 to pl. de L'Istiqlal and head to the top of the square. Bear left, then immediately right down a skinny, spindly street. Cross the first busy thoroughfare and pass the Mosque of Sidi Lezzaz. The next big street is **Tala Kebira,** the main artery that begins at Bab Boujeloud and runs the full length of the medina.

Dar Batha and Bab Boujeloud

A 19th-century palace conceals a well-kept and beautiful museum, the **Dar Batha.** The spacious Moorish mansion was headquarters for Sultan Hassan I and his playboy son Moulay Abd el-Aziz during the final years of decadence before the French occupation. The extraordinary collection highlights Moroccan folk art, including intricately illuminated Qur'anic manuscripts, a stamp collection, musical instruments, fine embroidery, Berber carpets, and excellent *mashrabiyya* and wood sculptures from the local *medersa* and mosques. During the *moussem* of Moulay Idriss in September, the museum hosts Moroccan music concerts.

To reach the Dar Batha from the *ville nouvelle,* take bus #9 in front of the Grand Hôtel or a *petit taxi* to pl. l'Istiqlal outside the medina near Bab Boujeloud. Look for the green tile roofs of the palace. Turn left at the corner from the bus stop, enter the square, and head up the hill on the first left. Red flags mark the entrance on the right. (Open Wed.-Sat. 9am-noon and 3-6pm. Admission 10dh.)

Fes el-Bali

Allow a full morning to tour Fes el-Bali (Old Fes). Begin at Tala Kebira, just inside Bab Boujeloud and to the left. The **medieval clock**, a carved wooden contraption on the left that overlooks the street from the second story of an ancient shop, is Fes's oldest timepiece (it dates from 1357). The circular bronze hammers strapped to its ornate façade pound out the hour.

Farther downhill on the right is the **Medrassa of Bou Inania,** the best-preserved Qu'ranic school in Morocco. Built under the Merinid Dynasty in the mid-14th century, its beautifully carved white plastered walls and *mihrab* remain in remarkably fine condition. A tiny canal separates the school from an adjoining mosque. (Open Sat.-Thurs. 9am-6pm, Fri. 8:30am-10am and 1:30-6pm. Admission 10dh.)

Farther down on Tala Kebira, past the **Tijania Zaouia** on the left, is the trim **Mosque of Sidi Ahmed Tijani,** an elegant turquoise-tiled minaret. Many side-street *fondouks* (two-story neighborhood *souks* set up in private courtyards) lurk in the side streets off Tala Kebira.

A bit farther down the main route is the small, whitewashed minaret of the **Mzara of Moulay Idriss,** an ancient house of worship where wise Sultan Moulay Idriss I predicted the founding of the city. Next door is the lively **drum-makers' fondouk.** Diagonally across the street in the **sheepskin fondouk,** untanned woolly hides are bartered by the dozen.

From here rue Tala Kebira bows slightly to the right and changes its identity to **rue ech Cherabliyyan**. A traditional **hamman** (bath) bubbles around the corner. Up ahead wallets, sandals, belts, bags, and other ex-animal skins convalesce in the **leather souk**.

From the *souk*, a right then a left leads to the **pl. Nejarine,** a small triangular plaza ruled by the dazzling tiled **Fontaine Nejarine.** Women gather here to socialize and collect household water while young children play. Just below, an arched doorway leads into the **Nejarine Fondouk,** a fabulous 18th-century shopping area of delicate *mashrabiyya* and handsome balconies. Across the way, woodsmiths chisel in the lively **carpenters' fondouk.**

At the opposite end of the plaza from the fountain is one corner of the great **Zaouia of Moulay Idriss II,** honoring the saint, sultan, and son of the founder of Fes. Inside the *zaouia,* the Mosque of Chorfa houses the saint's tomb. The faithful arrive each morning to worship under the intricate stalactite ceiling. A tiny brass star with a gold slot is set in the wall nearby. Through the slot you can touch the back of the tomb—a practice believed to channel *baraka* (good luck) from the saint to his followers. The **henna souk,** a steep side street up the western wall of the shrine, is a fragrant, spice-filled alley. Local women tattoo bright orange diamond patterns on their hands with natural dye, and many Berber women mark themselves with blue tattoos on the forehead and chin.

The **Medrassa el-Attarine,** left from the corner of Zaouia and downhill, is Fes' finest Merinid monument. The prayer hall is now open to all. (Open 9am-6pm. Admission 10dh.)

Turn right then left from the Madrassa to reach the splendid **Karaouyine Mosque,** the largest in northern Africa and the greatest symbol of Fes's past prestige. Every Friday, 2000 flock here to pray—though the mosque can hold up to 20,000 men and 2000 women (who worship around and behind the men). The Karaouyine nurtured many great minds, including that of Pope Sylvester II, who introduced algebra and the number system to Europe. Today the mosque is home to Karaouyine University, where a few hundred students debate Qur'anic law; founded in 859 AD, the mosque is one of the oldest universities in the world. Worshipers wade walk through the tiled canal to the right of the entrance to clean their feet before praying.

South, past the walls of the mosque, the **plaza Seffarine** is famous for deafening innocent travelers. **Medrassa Seffarine,** on the left of pl. Seffarine, is the oldest Merinid Qu'ranic school in Morocco (1280).

Around the Medrassa Seffarine to the left and through the slender cobbled sidestreet is the smell. A microscopic alley on the right leads from here straight down into the mammoth outdoor **leather tannery.** To tan a hide: 1. Soak skins in a hair-melting green liquid. 2. Rinse skins in washing machine/cement mixer hybrid. 3. Dunk hides in diluted pigeon excrement or waterlogged wheat husks (to make them more supple). 4. Saturate skin (by type) in yellow, brown, or red dye. Allow a year for the entire process.

To get to the smoky **wool-** and **silk-dyers' row** from the pl. Seffarine, take the road leading south from beside the Medrassa Seffarine, head left at the fork and make a sharp right at the river. Here, dyes boil over wood fires that blaze in old garbage cans. The finished skeins of brilliantly colored wool are so shiny that they appear wet even when dry.

Andalous Quarter

The Andalous Quarter is across the Oued Fes (river) from the heart of Fes el-Bali. Many of the Moors who fled from Muslim Spain (Andalusia) to Morocco during the 15th-century Reconquista settled around the great Almohad house of worship in Fes, the **Andalous Mosque.** The city's second-largest religious monument, its main attraction to non-Muslims is the grandiose 13th-century doorway. To find the mosque, head northwest from Bab Ftouh on the east end of the medina and take the first major left. From Fes el-Bali, cross the river at Port Bein el-Moudoun near the tanneries and head straight down rue Seffrah. The portal on the left side of the mosque offers the best view of the interior.

Fes el-Jdid

Christians and Jews, as well as Muslims, once lived in the Fes el-Jdid (New Fes), built by the Merinids in the 13th century. The ancient neighborhood still has narrow sidestreets, covered *souks,* and ornamental *mashrabiyya* balconies.

To the north, the arrow-straight **grande rue de Fels el-Jdid** traverses the area. To the south, the grande rue des Merinides cuts the adjacent *mellah.* **Bab Semmarin,** a chunky 20th-century gate, squats between the two areas. To reach Bab Semmarin from the *ville nouvelle,* take bus #4 or 9 from in front of the Grand Hôtel and tell the driver where to let you off. To walk from the *ville nouvelle* to the *mellah* (15min.), take av. Hassan II north past the PTT, veer left at the fork 2 blocks later on blvd. Moulay Hassan, and head straight for the Grand Place des Alaouites, where the *mellah* and grande rue des Merinides begin. To get here from Fes el-Bali, bus #9 returns by way of Bab Semmarin.

King Hassan II's sprawling modern palace, the **Dar el-Makhzen,** borders the **place des Alaouites.** The ostentatious brass doors of the palace open onto the plaza. Diagonally off the plaza, **grande rue des Merinides** runs up to Bab Semmarin on the other end of the *mellah.* Off this boulevard, the meter-wide side streets open into miniature underground tailors' shops, half-timbered houses, and sneaky alleyways.

At the top of grande rue des Merinides glitters the **jewelers' souk.** Cackling chickens, salty fish, dried okra, and shiny eggplants vie for attention in the animated **covered market,** inside Bab Semmarin at the entrance to Fes el-Jdid proper. Toward the top of the avenue, the *souks* are covered, shading rainbows of *kaftans* and gold-stitched *babouches.*

Bear left at the end of rue des Merinides into the **Petit Mechouar;** on the left is **Bab Dekaken,** the back entrance to the Dar el-Makhzen. Through **Bab es Seba,** an imperial gate opens onto the **Grand Méchouar,** a roomy plaza lined with streetlamps. From here it's easy to walk to Bab Boujeloud—turn through the opening to the right of **Bab el-Seba,** continue straight for 1/4km, and veer to the right after passing through a large arch at the end of road. The entrance to the refreshing **Boujeloud Gardens** is on the right. If you exit the gardens via the archway at far side, take a left, then a right, and walk downhill to reach Bab Boujeloud.

Circuit of the Medina

Borj Nord and Borj Sud, the surrounding hills, are an easy bus or *petit taxi* drive away. If driving, bear east from blvd. Moulay Hassan in the *ville nouvelle* toward Taza and Oujda; the highway winds along the city fortifications. After 4km, turn right toward **Borj Sud,** a 16th-century hilltop fortress guarding the southern end of Fes el Bali. The castle, built by Christian slaves, is largely in ruins but commands an excellent view of the city.

The main highway continues east to **Bab Ftouh,** which arches in a **medieval cemetery.** Farther east, close to the ramparts, is **Bab Khoukha.** From here the walls curve wildly to **Bab Sidi Boujida.**

A kink in the highway then leads to the **Jamai Palace,** an exquisite 19th-century dream house raised by Sultan Moulay Hassan's powerful vizier. A luxury hotel, the palace tarries within **Bab Guissa,** where a **pigeon and parakeet market** squawks every Friday morning.

To continue the circuit, keep to the outer road and follow the signs for Hôtel des Merinides, which overlooks the ruins of the **Merinid Tombs.** The tombs once formed the second-largest Merinid necropolis (after the Chellah in Rabat). The domiciles burrowed out of the base of the hill were the **lepers' quarters** in medieval times.

Borj Nord, a short walk down the road from Hôtel des Merinides, looks like a crumbling hilltop fortress over the northern end of the city. It houses the **Museum of Arms,** a cache of weapons which have killed thousands of people. The guided tour in French lasts over an hour. (Open Wed.-Mon. 9am-noon and 3-6pm. Admission 10dh.)

Ville Nouvelle

The main attraction of the *ville nouvelle* is the superb **Ensemble Artisanal** on blvd. Allah ben Abdallah at the southwestern end of av. Hassan II. Sumptuous Arab carpets, Berber blankets, and other handiwork fill the garden of the courtyard, where you can watch the artisans at work. In the weaving rooms, hundreds of young girls poke, thread, knot, snip, and pack spools of many-hued wool to create lavish works of art. (Open 8:30am-6:30pm.) Or follow local crowds into the busy, aromatic **municipal market** just off blvd. Mohammed V (see Food: *Ville Nouvelle).*

Entertainment

Catch live Moroccan music and belly dancing in the palatial **Restaurant Firadous's** *salon marocain,* in the Palais Jamai complex, on the right inside the medina's Bab Guissa. An entire evening, beginning with dinner at 8:30pm, costs a cool 140dh including cover. To dance, sashay to **Night Club Oriental** in the Grand Hôtel (tel. 62 55 11) in the center of the *ville nouvelle* and pay a 40dh cover, which includes one drink.

Rabat

Rabat is very strange, for Morocco. You can't stand on the city buses, you won't get lost, and, thanks to the King's unflagging interest in his own backyard, discreetly ubiquitous soldiers keep the city hustler- and hassle-free. To most Moroccans, Rabat means the capital: business, supplies, traffic, and possibly the cinema. Restaurants aren't particularly elegant, the gardens aren't especially fair, and the merchants aren't strikingly cordial. In short, Rabat is a modern city frequented for its facilities, not its charm. It's also the city in Morocco where Western women travelers may feel most comfortable.

Orientation and Practical Information

The town is well-organized and easy to navigate. **Avenue Mohammed V** parades north-south from the Grand Essouna Mosque, past the train station and the post office, and right through the **medina.** From the train station, turn left down this avenue to reach most of the budget hotels. Perpendicular to av. Mohammed V is **avenue Hassan II,** which runs east-west along the medina's southern walls. To the east is Rabat's sibling city **Salé;** to the west is the **route de Casablanca,** home of the inconvenient "central" bus station.

> **Tourist Office: National,** 22 rue al-Jazair (tel. 73 05 62). Far away but helpful. Turn right out of the train station, walk up av. Mohammed V to the Grand Essouna Mosque, turn left on av. Moulay Hassan, and bear right into rue al-Jazair. English-speaking staff. Sketchy maps of Rabat and other large cities. Open Mon.-Fri. 8am-3pm; mid-Sept. to June Mon.-Fri. 8:30am-6:30pm; Ramadan Mon.-Fri. 9am-3pm. **Syndicat d'Initiative,** rue Patrice Lumumba (tel. 232 72). From the post office, cross av. Mohammed V and head right along rue el-Kahira, which intersects rue Patrice Lumumba a few blocks down. More centrally located. Bare-bones office whose purpose is to arrange official guides. Very little else. Open 8am-6pm.
>
> **Embassies: U.S.,** 2 av. Marrakech (tel. 76 22 65). Look for the flag waving over blvd. Tarik Ibn Ziyad, which runs beside the fortifications on the southeastern edge of town along the river. Consulate open Mon.-Fri. 8:30-11:30am (8:30am-5:30pm for U.S. citizens). 24-hr. emergency phone. **Canadian,** 13 Joafar Essadik, Agday (tel. 77 13 76, 77 13 77). Open Mon.-Tues. and Thurs.-Fri. 8-11am. **Australian** citizens should go here as well. **U.K.,** 17 blvd. de la Tour Hassan (tel. 72 09 05). Open Mon.-Fri. 8-11:30am. Also handes citizens of **New Zealand. Algerian Visas:** Algerian **Consulate,** 10 rue d'Azrou off av. Fes (tel. 76 78 58). US and Canadian citizens must go to their own embassies first, then come with forms, 4 photos, and 100dh (US) or 400dh (Canada). U.K. citizens can obtain visas here or at home, but there's a 7-10 day wait in either case. Open Mon.-Fri. 8am-1pm.
>
> **Currency Exchange: Hôtel de la Tour Hassan,** 22 av. Chellah (tel. 72 14 01). From the train station, hop across pl. des Alaouites onto el-Forat, cross pl. du Golan (pl. de la Cathédrale) onto Laghouat, walk to the next block, and turn left onto av. Chellah. Official bank rates. Open 8am-noon and 2-6pm.
>
> **Post Office:** av. Mohammed V (tel. 72 07 31), left from the train station at rue Soekarno. Open Mon.-Fri. 8am-3:30pm; mid-Sept. to June Mon.-Fri. 8:30am-noon and 2-6:45pm.
>
> **Telephones:** rue Soekarno, facing post office. Open 24 hrs. Lines are shortest noon-3pm. Handy English-speaking assistant. Also receives Poste Restante (1.40dh per piece). **Telephone Code:** 07.
>
> **Flights: International Airport Mohammed V** (tel. (02) 33 90 40), in Casablanca. Buses leave for the airport from corner of av. Mohammed V and av. Moulay Youssef, across from the train station (7 per day, 1 1/2 hr., 50dh). **Royal Air Maroc,** 35 rue Abou Faris Amarini (tel. 70 97 00). Open Mon.-Fri. 8:30am-noon and 2:30-7pm, Sat. 8:30am-noon and 3-6pm. **Air France,** 281 av. Mohammed V (tel. 70 70 66). Open Mon.-Fri. 8:30am-12:15pm and 2:30-6:30pm, Sat. 9am-12:15pm. Also open for information Sat. 3-6pm.

Trains: av. Mohammed V at av. Moulay Youssef (tel. 76 56 67). 2nd-class to: Tangier (6 per day, 5 1/2 hr., 79dh); Fes (7 per day, 4hr., 62.50dh); Oujda (4 per day, 7hr., 158.50dh); Casablanca (13 per day, 1hr., 24.50dh). The trans-Maghreb train departs Rabat at 9:50pm, stops at Oujda at 8:30am the next day, arrives in Algiers at 8:25pm that night (274.50dh), and at Tunis at 7:30pm the day after that (438.50dh).

Buses: route de Casablanca (tel. 77 51 24), at pl. Mohammed Zerktouni. Shockingly far from the town center: take *petit taxi* (10dh) or bus #30 from av. Hassan near rue Mohammed V (2.40dh). All the bus companies operate from here. CTM tickets sold at windows #14 and 15; the other 13 windows belong to private companies. **CTM** to: Casablanca (6 per day, 1hr., 21.50dh); Fes (6 per day, 3 1/2 hr., 46.50dh) via Meknes (2 1/2 hr., 32.50 dh); Tangier (5 per day, 5hr., 66dh); Tetuan (2 per day, 62dh).

Taxis: Stands at the train station, in front of the bus station along av. Hassan II across from Bab Oudaias, and at the entrance to the medina by the corner of av. Hassan II and av. Mohammed V.

Car Rental: Hertz, 467 av. Mohammed V (tel. 76 92 27). Renault IV for 3 days with unlimited mileage is 1560dh. **Avis,** 7 Zankat (tel. 697 59), above Faris El Marin. Another office at the Rabat airport (tel. 76 75 03).

Luggage Storage: At the **train station** (2dh per locked bag). At the **bus station** (3dh per day). Open 6am-9pm.

English Bookstore: American Bookstore, 4 rue Tanja (tel. 76 10 16). Superb shelf on Morocco and Islam, classics, and other random books (5-25dh). A bizarre predominance of Henry James and Stephen King. Open Mon.-Fri. 9:30am-12:30pm and 2:30-6:30pm, Sat. 10am-1pm.

Library: George Washington Library, 35 av. al Fahs (tel. 75 07 88), in Souissi near Hôpital Avicenne. Current newspapers, periodicals, and a library. Open 10am-noon and 4-6pm.

Laundromat: Rabat Pressing, 67 av. Hassan II (tel. 72 63 61), at Allal ben Abdallah. Pants 12dh, jackets 16-20dh. Hotels usually offer cheaper service. Open Mon.-Sat. 8am-12:30pm and 2:30-7:30pm.

Late-Night Pharmacy: Pharmacie de Préfecture, av. Moulay Slimane (tel. 70 70 72). Take rue Abou Inane, which goes straight ahead from the train station; behind the big church, take a left downhill. Hanging red crescent moon outside. Open 8:30pm-8am.

Medical Services: Hôpital Avicenne, av. Ibn Sina (tel. 77 44 11), at the southern end of blvd. d'Argonne; in Souissi just south of Agdal. Emergency medical care free of charge to all. U.S. citizens can also go to the U.S. Embassy for medical care. **Ambulance:** tel. 15.

Police: rue Soekarno (tel. 19), 2 bl. down from the post office off av. Mohammed V.

Accommodations and Camping

Auberge de Jeunesse (HI), 43 rue Marassa (tel. 72 57 69), in the *ville nouvelle,* just outside the medina walls several bl. north of Bab el Had. Drab, cramped rooms around a groovy garden. Shopworn but clean; one of Morocco's better hostels. The staff speaks English and will watch your valuables at the front desk. No linen available, so bring your own. Reception open 7-9:30am, noon-3pm, and 7pm-midnight; winter 8-10am, noon-3pm, 6-10:30pm. HI cards sold on the spot (when they have them). 25dh per person. Breakfast included (8-9am).

In the Medina

While most of the town's action is the new city, the medina has cheaper beds. Search early in mid-summer. Be wary—the few hustlers of Rabat peddle "Rolex" watches here.

Hôtel Maghrib El-Jadid, 2 rue Sebbahi (tel. 73 22 07), at av. Mohammed V, right past entrance to the medina. New bright pink paint and modeling. Clean floors, cot-like beds. Rooftop terrace. English spoken. Singles 40dh. Doubles 60dh. Hot showers 5dh. **Hôtel Marrakech,** 10 rue Sebbahi (tel. 277 03), just past the above. Cooling tiled walls and as clean as the medina gets. Rooms verge on the miniature, but there's a fresh towel every day. Rustic toilets. Singles 40dh. Doubles 60dh. Showers 2dh.

Ville Nouvelle

Oh so many plushy hotels are along and just off av. Mohammed V and **av. Allal ben Abdellah.** From the train station's main entrance, turn left onto av. Mohammed V and walk toward the medina. Av. Allal ben Abdellah is one block to the right as you walk downhill.

Hôtel Capitol, 34 av. Allal ben Abdellah (tel. 73 12 36), classier than its prices would indicate. Spacious rooms with lovely reading chairs and beds to melt into. Fresh towels daily, laundry service available, and delectable continental breakfasts in the restaurant. Singles 60dh, with shower 74dh, with full bath 95dh. Doubles 74dh, with shower 95dh, with full bath 110dh. **Hôtel Central,** 2 rue el-Basra (tel. 70 73 56). From the train station, cross av. Mohammed V and walk 2 bl. toward the medina; take the 2nd right *immediatement* after Hôtel Balima. Rooms decorated in white and a sizzling hot pink. Sprawling beds and antique-seeming furniture. Huge front sitting room. Frequented by the few other foreigners in Rabat. Singles 63dh. Doubles 80-103dh, with shower 120dh.

Hôtel Majestic, 121 av. Hassan II (tel. 72 29 97), 2 bl. left of av. Mohammed V. Hardly majestic but not so bad. Rambling beds, clean, and well-located near the medina. Mainly Moroccan clientele. Singles 53dh, with shower 65dh. Doubles 60dh, with shower 68dh.

Hôtel Velleda, 106 av. Allal ben Abdellah, 4th fl. (tel. 76 95 31, 76 95 32). Barren but big rooms painted an unpleasant shade of yellow. Unidentifiable plants hulk in the sitting area. Sizeable breakfast and TV rooms; gloomy halls. Singles 54dh, with shower 75dh, with full bath 92dh. Doubles 64dh, with shower 92dh, with full bath 112dh.

Camping de la Plage (tel. 78 23 68), on the beach across from the Bou Regreg River in Salé. Taxi to the site 10-15dh. Running water, toilets, and a grocery store-*cum*-restaurant. The facilities are primitive and a bit shabby, but the prices rule. Reception open 24 hrs. 10.50dh per person, 5dh per tent and per car, slightly more for vans or larger vehicles. Cold showers and electricity included.

Food

A meal in the **medina** entails eating beside slabs of flayed lamb and dangling innards. Several inexpensive places stud **avenue Mohammed V.** At the nearby stalls, 18dh brings a plateful of tripe or a veal cutlet, salad, and bread. Certain sandwich shops also offer quick-grilled genitalia with *frites*—yummy yum. *Patisseries* sell Andalusian meat pastries (tangy chicken cooked in a flaky crust).

Budgeteers eat in two areas of the new city: 1) around av. Mohammed V and **avenue Allal ben Abdellah,** a block or two from the medina, and 2) around the train station, just off **avenue Moulay Youssef.** The covered **market** is between the entrance of the medina and pl. du Marché.

Restaurant el-Bahia, av. Hassan II (tel. 73 45 04), to the right going toward the medina on av. Mohammed V. Built into the walls of the medina. Interior court and fountain with goldfish. Appetizing food at bargain prices. Crowded at lunch. Lavish *salon marocain* upstairs boasts embroidered sofas and fluffy pillows. Popular dishes may run out by dinner time. Almond or grape juice 4.50dh. Fixed *menu* 23dh. Service charge 10%. Open 11am-11pm.

Restaurant Ghazzah, 3 rue Ghazza (tel. 72 45 53), across the street from Hôtel Splendide. Utilitarian decor (tables, chairs, wild-eyed peacock in silver-tipped cowboy boots, requisite photo of King Hassan II) and Moroccan clientele. Dining cubbyhole upstairs for short customers. Piquant, spicy chicken 24dh. Scrumpy *filet du merlan* (24dh), when they have it. Open 9am-11pm.

Restaurant le Fouquet's, 285 av. Mohammed V (tel. 76 80 07), across the street and downhill from the train station. Cozy and tableclothed in a blatant attempt to be French. Specialty fish dishes (65-80dh). *Menu du jour* 70dh. Open noon-4pm and 6-11pm.

Café-Restaurant La Clef (tel. 73 47 79), near the train station. Exiting the station, make a hairpin right onto av. Moulay Youssef, then down the 1st alley on the left. The *salon marocain* has low-slung couches. Yummy *tajine pigeon* (tender pigeon stewed with prunes, almonds, and onions) 38dh. Open noon-4pm and 7-11pm.

Restaurant Saadi, 81 av. Allal ben Abdellah (tel. 76 99 03), a right off rue Jeddah coming from av. Mohammed V in the arcade. A place to gorge. Succulent lamb or chicken *couscous* 70dh. *Menu du jour* (70dh) changes daily. Open 10am-11pm.

Sights

The city's landmark, the **Essouna Grand Mosque** at av. Mohammed V and av. Moulay Hassan is bedecked with gold-trimmed windows and sandy-hued arch. A tan and green minaret, pierced by arched windows on five levels, towers over the shingled roof. Intricately carved walls and arches are inside. (Entrance forbidden to non-Muslims.)

Avenue Moulay Hassan saunters over to the salmon pink Almohad **Bab el-Rouah** (Gate of the Winds), which sports Kufic inscriptions and arabesques on the arches. Inside the gate to the right is a gallery of contemporary, vaguely Gauguinesque Moroccan paintings. Exhibits change every few weeks, and you can occasionally glimpse the artists sipping mint tea in the corner, brushes in hand. (Open 8:30am-noon and 2:30-8pm.)

Back through Bab er Rouah and through the wall to the right, a tree-lined promenade leads to the **Dar el-Makhzen** (Royal Palace). Although it was begun in the 18th century, most of the present palace postdates the French occupation. Visitors aren't permitted inside and those who come too close will be chased away by disdainful armed guards, who wear the traditional *serouel* (pleated, baggy white pants), red sash, and blue turban with a diamond on the front. Photography is permitted.

Beyond the southern extremity of the palace grounds at the end of av. Yacoub el-Mansour loom the decrepit but still impressive remains of the **Chellah burial complex,** a fortified royal necropolis revered since the time of the Almohads. To get here from the palace, walk out the gate adjacent to the palace (**Bab Zaers,** not the entrance gate), and turn left. The ruins sprout hallucinatory trees, cacti, and exotic flowers, and are especially trippy at sunset when bathed in an unearthly, intensely orange glow. The views over the Bou Regreg River are euphoric. Down the path from the Chellah Gate is Hassan's **mausoleum;** his tombstone is the white prism in the back. The psychedelic tiled minaret is the highlight of the ruined **mosque.** The best-preserved chamber circles around a turquoise-and-emerald pit at the base of the minaret. The mosque is open to non-Muslims since it's no longer in use. There's also a public **park** where narrow footpaths wind through carefully tended gardens.

Across town along av. Abi Regreg (near the Pont Moulay Hassan to Salé) hulks the somber, elegant **Mausoleum of Mohammed V.** Surrounding the white marble tomb, a wreath of flowers and polished black marble honor the king who led the country from colonialism to independence. Turquoise and sapphire stained-glass windows ring the gold-leaf dome. Traditionally dressed guards lower the flag daily at 5pm. (Open 8am-last prayer: around 10pm, winter 8pm. Free.)

The imposing **Hassan Tower** is an unfinished minaret from the 12th century's largest Western mosque. Sultan Yacoub el-Mansour wanted to construct the three greatest towers in the world; he set up the Giralda minaret of Sevilla and the Koutoubia of Marrakech before aspiring to this lofty spire, but died before he finished this one. Still, at 55m the incomplete turret towers above both its famous siblings. (Interior closed to the public.)

In the northern corner of the medina along Tarik el-Marsa are the walls of the famed **Kasbah des Oudaias,** the *ribat* where, in the 10th century, a garrison of the Oudaia tribe watched the city. Andalusian refugees settled here in the 17th century. **Bab Oudaia,** at the top of the hill, is the more curious of the gates. The **Oudaias Gardens** inside are flower-strewn and serene. Also inside is the **Museum of Moroccan Arts,** parked in two separate parts of the 17th-century palace of Moulay Ismail. It contains an intriguing assemblage of musical instruments, including a psalterion (a harpsichord without a keyboard) and a double clarinet. The other room exhibits traditional Moroccan dress, ceramics, and jewelry. (Museum and garden open 10am-5pm; winter Wed.-Mon. 8:30am-noon and 3-6:30pm. Admission to museum 3dh.)

Although less crazy than others, Rabat's **medina** is bustling, enticing, and fun for a stroll. Enter via av. Mohammed V. To the left lies the **fruit and vegetable market.** Animal parts hang cheek by jowl with sneakers and videotapes on **rue Souiqa,** the first right off Mohammed V. **Rue Souiqa** eventually turns into **Souk es Sebat,** a narrow alley covered with straw mats as protection from the blazing sun. Renovated in 1887 by Moulay Hassan, the **Grand Mosque** adjoins the *souk.*

South of pl. de la Grande Mosquée, the **archeological museum** houses a collection of Volubilis bronze works (including a bust of Juba II), all cast before 25 BC. The museum also has exhibits on the Roman necropolis of Salé, Phoenician and Carthaginian relics, and the standard room of animal bones. To get here, walk down av. Mohammed V and turn left onto Abd Al Aziz at the Grand Mosque. The museum is on the next street off Abd Al Aziz. (Open Wed.-Mon. 8:30am-5pm; winter Wed.-Mon. 8:30am-noon and 2-6:30pm. Admission 10dh.)

Entertainment

Rabat nightlife means cinemas and pricey, pseudo-Euro discos. For something spicier, call the palatial **Tour Hassan Hôtel,** 22 av. Chellah (tel. 72 14 91), to find out if there will be a modern music performance that evening. Else, the outdoor tables of **Café Balima** (in front of Hôtel Balima on av. Mohammed V near the train station) are a relaxing spot to sip mint tea.

On March 3, there's the **Fête du Trone,** the anniversary of the king's accession; on July 9, the **Royal Birthday.** On November 6, swing by the **Fête de la Marche Verte,** which commemorates the 1975 return of the southwestern Sahara; and on November 18, give a hurrah in honor of independence.

Casablanca

Casablanca is such stuff as disappointments are made on. No Rick's Café Américain, no getaway plane at the airport, no one looking at you, kid, except the hustlers who prowl the port and the medina. The city is as bland and commercial as any other modern European town; use it as a service center and transportation hub.

Orientation and Practical Information

Almost 100km directly south of Rabat, Casablanca is easily accessible by plane, bus and train. Casa's two train stations confuse everyone. **Casa Port** is close to the youth hostel and the city center. **Casa Voyageurs** is close to nothing and is a 50-minute walk from Casa Port. If you have any choice, get off at Casa Port; if you don't, take a *petit taxi* to the city center (about 15dh). To get from Casa Port to the CTM bus station, cross the street, follow blvd. Mohammed El Hansali to the end (1km), turn left on av. de l'Armée Royale, and look out for the Hôtel Safir. The station is behind it and to the right.

The city's two main squares, **place des Nations Unies** and **place Mohammed V,** also puzzle travelers. The first spreads in front of the Hyatt Regency; the second is surrounded by neo-Islamic government buildings near the PTT.

> **Tourist Office:** 55 rue Omar Slaoui (tel. 27 95 33). From place Mohammed V, walk south along av. Hassan II, turn left onto rue Reitzer, then right onto rue Omar Slaoui. They have great maps of the city and southern deserts. Open Mon.-Thurs. 8:30am-noon and 2:30-6:30pm, Fri. 8:30-11am and 3-6:30pm; Ramadan Mon-Fri. 9am-4pm. **Syndicat d'Initiative,** 98 blvd. Mohammed V (tel 22 15 24). Facing the CTM station, walk 1 bl. right on av. des Forces Armées Royales, then left up rue Colbert. Stocked with good maps and lists of cinemas, health clubs and discos. Open Mon.-Sat. 9am-noon and 3-6:30pm, Sun. 9am-noon; Ramadan 9am-4pm.
>
> **Consulates: U.S.,** 8 blvd. Moulay Youssef (tel. 22 14 49). Open Mon.-Fri. 8am-4:30pm; off-season Mon.-Fri. 8am-5:30pm. **U.K.,** 60 blvd. d'Anfa (tel. 26 14 40, 26 14 41). Open Mon. 8:30am-12:30pm and 2-6pm, Tues.-Fri. 8:30am-12:30pm and 2-5:30pm.
>
> **Currency Exchange:** Larger hotels change money at official rates when banks are closed. Try the Hyatt Regency, Hôtel Suisse, or Hôtel Safir near the bus station.
>
> **American Express: Voyages Schwartz,** 112 av. du Prince Moulay Abdallah (tel. 22 29 47, 27 80 54; fax 27 31 33; telex 216 40). Standard services, except they don't receive wired money. Open Mon.-Fri. 8:30am-noon and 2:30-6:30pm, Sat 8:30am-noon; cash transactions only in morning.
>
> **Post Office:** Av. de Paris at av. Hassan II, near the neo-Islamic buildings. Send Poste Restante here. Open Mon.-Fri. 8am-3:30pm.

Telephones: Make collect or international calls from the post office. Open 8am-11pm. Pay phones on blvd. d'Anfa, just south of blvd. de Paris. **Telephone Code:** 07.

Flights: Aeroport Mohammed V (tel. 33 90 40). Shuttle buses (20dh) run between here and the CTM bus station. All international and most domestic flights. **Aeroport de Casablanca, ANFA** (tel. 91 20 00). Accessible by taxi only (about 150dh). Other domestic flights. **Royal Air Maroc Ticket Office,** 44 av. des Forces Armées Royales (tel. 31 41 41).

Trains: 2 stations. **Casa Port,** Port de Casablanca (tel. 22 30 11), 10min. from the youth hostel. Mainly northbound service. To Rabat (24 per day, 24.50dh). **Casa Voyageurs,** blvd. Ba Hammed (tel. 24 58 01), way the hell out there. Mainly southbound service. To Marrakech (4 per day, 5hr., 34dh) and El-Jadida (at 6:30am, 1hr., 24dh).

Buses: CTM, 23 rue Léon L'Africain (tel. 26 80 61), off rue Colbert. To: Rabat (20 per day, 1 1/2hr., 21.50dh); Essaouira via El-Jadida (2 per day, 5 1/2 hr., 76dh); Marrakech (5 per day, 56dh). Shuttle bus to the international airport (every hr. 7am-11pm, 45min., 20dh). Other bus companies leave from pl. Benjdia to Marrakech and points south.

Car Rental: Europcar, 44 av. des Force Armées Royales (tel. 31 37 37). Renault IV for 3 days with unlimited mileage 1500dh. Another office at the airport. **Hertz,** 25 rue de Foucauld (tel. 31 22 23) and at the airport, has slightly lower rates than Europcar and the lowest minimum age, 21.

English Bookstore: American Language Center Bookstore, blvd. Moulay Youssef (tel. 27 95 59), under the American Language Center at pl. de la Fraternité. Vasty array of novels and reference books. Open Mon.-Fri. 9:30am-12:30pm and 3:30-7:30pm, Sat. 10am-1pm.

Late-Night Pharmacy: Pharmacie de Nuit, pl. des Nations Unies (tel. 26 94 91). Open 8pm-8am.

Medical Services: Croissant Rouge Marocain, blvd. El Massira El Khadia (tel. 25 25 21). **Permanence,** blvd. d'Anfa, just south of blvd. de Paris. Open 8:30pm-8am.

Ambulance: tel. 15

Police: emergency tel. 19.

Accommodations and Food

The tourist office and *Syndicat* keep an exhaustive, graded list of hotels; the ratings help standardize price and quality. Many linger about **rue Colbert** and **av. des Forces Armées Royales**, near the bus station, the medina, and inexpensive food.

Auberge de Jeunesse (HI), 6 pl. Amiral Philibert (tel. 22 05 51), 3min. from Casa Port. Cross the street in front of the station, turn right, walk along the walls, then turn left up a small flight of stairs. French-speaking staff welcomes youths to a dusty, cluttered, and popular hostel. Astoundingly spacious, tiled sitting area with English-language newspapers. Reception open 8-10am and noon-11pm. 20dh per person; nonmembers 22.50dh. Cold shower included. Breakfast 5dh.

Hôtel Foucauld, 52 rue de Foucauld (tel. 22 76 66), off av. des Forces Armées Royales. Clean beds in dreary green rooms. Mattresses firm as unripe avocados. Some rooms have balconies overlooking the street. Relax in the *salon marocain*. Classy clientele. Singles 60dh. Doubles with shower 74dh. Doubles 74dh, with shower 95dh.

Hôtel George V, av. des Forces Armées Royales (tel. 31 24 48), across rue Angle from the Royal Mansour Hôtel. Clean, white, modern rooms with free towels and bars of soap. A few rough edges: hard beds, tepid hot water, lame TV room. Singles with shower 108dh. Doubles with shower 130dh. Breakfast 17dh.

In the *ville nouvelle*, budget fooderies concentrate on **rue Colbert.** In the medina, restaurants and food stands sprinkle the vicinity of **rue de Fes.** Shop for staples at the clean and sprawling **Central Market Halls,** 7 rue de Colbert.

Restaurant Widad, 9 rue de Fes. Enter the medina near the Hyatt Regency by blvd. Mohammed el-Hansali. Attentive service and truckloads of food for few *dirhams*. Salad, fruit, and mounds of *couscous* topped with 1/4-chicken stewed with vegetables 26dh. Open 11am-10pm.

International Seaman's Center, 118 blvd. Moulay Abderhamane (tel. 30 99 50). In an industrial wasteland 800m east of Casa Port, but worth the walk. Did we say there was no Rick's Cafe in Casablanca? Once for sailors only, this sprawling, inviting, casual bar welcomes foreigners. Friendly American management, outdoor patio, pool table, phones for international calls, and rock blaring all day long.

Sights

Casa is the only town in Morocco devoid of sights. (You can wander through the **old medina** or the **new medina**—the Habbous quarter—to buy Moroccan goods. For the truly stranded, the Rif Cinema is at the corner of rue Foucauld, and Parc de la Ligne on av. Hassan II is a good picnic spot.)

El-Jadida

Less windy than Essaouira, more old-fashioned than Agadir, less crowded than Mohammedia, this is the prime Atlantic resort in Morocco. With a charming medina, crenellated Portuguese battlements, palmy boulevards, and a first-rate beach, it's the ideal antidote to Marrekech or Rabat. Less than 100km south of Casablanca, El-Jadida is close enough to the major northern centers to have crowded beaches in the peak summer months.

Portugal started invading Morocco at El-Jadida in the 16th century. When Sultan Muhammad bin Abdallah reconquered Morocco in 1769, it was the last Portuguese citadel in the country to fall. After independence the city became both El-Jadida ("The New One") and a summer retreat for Marrakech's affluent families.

Orientation and Practical Information

The main centers are **place Mohammed V,** where the post office is, and **place el-Hansali,** which connects pl. Mohammed V to the old Portuguese medina.

Tourist Office: rue Ibn Khaldoun (tel. 34 27 04), down the street from Hôtel de Bruxelles and Hôtel de Provence. Follow signs from blvd. Mohammed V and the post office. English-speaking staff. No maps for you, but the map on the wall is useful. Open Mon.-Fri. 8:30am-3pm; mid-Sept. to June Mon.-Fri. 8am-noon and 2:30-6:30pm.

Currency Exchange: Hôtel Dar es Salaam des Doukkala, av. Ligue Arabe (tel. 34 35 75), facing the beach. Traveler's checks cashed for a 5% commission.

Post Office: pl. Mohammed V. Open for Poste Restante, **telephones,** and **telegrams** Mon.-Fri. 8am-3:30pm, Sat. 8am-11:30am; winter Mon.-Fri. 8:30am-12:15pm and 2:30-6:45pm, Sat. 8:30-11:30am.

Telephones: At the **post office.**

Trains: The new station is 6km south of town. Free bus from in front of the Portugese ramparts (7:45am) runs to the station. A similar free bus shuttles arrivals into El-Jadida immediately after a train pulls in. To Rabat (at 8:15am, 2hr.) continuing to Casablanca.

Buses: blvd. Mohammed V. To reach the city center from here, exit to the left on blvd. Mohammed V and continue to pl. Mohammed V (15min.). To: Casablanca (every 1/2 hr., 2hr., 18dh); Essaouira (at 7am, 5hr., 40.50dh). Private companies are half as swift and costly. Buses south to Essaouira begin in Casablanca and thus have very few seats left by the time they arrive in El-Jadida. Buy ticket as far in advance as possible to be assured of a seat.

Late-Night Pharmacy: av. Ligue Arabe off pl. Mohammed V. Look for the plaque next door to the Croissant Rouge Marocain (Red Cross). Open 10pm-9am.

Hospital: rue Sidi Bouzi (tel. 34 20 04, 34 20 05), near rue Boucharette at the southern edge of town.

Emergency: tel. 19.

Police: At bus station, around the corner from the all-night pharmacy, and at the beach (tel. 19).

Accommodations and Camping

How shocking that a quiet coastal town could have so many decent budget hotels. They drift around **place Mohammed V**, a few blocks from the sea. Call ahead to reserve a room in July and August.

> **Hôtel de Provence,** 42 rue Fquih Mohammed Errafi (tel. 34 23 47, 34 41 12). From the post office head 1 bl. away from the beach. A real gem. Expatriates occupy a good number of the regal rooms. Singles with shower 84dh. Doubles with shower 103dh. Continental breakfast 17dh.
>
> **Hôtel France,** rue Lescould (tel. 34 21 81), off pl. Hansali. Basically sanitary. This super-cheap, cavernous hotel has impossibly capacious rooms—more like vast mausoleums. Singles 25dh. Doubles 36dh.
>
> **Hôtel Royal,** 108 blvd. Mohammed V (tel. 34 11 00), between the post office and the bus station. Bright rooms with low, comfy beds. Tiled lobby, TV room. Sitting area with nautical-Gothic decor. Singles 50dh, with shower 65dh. Doubles 68dh, with shower 78dh.
>
> **Camping: Camping International** (tel. 34 27 55), a large site with standard facilities out av. des Nations Unies. 10dh per person, per tent, and per car.

Food

A few good restaurants near **place Mohammed V** whip up affordable, savory Moroccan dishes.

> **Restaurant la Broche,** 6 pl. el-Hansali (tel. 34 22 99), next to the Paris Cinema. Speedy service and intimate upstairs dining room. *Tajine* 25-30dh. Fish dishes 20-35dh. Spaghetti 25-35dh. Fresh banana juice 7dh. Open 7am-11pm.
>
> **Restaurant-Bar-Grill Royal,** in the eponymous hotel. *Charmant* patio and garden. Quiet and relaxing. Try *poulet roti* (16dh) or *tajine* (16dh). Beer 7dh. Open 9am-11pm.

Sights

Completed in 1502, the Portuguese-built **medina** was the first and last Portuguese stronghold in North Africa. Just before retreating, the Portuguese sprinkled the entire city with gunpowder and detonated it. When Sultan Moulay Abderrahman got around to renovating it in the 19th century, a *mellah* (Jewish quarter) sprung up in one area. Iron balconies, garlanded cornices, and pillared doorways fill all the nooks and crannies here.

Enter the medina through the sturdy, fortified gate that opens off pl. Sidi Muhammad bin Abdallah, at the top of blvd. de Suez. Immediately to the left off rue de Carreira kneels **l'Eglise Portuguese.** This 17th-century church has Spanish walls and a misfit of a French wooden roof.

Up rue de Carreira on the left, a yellow plaque marks the entrance to the **Portuguese Cisterns,** one of the few buildings that survived the Portuguese blow-up. The subterranean hall resembles a miniature cathedral. During frequent sieges, the cisterns held the city's water supply; the rainwater on the floor reflects the entire interior. Orson Welles used this haunting place as a backdrop for *Othello*. By the entrance, a diorama depicts the moats and drawbridges of the original Portuguese city. Ask the custodian to unlock the passage to a 16th-century fortress on the roof. (Cisterns open 9am-12:30pm and 3-7:30pm; winter Mon.-Fri. 9am-noon and 2-7pm. Admission 10dh plus a tip for the guide who gives the mandatory tour.)

Porta do Mar, the great archway at the end of rue de Carreira, leads to the harbor. The entrance to the ramparts, to the right of Porta do Mar, is locked; the trusty guide from the Cisterns will unlock it. Slightly north, at the top of the incline, the **Bastion de l'Ange** commands a view or the harbor. From here, walk along the walls to the **Bastion of St. Sebastian,** flanked by a Portuguese chapel, or stroll along the jetty to see the entire town.

In the center of the city at place Moussa, the Gothic **Church of the Assumption** is now an assembly hall. Nearby is the abandonded Portuguese **Tribunal,** converted into a synagogue after the resettlement of Jews here in 1815. Five km south of the city center is **Sidi Bouzid**—a less crowded and more scenic spot to join the chic soaking up some sun. A *grand taxi* there will cost 10dh per person, or 60dh if solo.

If you're hankering for some veggies, or fruit, or ram heads, or cow lungs, or bull genitalia, head to the **souk,** held on Wednesday near the lighthouse.

Near El-Jadida

Azemmour

Isolated yet amiable, the village of Azemmour giggles to itself at the juncture of the Oum el-Rbia (Rbia River) and the Atlantic, 16km north of El-Jadida. A series of 16th-century Portuguese ramparts overlook the river and wrap aroung the whitewashed medina in a rectangle of massive, crenellated walls. About 2km north of pl. du Souk, the smooth beach of **Haouzia** washes past a small eucalyptus forest. A bevy of placid beaches extends from here to Casablanca.

To get to the main square outside the medina from the bus stop, continue downhill and bear left at the fork. **Hôtel la Victoire,** blvd. Mohammed V (tel. 34 71 57) rents adequate singles (30dh) and doubles (40dh). The cafés in the square serve nothing fancier than brochettes. For information on renting private rooms, ask at the **Syndicat d'Initiative,** 1 block up from the hotel (open Mon.-Sat.). Near the center of town are the **post office** and the **pharmacy** (open 9am-12:30pm and 3:30-8pm). Several **buses** per day drive here from Casablanca. From El-Jadida they run every 1/2hr.

Boulaouane

Once the surrounding parched lands of Boulaouane were noted for their vineyards. In 1710 Sultan Moulay Ismail established the **Kasbah of Boulaouane** here to levy a tax on the fertile fields. Legend has it the sultan was so utterly thrilled with a woman named Halima that he impulsively gave her all the land in sight; from that day on she lived in her own palace within the Kasbah ramparts. After her death the sultan closed the castle and never returned to town again.

Try to catch one of the **markets** between Boulaouane and El-Jadida. The **souk**—household appliances and food—rocks on Sunday at **Had Od Frej,** Tuesday at **Sidi Bennour,** and Wednesday at **Aounat.**

A **bus** runs to Boulaouane via **Settat** from El-Jadida (6dh); a *grand taxi* drives for about 20dh per person. If you're traveling the 68km from El-Jadida by car, take the inconspicuous right turn immediately before the village of Boulaouane—signs mark the route from there.

Oualidia

Languishing beside a pensive lagoon and a sea-lapped shore, lonely Oualidia has the finest **beach** in the region and is a favorite haunt of Moroccan aristocracy. Few foreign tourists are aware that it exists. The bones of a 12th-century **kasbah** occupy a hilltop overlooking the lagoon. In 1947 Sultan Muhammad V built a waterside summer pavilion directly below. The lagoon is linked to the ocean by two narrow channels cut from the natural rock barrier.

The raised highway from Oualidia to Safi skirts cliffs overlooking both beaches and barren land. **Playa Beddauza,** halfway beween Oualidia and Safi near the village **Beddauza,** is a popular spot for unofficial camping. Watch your stuff. In town by the highway, **Auberge de la Lagune** (tel. 34 64 77) charges 95dh for singles with bath and 110dh for doubles with bath. Its terrace restaurant overlooks the ocean and serves a seafood feast (60dh). **Complex Champs** maintains a tourist complex of tentsites, hotel rooms, bungalows, parking lot, and a restaurant (45dh set menu). Camping costs 7dh per person, per small tent, and per car; 9dh per large tent. Hotel doubles are 130dh. Six-person bungalows rent for 300dh and include hot showers.

Daily **buses** run along the coastal road from El-Jadida (75km) and Safi (70km) to Oualidia.

Essaouria

To defend his band of pirates, powerful Sultan Muhammad bin Abdallah annihilated Mogador, Portugal, then fled to Essaouira and erected mighty ramparts. Théodore Cornut, a French prisoner forced into service as architect, designed the ingenious town fortifications.

Lovely Essaouira flaunts whitewashed walls and brilliant blue shutters, framed by medieval defensive walls. Jimi Hendrix came here in 1968 and triggered a mass migration in his wake. Over the next five years Essaouira achieved international notoriety as a hotspot for hippies. Now that most of the hash smoke has cleared, windsurfers whoop it up on the sandy beach in the gusty wind.

Orientation and Practical Information

Buses arrive at the new bus station, a 10-minute walk from the walls of the medina. To get from the station to **Bab Doukkala** (the main entrance to the medina), exit the front of the station, walk to your left, and take another left when this road ends.

Tourist Office: Allegedly to reopen in 1993 after a hiatus of 9 yrs. For a bad photocopy of a bad map, go to **Hôtel Beau Rivage.**

Currency Exchange: Hôtel les Iles, av. Mohammed V, outside the medina facing the beach. **Hôtel Beau Rivage,** pl. Moulay Hassan cashes traveler's checks (charge 5dh).

Post Office: av. el-Moqaquamah at Lalla Aicha, the 1st left after Hôtel les Isles when walking away from the medina. Near the big red and white radio tower. Open for Poste Restante, **telegrams,** and **telephones** Mon.-Fri. 8am-12:15pm and 2:30-6:30pm; Oct.-June 8am-noon.

Telephones: At the **post office. Telephone Code:** 047. International calls and **faxes** also at **Jack's** (see English-Language Periodicals below).

Buses: CTM (tel. 47 24 68). To Casablanca (2 per day, 6hr., 56dh) and Marrakech (at 7am, 4hr., 31dh).

Luggage Storage: At the **bus station** (3dh per bag). Open 24 hrs.

English-Language Periodicals: Jack's, pl. Moulay Hassan. Also has a small selection of used English paperbacks. Open 10am-2pm and 4-9:30pm.

Public Showers: Bain-Douche, next to Hôtel Tafraoute (see Accommodations below). Hot showers 2.50dh.

Hospital: av. el-Moqaquamah, next to the post office.

Police: tel. 19.

Accomodations and Camping

The medina swells with 25dh hotels.

Hôtel des Remparts, 18 rue Ibn Rochdi (tel. 47 22 82), in the medina to the right of pl. Moulay Hassan. A vast interior atrium with swooping swallows at dusk. Great view from Essaouira's highest terrace. Budgeters flock to this bargain like vultures, although beds are of questionable quality. English spoken. Singles 35dh, with shower 50dh. Doubles 55dh, with shower 70dh.

Hôtel Beau Rivage, pl. Moulay Hassan (tel. 47 29 25), in the center of things, directly opposite Jack's Bumper-Sticker Emporium. Pink rooms at penny-pinching prices. The atmosphere is young and hip, the location perfect. Owner cashes traveler's checks at all hours like an ATM, and also has photocopied maps of the town. Singles 39dh. Doubles 52dh.

Hôtel Sahara, av. de l'Istiqlal (tel. 47 22 92), near Porte Portugaise. Uninspired interior, utilitarian rooms. Very vanilla. Non-guests can drink tea and watch TV in the spiffy *salon marocain*. Night manager has habit of listening to TV at incredibly high volume. Singles 64dh, with shower 107dh. Doubles 80dh, with showers 133dh. Breakfast 17dh.

Camping: Municipal campground (tel. 47 38 17), off av. Mohammed V at the far end of the beach. Essentially a gravelly parking lot. 7dh per person.

Food

Restaurants congregate in the medina, at the port, and on the waterfront at **av. Mohammed V**. The so-called **Berber cafés** near Porte Portugaise, off av. de l'Istiqlal, have low tables, straw mats, and fresh fish *tajine* or *couscous* (about 18dh). After the second archway beyond the Porte Portugaise to the right, a handful of Berber cafés sell *kefta* and meatballs for 3dh apiece. Sit at the communal table and point to what you want, but establish prices before chewing.

During the day (even at breakfast), crispy fried sardines are peddled at the **port** (6-8 fish, bread, lemon, and tomatoes 6dh).

> **Café Restaurant Essalem,** pl. Moulay Hassan. Popular vegetarian hangout since the 60s. Rapturous dishes at fairly low prices. Owner gladly discusses the town's history and gestures at the table where Cat Stevens always sat studying Islam. *Menus* 25, 35, and 45dh. The *tajine de boeuf,* stewed with prunes and onions, is swoony. Open 8am-3pm and 5-11pm.
>
> **El Minzah,** av. de l'Istiqlal near Porte Portugaise. Seafood and Moroccan specialties in the appealing garden. Bargain 50dh *menu*. Open 7am-10:30pm.
>
> **Chez Sam,** at the end of the harbor overlooking the sea. Warped wood ceilings and Groton's Fish Sticks decor. Steaming pyramid of mussels 25dh. *Menu* 60dh. Fish dishes 40-60dh. Beer and wine. Open noon-2pm and 7pm-midnight.

Sights

Off pl. Moulay Hassan, rue Sidi Mohammed ben Abdallah leads to the heart of the medina. Some alleyways, originally used by escape artists and crafty smugglers, burrow beneath the massive vaults of the city's fortifications. The most dramatic portion of the medina is the sea-sprayed **kasbah** (Village Sqala), down the narrow alley across the street from the bus station. A stone ramp leads up to a lookout post, where a battery of Catalan cannon, gun turrets, and fortress ramparts withstand the pounding surf. Watch out for amorous stray dogs.

Below the kasbah rests the delightful **carpenter's district.** In the ramparts' cell-like caverns, skilled woodworkers lay ebony, silver, and lemonwood into the surfaces of fragrant thuya wood boxes. Carpenters sell their woodcrafts directly, although the selection and quality are better at the woodwork emporia on **rue Abdul Aziz el-Fechtaly** (off rue Sidi ben Abdallah in the medina).

Just inside the medina and next to the Centre Artisanal, the town **museum** hoards an eclectic group of farm implements, manuscripts (including a 13th-century Qu'ran), Andalusian musical instruments, and an exhibit on the musicology of the Hamadcha. (Closed, scheduled to reopen in 1993.)

Near Essaouira

Isle of Mogador

Like a mythological land from the tales of Tolkien, Mogador, the largest of the Isles Purpuraires, bears an ancient and tumultuous history. The Berber king of Mauritania, Juba II, set up dye factories on the islands around 100 BC. When red dye inevitably splashed on monuments, clothing, and vegetation, the islands earned their Latin name. In 1506, under King Manuel, the Portuguese contributed a fortress and Moulay Hassan added a prison. The islands are now fishily deserted. Visitors need special permission from *le bureau de province,* av. Mohammed V (by the parking lot outside medina walls) for 20dh. Charter a fishing **boat** to get there (200dh per day).

Diabat

Jimi Hendrix attempted to purchase the **beach** of Diabat from the Moroccan government, who politely refused his offer. The police closed down all the accomodations in Diabat—at least officially—after several tourists sleeping on the beach were killed (no connection with Jimi). Recently, however, a campground and one hotel grew near the beach, about 4km away. To walk to Diabat, sweep along Essaouira's beach to a cape

2km away. The audacious attempt the rocky access road off the coastal route to Agadir. Beware the perilous crossing on a dilapidated bridge.

Diabat's only remotely nearby hotel, **Auberge Tangaro,** is a ramshackle but cheery outfit with an adjacent restaurant, both run by a hospitable French proprietor. The meager **Camping Tangaro,** in the adjacent enclosure, is a good ground. Both the hotel and campground (6 1/2 km from Essaouira) are on the access road between the highway to Agadir and the Diabat beach—just follow the signs from the highway.

Cap Sim

Ten km south of Essaouira along the road to Agadir, rte. 6604 curves to a **beach** marked by a lone whitewashed *marabout* tomb. No buses come from Essaouira. Some take taxis. Some drive (follow the highway to Agadir south until the paved turn-off "Marabout Tomb of Sidi Kaouki"; turn onto it and continue another 11km to the coast). Some walk (4hr.). Halfway between the cape and Diabat beach, a washed-out dirt road (not for cars) winds there from Diabat.

The incongruous sight of camels plodding along the seashore isn't a mirage. You can haggle with camel drivers who occasionally hang out under the shady trees 100m behind the *marabout* tomb and, if you happen to catch them there, ride a camel along the beach to the **Dunes of Cap Sim.** The camel is your friend, but don't become too attached to one; camels carry syphilis. Most are muzzled.

Sidi Kaouki

Twenty-five km south of Essaouira, Sidi Kaouki is known to Europeans as the best **windsurfing** beach in the world. A blue and white sign points the way from the main road to the beach, where vans with "wind city" bumper stickers crowd the big parking lot near the sand's edge. Take care—this is not the crowded tourist beach at Essaouira and there are no lifeguards. A constant north-south wind blows waves of stinging sand down a shore filled only with windsurfers. No public transportation connects to Sidi Kaouki, although **grand taxis** make the round trip from Essaouira for about 150dh.

Jebel Amsittene

The summit of Jebel Amsittene (58km) makes a lovely daytrip from Essaouira. The solitary ancient watchtower at the summit provides shade from the intense sun as well as an excellent view of the Haha region. The beekeeper, who occasionally can be found near the summit, escorts visitors to the watchtower. Aside from this hermit, the mountain is uninhabited and accommodationless.

Local **buses** from Essaouira go far as the turn-off from the highway. From here it's a lonely grueling 9km trek to the top. To drive from Essaouira, take the highway toward Agadir until the village of **Smimou.** Continue another 7km along the highway, staying on the main dirt road (bear right at the first fork and left at the second); it will zip you right to the summit's watchtower. The track is stony and crumbling, but passable.

Marrakech

This gateway to the desert exerts an unshakable grip on travelers. Twisting through the streets of the medina are Berbers, Arab artisans, Western tourists, desert Blue People, and troupes of merchants and performers from Mali, Niger, and Mauritania. The Djemâa el-Fna is a cacophonous mix of snake charmers, musicians, dancers, doctors, dentists, acrobats, beggars, peddlers, hash vendors, and hustlers. In the intense summer heat, early morning and early evening are the best times for activity. Winter temperatures drop as cold air swings down from the snow-covered High Atlas.

Marrakech 595

Marrakech

MEDINA

Place Djemâa el Fna

rue de Bab Aguenaou
rue Bab Mouahidine
rue Oqba ben Nafaa
rue Sidi Mimoun
rue Fatima Zohra
rue Dar el Glaoui
avenue Mohammed V
avenue Houmman el Fetouaki
rue el Adala
Bab Nkob
rue Aboul el Abbes Sebti
Bab Jedid
Bab Agnaou
Bab Doukkala
rue Mohammed el Mellakh
avenue Ahmed Ouassim
City Walls
boulevard el Yarmouk
rue Haroun Errachid
Place de la Liberté
rue Echchouada
avenue el Qadissia
avenue el Menara
Place du XVI Novembre
avenue Moulay el Hassan
avenue President Kennedy
boulevard Moulay R'Chid
avenue Hassan II

1 Tourist Office
2 Post Office
3 Train Station
4 Bus Station
5 Koutoubia Mosque
6 Medrassa ben Youssef
7 Souks
8 Saadien Tombs
9 El-Badi Palace
10 Dar el Makhzen
11 Bahia Palace
12 Museum of Moroccan Art
13 Mouassin Fountain

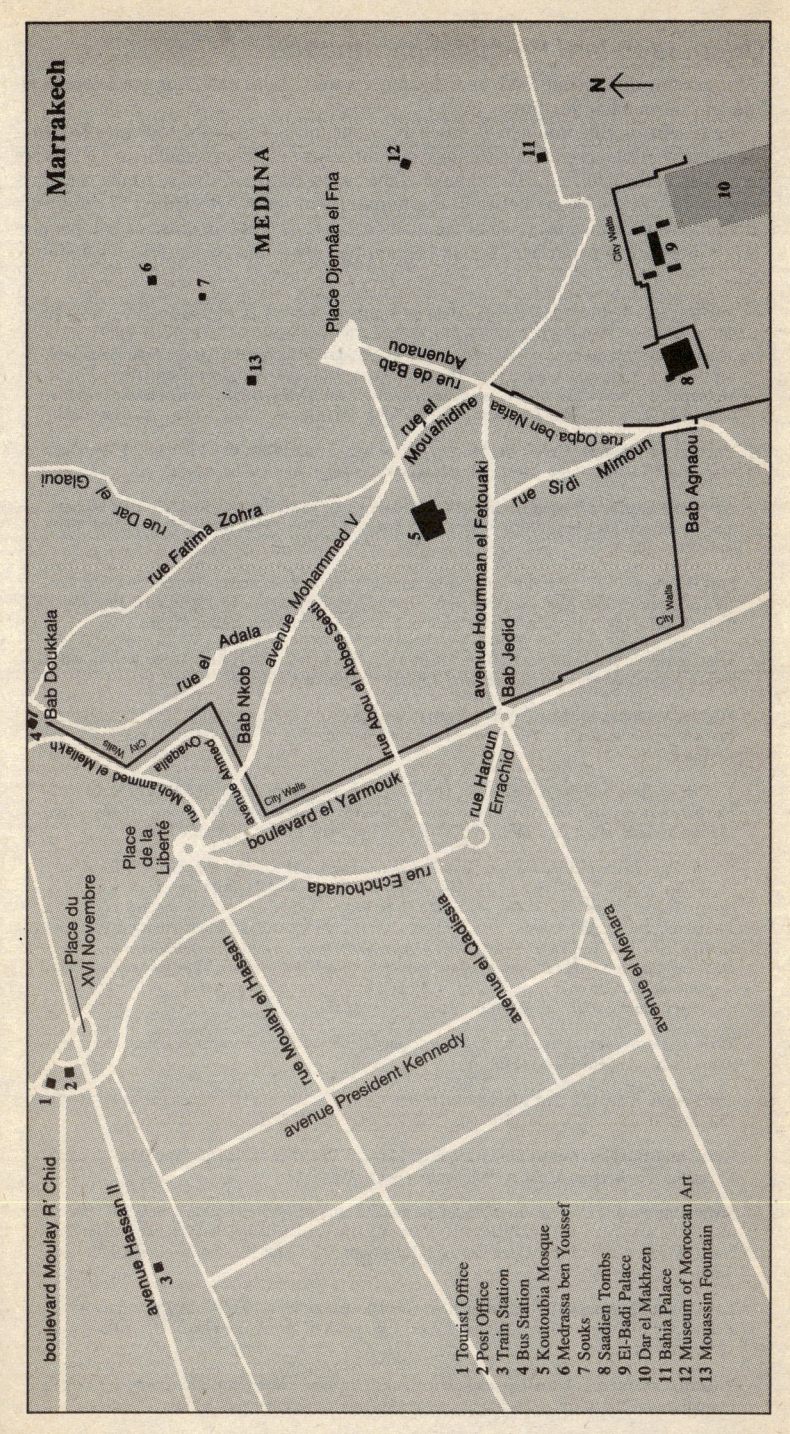

Orientation and Practical Information

All excitement, budget food, and cheap accommodations center on the **Djemâa el-Fna** and surrounding **medina**.

The **Guéliz** or **ville nouvelle** is down av. Mohammed V, past the towering **Koutoubia minaret**. The bus and train stations, administrative buildings, and luxury hotels are here. Also in the *ville nouvelle* are most of the car rentals, newsstands, banks, and travel agencies. Bus #1 runs between the minaret and the heart of the *ville nouvelle* (1.50dh). You can also take one of the many *petits taxis* (bargain down to 5dh per person) or horse-drawn carriages (again bargain fiercely to the posted price of 40dh per hr.).

Tourist Office: Office National Marocain du Tourisme (ONMT), av. Mohammed V (tel. 44 88 99), at pl. Abdel Moumen ben Ali. English spoken. The free brochures have good outlines of the medina *souks*. Multilingual maps. Official guides: 1/2-day 50dh, full day 100dh. Open 8am-3pm; Sept.-June 8:30am-noon and 2:30-6:30pm; Ramadan 9am-3pm. **Syndicat d'Initiative,** 176 av. Mohammed V (tel. 43 30 97), between the post office and ONMT. Binders full of useful information. Open Mon.-Sat. 8am-3pm; Sept. 13-June Mon.-Fri. 8am-noon and 3-7pm, Sat. 8am-noon.

Currency Exchange: Crédit du Maroc, 43 rue Bab Agnaou (tel. 44 22 35, 44 20 38). Open Mon.-Fri. 8:15am-1:45pm. Most luxury hotels will change money at late hours.

American Express: Voyages Schwartz, rue Mauritania, 2nd fl. (tel. 43 30 22), off av. Mohammed V, 2nd left after post office. Office open 6am-11pm; bank open Mon.-Fri. 8:30am-1:30pm and 2:30-4:30pm.

Post Office: pl. XVI Novembre, off av. Mohammed V. Poste Restante here is slow, and Saturdays are a madhouse. Open Mon.-Sat. 8am-3pm; winter Mon.-Sat. 8:30am-12:15pm and 2:30-6:45pm. **Branch office** in the Djemâa. Open Mon.-Fri. 8:30am-12:15pm and 2:30-6:45pm.

Telephones: In the main **post office.** Open Mon.-Fri. 8am-2:30pm. Also at the less crowded branch post office. Open Mon.-Fri. 8am-3:30pm. **Telephone Code:** 04.

Flights: Aeroport de Marrakech Menara (tel. 44 78 65, 44 79 10, 44 85 06), 5km south of town. Taxi service about 20dh; no bus. Domestic and international flights on Royal Air Maroc and Royal Air Inter.

Trains: av. Hassan II, 5min. west on av. Hassan II from av. Mohammed V and pl. XVI Novembre. The best way to head north. To: Casablanca (4 per day, 3hr., 66.50dh); Tangier (5 per day, 11hr., 135dh); Meknes (4 per day, 9hr., 137.50dh); Fes (6 per day, 10hr., 121.50-153.50dh).

Buses: Outside the medina walls by Bab Doukkala. The **CTM** window is next to #8. To: Agadir (2 per day, 59dh); Casablanca (4 per day, 56dh); Fes (2 per day, 106dh); Ouarzazate (2 per day, 88dh); Zagora (4 per day, 79dh); Essaouira (6 per day, 31dh). The **SATAS** window is #14. To Taroudannt at 5am and 4:30pm. One is direct (70dh) and the other is a mountain route that goes through the Tizi-n-Test Pass (55dh). Other windows represent private companies with lower prices, lower standards, and far more frequent service to certain destinations. Most private buses also stop outside the Bab er Rob, just south of Djemâa el-Fna, but seats are usually gone by then. To Setti-Fatma in the High Atlas start from here (every 1/2 hr., 11dh).

Taxis: Collective taxis leave from Bab er Rob and Djemâa el-Fna for nearby destinations, such as Asni (15dh) and Setti-Fatma (15dh).

Car Rental: Avis, 137 blvd. Mohammed V (tel. 43 37 27). Renault IV 2695dh per week. **Hertz,** 154 blvd. Mohammed V (tel. 43 46 80, 43 13 94). Renault IV 2730dh per week.

Horse-and-Buggies: Across from Banque du Maroc on the edge of the Djemâa el-Fna, along av. Mohammed V. Bargain to about 40dh per hr. per carriage.

Swimming Pool: Piscine Koutoubia, in the medina off av. Mohammed V, the next left heading toward the new city from the Koutoubia. Now officialy coed, although women may be outnumbered by a thousand to one. Open late June-early Sept. Wed.-Mon. 9:30am-noon and 2:30-6pm. Admission about 4dh.

Late-Night Pharmacy: In the fire station complex (tel. at fire station 43 04 15), corner of rue Kahlid Ben El Oualid and av. Nations Unies, 1 bl. north of Hôtel Marrakech. Open Tues.-Sun. 10:30pm-8am.

Medical Emergency: Doctor on call until 10pm at the above **late-night pharmacy.** It's best to avoid the government-run polyclinique; have a pharmacist recommend a private physician.

Police: tel. 19.

Accommodations and Camping

Apart from the youth hostel and campgrounds, which are far from the medina but close to the train station, all cheap accommodations are within a stone's throw of the Djemâa el-Fna.

Auberge de Jeunesse (HI), rue el-Jahid (tel. 44 77 13), handily 5min. from the train station in the *ville nouvelle*. Across av. Hassan II to the right, then the 1st left. Continue as straight as possible and then right at the eucalyptus tree lot; the hostel is at the end of the street. Spartan and tiled, it's exceptionally clean, with a courtyard and terrace. Cold showers only. Open 8-9am, noon-2pm, and 6-10pm. Officially members only. 15dh per person. Unofficially non-members 20dh.

Djemâa el-Fna

Hôtel CTM (tel. 44 43 49, 44 23 25), facing Djemâa el-Fna left of the Café du Grand Balcon. Occupying the site of the former CTM bus station, it retains some of its predecessor's charmless atmosphere. The courtyard and large terrace have a fabulous view of the Djemâa. Bright pink bedrooms are shabby and a bit saggy. The rooms in the back are quiet, but those facing the Djemâa are bigger. Parking available. Singles 52dh, with shower 77dh. Doubles 69dh, with shower 100dh. Breakfast on the terrace 16dh.

Hôtel Ali, rue Moulay Ismael (tel. 44 49 79; fax 43 36 09). The Club Med of the budget traveler. Clean, sufficient rooms a few doors from the Djemâa el-Fna. Melanomic sunbathing on the terrace. Some rooms have balconies. All rooms have modern bathrooms and A/C. The restaurant serves a satisfying 4-course meal (40-60dh). Singles with shower 85dh. Doubles with shower 120dh. Breakfast included. Popular terrace buffet-under-the-stars 7-11pm (50dh).

Hôtel de Foucauld, rue el-Mouahdine (tel. 44 54 99). Clean, painted rooms with marbled baths and balconies. Capacious rooftop terrace with view of minaret. Closest bar to the Djemâa. Singles with bath 103dh. Doubles with bath 125dh.

Hôtel Essaouira, 3 Derb Sidi Bouloukat, the 1st main right 150m down rue Riad Zitoune el-Kedim. The attractive courtyard imitates Essaouira's cool white and blue color scheme. Born-again bedrooms with new beds. 30dh per person.

Hôtel de France, 197 rue Riad Zitoune el-Kedim (tel. 44 30 67), not to be confused with the Hôtel-Café Restaurant de France overlooking the Djemâa el-Fna. Same two-tone palette as Hôtel Essaouira, but without the newness. Rambling. Slightly stuffy rooms due to roofed-in patio. Clean bathrooms. Singles 30dh. Doubles 60dh. Triples 60dh. Hot showers 5dh. Cold showers 3dh.

Hôtel Chella, 14 rue Riad Zitoune Kedim Derb Skaya (tel. 44 19 77), the 3rd right after rue Riad Zitoune el-Kedim. Charming courtyard with slender shady orange trees, Saharan murals, and bedrooms with green walls and cushy beds. Singles 30dh. Doubles 60dh. Hot showers 10dh. Cold showers 5dh.

Hôtel Gallia, 30 rue de la Recette (tel. 44 59 13). From the Djemâa, take the 2nd left on rue Bab Agnaou. Gorgeous Arab-style tiles and carvings ornament the interior. 2 airy treeful patios. Clean bedrooms, each with a different Moroccan blanket for a bedspread. TV room. Laundry service for a small fee. Singles 68dh, with shower 84dh. Doubles 84dh, with shower 103dh.

Hôtel El At Lal, 48 rue de la Recette, down the rue from the Gallia. A treasure trove of Arabic patterned tiles and arabesques on walls, floors, ceilings, toilet paper, etc. The entire place is scrubbed at least three times daily. When their rag and broom befall your room, expect your possessions to be put in perfect order. Singles 45dh. Doubles 70dh. Hot shower 7dh.

Ville Nouvelle

Hôtel des Voyageurs, 40 blvd. Mohammed Zerktouni (tel. 44 72 18), off blvd. Mohammed V., about 100m from ONMT tourist office. Old, dark, dull, and convenient. Central courtyard and beds spread with bright Moroccan blankets. Singles 50dh, with shower 65dh. Doubles 68dh, with shower 78dh.

Hôtel Koutoubia, 51 av. Mansour Eddahbi (tel. 43 09 21), at the corner of rue Yougoslavie and 4 bl. from ONMT tourist office. Pool! The stained-glass windows and carved arches bedazzle. Idyllic oasis of a courtyard and adequate rooms. Singles with shower 154dh. Doubles with shower 196dh.

Camping: Camping-Caravaning Municipal, in a partially wooded park near the train station. From the train station, walk east (left as you exit) to pl. Haile Selassie, make a right onto rue de France, and take the 2nd right. The sites are usually full, but it's so humongous that there's always room for another tent. Electricity 220V, shop, cold showers, and pool. The premises crawl with opportunists; be careful with your stuff. 10dh per person, 11dh per tent, 8dh per car.

Food

Along the fortifications surrounding the city, two **markets** peddle their fresh produce. These are a long walk by foot. A closer daily fruit and vegetable market is just outside **Bab Aghmat,** and **Bab el-Kemis** hosts a lively Thursday market.

Djemâa el-Fna

For often delicious bargains, devour the wares of the stalls of the Djemâa. The number of options increases three-fold in the evening, when vendors set up their benches. Settle prices before snarfing. If unsure of the correct price hang around and see how much the locals pay. Sample the succulent pulp of prickly cactus buds (not hallucinogenic), but first ask a pro to pinch off the ends and peel back the skin (1dh).

> **Café-Restaurant-Hôtel de France,** pl. Djemâa el-Fna. Typical mediocre *menu* (50dh) in attractive surroundings. The *salon marocain* is the coolest place to eat, while the rooftop has the best view by night and is the tallest in the old town. Open 6am-11pm; winter 5am-10pm.
>
> **Café-Patisserie Toubkal,** pl. Djemâa el-Fna across from the Hôtel CTM. Refresh your aching skull on the shady outdoor patio. Mmm, shish kebab done with fried onions and peppers (16dh). Steaks or brochettes with salad, bread, and fries 20dh. Open 7am-11pm.

The Medina

> **Café-Restaurant el-Baraka,** rue Bab Agnaou, 150m down from the Djemâa. Fair chicken, decent *couscous,* and peerless *tajine de la viande.* 3-course *menu* 30dh. Open 8am-11pm.
>
> **Restaurant Etoile de Marrakech,** rue Bab Agnaou, down the street from the above. Pleasing upstairs dining and a *terrasse panoramique* high above the bedlam. One of the only places in the area where you can order à la carte without hassle. *Clientèle touristique.* Daily *menu* 25dh. *Tajine* and *couscous* 25dh. Open 11am-11pm.

Ville Nouvelle

Plenty of uninspired four-course meals for 45-50dh.

> **La Taverne,** 23 blvd. Zerktouni (tel. 44 61 26), where the delectable French *menu* (80dh) changes daily. Open 11am-3pm and 7pm-midnight.

Sights

Djemâa el-Fna

Welcome to Djemâa el-Fna, the Assembly of the Dead. At night, it metamorphoses into a hectic outdoor circus peopled with characters from your most obscure nightmares and fantasies. This sideshow was once the spot where sultans had criminals beheaded. As a warning to troublemakers, executioners impaled the dried heads on spikes for public viewing. Today's audiences, often numbering in the thousands, cluster tightly around frenzied street performers. Storytellers, snake charmers, and dentists are merely a few of the entertainers. The snake-charmers are the most notorious extortionists. Don't let one drape a pit viper around your neck; they'll charge you to remove it.

After sunset the odder sorts clear out and the food vendors take over. By 8pm the square is carpeted with eager merchants plugging ceramics, weavings, carpets, clothing, and souvenirs. The crowds jostle on until midnight.

Almost every tour of Marrakech begins at the 12th-century **Koutoubia Mosque,** whose magnificent **minaret** presides over Djemâa el-Fna. The minaret, crowned by a lantern of three golden spheres, is the oldest and best surviving example of the art of the Almohads, who made Marrakech their capital (1130-1213) and at one time ruled the region from Spain to present-day Tunisia. In 1157, Abd el-Mumin acquired one of the four editions of the Qu'ran authorized by the caliph Uthman and used it as a talisman in battle and inspiration for the design of the second Koutoubia Mosque. Possession of this holy book turned Marrakech into a seat of religious learning. In fact, the name Koutoubia comes from the Arabic *kutubiyyin,* which means "of the books." As with most Moroccan mosques, entrance is forbidden to non-Muslims.

More than 2km of pink-tinged **fortifications** encircle the city on all sides. The Almoravid Sultan Ali ben Youssef comissioned most of these bulky battlements in the 12th century; they've been in the process of renovation for several centuries Thousands of Christian slave laborers lost their lives while building the walls; as they died (allegedly), their corpses were plastered into the mud-brick.

> **Bab Agnaou** is the most dazzling gate (3 bl. south of the Koutoubia minaret) and formerly portal to the Kasbah of Yacoub el-Mansour. Highly decorative, the 12-century gate was where mutilated corpses and heads of slain enemies were often displayed as trophies of war.
>
> **Bab el-Rob,** next to it, was the southern doorway to the city.
>
> **Marjorelle Gardens** shelter birds and spiny cacti north of the Bab el-Rob, above pl. Mourabite off av. d'el-Jadida. The exquisite landscaping was done by French artist Louis Marjorelle.
>
> **Bab el-Khemis,** site of a lively Thursday market, is in the northeast corner of Marrakech, a long swing around town. The bastion was reputedly designed and built by Andalusian architects and artisans.
>
> **Bab Aylen,** farther south, marks the spot where the Almohads suffered a crushing defeat in 1130 in their first attack on the Almoravid city.
>
> **Bab Aghmat,** the next gateway along the walls, watches over an extensive daily fruit and vegetable market.
>
> **Bab Ahmar,** an Alawite gate, opens onto the grounds of the royal palace.

The Medina

The Marrakech medina exists on an imperial scale. The salmon-colored houses are brighter, the streets and *souks* larger, and the smells more invigorating than in other medinas. Enter the medina to the left of Café el Fati. This is the medina's main thoroughfare, the enormous **Souk Smarine,** which takes a turn at the **potters' souk.** Follow the concentration of *souks;* Berber blankets, woven by families spinning wool in a tangle of dowels, string, and cards of yarn, pile the alleyways of the **fabric souk.**

Through the first major orange gateway, the first opening on the right leads to the **Zahba Kedima,** a small plaza flanked by the **spice souk** on one side and the **carpet souk** on the other. A mind-boggling array of panaceas stock the spice *souk*—goat hoof for hair treatment, ground-up ferrets for depression, and live chameleons for sexual frustration.

Continue through the bolts of silks and satins on the Souk Smarine until the road forks. The left road, the **Souk Attarine,** meanders past a few copper and silver merchants. The left path of the second fork leads to the center of the **woodworkers' souk,** where skilled artisans carve tiny chess pieces at an astonishing speed. The second street on the left passes through a section of **basketweavers.** Past the baskets, bubbling cauldrons of color cram the **dyers' souk** stalls. At the end of the street, northeast of the 16th-century Mosque of Mouassin, dust and grime camouflage the **Mouassin Fountain's** gilded cedar corbels and colorful carvings.

The residential area west of the fountain is more domestic. Small doorways open into two-story mini-*souks* in rectangular courtyards. These offshoots are the **fondouks,** neighborhood markets once surrounded on three sides by arcades of shops.

On the road that goes to the right where Souk Attarine forks, an endless selection of Moroccan slippers preens itself at the **babouche souk.** The right fork at the end of the street leads to the **cherratine souk,** which connects the *babouche souk* to the Souk el-Kbir (the right fork off Souk Smarine as you enter the medina). This street is the **leather souk**—not as large, but just as colorful and putrid as the one in Fes. In 1565, Sultan Moulay Abdallah el-Ghalib raised the **Medrassa of ben Youssef** in the center of the medina (backtrack to Souk Smarine, bear right at the fork onto Souk el-Kbir, and follow this to its end); it reigned as the largest Qu'ranic school in the Maghreb until it closed in 1956. Students used the central court's fountain and the corridor's basin for ablutions. Two stories of dorm rooms—once containing 900 students—surround the court. Youths attended *medrassa* free of charge, and after finishing their studies often continued at the Karaouiyue University in Fes. (*Medrassa* open Tues.-Sun. 8am-noon and 3-7pm; winter Tues.-Sun. 8am-noon and 2-6pm. Admission 10dh.)

Around the corner, beside the Ben-Youssef mosque, juts the squat, unpainted cupola of 12th-century **Koubba el-Ba'adiyn,** the oldest monument in town. The underside of the fanciful tower is carved in an excessive floral arabesque pattern. The guard can open an ancient wooden door to the subterranean cisterns. (Open 8:30am-noon and 2:30-6pm. Bang on the door to get in if it's closed. Free, but the custodian may charge 10dh plus tip.)

Turn right on the **Souk el-Kbir** to return to the **Djemâa el-Fna.** On the right on the decent toward the Djemâa, are the **Anciennes Kissarias,** parallel rows of spindly streets that connect the Souk Attarine and the *babouche souk* to the Souk el-Kmir. Here is the **clothing souk**—fezzes jostle fedoras, wool *djellabahs,* and polypropylene jumpsuits. On the left of the Souk el-Kmir glitters the **jewelers' souk:** hammered copperware, lacy silver bracelets, pewter perfume bottles, and gem-studded scabbards.

If you can stomach it, visit the bubbling cauldrons of the **tannery,** just inside Bab el-Debbagh (gate) in the northeast corner of the medina. Each vat holds a different chemical for each stage of leather production; children dive in to recover the skins and emerge covered with olive-purple slime.

Palaces

The **Saadien Tombs,** modeled after the interior of the Alhambra in Granada, constitute Morocco's most lavish mausoleum. The tombs served as the royal Saadien necropolis during the 16th and 17th centuries, until Moulay Ismail walled them off to efface the memory of his predecessors. In 1912 the burial complex was rediscovered. One **mausoleum** opulently brims with tiles and marble columns, crowned by a gleaming *mihrab.* Batches of brilliant green tile lather the less splendid second mausoleum. In the neighboring **Hall of the Twelve Columns,** trapezoidal tombs rise from a pool of polished marble. The shifty Saadien sultan made his fortune trading salt and sugar for equal weights of Sudanese gold and Italian marble. His four wives, 23 concubines, and the most favored of his hundreds of children are buried close by. The unmarked tombs belong to the women. (Open 8:30am-noon and 2:30-6pm. Admission 10dh. Multilingual tours.) To reach the Saadien Tombs, follow the signs from Bab el-Rob. The turquoise minaret of the **Mosque of the Kasbah,** Sultan Yacoub el-Mansour's own personal mosque, flags the way; veer right into the alley adjoining the mosque.

The **Bahia Palace** was constructed in the late 19th century by Sidi Moussa, grand vizier to Sultan Sidi Mohammed ben Abd er Rahman, and Sidi Moussa's son Ba Ahmed, chief adviser and favorite of Sultans Moulay el-Hassan and Moulay Abd el-Aziz. More powerful than the king himself, these two wallowed in the wealth of the kingdom despite the ugly colonial domination that impoverished the nation. On the eve of the European takeover of Morocco, they constructed the magnificent palace, whose name means "The Riches." Ample traces of their embarrassing greed remain: dazzling tilework, crimson curtains, and mahogany furniture fill a seemingly endless procession of reception halls, tea rooms, courtyards, and patios. Sultan Hassan II currently owns Bahia, Morocco's only royal palace open to the public. The **Court of Honor,** a 50m marble-paved corridor, is the roomiest chamber. In the **Moorish Garden** jasmine, mint, orange, grapefruit, and banana trees bloom. (Open 8:30-11:45am and 3-7pm; winter 8:30am-11:45am and 2:30-5:45pm. Free. Mandatory official museum tour; 5dh is a respectable contribution.) Facing the Hôtel CTM in the Djemâa, head left through an archway onto rue Riad Zitoun el-Kedim on the right; follow the main thoroughfare to the end, and bear left through pl. des Ferblantiers, curving around 180°. On the right, a reddish-brown archway opens into a long, tree-lined avenue leading to the palace door.

Dar Si Said, a 19th-century palace built by Si Said, brother of Grand Vizier Ba Ahmed and chamberlain of Sultan Moulay el-Hassan, houses the **Museum of Moroccan Art**. The collection features splendid Berber carpets, pottery, jewelry, Essaouiran ebony, and Saadien woodcarving. (Open Wed.-Mon. 8:30am-noon and 2:30-5:45pm.

Admission 10dh.) The gleaming Dar Si Said is located a tiny alley off rue Riad Zitoun el-Jadid, the 2nd right heading north toward the Djemâa el-Fna from the Bahia Palace.

Dar el-Makhzen puts Sultan Hassan II up for the night when he's in town. This sprawling ochre palace is roofed with rounded green tiles. The interior is closed to the public. Swing through the Bab Ahmar to glimpse the **Grand Méchouar**. It's a walled court where European diplomats and heads of state were once received amid much pomp. The **Agdal Gardens** are accessible via a roofed portal overlooking the Grand Méchouar. The 3km enclosure is filled with scrubby olive and fruit trees.

The **Menara Gardens,** a vast enclave of olive groves around an enormous pond, are most beautiful at sunset, when the mauve and tangerine light glints off the artificial lake. The cold green reservoir, 800m by 1200m, dates from the Almohad era. To reach the Gardens, head west through Bab el-Jedid and straight down av. Menara, the wide boulevard that resembles an airport landing strip. To the south (left) lies the expanse of the **Olive Grove of Bab Jedid,** a continuation of the Gardens.

El-Badi Palace is now simply a great open square. After a resounding victory over the Portuguese at the Battle of the Three Kings, Sultan Ahmed el-Mansour retired to Marrakech to construct this enormous festival palace (1578). A century later Moulay Ismail ordered its destruction. Some pools of water ringed by drooping orange trees, fragments of delicately carved stucco and sculpted cedar, and one solitary *minbar* are all that is left. (Open only during the el-Badi Festival in Sept.)

Entertainment

El-Bedi Palace is now the site of the annual **Folklore Festival,** which begins the second week of September and lasts for ten days. The extravaganza involves hundreds of performers, mostly acrobats and saber, rifle, and Ghedra dancers (toned down for the tourist audiences). The ONMT tourist office has performance schedules and sells tickets (30dh). In the evenings, three-hour sound and light shows light and sound up the palace pools (every night at 9pm, 40dh).

During the same ten days of this Folklore Festival, a fantasia is held outside Bab Jedid around 5 or 6pm. At the sound of a gunshot, former Berber soldiers emerge from pointy-topped tents and mount their Arabian stallions to re-enact the days when they swept down from the mountains to fight the French. With *koumiya* knives dangling at their sides and *moukkahla* muskets arched over their shoulders, the riders gallop down the field, swivel backwards on their stallions, and fire. For less seasonal entertainments, visit the several European-style discos attached to the luxury hotels in town. **Diamond Noir**, at Hôtel Marrakech, pl. de la Liberté (tel. 43 43 51), has no dress code and no cover charge (50dh per drink).

Glossary

General

Terms that recur frequently throughout this book are listed below in alphabetical order. The parentheses after a word indicate its abbreviation (if any) and its language. We abbreviate *castellano* (Castilian) as Cast.; *català* (Catalan) as Cat.; *galego* (Galician) as G; and *portugues* (Portuguese) as P.

abadía (Cast.)	abbey
acueducto (Cast.)	aqueduct
ajuntament (Cat.)	city hall
albergue (juvenil) (Cast.)	youth hostel
alcazaba (Cast.)	Muslim citadel
alcázar (Cast.)	Muslim fortress-palace
anfiteatro (Cast.)	amphitheater
aqueduto (P.)	aqueduct
arco (P.)	arch
autobús (Cast.)	bus
avenida (Av.; Cast., P.)	avenue
avinguda (Av.; Cat.)	avenue
ayuntamiento (Cast.)	city hall
azulejo (P.)	glazed tile
bahía (Cast.)	bay
barrio viejo (Cast.)	old city
baños (Cast.)	baths
biblioteca municipal (P.)	public library
cabo (P.)	cape (land, not clothing)
calle (C.; Cast.)	street
cámara municipal (P.)	town hall
capela (P.)	chapel
capilla mayor (Cast.)	chapel containing high altar
carrer (Cat.)	street
carrera (Cast.)	road
carretera (Ctra.; Cast.)	highway
casa do concello (G.)	city hall
casa particular (Cast. and P.)	lodging in a private home
casco antiguo (Cast.)	old city
castell (Cat.)	castle
castelo (P.)	castle
castillo (Cast.)	castle
catedral (Cast.)	cathedral
(el) centro (Cast.)	city center
ciudad nueva (Cast.)	new city
ciudad vieja (Cast.)	old city
ciutat vella (Cat.)	old city
claustre (Cat.)	cloister
claustro (Cast., P.)	cloister
colegiata (Cast.)	collegiate church
colexiata (G.)	collegiate church
colexio (G.)	school
convento (P.)	convent
coro (Cast, P.)	choir in a church
coro alto (P.)	upper choir

Glossary

cripta (Cast.)	crypt
cruz (Cast.)	cross
cuevas (Cast.)	caves
ermida (Cat.)	hermitage
ermita (Cast.)	hermitage
església (Cat.)	church
estacão (P.)	station (train or bus)
estación (Cast.)	station (train or bus)
fachada (Cast.)	façade
ferrocarriles (FFCC; Cast.)	trains
floresta (P.)	forest
fonte (P.)	fountain
fortaleza (P.)	fortress
fuente (Cast.)	fountain
glorieta (Cast.)	rotary
habitaciones (Cast.)	rooms
iglesia (Cast.)	church
igreja (P.)	church
igreja do seminário (P.)	seminary church
igrexa (G.)	church!
illes (Cat.)	islands
jardim botanico (P.)	botanical garden
jardim público (P.)	public garden
jardín público (Cast.)	public gardens
Judería (Cast.)	Jewish quarter
lavandería (Cast.)	laundromat
llotja (Cat.)	stock exchange
lonja (Cast.)	stock exchange
mercado (Cast., P.)	market (usually grocery market)
mercado municipal (Cast., P.)	local farmers' market
mercat (Cat.)	market
mesquita (P.)	mosque
mezquita (Cast.)	mosque
monestir (Cat.)	monastery
monte (Cast.)	mountain
mosteiro (G. and P.)	monastery
Mozarab (Cast.)	style of art developed by Christian artisans under Muslim rule
Mudejar (Cast.)	style of art developed by Muslims under Christian rule
museo (Cast.)	museum
museu (Cat. and P.)	museum
muralla (Cast.)	wall
palacio (Cast.)	palace
palau (Cat.)	palace
parador (*nacional*) (Cast.)	state-run hotel
parc (Cat.)	park
parque (Cast. and P.)	park
paseo (Po.; Cast.)	promenade
passeig (Pg.; Cat.)	promenade
patio (Cast.)	courtyard
plaça (Pl.; Cat.)	square
plaia (G.)	beach
platja (Cat.)	beach
playa (Cast.)	beach

plaza (Pl.; Cast.)	square
polideportivo (Cast.)	sports center
ponta (P.)	bridge
porta (P.)	gate
portal (Cast.)	entrance hall
pousada (P.)	a state-run hotel
pousada juventude (P.)	youth hostel
praça (Pr.; P.)	square
praza (Pr.; G.)	square
puente (Cast.)	bridge
quarto (P.)	lodging in a private house
real (Cast.)	royal
red (Cast.)	company
reina (Cast.)	queen
rey (Cast.)	king
ría (G.)	inlet or firth at mouth of a river
río (Cast.)	river
rio (P.)	river
riu (Cat.)	river
retablo (Cast.)	altarpiece, retable
ronda (Cast.)	rotary
rossio (P.)	rotary
rua (R.; P.)	street
rúa (R.; Cast., G.)	street
sala (Cast.)	room or hall
sardanas (Cast.)	folk dance
Semana Santa (Cast.)	Holy Week (week before Easter Sunday)
serra (Cat.)	mountain range
seu (Cat.)	cathedral
sillería (Cast.)	choir stalls
s/n (sin número) (Cast.)	unnumbered (in addresses)
tesoro (Cast.)	treasury of a church
tesouro (P.)	treasury of a church
torre (Cast., P.)	tower
torre de menagem (P.)	castle keep
universidade (P.)	university
valle (Cast.)	valley

Food, Drink, and Restaurant Terms

See Once There: Food for Spain and Portugal for fuller explanations. Terms that recur frequently throughout this book are listed below in alphabetical order. The parentheses after a word indicate its abbreviation (if any) and its language. We abbreviate *castellano* (Castilian) as Cast.; *català* (Catalan) as Cat.; *galego* (Galician) as G; and *portugues* (Portuguese) as P.

ajillo (Cast.)	garlic
atún (Cast.)	tuna
asado (Cast.)	anything grilled
bica (Cast.)	generic word for a mixed drink
bocadillo (Cast.)	*tapa* sandwiched between a hunk of bread
boquerones (Cast.)	smelts
caña (Cast.)	normal-sized beer
cerveza (Cast.)	beer (general term)

Glossary

champiñones (Cast.)	mushrooms
chocos (Cast.)	squid
chorizo (Cast.)	yummy sausage
churrasco (Cast.)	"barbecued" meat—cooked over an open flame
churros (Cast.)	¡lightly fried breakfast fritters!
cocido (Cast.)	stew with chickpeas
comedor (Cast.)	dining room
comida (Cast.)	lunchtime
copa (Cast.)	generic word for a mixed drink or cup
empanada (Cast.)	meat or vegetable turnover
ensalada (Cast.)	salad
fabada (Cast.)	bean stew
gambas (Cast.)	shrimp
gazpacho (Cast.)	duh
jamón (Cast.)	mountain-cured ham
jerez (Cast.)	sherry
lulas (G.)	squid
menú (Cast., Cat., and P.)	choice of 2 dishes, bread, beverage, and side order
mercado (Cast. and P.)	market (usually grocery market)
mercado municipal (Cast. and P.)	local farmers' market
mercat (Cat.)	market
merluza (Cast.)	hake (a white-fleshed fish)
para llevar (Cast.)	to go (take-away)
pescado (Cast.)	fish
pincho (Cast.)	*tapa* on a toothpick, like an hors d'oeuvre
plato del día (Cast.)	special of the day
platos combinados (Cast.)	entree and side order
pollo (Cast.)	chicken
prato do dia (P.)	special of the day
pratos combinados (P.)	entree and side order
queso (Cast.)	cheese
ración, pl. *raciones* (Cast.)	large size of *tapa*
serrano (Cast.)	anything smoked or cured
sidra (Cast.)	alcoholic cider
sopa (Cast.)	soup
taberna (Cast.)	*tapas* bar
tapa, pl. *tapas* (Cast.)	see Spain: Once There: Food
tasca (Cast.)	*tapas* bar
tubo (Cast.)	large-sized beer
zarzuela (Cat.)	seafood and tomato bouillabaisse

Appendices

Addresses

Spain and Portugal: "Av.", "C.", "R.", and "Trav." are abbreviations for street. "Po." and "Pg." are abbreviations for a promenade, "Pl." is a square, and "Glorieta" is a rotary. "Ctra." is the abbreviation for highway. The number of a building follows the street name, unlike in English. "s/n" means the building has no number. Floors are indicated with degree signs (°): "4th floor" is "4°". Note that the 4th floor to Europeans is the 5th floor to Americans, as Europeans don't count street level as the 1st floor.

Morocco: Because things are named in French, "av.", "blvd.", "rue", and "calle" mean street. "pl." is a plaza. Note that these aren't capitalized. The number of a building comes before the street name, as in English. When hunting for an address, keep in mind that many streets are being renamed in Arabic; "rue" and "calle" may be replaced by "zankat", "derb", or "sharia".

Country and City Codes (for telephone)

Spain: 34. Madrid: 1. Barcelona: 3. Sevilla: 5. Toledo: 25. Córdoba: 57. Granada: 58. València: 6. Pamplona: 48. Santiago de Compostela: 81.

Portugal: 351. Lisbon: 1. Porto: 2. Coimbra: 39.

Morocco: 212. Rabat: 7. Casablanca: 7. Tangier: 9. Marrakech: 4. Fes: 6.

U.S. and Canada: 1. **U.K.:** 44. London: 71. **Ireland:** 353. Dublin: 1. **Australia:** 61. Sydney: 2. Canberra: 6. **New Zealand:** 64.

Emergency Phone Numbers

Spain: 091.

Portugal: 115.

Morocco: 19.

Luggage Storage

Train and bus station lockers are usually operated by a token (*ficha* in Spanish) for which you pay. Less secure baggage checkrooms may also be found in train and bus stations.

Spain: *Consigna Automática* (lockers). *Consigna* (baggage check). The word for luggage is *equipaje*, for backpack *mochila*.

Portugal: *Depósito de Volumes* (baggage checkroom). Usually adjacent to the *chefe da estação* (station chief's office) on the platform. Pay when you reclaim your bag. 165$ per piece per 4 hr., 210$ per piece per 24 hrs.

Morocco: The baggage check at CTM bus depots is usually safe. If you don't have padlocks on the zippers, however, your bags may not be accepted. Private bus companies also have baggage checkrooms. They're generally trustworthy and accept any kind of bag.

Nude Sunbathing

Most towns on the Spanish and Portuguese coast have at least a few nude beaches; some beaches have a separate section for nude sunbathers. Nude sunbathing is most common in resort areas. In **Spain** look for *playa natural* or *playa de nudistas* signs. In **Morocco,** nude sunbathing is unacceptable.

Pharmacies

Listings of late-night or 24-hour pharmacies are included for every town under the Orientation and Practical Information listings. In Spain, pharmacies are identified by their standard signs bearing a green cross. At least one pharmacy will be open all night in a Spanish town, on a rotating system. To find out which one will be open, look for a notice posted in the windows and doors of any pharmacy, or check the *Farmacia de Guardia* listing on the second or third page of the local paper.

Time Differences

Spain: 6 hours after EST; 1 hour after GMT.

Portugal: 5 hours after EST; same as GMT. Daylight savings is on the last Sunday in March (clocks are set 1 hour faster) and the last Sunday in September (clocks are set 1 hour slower); i.e., spring ahead/fall back.

Morocco: Same as Spain.

Weights and Measures

1 millimeter (mm) = 0.04 inch	1 inch = 25mm
1 meter (m) = 1.09 yards	1 yard = 0.92m
1 kilometer (km) = 0.62 mile	1 mile = 1.61km
1 gram (g) = 0.04 ounce	1 ounce = 25g
1 kilogram (kg) = 2.2 pounds	1 pound = 0.45kg
1 liter = 1.06 quarts	1 quart = 0.94 liter

Clothing Sizes and Conversion

Men's Shirts (Collar Sizes)

U.S./U.K.:	14 1/2	15	15 1/2	16	16 1/2
Continent:	37	38	39	40	41

Men's Suits and Coats

U.S./U.K.:	38	40	42	44	46
Continent:	48	50	52	54	56

Women's Blouses and Sweaters

U.S.:	6	8	10	12	14
U.K.:	28	30	32	34	36
Continent:	34	36	38	40	42

Women's Dresses, Coats, and Skirts

U.S.:	4	6	8	10	12	14
U.K.:	6	8	10	12	14	16
Continent:	34	36	38	40	42	44

Men's Shoes

U.S.:	8	9	10	11	12
U.K.:	7	8	9	10	11
Continent:	41	42	43	44 1/2	46

Women's Shoes

U.S.:	6	7	8	9	10
U.K.:	4 1/2	5 1/2	6 1/2	7 1/2	8 1/2
Continent:	37	38	39	40	41

Calendar of Festivals and Holidays

Spain

Spring

late March: Week of Religious Music. Cuenca.

March 29-April 5: Semana Santa (Holy Week). National.

April 16-21: Feria de Abril. Sevilla.

April 23: St. George's Day and Cervantes Day. Barcelona.

May 1: May Day. National.

May 4-19: Patio Festival. Córdoba.

May 5-12: Horse Fair. Jerez de la Frontera.

May 12-30: San Isidro Festival. Madrid.

May 18-20: Rocío Pilgrimage. Almonte (near Huelva).

June 2: Corpus Christi. National, with special celebrations in Toledo, La Laguna (near Tenerife), and Granada.

June 14-July 2: International Music and Dance Festival. Granada.

Summer

June 21-24: Bonfires of San Juan. Alaçant.

July 1-14: Medieval Theater Festival. Hita (near Guadalajara).

July 6-14: Fiestas de San Fermín (Running of the Bulls). Pamplona.

July 16-30: International Jazz Festival. Donostia/San Sebastían.

July 25: Feast of Santiago. National.

July 25-28: Festival of Christians and Moors in Honor of Santa María. Vilajoiosa (near Alacant).

Aug.: Classical Drama Festival. Mérida (near Badajoz).

Aug. 15: Feast of the Assumption. National.

Autumn

early Sept.: Festival of Classical Drama and Comedy. Almagro (near Ciudad Real).

Sept. 4-9: Festival of Christians and Moors in Honor of Our Lady of Virtue. Villena (near Alacant).

mid-Sept.: Grape Harvest Festival. Jerez de la Frontera (near Cádiz).

late Sept.: International Film Festival. Donostia/San Sebastían.

Oct. 1-7: Festival Internacional de Cine Fantástico. Sitges (near Barcelona).

Oct. 12: Spain's National Day.

Oct. 27: The Saffron Rose Festival. Consuegra (near Toledo).

late Oct.: International Film Festival. Valladolid.

Nov. 1: All Saints' Day. National.

Appendices

Winter

Dec. 6: Constitution Day. National.

Dec. 8: Feast of the Immaculate Conception. National.

Dec. 25: Christmas Day. National.

Jan. 6: The Epiphany. National.

Feb. 3-17: Carnival. Santa Cruz de Tenerife.

Feb. 7-17: Carnival. Cádiz.

Feb. 9-12: Pero Palo Festival. Villanueva de la Vera (near Cáceres).

March 12-19: Fallas de San José. València.

Portugal

Spring

March 29-April 5: Semana Santa (Holy Week). National, with special celebrations in Braga, Ovar, and Povoa de Varzim.

March 25-April 25: Feira de Artesanato. Aveiro.

April 25: Liberty Day.

May: International Film Festival. Santarém.

May 1: Labor Day. National.

May 3-5: Festa das Cruzes (Festival of the Crosses). Barcelos.

May 4-6: Festivals for Senhor Santo Cristo. Ponta Delgada, S. Miguel Island, and Azores.

May 12-13: Pilgrimage. Fátima.

May-June: Music Festival. Algarve.

May 15-June 16: Book Fair. Lisboa.

May 30: Corpus Christi. National.

Summer

June 8-16: National Fair of Agriculture. Santarém.

June 10: Portugal's and Camões Day. National.

June 12-13: Festival of St. Anthony. Lisboa.

June-July: Music Festival. Sintra.

June 18: Corpus Christi (Corpo de Cristo). National.

June 22-24: Feira de São João. Évora.

June 23-24: Festa de São João. Porto, Figueira, and Braga.

June 29: Festa de São Pedro. Évora.

early July: Festa dos Tabuleiros. Tomar.

early July: Bienal de Escultura. Caldas da Rainha.

July: Feira do Ribatejo. Santarém.

July: Festa da Cerveja. Silves.

July: Sea Fair. Cascais.

July 4-Aug. 25: Handicrafts Fair. Estoril.

July 5-7: Colete Encarnado (Red Waistcoast Festival). Vila Franca de Xira (near Ribatejo).

July 12-21: International Handicraft Fair. Lisboa.

July 13-14: Gala dos Pequenos Cantores. Figueira.

July 14-Aug. 12: Festa da Ria. Aveiro.

July 20: Festival de Danças Folclóricas Luso-Espanhol. Marvão.

Aug. 3-5: Gualterianas Festival (St. Walter's). National.

Aug. 14-15: Our Lady of the Monte. Funchal, Madeira.

Aug. 15: Feast of the Assumption. National.

Aug. 17-20: Our Lady of Agony Festival. Viana do Castelo.

Aug. 22-Sept. 22: St. Matthew's Fair. Viseu.

Aug. 31-Sept. 3: Wine Harvest Festival. Palmela.

Autumn

Sept.: Cinema Festival. Figueira.

Sept.: Nossa Senhora da Estrela. Marvão.

Sept. 6-8: Folk Music Festival. Algarve.

Sept. 8-15: Our Lady of Nazaré. Nazaré.

Oct. 5: Republic Day. National.

Oct. 5-13: October Fair. Vila Franca de Xira.

Oct. 12-13: Pilgrimage. Fátima.

Oct. 24-Nov. 3: National Festival of Gastronomy. Santarém.

Nov. 1: All Saints' Day. National.

Winter

Dec. 1: Restorations of Independence. National.

Dec. 8: Feast of the Immaculate Conception. National.

Dec. 25: Christmas Day. National.

Dec. 31: Festival of St. Sylvester. Funchal, Madeira.

Feb. 9-13: Carnival. Loulé, Nazaré, and Ovar.

Climate

The following information is drawn from the International Association for Medical Assistance to Travelers (IAMAT)'s *World Climate Charts*. In each monthly listing, the first two numbers represent the average daily maximum and minimum temperatures in degrees **Celsius,** while the numbers in parentheses represent the same temperatures in degrees **Fahrenheit.** The remaining numbers indicate the mean relative **humidity percentage,** and the average number of days with a measurable amount of **precipitation.**

Spain

	Jan.		April		July		Oct.	
Avila	7/-2 78%	(45/28) 6	14/3 63%	(57-37) 8	28/13 45%	(82/55) 2	16/6 70%	(61/43) 7
Barcelona	13/6 68%	(55/43) 5	18/11 66%	(64/52) 9	28/21 65%	(82/70) 4	21/15 71%	(70/59) 9
Burgos	6/-1 88%	(43/30) 10	15/4 69%	(59/39) 11	26/12 63%	(79/54) 5	16/7 79%	(61/45) 11
Cáceres	11/4 79%	(52/39) 9	19/9 62%	(66/48) 8	34/19 38%	(93/66) 1	22/12 62%	(72/54) 7
Cádiz	15/9 78%	(59/48) 9	20/13 71%	(68/55) 6	27/20 72%	(81/68) 0	23/17 76%	(73/63) 7
Cuenca	8/-2 80%	(46/28) 7	16/3 68%	(61/37) 9	30/14 51%	(86/57) 3	18/6 71%	(64/43) 7
Granada	12/2 78%	(54/36) 8	20/7 68%	(68/45) 10	34/17 48%	(93/63) 1	23/10 69%	(73/50) 7
Madrid	9/2 79%	(48/36) 8	18/7 62%	(64/45) 9	31/17 46%	(88/63) 2	19/10 70%	(66/50) 8
Málaga	17/8 70%	(63/46) 7	21/13 67%	(70/55) 6	29/21 66%	(84/70) 0	23/16 72%	(73/61) 6
Palma	14/6 78%	(57/43) 8	19/10 72%	(66/50) 6	29/20 68%	(84/68) 1	18/10 77%	(64/50) 9
Santander	12/7 74%	(53/45) 16	15/10 77%	(59/50) 13	22/16 80%	(72/61) 11	18/12 78%	(64/54) 14
Santiago de Compostela	10/5 84%	(50/41) 21	18/8 70%	(64/46) 7	24/13 65%	(75/55) 1	21/11 77%	(70/52) 10
Sevilla	15/6 81%	(59/43) 8	24/11 71%	(75/52) 7	36/20 55%	(97/68) 0	26/14 74%	(79/57) 6
València	15/6 67%	(59/43) 5	20/10 64%	(68/50) 7	29/20 69%	(84/68) 2	23/13 70%	(73/55) 7
Zaragoza	10/2 74%	(50/36) 6	19/8 59%	(66/46) 8	31/18 54%	(88/64) 3	14/6 68%	(57/43) 6

Portugal

	Jan.		April		July		Oct.	
Bragança	8/0 85%	(46/32) 15	16/5 71%	(61/41) 10	28/13 62%	(82/55) 3	18/7 77%	(64/45) 10
Coimbra	14/5 75%	(57/41) 15	21/9 60%	(70/48) 13	29/15 57%	(84/59) 4	23/12 65%	(73/54) 13
Évora	12/6 76%	(54/43) 14	19/10 58%	(66/50) 10	30/16 39%	(86/61) 1	22/13 60%	(72/56) 9
Faro	15/9 76%	(59/48) 9	20/13 68%	(68/55) 6	28/20 63%	(82/68) 0	22/16 69%	(72/61) 6
Lisboa	14/8 78%	(57/46) 15	20/12 63%	(68/54) 10	27/17 55%	(81/63) 2	22/14 67%	(72/57) 9
Porto	13/5 78%	(55/41) 18	18/9 69%	(64/48) 13	25/15 67%	(77/59) 5	21/11 73%	(70/52) 15

Morocco

	Jan.		April		July		Oct.	
Essaouira	17/11	(63/51)	19/14	(66/57)	22/17	(71/63)	22/16	(71/61)
	77%	6	81%	5	92%	0	83%	3
Fes	16/4	(60/39)	23/9	(73/49)	36/18	(97/64)	26/13	(78/55)
	79%	8	73%	9	58%	1	64%	7
Marrakech	18/4	(65/40)	26/11	(79/52)	38/19	(101/67)	28/14	(83/57)
	77%	7	65%	6	53%	1	61%	4
Rabat	17/8	(63/46)	22/11	(71/52)	28/17	(82/63)	25/14	(77/58)
	81%	9	75%	7	74%	0	77%	6
Tangier	16/8	(60/47)	18/11	(65/51)	27/18	(80/64)	22/15	(72/59)
	76%	10	73%	8	67%	0	75%	8

INDEX

A
A Coruña (La Coruña) 164
A Garda 158
A Toxa (La Toja) 160
Abadía de Santo Domingo de Silos 145
Abamia 177
Agost 349
Aigüestortes 303
Aínsa 250
Alacant (Alicante) 345
Alba de Tormes 125
Albarracín 241
Albufeira 341
Alcalá de Henares 97
Alcobaca 492
Alcúdia 319
Alentejo 527
Algarve 545
Algatocín 416
Algeciras 416
Alicante (Alacant) 345
Aljustrel 501
Almagro 106
Almodóvar del Río 381
Almonte 430
Almuñécar 405
Alora 403
Andalucía 355
Andraitx 317
Aniezo 180
Antequera 410
Appendix 605
Aragón 229
Aragonese Pyrenees 243
Aranjuez 98
Architecture, Portugal 462
Architecture, Spain 53
Arcos de la Frontera 432
Arenas de Cabrales 178
Argamasilla de Alba 105
Art, Morocco 567
Art, Portugal 462
Art, Spain 52,
Artá 320
Asilah 574
Astorga 131
Asturian Coast 185
Asturias 171
ATMs 8
Aveiro 504
Avila 116
Ayerbe 246
Azemmour 591

B
Badajoz 445
Baeza 385
Baiona (Bayona) 157
Baleal 486
Balearic Islands (Illes Baleares) 310
Banos de Cerrato 140
Banyalbufar 317
Barcelona 253
Barcelos 518
Basque Country (Euskadi, País Vasco) 189
Batalha 499
Beddauza 591
Beira Baixa 493
Beira Alta 493
Beja 542
Belém 475
Benadolid 416
Benasque 251
Benjaón 415
Betanzos 167
BIJ 30
Bilbo (Bilbao) 190
Bornos 434
Boulaouane 591
Braga 512
Bragança 523
Buarcos 504
Bubión 399
Bulnes 179
Burgau 551
Burgos 140
Burguete 228
Bus, Morocco 558
Bus, Portugal 454
Bus, Spain 40
Busot 349

C
Caín 179
Cabo Fisterra (Cabo Finisterre) 162
Cabo de São Vicente 552
Cabo da Roca 480
Cabo Carvoeiro 487
Cabrera 321
Cáceres 435
Cadaqués 291
Cádiz 423
Caldas da Rainha 488
Calella 287
Calendar of Festivals and Holidays 607
Calp (Calpe) 350
Camariñas 163
Camarmeña 179
Cambados 160
Camping 14
Cangas 157
Cangas de Onís 176
Cantabria 171
Cantabrian Coast 185
Cap Sim 594
Capileira 399
Cariñena 236
Carmona 372
Carrapateira 552
Carrión de los Condes 139
Cartuja de Aula Dei 235
Casablanca 587
Cascais 481
Castelldefels 305
Castelo de Vide 542
Castilla y León 111
Castilla-La Mancha 100
Castillo Javier 225
Catalan Pyrenees 298
Catalonia (Catalunya) 252
Catalunya (Catalonia) 252
Catoira 160
Cazorla 386
Cedeira 169
Cée 163
Cercedilla 96
Charter Flights 28
Chipiona 428
Ciudad Rodrigo 125
Ciutadella (Ciudadela) 326
Climate 609
Clothing and Footwear 11
Clothing Sizes and Conversion 606
Clunia 144
Coca 116
Coimbra 494
Comillas 186
Commercial Airlines 27
Condeixa 498
Conímbriga 497
Consuegra 105
Córdoba 374
Corme 164
Costa del Sol 404
Costa Brava 282
Costa Daurada (Costa Dorada) 304
Costa Blanca 349
Costa de la Luz 426
Country and City Codes (for telephone) 605
Courier Flights 30
Covas 170
Covadonga 177
Crato 542
Credit Cards 8
Cueva de Santimamiñe 196
Cuevas de Altamira 186
Cuevas de la Pileta 415
Cullera 341
Currency and Exchange 7
Customs 32

D
Daroca 237
Deià 317
Denia 350
Diabat 593
Diabetics 17
Diets 17
Discount Clubs and Consolidators 28
Documents 2
Donostia (San Sebastián) 197
Douro 508
Drinks, Morocco 561
Drinks, Portugal 457
Drinks, Spain 46
Driving, Morocco 558
Driving, Portugal 454
Driving, Spain 41
Drugs 17

E
Ecija 373
Eivissa (Ibiza) 328
Eivissa City 328
El Burgo de Osma 149
El Castillo de Loarre 246
El Chorro Gorge 403
El Corte Inglés 48
El Escorial 92
El Grove 160
El-Jadida 589
El Palmar 341
El Pardo 80
El Puerto de Santa María 426
El Rocío 371
El Toboso 105
El Torcal 412
El Valle de los Caídos 96
Elche (Elx) 349
Elvas 536
Elx (Elche) 349
Embassies and Consulates in Portugal 452
Embassies and Consulates in Spain 36
Embassies and Consulates in Morocco 557
Embassies and Consulates 25
Emergency Phone Numbers 605
Empalme de Vera 235, 236
Empúries and L'Escala 289
Espinama 180
Esquivias 105
Essaouria 592
Estany de Sant Maurici 303
Estella 222
Estoril 481
Estremadura 478
Eurail 31
Euskadi (País Vasco, Basque Country) 189
Évora 533
Evoramonte 536
Exports 32
Extremadura 434
Ezaro 162

615

Index

F
Fado 476
Faro 545
Fátima 500
Fax, Portugal 458
Fax, Spain 47
Felanitx 322
Ferry 32
Fes 576
FEVE 40
Figueira da Foz 502
Figueres (Figueiras) 290
Finisterre (Fisterra) 162
Fisterra (Finisterre) 162
Flor da Rosa 542
Floresta de Bucaço 498
Food and Drink, Morocco 560
Food and Drink, Portugal 457
Food and Drink, Spain 44
Fornalutx 318
Frigiliana 407
Fuendetodos 235
Fuengirola 408
Fuente Dé 180
Fuenterrabía (Hondarribía) 205
Fuentevaqueros 396

G
Galiza (Galicia) 149
Gandía 344
Garganta del Chorro (El Chorro Gorge) 403
Gaucín 416
Gay and Lesbian Travelers 18
Geographical Organization 2
Gernika (Guernica) 194
Gerona (Girona) 293
Getares 418
Gibraltar 418
Girona (Gerona) 293
Glossary 602
Granada 387
Guadalajara 109
Guadalest 350
Guadalupe 443
Guadix 396
Guernica (Gernika) 194
Guimaráes 517

H
Halal Diets 17
Haouzia 591
Haro 215
Hashish 563
Health 15
Hecho 247
History, Morocco 565
History, Portugal 460
History, Spain 49
Hitchhiking, Morocco 559
Hitchhiking, Portugal 455
Hitchhiking, Spain 42
Hondarribía (Fuenterra-
bía) 205
Hostelling Organizations 6
Hoz de Arbayún 225
Hoz de Lumbier 225
Huesca 242
Hustlers and Guides 563

I
Ibiza (Eivissa) 328
Iglesia de San Juan de la Peña 246
Ilha da Armona 553
Ilhas Berlengas (Berlenga Islands) 487
Illes Baleares (Balearic Islands) 310
Imports 32
Inca 322
Insurance 10
International Driving Permit and Insurance Certificate 6
Invernales de Cabao 179
Irún 206
Isaba 227
Isle of Mogador 593
Iso 225
Itálica 372

J
Jaca 243
Jaén 381
Játiva (Xàtiva) 342
Jebel Amsittene 594
Jerez de los Caballeros 450
Jerez de la Frontera 430

K
Kortezubi 196
Kosher diets 17

L
La Alberca 125
La Coruña (A Coruña) 164
La Granja de San Ildefonso 115
La Herradura 405
La Línea 419
La Macarena 367
La Rioja 211
La Toja 160
La Vila Joiosa 349
Lagos 549
Lagos de Enol y Ercina 178
Lamas de Olo 527
Lanjarón 398
Laroles 400
Laroles 400
Las Alpujarras 398
Laxe 164
Leiria 498
Lekeitio (Lequeitio) 196
León 128
Li édana 225
Lisboa (Lisbon) 464
Literature, Morocco 567
Literature, Portugal 462
Literature, Spain 53
Llafranc 287
Llançà 292
Llanes 188
Llerena 450
Lloret de Mar 284
Lluc 318
Loarre 246
Logroño 211
Lorca 354
Los Pueblos Blancos 449
Los Cotos 97
Louro 161
Luggage 11
Lumbier 225
Luriezo 180
Luso 498

M
Madrid 56
Mafra 482
Mail, Morocco 561
Mail, Portugal 458
Mail, Spain 46
Málaga 400
Mallorca 311
Malpica 164
Manacor 322
Manises 341
Maò 323
Marbella 408
Maro 407
Marrakech 594
Marvão 541
Mateus 526
Medina Azahara 381
Menorca 322
Meranges 302
Mérida 447
Miño 167
Minho 508
Mogrovejo 180
Monasterio de Veruela 235
Monasterio de Leyre 226
Mondoñedo 170
Monestir Santes Creus 309
Monestir Poblet 309
Money 7
Money, Morocco 562
Money, Portugal 459
Money, Spain 48
Monsaraz 536
Montjuïc 272
Montserrat 280
Moped and Bicycle, Portugal 455
Moped and Bicycle, Spain 41
Mora de Rubielos 241
Moraira 350
Morella 341
MOROCCO 556
Muel 236
Murcia 351
Muros 161
Muxía 163

N
Navarra 211
Navarrese Pyrenees 224
Nazaré 489
Nerja 406
Noia (Noya) 161
Nude Sunbathing 606
Núria 300

O
O Castro de Baroña 161
O Grove (El Grove) 161
Óbidos 484
Ochagavía 227
Odeceixe 552
Olhão 553
Olite 221
Olivenza 451
Olvera 416
Ortigueira 169
Osuna 373
Oualidia 591
Oviedo 172
Oyambre 186

P
Packing 11
País Vasco (Euskadi, Basque Country) 189
Palafrugell 287
Palencia 136
Palma 312
Pampaneira 399
Pamplona 216
Panes 180
Papôa 487
Parc Nacional d'Aigüestortes i Estany de Sant Maurici 303
Paredes de Nava 140
Parque Nacional de Ordesa y Monte Perdido 248
Parque Nacional Peneda-Gerês 516
Parque Natural Sierra España 354
Passports 2
Pedraza 116
Pembes 180
Peña de Francia 125
Peniche 486
Petra 322
Pharmacies 606
Picos de Europa 176
Pitres 399
Planning Your Trip 2
Plasencia 438
Pollença 319
Poncebos 178
Ponte de Lima 522
Pontedeume 167
Pontevedra 159
Port d'Alcúdia 320
Port de Sóller 318
Portagem and Beira 541
Portalegre 539
Portbou 292
Porto Cristo 321
Porto do Son 161

Index 617

Porto (Oporto) 508
Porto Petro 321
PORTUGAL 452
Portugos 399
Potes 179
Prado Llano 397
Puente Viesgo 185
Puerto Banús 410
Puerto de Navacerrada 97
Puigcerdà 300
Purullena 396

Q
Queluz 480
Quesada 385

R
Rabat 583
Ría de Arousa 160
Ría de Muros e Noia 160
Rías Altas 168
Rías Baixas (Bajas) 155
Rías da Costa da Morte (Rías de la Costa de la Muerte) 162
Rías de Foz and Ribadeo 170
Rías de Cedeira, Ortigueira, and Viveiro 168
Ribadeo 170
Ribatejo 527
Río Miño 158
Ripoll 298
Roncal 266
Roncesvalles 228
Ronda 412
Rota 427
Rubielos de Mora 241
Ruiloba 187
Ruins of Numancia 148
Ruta del Vino 236

S
Sa Calobra 318
Safety 16
Sagres 551
Sagunt 340
Sahagún 132
Salamanca 119
Salema 551
Salinas 331
Salobreña 404
Salou 308
San Pedro de Cardeña 145
San Sebastián (Donostia) 197

San Millán de la Cogolla 215
San Vicente de la Barquera 187
Sangüesa 224
Sanlúcar de Barrameda 428
Sant Pere de Roda 292
Sant Antoni Abad 331
Sant Feliu de Guíxols 286
Sant Cugat del Vallès 282
Sant Pere de Roda 293
Santa Eulària des Riu 332
Santander 180
Santanyí 321
Santarém 527
Santiago de Compostela 150
Santillana del Mar 185
Santo Domingo de la Calzada 213
São Jacinto 506
Sarrià 274
Segovia 111
Sending Money Abroad 10
Senior Travelers 18
Setenil de las Bodegas 416
Settat 591
Setúbal 482
Sevilla 355
Sidi Kaouki 594
Sierra Nevada 397
Sierra de Torcal 412
Sierra de Torcal 412
Sierra de Guadarrama 96
Sigüenza 110
Sintra 478
Siresa 247
Sitges 304
Smimou 594
Sóller 318
Soria 146
Sos del Rey Católico 234
Southeastern Mallorca 321
SPAIN 36
Student and Youth Identification 4
Study 21

T
Tabarca 349
Tamariu 287
Tangier 569

Tapas 45
Tarazona 235
Tarifa 421
Tarragona 305
Tavira 553
Telegraph, Morocco 562
Telegraph, Portugal 458
Telegraph, Spain 47
Telephone, Morocco 562
Telephone, Portugal 459
Teruel 237
Tibidabo 274
Time Differences 606
Tipping, Morocco 562
Tipping, Portugal 460
Tipping, Spain 48
Toledo 100
Tomar 530
Torla 248
Torredembara 308
Torremolinos 407
Torrevieja 349
Tossa de Mar 282
Tourist Offices, Morocco 556
Tourist Offices, Portugal 452
Tourist Offices, Spain 36
Train, Morocco 557
Train, Portugal 452
Train, Spain 37
Trás-Os-Montes 523
Travel Services 25
Traveler's Checks 7
Travelers with Children 19
Travelers with Disabilities 20
Trevélez 399
Trujillo 440
Tudela 222
Túi 158

U
Ubeda 383
Ugijar 400Ugijar 400
Ujué 222

V
Val de Boí 303
Valcarlos 228
Valdoviño 168
Valençado do Minho 522
València 333
Valladolid 132
Valldemosa 317
Valle de Ansó 248

Valle de Benasque 251
Valle de Hecho 246
Valle de Oza 227
Valle de Salazar 227
Value-Added Tax (VAT), Morocco 562
Value-Added Tax (VAT), Portugal 459
Value-Added Tax (VAT), Spain 48
Vegetarian diets 17
Véjer de la Frontera 422
Veleta 397
Vera de Moncayo 235
Viana do Castelo 519
Vigo 155
Vila Real de Santo António 554
Vila Nova de Cerveira 521
Vila Real 525
Vilagarc 1 a de Arousa 160
Vilanova i la Geltru 305
Villajoyosa 349
Vinarós 342
Visas 4
Viseu 506
Vitoria-Gasteiz 207
Viveiro (Vivero) 169

W
Weights and Measures 606
When To Go 2
Women Travelers, 20
Work and Volunteering 22

X
Xàbia (Jávea) 350
Xàtiva (Játiva) 342
Xixona 349

Y
Yegen 400
Yesa 225
Youth Hostels, 42
Youth Hostels, Morocco 559
Youth Hostels, Portugal 455
Youth Hostels, Spain 66

Z
Zafra 449
Zahara de la Sierra 416
Zamarramala 115
Zamora 126
Zaragoza 230